WILLIAM SHAKESPEARE

THE HISTORIES, SONNETS AND POEMS

WILLIAM SHAKESPEARE

WILLIAM SHAKESPEARE

THE HISTORIES, SONNETS AND POEMS

ILLUSTRATED

GRAMERCY BOOKS
NEW YORK

This 2002 edition published by Gramercy Books, an imprint of Random House Value Publishing, a division of Random House, Inc., 280 Park Avenue, New York, NY 10017.

Gramercy is a registered trademark and the colophon is a trademark of Random House, Inc.

Printed in the United States of America

Cover design by Mary Helen Fink

Random House
New York • Toronto • London • Sydney • Auckland
www.randomhouse.com

Library of Congress Cataloging-in-Publication Data

Shakespeare, William, 1564-1616.
    [Selections. 2002]
    William Shakespeare, the histories, sonnets, and other poems : illustrated.
        p. cm.
    Previously published under title: William Shakespeare, the complete works. 1975.
    ISBN 0-517-22058-X
    1. Historical drama, English. 2. Sonnets, English. I. Title.

PR2762 2002
822.3'3—dc21

2002021616

987654321

CONTENTS

KING JOHN.

Act IV. Sc. 1.

KING JOHN

DRAMATIS PERSONÆ

KING JOHN.
PRINCE HENRY, *his Son; afterwards* KING HENRY III.
ARTHUR, *Duke of Bretagne, Son to* GEFFREY, *late Duke of Bretagne, the Elder Brother to* KING JOHN.
WILLIAM MARESHALL, *Earl of Pembroke.*
GEFFREY FITZ-PETER, *Earl of Essex, Chief Justiciary of England.*
WILLIAM LONGSWORD, *Earl of Salisbury.*
ROBERT BIGOT, *Earl of Norfolk.*
HUBERT DE BURGH, *Chamberlain to the* KING.
ROBERT FALCONBRIDGE, *Son to* SIR ROBERT FALCONBRIDGE.
PHILIP FALCONBRIDGE, *his Half-brother, Bastard Son to* KING RICHARD I.
JAMES GURNEY, *Servant to* LADY FALCONBRIDGE.

PETER *of Pomfret, a Prophet.*
PHILIP, *King of France.*
LOUIS, *the Dauphin.*
ARCHDUKE OF AUSTRIA.
CARDINAL PANDULPH, *the Pope's Legate.*
MELUN, *a French Lord.*
CHATILLON, *Ambassador from France to* KING JOHN.

ELINOR, *Widow of* KING HENRY II., *and Mother to* KING JOHN.
CONSTANCE, *Mother to* ARTHUR.
BLANCH, *Daughter to* ALPHONSO, *King of Castile, and Niece to* KING JOHN.
LADY FALCONBRIDGE, *Mother to the* BASTARD *and* ROBERT FALCONBRIDGE.

Lords, Citizens *of Angiers,* Sheriff, Heralds, Officers, Soldiers, Messengers, *and other* Attendants.

SCENE,—*Sometimes in* ENGLAND, *and sometimes in* FRANCE.

ACT I.

SCENE I.—NORTHAMPTON. *A Room of State in the Palace.*

Enter KING JOHN, QUEEN ELINOR, PEMBROKE, ESSEX, SALISBURY, *and others, with* CHATILLON.

K. John. Now, say, Chatillon, what would France with us?   [of France,
Chat. Thus, after greeting, speaks the King
In my behaviour, to the majesty,
The borrow'd majesty of England here.
Eli. A strange beginning;—borrow'd majesty!
K. John. Silence, good mother; hear the embassy.   [behalf
Chat. Philip of France, in right and true
Of thy deceased brother Geffrey's son,
Arthur Plantagenet, lays most lawful claim
To this fair island, and the territories,—
To Ireland, Poictiers, Anjou, Touraine, Maine;
Desiring thee to lay aside the sword
Which sways usurpingly these several titles,
And put the same into young Arthur's hand,
Thy nephew and right royal sovereign.
K. John. What follows, if we disallow of this?
Chat. The proud control of fierce and bloody war,
To enforce these rights so forcibly withheld.
K. John. Here have we war for war, and blood for blood,
Controlment for controlment: so answer France.

Chat. Then take my king's defiance from my mouth,
The furthest limit of my embassy.   [peace:
K. John. Bear mine to him, and so depart in
Be thou as lightning in the eyes of France;
For ere thou canst report I will be there,
The thunder of my cannon shall be heard:
So, hence! Be thou the trumpet of our wrath,
And sullen presage of your own decay.—
An honourable conduct let him have:—
Pembroke, look to 't. Farewell, Chatillon.
            [*Exeunt* CHATILLON *and* PEMBROKE.
Eli. What now, my son! have I not ever said
How that ambitious Constance would not cease
Till she had kindled France and all the world
Upon the right and party of her son?
That might have been prevented and made whole,
With very easy arguments of love;
Which now the manage of two kingdoms must
With fearful bloody issue arbitrate.
K. John. Our strong possession and our right for us.   [your right,
Eli. Your strong possession much more than
Or else it must go wrong with you and me:
So much my conscience whispers in your ear,
Which none but heaven and you and I shall hear.

Enter the Sheriff of Northamptonshire, *who whispers* ESSEX.

Essex. My liege, here is the strangest controversy,

I

Come from the country to be judg'd by you,
That e'er I heard: shall I produce the men?
  K. John. Let them approach.—
                     [*Exit* Sheriff.
Our abbeys and our priories shall pay
This expedition's charge.

Re-enter Sheriff, *with* ROBERT FALCONBRIDGE,
  and PHILIP, *his bastard Brother.*
           What men are you?
  Bast. Your faithful subject I, a gentleman
Born in Northamptonshire, and eldest son,
As I suppose, to Robert Falconbridge,—
A soldier, by the honour-giving hand
Of Cœur-de-lion knighted in the field.
  K. John. What art thou?
  Rob. The son and heir to that same Falcon-
    bridge.   [heir?
  K. John. Is that the elder, and art thou the
You came not of one mother, then, it seems.
  Bast. Most certain of one mother, mighty
    king,—
That is well known; and, as I think, one father:
But for the certain knowledge of that truth
I put you o'er to heaven and to my mother:—
Of that I doubt, as all men's children may.
  Eli. Out on thee, rude man! thou dost shame
    thy mother,
And wound her honour with this diffidence.
  Bast. I, madam? no, I have no reason for
    it,—
That is my brother's plea, and none of mine;
The which if he can prove, 'a pops me out
At least from fair five hundred pound a-year:
Heaven guard my mother's honour and my
    land!   [younger born,
  K. John. A good blunt fellow.—Why, being
Doth he lay claim to thine inheritance?
  Bast. I know not why, except to get the land.
But once he slander'd me with bastardy:
But whe'r I be as true begot or no,
That still I lay upon my mother's head;
But, that I am as well begot, my liege,—
Fair fall the bones that took the pains for me!—
Compare our faces, and be judge yourself.
If old Sir Robert did beget us both,
And were our father, and this son like him,—
O old Sir Robert, father, on my knee
I give heaven thanks I was not like to thee!
  K. John. Why, what a madcap hath heaven
    lent us here!
  Eli. He hath a trick of Cœur-de-lion's face;
The accent of his tongue affecteth him:
Do you not read some tokens of my son
In the large composition of this man?   [parts,
  K. John. Mine eye hath well examined his
And finds them perfect Richard.—Sirrah, speak,
What doth move you to claim your brother's
    land?   [father;
  Bast. Because he hath a half-face, like my
With that half-face would he have all my land:
A half-fac'd groat five hundred pound a-year!
  Rob. My gracious liege, when that my father
    liv'd,

Your brother did employ my father much,—
  Bast. Well, sir, by this you cannot get my
    land:
Your tale must be, how he employ'd my mother.
  Rob. And once despatch'd him in an embassy
To Germany, there with the emperor
To treat of high affairs touching that time.
The advantage of his absence took the king,
And in the meantime sojourn'd at my father's;
Where how he did prevail I shame to speak,—
But truth is truth: large lengths of seas and
    shores
Between my father and my mother lay,—
As I have heard my father speak himself,—
When this same lusty gentleman was got.
Upon his death-bed he by will bequeath'd
His lands to me; and took it, on his death,
That this, my mother's son, was none of his;
And if he were, he came into the world
Full fourteen weeks before the course of time.
Then, good my liege, let me have what is mine,
My father's land, as was my father's will.
  K. John. Sirrah, your brother is legitimate;
Your father's wife did after wedlock bear him;
And if she did play false, the fault was hers;
Which fault lies on the hazards of all husbands
That marry wives. Tell me, how if my brother,
Who, as you say, took pains to get this son,
Had of your father claim'd this son for his?
In sooth, good friend, your father might have
    kept
This calf, bred from his cow, from all the world;
In sooth, he might: then, if he were my
    brother's,   [father,
My brother might not claim him; nor your
Being none of his, refuse him. This concludes,—
My mother's son did get your father's heir;
Your father's heir must have your father's land.
  Rob. Shall, then, my father's will be of no
    force
To dispossess that child which is not his?
  Bast. Of no more force to dispossess me, sir,
Than was his will to get me, as I think.
  Eli. Whether hadst thou rather be a Falcon-
    bridge,
And like thy brother, to enjoy thy land,
Or the reputed son of Cœur-de-lion,
Lord of thy presence, and no land beside?
  Bast. Madam, an if my brother had my
    shape
And I had his, Sir Robert his, like him;
And if my legs were two such riding-rods,
My arms such eel-skins stuff'd, my face so thin
That in mine ear I durst not stick a rose
Lest men should say, *Look, where three-farthings
    goes!*
And, to his shape, were heir to all this land,
Would I might never stir from off this place,
I'd give it every foot to have this face;
I would not be Sir Nob in any case.
  Eli. I like thee well: wilt thou forsake thy
    fortune,
Bequeath thy land to him, and follow me?
I am a soldier, and now bound to France.

Bast. Brother, take you my land, I'll take
　my chance:
Your face hath got five hundred pound a-year;
Yet sell your face for fivepence, and 'tis dear.—
Madam, I'll follow you unto the death.
　Eli. Nay, I would have you go before me
　　thither.　　　　　　　　　　　　[way.
　Bast. Our country manners give our betters
　K. John. What is thy name?
　Bast. Philip, my liege; so is my name begun;
Philip, good old Sir Robert's wife's eldest son.
　K. John. From henceforth bear his name
　　whose form thou bear'st:
Kneel thou down Philip, but arise more great,—
Arise Sir Richard and Plantagenet.
　Bast. Brother by the mother's side, give me
　　your hand:
My father gave me honour, yours gave land.—
Now blessed be the hour, by night or day,
When I was got, Sir Robert was away!
　Eli. The very spirit of Plantagenet!—
I am thy grandam, Richard; call me so.
　Bast. Madam, by chance, but not by truth:
　　what though?
Something about, a little from the right,
　In at the window, or else o'er the hatch;
Who dares not stir by day must walk by night;
　And have is have, however men do catch:
Near or far off, well won is still well shot;
And I am I, howe'er I was begot.
　K. John. Go, Falconbridge; now hast thou
　　thy desire;
A landless knight makes thee a landed squire.—
Come, madam,—and come, Richard; we must
　　speed
For France, for France; for it is more than need.
　Bast. Brother, adieu: good fortune come to
　　thee!
For thou wast got i' the way of honesty.
　　　　　　　[Exeunt all except the BASTARD.
A foot of honour better than I was;
But many a many foot of land the worse.
Well, now can I make any Joan a lady:—
Good den, Sir Richard:—God-a-mercy, fellow:—
And if his name be George, I'll call him Peter:
For new-made honour doth forget men's names:
'Tis too respective and too sociable
For your conversion. Now your traveller,—
He and his toothpick at my worship's mess;
And when my knightly stomach is suffic'd,
Why then I suck my teeth, and catechize
My picked man of countries:—*My dear sir,*—
Thus, leaning on mine elbow, I begin,—
I shall beseech you—that is question now;
And then comes answer like an ABC-book:—
O sir, says answer, *at your best command;*
At your employment; at your service, sir:—
No sir, says question, *I, sweet sir, at yours:*
And so, ere answer knows what question
　　would,—
Saving in dialogue of compliment,
And talking of the Alps and Apennines,
The Pyrenean and the river Po,—
It draws towards supper in conclusion so.

But this is worshipful society,
And fits the mounting spirit like myself:
For he is but a bastard to the time,
That doth not smack of observation,—
And so am I, whether I smack or no;
And not alone in habit and device,
Exterior form, outward accoutrement,
But from the inward motion to deliver
Sweet, sweet, sweet poison for the age's tooth:
Which, though I will not practise to deceive,
Yet, to avoid deceit, I mean to learn;
For it shall strew the footsteps of my rising.—
But who comes in such haste before her?
What woman-post is this? hath she no husband,
That will take pains to blow a horn before her?

　　Enter LADY FALCONBRIDGE, *and* JAMES
　　　　　　GURNEY.

O me! it is my mother.—How now, good lady!
What brings you here to court so hastily?
　Lady F. Where is that slave, thy brother?
　　where is he
That holds in chase mine honour up and down?
　Bast. My brother Robert? old Sir Robert's
　　son?
Colbrand the giant, that same mighty man?
Is it Sir Robert's son that you seek so?
　Lady F. Sir Robert's son! Ay, thou un-
　　reverend boy,　　　　　　　　[Robert?
Sir Robert's son: why scorn'st thou at Sir
He is Sir Robert's son; and so art thou.
　Bast. James Gurney, wilt thou give us leave
　　awhile?
　Gur. Good leave, good Philip.
　Bast.　　　　　　Philip?—sparrow!—James,
There's toys abroad: anon I'll tell thee more.
　　　　　　　　　　　　　　[*Exit* GURNEY.
Madam, I was not old Sir Robert's son;
Sir Robert might have eat his part in me
Upon Good-Friday, and ne'er broke his fast:
Sir Robert could do well: marry, to confess,
Could not get me; Sir Robert could not do it,—
We know his handiwork:—therefore, good
　　mother,
To whom am I beholding for these limbs?
Sir Robert never holp to make this leg.
　Lady F. Hast thou conspired with thy
　　brother too,　　　　　　　　[honour?
That for thine own gain shouldst defend mine
What means this scorn, thou most untoward
　　knave?　　　　　　　　　　[isco-like:
　Bast. Knight, knight, good mother,—Basil-
What! am I dubb'd? I have it on my shoulder.
But, mother, I am not Sir Robert's son;
I have disclaim'd Sir Robert and my land;
Legitimation, name, and all is gone:
Then, good my mother, let me know my
　　father,—
Some proper man, I hope: who was it, mother?
　Lady F. Hast thou denied thyself a Falcon-
　　bridge?
　Bast. As faithfully as I deny the devil.
　Lady F. King Richard Cœur-de-lion was thy
　　father:

By long and vehement suit I was seduc'd
To make room for him in my husband's bed:—
Heaven lay not my transgression to my
    charge!—
Thou art the issue of my dear offence,
Which was so strongly urg'd, past my defence.
   Bast. Now, by this light, were I to get again,
Madam, I would not wish a better father.
Some sins do bear their privilege on earth,
And so doth yours; your fault was not your
    folly:
Needs must you lay your heart at his dispose,—
Subjected tribute to commanding love,—
Against whose fury and unmatched force
The aweless lion could not wage the fight,
Nor keep his princely heart from Richard's
    hand:
He that perforce robs lions of their hearts
May easily win a woman's. Ay, my mother,
With all my heart I thank thee for my father!
Who lives and dares but say, thou didst not well
When I was got, I'll send his soul to hell.
Come, lady, I will show thee to my kin;
  And they shall say, when Richard me begot,
If thou hadst said him nay, it had been sin:
  Who says it was, he lies; I say 'twas not.
                    [Exeunt.

ACT II.

SCENE I.—FRANCE. *Before the Walls of Angiers.*

Enter, on one side, the ARCHDUKE OF AUSTRIA
   and Forces; *on the other,* PHILIP, *King of*
   France, LOUIS, CONSTANCE, ARTHUR, *and*
   Forces.

   Lou. Before Angiers well met, brave Aus-
tria.—
Arthur, that great forerunner of thy blood,
Richard, that robb'd the lion of his heart,
And fought the holy wars in Palestine,
By this brave duke came early to his grave:
And, for amends to his posterity,
At our importance hither is he come
To spread his colours, boy, in thy behalf;
And to rebuke the usurpation
Of thy unnatural uncle, English John:
Embrace him, love him, give him welcome
    hither.   [death
   Arth. God shall forgive you Cœur-de-lion's
The rather that you give his offspring life,
Shadowing their right under your wings of war:
I give you welcome with a powerless hand,
But with a heart full of unstained love,—
Welcome before the gates of Angiers, duke.
   Lou. A noble boy! Who would not do thee
    right?
   Aust. Upon thy cheek lay I this zealous kiss,
As seal to this indenture of my love,—
That to my home I will no more return,
Till Angiers, and the right thou hast in France,
Together with that pale, that white-fac'd shore,
Whose foot spurns back the ocean's roaring
    tides,
And coops from other lands her islanders,—

Even till that England, hedg'd in with the main,
That water-walled bulwark still secure
And confident from foreign purposes,—
Even till that utmost corner of the west
Salute thee for her king: till then, fair boy,
Will I not think of home, but follow arms.
   Const. O, take his mother's thanks, a wid-
    ow's thanks,   [strength
Till your strong hand shall help to give him
To make a more requital to your love!
   Aust. The peace of heaven is theirs that lift
    their swords
In such a just and charitable war.
   K. Phi. Well, then, to work: our cannon
    shall be bent
Against the brows of this resisting town.—
Call for our chiefest men of discipline,
To cull the plots of best advantages:
We'll lay before this town our royal bones,
Wade to the market-place in Frenchman's
    blood,
But we will make it subject to this boy.
   Const. Stay for an answer to your embassy,
Lest unadvis'd you stain your swords with
    blood:
My Lord Chatillon may from England bring
That right in peace, which here we urge in war;
And then we shall repent each drop of blood
That hot rash haste so indirectly shed.
   K. Phi. A wonder, lady!—lo, upon thy wish,
Our messenger Chatillon is arriv'd!

Enter CHATILLON.

What England says, say briefly, gentle lord;
We coldly pause for thee; Chatillon, speak.
   Chat. Then turn your forces from this paltry
    siege,
And stir them up against a mightier task.
England, impatient of your just demands,
Hath put himself in arms: the adverse winds,
Whose leisure I have stay'd, have given him
    time
To land his legions all as soon as I;
His marches are expedient to this town,
His forces strong, his soldiers confident.
With him along is come the mother-queen,
An Até, stirring him to blood and strife;
With her her niece, the Lady Blanch of Spain;
With them a bastard of the king deceas'd:
And all the unsettled humours of the land,—
Rash, inconsiderate, fiery voluntaries,
With ladies' faces, and fierce dragons' spleens,—
Have sold their fortunes at their native homes,
Bearing their birthrights proudly on their
    backs,
To make a hazard of new fortunes here.
In brief, a braver choice of dauntless spirits,
Than now the English bottoms have waft o'er,
Did never float upon the swelling tide,
To do offence and scath in Christendom.
                  [Drums beat within.
The interruption of their churlish drums
Cuts off more circumstance: they are at hand,
To parley or to fight: therefore prepare.

K. Phi. How much unlook'd-for is this ex-
pedition!
Aust. By how much unexpected, by so much
We must awake endeavour for defence;
For courage mounteth with occasion:
Let them be welcome, then; we are prepar'd.

Enter KING JOHN, ELINOR, BLANCH, *the*
BASTARD, Lords, *and* Forces.

K. John. Peace be to France, if France in
peace permit
Our just and lineal entrance to our own!
If not, bleed France, and peace ascend to
heaven!
Whiles we, God's wrathful agent, do correct
Their proud contempt that beat his peace to
heaven.   [return
K. Phi. Peace be to England, if that war
From France to England, there to live in peace!
England we love; and for that England's sake
With burden of our armour here we sweat.
This toil of ours should be a work of thine;
But thou from loving England art so far,
That thou hast under-wrought his lawful king,
Cut off the sequence of posterity,
Outfaced infant state, and done a rape
Upon the maiden virtue of the crown.
Look here upon thy brother Geffrey's face;—
These eyes, these brows, were moulded out of
his:
This little abstract doth contain that large
Which died in Geffrey; and the hand of time
Shall draw this brief into as huge a volume.
That Geffrey was thy elder brother born,
And this his son; England was Geffrey's right,
And this is Geffrey's: in the name of God,
How comes it then, that thou art call'd a king,
When living blood doth in these temples beat,
Which owe the crown that thou o'ermasterest?
K. John. From whom hast thou this great
commission, France,
To draw my answer from thy articles?
K. Phi. From that supernal judge that stirs
good thoughts
In any breast of strong authority,
To look into the blots and stains of right.
That judge hath made me guardian to this boy:
Under whose warrant I impeach thy wrong;
And by whose help I mean to chástise it.
K. John. Alack, thou dost usurp authority.
K. Phi. Excuse,—it is to beat usurping
down.
Eli. Who is it thou dost call usurper, France?
Const. Let me make answer;—thy usurping
son.
Eli. Out, insolent! thy bastard shall be king,
That thou mayst be a queen, and check the
world!
Const. My bed was ever to thy son as true
As thine was to thy husband; and this boy
Liker in feature to his father Geffrey   [like
Than thou and John in manners,—being as
As rain to water, or devil to his dam.
My boy a bastard! By my soul, I think

His father never was so true begot:
It cannot be, an if thou wert his mother.
Eli. There's a good mother, boy, that blots
thy father.
Const. There's a good grandam, boy, that
would blot thee.
Aust. Peace!
Bast.   Hear the crier.
Aust.   What the devil art thou?
Bast. One that will play the devil, sir, with
you
An 'a man catch your hide and you alone.
You are the hare of whom the proverb goes,
Whose valour plucks dead lions by the beard:
I'll smoke your skin-coat an I catch you right;
Sirrah, look to 't; i' faith, I will, i' faith.
Blanch. O, well did he become that lion's
robe
That did disrobe the lion of that robe!
Bast. It lies as sightly on the back of him
As great Alcides' shoes upon an ass:—
But, ass, I'll take that burden from your back,
Or lay on that shall make your shoulders crack.
Aust. What cracker is this same that deafs
our ears
With this abundance of superfluous breath?
K. Phi. Louis, determine what we shall do
straight.   [ference.—
Lou. Women and fools, break off your con-
King John, this is the very sum of all,—
England and Ireland, Anjou, Touraine, Maine,
In right of Arthur, do I claim of thee:
Wilt thou resign them, and lay down thy arms?
K. John. My life as soon:—I do defy thee,
France.
Arthur of Bretagne, yield thee to my hand;
And out of my dear love, I'll give thee more
Than e'er the coward hand of France can win:
Submit thee, boy.
Eli.   Come to thy grandam, child.
Const. Do, child, go to it' grandam, child;
Give grandam kingdom, and it' grandam will
Give it a plum, a cherry, and a fig:
There's a good grandam.
Arth.   Good my mother, peace!
I would that I were low laid in my grave:
I am not worth this coil that's made for me.
Eli. His mother shames him so, poor boy,
he weeps.   [does or no!
Const. Now, shame upon you, whe'r she
His grandam's wrongs, and not his mother's
shames,   [poor eyes,
Draw those heaven-moving pearls from his
Which heaven shall take in nature of a fee:
Ay, with these crystal beads heaven shall be
brib'd
To do him justice, and revenge on you.
Eli. Thou monstrous slanderer of heaven
and earth!   [and earth!
Const. Thou monstrous injurer of heaven
Call not me slanderer; thou and thine usurp
The dominations, royalties, and rights   [son,
Of this oppressed boy: this is thy eldest son's
Infortunate in nothing but in thee:

Thy sins are visited in this poor child;
The canon of the law is laid on him,
Being but the second generation
Removed from thy sin-conceiving womb.
　K. John. Bedlam, have done.
　Const. 　　　　I have but this to say,—
That he is not only plagued for her sin,
But God hath made her sin and her the plague
On this removed issue, plagu'd for her,
And with her plague, her sin; his injury
Her injury,—the beadle to her sin;
All punish'd in the person of this child,
And all for her: a plague upon her!
　Eli. Thou unadvised scold, I can produce
A will that bars the title of thy son. 　[will;
　Const. Ay, who doubts that? a will! a wicked
A woman's will; a canker'd grandam's will!
　K. Phi. Peace, lady! pause, or be more temperate:
It ill beseems this presence to cry aim
To these ill-tuned repetitions.—
Some trumpet summon hither to the walls
These men of Angiers: let us hear them speak
Whose title they admit, Arthur's or John's.

Trumpet sounds. Enter Citizens *upon the walls.*

　1 *Cit.* Who is it that hath warn'd us to the walls?
　K. Phi. 'Tis France, for England.
　K. John. 　　　　England, for itself:—
You men of Angiers, and my loving subjects,—
　K. Phi. You loving men of Angiers, Arthur's subjects,
Our trumpet call'd you to this gentle parle.
　K. John. For our advantage; therefore hear us first.
These flags of France, that are advanced here
Before the eye and prospect of your town,
Have hither march'd to your endamagement:
The cannons have their bowels full of wrath,
And ready mounted are they to spit forth
Their iron indignation 'gainst your walls:
All preparation for a bloody siege
And merciless proceeding by these French
Confronts your city's eyes, your winking gates;
And, but for our approach, those sleeping stones,
That as a waist do girdle you about,
By the compulsion of their ordinance
By this time from their fixed beds of lime
Had been dishabited, and wide havoc made
For bloody power to rush upon your peace.
But, on the sight of us, your lawful king,—
Who painfully, with much expedient march,
Have brought a countercheck before your gates,
To save unscratch'd your city's threaten'd cheeks;
Behold, the French, amaz'd, vouchsafe a parle;
And now, instead of bullets wrapp'd in fire,
To make a shaking fever in your walls,
They shoot but calm words, folded up in smoke,
To make a faithless error in your ears:
Which trust accordingly, kind citizens,
And let us in, your king; whose labour'd spirits,

Forwearied in this action of swift speed,
Crave harbourage within your city-walls.
　K. Phi. When I have said, make answer to us both.
Lo, in this right hand, whose protection
Is most divinely vow'd upon the right
Of him it holds, stands young Plantagenet,
Son to the elder brother of this man,
And king o'er him and all that he enjoys:
For this down-trodden equity we tread
In war-like march these greens before your town;
Being no further enemy to you
Than the constraint of hospitable zeal
In the relief of this oppressed child
Religiously provokes. Be pleased, then,
To pay that duty which you truly owe
To him that owes it, namely, this young prince:
And then our arms, like to a muzzled bear,
Save in aspéct, have all offence seal'd up;
Our cannons' malice vainly shall be spent
Against the invulnerable clouds of heaven;
And with a blessed and unvex'd retire,
With unhack'd swords and helmets all unbruis'd,
We will bear home that lusty blood again
Which here we came to spout against your town,
And leave your children, wives, and you in peace.
But if you fondly pass our proffer'd offer,
'Tis not the rondure of your old-fac'd walls
Can hide you from our messengers of war,
Though all these English, and their discipline,
Were harbour'd in their rude circumference.
Then, tell us, shall your city call us lord
In that behalf which we have challeng'd it?
Or shall we give the signal to our rage,
And stalk in blood to our possession?
　1 *Cit.* In brief, we are the King of England's subjects:
For him, and in his right, we hold this town.
　K. John. Acknowledge then the king, and let me in.
　1 *Cit.* That can we not; but he that proves the king,
To him will we prove loyal: till that time
Have we ramm'd up our gates against the world.
　K. John. Doth not the crown of England prove the king?
And, if not that, I bring you witnesses,
Twice fifteen thousand hearts of England's breed,—
　Bast. Bastards, and else.
　K. John. To verify our title with their lives.
　K. Phi. As many and as well-born bloods as those,—
　Bast. Some bastards too.
　K. Phi. Stand in his face, to contradict his claim.
　1 *Cit.* Till you compound whose right is worthiest,
We for the worthiest hold the right from both.

K. John. Then God forgive the sin of all those souls
That to their everlasting residence,
Before the dew of evening fall, shall fleet,
In dreadful trial of our kingdom's king!
  K. Phi. Amen, Amen!—Mount, chevaliers! to arms!
  Bast. St. George, that swinged the dragon, and e'er since
Sits on his horse' back at mine hostess' door,
Teach us some fence!—Sirrah [*to* AUSTRIA], were I at home,
At your den, sirrah, with your lioness,
I would set an ox-head to your lion's hide,
And make a monster of you.
  Aust.   Peace! no more.
  Bast. O, tremble, for you hear the lion roar.
  K. John. Up higher to the plain; where we'll set forth
In best appointment all our regiments. [*field.*
  Bast. Speed, then, to take advantage of the
  K. Phi. It shall be so;—[*to* LOUIS] and at the other hill
Command the rest to stand.—God and our right!   [*Exeunt severally.*

After Excursions, enter a French Herald, *with trumpets, to the gates.*

  F. Her. You men of Angiers, open wide your gates,
And let young Arthur, Duke of Bretagne, in,
Who, by the hand of France, this day hath made
Much work for tears in many an English mother,
Whose sons lie scatter'd on the bleeding ground;
Many a widow's husband grovelling lies,
Coldly embracing the discolour'd earth;
And victory, with little loss, doth play
Upon the dancing banners of the French,
Who are at hand triumphantly display'd.
To enter conquerors, and to proclaim
Arthur of Bretagne England's king and yours.

Enter an English Herald, *with trumpets.*

  E. Her. Rejoice, you men of Angiers, ring your bells;   [proach,
King John, your king and England's, doth ap-
Commander of this hot malicious day:
Their armours, that march'd hence so silver-bright,
Hither return all gilt with Frenchmen's blood;
There stuck no plume in any English crest
That is removed by a staff of France;
Our colours do return in those same hands
That did display them when we first march'd forth;
And, like a jolly troop of huntsmen, come
Our lusty English, all with purpled hands,
Dy'd in the dying slaughter of their foes:
Open your gates, and give the victors way.
  1 Cit. Heralds, from off our towers, we might behold,

From first to last, the onset and retire
Of both your armies, whose equality
By our best eyes cannot be censured:
Blood hath bought blood, and blows have answer'd blows;
Strength match'd with strength, and power confronted power:
Both are alike; and both alike we like.
One must prove greatest: while they weigh so even
We hold our town for neither; yet for both.

Re-enter, on one side, KING JOHN, ELINOR, BLANCH, *the* BASTARD, *and* Forces; *at the other,* KING PHILIP, LOUIS, AUSTRIA, *and* Forces.

  K. John. France, hast thou yet more blood to cast away?
Say, shall the current of our right run on?
Whose passage, vex'd with thy impediment,
Shall leave his native channel, and o'erswell
With course disturb'd even thy confining shores,
Unless thou let his silver water keep
A peaceful progress to the ocean.
  K. Phi. England, thou hast not sav'd one drop of blood,
In this hot trial, more than we of France;
Rather, lost more: and by this hand I swear,
That sways the earth this climate overlooks,
Before we will lay down our just-borne arms,
We'll put thee down, 'gainst whom these arms we bear,
Or add a royal number to the dead,
Gracing the scroll that tells of this war's loss
With slaughter coupled to the name of kings
  Bast. Ha, majesty! how high thy glory towers
When the rich blood of kings is set on fire!
O, now doth Death line his dead chaps with steel;
The swords of soldiers are his teeth, his fangs;
And now he feasts, mousing the flesh of men,
In undetermin'd differences of kings.—
Why stand these royal fronts amazed thus?
Cry, havoc, kings! back to the stained field,
You equal potentates, fiery-kindled spirits!
Then let confusion of one part confirm
The other's peace; till then, blows, blood, and death!   [admit?
  K. John. Whose party do the townsmen yet
  K. Phi. Speak, citizens, for England; who's your king?   [the king.
  1 Cit. The king of England, when we know
  K. Phi. Know him in us, that here hold up his right.
  K. John. In us, that are our own great deputy,
And bear possession of our person here;
Lord of our presence, Angiers, and of you.
  1 Cit. A greater power than we denies all this;
And till it be undoubted, we do lock
Our former scruple in our strong-barr'd gates;
King'd of our fear, until our fears, resolv'd,

Be by some certain king purg'd and depos'd.

   Bast. By heaven, these scroyles of Angiers
      flout you, kings,
And stand securely on their battlements
As in a theatre, whence they gape and point
At your industrious scenes and acts of death.
Your royal presences be rul'd by me:—
Do like the mutines of Jerusalem,
Be friends awhile, and both conjointly bend
Your sharpest deeds of malice on this town:
By east and west let France and England mount
Their battering cannon, charged to the mouths,
Till their soul-fearing clamours have brawl'd
    down
The flinty ribs of this contemptuous city:
I'd play incessantly upon these jades,
Even till unfenced desolation
Leave them as naked as the vulgar air.
That done, dissever your united strengths,
And part your mingled colours once again:
Turn face to face, and bloody point to point;
Then, in a moment, fortune shall cull forth
Out of one side her happy minion,
To whom in favour she shall give the day,
And kiss him with a glorious victory.
How like you this wild counsel, mighty states?
Smacks it not something of the policy?

   K. John. Now, by the sky that hangs above
     our heads,
I like it well.—France, shall we knit our powers,
And lay this Angiers even with the ground;
Then, after, fight who shall be king of it?

   Bast. And if thou hast the mettle of a king,—
Being wrong'd, as we are, by this peevish
    town,—
Turn thou the mouth of thy artillery,
As we will ours, against these saucy walls;
And when that we have dash'd them to the
    ground,
Why, then defy each other, and, pell-mell,
Make work upon ourselves, for heaven or hell!

   K. Phi. Let it be so.—Say, where will you
     assault?   'struction

   K. John. We from the west will send de-
Into this city's bosom.

   Aust. I from the north.

   K. Phi.   Our thunder from the south
Shall rain their drift of bullets on this town.

   Bast. O prudent discipline! From north to
    south,—
Austria and France shoot in each other's
    mouth: [away!
I'll stir them to it. [*Aside.*]—Come, away,

   1 *Cit.* Hear us, great kings: vouchsafe awhile
    to stay,
And I shall show you peace and fair-fac'd
    league;
Win you this city without stroke or wound;
Rescue those breathing lives to die in beds,
That here come sacrifices for the field:
Perséver not, but hear me, mighty kings.

   K. John. Speak on, with favour; we are bent
    to hear.   [Lady Blanch,

   1 *Cit.* That daughter there of Spain, the

Is neice to England:—look upon the years
Of Louis the Dauphin, and that lovely maid:
If lusty love should go in quest of beauty,
Where should he find it fairer than in Blanch?
If zealous love should go in search of virtue,
Where should he find it purer than in Blanch?
If love ambitious sought a match of birth,
Whose veins bound richer blood than Lady
    Blanch?
Such as she is, in beauty, virtue, birth,
Is the young Dauphin every way complete,—
If not complete of, say he is not she;
And she again wants nothing, to name want,
If want it be not, that she is not he:
He is the half part of a blessed man,
Left to be finished by such a she;
And she a fair divided excellence,
Whose fulness of perfection lies in him.
O, two such silver currents, when they join
Do glorify the banks that bound them in;
And two such shores to two such streams made
    one,
Two such controlling bounds shall you be,
    kings,
To these two princes, if you marry them.
This union shall do more than battery can
To our fast-closed gates; for, at this match,
With swifter spleen than powder can enforce,
The mouth of passage shall we fling wide ope,
And give you entrance; but without this match,
The sea enraged is not half so deaf,
Lions more confident, mountains and rocks
More free from motion; no, not Death himself
In mortal fury half so peremptory,
As we to keep this city.

   Bast.   Here's a stay,
That shakes the rotten carcase of old Death
Out of his rags! Here's a large mouth, indeed,
That spits forth death and mountains, rocks
    and seas;
Talks as familiarly of roaring lions
As maids of thirteen do of puppy-dogs!
What cannoneer begot this lusty blood?
He speaks plain cannon,—fire and smoke and
    bounce;
He gives the bastinado with his tongue;
Our ears are cudgell'd; not a word of his
But buffets better than a fist of France:
Zounds! I was never so bethump'd with words
Since I first called my brother's father dad.

   Eli. Son, list to this conjunction, make this
    match;
Give with our niece a dowry large enough:
For by this knot thou shalt so surely tie
Thy now unsur'd assurance to the crown,
That yon green boy shall have no sun to ripe
The bloom that promiseth a mighty fruit.
I see a yielding in the looks of France;
Mark how they whisper: urge them while their
    souls
Are capable of this ambition,
Lest zeal, now melted by the windy breath
Of soft petitions, pity, and remorse,
Cool and congeal again to what it was.

1 Cit. Why answer not the double majesties
This friendly treaty of our threaten'd town?
    K. Phi. Speak England first, that hath been
    forward first ·
To speak unto this city: what say you?
    K. John. If that the Dauphin there, thy
    princely son,
Can in this book of beauty read, "I love,"
Her dowry shall weigh equal with a queen:
For Anjou, and fair Touraine, Maine, Poictiers,
And all that we upon this side the sea,—
Except this city now by us besieg'd,—
Find liable to our crown and dignity,
Shall gild her bridal bed; and make her rich
In titles, honours, and promotions,
As she in beauty, education, blood,
Holds hand with any princess of the world.
    K. Phi. What say'st thou, boy? look in the
    lady's face.
    Lou. I do, my lord, and in her eye I find
A wonder, or a wondrous miracle,
The shadow of myself form'd in her eye;
Which, being but the shadow of your son,
Becomes a sun, and makes your son a shadow:
I do protest I never lov'd myself
Till now infixed I beheld myself
Drawn in the flattering table of her eye.
                        [Whispers with BLANCH.
    Bast. [*Aside.*] Drawn in the flattering table
    of her eye!—
    Hang'd in the frowning wrinkle of her
    brow!—
And quarter'd in her heart!—he doth espy
    Himself love's traitor! This is pity now,
That, hang'd, and drawn, and quarter'd, there
    should be
In such a love so vile a lout as he.
    Blanch. My uncle's will in this respect is
    mine.
If he see aught in you that makes him like,
That anything he sees, which moves his liking,
I can with ease translate it to my will;
Or if you will, to speak more properly,
I will enforce it easily to my love.
Further, I will not flatter you, my lord,
That all I see in you is worthy love,
Than this,—that nothing do I see in you,
Though churlish thoughts themselves should
    be your judge,—
That I can find should merit any hate.
    K. John. What say these young ones?—
    What say you, my niece?   [do
    Blanch. That she is bound in honour still to
What you in wisdom still vouchsafe to say.
    K. John. Speak then, Prince Dauphin; can
    you love this lady?
    Lou. Nay, ask me if I can refrain from love;
For I do love her most unfeignedly.
    K. John. Then do I give Volquessen, Tou-
    raine, Maine,
Poictiers, and Anjou, these five provinces,
With her to thee; and this addition more,
Full thirty thousand marks of English coin.—
Philip of France, if thou be pleas'd withal,

Command thy son and daughter to join hands.
    K. Phi. It likes us well.—Young princes,
    close your hands.
    Aust. And your lips too; for I am well assur'd
That I did so when I was first assur'd.
    K. Phi. Now, citizens of Angiers, ope your
    gates,
Let in that amity which you have made;
For at Saint Mary's chapel presently
The rites of marriage shall be solemniz'd.—
Is not the Lady Constance in this troop?
I know she is not; for this match made up
Her presence would have interrupted much:
Where is she and her son? tell me, who knows.
    Lou. She is sad and passionate at your high-
    ness' tent.
    K. Phi. And, by my faith, this league that
    we have made
Will give her sadness very little cure.—
Brother of England, how may we content
This widow lady? In her right we came;
Which we, God knows, have turn'd another
    way,
To our own vantage.
    K. John.   We will heal up all;
For we'll create young Arthur Duke of Bretagne
And Earl of Richmond; and this rich fair town
We make him lord of.—Call the Lady Con-
    stance:
Some speedy messenger bid her repair
To our solemnity:—I trust we shall,
If not fill up the measure of her will?
Yet in some measure satisfy her so
That we shall stop her exclamation.
Go we, as well as haste will suffer us,
To this unlook'd-for, unprepared pomp.
           [*Exeunt all but the* BASTARD. *The* Citizens
                      retire from the Walls.
    Bast. Mad world! mad kings! mad composi-
    tion!
John, to stop Arthur's title in the whole,
Hath willingly departed with a part;
And France,—whose armour conscience buck-
    led on,
Whom zeal and charity brought to the field
As God's own soldier,—rounded in the ear
With that same purpose-changer, that sly devil;
That broker, that still breaks the pate of faith;
That daily break-vow; he that wins of all,
Of kings, of beggars, old men, young men,
    maids,—
Who having no external thing to lose
But the word maid, cheats the poor maid of
    that;
That smooth-fac'd gentleman, tickling com-
    modity,—
Commodity, the bias of the world;
The world, who of itself is peised well,
Made to run even upon even ground,
Till this advantage, this vile-drawing bias,
This sway of motion, this commodity,
Makes it take head from all indifferency,
From all direction, purpose, course, intent:
And this same bias, this commodity,

This bawd, this broker, this all-changing word,
Clapp'd on the outward eye of fickle France,
Hath drawn him from his own determin'd aid,
From a resolv'd and honourable war,
To a most base and vile-concluded peace.—
And why rail I on this commodity?
But for because he hath not woo'd me yet:
Not that I have the power to clutch my hand
When his fair angels would salute my palm;
But for my hand, as unattempted yet,
Like a poor beggar, raileth on the rich.
Well, whiles I am a beggar, I will rail,
And say, There is no sin but to be rich;
And, being rich, my virtue then shall be,
To say, There is no vice but beggary:
Since kings break faith upon commodity,
Gain, be my lord!—for I will worship thee.
         [*Exit.*

ACT III.

SCENE I.—FRANCE. *The* French King's *Tent.*

Enter CONSTANCE, ARTHUR, *and* SALISBURY.

  Const. Gone to be married! gone to swear a
     peace!
False blood to false blood join'd! gone to be
     friends!
Shall Louis have Blanch? and Blanch those
     provinces?
It is not so; thou hast misspoke, misheard;
Be well advis'd, tell o'er thy tale again:
It cannot be; thou dost but say 'tis so:
I trust I may not trust thee; for thy word
Is but the vain breath of a common man:
Believe me, I do not believe thee, man;
I have a king's oath to the contrary.
Thou shalt be punish'd for thus frighting me,
For I am sick, and capable of fears;
Oppress'd with wrongs, and therefore full of
     fears;
A widow, husbandless, subject to fears;
A woman, naturally born to fears;
And though thou now confess thou didst but
     jest,
With my vex'd spirits I cannot take a truce,
But they will quake and tremble all this day.
What dost thou mean by shaking of thy head?
Why dost thou look so sadly on my son?
What means that hand upon that breast of
     thine?
Why holds thine eye that lamentable rheum,
Like a proud river peering o'er its bounds?
Be these sad signs confirmers of thy words?
Then speak again,—not all thy former tale,
But this one word, whether thy tale be true.
  Sal. As true as I believe you think them false
That give you cause to prove my saying true.
  Const. O, if thou teach me to believe this
     sorrow,
Teach thou this sorrow how to make me die;
And let belief and life encounter so
As doth the fury of two desperate men,
Which in the very meeting fall and die!—

Louis marry Blanch! O boy, then where art
     thou?   [me?—
France friend with England! what becomes of
Fellow, be gone: I cannot brook thy sight;
This news hath made thee a most ugly man.
  Sal. What other harm have I, good lady,
     done,
But spoke the harm that is by others done?
  Const. Which harm within itself so heinous is,
As it makes harmful all that speak of it.
  Arth. I do beseech you, madam, be content.
  Const. If thou, that bid'st me be content,
     wert grim,
Ugly, and slanderous to thy mother's womb,
Full of unpleasing blots and sightless stains,
Lame, foolish, crooked, swart, prodigious,
Patch'd with foul moles and eye-offending
     marks,
I would not care, I then would be content;
For then I should not love thee; no, nor thou
Become thy great birth, nor deserve a crown.
But thou art fair; and at thy birth, dear boy,
Nature and fortune join'd to make thee great:
Of nature's gifts thou mayst with lilies boast,
And with the half-blown rose: but Fortune, O!
She is corrupted, chang'd, and won from thee;
She adulterates hourly with thine uncle John;
And with her golden hand hath pluck'd on
     France
To tread down fair respect of sovereignty,
And make his majesty the bawd to theirs.
France is a bawd to Fortune, and king John—
That strumpet Fortune, that usurping John!—·
Tell me, thou fellow, is not France forsworn?
Envenom him with words; or get thee gone,
And leave those woes alone, which I alone
Am bound to under-bear.
  Sal.   Pardon me, madam,
I may not go without you to the kings.
  Const. Thou mayst, thou shalt; I will not go
     with thee:
I will instruct my sorrows to be proud;
For grief is proud, and makes his honour stout.
To me, and to the state of my great grief,
Let kings assemble; for my grief's so great
That no supporter but the huge firm earth
Can hold it up: here I and sorrows sit;
Here is my throne, bid kings come bow to it.
         [*Seats herself on the ground.*

Enter KING JOHN, KING PHILIP, LOUIS,
     BLANCH, ELINOR, BASTARD, AUSTRIA, *and*
     Attendants.

  K. Phi. 'Tis true, fair daughter; and this
     blessed day
Ever in France shall be kept festival:
To solemnize this day the glorious sun
Stays in his course, and plays the alchemist,
Turning, with splendour of his precious eye,
The meagre cloddy earth to glittering gold:
The yearly course that brings this day about
Shall never see it bud a holiday.
  Const. A wicked day, and not a holy day!
         [*Rising.*

What hath this day deserv'd? what hath it
done,
That it in golden letters should be set
Among the high tides in the calendar?
Nay, rather turn this day out of the week,
This day of shame, oppression, perjury:
Or, if it must stand still, let wives with child
Pray that their burdens may not fall this day,
Lest that their hopes prodigiously be cross'd:
But on this day let seamen fear no wreck;
No bargains break that are not this day made:
This day, all things begun come to ill end,—
Yea, faith itself to hollow falsehood change!

    K. Phi. By heaven, lady, you shall have no
cause
To curse the fair proceedings of this day.
Have I not pawn'd to you my majesty?

    Const. You have beguil'd me with a counter-
feit   [tried,
Resembling majesty; which, being touch'd and
Proves valueless: you are forsworn, forsworn:
You came in arms to spill mine enemies' blood,
But now in arms you strengthen it with yours:
The grappling vigour and rough frown of war
Is cold in amity and painted peace,
And our oppression hath made up this league.—
Arm, arm, you heavens, against these perjur'd
kings!
A widow cries; be husband to me, heavens!
Let not the hours of this ungodly day
Wear out the day in peace; but, ere sunset,
Set armed discord 'twixt these perjur'd kings!
Hear me, O, hear me!

    Aust.   Lady Constance, peace.

    Const. War! war! no peace! peace is to me
a war.
O Lymoges! O Austria! thou dost shame
That bloody spoil: thou slave, thou wretch,
thou coward!
Thou little valiant, great in villany!
Thou ever strong upon the stronger side!
Thou Fortune's champion that dost never fight
But when her humorous ladyship is by
To teach thee safety!—thou art perjur'd too,
And sooth'st up greatness. What a fool art
thou,
A ramping fool, to brag, and stamp, and swear
Upon thy party! Thou cold-blooded slave,
Hast thou not spoke like thunder on my side?
Been sworn my soldier? bidding me depend
Upon thy stars, thy fortune, and thy strength?
And dost thou now fall over to my foes?
Thou wear a lion's hide! doff it for shame,
And hang a calf's-skin on those recreant limbs!

    Aust. O, that a man should speak those
words to me!   [limbs.

    Bast. And hang a calf's-skin on those recreant

    Aust. Thou dar'st not say so, villain, for thy
life.

    Bast. And hang a calf's-skin on those recre-
ant limbs.

    K. John. We like not this; thou dost forget
thyself.   [pope.

    K. Phi. Here comes the holy legate of the

               Enter PANDULPH.

    Pand. Hail, you anointed deputies of
heaven!—
To thee, King John, my holy errand is.
I Pandulph, of fair Milan cardinal,
And from Pope Innocent the legate here,
Do in his name religiously demand,
Why thou against the church, our holy mother,
So wilfully dost spurn; and, force perforce,
Keep Stephen Langton, chosen archbishop
Of Canterbury, from that holy see?
This, in our foresaid holy father's name,
Pope Innocent, I do demand of thee.

    K. John. What earthly name to interroga-
tories
Can task the free breath of a sacred king?
Thou canst not, cardinal, devise a name
So slight, unworthy, and ridiculous,
To charge me to an answer, as the pope.
Tell him this tale; and from the mouth of
England
Add thus much more,—That no Italian priest
Shall tithe or toll in our dominions:
But as we under heaven are supreme head,
So, under him, that great supremacy,
Where we do reign, we will alone uphold,
Without the assistance of a mortal hand:
So tell the pope; all reverence set apart
To him and his usurp'd authority.

    K. Phi. Brother of England, you blaspheme
in this.   [Christendom,

    K. John. Though you, and all the kings of
Are led so grossly by this meddling priest,
Dreading the curse that money may buy out;
And by the merit of vile gold, dross, dust,
Purchase corrupted pardon of a man,
Who in that sale sells pardon from himself;
Though you and all the rest, so grossly led,
This juggling witchcraft with revenue cherish;
Yet I, alone, alone do me oppose
Against the pope, and count his friends my
foes.

    Pand. Then, by the lawful power that I have,
Thou shalt stand curs'd and excommunicate:
And blessed shall he be that doth revolt
From his allegiance to an heretic;
And meritorious shall that hand be call'd,
Canonized, and worshipp'd as a saint,
That takes away by any secret course
Thy hateful life.

    Const.   O, lawful let it be
That I have room with Rome to curse awhile!
Good father cardinal, cry thou amen
To my keen curses: for without my wrong
There is no tongue hath power to curse him
right.   [my curse.

    Pand. There's law and warrant, lady, for

    Const. And for mine too: when law can do
no right,
Let it be lawful that law bar no wrong:
Law cannot give my child his kingdom here;
For he that holds his kingdom holds the law:
Therefore, since law itself is perfect wrong,

How can the law forbid my tongue to curse?

Pand. Philip of France, on peril of a curse,
Let go the hand of that arch-heretic;
And raise the power of France upon his head,
Unless he do submit himself to Rome.

Eli. Look'st thou pale, France; do not let
go thy hand.   [repent

Const. Look to that, devil; lest that France
And, by disjoining hands, hell lose a soul.

Aust. King Philip, listen to the cardinal.

Bast. And hang a calf's-skin on his recreant
limbs.   [wrongs,

Aust. Well, ruffian, I must pocket up these
Because—

Bast. Your breeches best may carry them.

K. John. Philip, what say'st thou to the
cardinal?   [cardinal?

Const. What should he say, but as the

Lou. Bethink you, father; for the difference
Is, purchase of a heavy curse from Rome,
Or the light loss of England for a friend:
Forego the easier.

Blanch.   That's the curse of Rome.

Const. O Louis, stand fast! the devil tempts
thee here
In likeness of a new uptrimmed bride.

Blanch. The Lady Constance speaks not
from her faith,
But from her need.

Const.   O, if thou grant my need,
Which only lives but by the death of faith,
That need must needs infer this principle,—
That faith would live again by death of need!
O, then, tread down my need, and faith mounts
up;
Keep my need up, and faith is trodden down!

K. John. The king is mov'd, and answers not
to this.   [well!

Const. O, be remov'd from him, and answer

Aust. Do so, King Philip; hang no more in
doubt.   [sweet lout.

Bast. Hang nothing but a calf's-skin, most

K. Phi. I am perplex'd, and know not what
to say.   [thee more,

Pand. What canst thou say, but will preplex
If thou stand excommunicate and curs'd?

K. Phi. Good reverend father, make my
person yours,
And tell me how you would bestow yourself.
This royal hand and mine are newly knit,
And the conjunction of our inward souls
Married in league, coupled and link'd together
With all religious strength of sacred vows;
The latest breath that gave the sound of words
Was deep-sworn faith, peace, amity, true love,
Between our kingdoms and our royal selves,
And even before this truce, but new before,—
No longer than we well could wash our hands,
To clap this royal bargain up of peace,—
Heaven knows, they were besmear'd and over-
stain'd
With slaughter's pencil, where revenge did
paint
The fearful difference of incensed kings:

And shall these hands, so lately purg'd of blood,
So newly joined in love, so strong in both,
Unyoke this seizure and this kind regreet?
Play fast and loose with faith? so jest with
heaven,
Make such unconstant children of ourselves,
As now again to snatch our palm from palm;
Unswear faith sworn; and on the marriage-bed
Of smiling peace to march a bloody host,
And make a riot on the gentle brow
Of true sincerity? O, holy sir,
My reverend father, let it not be so!
Out of your grace, devise, ordain, impose
Some gentle order; and then we shall be bless'd
To do your pleasure, and continue friends.

Pand. All form is formless, order orderless,
Save what is opposite to England's love.
Therefore, to arms! be champion of our church!
Or let the church, our mother, breathe her
curse,—
A mother's curse,—on her revolting son.
France, thou mayst hold a serpent by the
tongue,
A chafed lion by the mortal paw,
A fasting tiger safer by the tooth,   [hold.
Than keep in peace that hand which thou dost

K. Phi. I may disjoin my hand, but not my
faith.   [faith.

Pand. So mak'st thou faith an enemy to
And, like a civil war, sett'st oath to oath,
Thy tongue against thy tongue. O, let thy vow
First made to heaven, first be to heaven per-
form'd,—
That is, to be the champion of our church!
What since thou swor'st·is sworn against thy-
self,
And may not be performed by thyself:
For that which thou hast sworn to do amiss
Is not amiss when it is truly done;
And being not done, where doing tends to ill,
The truth is then most done not doing it:
The better act of purposes mistook
Is to mistake again; though indirect,
Yet indirection thereby grows direct,
And falsehood falsehood cures; as fire cools fire
Within the scorched veins of one new burn'd.
It is religion that doth make vows kept;
But thou hast sworn against religion,
By what thou swear'st against the thing thou
swear'st;
And mak'st an oath the surety for thy truth
Against an oath: the truth thou art unsure
To swear, swears only not to be forsworn;
Else what a mockery should it be to swear!
But thou dost swear only to be forsworn;
And most forsworn, to keep what thou dost
swear.
Therefore thy latter vows against thy first
Is in thyself rebellion to thyself;
And better conquest never canst thou make
Than arm thy constant and thy nobler parts
Against these giddy loose suggestions:
Upon which better part our prayers come in,
If thou vouchsafe them; but if not, then know

The peril of our curses light on thee,
So heavy as thou shalt not shake them off,
But in despair die under their black weight.
　Aust. Rebellion, flat rebellion!
　Bast.　　　　　　　　　　　　Will 't not be?
Will not a calf's-skin stop that mouth of thine?
　Lou. Father, to arms!
　Blanch.　　　　　　　Upon thy wedding-day?
Against the blood that thou hast married?
What, shall our feast be kept with slaughter'd
　　men?
Shall braying trumpets and loud churlish
　　drums,—
Clamours of hell,—be measures to our pomp?
O husband, hear me!—ay, alack, how new
Is husband in my mouth!—even for that name,
Which till this time my tongue did ne'er pro-
　　nounce,
Upon my knee I beg, go not to arms
Against mine uncle.
　Const.　　　　　　O, upon my knee,
Made hard with kneeling, I do pray to thee,
Thou virtuous Dauphin, alter not the doom
Forethought by heaven.
　Blanch. Now shall I see thy love: what mo-
　　tive may
Be stronger with thee than the name of wife?
　Const. That which upholdeth him that thee
　　upholds,
His honour:—O, thine honour, Louis, thine
　　honour!
　Lou. I muse your majesty doth seem so cold,
When such profound respects do pull you on.
　Pand. I will denounce a curse upon his head.
　K. Phi. Thou shalt not need.—England, I
　　will fall from thee.
　Const. O fair return of banish'd majesty!
　Eli. O foul revolt of French inconstancy!
　K. John. France, thou shalt rue this hour
　　within this hour.
　Bast. Old Time the clock-setter, that bald
　　sexton Time,
Is it as he will? well, then, France shall rue.
　Blanch. The sun's o'ercast with blood: fair
　　day, adieu!
Which is the side that I must go withal?
I am with both: each army hath a hand;
And in their rage, I having hold of both,
They whirl asunder and dismember me.
Husband, I cannot pray that thou mayst win;
Uncle, I needs must pray that thou mayst lose;
Father, I may not wish the fortune thine;
Grandam, I will not wish thy wishes thrive;
Whoever wins, on that side shall I lose;
Assured loss before the match be play'd.
　Lou. Lady, with me; with me thy fortune
　　lies.
　Blanch. There where my fortune lives, there
　　my life dies.
　K. John. Cousin, go draw our puissance to-
　　gether.—　　　　　　　[*Exit* BASTARD.
France, I am burn'd up with inflaming wrath;
A rage whose heat hath this condition,
That nothing can allay, nothing but blood,—

The blood, and dearest-valu'd blood of France.
　K. Phi. Thy rage shall burn thee up, and
　　thou shalt turn
To ashes, ere our blood shall quench that fire:
Look to thyself, thou art in jeopardy.
　K. John. No more than he that threats.—To
　　arms let's hie!　　　　　　[*Exeunt severally.*

SCENE II.—*The same. Plains near Angiers.*

Alarums. Excursions. Enter the BASTARD, *with*
AUSTRIA'S *head.*

　Bast. Now, by my life, this day grows won-
　　drous hot;
Some airy devil hovers in the sky,　　　[there,
And pours down mischief.—Austria's head lie
While Philip breathes.

Enter KING JOHN, ARTHUR, *and* HUBERT.

　K. John. Hubert, keep this boy.—Philip,
　　make up:
My mother is assailed in our tent,
And ta'en, I fear.
　Bast.　　　　　My lord, I rescu'd her;
Her highness is in safety, fear you not:
But on, my liege; for very little pains
Will bring this labour to an happy end.,
　　　　　　　　　　　　　　　[*Exeunt.*

SCENE III.—*The same.*

Alarums, Excursions, Retreat. Enter KING
JOHN, ELINOR, ARTHUR, *the* BASTARD,
HUBERT, *and* Lords.

　K. John. So shall it be; your grace shall stay
　　behind,　　　　　　　　　[*To* ELINOR.
So strongly guarded.—Cousin, look not sad:
　　　　　　　　　　　　　　[*To* ARTHUR.
Thy grandam loves thee; and thy uncle will
As dear be to thee as thy father was.　[grief!
　Arth. O, this will make my mother die with
　K. John. Cousin [*to the* BASTARD], away for
　　England; haste before:
And, ere our coming, see thou shake the bags
Of hoarding abbots; imprison'd angels
Set at liberty: the fat ribs of peace
Must by the hungry now be fed upon:
Use our commission in his utmost force.
　Bast. Bell, book, and candle shall not drive
　　me back,
When gold and silver becks me to come on.
I leave your highness.—Grandam, I will pray,—
If ever I remember to be holy,—
For your fair safety; so, I kiss your hand.
　Eli. Farewell, gentle cousin.
　K. John. Coz, farewell.　[*Exit* BASTARD.
　Eli. Come hither, little kinsman; hark a
　　word.　　　　[*She takes* ARTHUR *aside.*
　K. John. Come hither, Hubert. O my gentle
　　Hubert,
We owe thee much! within this wall of flesh
There is a soul counts thee her creditor,
And with advantage means to pay thy love:
And, my good friend, thy voluntary oath

Lives in this bosom, dearly cherished.
Give me thy hand. I had a thing to say,—
But I will fit it with some better time.
By heaven, Hubert, I am almost asham'd
To say what good respect I have of thee.
  Hub. I am much bounden to your majesty.
  K. John. Good friend, thou hast no cause to
    say so yet:
But thou shalt have; and creep time ne'er so
    slow,
Yet it shall come for me to do thee good.
I had a thing to say,—but let it go:
The sun is in the heaven, and the proud day,
Attended with the pleasures of the world,
Is all too wanton and too full of gawds
To give me audience:—if the midnight bell
Did, with his iron tongue and brazen mouth,
Sound one unto the drowsy ear of night;
If this same were a churchyard where we stand,
And thou possessed with a thousand wrongs;
Or if that surly spirit, melancholy,   [thick,—
Had bak'd thy blood, and made it heavy,
Which else runs tickling up and down the veins,
Making that idiot, laughter, keep men's eyes,
And strain their cheeks to idle merriment—
A passion hateful to my purposes;—
Or if that thou couldst see me without eyes,
Hear me without thine ears, and make reply
Without a tongue, using conceit alone,
Without eyes, ears, and harmful sound of
    words,—
Then, in despite of brooded watchful day,
I would into thy bosom pour my thoughts:
But, ah, I will not!—yet I love thee well;
And, by my troth, I think thou lov'st me well.
  Hub. So well that what you bid me under-
    take;
Though that my death were adjunct to my act,
By heaven, I would do it.
  K. John.   Do not I know thou wouldst?
Good Hubert, Hubert, Hubert, throw thine
    eye
On yon young boy: I'll tell thee what, my
    friend,
He is a very serpent in my way;
And wheresoe'er this foot of mine doth tread,
He lies before me:—dost thou understand me?
Thou art his keeper.
  Hub.   And I'll keep him so
That he shall not offend your majesty.
  K. John. Death.
  Hub.   My lord?
  K. John.   A grave.
  Hub.   He shall not live.
  K. John.   Enough.—
I could be merry now. Hubert, I love thee:
Well, I'll not say what I intend for thee:
Remember.—Madam, fare you well:
I'll send those powers o'er to your majesty.
  Eli. My blessing go with thee!
  K. John.   For England, cousin, go:
Hubert shall be your man, attend on you
With all true duty.—On toward Calais, ho!
                   [*Exeunt.*

SCENE IV.—*The same. The* French King's
Tent.

Enter KING PHILIP, LOUIS, PANDULPH, *and*
Attendants.

  K. Phi. So, by a roaring tempest on the
    flood,
A whole armado of convicted sail
Is scatter'd and disjoin'd from fellowship.
  Pand. Courage and comfort! all shall yet go
    well.   [run so ill.
  K. Phi. What can go well, when we have
Are we not beaten? Is not Angiers lost?
Arthur ta'en prisoner? divers dear friends slain?
And bloody England into England gone,
O'erbearing interruption, spite of France?
  Lou. What he hath won, that hath he forti-
    fied:
So hot a speed with such advice dispos'd,
Such temperate order in so fierce a cause,
Doth want example: who hath read or heard
Of any kindred action like to this?
  K. Phi. Well could I bear that England had
    this praise,
So we could find some pattern of our shame.—
Look, who comes here! a grave unto a soul;
Holding the eternal spirit, against her will,
In the vile prison of afflicted breath.

Enter CONSTANCE.

I pr'ythee, lady, go away with me.   [peace!
  Const. Lo, now! see the issue of your
  K. Phi. Patience, good lady! comfort, gentle
    Constance!
  Const. No, I defy all counsel, all redress,
But that which ends all counsel, true redress,
Death, death:—O amiable lovely death!
Thou odoriferous stench! sound rottenness!
Arise forth from the couch of lasting night,
Thou hate and terror to prosperity,
And I will kiss thy détestable bones;
And put my eyeballs in thy vaulty brows;
And ring these fingers with thy household
    worms;
And stop this gap of breath with fulsome dust,
And be a carrion monster like thyself:
Come, grin on me; and I will think thou smil'st,
And buss thee as thy wife! Misery's love,
O, come to me!
  K. Phi.   O fair affliction, peace!
  Const. No, no, I will not, having breath to
    cry:—
O, that my tongue were in the thunder's mouth!
Then with a passion would I shake the world:
And rouse from sleep that fell anatomy
Which cannot hear a lady's feeble voice,
Which scorns a modern invocation.
  Pand. Lady, you utter madness, and not
    sorrow.
  Const. Thou art not holy to belie me so;
I am not mad: this hair I tear is mine;
My name is Constance; I was Geffrey's wife;
Young Arthur is my son, and he is lost:

I am not mad;—I would to heaven I were!
For then, 'tis like I should forget myself:
O, if I could, what grief should I forget!—
Preach some philosophy to make me mad,
And thou shalt be canóniz'd, cardinal;
For, being not mad, but sensible of grief,
My reasonable part produces reason
How I may be deliver'd of these woes,
And teaches me to kill or hang myself:
If I were mad I should forget my son,
Or madly think a babe of clouts were he:
I am not mad; too well, too well I feel
The different plague of each calamity.
　　K. Phi. Bind up those tresses.—O, what
　　　love I note
In the fair multitude of those her hairs!
Where but by chance a silver drop hath fallen,
Even to that drop ten thousand wiry friends
Do glue themselves in sociable grief;
Like true, inseparable, faithful loves,
Sticking together in calamity.
　　Const. To England, if you will.
　　K. Phi.　　　　　　Bind up your hairs.
　　Const. Yes, that I will; and wherefore will
　　　I do it?
I tore them from their bonds, and cried aloud,
O that these hands could so redeem my son,
As they have given these hairs their liberty!
But now I envy at their liberty,
And will again commit them to their bonds,
Because my poor child is a prisoner.—
And, father cardinal, I have heard you say
That we shall see and know our friends in
　　heaven:
If that be true, I shall see my boy again;
For since the birth of Cain, the first male child,
To him that did but yesterday suspire,
There was not such a gracious creature born.
But now will canker sorrow eat my bud,
And chase the native beauty from his cheek,
And he will look as hollow as a ghost,
As dim and meagre as an ague's fit;
And so he'll die; and, rising so again,
When I shall meet him in the court of heaven
I shall not know him: therefore never, never
Must I behold my pretty Arthur more.
　　Pand. You hold too heinous a respect of
　　　grief.
　　Const. He talks to me that never had a son.
　　K. Phi. You are as fond of grief as of your
　　　child.　　　　　　　　　　　[child,
　　Const. Grief fills the room up of my absent
Lies in his bed, walks up and down with me,
Puts on his pretty looks, repeats his words,
Remembers me of all his gracious parts,
Stuffs out his vacant garments with his form;
Then have I reason to be fond of grief.
Fare you well: had you such a loss as I,
I could give better comfort than you do.—
I will not keep this form upon my head,
　　　　　　[*Tearing off her head-dress.*
When here is such disorder in my wit.
O Lord! my boy, my Arthur, my fair son!
My life, my joy, my food, my all the world!

My widow-comfort, and my sorrow's cure!
　　　　　　　　　　　　　　　[*Exit.*
　　K. Phi. I fear some outrage, and I'll follow
　　　her.　　　　　　　　　　　[*Exit.*
　　Lou. There's nothing in this world can make
　　　me joy:
Life is as tedious as a twice-told tale
Vexing the dull ear of a drowsy man;　　[taste,
And bitter shame hath spoil'd the sweet world's
That it yields naught but shame and bitterness.
　　Pand. Before the curing of a strong disease,
Even in the instant of repair and health,
The fit is strongest; evils that take leave,
On their departure most of all show evil:
What have you lost by losing of this day?
　　Lou. All days of glory, joy, and happiness.
　　Pand. If you had won it, certainly you had.
No, no; when Fortune means to men most good,
She looks upon them with a threatening eye.
'Tis strange to think how much King John hath
　　lost
In this which he accounts so clearly won:
Are not you griev'd that Arthur is his prisoner?
　　Lou. As heartily as he is glad he hath him.
　　Pand. Your mind is all as youthful as your
　　　blood.
Now hear me speak with a prophetic spirit;
For even the breath of what I mean to speak
Shall blow each dust, each straw, each little rub,
Out of the path which shall directly lead
Thy foot to England's throne; and therefore
　　mark.
John hath seiz'd Arthur; and it cannot be
That, whiles warm life plays in that infant's
　　veins,
The misplac'd John should entertain an hour,
One minute, nay, one quiet breath of rest:
A sceptre snatch'd with an unruly hand
Must be as boisterously maintain'd as gain'd;
And he that stands upon a slippery place
Makes nice of no vile hole to stay him up:
That John may stand, then Arthur needs must
　　fall;
So be it, for it cannot be but so.　　　[fall?
　　Lou. But what shall I gain by young Arthur's
　　Pand. You, in the right of Lady Blanch
　　　your wife,
May then make all the claim that Arthur did.
　　Lou. And lose it, life and all, as Arthur did.
　　Pand. How green you are, and fresh in this
　　　old world!　　　　　　　　　　[you;
John lays you plots; the times conspire with
For he that steeps his safety in true blood
Shall find but bloody safety and untrue.
This act, so evilly borne, shall cool the hearts
Of all his people, and freeze up their zeal,
That none so small advantage shall step forth
To check his reign, but they will cherish it;
No natural exhalation in the sky,
No scape of nature, no distemper'd day,
No common wind, no customed event,
But they will pluck away his natural cause,
And call them meteors, prodigies, and signs,
Abortives, présages, and tongues of heaven,

Plainly denouncing vengeance upon John.

Lou. May be he will not touch young Arthur's life,
But hold himself safe in his prisonment.

Pand. O, sir, when he shall hear of your approach,
If that young Arthur be not gone already,
Even at that news he dies; and then the hearts
Of all his people shall revolt from him,
And kiss the lips of unacquainted change;
And pick strong matter of revolt and wrath
Out of the bloody fingers' ends of John.
Methinks I see this hurly all on foot:
And, O, what better matter breeds for you
Than I have nam'd!—The bastard Falconbridge
Is now in England, ransacking the church,
Offending charity: if but a dozen French
Were there in arms, they would be as a call
To train ten thousand English to their side;
Or as a little snow, tumbled about
Anon becomes a mountain. O noble Dauphin,
Go with me to the king:—'tis wonderful
What may be wrought out of their discontent,
Now that their souls are topful of offence:
For England go:—I will whet on the king.

Lou. Strong reasons make strong actions: let us go:
If you say ay, the king will not say no.
                            [*Exeunt.*

ACT IV.

SCENE I.—NORTHAMPTON. *A Room in the Castle.*

Enter HUBERT *and two* Attendants.

Hub. Heat me these irons hot; and look thou stand
Within the arras: when I strike my foot
Upon the bosom of the ground, rush forth,
And bind the boy which you shall find with me
Fast to the chair: be heedful: hence, and watch.

1 *Attend.* I hope your warrant will bear out the deed.

Hub. Uncleanly scruples! Fear not you: look to 't.—   [*Exeunt* Attendants.
Young lad, come forth; I have to say with you.

Enter ARTHUR.

Arth. Good-morrow, Hubert.
Hub.   Good-morrow, little prince.
Arth. As little prince, having so great a title
To be more prince, as may be.—You are sad.
Hub. Indeed, I have been merrier.
Arth.   Mercy on me!
Methinks no body should be sad but I:
Yet, I remember, when I was in France,
Young gentlemen would be as sad as night,
Only for wantonness. By my christendom,
So I were out of prison, and kept sheep,
I should be as merry as the day is long;
And so I would be here, but that I doubt
My uncle practices more harm to me:
He is afraid of me, and I of him:

Is it my fault that I was Geffrey's son?
No, indeed, is 't not; and I would to heaven
I were your son, so you would love me, Hubert.

Hub. [*Aside.*] If I talk to him, with his innocent prate
He will awake my mercy, which lies dead:
Therefore I will be sudden and despatch.

Arth. Are you sick, Hubert? you look pale to-day:
In sooth, I would you were a little sick,
That I might sit all night and watch with you:
I warrant I love you more than you do me.

Hub. [*Aside.*] His words do take possession of my bosom.—
Read here, young Arthur.   [*Showing a paper.*
             [*Aside.*] How now, foolish rheum!
Turning dispiteous torture out of door!
I must be brief, lest resolution drop
Out at mine eyes in tender womanish tears.—
Can you not read it? is it not fair writ?

Arth. Too fairly, Hubert, for so foul effect.
Must you with hot irons burn out both mine eyes?

Hub. Young boy, I must.
Arth.   And will you?
Hub.   And I will.
Arth. Have you the heart? When your head did but ache
I knit my handkerchief about your brows,—
The best I had, a princess wrought it me,—
And I did never ask it you again;
And with my hand at midnight held your head;
And, like the watchful minutes to the hour,
Still and anon cheer'd up the heavy time,
Saying, *What lack you?* and, *Where lies your grief?*
Or, *What good love may I perform for you?*
Many a poor man's son would have lien still,
And ne'er have spoke a loving word to you;
But you at your sick service had a prince.
Nay, you may think my love was crafty love,
And call it cunning:—do, an if you will:
If heaven be pleas'd that you must use me ill,
Why, then you must.—Will you put out mine eyes?
These eyes that never did nor never shall
So much as frown on you?

Hub.   I have sworn to do it!
And with hot irons must I burn them out.

Arth. Ah, none but in this iron age would do it!
The iron of itself, though heat red hot,
Approaching near these eyes, would drink my tears,
And quench his fiery indignation,
Even in the matter of mine innocence;
Nay, after that, consume away in rust,
But for containing fire to harm mine eye.
Are you more stubborn-hard than hammer'd iron?
An if an angel should have come to me
And told me Hubert should put out mine eyes
I would not have believ'd him,—no tongue but Hubert's.

Hub. Come forth.   [*Stamps.*

Re-enter Attendants, *with cords, irons, &c.*

Do as I bid you.

Arth. O, save me, Hubert, save me! my eyes
are out
Even with the fierce looks of these bloody men.
Hub. Give me the iron, I say, and bind him
here.   [rough?
Arth. Alas, what need you be so boist'rous-
I will not struggle, I will stand stone-still.
For heaven's sake, Hubert, let me not be bound!
Nay, hear me, Hubert!—drive these men away,
And I will sit as quiet as a lamb;
I will not stir, nor wince, nor speak a word,
Nor look upon the iron angerly:
Thrust but these men away, and I'll forgive
you,
Whatever torment you do put me to.   [him.
Hub. Go, stand within; let me alone with
1 *Attend.* I am best pleas'd to be from such
a deed.   [*Exeunt* Attendants.
Arth. Alas, I then have chid away my friend!
He hath a stern look but a gentle heart:—
Let him come back, that his compassion may
Give life to yours.
Hub.   Come, boy, prepare yourself.
Arth. Is there no remedy?
Hub.   None, but to lose your eyes.
Arth. O heaven!—that there were but a
mote in yours,
A grain, a dust, a gnat, a wandering hair,
Any annoyance in that precious sense!
Then, feeling what small things are boisterous
there,
Your vile intent must needs seem horrible.
Hub. Is this your promise? go to, hold your
tongue.
Arth. Hubert, the utterance of a brace of
tongues
Must needs want pleading for a pair of eyes:
Let me not hold my tongue,—let me not,
Hubert!
Or, Hubert, if you will, cut out my tongue,
So I may keep mine eyes: O, spare mine eyes,
Though to no use but still to look on you!—
Lo, by my troth, the instrument is cold,
And would not harm me.
Hub.   I can heat it, boy.
Arth. No, in good sooth; the fire is dead with
grief,
Being create for comfort, to be us'd
In undeserv'd extremes: see else yourself;
There is no malice in this burning coal;
The breath of heaven hath blown his spirit out,
And strew'd repentant ashes on his head.
Hub. But with my breath I can revive it,
boy.
Arth. And if you do, you will but make it
blush,   [Hubert:
And glow with shame of your proceedings,
Nay, it, perchance, will sparkle in your eyes;
And, like a dog that is compell'd to fight,
Snatch at his master that doth tarre him on.

All things that you should use to do me wrong,
Deny their office: only you do lack
That mercy which fierce fire and iron extends,
Creatures of note for mercy-lacking uses.
Hub. Well, see to live; I will not touch thine
eyes
For all the treasure that thine uncle owes:
Yet am I sworn, and I did purpose, boy,
With this same very iron to burn them out.
Arth. O, now you look like Hubert! all this
while
You were disguised.
Hub.   Peace; no more. Adieu!
Your uncle must not know but you are dead;
I'll fill these dogged spies with false reports:
And, pretty child, sleep doubtless and secure,
That Hubert, for the wealth of all the world,
Will not offend thee.
Arth.   O heaven! I thank you, Hubert.
Hub. Silence; no more: go closely in with me:
Much danger do I undergo for thee.   [*Exeunt.*

SCENE II.—*The same. A Room of State in the
Palace.*

Enter KING JOHN, *crowned;* PEMBROKE, SALIS-
BURY, *and other* Lords. *The* KING *takes his
State.*

K. John. Here once again we sit, once again
crown'd,
And look'd upon, I hope, with cheerful eyes.
Pem. This once again, but that your high-
ness pleas'd,
Was once superfluous: you were crown'd before,
And that high royalty was ne'er pluck'd off;
The faiths of men ne'er stained with revolt;
Fresh expectation troubled not the land
With any long'd-for change or better state.
Sal. Therefore, to be possess'd with double
pomp,
To guard a title that was rich before,
To gild refined gold, to paint the lily,
To throw a perfume on the violet,
To smooth the ice, or add another hue
Unto the rainbow, or with taper-light
To seek the beauteous eye of heaven to garnish,
Is wasteful and ridiculous excess.   [done,
Pem. But that your royal pleasure must be
This act is as an ancient tale new told;
And in the last repeating troublesome,
Being urged at a time unseasonable.
Sal. In this, the antique and well-noted face
Of plain old form is much disfigured;
And, like a shifted wind unto a sail,
It makes the course of thoughts to fetch about;
Startles and frights consideration;
Makes sound opinion sick, and truth suspected,
For putting on so new a fashion'd robe.   ·
Pem. When workmen strive to do better
than well,
They do confound their skill in convetousness;
And oftentimes excusing of a fault
Doth make the fault the worse by the excuse,—
As patches set upon a little breach

Discredit more in hiding of the fault
Than did the fault before it was so patch'd.
Sal. To this effect, before you were new-
crown'd, [highness
We breath'd our counsel: but it pleas'd your
To overbear it; and we are all well pleas'd,
Since all and every part of what we would
Doth make a stand at what your highness will.
K. John. Some reasons of this double coro-
nation
I have possess'd you with, and think them
strong;
And more, more strong, when lesser is my fear,
I shall indue you with: meantime but ask
What you would have reform'd that is not well,
And well shall you perceive how willingly
I will both hear and grant you your requests.
Pem. Then I,—as one that am the tongue
of these,
To sound the purposes of all their hearts,—
Both for myself and them,—but, chief of all,
Your safety, for the which myself and them
Bend their best studies,—heartily request
The enfranchisement of Arthur; whose restraint
Doth move the murmuring lips of discontent
To break into this dangerous argument,—
If what in rest you have in right you hold,
Why, then, your fears,—which, as they say,
attend
The steps of wrong,—should move you to mew
up
Your tender kinsman, and to choke his days
With barbarous ignorance, and deny his youth
The rich advantage of good exercise?
That the time's enemies may not have this
To grace occasions, let it be our suit
That you have bid us ask his liberty;
Which for our goods we do no further ask
Than whereupon our weal, on you depending,
Counts it your weal he have his liberty.
K. John. Let it be so: I do commit his youth
To your direction.

Enter HUBERT.

Hubert, what news with you? [deed;
Pem. This is the man should do the bloody
He show'd his warrant to a friend of mine:
The image of a wicked heinous fault
Lives in his eye; that close aspèct of his
Doth show the mood of a much-troubled breast;
And I do fearfully believe 'tis done
What we so fear'd he had a charge to do. [go
Sal. The colour of the king doth come and
Between his purpose and his conscience,
Like heralds 'twixt two dreadful battles set:
His passion is so ripe it needs must break.
Pem. And when it breaks, I fear will issue
thence
The foul corruption of a sweet child's death.
K. John. We cannot hold mortality's strong
hand:—
Good lords, although my will to give is living,
The suit which you demand is gone and dead:
He tells us Arthur is deceas'd to-night.

Sal. Indeed, we fear'd his sickness was past
cure. [he was,
Pem. Indeed, we heard how near his death
Before the child himself felt he was sick:
This must be answer'd either here or hence.
K. John. Why do you bend such solemn
brows on me?
Think you I bear the shears of destiny?
Have I commandment on the pulse of life?
Sal. It is apparent foul-play; and 'tis shame
That greatness should so grossly offer it:
So thrive it in your game! and so, farewell.
Pem. Stay yet, Lord Salisbury; I'll go with
thee,
And find the inheritance of this poor child,
His little kingdom of a forced grave. [isle,
That blood which ow'd the breadth of all this
Three foot of it doth hold:—bad world the
while! [out
This must not be thus borne: this will break
To all our sorrows, and ere long, I doubt.
[*Exeunt* Lords.
K. John. They burn in indignation. I repent:
There is no sure foundation set on blood;
No certain life achiev'd by other's death.—

Enter a Messenger.

A fearful eye thou hast: where is that blood
That I have seen inhabit in those cheeks?
So foul a sky clears not without a storm:
Pour down thy weather:—how goes all in
France? [such a power
Mess. From France to England.—Never
For any foreign preparation
Was levied in the body of a land.
The copy of your speed is learn'd by them;
For when you should be told they do prepare,
The tidings come that they are all arriv'd.
K. John. O, where hath our intelligence been
drunk? [care,
Where hath it slept? Where is my mother's
That such an army could be drawn in France,
And she not hear of it?
Mess. My liege, her ear
Is stopp'd with dust; the first of April died
Your noble mother: and, as I hear, my lord,
The Lady Constance in a frenzy died [tongue
Three days before; but this from rumour's
I idly heard,—if true or false I know not.
K. John. Withhold thy speed, dreadful oc-
casion!
O, make a league with me, till I have pleas'd
My discontented peers!—What! mother dead
How wildly, then, walks my estate in France!—
Under whose conduct came those powers of
France
That thou for truth giv'st out are landed here?
Mess. Under the Dauphin.
K. John. Thou hast made me giddy
With these ill tidings.

Enter the BASTARD *and* PETER *of Pomfret.*
Now, what says the world
To your proceedings? do not seek to stuff

My head with more ill news, for it is full.

  Bast. But if you be afeared to hear the worst,
Then let the worst, unheard, fall on your
    head.

  K. John. Bear with me, cousin; for I was
    amaz'd
Under the tide: but now I breathe again
Aloft the flood; and can give audience
To any tongue, speak it of what it will.

  Bast. How I have sped among the clergymen,
The sums I have collected shall express.
But as I travell'd hither through the land,
I find the people strangely fantasied;
Possess'd with rumours, full of idle dreams.
Not knowing what they fear, but full of fear:
And here's a prophet that I brought with me
From forth the streets of Pomfret, whom I
    found
With many hundreds treading on his heels;
To whom he sung, in rude harsh-sounding
    rhymes,
That, ere the next Ascension-day at noon,
Your highness should deliver up your crown.

  K. John. Thou idle dreamer, wherefore didst
    thou so?   [out so.

  Peter. Foreknowing that the truth will fall

  K. John. Hubert, away with him; imprison
    him;
And on that day at noon, whereon he says
I shall yield up my crown, let him be hang'd.
Deliver him to safety; and return,
For I must use thee.

              [*Exit* HUBERT *with* PETER.
              O my gentle cousin,
Hear'st thou the news abroad, who are arriv'd?

  Bast. The French, my lord; men's mouths
    are full of it:
Besides, I met Lord Bigot and Lord Salis-
    bury,—
With eyes as red as new-enkindled fire,—
And others more, going to seek the grave
Of Arthur, whom they say is kill'd to-night
On your suggestion.

  K. John.   Gentle kinsman, go
And thrust thyself into their companies:
I have a way to win their loves again:
Bring them before me.

  Bast.   I will seek them out.

  K. John. Nay, but make haste; the better
    foot before.
O, let me have no subject enemies
When adverse foreigners affright my towns
With dreadful pomp of stout invasion!
Be Mercury, set feathers to thy heels,
And fly like thought from them to me again.

  Bast. The spirit of the time shall teach me
    speed.

  K. John. Spoke like a spriteful noble gentle-
    man.   [*Exit* BASTARD.
Go after him; for he perhaps shall need
Some messenger betwixt me and the peers;
And be thou he.

  Mess. With all my heart, my liege.   [*Exit.*

  K. John. My mother dead!

Re-enter HUBERT.

  Hub. My lord, they say five moons were
    seen to-night;
Four fixed; and the fifth did whirl about
The other four in wondrous motion.

  K. John. Five moons!

  Hub. Old men and beldams in the streets
Do prophesy upon it dangerously: [mouths:
Young Arthur's death is common in their
And when they talk of him, they shake their
    heads,
And whisper one another in the ear;
And he that speaks doth gripe the hearer's
    wrist;
Whilst he that hears makes fearful action,
With wrinkled brows, with nods, with rolling
    eyes.
I saw a smith stand with his hammer, thus,
The whilst his iron did on the anvil cool,
With open mouth swallowing a tailor's news;
Who, with his shears and measure in his hand,
Standing on slippers,—which his nimble haste
Had falsely thrust upon contráry feet,—
Told of a many thousand warlike French
That were embattailed and rank'd in Kent?
Another lean unwash'd artificer
Cuts off his tale, and talks of Arthur's death?

  K. John. Why seek'st thou to possess me
    with these fears?
Why urgest thou so oft young Arthur's death?
Thy hand hath murder'd him: I had a mighty
    cause   [kill him.
To wish him dead, but thou hadst none to

  Hub. No hand, my lord! why, did you not
    provoke me?   [tended

  K. John. It is the curse of kings to be at-
By slaves that take their humours for a warrant
To break within the bloody house of life;
And, on the winking of authority,
To understand a law; to know the meaning
Of dangerous majesty, when perchance it frowns
More upon humour than advis'd respect.

  Hub. Here is your hand and seal for what I
    did.

  K. John. O, when the last account 'twixt
    heaven and earth
Is to be made, then shall this hand and seal
Witness against us to damnation!
How oft the sight of means to do ill deeds
Make ill deeds done! Hadst not thou been by,
A fellow by the hand of nature mark'd,
Quoted, and sign'd, to do a deed of shame,
This murder had not come into my mind:
But, taking note of thy abhorr'd aspèct,
Finding thee fit for bloody villany,
Apt, liable to be employ'd in danger,
I faintly broke with thee of Arthur's death;
And thou, to be endeared to a king,
Made it no conscience to destroy a prince.

  Hub. My lord,—

  K. John. Hadst thou but shook thy head, or
    made a pause,
When I spake darkly what I purpos'd,

Or turn'd an eye of doubt upon my face,
As bid me tell my tale in express words,
Deep shame had struck me dumb, made me
    break off,
And those thy fears might have wrought fears
    in me:
But thou didst understand me by my signs,
And didst in signs again parley with sin;
Yea, without stop, didst let thy heart consent,
And consequently thy rude hand to act
The deed, which both our tongues held vile to
    name.—
Out of my sight, and never see me more!
My nobles leave me; and my state is brav'd,
Even at my gates, with ranks of foreign powers:
Nay, in the body of this fleshly land,
This kingdom, this confine of blood and breath,
Hostility and civil tumult reigns
Between my conscience and my cousin's death.
    Hub. Arm you against your other enemies,
I'll make a peace between your soul and you.
Young Arthur is alive: this hand of mine
Is yet a maiden and an innocent hand,
Not painted with the crimson spots of blood.
Within this bosom never enter'd yet
The dreadful motion of a murderous thought;
And you have slander'd nature in my form,—
Which, howsoever rude exteriorly,
Is yet the cover of a fairer mind
Than to be butcher of an innocent child.
    K. John. Doth Arthur live? O, haste thee
        to the peers,
Throw this report on their incensed rage,
And make them tame to their obedience!
Forgive the comment that my passion made
Upon thy feature; for my rage was blind,
And foul imaginary eyes of blood
Presented thee more hideous than thou art.
O, answer not; but to my closet bring
The angry lords with all expedient haste:
I cónjure thee but slowly; run more fast.
                                        [*Exeunt.*

SCENE III.—*The same. Before the Castle.*

Enter ARTHUR, *on the Walls.*

    Arth. The wall is high, and yet will I leap
        down:—
Good ground, be pitiful, and hurt me not!—
There's few or none do know me: if they did,
This ship-boy's semblance hath disguis'd me
    quite.
I am afraid; and yet I'll venture it.
If I get down, and do not break my limbs,
I'll find a thousand shifts to get away:
As good to die and go, as die and stay.
                                    [*Leaps down.*
O me! my uncle's spirit is in these stones:—
Heaven take my soul, and England keep my
    bones!   [*Dies.*

Enter PEMBROKE, SALISBURY, *and* BIGOT.

    Sal. Lords, I will meet him at Saint Ed-
        mund's-Bury:
It is our safety, and we must embrace
This gentle offer of the perilous time.

    Pem. Who brought that letter from the
        cardinal?   [France;
    Sal. The Count Melun, a noble lord of
Whose private with me of the Dauphin's love
Is much more general than these lines import.
    Big. To-morrow morning let us meet him,
        then.
    Sal. Or rather than set forward; for 'twill be
Two long days' journey, lords, or e'er we meet.

Enter the BASTARD.

    Bast. Once more to-day well met, distem-
        per'd lords!
The king by me requests your presence straight.
    Sal. The king hath dispossess'd himself of us:
We will not line his thin bestained cloak
With our pure honours, nor attend the foot
That leaves the print of blood where'er it walks.
Return and tell him so: we know the worst.
    Bast. Whate'er you think, good words, I
        think, were best.   [now.
    Sal. Our griefs, and not our manners, reason
    Bast. But there is little reason in your grief;
Therefore 'twere reason you had manners now.
    Pem. Sir, sir, impatience hath his privilege.
    Bast. 'Tis true,—to hurt his master, no man
        else.
    Sal. This is the prison:—what is he lies here?
                                [*Seeing* ARTHUR.
    Pem. O death, made proud with pure and
        princely beauty!
The earth had not a hole to hide this deed.
    Sal. Murder, as hating what himself hath
        done,
Doth lay it open to urge on revenge.   [grave,
    Big. Or, when he doom'd this beauty to a
Found it too precious-princely for a grave.
    Sal. Sir Richard, what think you? Have you
        beheld,
Or have you read or heard? or could you think?
Or do you almost think, although you see,
That you do see? could thought, without this
        object,
Form such another? This is the very top,
The height, the crest, or crest unto the crest
Of murder's arms: this is the bloodiest shame,
The wildest savagery, the vilest stroke,
That ever wall-ey'd wrath or staring rage
Presented to the tears of soft remorse. [this.
    Pem. All murders past do stand excus'd in
And this, so sole and so unmatchable,
Shall give a holiness, a purity,
To the yet unbegotten sin of times;
And prove a deadly bloodshed but a jest,
Exampled by this heinous spectacle.
    Bast. It is a damned and a bloody work;
The graceless action of a heavy hand,—
If that it be the work of any hand.
    Sal. If that it be the work of any hand?—
We had a kind of light what would ensue:
It is the shameful work of Hubert's hand;
The practice and the purpose of the king:—
From whose obedience I forbid my soul,
Kneeling before this ruin of sweet life,

And breathing to his breathless excellence
The incense of a vow, a holy vow,
Never to taste the pleasures of the world,
Never to be infected with delight,
Nor conversant with ease and idleness,
Till I have set a glory to this hand,
By giving it the worship of revenge.   [words.
  Pem. Big. Our souls religiously confirm thy

Enter HUBERT.

  Hub. Lords, I am hot with haste in seeking
you:
Arthur doth live; the king hath sent for you.
  Sal. O, he is bold, and blushes not at
death:—
Avaunt, thou hateful villain, get thee gone!
  Hub. I am no villain.
  Sal.   Must I rob the law?
                          [*Drawing his sword.*
  Bast. Your sword is bright, sir; put it up
again.   [skin.
  Sal. Not till I sheathe it in a murderer's
  Hub. Stand back, Lord Salisbury,—stand
back, I say;   [yours.
By heaven, I think my sword's as sharp as
I would not have you, lord, forget yourself,
Nor tempt the danger of my true defence;
Lest I, by marking of your rage, forget
Your worth, your greatness, and nobility.
  Big. Out, dunghill! dar'st thou brave a
nobleman?
  Hub. Not for my life: but yet I dare defend
My innocent life against an emperor.
  Sal. Thou art a murderer.
  Hub.   Do not prove me so;
Yet I am none: whose tongue soe'er speaks
false,
Not truly speaks; who speaks not truly, lies.
  Pem. Cut him to pieces.
  Bast.   Keep the peace, I say.
  Sal. Stand by, or I shall gall you, Falcon-
bridge.   [bury.
  Bast. Thou wert better gall the devil, Salis-
If thou but frown on me, or stir thy foot,
Or teach thy hasty spleen to do me shame,
I'll strike thee dead. Put up thy sword betime;
Or I'll so maul you and your toasting-iron
That you shall think the devil is come from hell.
  Big. What wilt thou do, renowned Falcon-
bridge?
Second a villain and a murderer?
  Hub. Lord Bigot, I am none.
  Big.   Who kill'd this prince?
  Hub. 'Tis not an hour since I left him well:
I honour'd him, I lov'd him; and will weep
My date of life out for his sweet life's loss.
  Sal. Trust not those cunning waters of his
eyes,
For villany is not without such rheum;
And he, long traded in it, makes it seem
Like rivers of remorse and innocency.
Away with me, all you whose souls abhor
The uncleanly savours of a slaughter-house;
For I am stifled with this smell of sin.

  Big. Away toward Bury, to the Dauphin
there!   [out.
  Pem. There, tell the king, he may inquire us
                          [*Exeunt* Lords.
  Bast. Here's a good world!—Knew you of
this fair work?
Beyond the infinite and boundless reach
Of mercy, if thou didst this deed of death,
Art thou damn'd, Hubert.
  Hub.   Do but hear me, sir.
  Bast. Ha! I'll tell thee what;   [black;
Thou'rt damn'd as black—nay, nothing is so
Thou art more deep damn'd than Prince
Lucifer:
There is not yet so ugly a fiend of hell
As thou shalt be, if thou didst kill this child.
  Hub. Upon my soul,—
  Bast.   If thou didst but consent
To this most cruel act, do but despair;
And if thou want'st a cord, the smallest thread
That ever spider twisted from her womb
Will serve to strangle thee; a rush will be
A beam to hang thee on; or wouldst thou
drown thyself,
Put but a little water in a spoon,
And it shall be as all the ocean,
Enough to stifle such a villain.up.
I do suspect thee very grievously.
  Hub. If I in act, consent, or sin of thought
Be guilty of the stealing that sweet breath
Which was embounded in this beauteous clay,
Let hell want pains enough to torture me!
I left him well.
  Bast.   Go, bear him in thine arms.—
I am amaz'd, methinks, and lose my way
Among the thorns and dangers of this world.—
How easy dost thou take all England up!
From forth this morsel of dead royalty,
The life, the right, and truth of all this realm
Is fled to heaven; and England now is left
To tug and scamble, and to part by the teeth
The unow'd interest of proud-swelling state.
Now for the bare-pick'd bone of majesty
Doth dogged war bristle his angry crest,
And snarleth in the gentle eyes of peace:
Now powers from home and discontents at home
Meet in one line; and vast confusion waits,
As doth a raven on a sick-fallen beast,
The imminent decay of wrested pomp.
Now happy he whose cloak and cincture can
Hold out this tempest.—Bear away that child,
And follow me with speed: I'll to the king:
A thousand businesses are brief in hand,
And heaven itself doth frown upon the land.
                                        [*Exeunt.*

ACT V.

SCENE I.—NORTHAMPTON. *A Room in the
Palace.*

Enter KING JOHN, PANDULPH *with the crown,
and* Attendants.

  K. John. Thus have I yielded up into your
hand
The circle of my glory.

Pand.   Take again
     [*Giving* KING JOHN *the crown.*
From this my hand, as holding of the pope,
Your sovereign greatness and authority.
    K. John. Now keep your holy word: go
      meet the French;
And from his holiness use all your power
To stop their marches 'fore we are inflam'd.
Our discontented counties do revolt;
Our people quarrel with obedience;
Swearing allegiance and the love of soul
To stranger blood, to foreign royalty.
This inundation of mistemper'd humour
Rests by you only to be qualified.
Then pause not; for the present time's so sick
That present medicine must be minister'd,
Or overthrow incurable ensues.
    Pand. It was my breath that blew this tem-
      pest up,
Upon your stubborn usage of the pope:
But since you are a gentle convertite,
My tongue shall hush again this storm of war,
And make fair weather in your blustering land.
On this Ascension-day, remember well,
Upon your oath of service to the pope,
Go I to make the French lay down their arms.
               [*Exit.*
    K. John. Is this Ascension-day? Did not the
      prophet
Say that before Ascension-day at noon
My crown I should give off? Even so I have:
I did suppose it should be on constraint;
But, heaven be thank'd, it is but voluntary.

        Enter the BASTARD.

    Bast. All Kent hath yielded; nothing there
      holds out
But Dover Castle: London hath receiv'd,
Like a kind host, the Dauphin and his powers:
Your nobles will not hear you, but are gone
To offer service to your enemy;
And wild amazement hurries up and down
The little number of your doubtful friends.
    K. John. Would not my lords return to me
      again,
After they heard young Arthur was alive?
    Bast. They found him dead, and cast into
      the streets;
An empty casket, where the jewel of life
By some damn'd hand was robb'd and ta'en
      away.
    K. John. That villain Hubert told me he did
      live.
    Bast. So, on my soul, he did, for aught he
      knew.
But wherefore do you droop? why look you sad?
Be great in act, as you have been in thought;
Let not the world see fear and sad distrust
Govern the motion of a kingly eye:
Be stirring as the time; be fire with fire;
Threaten the threatener, and outface the brow
Of bragging horror: so shall inferior eyes,
That borrow their behaviours from the great,
Grow great by your example, and put on

The dauntless spirit of resolution.
Away, and glister like the god of war
When he intendeth to become the field:
Show boldness and aspiring confidence.
What, shall they seek the lion in his den,
And fright him there? and make him tremble
      there?
O, let it not be said!—Forage, and run
To meet displeasure further from the doors,
And grapple with him ere he come so nigh.
    K. John. The legate of the pope hath been
      with me,
And I have made a happy peace with him;
And he hath promis'd to dismiss the powers
Led by the Dauphin.
    Bast.   O inglorious league!
Shall we, upon the footing of our land,
Send fair-play orders, and make compromise,
Insinuation, parley, and base truce,
To arms invasive? shall a beardless boy,
A cocker'd silken wanton, brave our fields,
And flesh his spirit in a warlike soil,
Mocking the air with colours idly spread,
And find no check? Let us, my liege, to arms:
Perchance the cardinal cannot make your
      peace;
Of, if he do, let it at least be said,
They saw we had a purpose of defence.
    K. John. Have thou the ordering of this
      present time.   [I know,
    Bast. Away, then, with good courage! yet,
Our party may well meet a prouder foe.
               [*Exeunt.*

   SCENE II.—*Near* ST. EDMUND'S-BURY.
        The French Camp.

  Enter, in arms, LOUIS, SALISBURY, MELUN,
    PEMBROKE, BIGOT, *and* Soldiers.

    Lou. My Lord Melun, let this be copied out,
And keep it safe for our remembrance:
Return the precedent to these lords again;
That, having our fair order written down,
Both they and we, perusing o'er these notes,
May know wherefore we took the sacrament,
And keep our faiths firm and inviolable.
    Sal. Upon our sides it never shall be broken.
And, noble Dauphin, albeit we swear
A voluntary zeal and unurg'd faith
To your proceedings; yet, believe me, prince,
I am not glad that such a sore of time
Should seek a plaster by contemn'd revolt,
And heal the inveterate canker of one wound
By making many. O, it grieves my soul
That I must draw this metal from my side
To be a widow-maker! O, and there
Where honourable rescue and defence
Cries out upon the name of Salisbury!
But such is the infection of the time,
That, for the health and physic of our right,
We cannot deal but with the very hand
Of stern injustice and confused wrong.—
And is 't not pity, O my grieved friends!
That we, the sons and children of this isle,
Were born to see so sad an hour as this;

Wherein we step after a stranger-march
Upon her gentle bosom, and fill up
Her enemies' ranks—I must withdraw and weep
Upon the spot of this enforc'd cause—
To grace the gentry of a land remote,
And follow unacquainted colours here?
What, here?—O nation, that thou couldst re-
move!
That Neptune's arms, who clippeth thee about,
Would bear thee from the knowledge of thyself,
And grapple thee unto a pagan shore,   [bine
Where these two Christian armies might com-
The blood of malice in a vein of league,
And not to spend it so unneighbourly!

   Lou. A noble temper dost thou show in this;
And great affections wrestling in thy bosom
Do make an earthquake of nobility.
O, what a noble combat hast thou fought
Between compulsion and a brave respect!
Let me wipe off this honourable dew
That silverly doth progress on thy cheeks:
My heart hath melted at a lady's tears,
Being an ordinary inundation;
But this effusion of such manly drops,
This shower, blown up by tempest of the soul,
Startles mine eyes, and makes me more amaz'd
Than had I seen the vaulty top of heaven
Figur'd quite o'er with burning meteors.
Lift up thy brow, renowned Salisbury,
And with a great heart heave away this storm:
Commend these waters to those baby eyes
That never saw the giant world enrag'd,
Nor met with fortune other than at feasts,
Full warm of blood, of mirth, of gossiping.
Come, come; for thou shalt thrust thy hand as
deep
Into the purse of rich prosperity
As Louis himself:—so, nobles, shall you all,
That knit your sinews to the strength of mine.—
And even there, methinks, an angel spake:
Look, where the holy legate comes apace,
To give us warrant from the hand of heaven,
And on our actions set the name of right
With holy breath.

Enter PANDULPH, attended.

   Pand. Hail, noble prince of France!
The next is this,—King John hath reconcil'd
Himself to Rome; his spirit is come in,
That so stood out against the holy church,
The great metropolis and see of Rome:
Therefore thy threatening colours now wind up,
And tame the savage spirit of wild war,
That, like a lion foster'd up at hand,
It may lie gently at the foot of peace,
And be no further harmful than in show.

   Lou. Your grace shall pardon me, I will not
back:
I am too high-born to be propertied,
To be a secondary at control,
Or useful serving-man and instrument
To any sovereign state throughout the world.
Your breath first kindled the dead coal of wars
Between this chastis'd kingdom and myself,

And brought in matter that should feed this
fire;
And now 'tis far too huge to be blow out
With that same weak wind which enkindled it.
You taught me how to know the face of right,
Acquainted me with interest to this land,
Yea, thrust this enterprise into my heart;
And come ye now to tell me John hath made
His peace with Rome? What is that peace to
me?
I, by the honour of my marriage-bed,
After young Arthur, claim this land for mine;
And, now it is half-conquer'd, must I back
Because that John hath made his peace with
Rome?   [borne,
Am I Rome's slave? What penny hath Rome
What men provided, what munition sent,
To underprop this action? Is't not I
That undergo this charge? who else but I,
And such as to my claim are liable,
Sweat in this business and maintain this war.
Have I not heard these islanders shout out,
Vive le roi! as I have bank'd their towns?
Have I not here the best cards for the game,
To win this easy match play'd for a crown?
And shall I now give o'er the yielded set?
No, no, on my soul, it never shall be said.

   Pand. You look but on the outside of this
work.

   Lou. Outside or inside, I will not return
Till my attempt so much be glorified
As to my ample hope was promised
Before I drew this gallant head of war,
And cull'd these fiery spirits from the world,
To outlook conquest, and to win renown
Even in the jaws of danger and of death.—
                  [Trumpet sounds.
What lusty trumpet thus doth summon us?

Enter the BASTARD, attended.

   Bast. According to the fair play of the world,
Let me have audience; I am sent to speak:—
My holy lord of Milan, from the king
I come, to learn how you have dealt for him;
And, as you answer, I do know the scope
And warrant limited unto my tongue.

   Pand. The Dauphin is too wilful-opposite,
And will not temporize with my entreaties;
He flatly says he'll not lay down his arms.

   Bast. By all the blood that ever fury breath'd,
The youth says well.—Now hear our English
king;
For thus his royalty doth speak in me.
He is prepar'd; and reason too he should:
This apish and unmannerly approach,
This harness'd masque and unadvised revel,
This unhair'd sauciness and boyish troops,
The king doth smile at; and is well prepar'd
To whip this dwarfish war, these pigmy arms,
From out the circle of his territories.   [door,
That hand which had the strength, even at your
To cudgel you, and make you take the hatch;
To dive, like buckets, in concealed wells;
To crouch in litter of your stable planks;

To lie, like pawns, lock'd up in chests and
    trunks;
To hug with swine; to seek sweet safety out
In vaults and prisons; and to thrill and shake
Even at the crying of your nation's crow,
Thinking his voice an armed Englishman;—
Shall that victorious hand be feebled here,
That in your chambers gave you chastisement?
No: know the gallant monarch is in arms;
And like an eagle o'er his aery towers,
To souse annoyance that comes near his nest.—
And you degenerate, you ingrate revolts,
You bloody Neroes, ripping up the womb
Of your dear mother England, blush for shame;
For your own ladies and pale-visag'd maids,
Like Amazons, come tripping after drums,—
Their thimbles into armed gauntlets chang'd,
Their needles to lances, and their gentle hearts
To fierce and bloody inclination.   [in peace;
    Lou. There end thy brave, and turn thy face
We grant thou canst outscold us; fare thee well;
We hold our time too precious to be spent
With such a brabbler.
    Pand.   Give me leave to speak.
    Bast. No, I will speak.
    Lou.   We will attend to neither.—
Strike up the drums; and let the tongue of war
Plead for our interest and our being here.
    Bast. Indeed, your drums, being beaten, will
    cry out;
And so shall you, being beaten: do but start
An echo with the clamour of thy drum,
And even at hand a drum is ready brac'd
That shall reverberate all as loud as thine;
Sound but another, and another shall,
As loud as thine, rattle the welkin's ear,
And mock the deep-mouth'd thunder: for at
    hand,—
Not trusting to this halting legate here,
Whom he hath us'd rather for sport than need,—
Is warlike John; and in his forehead sits
A bare-ribb'd death, whose office is this day
To feast upon whole thousands of the French.
    Lou. Strike up our drums, to find this danger
    out.
    Bast. And thou shalt find it, Dauphin, do
    not doubt.   [*Exeunt.*

SCENE III.—*The same. A Field of Battle.*

Alarums. Enter KING JOHN *and* HUBERT.

    K. John. How goes the day with us? O,
    tell me, Hubert.
    Hub. Badly, I fear. How fares your majesty?
    K. John. This fever, that hath troubled me
    so long,
Lies heavy on me;—O, my heart is sick!

Enter a Messenger.

    Mess. My lord, your valiant kinsman, Fal-
    conbridge,
Desires your majesty to leave the field,
And send him word by me which way you go.
    K. John. Tell him, toward Swinstead, to the
    abbey there.

    Mess. Be of good comfort; for the great
    supply
That was expected by the Dauphin here
Are wreck'd three nights ago on Goodwin
    Sands.   [now:
This news was brought to Richard but even
The French fight colding, and retire themselves.
    K. John. Ay me! this tyrant fever burns me
    up,
And will not let me welcome this good news.—
Set on toward Swinstead: to my litter straight;
Weakness possesseth me, and I am faint.
                           [*Exeunt.*

SCENE IV.—*The same. Another part of the same.*

Enter SALISBURY, PEMBROKE, *and others.*

    Sal. I did not think the king so stor'd with
    friends.
    Pem. Up once again; put spirit in the French:
If they miscarry we miscarry too.
    Sal. That misbegotten devil, Falconbridge,
In spite of spite, alone upholds the day.
    Pem. They say King John, sore sick, hath
    left the field.

Enter MELUN *wounded, and led by* Soldiers.

    Mel. Lead me to the revolts of England here.
    Sal. When we were happy we had other
    names.
    Pem. It is the Count Melun.
    Sal.   Wounded to death.
    Mel. Fly, noble English, you are bought and
    sold;
Unthread the rude eye of rebellion,
And welcome home again discarded faith.
Seek out King John, and fall before his feet;
For if the French be lords of this loud day,
He means to recompense the pains you take
By cutting off your heads: thus hath he sworn,
And I with him, and many more with me,
Upon the altar at Saint Edmund's-Bury;
Even on that altar where we swore to you
Dear amity and everlasting love.
    Sal. May this be possible? may this be true?
    Mel. Have I not hideous death within my
    view,
Retaining but a quantity of life,
Which bleeds away even as a form of wax
Resolveth from his figure 'gainst the fire?
What in the world should make me now deceive,
Since I must lose the use of all deceit?
Why should I then be false, since it is true
That I must die here, and live hence by truth?
I say again, if Louis do win the day,
He is forsworn if e'er those eyes of yours
Behold another day break in the east:
But even this night,—whose black contagious
    breath
Already smokes about the burning crest
Of the old, feeble, and day-wearied sun,—
Even this ill night, your breathing shall expire;
Paying the fine of rated treachery
Even with a treacherous fine of all your lives,
If Louis by your assistance win the day.

Commend me to one Hubert, with your king;
The love of him,—and this respect besides,
For that my grandsire was an Englishman,—
Awakes my conscience to confess all this.
In lieu whereof, I pray you, bear me hence
From forth the noise and rumour of the field,
Where I may think the remnant of my thoughts
In peace, and part this body and my soul
With contemplation and devout desires. [soul

Sal. We do believe thee:—and beshrew my
But I do love the favour and the form
Of this most fair occasion, by the which
We will entread the steps of damned flight;
And, like a bated and retired flood,
Leaving our rankness and irregular course,
Stoop low within those bounds we have o'er-
　　look'd,
And calmly run on in obedience,
Even to our ocean, to our great King John.—
My arm shall give thee help to bear thee hence;
For I do see the cruel pangs of death　[flight,
Right in thine eye.—Away, my friends! New
And happy newness, that intends old right.
　　　　　　[*Exeunt, leading off* MELUN.

SCENE V.—*The same. The French Camp.*

Enter LOUIS *and his train.*

Lou. The sun of heaven methought was loth
　　to set,
But stay'd, and made the western welkin blush,
When the English measur'd backward their
　　own ground
In faint retire. O, bravely came we off,
When with a volley of our needless shot,
After such bloody toil, we bid good-night;
And wound our tattering colours clearly up,
Last in the field, and almost lords of it!

Enter a Messenger.

Mess. Where is my prince, the Dauphin?
Lou.　　　　Here:—what news?
Mess. The Count Melun is slain; the English
　　lords,
By his persuasion are again fallen off;
And your supply, which you have wish'd so long,
Are cast away and sunk on Goodwin Sands.
Lou. Ah, foul shrewd news!—beshrew thy
　　very heart!—
I did not think to be so sad to-night
As this hath made me.—Who was he that said
King John did fly an hour or two before
The stumbling night did part our weary powers?
Mess. Whoever spoke it, it is true, my lord.
Lou. Well; keep good quarter and good care
　　to-night;
The day shall not be up so soon as I,
To try the fair adventure of to-morrow.
　　　　　　　　　　　　　　　[*Exeunt.*

SCENE VI.—*An open Place in the neighbourhood of Swinstead Abbey.*

Enter the BASTARD *and* HUBERT, *meeting.*

Hub. Who's there? speak, ho! speak quickly,
or I shoot.

Bast. A friend.—What art thou?
Hub.　　　　　Of the part of England.
Bast. Whither dost thou go?
Hub. What's that to thee? Why may I not
　　demand
Of thine affairs, as well as thou of mine?
Bast. Hubert, I think.
Hub.　　　Thou hast a perfect thought:
I will, upon all hazards, well believe　[well.
Thou art my friend, that know'st my tongue so
Who art thou?
Bast.　　　Who thou wilt: an if thou please,
Thou mayst befriend me so much as to think
I come one way of the Plantagenets.
Hub. Unkind remembrance! thou and eye-
　　less night　　　　　　　　　　　　[me,
Have done me shame:—brave soldier, pardon
That any accent breaking from thy tongue
Should 'scape the true acquaintance of mine ear.
Bast. Come, come; sans compliment, what
　　news abroad?　　　　　　　　　　[night,
Hub. Why, here walk I, in the black brow of
To find you out.
Bast.　　　Brief, then; and what's the news?
Hub. O, my sweet sir, news fitting to the
　　night,
Black, fearful, comfortless, and horrible.
Bast. Show me the very wound of this ill
　　news;
I am no woman, I'll not swoon at it.
Hub. The king, I fear, is poison'd by a monk:
I left him almost speechless and broke out
To acquaint you with this evil, that you might
The better arm you to the sudden time,
Than if you had at leisure known of this.
Bast. How did he take it; who did taste to
　　him?
Hub. A monk, I tell you; a resolved villain,
Whose bowels suddenly burst out: the king
Yet speaks, and peradventure may recover.
Bast. Who didst thou leave to tend his
　　majesty?　　　　　　　　　　[come back,
Hub. Why, know you not? the lords are all
And brought Prince Henry in their company;
At whose request the king hath pardon'd them,
And they are all about his majesty.　[heaven,
Bast. Withhold thine indignation, mighty
And tempt us not to bear above our power!—
I'll tell thee, Hubert, half my power this night,
Passing these flats, are taken by the tide,—
These Lincoln washes have devoured them;
Myself, well-mounted, hardly have escap'd.
Away, before! conduct me to the king;
I doubt he will be dead or ere I come. [*Exeunt.*

SCENE VII.—*The Orchard of Swinstead Abbey.*

Enter PRINCE HENRY, SALISBURY, *and* BIGOT.

P. Hen. It is too late: the life of all his blood
Is touch'd corruptibly; and his pure brain,—
Which some suppose the soul's frail dwelling-
　　house,—
Doth, by the idle comments that it makes,
Foretell the ending of mortality.

Enter PEMBROKE.

Pem. His highness yet doth speak; and holds belief
That, being brought into the open air,
It would allay the burning quality
Of that fell poison which assaileth him.
  P. Hen. Let him be brought into the orchard here.—
Doth he still rage?   [*Exit* BIGOT.
  Pem.   He is more patient
Than when you left him; even now he sung.
  P. Hen. O vanity of sickness! fierce extremes
In their continuance will not feel themselves.
Death, having prey'd upon the outward parts,
Leaves them invisible; and his siege is now
Against the mind, the which he pricks and wounds
With many legions of strange fantasies,
Which, in their throng and press to that last hold,   [should sing.—
Confound themselves. 'Tis strange that death
I am the cygnet to this pale faint swan,
Who chants a doleful hymn to his own death;
And from the organ-pipe of frailty sings
His soul and body to their lasting rest.   [born
  Sal. Be of good comfort, prince; for you are
To set a form upon that indigest
Which he hath left so shapeless and so rude.

Re-enter BIGOT *and* Attendants, *who bring in* KING JOHN *in a chair.*

  K. John. Ay, marry, now my soul hath elbow-room;
It would not out at windows nor at doors.
There is so hot a summer in my bosom
That all my bowels crumble up to dust;
I am a scribbled form, drawn with a pen
Upon a parchment; and against this fire
Do I shrink up.
  P. Hen.   How fares your majesty?
  K. John. Poison'd,—ill fare;—dead, forsook, cast off:
And none of you will bid the winter come,
To thrust his icy fingers in my maw;
Nor let my kingdom's rivers take their course
Through my burn'd bosom; nor entreat the north
To make his bleak winds kiss my parched lips,
And comfort me with cold:—I do not ask you much;
I beg cold comfort; and you are so strait,
And so ingrateful, you deny me that.
  P. Hen. O, that there were some virtue in my tears,
That might relieve you!
  K. John.   The salt in them is hot.—
Within me is a hell; and there the poison
Is, as a fiend, confin'd to tyrannize
On unreprievable condemned blood.

         Enter the BASTARD.

  Bast. O, I am scalded with my violent motion,
And spleen of speed to see your majesty!
  K. John. O cousin, thou art come to set mine eye:
The tackle of my heart is crack'd and burn'd;
And all the shrouds, wherewith my life should sail,
Are turned to one thread, one little hair:
My heart hath one poor string to stay it by,
Which holds but till thy news be uttered;
And then all this thou seest is but a clod,
And model of confounded royalty.
  Bast. The Dauphin is preparing hitherward,
Where heaven he knows how we shall answer him;
For in a night the best part of my power,
As I upon advantage did remove,
Were in the washes all unwarily
Devoured by the unexpected flood.
            [*The* KING *dies.*
  Sal. You breathe these dead news in as dead an ear.   [thus.
My liege! my lord!—But now a king,—now
  P. Hen. Even so must I run on, and even so stop,
What surety of the world, what hope, what stay,
When this was now a king, and now is clay!
  Bast. Art thou gone so? I do but stay behind
To do the office for thee of revenge,
And then my soul shall wait on thee to heaven,
As it on earth hath been thy servant still.—
Now, now, you stars that move in your right spheres,   [faiths;
Where be your powers? Show now your mended
And instantly return with me again,
To push destruction and perpetual shame
Out of the weak door of our fainting land.
Straight let us seek, or straight we shall be sought;
The Dauphin rages at our very heels.
  Sal. It seems you know not, then, so much as we:
The Cardinal Pandulph is within at rest,
Who half an hour since came from the Dauphin,
And brings from him such offers of our peace
As we with honour and respect may take,
With purpose presently to leave this war.
  Bast. He will the rather do it when he sees
Ourselves well sinewed to our defence.
  Sal. Nay, it is in a manner done already;
For many carriages he hath despatch'd
To the sea-side, and put his cause and quarrel
To the disposing of the cardinal:
With whom yourself, myself, and other lords,
If you think meet, this afternoon will post
To cónsummate this business happily.
  Bast. Let it be so:—And you, my noble prince,
With other princes that may best be spar'd,
Shall wait upon your father's funeral.
  P. Hen. At Worcester must his body be interr'd;
For so he will'd it.
  Bast.   Thither shall it, then:

And happily may your sweet self put on
The lineal state and glory of the land!
To whom, with all submission, on my knee,
I do bequeath my faithful services
And true subjection everlastingly.
   Sal. And the like tender of our love we make,
To rest without a spot for evermore.
     P. Hen. I have a kind soul that would give
     you thanks,
And knows not how to do it but with tears.

   Bast. O, let us pay the time but needful woe,
Since it hath been beforehand with our griefs.—
This England never did, nor never shall,
Lie at the proud foot of a conqueror,
But when it first did help to wound itself.
Now these her princes are come home again,
Come the three corners of the world in arms,
And we shall shock them: nought shall make
     us rue,
If England to itself do rest but true. [*Exeunt.*

KING
RICHARD
SECOND.

Act II. Sc. 1.

THE LIFE AND DEATH OF KING RICHARD II.

DRAMATIS PERSONÆ

KING RICHARD THE SECOND.
EDMUND OF LANGLEY, *Duke of York,* } *Uncles to the King.*
JOHN OF GAUNT, *Duke of Lancaster,*
HENRY, *surnamed* BOLINGBROKE, *Duke of Hereford, Son to* JOHN OF GAUNT, *afterwards* KING HENRY IV.
DUKE OF AUMERLE, *Son to the Duke of York.*
THOMAS MOWBRAY, *Duke of Norfolk.*
DUKE OF SURREY.
EARL OF SALISBURY.
EARL BERKLEY.
BUSHY,
BAGOT, } *Creatures to* KING RICHARD.
GREEN,
EARL OF NORTHUMBERLAND.
HENRY PERCY, *his Son.*

LORD ROSS.
LORD WILLOUGHBY.
LORD FITZWATER.
BISHOP OF CARLISLE.
ABBOT OF WESTMINSTER.
Lord Marshal.
SIR PIERCE OF EXTON.
SIR STEPHEN SCROOP.
Captain *of a Band of Welshmen.*

QUEEN *to* KING RICHARD.
DUCHESS OF GLOSTER.
DUCHESS OF YORK.
Lady *attending on the* QUEEN.

Lords, Heralds, Officers, Soldiers, Two Gardeners, Keeper, Messenger, Groom, *and other* Attendants.

SCENE,—*Dispersedly in* ENGLAND *and* WALES.

ACT I.

SCENE I.—LONDON. *A Room in the Palace.*

Enter KING RICHARD, *attended;* JOHN OF GAUNT, *and other* Nobles.

K. Rich. Old John of Gaunt, time-honour'd Lancaster,
Hast thou, according to thy oath and band,
Brought hither Henry Hereford, thy bold son,
Here to make good the boisterous late appeal,
Which then our leisure would not let us hear,
Against the Duke of Norfolk, Thomas Mowbray?
   Gaunt. I have, my liege.   [sounded him,
   K. Rich. Tell me, moreover, hast thou
If he appeal the duke on ancient malice;
Or worthily, as a good subject should,
On some known ground of treachery in him?
   Gaunt. As near as I could sift him on that argument,—
On some apparent danger seen in him,
Aim'd at your highness,—no inveterate malice.
   K. Rich. Then call them to our presence: face to face.
And frowning brow to brow, ourselves will hear
The accuser and the accused freely speak:—
      [*Exeunt some* Attendants.
High-stomach'd are they both, and full of ire,
In rage deaf as the sea, hasty as fire.

Re-enter Attendants, *with* BOLINGBROKE *and* NORFOLK.

   Boling. Many years of happy days befall
My gracious sovereign, my most loving liege!
   Nor. Each day still better other's happiness;
Until the heavens, envying earth's good hap,
Add an immortal title to your crown!
   K. Rich. We thank you both: yet one but flatters us,
As well appeareth by the cause you come;
Namely, to appeal each other of high treason.—
Cousin of Hereford, what dost thou object
Against the Duke of Norfolk, Thomas Mowbray?   [speech!—
   Boling. First,—heaven be the record to my
In the devotion of a subject's love,
Tendering the precious safety of my prince,
And free from other misbegotten hate,
Come I appellant to this princely presence.—
Now, Thomas Mowbray, do I turn to thee;
And mark my greeting well; for what I speak,
My body shall make good upon this earth
Or my divine soul answer it in heaven.
Thou are a traitor and a miscreant;
Too good to be so, and too bad to live;
Since the more fair and crystal is the sky,
The uglier seem the clouds that in it fly.
Once more, the more to aggravate the note,
With a foul traitor's name stuff I thy throat;
And wish,—so please my sovereign,—ere I move,   [may prove.
What my tongue speaks, my right-drawn sword
   Nor. Let not my cold words here accuse my zeal;
'Tis not the trial of a woman's war,
The bitter clamour of two eager tongues,

Can arbitrate this cause betwixt us twain:
The blood is hot that must be cool'd for this:
Yet can I not of such tame patience boast
As to be hush'd, and naught at all to say: [me
First, the fair reverence of your highness curbs
From giving reins and spurs to my free speech;
Which else would post until it had return'd
These terms of treason doubled down his throat.
Setting aside his high blood's royalty,
And let him be no kinsman to my liege
I do defy him, and I spit at him;
Call him a slanderous coward and a villain:
Which to maintain, I would allow him odds;
And meet him, were I tied to run a-foot
Even to the frozen ridges of the Alps,
Or any other ground inhabitable,
Wherever Englishman durst set his foot.
Meantime let this defend my loyalty,—
By all my hopes, most falsely doth he lie.

Boling. Pale trembling coward, there I
    throw my gage,
Disclaiming here the kindred of the king;
And lay aside my high blood's royalty, [cept.
Which fear, not reverence, makes thee to ex-
If guilty dread hath left thee so much strength
As to take up mine honour's pawn, then stoop:
By that and all the rites of knighthood else,
Will I make good against thee, arm to arm,
What I have spoke, or thou canst worst devise.

Nor. I take it up; and by that sword I swear,
Which gently laid my knighthood on my
    shoulder,
I'll answer thee in any fair degree,
Or chivalrous design of knightly trial:
And when I mount, alive may I not light,
If I be traitor or unjustly fight!

K. Rich. What doth our cousin lay to Mow-
    bray's charge?
It must be great, that can inherit us
So much as of a thought of ill in him.

Boling. Look, what I speak my life shall
    prove it true;— [nobles,
That Mowbray hath receiv'd eight thousand
In name of lendings for your highness' soldiers,
The which he hath detain'd for lewd employ-
    ments,
Like a false traitor and injurious villain.
Besides, I say, and will in battle prove,—
Or here, or elsewhere to the farthest verge
That ever was survey'd by English eye,—
That all the treasons for these eighteen years
Complotted and contrived in this land
Fetch'd from false Mowbray their first head
    and spring.
Further, I say,—and further will maintain
Upon his bad life to make all this good,—
That he did plot the Duke of Gloster's death;
Suggest his soon-believing adversaries,
And consequently, like a traitor coward,
Sluic'd out his innocent soul through streams
    of blood:
Which blood, like sacrificing Abel's, cries,
Even from the tongueless caverns of the earth,
To me for justice and rough chastisement;

And, by the glorious worth of my descent,
This arm shall do it, or this life be spent!

K. Rich. How high a pitch his resolution
    soars!—
Thomas of Norfolk, what say'st thou to this?

Nor. O, let my sovereign turn away his face,
And bid his ears a little while be deaf,
Till I have told this slander of his blood,
How God and good men hate so foul a liar.

K. Rich. Mowbray, impartial are our eyes
    and ears:
Were he my brother, nay, my kingdom's heir,—
As he is but my father's brother's son,—
Now, by my sceptre's awe, I make a vow,
Such neighbour-nearness to our sacred blood
Should nothing privilege him, nor partialize
The unstooping firmness of my upright soul:
He is our subject, Mowbray, so art thou;
Free speech and fearless I to thee allow.

Nor. Then, Bolingbroke, as low as to thy
    heart, [liest!
Through the false passage of thy throat, thou
Three parts of that receipt I had for Calais
Disburs'd I duly to his highness' soldiers;
The other part reserv'd I by consent,
For that my sovereign liege was in my debt
Upon remainder of a dear account,
Since last I went to France to fetch his queen:
Now swallow down that lie!—For Gloster's
    death,—
I slew him not; but, to mine own disgrace,
Neglected my sworn duty in that case.—
For you, my noble Lord of Lancaster,
The honourable father to my foe,
Once did I lay an ambush for your life,
A trespass that doth vex my grieved soul:
But, ere I last receiv'd the sacrament,
I did confess it; and exactly begg'd
Your grace's pardon, and I hope I had it.
This is my fault: as for the rest appeal'd,
It issues from the rancour of a villain,
A recreant and most degenerate traitor:
Which in myself I boldly will defend;
And interchangeably hurl down my gage
Upon this overweening traitor's foot,
To prove myself a loyal gentleman
Even in the best blood chamber'd in his bosom.
In haste whereof, most heartily I pray
Your highness to assign our trial day.

K. Rich. Wrath-kindled gentlemen, be rul'd
    by me;
Let's purge this choler without letting blood;
This we prescribe, though no physician;
Deep malice makes too deep incision:
Forget, forgive; conclude, and be agreed;
Our doctors say this is no time to bleed.—
Good uncle, let this end where it begun;
We'll calm the Duke of Norfolk, you your son.

Gaunt. To be a make-peace shall become
    my age:— [gage.
Throw down, my son, the Duke of Norfolk's

K. Rich. And, Norfolk, throw down his.

Gaunt.   When, Harry? when?
Obedience bids I should not bid again.

K. Rich. Norfolk, throw down; we bid; there
　　is no boot.
Nor. Myself I throw, dread sovereign at thy
　　foot:
My life thou shalt command, but not my shame:
The one my duty owes; but my fair name,—
Despite of death, that lives upon my grave,—
To dark dishonour's use thou shalt not have.
I am disgrac'd, impeach'd, and baffled here;
Pierc'd to the soul with slander's venom'd
　　spear,
The which no balm can cure but his heart-blood
Which breath'd this poison.
　　K. Rich.　　　　Rage must be withstood:
Give me his gage:—lions make leopards tame.
　　Nor. Yea, but not change his spots: take
　　　　but my shame,
And I resign my gage. My dear dear lord,
The purest treasure mortal times afford
Is spotless reputation; that away,
Men are but gilded loam or painted clay.
A jewel in a ten-times-barr'd-up chest
Is a bold spirit in a loyal breast.
Mine honour is my life; both grow in one;
Take honour from me, and my life is done:
Then, dear my liege, mine honour let me try;
In that I live, and for that will I die.
　　K. Rich. Cousin, throw down your gage; do
　　　　you begin.　　　　　　　[foul sin!
　　Boling. O, God defend my soul from such
Shall I seem crest-fallen in my father's sight?
Or with pale beggar-fear impeach my height
Before this outdar'd dastard? Ere my tongue
Shall wound mine honour with such feeble
　　wrong,
Or sound so base a parle, my teeth shall tear
The slavish motive of recanting fear;
And spit it bleeding in his high disgrace,
Where shame doth harbour, even in Mow-
　　bray's face!　　　　　　　[*Exit* GAUNT.
　　K. Rich. We were not born to sue, but to
　　　　command:—
Which since we cannot do to make you friends,
Be ready, as your lives shall answer it,
At Coventry, upon Saint Lambert's day:
There shall your swords and lances arbitrate
The swelling difference of your settled hate:
Since we can not atone you, we shall see
Justice design the victor's chivalry.—
Lord marshal, command our officers-at-arms
Be ready to direct these home-alarms. [*Exeunt.*

SCENE II.—*The same. A Room in the* DUKE OF
　　LANCASTER'S *Palace.*

Enter GAUNT *and* DUCHESS OF GLOSTER.

　　Gaunt. Alas, the part I had in Gloster's blood
Doth more solicit me than your exclaims,
To stir against the butchers of his life.
But since correction lieth in those hands
Which made the fault that we cannot correct,
Put we our quarrel to the will of heaven;
Who, when they see the hours ripe on earth,
Will rain hot vengeance on offenders' heads.

　　Duch. Finds brotherhood in thee no sharper
　　　　spur?
Hath love in thy old blood no living fire?
Edward's seven sons, whereof thyself art one,
Were as seven vials of his sacred blood,
Or seven fair branches springing from one root:
Some of those seven are dried by nature's
　　course,
Some of those branches by the Destinies cut;
But Thomas, my dear lord, my life, my Glos-
　　ter,—
One vial full of Edward's sacred blood,
One flourishing branch of his most royal root,
Is crack'd, and all the precious liquor spilt;
Is hack'd down, and his summer-leaves all
　　faded,
By envy's hand and murder's bloody axe.
Ah, Gaunt, his blood was thine! that bed, that
　　womb,
That mettle, that self-mould, that fashion'd
　　thee,
Made him a man; and though thou liv'st and
　　breath'st,
Yet art thou slain in him: thou dost consent
In some large measure to thy father's death,
In that thou seest thy wretched brother die,
Who was the model of thy father's life.
Call it not patience, Gaunt,—it is despair:
In suffering thus thy brother to be slaughter'd,
Thou show'st the naked pathway to thy life,
Teaching stern murder how to butcher thee:
That which in mean men we entitle patience,
Is pale cold cowardice in noble breasts.
What shall I say? to safeguard thine own life,
The best way is to venge my Gloster's death.
　　Gaunt. God's is the quarrel; for God's sub-
　　　　stitute,
His deputy anointed in his sight,
Hath caus'd his death: the which, if wrongfully,
Let heaven revenge; for I may never lift
An angry arm against his minister.
　　Duch. Where, then, alas, may I complain
　　　　myself?
　　Gaunt. To God, the widow's champion and
　　　　defence.　　　　　　　　　　[Gaunt.
　　Duch. Why, then, I will. Farewell, old
Thou go'st to Coventry, there to behold
Our cousin Hereford and fell Mowbray fight:
O, sit my husband's wrongs on Hereford's
　　spear,
That it may enter butcher Mowbray's breast!
Or, if misfortune miss the first career,
Be Mowbray's sins so heavy in his bosom
That they may break his foaming courser's
　　back,
And throw the rider headlong in the lists,
A caitiff recreant to my cousin Hereford!
Farewell, old Gaunt; thy sometimes brother's
　　wife,
With her companion grief must end her life.
　　Gaunt. Sister, farewell: I must to Coventry:
As much good stay with thee as go with me!
　　Duch. Yet one word more:—grief boundeth
　　　　where it falls,

Not with the empty hollowness, but weight:
I take my leave before I have begun;
For sorrow ends not when it seemeth done.
Commend me to my brother, Edmund York.
Lo, this is all:—nay, yet depart not so;
Though this be all, do not so quickly go;
I shall remember more. Bid him—O, what?—
With all good speed at Plashy visit me.
Alack, and what shall good old York there see,
But empty lodgings and unfurnish'd walls,
Unpeopled offices, untrodden stones?
And what hear there for welcome but my
   groans?
Therefore commend me; let him not come there
To seek out sorrow that dwells everywhere.
Desolate, desolate, will I hence and die:
The least leave of thee takes my weeping eye!
                              [*Exeunt.*

SCENE III.—*Gosford Green, near Coventry.*

*Lists set out, and a throne. Heralds, &c., attend-
ing. Enter the* Lord Marshal, *and* AUMERLE.

Mar. My Lord Aumerle, is Harry Hereford
   arm'd?   [in.
Aum. Yea, at all points; and longs to enter
Mar. The Duke of Norfolk, sprightfully and
   bold,   [pet.
Stays but the summons of the appellant's trum-
Aum. Why, then, the champions are pre-
   par'd, and stay
For nothing but his majesty's approach.

Flourish of trumpets. Enter KING RICHARD,
who takes his seat on his throne; GAUNT *and
several* Noblemen, *who take their places. A
trumpet is sounded, and answered by another
trumpet within. Then enter* NORFOLK *in armour, preceded by a* Herald.

K. Rich. Marshal, demand of yonder cham-
   pion
The cause of his arrival here in arms:
Ask him his name; and orderly proceed
To swear him in the justice of his cause.
Mar. In God's name and the king's, say
   who thou art,
And why thou com'st thus knightly clad in
   arms;
Against what man thou com'st, and what thy
   quarrel:
Speak truly, on thy knighthood and thine oath;
And so defend thee heaven and thy valour!
Nor. My name is Thomas Mowbray, Duke
   of Norfolk;
Who hither come engaged by my oath,—
Which God defend a knight should violate!—
Both to defend my loyalty and truth
To God, my king, and his succeeding issue,
Against the Duke of Hereford that appeals me;
And, by the grace of God and this mine arm,
To prove him in defending of myself,
A traitor to my God, my king, and me:
And as I truly fight, defend me heaven!

Trumpet sounds. Enter BOLINGBROKE *in armour, preceded by a* Herald.

K. Rich. Marshal, ask yonder knight in arms,
Both who he is, and why he cometh hither
Thus plated in habiliments of war;
And formally, according to our law,
Depose him in the justice of his cause.
Mar. What is thy name? and wherefore
   com'st thou hither,
Before King Richard in his royal lists?
Against whom comest thou? and what's thy
   quarrel?
Speak like a true knight, so defend thee heaven!
Boling. Harry of Hereford, Lancaster, and
   Derby,
Am I; who ready here do stand in arms,
To prove, by God's grace and my body's valour,
In lists, on Thomas Mowbray, Duke of Norfolk,
That he's a traitor, foul and dangerous,
To God of Heaven, King Richard, and to me:
And as I truly fight, defend me heaven!
Mar. On pain of death, no person be so bold
Or daring-hardy as to touch the lists,
Except the marshal and such officers
Appointed to direct these fair designs.
Boling. Lord marshal, let me kiss my sove-
   reign's hand,
And bow my knee before his majesty:
For Mowbray and myself are like two men
That vow a long and weary pilgrimage;
Then let us take a ceremonious leave
And loving farewell of our several friends.
Mar. The appellant in all duty greets your
   highness,
And craves to kiss your hand and take his leave.
K. Rich. We will descend and fold him in
   our arms.—
Cousin of Hereford, as thy cause is right,
So be thy fortune in this royal fight!
Farewell, my blood; which if to-day thou shed,
Lament we may, but not revenge thee dead.
Boling. O, let no noble eye profane a tear
For me, if I be gor'd with Mowbray's spear:
As confident as is the falcon's flight
Against a bird, do I with Mowbray fight.—
My loving lord, I take my leave of you;—
Of you, my noble cousin, Lord Aumerle,
Not sick, although I have to do with death,
But lusty, young, and cheerly drawing breath.—
Lo, as at English feasts, so I regreet
The daintiest last, to make the end more sweet:—
O thou, the earthly author of my blood,—
                              [*To* GAUNT.
Whose youthful spirit, in me regenerate,
Doth with a twofold vigour lift me up
To reach at victory above my head,—
Add proof unto mine armour with thy prayers;
And with thy blessings steel my lance's point,
That it may enter Mowbray's waxen coat,
And furbish new the name of John o' Gaunt,
Even in the lusty 'haviour of his son. [perous!
Gaunt. God in thy good cause make thee pros-
Be swift like lightning in the execution;

And let thy blows, doubly redoubled,
Fall like amazing thunder on the casque
Of thy advérse pernicious enemy:
Rouse up thy youthful blood, be valiant and live.
  Boling. Mine innocency and Saint George to
    thrive!
  Nor. However God or fortune cast my lot,
There lives or dies, true to King Richard's throne,
A loyal, just, and upright gentleman:
Never did captive with a freer heart
Cast off his chains of bondage, and embrace
His golden uncontroll'd enfranchisement,
More than my dancing soul doth celebrate
This feast of battle with mine adversary.—
Most mighty liege,—and my companion peers,—
Take from my mouth the wish of happy years:
As gentle and as jocund as to jest
Go I to fight: truth hath a quiet breast.
  K. Rich. Farewell, my lord: securely I espy
Virtue with valour couched in thine eye.—
Order the trial, marshal, and begin. [Derby,
  Mar. Harry of Hereford, Lancaster, and
Receive thy lance; and God defend the right!
  Boling. Strong as a tower in hope, I cry amen.
  Mar. Go bear this lance [*to an* Officer] to
    Thomas, Duke of Norfolk. [Derby,
  1 *Her.* Harry of Hereford, Lancaster, and
Stands here for God, his sovereign, and himself,
On pain to be found false and recreant,
To prove the Duke of Norfolk, Thomas Mow-
    bray,
A traitor to his God, his king, and him;
And dares him to set forward to the fight.
  2 *Her.* Here standeth Thomas Mowbray,
    Duke of Norfolk,
On pain to be found false and recreant,
Both to defend himself, and to approve
Henry of Hereford, Lancaster, and Derby,
To God, his sovereign, and to him disloyal;
Courageously, and with a free desire,
Attending but the signal to begin.
  Mar. Sound, trumpets; and set forward,
    combatants. [*A charge sounded.*
Stay, the king hath thrown his warder down.
  K. Rich. Let them lay by their helmets and
    their spears,
And both return back to their chairs again:—
Withdraw with us:—and let the trumpets sound
While we return these dukes what we decree.—
               [*A long flourish.*
Draw near, [*To the combatants.*
And list what with our council we have done.
For that our kingdom's earth should not be soil'd
With that dear blood which it hath fostered;
And for our eyes do hate the dire aspéct
Of civil wounds plough'd up with neighbours'
    swords;
And for we think the eagle-winged pride
Of sky-aspiring and ambitious thoughts,
With rival-hating envy, set on you
To wake our peace, which in our country's cradle
Draws the sweet infant breath of gentle sleep;
Which so rous'd up with boisterous untun'd
    drums,

With harsh-resounding trumpets' dreadful bray,
And grating shock of wrathful iron arms,
Might from our quiet confines fright fair peace,
And make us wade even in our kindred's blood;—
Therefore, we banish you our territories:—
You, cousin Hereford, upon pain of life,
Till twice five summers have enrich'd our fields
Shall not regreet our fair dominions,
But tread the stranger paths of banishment.
  Boling. Your will be done: this must my
    comfort be,— [me;
That sun that warms you here shall shine on
And those his golden beams to you here lent
Shall point on me and gild my banishment.
  K. Rich. Norfolk, for thee remains a heavier
    doom,
Which I with some unwillingness pronounce:
The sly-slow hours shall not determinate
The dateless limit of thy dear exile;—
The hopeless word of—never to return
Breathe I against thee, upon pain of life.
  Nor. A heavy sentence, my most gracious
    liege, [mouth:
And all unlook'd-for from your highness'
A dearer merit, not so deep a maim
As to be cast forth in the common air,
Have I deserved at your highness' hands.
The language I have learn'd these forty years,
My native English, now I must forego:
And now my tongue's use is to me no more
Than an unstring'd viol or a harp;
Or like a cunning instrument cas'd up,
Or, being open, put into his hands
That knows no touch to tune the harmony:
Within my mouth you have engaol'd my tongue,
Doubly portcullis'd with my teeth and lips;
And dull, unfeeling, barren ignorance
Is made my gaoler to attend on me.
I am too old to fawn upon a nurse,
Too far in years to be a pupil now:
What is thy sentence, then, but speechless death,
Which robs my tongue from breathing native
    breath? [sionate:
  K. Rich. It boots thee not to be compas-
After our sentence plaining comes too late.
  Nor. Then thus I turn me from my country's
    light,
To dwell in solemn shades of endless night.
                 [*Retiring.*
  K. Rich. Return again, and take an oath
    with thee.
Lay on our royal sword your banish'd hands;
Swear by the duty that you owe to God,—
Our part therein we banish with yourselves,—
To keep the oath that we administer:—
You never shall—so help you truth and God!—
Embrace each other's love in banishment;
Nor never look upon each other's face;
Nor never write, regreet, nor reconcile
This lowering tempest of your home-bred hate;
Nor never by advised purpose meet
To plot, contrive, or complot any ill
'Gainst us, our state, our subjects, or our land.
  Boling. I swear.

Nor. And I, to keep all this.

Boling. Norfolk, so far as to mine enemy;—
By this time, had the king permitted us,
One of our souls had wander'd in the air,
Banish'd this frail sepulchre of our flesh,
As now our flesh is banish'd from this land:
Confess thy treasons, ere thou fly the realm;
Since thou hast far to go, bear not along
The clogging burden of a guilty soul.

Nor. No, Bolingbroke: if ever I were traitor,
My name be blotted from the book of life,
And I from heaven banish'd, as from hence!
But what thou art, God, thou, and I do know;
And all too soon, I fear, the king shall rue.—
Farewell, my liege.—Now no way can I stray:
Save back to England, all the world's my way.
                                                        [*Exit.*

K. Rich. Uncle, even in the glasses of thine eyes
I see thy grieved heart: thy sad aspéct
Hath from the number of his banish'd years
Pluck'd four away.—[*To* BOLING.] Six frozen winters spent,
Return with welcome home from banishment.

Boling. How long a time lies in one little word!
Four lagging winters and four wanton springs
End in a word: such is the breath of kings.

Gaunt. I thank my liege that in regard of me
He shortens four years of my son's exile:
But little vantage shall I reap thereby;
For, ere the six years that he hath to spend
Can change their moons and bring their times about,
My oil-dried lamp and time bewasted light
Shall be extinct with age and endless night;
My inch of taper will be burnt and done,
And blindfold death not let me see my son.

K. Rich. Why, uncle, thou hast many years to live.

Gaunt. But not a minute, king, that thou canst give:
Shorten my days thou canst with sullen sorrow,
And pluck nights from me, but not lend a morrow;
Thou canst help time to furrow me with age,
But stop no wrinkle in his pilgrimage;
Thy word is current with him for my death,
But dead, thy kingdom cannot buy my breath.

K. Rich. Thy son is banish'd upon good advice,
Whereto thy tongue a party-verdict gave:
Why at our justice seem'st thou, then, to lower?

Gaunt. Things sweet to taste prove in digestion sour.
You urg'd me as a judge; but I had rather
You would have bid me argue like a father.
O, had it been a stranger, not my child,
To smooth his fault I should have been more mild:
A partial slander sought I to avoid,
And in the sentence my own life destroy'd.
Alas, I look'd when some of you should say,
I was too strict to make mine own away;

But you gave leave to mine unwilling tongue
Against my will to do myself this wrong.

K. Rich. Cousin, farewell;—and, uncle, bid him so:
Six years we banish him, and he shall go.
                        [*Flourish. Exeunt* K. RICH. *and* Train.

Aum. Cousin, farewell: what presence must not know,
From where you do remain let paper show.

Mar. My lord, no leave take I; for I will ride
As far as land will let me by your side.

Gaunt. O, to what purpose dost thou hoard thy words,
That thou return'st no greeting to thy friends?

Boling. I have too few to take my leave of you,
When the tongue's office should be prodigal
To breathe the abundant dolour of the heart.

Gaunt. Thy grief is but thy absence for a time.

Boling. Joy absent, grief is present for that time.

Gaunt. What is six winters? they are quickly [gone.

Boling. To men in joy; but grief makes one hour ten. [pleasure.

Gaunt. Call it a travel that thou tak'st for

Boling. My heart will sigh when I miscall it so,
Which finds it an enforced pilgrimage.

Gaunt. The sullen passage of thy weary steps
Esteem a foil, wherein thou art to set
The precious jewel of thy home-return.

Boling. Nay, rather, every tedious stride I make
Will but remember me what a deal of world
I wander from the jewels that I love.
Must I not serve a long apprenticehood
To foreign passages; and in the end,
Having my freedom, boast of nothing else
But that I was a journeyman to grief? [visits

Gaunt. All places that the eye of heaven
Are to a wise man ports and happy heavens,
Teach thy necessity to reason thus;
There is no virtue like necessity.
Think not the king did banish thee,
But thou the king: woe doth the heavier sit
Where it perceives it is but faintly borne.
Go, say I sent thee forth to purchase honour
And not the king exil'd thee; or suppose
Devouring pestilence hangs in our air,
And thou art flying to a fresher clime:
Look, what thy soul holds dear, imagine it
To lie that way thou go'st, not whence thou com'st:
Suppose the singing-birds musicians, [strew'd,
The grass whereon thou tread'st the presence
The flowers fair ladies, and thy steps no more
Than a delightful measure or a dance;
For gnarling sorrow hath less power to bite
The man that mocks at it and sets it light.

Boling. O, who can hold a fire in his hand
By thinking on the frosty Caucasus?
Or cloy the hungry edge of appetite
By bare imagination of a feast?

Or wallow naked in December snow
By thinking on fantastic summer's heat?
O, no! the apprehension of the good
Gives but the greater feeling to the worse:
Fell sorrow's tooth doth never rankle more
Than when it bites, but lanceth not the sore.
　Gaunt. Come, come, my son, I'll bring thee
　　on thy way:
Had I thy youth and cause, I would not stay.
　Boling. Then, England's ground, farewell;
　　sweet soil, adieu;
My mother, and my nurse, that bears me yet!
Where'er I wander, boast of this I can,—
Though banish'd, yet a true-born Englishman.
　　　　　　　　　　　　　　　　　　[*Exeunt.*

SCENE IV.—*The Court.*

Enter KING RICHARD, BAGOT, *and* GREEN;
　　　AUMERLE *following.*

　K. Rich. We did observe.—Cousin Aumerle,
How far brought you high Hereford on his
　way?　　　　　　　　　　　　　　　[him so,
　Aum. I brought high Hereford, if you call
But to the next highway, and there I left him.
　K. Rich. And say, what store of parting
　　tears were shed?　　　　　　　　　[east wind,
　Aum. Faith, none for me; except the north-
Which then blew bitterly against our faces,
Awak'd the sleeping rheum, and so by chance
Did grace our hollow parting with a tear.
　K. Rich. What said our cousin when you
　　parted with him?
　Aum. "Farewell:"
And, for my heart disdained that my tongue
Should so profane the word, that taught me
　　craft
To counterfeit oppression of such grief,
That words seem'd buried in my sorrow's grave.
Marry, would the word "farewell" have
　　lengthen'd hours,
And added years to his short banishment,
He should have had a volume of farewells;
But since it would not, he had none of me.
　K. Rich. He is our cousin, cousin; but 'tis
　　doubt,
When time shall call him home from banish-
　　ment,
Whether our kinsman come to see his friends.
Ourself, and Bushy, Bagot here, and Green,
Observ'd his courtship to the common people;
How he did seem to dive into their hearts
With humble and familiar courtesy;
What reverence he did throw away on slaves;
Wooing poor craftsmen with the craft of smiles,
And patient underbearing of his fortune,
As 'twere to banish their affects with him.
Off goes his bonnet to an oyster-wench;
A brace of draymen bid God speed him well,
And had the tribute of his supple knee,
With *Thanks, my countrymen, my loving friends;*
As were our England in reversion his,
And he our subjects' next degree in hope.
　Green. Well, he is gone; and with him go
　　these thoughts.

Now for the rebels which stand out in Ire-
　land,—
Expedient manage must be made, my liege,
Ere further leisure yield them further means
For their advantage and your highness' loss.
　K. Rich. We will ourself in person to this
　　war:
And, for our coffers,—with too great a court
And liberal largess,—are grown somewhat light,
We are enforc'd to farm our royal realm;
The revenue whereof shall furnish us
For our affairs in hand. If that come short,
Our substitutes at home shall have blank
　　charters;　　　　　　　　　　　　　　[rich,
Whereto, when they shall know what men are
They shall subscribe them for large sums of
　　gold,
And send them after to supply our wants;
For we will make for Ireland presently.

Enter BUSHY.

Bushy, what news?
　Bushy. Old John of Gaunt is grievous sick,
　　my lord,
Suddenly taken; and hath sent post-haste
To entreat your majesty to visit him.
　K. Rich. Where lies he?
　Bushy. At Ely House.　　　　　　[mind
　K. Rich. Now put it, God, in his physician's
To help him to his grave immediately!
The lining of his coffers shall make coats
To deck our soldiers for these Irish wars.—
Come, gentlemen, let's all go visit him:
Pray God we may make haste, and come too
　　late!　　　　　　　　　　　　　　[*Exeunt.*

ACT II.

SCENE I.—LONDON. *A Room in* ELY HOUSE.

GAUNT *on a couch; the* DUKE OF YORK *and
　　others standing by him.*

　Gaunt. Will the king come, that I may
　　breathe my last
In wholesome counsel to his unstaid youth?
　York. Vex not yourself, nor strive not with
　　your breath;
For all in vain comes counsel to his ear. [men
　Gaunt. O, but they say the tongues of dying
Enforce attention like deep harmony:
Where words are scarce, they are seldom spent
　　in vain;　　　　　　　　　　　　　　[in pain
For they breathe truth that breathe their words
He that no more must say is listen'd more
　Than they whom youth and ease have taught
　　to glose;　　　　　　　　　　　　　[before;
More are men's ends mark'd than their lives
　The setting sun, and music at the close,
As the last taste of sweets, is sweetest last,
Writ in remembrance more than things long
　　past;　　　　　　　　　　　　　　[hear,
Though Richard my life's counsel would not
My death's sad tale may yet undeaf his ear.
　York. No; it is stopp'd with other flattering
　　sounds,

As, praises of his state: then there are found
Lascivious metres, to whose venom-sound
The open ear of youth doth always listen;
Report of fashions in proud Italy,
Whose manners still our tardy apish nation
Limps after, in base imitation.
Where doth the world thrust forth a vanity,—
So it be new, there's no respect how vile,—
That is not quickly buzz'd into his ears?
Then all too late comes counsel to be heard,
Where will doth mutiny with wit's regard.
Direct not him, whose way himself will choose:
'Tis breath thou lack'st, and that breath wilt
　　　thou lose.　　　　　　　　　[inspir'd,
　　Gaunt. Methinks I am a prophet new
And thus, expiring, do foretell of him:
His rash fierce blaze of riot cannot last,
For violent fires soon burn out themselves;
Small showers last long, but sudden storms are
　　short;
He tires betimes that spurs too fast betimes;
With eager feeding food doth choke the feeder:
Light vanity, insatiate cormorant,
Consuming means, soon preys upon itself.
This royal throne of kings, this scepter'd isle
This earth of majesty, this seat of Mars,
This other Eden, demi-paradise;
This fortress built by Nature for herself
Against infection and the hand of war;
This happy breed of men, this little world;
This precious stone set in the silver sea,
Which serves it in the office of a wall,
Or as a moat defensive to a house,
Against the envy of less happier lands;
This blessed plot, this earth, this realm, this
　　England,
This nurse, this teeming womb of royal kings,
Fear'd by their breed, and famous by their
　　birth,
Renowned for their deeds as far from home,—
For Christian service and true chivalry,—
As is the sepulchre in stubborn Jewry
Of the world's ransom, blessed Mary's Son;—
This land of such dear souls, this dear dear land,
Dear for her reputation through the world,
Is now leas'd out,—I die pronouncing it,—
Like to a tenement or pelting farm:
England, bound in with the triumphant sea,
Whose rocky shore beats back the envious siege
Of watery Neptune, is now bound in with
　　shame,
With inky blots, and rotten parchment bonds:
That England, that was wont to conquer others,
Hath made a shameful conquest of itself.
Ah, would the scandal vanish with my life,
How happy then were my ensuing death!

Enter KING RICHARD *and* QUEEN, AUMERLE,
　　BUSHY, GREEN, BAGOT, ROSS, *and* WIL-
　　LOUGHBY.

　　York. The king is come: deal mildly with
　　　his youth;　　　　　　　　　　[more.
For young hot colts, being rag'd, do rage the

　　K. Rich. What comfort, man? How is't with
　　　aged Gaunt?　　　　　　　　　[position!
　　Gaunt. O, how that name befits my com-
Old Gaunt, indeed; and gaunt in being old:
Within me grief hath kept a tedious fast;
And who abstains from meat that is not gaunt?
For sleeping England long time have I watch'd;
Watching breeds leanness, leanness is all gaunt:
The pleasure that some fathers feeds upon
Is my strict fast,—I mean my children's looks;
And therein fasting, hast thou made me gaunt:
Gaunt am I for the grave, gaunt as a grave,
Whose hollow womb inherits naught but bones.
　　K. Rich. Can sick men play so nicely with
　　　their names?
　　Gaunt. No, misery makes sport to mock
　　　itself:
Since thou dost seek to kill my name in me,
I mock my name, great king, to flatter thee.
　　K. Rich. Should dying men flatter with those
　　　that live?　　　　　　　　　　[die.
　　Gaunt. No, no; men living flatter those that
　　K. Rich. Thou, now a-dying, say'st thou
　　　flatter'st me.
　　Gaunt. O, no! thou diest, though I the sicker
　　　be.　　　　　　　　　　　　[thee ill.
　　K. Rich. I am in health, I breathe, and see
　　Gaunt. Now, He that made me knows I see
　　　thee ill;
Ill in myself to see, and in thee seeing ill.
Thy death-bed is no lesser than the land
Wherein thou liest in reputation sick;
And thou, too careless patient as thou art,
Committ'st thy anointed body to the cure
Of those physicians that first wounded thee:
A thousand flatterers sit within thy crown,
Whose compass is no bigger than thy head;
And yet, encaged in so small a verge,
The waste is no whit lesser than thy land.
O, had thy grandsire, with a prophet's eye,
Seen how his son's son should destroy his sons,
From forth thy reach he would have laid thy
　　shame,
Deposing thee before thou wert possess'd,
Which art possess'd now to depose thyself.
Why, cousin, wert thou regent of the world,
It were a shame to let this land by lease;
But for thy world enjoying but this land,
Is it not more than shame to shame it so?
Landlord of England art thou now, not king:
Thy state of law is bondslave to the law;
And—
　　K. Rich. And thou a lunatic lean-witted fool,
Presuming on an ague's privilege,
Dar'st with thy frozen admonition
Make pale our cheek, chasing the royal blood
With fury from his native residence.
Now by my seat's right royal majesty,
Wert thou not brother to great Edward's son,
This tongue that runs so roundly in thy head
Should run thy head from thy unreverend
　　shoulders.　　　　　　　　　[ward's son,
　　Gaunt. O, spare me not, my brother Ed-
For that I was his father Edward's son;—

　　Queen. How fares our noble uncle, Lancaster?

That blood already, like the pelican,
Hast thou tapp'd out, and drunkenly carous'd:
My brother Gloster, plain well-meaning soul—
Whom fair befall in heaven 'mongst happy
　　souls!—
May be a precedent and witness good [blood:
That thou respect'st not spilling Edward's
Join with the present sickness that I have:
And thy unkindness be like crooked age,
To crop at once a too-long wither'd flower.
Live in thy shame, but die not shame with
　　thee!—
These words hereafter thy tormentors be!—
Convey me to my bed, then to my grave.
Love they to live that love and honour have.
　　　　[*Exit, borne out by his* Attendants.
　　K. Rich. And let them die that age and
　　　sullens have;
For both hast thou, and both become the grave.
　　York. I do beseech your majesty, impute his
　　words
To wayward sickliness and age in him:
He loves you, on my life, and holds you dear
As Harry Duke of Hereford, were he here.
　　K. Rich. Right, you say true: as Hereford's
　　love, so his;
As theirs, so mine; and all be as it is.

　　　　Enter NORTHUMBERLAND.

　　North. My liege, old Gaunt commends him
　　to your majesty.
　　K. Rich. What says he?
　　North.　　　Nay, nothing; all is said:
His tongue is now a stringless instrument;
Words, life, and all, old Lancaster hath spent.
　　York. Be York the next that must be bank-
　　rupt so!
Though death be poor, it ends a mortal woe.
　　K. Rich. The ripest fruit first falls, and so
　　doth he;
His time is spent, our pilgrimage must be:
So much for that.—Now for our Irish wars:
We must supplant those rough rug-headed kerns,
Which live like venom, where no venom else,
But only they, hath privilege to live.
And for these great affairs do ask some charge:
Towards our assistance we do seize to us
The plate, coin, revenues, and movables,
Whereof our uncle Gaunt did stand possess'd.
　　York. How long shall I be patient? ah, how
　　long
Shall tender duty make me suffer wrong?
Not Gloster's death, nor Hereford's banish-
　　ment,　　　　　　　　　　　　[wrongs,
Not Gaunt's rebukes, nor England's private
Nor the prevention of poor Bolingbroke
About his marriage, nor my own disgrace,
Have ever made me sour my patient cheek,
Or bend one wrinkle on my sovereign's face.
I am the last of noble Edward's sons,
Of whom thy father, Prince of Wales, was first:
In war was never lion rag'd more fierce,
In peace was never gentle lamb more mild,
Than was that young and princely gentleman.

His face thou hast, for even so look'd he,
Accomplish'd with the number of thy hours;
But when he frown'd, it was against the French,
And not against his friends: his noble hand
Did win what he did spend, and spent not that
Which his triumphant father's hand had won:
His hands were guilty of no kindred's blood,
But bloody with the enemies of his kin.
O Richard! York is too far gone with grief,
Or else he never would compare between.
　　K. Rich. Why, uncle, what's the matter?
　　York.　　　　　　O my liege,
Pardon me, if you please; if not, I, pleas'd
Not to be pardon'd, am content withal.
Seek you to seize, and gripe into your hands,
The royalties and rights of banish'd Hereford?
Is not Gaunt dead? and doth not Hereford live?
Was not Gaunt just? and is not Harry true?
Did not the one deserve to have an heir?
Is not his heir a well-deserving son?　　[Time
Take Hereford's rights away, and take from
His charters and his customary rights;
Let not to-morrow, then, ensue to-day;
Be not thyself,—for how art thou a king
But by fair sequence and succession?
Now, afore God—God forbid I say true!—
If you do wrongfully seize Hereford's rights,
Call in the letters-patents that he hath
By his attorneys-general to sue
His livery, and deny his offer'd homage,
You pluck a thousand dangers on your head,
You lose a thousand well-disposed hearts,
And prick my tender patience to those thoughts
Which honour and allegiance cannot think.
　　K. Rich. Think what you will, we seize into
　　our hands
His plate, his goods, his money, and his lands.
　　York. I'll not be by the while: my liege,
　　farewell:
What will ensue hereof, there's none can tell:
But by bad courses may be understood
That their events can never fall out good.
　　　　　　　　　　　　　　　[*Exit.*
　　K. Rich. Go, Bushy, to the Earl of Wiltshire
　　straight:
Bid him repair to us to Ely House
To see this business. To-morrow next
We will for Ireland; and 'tis time, I trow:
And we create, in absence of ourself,
Our uncle York lord governor of England;
For he is just, and always lov'd us well.—
Come on, our queen: to-morrow must we part;
Be merry, for our time of stay is short.
　　　　[*Flourish. Exeunt* KING, QUEEN, BUSHY,
　　　　　　AUMERLE, GREEN, *and* BAGOT.
　　North. Well, lords, the Duke of Lancaster
　　is dead.
　　Ross. And living too; for now his son is duke.
　　Willo. Barely in title, not in revenue.
　　North. Richly in both, if justice had her
　　right.
　　Ross. My heart is great; but it must break
　　with silence,
Ere 't be disburden'd with a liberal tongue.

North. Nay, speak thy mind; and let him
ne'er speak more
That speaks thy words again to do thee harm!
Willo. Tends that thou wouldst speak to the
Duke of Hereford?
If it be so, out with it boldly, man;
Quick is mine ear to hear of good towards him.
Ross. No good at all, that I can do for him;
Unless you call it good to pity him,
Bereft and gelded of his patrimony.
North. Now, afore God, 'tis shame such
wrongs are borne
In him, a royal prince, and many more
Of noble blood in this declining land.
The king is not himself, but basely led
By flatterers; and what they will inform,
Merely in hate, 'gainst any of us all,
That will the king severely prosecute
'Gainst us, our lives, our children, and our
heirs.
Ross. The commons hath be pill'd with
grievous taxes,
And quite lost their hearts: the nobles hath he
fin'd
For ancient quarrels, and quite lost their hearts.
Willo. And daily new exactions are devis'd,—
As blanks, benevolences, and I wot not what:
But what, o' God's name, doth become of this?
North. Wars have not wasted it, for warr'd
he hath not,
But basely yielded upon compromise
That which his ancestors achiev'd with blows:
More hath he spent in peace than they in wars.
Ross. The Earl of Wiltshire hath the realm
in farm.
Willo. The king's grown bankrupt, like a
broken man.   [over him.
North. Reproach and dissolution hangeth
Ross. He hath not money for these Irish
wars,
His burdenous taxations notwithstanding,
But by the robbing of the banish'd duke.
North. His noble kinsman:—most degener-
ate king!
But, lords, we hear this fearful tempest sing,
Yet seek no shelter to avoid the storm;
We see the wind set sore upon our sails,
And yet we strike not, but securely perish.
Ross. We see the very wreck that we must
suffer;
And unavoided is the danger now,
For suffering so the causes of our wreck.
North. Not so; even through the hollow eyes
of death
I spy life peering; but I dare not say
How near the tidings of our comfort is.
Willo. Nay, let us share thy thoughts, as
thou dost ours.   [land:
Ross. Be confident to speak, Northumber-
We three are but thyself; and, speaking so,
Thy words are but as thoughts; therefore, be
bold.
North. Then thus:—I have from Port le
Blanc, a bay

In Brittany, receiv'd intelligence   [Cobham,
That Harry Duke of Hereford, Renald Lord
That late broke from the Duke of Exeter,
His brother, Archbishop late of Canterbury,
Sir Thomas Erpingham, Sir John Ramston,
Sir John Norbery, Sir Robert Waterton, and
Francis Quoint,—   [tagne,
All these, well furnish'd by the Duke of Bre-
With eight tall ships, three thousand men of
war,
Are making hither with all due expedience,
And shortly mean to touch our northern shore:
Perhaps they had ere this, but that they stay
The first departing of the king for Ireland.
If, then, we shall shake off our slavish yoke,
Imp out our drooping country's broken wing,
Redeem from broking pawn the blemish'd crown,
Wipe off the dust that hides our sceptre's gilt,
And make high majesty look like itself,
Away with me in post to Ravenspurg;
But if you faint, as fearing to do so,
Stay and be secret, and myself will go.
Ross. To horse, to horse! urge doubts to
them that fear.
Willo. Hold out my horse, and I will first
be there.   [*Exeunt.*

SCENE II.—*The same. A Room in the Palace.*

Enter QUEEN, BUSHY, *and* BAGOT.

Bushy. Madam, your majesty is too much
sad:
You promis'd, when you parted with the king,
To lay aside life-harming heaviness,
And entertain a cheerful disposition.   [myself,
Queen. To please the king, I did; to please
I cannot do it; yet I know no cause
Why I should welcome such a guest as grief,
Save bidding farewell to so sweet a guest
As my sweet Richard: yet, again, methinks
Some unborn sorrow, ripe in fortune's womb,
Is coming towards me; and my inward soul
With nothing trembles: at some thing it grieves,
More than with parting from my lord the king.
Bushy. Each substance of a grief hath
twenty shadows,
Which show like grief itself, but are not so;
For sorrow's eye, glazed with blinding tears,
Divides one thing entire to many objects;
Like perspectives, which, rightly gaz'd upon,
Show nothing but confusion,—ey'd awry,
Distinguish form: so your sweet majesty,
Looking awry upon your lord's departure,
Finds shapes of grief, more than himself, to
wail;
Which, look'd on as it is, is naught but shadows
Of what it is not. Then, thrice-gracious queen,
More than your lord's departure weep not,—
more's not seen;
Or if it be, 'tis with false sorrow's eye,
Which for things true weeps things imaginary.
Queen. It may be so; but yet my inward soul
Persuades me it is otherwise: howe'er it be,
I cannot but be sad; so heavy sad,   [think,—

As,—though, on thinking, on no thought I
Makes me with heavy nothing faint and shrink.
 Bushy. 'Tis nothing but conceit, my gracious
  lady.   [riv'd
 Queen. 'Tis nothing less: conceit is still de-
From some forefather grief; mine is not so,
For nothing hath begot my something grief;
Or something hath the nothing that I grieve:
'Tis in reversion that I do possess;
But what it is, that is not yet known; what
I cannot name; 'tis nameless woe, I wot.

Enter GREEN.

 Green. God save your majesty!—and well
  met, gentlemen:—
I hope the king is not yet shipp'd for Ireland.
 Queen. Why hop'st thou so? 'tis better hope
  he is;
For his designs crave haste, his haste good
  hope:
Then wherefore dost thou hope he is not
  shipp'd?
 Green. That he, our hope, might have retir'd
  his power,
And driven into despair an enemy's hope,
Who strongly hath set footing in this land:
The banish'd Bolingbroke repeals himself,
And with uplifted arms is safe arriv'd
At Ravenspurg.
 Queen.   Now God in heaven forbid!
 Green. O madam, 'tis too true: and that is
  worse,   [Henry Percy,
The Lord Northumberland, his son young
The Lords of Ross, Beaumond, and Willoughby,
With all their powerful friends, are fled to him.
 Bushy. Why have you not proclaim'd
  Northumberland,
And all the rest of the revolted faction,
Traitors?   [Worcester
 Green. We have: whereupon the Earl of
Hath broke his staff, resign'd his stewardship,
And all the household servants fled with him
To Bolingbroke.   [my woe,
 Queen. So, Green, thou art the midwife to
And Bolingbroke my sorrow's dismal heir;
Now hath my soul brought forth her prodigy;
And I, a gasping new-deliver'd mother,
Have woe to woe, sorrow to sorrow join'd.
 Bushy. Despair not, madam.
 Queen.   Who shall hinder me?
I will despair, and be at enmity
With cozening hope,—he is a flatterer,
A parasite, a keeper-back of death,
Who gently would dissolve the bands of life,
Which false hope lingers in extremity.
 Green. Here comes the Duke of York.
 Queen. With signs of war about his aged
  neck:
O, full of careful business are his looks!

Enter YORK.

Uncle, for God's sake, speak comfortable words.
 York. Should I do so, I should belie my
  thoughts:

Comfort's in heaven; and we are on the earth,
Where nothing lives but crosses, care, and grief.
Your husband, he is gone to save far off,
Whilst others come to make him lose at home:
Here am I left to underprop his land,
Who, weak with age, cannot support myself:
Now comes the sick hour that his surfeit made;
Now shall he try his friends that flatter'd him.

Enter a Servant.

 Serv. My lord, your son was gone before I
  came.
 York. He was?—Why, so!—go all which way
  it will!—
The nobles they are fled, the commons they are
  cold,
And will, I fear, revolt on Hereford's side.—
Sirrah, get thee to Plashy, to my sister Gloster;
Bid her send me presently a thousand pound:—
Hold, take my ring.   [ship,
 Serv. My lord, I had forgot to tell your lord-
To-day, as I came by, I called there;—
But I shall grieve you to report the rest.
 York. What is't, knave?
 Serv. An hour before I came, the duchess died.
 York. God for his mercy! what a tide of woes
Comes rushing on this woeful land at once!
I know not what to do:—I would to God,—
So my untruth had not provok'd him to it,—
The king had cut off my head with my brother's.
What, are there no posts despatch'd for Ire-
  land?—
How shall we do for money for these wars?—
Come, sister,—cousin, I would say,—pray,
  pardon me.
Go, fellow [*to the* Servant], get thee home, pro-
  vide some carts,
And bring away the armour that is there.—
          [*Exit* Servant.
Gentlemen, will you go muster men? If I know
How or which way to order these affairs,
Thus thrust disorderly into my hands,
Never believe me. Both are my kinsmen:—
The one's my sovereign, whom both my oath
And duty bids defend; the other, again,
Is my kinsman, whom the king hath wrong'd,
Whom conscience and my kindred bids to right.
Well, somewhat we must do.—Come, cousin,
  I'll   [your men,
Dispose of you.—Gentlemen, go, muster up
And meet me presently at Berkley Castle.
I should to Plashy too;—
But time will not permit:—all is uneven,
And everything is left at six and seven.
     [*Exeunt* YORK *and* QUEEN.
 Bushy. The wind sits fair for news to go to
  Ireland,
But none returns. For us to levy power
Proportionable to the enemy
Is all impossible.   [love
 Green. Besides, our nearness to the king in
Is near the hate of those love not the king.
 Bagot. And that's the wavering commons:
  for their love

Lies in their purses; and whoso empties them,
By so much fills their hearts with deadly hate.
Bushy. Wherein the king stands generally
condemn'd.
Bagot. If judgment lie in them, then so do we,
Because we ever have been near the king.
Green. Well, I will for refuge straight to
Bristol Castle:
The Earl of Wiltshire is already there. [office
Bushy. Thither will I with you: for little
The hateful commons will perform for us,
Except like curs to tear us all to pieces.—
Will you go along with us?
Bagot. No; I will to Ireland to his majesty.
Farewell: if heart's presages be not vain,
We three here part that ne'er shall meet again.
Bushy. That's as York thrives to beat back
Bolingbroke.   [takes
Green. Alas, poor duke! the task he under-
Is numbering sands, and drinking oceans dry:
Where one on his side fights, thousands will fly.
Farewell at once,—for once, for all, and ever.
Bushy. Well, we may meet again.
Bagot.   I fear me, never. [*Exeunt.*

SCENE III.—*The Wilds in Glostershire.*

Enter BOLINGBROKE *and* NORTHUMBERLAND,
with Forces.

Boling. How far is it, my lord, to Berkley
now?
North. Believe me, noble lord,
I am a stranger here in Glostershire:
These high wild hills and rough uneven ways
Draw out our miles, and make them wearisome;
And yet your fair discourse hath been as sugar,
Making the hard way sweet and délectable.
But I bethink me what a weary way
From Ravenspurg to Cotswold will be found
In Ross and Willoughby, wanting your company,
Which, I protest, hath very much beguil'd
The tediousness and process of my travel:
But theirs is sweeten'd with the hope to have
The present benefit which I possess;
And hope to joy is little less in joy
Than hope enjoy'd: by this the weary lords
Shall make their way seem short; as mine hath
done
By sight of what I have, your noble company.
Boling. Of much less value is my company
Than your good words.—But who comes here?
North. It is my son, young Harry Percy,
Sent from my brother Worcester, whencesoever.

Enter HARRY PERCY.

Harry, how fares your uncle?
Percy. I had thought, my lord, to have
learned his health of you.
North. Why, is he not with the queen?
Percy. No, my good lord; he hath forsook
the court,
Broken his staff of office, and dispers'd
The household of the king.
North.   What was his reason?

He was not so resolv'd when last we spake to-
gether.
Percy. Because your lordship was proclaimed
traitor.
But he, my lord, is gone to Ravenspurg,
To offer service to the Duke of Hereford;
And sent me o'er by Berkley, to discover
What power the Duke of York had levied there
Then with direction to repair to Ravenspurg.
North. Have you forgot the Duke of Here-
ford, boy?   [forgot
Percy. No, my good lord; for that is not
Which ne'er I did remember: to my knowledge,
I never in my life did look on him.
North. Then learn to know him now; this is
the duke.   [service,
Percy. My gracious lord, I tender you my
Such as it is, being tender, raw, and young;
Which elder days shall ripen, and confirm
To more approved service and desert.   [sure
Boling. I thank thee, gentle Percy; and be
I count myself in nothing else so happy
As in a soul remembering my good friends;
And, as my fortune ripens with thy love,
It shall be still thy true love's recompence:
My heart this covenant makes, my hand thus
seals it.
North. How far is it to Berkley? and what stir
Keeps good old York there with his men of war?
Percy. There stands the castle, by yon tuft
of trees,   [heard:
Mann'd with three hundred men, as I have
And in it are the Lords of York, Berkley, and
Seymour,—
None else of name and noble estimate.
North. Here come the Lords of Ross and
Willoughby,
Bloody with spurring, fiery-red with haste.

Enter ROSS *and* WILLOUGHBY.

Boling. Welcome, my lords. I wot your love
pursues
A banish'd traitor: all my treasury
Is yet but unfelt thanks, which, more enrich'd,
Shall be your love and labour's recompence.
Ross. Your presence makes us rich, most
noble lord.   [tain it.
Willo. And far surmounts our labour to at-
Boling. Evermore thanks, the exchequer of
the poor;
Which, till my infant fortune comes to years,
Stands for my bounty.—But, who comes here?
North. It is my Lord of Berkley, as I guess.

Enter BERKLEY.

Berk. My Lord of Hereford, my message is
to you.
Boling. My lord, my answer is—to Lan-
caster;
And I am come to seek that name in England;
And I must find that title in your tongue,
Before I make reply to aught you say.
Berk. Mistake me not, my lord; 'tis not my
meaning

To raze one title of your honour out:—
To you, my lord, I come,—what lord you will,—
From the most gracious regent of this land,
The Duke of York, to know what pricks you on
To take advantage of the absent time,
And fright our native peace with self-born arms.

Boling. I shall not need transport my words
     by you;
Here comes his grace in person.

     Enter YORK, *attended.*

               My noble uncle!   [*Kneels.*
York. Show me thy humble heart, and not
     thy knee,
Whose duty is deceivable and false.
Boling. My gracious uncle!—
York.   Tut, tut!
Grace me no grace, nor uncle me no uncle:
I am no traitor's uncle; and that word—grace,
In an ungracious mouth is but profane.
Why have those banish'd and forbidden legs
Dar'd once to touch a dust of England's ground?
But, then, more why,—why have they dar'd to
     march
So many miles upon her peaceful bosom,
Frighting her pale-fac'd villages with war
And ostentation of despised arms?
Com'st thou because the anointed king is hence?
Why, foolish boy, the king is left behind,
And in my loyal bosom lies his power.
Were I but now the lord of such hot youth
As when brave Gaunt thy father, and myself,
Rescued the Black Prince, that young Mars of
     men,
From forth the ranks of many thousand French,
O, then, how quickly should this arm of mine,
Now prisoner to the palsy, chástise thee,
And minister correction to thy fault!   [fault;
Boling. My gracious uncle, let me know my
On what condition stands it and wherein?
York. Even in condition of the worst de-
     gree,—
In gross rebellion and detested treason:
Thou art a banish'd man; and here art come
Before the expiration of thy time,
In braving arms against thy sovereign.
Boling. As I was banish'd, I was banish'd
     Hereford;
But as I come, I come for Lancaster.
And, noble uncle, I beseech your grace
Look on my wrongs with an indifferent eye:
You are my father, for methinks in you
I see old Gaunt alive; O, then, my father,
Will you permit that I shall stand condemn'd
A wandering vagabond; my rights and royalties
Pluck'd from my arms perforce, and given away
To upstart unthrifts? Wherefore was I born?
If that my cousin king be king of England,
It must be granted I am Duke of Lancaster.
You have a son, Aumerle, my noble kinsman;
Had you first died, and he been thus trod down,
He should have found his uncle Gaunt a father,
To rouse his wrongs, and chase them to the bay.
I am denied to sue my livery here,

And yet my letters-patents give me leave:
My father's goods are all distrain'd and sold;
And these and all are all amiss employ'd,
What would you have me do? I am a subject,
And challenge law: attorneys are denied me;
And therefore personally I lay my claim
To my inheritance of free descent.   [abus'd.
North. The noble duke hath been too much
Ross. It stands your grace upon to do him
     right.
Willo. Base men by his endowments are
     made great.
York. My lords of England, let me tell you
     this:—
I have had feeling of my cousin's wrongs,
And labour'd all I could to do him right:
But in this kind to come, in braving arms,
Be his own carver, and cut out his way,
To find out right with wrong,—it may not be;
And you that do abet him in this kind
Cherish rebellion, and are rebels all.
North. The noble duke hath sworn his com-
     ing is
But for his own; and for the right of that
We all have strongly sworn to give him aid;
And let him ne'er see joy that breaks that oath!
York. Well, well, I see the issue of these
     arms;—
I cannot mend it, I must needs confess,
Because my power is weak and all ill left:
But if I could, by him that gave me life,
I would attach you all, and make you stoop
Unto the sovereign mercy of the king;
But since I cannot, be it known to you
I do remain as neuter. So, fare you well;—
Unless you please to enter in the castle,
And there repose you for this night.
Boling. An offer, uncle, that we will accept
But we must win your grace to go with us
To Bristol Castle, which they say is held
By Bushy, Bagot, and their complices,
The caterpillars of the commonwealth,
Which I have sworn to weed and pluck away.
York. It may be I will go with you:—but
     yet I'll pause;
For I am loth to break our country's laws.
Nor friends nor foes, to me welcome you are:
Things past redress are now with me past care.
                              [*Exeunt.*

     SCENE IV.—*A Camp in Wales.*

     Enter SALISBURY *and a* Captain.

Cap. My Lord of Salisbury, we have stay'd
     ten days,
And hardly kept our countrymen together,
And yet we hear no tidings from the king;
Therefore we will disperse ourselves: farewell.
Sal. Stay yet another day, thou trusty
     Welshman:
The king reposeth all his confidence
In thee.   [not stay.
Cap. 'Tis thought the king is dead; we will
The bay trees in our country all are wither'd,
And meteors fright the fixed stars of heaven;

The pale-fac'd moon looks bloody on the earth,
And lean-look'd prophets whisper fearful
    change;   [leap,—
Rich men look sad, and ruffians dance and
The one in fear to lose what they enjoy,
The other to enjoy by rage and war:
These signs forerun the death or fall of kings.—
Farewell: our countrymen are gone and fled,
As well assur'd Richard their king is dead.
                              [*Exit.*

    Sal. Ah, Richard, with the eyes of heavy
    mind,
I see thy glory, like a shooting star,
Fall to the base earth from the firmament!
The sun sets weeping in the lowly west,
Witnessing storms to come, woe, and unrest;
Thy friends are fled, to wait upon thy foes;
And crossly to thy good all fortune goes.
                              [*Exit.*

ACT III.

SCENE I.—BOLINGBROKE'S *Camp at Bristol.*

Enter BOLINGBROKE, YORK, NORTHUMBER-
LAND, PERCY, WILLOUGHBY, ROSS: *Officers
behind, with* BUSHY *and* GREEN, *prisoners.*

    Boling. Bring forth these men.—
Bushy and Green, I will not vex your souls,—
Since presently your souls must part your
    bodies,—
With too much urging your pernicious lives,
For 'twere no charity; yet, to wash your blood
From off my hands, here, in the view of men,
I will unfold some causes of your deaths.
You have misled a prince, a royal king,
A happy gentleman in blood and lineaments,
By you unhappied and disfigur'd clean:
You have in manner with your sinful hours
Made a divorce betwixt his queen and him;
Broke the possession of a royal bed,
And stain'd the beauty of a fair queen's cheeks
With tears drawn from her eyes by your foul
    wrongs.
Myself,—a prince by fortune of my birth,
Near to the king in blood, and near in love
Till you did make him misinterpret me,—
Have stoop'd my neck under your injuries,
And sigh'd my English breath in foreign clouds,
Eating the bitter bread of banishment,
Whilst you have fed upon my signories,
Dispark'd my parks, and fell'd my forest-
    woods,   [coat,
From my own windows torn my household
Raz'd out my impress, leaving me no sign,
Save men's opinions and my living blood,
To show the world I am a gentleman.
This and much more, much more than twice
    all this,
Condemns you to the death.—See them de-
    liver'd over
To execution and the hand of death.
    Bushy. More welcome is the stroke of death
    to me   [well.
Than Bolingbroke to England.—Lords, fare-

    Green. My comfort is, that heaven will take
    our souls,
And plague injustice with the pains of hell.
    Boling. My Lord Northumberland, see them
    despatch'd.
    [*Exeunt* NORTH. *and others, with* Prisoners.
Uncle, you say the queen is at your house;
For God's sake, fairly let her be entreated:
Tell her I send to her my kind commends;
Take special care my greetings be deliver'd.
    York. A gentleman of mine I have despatch'd
With letters of your love to her at large.
    Boling. Thanks, gentle uncle.—Come, lords,
    away,
To fight with Glendower and his complices:
Awhile to work, and after holiday.   [*Exeunt.*

SCENE II.—*The Coast of* WALES. *A Castle in
view.*

Flourish; drums and trumpets. Enter KING
RICHARD, *the* BISHOP OF CARLISLE, AU-
MERLE, *and* Soldiers.

    K. Rich. Barkloughly Castle call they this
    at hand?
    Aum. Yea, my lord. How brooks your grace
    the air,
After your late tossing on the breaking seas?
    K. Rich. Needs must I like it well: I weep
    for joy
To stand upon my kingdom once again.—
Dear earth, I do salute thee with my hand,
Though rebels wound thee with their horses'
    hoofs:
As a long-parted mother with her child
Plays fondly with her tears and smiles in
    meeting,
So, weeping-smiling, greet I thee, my earth,
And do thee favour with my royal hands.
Feed not thy sovereign's foe, my gentle earth,
Nor with thy sweets comfort his rav'nous sense;
But let thy spiders, that suck up thy venom,
And heavy-gaited toads, lie in their way,
Doing annoyance to the treacherous feet
Which with usurping steps do trample thee:
Yield stinging nettles to mine enemies;
And when they from thy bosom pluck a flower,
Guard it, I pray thee, with a lurking adder,
Whose double tongue may with a mortal touch
Throw death upon thy sovereign's enemies.—
Mock not my senseless conjuration, lords:
This earth shall have a feeling, and these stones
Prove armed soldiers, ere her native king
Shall falter under foul rebellion's arms!
    Car. Fear not, my lord; that Power that
    made you king
Hath power to keep you king in spite of all.
The means that heaven yields must be embrac'd
And not neglected; else, if heaven would,
And we will not, heaven's offer we refuse,
The proffer'd means of succour and redress.
    Aum. He means, my lord, that we are too
    remiss;
Whilst Bolingbroke, through our security,

Grows strong and great in substance and in
   friends.   [thou not
  K. Rich. Discomfortable cousin! know'st
That when the searching eye of heaven is hid
Behind the globe that lights the lower world,
Then thieves and robbers range abroad unseen,
In murders and in outrage, boldly here;
But when, from under this terrestrial ball,
He fires the proud tops of the eastern pines,
And darts his light through every guilty hole,
Then murders, treasons, and detested sins,
The cloak of night being pluck'd from off their
   backs,
Stand bare and naked, trembling at themselves?
So when this thief, this traitor, Bolingbroke,—
Who all this while hath revell'd in the night,
Whilst we were wandering with the antipodes,—
Shall see us rising in our throne, the east,
His treasons will sit blushing in his face,
Not able to endure the sight of day,
But self-affrighted tremble at his sin.
Not all the water in the rough rude sea
Can wash the balm from an anointed king;
The breath of worldly men cannot depose
The deputy elected by the Lord;
For every man that Bolingbroke hath press'd
To lift shrewd steel against our golden crown,
God for his Richard hath in heavenly pay
A glorious angel: then, if angels fight,   [right.
Weak man must fall; for heaven still guards the

Enter SALISBURY.

Welcome, my lord: how far off lies your power?
  Sal. Nor near nor further off, my gracious
   lord,   [tongue,
Than this weak arm: discomfort guides my
And bids me speak of nothing but despair.
One day too late, I fear, my noble lord,
Hath clouded all thy happy days on earth:
O, call back yesterday, bid time return,
And thou shalt have twelve thousand fighting
   men!
To-day, to-day, unhappy day, too late,
O'erthrows thy joys, friends, fortune, and thy
   state;
For all the Welshmen, hearing thou wert dead,
Are gone to Bolingbroke, dispers'd, and fled.
  Aum. Comfort, my liege: why looks your
   grace so pale?
  K. Rich. But now the blood of twenty thou-
   sand men
Did triumph in my face, and they are fled;
And, till so much blood thither come again,
Have I not reason to look pale and dead?
All souls that will be safe fly from my side;
For time hath set a blot upon my pride.   [are.
  Aum. Comfort, my liege; remember who you
  K. Rich. I had forgot myself: am I not king?
Awake, thou sluggard majesty! thou sleep'st.
Is not the king's name forty thousand names?
Arm, arm, my name! a puny subject strikes
At thy great glory.—Look not to the ground,
Ye favourites of a king: are we not high?
High be our thoughts: I know my uncle York

Hath power enough to serve our turn.—But
  who comes here?

Enter SCROOP.

  Scroop. More health and happiness betide
   my liege
Than can my care-tun'd tongue deliver him.
  K. Rich. Mine ear is open and my heart
   prepar'd:
The worst is worldly loss thou canst unfold.
Say, is my kingdom lost? why, 'twas my care;
And what loss is it to be rid of care?
Strives Bolingbroke to be as great as we?
Greater he shall not be; if he serve God,
We'll serve him too, and be his fellow so:
Revolt our subjects? that we cannot mend;
They break their faith to God, as well as us:
Cry woe, destruction, ruin, loss, decay;
The worst is death, and death will have his day!
  Scroop. Glad am I that your highness is so
   arm'd
To bear the tidings of calamity.
Like an unseasonable stormy day,
Which makes the silver rivers drown their
   shores,
As if the world were all dissolv'd to tears;
So high above his limits swells the rage
Of Bolingbroke, covering your fearful land
With hard bright steel, and hearts harder than
   steel.
White-beards have arm'd their thin and hair-
   less scalps   [voices,
Against thy majesty; and boys, with women's
Strive to speak big, and clap their female joints
In stiff unwieldy arms against thy crown:
Thy very beadsmen learn to bend their bows
Of double-fatal yew against thy state;
Yea, distaff-women manage rusty bills
Against thy seat: both old and young rebel,
And all goes worse than I have power to tell.
  K. Rich. Too well, too well thou tell'st a
   tale so ill.
Where is the Earl of Wiltshire? where is Bagot?
What is become of Bushy, where is Green?
That they have let the dangerous enemy
Measure our confines with such peaceful steps?
If we prevail, their heads shall pay for it:
I warrant they have made peace with Boling-
   broke.
  Scroop. Peace have they made with him,
   indeed, my lord.   [redemption!
  K. Rich. O villains, vipers, damn'd without
Dogs, easily won to fawn on any man!
Snakes, in my heart-blood warm'd, that sting
   my heart!   [Judas!
Three Judases, each one thrice worse than
Would they make peace? terrible hell make war
Upon their spotted souls for this offence!
  Scroop. Sweet love, I see, changing his prop-
   erty,
Turns to the sourest and most deadly hate:—
Again uncurse their souls; their peace is made
With heads, and not with hands: those whom
   you curse

Have felt the worst of death's destroying wound,
And lie full low, grav'd in the hollow ground.

Aum. Is Bushy, Green, and the Earl of Wiltshire dead? [heads.

Scroop. Yea, all of them at Bristol lost their

Aum. Where is the duke my father with his power?

K. Rich. No matter where;—of comfort, no man speak:
Let's talk of graves, of worms, and epitaphs;
Make dust our paper, and with rainy eyes
Write sorrow on the bosom of the earth.
Let's choose executors, and talk of wills:
And yet not so,—for what can we bequeath,
Save our deposed bodies to the ground?
Our lands, our lives, and all are Bolingbroke's,
And nothing can we call our own but death,
And that small model of the barren earth
Which serves as paste and cover to our bones.
For God's sake, let us sit upon the ground,
And tell sad stories of the death of kings:—
How some have been depos'd; some slain in war;
Some haunted by the ghosts they have depos'd;
Some poison'd by their wives; some sleeping kill'd;
All murder'd:—for within the hollow crown
That rounds the mortal temples of a king
Keeps Death his court; and there the antic sits,
Scoffing his state, and grinning at his pomp;
Allowing him a breath, a little scene,
To monarchize, be fear'd, and kill with looks;
Infusing him with self and vain conceit,—
As if this flesh, which walls about our life,
Were brass impregnable; and humour'd thus,
Comes at the last, and with a little pin
Bores through his castle-wall, and—farewell, king! [blood
Cover your heads, and mock not flesh and
With solemn reverence; throw away respect,
Tradition, form, and ceremonious duty;
For you have but mistook me all this while:
I live with bread like you, feel want, taste grief,
Need friends:—subjected thus,
How can you say to me, I am a king?

Car. My lord, wise men ne'er sit and wail their woes,
But presently prevent the ways to wail.
To fear the foe, since fear oppresseth strength,
Gives, in your weakness, strength unto your foe,
And so your follies fight against yourself.
Fear, and be slain; no worse can come to fight:
And fight and die is death destroying death;
Where fearing dying pays death servile breath.

Aum. My father hath a power; inquire of him;
And learn to make a body of a limb.

K. Rich. Thou chid'st me well:—proud Bolingbroke, I come [doom.
To change blows with thee for our day of
This ague-fit of fear is over-blown;
An easy task it is to win our own.—

Say, Scroop, where lies our uncle with his power?
Speak sweetly, man, although thy looks be sour. [sky

Scroop. Men judge by the complexion of the
The state and inclination of the day:
So may you by my dull and heavy eye,
My tongue hath but a heavier tale to say.
I play the torturer, by small and small
To lengthen out the worst that must be spoken:—
Your uncle York is join'd with Bolingbroke;
And all your northern castles yielded up,
And all your southern gentlemen in arms
Upon his party.

K. Rich. Thou hast said enough.—
Beshrew thee, cousin, which didst lead me forth [*To* AUMERLE.
Of that sweet way I was in to despair!
What say you now? what comfort have we now?
By heaven, I'll hate him everlastingly
That bids me be of comfort any more.
Go to Flint Castle: there I'll pine away;
A king, woe's slave, shall kingly woe obey.
That power I have, discharge; and let them go
To ear the land that hath some hope to grow,
For I have none:—let no man speak again
To alter this, for counsel is but vain.

Aum. My liege, one word.

K. Rich. He does me double wrong
That wounds me with the flatteries of his tongue.
Discharge my followers: let them hence away,
From Richard's night to Bolingbroke's fair day. [*Exeunt.*

SCENE III.—WALES. *Before Flint Castle.*

Enter, with drum and colours, BOLINGBROKE *and* Forces; YORK, NORTHUMBERLAND, *and others.*

Boling. So that by this intelligence we learn
The Welshmen are dispers'd; and Salisbury
Is gone to meet the king, who lately landed
With some few private friends upon this coast.

North. The news is very fair and good, my lord:
Richard not far from hence hath hid his head.

York. It would beseem the Lord Northumberland
To say, King Richard:—alack the heavy day
When such a sacred king should hide his head.

North. Your grace mistakes; only to be brief,
Left I his title out.

York. The time hath been,
Would you have been so brief with him, he would
Have been so brief with you, to shorten you,
For taking so the head, your whole head's length. [should.

Boling. Mistake not, uncle, further than you

York. Take not, good cousin, further than you should, [heads.
Lest you mistake: the heavens are o'er our

Boling. I know it, uncle; and oppose not myself
Against their will.—But who comes here?

Enter PERCY.

Well, Harry: what, will not this castle yield?
　Percy. The castle royally is mann'd, my lord,
Against thy entrance.
　Boling. Royally!
Why, it contains no king?
　Percy.　　　　　　Yes, my good lord,
It doth contain a king; King Richard lies
Within the limits of yond lime and stone:
And with him are the Lord Aumerle, Lord
　Salisbury,
Sir Stephen Scroop; besides a clergyman
Of holy reverence, who I cannot learn.
　North. O, belike it is the Bishop of Carlisle.
　Boling. Noble lord,
　　　　　　　　[*To* NORTHUMBERLAND.
Go to the rude ribs of that ancient castle;
Through brazen trumpet send the breath of
　parle
Into his ruin'd ears, and thus deliver:—
Harry Bolingbroke
On both his knees doth kiss King Richard's
　hand,
And sends allegiance and true faith of heart
To his most royal person; hither come
Even at his feet to lay my arms and power,
Provided that, my banishment repeal'd,
And lands restor'd again, be freely granted:
If not, I'll use the advantage of my power,
And lay the summer's dust with showers of
　blood
Rain'd from the wounds of slaughter'd Eng-
　lishmen:
The which, how far off from the mind of Bol-
　ingbroke
It is, such crimson tempest should bedrench
The fresh green lap of fair King Richard's land,
My stooping duty tenderly shall show.
Go, signify as much, while here we march
Upon the grassy carpet of this plain.—
　　　　[NORTH. *advances to the Castle, with a
　　　　　trumpet.*
Let's march without the noise of threat'ning
　drum,
That from the castle's tatter'd battlements
Our fair appointments may be well perus'd.
Methinks King Richard and myself should meet
With no less terror than the elements
Of fire and water, when their thund'ring shock
At meeting tears the cloudy cheeks of heaven.
Be he the fire, I'll be the yielding water:
The rage be his, while on the earth I rain
My waters,—on the earth, and not on him.
March on, and mark King Richard how he looks.

*A parle sounded, and answered by another trump-
et within. Flourish. Enter on the walls* KING
RICHARD, *the* BISHOP OF CARLISLE, AUM-
ERLE, SCROOP, *and* SALISBURY.

See, see, King Richard doth himself appear,
As doth the blushing discontented sun
From out the fiery portal of the east,
When he perceives the envious clouds are bent
To dim his glory, and to stain the track
Of his bright passage to the occident.
　York. Yet looks he like a king: behold, his
　　eye,
As bright as is the eagle's, lightens forth
Controlling majesty:—alack, alack, for woe,
That any harm should stain so fair a show!
　K. Rich. We are amaz'd; and thus long have
　　we stood
To watch the fearful bending of thy knee,
　　　　　　　　[*To* NORTHUMBERLAND.
Because we thought ourself thy lawful king:
And if we be, how dare thy joints forget
To pay their awful duty to our presence?
If we be not, show us the hand of God
That hath dismissed us from our stewardship;
For well we know, no hand of blood and bone
Can gripe the sacred handle of our sceptre,
Unless he do profane, steal, or usurp.
And though you think that all, as you have
　done,
Have torn their souls by turning them from us,
And we are barren and bereft of friends;
Yet know,—my master, God ' omnipotent,
Is mustering in his clouds, on our behalf,
Armies of pestilence; and they shall strike
Your children yet unborn and unbegot,
That lift your vassal hands against my head,
And threat the glory of my precious crown.
Tell Bolingbroke,—for yond methinks he is,—
That every stride he makes upon my land
Is dangerous treason: he is come to ope
The purple testament of bleeding war;
But ere the crown he looks for live in peace,
Ten thousand bloody crowns of mothers' sons
Shall ill become the flower of England's face,
Change the complexion of her maid-pale peace
To scarlet indignation, and bedew
Her pastures' grass with faithful English blood.
　North. The king of heaven forbid our lord
　　the king
Should so with civil and uncivil arms
Be rush'd upon! Thy thrice-noble cousin,
Harry Bolingbroke, doth humbly kiss thy hand;
And by the honourable tomb he swears,
That stands upon your royal grandsire's bones,
And by the royalties of both your bloods,—
Currents that spring from one most gracious
　head,—
And by the buried hand of warlike Gaunt,
And by the worth and honour of himself,
Comprising all that may be sworn or said,—
His coming hither hath no further scope
Than for his lineal royalties, and to beg
Enfranchisement immediate on his knees:
Which on thy royal party granted once,
His glittering arms he will commend to rust,
His barbed steeds to stables, and his heart
To faithful service of your majesty.
This swears he, as he is a prince, is just;
And, as I am a gentleman, I credit him.

K. Rich. Northumberland, say thus the king
returns:—
His noble cousin is right welcome hither;
And all the number of his fair demands
Shall be accomplish'd without contradiction:
With all the gracious utterance thou hast
Speak to his gentle hearing kind commends.—
We do debase ourself, cousin, do we not,
[*To* AUMERLE.
To look so poorly, and to speak so fair?
Shall we call back Northumberland, and send
Defiance to the traitor, and so die?
Aum. No, good my lord; let's fight with
gentle words
Till time lend friends, and friends their helpful
swords.
K. Rich. O God, O God! that e'er this tongue
of mine,
That laid the sentence of dread banishment
On yond proud man, should take it off again
With words of sooth! O that I were as great
As is my grief, or lesser than my name!
Or that I could forget what I have been!
Or not remember what I must be now!
Swell'st thou, proud heart? I'll give thee scope
to beat,
Since foes have scope to beat both thee and me.
Aum. Northumberland comes back from
Bolingbroke.
K. Rich. What must the king do now? must
he submit?
The king shall do it: must he be depos'd?
The king shall be contented: must he lose
The name of king? o' God's name, let it go:
I'll give my jewels for a set of beads,
My gorgeous palace for a hermitage,
My gay apparel for an alms-man's gown,
My figur'd goblets for a dish of wood,
My sceptre for a palmer's walking staff,
My subjects for a pair of carved saints,
And my large kingdom for a little grave,
A little little grave, an obscure grave;—
Or I'll be buried in the king's highway,
Some way of common trade, where subjects'
feet
May hourly trample on their sovereign's head;
For on my heart they tread now whilst I live;
And buried once, why not upon my head?—
Aumerle, thou weep'st,—my tender-hearted
cousin!—
We'll make foul weather with despised tears;
Our sighs and they shall lodge the summer corn,
And make a dearth in this revolting land.
Or shall we play the wantons with our woes,
And make some pretty match with shedding
tears?
As thus;—to drop them still upon one place,
Till they have fretted us a pair of graves
Within the earth; and, therein laid,—there lies
Two kinsmen digg'd their graves with weeping
eyes.
Would not this ill do well?—Well, well, I see
I talk but idly, and you mock at me.—
Most mighty prince, my Lord Northumberland,

What says King Bolingbroke? will his majesty
Give Richard leave to live till Richard die?
You make a leg, and Bolingbroke says ay.
North. My lord, in the base court he doth
attend [down?
To speak with you;—may it please you to come
K. Rich. Down, down I come; like glister-
ing Phaeton,
Wanting the manage of unruly jades.
[NORTH. *retires to* BOLING.
In the base court? Base court, where kings
grow base,
To come at traitors' calls, and do them grace.
In the base court? Come down? Down, court!
down, king!
For night-owls shriek where mounting larks
should sing. [*Exeunt from above.*
Boling. What says his majesty?
North. Sorrow and grief of heart
Makes him speak fondly, like a frantic man:
Yet he is come.

Enter KING RICHARD, *and his* Attendants,
below.

Boling. Stand all apart,
And show fair duty to his majesty.—
My gracious lord,— [*Kneeling.*
K. Rich. Fair cousin, you debase your
princely knee
To make the base earth proud with kissing it;
Me rather had my heart might feel your love
Than my unpleas'd eye see your courtesy.
Up, cousin, up;—your heart is up, I know,
Thus high at least [*touching his own head*], al-
though your knee be low. [own.
Boling. My gracious lord, I come but for mine
K. Rich. Your own is yours, and I am yours,
and all. [lord,
Boling. So far be mine, my most redoubted
As my true service shall deserve your love.
K. Rich. Well you deserve:—they well de-
serve to have
That know the strong'st and surest way to get.—
Uncle, give me your hand: nay, dry your eyes;
Tears show their love, but want their remedies.—
Cousin, I am too young to be your father,
Though you are old enough to be my heir.
What you will have, I'll give, and willing too;
For do we must what force will have us do.—
Set on towards London:—cousin, is it so?
Boling. Yea, my good lord.
K. Rich. Then I must not say no.
[*Flourish. Exeunt.*

SCENE IV.—LANGLEY. *The* DUKE OF YORK'S
Garden.

Enter the QUEEN *and two* Ladies.

Queen. What sport shall we devise here in
this garden,
To drive away the heavy thought of care?
1 *Lady.* Madam, we'll play at bowls.
Queen. 'Twill make me think
The world is full of rubs, and that my fortune
Runs against the bias.

1 *Lady*.　　　　Madam, we'll dance.
Queen. My legs can keep no measure in de-
　　light,
When my poor heart no measure keeps in grief;
Therefore, no dancing, girl; some other sport.
1 *Lady*. Madam, we'll tell tales.
Queen.　　　　　　Of sorrow or of joy?
1 *Lady*. Of either, madam.
Queen.　　　　　　Of neither, girl:
For if of joy, being altogether wanting,
It doth remember me the more of sorrow;
Or if of grief, being altogether had,
It adds more sorrow to my want of joy:
For what I have, I need not to repeat;
And what I want, it boots not to complain.
1 *Lady*. Madam, I'll sing.
Queen.　　　　'Tis well that thou hast cause;
But thou shouldst please me better wouldst
　　thou weep.　　　　　　　　[you good.
1 *Lady*. I could weep, madam, would it do
Queen. And I could weep, would weeping do
　　me good,
And never borrow any tear of thee.—
But stay, here come the gardeners:
Let's step into the shadow of these trees.
My wretchedness unto a row of pins,
They'll talk of state; for every one doth so
Against a change: woe is forerun with woe.
　　　　　　　[QUEEN *and* Ladies *retire*.

Enter a Gardener *and two* Servants.

Gard. Go, bind thou up yond dangling apri-
　　cocks,
Which, like unruly children, make their sire
Stoop with oppression of their prodigal weight:
Give some supportance to the bending twigs.—
Go thou, and like an executioner
Cut off the heads of too-fast-growing sprays,
That look too lofty in our commonwealth:
All must be even in our government.—
You thus employ'd, I will go root away
The noisome weeds, that without profit suck
The soil's fertility from wholesome flowers.
1 *Serv*. Why should we, in the compass of a
　　pale,
Keep law and form and due proportion,
Showing, as in a model, our firm estate,
When our sea-walled garden, the whole land,
Is full of weeds; her fairest flowers chok'd up,
Her fruit-trees all unprun'd, her hedges ruin'd,
Her knots disorder'd, and her wholesome herbs
Swarming with caterpillars?
Gard.　　　　　　Hold thy peace:—
He that hath suffer'd this disorder'd spring
Hath now himself met with the fall of leaf:
The weeds that his broad-spreading leaves did
　　shelter,
That seem'd in eating him to hold him up,
Are pluck'd up root and all by Bolingbroke,—
I mean the Earl of Wiltshire, Bushy, Green.
1 *Serv*. What, are they dead?
Gard.　　　　　They are; and Bolingbroke
Hath seiz'd the wasteful king.—Oh! what pity
　　is it.

That he had not so trimm'd and dress'd his land
As we this garden! We at time of year
Do wound the bark, the skin of our fruit-trees,
Lest, being over-proud in sap and blood,
With too much richness it confound itself:
Had he done so to great and growing men,
They might have liv'd to bear, and he to taste
Their fruits of duty. Superfluous branches
We lop away, that bearing boughs may live:
Had he done so, himself had borne the crown,
Which waste of idle hours hath quite thrown
　　down.
1 *Serv*. What, think you, then, the king shall
　　be depos'd?
Gard. Depress'd he is already; and depos'd
'Tis doubt he will be: letters came last night
To a dear friend of the good Duke of York's,
That tell black tidings.
Queen. O, I am press'd to death through
　　want of speaking!—
Thou, old Adam's likeness [*coming forward with*
　　Ladies], set to dress this garden,
How dares thy harsh-rude tongue sound these
　　unpleasing news?
What Eve, what serpent, hath suggested thee
To make a second fall of cursed man?
Why dost thou say King Richard is depos'd?
Dar'st thou, thou little better thing than earth,
Divine his downfall? Say, where, when, and
　　how
Cam'st thou by this ill tidings? speak, thou
　　wretch,
Gard. Pardon me, madam: little joy have I
To breathe these news; yet what I say is true.
King Richard, he is in the mighty hold
Of Bolingbroke: their fortunes both are weigh'd:
In your lord's scale is nothing but himself,
And some few vanities that make him light;
But in the balance of great Bolingbroke,
Besides himself, are all the English peers,
And with that odds he weighs King Richard
　　down.
Post you to London, and you'll find it so;
I speak no more than every one doth know.
Queen. Nimble mischance, that art so light
　　of foot,
Doth not thy embassage belong to me,
And am I last that knows it? O, thou think'st
To serve me last, that I may longest keep
Thy sorrow in my breast.—Come, ladies, go
To meet at London London's king in woe.—
What, was I born to this, that my sad look
Should grace the triumph of great Bolingbroke?
Gardener, for telling me this news of woe,
I would the plants thou graft'st may never
　　grow.　　　　　[*Exeunt* QUEEN *and* Ladies.
Gard. Poor queen! so that thy state might
　　be no worse,
I would my skill were subject to thy curse.—
Here did she fall a tear; here, in this place,
I'll set a bank of rue, sour herb of grace:
Rue, even for ruth, here shortly shall be seen,
In the remembrance of a weeping queen.
　　　　　　　　　　　　[*Exeunt*.

ACT IV.

SCENE I.—LONDON. *Westminster Hall. The Lords spiritual on the right side of the throne; the Lords temporal on the left; the Commons below.*

Enter BOLINGBROKE, AUMERLE, SURREY, NORTHUMBERLAND, PERCY, FITZWATER, *another* Lord, *the* BISHOP OF CARLISLE, *the* ABBOT OF WESTMINSTER, *and* Attendants. Officers *behind, with* BAGOT.

Boling. Call forth Bagot.—
Now, Bagot, freely speak thy mind;
What thou dost know of noble Gloster's death;
Who wrought it with the king, and who perform'd
The bloody office of his timeless end.
Bagot. Then set before my face the Lord Aumerle. [that man.
Boling. Cousin, stand forth, and look upon
Bagot. My Lord Aumerle, I know your daring tongue
Scorns to unsay what once it hath deliver'd.
In that dead time when Gloster's death was plotted
I heard you say,—*Is not my arm of length,*
That reacheth from the restful English Court
As far as Calais, to my uncle's head?
Amongst much other talk, that very time,
I heard you say that you had rather refuse
The offer of an hundred thousand crowns
Than Bolingbroke's return to England;
Adding withal, how blest this land would be
In this your cousin's death.
Aum. Princes, and noble lords,
What answer shall I make to this base man?
Shall I so much dishonour my fair stars,
On equal terms to give him chastisement?
Either I must, or have mine honour soil'd
With the attainder of his slanderous lips.—
There is my gage, the manual seal of death,
That marks thee out for hell: I say, thou liest,
And will maintain what thou hast said is false
In thy heart-blood, though being all too base
To stain the temper of my knightly sword.
Boling. Bagot, forbear; thou shalt not take it up. [best
Aum. Excepting one, I would he were the
In all this presence that hath moved me so.
Fitz. If that thy valour stand on sympathy,
There is my gage, Aumerle, in gage to thine:
By that fair sun that shows me where thou stand'st, [it,
I heard thee say, and vauntingly thou spak'st
That thou wert cause of noble Gloster's death.
If thou deny'st it twenty times, thou liest;
And I will turn thy falsehood to thy heart,
Where it was forged, with my rapier's point.
Aum. Thou dar'st not, coward, live to see that day. [hour.
Fitz. Now, by my soul, I would it were this
Aum. Fitzwater, thou art damn'd to hell for this. [true
Percy. Aumerle, thou liest; his honour is as

In this appeal as thou art all unjust;
And that thou art so, there I throw my gage,
To prove it on thee to the extremest point
Of mortal breathing: seize it, if thou dar'st.
Aum. And if I do not, may my hands rot off,
And never brandish more revengeful steel
Over the glittering helmet of my foe!
Lord. I task the earth to the like, forsworn Aumerle;
And spur thee on with full as many lies
As may be holla'd in thy treacherous ear
From sun to sun: there is my honour's pawn;
Engage it to the trial, if thou dar'st.
Aum. Who sets me else? by heaven, I'll throw at all:
I have a thousand spirits in one breast,
To answer twenty thousand such as you. [well
Surrey. My Lord Fitzwater, I do remember
The very time Aumerle and you did talk.
Fitz. 'Tis very true: you were in presence then;
And you can witness with me this is true.
Surrey. As false, by heaven, as heaven itself is true.
Fitz. Surrey, thou liest.
Surrey. Dishonourable boy!
That lie shall lie so heavy on my sword
That it shall render vengeance and revenge
Till thou the lie-giver and that lie do lie
In earth as quiet as thy father's skull:
In proof whereof, there is mine honour's pawn;
Engage it to the trial, if thou dar'st. [horse!
Fitz. How fondly dost thou spur a forward
If I dare eat, or drink, or breathe, or live
I dare meet Surrey in a wilderness,
And spit upon him, whilst I say he lies,
And lies, and lies: there is my bond of faith,
To tie thee to my strong correction.—
As I intend to thrive in this new world,
Aumerle is guilty of my true appeal:
Besides, I heard the banish'd Norfolk say
That thou, Aumerle, didst send two of thy men
To execute the noble duke at Calais. [a gage,
Aum. Some honest Christian trust me with
That Norfolk lies: here do I throw down this,
If he may be repeal'd, to try his honour. [gage
Boling. These differences shall all rest under
Till Norfolk be repeal'd: repeal'd he shall be,
And, though mine enemy, restor'd again
To all his lands and signories: when he's return'd,
Against Aumerle we will enforce his trial.
Car. That honourable day shall ne'er be seen.—
Many a time hath banish'd Norfolk fought
For Jesu Christ in glorious Christian field,
Streaming the ensign of the Christian cross
Against black pagans, Turks, and Saracens:
And toil'd with works of war, retir'd himself
To Italy; and there, at Venice, gave
His body to that pleasant country's earth,
And his pure soul unto his captain Christ,
Under whose colours he had fought so long.
Boling. Why, bishop, is Norfolk dead?

Car. As surely as I live, my lord.

Boling. Sweet peace conduct his sweet soul
　　to the bosom
Of good old Abraham!—Lords appellants,
Your differences shall all rest under gage
Till we assign you to your days of trial.

Enter YORK, *attended.*

York. Great Duke of Lancaster, I come to
　　thee　　　　　　　　　　　　　　[soul
From plume-pluck'd Richard; who with willing
Adopts thee heir, and his high sceptre yields
To the possession of thy royal hand:
Ascend his throne, descending now from him,—
And long live Henry, of that name the fourth!

Boling. In God's name, I'll ascend the regal
　　throne.

Car. Marry, God forbid!—
Worst in this royal presence may I speak,
Yet best beseeming me to speak the truth.
Would God that any in this noble presence
Were enough noble to be upright judge
Of noble Richard! then true nobless would
Learn him forbearance from so foul a wrong.
What subject can give sentence on his king?
And who sits here that is not Richard's subject?
Thieves are not judg'd but they are by to hear,
Although apparent guilt be seen in them;
And shall the figure of God's majesty,
His captain, steward, deputy elect,
Anointed, crowned, planted many years,
Be judg'd by subject and inferior breath,
And he himself not present? O, forfend it, God,
That, in a Christian climate, souls refin'd
Should show so heinous, black, obscene a deed!
I speak to subjects, and a subject speaks,
Stirr'd up by God, thus boldly for his king.
My Lord of Hereford here, whom you call king,
Is a foul traitor to proud Hereford's king;
And if you crown him, let me prophesy,—
The blood of English shall manure the ground,
And future ages groan for this foul act;
Peace shall go sleep with Turk and infidels,
And in this seat of peace tumultuous wars
Shall kin with kin and kind with kind confound;
Disorder, horror, fear, and mutiny,
Shall here inhabit, and this land be call'd
The field of Golgotha and dead men's skulls.
Or, if you raise this house against this house,
It will the woefullest division prove
That ever fell upon this cursed earth,
Prevent, resist it, let it not be so,
Lest child, child's children, cry against you woe!

North. Well have you argu'd, sir; and, for
　　your pains,
Of capital treason we arrest you here.—
My Lord of Westminster, be it your charge
To keep him safely till his day of trial.—
May't please you, lords, to grant the commons'
　　suit?

Boling. Fetch hither Richard, that in com-
　　mon view
He may surrender; so we shall proceed
Without suspicion.

York. 　　　　　I will be his conduct. [*Exit.*

Boling. Lords, you that are here under our
　　arrest,
Procure your sureties for your days of answer.—
Little are we beholden to your love,
　　　　　　　　　　　　　　[*To* CARLISLE.
And little look'd for at your helping hands.

Re-enter YORK, *with* KING RICHARD, *and*
Officers *bearing the crown, &c.*

K. Rich. Alack, why am I sent for to a king,
Before I have shook off the regal thoughts
Wherewith I reign'd? I hardly yet have learn'd
To insinuate, flatter, bow, and bend my limbs:
Give sorrow leave awhile to tutor me
To this submission. Yet I well remember
The favours of these men: were they not mine?
Did they not sometime cry, All hail! to me?
So Judas did to Christ: but he, in twelve,
Found truth in all but one; I, in twelve thou-
　　sand, none.
God save the king!—Will no man say amen?
Am I both priest and clerk? well then, amen.
God save the king! although I be not he;
And yet, amen, if heaven do think him me.—
To do what service am I sent for hither?

York. To do that office of thine own good-
　　will
Which tired majesty did make thee offer,—
The resignation of thy state and crown
To Henry Bolingbroke.

K. Rich. Give me the crown.—Here, cousin,
　　seize the crown;
On this side my hand, and on that side yours.
Now is this golden crown like a deep well
That owes two buckets, filling one another;
The emptier ever dancing in the air,
The other down, unseen, and full of water:
That bucket down and full of tears am I,
Drinking my griefs, whilst you mount up on
　　high.　　　　　　　　　　　　[resign.

Boling. I thought you had been willing to
　　resign.

K. Rich. My crown I am; but still my griefs
　　are mine:
You may my glories and my state depose,
But not my griefs; still am I king of those.

Boling. Part of your cares you give me with
　　your crown.

K. Rich. Your cares set up do not pluck my
　　cares down.
My care is, loss of care, by old care done;
Your care is, gain of care, by new care won:
The cares I give, I have, though given away;
They tend the crown, yet still with me they
　　stay.　　　　　　　　　　　　[crown?

Boling. Are you contented to resign the

K. Rich. Ay, no;—no, ay; for I must noth-
　　ing be;
Therefore no no, for I resign to thee.
Now mark me, how I will undo myself:—
I give this heavy weight from off my head,
And thus unwieldy sceptre from my hand,
The pride of kingly sway from out my heart;
With mine own tears I wash away my balm,

With mine own hands I give away my crown,
With mine own tongue deny my sacred state,
With mine own breath release all duty's rites:
All pomp and majesty I do forswear;
My manors, rents. revenues I forego;
My acts, decrees, and statutes I deny:
God pardon all oaths that are broke to me!
God keep all vows unbroke that swear to thee!
Make me, that nothing have, with nothing
    griev'd,
And thou with all pleas'd, that hast all achiev'd!
Long mayst thou live in Richard's seat to sit,
And soon lie Richard in an earthy pit!
God save King Henry, unking'd Richard says,
And send him many years of sunshine days!—
What more remains?
    North.   No more, but that you read
                    [*Offering a paper.*
These accusations, and these grievous crimes
Committed by your person and your followers
Against the state and profit of this land;
That, by confessing them, the souls of men
May deem that you are worthily depos'd.
    K. Rich. Must I do so? and must I ravel out
My weav'd up follies? Gentle Northumberland,
If thy offences were upon record,
Would it not shame thee in so fair a troop
To read a lecture of them? If thou wouldst,
There shouldst thou find one heinous article,—
Containing the deposing of a king,
And cracking the strong warrant of an oath,—
Mark'd with a blot, damn'd in the book of
    heaven:—
Nay, all of you that stand and look upon,
Whilst that my wretchedness doth bait my-
    self,—
Though some of you, with Pilate, wash your
    hands,
Showing an outward pity; yet you Pilates
Have here deliver'd me to my sour cross,
And water cannot wash away your sin.
    North. My lord, despatch; read o'er these
    articles.   [see:
    K. Rich. Mine eyes are full of tears, I cannot
And yet salt water blinds them not so much
But they can see a sort of traitors here.
Nay, if I turn mine eyes upon myself,
I find myself a traitor with the rest;
For I have given here my soul's consent
To undeck the pompous body of a king;
Make glory base, and sovereignty a slave,
Proud majesty a subject, state a peasant.
    North. My lord,—   [sulting man,
    K. Rich. No lord of thine, thou haught in-
Nor no man's lord; I have no name, no title,—
No, not that name was given me at the font,—
But 'tis usurp'd:—alack the heavy day,
That I have worn so many winters out,
And know not now what name to call myself!
O that I were a mockery-king of snow,
Standing before the sun of Bolingbroke,
To melt myself away in water-drops!—
Good king,—great king,—and yet not greatly
    good,—

And if my word be sterling yet in England,
Let it command a mirror hither straight,
That it may show me what a face I have,
Since it is bankrupt of his majesty.
    Boling. Go some of you and fetch a looking-
    glass.   [*Exit an* Attendant.
    North. Read o'er this paper while the glass
    doth come.   [come to hell!
    K. Rich. Fiend, thou torment'st me ere I
    Boling. Urge it no more, my Lord Northum-
    berland.   [isfied.
    North. The commons will not, then, be sat-
    K. Rich. They shall be satisfied: I'll read
    enough,
When I do see the very book indeed
Where all my sins are writ, and that's myself.

            Re-enter Attendant *with a glass.*

Give me the glass, and therein will I read.—
No deeper wrinkles yet? hath sorrow struck
So many blows upon this face of mine,
And made no deeper wounds?—O flattering
    glass,
Like to my followers in prosperity,
Thou dost beguile me! Was this face the face
That every day under his household roof
Did keep ten thousand men? Was this the face
That, like the sun, did make beholders wink?
Was this the face that fac'd so many follies,
And was at last out-fac'd by Bolingbroke?
A brittle glory shineth in this face:
As brittle as the glory is the face;
            [*Dashes the glass against the ground.*
For there it is, crack'd in a hundred shivers.—
Mark, silent king, the moral of this sport,—
How soon my sorrow hath destroy'd my face.
    Boling. The shadow of your sorrow hath
    destroy'd
The shadow of your face.
    K. Rich.   Say that again.
The shadow of my sorrow! Ha! let's see:—
'Tis very true, my grief lies all within;
And these external manners of laments
Are merely shadows to the unseen grief
That swells with silence in the tortur'd soul;
There lies the substance: and I thank thee,
    king,
For thy great bounty, that not only giv'st
Me cause to wail, but teachest me the way
How to lament the cause. I'll beg one boon,
And then be gone and trouble you no more.
Shall I obtain it?
    Boling.   Name it, fair cousin.
    K. Rich. Fair cousin! Why, I am greater
    than a king:
For when I was a king, my flatterers
Were then but subjects; being now a subject,
I have a king here to my flatterer.
Being so great, I have no need to beg.
    Boling. Yet ask.
    K. Rich. And shall I have?
    Boling. You shall.
    K. Rich. Then give me leave to go.
    Boling. Whither?

K. Rich. Whither you will, so I were from
your sights. [Tower.
Boling. Go, some of you convey him to the
K. Rich. O, good! Convey?—conveyers are
you all.
That rise thus nimbly by a true king's fall.
[*Exeunt* K. RICH., *some Lords, and a* Guard.
Boling. On Wednesday next we solemnly set
down
Our coronation: lords, prepare yourselves.
[*Exeunt all but the* ABBOT OF WESTMINSTER,
BISHOP OF CARLISLE, *and* AUMERLE.
Abbot. A woeful pageant have we here be-
·held.
Car. The woe's to come; the children yet un-
born
Shall feel this day as sharp to them as thorn.
Aum. You holy clergymen, is there no plot
To rid the realm of this pernicious blot?
Abbot. Before I freely speak my mind herein,
You shall not only take the sacrament
To bury mine intents, but also to effect
Whatever I shall happen to devise.
I see your brows are full of discontent,
Your hearts of sorrow, and your eyes of tears:
Come home with me to supper; I will lay
A plot shall show us all a merry day. [*Exeunt.*

ACT V.

SCENE I.—LONDON. *A Street leading to the
Tower.*

Enter QUEEN *and* Ladies.

Queen. This way the king will come; this is
the way
To Julius Cæsar's ill-erected tower,
To whose flint bosom my condemned lord
Is doom'd a prisoner by proud Bolingbroke:
Here let us rest, if this rebellious earth
Have any resting for her true king's queen.—
But soft, but see, or rather do not see,
My fair rose wither: yet look up, behold,
That you in pity may dissolve to dew,
And wash him fresh again with true-love tears.

Enter KING RICHARD *and* Guards.

Ah, thou, the model where old Troy did stand;
Thou map of honour; thou King Richard's
tomb,
And not King Richard; thou most beauteous
inn,
Why should hard-favour'd grief be lodg'd in
thee,
When triumph is become an alehouse guest?
K. Rich. Join not with grief, fair woman, do
not so,
To make my end too sudden: learn, good soul,
To think our former state a happy dream;
From which awak'd, the truth of what we are
Shows us but this: I am sworn brother, sweet,
To grim Necessity; and he and I [France,
Will keep a league till death. Hie thee to
And cloister thee in some religious house:
Our holy lives must win a new world's crown,

Which our profane hours here have stricken
down. [and mind
Queen. What, is my Richard both in shape
Transform'd and weaken'd? Hath Bolingbroke
Depos'd thine intellect? Hath he been in thy
heart?
The lion, dying, thrusteth forth his paw,
And wounds the earth, if nothing else, with rage
To be o'erpower'd; and wilt thou, pupil-like,
Take thy correction mildly, kiss the rod,
And fawn on rage with base humility,
Which art a lion and a king of beasts?
K. Rich. A king of beasts, indeed; if aught
but beasts,
I had been still a happy king of men.
Good sometime queen, prepare thee hence for
France:
Think I am dead; and that even here thou
tak'st,
As from my death-bed, my last living leave.
In winter's tedious nights sit by the fire
With good old folks, and let them tell thee tales
Of woeful ages long ago betid;
And ere thou bid good-night, to quit their grief
Tell thou the lamentable tale of me,
And send the hearers weeping to their beds:
For why, the senseless brands will sympathize
The heavy accent of thy moving tongue,
And in compassion weep the fire out;
And some will mourn in ashes, some coal-black,
For the deposing of a rightful king.

Enter NORTHUMBERLAND *attended.*

North. My lord, the mind of Bolingbroke is
chang'd;
You must to Pomfret, not unto the Tower.—
And, madam, there is order ta'en for you;
With all swift speed you must away to France.
K. Rich. Northumberland, thou ladder
wherewithal
The mounting Bolingbroke ascends my throne,
The time shall not be many hours of age
More than it is, ere foul sin, gathering head,
Shall break into corruption: thou shalt think,
Though he divide the realm, and give thee half,
It is too little, helping him to all; [the way
And he shall think that thou, which know'st
To plant unrightful kings, wilt know again,
Being ne'er so little urg'd, another way
To pluck him headlong from the usurped
throne.
The love of wicked friends converts to fear;
That fear to hate; and hate turns one or both
To worthy danger and deserved death.
North. My guilt be on my head, and there
an end. [with.
Take leave, and part; for you must part forth-
K. Rich. Doubly divorc'd!—Bad men, ye
violate
A twofold marriage,—'twixt my crown and me,
And then betwixt me and my married wife.—
Let me unkiss the oath 'twixt thee and me;
And yet not so, for with a kiss 'twas made.—
Part us, Northumberland; I towards the north,

Where shivering cold and sickness pines the
   clime;   [pomp,
My wife to France, from whence, set forth in
She came adorned hither like sweet May,
Sent back like Hallowmas or short'st of day.
   Queen. And must we be divided? must we
      part?
   K. Rich. Ay, hand from hand, my love, and
      heart from heart.   [with me.
   Queen. Banish us both, and send the king
North. That were some love, but little policy.
   Queen. Then whither he goes thither let me
      go.   [woe.
   K. Rich. So two, together weeping, make one
Weep thou for me in France, I for thee here;
Better far off than near, be ne'er the near.
Go, count thy way with sighs; I, mine with
   groans.   [moans.
   Queen. So longest way shall have the longest
   K. Rich. Twice for one step I'll groan, the
      way being short,
And piece the way out with a heavy heart.
Come, come, in wooing sorrow let's be brief,
Since, wedding it, there is such length in grief.
One kiss shall stop our mouths, and dumbly
   part;
Thus give I mine, and thus take I thy heart.
                                       [*They kiss.*
   Queen. Give me mine own again; 'twere no
      good part
To take on me to keep and kill thy heart.
                                 [*They kiss again.*
So, now I have mine own again, be gone,
That I may strive to kill it with a groan.
   K. Rich. We make woe wanton with this
      fond delay:
Once more, adieu; the rest let sorrow say.
                                       [*Exeunt.*

SCENE II.—*The same. A Room in the* DUKE OF
               YORK'S *Palace.*

           Enter YORK *and his* DUCHESS.

   Duch. My lord, you told me you would tell
      the rest,
When weeping made you break the story off
Of our two cousins coming into London.
   York. Where did I leave?
   Duch.   At that sad stop, my lord,
Where rude misgovern'd hands from windows'
   tops   [head.
Threw dust and rubbish on King Richard's
   York. Then, as I said, the duke, great
      Bolingbroke,—
Mounted upon a hot and fiery steed,
Which his aspiring rider seem'd to know,—
With slow but stately pace kept on his course,
While all tongues cried, *God save thee, Boling-
   broke!*
You would have thought the very windows
   spake,
So many greedy looks of young and old
Through casements darted their desiring eyes
Upon his visage; and that all the walls
With painted imagery had said at once,

Jesu preserve thee! welcome, Bolingbroke!
Whilst he, from one side to the other turning,
Bareheaded, lower than his proud steed's neck,
Bespake them this,—*I thank you, countrymen:*
And thus still doing, thus he pass'd along.
   Duch. Alas, poor Richard! where rode he
      the whilst?
   York. As in a theatre the eyes·of men,
After a well-grac'd actor leaves the stage,
Are idly bent on him that enters next,
Thinking his prattle to be tedious;   [eyes
Even so, or with much more contempt, men's
Did scowl on Richard; no man cried, *God save
   him!*
No joyful tongue gave him his welcome home:
But dust was thrown upon his sacred head;
Which with such gentle sorrow he shook off,—
His face still combating with tears and smiles,
The badges of his grief and patience,—
That had not God, for some strong purpose,
   steel'd
The hearts of men, they must perforce have
   melted,
And barbarism itself have pitied him.
But heaven hath a hand in these events,
To whose high will we bound our calm contents.
To Bolingbroke are we sworn subjects now,
Whose state and honour I for aye allow.
   Duch. Here comes my son Aumerle.
   York.   Aumerle that was;
But that is lost for being Richard's friend,
And, madam, you must call him Rutland now:
I am in Parliament pledge for his truth
And lasting fealty to the new-made king.

                 Enter AUMERLE.

   Duch. Welcome, my son: who are the violets
      now
That strew the green lap of the new-come
   spring?
   Aum. Madam, I know not, nor I greatly
      care not:
God knows I had as lief be none as one.
   York. Well, bear you well in this new spring
      of time,
Lest you be cropp'd before you come to prime.
What news from Oxford? hold those justs and
   triumphs?
   Aum. For aught I know, my lord, they do.
   York. You will be there, I know.
   Aum. If God prevent it not, I purpose so.
   York. What seal is that that hangs without
      thy bosom?
Yea, look'st thou pale? let me see the writing.
   Aum. My lord, 'tis nothing.
   York.   No matter, then, who sees it.
I will be satisfied; let me see the writing.
   Aum. I do beseech your grace to pardon me:
It is a matter of small consequence,
Which for some reasons I would not have seen.
   York. Which for some reasons, sir, I mean
      to see.
I fear, I fear,—
   Duch.   What should you fear?

'Tis nothing but some bond that he is enter'd
into
For gay apparel against the triumph-day.
York. Bound to himself! what doth he with
a bond
That he is bound to? Wife, thou art a fool.—
Boy, let me see the writing.
Aum. I do beseech you, pardon me; I may
not show it.
York. I will be satisfied; let me see it, I say.
[*Snatches it, and reads.*
Treason! foul treason!—villain! traitor! slave!
Duch. What's the matter, my lord?
York. Ho! who's within there?

Enter a Servant.

Saddle my horse.
God for his mercy, what treachery is here!
Duch. Why, what is 't, my lord?
York. Give me my boots, I say; saddle my
horse.—
Now, by mine honour, by my life, my troth,
I will appeach the villain. [*Exit* Servant.
Duch. What's the matter?
York. Peace, foolish woman.
Duch. I will not peace.—What is the matter,
son?
Aum. Good mother, be content; it is no more
Than my poor life must answer.
Duch. Thy life answer!
York. Bring me my boots:—I will unto the
king.

Re-enter Servant *with boots.*

Duch. Strike him, Aumerle.—Poor boy, thou
art amaz'd.
Hence, villain! never more come in my sight.
[*To the* Servant.
York. Give me my boots, I say.
Duch. Why, York, what wilt thou do?
Wilt thou not hide the trespass of thine own?
Have we more sons? or are we like to have?
Is not my teeming date drunk up with time?
And wilt thou pluck my fair son from mine age,
And rob me of a happy mother's name?
Is he not like thee? is he not thine own?
York. Thou fond mad woman,
Wilt thou conceal this dark conspiracy?
A dozen of them here have ta'en the sacrament
And interchangeably set down their hands
To kill the king at Oxford.
Duch. He shall be none;
We'll keep him here: then what is that to him?
York. Away, fond woman! were he twenty
times my son
I would appeach him.
Duch. Hadst thou groan'd for him
As I have done, thou wouldst be more pitiful.
But now I know thy mind; thou dost suspect
That I have been disloyal to thy bed,
And that he is a bastard, not thy son:
Sweet York, sweet husband, be not of that
mind:
He is as like thee as a man may be,

Not like to me, nor any of my kin,
And yet I love him.
York. Make way, unruly woman!
[*Exit.*
Duch. After, Aumerle! mount thee upon his
horse;
Spur post, and get before him to the king,
And beg thy pardon ere he do accuse thee.
I'll not be long behind; though I be old,
I doubt not but to ride as fast as York;
And never will I rise up from the ground
Till Bolingbroke have pardon'd thee. Away, be
gone! [*Exeunt.*

SCENE III.—WINDSOR. *A Room in the Castle.*

Enter BOLINGBROKE *as King,* PERCY, *and
other* Lords.

Boling. Can no man tell of my unthrifty son?
'Tis full three months since I did see him last:—
If any plague hang over us, 'tis he.
I would to God, my lords, he might be found:
Inquire at London, 'mongst the taverns there,
For there, they say, he daily doth frequent,
With unrestrained loose companions,—
Even such, they say, as stand in narrow lanes,
And beat our watch, and rob our passengers;
While he, young, wanton, and effeminate boy,
Takes on the point of honour to support
So dissolute a crew.
Percy. My lord, some two days since I saw
the prince,
And told him of these triumphs held at Oxford.
Boling. And what said the gallant?
Percy. His answer was,—he would unto the
stews,
And from the common'st creature pluck a glove,
And wear it as a favour; and with that
He would unhorse the lustiest challenger.
Boling. As dissolute as desperate: yet
through both
I see some sparkles of a better hope,
Which elder days may happily bring forth.—
But who comes here?

Enter AUMERLE *hastily.*

Aum. Where is the king?
Boling. What means
Our cousin, that he stares and looks so wildly?
Aum. God save your grace! I do beseech
your majesty,
To have some conference with your grace alone.
Boling. Withdraw yourselves, and leave us
here alone.
[*Exeunt* PERCY *and* Lords.
What is the matter with our cousin now?
Aum. For ever may my knees grow to the
earth, [*Kneels.*
My tongue cleave to my roof within my mouth,
Unless a pardon ere I rise or speak.
Boling. Intended or committed was this
fault?
If but the first, how heinous e'er it be,
To win thy after-love I pardon thee.

Aum. Then give me leave that I may turn
the key,
That no man enter till my tale be done.
Boling. Have thy desire.
                              [AUMERLE *locks the door.*
York. [*Within.*] My liege, beware; look to
thyself;
Thou hast a traitor in thy presence there.
Boling. Villain, I'll make thee safe.
                                          [*Drawing.*
Aum. Stay thy revengeful hand;
Thou hast no cause to fear.
York. [*Within.*] Open the door, secure, fool-
hardy king:
Shall I, for love, speak treason to thy face?
Open the door, or I will break it open.
    [BOLING. *opens the door and locks it again.*

Enter YORK.

Boling. What is the matter, uncle? speak;
Recover breath; tell us how near is danger,
That we may arm us to encounter it.
York. Peruse this writing here, and thou
shalt know
The treason that my haste forbids me show.
Aum. Remember, as thou read'st, thy pro-
mise pass'd:
I do repent me; read not my name there;
My heart is not confederate with my hand.
York. It was, villain, ere thy hand did set it
down.—
I tore it from the traitor's bosom, king;
Fear, and not love, begets his penitence:
Forget to pity him, lest thy pity prove
A serpent that will sting thee to the heart.
Boling. O heinous, strong, and bold con-
spiracy!—
O loyal father of a treacherous son!
Thou sheer, immaculate, and silver fountain,
From whence this stream through muddy pas-
sages
Hath held his current and defil'd himself!
Thy overflow of good converts to bad;
And thy abundant goodness shall excuse
This deadly blot in thy digressing son.
York. So shall my virtue be his vice's bawd;
And he shall spend mine honour with his shame,
As thriftless sons their scraping fathers' gold.
Mine honour lives when his dishonour dies,
Or my sham'd life in his dishonour lies:
Thou kill'st me in his life; giving him breath,
The traitor lives, the true man's put to death.
Duch. [*Within.*] What ho, my liege! for God's
sake, let me in.
Boling. What shrill-voic'd suppliant makes
this eager cry?
Duch. A woman, and thine aunt, great king;
'tis I.
Speak with me, pity me, open the door:
A beggar begs that never begg'd before.
Boling. Our scene is alter'd from a serious
thing,
And now chang'd to *The Beggar and the
King.*—

My dangerous cousin, let your mother in:
I know she's come to pray for your foul sin.
                          [AUMERLE *unlocks the door.*
York. If thou do pardon, whosoever pray,
More sins, for this forgiveness, prosper may.
This fester'd joint cut off, the rest rests sound:
This let alone will all the rest confound.

Enter DUCHESS.

Duch. O king, believe not this hard-hearted
man!
Love, loving not itself, none other can.
York. Thou frantic woman, what dost thou
make here?
Shall thy old dugs once more a traitor rear?
Duch. Sweet York, be patient.—Hear me,
gentle liege.   [*Kneels.*
Boling. Rise up, good aunt.
Duch.   Not yet, I thee beseech:
For ever will I walk upon my knees,
And never see day that the happy sees
Till thou give joy; until thou bid me joy,
By pardoning Rutland, my transgressing boy.
Aum. Unto my mother's prayers I bend my
  . knee.   [*Kneels.*
York. Against them both, my true joints
bended be.   [*Kneels.*
Ill mayst thou thrive, if thou grant any grace!
Duch. Pleads he in earnest? look upon his
face;
His eyes do drop no tears, his prayers are in
jest;
His words come from his mouth, ours from our
breast:
He prays but faintly, and would be denied;
We pray with heart and soul, and all beside:
His weary joints would gladly rise, I know;
Our knees shall kneel till to the ground they
grow:
His prayers are full of false hypocrisy;
Ours of true zeal and deep integrity.
Our prayers do out-pray his; then let them have
That mercy which true prayers ought to have.
Boling. Good aunt, stand up.
Duch.   Nay, do not say *stand up;*
But *pardon* first, and afterwards *stand up.*
An if I were thy nurse, thy tongue to teach,
Pardon should be the first word of thy speech.
I never long'd to hear a word till now;
Say *pardon,* king; let pity teach thee how:
The word is short, but not so short as sweet;
No word like *pardon,* for kings' mouths so meet.
York. Speak it in French, king; say *par-
donnez-moi.*
Duch. Dost thou teach pardon pardon to
destroy?
Ah, my sour husband, my hard-hearted lord,
That sett'st the word itself against the word!—
Speak *pardon* as 'tis current in our land;
The chopping French we do not understand.
Thine eye begins to speak, set thy tongue there:
Or in thy piteous heart plant thou thine ear;
That hearing how our plaints and prayers do
pierce,

Pity may move thee *pardon* to rehearse.
Boling. Good aunt, stand up.
Duch.　　　　　　I do not sue to stand;
Pardon is all the suit I have in hand.
Boling. I pardon him, as God shall pardon
me.
Duch. O happy vantage of a kneeling knee!
Yet am I sick for fear: speak it again;
Twice saying *pardon* doth not pardon twain,
But makes one pardon strong.
Boling.　　　　　　With all my heart
I pardon him.
Duch.　　　A god on earth thou art.
Boling. But for our trusty brother-in-law,
and the abbot,
With all the rest of that consorted crew,
Destruction straight shall dog them at the
heels.
Good uncle, help to order several powers
To Oxford, or where'er these traitors are:
They shall not live within this world, I swear,
But I will have them, if I once know where.
Uncle, farewell:—and, cousin mine, adieu:
Your mother well hath pray'd, and prove you
true.
Duch. Come, my old son:—I pray God make
thee new.　　　　　　　　　[*Exeunt.*

SCENE IV.—*Another Room in the Castle.*

Enter SIR PIERCE OF EXTON *and a* Servant.

Exton. Didst thou not mark the king, what
words he spake?
Have I no friend will rid me of this living fear?
Was it not so?
Serv.　　　　Those were his very words.
Exton. Have I no friend? quoth he: he spake
it twice,
And urg'd it twice together,—did he not?
Serv. He did.
Exton. And, speaking it, he wistly look'd on
me,
As who should say,—I would thou wert the man
That would divorce this terror from my heart,—
Meaning the king at Pomfret. Come, let's go:
I am the king's friend, and will rid his foe.
　　　　　　　　　　　　　　　[*Exeunt.*

SCENE V.—POMFRET. *The Dungeon of the
Castle.*

Enter KING RICHARD.

·*K. Rich.* I have been studying how I may
compare
This prison where I live unto the world:
And, for because the world is populous,
And here is not a creature but myself,
I cannot do it;—yet I'll hammer't out.
My brain I'll prove the female to my soul,
My soul the father: and these two beget
A generation of still-breeding thoughts,
And these same thoughts people this little
world,
In humours like the people of this world,
For no thought is contented. The better sort,—
As thoughts of things divine,—are intermix'd

With scruples, and do set the word itself
Against the word:
As thus,—*Come, little ones;* and then again,—
It is as hard to come as for a camel
To thread the postern of a needle's eye.
Thoughts tending to ambition, they do plot
Unlikely wonders: how these vain weak nails
May tear a passage through the flinty ribs
Of this hard world, my ragged prison walls;
And, for they cannot, die in their own pride.
Thoughts tending to content flatter themselves
That they are not the first of fortune's slaves,
Nor shall not be the last; like silly beggars,
Who, sitting in the stocks, refuge their shame,
That many have, and others must sit there;
And in this thought they find a kind of ease,
Bearing their own misfortune on the back
Of such as have before endur'd the like.
Thus play I, in one person, many people,
And none contented: sometimes am I king;
Then treason makes me wish myself a beggar,
And so I am: then crushing penury
Persuades me I was better when a king;
Then am I king'd again: and by and by
Think that I am unking'd by Bolingbroke,
And straight am nothing:—but whate'er I am,
Nor I, nor any man that but man is,
With nothing shall be pleas'd till he be eas'd
With being nothing.—Music do I hear?
　　　　　　　　　　　　　　　[*Music.*
Ha, ha! keep time:—how sour sweet music is
When time is broke and no proportion kept!
So is it in the music of men's lives.
And here have I the daintiness of ear
To check time broke in a disorder'd string;
But, for the concord of my state and time,
Had not an ear to hear my true time broke.
I wasted time, and now doth time waste me;
For now hath time made me his numbering
clock:
My thoughts are minutes; and, with sighs, they
jar
Their watches on unto mine eyes, the outward
watch,
Whereto my finger, like a dial's point,
Is pointing still, in cleansing them from tears.
Now, sir, the sound that tells what hour it is,
Are clamorous groans that strike upon my
heart,
Which is the bell: so sighs, and tears, and
groans,
Show minutes, times, and hours:—but my time
Runs posting on in Bolingbroke's proud joy,
While I stand fooling here, his Jack o' the clock.
This music mads me; let it sound no more;
For though it have holp madmen to their wits,
In me it seems it will make wise men mad.
Yet blessing on his heart that gives it me!
For 'tis a sign of love; and love to Richard
Is a strange brooch in this all-hating world.

Enter Groom.

Groom. Hail, royal prince!
K. Rich.　　　　　　Thanks, noble peer;

The cheapest of us is ten groats too dear.
What art thou? and how com'st thou hither,
Where no man ever comes, but that sad dog
That brings me food to make misfortune live?
  Groom. I was a poor groom of thy stable,
    king,
When thou wert king; who, travelling towards
    York,—
With much ado at length have gotten leave
To look upon my sometimes royal master's
    face.
O, how it yearn'd my heart, when I beheld,
In London streets, that coronation-day,
When Bolingbroke rode on roan Barbary,—
That horse that thou so often hast bestrid,
That horse that I so carefully have dress'd!
  K. Rich. Rode he on Barbary? Tell me,
    gentle friend,
How went he under him?   [ground.
  Groom. So proudly as if he disdain'd the
  K. Rich. So proud that Bolingbroke was on
    his back!
That jade hath eat bread from my royal hand;
This hand hath made him proud with clapping
    him.
Would he not stumble? would he not fall
    down,—   [neck
Since pride must have a fall,—and break the
Of that proud man that did usurp his back?
Forgiveness, horse! why do I rail on thee,
Since thou, created to be aw'd by man,
Wast born to bear? I was not made a horse;
And yet I bear a burden like an ass,
Spur-gall'd and tir'd by jauncing Bolingbroke.

Enter Keeper *with a dish.*

  Keep. Fellow, give place; here is no longer
    stay.   [*To the* Groom.
  K. Rich. If thou love me, 'tis time thou wert
    away.
  Groom. What my tongue dares not, that my
    heart shall say.   [*Exit.*
  Keep. My lord, wilt please you to fall to?
  K. Rich. Taste of it first as thou art wont to
    do.
  Keep. My lord, I dare not. Sir Pierce of Ex-
    ton,
Who lately came from the king, commands the
    contrary.
  K. Rich. The devil take Henry of Lancaster
    and thee!
Patience is stale, and I am weary of it.
                            [*Beats the* Keeper.
  Keep. Help, help, help!

Enter EXTON *and Servants, armed.*

  K. Rich. How now! what means death in
    this rude assault?
Villain, thine own hand yields thy death's in-
    strument.
                [*Snatching a weapon, and killing one.*
Go thou, and fill another room in hell.
          [*He kills another, then* EXTON *strikes
                    him down.*

That hand shall burn in never-quenching fire
That staggers thus my person.—Exton, thy
    fierce hand
Hath with the king's blood stain'd the king's
    own land.
Mount, mount, my soul! thy seat is up on high;
Whilst my gross flesh sinks downward, here to
    die.   [*Dies.*
  Exton. As full of valour as of royal blood:
Both have I split;—O, would the deed were
    good!
For now the devil, that told me I did well,
Says that this deed is chronicled in hell.
This dead king to the living king I'll bear:—
Take hence the rest, and give them burial here.
                            [*Exeunt.*

SCENE VI.—WINDSOR. *A Room in the Castle.*

  Flourish. Enter BOLINGBROKE *as King,*
    YORK, LORDS, *and* Attendants.

  Boling. Kind uncle York, the latest news we
    hear
Is that the rebels have consum'd with fire
Our town of Cicester in Glostershire;
But whether they be ta'en or slain we hear not.

Enter NORTHUMBERLAND.

Welcome, my lord: what is the news?
  North. First, to thy sacred state wish I all
    happiness.
The next news is, I have to London sent
The heads of Salisbury, Spencer, Blunt, and
    Kent:
The manner of their taking may appear
At large discoursed in this paper here.
                        [*Presenting a paper.*
  Boling. We thank thee, gentle Percy, for thy
    pains;
And to thy worth will add right worthy gains.

Enter FITZWATER.

  Fitz. My lord, I have from Oxford sent to
    London
The heads of Brocas and Sir Bennet Seely;
Two of the dangerous consorted traitors
That sought at Oxford thy dire overthrow.
  Boling. Thy pains, Fitzwater, shall not be
    forgot;
Right noble is thy merit, well I wot.

Enter PERCY, *with the* BISHOP OF CARLISLE.

  Percy. The grand conspirator, Abbot of
    Westminster,
With clog of conscience and sour melancholy,
Hath yielded up his body to the grave;
But here is Carlisle living, to abide
Thy kingly doom and sentence of his pride.
  Boling. Carlisle, this is your doom:—
Choose out some secret place, some reverend
    room,
More than thou hast, and with it joy thy life;
So, as thou liv'st in peace, die free from strife:
For though mine enemy thou hast ever been,
High sparks of honour in thee have I seen.

Enter EXTON, *with* Attendants, *bearing a coffin.*

Exton. Great king, within this coffin I pre-
    sent
Thy buried fear: herein all breathless lies
The mightiest of thy greatest enemies,
Richard of Bordeaux, by me hither brought.

Boling. Exton, I thank thee not; for thou
    hast wrought
A deed of slander, with thy fatal hand,
Upon my head and all this famous land.

Exton. From your own mouth, my lord, did
    I this deed.   [need,

Boling. They love not poison that do poison
Nor do I thee: though I did wish him dead,
I hate the murderer, love him murdered.

The guilt of conscience take thou for thy la-
    bour,
But neither my good word nor princely favour:
With Cain go wander through the shade of
    night,
And never show thy head by day nor light.—
Lords, I protest, my soul is full of woe,
That blood should sprinkle -me to make me
    grow:
Come, mourn with me for that I do lament.
And put on sullen black incontinent:
I'll make a voyage to the Holy Land,
To wash this blood off from my guilty hand:—
March sadly after; grace my mournings here,
In weeping after this untimely bier.   [*Exeunt.*

King
HENRY THE FOURTH.
Part I.

Act II. Sc. 4.

KING HENRY IV.

FIRST PART

DRAMATIS PERSONÆ

KING HENRY THE FOURTH.
HENRY, *Prince of Wales,* } *Sons to the*
PRINCE JOHN *of Lancaster,* } KING.
EARL OF WESTMORELAND, } *Friends to the*
SIR WALTER BLUNT, } KING.
THOMAS PERCY, *Earl of Worcester.*
HENRY PERCY, *Earl of Northumberland.*
HENRY PERCY, *surnamed* HOTSPUR, *his Son.*
EDMUND MORTIMER, *Earl of March.*
SCROOP, *Archbishop of York.*
SIR MICHAEL, *a Friend to the Archbishop.*
ARCHIBALD, *Earl of Douglas.*
OWEN GLENDOWER.
SIR RICHARD VERNON.
SIR JOHN FALSTAFF.

POINS.
GADSHILL.
PETO.
BARDOLPH.

LADY PERCY, *Wife to* HOTSPUR, *and Sister to*
MORTIMER.
LADY MORTIMER, *Daughter to* GLENDOWER,
and Wife to MORTIMER.
MRS. QUICKLY, *Hostess of a Tavern in East-
cheap.*

Lords, Officers, Sheriff, Vintner, Chamberlain, Drawers, Two Carriers, Travellers,
and Attendants.

SCENE,—ENGLAND.

ACT I.

SCENE I.—LONDON. *A Room in the Palace.*

Enter KING HENRY, WESTMORELAND, SIR
WALTER BLUNT, *and others.*

K. Hen. So shaken as we are, so wan with
care,
Find we a time for frighted peace to pant,
And breathe short-winded accents of new broils
To be commenc'd in strands afar remote.
No more the thirsty entrance of this soil
Shall daub her lips with her own children's
blood;
No more shall trenching war channel her fields,
Nor bruise her flowerets with the armed hoofs
Of hostile paces: those opposed eyes
Which, like the meteors of a troubled heaven,
All of one nature, of one substance bred,
Did lately meet in the intestine shock
And furious close of civil butchery,
Shall now, in mutual well-beseeming ranks,
March all one way, and be no more oppos'd
Against acquaintance, kindred, and allies.
The edge of war, like an ill-sheathed knife,
No more shall cut his master. Therefore,
friends,
As far as to the sepulchre of Christ,—
Whose soldier now, under whose blessed cross
We are impressed and engag'd to fight,—
Forthwith a power of English shall we levy;
Whose arms were moulded in their mothers'
womb
To chase these pagans in those holy fields
Over whose acres walk'd those blessed feet
Which fourteen hundred years ago were nail'd
For our advantage on the bitter cross.

But this our purpose is a twelvemonth old,
And bootless 'tis to tell you we will go:
Therefore we meet not now.—Then let me hear
Of you, my gentle cousin Westmoreland,
What yesternight our council did decree
In forwarding this dear expedience.
West. My liege, this haste was hot in ques-
tion,
And many limits of the charge set down
But yesternight: when, all athwart, there
came
A post from Wales loaden with heavy news;
Whose worst was,—that the noble Mortimer
Leading the men of Herefordshire to fight
Against the irregular and wild Glendower,
Was by the rude hands of that Welshman taken,
A thousand of his people butchered;
Upon whose dead corpse there was such misuse,
Such beastly, shameless transformation,
By those Welshwomen done, as may not be
Without much shame re-told or spoken of.
K. Hen. It seems, then, that the tidings of
this broil
Brake off our business for the Holy Land.
West. This, match'd with other, did, my
gracious Lord;
For more uneven and unwelcome news
Came from the north, and thus it did import:
On Holy-rood day, the gallant Hotspur there,
Young Harry Percy, and brave Archibald,
That ever valiant and approved Scot,
At Holmedon met,
Where they did spend a sad and bloody hour;
As by discharge of their artillery,
And shape of likelihood, the news was told;
For he that brought them, in the very heat

And pride of their contention did take horse,
Uncertain of the issue any way.   [friend,

K. Hen. Here is a dear and true-industrious
Sir Walter Blunt, new lighted from his horse,
Stain'd with the variation of each soil
Betwixt that Holmedon and this seat of ours;
And he hath brought us smooth and welcome
    news.
The Earl of Douglas is discomfited:
Ten thousand bold Scots, two-and-twenty
    knights,
Balk'd in their own blood, did Sir Walter see
On Holmedon's plains: of prisoners, Hotspur
    took
Mordake, Earl of Fife and eldest son
To beaten Douglas; and the Earls of Athol,
Of Murray, Angus, and Menteith.
And is not this an honourable spoil?
A gallant prize? ha, cousin, is it not?

West.   In faith,
It is a conquest for a prince to boast of.

K. Hen. Yea, there thou mak'st me sad, and
mak'st me sin,
In envy that my Lord Northumberland
Should be the father to so blest a son,—
A son who is the theme of honour's tongue;
Amongst a grove, the very straightest plant;
Who is sweet fortune's minion and her pride:
Whilst I, by looking on the praise of him,
See riot and dishonour stain the brow
Of my young Harry. O that it could be prov'd
That some night-tripping fairy had exchang'd
In cradle-clothes our children where they lay,
And call'd mine Percy, his Plantagenet!
Then would I have his Harry, and he mine:
But let him from my thoughts.—What think
    you, coz,
Of this young Percy's pride? The prisoners,
Which he in this adventure hath surpris'd,
To his own use he keeps; and sends me word,
I shall have none but Mordake Earl of Fife.

West. This is his uncle's teaching, this is
    Worcester,
Malevolent to you in all aspécts;
Which makes him prune himself, and bristle up
The crest of youth against your dignity.

K. Hen. But I have sent for him to answer
    this;
And for this cause awhile we must neglect
Our holy purpose to Jerusalem.
Cousin, on Wednesday next our council we
Will hold at Windsor,—so inform the lords:
But come yourself with speed to us again;
For more is to be said and to be done
Than out of anger can be uttered.

West. I will, my liege.   [*Exeunt.*

SCENE II.—*The same. Another Room in the
Palace.*

Enter PRINCE HENRY *and* FALSTAFF.

Fal. Now, Hal, what time of day is it, lad?

P. Hen. Thou art so fat-witted, with drinking of old sack, and unbuttoning thee after supper, and sleeping upon benches after noon, that

thou hast forgotten to demand that truly which
thou wouldst truly know. What a devil hast
thou to do with the time of the day? unless
hours were cups of sack, and minutes capons,
and cocks the tongues of bawds, and dials the
signs of leaping houses, and the blessed sun
himself a fair hot wench in flame-coloured taf-
feta,—I see no reason why thou shouldst be so
superfluous to demand the time of the day.

Fal. Indeed, you come near me now, Hal;
for we that take purses go by the moon and the
seven stars, and not by Phœbus,—he, *that wandering knight so fair.* And, I pr'ythee, sweet
wag, when thou art king,—as, God save thy
grace, (majesty, I should say; for grace thou
wilt have none,)—

P. Hen. What, none?

Fal. No, by my troth; not so much as will
serve to be prologue to an egg and butter.

P. Hen. Well, how then? come, roundly,
roundly.

Fal. Marry, then, sweet wag, when thou art
king, let not us that are squires of the night's
body be called thieves of the day's beauty: let
us be Diana's foresters, gentlemen of the shade,
minions of the moon; and let men say we be
men of good government, being governed, as
the sea is, by our noble and chaste mistress the
moon, under whose countenance we steal.

P. Hen. Thou sayest well, and it holds well
too; for the fortune of us that are the moon's
men doth ebb and flow like the sea, being governed, as the sea is, by the moon. As, for proof,
now: a purse of gold most resolutely snatched
on Monday night, and most dissolutely spent
on Tuesday morning; got with swearing *lay by,*
and spent with crying *bring in;* now in as low
an ebb as the foot of the ladder, and by and by
in as high a flow as the ridge of the gallows.

Fal. By the Lord, thou sayest true, lad. And
is not my hostess of the tavern a most sweet
wench?

P. Hen. As the honey of Hybla, my old lad
of the castle. And is not a buff jerkin a most
sweet robe of durance?

Fal. How now, how now, mad wag! what,
in thy quips and thy quiddities? what a plague
have I to do with a buff jerkin?

P. Hen. Why, what a pox have I to do with
my hostess of the tavern?

Fal. Well, thou hast called her to a reckoning many a time and oft.

P. Hen. Did I ever call for thee to pay thy
part?

Fal. No; I'll give thee thy due, thou hast
paid all there.

P. Hen. Yea, and elsewhere, so far as my
coin would stretch; and where it would not, I
have used my credit.

Fal. Yea, and so used it that, were it not
here apparent that thou art heir-apparent,—
but, I pr'ythee, sweet wag, shall there be gallows standing in England when thou art king?
and resolution thus fobbed as it is with the

rusty curb of old father antic the law? Do not thou, when thou art king, hang a thief.

P. Hen. No; thou shalt.

Fal. Shall I? O rare! By the Lord, I'll be a brave judge.

P. Hen. Thou judgest false already: I mean, thou shalt have the hanging of the thieves, and so become a rare hangman.

Fal. Well, Hal, well; and in some sort it jumps with my humour as well as waiting in the court, I can tell you.

P. Hen. For obtaining of suits?

Fal. Yea, for obtaining of suits, whereof the hangman hath no lean wardrobe. 'Sblood, I am as melancholy as a gib-cat or a lugged bear.

P. Hen. Or an old lion, or a lover's lute.

Fal. Yea, or the drone of a Lincolnshire bag-pipe.

P. Hen. What sayest thou to a hare, or the melancholy of Moor-ditch?

Fal. Thou hast the most unsavoury similes, and art, indeed, the most comparative, rascallest,—sweet young prince,—but, Hal, I pr'ythee, trouble me no more with vanity. I would to God thou and I knew where a commodity of good names were to be bought. An old lord of the council rated me the other day in the street about you, sir,—but I marked him not; and yet he talked very wisely,—but I regarded him not; and yet he talked wisely, and in the street too.

P. Hen. Thou didst well; for wisdom cries out in the streets, and no man regards it.

Fal. O, thou hast damnable iteration, and art, indeed, able to corrupt a saint. Thou hast done much harm upon me, Hal,—God forgive thee for it! Before I knew thee, Hal, I knew nothing; and now am I, if a man should speak truly, little better than one of the wicked. I must give over this life, and I will give it over; by the Lord, an I do not, I am a villain: I'll be damned for never a king's son in Christendom.

P. Hen. Where shall we take a purse to-morrow, Jack?

Fal. Where thou wilt, lad; I'll make one; an I do not, call me villain, and baffle me.

P. Hen. I see a good amendment of life in thee,—from praying to purse-taking.

Enter POINS *at a distance.*

Fal. Why, Hal, 'tis my vocation, Hal; 'tis no sin for a man to labour in his vocation.—Poins!—Now shall we know if Gadshill have set a match.—O, if men were to be saved by merit, what hole in hell were hot enough for him? This is the most omnipotent villain that ever cried *stand* to a true man.

P. Hen. Good-morrow, Ned.

Poins. Good-morrow, sweet Hal.—What says Monsieur Remorse? What says Sir John Sack-and-sugar? Jack, how agrees the devil and thee about thy soul, that thou soldest him on Good-Friday last for a cup of Madeira and a cold capon's leg?

P. Hen. Sir John stands to his word,—the devil shall have his bargain; for he was never yet a breaker of proverbs,—he will give the devil his due.

Poins. Then art thou damned for keeping thy word with the devil.

P. Hen. Else he had been damned for cozening the devil.

Poins. But, my lads, my lads, to-morrow morning, by four o'clock, early at Gadshill! there are pilgrims going to Canterbury with rich offerings, and traders riding to London with fat purses: I have visards for you all; you have horses for yourselves: Gadshill lies to-night in Rochester: I have bespoke supper to-morrow night in Eastcheap: we may do it as secure as sleep. If you will go, I will stuff your purses full of crowns; if you will not, tarry at home and be hanged.

Fal. Hear ye, Yedward; if I tarry at home and go not, I'll hang you for going.

Poins. You will, chops?

Fal. Hal, wilt thou make one?

P. Hen. Who, I rob? I a thief? not I, by my faith.

Fal. There's neither honesty, manhood, nor good fellowship in thee, nor thou camest not of the blood royal, if thou darest not stand for ten shillings.

P. Hen. Well, then, once in my days I'll be a madcap.

Fal. Why, that's well said.   [home.

P. Hen. Well, come what will, I'll tarry at

Fal. By the Lord, I'll be a traitor, then, when thou art king.

P. Hen. I care not.

Poins. Sir John, I pr'ythee, leave the prince and me alone: I will lay him down such reasons for this adventure that he shall go.

Fal. Well, God give thee the spirit of persuasion, and him the ears of profiting, that what thou speakest may move, and what he hears may be believed, that the true prince may, for recreation sake, prove a false thief; for the poor abuses of the time want countenance. Farewell: you shall find me in Eastcheap.

P. Hen. Farewell, thou latter spring! Farewell, All-hallown summer!   [*Exit* FALSTAFF.

Poins. Now, my good sweet honey-lord, ride with us to-morrow: I have a jest to execute that I cannot manage alone. Falstaff, Bardolph, Peto, and Gadshill, shall rob those men that we have already waylaid; yourself and I will not be there; and when they have the booty, if you and I do not rob them, cut this head from my shoulders.

P. Hen. But how shall we part with them in setting forth?

Poins. Why, we will set forth before or after them, and appoint them a place of meeting, wherein it is at our pleasure to fail; and then will they adventure upon the exploit themselves; which they shall have no sooner achieved, but we'll set upon them.

P. Hen. Ay, but 'tis like that they will know us by our horses, by our habits, and by every other appointment, to be ourselves.

Poins. Tut, our horses they shall not see,—I'll tie them in the wood; our visards we will change after we leave them; and, sirrah, I have cases of buckram for the nonce, to immask our noted outward garments.

P. Hen. But I doubt they will be too hard for us.

Poins. Well, for two of them, I know them to be as true-bred cowards as ever turned back; and for the third, if he fight longer than he sees reason, I'll forswear arms. The virtue of this jest will be the incomprehensible lies that this same fat rogue will tell us when we meet at supper: how thirty, at least, he fought with; what wards, what blows, what extremities he endured; and in the reproof of this lies the jest.

P. Hen. Well, I'll go with thee: provide us all things necessary, and meet me to-morrow night in Eastcheap; there I'll sup. Farewell.

Poins. Farewell, my lord.   [*Exit* POINS.

P. Hen. I know you all, and will awhile uphold
The unyok'd humour of your idleness:
Yet herein will I imitate the sun,
Who doth permit the base contagious clouds
To smother up his beauty from the world,
That, when he please again to be himself,
Being wanted, he may be more wonder'd at
By breaking through the foul and ugly mists
Of vapours that did seem to strangle him.
If all the year were playing holidays,
To sport would be as tedious as to work;
But when they seldom come, they wish'd-for come,
And nothing pleaseth but rare accidents.
So, when this loose behaviour I throw off,
And pay the debt I never promised,
By how much better than my word I am,
By so much shall I falsify men's hopes;
And, like bright metal on a sullen ground,
My reformation, glittering o'er my fault,
Shall show more goodly and attract more eyes
Than that which hath no foil to set it off.
I'll so offend, to make offence a skill;
Redeeming time when men think least I will.
[*Exit.*

SCENE III.—*The same. Another Room in the Palace.*

Enter KING HENRY, NORTHUMBERLAND, WORCESTER, HOTSPUR, SIR WALTER BLUNT, *and others.*

K. Hen. My blood hath been too cold and temperate,
Unapt to stir at these indignities,
And you have found me; for accordingly
You tread upon my patience: but be sure
I will from henceforth rather be myself,
Mighty and to be fear'd, than my condition;
Which hath been smooth as oil, soft as young down,

And therefore lost that title of respect
Which the proud soul ne'er pays but to the proud.

Wor. Our house, my sovereign liege, little deserves
The scourge of greatness to be used on it;
And that same greatness, too which our own hands
Have holp to make so portly.

North. My lord,—

K. Hen. Worcester, get thee gone; for I see danger
And disobedience in thine eye: O, sir,
Your presence is too bold and peremptory
And majesty might never yet endure
The moody frontier of a servant brow.
You have good leave to leave us: when we need
Your use and counsel we shall send for you.
[*Exit* WORCESTER.
You were about to speak.
[*To* NORTHUMBERLAND.

North.   Yea, my good lord.
Those prisoners in your highness' name demanded,
Which Harry Percy here at Holmedon took,
Were, as he says, not with such strength denied
As is delivered to your majesty:
Either envy, therefore, or misprision
Is guilty of this fault, and not my son.

Hot. My liege, I did deny no prisoners.
But I remember when the fight was done,
When I was dry with rage and extreme toil,
Breathless and faint, leaning upon my sword,
Came there a certain lord, neat, trimly dress'd,
Fresh as a bridegroom; and his chin new reap'd
Show'd like a stubble-land at harvest-home;
He was perfum'd like a milliner;
And 'twixt his finger and his thumb he held
A pouncet-box, which ever and anon
He gave his nose, and took't away again;—
Who therewith angry, when it next came there,
Took it in snuff:—and still he smil'd and talk'd;
And as the soldiers bore dead bodies by,
He call'd them untaught knaves, unmannerly,
To bring a slovenly unhandsome corse
Betwixt the wind and his nobility.
With many holiday and lady terms
He question'd me; among the rest, demanded
My prisoners in your majesty's behalf.
I, then all smarting with my wounds being cold,
To be so pester'd with a popinjay,
Out of my grief and my impatience,
Answer'd neglectingly, I know not what,—
He should, or he should not;—for he made me mad
To see him shine so brisk, and smell so sweet,
And talk so like a waiting-gentlewoman
Of guns, and drums, and wounds,—God save the mark!—
And telling me the sovereign'st thing on earth
Was parmaceti for an inward bruise;
And that it was great pity, so it was,
This villanous saltpetre should be digg'd
Out of the bowels of the harmless earth,

Which many a good tall fellow had destroy'd
So cowardly; and but for these vile guns
He would himself have been a soldier.
This bald unjointed chat of his, my lord,
I answer'd indirectly, as I said;
And I beseech you, let not his report
Come current for an accusation
Betwixt my love and your high majesty.

　　Blunt. The circumstance consider'd, good
　　　　my lord,
Whatever Harry Percy then had said
To such a person, and in such a place,
At such a time, with all the rest re-told,
May reasonably die, and never rise
To do him wrong, or any way impeach
What then he said, so he unsay it now.

　　K. Hen. Why, yet he doth deny his prisoners,
But with proviso and exception,—
That we at our own charge shall ransom straight
His brother-in-law, the foolish Mortimer;
Who, on my soul, hath wilfully betray'd
The lives of those that he did lead to fight
Against the great magician, damn'd Glendower,
Whose daughter, as we hear, that Earl of March
Hath lately married. Shall our coffers, then,
Be emptied to redeem a traitor home?
Shall we buy treason? and indent with fears,
When they have lost and forfeited themselves?
No, on the barren mountains let him starve;
For I shall never hold that man my friend
Whose tongue shall ask me for one penny cost
To ransom home revolted Mortimer.

　　Hot. Revolted Mortimer!
He never did fall off, my sovereign liege,
But by the chance of war:—to prove that true,
Needs no more but one tongue for all those
　　　　wounds,　　　　　　　　　　　[took,
Those mouthed wounds, which valiantly he
When on the gentle Severn's sedgy bank,
In single opposition, hand to hand,
He did confound the best part of an hour
In changing hardiment with great Glendower:
Three times they breath'd, and three times did
　　　　they drink,
Upon agreement, of swift Severn's flood;
Who then, affrighted with their bloody looks,
Ran fearfully among the trembling reeds,
And hid his crisp head in the hollow bank
Blood-stained with these valiant combatants.
Never did base and rotten policy
Colour her working with such deadly wounds;
Nor could the noble Mortimer
Receive so many, and all willingly:
Then let him not be slander'd with revolt.

　　K. Hen. Thou dost belie him, Percy, thou
　　　　dost belie him;
He never did encounter with Glendower:
I tell thee,
He durst as well have met the devil alone
As Owen Glendower for any enemy.
Art thou not asham'd? But, sirrah, henceforth
Let me not hear you speak of Mortimer:
Send me your prisoners with the speediest
　　　　means,

Or you shall hear in such a kind from me
As will displease you.—My Lord Northumber-
　　　　land,
We license your departure with your son.—
Send us your prisoners, or you'll hear of it.
　　　　　[*Exeunt* K. HENRY, BLUNT, *and* Train.

　　Hot. And if the devil come and roar for
　　　　them,
I will not send them:—I will after straight,
And tell him so; for I will ease my heart,
Albeit I make a hazard of my head.

　　North. What, drunk with choler? stay, and
　　　　pause awhile:
Here comes your uncle.

Re-enter WORCESTER.)

　　Hot.　　　　　　　Speak of Mortimer!
Zounds, I will speak of him; and let my soul
Want mercy, if I do not join with him:
Yea, on his part I'll empty all these veins,
And shed my dear blood drop by drop i' the
　　　　dust,
But I will lift the down-trod Mortimer
As high i' the air as this unthankful king,
As this ingrate and canker'd Bolingbroke.

　　North. Brother, the king hath made your
　　　　nephew mad.　　　　[*To* WORCESTER.

　　Wor. Who struck this heat up after I was
　　　　gone?

　　Hot. He will, forsooth, have all my prisoners;
And when I urg'd the ransom once again
Of my wife's brother, then his cheek look'd pale,
And on my face he turn'd an eye of death,
Trembling even at the name of Mortimer.

　　Wor. I cannot blame him: was he not pro-
　　　　claim'd
By Richard that dead is the next of blood?

　　North. He was: I heard the proclamation:
And then it was when the unhappy king—
Whose wrongs in us God pardon!—did set forth
Upon his Irish expedition;
From whence he intercepted did return
To be depos'd, and shortly murdered.

　　Wor. And for whose death we in the world's
　　　　wide mouth
Live scandaliz'd and foully spoken of.

　　Hot. But, soft, I pray you; did King Richard
　　　　then
Proclaim my brother Edmund Mortimer
Heir to the crown?

　　North.　　　　　He did; myself did hear it.

　　Hot. Nay, then I cannot blame his cousin
　　　　king,
That wish'd him on the barren mountains
　　　　starve.
But shall it be that you that set the crown
Upon the head of this forgetful man,
And for his sake wear the detested blot
Of murderous subornation,—shall it be
That you a world of curses undergo,
Being the agents, or base second means,
The cords, the ladder, or the hangman rather?—
O, pardon me, that I descend so low
To show the line and the predicament

Wherein you range under this subtle king;—
Shall it, for shame, be spoken in these days,
Or fill up chronicles in time to come,
That men of your nobility and power
Did 'gage them both in an unjust behalf,—
As both of you, God pardon it! have done,—
To put down Richard, that sweet lovely rose,
And plant this thorn, this canker, Bolingbroke?
And shall it, in more shame, be further spoken
That you are fool'd, discarded, and shook off
By him for whom these shames ye underwent?
No; yet time serves, wherein you may redeem
Your banish'd honours, and restore yourselves
Into the good thoughts of the world again,—
Revenge the jeering and disdain'd contempt
Of this proud king, who studies day and night
To answer all the debt he owes to you
Even with the bloody payment of your deaths:
Therefore, I say,—

Wor.   Peace, cousin; say no more:
And now I will unclasp a secret book,
And to your quick-conceiving discontents
I'll read you matter deep and dangerous;
As full of peril and adventurous spirit
As to o'er-walk a current roaring loud
On the unsteadfast footing of a spear.

Hot. If he fall in, good-night!—or sink or
    swim:—
Send danger from the east unto the west,
So honour cross it from the north to south,
And let them grapple.—O, the blood more stirs
To rouse a lion than to start a hare!

North. Imagination of some great exploit
Drives him beyond the bounds of patience.

Hot. By heaven, methinks it were an easy
    leap
To pluck bright honour from the pale-fac'd
    moon;
Or dive into the bottom of the deep,
Where fathom-line could never touch the
    ground,
And pluck up drowned honour by the locks;
So he that doth redeem her thence might wear
Without corrival all her dignities:
But out upon this half-fac'd fellowship!

Wor. He apprehends a world of figures here,
But not the form of what he should attend.—
Good cousin, give me audience for awhile.

Hot. I cry you mercy.

Wor.   Those same noble Scots
That are your prisoners,—

Hot.   I'll keep them all;
By heaven, he shall not have a Scot of them;
No, if a Scot would save his soul, he shall not:
I'll keep them, by this hand.

Wor.   You start away,
And lend no ear unto my purposes.—
Those prisoners you shall keep.

Hot.   Nay, I will; that's flat:—
He said he would not ransom Mortimer;
Forbad my tongue to speak of Mortimer;
But I will find him when he lies asleep,
And in his ear I'll holla—*Mortimer!*
Nay,

I'll have a starling shall be taught to speak
Nothing but *Mortimer*, and give it him,
To keep his anger still in motion.

Wor. Hear you, cousin; a word.

Hot. All studies here I solemnly defy,
Save how to gall and pinch this Bolingbroke:
And that same sword-and-buckler Prince of
    Wales,—
But that I think his father loves him not,
And would be glad he met with some mischance,
I'd have him poison'd with a pot of ale.

Wor. Farewell, kinsman: I will talk to you
When you are better temper'd to attend.

North. Why, what a wasp-tongue and im-
    patient fool
Art thou to break into this woman's mood,
Tying thine ear to no tongue but thine own!

Hot. Why, look you, I am whipp'd and
    scourg'd with rods,
Nettled, and stung with pismires, when I hear
Of this vile politician, Bolingbroke.
In Richard's time,—what do ye call the place?—
A plague upon't—it is in Glostershire;—
'Twas where the madcap duke his uncle kept,—
His uncle York:—where I first bow'd my knee
Unto this king of smiles, this Bolingbroke,
When you and he came back from Ravenspurg.

North. At Berkley Castle.

Hot. You say true:—
Why, what a candy deal of courtesy
This fawning greyhound then did proffer me!
Look, *when his infant fortune came to age*,
And, *gentle Harry Percy*, and, *kind cousin*,—
O, the devil take such cozeners!—God forgive
    me!—
Good uncle, tell your tale; for I have done.

Wor. Nay, if you have not, to't again;
We'll stay your leisure.

Hot.   I have done, i' faith.

Wor. Then once more to your Scottish
    prisoners.
Deliver them up without their ransom straight,
And make the Douglas' son your only mean
For powers in Scotland; which, for divers
    reasons
Which I shall send you written, be assur'd,
Will easily be granted.—You, my lord,
                    [*To* NORTHUMBERLAND.
Your son in Scotland being thus employ'd,
Shall secretly into the bosom creep
Of that same noble prelate, well belov'd,
The archbishop.

Hot. Of York, is't not?

Wor. True; who bears hard
His brother's death at Bristol, the Lord Scroop.
I speak not this in estimation,
As what I think might be, but what I know
Is ruminated, plotted, and set down,
And only stays but to behold the face
Of that occasion that shall bring it on.

Hot. I smell it: upon my life, it will do well.

North. Before the game's a-foot, thou still
    lett'st slip.   [plot:—

Hot. Why, it cannot choose but be a noble

And then the power of Scotland and of York.—
To join with Mortimer, ha?

Wor.   And so they shall.

Hot. In faith, it is exceedingly well aim'd.

Wor. And 'tis no little reason bids us speed,
To save our heads by raising of a head;
For, bear ourselves as even as we can,
The king will always think him in our debt,
And think we think ourselves unsatisfied,
Till he hath found a time to pay us home:
And see already how he doth begin
To make us strangers to his looks of love.

Hot. He does, he does: we'll be reveng'd on
 him.

Wor. Cousin, farewell:—no further go in this
Than I by letters shall direct your course.
When time is ripe,—which will be suddenly,—
I'll steal to Glendower and Lord Mortimer;
Where you and Douglas, and our powers at
 once,—
As I will fashion it,—shall happily meet,
To bear our fortunes in our own strong arms,
Which now we hold at much uncertainty.

North. Farewell, good brother: we shall
 thrive, I trust.

Hot. Uncle, adieu:—O, let the hours be short,
Till fields and blows and groans applaud our
 sport.   [*Exeunt.*

ACT II.

SCENE I.—ROCHESTER. *An Inn Yard.*

Enter a Carrier *with a lantern in his hand.*

1 *Car.* Heigh-ho! an't be not four by the
day, I'll be hanged: Charles' wain is over the
new chimney, and yet our horse not packed.—
What, ostler!

Ost. [*Within.*] Anon, anon.

1 *Car.* I pr'ythee, Tom, beat Cut's saddle,
put a few flocks in the point; the poor jade is
wrong in the withers out of all cess.

Enter another Carrier.

2 *Car.* Peas and beans are as dank here as a
dog, and that is the next way to give poor jades
the bots: this house is turned upside down since
Robin ostler died.

1 *Car.* Poor fellow! never joyed since the
price of oats rose; it was the death of him.

2 *Car.* I think this be the most villanous
house in all London road for fleas: I am stung
like a tench.

1 *Car.* Like a tench! by the mass, there is
ne'er a king in Christendom could be better bit
than I have been since the first cock.

2 *Car.* Why, they will allow us ne'er a jorden, and then we leak in your chimney; and
your chamber-lie breeds fleas like a loach.

1 *Car.* What, ostler! come away, and be
hanged; come away.

2 *Car.* I have a gammon of bacon and two
races of ginger, to be delivered as far as Char-
ing-cross.

1 *Car.* 'Odsbody! the turkeys in my pannier
are quite starved.—What, ostler!—A plague on

thee! hast thou never an eye in thy head?
canst not hear? An 'twere not as good a deed
as drink, to break the pate of thee, I am a very
villain.—Come, and be hanged:—hast no faith
in thee?

Enter GADSHILL.

Gads. Good-morrow, carriers. What's
o'clock?

1 *Car.* I think it be two o'clock.

Gads. I pr'ythee, lend me thy lantern, to see
my gelding in the stable.

1 *Car.* Nay, soft, I pray ye; I know a trick
worth two of that, i' faith.

Gads. I pr'ythee, lend me thine.

2 *Car.* Ay, when? canst tell?—Lend me thy
lantern, quoth a?—marry, I'll see thee hanged
first.

Gads. Sirrah carrier, what time do you mean
to come to London?

2 *Car.* Time enough to go to bed with a
candle, I warrant thee.—Come, neighbour
Mugs, we'll call up the gentlemen: they will
along with company, for they have great
charge.   [*Exeunt* Carriers.

Gads. What, ho! chamberlain!

Cham. [*Within.*] At hand, quoth pick-purse.

Gads. That's even as fair as—at hand, quoth
the chamberlain; for thou variest no more from
picking of purses than giving direction doth
from labouring; thou layest the plot how.

Enter Chamberlain.

Cham. Good-morrow, Master Gadshill. It
holds current that I told you yesternight:—
there's a franklin in the wild of Kent hath
brought three hundred marks with him in gold:
I heard him tell it to one of his company last
night at supper; a kind of auditor; one that
hath abundance of charge too, God know what.
They are up already, and call for eggs and
butter: they will away presently.

Gads. Sirrah, if they meet not with Saint
Nicholas' clerks, I'll give thee this neck.

Cham. No, I'll none of it: I pr'ythee, keep
that for the hangman; for I know thou wor-
shippest Saint Nicholas as truly as a man of
falsehood may.

Gads. What talkest thou to me of the hangman? If I hang, I'll make a fat pair of gallows;
for if I hang, old Sir John hangs with me; and
thou knowest he's no starveling. Tut! there
are other Trojans that thou dreamest not of,
the which, for sport-sake, are content to do the
profession some grace; that would, if matters
should be looked into, for their own credit-sake,
make all whole. I am joined with no foot land-
rakers, no long-staff sixpenny strikers, none of
these mad mustachio purple-hued malt-worms;
but with nobility and tranquillity; burgomas-
ters and great oneyers, such as can hold in, such
as will strike sooner than speak, and speak
sooner than drink, and drink sooner than pray:
and yet I lie; for they pray continually to their

saint, the commonwealth; or, rather, not pray to her, but prey on her; for they ride up and down on her, and make her their boots.

Cham. What, the commonwealth their boots? will she hold out water in foul way?

Gads. She will, she will; justice hath liquored her. We steal as in a castle, cock-sure; we have the receipt of fern-seed,—we walk invisible.

Cham. Nay, by my faith, I think you are more beholding to the night than to fern-seed for your walking invisible.

Gads. Give me thy hand: thou shalt have a share in our purchase, as I am a true man.

Cham. Nay, rather let me have it, as you are a false thief.

Gads. Go to; *homo* is a common name to all men. Bid the ostler bring my gelding out of the stable. Farewell, you muddy knave. [*Exeunt.*

SCENE II.—*The Road by Gadshill.*

Enter PRINCE HENRY *and* POINS; BARDOLPH *and* PETO *at some distance.*

Poins. Come, shelter, shelter: I have removed Falstaff's horse, and he frets like a gummed velvet.

P. Hen. Stand close. [*They retire.*

Enter FALSTAFF.

Fal. Poins! Poins, and be hanged! Poins!

P. Hen. [*Coming forward.*] Peace, ye fat-kidneyed rascal! what a brawling dost thou keep!

Fal. Where's Poins, Hal?

P. Hen. He is walked up to the top of the hill: I'll go seek him. [*Pretends to seek* POINS.

Fal. I am accursed to rob in that thief's company: the rascal hath removed my horse, and tied him I know not where. If I travel but four foot by the squire further a-foot, I shall break my wind. Well, I doubt not but to die a fair death for all this, if I 'scape hanging for killing that rogue. I have forsworn his company hourly any time this two-and-twenty year, and yet I am bewitched with the rogue's company. If the rascal have not given me medicines to make me love him, I'll be hanged; it could not be else; I have drunk medicines.—Poins!—Hal!—a plague upon you both!—Bardolph!—Peto!—I'll starve, ere I'll rob a foot further. An 'twere not as good a deed as drink, to turn true man, and leave these rogues, I am the veriest varlet that ever chewed with a tooth. Eight yards of uneven ground is three-score and ten miles a-foot with me; and the stony-hearted villains know it well enough: a plague upon't, when thieves cannot be true to one another! [*They whistle.*] Whew!—a plague upon you all! Give me my horse, you rogues; give me my horse, and be hanged.

P. Hen. [*Coming forward.*] Peace, ye fat-guts! lie down; lay thine ear close to the ground, and list if thou canst hear the tread of travellers.

Fal. Have you any levers to lift me up again,

being down? 'Sblood, I'll not bear mine own flesh so far a-foot again for all the coin in thy father's exchequer. What a plague mean ye to colt me thus?

P. Hen. Thou liest; thou art not colted, thou art uncolted.

Fal. I pr'ythee, good Prince Hal, help me to my horse, good king's son.

P. Hen. Out, you rogue! shall I be your ostler?

Fal. Go, hang thyself in thine own heir-apparent garters! If I be ta'en, I'll peach for this. An I have not ballads made on you all, and sung to filthy tunes, let a cup of sack be my poison:—when a jest is so forward, and a-foot too!—I hate it.

Enter GADSHILL.

Gads. Stand.

Fal. So I do, against my will.

Poins. O, 'tis our setter: I know his voice. [*Coming forward with* BARD. *and* PETO.

Bard. What news?

Gads. Case ye, case ye; on with your vis-ards: there's money of the king's coming down the hill; 'tis going to the king's exchequer.

Fal. You lie, you rogue; 'tis going to the king's tavern.

Gads. There's enough to make us all.

Fal. To be hanged.

P. Hen. Sirs, you four shall front them in the narrow lane; Ned Poins and I will walk lower: if they 'scape from your encounter, then they light on us.

Peto. How many be there of them?

Gads. Some eight or ten.

Fal. Zounds, will they not rob us?

P. Hen. What, a coward, Sir John Paunch?

Fal. Indeed, I am not John of Gaunt, your grandfather; but yet no coward, Hal.

P. Hen. Well, we leave that to the proof.

Poins. Sirrah Jack, thy horse stands behind the hedge: when thou needest him, there thou shalt find him. Farewell, and stand fast.

Fal. Now cannot I strike him, if I should be hanged.

P. Hen. [*Aside to* POINS.] Ned, where are our disguises?

Poins. Here, hard by: stand close. [*Exeunt* P. HENRY *and* POINS.

Fal. Now, my masters, happy man be his dole, say I: every man to his business.

Enter Travellers.

1 *Trav.* Come, neighbour: the boy shall lead our horses down the hill; we'll walk a-foot awhile, and ease our legs.

Fal., Gads., &c. Stand!

Trav. Jesu bless us!

Fal. Strike; down with them; cut the vil-lains' throats:—ah, whoreson caterpillars! bacon-fed knaves! they hate us youth:—down with them; fleece them.

Trav. O, we are undone, both we and ours for ever!

Fal. Hang ye, gorbellied knaves, are ye undone? No, ye fat chuffs; I would your store were here! On, bacons on! What, ye knaves! young men must live. You are grand-jurors, are ye? we'll jure ye, i' faith.

[*Exeunt* FAL., *&c., driving the Travellers out.*

Re-enter PRINCE HENRY *and* POINS.

P. Hen. The thieves have bound the true men. Now could thou and I rob the thieves, and go merrily to London, it would be argument for a week, laughter for a month, and a good jest for ever.

Poins. Stand close; I hear them coming.

Re-enter FALSTAFF, GADSHILL, BARDOLPH, *and* PETO.

Fal. Come, my masters, let us share, and then to horse before day. An the Prince and Poins be not two arrant cowards, there's no equity stirring: there's no more valour in that Poins than in a wild duck.

P. Hen. Your money!

[*Rushing out upon them.*

Poins. Villains!

[GADS., BARD., *and* PETO *run away; and* FAL. *also, after a blow or two, leaving the booty.*

P. Hen. Got with much ease. Now merrily to horse:

The thieves are scatter'd, and possess'd with fear
So strongly that they dare not meet each other;
Each takes his fellow for an officer.
Away, good Ned. Falstaff sweats to death,
And lards the lean earth as he walks along:
Were't not for laughing, I should pity him.

Poins. How the rogue roar'd! [*Exeunt.*

SCENE III.—WARKWORTH. *A Room in the Castle.*

Enter HOTSPUR, *reading a letter.*

Hot. —*But, for mine own part, my lord, I could be well contented to be there, in respect of the love I bear your house.*—He could be contented,—why is he not, then? In respect of the love he bears our house:—he shows in this, he loves his own barn better than he loves our house. Let me see some more. *The purpose you undertake is dangerous.*—Why, that's certain: 'tis dangerous to take a cold, to sleep, to drink; but I tell you, my lord fool, out of this nettle, danger, we pluck this flower, safety. *The purpose you undertake is dangerous; the friends you have named uncertain; the time itself unsorted; and your whole plot too light for the counterpoise of so great an opposition.*—Say you so, say you so? I say unto you again, you are a shallow, cowardly hind, and you lie. What a lack-brain is this! By the Lord, our plot is a good plot as ever was laid; our friends true and constant: a good plot, good friends, and full of expectation;

an excellent plot, very good friends. What a frosty-spirited rogue is this! Why, my Lord of York commends the plot and the general course of the action. Zounds, an I were now by this rascal, I could brain him with his lady's fan. Is there not my father, my uncle, and myself? Lord Edmund Mortimer, my Lord of York, and Owen Glendower? Is there not, besides, the Douglas? Have I not all their letters to meet me in arms by the ninth of the next month? and are they not some of them set forward already? What a pagan rascal is this! an infidel! Ha! you shall see now, in very sincerity of fear and cold heart, will he to the king, and lay open all our proceedings. O, I could divide myself, and go to buffets, for moving such a dish of skimmed milk with so honourable an action! Hang him! Let him tell the king: we are prepared. I will set forward to-night.

Enter LADY PERCY.

How now, Kate! I must leave you within these two hours.

Lady. O, my good lord, why are you thus alone?
For what offence have I this fortnight been
A banish'd woman from my Harry's bed?
Tell me, sweet lord, what is't that takes from thee
Thy stomach, pleasure, and thy golden sleep?
Why dost thou bend thine eyes upon the earth,
And start so often when thou sitt'st alone?
Why hast thou lost the fresh blood in thy cheeks,
And given my treasures and my rights of thee
To thick-ey'd musing and curs'd melancholy?
In thy faint slumbers I by thee have watch'd,
And heard thee murmur tales of iron wars;
Speak terms of manage to thy bounding steed;
Cry, *Courage!—to the field!*—And thou hast talk'd
Of sallies and retires, of trenches, tents,
Of palisadoes, frontiers, parapets,
Of basilisks, of cannon, culverin,
Of prisoners' ransom, and of soldiers slain,
And all the currents of a heady fight.
Thy spirit within thee hath been so at war,
And thus hath so bestirr'd thee in thy sleep
That beads of sweat have stood upon thy brow,
Like bubbles in a late disturbed stream;
And in thy face strange motions have appear'd,
Such as we see when men restrain their breath
On some great sudden hest. O, what portents are these?
Some heavy business hath my lord in hand,
And I must know it, else he loves me not.

Hot. What, ho!

Enter a Servant.

Is Gilliams with the packet gone?

Serv. He is, my lord, an hour ago.

Hot. Hath Butler brought those horses from the sheriff?

Serv. One horse, my lord, he brought even now.

Hot. What horse? a roan, a crop-ear, is it not?

Serv. It is, my lord.

Hot.   That roan shall be my throne. Well, I will back him straight: O *esperance!*— Bid Butler lead him forth into the park.

                  [*Exit* Servant.

Lady. But hear you, my lord.

Hot.   What say'st thou, my lady?

Lady. What is it carries you away?

Hot. Why, my horse, my love,—my horse.

Lady.   Out, you mad-headed ape! A weasel hath not such a deal of spleen As you are toss'd with. In faith, I'll know your business, Harry,—that I will. I fear my brother Mortimer doth stir About his title, and hath sent for you To line his enterprise: but if you go,—

Hot. So far a-foot, I shall be weary, love.

Lady. Come, come, you paraquito, answer me Directly to this question that I ask: In faith, I'll break thy little finger, Harry, An if thou wilt not tell me all things true.

Hot. Away, Away, you trifler!—Love?—I love thee not, I care not for thee, Kate: this is no world To play with mammets and to tilt with lips: We must have bloody noses and crack'd crowns, And pass them current too.—Gods me, my horse!— What say'st thou, Kate? what wouldst thou have with me?

Lady. Do you not love me? do you not, indeed? Well, do not, then; for since you love me not, I will not love myself. Do you not love me? Nay, tell me if you speak in jest or no.

Hot. Come, wilt thou see me ride? And when I am o' horseback, I will swear I love thee infinitely. But hark you, Kate; I must not have you henceforth question me Whither I go, nor reason whereabout: Whither I must, I must; and, to conclude, This evening must I leave you, gentle Kate. I know you wise; but yet no further wise Than Harry Percy's wife: constant you are; But yet a woman: and for secrecy, No lady closer; for I well believe Thou wilt not utter what thou dost not know,— And so far will I trust thee, gentle Kate.

Lady. How! so far?   [Kate:

Hot. Not an inch further. But hark you, Whither I go, thither shall you go too; To-day will I set forth, to-morrow you.— Will this content you, Kate?

Lady.   It must, of force. [*Exeunt.*

SCENE IV.—EASTCHEAP. *A Room in the Boar's Head Tavern.*

Enter PRINCE HENRY.

P. Hen. Ned, pr'ythee, come out of that fat room, and lend me thy hand to laugh a little.

Enter POINS.

Poins. Where hast been, Hal?

P. Hen. With three or four loggerheads amongst three or fourscore hogsheads. I have sounded the very base string of humility. Sirrah, I am sworn brother to a leash of drawers; and can call them all by their Christian names, as—Tom, Dick, and Francis. They take it already upon their salvation, that though I be but Prince of Wales, yet I am the king of courtesy; and tell me flatly I am no proud Jack, like Falstaff, but a Corinthian, a lad of mettle, a good boy,—by the Lord, so they call me,—and when I am king of England I shall command all the good lads in Eastcheap. They call drinking deep, dying scarlet; and when you breathe in your watering, they cry *hem!* and bid you play it off. To conclude, I am so good a proficient in one quarter of an hour, that I can drink with any tinker in his own language during my life. I tell thee, Ned, thou hast lost much honour, that thou wert not with me in this action. But, sweet Ned,—to sweeten which name of Ned, I give thee this pennyworth of sugar, clapped even now into my hand by an under-skinker; one that never spake other English in his life than, *Eight shillings and six-pence,* and *You are welcome;* with this shrill addition, *Anon, anon, sir! Score a pint of bastard in the Half-moon,* or so. But, Ned, to drive away the time till Falstaff come, I pr'ythee, do thou stand in some by-room, while I question my puny drawer to what end he gave me the sugar; and do thou never leave calling *Francis,* that his tale to me may be nothing but *anon.* Step aside, and I'll show thee a precedent.   [*Exit* POINS.

Poins. [*Within.*] Francis!

P. Hen. Thou art perfect.

Poins. [*Within.*] Francis!

Enter FRANCIS.

Fran. Anon, anon, sir.—Look down into the Pomegranate, Ralph.

P. Hen. Come hither, Francis.

Fran. My lord?

P. Hen. How long hast thou to serve, Francis?

Fran. Forsooth, five years, and as much as to,—

Poins. [*Within.*] Francis!

Fran. Anon, anon, sir.

P. Hen. Five years! by'r lady, a long lease for the clinking of pewter. But, Francis, darest thou be so valiant as to play the coward with thy indenture, and show it a fair pair of heels and run from it?

Fran. O Lord, sir, I'll be sworn upon all the books in England, I could find in my heart,—

Poins. [*Within.*] Francis!

Fran. Anon, anon, sir.

P. Hen. How old art thou, Francis?

Fran. Let me see,—about Michaelmas next I shall be,—

Poins. [*Within.*] Francis!

Fran. Anon, sir,—Pray you, stay a little, my lord.

P. Hen. Nay, but hark you, Francis: for the sugar thou gavest me,—'twas a pennyworth, was't not?

Fran. O Lord, sir, I would it had been two!

P. Hen. I will give thee for it a thousand pound: ask me when thou wilt, and thou shalt have it.

Poins. [*Within.*] Francis!

Fran. Anon, anon.

P. Hen. Anon, Francis? No, Francis; but to-morrow, Francis; or, Francis, on Thursday; or, indeed, Francis, when thou wilt. But, Francis,—

Fran. My lord?

P. Hen. Wilt thou rob this leathern-jerkin, crystal-button, nott-pated, agate-ring, puke-stocking, caddis-garter, smooth-tongue, Spanish-pouch,—

Fran. O Lord, sir, who do you mean?

P. Hen. Why, then, your brown bastard is your only drink; for, look you, Francis, your white canvas doublet will sully: in Barbary, sir, it cannot come to so much.

Fran. What, sir?

Poins. [*Within.*] Francis!

P. Hen. Away, you rogue! dost thou not hear them call?

[*Here they both call him;* FRANCIS *stands amazed, not knowing which way to go.*

Enter Vintner.

Vint. What, standest thou still, and hearest such a calling? Look to the guests within. [*Exit* FRAN.] My lord, old Sir John, with half-a-dozen more, are at the door: shall I let them in?

P. Hen. Let them alone awhile, and then open the door. [*Exit* Vintner.] Poins!

Re-enter POINS.

Poins. Anon, anon, sir.

P. Hen. Sirrah, Falstaff and the rest of the thieves are at the door: shall we be merry?

Poins. As merry as crickets, my lad. But hark ye; what cunning match have you made with this jest of the drawer? come, what's the issue?

P. Hen. I am now of all humours that have showed themselves humours since the old days of goodman Adam to the pupil-age of this present twelve o'clock at midnight.—What's o'clock, Francis?

Fran. [*Within.*] Anon, anon, sir.

P. Hen. That ever this fellow should have fewer words than a parrot, and yet the son of a woman! His industry is upstairs and downstairs; his eloquence the parcel of a reckoning. I am not yet of Percy's mind, the Hotspur of the north; he that kills me some six or seven dozen Scots at a breakfast, washes his hands, and says to his wife, *Fie upon this quiet life! I want work.* O my sweet Harry, says she, *how many hast thou killed to-day?* Give my roan horse *a drench,* says he; and answers, *Some fourteen,* an hour after,—*a trifle, a trifle.* I pr'ythee, call in Falstaff: I'll play Percy, and that damned brawn shall play Dame Mortimer his wife. *Rivo* says the drunkard. Call in ribs, call in tallow.

Enter FALSTAFF, GADSHILL, BARDOLPH, *and* PETO; *followed by* FRANCIS *with wine.*

Poins. Welcome, Jack: where hast thou been?

Fal. A plague of all cowards, I say, and a vengeance too! marry, and amen!—Give me a cup of sack, boy.—Ere I lead this life long, I'll sew nether-stocks, and mend them and foot them too. A plague of all cowards!—Give me a cup of sack, rogue.—Is there no virtue extant? [*He drinks.*

P. Hen. Didst thou never see Titan kiss a dish of butter? pitiful-hearted Titan, that melted at the sweet tale of the sun! if thou didst, then behold that compound.

Fal. You rogue, here's lime in this sack too: there is nothing but roguery to be found in villanous man: yet a coward is worse than a cup of sack with lime in it,—a villanous coward.—Go thy ways, old Jack; die when thou wilt, if manhood, good manhood, be not forgot upon the face of the earth, then am I a shotten herring. There live not three good men unhanged in England; and one of them is fat, and grows old: God help the while! a bad world, I say. I would I were a weaver; I could sing psalms or anything. A plague of all cowards, I say still.

P. Hen. How now, woolsack! what mutter you?

Fal. A king's son! If I do not beat thee out of thy kingdom with a dagger of lath, and drive all thy subjects afore thee like a flock of wild geese, I'll never wear hair on my face more. You Prince of Wales!

P. Hen. Why, you whoreson round man, what's the matter?

Fal. Are you not a coward? answer me to that:—and Poins there?

Poins. Zounds, ye fat paunch, an ye call me coward, I'll stab thee.

Fal. I call thee coward! I'll see thee damned ere I call thee coward: but I would give a thousand pound I could run as fast as thou canst. You are straight enough in the shoulders,—you care not who sees your back: call you that backing of your friends? A plague upon such backing! give me them that will face me.—Give me a cup of sack:—I am a rogue if I drunk to-day.

P. Hen. O villain! thy lips are scarce wiped since thou drunkest last.

Fal. All's one for that. A plague of all cowards, still say I. [*He drinks.*

P. Hen. What's the matter?

Fal. What's the matter! there be four of us here have ta'en a thousand pound this day morning.

P. Hen. Where is it, Jack? where is it?

Fal. Where is it! taken from us it is: a hundred upon poor four of us.

P. Hen. What, a hundred, man?

Fal. I am a rogue, if I were not at half-sword with a dozen of them two hours together. I have 'scaped by miracle. I am eight times thrust through the doublet, four through the hose; my buckler cut through and through; my sword hacked like a hand-saw,—*ecce signum!* I never dealt better since I was a man: all would not do. A plague of all cowards!—Let them speak: if they speak more or less than truth, they are villains, and the sons of darkness.

P. Hen. Speak, sirs; how was it?

Gads. We four set upon some dozen,—

Fal. Sixteen at least, my lord.

Gads. And bound them.

Peto. No, no, they were not bound.

Fal. You rogue, they were bound, every man of them; or I am a Jew else, an Ebrew Jew.

Gads. As we were sharing, some six or seven fresh men set upon us,—

Fal. An unbound the rest, and then come in the other.

P. Hen. What, fought ye with them all?

Fal. All! I know not what ye call all; but if I fought not with fifty of them, I am a bunch of radish: if there were not two or three and fifty upon poor old Jack, then am I no two-legged creature.

P. Hen. Pray God, you have not murdered some of them.

Fal. Nay, that's past praying for: I have peppered two of them; two I am sure I have paid,—two rogues in buckram suits. I tell thee what, Hal,—if I tell thee a lie, spit in my face, call me horse. Thou knowest my old ward;— here I lay, and thus I bore my point. Four rogues in buckram let drive at me,—

P. Hen. What, four? thou saidst but two even now.

Fal. Four, Hal; I told thee four.

Poins. Ay, ay, he said four.

Fal. These four came all a-front, and mainly thrust at me. I made me no more ado but took all their seven points in my target, thus.

P. Hen. Seven? why, there were but four even now in buckram.

Poins. Ay, four in buckram suits.

Fal. Seven, by these hilts, or I am a villain else.

P. Hen. Pr'ythee, let him alone; we shall have more anon.

Fal. Dost thou hear me, Hal?

P. Hen. Ay, and mark thee too, Jack.

Fal. Do so, for it is worth the listening to. These nine in buckram that I told thee of,—

P. Hen. So, two more already.

Fal. Their points being broken,—

Poins. Down fell their hose.

Fal. Began to give me ground: but I followed me close, came in foot and hand; and with a thought seven of the eleven I paid.

P. Hen. O monstrous! eleven buckram men grown out of two!

Fal. But, as the devil would have it, three misbegotten knaves in Kendal green came at my back and let drive at me;—for it was so dark, Hal, that thou couldst not see thy hand.

P. Hen. These lies are like the father that begets them,—gross as a mountain, open, palpable. Why, thou clay-brained guts, thou nott-pated fool, thou whoreson, obscene, greasy tallow-keech,—

Fal. What, art thou mad? art thou mad? is not the truth the truth?

P. Hen. Why, how couldst thou know these men in Kendal green, when it was so dark thou couldst not see thy hand? come, tell us your reason: what sayest thou to this?

Poins. Come, your reason, Jack,—your reason.

Fal. What, upon compulsion? No; were I at the strappado, or all the racks in the world, I would not tell you on compulsion. Give you a reason on compulsion! if reasons were as plenty as blackberries I would give no man a reason upon compulsion, I.

P. Hen. I'll be no longer guilty of this sin; this sanguine coward, this bed-presser, this horse back-breaker, this huge hill of flesh,—

Fal. Away, you starveling, you elf-skin, you dried neat's tongue, bull's pizzle, you stock-fish,—O for breath to utter what is like thee!— you tailor's yard, you sheath, you bow-case, you vile standing-tuck,—

P. Hen. Well, breathe awhile, and then to it again: and when thou hast tired thyself in base comparisons, hear me speak but this.

Poins. Mark, Jack.

P. Hen. We two saw you four set on four; you bound them, and were masters of their wealth.—Mark now, how a plain tale shall put you down.—Then did we two set on you four; and, with a word, out-faced you from your prize, and have it; yea, and can show it you here in the house:—and, Falstaff, you carried your guts away as nimbly, with as quick dexterity, and roared for mercy, and still ran and roared, as ever I heard bull-calf. What a slave art thou, to hack thy sword as thou hast done, and then say it was in fight! What trick, what device, what starting-hole, canst thou now find out to hide thee from this open and apparent shame?

Poins. Come, let's hear, Jack; what trick hast thou now?

Fal. By the Lord, I knew ye as well as he that made ye. Why, hear ye, my masters: was it for me to kill the heir-apparent? Should I turn upon the true prince? Why, thou knowest I am as valiant as Hercules: but beware instinct; the lion will not touch the true prince. Instinct is a great matter; I was a coward on instinct. I shall think the better of myself and thee during my life; I for a valiant lion, and thou for a true prince. But, by the Lord, lads, I am glad you have the money.—Hostess, clap to the doors [to Hostess within]:—watch to-night, pray to-morrow.—Gallants, lads, boys, hearts of gold, all the titles of good fellowship come to you! What, shall we be merry? Shall we have a play extempore?

P. Hen. Content;—and the argument shall be thy running away.

Fal. Ah, no more of that, Hal, an thou lovest me!

Enter Hostess.

Host. O Jesu, my lord the prince,—

P. Hen. How now, my lady the hostess!—What sayest thou to me?

Host. Marry, my lord, there is a nobleman of the court at door would speak with you: he says he comes from your father.

P. Hen. Give him as much as will make him a royal man, and send him back again to my mother.

Fal. What manner of man is he?

Host. An old man.

Fal. What doth gravity out of his bed at midnight?—Shall I give him his answer?

P. Hen. Pr'ythee, do, Jack.

Fal. Faith, and I'll send him packing. [*Exit.*

P. Hen. Now, sirs:—by'r lady, you fought fair;—so did you, Peto;—so did you, Bardolph: you are lions too, you ran away upon instinct, you will not touch the true prince; no,—fie!

Bard. Faith, I ran when I saw others run.

P. Hen. Tell me now in earnest, how came Falstaff's sword so hacked?

Peto. Why, he hacked it with his dagger; and said he would swear truth out of England, but he would make you believe it was done in fight; and persuaded us to do the like.

Bard. Yea, and to tickle our noses with speargrass to make them bleed; and then to beslubber our garments with it, and swear it was the blood of true men. I did that I did not this seven year before,—I blushed to hear his monstrous devices.

P. Hen. O villain, thou stolest a cup of sack eighteen years ago, and wert taken with the manner, and ever since thou hast blushed extempore. Thou hadst fire and sword on thy side, and yet thou rannest away: what instinct hadst thou for it?

Bard. My lord, do you see these meteors? do you behold these exhalations?

P. Hen. I do.

Bard. What think you they portend?

P. Hen. Hot livers and cold purses.

Bard. Choler, my lord, if rightly taken.

P. Hen. No, if rightly taken, halter.—Here comes lean Jack, here comes bare-bone.

Re-enter FALSTAFF.

How now, my sweet creature of bombast! How long is't ago, Jack, since thou sawest thine own knee?

Fal. My own knee! when I was about thy years, Hal, I was not an eagle's talon in the waist; I could have crept into any alderman's thumb-ring: a plague of sighing and grief! it blows a man up like a bladder—There's villanous news abroad: here was Sir John Bracy from your father; you must to the court in the morning. That same mad fellow of the north, Percy; and he of Wales, that gave Amaimon the bastinado, and made Lucifer cuckold, and swore the devil his true liegeman upon the cross of a Welsh hook,—what, a plague, call you him?—

Poins. O, Glendower.

Fal. Owen, Owen,—the same; and his son-in-law, Mortimer; and old Northumberland; and that sprightly Scot of Scots, Douglas, that runs o' horseback up a hill perpendicular,—

P. Hen. He that rides at high speed, and with his pistol kills a sparrow flying?

Fal. You have hit it.

P. Hen. So did he never the sparrow.

Fal. Well, that rascal hath good mettle in him; he will not run;—

P. Hen. Why, what a rascal art thou, then, to praise him so for running.

Fal. O' horseback, ye cuckoo; but a-foot he will not budge a foot.

P. Hen. Yes, Jack, upon instinct.

Fal. I grant ye, upon instinct.—Well, he is there too, and one Mordake, and a thousand blue-caps more: Worcester is stolen away to-night; thy father's beard is turned white with the news: you may buy land now as cheap as stinking mackerel.

P. Hen. Why, then, it is like, if there come a hot June, and this civil buffeting hold, we shall buy maidenheads as they buy hob-nails, by the hundreds.

Fal. By the mass, lad, thou sayest true; it is like we shall have good trading that way.—But tell me, Hal, art thou not horribly afeard? thou being heir-apparent, could the world pick thee out three such enemies again as that fiend Douglas, that spirit Percy, and that devil Glendower? Art thou not horribly afraid? doth not thy blood thrill at it?

P. Hen. Not a whit, i' faith; I lack some of thy instinct.

Fal. Well, thou wilt be horribly chid to-morrow when thou comest to thy father: if thou love me, practise an answer.

P. Hen. Do thou stand for my father! and examine me upon the particulars of my life.

Fal. Shall I? content:—this chair shall be my state, this dagger my sceptre, and this cushion my crown.

P. Hen. Thy state is taken for a joint-stool, thy golden sceptre for a leaden dagger, and thy precious rich crown for a pitiful bald crown!

Fal. Well, an the fire of grace be not quite out of thee, now shalt thou be moved.—Give me a cup of sack to make mine eyes look red, that it may be thought I have wept; for I must speak in passion, and I will do it in King Cambyses' vein.

P. Hen. Well, here is my leg.

Fal. And here is my speech.—Stand aside, nobility.

Host. O Jesu, this is excellent sport, i' faith!

Fal. Weep not, sweet queen; for trickling tears are vain.

Host. O, the father, how he holds his countenance!

Fal. For God's sake, lords, convey my tristful queen;

For tears do stop the floodgates of her eyes.

Host. O Jesu, he doth it as like one of these harlotry players as ever I see!

Fal. Peace, good pint-pot; peace, good tickle-brain.—Harry, I do not only marvel where thou spendest thy time, but also how thou art accompanied: for though the camomile, the more it is trodden on, the faster it grows, yet youth, the more it is wasted, the sooner it wears. That thou art my son, I have partly thy mother's word, partly my own opinion; but chiefly a villanous trick of thine eye, and a foolish hanging of thy nether lip, that doth warrant me. If, then, thou be son to me, here lies the point;—why, being son to me, art thou so pointed at? Shall the blessed sun of heaven prove a micher, and eat blackberries? a question not to be asked. Shall the son of England prove a thief, and take purses? a question to be asked. There is a thing, Harry, which thou hast often heard of, and it is known to many in our land by the name of pitch: this pitch, as ancient writers do report, doth defile; so doth the company thou keepest: for, Harry, now I do not speak to thee in drink, but in tears; not in pleasure, but in passion; not in words only, but in woes also:—and yet there is a virtuous man whom I have often noted in thy company, but I know not his name.

P. Hen. What manner of man, an it like your majesty?

Fal. A goodly portly man, i' faith, and a corpulent; of a cheerful look, a pleasing eye, and a most noble carriage; and, as I think, his age some fifty, or, by'r lady, inclining to threescore; and now I remember me, his name is Falstaff: if that man should be lewdly given, he deceiveth me; for, Harry, I see virtue in his looks. If, then, the tree may be known by the fruit, as the fruit by the tree, then, peremptorily I speak it, there is virtue in that Falstaff: him keep with, the rest banish. And tell me now, thou naughty varlet, tell me, where hast thou been this month?

P. Hen. Dost thou speak like a king? Do thou stand for me, and I'll play my father.

Fal. Depose me? if thou dost it half so gravely, so majestically, both in word and matter, hang me up by the heels for a rabbit-sucker or a poulter's hare.

P. Hen. Well, here I am set.

Fal. And here I stand:—judge, my masters.

P. Hen. Now, Harry, whence come you?

Fal. My noble lord, from Eastcheap.

P. Hen. The complaints I hear of thee are grievous.

Fal. 'Sblood, my lord, they are false:—nay, I'll tickle ye for a young prince, i' faith.

P. Hen. Swearest thou, ungracious boy? henceforth ne'er look on me. Thou art violently carried away from grace: there is a devil haunts thee, in the likeness of a fat old man,—a tun of man is thy companion. Why dost thou converse with that trunk of humours, that bolting-hutch of beastliness, that swollen parcel of dropsies, that huge bombard of sack, that stuffed cloak-bag of guts, that roasted Manningtree ox, with the pudding in his belly, that reverend vice, that gray iniquity, that father ruffian, that vanity in years? Wherein is he good, but to taste sack and drink it? wherein neat and cleanly, but to carve a capon and eat it? wherein cunning, but in craft? wherein crafty, but in villany? wherein villanous, but in all things? wherein worthy, but in nothing?

Fal. I would your grace would take me with you: whom means your grace?

P. Hen. That villanous abominable misleader of youth, Falstaff, that old white-bearded Satan.

Fal. My lord, the man I know.

P. Hen. I know thou dost.

Fal. But to say I know more harm in him than in myself, were to say more than I know. That he is old,—the more the pity,—his white hairs do witness it; but that he is,—saving your reverence,—a whoremaster, that I utterly deny. If sack and sugar be a fault, God help the wicked! If to be old and merry be a sin, then many an old host that I know is damned: if to be fat be to be hated, then Pharaoh's lean kine are to be loved. No, my good lord; banish Peto, banish Bardolph, banish Poins: but, for sweet Jack Falstaff, kind Jack Falstaff, true Jack Falstaff, valiant Jack Falstaff, and therefore more valiant, being, as he is, old Jack Falstaff, banish not him thy Harry's company, banish not him thy Harry's company:—banish plump Jack, and banish all the world.

P. Hen. I do, I will.   [*A knocking heard.*

[*Exeunt* HOST., FRAN., *and* BARD.

Re-enter BARDOLPH, *running.*

Bard. O, my lord, my lord! the sheriff with a most monstrous watch is at the door.

Fal. Out, you rogue!—play out the play: I have much to say in the behalf of that Falstaff.

Re-enter Hostess, *hastily.*

Host. O Jesu, my lord, my lord,—

P. Hen. Heigh, heigh! the devil rides upon a fiddle-stick: what's the matter?

Host. The sheriff and all the watch are at the door: they are come to search the house. Shall I let them in?

Fal. Dost thou hear, Hal? never call a true piece of gold a counterfeit: thou art essentially mad, without seeming so.

P. Hen. And thou a natural coward, without instinct.

Fal. I deny your *major:* if you will deny the sheriff, so; if not, let him enter: if I become not a cart as well as another man, a plague on my bringing up! I hope I shall as soon be strangled with a halter as another.

P. Hen. Go, hide thee behind the arras:— the rest walk up above. Now, my masters, for a true face and good conscience.

Fal. Both which I have had; but their date is out, and therefore I'll hide me.

　　　[*Exeunt all but the* PRINCE *and* POINS.

P. Hen. Call in the sheriff.

Enter Sheriff *and* Carrier.

Now, master sheriff, what is your will with me?

Sher. First, pardon me, my lord. A hue and cry
Hath followed certain men unto this house.

P. Hen. What men?

Sher. One of them is well known, my gracious lord,—
A gross fat man.

Car. 　　　　As fat as butter.

P. Hen. The man, I do assure you, is not here;
For I myself at this time have employ'd him.
And, sheriff, I will engage my word to thee,
That I will, by to-morrow dinner-time,
Send him to answer thee, or any man,
For anything he shall be charg'd withal:
And so, let me entreat you leave the house.

Sher. I will, my lord. There are two gentlemen
Have in this robbery lost three hundred marks.

P. Hen. It may be so: if he have robb'd these men
He shall be answerable; and so, farewell.

Sher. Good-night, my noble lord.

P. Hen. I think it is good-morrow, is it not?

Sher. Indeed, my lord, I think it be two o'clock.　　[*Exeunt* Sheriff *and* Carrier.

P. Hen. This oily rascal is known as well as Paul's. Go, call him forth.

Poins. Falstaff!—fast asleep behind the arras, and snorting like a horse.

P. Hen. Hark, how hard he fetches breath. Search his pockets. [POINS *searches.*] What hast thou found?

Poins. Nothing but papers, my lord.

P. Hen. Let's see what they be: read them.

Poins. [*Reads.*] Item, A capon, . . 　2s. 2d.
Item, Sauce, ... 　os. 4d.
Item, Sack, two gallons, . . . 　5s. 8d.
Item, Anchovies and sack after
　　　supper, ... 　2s. 6d.
Item, Bread, ... 　os. o½d.

P. Hen. O monstrous! but one halfpennyworth of bread to this intolerable deal of sack!—What there is else, keep close; we'll read it at more advantage: there let him sleep till day. I'll to the court in the morning. We must all to the wars, and thy place shall be honourable. I'll procure this fat rogue a charge of foot; and I know his death will be a march of twelve-score. The money shall be paid back again with advantage. Be with me betimes in the morning; and so, good-morrow, Poins.

Poins. Good-morrow, good my lord.

　　　　　　　　　　　　　　　[*Exeunt.*

ACT III.

SCENE I.—BANGOR. *A Room in the*
ARCHDEACON'S *House.*

Enter HOTSPUR, WORCESTER, MORTIMER,
and GLENDOWER.

Mort. These promises are fair, the parties sure,
And our induction full of prosperous hope.

Hot. Lord Mortimer,—and cousin Glendower,—
Will you sit down?—
And uncle Worcester:—a plague upon it!
I have forgot the map.

Glend. 　　　No, here it is.
Sit, cousin Percy; sit, good cousin Hotspur,—
For by that name as oft as Lancaster
Doth speak of you, his cheek looks pale, and with
A rising sigh he wishes you in heaven.

Hot. And you in hell, as often as he hears
Owen Glendower spoke of.

Glend. I cannot blame him: at my nativity
The front of heaven was full of fiery shapes,
Of burning cressets; and at my birth
The frame and huge foundation of the earth
Shak'd like a coward.

Hot. 　　　Why, so it would have done,
At the same season, if your mother's cat
Had but kitten'd, though yourself had ne'er been born.

Glend. I say the earth did shake when I was born.

Hot. And I say the earth was not of my mind,
If you suppose as fearing you it shook.

Glend. The heavens were all on fire, the earth did tremble.

Hot. O, then the earth shook to see the heavens on fire,
And not in fear of your nativity.
Diseased nature oftentimes breaks forth
In strange eruptions; oft the teeming earth
Is with a kind of colic pinch'd and vex'd
By the imprisoning of unruly wind
Within her womb; which, for enlargement striving,
Shakes the old beldame earth, and topples down
Steeples and moss-grown towers. At your birth,

Our grandam earth, having this distempera-
   ture,
In passion shook.
   Glend.   Cousin, of many men
I do not bear these crossings. Give me leave
To tell you once again that at my birth
The front of heaven was full of fiery shapes;
The goats ran from the mountains, and the
   herds
Were strangely clamorous to the frighted fields.
These signs have mark'd me extraordinary;
And all the courses of my life do show
I am not in the roll of common men.
Where is he living,—clipp'd in with the sea
That chides the banks of England, Scotland,
   Wales,—
Which calls me pupil, or hath read to me?
And bring him out that is but woman's son
Can trace me in the tedious ways of art,
And hold me pace in deep experiments.
   Hot. I think there is no man speaks better
   Welsh.—
I'll to dinner.
   Mort. Peace, cousin Percy; you will make
   him mad.
   Glend. I can call spirits from the vasty deep.
   Hot. Why, so can I, or so can any man;
But will they come when you do call for them?
   Glend. Why, I can teach thee, cousin, to
   command
The devil.
   Hot. And I can teach thee, coz, to shame
   the devil
By telling truth: tell truth, and shame the
   devil!
If thou have power to raise him, bring him
   hither,
And I'll be sworn I have power to shame him
   hence.
O, while you live, tell truth, and shame the
   devil!
   Mort. Come, come,
No more of this unprofitable chat.
   Glend. Three times hath Henry Bolingbroke
   made head
Against my power; thrice from the banks of
   Wye
And sandy-bottom'd Severn have I sent him
Bootless home and weather-beaten back.
   Hot. Home without boots, and in foul
   weather too!
How 'scapes he agues, in the devil's name?
   Glend. Come, here's the map: shall we di-
   vide our right
According to our threefold order ta'en?
   Mort. The archdeacon hath divided it
Into three limits very equally:
England, from Trent and Severn hitherto,
By south and east is to my part assign'd:
All westward, Wales beyond the Severn shore,
And all the fertile land within that bound,
To Owen Glendower:—and, dear coz, to you
The remnant northward, lying off from Trent.
And our indentures tripartite are drawn;

Which being sealed interchangeably,—
A business that this night may execute,—
To-morrow, cousin Percy, you, and I,
And my good Lord Worcester, will set forth
To meet your father and the Scottish power,
As is appointed us, at Shrewsbury.
My father Glendower is not ready yet,
Nor shall we need his help these fourteen
   days:—
Within that space [*to* GLEND.] you may have
   drawn together
Your tenants, friends, and neighbouring gen-
   tlemen.
   Glend. A shorter time shall send me to you,
   lords:
And in my conduct shall your ladies come;
From whom you now must steal, and take no
   leave;
For there will be a world of water shed
Upon the parting of your wives and you.
   Hot. Methinks my moiety, north from Bur-
   ton here,
In quantity equals not one of yours:
See how this river comes me cranking in,
And cuts me from the best of all my land
A huge half-moon, a monstrous cantle out.
I'll have the current in this place damm'd up;
And here the smug and silver Trent shall run
In a new channel, fair and evenly:
It shall not wind with such a deep indent,
To rob me of so rich a bottom here.
   Glend. Not wind! it shall, it must; you see
   it doth.
   Mort. Yea.
But mark how he bears his course and runs
   me up
With like advantage on the other side;
Gelding the opposed continent as much
As on the other side it takes from you.
   Wor. Yea, but a little charge will trench
   him here,
And on this north side win this cape of land;
And then he runs straight and even.
   Hot. I'll have it so: a little charge will do it.
   Glend. I will not have it alter'd.
   Hot.   Will not you?
   Glend. No, nor you shall not.
   Hot.   Who shall say me nay?
   Glend. Why, that will I.
   Hot.   Let me not understand you, then;
Speak it in Welsh.
   Glend. I can speak English, lord, as well as
   you;
For I was train'd up in the English court;
Where, being but young, I framed to the harp
Many an English ditty, lovely well,
And gave the tongue a helpful ornament,—
A virtue that was never seen in you.
   Hot. Marry, and I am glad of it with all my
   heart;
I had rather be a kitten and cry mew,
Than one of these same metre ballad-mongers;
I had rather hear a brazen candlestick turn'd,
Or a dry wheel grate on the axle-tree;

And that would set my teeth nothing on edge,
Nothing so much as mincing poetry:—
'Tis like the forc'd gait of a shuffling nag.
   Glend. Come, you shall have Trent turn'd.
   Hot. I do not care; I'll give thrice so much
    land
To any well-deserving friend;
But in the way of bargain, mark ye me,
I'll cavil on the ninth part of a hair.
Are the indentures drawn? shall we be gone?
   Glend. The moon shines fair; you may away
    by night:
I'll haste the writer, and withal
Break with your wives of your departure hence:
I am afraid my daughter will run mad,
So much she doteth on her Mortimer.   [*Exit.*
   Mort. Fie, cousin Percy! how you cross my
    father!
   Hot. I cannot choose: sometimes he angers
    me
With telling me of the moldwarp and the ant,
Of the dreamer Merlin and his prophecies,
And of a dragon and a finless fish,
A clip-wing'd griffin and a moulten raven,
A couching lion and a ramping cat,
And such a deal of skimble-skamble stuff
As puts me from my faith. I tell you what,—
He held me last night at least nine hours
In reckoning up the several devils' names
That were has lackeys: I cried *hum,* and *well,*
    go to,
But mark'd him not a word. O, he's as tedious
As is a tired horse, a railing wife;
Worse than a smoky house:—I had rather live
With cheese and garlic in a windmill, far,
Than feed on cates and have him talk to me
In any summer-house in Christendom.
   Mort. In faith, he is a worthy gentleman;
Exceedingly well read, and profited
In strange concealments; valiant as a lion,
And wondrous affable; and as bountiful
As mines of India. Shall I tell you, cousin?
He holds your temper in a high respect,
And curbs himself even of his natural scope
When you do cross his humour; faith, he does:
I warrant you, that man is not alive
Might so have tempted him as you have done,
Without the taste of danger and reproof:
But do not use it oft, let me entreat you.
   Wor. In faith, my lord, you are too wilful-
    blame;
And since your coming hither have done enough
To put him quite beside his patience.
You must needs learn, lord, to amend this
    fault: [blood,—
Though sometimes it shows greatness, courage,
And that's the dearest grace it renders you,—
Yet oftentimes it doth present harsh rage,
Defect of manners, want of government,
Pride, haughtiness, opinion, and disdain:
The least of which, haunting a nobleman,
Loseth men's hearts, and leaves behind a stain
Upon the beauty of all parts besides,
Beguiling them of commendation.

   Hot. Well, I am school'd: good manners be
    your speed!
Here come our wives, and let us take our leave.

  Re-enter GLENDOWER, *with* LADY MORTIMER
      and LADY PERCY.

   Mort. This is the deadly spite that angers
    me,—
My wife can speak no English, I no Welsh.
   Glend. My daughter weeps: she will not part
    with you:
She'll be a soldier too, she'll to the wars.
   Mort. Good father, tell her that she and my
    aunt Percy
Shall follow in your conduct speedily.
    [GLEND. *speaks to* LADY MORT. *in Welsh,*
       and she answers him in the same.
   Glend. She's desperate here; a peevish, self-
    will'd harlotry,
One that no persuasion can do good upon.
    [LADY MORT. *speaks to* MORT. *in Welsh*
   Mort. I understand thy looks: that pretty
    Welsh
Which thou pour'st down from these welling
    heavens,
I am too perfect in; and, but for shame,
In such a parley should I answer thee.
             [LADY MORT. *speaks again.*
I understand thy kisses, and thou mine,
And that's a feeling disputation:
But I will never be a truant, love,
Till I have learned thy language; for thy tongue
Makes Welsh as sweet as ditties highly penn'd,
Sung by a fair queen in a summer's bower,
With ravishing division, to her lute.
   Glend. Nay, if you melt, then will she run
    mad.   [LADY MORT. *speaks again.*
   Mort. O, I am ignorance itself in this!
   Glend. She bids you on the wanton rushes
    lay you down,
And rest your gentle head upon her lap,
And she will sing the song that pleaseth you,
And on your eyelids crown the god of sleep,
Charming your blood with pleasing heaviness;
Making such difference betwixt wake and sleep
As is the difference betwixt day and night,
The hour before the heavenly harness'd team
Begins his golden progress in the east.
   Mort. With all my heart I'll sit and hear her
    sing:
By that time will our book, I think, be drawn.
   Glend. Do so;
And those musicians that shall play to you
Hang in the air a thousand leagues from hence;
And straight they shall be here: sit, and attend.
   Hot. Come, Kate, thou art perfect in lying
down: come, quick, quick, that I may lay my
head in thy lap.
   Lady P. Go, ye giddy goose.
                 [*The music plays.*
   Hot. Now I perceive the devil understands
    Welsh;
And 'tis no marvel he's so humorous.
By'r lady, he's a good musician.

Lady P. Then should you be nothing but musical; for you are altogether governed by humours. Lie still, ye thief, and hear the lady sing in Welsh.

Hot. I had rather hear *Lady*, my brach, howl in Irish.

Lady P. Wouldst thou have thy head broken?

Hot. No.

Lady P. Then be still.

Hot. Neither; 'tis a woman's fault.

Lady P. Now God help thee!

Hot. To the Welsh lady's bed.

Lady P. What's that?

Hot. Peace! she sings.

[*A Welsh Song sung by* LADY MORT.

Hot. Come, Kate, I'll have your song too.

Lady P. Not mine, in good sooth.

Hot. Not yours, in good sooth! 'Heart, you swear like a comfit-maker's wife! *Not you, in good sooth;* and, *As true as I live;* and, *As God shall mend me;* and, *As sure as day:* And giv'st such sarcenet surety for thy oaths, As if thou never walk'dst further than Finsbury. Swear me, Kate, like a lady as thou art, A good mouth-filling oath; and leave *in sooth,* And such protest of pepper-gingerbread, To velvet guards and Sunday-citizens. Come, sing.

Lady P. I will not sing.

Hot. 'Tis the next way to turn tailor, or be redbreast teacher. An the indentures be drawn, I'll away within these two hours; and so, come in when ye will. [*Exit.*

Glend. Come, come, Lord Mortimer; you are as slow As hot Lord Percy is on fire to go. By this our book is drawn; we will but seal, And then to horse immediately.

Mort.   With all my heart.
[*Exeunt.*

SCENE II.—LONDON. *A Room in the Palace.*

Enter KING HENRY, PRINCE HENRY, *and* Lords.

K. Hen. Lords, give us leave; the Prince of Wales and I Must have some conference; but be near at hand, For we shall presently have need of you.
[*Exeunt* Lords.
I know not whether God will have it so, For some displeasing service I have done, That, in his secret doom, out of my blood He'll breed revengement and a scourge for me; But thou dost, in thy passages of life, Make me believe that thou art only mark'd For the hot vengeance and the rod of heaven To punish my mistreadings. Tell me else, Could such inordinate and low desires, Such poor, such bare, such lewd, such mean attempts, Such barren pleasures, rude society,

As thou art match'd withal and grafted to, Accompany the greatness of thy blood, And hold their level with thy princely heart?

P. Hen. So please your majesty, I would I could Quit all offences with as clear excuse, As well as I am doubtless I can purge Myself of many I am charg'd withal: Yet such extenuation let me beg, As, in reproof of many tales devis'd,— Which oft the ear of greatness needs must hear,— By smiling pick-thanks and base newsmongers, I may, for some things true, wherein my youth Hath faulty wander'd and irregular, Find pardon on my true submission.

K. Hen. God pardon thee!—yet let me wonder, Harry, At thy affections, which do hold a wing Quite from the flight of all thy ancestors. Thy place in council thou hast rudely lost, Which by thy younger brother is supplied; And art almost an alien to the hearts Of all the court and princes of my blood: The hope and expectation of thy time Is ruin'd; and the soul of every man Prophetically does forethink thy fall. Had I so lavish of my presence been, So common-hackney'd in the eyes of men, So stale and cheap to vulgar company,— Opinion, that did help me to the crown, Had still kept loyal to possession, And left me in reputeless banishment, A fellow of no mark nor likelihood. By being seldom seen, I could not stir But, like a comet, I was wonder'd at; That men would tell their children, *This is he;* Others would say,—*Where, which is Bolingbroke?* And then I stole all courtesy from heaven, And dress'd myself in such humility That I did pluck allegiance from men's hearts, Loud shouts and salutations from their mouths, Even in the presence of the crowned king. Thus did I keep my person fresh and new; My presence, like a robe pontifical, Ne'er seen but wonder'd at: and so my state, Seldom but sumptuous, showed like a feast, And won by rareness such solemnity. The skipping king, he ambled up and down With shallow jesters and rash bavin wits, Soon kindled and soon burn'd: carded his state; Mingled his royalty with carping fools; Had his great name profaned with their scorns; And gave his countenance, against his name, To laugh at gibing boys, and stand the push Of every beardless vain comparative; Grew a companion to the common streets, Enfeoff'd himself to popularity; That, being daily swallow'd by men's eyes, They surfeited with honey, and began To loathe the taste of sweetness, whereof a little More than a little is by much too much. So, when he had occasion to be seen,

He was but as the cuckoo is in June,
Heard, not regarded,—seen, but with such
eyes,
As, sick and blunted with community,
Afford no extraordinary gaze,
Such as is bent on sun-like majesty
When it shines seldom in admiring eyes:
But rather drowz'd, and hung their eyelids
down,
Slept in his face, and render'd such aspéct
As cloudy men use to their adversaries,
Being with his presence glutted, gorg'd, and
full.
And in that very line, Harry, stand'st thou;
For thou hast lost thy princely privilege
With vile participation: not an eye
But is a-weary of thy common sight,
Save mine, which hath desir'd to see thee more;
Which now doth that I would not have it do,—
Make blind itself with foolish tenderness.
   P. Hen. I shall hereafter, my thrice-gracious
lord,
Be more myself.
   K. Hen.   For all the world,
As thou art to this hour, was Richard then
When I from France set foot at Ravenspurg;
And even as I was then is Percy now.
Now, by my sceptre, and my soul to boot,
He hath more worthy interest to the state
Than thou, the shadow of succession:
For, of no right, nor colour like to right,
He doth fill fields with harness in the realm;
Turns head against the lion's armed jaws;
And, being no more in debt to years than thou,
Leads ancient lords and reverend bishops on
To bloody battles and to bruising arms.
What never-dying honour hath he got
Against renowned Douglas! whose high deeds,
Whose hot incursions, and great name in arms,
Holds from all soldiers chief majority
And military title capital
Through all the kingdoms that acknowledge
Christ:
Thrice hath this Hotspur Mars in swathing-
clothes,
This infant warrior, in his enterprises
Discomfited great Douglas; ta'en him once,
Enlarged him, and made a friend of him,
To fill the mouth of deep defiance up,
And shake the peace and safety of our throne.
And what say you to this? Percy, Northumber-
land,
The Archbishop's grace of York, Douglas,
Mortimer,
Capitulate against us, and are up.
But wherefore do I tell these news to thee?
Why, Harry, do I tell thee of my foes,
Which art my near'st and dearest enemy?
Thou that art like enough,—through vassal
fear,
Base inclination, and the start of spleen,—
To fight against me under Percy's pay,
To dog his heels, and court'sy at his frowns,
To show how much thou art degenerate.

   P. Hen. Do not think so, you shall not find
it so:
And God forgive them that have so much
sway'd
Your majesty's good thoughts away from me!
I will redeem all this on Percy's head,
And, in the closing of some glorious day,
Be bold to tell you that I am your son;
When I will wear a garment all of blood,
And stain my favours in a bloody mask,
Which, wash'd away, shall scour my shame
with it:
And that shall be the day, whene'er it lights,
That this same child of honour and renown,
This gallant Hotspur, this all-praised knight,
And your unthought-of Harry chance to meet.
For every honour sitting on his helm,
Would they were multitudes, and on my head
My shames redoubled! for the time will come
That I shall make this northern youth ex-
change
His glorious deeds for my indignities.
Percy is but my factor, good my lord,
To engross up glorious deeds on my behalf;
And I will call him to so strict account,
That he shall render every glory up,
Yea, even the slightest worship of his time,
Or I will tear the reckoning from his heart.
This, in the name of God, I promise here:
The which if he be pleas'd I shall perform,
I do beseech your majesty, may salve
The long-grown wounds of my intemperance:
If not, the end of life cancels all bands:
And I will die a hundred thousand deaths
Ere break the smallest parcel of this vow.
   K. Hen. A hundred thousand rebels die in
this:—   [herein.
Thou shalt have charge and sovereign trust

Enter SIR WALTER BLUNT.

How now, good Blunt! thy looks are full of
speed.   [speak of.
   Blunt. So hath the business that I come to
Lord Mortimer of Scotland hath sent word
That Douglas and the English rebels met
The eleventh of this month at Shrewsbury:
A mighty and a fearful head they are,
If promises be kept on every hand,
As ever offer'd foul play in a state.
   K. Hen. The Earl of Westmoreland set forth
to-day;
With him my son, Lord John of Lancaster;
For this advertisement is five days old:—
On Wednesday next, Harry, you shall set for-
ward;
On Thursday we ourselves will march:
Our meeting is Bridgenorth: and, Harry, you
Shall march through Glostershire; by which
account,
Our business valued, some twelve days hence
Our general forces at Bridgenorth shall meet.
Our hands are full of business: let's away;
Advantage feeds him fat while men delay.
                                          [*Exeunt.*

SCENE III.—EASTCHEAP. *A Room in the Boar's Head Tavern.*

Enter FALSTAFF *and* BARDOLPH.

Fal. Bardolph, am I not fallen away vilely since this last action? do I not bate? do I not dwindle? Why, my skin hangs about me like an old lady's loose gown; I am withered like an old apple-john. Well, I'll repent, and that suddenly, while I am in some liking; I shall be out of heart shortly, and then I shall have no strength to repent. An I have not forgotten what the inside of a church is made of, I am a pepper-corn, a brewer's horse: the inside of a church! Company, villanous company, hath been the spoil of me.

Bard. Sir John, you are so fretful, you cannot live long.

Fal. Why, there is it: come, sing me a bawdy song; make me merry. I was as virtuously given as a gentleman need to be; virtuous enough; swore little; diced not above seven times a week; went to a bawdy-house not above once in a quarter—of an hour; paid money that I borrowed—three or four times: lived well, and in good compass: and now I live out of all order, out of all compass.

Bard. Why, you are so fat, Sir John, that you must needs be out of all compass,—out of all reasonable compass, Sir John.

Fal. Do thou amend thy face, and I'll amend my life: thou art our admiral, thou bearest the lantern in the poop,—but 'tis in the nose of thee; thou art the Knight of the Burning Lamp.

Bard. Why, Sir John, my face does you no harm.

Fal. No, I'll be sworn; I make as good use of it as many a man doth of a Death's head or a *memento mori:* I never see thy face but I think upon hell-fire, and Dives that lived in purple; for there he is in his robes, burning, burning. If thou wert any way given to virtue, I would swear by thy face; my oath should be, *By this fire, that's God's angel;* but thou art altogether given over; and wert indeed, but for the light in thy face, the son of utter darkness. When thou rannest up Gadshill in the night to catch my horse, if I did not think thou hadst been an *ignis fatuus* or a ball of wildfire, there's no purchase in money. O, thou art a perpetual triumph, an everlasting bonfire light! Thou hast saved me a thousand marks in links and torches, walking with thee in the night betwixt tavern and tavern: but the sack that thou hast drunk me would have bought me lights as good cheap at the dearest chandler's in Europe. I have maintained that salamander of yours with fire any time this two-and-thirty years; God reward me for it!

Bard. 'Sblood, I would my face were in your belly!

Fal. God-a-mercy! so should I be sure to be heart-burn'd.

Enter Hostess.

How now, Dame Partlet the hen! have you inquired yet who picked my pocket?

Host. Why, Sir John, what do you think, Sir John? do you think I keep thieves in my house? I have searched, I have inquired, so has my husband, man by man, boy by boy, servant by servant: the tithe of a hair was never lost in my house before.

Fal. You lie, hostess: Bardolph was shaved, and lost many a hair; and I'll be sworn my pocket was picked. Go to, you are a woman, go.

Host. Who, I? no; I defy thee: God's light, I was never called so in mine own house before.

Fal. Go to, I know you well enough.

Host. No, Sir John; you do not know me, Sir John. I know you, Sir John: you owe me money, Sir John; and now you pick a quarrel to beguile me of it: I bought you a dozen of shirts to your back.

Fal. Dowlas, filthy dowlas: I have given them away to bakers' wives, and they have made bolters of them.

Host. Now, as I am a true woman, holland of eight shillings an ell. You owe money here besides, Sir John, for your diet and by-drinkings, and money lent you, four-and-twenty pound.

Fal. He had his part of it; let him pay.

Host. He? alas, he is poor; he hath nothing.

Fal. How! poor? look upon his face; what call you rich? let them coin his nose, let them coin his cheeks: I'll not pay a denier. What, will you make a younker of me? shall I not take mine ease in mine inn, but I shall have my pocket picked? I have lost a seal-ring of my grandfather's worth forty mark.

Host. O Jesu, I have heard the prince tell him, I know not how oft, that that ring was copper!

Fal. How! the prince is a Jack, a sneak-cup: 'sblood, an he were here I would cudgel him like a dog if he would say so.

Enter PRINCE HENRY *and* POINS, *marching.* FALSTAFF *meets the* PRINCE, *playing on his truncheon like a fife.*

Fal. How now, lad! is the wind in that door, i' faith? must we all march?

Bard. Yea, two and two, Newgate-fashion.

Host. My lord, I pray you, hear me.

P. Hen. What sayest thou, Mistress Quickly? How does thy husband? I love him well; he is an honest man.

Host. Good my lord, hear me.

Fal. Pr'ythee, let her alone, and list to me.

P. Hen. What sayest thou, Jack?

Fal. The other night I fell asleep here behind the arras, and had my pocket picked: this house is turned bawdy-house; they pick pockets.

P. Hen. What didst thou lose, Jack?

Fal. Wilt thou believe me, Hal? three or four bonds of forty pound a-piece, and a seal-ring of my grandfather's.

P. Hen. A trifle, some eight-penny matter.

Host. So I told him, my lord; and I said I heard your grace say so: and, my lord, he speaks most vilely of you, like a foul-mouthed man as he is, and said he would cudgel you.

P. Hen. What! he did not?

Host. There's neither faith, truth, nor womanhood in me else.

Fal. There's no more faith in thee than in a stewed prune; nor no more truth in thee than in a drawn fox; and for womanhood, Maid Marian may be the deputy's wife of the ward to thee. Go, you thing, go.

Host. Say, what thing? what thing?

Fal. What thing! why, a thing to thank God on.

Host. I am no thing to thank God on, I would thou shouldst know it; I am an honest man's wife; and, setting thy knighthood aside, thou art a knave to call me so.

Fal. Setting thy womanhood aside, thou art a beast to say otherwise.

Host. Say, what beast, thou knave, thou?

Fal. What beast! why, an otter,

P. Hen. An otter, Sir John! why an otter?

Fal. Why, she's neither fish nor flesh; a man knows not where to have her.

Host. Thou art an unjust man in saying so: thou or any man knows where to have me, thou knave, thou!

P. Hen. Thou sayest true, hostess; and he slanders thee most grossly.

Host. So he doth you, my lord; and said this other day you ought him a thousand pound.

P. Hen. Sirrah, do I owe you a thousand pound?

Fal. A thousand pound, Hal! a million: thy love is worth a million; thou owest me thy love.

Host. Nay, my lord, he call'd you Jack, and said he would cudgel you.

Fal. Did I, Bardolph?

Bard. Indeed, Sir John, you said so.

Fal. Yea,—if he said my ring was copper.

P. Hen. I say 'tis copper: darest thou be as good as thy word now?

Fal. Why, Hal, thou knowest, as thou art but man, I dare: but as thou art prince, I fear thee, as I fear the roaring of the lion's whelp.

P. Hen. And why not as the lion?

Fal. The king himself is to be feared as the lion: dost thou think I'll fear thee as I fear thy father? nay, an I do, I pray God my girdle break.

P. Hen. O, if it should, how would thy guts fall about thy knees! But, sirrah, there's no room for faith, truth, nor honesty, in this bosom of thine,—it is all filled up with guts and midriff. Charge an honest woman with picking thy pocket! Why, thou whoreson, impudent, embossed rascal, if there were anything in thy pocket but tavern-reckonings, memorandums of bawdy-houses, and one poor penny-worth of sugar-candy to make thee long-winded,—if thy pocket were enriched with any other injuries but these, I am a villain: and yet you will stand to it; you will not pocket-up wrong: art thou not ashamed?

Fal. Dost thou hear, Hal? thou knowest in the state of innocency Adam fell; and what should poor Jack Falstaff do in the days of villany? Thou seest I have more flesh than another man, and therefore more frailty. You confess, then, you picked my pocket?

P. Hen. It appears so by the story.

Fal. Hostess, I forgive thee: go, make ready breakfast; love thy husband, look to thy servants, cherish thy guests: thou shalt find me tractable to any honest reason: thou seest I am pacified.—Still?—Nay, pr'ythee, be gone. [*Exit* Hostess.] Now, Hal, to the news at court: for the robbery, lad,—how is that answered?

P. Hen. O, my sweet beef, I must still be good angel to thee:—the money is paid back again.

Fal. O, I do not like that paying back: 'tis a double labour.

P. Hen. I am good friends with my father, and may do anything.

Fal. Rob me the exchequer the first thing thou doest, and do it with unwashed hands too

Bard. Do, my lord.   [of foot.

P. Hen. I have procured thee, Jack, a charge

Fal. I would it had been of horse. Where shall I find one that can steal well? O for a fine thief, of the age of two-and-twenty or thereabouts! I am heinously unprovided. Well, God be thanked for these rebels,—they offend none but the virtuous: I laud them, I praise them.

P. Hen. Bardolph,—

Bard. My lord.   [Lancaster,

P. Hen. Go bear this letter to Lord John of
To my brother John; this to my Lord of West-
    moreland.   [*Exit* BARDOLPH.
Go, Poins, to horse, to horse; for thou and I
Have thirty miles to ride yet ere dinner-time.—
                             [*Exit* POINS.
Jack, meet me to-morrow in the Temple-hall
At two o'clock in the afternoon: [receive
There shalt thou know thy charge, and there
Money and order for their furniture.
The land is burning; Percy stands on high;
And either they or we must lower lie. [*Exit.*

Fal. Rare words! brave world!—Hostess,
    my breakfast; come:—
O, I could wish this tavern were my drum!
                             [*Exit.*

ACT IV.

SCENE I.—*The Rebel Camp near Shrewsbury.*

Enter HOTSPUR, WORCESTER, *and* DOUGLAS.

Hot. Well said, my noble Scot: if speaking
    truth
In this fine age were not thought flattery,
Such attribution should the Douglas have,
As not a soldier of this season's stamp
Should go so general current through the world.
By heaven, I cannot flatter; I defy
The tongues of soothers; but a braver place
In my heart's love hath no man than yourself:

Nay, task me to my word; approve me, lord.
Doug. Thou art the king of honour:
No man so potent breathes upon the ground
But I will beard him.
Hot.   Do so, and 'tis well.—

Enter a Messenger *with letters.*

What letters hast thou there?—I can but thank
      you.
Mess. These letters come from your father,—
Hot. Letters from him! why comes he not
      himself?   [ous sick.
Mess. He cannot come, my lord; he's griev-
Hot. Zounds! how has he the leisure to be
      sick
In such a justling time? Who leads his power?
Under whose government come they along?
Mess. His letters bear his mind, not I, my
      lord.   [bed?
Wor. I pr'ythee, tell me, doth he keep his
Mess. He did, my lord, four days ere I set
      forth;
And at the time of my departure thence
He was much fear'd by his physicians.
Wor. I would the state of time had first been
      whole
Ere he by sickness had been visited:
His health was never better worth than now.
Hot. Sick now! droop now! this sickness doth
      infect
The very life-blood of our enterprise;
'Tis catching hither, even to our camp.—
He writes me here that inward sickness,—
And that his friends by deputation could not
So soon be drawn; nor did he think it meet
To lay so dangerous and dear a trust
On any soul remov'd, but on his own.
Yet doth he give us bold advertisement,
That with our small conjunction we should on,
To see how fortune is dispos'd to us;
For, as he writes, there is no quailing now,
Because the king is certainly possess'd
Of all our purposes. What say you to it?
Wor. Your father's sickness is a maim to us.
Hot. A perilous gash, a very limb lopp'd
      off:—
And yet, in faith, 'tis not; his present want
Seems more than we shall find it:—were it good
To set the exact wealth of all our states
All at one cast? to set so rich a main
On the nice hazard of one doubtful hour?
It were not good; for therein should we read
The very bottom and the soul of hope,
The very list, the very utmost bound
Of all our fortunes.
Doug.   Faith, and so we should;
Where now remains a sweet reversion:
We may boldly spend upon the hope of what
Is to come in:
A comfort of retirement lives in this.
Hot. A rendezvous, a home to fly unto,
If that the devil and mischance look big
Upon the maidenhead of our affairs.   [here.
Wor. But yet I would your father had been

The quality and hair of our attempt
Brooks no division: it will be thought
By some, that know not why he is away,
That wisdom, loyalty, and mere dislike
Of our proceedings, kept the earl from hence:
And think how such an apprehension
May turn the tide of fearful faction,
And breed a kind of question in our cause;
For well you know we of the offering side
Must keep aloof from strict arbitrement,
And stop all sight-holes, every loop from whence
The eye of reason may pry in upon us:
This absence of your father's draws a curtain
That shows the ignorant a kind of fear
Before not dreamt of.
Hot.   You strain too far.
I, rather, of his absence make this use:—
It lends a lustre and more great opinion,
A larger dare to our great enterprise,
Than if the earl were here: for men must think,
If we, without his help, can make a head
To push against the kingdom, with his help
We shall o'erturn it topsy-turvy down.—
Yet all goes well, yet all our joints are whole.
Doug. As heart can think: there is not such
      a word
Spoke of in Scotland as this term of fear.

Enter Sir Richard Vernon.

Hot. My cousin Vernon! welcome, by my
      soul.   [lord.
Ver. Pray God my news be worth a welcome,
The Earl of Westmoreland, seven thousand
      strong,
Is marching hitherwards; with him Prince
      John.
Hot. No harm:—what more?
Ver.   And further, I have learn'd
The king himself in person is set forth,
Or hitherwards intended speedily,
With strong and mighty preparation.   [son,
Hot. He shall be welcome too. Where is his
The nimble-footed madcap Prince of Wales
And his comrades, that daff'd the world aside,
And bid it pass?
Ver.   All furnish'd, all in arms;
All plum'd like estridges, that wing the wind;
Bated like eagles having lately bath'd;
Glittering in golden coats, like images;
As full of spirit as the month of May,
And gorgeous as the sun at midsummer;
Wanton as youthful goats, wild as young bulls.
I saw young Harry,—with his beaver on,
His cuisses on his thighs, gallantly arm'd,—
Rise from the ground like feather'd Mercury,
And vaulted with such ease into his seat,
As if an angel dropp'd down from the clouds,
To turn and wind a fiery Pegasus,
And witch the world with noble horsemanship.
Hot. No more, no more; worse than the sun
      in March,
This praise doth nourish agues. Let them come.
They come like sacrifices in their trim,
And to the fire-ey'd maid of smoky war,

All hot and bleeding, will we offer them:
The mailed Mars shall on his altar sit,
Up to the ears in blood. I am on fire
To hear this rich reprisal is so nigh.
And yet not ours.—Come, let me taste my
    horse,
Who is to bear me, like a thunderbolt,
Against the bosom of the Prince of Wales:
Harry to Harry shall, hot horse to horse,
Meet, and ne'er part till one drop down a
    corse.—
O that Glendower were come!
    Ver.   There is more news:
I learn'd in Worcester, as I rode along,
He cannot draw his power this fourteen days.
    Doug. That's the worst tidings that I hear
of yet.
    Wor. Ay, by my faith, that bears a frosty
sound.
    Hot. What may the king's whole battle reach
unto?
    Ver. To thirty thousand.
    Hot.   Forty let it be:
My father and Glendower being both away,
The powers of us may serve so great a day.
Come, let us take a muster speedily:
Doomsday is near; die all, die merrily.
    Doug. Talk not of dying; I am out of fear
Of death or death's hand for this one half-year.
                             [*Exeunt.*

SCENE II.—*A public Road near Coventry.*

Enter FALSTAFF *and* BARDOLPH.

    Fal. Bardolph, get thee before to Coventry;
fill me a bottle of sack: our soldiers shall march
through; we'll to Sutton-Cop-hill to-night.
    Bard. Will you give me money, captain?
    Fal. Lay out, lay out.
    Bard. This bottle makes an angel.
    Fal. An if it do, take it for thy labour; and
if it make twenty, take them all; I'll answer
the coinage. Bid my lieutenant Peto meet me
at the town's end.
    Bard. I will, captain: farewell.   [*Exit.*
    Fal. If I be not ashamed of my soldiers, I
am a soused gurnet. I have misused the king's
press damnably. I have got, in exchange of a
hundred and fifty soldiers, three hundred and
odd pounds. I press me none but good house-
holders, yeomen's sons; inquire me out contracted bachelors, such as had been asked twice
on the bans; such a commodity of warm slaves
as had as lief hear the devil as a drum; such as
fear the report of a caliver worse than a struck
fowl or a hurt wild-duck. I pressed me none
but such toasts-and-butter, with hearts in their
bellies no bigger than pins' heads, and they
have bought out their services; and now my
whole charge consists of ancients, corporals,
lieutenants, gentlemen of companies, slaves as
ragged as Lazarus in the painted cloth, where
the glutton's dogs licked his sores; and such
as, indeed, were never soldiers, but discarded

unjust serving-men, younger sons to younger
brothers, revolted tapsters, and ostlers trade-
fallen; the cankers of a calm world and a long
peace; ten times more dishonourable ragged
than an old-faced ancient: and such have I, to
fill up the rooms of them that have bought out
their services, that you would think that I had
a hundred and fifty tattered prodigals lately
come from swine-keeping, from eating draff and
husks. A mad fellow met me on the way, and
told me I had unloaded all the gibbets, and
pressed the dead bodies. No eye hath seen such
scarecrows. I'll not march through Coventry
with them, that's flat:—nay, and the villains
march wide betwixt the legs, as if they had
gyves on; for, indeed, I had the most of them
out of prison. There's but a shirt and a half in
all my company; and the half-shirt is two nap-
kins tacked together and thrown over the
shoulders like a herald's coat without sleeves;
and the shirt, to say the truth, stolen from my
host at Saint Alban's, or the red-nose innkeeper
of Daventry. But that's all one; they'll find
linen enough on every hedge.

Enter PRINCE HENRY *and* WESTMORELAND.

    P. Hen. How now, blown Jack! how now,
quilt!
    Fal. What, Hal! how now, mad wag! what
a devil dost thou in Warwickshire?—My good
Lord of Westmoreland, I cry you mercy: I
thought your honour had already been at
Shrewsbury.
    West. Faith, Sir John, 'tis more than time
that I were there, and you too; but my powers
are there already. The king, I can tell you,
looks for us all: we must away all night.
    Fal. Tut, never fear me: I am as vigilant as
a cat to steal cream.
    P. Hen. I think, to steal cream, indeed; for
thy theft hath already made thee butter. But
tell me, Jack, whose fellows are these that come
after?
    Fal. Mine, Hal, mine.
    P. Hen. I did never see such pitiful rascals.
    Fal. Tut, tut; good enough to toss; food for
powder, food for powder; they'll fill a pit as
well as better: tush, man, mortal men, mortal
men.
    West. Ay, but, Sir John, methinks they are
exceeding poor and bare,—too beggarly.
    Fal. Faith, for their poverty, I know not
where they had that; and for their bareness, I
am sure they never learned of me.
    P. Hen. No, I'll be sworn; unless you call
three fingers on the ribs bare. But, sirrah, make
haste: Percy is already in the field.
    Fal. What, is the king encamped?
    West. He is, Sir John: I fear we shall stay
too long.
    Fal. Well,
To the latter end of a fray and the beginning of
    a feast
Fits a dull fighter and a keen guest.   [*Exeunt.*

SCENE III.—*The Rebel Camp near Shrewsbury.*

Enter HOTSPUR, WORCESTER, DOUGLAS, *and* VERNON.

Hot. We'll fight with him to-night.
Wor.   It may not be.
Doug. You give him, then, advantage.
Ver.   Not a whit.
Hot. Why say you so? looks he not for supply?
Ver. So do we.
Hot.   His is certain, ours is doubtful.
Wor. Good cousin, be advis'd; stir not to-night.
Ver. Do not, my lord.
Doug.   You do not counsel well:
You speak it out of fear and cold heart.
Ver. Do me no slander, Douglas: by my life,—
And I dare well maintain it with my life,—
If well-respected honour bid me on,
I hold as little counsel with weak fear
As you, my lord, or any Scot that lives:—
Let it be seen to-morrow in the battle
Which of us fears.
Doug.   Yea, or to-night.
Ver.   Content.
Hot. To-night, say I.   [much,
Ver. Come, come, it may not be. I wonder
Being men of such great leading as you are,
That you foresee not what impediments
Drag back our expedition: certain horse
Of my cousin Vernon's are not yet come up:
Your uncle Worcester's horse came but to-day;
And now their pride and mettle is asleep,
Their courage with hard labour tame and dull,
That not a horse is half the half of himself.
Hot. So are the horses of the enemy
In general, journey-bated and brought low:
The better part of ours is full of rest.
Wor. The number of the king exceedeth ours.
For God's sake, cousin, stay till all come in.

[*The trumpet sounds a parley.*

Enter SIR WALTER BLUNT.

Blunt. I come with gracious offers from the king,
If you vouchsafe me hearing and respect.
Hot. Welcome, Sir Walter Blunt; and would to God
You were of our determination!
Some of us love you well; and even those some
Envy your great deservings and good name,
Because you are not of our quality,
But stand against us like an enemy. [stand so,
Blunt. And God defend but still I should
So long as out of limit and true rule
You stand against anointed majesty!
But, to my charge.—The king hath sent to know
The nature of your griefs; and whereupon
You conjure from the breast of civil peace
Such bold hostility; teaching his duteous land
Audacious cruelty. If that the king

Have any way your good deserts forgot,—
Which he confesseth to be manifold,—
He bids you name your griefs; and with all speed
You shall have your desires with interest,
And pardon absolute for yourself, and these
Herein misled by your suggestion.   [king
Hot. The king is kind; and well we know the
Knows at what time to promise, when to pay.
My father and my uncle and myself
Did give him that same royalty he wears;
And when he was not six-and-twenty strong,
Sick in the world's regard, wretched and low,
A poor unminded outlaw sneaking home,
My father gave him welcome to the shore;
And when he heard him swear, and vow to God,
He came but to be Duke of Lancaster,
To sue his livery and beg his peace,
With tears of innocency and terms of zeal,—
My father, in kind heart and pity mov'd,
Swore him assistance, and perform'd it too.
Now, when the lords and barons of the realm
Perceiv'd Northumberland did lean to him,
The more and less came in with cap and knee;
Met him in boroughs, cities, villages;
Attended him on bridges, stood in lanes,
Laid gifts before him, proffer'd him their oaths,
Gave him their heirs as pages, follow'd him
Even at the heels in golden multitudes.
He presently,—as greatness knows itself,—
Steps me a little higher than his vow
Made to my father, while his blood was poor,
Upon the naked shore at Ravenspurg;
And now, forsooth, takes on him to reform
Some certain edicts, and some strait decrees,
That lie too heavy on the commonwealth;
Cries out upon abuses, seems to weep
Over his country's wrongs; and, by this face,
This seeming brow of justice, did he win
The hearts of all that he did angle for:
Proceeded further; cut me off the heads
Of all the favourites that the absent king
In deputation left behind him here,
When he was personal in the Irish war.
Blunt. Tut, I came not to hear this.
Hot.   Then to the point.
In short time after, he depos'd the king;
Soon after that, depriv'd him of his life;
And, in the neck of that, task'd the whole state:
To make that worse, suffer'd his kinsman March,—
Who is, if every owner were well plac'd,
Indeed his king,—to be incag'd in Wales
There without ransom to lie forfeited;
Disgrac'd me in my happy victories;
Sought to entrap me by intelligence;
Rated my uncle from the council-board;
In rage dismiss'd my father from the court;
Broke oath on oath, committed wrong on wrong;
And, in conclusion, drove us to seek out
This head of safety; and withal to pry
Into his title, the which we find
Too indirect for long continuance.
Blunt. Shall I return this answer to the king?

Hot. Not so, Sir Walter: we'll withdraw
 awhile.
Go to the king; and let there be impawn'd
Some surety for a safe return again,
And in the morning early shall my uncle
Bring him our purposes: and so, farewell.
 Blunt. I would you would accept of grace
 and love.
 Hot. And may be so we shall.
 Blunt.   Pray God you do!
                              [*Exeunt.*

SCENE IV.—YORK. *A Room in the* ARCH-
         BISHOP'S *House.*

Enter the ARCHBISHOP OF YORK, *and* SIR
         MICHAEL.

 Arch. Hie, good Sir Michael; bear this sealed
  brief
With winged haste to the lord marshal;
This to my cousin Scroop; and all the rest
To whom they are directed. If you knew
How much they do import, you would make
  haste.
 Sir M. My good lord,
I guess their tenor.
 Arch.   Like enough you do.
To-morrow, good Sir Michael, is a day
Wherein the fortune of ten thousand men
Must bide the touch; for, sir, at Shrewsbury,
As I am truly given to understand,
The king, with mighty and quick-raised power,
Meets with Lord Harry: and I fear, Sir
  Michael,
What with the sickness of Northumberland,—
Whose power was in the first proportion,—
And what with Owen Glendower's absence
  thence,—
Who with them was a rated sinew too,
And comes not in, o'erruled by prophecies,—
I fear the power of Percy is too weak
To wage an instant trial with the king.
 Sir M. Why, my good lord, you need not
  fear; there is Douglas,
And Lord Mortimer.
 Arch.   No, Mortimer is not there.
 Sir M. But there is Mordake, Vernon, Lord
  Harry Percy,
And there is my Lord of Worcester; and a head
Of gallant warriors, noble gentlemen.
 Arch. And so there is; but yet the king hath
  drawn
The special head of all the land together:—
The Prince of Wales, Lord John of Lancaster,
The noble Westmoreland, and warlike Blunt;
And many more corrivals and dear men
Of estimation and command in arms.
 Sir M. Doubt not, my lord, they shall be
  well oppos'd.
 Arch. I hope no less, yet needful 'tis to fear;
And, to prevent the worst, Sir Michael, speed:
For if Lord Percy thrive not, ere the king
Dismiss his power, he means to visit us,—
For he hath heard of our confederacy,—

And 'tis but wisdom to make strong against
  him:
Therefore make haste. I must go write again
To other friends; and so, farewell, Sir Michael.
                              [*Exeunt severally.*

ACT V.

SCENE I.—*The* KING'S *Camp near Shrewsbury.*

Enter KING HENRY, PRINCE HENRY, PRINCE
 JOHN OF LANCASTER, SIR WALTER BLUNT,
 and SIR JOHN FALSTAFF.

 K. Hen. How bloodily the sun begins to peer
Above yon bosky hill! the day looks pale
At his distemperature.
 P. Hen.   The southern wind
Doth play the trumpet to his purposes;
And by his hollow whistling in the leaves
Foretells a tempest and a blustering day.
 K. Hen. Then with the losers let it sympa-
  thize,
For nothing can seem foul to those that win.
                              [*Trumpet sounds.*

Enter WORCESTER *and* VERNON.

How now, my Lord of Worcester! 'tis not well
That you and I should meet upon such terms
As now we meet. You have deceiv'd our trust;
And made us doff our easy robes of peace,
To crush our old limbs in ungentle steel;
This is not well, my lord, this is not well.
What say you to it? will you again unknit
This churlish knot of all-abhorred war?
And move in that obedient orb again
Where you did give a fair and natural light;
And be no more an exhal'd meteor,
A prodigy of fear, and a portent
Of broached mischief to the unborn times?
 Wor. Hear me, my liege:
For mine own part, I could be well content
To entertain the lag-end of my life
With quiet hours; for, I do protest,
I have not sought the day of this dislike.
 K. Hen. You have not sought it! how comes
  it, then?
 Fal. Rebellion lay in his way, and he found it.
 P. Hen. Peace, chewet, peace!   [*looks*
 Wor. It pleas'd your majesty to turn your
Of favour from myself and all our house;
And yet I must remember you, my lord,
We were the first and dearest of your friends.
For you my staff of office did I break
In Richard's time; and posted day and night
To meet you on the way, and kiss your hand,
When yet you were in place and in account
Nothing so strong and fortunate as I.
It was myself, my brother, and his son,
That brought you home, and boldly did out-
  dare
The dangers of the time: you swore to us,—
And you did swear that oath at Doncaster,—
That you did nothing purpose 'gainst the state;
Nor claim no further than your new-fall'n right,
The seat of Gaunt, dukedom of Lancaster:

To this we swore our aid. But in short space
It rain'd down fortune showering on your head;
And such a flood of greatness fell on you,—
What with our help, what with the absent king,
What with the injuries of a wanton time,
The seeming sufferances that you had borne,
And the contrarious winds that held the king
So long in his unlucky Irish wars
That all in England did repute him dead,—
And, from this swarm of fair advantages,
You took occasion to be quickly woo'd
To gripe the general sway into your hand;
Forgot your oath to us at Doncaster;
And, being fed by us, you us'd us so
As that ungentle gull, the cuckoo's bird,
Useth the sparrow,—did oppress our nest,
Grew by our feeding to so great a bulk   [sight
That even our love durst not come near your
For fear of swallowing; but with nimble wing
We were enforc'd, for safety-sake, to fly
Out of your sight, and raise this present head:
Whereby we stand opposed by such means
As you yourself have forg'd against yourself;
By unkind usage, dangerous countenance,
And violation of all faith and troth
Sworn to us in your younger enterprise.
    K. Hen. These things, indeed, you have ar-
        ticulated,
Proclaim'd at market-crosses, read in churches;
To face the garment of rebellion
With some fine colour that may please the eye
Of fickle changelings and poor discontents,
Which gape and rub the elbow at the news
Of hurlyburly innovation:
And never yet did insurrection want
Such water-colours to impaint his cause;
Nor moody beggars, starving for a time
Of pellmell havoc and confusion.   [a soul
    P. Hen. In both our armies there is many
Shall pay full dearly for this encounter,
If once they join in trial. Tell your nephew,
The Prince of Wales doth join with all the
        world
In praise of Henry Percy: by my hopes,
This present enterprise set off his head,
I do not think a braver gentleman,
More active-valiant or more valiant-young,
More daring or more bold, is now alive
To grace this latter age with noble deeds.
For my part, I may speak it to my shame,
I have a truant been to chivalry;
And so I hear he doth account me too:
Yet this before my father's majesty,—
I am content that he shall take the odds
Of his great name and estimation,
And will, to save the blood on either side,
Try fortune with him in a single fight.
    K. Hen. And, Prince of Wales, so dare we
        venture thee,
Albeit considerations infinite
Do make against it.—No, good Worcester, no,
We love our people well; even those we love
That are misled upon your cousin's part;
And, will they take the offer of our grace,

Both he, and they, and you, yea, every man
Shall be my friend again, and I'll be his:
So tell your cousin, and bring me word
What he will do: but if he will not yield,
Rebuke and dread correction wait on us,
And they shall do their office. So, be gone;
We will not now be troubled with reply:
We offer fair; take it advisedly.
                        [*Exeunt* WOR. *and* VER.
    P. Hen. It will not be accepted, on my life:
The Douglas and the Hotspur both together
Are confident against the world in arms.
    K. Hen. Hence, therefore, every leader to
        his charge;
For, on their answer, will we set on them:
And God befriend us, as our cause is just!
            [*Exeunt* KING, BLUNT, *and* P. JOHN.
    Fal. Hal, if thou see me down in the battle,
and bestride me, so; 'tis a point of friendship.
    P. Hen. Nothing but a colossus can do thee
that friendship. Say thy prayers, and farewell.
    Fal. I would it were bed-time, Hal, and all
well.
    P. Hen. Why, thou owest God a death.
                        [*Exit.*
    Fal. 'Tis not due yet; I would be loth to
pay him before his day. What need I be so
forward with him that calls not on me? Well,
'tis no matter; honour pricks me on. Yea, but
how if honour prick me off when I come on?
how then? Can honour set-to a leg? no: or an
arm? no: or take away the grief of a wound?
no. Honour hath no skill in surgery, then? no.
What is honour? a word. What is in that word,
honour? What is that honour? air. A trim reckoning!—Who hath it? he that died o' Wednesday. Doth he feel it? no. Doth he hear it? no.
Is it insensible, then? yea, to the dead. But
will it not live with the living? no. Why? de-
traction will not suffer it:—therefore I'll none
of it: honour is a mere scutcheon: and so ends
my catechism.   [*Exit.*

SCENE II.—*The Rebel Camp.*

Enter WORCESTER *and* VERNON.

    Wor. O, no, my nephew must not know, Sir
        Richard,
The liberal kind offer of the king.
    Ver. 'Twere best he did.
    Wor.   Then are we all undone.
It is not possible, it cannot be,
The king should keep his word in loving us;
He will suspect us still, and find a time
To punish this offence in other faults:
Suspicion shall be all stuck full of eyes:
For treason is but trusted like the fox,
Who, ne'er so tame, so cherish'd, and lock'd up,
Will have a wild trick of his ancestors.
Look how we can, or sad or merrily,
Interpretation will misquote our looks;
And we shall feed like oxen at a stall,
The better cherish'd still the nearer death.
My nephew's trespass may be well forgot,—

It hath the excuse of youth and heat of blood,
And an adopted name of privilege,—
A hare-brain'd Hotspur, govern'd by a spleen.
All his offences live upon my head
And on his father's: we did train him on;
And, his corruption being ta'en from us,
We, as the spring of all, shall pay for all.
Therefore, good cousin, let not Harry know,
In any case the offer of the king.

Ver. Deliver what you will, I'll say 'tis so.
Here comes your cousin.

Enter HOTSPUR *and* DOUGLAS; Officers *and*
Soldiers *behind.*

Hot. My uncle is return'd:—deliver up
My Lord of Westmoreland.—Uncle, what
news?
Wor. The king will bid you battle presently.
Doug. Defy him by the Lord of Westmoreland.
Hot. Lord Douglas, go you and tell him so.
Doug. Marry, and shall, and very willingly.
[*Exit.*
Wor. There is no seeming mercy in the king.
Hot. Did you beg any? God forbid!
Wor. I told him gently of our grievances,
Of his oath-breaking; which he mended thus,—
By now forswearing that he is forsworn:
He calls us rebels, traitors; and will scourge
With haughty arms this hateful name in us.

Re-enter DOUGLAS.

Doug. Arm, gentlemen; to arms! for I have
thrown
A brave defiance in King Henry's teeth,
And Westmoreland, that was engag'd, did bear
it;
Which cannot choose but bring him quickly on.
Wor. The Prince of Wales stepp'd forth before the king,
And, nephew, challeng'd you to single fight.
Hot. O, would the quarrel lay upon our
heads!
And that no man might draw short breath today
But I and Harry Monmouth! Tell me, tell me,
How show'd his tasking? seem'd it in contempt?
Ver. No, by my soul; I never in my life
Did hear a challenge urg'd more modestly,
Unless a brother should a brother dare
To gentle exercise and proof of arms.
He gave you all the duties of a man;
Trimm'd up your praises with a princely
tongue;
Spoke your deservings like a chronicle;
Making you ever better than his praise,
By still dispraising praise valu'd with you:
And, which became him like a prince indeed,
He made a blushing cital of himself;
And chid his truant youth with such a grace,
As if he master'd there a double spirit,
Of teaching and of learning instantly.
There did he pause: but let me tell the world,—
If he outlive the envy of this day,

England did never owe so sweet a hope,
So much misconstru'd in his wantonness.
Hot. Cousin, I think thou art enamoured
Upon his follies: never did I hear
Of any prince so wild o' liberty.
But be he as he will, yet once ere night
I will embrace him with a soldier's arm,
That he shall shrink under my courtesy.—
Arm, arm with speed:—and, fellows, soldiers,
friends,
Better consider what you have to do
Than I, that have not well the gift of tongue,
Can lift your blood up with persuasion.

Enter a Messenger.

Mess. My lord, here are letters for you.
Hot. I cannot read them now.—
O gentlemen, the time of life is very short!
To spend that shortness basely were too long,
If life did ride upon a dial's point,
Still ending at the arrival of an hour.
An if we live, we live to tread on kings;
If die, brave death, when princes die with us!
Now, for our consciences,—the arms are fair,
When the intent of bearing them is just.

Enter another Messenger.

Mess. My lord, prepare; the king comes on
apace.   [tale,
Hot. I thank him that he cuts me from my
For I profess not talking; only this,—
Let each man do his best: and here draw I
A sword, whose temper I intend to stain
With the best blood that I can meet withal
In the adventure of this perilous day.
Now,—*Esperance!*—Percy!—and set on.—
Sound all the lofty instruments of war,
And by that music let us all embrace:
For, heaven to earth, some of us never shall
A second time do such a courtesy.
[*The trumpets sound. They embrace, and
exeunt.*

SCENE III.—*Plain near Shrewsbury.*

*Excursions, and parties fighting. Alarum to the
battle. Then enter* DOUGLAS *and* BLUNT,
meeting.

Blunt. What is thy name, that in the battle
thus
Thou crossest me? What honour dost thou seek
Upon my head?
Doug. Know, then, my name is Douglas;
And I do haunt thee in the battle thus
Because some tell me that thou art a king.
Blunt. They tell thee true.   [bought
Doug. The Lord of Stafford dear to-day hath
Thy likeness; for, instead of thee, King Harry,
The sword hath ended him: so shall it thee,
Unless thou yield thee as my prisoner.
Blunt. I was not born a yielder, thou proud
Scot;
And thou shalt find a king that will revenge
Lord Stafford's death.
[*They fight, and* BLUNT *is slain.*

Enter HOTSPUR.

Hot. O Douglas, hadst thou fought at
    Holmedon thus,
I never had triúmph'd upon a Scot.
Doug. All's done, all's won; here breathless
    lies the king.
Hot. Where?
Doug. Here.
Hot. This, Douglas? no; I know this face
    full well:
A gallant knight he was, his name was Blunt;
Semblably furnish'd like the king himself.
Doug. A fool go with thy soul, whither it
    goes!
A borrow'd title hast thou bought too dear:
Why didst thou tell me that thou wert a king?
Hot. The king hath many masking in his
    coats.
Doug. Now, by my sword, I will kill all his
    coats;
I'll murder all his wardrobe, piece by piece,
Until I meet the king.
Hot.   Up, and away!
Our soldiers stand full fairly for the day.
                                    [*Exeunt.*

Other alarums. Enter FALSTAFF.

Fal. Though I could 'scape shot-free at London, I fear the shot here: here's no scoring but
upon the pate.—Soft! who art thou? Sir
Walter Blunt:—there's honour for you: here's
no vanity!—I am as hot as molten lead, and as
heavy too: God keep lead out of me! I need
no more weight than mine own bowels.—I have
led my raggamuffins where they are peppered:
there's not three of my hundred and fifty left
alive; and they are for the town's end, to beg
during life.—But who comes here?

Enter PRINCE HENRY.

P. Hen. What, stand'st thou idle here? lend
me thy sword:
Many a nobleman lies stark and stiff
Under the hoofs of vaunting enemies,
Whose deaths are unreveng'd: pr'ythee, lend
me thy sword.
Fal. O Hal, I pr'ythee, give me leave to
breathe awhile.—Turk Gregory never did such
deeds in arms as I have done this day. I have
paid Percy, I have made him sure.
P. Hen. He is, indeed; and living to kill
thee. Lend me thy sword, I pr'ythee.
Fal. Nay, before God, Hal, if Percy be
alive thou gettest not my sword; but take my
pistol, if thou wilt.
P. Hen. Give it me: what, is it in the case?
Fal. Ay, Hal; 'tis hot, 'tis hot; there's that
will sack a city.
        [*The* PRINCE *draws out a bottle of sack.*
P. Hen. What, is't a time to jest and dally
now?   [*Throws it at him, and exit.*
Fal. Well, if Percy be alive, I'll pierce him.
If he do come in my way, so; if he do not, if

I come in his willingly, let him make a car-
bonado of me. I like not such grinning honour
as Sir Walter hath: give me life: which if I
can save, so; if not, honour comes unlooked
for, and there's an end.   [*Exit.*

SCENE IV.—*Another part of the Field.*

Alarums. Excursions. Enter KING HENRY,
PRINCE HENRY, PRINCE JOHN, *and* WEST-
MORELAND.

K. Hen. I pr'ythee,
Harry, withdraw thyself; thou bleed'st too
    much.—
Lord John of Lancaster, go you with him.
P. John. Not I, my lord, unless I did bleed
    too.
P. Hen. I do beseech your majesty, make up,
Lest your retirement do amaze your friends.
K. Hen. I will do so.—   [tent.
My Lord of Westmoreland, lead him to his
West. Come, my lord, I will lead you to
    your tent.   [your help:
P. Hen. Lead me, my lord? I do not need
And God forbid a shallow scratch should drive
The Prince of Wales from such a field as this,
Where stain'd nobility lies trodden on,
And rebels' arms triúmph in massacres!
P. John. We breathe too long:—come,
    cousin Westmoreland,
Our duty this way lies; for God's sake, come.
                    [*Exeunt* P. JOHN *and* WEST.
P. Hen. By heaven, thou hast deceiv'd me,
    Lancaster;
I did not think thee lord of such a spirit:
Before, I lov'd thee as a brother, John;
But now I do respect thee as my soul.
K. Hen. I saw him hold Lord Percy at the
    point
With lustier maintenance than I did look for
Of such an ungrown warrior.
P. Hen.   O, this boy
Lends mettle to us all.   [*Exit.*

Alarums. Enter DOUGLAS.

Doug. Another king! they grow like Hydra's
    heads:
I am the Douglas, fatal to all those
That wear those colours on them:—What art
    thou,
That counterfeit'st the person of a king?
K. Hen. The king himself, who, Douglas,
    grieves at heart,
So many of his shadows thou hast met,
And not the very king. I have two boys
Seek Percy and thyself about the field:
But, seeing thou fall'st on me so luckily,
I will assay thee; so, defend thyself!
Doug. I fear, thou art another counterfeit;
And yet, in faith, thou bear'st thee like a king:
But mine I am sure thou art, whoe'er thou be,
And thus I win thee.
        [*They fight; the* KING *being in danger,*
                re-enter P. HENRY.

P. Hen. Hold up thy head, vile Scot, or
　　thou art like
Never to hold it up again! the spirits
Of Shirley, Stafford, Blunt, are in my arms:
It is the Prince of Wales that threatens thee;
Who never promiseth but he means to pay.
　　　　　[*They fight;* DOUGLAS *flies.*
Cheerly, my lord: how fares your grace?—
Sir Nicholas Gawsey hath for succour sent,
And so hath Clifton: I'll to Clifton straight.
　K. Hen. Stay, and breathe awhile:—
Thou hast redeem'd thy lost opinion;
And show'd thou mak'st some tender of my life
In this fair rescue thou hast brought to me.
　P. Hen. O God, they did me too much injury
That ever said I hearken'd for your death!
If it were so, I might have let alone
The insulting hand of Douglas over you,
Which would have been as speedy in your end
As all the poisonous potions in the world,
And sav'd the treacherous labour of your son.
　K. Hen. Make up to Clifton, I'll to Sir
　　Nicholas Gawsey.　　　　　[*Exit.*

　　　　　Enter HOTSPUR.

Hot. If I mistake not, thou art Harry Mon-
　　mouth.
P. Hen. Thou speak'st as if I would deny my
　　name.
Hot. My name is Harry Percy.
P. Hen.　　　　　　　　Why, then I see
A very valiant rebel of the name.
I am the Prince of Wales; and think not, Percy,
To share with me in glory any more:
Two stars keep not their motion in one sphere;
Nor can one England brook a double reign,
Of Harry Percy and the Prince of Wales.
　Hot. Nor shall it, Harry, for the hour is come
To end the one of us; and would to God
Thy name in arms were now as great as mine!
　P. Hen. I'll make it greater ere I part from
　　thee;
And all the budding honours on thy crest
I'll crop, to make a garland for my head.
　Hot. I can no longer brook thy vanities.
　　　　　　　　　　　　　[*They fight.*

　　　　　Enter FALSTAFF.

Fal. Well said, Hal! to it, Hal!—Nay, you
shall find no boy's play here, I can tell you.

Re-enter DOUGLAS; *he fights with* FALSTAFF,
who falls down as if he were dead, and exit
DOUGLAS. HOTSPUR *is wounded, and falls.*

Hot. O, Harry, thou hast robb'd me of my
　　youth!
I better brook the loss of brittle life
Than those proud titles thou hast won of me;
They wound my thoughts worse than thy
　　sword my flesh:—
But thought's the slave of life, and life time's
　　fool;
And time, that takes survey of all the world,
Must have a stop. O, I could prophesy,

But that the earthy and cold hand of death
Lies on my tongue:—No, Percy, thou art dust,
And food for—　　　　　　　　[*Dies.*
　P. Hen. For worms, brave Percy: fare thee
　　well, great heart!—
Ill-weav'd ambition, how much art thou
　　shrunk!
When that this body did contain a spirit,
A kingdom for it was too small a bound;
But now two paces of the vilest earth
Is room enough:—this earth that bears thee
　　dead
Bears not alive so stout a gentleman.
If thou wert sensible of courtesy,
I should not make so dear a show of zeal:—
But let my favours hide thy mangled face;
And, even in thy behalf, I'll thank myself
For doing these fair rites of tenderness.
Adieu, and take thy praise with thee to heaven!
Thy ignominy sleep with thee in the grave,
But not remember'd in thy epitaph!—
　　　　　　[*He sees* FAL. *on the ground.*
What, old acquaintance! could not all this flesh
Keep in a little life? Poor Jack, farewell!
I could have better spar'd a better man.
O, I should have a heavy miss of thee,
If I were much in love with vanity.
Death hath not struck so fat a deer to-day,
Though many dearer, in this bloody fray.
Embowell'd will I see thee by and by:
Till then in blood by noble Percy lie.　[*Exit.*
　Fal. [*Rising slowly.*] Embowelled! if thou
embowel me to-day, I'll give you leave to
powder me and eat me too to-morrow. 'Sblood,
'twas time to counterfeit, or that hot termagant
Scot had paid me scot and lot too. Counterfeit? I lie, I am no counterfeit: to die is to be
a counterfeit; for he is but the counterfeit of a
man who hath not the life of a man; but to
counterfeit dying, when a man thereby liveth,
is to be no counterfeit, but the true and perfect
image of life indeed. The better part of valour
is discretion; in the which better part I have
saved my life. Zounds, I am afraid of this
gunpowder Percy, though he be dead; how if
he should counterfeit too, and rise? I am afraid
he would prove the better counterfeit. Therefore I'll make him sure: yea, and I'll swear I
killed him. Why may not he rise as well as I?
Nothing confutes me but eyes, and nobody
sees me. Therefore, sirrah [*stabbing him*], with
a new wound in your thigh, come you along
with me.　　　　　[*Takes* HOTSPUR *on his back.*

　Re-enter PRINCE HENRY *and* PRINCE JOHN.

　P. Hen. Come, brother John, full bravely
　　hast thou flesh'd
Thy maiden sword.
　P. John.　　　But, soft! whom have we here?
Did you not tell me this fat man was dead?
　P. Hen. I did; I saw him dead, breathless
　　and bleeding
On the ground.—
Art thou alive? or is it fantasy

That plays upon our eyesight? I pr'ythee,
    speak;
We will not trust our eyes without our ears:—
Thou art not what thou seem'st.

Fal. No, that's certain; I am not a double
man: but if I be not Jack Falstaff, then am I
a Jack. There is Percy [*throwing the body down*]:
if your father will do me any honour, so; if not,
let him kill the next Percy himself. I look to be
either earl or duke, I can assure you.

P. Hen. Why, Percy I killed myself, and
saw thee dead.

Fal. Didst thou?—Lord, Lord, how this
world is given to lying!—I grant you I was
down and out of breath, and so was he; but we
rose both at an instant, and fought a long hour
by Shrewsbury clock. If I may be believed, so;
if not, let them that should reward valour bear
the sin upon their own heads. I'll take it upon
my death, I gave him this wound in the thigh:
if the man were alive, and would deny it,
zounds, I would make him eat a piece of my
sword.

P. John. This is the strangest tale that e'er
    I heard.

P. Hen. This is the strangest fellow, brother
    John.—
Come, bring your luggage nobly on your back:
For my part, if a lie may do thee grace,
I'll gild it with the happiest terms I have.
                        [*A retreat is sounded.*
The trumpet sounds retreat; the day is ours.
Come, brother, let's to the highest of the field,
To see what friends are living, who are dead.
                [*Exeunt* P. HENRY *and* P. JOHN.

Fal. I'll follow, as they say, for reward. He
that rewards me, God reward him! If I do
grow great, I'll grow less; for I'll purge, and
leave sack, and live cleanly, as a nobleman
should do.   [*Exit, bearing off the body.*

SCENE V.—*Another part of the Field.*

The Trumpets sound. Enter KING HENRY,
PRINCE HENRY, PRINCE JOHN, WESTMORE-
LAND, *and others, with* WORCESTER *and*
VERNON *prisoners.*

K. Hen. Thus ever did rebellion find re-
    buke.—
Ill-spirited Worcester! did we not send grace,
Pardon, and terms of love to all of you?
And wouldst thou turn our offers contrary?
Misuse the tenor of thy kinsman's trust?

Three knights upon our party slain to-day,
A noble earl, and many a creature else,
Had been alive this hour,
If, like a Christian, thou hadst truly borne
Betwixt our armies true intelligence.

Wor. What I have done my safety urg'd me
    to,
And I embrace this fortune patiently,
Since not to be avoided it falls on me.

K. Hen. Bear Worcester to the death, and
    Vernon too:
Other offenders we will pause upon.
                [*Exeunt* WOR. *and* VER., *guarded.*
How goes the field?

P. Hen. The noble Scot, Lord Douglas,
    when he saw
The fortune of the day quite turn'd from him,
The noble Percy slain, and all his men
Upon the foot of fear,—fled with the rest;
And falling from a hill, he was so bruis'd
That the pursuers took him. At my tent
The Douglas is; and I beseech your grace
I may dispose of him.

K. Hen. With all my heart.

P. Hen. Then, brother John of Lancaster, to
    you
This honourable bounty shall belong:
Go to the Douglas, and deliver him
Up to his pleasure, ransomless and free:
His valour, shown upon our crests to-day,
Hath taught us how to cherish such high
    deeds
Even in the bosom of our adversaries.

P. John. I thank your grace for this high
    courtesy,
Which I shall give away immediately.

K. Hen. Then this remains,—that we divide
    our power.—
You, son John, and my cousin Westmoreland,
Towards York shall bend you with your dearest
    speed,
To meet Northumberland and the prelate
    Scroop,
Who, as we hear, are busily in arms:
Myself,—and you, son Harry,—will towards
    Wales,
To fight with Glendower and the Earl of
    March.
Rebellion in this land shall lose his sway,
Meeting the check of such another day:
And since this business so fair is done,
Let us not leave till all our own be won.
                                        [*Exeunt.*

KING HENRY IV
PART II.

Act IV. Sc. 4.

KING HENRY IV.

SECOND PART

DRAMATIS PERSONÆ

KING HENRY THE FOURTH.
HENRY, *Prince of Wales, afterwards* KING HENRY V.,
THOMAS, *Duke of Clarence,*
PRINCE JOHN OF LANCASTER, *afterwards* (Henry V.) *Duke of Bedford,*
PRINCE HUMPHREY OF GLOSTER, *afterwards* (Henry V.) *Duke of Gloster,* } *his* Sons.

EARL OF WARWICK,
EARL OF WESTMORELAND,
EARL OF SURREY,
GOWER,
HARCOURT, } *of the* KING's *party.*
Lord Chief-Justice *of the King's Bench.*
A Gentleman *attending on the* Chief-Justice.

EARL OF NORTHUMBERLAND,
SCROOP, *Archbishop of York,*
LORD MOWBRAY,
LORD HASTINGS,
LORD BARDOLPH,
SIR JOHN COLEVILE, } *Enemies to the* KING.

TRAVERS *and* MORTON, *Retainers of* NORTHUMBERLAND.
FALSTAFF, BARDOLPH, PISTOL, *and* Page.
POINS *and* PETO, *Attendants on* PRINCE HENRY.
SHALLOW *and* SILENCE, *Country Justices.*
DAVY, *Servant to* SHALLOW.
MOULDY, SHADOW, WART, FEEBLE, *and* BULLCALF, *Recruits.*
FANG *and* SNARE, *Sheriff's Officers.*
Rumour.
A Porter.
A Dancer, *Speaker of the Epilogue.*

LADY NORTHUMBERLAND.
LADY PERCY.
MISTRESS QUICKLY, *Hostess of a Tavern in Eastcheap.*
DOLL TEARSHEET.

Lords *and other* Attendants; Officers, Soldiers, Messengers, Drawers, Beadles, Grooms, &c.

SCENE,—ENGLAND.

INDUCTION.

WARKWORTH. *Before* NORTHUMBERLAND'S *Castle.*

Enter Rumour, *painted full of tongues.*

Rum. Open your ears; for which of you will stop
The vent of hearing when loud Rumour speaks?
I, from the orient to the drooping west,
Making the wind my post-horse, still unfold
The acts commenced on this ball of earth:
Upon my tongues continual slanders ride,
The which in every language I pronounce,
Stuffing the ears of men with false reports.
I speak of peace, while covert enmity,
Under the smile of safety, wounds the world:
And who but Rumour, who but only I,
Make fearful musters and prepar'd defence;
Whilst the big year, swoln with some other grief,
Is thought with child by the stern tyrant war,
And no such matter? Rumour is a pipe
Blown by surmises, jealousies, conjectures;
And of so easy and so plain a stop
That the blunt monster with uncounted heads,
The still-discordant wavering multitude,
Can play upon it. But what need I thus
My well-known body to anatomize
Among my household? Why is Rumour here?

I run before King Harry's victory;
Who, in a bloody field by Shrewsbury,
Hath beaten down young Hotspur and his troops,
Quenching the flame of bold rebellion
Even with the rebel's blood. But what mean I
To speak so true at first? my office is
To noise abroad that Harry Monmouth fell
Under the wrath of noble Hotspur's sword;
And that the king before the Douglas' rage
Stoop'd his anointed head as low as death.
This have I rumour'd through the peasant towns
Between that royal field of Shrewsbury
And this worm-eaten hold of ragged stone,
Where Hotspur's father, old Northumberland,
Lies crafty-sick: the posts come tiring on,
And not a man of them brings other news
Than they have learn'd of me: from Rumour's tongues
They bring smooth comforts false, worse than true wrongs. [*Exit.*

ACT I.

SCENE I.—*The same.*

The Porter *before the Gate; enter* LORD BARDOLPH.

L. Bard. Who keeps the gate here, ho?—
Where is the earl?

Port. What shall I say you are?

L. Bard.   Tell thou the earl
That the Lord Bardolph doth attend him here.

Port. His lordship is walk'd forth into the
    orchard:
Please it your honour, knock but at the gate,
And he himself will answer.

L. Bard.   ·Here comes the earl.
                              [*Exit* Porter.

Enter NORTHUMBERLAND.

North. What news, Lord Bardolph? every
    minute now
Should be the father of some stratagem:
The times are wild; contention, like a horse,
Full of high feeding, madly hath broke loose
And bears down all before him.

L. Bard.   Noble earl,
I bring you certain news from Shrewsbury.

North. Good, an God will!

L. Bard.   As good as heart can wish:—
The king is almost wounded to the death;
And, in the fortune of my lord your son,
Prince Harry slain outright; and both the
    Blunts
Kill'd by the hand of Douglas: young Prince
    John,
And Westmoreland, and Stafford, fled the field;
And Harry Monmouth's brawn, the hulk Sir
    John,
Is prisoner to your son: O, such a day,
So fought, so follow'd, and so fairly won,
Came not till now to dignify the times,
Since Cæsar's fortunes!

North.   How is this deriv'd?
Saw you the field? came you from Shrewsbury?

L. Bard. I spake with one, my lord, that
    came from thence;
A gentleman well bred and of good name,
That freely render'd me these news for true.

North. Here comes my servant Travers,
    whom I sent
On Tuesday last to listen after news.

L. Bard. My lord, I over-rode him on the
    way;
And he is furnish'd with no certainties
More than he haply may retail from me.

Enter TRAVERS.

North. Now, Travers, what good tidings
    come with you?

Tra. My lord, Sir John Umfrevile turn'd me
    back
With joyful tidings; and, being better hors'd,
Out-rode me. After him came spurring hard
A gentleman, almost forspent with speed,
That stopp'd by me to breathe his bloodied
    horse.
He ask'd the way to Chester; and of him
I did demand what news from Shrewsbury.
He told me that rebellion had bad luck,
And that young Harry Percy's spur was cold.
With that, he gave his able horse the head,
And, bending forward, struck his armed heels

Against the panting sides of his poor jade
Up to the rowel-head; and starting so,
He seem'd in running to devour the way,
Staying no longer question.

North.   Ha!—Again:
Said he young Harry Percy's spur was cold?
Of Hotspur, coldspur? that rebellion
Had met ill-luck?

L. Bard.   My lord, I'll tell you what;
If my young lord your son have not the day,
Upon mine honour, for a silken point
I'll give my barony: never talk of it.

North. Why should the gentleman that rode
    by Travers
Give, then, such instances of loss?

L. Bard.   Who, he?
He was some hilding fellow, that had stolen
The horse he rode on; and, upon my life,
Spoke at a venture.—Look, here comes more
    news.

Enter MORTON.

North. Yea, this man's brow, like to a title-
    leaf,
Foretells the nature of a tragic volume:
So looks the strand, whereon the imperious
    flood
Hath left a witness'd usurpation,—
Say, Morton, didst thou come from Shrews-
    bury?

Mor. I ran from Shrewsbury, my noble lord;
Where hateful death put on his ugliest mask
To fright our party.

North.   How doth my son and brother?
Thou tremblest; and the whiteness in thy cheek
Is apter than thy tongue to tell thy errand.
Even such a man, so faint, so spiritless,
So dull, so dead in look, so woe-begone,
Drew Priam's curtain in the dead of night,
And would have told him half his Troy was
    burn'd;
But Priam found the fire ere he his tongue,
And I my Percy's death ere thou report'st it.
This thou wouldst say,—Your son did thus and
    thus;
Your brother thus; so fought the noble Douglas;
Stopping my greedy ear with their bold deeds:
But in the end to stop mine ear indeed,
Thou hast a sigh to blow away this praise,
Ending with—brother, son, and all are dead.

Mor. Douglas is living, and your brother,
    yet;
But, for my lord your son,—

North.   Why, he is dead.
See what a ready tongue suspicion hath!
He that but fears the thing he would not know
Hath by instinct knowledge from others' eyes
That what he fear'd is chanced. Yet speak,
    Morton;
Tell thou thy earl his divination lies,
And I will take it as a sweet disgrace,
And make thee rich for doing me such wrong.

Mor. You are too great to be by me gain-
    said:

Your spirit is too true, your fears too certain.

North. Yet, for all this, say not that Percy's
    dead.
I see a strange confession in thine eye:
Thou shak'st thy head, and hold'st it fear or sin
To speak a truth. If he be slain, say so;
The tongue offends not that reports his death:
And he doth sin that doth belie the dead;
Not he which says the dead is not alive.
Yet the first bringer of unwelcome news
Hath but a losing office; and his tongue
Sounds ever after as a sullen bell,
Remember'd knolling a departing friend.

L. Bard. I cannot think, my lord, your son
    is dead.

Mor. I am sorry I should force you to believe
That which I would to God I had not seen;
But these mine eyes saw him in bloody state,
Rend'ring faint quittance, wearied and out-
    breath'd,   [down
To Harry Monmouth; whose swift wrath beat
The never-daunted Percy to the earth,
From whence with life he never more sprang up.
In few, his death,—whose spirit lent a fire
Even to the dullest peasant in his camp,—
Being bruited once, took fire and heat away
From the best-temper'd courage in his troops;
For from his metal was his party steel'd;
Which once in him abated, all the rest
Turn'd on themselves, like dull and heavy lead:
And as the thing that's heavy in itself,
Upon enforcement, flies with greatest speed,
So did our men, heavy in Hotspur's loss,
Lend to this weight such lightness with their
    fear,
That arrows fled not swifter toward their aim
Than did our soldiers, aiming at their safety,
Fly from the field. Then was that noble
    Worcester
Too soon ta'en prisoner; and that furious Scot,
The bloody Douglas, whose well-labouring
    sword   [king,
Had three times slain the appearance of the
'Gan vail his stomach, and did grace the shame
Of those that turn'd their backs; and in his
    flight,
Stumbling in fear, was took. The sum of all
Is, that the king hath won; and hath sent out
A speedy power to encounter you, my lord,
Under the conduct of young Lancaster
And Westmoreland. This is the news at full.

North. For this I shall have time enough to
    mourn.
In poison there is physic; and these news,
Having been well, that would have made me
    sick,
Being sick, have in some measure made me
    well: [joints,
And as the wretch, whose fever-weaken'd
Like strengthless hinges, buckle under life,
Impatient of his fit, breaks like a fire
Out of his keeper's arms; even so my limbs,
Weaken'd with grief, being now enrag'd with
    grief,

Are thrice themselves. Hence, therefore, thou
    nice crutch!
A scaly gauntlet now, with joints of steel,
Must glove this hand: and hence, thou sickly
    quoif!
Thou art a guard too wanton for the head
Which princes, flesh'd with conquest, aim to
    hit.
Now bind my brows with iron, and approach
The rugged'st hour that time and spite dare
    bring
To frown upon the enrag'd Northumberland!
Let heav'n kiss earth! Now let not Nature's
    hand
Keep the wild flood confin'd! let order die!
And let this world no longer be a stage
To feed contention in a lingering act;
But let one spirit of the first-born Cain
Reign in all bosoms, that, each heart being set
On bloody courses, the rude scene may end,
And darkness be the burier of the dead!

Tra. This strained passion doth you wrong,
    my lord.

L. Bard. Sweet earl, divorce not wisdom
    from your honour.

Mor. The lives of all your loving complices
Lean on your health; the which, if you give o'er
To stormy passion, must perforce decay.
You cast the event of war, my noble lord,
And summ'd the account of chance, before you
    said,
Let us make head. It was your presurmise
That in the dole o' blows your son might drop:
You knew he walk'd o'er perils on an edge,
More likely to fall in than to get o'er;
You were advis'd his flesh was capable
Of wounds and scars; and that his forward
    spirit
Would lift him where most trade of danger
    rang'd:
Yet did you say,—Go forth; and none of this
Though strongly apprehended, could restrain
The stiff-borne action. What hath, then, be-
    fallen,
Or what hath this bold enterprise brought forth,
More than that being which was like to be?

L. Bard. We all that are engaged to this loss
Knew that we ventur'd on such dangerous seas,
That if we wrought out life, 'twas ten to one:
And yet we ventur'd, for the gain propos'd
Chok'd the respect of likely peril fear'd;
And since we are o'erset, venture again.
Come, we will all put forth, body and goods.

Mor. 'Tis more than time: and, my most
    noble lord,
I hear for certain, and do speak the truth,—
The gentle Archbishop of York is up
With well-appointed powers: he is a man
Who with a double surety binds his followers.
My lord your son had only but the corpse,
But shadows and the shows of men, to fight:
For that same word, rebellion, did divide
The action of their bodies from their souls;
And they did fight with queasiness, constrain'd,

As men drink potions; that their weapons only
Seem'd on our side, but, for their spirits and
   souls,
This word, rebellion, it had froze them up,
As fish are in a pond. But now the archbishop
Turns insurrection to religion:
Suppos'd sincere and holy in his thoughts,
He's follow'd both with body and with mind;
And doth enlarge his rising with the blood
Of fair King Richard, scrap'd from Pomfret
   stones;
Derives from heaven his quarrel and his cause;
Tells them he doth bestride a bleeding land,
Gasping for life under great Bolingbroke;
And more and less do flock to follow him.

   North. I knew of this before; but, to speak
     truth,
This present grief had wip'd it from my mind.
Go in with me; and counsel every man
The aptest way for safety and revenge?
Get posts and letters, and make friends with
   speed,—
Never so few, and never yet more need.
                          [Exeunt.

SCENE II.—LONDON. *A Street.*

Enter SIR JOHN FALSTAFF, *with his* Page
   bearing his sword and buckler.

   Fal. Sirrah, you giant, what says the doctor
to my water?
   Page. He said, sir, the water itself was a good
healthy water; but, for the party that owed it,
he might have more diseases than he knew of.
   Fal. Men of all sorts take a pride to gird at
me: the brain of this foolish-compounded clay,
man, is not able to invent anything that tends
to laughter, more than I invent or is invented
on me: I am not only witty in myself, but the
cause that wit is in other men. I do here walk
before thee like a sow that hath overwhelmed
all her litter but one. If the prince put thee
into my service for any other reason than to set
me off, why then I have no judgment. Thou
whoreson mandrake, thou art fitter to be worn
in my cap than to wait at my heels. I was never
manned with an agate till now: but I will set
you neither in gold nor silver, but in vile apparel, and send you back again to your master,
for a jewel,—the juvenal, the prince your master, whose chin is not yet fledged. I will sooner
have a beard grow in the palm of my hand than
he shall get one on his cheek; and yet he will
not stick to say his face is a face-royal: God
may finish it when he will, it is not a hair amiss
yet: he may keep it still as a face-royal, for a
barber shall never earn sixpence out of it; and
yet he will be crowing as if he had writ man
ever since his father was a bachelor. He may
keep his own grace, but he is almost out of
mine, I can assure him.—What said Master
Dumbleton about the satin for my short cloak
and my slops?
   Page. He said, sir, you should procure him

better assurance than Bardolph: he would not
take his bond and yours; he liked not the
security.
   Fal. Let him be damned, like the glutton!
may his tongue be hotter!—A whoreson Achi-
tophel! a rascally yea-forsooth knave! to bear
a gentleman in hand, and then stand upon
security!—The whoreson smooth-pates do now
wear nothing but high shoes, and bunches of
keys at their girdles; and if a man is thorough
with them in honest taking up, then they must
stand upon security. I had as lief they would
put ratsbane in my mouth as offer to stop it
with security. I looked he should have sent me
two-and-twenty yards of satin, as I am a true
knight, and he sends me security. Well, he may
sleep in security; for he hath the horn of abundance, and the lightness of his wife shines
through it: and yet cannot he see, thou he have
his own lantern to light him.—Where's Bardolph?
   Page. He's gone into Smithfield to buy your
worship a horse.
   Fal. I bought him in Paul's, and he'll buy
me a horse in Smithfield: an I could get me
but a wife, in the stews, I were manned, horsed,
and wived.
   Page. Sir, here comes the nobleman that
committed the prince for striking him about
Bardolph.
   Fal. Wait close; I will not see him.

Enter the Lord Chief-Justice *and an* Attendant.

   Ch. Just. What's he that goes there?
   Atten. Falstaff, an't please your lordship.
   Ch. Just. He that was in question for the
robbery?
   Atten. He, my lord: but he hath since done
good service at Shrewsbury; and, as I hear, is
now going with some charge to the Lord John
of Lancaster.
   Ch. Just. What, to York? Call him back
again.
   Atten. Sir John Falstaff!
   Fal. Boy, tell him I am deaf.
   Page. You must speak louder; my master is
deaf.
   Ch. Just. I am sure he is, to the hearing of
anything good.—Go, pluck him by the elbow;
I must speak with him.
   Atten. Sir John,—
   Fal. What! a young knave, and begging!
Is there not wars? is there not employment?
Doth not the king lack subjects? Do not the
rebels need soldiers? Though it be a shame to
be on any side but one, it is worse shame to beg
than to be on the worst side, were it worse than
the name of rebellion can tell how to make it.
   Atten. You mistake me, sir.
   Fal. Why, sir, did I say you were an honest
man? setting my knighthood and my soldier-
ship aside, I had lied in my throat if I had
said so.
   Atten. I pray you, sir, then set your knight

hood and your soldiership aside; and give me leave to tell you, you lie in your throat, if you say I am any other than an honest man.

Fal. I give thee leave to tell me so! I lay aside that which grows to me! If thou gettest any leave of me, hang me; if thou takest leave, thou wert better be hanged. You hunt-counter, hence! avaunt!

Atten. Sir, my lord would speak with you.

Ch. Just. Sir John Falstaff, a word with you.

Fal. My good lord!—God give your lordship good time of day. I am glad to see your lordship abroad: I heard say your lordship was sick: I hope your lordship goes abroad by advice. Your lordship, though not clean past your youth, hath yet some smack of age in you, some relish of the saltness of time; and I most humbly beseech your lordship to have a reverend care of your health.

Ch. Just. Sir John, I sent for you before your expedition to Shrewsbury.

Fal. An't please your lordship, I hear his majesty is returned with some discomfort from Wales.

Ch. Just. I talk not of his majesty:—you would not come when I sent for you.

Fal. And I hear, moreover, his highness is fallen into this same whoreson apoplexy.

Ch. Just. Well, God mend him! I pray you let me speak with you.

Fal. This apoplexy is, as I take it, a kind of lethargy, an't please your lordship; a kind of sleeping in the blood, a whoreson tingling.

Ch. Just. What tell you me of it? be it as it is.

Fal. It hath its original from much grief, from study, and perturbation of the brain: I have read the cause of his effects in Galen; it is a kind of deafness.

Ch. Just. I think you are fallen into the disease; for you hear not what I say to you.

Fal. Very well, my lord, very well: rather, an't please you, it is the disease of not listening, the malady of not marking, that I am troubled withal.

Ch. Just. To punish you by the heels would amend the attention of your ears; and I care not if I do become your physician.

Fal. I am as poor as Job, my lord, but not so patient: your lordship may minister the potion of imprisonment to me in respect of poverty; but how I should be your patient to follow your prescriptions, the wise may make some dram of a scruple, or, indeed, a scruple itself.

Ch. Just. I sent for you when there were matters against you for your life, to come speak with me.

Fal. As I was then advised by my learned counsel in the laws of this land-service, I did not come.

Ch. Just. Well, the truth is, Sir John, you live in great infamy.

Fal. He that buckles him in my belt cannot live in less.

Ch. Just. Your means are very slender, and your waste is great.

Fal. I would it were otherwise; I would my means were greater and my waist slenderer.

Ch. Just. You have misled the youthful prince.

Fal. The young prince hath misled me: I am the fellow with the great belly, and he my dog.

Ch. Just. Well, I am loth to gall a new-healed wound: your day's service at Shrewsbury hath a little gilded over your night's exploit on Gadshill: you may thank the unquiet time for your quiet o'erposting that action.

Fal. My lord,—

Ch. Just. But since all is well, keep it so: wake not a sleeping wolf.

Fal. To wake a wolf is as bad as to smell a fox.

Ch. Just. What! you are as a candle, the better part burnt out.

Fal. A wassail candle, my lord; all tallow: if I did say of wax, my growth would approve the truth.

Ch. Just. There is not a white hair on your face but should have his effect of gravity.

Fal. His effect of gravy, gravy, gravy.

Ch. Just. You follow the young prince up and down, like his ill angel.

Fal. Not so, my lord; your ill angel is light; but I hope he that looks upon me will take me without weighing: and yet, in some respects, I grant, I cannot go:—I cannot tell. Virtue is of so little regard in these costermonger times that true valour is turned bear-herd: pregnancy is made a tapster, and hath his quick wit wasted in giving reckonings: all the other gifts appertinent to man, as the malice of this age shapes them, are not worth a gooseberry. You that are old consider not the capacities of us that are young; you measure the heat of our livers with the bitterness of your galls: and we that are in the vaward of our youth, I must confess, are wags too.

Ch. Just. Do you set down your name in the scroll of youth, that are written down old with all the characters of age? Have you not a moist eye? a dry hand? a yellow cheek? a white beard? a decreasing leg? an increasing belly? Is not your voice broken? your wind short? your chin double? your wit single? and every part about you blasted with antiquity? and will you yet call yourself young? Fie, fie, fie, Sir John!

Fal. My lord, I was born about three of the clock in the afternoon, with a white head, and something a round belly. For my voice,—I have lost it with hollaing and singing of anthems. To approve my youth further, I will not; the truth is, I am only old in judgment and understanding; and he that will caper with me for a thousand marks, let him lend me the money, and have at him. For the box o' the ear that the prince gave you,—he gave it like a rude prince, and you took it like a sensible lord. I have checked him for it; and the young lion repents; marry, not in ashes and sackcloth, but in new silk and old sack.

Ch. Just. Well, God send the prince a better companion!

Fal. God send the companion a better prince! I cannot rid my hands of him.

Ch. Just. Well, the king hath severed you and Prince Harry: I hear you are going with Lord John of Lancaster against the archbishop and the Earl of Northumberland.

Fal. Yea; I thank your pretty sweet wit for it. But look you, pray, all you that kiss my Lady Peace at home, that our armies join not in a hot day; for, by the Lord, I take but two shirts out with me, and I mean not to sweat extraordinarily: if it be a hot day, and I brandish anything but my bottle, I would I might never spit white again. There is not a dangerous action can peep out his head but I am thrust upon it: well, I cannot last ever: but it was alway yet the trick of our English nation, if they have a good thing, to make it too common. If you will needs say I am an old man, you should give me rest. I would to God my name were not so terrible to the enemy as it is: I were better to be eaten to death with rust than to be scoured to nothing with perpetual motion.

Ch. Just. Well, be honest, be honest; and God bless your expedition!

Fal. Will your lordship lend me a thousand pound to furnish me forth?

Ch. Just. Not a penny, not a penny; you are too impatient to bear crosses. Fare you well: commend me to my cousin Westmoreland.

[*Exeunt* Chief-Justice *and* Attendant.

Fal. If I do, fillip me with a three-man beetle.—A man can no more separate age and covetousness than he can part young limbs and lechery: but the gout galls the one, and the pox pinches the other; and so both the diseases prevent my curses.—Boy!—

Page. Sir?

Fal. What money is in my purse?

Page. Seven groats and two pence.

Fal. I can get no remedy against this consumption of the purse: borrowing only lingers and lingers it out, but the disease is incurable. —Go bear this letter to my Lord of Lancaster; this to the prince; this to the Earl of Westmoreland; and this to old Mistress Ursula, whom I have weekly sworn to marry since I perceive the first white hair on my chin. About it; you know where to find me. [*Exit* Page.] A pox of this gout! or, a gout of this pox! for the one or the other plays the rogue with my great toe. It is no matter if I do halt; I have the wars for my colour, and my pension shall seem the more reasonable. A good wit will make use of anything. I will turn diseases to commodity.

[*Exit.*

SCENE III.—YORK. *A Room in the* ARCH-BISHOP's *Palace.*

Enter the ARCHBISHOP OF YORK, *the* LORDS HASTINGS, MOWBRAY, *and* BARDOLPH.

Arch. Thus/ have you heard our cause and know our means;
And, my most noble friends, I pray you all
Speak plainly your opinions of our hopes:—
And first, lord marshal, what say you to it?

Mowb. I well allow the occasion of our arms,
But gladly would be better satisfied
How, in our means, we should advance ourselves
To look with forehead bold and big enough
Upon the power and puissance of the king.

Hast. Our present musters grow upon the file
To five-and-twenty thousand men of choice;
And our supplies live largely in the hope
Of great Northumberland, whose bosom burns
With an incensed fire of injuries.

L. Bard. The question, then, Lord Hastings, standeth thus;—
Whether our present five-and-twenty thousand
May hold up head without Northumberland?

Hast. With him, we may.

L. Bard.   Ay, marry, there's the point:
But if without him we be thought too feeble,
My judgment is, we should not step too far
Till we had his assistance by the hand;
For, in a theme so bloody-fac'd as this,
Conjecture, expectation, and surmise
Of aids uncertain, should not be admitted.

Arch. 'Tis very true, Lord Bardolph; for, indeed,
It was young Hotspur's case at Shrewsbury.

L. Bard. It was, my lord; who lin'd himself with hope,
Eating the air on promise of supply,
Flattering himself with project of a power
Much smaller than the smallest of his thoughts:
And so, with great imagination,
Proper to madmen, led his powers to death,
And, winking, leap'd into destruction.

Hast. But, by your leave, it never yet did hurt
To lay down likelihoods and forms of hope.

L. Bard. Yes, in this present quality of war;—
Indeed, the instant action,—a cause on foot,—
Lives so in hope, as in an early spring
We see the appearing buds; which, to prove fruit,
Hope gives not so much warrant, as despair
That frosts will bite them. When we mean to build,
We first survey the plot, then draw the model;
And when we see the figure of the house,
Then must we rate the cost of the erection;
Which, if we find outweighs ability,
What do we then but draw anew the model
In fewer offices, or at least desist   [work,—
To build at all? Much more, in this great

Which is almost to pluck a kingdom down
And set another up,—should we survey
The plot of situation and the model,
Consent upon a sure foundation,
Question surveyors, know our own estate,
How able such a work to undergo,
To weigh against his opposite; or else,
We fortify in paper and in figures,
Using the names of men instead of men:
Like one that draws the model of a house
Beyond his power to build it; who, half through,
Gives o'er, and leaves his part-created cost
A naked subject to the weeping clouds,
And waste for churlish winter's tyranny.

Hast. Grant that our hopes,—yet likely of
    fair birth,—
Should be still-born, and that we now possess'd
The utmost man of expectation;
I think we are a body strong enough,
Even as we are, to equal with the king.

L. Bard. What, is the king but five-and-
    twenty thousand?

Hast. To us no more; nay, not so much, Lord
    Bardolph;
For his divisions, as the times do brawl,
Are in three heads: one power against the
    French,
And one against Glendower; perforce a third
Must take up us: so is the unfirm king
In three divided; and his coffers sound
With hollow poverty and emptiness.

Arch. That he should draw his several
    strengths together,
And come against us in full puissance,
Need not be dreaded.

Hast.   If he should do so,
He leaves his back unarm'd, the French and
    Welsh
Baying him at the heels: never fear that.

L. Bard. Who is it like should lead his forces
    hither?

Hast. The Duke of Lancaster and West-
    moreland;   [mouth:
Against the Welsh, himself and Harry Mon-
But who is substituted 'gainst the French,
I have no certain notice.

Arch.   Let us on,
And publish the occasion of our arms.
The commonwealth is sick of their own choice;
Their over-greedy love hath surfeited:
An habitation giddy and unsure
Hath he that buildeth on the vulgar heart.
O thou fond many! with what loud applàuse
Didst thou beat heaven with blessing Boling-
    broke,
Before he was what thou wouldst have him be!
And being now trimm'd in thine own desires,
Thou, beastly feeder, art so full of him
That thou provok'st thyself to cast him up.
So, so, thou common dog, didst thou disgorge
Thy glutton bosom of the royal Richard;
And now thou wouldst eat thy dead vomit up,
And howl'st to find it. What trust is in these
    times?

They that, when Richard liv'd, would have him
    die,
Are now become enamour'd on his grave:
Thou, that threw'st dust upon his goodly head,
When through proud London he came sighing
    on
After the admired heels of Bolingbroke,
Cry'st now, *O earth yield us that king again,
And take thou this!* O thoughts of men accurst!
Past, and to come, seems best; things present,
    worst.

Mowb. Shall we go draw our numbers, and
    set on?

Hast. We are time's subjects, and time bids
    be gone.   [*Exeunt.*

ACT II.

SCENE I.—LONDON. *A Street.*

Enter Hostess, FANG *and his* Boy *with her,
and* SNARE *following.*

Host. Master Fang, have you entered the
action?

Fang. It is entered.

Host. Where is your yeoman? Is it a lusty
yeoman? will he stand to it?

Fang. Sirrah, where's Snare?

Host. O Lord, ay! good Master Snare.

Snare. Here, here.

Fang. Snare, we must arrest Sir John Falstaff.

Host. Yea, good Master Snare; I have entered him and all.

Snare. It may chance cost some of us our
lives, for he will stab.

Host. Alas the day! take heed of him; he
stabbed me in mine own house, and that most
beastly: in good faith, he cares not what mischief he doth, if his weapon be out: he will foin
like any devil; he will spare neither man,
woman, nor child.

Fang. If I can close with him, I care not for
his thrust.

Host. No, nor I neither: I'll be at your elbow.

Fang. An I but fist him once; an he come
but within my vice,—

Host. I am undone by his going; I warrant
you, he is an infinitive thing upon my score:—
good Master Fang, hold him sure;—good Master Snare, let him not 'scape. He comes con-
tinuantly to Pie-corner,—saving your manhoods,—to buy a saddle; and he is indited to
dinner to the Lubber's Head in Lumbert Street,
to Master Smooth's the silkman: I pray ye,
since my exion is entered, and my case so
openly known to the world, let him be brought
in to his answer. A hundred mark is a long one
for a poor lone woman to bear: and I have
borne, and borne, and borne; and have been
fubbed off, and fubbed off, and fubbed off,
from this day to that day, that it is a shame to
be thought on. There is no honesty in such
dealing; unless a woman should be made an ass

and a beast, to bear every knave's wrong. Yonder he comes; and that arrant malmsey-nose knave, Bardolph, with him. Do your offices, do your offices, Master Fang and Master Snare; do me, do me, do me your offices.

Enter Sir John Falstaff, Page, *and* Bardolph.

Fal. How now! whose mare's dead? what's the matter?

Fang. Sir John, I arrest you at the suit of Mistress Quickly.

Fal. Away, varlets!—Draw, Bardolph: cut me off the villain's head; throw the quean in the channel.

Host. Throw me in the channel! I'll throw thee in the channel. Wilt thou? wilt thou? thou bastardly rogue!—Murder, murder! O thou honeysuckle villain! wilt thou kill God's officers and the king's? O thou honey-seed rogue! thou art a honey-seed; a man-queller and a woman-queller.

Fal. Keep them off, Bardolph.

Fang. A rescue! a rescue!

Host. Good people, bring a rescue or two.— Thou wo't, wo't thou? thou wo't, wo't thou? do, do, thou rogue! do, thou hemp-seed!

Fal. Away, you scullion! you rampallian! you fustilarian! I'll tickle your catastrophe.

Enter the Lord Chief-Justice, *attended.*

Ch. Just. What is the matter? keep the peace here, ho!

Host. Good my lord, be good to me! I beseech you, stand to me!

Ch. Just. How now, Sir John! what, are you brawling here?

Doth this become your place, your time, and business?

You should have been well on your way to York.—

Stand from him, fellow: wherefore hang'st thou on him?

Host. O my most worshipful lord, an't please your grace, I am a poor widow of Eastcheap, and he is arrested at my suit.

Ch. Just. For what sum?

Host. It is more than for some, my lord; it is for all,—all I have. He hath eaten me out of house and home; he hath put all my substance into that fat belly of his:—but I will have some of it out again, or I will ride thee o' nights like the mare.

Fal. I think I am as like to ride the mare, if I have any vantage of ground to get up.

Ch. Just. How comes this, Sir John? Fie! What man of good temper would endure this tempest of exclamation? Are you not ashamed to enforce a poor widow to so rough a course to come by her own?

Fal. What is the gross sum that I owe thee?

Host. Marry, if thou wert an honest man, thyself and the money too. Thou didst swear to me upon a parcel-gilt goblet, sitting in my

Dolphin-chamber, at the round table, by a sea-coal fire, upon Wednesday in Whitsun-week, when the prince broke thy head for liking his father to a singing-man of Windsor.—thou didst swear to me then, as I was washing thy wound, to marry me, and make me my lady thy wife. Canst thou deny it? Did not goodwife Keech, the butcher's wife, come in then, and call me gossip Quickly? coming in to borrow a mess of vinegar; telling us she had a good dish of prawns; whereby thou didst desire to eat some; whereby I told thee they were ill for a green wound? And didst thou not, when she was gone down stairs, desire me to be no more so familiarity with such poor people; saying that ere long they should call me madam? And didst thou not kiss me, and bid me fetch thee thirty shillings? I put thee now to thy book-oath: deny it, if thou canst!

Fal. My lord, this is a poor mad soul; and she says, up and down the town, that her eldest son is like you: she hath been in good case, and, the truth is, poverty hath distracted her. But for these foolish officers, I beseech you I may have redress against them.

Ch. Just. Sir John, Sir John, I am well acquainted with your manner of wrenching the true cause the false way. It is not a confident brow, nor the throng of words that come with such more than impudent sauciness from you, can thrust me from a level consideration: you have, as it appears to me, practised upon the easy yielding spirit of this woman, and made her serve your uses both in purse and in person.

Host. Yea, in troth, my lord.

Ch. Just. Pr'ythee, peace.—Pay her the debt you owe her, and unpay the villany you have done with her: the one you may do with sterling money, and the other with current repentance.

Fal. My lord, I will not undergo this sneap without reply. You call honourable boldness impudent sauciness: if a man will make court'sy, and say nothing, he is virtuous:—no, my lord, my humble duty remembered, I will not be your suitor. I say to you, I do desire deliverance from these officers, being upon hasty employment in the king's affairs.

Ch. Just. You speak as having power to do wrong: but answer in the effect of your reputation, and satisfy the poor woman.

Fal. Come hither, hostess. [*Takes her aside.*

Enter Gower.

Ch. Just. Now, Master Gower,—what news?

Gow. The king, my lord, and Harry Prince of Wales

Are near at hand: the rest this paper tells.
[*Gives a letter.*

Fal. As I am a gentleman,—

Host. Nay, you said so before.

Fal. As I am a gentleman:—come, no more words of it.

Host. By this heavenly ground I tread on, I

must be fain to pawn both my plate and the tapestry of my dining-chambers.

Fal. Glasses, glasses, is the only drinking: and for thy walls,—a pretty slight drollery, or the story of the Prodigal, or the German hunting in water-work, is worth a thousand of these bed-hangings and these fly-bitten tapestries. Let it be ten pound, if thou canst. Come, an it were not for thy humours, there is not a better wench in England. Go, wash thy face, and draw thy action. Come, thou must not be in this humour with me; dost not know me? come, come, I know thou wast set on to this.

Host. Pray thee, Sir John, let it be but twenty nobles: i' faith, I am loth to pawn my plate, so God save me, la.

Fal. Let it alone; I'll make other shift: you'll be a fool still.

Host. Well, you shall have it, though I pawn my gown. I hope you'll come to supper. You'll pay me all together?

Fal. Will I live?—Go, with her, with her [*to* BARDOLPH]; hook on, hook on.

Host. Will you have Doll Tearsheet meet you at supper?

Fal. No more words; let's have her.

[*Exeunt* HOST., BARD., Officers, *and* Page.

Ch. Just. I have heard better news.

Fal. What's the news, my good lord?

Ch. Just. Where lay the king last night?

Gow. At Basingstoke, my lord.

Fal. I hope, my lord, all's well: what's the news, my lord?

Ch. Just. Come all his forces back? [horse,

Gow. No; fifteen hundred foot, five hundred Are march'd up to my Lord of Lancaster, Against Northumberland and the archbishop.

Fal. Comes the king back from Wales, my noble lord? [ently:

Ch. Just. You shall have letters of me pres-Come, go along with me, good master Gower.

Fal. My lord!

Ch. Just. What's the matter?

Fal. Master Gower, shall I entreat you with me to dinner?

Gow. I must wait upon my good lord here, —I thank you, good Sir John.

Ch. Just. Sir John, you loiter here too long, being you are to take soldiers up in counties as you go.

Fal. Will you sup with me, Master Gower?

Ch. Just. What foolish master taught you these manners, Sir John?

Fal. Master Gower, if they become me not, he was a fool that taught them me.—This is the right fencing grace, my lord; tap for tap, and so part fair.

Ch. Just. Now, the Lord lighten thee! thou art a great fool. [*Exeunt.*

SCENE II.—*The same. Another Street.*

Enter PRINCE HENRY *and* POINS.

P. Hen. Before God, I am exceeding weary.

Poins. Is it come to that? I had thought weariness durst not have attached one of so high blood.

P. Hen. Faith, it does me; though it discolours the complexion of my greatness to acknowledge it. Doth it not show vilely in me to desire small beer?

Poins. Why, a prince should not be so loosely studied as to remember so weak a composition.

P. Hen. Belike, then, my appetite was not princely got; for, by my troth, I do now remember the poor creature, small beer. But, indeed, these humble considerations make me out of love with my greatness. What a disgrace is it to me to remember thy name? or to know thy face to-morrow? or to take note how many pair of silk stockings thou hast; viz., these, and those that were thy peach-coloured ones? or to bear the inventory of thy shirts, as, one for superfluity, and one other for use?—but that the tennis court-keeper knows better than I; for it is a low ebb of linen with thee when thou keepest not racket there; as thou hast not done a great while, because the rest of thy low-countries have made a shift to eat up thy holland: and God knows, whether those that bawl out the ruins of thy linen shall inherit his kingdom: but the midwives say the children are not in the fault; whereupon the world increases, and kindreds are mightily strengthened.

Poins. How ill it follows, after you have laboured so hard, you should talk so idly! Tell me, how many good young princes would do so, their fathers being so sick as yours at this time is?

P. Hen. Shall I tell thee one thing, Poins?

Poins. Yes, faith; and let it be an excellent good thing.

P. Hen. It shall serve among wits of no higher breeding than thine.

Poins. Go to; I stand the push of your one thing that you will tell.

P. Hen. Marry, I tell thee,—it is not meet that I should be sad, now my father is sick: albeit I could tell to thee,—as to one it pleases me, for fault of a better, to call my friend,—I could be sad and sad indeed too.

Poins. Very hardly upon such a subject.

P. Hen. By this hand, thou think'st me as far in the devil's book as thou and Falstaff for obduracy and persistency: let the end try the man. But I tell thee, my heart bleeds inwardly that my father is so sick: and keeping such vile company as thou art hath in reason taken from me all ostentation of sorrow.

Poins. The reason?

P. Hen. What wouldst thou think of me if I should weep?

Poins. I would think thee a most princely hypocrite.

P. Hen. It would be every man's thought; and thou art a blessed fellow to think as every man thinks: never a man's thought in the world keeps the road-way better than thine: every man would think me an hypocrite indeed. And

What accites your most worshipful thought to think so?

Poins. Why, because you have been so lewd, and so much engraffed to Falstaff.

P. Hen. And to thee.

Poins. By this light, I am well spoke on; I can hear it with mine own ears: the worst that they can say of me is that I am a second brother, and that I am a proper fellow of my hands; and those two things, I confess, I cannot help.—By the mass, here comes Bardolph.

P. Hen. And the boy that I gave Falstaff: he had him from me Christian; and look, if the fat villain have not transformed him ape.

Enter BARDOLPH *and* Page.

Bard. God save your grace!

P. Hen. And yours, most noble Bardolph!

Bard. Come, you virtuous ass [*to the* Page], you bashful fool, must you be blushing? wherefore blush you now? What a maidenly man-at-arms are you become? Is it such a matter to get a pottle-pot's maidenhead?

Page. He called me even now, my lord, through a red lattice, and I could discern no part of his face from the window: at last I spied his eyes; and methought he had made two holes in the alewife's new red petticoat, and so peeped through.

P. Hen. Hath not the boy profited?

Bard. Away, you whoreson upright rabbit, away!

Page. Away, you rascally Althæa's dream, away!

P. Hen. Instruct us, boy; what dream, boy?

Page. Marry, my lord, Althæa dreamed she was delivered of a fire-brand; and therefore I call him her dream.

P. Hen. A crown's worth of good interpretation:—there it is, boy.   [*Gives him money.*

Poins. O that this good blossom could be kept from cankers!—Well, there is sixpence to preserve thee.

Bard. An you do not make him be hanged among you, the gallows shall have wrong.

P. Hen. And how doth thy master, Bardolph?

Bard. Well, my lord. He heard of your grace's coming to town; there's a letter for you.

Poins. Delivered with good respect.—And how doth the martlemas, your master?

Bard. In bodily health, sir.

Poins. Marry, the immortal part needs a physician; but that moves not him: though that be sick, it dies not.

P. Hen. I do allow this wen to be as familiar with me as my dog: and he holds his place; for look you how he writes.

Poins. [*Reads.*] *John Falstaff, knight,*—every man must know that, as oft as he has occasion to name himself: even like those that are kin to the king; for they never prick their finger but they say, *There is some of the king's blood spilt.*—*How comes that?* says he, that

takes upon him not to conceive. The answer is as ready as a borrower's cap, *I am the king's poor cousin, sir.*

P. Hen. Nay, they will be kin to us, or they will fetch it from Japhet. But to the letter:—

Poins. [*Reads.*] *Sir John Falstaff, knight, to the son of the king, nearest his father, Harry Prince of Wales, greeting.*—Why, this is a certificate.

P. Hen. Peace!

Poins. [*Reads.*] *I will imitate the honourable Romans in brevity:*—sure he means brevity in breath, short-winded.—*I commend me to thee, I commend thee, and I leave thee. Be not too familiar with Poins; for he misuses thy favours so much that he swears thou art to marry his sister Nell. Repent at idle times as thou mayest, and so, farewell.*

> *Thine, by yea and no, (which is as much as to say, as thou usest him,)* JACK FALSTAFF, *with my familiars;* JOHN, *with my brothers and sisters; and* SIR JOHN *with all Europe.*

My lord, I will steep this letter in sack, and make him eat it.

P. Hen. That's to make him eat twenty of his words. But do you use me thus, Ned? must I marry your sister?

Poins. God send the wench have no worse fortune! but I never said so.

P. Hen. Well, thus we play the fools with the time; and the spirits of the wise sit in the clouds and mock us.—Is your master here in London?

Bard. Yes, my lord.

P. Hen. Where sups he? doth the old boar feed in the old frank?

Bard. At the old place, my lord,—in Eastcheap.

P. Hen. What company?

Page. Ephesians, my lord,—of the old church.

P. Hen. Sup any women with him?

Page. None, my lord, but old Mistress Quickly and Mistress Doll Tearsheet.

P. Hen. What pagan may that be?

Page. A proper gentlewoman, sir, and a kinswoman of my master's.

P. Hen. Even such kin as the parish heifers are to the town bull.—Shall we steal upon them, Ned, at supper?

Poins. I am your shadow, my lord; I'll follow you.

P. Hen. Sirrah, you boy,—and Bardolph,—no word to your master that I am yet come to town: there's for your silence.

Bard. I have no tongue, sir.

Page. And for mine, sir,—I will govern it.

P. Hen. Fare ye well; go. [*Exeunt* BARDOLPH *and* Page.]—This Doll Tearsheet should be some road.

Poins. I warrant you, as common as the way between Saint Alban's and London.

P. Hen. How might we see Falstaff bestow

himself to-night in his true colours, and not ourselves be seen?

Poins. Put on two leathern jerkins and aprons, and wait upon him at his table as drawers.

P. Hen. From a god to a bull? a heavy descension! it was Jove's case. From a prince to a prentice? a low transformation! that shall be mine; for in everything the purpose must weigh with the folly.—Follow me, Ned. *[Exeunt.*

SCENE III.—WARKWORTH. *Before the Castle.*

Enter NORTHUMBERLAND, LADY NORTHUMBERLAND, *and* LADY PERCY.

North. I pray thee, loving wife, and gentle daughter,
Give even way unto my rough affairs:
Put not you on the visage of the times,
And be, like them, to Percy troublesome.

Lady N. I have given over, I will speak no more:
Do what you will; your wisdom be your guide.

North. Alas, sweet wife, my honour is at pawn;
And, but my going, nothing can redeem it.

Lady P. O, yet, for God's sake, go not to these wars!
The time was, father, that you broke your word,
When you were more endear'd to it than now;
When your own Percy, when my heart-dear Harry,
Threw many a northward look to see his father
Bring up his powers; but he did long in vain.
Who then persuaded you to stay at home?
There were two honours lost,—yours and your son's.
For yours,—may heavenly glory brighten it!
For his,—it stuck upon him, as the sun
In the grey vault of heaven: and by his light
Did all the chivalry of England move
To do brave acts: he was, indeed, the glass
Wherein the noble youth did dress themselves:
He had no legs that practis'd not his gait;
And speaking thick, which nature made his blemish,
Became the accents of the valiant;
For those that could speak low and tardily
Would turn their own perfection to abuse
To seem like him: so that in speech, in gait,
In diet, in affections of delight,
In military rules, humours of blood,
He was the mark and glass, copy and book,
That fashion'd others. And him,—O wondrous him!
O miracle of men!—him did you leave,—
Second to none, unseconded by you,—
To look upon the hideous god of war
In disadvantage; to abide a field
Where nothing but the sound of Hotspur's name
Did seem defensible:—so you left him.
Never, O never, do his ghost the wrong

To hold your honour more precise and nice
With others than with him! let them alone:
The marshal and the archbishop are strong:
Had my sweet Harry had but half their numbers,
To-day might I, hanging on Hotspur's neck,
Have talk'd of Monmouth's grave.

North. Beshrew your heart,
Fair daughter, you do draw my spirits from me
With new lamenting ancient oversights.
But I must go, and meet with danger there;
Or it will seek me in another place,
And find me worse provided.

Lady N. O, fly to Scotland,
Till that the nobles and the armed commons
Have of their puissance made a little taste.

Lady P. If they get ground and vantage of the king,
Then join you with them, like a rib of steel,
To make strength stronger; but, for all our loves,
First let them try themselves. So did your son;
He was so suffer'd: so came I a widow;
And never shall have length of life enough
To rain upon remembrance with mine eyes,
That it may grow and sprout as high as heaven,
For recordation to my noble husband.

North. Come, come, go in with me. 'Tis with my mind
As with the tide swell'd up unto its height,
That makes a still-stand, running neither way.
Fain would I go to meet the archbishop,
But many thousand reasons hold me back.
I will resolve for Scotland: there am I,
Till time and vantage crave my company. *[Exeunt.*

SCENE IV.—LONDON. *A Room in the Boar's Head Tavern in Eastcheap.*

Enter two Drawers.

1 *Draw.* What the devil hast thou brought there? apple-johns? thou know'st Sir John cannot endure an apple-john.

2 *Draw.* Mass, thou sayest true. The prince once set a dish of apple-johns before him, and told him there were five more Sir Johns; and, putting off his hat, said, *I will now take my leave of these six dry, round, old, withered knights.* It angered him to the heart: but he hath forgot that.

1 *Draw.* Why, then, cover, and set them down: and see if thou canst find out Sneak's noise: Mistress Tearsheet would fain hear some music. Despatch:—the room where they supped is too hot; they'll come in straight.

2 *Draw.* Sirrah, here will be the prince and Master Poins anon; and they will put on two of our jerkins and aprons; and Sir John must not know of it: Bardolph hath brought word.

1 *Draw.* By the mass, here will be old utis: it will be an excellent stratagem.

2 *Draw.* I'll see if I can find out Sneak. *[Exit.*

Enter Hostess *and* DOLL TEARSHEET.

Host. I' faith, sweetheart, methinks now you are in an excellent good temperality: your pulsidge beats as extraordinarily as heart would desire; and your colour, I warrant you, is as red as any rose: but, i' faith, you have drunk too much canaries; and that's a marvellous searching wine, and it perfumes the blood ere one can say, What's this?—How do you now?

Doll. Better than I was:—hem.

Host. Why, that's well said; a good heart's worth gold.—Look, here comes Sir John.

Enter FALSTAFF *singing.*

Fal. When Arthur first in court—Empty the jorden. [*Exit* 1 Drawer.]—And was a worthy king.—How now, Mistress Doll!

Host. Sick of a calm; yea, good sooth.

Fal. So is all her sect; an they be once in a calm, they are sick.

Doll. You muddy rascal, is that all the comfort you give me?

Fal. You make fat rascals, Mistress Doll.

Doll. I make them! gluttony and diseases make them; I make them not.

Fal. If the cook help to make the gluttony, you help to make the diseases, Doll: we catch of you, Doll, we catch of you; grant that, my poor virtue, grant that.

Doll. Yea, joy,—our chains and our jewels.

Fal. Your brooches, pearls, and ouches:—for to serve bravely is to come halting off, you know: to come off the breach with his pike bent bravely, and to surgery bravely; to venture upon the charged chambers bravely,—

Doll. Hang yourself, you muddy conger, hang yourself!

Host. By my troth, this is the old fashion; you two never meet but you fall to some discord: you are both, in good troth, as rheumatic as two dry toasts; you cannot one bear with another's confirmities. What the good-year! one must bear, and that must be you [*to* DOLL]: you are the weaker vessel, as they say, the emptier vessel.

Doll. Can a weak empty vessel bear such a huge full hogshead? there's a whole merchant's venture of Bourdeaux stuff in him; you have not seen a hulk better stuffed in the hold.— Come, I'll be friends with thee, Jack: thou are going to the wars; and whether I shall ever see thee again or no, there is nobody cares.

Re-enter First Drawer.

1 *Draw.* Sir, Ancient Pistol is below, and would speak with you.

Doll. Hang him, swaggering rascal! let him not come hither: it is the foul-mouth'dst rogue in England.

Host. If he swagger, let him not come here: no, by my faith; I must live amongst my neighbours; I'll no swaggerers: I am in good name and fame with the very best:—shut the door;—there comes no swaggerers here: I have not lived all this while to have swaggering now: —shut the door, I pray you.

Fal. Dost thou hear, hostess?—

Host. Pray you, pacify yourself, Sir John: there comes no swaggerers here.

Fal. Dost thou hear? it is mine ancient.

Host. Tilly-fally, Sir John, never tell me: your ancient swaggerer comes not in my doors. I was before Master Tisick, the deputy, the other day; and, as he said to me,—it was no longer ago than Wednesday last,—*Neighbour Quickly,* says he;—Master Dumb, our minister, was by then;—*Neighbour Quickly,* says he, *receive those that are civil; for,* saith he, *you are in an ill-name;*—now he said so, I can tell whereupon; *for,* says he, *you are an honest woman, and well thought on; therefore take heed what guests you receive: receive,* says he, *no swaggering companions.*—There comes none here;— you would bless you to hear what he said:— no, I'll no swaggerers.

Fal. He's no swaggerer, hostess; a tame cheater, i' faith; you may stroke him as gently as a puppy greyhound: he will not swagger with a Barbary hen, if her feathers turn back in any show of resistance.—Call him up, drawer.

[*Exit* 1 Drawer.

Host. Cheater, call you him? I will bar no honest man my house, nor no cheater: but I do not love swaggering; by my troth, I am the worse when one says swagger: feel, masters, how I shake; look you, I warrant you.

Doll. So you do, hostess.

Host. Do I? yea, in very truth, do I, an 'twere an aspen leaf: I cannot abide swaggerers.

Enter PISTOL, BARDOLPH, *and* Page.

Pist. God save you, Sir John!

Fal. Welcome, Ancient Pistol. Here, Pistol, I charge you with a cup of sack: do you discharge upon mine hostess.

Pist. I will discharge upon her, Sir John, with two bullets.

Fal. She is pistol-proof, sir; you shall hardly offend her.

Host. Come, I'll drink no proofs nor no bullets; I'll drink no more than will do me good, for no man's pleasure, I.

Pist. Then to you, Mrs. Dorothy; I will charge you.

Doll. Charge me! I scorn you, scurvy companion. What! you poor, base, rascally, cheating, lack-linen mate! Away, you mouldy rogue, away! I am meat for your master.

Pist. I know you, Mistress Dorothy.

Doll. Away, you cut-purse rascal! you filthy bung, away! by this wine, I'll thrust my knife in your mouldy chaps, an you play the saucy cuttle with me. Away, you bottle-ale rascal! you basket-hilt stale juggler, you!—Since when, I pray you, sir?—God's light, with two points on your shoulder? much!

Pist. I will murder your ruff for this.

Fal. No more, Pistol; I would not have you go off here: discharge yourself of our company, Pistol.

Host. No, good Captain Pistol; not here, sweet captain.

Doll. Captain! thou abominable damned cheater, art thou not ashamed to be called captain? If captains were of my mind, they would truncheon you out, for taking their names upon you before you have earned them. You a captain! you slave, for what? for tearing a poor whore's ruff in a bawdy-house?—He a captain! hang him, rogue! He lives upon mouldy stewed prunes and dried cakes. A captain! God's light, these villains will make the word as odious as the word occupy; which was an excellent good word before it was ill-sorted: therefore captains had need look to it.

Bard. Pray thee, go down, good ancient.

Fal. Hark thee hither, Mistress Doll.

Pist. Not I: I tell thee what, Corporal Bardolph,—I could tear her:—I'll be revenged on her.

Page. Pray thee, go down.

Pist. I'll see her damned first;—to Pluto's damned lake, by this hand, to the infernal deep, with Erebus and tortures vile also. Hold hook and line, say I. Down, down, dogs! down, faitors! Have we not Hiren here?

Host. Good Captain Peesel, be quiet; it is very late, i' faith: I beseek you now, aggravate your choler.

Pist. These be good humours, indeed! Shall packhorses,
And hollow pamper'd jades of Asia,
Which cannot go but thirty miles a-day,
Compare with Cæsars, and with Cannibals,
And Trojan Greeks? nay, rather damn them with
King Cerberus; and let the welkin roar.
Shall we fall foul for toys?

Host. By my troth, captain, these are very bitter words.

Bard. Be gone, good ancient: this will grow to a brawl anon.

Pist. Die men like dogs! give crowns like pins! Have we not Hiren here?

Host. O' my word, captain; there's none such here. What the good-year! do you think I would deny her? for Godsake, be quiet.

Pist. Then feed and be fat, my fair Calipolis. Come, give me some sack.
Se fortuna mi tormenta, lo sperare mi contenta.—
Fear we broadsides? no, let the fiend give fire:
Give me some sack:—and, sweetheart, lie thou there.   [*Laying down his sword.*
Come we to full points here; and are *et-ceteras* nothing?

Fal. Pistol, I would, be quiet.

Pist. Sweet knight, I kiss thy neif: what! we have seen the seven stars.

Doll. Thrust him downstairs; I cannot endure such a fustian rascal.

Pist. Thrust him down stairs! know we not Galloway nags?

Fal. Quoit him down, Bardolph, like a shove-groat shilling: nay, an he do nothing but speak nothing, he shall be nothing here.

Bard. Come, get you down stairs.

Pist. What! shall we have incision? shall we imbrue?—   [*Snatching up his sword.*
Then death rock me asleep, abridge my doleful days!
Why, then, let grievous, ghastly, gaping wounds
Untwine the Sisters Three! Come, Atropos, I say!

Host. Here's goodly stuff toward!

Fal. Give me my rapier, boy.

Doll. I pray thee, Jack, I pray thee, do not draw.

Fal. Get you down stairs.
       [*Drawing, and driving* PIST. *out.*

Host. Here's a goodly tumult! I'll forswear keeping house afore I'll be in these tirrits and frights. So; murder, I warrant now.—Alas, alas! put up your naked weapons, put up your naked weapons.   [*Exeunt* PIST. *and* BARD.

Doll. I pray thee, Jack, be quiet; the rascal is gone.—Ah, you whoreson little valiant villain, you!

Host. Are you not hurt i' the groin? methought he made a shrewd thrust at your belly.

Re-enter BARDOLPH.

Fal. Have you turned him out of doors?

Bard. Yes, sir. The rascal's drunk: you have hurt him, sir, in the shoulder.

Fal. A rascal! to brave me!

Doll. Ah, you sweet little rogue, you! Alas, poor ape, how thou sweatest! come, let me wipe thy face;—come on, you whoreson chops:—ah, rogue! i' faith, I love thee. Thou art as valorous as Hector of Troy, worth five of Agamemnon, and ten times better than the nine worthies: ah, villain!

Fal. A rascally slave! I will toss the rogue in a blanket.

Doll. Do, if thou darest for thy heart: if thou dost, I'll canvass thee between a pair of sheets.

Enter Musicians.

Page. The music is come, sir.

Fal. Let them play;—play, sirs.—Sit on my knee, Doll.—A rascal-bragging slave! the rogue fled from me like quicksilver.

Doll. I' faith, and thou followedst him like a church. Thou whoreson little tidy Bartholomew boar-pig, when wilt thou leave fighting o' days and foining o' nights, and begin to patch up thine old body for heaven?

Enter, behind, PRINCE HENRY *and* POINS *disguised as Drawers.*

Fal. Peace, good Doll! do not speak like a

Death's-head; do not bid me remember mine end.

Doll. Sirrah, what humour is the prince of?

Fal. A good shallow young fellow: he would have made a good pantler; he would have chipped bread well.

Doll. They say Poins has a good wit.

Fal. He a good wit? hang him, baboon! his wit is as thick as Tewksbury mustard; there is no more conceit in him than is in a mallet.

Doll. Why does the prince love him so, then?

Fal. Because their legs are both of a bigness; and he plays at quoits well; and eats conger and fennel; and drinks off candles' ends for flap-dragons; and rides the wild mare with the boys; and jumps upon joint-stools; and swears with a good grace; and wears his boot very smooth, like unto the sign of the leg; and breeds no bate with telling of discreet stories; and such other gambol faculties he has, that show a weak mind and an able body, for the which the prince admits him: for the prince himself is such another; the weight of a hair will turn the scales between their avoirdupois.

P. Hen. Would not this nave of a wheel have his ears cut off?

Poins. Let us beat him before his whore.

P. Hen. Look, whether the withered elder hath not his poll clawed like a parrot.

Poins. Is it not strange that desire should so many years outlive performance?

Fal. Kiss me, Doll.

P. Hen. Saturn and Venus this year in conjunction! what says the almanac to that?

Poins. And, look, whether the fiery Trigon, his man, be not lisping to his master's old tables, his note-book, his counsel-keeper.

Fal. Thou dost give me flattering busses.

Doll. By my troth, I kiss thee with a most constant heart.

Fal. I am old, I am old.

Doll. I love thee better than I love e'er a scurvy young boy of them all.

Fal. What stuff wilt thou have a kirtle of? I shall receive money on Thursday; thou shalt have a cap to-morrow. A merry song, come: it grows late; we will to bed. Thou wilt forget me when I am gone.

Doll. By my troth, thou wilt set me a weeping, an thou sayest so: prove that ever I dress myself handsome till thy return:—well, harken the end.

Fal. Some sack, Francis.

P. Hen., Poins. Anon, anon, sir.

[*Advancing.*

Fal. Ha! a bastard son of the king's?—And art not thou Poins, his brother?

P. Hen. Why, thou globe of sinful continents, what a life dost thou lead!

Fal. A better than thou: I am a gentleman; thou art a drawer.

P. Hen. Very true, sir, and I come to draw you out by the ears.

Host. O, the Lord preserve thy good grace!

by my troth, welcome to London. Now, the Lord bless that sweet face of thine! O Jesu, are you come from Wales?

Fal. Thou whoreson mad compound of majesty,—by this light flesh and corrupt blood, thou art welcome.

[*Leaning his hand upon* DOLL.

Doll. How, you fat fool! I scorn you.

Poins. My lord, he will drive you out of your revenge, and turn all to a merriment, if you take not the heat.

P. Hen. You whoreson candle-mine, you, how vilely did you speak of me even now before this honest, virtuous, civil, gentlewoman!

Host. God's blessing on your good heart! and so she is, by my troth.

Fal. Didst thou hear me?

P. Hen. Yes; and you knew me, as you did when you ran away by Gadshill: you knew I was at your back, and spoke it on purpose to try my patience.

Fal. No, no, no; not so; I did not think thou wast within hearing.

P. Hen. I shall drive you, then, to confess the wilful abuse, and then I know how to handle you.

Fal. No abuse, Hal, on mine honour; no abuse.

P. Hen. Not! to dispraise me, and call me pantler, and bread-chipper, and I know not what!

Fal. No abuse, Hal.

Poins. No abuse!

Fal. No abuse, Ned, in the world; honest Ned, none. I dispraised him before the wicked, that the wicked might not fall in love with him;—in which doing, I have done the part of a careful friend and a true subject, and thy father is to give me thanks for it. No abuse, Hal;—none, Ned, none;—no, faith, boys, none.

P. Hen. See now, whether pure fear and entire cowardice doth not make thee wrong this virtuous gentlewoman to close with us? is she of the wicked? is thine hostess here of the wicked? or is thy boy of the wicked? or honest Bardolph, whose zeal burns in his nose, of the wicked?

Poins. Answer, thou dead elm, answer.

Fal. The fiend hath pricked down Bardolph irrecoverable; and his face is Lucifer's privy-kitchen, where he doth nothing but roast malt-worms. For the boy,—there is a good angel about him; but the devil outbids him too.

P. Hen. For the women?

Fal. For one of them,—she is in hell already, and burns, poor soul! For the other,—I owe her money; and whether she be damned for that, I know not.

Host. No, I warrant you.

Fal. No, I think thou art not; I think thou art quit for that. Marry, there is another indictment upon thee for suffering flesh to be eaten in thy house, contrary to the law; for the which I think thou wilt howl

Host. All victuallers do so: what's a joint of mutton or two in a whole Lent?

P. Hen. You, gentlewoman,—

Doll. What says your grace?

Fal. His grace says that which his flesh rebels against. *[Knocking within.*

Host. Who knocks so loud at door? Look to the door there, Francis.

Enter PETO.

P. Hen. Peto, how now! what news?

Pet. The king your father is at Westminster;
And there are twenty weak and wearied posts
Come from the north: and as I came along
I met and overtook a dozen captains,
Bare-headed, sweating, knocking at the taverns,
And asking every one for Sir John Falstaff.

P. Hen. By heaven, Poins, I feel me much to blame,
So idly to profane the precious time;
When tempest of commotion, like the south,
Borne with black vapour, doth begin to melt,
And drop upon our bare unarmed heads.
Give me my sword and cloak.—Falstaff, good-night.

[Exeunt P. HEN., POINS, PETO, *and* BARD.

Fal. Now comes in the sweetest morsel of the night, and we must hence, and leave it unpicked. *[Knocking within.]* More knocking at the door!

Re-enter BARDOLPH.

How now! what's the matter?

Bard. You must away to court, sir, presently; a dozen captains stay at door for you.

Fal. Pay the musicians, sirrah *[to the* Page]. —Farewell, hostess;—farewell, Doll.—You see, my good wenches, how men of merit are sought after: the undeserver may sleep, when the man of action is called on. Farewell, good wenches: if I be not sent away post, I will see you again ere I go.

Doll. I cannot speak;—if my heart be not ready to burst,—well, sweet Jack, have a care of thyself.

Fal. Farewell, farewell.

[Exeunt FALSTAFF *and* BARDOLPH.

Host. Well, fare thee well: I have known thee these twenty-nine years, come peascod-time; but an honester and truer-hearted man,— well, fare thee well.

Bard. *[Within.]* Mistress Tearsheet,—

Host. What's the matter?

Bard. *[Within.]* Bid Mistress Tearsheet come to my master.

Host. O, run, Doll, run; run, good Doll.

[Exeunt.

ACT III.

SCENE I.—WESTMINSTER. *A Room in the Palace.*

Enter KING HENRY *in his nightgown, with a Page*

K. Hen. Go call the Earls of Surrey and of Warwick;
But, ere they come, bid them o'er-read these letters,
And well consider of them: make good speed.

[Exit Page.

How many thousand of my poorest subjects
Are at this hour asleep!—O sleep, O gentle sleep,
Nature's soft nurse, how have I frighted thee,
That thou no more wilt weigh my eyelids down,
And steep my senses in forgetfulness?
Why rather, sleep, liest thou in smoky cribs,
Upon uneasy pallets stretching thee,
And hush'd with buzzing night-flies to thy slumber,
Than in the perfum'd chambers of the great,
Under high canopies of costly state,
And lull'd with sounds of sweetest melody?
O thou dull god, why liest thou with the vile
In loathsome beds, and leav'st the kingly couch
A watch-case or a common 'larum bell?
Wilt thou upon the high and giddy mast
Seal up the ship-boy's eyes, and rock his brains
In cradle of the rude imperious surge,
And in the visitation of the winds,
Who take the ruffian billows by the top,
Curling their monstrous heads, and hanging them
With deafening clamour in the slippery shrouds,
That, with the hurly, death itself awakes?
Canst thou, O partial sleep, give thy repose
To the wet sea-boy in an hour so rude;
And in the calmest and most stillest night,
With all appliances and means to boot,
Deny it to a king? Then, happy low, lie down!
Uneasy lies the head that wears a crown.

Enter WARWICK *and* SURREY.

War. Many good-morrows to your majesty!

K. Hen. Is it good-morrow, lords?

War. 'Tis one o'clock, and past.

K. Hen. Why, then, good-morrow to you all, my lords.
Have you read o'er the letters that I sent you?

War. We have, my liege.

K. Hen. Then you perceive the body of our kingdom
How foul it is; what rank diseases grow,
And with what danger, near the heart of it.

War. It is but as a body yet distemper'd;
Which to his former strength may be restor'd
With good advice and little medicine:—
My lord Northumberland will soon be cool'd.

K. Hen. O God! that one might read the book of fate,
And see the revolution of the times
Make mountains level, and the continent,—
Weary of solid firmness,—melt itself
Into the sea! and, other times, to see
The beachy girdle of the ocean
Too wide for Neptune's hips; how chances mock,
And changes fill the cup of alteration

With divers liquors! Oh, if this were seen,
The happiest youth,—viewing his progress
    through,
What perils past, what crosses to ensue,—
Would shut the book, and sit him down and die.
'Tis not ten years gone   [friends,
Since Richard and Northumberland, great
Did feast together, and in two years after
Were they at wars. It is but eight years since
This Percy was the man nearest my soul;
Who like a brother toil'd in my affairs,
And laid his love and life under my foot;
Yea, for my sake, even to the eyes of Richard
Gave him defiance. But which of you was by,—
You, cousin Nevil, as I may remember,—
              [*To* WARWICK.
When Richard,—with his eye brimful of tears,
Then check'd and rated by Northumberland,—
Did speak these words, now prov'd a prophecy?
*Northumberland, thou ladder by the which
My cousin Bolingbroke ascends my throne,*—
Though then, God knows, I had no such intent,
But that necessity so bow'd the state
That I and greatness were compell'd to kiss:—
The time shall come, thus did he follow it,
*The time will come, that foul sin, gathering head,
Shall break into corruption*—so went on,
Foretelling this same time's condition,
And the division of our amity.
  War. There is a history in all men's lives,
Figuring the nature of the times deceas'd;
The which observ'd, a man may prophesy,
With a near aim, of the main chance of things
As yet not come to life, which in their seeds
And weak beginnings lie intreasured.
Such things become the hatch and brood of
    time;
And, by the necessary form of this,
King Richard might create a perfect guess
That great Northumberland, then false to him,
Would of that seed grow to a greater falseness;
Which should not find a ground to root upon,
Unless on you.
  K. Hen. Are these things, then, necessities?
Then let us meet them like necessities;—
And that the same word even now cries out
    on us:
They say the bishop and Northumberland
Are fifty thousand strong.
  War.   It cannot be, my lord;
Rumor doth double, like the voice and echo,
The numbers of the fear'd. Please it your grace
To go to bed. Upon my life, my lord,
The powers that you already have sent forth
Shall bring this prize in very easily.
To comfort you the more, I have receiv'd
A certain instance that Glendower is dead.
Your majesty hath been this fortnight ill;
And these unseason'd hours perforce must add
Unto your sickness.
  K. Hen.   I will take your counsel:
And, were these inward wars once out of hand,
We would, dear lords, unto the Holy Land.
                   [*Exeunt.*

SCENE II.—*Court before* JUSTICE SHALLOW'S
    House in Gloucestershire.

Enter SHALLOW *and* SILENCE, *meeting;*
  MOULDY, SHADOW, WART, FEEBLE, BULL-
  CALF, *and* Servants, *behind.*

  Shal. Come on, come on, come on, sir; give
me your hand, sir, give me your hand, sir: an
early stirrer, by the rood. And how doth my
good cousin Silence?
  Sil. Good-morrow, good cousin Shallow.
  Shal. And how doth my cousin, your bedfellow? and your fairest daughter and mine, my
god-daughter Ellen?
  Sil. Alas, a black ousel, cousin Shallow!
  Shal. By yea and nay, sir, I dare say my
cousin William is become a good scholar: he
is at Oxford still, is he not?
  Sil. Indeed, sir, to my cost.
  Shal. He must, then, to the inns of court
shortly: I was once of Clement's-inn; where I
think they will talk of mad Shallow yet.
  Sil. You were called lusty Shallow then,
cousin.
  Shal. By the mass, I was called anything;
and I would have done anything indeed, too,
and roundly too. There was I, and little John
Doit of Staffordshire, and black George Bare,
and Francis Pickbone, and Will Squele a Cotswold man,—you had not four such swinge-
bucklers in all the inns of court again: and, I
may say to you, we knew where the *bona-robas*
were, and had the best of them all at commandment. Then was Jack Falstaff, now Sir John,
a boy, and page to Thomas Mowbray, Duke of
Norfolk.
  Sil. This Sir John, cousin, that comes hither
anon about soldiers?
  Shal. The same Sir John, the very same. I
saw him break Skogan's head at the court gate,
when he was a crack not thus high: and the
very same day did I fight with one Sampson
Stockfish, a fruiterer, behind Gray's-inn. Jesu,
Jesu, the mad days that I have spent! and to see
how many of mine old acquaintance are dead!
  Sil. We shall all follow, cousin.
  Shal. Certain, 'tis certain; very sure, very
sure: death, as the Psalmist saith, is certain to
all; all shall die.—How a good yoke of bullocks
at Stamford fair?
  Sil. Truly, cousin, I was not there.
  Shal. Death is certain.—Is old Double of
your town living yet?
  Sil. Dead, sir.
  Shal. Jesu, Jesu, dead!—he drew a good
bow; and dead!—he shot a fine shoot:—John
of Gaunt loved him well, and betted much
money on his head. Dead!—he would have
clapp'd in the clout at twelve score, and carried
you a forehand shaft a fourteen and fourteen
and a half, that it would have done a man's
heart good to see.—How a score of ewes now?
  Sil. Thereafter as they be: a score of good
ewes may be worth ten pounds.

Shal. And is old Double dead?

Sil. Here come two of Sir John Falstaff's men, as I think.

Enter BARDOLPH *and one with him.*

Bard. Good-morrow, honest gentlemen: I beseech you, which is Justice Shallow?

Shal. I am Robert Shallow, sir, a poor esquire of this county, and one of the king's justices of the peace: what is your good pleasure with me?

Bard. My captain, sir, commends him to you; my captain, Sir John Falstaff,—a tall gentleman, by heaven, and a most gallant leader.

Shal. He greets me well, sir; I knew him a good backsword man: how doth the good knight? may I ask how my lady his wife doth?

Bard. Sir, pardon; a soldier is better accommodated than with a wife.

Shal. It is well said, in faith, sir; and it is well said indeed too. Better accommodated!—it is good; yea, indeed, is it: good phrases are surely, and ever were, very commendable. Accommodated!—it comes from *accommodo:* very good; a good phrase.

Bard. Pardon me, sir; I have heard the word. Phrase call you it? By this good day, I know not the phrase; but I will maintain the word with my sword to be a soldier-like word, and a word of exceeding good command. Accommodated; that is, when a man is, as they say, accommodated; or, when a man is, being, whereby he may be thought to be accommodated; which is an excellent thing.

Shal. It is very just.—Look, here comes good Sir John.

Enter FALSTAFF.

Give me your good hand, give me your worship's good hand: by my troth, you look well and bear your years very well: welcome, good Sir John.

Fal. I am glad to see you well, good Master Robert Shallow:—Master Surecard, as I think?

Shal. No, Sir John, it is my cousin Silence, in commission with me.

Fal. Good Master Silence, it well befits you should be of the peace.

Sil. Your good worship is welcome.

Fal. Fie! this is hot weather.—Gentlemen, have you provided me here half a dozen sufficient men?

Shal. Marry, have we, sir. Will you sit?

Fal. Let me see them, I beseech you.

Shal. Where's the roll? where's the roll? where's the roll?—let me see, let me see. So, so, so, so:—yea, marry, sir:—Ralph Mouldy!—let them appear as I call; let them do so, let them do so.—Let me see; where is Mouldy?

Moul. Here, an't please you.

Shal. What think you, Sir John? a good limbed fellow; young, strong, and of good friends.

Fal. Is thy name Mouldy?

Moul. Yea, an't please you.

Fal. 'Tis the more time thou wert used.

Shal. Ha, ha, ha! most excellent, i' faith! things that are mouldy lack use: very singular good!—in faith, well said, Sir John; very well said.

Fal. Prick him. [*To* SHALLOW.

Moul. I was pricked well enough before, an you could have let me alone: my old dame will be undone now for one to do her husbandry and her drudgery: you need not to have pricked me; there are other men fitter to go out than I.

Fal. Go to; peace, Mouldy; you shall go. Mouldy, it is time you were spent.

Moul. Spent!

Shal. Peace, fellow, peace; stand aside: know you where you are?—For the other, Sir John:—let me see;—Simon Shadow!

Fal. Yea, marry, let me have him to sit under: he's like to be a cold soldier.

Shal. Where's Shadow?

Shad. Here, sir.

Fal. Shadow, whose son art thou?

Shad. My mother's son, sir.

Fal. Thy mother's son! like enough; and thy father's shadow: so the son of the female is the shadow of the male: it is often so, indeed; but not much of the father's substance.

Shal. Do you like him, Sir John?

Fal. Shadow will serve for summer,—prick him; for we have a number of shadows to fill up the muster-book.

Shal. Thomas Wart!

Fal. **Where's** he?

Wart. Here, sir.

Fal. Is thy name Wart?

Wart. Yea, sir.

Fal. Thou are a very ragged wart.

Shal. Shall I prick him, Sir John?

Fal. It were superfluous; for his apparel is built upon his back, and the whole frame stands upon pins: prick him no more.

Shal. Ha, ha, ha!—you can do it, sir; you can do it: I commend you well.—Francis Feeble!

Fee. Here, sir.

Fal. What trade art thou, Feeble?

Fee. A woman's tailor, sir.

Shal. Shall I prick him, sir?

Fal. You may: but if he had been a man's tailor, he would have pricked you.—Wilt thou make as many holes in an enemy's battle as thou hast done in a woman's petticoat?

Fee. I will do my good will, sir; you can have no more.

Fal. Well said, good woman's tailor! well said, courageous Feeble! Thou wilt be as valiant as the wrathful dove or most magnanimous mouse.—Prick the woman's tailor well, Master Shallow; deep, Master Shallow.

Fee. I would Wart might have gone, sir.

Fal. I would thou wert a man's tailor, that thou mightst mend him, and make him fit to go. I cannot put him to a private soldier, that is the leader of so many thousands: let that suffice, most forcible Feeble.

Fee. It shall suffice, sir.

Fal. I am bound to thee, Reverend Feeble.—Who is next?

Shal. Peter Bullcalf of the green!

Fal. Yea, marry, let us see Bullcalf.

Bull. Here, sir.

Fal. 'Fore God, a likely fellow!—Come, prick me, Bullcalf, till he roar again.

Bull. O lord! good my lord captain,—

Fal. What, dost thou roar before thou art pricked?

Bull. O lord, sir! I am a diseased man.

Fal. What disease hast thou?

Bull. A whoreson cold, sir,—a cough, sir,—which I caught with ringing in the king's affairs upon his coronation day, sir.

Fal. Come, thou shalt go to the wars in a gown; we will have away thy cold; and I will take such order that thy friends shall ring for thee.—Is here all?

Shal. Here is two more called than your number; you must have but four here, sir:—and so, I pray you, go in with me to dinner.

Fal. Come, I will go drink with you, but I cannot tarry dinner. I am glad to see you, by my troth, Master Shallow.

Shal. O, Sir John, do you remember since we lay all night in the windmill in Saint George's Fields?

Fal. No more of that, good Master Shallow, no more of that.

Shal. Ha, it was a merry night. And is Jane Nightwork alive?

Fal. She lives, Master Shallow.

Shal. She never could away with me.

Fal. Never, never; she would always say she could not abide Master Shallow.

Shal. By the mass, I could anger her to the heart. She was then a bona-roba. Doth she hold her own well?

Fal. Old, old, Master Shallow.

Shal. Nay, she must be old; she cannot choose but be old; certain she's old; and had Robin Nightwork, by old Nightwork, before I came to Clement's-inn.

Sil. That's fifty-five year ago.

Shal. Ha, cousin Silence, that thou hadst seen that that this knight and I have seen!—Ha, Sir John, said I well?

Fal. We have heard the chimes at midnight, Master Shallow.

Shal. That we have, that we have, that we have; in faith, Sir John, we have: our watch-word was, *Hem, boys!*—Come, let's to dinner; come, let's to dinner:—O, the days that we have seen!—come, come.

[*Exeunt* FAL., SHAL., *and* SIL.

Bull. Good Master Corporate Bardolph, stand my friend; and here is four Harry ten shillings in French crowns for you. In very truth, sir, I had as lief be hanged, sir, as go:

and yet, for mine own part, sir, I do not care; but rather, because I am unwilling, and, for mine own part, have a desire to stay with my friends; else, sir, I did not care for mine own part, so much.

Bard. Go to; stand aside.

Moul. And, good master corporal captain, for my old dame's sake, stand my friend: she has nobody to do anything about her when I am gone; and she is old, and cannot help herself: you shall have forty, sir.

Bard. Go to; stand aside.

Fee. By my troth, I care not; a man can die but once; we owe God a death: I'll ne'er bear a base mind: an't be my destiny, so; an't be not, so: no man's too good to serve his prince; and, let it go which way it will, he that dies this year is quit for the next.

Bard. Well said; thou'rt a good fellow.

Fee. Faith, I'll bear no base mind.

Re-enter FALSTAFF *and* Justices.

Fal. Come, sir, which men shall I have?

Shal. Four of which you please.

Bard. Sir, a word with you:—I have three pound to free Mouldy and Bullcalf.

Fal. Go to; well.

Shal. Come, Sir John, which four will you have?

Fal. Do you choose for me.

Shal. Marry, then,—Mouldy, Bullcalf, Feeble, and Shadow.

Fal. Mouldy and Bullcalf:—for you, Mouldy, stay at home till you are past service: and for your part, Bullcalf,—grow till you come unto it: I will none of you.

Shal. Sir John, Sir John, do not yourself wrong: they are your likeliest men, and I would have you served with the best.

Fal. Will you tell me, Master Shallow, how to choose a man? Care I for the limb, the thews, the stature, bulk, and big assemblance of a man! Give me the spirit, Master Shallow. —Here's Wart;—you see what a ragged appearance it is: he shall charge you and discharge you, with the motion of a pewterer's hammer; come off, and on, swifter than he that gibbets on the brewer's bucket. And this same half-faced fellow, Shadow,—give me this man: he presents no mark to the enemy; the foeman may with as great aim level at the edge of a penknife. And, for a retreat,—how swiftly will this Feeble, the woman's tailor, run off! O, give me the spare men, and spare me the great one.—Put me a caliver into Wart's hand, Bardolph.

Bard. Hold, Wart, traverse; thus, thus, thus.

Fal. Come, manage me your caliver. So:—very well:—go to:—very good:—exceeding good.—O, give me always a little, lean, old, chapped, bald shot.—Well said, i' faith, Wart; thou'rt a good scab: hold, there's a tester for thee.

Shal. He is not his craft's-master, he doth not do it right. I remember at Mile-end Green, —when I lay at Clement's-inn,—I was then Sir Dagonet in Arthur's show,—there was a little quiver fellow, and he would manage you his piece thus; and he would about and about, and come you in and come you in: *rah, tah, tah,* would he say; *bounce* would he say; and away again would he go, and again would he come: —I shall never see such a fellow.

Fal. These fellows will do well, Master Shallow.—God keep you, Master Silence: I will not use many words with you.—Fare you well, gentlemen both: I thank you: I must a dozen mile to-night.—Bardolph, give the soldiers coats.

Shal. Sir John, heaven bless you, and prosper your affairs, and send us peace! as you return, visit my house; let our old acquaintance be renewed: peradventure I will with you to the court.

Fal. 'Fore God, I would you would, Master Shallow.

Shal. Go to; I have spake at a word. Fare you well. [*Exeunt* SHAL. *and* SIL.

Fal. Fare you well, gentle gentlemen. On, Bardolph; lead the men away. [*Exeunt* BARDOLPH, Recruits, &c.] As I return, I will fetch off these justices: I do see the bottom of Justice Shallow. Lord, Lord, how subject we old men are to this vice of lying! This same starved Justice hath done nothing but prate to me of the wildness of his youth, and the feats he hath done about Turnbull Street; and every third word a lie, duer paid to the hearer than the Turk's tribute. I do remember him at Clement's-inn, like a man made after supper of a cheese-paring: when he was naked, he was, for all the world, like a forked radish, with a head fantastically carved upon it with a knife: he was so forlorn that his dimensions to any thick sight were invincible: he was the very genius of famine: yet lecherous as a monkey, and the whores called him mandrake: he came ever in the reward of the fashion; and sung those tunes to the overscutched huswifes that he heard the carmen whistle, and sware they were his fancies or his good-nights. And now is this Vice's dagger become a squire, and talks as familiarly of John of Gaunt as if he had been sworn brother to him; and I'll be sworn he never saw him but once in the Tilt-yard; and then he burst his head for crowding among the marshal's men. I saw it, and told John of Gaunt he beat his own name; for you might have thrust him and all his apparel into an ell-skin; the case of a treble hautboy was a mansion for him, a court: —and now has he land and beeves. Well, I will be acquainted with him if I return; and it shall go hard but I will make him a philosopher's two stones to me: if the young dace be a bait for the old pike, I see no reason, in the law of nature, but I may snap at him. Let time shape, and there an end. [*Exit.*

ACT IV.

SCENE I.—*A Forest in Yorkshire.*

Enter the ARCHBISHOP OF YORK, MOWBRAY, HASTINGS, *and others.*

Arch. What is this forest call'd?

Hast. 'Tis Gualtree Forest, an't shall please your grace.

Arch. Here stand, my lords; and send discoverers forth
To know the numbers of our enemies.

Hast. We have sent forth already.

Arch.   'Tis well done.
My friends and brethren in these great affairs,
I must acquaint you that I have receiv'd
New-dated letters from Northumberland;
Their cold intent, tenour, and substance, thus:—
Here doth he wish his person, with such powers
As might hold sortance with his quality,
The which he could not levy; whereupon
He is retir'd, to ripe his growing fortunes,
To Scotland; and concludes in hearty prayers
That your attempts may over-live the hazard
And fearful meeting of their opposite.

Mowb. Thus do the hopes we have in him touch ground,
And dash themselves to pieces.

Enter a Messenger.

Hast.   Now, what news?

Mess. West of this forest, scarcely off a mile,
In goodly form comes on the enemy;
And, by the ground they hide, I judge their number
Upon or near the rate of thirty thousand.

Mowb. The just proportion that we gave them out.
Let us sway on, and face them in the field.

Arch. What well-appointed leader fronts us here?

Mowb. I think it is my Lord of Westmoreland.

Enter WESTMORELAND.

West. Health and fair greeting from our general
The prince, Lord John and Duke of Lancaster.

Arch. Say, on, my Lord of Westmoreland, in peace,
What doth concern your coming.

West.   Then, my lord,
Unto your grace do I in chief address
The substance of my speech. If that rebellion
Came like itself, in base and abject routs,
Led on by bloody youth, guarded with rags,
And countenanc'd by boys and beggary,—
I say, if damn'd commotion so appear'd,
In his true, native, and most proper shape,
You, reverend father, and these noble lords,
Had not been here, to dress the ugly form
Of base and bloody insurrection
With your fair honours. You, lord archbishop,—

Whose see is by a civil peace maintain'd;
Whose beard the silver hand of peace hath
    touch'd;
Whose learning and good letters peace hath
    tutor'd;
Whose white investments figure innocence,
The dove and very blessed spirit of peace,—
Wherefore do you so ill translate yourself
Out of the speech of peace, that bears such
    grace,
Into the harsh and boisterous tongue of war;
Turning your books to greaves, your ink to
    blood,
Your pens to lances, and your tongue divine
To a loud trumpet and a point of war?
   Arch. Wherefore do I this?—so the question
    stands.
Briefly to this end:—we are all diseas'd;
And with our surfeiting and wanton hours
Have brought ourselves into a burning fever,
And we must bleed for it: of which disease
Our late king, Richard, being infected, died.
But, my most noble Lord of Westmoreland,
I take not on me here as a physician;
Nor do I, as an enemy to peace,
Troop in the throngs of military men;
But, rather, show awhile like fearful war,
To diet rank minds sick of happiness,
And purge the obstructions which begin to stop
Our very veins of life. Hear me more plainly.
I have in equal balance justly weigh'd
What wrongs our arms may do, what wrongs
    we suffer,
And find our griefs heavier than our offences.
We see which way the stream of time doth run,
And are enforc'd from our most quiet sphere
By the rough torrent of occasion;
And have the summary of all our griefs,
When time shall serve, to show in articles;
Which long ere this we offer'd to the king,
And might by no suit gain our audience:
When we are wrong'd, and would unfold our
    griefs,
We are denied access unto his person
Even by those men that most have done us
    wrong.
The dangers of the days but newly gone,—
Whose memory is written on the earth
With yet appearing blood,—and the examples
Of every minute's instance,—present now,—
Have put us in these ill-beseeming arms;
Not to break peace, or any branch of it,
But to establish here a peace indeed,
Concurring both in name and quality.
   West. When ever yet was your appeal
    denied;
Wherein have you been galled by the king;
What peer hath been suborn'd to grate on
    you;—
That you should seal this lawless bloody book
Of forg'd rebellion with a seal divine,
And consecrate commotion's bitter edge?
   Arch. My brother general, the common-
    wealth,

To brother born an household cruelty,
I make my quarrel in particular.
   West. There is no need of any such redress;
Or if there were, it not belongs to you.
   Mowb. Why not to him in part, and to us all
That feel the bruises of the days before,
And suffer the condition of these times
To lay a heavy and unequal hand
Upon our honours?
   West.   O, my good Lord Mowbray,
Construe the times to their necessities,
And you shall say indeed, it is the time,
And not the king, that doth you injuries.
Yet, for your part, it not appears to me,
Either from the king or in the present time,
That you should have an inch of any ground
To build a grief on: were you not restor'd
To all the Duke of Norfolk's signiories,
Your noble and right-well-remember'd father's?
   Mowb. What thing, in honour, had my
    father lost,
That need to be reviv'd and breath'd in me?
The king, that lov'd him, as the state stood
    then,
Was, force perforce, compell'd to banish him,
And then that Henry Bolingbroke and he,—
Being mounted and both roused in their seats,
Their neighing coursers daring of the spur,
Their armed staves in charge, their beavers
    down,
Their eyes of fire sparkling through sights of
    steel,
And the loud trumpet blowing them together,—
Then, then, when there was nothing could have
    stay'd
My father from the breast of Bolingbroke,
O, when the king did throw his warder down,
His own life hung upon the staff he threw;
Then threw he down himself, and all their lives
That by indictment and by dint of sword
Have since miscarried under Bolingbroke.
   West. You speak, Lord Mowbray, now you
    know not what.
The Earl of Hereford was reputed then
In England the most valiant gentleman:
Who knows on whom fortune would then have
    smil'd?
But if your father had been victor there,
He ne'er had borne it out of Coventry,
For all the country, in a general voice,
Cried hate upon him; and all their prayers and
    love
Were set on Hereford, whom they doted on,
And bless'd and grac'd indeed, more than the
    king.
But this is mere digression from my purpose.—
Here come I from our princely general
To know your griefs; to tell you from his grace
That he will give you audience; and wherein
It shall appear that your demands are just,
You shall enjoy them,—everything set off
That might so much as think you enemies.
   Mowb. But he hath forc'd us to compel this
    offer;

And it proceeds from policy, not love.

West. Mowbray, you overween to take it so;
This offer comes from mercy, not from fear:
For, lo! within a ken, our army lies:
Upon mine honour, all too confident
To give admittance to a thought of fear.
Our battle is more full of names than yours,
Our men more perfect in the use of arms,
Our armour all as strong, our cause the best;
Then reason will our hearts should be as good:
Say you not, then, our offer is compell'd.

Mowb. Well, by my will we shall admit no
parley.

West. That argues but the shame of your
offence:
A rotten case abides no handling.

Hast. Hath the Prince John a full commis-
sion,
In very ample virtue of his father,
To hear and absolutely to determine
Of what conditions we shall stand upon?

West. That is intended in the general's
name:
I muse you make so slight a question.

Arch. Then take, my Lord of Westmoreland,
this schedule,
For this contains our general grievances:
Each several article herein redress'd,
All members of our cause, both here and hence,
That are insinew'd to this action,
Acquitted by a true substantial form,
And present execution of our wills
To us and to our purposes consign'd,—
We come within our awful banks again,
And knit our powers to the arm of peace.

West. This will I show the general. Please
you, lords,
In sight of both our battles we may meet;
And either end in peace,—which God so
frame!—
Or to the place of difference call the swords
Which must decide it.

Arch.   My lord, we will do so.
                         [*Exit* WESTMORELAND.

Mowb. There is a thing within my bosom
tells me
That no conditions of our peace can stand.

Hast. Fear you not that: if we can make our
peace
Upon such large terms and so absolute
As our conditions shall consist upon,
Our peace shall stand as firm as rocky moun-
tains.

Mowb. Ay, but our valuation shall be such,
That every slight and false-derived cause,
Yea, every idle, nice, and wanton reason,
Shall to the king taste of this action;
That, were our royal faiths martyrs in love,
We shall be winnow'd with so rough a wind
That even our corn shall seem as light as chaff,
And good from bad find no partition.

Arch. No, no, my lord. Note this,—the king
is weary
Of dainty and such picking grievances:

For he hath found, to end one doubt by death
Revives two greater in the heirs of life;
And therefore will he wipe his tables clean,
And keep no tell-tale to his memory,
That may repeat and history his loss
To new remembrance: for full well he knows
He cannot so precisely weed this land
As his misdoubts present occasion:
His foes are so enrooted with his friends
That, plucking to unfix an enemy,
He doth unfasten so and shake a friend.
So that this land, like an offensive wife
That hath enrag'd him on to offer strokes,
As he is striking, holds his infant up,
And hangs resolv'd correction in the arm
That was uprear'd to execution.

Hast. Besides, the king hath wasted all his
rods
On late offenders, that he now doth lack
The very instruments of chastisement:
So that his power, like to a fangless lion,
May offer, but not hold.

Arch.   'Tis very true:
And therefore be assur'd, my good lord mar-
shal,
If we do now make our atonement well,
Our peace will, like a broken limb united,
Grow stronger for the breaking.

Mowb.   Be it so,
Here is return'd my Lord of Westmoreland.

Re-enter WESTMORELAND.

West. The prince is here at hand: pleaseth
your lordship
To meet his grace just distance 'tween our
armies?

Mowb. Your grace of York, in God's name,
then, set forward.

Arch. Before, and greet his grace:—my lord,
we come.   [*Exeunt.*

SCENE II.—*Another part of the Forest.*

Enter, from one side, MOWBRAY, *the* ARCH-
BISHOP, HASTINGS, *and others: from the other
side,* PRINCE JOHN OF LANCASTER, WEST-
MORELAND, *Officers and* Attendants.

P. John. You are well encounter'd here, my
cousin Mowbray:
Good-day to you, gentle lord archbishop;
And so to you, Lord Hastings,—and to all.—
My Lord of York, it better show'd with you
When that your flock, assembled by the bell,
Encircled you to hear with reverence
Your exposition on the holy text,
Than now to see you here an iron man,
Cheering a rout of rebels with your drum,
Turning the word to sword, and life to death.
That man that sits within a monarch's heart,
And ripens in the sunshine of his favour,
Would he abuse the countenance of the king,
Alack, what mischiefs might he set abroach
In shadow of such greatness! With you, lord
bishop,
It is even so. Who hath not heard it spoken

How deep you were within the books of God?
To us the speaker in his parliament;
To us the imagin'd voice of God himself;
The very opener and intelligencer
Between the grace, the sanctities of heaven,
And our dull workings. O, who shall believe
But you misuse the reverence of your place,
Employ the countenance and grace of heaven,
As a false favourite doth his prince's name,
In deeds dishonourable? You have taken up,
Under the counterfeited seal of God,
The subjects of his substitute, my father,
And both against the peace of heaven and him
Have here up-swarm'd them.

Arch.   Good my Lord of Lancaster,
I am not here against your father's peace;
But as I told my lord of Westmoreland,
The time misorder'd doth, in common sense,
Crowd us and crush us to this monstrous form,
To hold our safety up. I sent your grace
The parcels and particulars of our grief,—
The which hath been with scorn shov'd from
the court,—
Whereon this Hydra son of war is born;
Whose dangerous eyes may well be charm'd
asleep
With grant of our most just and right desires,
And true obedience, of this madness cur'd,
Stoop tamely to the foot of majesty.

Mowb. If not, we ready are to try our fortunes
To the last man.

Hast.   And though we here fall down,
We have supplies to second our attempt:
If they miscarry, theirs shall second them;
And so success of mischief shall be born,
And heir from heir shall hold this quarrel up
Whiles England shall have generation.

P. John. You are too shallow, Hastings,
much too shallow,
To sound the bottom of the after-times.

West. Pleaseth your grace to answer them
directly,
How far-forth you do like their articles.

P. John. I like them all, and do allow them
well;
And swear here, by the honour of my blood,
My father's purposes have been mistook;
And some about him have too lavishly
Wrested his meaning and authority.—
My lord; these griefs shall be with speed re-
dress'd;
Upon my soul, they shall. If this may please
you,
Discharge your powers unto their several coun-
ties,
As we will ours: and here, between the armies,
Let's drink together friendly, and embrace,
That all their eyes may bear those tokens home
Of our restored love and amity.

Arch. I take your princely word for these
redresses.

P. John. I give it you, and will maintain my
word:

And thereupon I drink unto your grace.

Hast. Go, captain [_to an_ Officer], and deliver
to the army
This news of peace; let them have pay, and
part:
I know it will well please them. Hie thee,
captain.   [_Exit_ Officer.

Arch. To you, my noble Lord of Westmoreland.

West. I pledge your grace; and, if you knew
what pains
I have bestow'd to breed this present peace,
You would drink freely: but my love to you
Shall show itself more openly hereafter.

Arch. I do not doubt you.

West.   I am glad of it.—
Health to my lord and gentle cousin, Mowbray.

Mowb. You wish me health in very happy
season;
For I am, on the sudden, something ill.

Arch. Against ill chances men are ever
merry;
But heaviness foreruns the good event.

West. Therefore be merry, coz; since sudden
sorrow
Serves to say thus,—Some good thing comes
to-morrow.

Arch. Believe me, I am passing light in spirit.

Mowb. So much the worse, if your own rule
be true.   [_Shouts within._

P. John. The word of peace is render'd;
hark, how they shout!

Mowb. This had been cheerful after victory.

Arch. A peace is of the nature of a conquest;
For then both parties nobly are subdued,
And neither party loser.

P. John.   Go, my lord,
And let our army be discharged too.
                  [_Exit_ WESTMORELAND.
And, good my lord, so please you let your trains
March by us, that we may peruse the men
We should have cop'd withal.

Arch.   Go, good Lord Hastings,
And, ere they be dismissed, let them march by.
                  [_Exit_ HASTINGS.

P. John. I trust, my lords, we shall lie to-
night together.

Re-enter WESTMORELAND.

Now, cousin, wherefore stands our army still?

West. The leaders, having charge from you
to stand,
Will not go off until they hear you speak.

P. John. They know their duties.

Re-enter HASTINGS.

Hast. My lord, our army is dispers'd already:
Like youthful steers unyok'd, they take their
courses   [up,
East, west, north, south; or, like a school broke
Each hurries toward his home and sporting-
place.

West. Good tidings, my Lord Hastings; for
the which

I do arrest thee, traitor, of high treason:—
And you, lord archbishop,—and you, Lord
Mowbray.—
Of capital treason I attach you both.

Mowb. Is this proceeding just and honourable?

West. Is your assembly so?

Arch. Will you thus break your faith?

P. John. I pawn'd thee none:
I promis'd you redress of these same grievances
Whereof you did complain; which, by mine
honour,
I will perform with a most Christian care.
But for you, rebels,—look to taste the due
Meet for rebellion and such acts as yours.
Most shallowly did you these arms commence,
Fondly brought here, and foolishly sent hence.—
Strike up our drums, pursue the scatter'd stray:
God, and not we, hath safely fought to-day.—
Some guard these traitors to the block of death,
Treason's true bed and yielder-up of breath.

[*Exeunt.*

SCENE III.—*Another part of the Forest.*

Alarums: excursions. Enter FALSTAFF *and*
COLEVILE, *meeting.*

Fal. What's your name, sir? of what condition are you, and of what place, I pray?

Cole. I am a knight, sir; and my name is
Colevile of the dale.

Fal. Well, then, Colevile is your name, a
knight is your degree, and your place the dale:
Colevile shall be still your name, a traitor your
degree, and the dungeon your dale,—a dale
deep enough; so shall you be still Colevile of
the dale.

Cole. Are not you Sir John Falstaff?

Fal. As good a man as he, sir, whoe'er I am.
Do ye yield, sir? or shall I sweat for you? If
I do sweat, they are the drops of thy lovers, and
they weep for thy death; therefore rouse up
fear and trembling, and do observance to my
mercy.

Cole. I think you are Sir John Falstaff; and
in that thought yield me.

Fal. I have a whole school of tongues in this
belly of mine; and not a tongue of them all
speaks any other word but my name. An I had
but a belly of any indifferency, I were simply
the most active fellow in Europe: my womb,
my womb, my womb undoes me.—Here comes
our general.

Enter PRINCE JOHN OF LANCASTER,
WESTMORELAND, *and others.*

P. John. The heat is past, follow no farther
now:—
Call in the powers, good cousin Westmoreland.

[*Exit* WESTMORELAND.

Now, Falstaff, where have you been all this
while?
When everything is ended, then you come:
These tardy tricks of yours will, on my life,
One time or other break some gallows' back.

Fal. I would be sorry, my lord, but it should
be thus: I never knew yet but rebuke and check
was the reward of valour. Do you think me a
swallow, an arrow, or a bullet? have I, in my
poor and old motion, the expedition of thought?
I have speeded hither with the very extremest
inch of possibility; I have foundered nine-score
and odd posts: and here, travel tainted as I am,
have, in my pure and immaculate valour, taken
Sir John Colevile of the dale, a most furious
knight and valorous enemy. But what of that?
he saw me, and yielded; that I may justly say
with the hook-nosed fellow of Rome,—I came,
saw, and overcame.

P. John. It was more of his courtesy than
your deserving.

Fal. I know not:—here he is, and here I
yield him: and I beseech your grace, let it be
booked with the rest of this day's deeds; or,
by the Lord, I will have it in a particular ballad
else, with mine own picture on the top of it,
Colevile kissing my foot: to the which course
if I be enforced, if you do not all show like gilt
two-pences to me, and I, in the clear sky of
fame, o'ershine you as much as the full moon
doth the cinders of the element, which show
like pins' heads to her, believe not the word of
the noble: therefore let me have right, and let
desert mount.

P. John. Thine's too heavy to mount.

Fal. Let it shine, then.

P. John. Thine's too thick to shine.

Fal. Let it do something, my good lord, that
may do me good, and call it what you will.

P. John. Is thy name Colevile?

Cole. It is, my lord.

P. John. A famous rebel art thou, Colevile.

Fal. And a famous true subject took him.

Cole. I am, my lord, but as my betters are
That led me hither: had they been rul'd by me,
You should have won them dearer than you
have.

Fal. I know not how they sold themselves:
but thou, like a kind fellow, gavest thyself
away gratis; and I thank thee for thee.

Re-enter WESTMORELAND.

P. John. Now, have you left pursuit?

West. Retreat is made, and execution stay'd.

P. John. Send Colevile, with his confeder-
ates,
To York, to present execution:—
Blunt, lead him hence; and see you guard him
sure. [*Exeunt some with* COLEVILE.
And now despatch we toward the court, my
lords.
I hear the king, my father, is sore sick:
Our news shall go before us to his majesty,—
Which, cousin, you shall bear,—to comfort him;
And we with sober speed will follow you.

Fal. My lord, I beseech you, give me leave
to go
Through Glostershire: and, when you come to
court,

Stand, my good lord, pray, in your good report.

P. John. Fare you well, Falstaff: I, in my condition,
Shall better speak of you than you deserve.

                                [Exeunt all but FAL.

Fal. I would you had but the wit: 'twere better than your dukedom. Good faith, this same young sober-blooded boy doth not love me; nor a man cannot make him laugh;—but that's no marvel; he drinks no wine. There's never any of these demure boys come to any proof; for thin drink doth so over-cool their blood, and making many fish-meals, that they fall into a kind of male green-sickness; and then, when they marry, they get wenches: they are generally fools and cowards;—which some of us should be too, but for inflammation. A good sherris-sack hath a twofold operation in it. It ascends me into the brain; dries me there all the foolish and dull and crudy vapours which environ it; makes it apprehensive, quick, forgetive, full of nimble, fiery, and delectable shapes; which delivered o'er to the voice,—the tongue,—which is the birth, becomes excellent wit. The second property of your excellent sherris is,—the warming of the blood; which, before cold and settled, left the liver white and pale, which is the badge of pusillanimity and cowardice: but the sherris warms it, and makes it course from the inwards to the parts extreme: it illumineth the face; which, as a beacon, gives warning to all the rest of this little kingdom, man, to arm; and then the vital commoners and inland petty spirits muster me all to their captain, the heart, who, great and puffed up with this retinue, doth any deed of courage: and this valour comes of sherris. So that skill in the weapon is nothing without sack, for that sets it a-work; and learning, a mere hoard of gold kept by a devil till sack commences it and sets it in act and use. Hereof comes it that Prince Harry is valiant; for the cold blood he did naturally inherit of his father, he hath, like lean, sterile, and bare land, manured, husbanded, and tilled, with excellent endeavour of drinking good and good store of fertile sherris, that he is become very hot and valiant. If I had a thousand sons, the first human principle I would teach them should be,—to forswear thin potations, and to addict themselves to sack.

                Enter BARDOLPH.

How now, Bardolph!

Bard. The army is discharged all, and gone.

Fal. Let them go. I'll through Glostershire: and there will I visit Master Robert Shallow, Esquire: I have him already tempering between my finger and my thumb, and shortly will I seal with him. Come away.   *[Exeunt.*

SCENE IV.—WESTMINSTER. *A Room in the Palace.*

Enter KING HENRY, CLARENCE, PRINCE HUMPHREY, WARWICK, *and others.*

K. Hen. Now, lords, if God doth give successful end
To this debate that bleedeth at our doors,
We will our youth lead on to higher fields,
And draw no swords but what are sanctified.
Our navy is address'd, our power collected,
Our substitutes in absence well invested,
And everything lies level to our wish:
Only, we want a little personal strength;
And pause us till these rebels, now afoot,
Come underneath the yoke of government.

War. Both which we doubt not but your majesty
Shall soon enjoy.

K. Hen.   Humphrey, my son of Gloster,
Where is the prince your brother?

P. Humph. I think he's gone to hunt, my lord, at Windsor.

K. Hen. And how accompanied?

P. Humph.   I do not know, my lord.

K. Hen. Is not his brother, Thomas of Clarence, with him?

P. Humph. No, my good lord, he is in presence here.

Cla. What would my lord and father?

K. Hen. Nothing but well to thee, Thomas of Clarence.
How chance thou art not with the prince thy brother?
He loves thee, and thou dost neglect him, Thomas;
Thou hast a better place in his affection
Than all thy brothers: cherish it, my boy;
And noble offices thou mayst effect
Of mediation, after I am dead,
Between his greatness and thy other brethren:
Therefore omit him not; blunt not his love,
Nor lose the good advantage of his grace
By seeming cold or careless of his will;
For he is gracious if he be observ'd:
He hath a tear for pity, and a hand
Open as day for melting charity:
Yet notwithstanding, being incens'd, he's flint;
As humorous as winter, and as sudden
As flaws congealed in the spring of day.
His temper, therefore, must be well observ'd
Chide him for faults, and do it reverently,
When you perceive his blood inclin'd to mirth;
But, being moody, give him line and scope,
Till that his passions, like a whale on ground,
Confound themselves with working. Learn this, Thomas,
And thou shalt prove a shelter to thy friends,
A hoop of gold to bind thy brothers in,
That the united vessel of their blood,
Mingled with venom of suggestion,—
As, force perforce, the age will pour it in,—
Shall never leak, though it do work as strong
As aconitum or rash gunpowder.   [love.

Cla. I shall observe him with all care and

K. Hen. Why art thou not at Windsor with him, Thomas?

Cla. He is not there to-day; he dines in London.

K. Hen. And how accompanied? canst thou tell that?

Cla. With Poins, and other his continual followers.

K. Hen. Most subject is the fattest soil to weeds;
And he, the noble image of my youth,
Is overspread with them: therefore my grief
Stretches itself beyond the hour of death:
The blood weeps from my heart when I do shape,
In forms imaginary, the unguided days
And rotten times that you shall look upon
When I am sleeping with my ancestors.
For when his headstrong riot hath no curb,
When rage and hot blood are his counsellors,
When means and lavish manners meet together,
O, with what wings shall his affections fly
Towards fronting peril and oppos'd decay!

Wor. My gracious lord, you look beyond him quite:
The prince but studies his companions
Like a strange tongue; wherein, to gain the language,
'Tis needful that the most immodest word
Be look'd upon and learn'd; which once attain'd,
Your highness knows, comes to no further use
But to be known and hated. So, like gross terms,
The prince will, in the perfectness of time,
Cast off his followers; and their memory
Shall as a pattern or a measure live,
By which his grace must mete the lives of others,
Turning past evils to advantages.

K. Hen. 'Tis seldom when the bee doth leave her comb
In the dead carrion,—

Enter WESTMORELAND.

Who's here? Westmoreland?

West. Health to my sovereign, and new happiness
Added to that that I am to deliver!
Prince John, your son, doth kiss your grace's hand:
Mowbray, the Bishop Scroop, Hastings, and all,
Are brought to the correction of your law;
There is not now a rebel's sword unsheathed,
But peace puts forth her olive everywhere:
The manner how this action hath been borne,
Here at more leisure may your highness read,
With every course in his particular.

K. Hen. O, Westmoreland, thou art a summer bird,
Which ever in the haunch of winter sings
The lifting-up of day. Look, here's more news.

Enter HARCOURT.

Har. From enemies heaven keep your majesty;
And, when they stand against you, may they fall
As those that I am come to tell you of!

The Earl Northumberland and the Lord Bardolph,
With a great power of English and of Scots,
Are by the sheriff of Yorkshire overthrown:
The manner and true order of the fight
This packet, please it you, contains at large.

K. Hen. And wherefore should these good news make me sick?
Will fortune never come with both hands full,
But write her fair words still in foulest letters?
She either gives a stomach, and no food,—
Such are the poor, in health; or else a feast,
And takes away the stomach,—such are the rich,
That have abundance, and enjoy it not.
I should rejoice now at this happy news;
And now my sight fails, and my brain is giddy:—
O me! come near me, now I am much ill. [*Swoons.*

P. Humph. Comfort, your majesty!

Cla. O my royal father!

West. My sovereign lord, cheer up yourself, look up.

War. Be patient, princes; you do know, these fits
Are with his highness very ordinary.
Stand from him, give him air; he'll straight be well.

Cla. No, no: he cannot long hold out these pangs:
The incessant care and labour of his mind
Hath wrought the mure, that should confine it in,
So thin, that life looks through, and will break out.

P. Humph. The people fear me; for they do observe
Unfather'd heirs and loathly births of nature:
The seasons change their manners, as the year
Had found some months asleep, and leap'd them over.

Cla. The river hath thrice flow'd, no ebb between;
And the old folk, time's doting chronicles,
Say it did so a little time before
That our great grandsire, Edward, sick'd and died.

War. Speak lower, princes, for the king recovers.

P. Humph. This apoplexy will certain be his end. [me hence

K. Hen. I pray you, take me up, and bear
Into some other chamber: softly, pray.
[*They convey the* KING *into an inner part of the room, and place him on a bed.*
Let there be no noise made, my gentle friends;
Unless some dull and favourable hand
Will whisper music to my weary spirit.

War. Call for the music in the other room.

K. Hen. Set me the crown upon my pillow here.

Cla. His eye is hollow, and he changes much.

War. Less noise, less noise!

Enter PRINCE HENRY.

P. Hen. Who saw the Duke of Clarence?
Cla. I am here, brother, full of heaviness.
P. Hen. How now! rain within doors, and
 none abroad!
How doth the king?
P. Humph. Exceeding ill.
P. Hen.   Heard he the good news yet?
Tell it him.
P. Humph. He alter'd much upon the hear-
 ing it.
P. Hen. If he be sick
With joy, he will recover without physic.
War. Not so much noise, my lords;—sweet
 prince, speak low;
The king your father is dispos'd to sleep.
Cla. Let us withdraw into the other room.
War. Will't please your grace to go along
 with us?
P. Hen. No; I will sit and watch here by the
 king.   [*Exeunt all but* P. HENRY.
Why doth the crown lie there upon his pillow,
Being so troublesome a bedfellow?
O polish'd perturbation! golden care!
That keep'st the ports of slumber open wide
To many a watchful night!—sleep with it now!
Yet not so sound and half so deeply sweet
As he whose brow with homely biggin bound
Snores out the watch of night. O majesty!
When thou dost pinch thy bearer, thou dost sit
Like a rich armour worn in heat of day,
That scalds with safety. By his gates of breath·
There lies a downy feather which stirs not:
Did he suspire, that light and weightless down
Perforce must move.—My gracious lord! my
 father!—
This sleep is sound indeed; this is a sleep
That from this golden rigol hath divorc'd
So many English kings. Thy due from me
Is tears and heavy sorrows of the blood,
Which nature, love, and filial tenderness
Shall, O dear father, pay thee plenteously:
My due from thee is this imperial crown,
Which, as immediate from thy place and
 blood,
Derives itself to me. Lo, here it sits,—
    [*Putting it on his head.*
Which God shall guard: and put the world's
 whole strength
Into one giant arm, it shall not force
This lineal honour from me: this from thee
Will I to mine leave, as 'tis left to me. [*Exit.*
K. Hen. Warwick! Gloster! Clarence!

Re-enter WARWICK *and the rest.*

Cla..   Doth the king call?
War. What would your majesty? how fares
 your grace?
K. Hen. Why did you leave me here alone,
 my lords?
Cla. We left the prince my brother here, my
 liege,
Who undertook to sit and watch by you.

K. Hen. The Prince of Wales! Where is he?
 let me see him:
He is not here.
War. This door is open; he is gone this way.
P. Humph. He came not through the cham-
 ber where we stay'd.
K. Hen. Where is the crown? who took it
 from my pillow?
War. When we withdrew, my liege, we left
 it here.
K. Hen. The prince hath ta'en it hence:—
 go, seek him out.
Is he so hasty that he doth suppose
My sleep my death?
Find him, my Lord of Warwick; chide him
 hither.
        [*Exit* WARWICK.
This part of his conjoins with my disease,
And helps to end me.—See, sons, what things
 you are!
How quickly nature falls into revolt
When gold becomes her object!
For this the foolish over-careful fathers
Have broke their sleep with thoughts, their
 brains with care,
Their bones with industry;
For this they have engrossed and pil'd up
The canker'd heaps of strange-achieved gold;
For this they have been thoughtful to invest
Their sons with arts and martial exercises:
When, like the bee, tolling from every flower
The virtuous sweets,
Our thighs with wax, our mouths with honey
 pack'd,
We bring it to the hive: and, like the bees,
Are murder'd for our pains. This bitter taste
Yield his engrossments to the ending father.

Re-enter WARWICK.

Now, where is he that will not stay so long
Till his friend sickness hath determin'd me?
War. My lord, I found the prince in the
 next room,
Washing with kindly tears his gentle cheeks;
With such a deep demeanour in great sorrow,
That tyranny, which never quaff'd but blood,
Would, by beholding him, have wash'd his knife
With gentle eye-drops. He is coming hither.
K. Hen. But wherefore did he take away
 the crown?

Re-enter PRINCE HENRY.

Lo, where he comes.—Come hither to me,
 Harry.—
Depart the chamber, leave us here alone.
   [*Exeunt* CLAR., P. HUMPH., Lords, *&c.*
P. Hen. I never thought to hear you speak
 again.
K. Hen. Thy wish was father, Harry, to that
 thought:
I stay too long by thee, I weary thee.
Dost thou so hunger for my empty chair
That thou wilt needs invest thee with mine
 honours

Before thy hour be ripe? O foolish youth!
Thou seek'st the greatness that will overwhelm
    thee.
Stay but a little; for my cloud of dignity
Is held from falling with so weak a wind
That it will quickly drop: my day is dim.
Thou hast stolen that which, after some few
    hours,
Were thine without offence; and at my death
Thou hast seal'd up my expectation:
Thy life did manifest thou lov'dst me not,
And thou wilt have me die assur'd of it.
Thou hid'st a thousand daggers in thy thoughts,
Which thou hast whetted on thy stony heart,
To stab at half an hour of my life.
What! canst thou not forbear me half an hour?
Then, get thee gone, and dig my grave thyself;
And bid the merry bells ring to thine ear,
That thou art crowned, not that I am dead.
Let all the tears that should bedew my hearse
Be drops of balm to sanctify thy head:
Only compound me with forgotten dust;
Give that which gave thee life unto the worms.
Pluck down my officers, break my decrees;
For now a time is come to mock at form:—
Harry the fifth is crown'd:—up, vanity!
Down, royal state! all you sage counsellors,
    hence!
And to the English court assemble now,
From every region, apes of idleness!
Now, neighbour confines, purge you of your
    scum:
Have you a ruffian that will swear, drink, dance,
Revel the night, rob, murder, and commit
The oldest sins the newest kind of ways?
Be happy, he will trouble you no more;
England shall double-gild his treble guilt,—
England shall give him office, honour, might;
For the fifth Harry from curb'd license plucks
The muzzle of restraint, and the wild dog
Shall flesh his tooth in every innocent.
O my poor kingdom, sick with civil blows!
When that my care could not withold thy riots,
What wilt thou do when riot is thy care?
O, thou wilt be a wilderness again,
Peopled with wolves, thy old inhabitants!

    P. Hen. O, pardon me, my liege! but for my
      tears,   [*Kneeling.*
The moist impediments unto my speech,
I had forestall'd this dear and deep rebuke
Ere you with grief had spoke and I had heard
The course of it so far. There is your crown;
And He that wears the crown immortally
Long guard it yours! If I affect it more
Than as your honour and as your renown,
Let me no more from this obedience rise,—
Which my most inward and true duteous spirit
Teacheth,—this prostrate and exterior bending!
God witness with me, when I here came in,
And found no course of breath within your
    majesty,
How cold it struck my heart! If I do feign,
O, let me in my present wildness die,
And never live to show the incredulous world

The noble change that I have purposed!
Coming to look on you, thinking you dead,—
And dead almost, my liege, to think you were,—
I spake unto the crown as having sense,
And thus upbraided it: *The care on the depend-*
    ing
Hath fed upon the body of my father;
Therefore, thou, best of gold, art worst of gold:
Other, less fine in carat, is more precious,
Preserving life in medicine potable;
But thou, most fine, most honour'd, most re-
    nown'd,
Hast eat thy bearer up. Thus, my most royal
    liege,
Accusing it, I put it on my head,
To try with it, as with an enemy
That had before my face murder'd my father,—
The quarrel of a true inheritor.
But if it did infect my blood with joy,
Or swell my thoughts to any strain of pride;
If any rebel or vain spirit of mine
Did with the least affection of a welcome
Give entertainment to the might of it,
Let God for ever keep it from my head,
And make me as the poorest vassal is,
That doth with awe and terror kneel to it!

    K. Hen. O my son,
God put it in thy mind to take it hence,
That thou mightst win the more thy father's
    love,
Pleading so wisely in excuse of it!
Come hither, Harry, sit thou by my bed;
And hear, I think, the very latest counsel
That ever I shall breathe. God knows, my son,
By what by-paths and indirect crook'd ways
I met this crown; and I myself know well
How troublesome it sat upon my head:
To thee it shall descend with better quiet,
Better opinion, better confirmation;
For all the soil of the achievement goes
With me into the earth. It seem'd in me
But as an honour snatch'd with boisterous
    hand;
And I had many living to upbraid
My gain of it by their assistances;
Which daily grew to quarrel and to bloodshed,
Wounding supposed peace: all these bold fears
Thou see'st with peril I have answered;
For all my reign hath been but as a scene
Acting that argument: and now my death
Changes the mode; for what in me was pur-
    chas'd,
Falls upon thee in a more fairer sort;
So thou the garland wear'st successively.
Yet, though thou stand'st more sure than I
    could do,
Thou art not firm enough, since griefs are green;
And all my friends, which thou must make thy
    friends,
Have but their stings and teeth newly ta'en out;
By whose fell working I was first advanc'd,
And by whose power I well might lodge a fear
To be again displac'd: which to avoid,
I cut them off, and had a purpose now

To lead out many to the Holy Land,
Lest rest and lying still might make them look
Too near unto my state. Therefore, my Harry,
Be it thy course to busy giddy minds   [out,
With foreign quarrels; that action, hence borne
May waste the memory of the former days.
More would I, but my lungs are wasted so,
That strength of speech is utterly denied me.
How I came by the crown, O God forgive;
And grant it may with thee in true peace live!
    P. Hen. My gracious liege,
You won it, wore it, kept it, gave it me;
Then plain and right must my possession be:
Which I with more than with a common pain
'Gainst all the world will rightfully maintain.
    K. Hen. Look, look, here comes my John of
          Lancaster.

Enter PRINCE JOHN OF LANCASTER,
          WARWICK, Lords, *and others.*

    P. John. Health, peace and happiness to my
          royal father!
    K. Hen. Thou bring'st me happiness and
          peace, son John;
But health, alack, with youthful wings is flown
From this bare wither'd trunk: upon thy sight,
My worldly business makes a period.—
Where is my Lord of Warwick?
    P. Hen.   My Lord of Warwick!
    K. Hen. Doth any name particular belong
Unto the lodging where I first did swoon?
    War. 'Tis call'd Jerusalem, my noble lord.
    K. Hen. Laud be to God!—even there my
          life must end.
It hath been prophesied to me many years,
I should not die but in Jerusalem;
Which vainly I suppos'd the Holy Land:—
But bear me to that chamber; there I'll lie;
In that Jerusalem shall Harry die.   [*Exeunt.*

ACT V.

SCENE I.—GLOUCESTERSHIRE. *A Hall in*
          SHALLOW'S *House.*

Enter SHALLOW, FALSTAFF, BARDOLPH, *and*
          Page.

    Shal. By cock and pie, sir, you shall not
away to-night.—What, Davy, I say!
    Fal. You must excuse me, Master Robert
Shallow.
    Shal. I will not excuse you; you shall not be
excused; excuses shall not be admitted; there is
no excuse shall serve; you shall not be excused.
—Why, Davy!

Enter DAVY.

    Davy. Here, sir.
    Shal. Davy, Davy, Davy,—let me see,
Davy; let me see:—yea, marry, William cook,
bid him come hither.—Sir John, you shall not
be excused.
    Davy. Marry, sir, thus;—those precepts can-
not be served: and, again, sir,—shall we sow
the headland with wheat?

    Shal. With red wheat, Davy. But for Wil-
liam cook:—are there no young pigeons?
    Davy. Yes, sir.—Here is now the smith's
note for shoeing and plough-irons.
    Shal. Let it be cast, and paid.—Sir John,
you shall not be excused.
    Davy. Now, sir, a new link to the bucket
must needs be had:—and, sir, do you mean to
stop any of William's wages about the sack he
lost the other day at Hinckley fair?
    Shal. He shall answer it.—Some pigeons,
Davy, a couple of short-legged hens, a joint of
mutton, and any pretty little tiny kickshaws,
tell William cook.
    Davy. Doth the man of war stay all night,
sir?
    Shal. Yea, Davy, I will use him well: a
friend i' the court is better than a penny in
purse. Use his men well, Davy; for they are
arrant knaves, and will backbite.
    Davy. No worse than they are back-bitten,
sir; for they have marvellous foul linen.
    Shal. Well conceited, Davy:—about thy
business, Davy.
    Davy. I beseech you, sir, to countenance
William Visor of Wincot against Clement
Perkes of the hill.
    Shal. There are many complaints, Davy,
against that Visor: that Visor is an arrant
knave, on my knowledge.
    Davy. I grant your worship that he is a
knave, sir; but yet, God forbid, sir, but a knave
should have some countenance at his friend's
request. An honest man, sir, is able to speak for
himself, when a knave is not. I have served
your worship truly, sir, this eight years; and if
I cannot once or twice in a quarter bear out a
knave against an honest man, I have but a very
little credit with your worship. The knave is
mine honest friend, sir; therefore, I beseech
your worship, let him be countenanced.
    Shal. Go to; I say, he shall have no wrong.
Look about, Davy. [*Exit* DAVY.] Where are
you, Sir John? Come, come, come, off with
your boots.—Give me your hand, Master Bardolph.
    Bard. I am glad to see your worship.
    Shal. I thank thee with all my heart, kind
Master Bardolph:—and welcome, my tall fellow [*to the* Page].—Come, Sir John.
    Fal. I'll follow you, good Master Robert
Shallow. [*Exit* SHALLOW.] Bardolph, look to
our horses. [*Exeunt* BARDOLPH *and* Page.] If
I were sawed into quantities, I should make
four dozen of such bearded hermits' staves as
Master Shallow. It is a wonderful thing to see
the semblance coherence of his men's spirits
and his: they, by observing of him, do bear
themselves like foolish justices; he, by conversing with them, is turned into a justice-like serv-
ingman: their spirits are so married in conjunction with the participation of society that they
flock together in consent, like so many wild
geese. If I had a suit to Master Shallow, I

would humour his men with the imputation of being near their master: if to his men, I would curry with Master Shallow that no man could better command his servants. It is certain that either wise bearing or ignorant carriage is caught, as men take diseases, one of another: therefore, let men take heed of their company. I will devise matter enough out of this Shallow to keep Prince Harry in continual laughter the wearing out of six fashions,—which is four terms, or two actions,—and he shall laugh without *intervallums*. O, it is much that a lie with a slight oath, and a jest with a sad brow, will do with a fellow that never had the ache in his shoulders! O, you shall see him laugh till his face be like a wet cloak ill laid up!

Shal. [*Within*.] Sir John!

Fal. I come, Master Shallow; I come, Master Shallow.   [*Exit*.

SCENE II.—WESTMINSTER. *A Room in the Palace*.

Enter, severally, WARWICK *and the* Lord Chief-Justice.

War. How now, my lord chief-justice! whither away?

Ch. Just. How doth the king?

War. Exceedingly well; his cares are now all ended.

Ch. Just. I hope, not dead.

War.   He's walk'd the way of nature; And to our purposes he lives no more.

Ch. Just. I would his majesty had call'd me with him:
The service that I truly did his life
Hath left me open to all injuries.

War. Indeed I think the young king loves you not.   [myself

Ch. Just. I know he doth not; and do arm
To welcome the condition of the time;
Which cannot look more hideously upon me
Than I have drawn it in my fantasy.

War. Here come the heavy issue of dead Harry:
O that the living Harry had the temper
Of him, the worst of these three gentlemen!
How many nobles then should hold their places,
That must strike sail to spirits of vile sort!

Ch. Just. O God, I fear all will be overturn'd.

Enter PRINCE JOHN, PRINCE HUMPHREY, CLARENCE, WESTMORELAND, *and others*.

P. John. Good-morrow, cousin Warwick, good-morrow.

P. Humph., Cla. Good-morrow, cousin.

P. John. We meet like men that had forgot to speak.

War. We do remember; but our argument Is all too heavy to admit much talk.

P. John. Well, peace be with him that hath made us heavy!

Ch. Just. Peace be with us, lest we be heavier!

P. Humph. O, good my lord, you have lost a friend indeed;

And I dare swear you borrow not that face
Of seeming sorrow,—it is sure your own.

P. John. Though no man be assur'd what grace to find,
You stand in coldest expectation:
I am the sorrier; would 'twere otherwise.

Cla. Well, you must now speak Sir John Falstaff fair;
Which swims against your stream of quality.

Ch. Just. Sweet princes, what I did, I did in honour,
Led by the impartial conduct of my soul;
And never shall you see that I will beg
A ragged and forestall'd remission.
If truth and upright innocency fail me,
I'll to the king my master that is dead,
And tell him who hath sent me after him.

War. Here comes the prince.

Enter KING HENRY V.

Ch. Just. Good-morrow; and God save your majesty!

King. This new and gorgeous garment, majesty,
Sits not so easy on me as you think.—
Brothers, you mix your sadness with some fear:
This is the English, not the Turkish court;
Not Amurath an Amurath succeeds,
But Harry Harry. Yet be sad, good brothers,
For, to speak truth, it very well becomes you:
Sorrow so royally in you appears
That I will deeply put the fashion on,
And wear it in my heart: why, then, be sad;
But entertain no more of it, good brothers,
Than a joint burden laid upon us all.
For me, by heaven, I bid you be assur'd,
I'll be your father and your brother too;
Let me but bear your love, I'll bear your cares:
Yet weep that Harry's dead; and so will I;
But Harry lives, that shall convert those tears,
By number, into hours of happiness.

P. John, &c. We hope no other from your majesty.

King. You all look strangely on me:—and you most;   [*To the* Chief-Justice.
You are, I think, assur'd I love you not.

Ch. Just. I am assur'd, if I be measur'd rightly,
Your majesty hath no just cause to hate me.

King. No!
How might a prince of my great hopes forget
So great indignities you laid upon me?
What! rate, rebuke, and roughly send to prison
The immediate heir of England! Was this easy?
May this be wash'd in Lethe, and forgotten?

Ch. Just. I then did use the person of your father;
The image of his power lay then in me:
And, in the administration of his law,
Whiles I was busy for the commonwealth,
Your highness pleased to forget my place,
And majesty and power of law and justice,
The image of the king whom I presented,
And struck me in my very seat of judgment;

Whereon, as an offender to your father,
I gave bold way to my authority,
And did commit you. If the deed were ill,
Be you contented, wearing now the garland,
To have a son set your decrees at naught,
To pluck down justice from your awful bench,
To trip the course of law, and blunt the sword
That guards the peace and safety of your person;
Nay, more, to spurn at your most royal image,
And mock your workings in a second body.
Question your royal thoughts, make the case yours;
Be now the father, and propose a son;
Hear your own dignity so much profan'd,
See your most dreadful laws so loosely slighted,
Behold yourself so by a son disdain'd;
And then imagine me taking your part,
And, in your power, soft silencing your son:
After this cold considerance, sentence me;
And, as you are a king, speak in your state
What I have done that misbecame my place,
My person, or my liege's sovereignty.

King. You are right, justice, and you weigh this well;
Therefore still bear the balance and the sword:
And I do wish your honours may increase
Till you do live to see a son of mine
Offend you, and obey you, as I did.
So shall I live to speak my father's words
Happy am I, that have a man so bold,
That dares do justice on my proper son;
And not less happy, having such a son,
That would deliver up his greatness so
Into the hands of justice.—You did commit me:
For which I do commit into your hand
The unstain'd sword that you have us'd to bear;
With this remembrance,—that you use the same
With the like bold, just, and impartial spirit
As you have done 'gainst me. There is my hand;
You shall be as a father to my youth:
My voice shall sound as you do prompt mine ear;
And I will stoop and humble my intents
To your well-practis'd wise directions.—
And, princes all, believe me, I beseech you;—
My father is gone wild into his grave,
For in his tomb lie my affections;
And with his spirit sadly I survive,
To mock the expectation of the world,
To frustrate prophecies, and to raze out
Rotten opinion, who hath writ me down
After my seeming. The tide of blood in me
Hath proudly flow'd in vanity till now:
Now doth it turn, and ebb back to the sea,
Where it shall mingle with the state of floods,
And flow henceforth in formal majesty.
Now call we our high court of parliament:
And let us choose such limbs of noble counsel,
That the great body of our state may go
In equal rank with the best-govern'd nation;
That war or peace, or both at once, may be
As things acquainted and familiar to us;

In which you, father, shall have foremost hand.
       [*To the* Lord Chief-Justice.
Our coronation done, we will accite,
As I before remember'd, all our state:
And,—God consigning to my good intents,—
No prince nor peer shall have just cause to say,
God shorten Harry's happy life one day.
          [*Exeunt.*

SCENE III.—GLOUCESTERSHIRE. *The Garden*
of SHALLOW'S *House.*

Enter FALSTAFF, SHALLOW, SILENCE,
BARDOLPH, *the* Page, *and* DAVY.

Shal. Nay, you shall see mine orchard, where, in an arbour, we will eat a last year's pippin of my own graffing, with a dish of carraways, and so forth:—come, cousin Silence:—and then to bed.

Fal. 'Fore God, you have here a goodly dwelling and a rich.

Shal. Barren, barren,—barren; beggars all, beggars all, Sir John:—marry, good air.—Spread, Davy; spread, Davy: well said, Davy.

Fal. This Davy serves you for good uses; he is your serving-man and your husband.

Shal. A good varlet, a good varlet, a very good varlet, Sir John:—by the mass, I have drunk too much sack at supper:—a good varlet. Now sit down, now sit down:—come, cousin.

Sil. Ah, sirrah! quoth-a,—we shall
Do nothing but eat, and make good cheer,
         [*Singing.*
And praise heaven for the merry year;
When flesh is cheap, and females dear,
And lusty lads roam here and there,
  So merrily,
   And ever among so merrily.

Fal. There's a merry heart!—Good Master Silence, I'll give you a health for that anon.

Shal. Give Master Bardolph some wine, Davy.

Davy. Sweet sir, sit [*seating* BARDOLPH *and the* Page *at another table*]; I'll be with you anon; most sweet sir, sit.—Master Page, good Master Page, sit.—Proface! What you want in meat, we'll have in drink. But you must bear; the heart's all.   [*Exit.*

Shal. Be merry, Master Bardolph;—and, my little soldier there, be merry.

Sil. *Be merry, be merry, my wife has all;*
         [*Singing.*
For women are shrews, both short and tall;
'Tis merry in hall when beards wag all,
  And welcome merry shrove-tide.
Be merry, be merry, &c.

Fal. I did not think Master Silence had been a man of this mettle.

Sil. Who, I? I have been merry twice and once ere now.

Re-enter DAVY.

Davy. There is a dish of leather-coats for you.   [*Setting them before* BARD.

Shal. Davy,—

Davy. Your worship?—I'll be with you straight [*to* BARD.]—A cup of wine, sir?

Sil. *A cup of wine that's brisk and fine,*
[*Singing.*
And drink unto the leman mine;
And a merry heart gives long-a.

Fal. Well, said, Master Silence.

Sil. And we shall be merry;—now comes in the sweet of the night.

Fal. Health and long life to you, Master Silence

Sil. *Fill the cup, and let it come;* [*Singing.*
I'll pledge you a mile to the bottom.

Shal. Honest Bardolph, welcome: if thou wantest anything, and wilt not call, beshrew thy heart.—Welcome, my little tiny thief [*to the* Page]; and welcome indeed too.—I'll drink to Master Bardolph, and to all the cavaleroes about London.

Davy. I hope to see London once ere I die.

Bard. An I might see you there, Davy,—

Shal. By the mass, you'll crack a quart together,—ha! will you not, Master Bardolph?

Bard. Yea, sir, in a pottle-pot.

Shal. By God's liggens, I thank thee:—the knave will stick by thee, I can assure thee that: he will not out; he is true bred.

Bard. And I'll stick by him, sir.

Shal. Why, there spoke a king. Lack nothing: be merry. [*Knocking heard.*] Look who's at door there, ho! who knocks?　[*Exit* DAVY.

Fal. Why, now you have done me right.
[*To* SIL., *who has drunk a bumper.*

Sil.　Do me right,　[*Singing.*
And dub me knight:
Samingo.
Is't not so?

Fal. 'Tis so.　[*do somewhat.*

Sil. Is't so? Why, then, say an old man can

Re-enter DAVY.

Davy. An it please your worship, there's one Pistol come from the court with news.

Fal. From the court! let him come in.

Enter PISTOL.

How now, Pistol!

Pist. Sir John, God save you!

Fal. What wind blew you hither, Pistol?

Pist. Not the ill wind which blows no man to good.—Sweet knight, thou art now one of the greatest men in the realm.

Sil. By'r lady, I think he be, but goodman Puff of Barson.

Pist. Puff?
Puff in thy teeth, most recreant coward base!—
Sir John, I am thy Pistol and thy friend,
And helter-skelter have I rode to thee;
And tidings do I bring, and lucky joys,
And golden times, and happy news of price.

Fal. I pr'ythee now, deliver them like a man of this world.　[*base!*

Pist. A foutra for the world and worldlings I speak of Africa and golden joys.

Fal. O base Assyrian knight, what is thy news?
Let King Cophetua know the truth thereof.

Sil. *And Robin Hood, Scarlet, and John.*
[*Singing.*

Pist. Shall dunghill curs confront the Helicons?
And shall good news be baffled?
Then, Pistol, lay thy head in Furies' lap.

Shal. Honest gentleman, I know not your breeding.

Pist. Why, then, lament, therefore.

Shal. Give me pardon, sir:—if, sir, you come with news from the court, I take it there is but two ways; either to utter them, or to conceal them. I am, sir, under the king, in some authority.

Pist. Under which king, bezonian? speak, or die.

Shal. Under King Harry.

Pist. Harry the fourth? or fifth?

Shal. Harry the fourth.

Pist.　A foutra for thine office!—
Sir John, thy tender lambkin now is king;
Harry the fifth's the man. I speak the truth:
When Pistol lies, do this; and fig me, like
The bragging Spaniard.

Fal. What! is the old king dead?

Pist. As nail in door: the things I speak are just.

Fal. Away, Bardolph! saddle my horse.—Master Robert Shallow, choose what office thou wilt in the land,'tis thine.—Pistol, I will double-charge thee with dignities.

Bard. O joyful day!
I would not take a knighthood for my fortune.

Pist. What, I do bring good news?

Fal. Carry Master Silence to bed.—Master Shallow, my Lord Shallow, be what thou wilt; I am fortune's steward. Get on thy boots: we'll ride all night:—O sweet Pistol!—away, Bardolph! [*Exit* BARDOLPH.]—Come, Pistol, utter more to me; and, withal, devise something to do thyself good.—Boot, boot, Master Shallow: I know the young king is sick for me. Let us take any man's horses; the laws of England are at my commandment. Happy are they which have been my friends; and woe unto my Lord Chief-Justice!

Pist. Let vultures vile seize on his lungs also!
Where is the life that late I led? say they:
Why, here it is;—welcome this pleasant day!
[*Exeunt.*

SCENE IV.—LONDON. *A Street.*

Enter Beadles, *dragging in* HOSTESS QUICKLY *and* DOLL TEARSHEET.

Host. No, thou arrant knave; I would I might die, that I might have thee hanged: thou hast drawn my shoulder out of joint.

1 *Bead.* The constables have delivered her over to me; and she shall have whipping-cheer enough, I warrant her: there hath been a man or two lately killed about her.

Doll. Nut-hook, nut-hook, you lie. Come on; I'll tell thee what, thou damned tripe-visaged rascal, an the child I now go with do miscarry, thou hadst better thou hadst struck thy mother, thou paper-faced villain.

Host. O the Lord, that Sir John were come! he would make this a bloody day to somebody. But I pray God the fruit of her womb miscarry!

1 Bead. If it do, you shall have a dozen of cushions again; you have but eleven now. Come, I charge you both go with me; for the man is dead that you and Pistol beat among you.

Doll. I'll tell thee what, thou thin man in a censer, I will have you as soundly swinged for this,—you blue-bottle rogue, you filthy famished corrections, if you be not swinged, I'll forswear half-kirtles.

1 Bead. Come, come, you she knight-errant, come.

Host. O God, that right should thus overcome might! Well, of sufferance comes ease.

Doll. Come, you rogue, come; bring me to a justice.

Host. Ay, come, you starved bloodhound.

Doll. Goodman death, goodman bones!

Host. Thou atomy, thou!

Doll. Come, you thin thing; come, you rascal.

1 Bead. Very well. [*Exeunt.*

SCENE V.—*A public Place near Westminster Abbey.*

Enter two Grooms, *strewing rushes.*

1 Groom. More rushes, more rushes.

2 Groom. The trumpets have sounded twice.

1 Groom. It will be two o'clock ere they come from the coronation: despatch, despatch.

[*Exeunt.*

Enter FALSTAFF, SHALLOW, PISTOL, BARDOLPH, *and the* Page.

Fal. Stand here by me, Master Robert Shallow; I will make the king do you grace: I will leer upon him, as he comes by; and do but mark the countenance that he will give me.

Pist. God bless thy lungs, good knight.

Fal. Come here, Pistol; stand behind me.— O, if I had had time to have made new liveries, I would have bestowed the thousand pound I borrowed of you [*to* SHALLOW]. But 'tis no matter; this poor show doth better: this doth infer the zeal I had to see him,—

Shal. It doth so.

Fal. It shows my earnestness of affection,—

Shal. It doth so.

Fal. My devotion,—

Shal. It doth, it doth, it doth.

Fal. As it were, to ride day and night; and not to deliberate, not to remember, not to have patience to shift me,—

Shal. It is most certain.

Fal. But to stand stained with travel, and sweating with desire to see him; thinking of nothing else, putting all affairs else in oblivion, as if there were nothing else to be done but to see him.

Pist. 'Tis *semper idem,* for *absque hoc nihil est:* 'tis all in every part.

Shal. 'Tis so, indeed. [liver,

Pist. My knight, I will inflame thy noble And make thee rage.
Thy Doll, and Helen of thy noble thoughts,
Is in base durance and contagious prison;
Haul'd thither
By most mechanical and dirty hand:—
Rouse up revenge from ebon den with fell Alecto's snake,
For Doll is in. Pistol speaks naught but truth.

Fal. I will deliver her.
[*Shouts within, and the trumpets sound*

Pist. There roar'd the sea, and trumpets clangor sounds.

Enter the KING *and his* Train, *the* Chief-Justice *among them.*

Fal. God save thy grace, King Hal; my royal Hal!

Pist. The heavens thee guard and keep, most royal imp of fame!

Fal. God save thee, my sweet boy!

King. My lord chief-justice, speak to that vain man.

Ch. Just. Have you your wits? know you what 'tis you speak?

Fal. My king! my Jove! I speak to thee, my heart!

King. I know thee not, old man: fall to thy prayers;
How ill white hairs become a fool and jester!
I have long dream'd of such a kind of man,
So surfeit-swell'd, so old, and so profane;
But, being awake, I do despise my dream.
Make less thy body hence, and more thy grace;
Leave gormandizing; know the grave doth gape
For thee thrice wider than for other men.—
Reply not to me with a fool-born jest:
Presume not that I am the thing I was;
For God doth know, so shall the world perceive,
That I have turn'd away my former self;
So will I those that kept me company.
When thou dost hear I am as I have been,
Approach me, and thou shalt be as thou wast,
The tutor and the feeder of my riots:
Till then I banish thee, on pain of death,—
As I have done the rest of my misleaders,—
Not to come near our person by ten mile.
For competence of life I will allow you,
That lack of means enforce you not to evil:
And, as we hear you do reform yourselves,
We will, according to your strength and qualities,
Give you advancement.—Be it your charge, my lord,
To see perform'd the tenor of our word.—
Set on. [*Exeunt* KING *and his* Train.

Fal. Master Shallow, I owe you a thousand pound.

Shal. Yèa, marry, Sir John; which I beseech you to let me have home with me.

Fal. That can hardly be, Master Shallow. Do not you grieve at this; I shall be sent for in private to him: look you, he must seem thus to the world: fear not your advancement; I will be the man yet that shall make you great.

Shal. I cannot perceive how,—unless you give me your doublet, and stuff me out with straw. I beseech you, good Sir John, let me have five hundred of my thousand.

Fal. Sir, I will be as good as my word: this that you heard was but a colour.

Shal. A colour, I fear, that you will die in, Sir John.

Fal. Fear no colours: go with me to dinner. Come, Lieutenant Pistol;—come, Bardolph:— I shall be sent for soon at night.

Re-enter PRINCE JOHN, *the* Chief-Justice, Officers, &c.

Ch. Just. Go, carry Sir John Falstaff to the Fleet;
Take all his company along with him.

Fal. My lord, my lord,—

Ch. Just. I cannot now speak: I will hear you soon.—
Take them away.

Pist. *Se fortuna mi tormenta, lo sperare mi contenta.*

[*Exeunt* FAL., SHAL., PIST., BARD., Page, *and* Officers.

P. John. I like this fair proceeding of the king's:
He hath intent his wonted followers
Shall all be very well provided for;
But all are banish'd till their conversations
Appear more wise and modest to the world.

Ch. Just. And so they are.

P. John. The king hath call'd his parliament, my lord.

Ch. Just. He hath.

P. John. I will lay odds that, ere this year expire,

We bear our civil swords and native fire
As far as France: I heard a bird so sing,
Whose music, to my thinking, pleas'd the king.
Come, will you hence? [*Exeunt.*

EPILOGUE.—*Spoken by a Dancer.*

First my fear; then my court'sy; last my speech. My fear is, your displeasure; my court'sy, my duty; and my speech, to beg your pardons. If you look for a good speech now, you undo me: for what I have to say is of mine own making; and what, indeed, I should say will, I doubt, prove mine own marring. But to the purpose, and so to the venture.—Be it known to you,—as it is very well,—I was lately here in the end of a displeasing play, to pray your patience for it, and to promise you a better. I did mean, indeed, to pay you with this; which, if, like an ill venture, it come unluckily home, I break, and you, my gentle creditors, lose. Here I promised you I would be, and here I commit my body to your mercies: bate me some, and I will pay you some, and, as most debtors do, promise you infinitely.

If my tongue cannot entreat you to acquit me, will you command me to use my legs? and yet that were but light payment,—to dance out of your debt. But a good conscience will make any possible satisfaction, and so will I. All the gentlewomen here have forgiven me: if the gentlemen will not, then the gentlemen do not agree with the gentlewomen, which was never seen before in such an assembly.

One word more, I beseech you. If you be not too much cloyed with fat meat, our humble author will continue the story, with Sir John in it, and make you merry with fair Katherine of France: where, for anything I know, Falstaff shall die of a sweat, unless already he be killed with your hard opinions; for Oldcastle died a martyr, and this is not the man. My tongue is weary; when my legs are too, I will bid you good-night: and so kneel down before you;— but, indeed, to pray for the queen.

KING HENRY V.

Act IV. Sc. 7.

KING HENRY V.

DRAMATIS PERSONÆ

KING HENRY THE FIFTH.
DUKE OF GLOSTER,
DUKE OF BEDFORD, } *Brothers to the* KING.
DUKE OF EXETER, *Uncle to the* KING.
DUKE OF YORK, *Cousin to the* KING.
EARLS OF SALISBURY, WESTMORELAND, *and* WARWICK.
ARCHBISHOP OF CANTERBURY.
BISHOP OF ELY.
EARL OF CAMBRIDGE,
LORD SCROOP, } *Conspirators against the* KING.
SIR THOMAS GREY,
SIR THOMAS ERPINGHAM, GOWER, FLUELLEN, MACMORRIS, JAMY, *Officers in* KING HENRY'S *Army.*
BATES, COURT, WILLIAMS, *Soldiers in the same.*
NYM, BARDOLPH, PISTOL, *formerly Servants to* FALSTAFF, *now Soldiers in the same.*
Boy, *Servant to them.*
A Herald.

Chorus.

CHARLES THE SIXTH, *King of France.*
LOUIS, *the Dauphin.*
DUKES OF BURGUNDY, ORLEANS, *and* BOURBON.
The Constable of France.
RAMBURES *and* GRANDPREE, *French Lords.*
Governor of Harfleur.
MONTJOY, *a French Herald.*
Ambassadors to the King of England.

ISABEL, *Queen of France.*
KATHARINE, *Daughter to* CHARLES *and* ISABEL.
ALICE, *a Lady attending on the* PRINCESS KATHARINE.
QUICKLY, PISTOL'S *Wife, an Hostess.*

Lords, Ladies, Officers, French *and* English Soldiers, Messengers, *and* Attendants.

SCENE,—*At the beginning of the Play, lies in* ENGLAND; *but afterwards wholly in* FRANCE.

Enter Chorus.

Chor. O for a Muse of fire, that would ascend
The brightest heaven of invention!
A kingdom for a stage, princes to act,
And monarchs to behold the swelling scene!
Then should the warlike Harry, like himself,
Assume the port of Mars; and at his heels,
Leash'd in like hounds, should famine, sword,
   and fire,
Crouch for employment. But pardon, gentles all,
The flat unraised spirit that hath dar'd
On this unworthy scaffold to bring forth
So great an object: can this cockpit hold
The vasty fields of France? or may we cram
Within this wooden O the very casques
That did affright the air at Agincourt?
O, pardon! since a crooked figure may
Attest in little place a million;
And let us, ciphers to this great acompt,
On your imaginary forces work.
Suppose within the girdle of these walls
Are now confin'd two mighty monarchies,
Whose high upreared and abutting fronts
The perilous narrow ocean parts asunder:
Piece out our imperfections with your thoughts:
Into a thousand parts divide one man,
And make imaginary puissance;
Think, when we talk of horses, that you see
   them
Printing their proud hoof i' the receiving earth;

For 'tis your thoughts that now must deck our
   kings,
Carry them here and there; jumping o'er times,
Turning the accomplishment of many years
Into an hour-glass: for the which supply,
Admit me Chorus to this history;
Who, prologue-like, your humble patience pray,
Gently to hear, kindly to judge, our play.

ACT I.

SCENE I.—LONDON. *An Ante-chamber in the* KING'S *Palace.*

Enter the ARCHBISHOP OF CANTERBURY *and the* BISHOP OF ELY.

Cant. My lord, I'll tell you,—that self bill
   is urg'd,
Which in the eleventh year of the last king's
   reign
Was like, and had indeed against us pass'd,
But that the scambling and unquiet time
Did push it out of further question.   [now?
  Ely. But how, my lord, shall we resist it
  Cant. It must be thought on. If it pass
   against us,
We lose the better half of our possession:
For all the temporal lands, which men devout
By testament have given to the church,
Would they strip from us; being valu'd thus,—
As much as would maintain, to the king's
   honour,

Full fifteen earls and fifteen hundred knights,
Six thousand and two hundred good esquires;
And, to relief of lazars and weak age,
Of indigent faint souls past corporal toil,
A hundred alms-houses right well supplied;
And to the coffers of the king, beside,
A thousand pounds by the year: thus runs the
　　bill.
Ely. This would drink deep.
Cant.　　　'Twould drink the cup and all.
Ely. But what prevention?
Cant. The king is full of grace and fair re-
　　gard.
Ely. And a true lover of the holy church.
Cant. The courses of his youth promis'd it
　　not.
The breath no sooner left his father's body
But that his wildness, mortified in him,
Seem'd to die too: yea, at that very moment,
Consideration, like an angel, came,
And whipp'd the offending Adam out of him,
Leaving his body as a paradise,
To envelop and contain celestial spirits.
Never was such a sudden scholar made;
Never came reformation in a flood,
With such a heady current, scouring faults;
Nor never Hydra-headed wilfulness
So soon did lose his seat, and all at once,
As in this king.
Ely.　　　　We are blessed in the change.
Cant. Hear him but reason in divinity,
And, all-admiring, with an inward wish
You would desire the king were made a prelate:
Hear him debate of commonwealth affairs,
You would say, it hath been all-in-all his study:
List his discourse of war, and you shall hear
A fearful battle render'd you in music:
Turn him to any cause of policy,
The Gordian knot of it he will unloose,
Familiar as his garter:—that, when he speaks,
The air, a charter'd libertine, is still,
And the mute wonder lurketh in men's ears,
To steal his sweet and honeyed sentences;
So that the art and practice part of life
Must be the mistress to this theoric:
Which is a wonder how his grace should glean
　　it,
Since his addiction was to courses vain;
His companies unletter'd, rude, and shallow;
His hours fill'd up with riots, banquets, sports;
And never noted in him any study,
Any retirement, any sequestration
From open haunts and popularity.
Ely. The strawberry grows underneath the
　　nettle,
And wholesome berries thrive and ripen best
Neighbour'd by fruit of baser quality:
And so the prince obscur'd his contemplation
Under the veil of wildness; which, no doubt,
Grew like the summer grass, fastest by night,
Unseen, yet crescive in his faculty.
Cant. It must be so; for miracles are ceas'd;
And therefore we must needs admit the means
How things are perfected.

Ely.　　　　　　But, my good lord,
How now for mitigation of this bill
Urg'd by the commons? Doth his majesty
Incline to it, or no?
Cant.　　　　　　He seems indifferent;
Or, rather, swaying more upon our part
Than cherishing the exhibitors against us:
For I have made an offer to his majesty,—
Upon our spiritual convocation,
And in regard of causes now in hand,
Which I have open'd to his grace at large,
As touching France,—to give a greater sum
Than ever at one time the clergy yet
Did to his predecessors part withal.
Ely. How did this offer seem receiv'd, my
　　lord?
Cant. With good acceptance of his majesty;
Save that there was not time enough to hear,—
As, I perceiv'd, his grace would fain have
　　done,—
The severals and unhidden passages
Of his true titles to some certain dukedoms,
And, generally, to the crown and seat of France,
Deriv'd from Edward, his great-grandfather.
Ely. What was the impediment that broke
　　this off?
Cant. The French ambassador upon that
　　instant
Crav'd audience: and the hour, I think, is come
To give him hearing: is it four o'clock?
Ely.　　　　　　　　　It is.
Cant. Then go we in, to know his embassy;
Which I could, with a ready guess, declare,
Before the Frenchman speak a word of it.
Ely. I'll wait upon you; and I long to hear it.
　　　　　　　　　　　　　　[*Exeunt.*

SCENE II.—*The same. A Room of State in the
　　　　　　　same.*

Enter KING HENRY, GLOSTER, BEDFORD,
　　EXETER, WARWICK, WESTMORELAND, *and*
　　Attendants.

K. Hen. Where is my gracious Lord of
　　Canterbury?
Exe. Not here in presence.
K. Hen. Send for him, good uncle.
West. Shall we call in the ambassador, my
　　liege?
K. Hen. Not yet, my cousin; we would be
　　resolv'd,
Before we hear him, of some things of weight,
That task our thoughts, concerning us and
　　France.

Enter the ARCHBISHOP OF CANTERBURY *and*
　　　　　BISHOP OF ELY.

Cant. God and his angels guard your sacred
　　throne,
And make you long become it!
K. Hen.　　　　　Sure, we thank you.
My learned lord, we pray you to proceed,
And justly and religiously unfold
Why the law Salique, that they have in France,
Or should, or should not, bar us in our claim:

And God forbid, my dear and faithful lord,
That you should fashion, wrest, or bow your
    reading,
Or nicely charge your understanding soul
With opening titles miscreate, whose right
Suits not in native colours with the truth;
For God doth know how many, now in health,
Shall drop their blood in approbation
Of what your reverence shall incite us to:
Therefore take heed how you impawn our
    person,
How you awake the sleeping sword of war:
We charge you, in the name of God, take heed;
For never two such kingdoms did contend
Without much fall of blood; whose guiltless
    drops
Are every one a woe, a sore complaint
'Gainst him whose wrongs give edge unto the
    swords
That make such waste in brief mortality.
Under this conjuration, speak, my lord;
For we will hear, note, and believe in heart
That what you speak is in your conscience
    wash'd
As pure as sin with baptism.
    Cant. Then hear me, gracious sovereign,—
    and you peers,
That owe yourselves, your lives, and services
To this imperial throne.—There is no bar
To make against your highness' claim to France
But this, which they produce from Phara-
    mond,—
In terram Salicam muliers ne succedant,
No woman shall succeed in Salique land:
Which Salique land the French unjustly gloze
To be the realm of France, and Pharamond
The founder of this law and female bar.
Yet their own authors faithfully affirm
That the land Salique is in Germany,
Between the floods of Sala and of Elbe;
Where Charles the Great, having subdu'd the
    Saxons,
There left behind and settled certain French;
Who, holding in disdain the German women
For some dishonest manners of their life,
Establish'd then this law,—to wit, no female
Should be inheritrix in Salique land:
Which Salique, as I said, 'twixt Elbe and Sala,
Is at this day in Germany called Meisen.
Then doth it well appear, the Salique law
Was not devised for the realm of France:
Nor did the French possess the Salique land
Until four hundred one-and-twenty years
After defunction of King Pharamond,
Idly suppos'd the founder of this law;
Who died within the year of our redemption
Four hundred twenty-six; and Charles the
    Great
Subdu'd the Saxons, and did seat the French
Beyond the river Sala, in the year
Eight hundred five. Besides, their writers say,
King Pepin, which deposed Childeric,
Did, as heir general, being descended
Of Blithild, which was daughter to King Clothair,

Make claim and title to the crown of France.
Hugh Capet also,—who usurp'd the crown
Of Charles the Duke of Lorraine, sole heir male
Of the true line and stock of Charles the
    Great,—
To fine his title with some show of truth,—
Though, in pure truth, it was corrupt and
    naught,—
Convey'd himself as heir to the Lady Lingare,
Daughter to Charlemain, who was the son
To Louis the emperor, and Louis the son
Of Charles the Great. Also King Louis the
    Tenth,
Who was sole heir to the usurper Capet,
Could not keep quiet in his conscience,
Wearing the crown of France, till satisfied
That fair Queen Isabel, his grandmother,
Was lineal of the Lady Ermengare,
Daughter to Charles the foresaid Duke of Lor-
    raine:
By the which marriage the line of Charles the
    Great
Was re-united to the Crown of France.
So that, as clear as is the summer's sun,
King Pepin's title, and Hugh Capet's claim,
King Louis his satisfaction, all appear
To hold in right and title of the female:
So do the kings of France unto this day;
Howbeit they would hold up this Salique law
To bar your highness claiming from the female;
And rather choose to hide them in a net
Than amply to imbar their crooked titles
Usurp'd from you and your progenitors.
    K. Hen. May I with right and conscience
    make this claim?
    Cant. The sin upon my head, dread sover-
    eign!
For in the book of Numbers is it writ,—
When the man dies, let the inheritance
Descend unto the daughter. Gracious lord,
Stand for your own; unwind your bloody flag;
Look back unto your mighty ancestors.
Go, my dread lord, to your great-grandsire's
    tomb,
From whom you claim; invoke his warlike
    spirit,
And your great-uncle's, Edward the Black
    Prince,
Who on the French ground play'd a tragedy,
Making defeat on the full power of France,
Whiles his most mighty father on a hill
Stood smiling to behold his lion's whelp
Forage in blood of French nobility.
O noble English, that could entertain
With half their forces the full pride of France,
And let another half stand laughing by,
All out of work and cold for action!
    Ely. Awake remembrance of these valiant
    dead,
And with your puissant arm renew their feats:
You are their heir; you sit upon their throne;
The blood and courage that renowned them
Runs in your veins; and my thrice-puissant
    liege

Is in the very May-morn of his youth,
Ripe for exploits and mighty enterprises.
Exe. Your brother kings and monarchs of the earth
Do all expect that you should rouse yourself,
As did the former lions of your blood.
West. They know your grace hath cause and means and might:—
So hath your highness; never king of England
Had nobles richer and more loyal subjects,
Whose hearts have left their bodies here in England,
And lie pavilion'd in the fields of France.
Cant. O, let their bodies follow, my dear liege,
With blood and sword and fire to win your right:
In aid whereof we of the spiritualty
Will raise your highness such a mighty sum
As never did the clergy at one time
Bring in to any of your ancestors.
K. Hen. We must not only arm to invade the French,
But lay down our proportions to defend
Against the Scot, who will make road upon us
With all advantages.
Cant. They of those marches, gracious sovereign,
Shall be a wall sufficient to defend
Our inland from the pilfering borderers.
K. Hen. We do not mean the coursing snatchers only,
But fear the main intendment of the Scot,
Who hath been still a giddy neighbour to us;
For you shall read that my great-grandfather
Never went with his forces into France
But that the Scot on his unfurnish'd kingdom
Came pouring, like the tide into a breach,
With ample and brim fulness of his force;
Galling the gleaned land with hot essays,
Girding with grievous siege castles and towns;
That England, being empty of defence,
Hath shook and trembled at the ill neighbourhood.
Cant. She hath been then more fear'd than harm'd, my liege;
For hear her but exampled by herself:—
When all her chivalry hath been in France,
And she a mourning widow of her nobles,
She hath herself not only well defended,
But taken, and impounded as a stray,
The king of Scots; whom she did send to France,
To fill King Edward's fame with prisoner kings,
And make her chronicle as rich with praise
As is the ooze and bottom of the sea
With sunken wreck and sumless treasuries.
West. But there's a saying, very old and true,—
  If that you will France win,
  Then with Scotland first begin:
For once the eagle England being in prey,
To her unguarded nest the weasel Scot
Comes sneaking, and so sucks her princely eggs;

Playing the mouse in absence of the cat,
To tear and havoc more than she can eat.
Exe. It follows, then, the cat must stay at home:
Yet that is but a curs'd necessity,
Since we have locks to safeguard necessaries,
And pretty traps to catch the petty thieves.
While that the armed hand doth fight abroad,
The advised head defends itself at home;
For government, though high, and low, and lower,
Put into parts, doth keep in one concent;
Congruing in a full and natural close,
Like music.
Cant.   Therefore doth heaven divide
The state of man in divers functions,
Setting endeavour in continual motion;
To which is fixed, as an aim or butt,
Obedience: for so work the honey bees;
Creatures that, by a rule in nature, teach
The act of order to a peopled kingdom.
They have a king, and officers of sorts:
Where some, like magistrates, correct at home;
Others, like merchants, venture trade abroad;
Others, like soldiers, armed in their stings,
Make boot upon the summer's velvet buds;
Which pillage they with merry march bring home
To the tent-royal of their emperor:
Who, busied in his majesty, surveys
The singing masons building roofs of gold;
The civil citizens kneading up the honey;
The poor mechanic porters crowding in
Their heavy burdens at his narrow gate;
The sad-ey'd justice, with his surly hum,
Delivering o'er to executors pale
The lazy yawning drone. I this infer,—
That many things, having full reference
To one concent, may work contrariously:
As many arrows, loosed several ways,
Fly to one mark;
As many several ways meet in one town;
As many fresh streams meet in one salt sea;
As many lines close in the dial's centre:
So may a thousand actions, once afoot,
End in one purpose, and be all well borne
Without defeat. Therefore to France, my liege.
Divide your happy England into four;
Whereof take you one quarter into France,
And you withal shall make all Gallia shake.
If we, with thrice such powers left at home,
Cannot defend our own doors from the dog,
Let us be worried, and our nation lose
The name of hardiness and policy.
K. Hen. Call in the messengers sent from the Dauphin.   [*Exit an* Attendant.
Now are we well resolv'd: and, by God's help
And yours, the noble sinews of our power,
France being ours, we'll bend it to our awe,
Or break it all to pieces: or there we'll sit,
Ruling in large and ample empery
O'er France and all her almost kingly dukedoms,
Or lay these bones in an unworthy urn,

Tombless, with no remembrance over them:
Either our history shall with full mouth
Speak freely of our acts, or else our grave,
Like Turkish mute, shall have a tongueless
  mouth,
Not worshipp'd with a waxen epitaph.

Enter Ambassadors *of France.*

Now are we well prepar'd to know the pleasure
Of our fair cousin Dauphin; for we hear
Your greeting is from him, not from the king.
  1 *Amb.* May it please your majesty to give
    us leave
Freely to render what we have in charge;
Or shall we sparingly show you far off
The Dauphin's meaning and our embassy?
  K. Hen. We are no tyrant, but a Christian
    king;
Unto whose grace our passion is as subject
As are our wretches fetter'd in our prisons:
Therefore with frank and with uncurbed plain-
  ness
Tell us the Dauphin's mind.
  1 *Amb.*   Thus, then, in few.
Your highness, lately sending into France,
Did claim some certain dukedoms, in the right
Of your great predecessor, King Edward the
  Third.
In answer of which claim, the prince our master
Says, that you savour too much of your youth;
And bids you be advis'd there's naught in
  France
That can be with a nimble galliard won;—
You cannot revel into dukedoms there.
He therefore sends you, meeter for your spirit,
This tun of treasure; and, in lieu of this,
Desires you let the dukedoms that you claim
Hear no more of you. This the Dauphin speaks.
  K. Hen. What treasure, uncle?
  Exe.   Tennis-balls, my liege.
  K. Hen. We are glad the Dauphin is so
    pleasant with us;
His present and your pains we thank you for:
When we have match'd our rackets to these
  balls,
We will, in France, by God's grace, play a set
Shall strike his father's crown into the hazard.
Tell him he hath made a match with such a
  wrangler
That all the courts of France will be disturb'd
With chases. And we understand him well,
How he comes o'er us with our wilder days,
Not measuring what use we made of them.
We never valu'd this poor seat of England;
And therefore, living hence, did give ourself
To barbarous license; as 'tis ever common
That men are merriest when they are from
  home.
But tell the Dauphin, I will keep my state;
Be like a king, and show my sail of greatness,
When I do rouse me in my throne of France:
For that I have laid by my majesty,
And plodded like a man for working-days;
But I will rise there with so full a glory

That I will dazzle all the eyes of France,
Yea, strike the Dauphin blind to look on us.
And tell the pleasant prince this mock of his
Hath turn'd his balls to gun-stones; and his soul
Shall stand sore charged for the wasteful ven-
  geance
That shall fly with them; for many a thousand
  widows
Shall this his mock mock out of their dear
  husbands;
Mock mothers from their sons, mock castles
  down;
And some are yet ungotten and unborn
That shall have cause to curse the Dauphin's
  scorn.
But this lies all within the will of God,
To whom I do appeal; and in whose name,
Tell you the Dauphin, I am coming on,
To venge me as I may, and to put forth
My rightful hand in a well-hallow'd cause.
So, get you hence in peace; and tell the Dauphin
His jest will savour but of shallow wit,
When thousands weep, more than did laugh
  at it.—
Convey them with safe conduct.—Fare you
  well.   [*Exeunt* Ambassadors.
  Exe. This was a merry message.
  K. Hen. We hope to make the sender blush
    at it.
Therefore, my lords, omit no happy hour
That may give furtherance to our expedition;
For we have now no thought in us but France,
Save those to God, that run before our business.
Therefore let our proportions for these wars
Be soon collected, and all things thought upon
That may with reasonable swiftness add
More feathers to our wings; for, God before,
We'll chide this Dauphin at his father's door.
Therefore let every man now task his thought,
That this fair action may on foot be brought.
                                      [*Exeunt.*

Enter Chorus.

  Chor. Now all the youth of England are on
    fire,
And silken dalliance in the wardrobe lies:
Now thrive the armourers, and honour's thought
Reigns solely in the breast of every man:
They sell the pasture now to buy the horse;
Following the mirror of all Christian kings,
With winged heels, as English Mercuries,
For now sits Expectation in the air;
And hides a sword from hilts unto the point
With crowns imperial, crowns, and coronets,
Promis'd to Harry and his followers.
The French, advis'd by good intelligence
Of this most dreadful preparation,
Shake in their fear; and with pale policy
Seek to divert the English purposes.
O England!—model to thy inward greatness,
Like little body with a mighty heart,—
What mightst thou do, that honour would
  thee do,
Were all thy children kind and natural!

But see thy fault! France hath in thee found
 out
A nest of hollow bosoms, which he fills
With treacherous crowns; and three corrupted
 men,—
One, Richard Earl of Cambridge; and the
 second,
Henry Lord Scroop of Masham; and the third,
Sir Thomas Grey, knight, of Northumber-
 land,—
Have, for the guilt of France,—O guilt in-
 deed!—
Confirm'd conspiracy with fearful France;
And by their hands this grace of kings must
 die,—
If hell and treason hold their promises,—
Ere he take ship for France, and in South-
 ampton.
Linger your patience on; and well digest
The abuse of distance, while we force a play.
The sum is paid; the traitors are agreed;
The king is set from London; and the scene
Is now transported, gentles, to Southampton,—
There is the play-house now, there must you
 sit:
And thence to France shall we convey you safe,
And bring you back, charming the narrow seas
To give you gentle pass; for, if we may,
We'll not offend one stomach with our play.
But, till the king come forth, and not till then,
Unto Southampton do we shift our scene.
           [*Exit.*

ACT II.

SCENE I.—LONDON. *Before the Boar's Head
Tavern, Eastcheap.*

Enter, severally, NYM *and* BARDOLPH.

Bard. Well met, Corporal Nym.

Nym. Good-morrow, Lieutenant Bardolph.

Bard. What, are Ancient Pistol and you
friends yet?

Nym. For my part, I care not: I say little;
but when time shall serve, there shall be smiles;
—but that shall be as it may. I dare not fight;
but I will wink, and hold out mine iron: it is
a simple one; but what though? it will toast
cheese: and it will endure cold as another man's
sword will, and there's the humour of it.

Bard. I will bestow a breakfast to make you
friends; and we'll be all three sworn brothers
to France: let it be so, good Corporal Nym.

Nym. Faith, I will live so long as I may,
that's the certain of it; and when I cannot live
any longer, I will do as I may: that is my rest,
that is the rendezvous of it.

Bard. It is certain, corporal, that he is married to Nell Quickly: and, certainly, she did you
wrong; for you were troth-plight to her.

Nym. I cannot tell:—things must be as they
may: men may sleep, and they may have their
throats about them at that time; and, some
say, knives have edges. It must be as it may:
though patience be a tired mare, yet she will

plod. There must be conclusions. Well, I cannot tell.

Bard. Here comes Ancient Pistol and his
wife:—good corporal, be patient here.

Enter PISTOL *and* Hostess.

How now, mine host Pistol!

Pist. Base tike, call'st thou me host?
Now, by this hand, I swear, I scorn the term;
Nor shall my Nell keep lodgers.

Host. No, by my troth, not long; for we
cannot lodge and board a dozen or fourteen
gentlewomen that live honestly by the prick of
their needles, but it will be thought we keep a
bawdy-house straight. [NYM *draws his sword.*]
O well-a-day, Lady, if he be not drawn! now
we shall see wilful adultery and murder committed.

Bard. Good lieutenant,—good corporal,—
offer nothing here.

Nym. Pish!

Pist. Pish for thee, Iceland dog! thou prick-
 ear'd cur of Iceland!

Host. Good Corporal Nym, show thy valour,
and put up your sword.

Nym. Will you shog off? I would have you
solus.   [*Sheathing his sword.*

Pist. Solus, egregious dog? O viper vile!
The *solus* in thy most marvellous face;
The *solus* in thy teeth, and in thy throat,
And in thy hateful lungs, yea, in thy maw,
 perdy;
And, which is worse, within thy nasty mouth!
I do retort the *solus* in thy bowels;
For I can take, and Pistol's cock is up,
And flashing fire will follow.

Nym. I am not Barbason; you cannot conjure me. I have an humour to knock you indif-
ferently well. If you grow foul with me, Pistol,
I will scour you with my rapier, as I may, in
fair terms: if you would walk off I would prick
your guts a little, in good terms, as I may: and
that's the humour of it.

Pist. O braggart vile and damned furious
 wight!
The grave doth gape and doting death is near;
Therefore exhale. [PISTOL *and* NYM *draw.*

Bard. Hear me, hear me what I say:—he
that strikes the first stroke I'll run him up to
the hilts, as I am a soldier. [*Draws.*

Pist. An oath of mickle might; and fury
 shall abate.
Give me thy fist, thy fore-foot to me give:
Thy spirits are most tall.

Nym. I will cut thy throat one time or other,
in fair terms: that is the humour of it.

Pist. Coupe la gorge! That's the word.—I
 thee defy again.
O hound of Crete, think'st thou my spouse to
 get?
No; to the spital go,
And from the powdering tub of infamy
Fetch forth the lazar kite of Cressid's kind,
Doll Tearsheet she by name, and her espouse.

I have, and I will hold, the *quondam* Quickly
For the only she; and—*Pauca*, there's enough.
Go to.

Enter the Boy.

Boy. Mine host Pistol, you must come to
my master,—and you, hostess:—he is very
sick, and would to bed.—Good Bardolph, put
thy nose between his sheets, and do the office of
a warming-pan. Faith, he's very ill.

Bard. Away, you rogue.

Host. By my troth, he'll yield the crow a
pudding one of these days: the king has killed
his heart.—Good husband, come home presently.   [*Exeunt* Hostess *and* Boy.

Bard. Come, shall I make you two friends?
We must to France together: why the devil
should we keep knives to cut one another's
throats?

Pist. Let floods o'erswell and fiends for food
howl on!

Nym. You'll pay me the eight shillings I
won of you at betting?

Pist. Base is the slave that pays.

Nym. That now I will have: that's the
humour of it.

Pist. As manhood shall compound: push
home.   [PISTOL *and* NYM *draw.*

Bard. By this sword, he that makes the first
thrust I'll kill him; by this sword, I will.

Pist. Sword is an oath, and oaths must have
their course.

Bard. Corporal Nym, an thou wilt be friends,
be friends: an thou wilt not, why, then, be
enemies with me too. Pr'ythee, put up.

Nym. I shall have my eight shillings I won
of you at betting?

Pist. A noble shalt thou have, and present
pay;
And liquor likewise will I give to thee,
And friendship shall combine, and brotherhood:
I'll live by Nym and Nym shall live by me;—
Is not this just?—for I shall sutler be
Unto the camp, and profits will accrue.
Give me thy hand.

Nym. I shall have my noble?

Pist. In cash most justly paid.

Nym. Well, then, that's the humour of it.

Re-enter Hostess.

Host. As ever you came of women, come in
quickly to Sir John. Ah, poor heart! he is so
shaken of a burning quotidian tertian that it is
most lamentable to behold. Sweet men, come
to him.

Nym. The king hath run bad humours on
the knight; that's the even of it.

Pist. Nym, thou hast spoke the right;
His heart is fracted and corroborate.

Nym. The king is a good king: but it must
be as it may; he passes some humours and
careers.

Pist. Let us condole the knight; for, lamb-
kins, we will live.   [*Exeunt.*

SCENE II.—SOUTHAMPTON. *A Council Chamber*.

Enter EXETER, BEDFORD, *and* WESTMORELAND.

Bed. 'Fore God, his grace is bold, to trust
these traitors.

Exe. They shall be apprehended by and by

West. How smooth and even they do beat
themselves!
As if allegiance in their bosom sat,
Crowned with faith and constant loyalty.

Bed. The king hath note of all that they intend,
By interception which they dream not of.

Exe. Nay, but the man that was his bed-
fellow,
Whom he hath dull'd and cloy'd with gracious
favours,—
That he should, for a foreign purse, so sell
His sovereign's life to death and treachery!

Trumpet sounds. Enter KING HENRY, SCROOP,
CAMBRIDGE, GREY, Lords, *and* Attendants.

K. Hen. Now sits the wind fair, and we will
aboard.
My Lord of Cambridge,—and my kind Lord of
Masham,—
And you, my gentle knight,—give me your
thoughts:
Think you not that the powers we bear with us
Will cut their passage through the force of
France,
Doing the execution and the act
For which we have in head assembled them?

Scroop. No doubt, my liege, if each man do
his best.

K. Hen. I doubt not that; since we are well
persuaded
We carry not a heart with us from hence
That grows not in a fair consent with ours,
Nor leave not one behind that doth not wish
Success and conquest to attend on us.

Cam. Never was monarch better fear'd and
lov'd
Than is your majesty: there's not, I think, a
subject
That sits in heart-grief and uneasiness
Under the sweet shade of your government.

Grey. True: those that were your father's
enemies
Have steep'd their galls in honey, and do serve
you
With hearts create of duty and of zeal.

K. Hen. We therefore have great cause of
thankfulness;
And shall forget the office of our hand
Sooner than quittance of desert and merit
According to the weight and worthiness.

Scroop. So service shall with steel'd sinews
toil,
And labour shall refresh itself with hope,
To do your grace incessant services.

K. Hen. We judge no less.—Uncle of Exeter

Enlarge the man committed yesterday,
That rail'd against our person: we consider
It was excess of wine that set him on;
And on his more advice we pardon him.

  Scroop. That's mercy, but too much security:
Let him be punish'd, sovereign; lest example
Breed, by his sufferance, more of such a kind.

  K. Hen. O, let us yet be merciful.

  Cam. So may your highness, and yet punish
    too.

  Grey. Sir, you show great mercy if you give
    him life,
After the taste of much correction.

  K. Hen. Alas, your too much love and care
    of me
Are heavy orisons 'gainst this poor wretch!
If little faults, proceeding on distemper,
Shall not be wink'd at, how shall we stretch
    our eye
When capital crimes, chew'd, swallow'd, and
    digested,
Appear before us?—We'll yet enlarge that man,
Though Cambridge, Scroop, and Grey, in their
    dear care
And tender preservation of our person,
Would have him punish'd. And now to our
    French causes:
Who are the late commissioners?

  Cam. I one, my lord:
Your highness bade me ask for it to-day.

  Scroop. So did you me, my liege.

  Grey. And me, my royal sovereign.

  K. Hen. Then, Richard Earl of Cambridge,
    there is yours;—
There yours, Lord Scroop of Masham;—and,
    sir knight,
Grey of Northumberland, this same is yours:—
Read them, and know I know your worthi-
    ness.—
My Lord of Westmoreland,—and uncle Ex-
    eter,—
We will aboard to-night.—Why, how now,
    gentlemen!
What see you in those papers, that you lose
So much complexion?—Look ye, how they
    change!
Their cheeks are paper.—Why, what read you
    there
That hath so cowarded and chas'd your blood
Out of appearance?

  Cam.   I do confess my fault,
And do submit me to your highness' mercy.

  Grey, Scroop. To which we all appeal.

  K. Hen. The mercy that was quick in us but
    late
By your own counsel is suppress'd and kill'd:
You must not dare, for shame, to talk of mercy;
For your own reasons turn into your bosoms,
As dogs upon their masters, worrying you.—
See you, my princes and my noble peers,
These English monsters! My Lord of Cam-
    bridge here,—
You know how apt our love was to accord
To furnish him with all appertinents

Belonging to his honour; and this man
Hath, for a few light crowns, lightly conspir'd,
And sworn unto the practices of France,
To kill us here in Hampton: to the which
This knight, no less for bounty bound to us
Than Cambridge is, hath likewise sworn.—
    But, O,   [cruel,
What shall I say to thee, Lord Scroop? thou
Ingrateful, savage, and inhuman creature!
Thou that didst bear the key of all my counsels,
That knew'st the very bottom of my soul,
That almost mightst have coin'd me into gold,
Wouldst thou have practis'd on me for thy
    use,—
May it be possible that foreign hire
Could out of thee extract one spark of evil
That might annoy my finger? 'tis so strange
That, though the truth of it stands off as gross
As black from white, my eye will scarcely see it.
Treason and murder ever kept together,
As two yoke-devils sworn to either's purpose,
Working so grossly in a natural cause
That admiration did not whoop at them:
But thou, 'gainst all proportion, didst bring in
Wonder to wait on treason and on murder:
And whatsoever cunning fiend it was
That wrought upon thee so preposterously
Hath got the voice in hell for excellence: .
And other devils, that suggest by treasons,
Do botch and bungle up damnation
With patches, colours, and with forms being
    fetch'd
From glistering semblances of piety;
But he that temper'd thee bade thee stand up,
Gave thee no instance why thou shouldst do
    treason,
Unless to dub thee with the name of traitor.
If that same demon that hath gull'd thee thus
Should with his lion gait walk the whole world,
He might return to vasty Tartar back,
And tell the legions, *I can never win*
A soul so easy as that Englishman's.
O, how hast thou with jealousy infected
The sweetness of affiance! Show men dutiful?
Why, so didst thou: seem they grave and
    learned?
Why, so didst thou: come they of noble family?
Why, so didst thou: seem they religious?
Why, so didst thou: or are they spare in diet;
Free from gross passion, or of mirth or anger;
Constant in spirit, not swerving with the blood;
Garnish'd and deck'd in modest complement;
Not working with the eye without the ear,
And but in purged judgment trusting neither?
Such and so finely bolted didst thou seem:
And thus thy fall hath left a kind of blot,
To mark the full-fraught man and best indu'd
With some suspicion. I will weep for thee;
For this revolt of thine, methinks, is like
Another fall of man.—Their faults are open:
Arrest them to the answer of the law;—
And God acquit them of their practices!

  Exe. I arrest thee of high treason, by the
name of Richard Earl of Cambridge.

I arrest thee of high treason, by the name of Henry Lord Scroop of Masham.

I arrest thee of high treason, by the name of Thomas Grey, knight, of Northumberland.

Scroop. Our purposes God justly hath discover'd;
And I repent my fault more than my death;
Which I beseech your highness to forgive,
Although my body pay the price of it.

Cam. For me,—the gold of France did not seduce;
Although I did admit it as a motive
The sooner to effect what I intended:
But God be thanked for prevention;
Which I in sufferance heartily will rejoice,
Beseeching God and you to pardon me.

Grey. Never did faithful subject more rejoice
At the discovery of most dangerous treason
Than I do at this hour joy o'er myself,
Prevented from a damned enterprise:
My fault, but not my body, pardon, sovereign.

K. Hen. God quit you in his mercy! Hear your sentence.
You have conspir'd against our royal person,
Join'd with an enemy proclaim'd, and from his coffers
Receiv'd the golden earnest of our death;
Wherein you would have sold your king to slaughter,
His princes and his peers to servitude,
His subjects to oppression and contempt,
And his whole kingdom into desolation.
Touching our person seek we no revenge;
But we our kingdom's safety must so tender,
Whose ruin you have sought, that to her laws
We do deliver you. Get you, therefore, hence,
Poor miserable wretches, to your death:
The taste whereof God of his mercy give you
Patience to endure, and true repentance
Of all your dear offences!—Bear them hence.

[Exeunt Conspirators, guarded.

Now, lords, for France; the enterprise whereof
Shall be to you, as us, like glorious.
We doubt not of a fair and lucky war:
Since God so graciously hath brought to light
This dangerous treason, lurking in our way
To hinder our beginnings, we doubt not now
But every rub is smoothed on our way.
Then, forth, dear countrymen: let us deliver
Our puissance into the hand of God,
Putting it straight in expedition.
Cheerly to sea; the signs of war advance:
No king of England, if not king of France.

[Exeunt.

SCENE III.—LONDON. *The* Hostess's *House in Eastcheap.*

Enter PISTOL, Hostess, NYM, BARDOLPH, *and* Boy.

Host. Pr'ythee, honey-sweet husband, let me bring thee to Staines.

Pist. No; for my manly heart doth yearn.—Bardolph, be blithe;—Nym, rouse thy vaunting veins;—

Boy, bristle thy courage up;—for Falstaff he is dead,
And we must yearn therefore.

Bard. Would I were with him, wheresome'er he is, either in heaven or in hell!

Host. Nay, sure, he's not in hell: he's in Arthur's bosom, if ever man went to Arthur's bosom. 'A made a finer end, and went away, an it had been any christom child; 'a parted even just between twelve and one, even at the turning o' the tide: for after I saw him fumble with the sheets, and play with flowers, and smile upon his fingers' ends, I knew there was but one way; for his nose was as sharp as a pen, and 'a babbled of green fields. *How now, Sir John!* quoth I: *what, man! be o' good cheer.* So 'a cried out—*God, God, God!* three or four times. Now I, to comfort him, bid him 'a should not think of God; I hoped there was no need to trouble himself with any such thoughts yet. So 'a bade me lay more clothes on his feet: I put my hand into the bed and felt them, and they were as cold as any stone; then I felt to his knees, and so upward and upward, and all was as cold as any stone.

Nym. They say he cried out of sack.

Host. Ay, that 'a did.

Bard. And of women.

Host. Nay, that 'a did not.

Boy. Yes, that 'a did; and said they were devils incarnate.

Host. 'A could never abide carnation; 'twas a colour he never liked.

Boy. 'A said once, the devil would have him about women.

Host. 'A did in some sort, indeed, handle women; but then he was rheumatic, and talked of the whore of Babylon.

Boy. Do you not remember, 'a saw a flea stick upon Bardolph's nose, and 'a said it was a black soul burning in hell?

Bard. Well, the fuel is gone that maintained that fire: that's all the riches I got in his service.

Nym. Shall we shog? the king will be gone from Southampton.

Pist. Come, let's away.—My love, give me thy lips.
Look to my chattels and my moveables:
Let senses rule; the word is, Pitch and pay;
Trust none;
For oaths are straws, men's faiths are wafer-cakes,
And holdfast is the only dog, my duck:
Therefore *caveto* be thy counsellor.
Go, clear thy crystals.—Yoke-fellows in arms,
Let us to France; like horse-leeches, my boys,
To suck, to suck, the very blood to suck!

Boy. And that is but unwholesome food, they say.

Pist. Touch her soft mouth and march.

Bard. Farewell, hostess. *[Kissing her.*

Nym. I cannot kiss, that is the humour of it; but, adieu.

Pist. Let housewifery appear: keep close, I thee command.

Host. Farewell; adieu.　　　　　　[*Exeunt.*

SCENE IV.—FRANCE. *A Room in the* FRENCH KING's *Palace.*

Flourish. Enter the FRENCH KING, *attended; the* DAUPHIN, *the* DUKE OF BURGUNDY, *the* Constable, *and others.*

Fr. King. Thus come the English with full power upon us;
And more than carefully it us concerns
To answer royally in our defences.
Therefore the Dukes of Berri and of Bretagne,
Of Brabant and of Orleans, shall make forth,—
And you, Prince Dauphin,—with all swift despatch,
To line and new repair our towns of war
With men of courage and with means defendant;
For England his approaches makes as fierce
As waters to the sucking of a gulf.
It fits us, then, to be as provident
As fear may teach us, out of late examples
Left by the fatal and neglected English
Upon our fields.

Dau.　　　　My most redoubted father,
It is most meet we arm us 'gainst the foe;
For peace itself should not so dull a kingdom,—
Though war, nor no known quarrel, were in question,—
But that defences, musters, preparations,
Should be maintain'd, assembled, and collected,
As were a war in expectation.
Therefore, I say, 'tis meet we all go forth
To view the sick and feeble parts of France:
And let us do it with no show of fear;　　[land
No, with no more than if we heard that Eng-
Were busied with a Whitsun morris-dance:
For, my good liege, she is so idly king'd,
Her sceptre so fantastically borne
By a vain, giddy, shallow, humorous youth,
That fear attends her not.

Con.　　　　O peace, Prince Dauphin!
You are too much mistaken in this king:
Question your grace the late ambassadors,—
With what great state he heard their embassy,
How well supplied with noble counsellors,
How modest in exception, and withal
How terrible in constant resolution,—
And you shall find his vanities forespent.
Were but the outside of the Roman Brutus,
Covering discretion with a coat of folly;
As gardeners do with ordure hide those roots
That shall first spring and be most delicate.

Dau. Well, 'tis not so, my lord high-constable;
But though we think it so, it is no matter:
In cases of defence 'tis best to weigh
The enemy more mighty than he seems:
So the proportions of defence are fill'd;
Which, of a weak and niggardly projection,
Doth like a miser spoil his coat with scanting
A little cloth.

Fr. King. Think we King Harry strong;
And, princes, look you strongly arm to meet him.
The kindred of him hath been flesh'd upon us;
And he is bred out of that bloody strain
That haunted us in our familiar paths:
Witness our too-much memorable shame
When Cressy battle fatally was struck,
And all our princes captiv'd by the hand
Of that black name, Edward Black Prince of Wales;
Whiles that his mountain sire,—on mountain standing,
Up in the air, crown'd with the golden sun,—
Saw his heroical seed, and smil'd to see him,
Mangle the work of nature, and deface
The patterns that by God and by French fathers
Had twenty years been made. This is a stem
Of that victorious stock; and let us fear
The native mightiness and fate of him.

Enter a Messenger.

Mess. Ambassadors from Harry King of England
Do crave admittance to your majesty.

Fr. King. We'll give them present audience.
Go, and bring them.
　　　　　[*Exeunt* Mess. *and certain* Lords.
You see this chase is hotly follow'd, friends.

Dau. Turn head and stop pursuit; for coward dogs
Most spend their mouths when what they seem to threaten
Runs far before them. Good my sovereign,
Take up the English short; and let them know
Of what a monarchy you are the head:
Self-love, my liege, is not so vile a sin
As self-neglecting.

Re-enter Lords, *with* EXETER *and* Train.

Fr. King.　　　From our brother England?

Exe. From him; and thus he greets your majesty.
He wills you, in the name of God Almighty,
That you divest yourself, and lay apart
The borrow'd glories that by gift of heaven,
By law of nature and of nations, 'long
To him and to his heirs; namely, the crown,
And all wide stretched honours that pertain,
By custom and the ordinance of times,
Unto the crown of France. That you may know
'Tis no sinister nor no awkward claim,
Pick'd from the worm-holes of long-vanish'd days,
Nor from the dust of old oblivion rak'd,
He sends you this most memorable line,
　　　　　　　　　　　　[*Gives a paper.*
In every branch truly demonstrative;
Willing you overlook this pedigree:
And when you find him evenly deriv'd
From his most fam'd of famous ancestors,
Edward the Third, he bids you then resign
Your crown and kingdom, indirectly held

From him the native and true challenger.

Fr. King. Or else what follows?

Exe. Bloody constraint; for if you hide the crown
Even in your hearts, there will he rake for it:
Therefore in fierce tempest is he coming,
In thunder and in earthquake, like a Jove,—
That if requiring fail, he will compel;—
And bids you, in the bowels of the Lord,
Deliver up the crown; and to take mercy
On the poor souls for whom this hungry war
Opens his vasty jaws: and on your head
Turns he the widows' tears, the orphans' cries,
The dead men's blood, the pining maidens' groans,
For husbands, fathers, and betrothed lovers,
That shall be swallow'd in this controversy.
This is his claim, his threatening, and my message;
Unless the Dauphin be in presence here,
To whom expressly I bring greeting too.

Fr. King. For us, we will consider of this further:
To-morrow shall you bear our full intent
Back to our brother England.

Dau. For the Dauphin,
I stand here for him: what to him from England?

Exe. Scorn and defiance; slight regard, contempt,
And anything that may not misbecome
The mighty sender, doth he prize you at.
Thus says my king: an if your father's highness
Do not, in grant of all demands at large,
Sweeten the bitter mock you sent his majesty,
He'll call you to so hot an answer for it
That caves and womby vaultages of France
Shall chide your trespass and return your mock
In second accent of his ordinance.

Dau. Say, if my father render fair return,
It is against my will; for I desire
Nothing but odds with England: to that end,
As matching to his youth and vanity,
I did present him with the Paris balls.

Exe. He'll make your Paris Louvre shake for it,
Were it the mistress court of mighty Europe:
And, be assur'd, you'll find a difference,—
As we, his subjects, have in wonder found,—
Between the promise of his greener days
And these he masters now: now he weighs time
Even to the utmost grain:—that you shall read
In your own losses if he stay in France.

Fr. King. To-morrow shall you know our mind at full.

Exe. Despatch us with all speed, lest that our king
Come here himself to question our delay;
For he is footed in this land already.

Fr. King. You shall be soon despatch'd with fair conditions:
A night is but small breath and little pause
To answer matters of this consequence.

[*Exeunt.*

Enter Chorus.

Cho. Thus with imagin'd wing our swift scene flies,
In motion of no less celerity
Than that of thought. Suppose that you have seen
The well-appointed king at Hampton pier
Embark his royalty; and his brave fleet
With silken streamers the young Phœbus fanning:
Play with your fancies; and in them behold
Upon the hempen tackle ship-boys climbing,
Hear the shrill whistle which doth order give
To sounds confus'd; behold the threaden sails,
Borne with the invisible and creeping wind,
Draw the huge bottoms through the furrow'd sea,
Breasting the lofty surge: O, do but think
You stand upon the rivage and behold
A city on the inconstant billows dancing;
For so appears this fleet majestical,
Holding due course to Harfleur. Follow, follow!
Grapple your minds to sternage of this navy;
And leave your England, as dead midnight still,
Guarded with grandsires, babies, and old women,
Either past or not arrived to pith and puissance;
For who is he, whose chin is but enrich'd
With one appearing hair, that will not follow
These cull'd and choice-drawn cavaliers to France?
Work, work your thoughts, and therein see a siege;
Behold the ordnance on their carriages,
With fatal mouths gaping on girded Harfleur.
Suppose the ambassador from the French comes back;
Tells Harry that the king doth offer him
Katharine his daughter; and with her, to dowry,
Some petty and unprofitable dukedomes.
The offer likes not: and the nimble gunner
With linstock now the devilish cannon touches,
[*Alarum, and chambers go off, within.*
And down goes all before them. Still be kind,
And eke out our performance with your mind.
[*Exit.*

ACT III.

SCENE I.—FRANCE. *Before Harfleur.*

Alarums. Enter KING HENRY, EXETER, BEDFORD, GLOSTER, *and* Soldiers, *with scaling-ladders.*

K. Hen. Once more unto the breach, dear friends, once more;
Or close the wall up with our English dead!
In peace there's nothing so becomes a man
As modest stillness and humility:
But when the blast of war blows in our ears,
Then imitate the action of the tiger;
Stiffen the sinews, summon up the blood,

Disguise fair nature with hard-favour'd rage;
Then lend the eye a terrible aspèct;
Let it pry through the portage of the head [it
Like the brass cannon; let the brow o'erwhelm
As fearfully as doth a galled rock
O'erhang and jutty his confounded base,
Swill'd with the wild and wasteful ocean.
Now set the teeth and stretch the nostril wide;
Hold hard the breath, and bend up every spirit
To his full height!—On, on, you noble English,
Whose blood is fet from fathers of war-proof!—
Fathers that, like so many Alexanders,
Have in these parts from morn till even fought,
And sheath'd their swords for lack of argu-
    ment:—
Dishonour not your mothers; now attest
That those whom you call'd fathers did beget
    you!
Be copy now to men of grosser blood,
And teach them how to war!—And you, good
    yeomen,
Whose limbs were made in England, show us
    here
The mettle of your pasture; let us swear
That you are worth your breeding: which I
    doubt not;
For there is none of you so mean and base,
That hath not noble lustre in your eyes.
I see you stand like greyhounds in the slips,
Straining upon the start. The game's afoot:
Follow your spirit; and upon this charge
Cry—God for Harry! England! and Saint
    George!
[*Exeunt. Alarum, and chambers go off, within.*

Enter NYM, BARDOLPH, PISTOL, *and* Boy.

Bard. On, on, on, on, on! to the breach, to
the breach!

Nym. Pray thee, corporal, stay: the knocks
are too hot; and, for mine own part, I have not
a case of lives: the humour of it is too hot, that
is the very plain-song of it.

Pist. The plain-song is most just; for humours do abound:

Knocks go and come; God's vassals drop and die;
    And sword and shield
    In bloody field
Doth win immortal fame.

Boy. Would I were in an alehouse in London! I would give all my fame for a pot of ale
and safety.

Pist. And I:

    If wishes would prevail with me,
    My purpose should not fail with me,
      But thither would I hie.

Boy. As duly, but not as truly,
    As bird doth sing on bough.

Enter FLUELLEN.

Flu. Up to the preach, you dogs! avaunt,
you cullions!   [*Driving them forward.*
  Pist. Be merciful, great duke, to men of
mould!

Abate thy rage, abate thy manly rage!
Abate thy rage, great duke!
Good bawcock, bate thy rage! use lenity, sweet
    chuck!
  Nym. These be good humours!—your honour wins bad humours.
    [*Exeunt* NYM, PISTOL, *and* BARDOLPH,
      followed by FLUELLEN.
  Boy. As young as I am, I have observed
these three swashers. I am boy to them all
three: but all they three, though they would
serve me, could not be man to me; for, indeed,
three such antics do not amount to a man. For
Bardolph,—he is white-livered and red-faced;
by the means whereof 'a faces it out, but fights
not. For Pistol,—he hath a killing tongue and
a quiet sword; by the means whereof 'a breaks
words and keeps whole weapons. For Nym,—
he hath heard that men of few words are the
best men; and therefore he scorns to say his
prayers lest 'a should be thought a coward: but
his few bad words are matched with as few
good deeds; for 'a never broke any man's head
but his own, and that was against a post when
he was drunk. They will steal anything, and
call it purchase. Bardolph stole a lute-case,
bore it twelve leagues, and sold it for three
halfpence. Nym and Bardolph are sworn
brothers in filching; and in Calais they stole a
fire-shovel: I knew by that piece of service the
men would carry coals. They would have me
as familiar with men's pockets as their gloves
or their handkerchers: which makes much
against my manhood, if I should take from
another's pocket to put into mine; for it is plain
pocketing up of wrongs. I must leave them,
and seek some better service: their villany goes
against my weak stomach, and therefore I must
cast it up.   [*Exit.*

Re-enter FLUELLEN, GOWER *following.*

  Gow. Captain Fluellen, you must come presently to the mines; the Duke of Gloster would
speak with you.
  Flu. To the mines! tell you the duke it is
not so goot to come to the mines; for, look you,
the mines is not according to the disciplines of
the war: the concavities of it is not sufficient;
for, look you, th' athversary,—you may discuss unto the duke, look you,—is digt himself
four yard under the countermines; by Cheshu,
I think 'a will plow up all, if there is not better
directions.
  Gow. The Duke of Gloster, to whom the
order of the siege is given, is altogether directed
by an Irishman,—a very valiant gentleman, i'
faith.
  Flu. It is Captain Macmorris, is it not?
  Gow. I think it be.
  Flu. By Cheshu, he is an ass, as in the 'orld:
I will verify as much in his peard: he has no
more directions in the true disciplines of the
wars, look you, of the Roman disciplines, than
is a puppy-dog.

Gow. Here 'a comes; and the Scots captain, Captain Jamy, with him.

Flu. Captain Jamy is a marvellous falorous gentleman, that is certain, and of great expedition and knowledge in the ancient wars, upon my particular knowledge of his directions: by Cheshu, he will maintain his argument as well as any military man in the 'orld, in the disciplines of the pristine wars of the Romans.

Enter MACMORRIS *and* JAMY, *at a distance.*

Jamy. I say gud-day, Captain Fluellen.

Flu. God-den to your worship, goot Captain Jamy.

Gow. How now, Captain Macmorris! have you quit the mines? have the pioneers given o'er?

Mac. By Chrish la, tish ill done: the work ish give over, the trumpet sound the retreat. By my hand, I swear, and by my father's soul, the work ish ill done; it ish give over: I would have blowed up the town, so Chrish save me, la, in an hour: O, tish ill done, tish ill done; by my hand, tish ill done!

Flu. Captain Macmorris, I peseech you now, will you voutsafe me, look you, a few disputations with you, as partly touching or concerning the disciplines of the war, the Roman wars, in the way of argument, look you, and friendly communication; partly to satisfy my opinion, and partly for the satisfaction, look you, of my mind, as touching the direction of the military discipline; that is the point.

Jamy. It sall be very gud, gud feith, gud captains bath: and I sall quit you with gud leve, as I may pick occasion; that sall I, mary.

Mac. It is no time to discourse, so Chrish save me: the day is hot, and the weather, and the wars, and the king, and the dukes: it is no time to discourse. The town is beseeched, and the trumpet call us to the breach; and we talk and, by Chrish, do nothing: 'tis shame for us all: so God sa' me, 'tis shame to stand still; it is shame, by my hand: and there is throats to be cut, and works to be done; and there ish nothing done, so Chrish sa' me, la.

Jamy. By the mess, ere theise eyes of mine take themselves to slumber, aile do gud service, or aile lig i' the grund for it; ay, or go to death; and aile pay 't as valorously as I may, that sall I surely do, that is the breff and the long. Mary, I wad full fain heard some question 'tween you tway.

Flu. Captain Macmorris, I think, look you, under your correction, there is not many of your nation,—

Mac. Of my nation! What ish my nation? what ish my nation? Who talks of my nation ish a villain, and a basterd, and a knave, and a rascal.

Flu. Look you, if you take the matter otherwise than is meant, Captain Macmorris, peradventure I shall think you do not use me with that affability as in discretion you ought to use

me, look you; being as goot a man as yourself, both in the disciplines of war and in the derivation of my birth, and in other particularities.

Mac. I do not know you so good a man as myself: so Chrish save me, I will cut off your head.

Gow. Gentlemen both, you will mistake each other.

Jamy. Au! that's a foul fault.

[*A parley sounded.*

Gow. The town sounds a parley.

Flu. Captain Macmorris, when there is more petter opportunity to be required, look you, I will be so pold as to tell you I know the disciplines of war; and there is an end. [*Exeunt.*

SCENE II.—*The same. Before the Gates of Harfleur.*

The Governor *and some* Citizens *on the walls; the* English Forces *below. Enter* KING HENRY *and his* Train.

K. Hen. How yet resolves the governor of the town?
This is the latest parley we will admit:
Therefore, to our best mercy give yourselves;
Or like to men proud of destruction,
Defy us to our worst: for as I am a soldier,—
A name that, in my thoughts, becomes me best,—
If I begin the battery once again,
I will not leave the half-achieved Harfleur
Till in her ashes she lie buried.
The gates of mercy shall be all shut up;
And the flesh'd soldier,—rough and hard of heart,—
In liberty of bloody hand shall range
With conscience wide as hell; mowing like grass
Your fresh-fair virgins and your flowering infants.
What is it then to me if impious war,—
Array'd in flames, like to the prince of fiends,—
Do, with his smirch'd complexion, all fell feats
Enlink'd to waste and desolation?
What is 't to me when you yourselves are cause,
If your pure maidens fall into the hand
Of hot and forcing violation?
What rein can hold licentious wickedness
When down the hill he holds his fierce career?
We may as bootless spend our vain command
Upon the enraged soldiers in their spoil,
As send précepts to the Leviathan   [fleur,
To come ashore. Therefore, you men of Har-
Take pity of your town and of your people
Whiles yet my soldiers are in my command;
Whiles yet the cool and temperate wind of grace
O'erblows the filthy and contagious clouds
Of heady murder, spoil, and villany.
If not, why, in a moment look to see
The blind and bloody soldier with foul hand
Defile the locks of your shrill-shrieking daughters;
Your fathers taken by the silver beards,
And their most reverend heads dash'd to the walls;

Your naked infants spitted upon pikes,
Whiles the mad mothers with their howls con-
    fus'd
Do break the clouds, as did the wives of Jewry
At Herod's bloody-hunting slaughtermen.
What say you? will you yield, and this avoid?
Or, guilty in defence, be thus destroy'd?

Gov. Our expectation hath this day an end:
The Dauphin, whom of succour we entreated,
Returns us that his powers are not yet ready
To raise so great a siege. Therefore, great king,
We yield our town and lives to thy soft mercy.
Enter our gates; dispose of us and ours;
For we no longer are defensible.

K. Hen. Open your gates.—Come, uncle
    Exeter,
Go you and enter Harfleur; there remain,
And fortify it strongly 'gainst the French:
Use mercy to them all. For us, dear uncle,—
The winter coming on, and sickness growing
Upon our soldiers,—we will retire to Calais.
To-night in Harfleur will we be your guest;
To-morrow for the march are we addrest.

    [*Flourish. The* KING, *&c., enter the Town.*

SCENE III.—ROUEN. *A Room in the Palace.*

Enter KATHARINE *and* ALICE.

Kath. Alice, *tu as été en Angleterre, et tu
parles bien le langage.*

Alice. Un peu, madame.

*Kath. Je te prie, m'enseignez; il faut que
j'apprenne à parler. Comment appelez-vous la
main en Anglais?*

Alice. La main? elle est appelée *de* hand.

Kath. De hand. *Et les doigts?*

*Alice. Les doigts? ma foi, j'oublie les doigts;
mais je me souviendrai. Les doigts? je pense
qu'ils sont appelés* de fingres; *oui,* de fingres.

Kath. La main, de hand; *les doigts,* de
fingres. *Je pense que je suis le bon écolier; j'ai
gagné deux mots d'Anglais vîtement. Comment
appelez-vous les ongles?*

Alice. Les ongles? les appelons de nails.

Kath. De nails. *Ecoutez; dites-moi, si je parle
bien:* de hand, de fingres, *et de* nails.

*Alice. C'est bien dit, madame; il est fort bon
Anglais.*

Kath. Dites-moi l'Anglais pour le bras.

Alice. De arm, *madame.*

Kath. Et le coude?

Alice. De elbow.

Kath. De elbow. *Je m'en fais la répétition
de tous les mots que vous m'avez appris dès à
présent.*

*Alice. Il est trop difficile, madame, comme je
pense.*

Kath. Excusez-moi, Alice; écoutez: de hand,
de fingres, de nails, de arm, de bilbow.

Alice. De elbow, *madame.*

Kath. O Seigneur Dieu, je m'en oublie! de
elbow. *Comment appelez-vous le col?*

Alice. De neck, *madame.*

Kath. De nick. *Et le menton?*

Alice. De chin.

Kath. De sin. *Le* col, *de* nick; *le menton,*
de sin.

*Alice. Oui. Sauf votre honneur, en vérité, vous
pronouncez les mots aussi droit que les natifs
d'Angleterre.*

*Kath. Je ne doute point d'apprendre, par la
grace de Dieu, et en peu de temps.*

*Alice. N'avez-vous pas déjà oublié ce que je
vous ai enseigné?*

Kath. Non, je reciterai à vous promptement:
de hand, de fingres, de mails,—

Alice. De nails, *madame.*

Kath. De nails, de arm, de ilbow.

Alice. Sauf votre honneur, de elbow.

Kath. Ainsi dis-je; de elbow, de nick, *et de*
sin. *Comment appelez-vous le pied et la robe?*

Alice. De foot, *madame; et de* coun.

Kath. De foot *et de* coun! *O Seigneur Dieu!
ce sont mots de son mauvais, corruptible, gros, et
impudique, et non pour les dames d'honneur à
user; je ne voudrais prononcer ces mots devant
les seigneurs de France pour tout le monde. Il
faut* de foot *et de* coun *néanmoins. Je reciterai
une autre fois ma leçon ensemble:* de hand, de
fingres, de nails, de arm, de elbow, de nick, de
sin, de foot, de coun.

Alice. Excellent, madame!

*Kath. C'est assez pour une fois: allons-nous
à dîner.*

    [*Exeunt.*

SCENE IV.—*The same. Another Room in
the same.*

Enter the FRENCH KING, *the* DAUPHIN, DUKE
OF BOURBON, *the* Constable of France, *and
others.*

Fr. King. 'Tis certain he hath pass'd the
    river Somme.

Con. And if he be not fought withal, my lord,
Let us not live in France; let us quit all,
And give our vineyards to a barbarous people.

Dau. O Dieu vivant! shall a few sprays of us,
The emptying of our fathers' luxury,
Our scions, put in wild and savage stock,
Spurt up so suddenly into the clouds,
And overlook their grafters?

Bour. Normans, but bastard Normans, Nor-
    man bastards!
Mort de ma vie! if they march along
Unfought withal, but I will sell my dukedom
To buy a slobbery and a dirty farm
In that nook-shotten isle of Albion.

Con. Dieu de batailles! where have they this
    mettle?
Is not their climate foggy, raw, and dull;
On whom, as in despite, the sun looks pale,
Killing their fruit with frowns? Can sodden
    water,   [broth,
A drench for sur-rein'd jades, their barley-
Decoct their cold blood to such valiant heat?
And shall our quick blood, spirited with wine,
Seem frosty? O, for honour of our land,
Let us not hang like roping icicles
Upon our houses' thatch, whiles a more frosty
    people

Sweat drops of gallant youth in our rich
    fields,—
Poor we may call them in their native lords!
    Dau. By faith and honour,
Our madams mock at us, and plainly say
Our mettle is bred out, and they will give
Their bodies to the lust of English youth
To new-store France with bastard warriors.
    Bour. They bid us to the English dancing-
        schools,
And teach lavoltas high and swift corantos;
Saying our grace is only in our heels,
And that we are most lofty runaways.
    Fr. King. Where is Montjoy, the herald?
        speed him hence:
Let him greet England with our sharp defi-
    ance.—
Up, princes! and, with spirit of honour edg'd
More sharper than your swords, hie to the field:
Charles De-la-bret, high-constable of France;
You Dukes of Orleans, Bourbon, and of Berri,
Alençon, Brabant, Bar, and Burgundy;
Jaques Chatillon, Rambures, Vaudemont,
Beaumont, Grandpree, Roussi, and Fauconberg,
Foix, Lestrale, Bouciqualt, and Charolois;
High dukes, great princes, barons, lords, and
    knights,
For your great seats, now quit you of great
    shames.
Bar Harry England, that sweeps through our
    land
With pennons painted in the blood of Harfleur:
Rush on his host as doth the melted snow
Upon the valleys, whose low vassal seat
The Alps doth spit and void his rheum upon:
Go down upon,—you have power enough,—
And in a captive chariot into Rouen
Bring him our prisoner.
    Con.   This becomes the great.
Sorry am I his numbers are so few,
His soldiers sick, and famish'd in their march;
For I am sure, when he shall see our army,
He'll drop his heart into the sink of fear,
And for achievement offer us his ransom.
    Fr. King. Therefore, lord constable, haste
        on Montjoy;
And let him say to England that we send
To know what willing ransom he will give.—
Prince Dauphin, you shall stay with us in
    Rouen.
    Dau. Not so, I do beseech your majesty.
    Fr. King. Be patient; for you shall remain
        with us.—
Now forth, lord constable and princes all,
And quickly bring us word of England's fall.
                                        [*Exeunt.*

SCENE V.—*The English Camp in Picardy.*

    Enter, severally, GOWER *and* FLUELLEN.

    Gow. How now, Captain Fluellen! come you
from the bridge?
    Flu. I assure you there is very excellent serv-
ices committed at the pridge.
    Gow. Is the Duke of Exeter safe?

    Flu. The Duke of Exeter is as magnanimous
as Agamemnon; and a man that I love and
honour with my soul, and my heart, and my
duty, and my life, and my living, and my utter-
most power: he is not,—God be praised and
plessed!—any hurt in the 'orld; but keeps the
pridge most valiantly, with excellent discipline.
There is an auncient there at the pridge,—I
think in my very conscience he is as valiant a
man as Mark Antony; and he is a man of no
estimation in the 'orld; but I did see him do
as gallant service.
    Gow. What do you call him?
    Flu. He is called Auncient Pistol.
    Gow. I know him not.
    Flu. Here is the man.

                Enter PISTOL.

    Pist. Captain, I thee beseech to do me fa-
        vours:
The Duke of Exeter doth love thee well.
    Flu. Ay, I praise Got; and I have merited
some love at his hands.
    Pist. Bardolph, a soldier, firm and sound of
        heart,
Of buxom valour, hath by cruel fate
And giddy Fortune's furious fickle wheel,—
That goddess blind,
That stands upon the rolling restless stone,—
    Flu. By your patience, Auncient Pistol. For-
tune is painted plind, with a muffler afore her
eyes, to signify to you that Fortune is plind;
and she is painted also with a wheel, to signify
to you, which is the moral of it, that she is
turning, and inconstant, and mutability, and
variation: and her foot, look you, is fixed upon
a spherical stone, which rolls, and rolls and
rolls.—In good truth, the poet makes a most
excellent description of it: Fortune is an excellent moral.
    Pist. Fortune is Bardolph's foe, and frowns
        on him;   [be,—
For he hath stol'n a pax, and hanged must 'a
A damned death!
Let gallows gape for dog; let man go free,
And let not hemp his windpipe suffocate:
But Exeter hath given the doom of death
For pax of little price.
Therefore, go speak,—the duke will hear thy
        voice;
And let not Bardolph's vital thread be cut
With edge of penny cord and vile reproach:
Speak, captain, for his life, and I will thee re-
        quite.
    Flu. Auncient Pistol, I do partly understand
your meaning.
    Pist. Why, then, rejoice therefore.
    Flu. Certainly, Auncient, it is not a thing to
rejoice at: for if, look you, he were my prother
I would desire the duke to use his goot pleasure,
and put him to execution; for discipline ought
to be used.   [friendship!
    Pist. Die and be damn'd! and fico for thy
    Flu. It is well.

Pist. The fig of Spain! [*Exit.*

Flu. Very goot.

Gow. Why, this is an arrant counterfeit rascal; I remember him now; a bawd, a cutpurse.

Flu. I'll assure you, 'a uttered as prave 'ords at the pridge as you shall see in a summer's day. But it is very well; what he has spoke to me, that is well, I warrant you, when time is serve.

Gow. Why, 'tis a gull, a fool, a rogue, that now and then goes to the wars, to grace himself, at his return into London, under the form of a soldier. And such fellows are perfect in the great commanders' names: and they will learn you by rote where services were done;—at such and such a sconce, at such a breach, at such a convoy; who came off bravely, who was shot, who disgraced, what terms the enemy stood on; and this they con perfectly in the phrase of war, which they trick up with new-tuned oaths: and what a beard of the general's cut, and a horrid suit of the camp, will do among foaming bottles and ale-washed wits, is wonderful to be thought on. But you must learn to know such slanders of the age, or else you may be marvellously mistook.

Flu. I tell you what, Captain Gower, I do perceive he is not the man that he would gladly make show to the 'orld he is: if I find a hole in his coat I will tell him my mind. [*Drum within.*] Hark you, the king is coming; and I must speak with him from the pridge.

Enter KING HENRY, GLOSTER, *and* Soldiers.

Got bless your majesty!

K. Hen. How now, Fluellen! cam'st thou from the bridge?

Flu. Ay, so please your majesty. The Duke of Exeter has very gallantly maintained the pridge: the French is gone off, look you; and there is gallant and most prave passages: marry, th' athversary was have possession of the pridge; but he is enforced to retire, and the Duke of Exeter is master of the pridge: I can tell your majesty the duke is a prave man.

K. Hen. What men have you lost, Fluellen?

Flu. The perdition of th' athversary hath been very great, reasonable great: marry, for my part, I think the duke hath lost never a man, but one that is like to be executed for robbing a church,—one Bardolph, if your majesty know the man: his face is all bubukles, and whelks, and knobs, and flames of fire; and his lips plows at his nose, and it is like a coal of fire, sometimes plue and sometimes red; but his nose is executed and his fire's out.

K. Hen. We would have all such offenders so cut off:—and we give express charge that in our marches through the country there be nothing compelled from the villages, nothing taken but paid for, none of the French upbraided or abused in disdainful language; for when lenity and cruelty play for a kingdom the gentler gamester is the soonest winner.

Tucket sounds. Enter MONTJOY.

Mont. You know me by my habit.

K. Hen. Well, then, I know thee: what shall I know of thee?

Mont. My master's mind.

K. Hen. Unfold it.

Mont. Thus says my king:—Say thou to Harry of England: Though we seemed dead we did but sleep; advantage is a better soldier than rashness. Tell him we could have rebuked him at Harfleur, but that we thought not good to bruise an injury till it were full ripe:—now we speak upon our cue, and our voice is imperial: England shall repent his folly, see his weakness, and admire our sufferance. Bid him, therefore, consider of his ransom; which must proportion the losses we have borne, the subjects we have lost, the disgrace we have digested; which, in weight to re-answer, his pettiness would bow under. For our losses his exchequer is too poor; for the effusion of our blood the muster of his kingdom too faint a number; and for our disgrace his own person, kneeling at our feet, but a weak and worthless satisfaction. To this add defiance: and tell him, for conclusion, he hath betrayed his followers, whose condemnation is pronounced. So far my king and master; so much my office.

K. Hen. What is thy name? I know thy quality.

Mont. Montjoy.

K. Hen. Thou dost thy office fairly. Turn thee back,
And tell thy king,—I do not seek him now;
But could be willing to march on to Calais
Without impeachment: for, to say the sooth,—
Though 'tis no wisdom to confess so much
Unto an enemy of craft and vantage,—
My people are with sickness much enfeebled;
My numbers lessen'd; and those few I have
Almost no better than so many French;
Who, when they were in health, I tell thee, herald,
I thought upon one pair of English legs
Did march three Frenchmen.—Yet, forgive me, God,
That I do brag thus!—this your air of France
Hath blown that vice in me; I must repent.
Go, therefore, tell thy master here I am;
My ransom is this frail and worthless trunk;
My army but a weak and sickly guard:
Yet, God before, tell him we will come on,
Though France himself, and such another neighbour,
Stand in our way. There's for thy labour, Montjoy.
Go, bid thy master well advise himself:
If we may pass, we will; if we be hinder'd,
We shall your tawny ground with your red blood
Discolour: and so, Montjoy, fare you well.
The sum of all our answer is but this:
We would not seek a battle as we are;

Nor as we are, we say, we will not shun it:
So tell your master.

Mont. I shall deliver so. Thanks to your
highness. 　　　　　　　　　　　[*Exit.*

Glo. I hope they will not come upon us now.

K. Hen. We are in God's hand, brother, not
in theirs.

March to the bridge; it now draws toward
night:—

Beyond the river we'll encamp ourselves;
And on to-morrow bid them march away.
　　　　　　　　　　　　　　[*Exeunt.*

SCENE VI.—*The French Camp near Agincourt.*

Enter the Constable of France, *the* LORD RAM-
BURES, *the* DUKE OF ORLEANS, *the* DAUPHIN,
and others.

Con. Tut! I have the best armour of the
world.—Would it were day!

Orl. You have an excellent armour; but let
my horse have his due.

Con. It is the best horse of Europe.

Orl. Will it never be morning?

Dau. My Lord of Orleans and my lord high-
constable, you talk of horse and armour,—

Orl. You are as well provided of both as any
prince in the world.

Dau. What a long night is this!—I will not
change my horse with any that treads but on
four pasterns. *Ca, ha!* he bounds from the
earth as if his entrails were hairs; *le cheval
volant,* the Pegasus, *qui a les narines de feu!*
When I bestride him I soar, I am a hawk: he
trots the air; the earth sings when he touches
it; the basest horn of his hoof is more musical
than the pipe of Hermes.

Orl. He's of the colour of the nutmeg.

Dau. And of the heat of the ginger. It is a
beast for Perseus: he is pure air and fire; and
the dull elements of earth and water never appear in him, but only in patient stillness while
his rider mounts him: he is indeed a horse; and
all other jades you may call beasts.

Con. Indeed, my lord, it is a most absolute
and excellent horse.

Dau. It is the prince of palfreys; his neigh
is like the bidding of a monarch, and his countenance enforces homage.

Orl. No more, cousin.

Dau. Nay, the man hath no wit that cannot,
from the rising of the lark to the lodging of the
lamb, vary deserved praise on my palfrey: it
is a theme as fluent as the sea; turn the sands
into eloquent tongues, and my horse is argument for them all: 'tis a subject for a sovereign
to reason on, and for a sovereign's sovereign to
ride on; and for the world,—familiar to us and
unknown,—to lay apart their particular functions and wonder at him. I once writ a sonnet
in his praise, and began thus: *Wonder of
nature,*—

Orl. I have heard a sonnet begin so to one's
mistress.

Dau. Then did they imitate that which I

composed to my courser: for my horse is my
mistress.

Orl. Your mistress bears well.

Dau. Me well; which is the prescript praise
and perfection of a good and particular mistress.

Con. Nay, for methought yesterday your
mistress shrewdly shook your back.

Dau. So, perhaps, did yours.

Con. Mine was not bridled.

Dau. O, then, belike she was old and gentle;
and you rode like a kern of Ireland, your
French hose off and in your strait strossers.

Con. You have good judgment in horsemanship.

Dau. Be warned by me, then: they that ride
so, and ride not warily, fall into foul bogs. I
had rather have my horse to my mistress.

Con. I had as lief have my mistress a jade.

Dau. I tell thee, constable, my mistress
wears his own hair.

Con. I could make as true a boast as that if
I had a sow to my mistress.

Dau. *Le chien est retourné à son propre
vomissement, et la truie lavée au bourbier:* thou
makest use of anything.

Con. Yet do I not use my horse for my mistress; or any such proverb so little kin to the
purpose.

Ram. My lord constable, the armour that I
saw in your tent to-night, are those stars or
suns upon it?

Con. Stars, my lord.

Dau. Some of them will fall to-morrow, I
hope.

Con. And yet my sky shall not want.

Dau. That may be, for you bear a many
superfluously, and 'twere more honour some
were away.

Con. Even as your horse bears your praises;
who would trot as well were some of your brags
dismounted.

Dau. Would I were able to load him with
his desert!—Will it never be day?—I will trot
to-morrow a mile, and my way shall be paved
with English faces.

Con. I will not say so, for fear I should be
faced out of my way: but I would it were
morning; for I would fain be about the ears of
the English.

Ram. Who will go to hazard with me for
twenty prisoners?

Con. You must first go yourself to hazard
ere you have them.

Dau. 'Tis midnight; I'll go arm myself.
　　　　　　　　　　　　　　[*Exit.*

Orl. The Dauphin longs for morning.

Ram. He longs to eat the English.

Con. I think he will eat all he kills.

Orl. By the white hand of my lady, he's a
gallant prince.

Con. Swear by her foot, that she may tread
out the oath.

Orl. He is, simply, the most active gentleman of France.

Con. Doing is activity; and he will still be doing.

Orl. He never did harm that I heard of.

Con. Nor will do none to-morrow: he will keep that good name still.

Orl. I know him to be valiant.

Con. I was told that by one that knows him better than you.

Orl. What's he?

Con. Marry, he told me so himself; and he said he cared not who knew it.

Orl. He needs not; it is no hidden virtue in him.

Con. By my faith, sir, but it is; never anybody saw it but his lackey: 'tis a hooded valour: and when it appears it will bate.

Orl. Ill-will never said well.

Con. I will cap that proverb with—There is flattery in friendship.

Orl. And I will take up that with—Give the devil his due.

Con. Well placed: there stands your friend for the devil: have at the very eye of that proverb with—A pox of the devil.

Orl. You are the better at proverbs by how much—A fool's bolt is soon shot.

Con. You have shot over.

Orl. 'Tis not the first time you were overshot.

Enter a Messenger.

Mess. My lord high-constable, the English lie within fifteen hundred paces of your tents.

Con. Who hath measured the ground?

Mess. The Lord Grandpree.

Con. A valiant and most expert gentleman. —Would it were day!—Alas, poor Harry of England! he longs not for the dawning as we do.

Orl. What a wretched and peevish fellow is this King of England, to mope with his fat-brained followers so far out of his knowledge!

Con. If the English had any apprehension they would run away.

Orl. That they lack; for if their heads had any intellectual armour they could never wear such heavy head-pieces.

Ram. That island of England breeds very valiant creatures; their mastiffs are of unmatchable courage.

Orl. Foolish curs, that run winking into the mouth of a Russian bear, and have their heads crush like rotten apples! You may as well say, that's a valiant flea that dare eat his breakfast on the lip of a lion.

Con. Just, just; and the men do sympathize with the mastiffs in robustious and rough coming-on, leaving their wits with their wives: and then give them great meals of beef, and iron and steel, they will eat like wolves and fight like devils.

Orl. Ay, but these English are shrewdly out of beef.

Con. Then shall we find to-morrow they have only stomachs to eat, and none to fight. Now is it time to arm: come, shall we about it?

Orl. It is now two o'clock: but, let me see,—
by ten
We shall have each a hundred Englishmen:
[*Exeunt.*

Enter Chorus.

Chor. Now entertain conjecture of a time
When creeping murmur and the poring dark
Fills the wide vessel of the universe.
From camp to camp, through the foul womb of night
The hum of either army stilly sounds,
That the fix'd sentinels almost receive
The secret whispers of each other's watch:
Fire answers fire, and through their paly flames
Each battle sees the other's umber'd face:
Steed threatens steed, in high and boastful neighs
Piercing the night's dull ear; and from the tents
The armourers, accomplishing the knights,
With busy hammers closing rivets up,
Give dreadful note of preparation:
The country cocks do crow, the clocks do toll,
And the third hour of drowsy morning name.
Proud of their numbers and secure in soul,
The confident and over-lusty French
Do the low-rated English play at dice;
And chide the cripple tardy-gaited night,
Who, like a foul and ugly witch, doth limp
So tediously away. The poor condemned English,
Like sacrifices, by their watchful fires
Sit patiently, and inly ruminate
The morning's danger; and their gesture sad
Investing lank-lean cheeks and war-worn coats
Presenteth them unto the gazing moon
So many horrid ghosts. O, now, who will behold
The royal captain of this ruin'd band   [tent,
Walking from watch to watch, from tent to
Let him cry, Praise and glory on his head!
For forth he goes and visits all his host;
Bids them good-morrow with a modest smile,
And calls them brothers, friends, and countrymen.
Upon his royal face there is no note
How dread an army hath enrounded him;
Nor doth he dedicate one jot of colour
Unto the weary and all-watched night;
But freshly looks, and over-bears attaint
With cheerful semblance and sweet majesty;
That every wretch, pining and pale before,
Beholding him, plucks comfort from his looks:
A largess universal, like the sun,
His liberal eye doth give to every one,
Thawing cold fear. Then, mean and gentle all,
Behold, as may unworthiness define,
A little touch of Harry in the night:
And so our scene must to the battle fly;
Where,—O for pity!—we shall much disgrace
With four or five most vile and ragged foils,
Right ill-dispos'd in brawl ridiculous,
The name of Agincourt. Yet sit and see;
Minding true things by what their mockeries
be.   [*Exit.*

ACT IV.

SCENE I.—FRANCE. *The English Camp at Agincourt.*

Enter KING HENRY, BEDFORD, *and* GLOSTER.

K. Hen. Gloster, 'tis true that we are in great danger;
The greater therefore should our courage be.—
Good-morrow, brother Bedford.—God Almighty!
There is some soul of goodness in things evil,
Would men observingly distil it out;
For our bad neighbour makes us early stirrers,
Which is both healthful and good husbandry:
Besides, they are our outward consciences
And preachers to us all: admonishing
That we should dress us fairly for our end.
Thus may we gather honey from the weed,
And make a moral of the devil himself.

Enter ERPINGHAM.

Good-morrow, old Sir Thomas Erpingham:
A good soft pillow for that good white head
Were better than a churlish turf of France.

Erp. Not so, my liege: this lodging likes me better,
Since I may say, Now lie I like a king.

K. Hen. 'Tis good for men to love their present pains
Upon example; so the spirit is eas'd:
And when the mind is quicken'd, out of doubt
The organs, though defunct and dead before,
Break up their drowsy grave, and newly move
With casted slough and fresh legerity.
Lend me thy cloak, Sir Thomas.—Brothers both,
Commend me to the princes in our camp;
Do my good-morrow to them; and anon
Desire them all to my pavilion.

Glo. We shall, my liege.
            [*Exeunt* GLOSTER *and* BEDFORD.

Erp. Shall I attend your grace?

K. Hen.   No, my good knight;
Go with my brothers to my lords of England:
I and my bosom must debate awhile,
And then I would no other company.

Erp. The Lord in heaven bless thee, noble Harry!   [*Exit.*

K. Hen. God-a-mercy, old heart! thou speak'st cheerfully.

Enter PISTOL.

Pist. Qui va là?

K. Hen. A friend.

Pist. Discuss unto me; art thou officer?
Or art thou base, common, and popular?

K. Hen. I am a gentleman of a company.

Pist. Trail'st thou the puissant pike?

K. Hen. Even so. What are you?

Pist. As good a gentleman as the emperor.

K. Hen. Then you are a better than the king.

Pist. The king's a bawcock and a heart of gold,
A lad of life, an imp of fame;

Of parents good, of fist most valiant:
I kiss his dirty shoe, and from my heart-strings
I love the lovely bully.—What is thy name?

K. Hen. Harry *le Roi.*

Pist. *Le Roy!* a Cornish name: art thou of Cornish crew?

K. Hen. No, I am a Welshman.

Pist. Know'st thou Fluellen?

K. Hen. Yes.

Pist. Tell him, I'll knock his leek about his pate
Upon Saint Davy's day.

K. Hen. Do not you wear your dagger in your cap that day, lest he knock that about yours.

Pist. Art thou his friend?

K. Hen. And his kinsman too.

Pist. The *fico* for thee, then!

K. Hen. I thank you: God be with you!

Pist. My name is Pistol called.   [*Exit.*

K. Hen. It sorts well with your fierceness.

Enter FLUELLEN *and* GOWER, *severally.*

Gow. Captain Fluellen!

Flu. So! in the name of Cheshu Christ, speak fewer. It is the greatest admiration in the universal 'orld when the true and auncient prerogatifs and laws of the wars is not kept: if you would take the pains but to examine the wars of Pompey the Great, you shall find, I warrant you, that there is no tiddle-taddle nor pibble-pabble in Pompey's camp; I warrant you, you shall find the ceremonies of the wars, and the cares of it, and the forms of it, and the sobriety of it, and the modesty of it, to be otherwise.

Gow. Why, the enemy is loud; you hear him all night.

Flu. If the enemy is an ass, and a fool, and a prating coxcomb, is it meet, think you, that we should also, look you, be an ass, and a fool, and a prating coxcomb,—in your own conscience, now?

Gow. I will speak lower.

Flu. I pray you and peseech you that you will.   [*Exeunt* GOWER *and* FLUELLEN.

K. Hen. Though it appear a little out of fashion,
There is much care and valour in this Welshman.

Enter BATES, COURT, *and* WILLIAMS.

Court. Brother John Bates, is not that the morning which breaks yonder?

Bates. I think it be: but we have no great cause to desire the approach of day.

Will. We see yonder the beginning of the day, but I think we shall never see the end of it.—Who goes there?

K. Hen. A friend.

Will. Under what captain serve you?

K. Hen. Under Sir Thomas Erpingham.

Will. A good old commander and a most kind gentleman: I pray you, what thinks he of our estate?

K. Hen. Even as men wrecked upon a sand, that look to be washed off the next tide.

Bates. He hath not told his thought to the king?

K. Hen. No; nor it is not meet he should. For though I speak it to you, I think the king is but a man as I am: the violet smells to him as it doth to me; the element shows to him as it doth to me; all his senses have but human conditions: his ceremonies laid by, in his nakedness he appears but a man; and though his affections are higher mounted than ours, yet, when they stoop, they stoop with the like wing. Therefore when he sees reason of fears, as we do, his fears, out of doubt, be of the same relish as ours are: yet, in reason, no man should possess him with any appearance of fear, lest he, by showing it, should dishearten his army.

Bates. He may show what outward courage he will; but I believe, as cold a night as 'tis, he could wish himself in the Thames up to the neck;—and so I would he were, and I by him, at all adventures, so we were quit here.

K. Hen. By my troth, I will speak my conscience of the king: I think he would not wish himself anywhere but where he is.

Bates. Then I would he were here alone; so should he be sure to be ransomed, and a many poor men's lives saved.

K. Hen. I dare say you love him not so ill, to wish him here alone, howsoever you speak this, to feel other men's minds: methinks I could not die anywhere so contented as in the king's company,—his cause being just and his quarrel honourable.

Will. That's more than we know.

Bates. Ay, or more than we should seek after; for we know enough if we know we are the king's subjects: if his cause be wrong, our obedience to the king wipes the crime of it out of us.

Will. But if the cause be not good, the king himself hath a heavy reckoning to make when all those legs and arms and heads, chopped off in a battle, shall join together at the latter day and cry all, We died at such a place; some swearing; some crying for a surgeon; some upon their wives left poor behind them; some upon the debts they owe; some upon their children rawly left. I am afeared there are few die well that die in a battle; for how can they charitably dispose of anything when blood is their argument? Now, if these men do not die well, it will be a black matter for the king that led them to it; who to disobey were against all proportion of subjection.

K. Hen. So if a son, that is by his father sent about merchandise do sinfully miscarry upon the sea, the imputation of his wickedness, by your rule, should be imposed upon his father that sent him: or if a servant, under his master's command, transporting a sum of money, be assailed by robbers, and die in many irreconciled iniquities, you may call the business of the master the author of the servant's damnation: —but this is not so: the king is not bound to answer the particular endings of his soldiers, the father of his son, nor the master of his servant; for they purpose not their death when they purpose their services. Besides, there is no king, be his cause never so spotless, if it come to the arbitrement of swords, can try it out with all unspotted soldiers: some peradventure have on them the guilt of premeditated and contrived murder; some of beguiling virgins with the broken seals of perjury; some making the wars their bulwark that have before gored the gentle bosom of peace with pillage and robbery. Now, if these men have defeated the law and outrun native punishment, though they can outstrip men they have no wings to fly from God: war is his beadle, war is his vengeance; so that here men are punished for before-breach of the king's laws in now the king's quarrel: where they feared the death they have borne life away; and where they would be safe they perish: then if they die unprovided, no more is the king guilty of their damnation than he was before guilty of those impieties for the which they are now visited. Every subject's duty is the king's; but every subject's soul is his own. Therefore should every soldier in the wars do as every sick man in his bed,—wash every mote out of his conscience: and dying so, death is to him advantage; or not dying, the time was blessedly lost wherein such preparation was gained: and in him that escapes it were not sin to think that, making God so free an offer, he let him outlive that day to see his greatness, and to teach others how they should prepare.

Will. 'Tis certain, every man that dies ill, the ill upon his own head,—the king is not to answer for it.

Bates. I do not desire he should answer for me; and yet I determine to fight lustily for him.

K. Hen. I myself heard the king say he would not be ransomed.

Will. Ay, he said so, to make us fight cheerfully: but when our throats are cut he may be ransomed, and we ne'er the wiser.

K. Hen. If I live to see it I will never trust his word after.

Will. You pay him then! That's a perilous shot out of an elder-gun, that a poor and a private displeasure can do against a monarch! you may as well go about to turn the sun to ice with fanning in his face with a peacock's feather. You'll never trust his word after! come, 'tis a foolish saying.

K. Hen. Your reproof is something too round: I should be angry with you if the time were convenient.

Will. Let it be a quarrel between us if you live.

K. Hen. I embrace it.

Will. How shall I know thee again?

K. Hen. Give me any gage of thine, and I will wear it in my bonnet: then, if ever thou

darest acknowledge it, I will make it my quarrel.

Will. Here's my glove: give me another of
thine.

K. Hen. There.

Will. This will I also wear in my cap: if
ever thou come to me and say, after to-morrow,
This is my glove, by this hand I will take ·thee
a box on the ear.

K. Hen. If ever I live to see it I will challenge it.

Will. Thou darest as well be hanged.

K. Hen. Well, I will do it though I take
thee in the king's company.

Will. Keep thy word: fare thee well.

Bates. Be friends, you English fools, be
friends: we have French quarrels enow, if you
could tell how to reckon.

K. Hen. Indeed, the French may lay twenty
French crowns to one they will beat us; for they
bear them on their shoulders: but it is no English treason to cut French crowns; and to-
morrow the king himself will be a clipper.
                              [*Exeunt* Soldiers.

Upon the king!—let us our lives, our souls, ·
Our debts, our careful wives, our children, and
Our sins lay on the king! We must bear all.
O hard condition, twin-born with greatness,
Subject to the breath of every fool,
Whose sense no more can feel but his own
      wringing.
What infinite heart's-ease must kings neglect
That private men enjoy!
And what have kings that privates have not
      too,
Save ceremony,—save general ceremony?
And what art thou, thou idol ceremony?
What kind of god art thou, that suffer'st more
Of mortal griefs than do thy worshippers?
What are thy rents? what are thy comings-in?
O ceremony, show me but thy worth!
What is thy soul of adoration?
Art thou aught else but place, degree, and
      form,
Creating awe and fear in other men?
Wherein thou art less happy being fear'd
Than they in fearing.
What drink'st thou oft, instead of homage
      sweet,
But poison'd flattery? O, be sick, great great-
      ness,
And bid thy ceremony give thee cure!
Think'st thou the fiery fever will go out
With titles blown from adulation?
Will it give place to flexure and low bending?
Canst thou, when thou command'st the beg-
      gar's knee,
Command the health of it? No, thou proud
      dream,
That play'st so subtly with a king's repose:
I am a king that find thee; and I know
'Tis not the balm, the sceptre, and the ball,
The sword, the mace, the crown imperial,
The intertissued robe of gold and pearl,

The farced title running 'fore the king,
The throne he sits on, nor the tide of pomp
That beats upon the high shore of this world,—
No, not all these, thrice gorgeous ceremony,
Not all these, laid in bed majestical,
Can sleep so soundly as the wretched slave
Who, with a body fill'd and vacant mind,
Gets him to rest, cramm'd with distressful
      bread;
Never sees horrid night, the child of hell;
But, like a lackey, from the rise to set
Sweats in the eye of Phœbus, and all night
Sleeps in Elysium; next day, after dawn,
Doth rise and help Hyperion to his horse;
And follows so the ever-running year,
With profitable labour, to his grave:
And but for ceremony, such a wretch, [sleep,
Winding up days with toil and nights with
Had the fore-hand and vantage of a king.
The slave, a member of the country's peace,
Enjoys it; but in gross brain little wots
What watch the king keeps to maintain the
      peace
Whose hours the peasant best advantages.

Enter ERPINGHAM.

Erp. My lord, your nobles, jealous of your
      absence,
Seek through your camp to find you.

K. Hen.   Good old knight,
Collect them all together at my tent:
I'll be before thee.

Erp.   I shall do't, my lord. [*Exit.*

K. Hen. O God of battles! steel my soldiers'
      hearts;
Possess them not with fear; take from them now
The sense of reckoning, if the opposed numbers
Pluck their hearts from them!—Not to-day, O
      Lord,
O, not to-day, think not upon the fault
My father made in compassing the crown!
I Richard's body have interred new,
And on it have bestow'd more contrite tears
Than from it issu'd forced drops of blood:
Five hundred poor I have in yearly pay,
Who twice a day their wither'd hands hold up
Toward heaven, to pardon blood; and I have
      built
Two chantries, where the sad and solemn priests
Sing still for Richard's soul. More will I do;
Though all that I can do is nothing worth,
Since that my penitence comes after all,
Imploring pardon.

Enter GLOSTER.

Glo. My liege!

K. Hen. My brother Gloster's voice?—Ay;
I know thy errand, I will go with thee:—
The day, my friends, and all things stay for me.
                                    [*Exeunt.*

SCENE II.—*The French Camp.*

Enter DAUPHIN, ORLEANS, RAMBURES, *and
      others.*

Orl. The sun doth gild our armour; up, my
　　lords!

Dau. *Montez à cheval!*—My horse! *varlet,
　　laquais!* ha!

Orl. O brave spirit!

Dau. *Via!—les eaux et la terre,—*

Orl. *Rienpuis? l'air et le feu,—*

Dau. *Ciel!* cousin Orleans.

Enter Constable.

Now, my lord constable!

Con. Hark, how our steeds for present ser-
　　vice neigh!

Dau. Mount them, and make incision in
　　their hides,

That their hot blood may spin in English eyes,

And dout them with superfluous courage, ha!

Ram. What, will you have them weep our
　　horses' blood?

How shall we, then, behold their natural tears?

Enter a Messenger.

Mess. The English are embattled, you French
　　peers.　　　　　　　　　　[to horse!

Con. To horse, you gallant princes! straight

Do but behold yon poor and starved band,

And your fair show shall suck away their souls,

Leaving them but the shales and husks of men.

There is not work enough for all our hands;

Scarce blood enough in all their sickly veins

To give each naked curtle-axe a stain,

That our French gallants shall to-day draw out,

And sheathe for lack of sport: let us but blow
　　on them,

The vapour of our valour will o'erturn them.

'Tis positive 'gainst all exceptions, lords,

That our superfluous lackeys and our peas-
　　ants,—

Who in unnecessary action swarm

About our squares of battle,—were enow

To purge this field of such a hilding foe;

Though we upon this mountain's basis by

Took stand for idle speculation,—

But that our honours must not. What's to say?

A very little little let us do,

And all is done. Then let the trumpets sound

The tucket-sonance and the note to mount:

For our approach shall so much dare the field

That England shall couch down in fear and
　　yield.

Enter GRANDPREE.

Grand. Why do you stay so long, my lords
　　of France?

Yond island carrions, desperate of their bones,

Ill-favouredly become the morning field:

Their ragged curtains poorly are let loose,

And our air shakes them passing scornfully:

Big Mars seems bankrupt in their beggar'd
　　host,

And faintly through a rusty beaver peeps:

The horsemen sit like fixed candlesticks,

With torch-staves in their hand; and their poor
　　jades

Lob down their heads, dropping the hides and
　　hips,

The gum down-roping from their pale-dead
　　eyes,

And in their pale dull mouths the gimmel-bit

Lies foul with chew'd grass, still and motionless;

And their exécutors, the knavish crows,

Fly o'er them, all impatient for their hour.

Description cannot suit itself in words

To demonstrate the life of such a battle

In life so lifeless as it shows itself.

Con. They have said their prayers and they
　　stay for death.

Dau. Shall we go send them dinners and
　　fresh suits,

And give their fasting horses provender,

And after fight with them?

Con. I stay but for my guidon:—to the
　　field!—

I will the banner from a trumpet take,

And use it for my haste. Come, come, away!

The sun is high, and we outwear the day.

　　　　　　　　　　　　　　　[*Exeunt.*

SCENE III.—*The English Camp.*

Enter the English Host; GLOSTER, BEDFORD,
EXETER, SALISBURY, *and* WESTMORELAND.

Glo. Where is the king?

Bed. The king himself is rode to view their
　　battle.

West. Of fighting men they have full three-
　　score thousand.

Exe. There's five to one; besides, they all are
　　fresh.

Sal. God's arm strike with us! 'tis a fearful
　　odds.

God b' wi' you, princes all; I'll to my charge:

If we no more meet till we meet in heaven,

Then joyfully,—my noble Lord of Bedford,—

My dear Lord Gloster,—and my good Lord
　　Exeter,—

And my kind kinsman,—warriors all, adieu!

Bed. Farewell, good Salisbury; and good
　　luck go with thee!

Exe. Farewell, kind lord; fight valiantly to-
　　day:

And yet I do thee wrong to mind thee of it,

For thou art fram'd of the firm truth of valour.

　　　　　　　　　　　　[*Exit* SALISBURY.

Bed. He is as full of valour as of kindness;

Princely in both.

West.　　　　　　O that we now had here

Enter KING HENRY.

But one ten thousand of those men in England

That do no work to-day!

K. Hen.　　　　　What's he that wishes so?

My cousin Westmoreland?—No, my fair cousin:

If we are mark'd to die, we are enow

To do our country loss; and if to live,

The fewer men the greater share of honour.

God's will! I pray thee, wish not one man more.

By Jove, I am not covetous for gold;

Nor care I who doth feed upon my cost;

It yearns me not if men my garments wear;
Such outward things dwell not in my desires:
But if it be a sin to covet honour,
I am the most offending soul alive.
No, faith, my coz, wish not a man from England:
God's peace! I would not lose so great an
  honour,
As one man more, methinks, would share from
  me,
For the best hope I have. O do not wish one
  more!
Rather proclaim it, Westmoreland, through my
  host,
That he which hath no stomach to this fight,
Let him depart; his passport shall be made,
And crowns for convoy put into his purse:
We would not die in that man's company
That fears his fellowship to die with us.
This day is call'd the feast of Crispian:
He that outlives this day, and comes safe home,
Will stand a tip-toe when this day is nam'd,
And rouse him at the name of Crispian.
He that shall live this day, and see old age,
Will yearly on the vigil feast his neighbours,
And say, To-morrow is Saint Crispian:
Then will he strip his sleeve and show his scars,
And say, These wounds I had on Crispin's day.
Old men forget; yet all shall be forgot,
But he'll remember with advantages
What feats he did that day: then shall our
  names,
Familiar in their mouths as household words,—
Harry the king, Bedford and Exeter,
Warwick and Talbot, Salisbury and Gloster,—
Be in their flowing cups freshly remember'd.
This story shall the good man teach his son;
And Crispin Crispian shall ne'er go by,
From this day to the ending of the world,
But we in it shall be remembered,—
We few, we happy few, we band of brothers;
For he to-day that sheds his blood with me
Shall be my brother; be he ne'er so vile,
This day shall gentle his condition:
And gentlemen in England now a-bed
Shall think themselves accurs'd they were not
  here,
And hold their manhoods cheap while any
  speaks
That fought with us upon Saint Crispin's day.

Re-enter SALISBURY.

Sal. My sovereign lord, bestow yourself
  with speed:
The French are bravely in their battles set,
And will with all expedience charge on us.
  K. Hen. All things are ready if our minds
  be so.
  West. Perish the man whose mind is backward now!
  K. Hen. Thou dost not wish more help from
  England, coz?
  West. God's will! my liege, would you and
  I alone,

Without more help, could fight this royal battle!
  K. Hen. Why, now thou hast unwish'd five
  thousand men;
Which likes me better than to wish us one.—
You know your places: God be with you all!

Tucket. Enter MONTJOY.

  Mont. Once more I come to know of thee,
  King Harry,
If for thy ransom thou wilt now compound,
Before thy most assured overthrow:
For certainly thou art so near the gulf
Thou needs must be englutted. Besides, in
  mercy,
The constable desires thee thou wilt mind
Thy followers of repentance; that their souls
May make a peaceful and a sweet retire
From off these fields, where, wretches, their
  poor bodies
Must lie and fester.
  K. Hen.   Who hath sent thee now?
  Mont. The constable of France.
  K. Hen. I pray thee, bear my former answer
  back:
Bid them achieve me, and then sell my bones.
Good God! why should they mock poor fellows
  thus?
The man that once did sell the lion's skin
While the beast liv'd was kill'd with hunting
  him.
A many of our bodies shall no doubt
Find native graves; upon the which, I trust,
Shall witness live in brass of this day's work:
And those that leave their valiant bones in
  France,
Dying like men, though buried in your dunghills,
They shall be fam'd; for there the sun shall
  greet them
And draw their honours reeking up to heaven,
Leaving their earthly parts to choke your clime.
The smell whereof shall breed a plague in
  France.
Mark, then, abounding valour in our English,
That, being dead, like to the bullet's grazing,
Break out into a second course of mischief,
Killing in relapse of mortality.
Let me speak proudly:—tell the constable
We are but warriors for the working-day;
Our gayness and our gilt are all besmirch'd
With rainy marching in the painful field;
There's not a piece of feather in our host,—
Good argument, I hope, we will not fly,—
And time hath worn us into slovenry:
But, by the mass, our hearts are in the trim;
And my poor soldiers tell me yet ere night
They'll be in fresher robes; or they will pluck
The gay new coats o'er the French soldiers'
  heads,
And turn them out of service. If they do this,—
As, if God please, they shall,—my ransom then
Will soon be levied. Herald, save thou thy
  labour;
Come thou no more for ransom, gentle herald:

They shall have none, I swear, but these my
    joints,—
Which if they have as I will leave 'em them,
Shall yield them little, tell the constable.

    Mont. I shall, King Harry. And so, fare thee
    well:
Thou never shalt hear herald any more. [*Exit.*

    K. Hen. I fear thou wilt once more come
    again for ransom.

        Enter the DUKE OF YORK.

    York. My Lord, most humbly on my knee
    I beg
The leading of the vaward.

    K. Hen. Take it, brave York.—Now, sol-
    diers, march away:—
And how thou pleasest, God, dispose the day!
                        [*Exeunt.*

    SCENE IV.—*The Field of Battle.*

Alarums. Excursions. Enter French Soldier,
    PISTOL, *and* Boy.

    Pist. Yield, cur!

    Fr. Sol. *Je pense que vous êtes le gentil-homme
de bonne qualité.*

    Pist. Quality! Callino, castore me! art thou
a gentleman? what is thy name? discuss.

    Fr. Sol. *O Seigneur Dieu!*

    Pist. O, Signieur Dew should be a gentle-
man:—
Perpend my words, O Signieur Dew, and
    mark;—
O Signieur Dew, thou diest on point of fox,
Except, O Signieur, thou do give to me
Egregious ransom.   [*moi!*

    Fr. Sol. *O prennez miséricorde! ayez pitié de*

    Pist. Moy shall not serve; I will have forty
    moys;
Or I will fetch thy rim out at thy throat
In drops of crimson blood.

    Fr. Sol. *Est-il impossible d'échapper la force
de ton bras?*

    Pist. Brass, cur!
Thou damned and luxurious mountain-goat,
Offer'st me brass?

    Fr. Sol. *O pardonnez-moi!*

    Pist. Say'st thou me so? is that a ton of
    moys?
Come hither, boy: ask me this slave in French
What is his name.

    Boy. *Ecoutez: comment êtes-vous appelé?.*

    Fr. Sol. *Monsieur le Fer.*

    Boy. He says his name is Master Fer.

    Pist. Master Fer! I'll fer him, and firk him,
and ferret him:—discuss the same in French
unto him.

    Boy. I do not know the French for fer, and
ferret, and firk.

    Pist. Bid him prepare; for I will cut his
throat.

    Fr. Sol. *Que dit-il, monsieur?*

    Boy. *Il me commande de vous dire que vous
faites vous prêt; car ce soldat ici est disposé tout
à cette heure de couper votre gorge.*

    Pist. *Oui, coupe la gorge, par ma foi, pesant,*
Unless thou give me crowns, brave crowns;
Or mangled shalt thou be by this my sword.

    Fr. Sol. *O, je vous supplie, pour l'amour de
Dieu, me pardonner! Je suis gentilhomme de
bonne maison: gardez ma vie, et je vous donnerai
deux cents écus.*

    Pist. What is his words?

    Boy. He prays you to save his life: he is a
gentleman of a good house; and for his ransom
he will give you two hundred crowns.

    Pist. Tell him·my fury shall abate, and I
The crowns will take.

    Fr. Sol. *Petit monsieur, que dit-il?*

    Boy. *Encore qu'il est contre son jurement de
pardonner aucun prisonnier, néanmoins, pour
les écus que vous l'avez promis, il est content de
vous donner la liberté, le franchisement.*

    Fr. Sol. *Sur mes genoux je vous donne mille
remercîmens; et je m'estine heureux que je suis
tombé entre les mains d'un chevalier, je pense, le
plus brave, vaillant, et très distingué seigneur
d'Angleterre.*

    Pist. Expound unto me, boy.

    Boy. He gives you, upon his knees, a thou-
sand thanks; and he esteems himself happy
that he hath fallen into the hands of one,—as
he thinks,—the most brave, valorous, and
thrice-worthy signieur of England.

    Pist. As I suck blood, I will some mercy
show.—Follow me!   [*Exit.*

    Boy. *Suivez-vous le grand capitaine.* [*Exit*
French Soldier.] I did never know so full a
voice issue from so empty a heart: but the saying is true,—the empty vessel makes the greatest sound. Bardolph and Nym had ten times
more valour than this roaring devil i' the old
play, that every one may pare his nails with a
wooden dagger; and they are both hanged; and
so would this be if he durst steal anything ad-
venturously. I must stay with the lackeys, with
the luggage of our camp: the French might
have a good prey of us if he knew of it; for there
is none to guard it but boys.   [*Exit.*

    SCENE V.—*Another part of the Field of Battle.*

Alarums. Enter DAUPHIN, ORLEANS, BOURBON,
    Constable, RAMBURES, *and others.*

    Con. *O diable!*

    Orl. *O seigneur! le jour est perdu, tout est
perdu!*

    Dau. *Mort de ma vie!* all is confounded, all!
Reproach and everlasting shame
Sits mocking in our plumes.—*O méchante for-
    tune!*—
Do not run away.   [*A short alarum.*

    Con.   Why, all our ranks are broke.

    Dau. O perdurable shame!—let's stab our-
selves.
Be these the wretches that we play'd at dice for?

    Orl. Is this the king we sent to for his
    ransom?

    Bour. Shame, and eternal shame, nothing
    but shame!

Let us die in honour: once more back again;
And he that will not follow Bourbon now,
Let him go hence, and with his cap in hand,
Like a base pander, hold the chamber-door
Whilst by a slave, no gentler than my dog,
His fairest daughter is contaminated.

Con. Disorder, that hath spoil'd us, friend
    us now!
Let us on heaps go offer up our lives
Unto these English, or else die with fame.

Orl. We are enow yet living in the field
To smother up the English in our throngs,
If any order might be thought upon.

Bour. The devil take order now! I'll to the
    throng:
Let life be short, else shame will be too long.
                                              [*Exeunt.*

SCENE VI.—*Another part of the Field.*

Alarums. Enter KING HENRY *and* Forces,
        EXETER, *and others.*

K. Hen. Well have we done, thrice-valiant
    countrymen:
But all's not done; yet keep the French the field.

Exe. The Duke of York commends him to
    your majesty.

K. Hen. Lives he, good uncle? thrice within
    this hour
I saw him down; thrice up again, and fighting;
From helmet to the spur all blood he was.

Exe. In which array, brave soldier, doth he lie
Larding the plain; and by his bloody side,—
Yoke-fellow to his honour-owing wounds,—
The noble Earl of Suffolk also lies.
Suffolk first died: and York, all haggled over,
Comes to him, where in gore he lay insteep'd,
And takes him by the beard; kisses the gashes
That bloodily did yawn upon his face;
And cries aloud, *Tarry, dear cousin Suffolk!*
My soul shall thine keep company to heaven;
Tarry, sweet soul, for mine, then fly a-breast;
As in this glorious and well-foughten field
We kept together in our chivalry!
Upon these words I came and cheer'd him up:
He smil'd me in the face, raught me his hand,
And, with a feeble grip, says, *Dear my lord,*
Commend my service to my sovereign.
So did he turn, and over Suffolk's neck
He threw his wounded arm, and kiss'd his lips;
And so, espous'd to death, with blood he seal'd
A testament of noble-ending love.
The pretty and sweet manner of it forc'd
Those waters from me which I would have
    stopp'd;
But I had not so much of man in me,
And all my mother came into mine eyes,
And gave me up to tears.

K. Hen.   I blame you not;
For, hearing this, I must perforce compound
With mistful eyes, or they will issue too.—
                                              [*Alarum.*
But, hark! what new alarum is this same?—
The French have reinforc'd their scatter'd
    men:—

Then every soldier kill his prisoners;
Give the word through.   [*Exeunt.*

SCENE VII.—*Another part of the Field.*

Alarums. Enter FLUELLEN *and* GOWER.

Flu. Kill the poys and the luggage! 'tis expressly against the law of arms: 'tis as arrant a
piece of knavery, mark you now, as can be
offered; in your conscience, now, is it not?

Gow. 'Tis certain there's not a boy left alive;
and the cowardly rascals that ran from the
battle have done this slaughter: besides, they
have burned and carried away all that was in
the king's tent; wherefore the king, most
worthily, hath caused every soldier to cut his
prisoner's throat. O, 'tis a gallant king!

Flu. Ay, he was porn at Monmouth, Captain
Gower. What call you the town's name where
Alexander the pig was porn?

Gow. Alexander the Great.

Flu. Why, I pray you, is not pig great? the
pig, or the great, or the mighty, or the huge, or
the magnanimous, are all one reckonings, save
the phrase is a little variations.

Gow. I think Alexander the Great was born
in Macedon: his father was called Philip of
Macedon, as I take it.

Flu. I think it is in Macedon where Alexander is porn. I tell you, captain, if you look
in the maps of the 'orld, I warrant you shall
find, in the comparisons between Macedon and
Monmouth, that the situations, look you, is
both alike. There is a river in Macedon; and
there is also moreover a river at Monmouth: it
is called Wye at Monmouth; but it is out of my
prains what is the name of the other river; but
'tis all one, 'tis alike as my fingers is to my
fingers, and there is salmons in both. If you
mark Alexander's life well, Harry of Monmouth's life is come after it indifferent well; for
there is figures in all things. Alexander,—Got
knows, and you know,—in his rages, and his
furies, and his wraths, and his cholers, and his
moods, and his displeasures, and his indigna-
tions, and also being a little intoxicates in his
prains, did, in his ales and his angers, look you,
kill his pest friend, Clytus.

Gow. Our king is not like him in that: he
never killed any of his friends.

Flu. It is not well done, mark you now, to
take the tales out of my mouth ere it is made
and finished. I speak but in the figures and
comparisons of it: as Alexander is kill his friend
Clytus, being in his ales and his cups; so also
Harry Monmouth, being in his right wits and
his goot judgments, turned away the fat knight
with the great pelly-doublet: he was full of
jests, and gipes, and knaveries, and mocks; I
have forgot his name.

Gow. Sir John Falstaff.

Flu. That is he:—I can tell you there is goot
men porn at Monmouth.

Gow. Here comes his majesty.

Alarum. Enter KING HENRY, *with a part of the* English Forces; WARWICK, GLOSTER, EX- ETER, *and others.*

K. Hen. I was not angry since I came to France
Until this instant.—Take a trumpet, herald;
Ride thou unto the horsemen on yond hill:
If they will fight with us, bid them come down,
Or void the field; they do offend our sight:
If they'll do neither, we will come to them,
And make them skirr away as swift as stones
Enforced from the old Assyrian slings:
Besides, we'll cut the throats of those we have;
And not a man of them that we shall take
Shall taste our mercy:—go and tell them so.
　　Exe. Here comes the herald of the French, my liege.
　　Glo. His eyes are humbler than they us'd to be.

　　　　　　Enter MONTJOY.

K. Hen. How now! what means this, herald?
know'st thou not
That I have fin'd these bones of mine for ransom?
Com'st thou again for ransom?
　　Mont.　　　　　　No, great king:
I come to thee for charitable license,
That we may wander o'er this bloody field
To book our dead, and then to bury them;
To sort our nobles from our common men;
For many of our princes,—woe the while!—
Lie drown'd and soak'd in mercenary blood;—
So do our vulgar drench their peasant limbs
In blood of princes;—and their wounded steeds
Fret fetlock deep in gore, and with wild rage
Yerk out their armed heels at their dead mas- ters,
Killing them twice. O, give us leave, great king,
To view the field in safety, and dispose
Of their dead bodies!
　　K. Hen.　　　　I tell thee truly, herald,
I know not if the day be ours or no;
For yet a many of your horsemen peer
And gallop o'er the field.
　　Mont.　　　　　The day is yours.
　　K. Hen. Praised be God, and not our strength, for it!—
What is this castle call'd that stands hard by?
　　Mont. They call it Agincourt.
　　K. Hen. Then call we this the field of Agin- court,
Fought on the day of Crispin Crispianus.
　　Flu. Your grandfather of famous memory, an't please your majesty, and your great-uncle Edward the Plack Prince of Wales, as I have read in the chronicles, fought a most prave pattle here in France.
　　K. Hen. They did, Fluellen.
　　Flu. Your majesty says very true: if your majesties is remembered of it, the Welshmen did goot service in a garden where leeks did grow, wearing leeks in their Monmouth caps;

which, your majesty knows, to this hour is an honourable padge of the service; and I do pe- lieve your majesty takes no scorn to wear the leek upon Saint Tavy's day.
　　K. Hen. I wear it for a memorable honour; For I am Welsh, you know, good countryman.
　　Flu. All the water in Wye cannot wash your majesty's Welsh plood out of your pody, I can tell you that: Got pless it and preserve it as long as it pleases his grace and his majesty too!
　　K. Hen. Thanks, good my countryman.
　　Flu. By Chesu, I am your majesty's coun- tryman, I care not who know it; I will confess it to all the 'orld: I need not be ashamed of your majesty, praised be Got, so long as your maj- esty is an honest man.
　　K. Hen. God keep me so!—Our heralds go with him:
Bring me just notice of the numbers dead
On both our parts.—Call yonder fellow hither.
　　　　［*Points to* WILL. *Exeunt* MONT. *and others.*
　　Exe. Soldier, you must come to the king.
　　K. Hen. Soldier, why wearest thou that glove in thy cap?
　　Will. An't please your majesty, 'tis the gage of one that I should fight withal, if he be alive.
　　K. Hen. An Englishman?
　　Will. An't please your majesty, a rascal that swaggered with me last night; who, if alive and ever dare to challenge this glove, I have sworn to take him a box o' the ear: or if I can see my glove in his cap,—which he swore, as he was a soldier, he would wear if alive,—I will strike it out soundly.
　　K. Hen. What think you, Captain Fluellen? is it fit this soldier keep his oath?
　　Flu. He is craven and a villain else, an't please your majesty, in my conscience.
　　K. Hen. It may be his enemy is a gentleman of great sort, quite from the answer of his de- gree.
　　Flu. Though he be as goot a gentleman as the tevil is, as Lucifer and Belzebub himself, it is necessary, look your grace, that he keep his vow and his oath: if he be perjured, see you now, his reputation is as arrant a villain and a Jack sauce as ever his plack shoe trod upon Got's ground and his earth, in my conscience, la.
　　K. Hen. Then keep thy vow, sirrah, when thou meefest the fellow.
　　Will. So I will, my liege, as I live.
　　K. Hen. Who servest thou under?
　　Will. Under Captain Gower, my liege.
　　Flu. Gower is a goot captain, and is goot knowledge and literatured in the wars.
　　K. Hen. Call him hither to me, soldier.
　　Will. I will, my liege.　　　　　［*Exit.*
　　K. Hen. Here, Fluellen; wear thou this fa- vour for me, and stick it in thy cap: when Alençon and myself were down together I pluck'd this glove from his helm: if any man challenge this, he is a friend to Alençon and an enemy to our person; if thou encounter any such, apprehend him, and thou dost love me

Flu. Your grace does me as great honours as can be desired in the hearts of his subjects: I would fain see the man that has but two legs that shall find himself aggriefed at this glove, that is all; but I would fain see it once, and please Got of his grace that I might see it.

K. Hen. Knowest thou Gower?

Flu. He is my dear friend, and please you.

K. Hen. Pray thee, go seek him, and bring him to my tent.

Flu. I will fetch him.　　　[*Exit.*

K. Hen. My Lord of Warwick and my brother Gloster,
Follow Fluellen closely at the heels:
The glove which I have given him for a favour
May haply purchase him a box o' the ear;
It is the soldier's; I, by bargain, should
Wear it myself. Follow, good cousin Warwick:
If that the soldier strike him,—as I judge
By his blunt bearing he will keep his word,—
Some sudden mischief may arise of it;
For I do know Fluellen valiant,
And, touch'd with choler, hot as gunpowder,
And quickly will return an injury:
Follow, and see there be no harm between them.—
Go you with me, uncle of Exeter.　　[*Exeunt.*

SCENE VIII.—*Before* KING HENRY'S *Pavillion.*

Enter GOWER *and* WILLIAMS.

Will. I warrant it is to knight you, captain.

Enter FLUELLEN.

Flu. Got's will and his pleasure, captain, I peseech you now, come apace to the king: there is more goot toward you peradventure than is in your knowledge to dream of.

Will. Sir, know you this glove?

Flu. Know the glove! I know the glove is a glove.

Will. I know this; and thus I challenge it.
　　　　　　　　　　　　　[*Strikes him.*

Flu. 'Sblood, an arrant traitor as any's in the universal 'orld, or in France, or in England!

Gow. How now, sir! you villain!

Will. Do you think I'll be forsworn?

Flu. Stand away, Captain Gower; I will give treason his payment into plows, I warrant you.

Will. I am no traitor.

Flu. That's a lie in thy throat.—I charge you in his majesty's name, apprehend him: he's a friend of the Duke Alençon's.

Enter WARWICK *and* GLOSTER.

War. How now, how now! what's the matter?

Flu. My Lord of Warwick, here is,—praised be Got for it!—a most contagious treason come to light, look you, as you shall desire in a summer's day.—Here is his majesty.

Enter KING HENRY *and* EXETER.

K. Hen. How now! what's the matter?

Flu. My liege, here is a villain and a traitor, that, look your grace, has struck the glove which your majesty is take out of the helmet of Alençon.

Will. My liege, this was my glove; here is the fellow of it; and he that I gave it to in change promised to wear it in his cap: I promised to strike him if he did: I met this man with my glove in his cap, and I have been as good as my word.

Flu. Your majesty hear now,—saving your majesty's manhood,—what an arrant, rascally, beggarly, lousy knave it is: I hope your majesty is pear me testimony and witness, and will avouchment, this is the glove of Alençon that your majesty is give me, in your conscience, now.

K. Hen. Give me thy glove, soldier: look, here is the fellow of it.
'Twas I, indeed, thou promisedst to strike;
And thou hast given me most bitter terms.

Flu. An please your majesty, let his neck answer for it if there is any martial law in the 'orld.

K. Hen. How canst thou make me satisfaction?

Will. All offences, my liege, come from the heart: never came any from mine that might offend your majesty.

K. Hen. It was ourself thou didst abuse.

Will. Your majesty came not like yourself: you appeared to me but as a common man; witness the night, your garments, your lowliness; and what your highness suffered under that shape I beseech you take it for your own fault, and not mine: for had you been as I took you for, I made no offence; therefore, I beseech your highness, pardon me.

K. Hen. Here, uncle Exeter, fill this glove with crowns,
And give it to this fellow.—Keep it, fellow;
And wear it for an honour in thy cap
Till I do challenge it.—Give him the crowns:—
And, captain, you must needs be friends with him.

Flu. By this day and this light, the fellow has mettle enough in his pelly:—hold, there is twelve pence for you; and I pray you to serve Got, and keep you out of prawls, and prabbles, and quarrels, and dissensions, and, I warrant you, it is the petter for you.

Will. I will none of your money.

Flu. It is with a goot will; I can tell you it will serve you to mend your shoes: come, wherefore should you be so pashful? your shoes is not so goot: 'tis a goot silling, I warrant you, or I will change it.

Enter an English Herald.

K. Hen. Now, herald,—are the dead number'd?

Her. Here is the number of the slaughter'd French.　　　　　　[*Delivers a paper.*

K. Hen. What prisoners of good sort are taken, uncle?

Exe. Charles Duke of Orleans, nephew to the king;
John Duke of Bourbon, and Lord Bouciqualt:
Of other lords and barons, knights and squires,
Full fifteen hundred, besides common men.

K. Hen. This note doth tell me of ten thousand French
That in the field lie slain: of princes, in this number,
And nobles bearing banners, there lie dead
One hundred twenty-six: added to these,
Of knights, esquires, and gallant gentlemen,
Eight thousand and four hundred; of the which
Five hundred were but yesterday dubb'd knights:
So that, in these ten thousand they have lost,
There are but sixteen hundred mercenaries;
The rest are princes, barons, lords, knights, squires,
And gentlemen of blood and quality.
The names of those their nobles that lie dead,—
Charles De-la-bret, high-constable of France;
Jaques of Chatillon, admiral of France;
The master of the cross-bows, Lord Rambures;
Great-master of France, the brave Sir Guischard Dauphin;
John Duke of Alençon; Antony Duke of Brabant,
The brother to the Duke of Burgundy;
And Edward Duke of Bar: of lusty earls,
Grandpree and Roussi, Fauconberg and Foix,
Beaumont and Marle, Vaudemont and Lestrale.
Here was a royal fellowship of death!—
Where is the number of our English dead?

[*Herald presents another paper.*
Edward the Duke of York, the Earl of Suffolk,
Sir Richard Ketly, Davy Gam, esquire:
None else of name; and of all other men
But five-and-twenty.—O God, thy arm was here;
And not to us, but to thy arm alone,
Ascribe we all!—When, without stratagem,
But in plain shock and even play of battle,
Was ever known so great and little loss
On one part and on the other?—Take it, God,
For it is none but thine!

Exe.   'Tis wonderful!

K. Hen. Come, go we in procession to the village:
And be it death proclaimed through our host
To boast of this, or take that praise from God
Which is his only.

Flu. Is it not lawful, an please your majesty, to tell how many is killed?

K. Hen. Yes, captain; but with this acknowledgment,
That God fought for us.

Flu. Yes, my conscience, he did us great goot.

K. Hen. Do we all holy rites:
Let there be sung *Non nobis* and *Te Deum;*
The dead with charity enclos'd in clay:
We'll then to Calais; and to England then;
Where ne'er from France arriv'd more happy men.   [*Exeunt.*

Enter Chorus.

Chor. Vouchsafe to those that have not read the story,
That I may prompt them: and of such as have,
I humbly pray them to admit the excuse
Of time, of numbers, and due course of things,
Which cannot in their huge and proper life
Be here presented. Now we bear the king
Toward Calais: grant him there; there seen,
Heave him away upon your winged thoughts
Athwart the sea. Behold, the English beach
Pales in the flood with men, with wives, and boys,
Whose shouts and claps out-voice the deepmouth'd sea,
Which, like a mighty whiffler, 'fore the king
Seems to prepare his way: so let him land;
And solemnly see him set on to London.
So swift a pace hath thought that even now
You may imagine him upon Blackheath;
Where that his lords desire him to have borne
His bruised helmet and his bended sword
Before him through the city: he forbids it,
Being free from vainness and self-glorious pride;
Giving full trophy, signal, and ostent,
Quite from himself to God. But now behold,
In the quick forge and working-house of thought,
How London doth pour out her citizens!
The mayor and all his brethren, in best sort,—
Like to the senators of the antique Rome,
With the plebeians swarming at their heels,—
Go forth, and fetch their conquering Cæsar in:
As, by a lower but by loving likelihood,
Were now the general of our gracious empress,—
As in good time he may,—from Ireland coming,
Bringing rebellion broached on his sword,
How many would the peaceful city quit
To welcome him! much more, and much more cause,
Did they this Harry. Now in London place him;—
As yet the lamentation of the French
Invites the King of England's stay at home;
The emperor's coming in behalf of France,
To order peace between them;—and omit
All the occurrences, whatever chanc'd,
Till Harry's back-return again to France:
There must we bring him; and myself have play'd
The interim, by remembering you 'tis past.
Then brook abridgment; and your eyes advance,
After your thoughts, straight back again to France.   [*Exit.*

ACT V.

SCENE I.—FRANCE. *An English Court of Guard.*

Enter FLUELLEN *and* GOWER.

Gow. Nay, that's right; but why wear you your leek to-day? Saint Davy's day is past.

Flu. There is occasions and causes why and wherefore in all things: I will tell you, as my friend, Captain Gower:—the rascally, scald, peggarly, lousy, pragging knave, Pistol,—which you and yourself, and all the 'orld, know to be no petter than a fellow, look you now, of no merits,—he is come to me, and prings me pread and salt yesterday, look you, and pid me eat my leek: it was in a place where I could not preed no contention with him; but I will be so pold as to wear it in my cap till I see him once again, and then I will tell him a little piece of my desires.

Gow. Why, here he comes, swelling like a turkey-cock.

Flu. 'Tis no matter for his swellings nor his turkey-cocks.

Enter PISTOL.

Got pless you, Auncient Pistol! you scurvy, lousy knave, Got pless you!

Pist. Ha! art thou bedlam? dost thou thirst, base Trojan,
To have me fold up Parca's fatal web?
Hence! I am qualmish at the smell of leek.

Flu. I peseech you heartily, scurvy, lousy knave, at my desires, and my requests, and my petitions, to eat, look you, this leek: because, look you, you do not love it, nor your affections, and your appetites, and your digestions, does not agree with it, I would desire you to eat it.

Pist. Not for Cadwallader and all his goats.

Flu. There is one goat for you. [*Strikes him.*] Will you be so goot, scald knave, as eat it?

Pist. Base Trojan, thou shalt die.

Flu. You say very true, scald knave,—when Got's will is: I will desire you to live in the meantime and eat your victuals: come, there is sauce for it. [*Striking him again.*] You called me yesterday mountain-squire; but I will make you to-day a squire of low degree. I pray you, fall to: if you can mock a leek you can eat a leek.

Gow. Enough, captain: you have astonished him.

Flu. I say, I will make him eat some part of my leek, or I will peat his pate four days.—Pite, I pray you; it is goot for your green wound and your ploody coxcomb.

Pist. Must I bite?

Flu. Yes, certainly, and out of doubt, and out of question too, and ambiguities.

Pist. By this leek, I will most horribly revenge: I eat, and eke, I swear—

Flu. Eat, I pray you: will you have some more sauce to your leek? there is not enough leek to swear by.

Pist. Quiet thy cudgel; thou dost see I eat.

Flu. Much goot do you, scald knave, heartily. Nay, pray you, throw none away; the skin is goot for your proken coxcomb. When you take occasions to see leeks hereafter, I pray you, mock at 'em; that is all.

Pist. Good.

Flu. Ay, leeks is goot:—hold you, there is a groat to heal your pate.

Pist. Me a groat!

Flu. Yes, verily and in truth, you shall take it; or I have another leek in my pocket which you shall eat.

Pist. I take thy groat in earnest of revenge.

Flu. If I owe you anything I will pay you in cudgels: you shall be a woodmonger, and buy nothing of me but cudgels. God b' wi' you, and keep you, and heal your pate.   [*Exit.*

Pist. All hell shall stir for this.

Gow. Go, go; you are a counterfeit cowardly knave. Will you mock at an ancient tradition, —begun upon an honourable respect, and worn as a memorable trophy of predeceased valour,— and dare not avouch in your deeds any of your words? I have seen you gleeking and galling at this gentleman twice or thrice. You thought, because he could not speak English in the native garb, he could not therefore handle an English cudgel: you find it otherwise; and henceforth let a Welsh correction teach you a good English condition. Fare ye well.   [*Exit.*

Pist. Doth Fortune play the huswife with me now?
News have I that my Nell is dead i' the spital
Of malady of France;
And there my rendezvous is quite cut off.
Old I do wax; and from my weary limbs
Honour is cudgell'd. Well, bawd will I turn,
And something lean to cutpurse of quick hand.
To England will I steal, and there I'll steal:
And patches will I get unto these scars,
And swear I got them in the Gallia wars. [*Exit.*

SCENE II.—TROYES *in Champagne.*
An Apartment in the FRENCH KING'S Palace.

Enter at one door, KING HENRY, BEDFORD, GLOSTER, EXETER, WARWICK, WESTMORELAND, *and other* Lords; *at another, the* FRENCH KING, QUEEN ISABEL, *the* PRINCESS KATHARINE, Lords, Ladies, &c., *the* DUKE OF BURGUNDY, *and his* Train.

K. Hen. Peace to this meeting, wherefore we are met!
Unto our brother France, and to our sister,
Health and fair time of day;—joy and good wishes
To our most fair and princely cousin Katharine;—
And,—as a branch and member of this royalty,
By whom this great assembly is contriv'd,—
We do salute you, Duke of Burgundy;—
And, princes French, and peers, health to you all!

Fr. King. Right joyous are we to behold your face,
Most worthy brother England; fairly met:—
So are you, princes English, every one.

Q. Isa. So happy be the issue, brother England,
Of this good day and of this gracious meeting

As we are now glad to behold your eyes;
Your eyes, which hitherto have borne in them
Against the French, that met them in their bent,
The fatal balls of murdering basilisks:
The venom of such looks, we fairly hope,
Have lost their quality; and that this day
Shall change all griefs and quarrels into love.
  K. Hen. To cry amen to that, thus we appear.
  Q. Isa. You English princes all, I do salute
you.
  Bur. My duty to you both, on equal love.
Great Kings of France and England! That I
  have labour'd   [ours,
With all my wits, my pains, and strong endeav-
To bring your most imperial majesties
Unto this bar and royal interview,
Your mightiness on both parts best can witness.
Since then my office hath so far prevail'd
That face to face and royal eye to eye
You have congreeted, let it not disgrace me
If I demand, before this royal view,
What rub or what impediment there is
Why that the naked, poor, and mangled Peace,
Dear nurse of arts, plenties, and joyful births,
Should not, in this best garden of the world,
Our fertile France, put up her lovely visage?
Alas, she hath from France too long been chas'd!
And all her husbandry doth lie on heaps,
Corrupting in its own fertility.
Her vine, the merry cheerer of the heart,
Unpruned dies; her hedges even-pleach'd,
Like prisoners wildly overgrown with hair,
Put forth disorder'd twigs; her fallow leas
The darnel, hemlock, and rank fumitory
Doth root upon, while that the coulter rusts,
That should deracinate such savagery;
The even mead, that erst brought sweetly forth
The freckled cowslip, burnet, and green clover,
Wanting the scythe, all uncorrected, rank,
Conceives by idleness, and nothing teems
But hateful docks, rough thistles, kecksies, burs,
Losing both beauty and utility.
And as our vineyards, fallows, meads, and
  hedges,
Defective in their natures, grow to wildness,
Even so our houses and ourselves and children
Have lost, or do not learn for want of time,
The sciences that should become our country;
But grow, like savages,—as soldiers will,
That nothing do but meditate on blood,—
To swearing and stern looks, diffus'd attire,
And everything that seems unnatural.
Which to reduce into our former favour
You are assembl'd: and my speech entreats
That I may know the let why gentle Peace
Should not expel these inconveniences,
And bless us with her former qualities.
  K. Hen. If, Duke of Burgundy, you would
    the peace
Whose want gives growth to the imperfections
Which you have cited, you must buy that peace
With full accord to all our just demands;
Whose tenors and particular effects
You have, enschedul'd briefly, in your hands.

  Bur. The king hath heard them; to the
    which as yet
There is no answer made.
  K. Hen.   Well, then, the peace
Which you before so urg'd lies in his answer.
  Fr. King. I have but with a cursory eye
O'erglanc'd the articles: pleaseth your grace
To appoint some of your council presently
To sit with us once more, with better heed
To re-survey them, we will suddenly
Pass our accept and peremptory answer.
  K. Hen. Brother, we shall.—Go, uncle
    Exeter,—
And brother Clarence,—and you, brother
    Gloster,—
Warwick,—and Huntington,—go with the king;
And take with you free power to ratify,
Augment, or alter, as your wisdoms best
Shall see advantageable for our dignity,
Anything in or out of our demands;
And we'll consign thereto.—Will you, fair sister,
Go with the princes or stay here with us?
  Q. Isa. Our gracious brother, I will go with
    them;
Haply a woman's voice may do some good
When articles too nicely urg'd be stood on.
  K. Hen. Yet leave our cousin Katharine
    here with us:
She is our capital demand, compris'd
Within the fore-rank of our articles.
  Q. Isa. She hath good leave.
    [*Exeunt all but* K. HEN., KATH., *and* ALICE.
  K. Hen.   Fair Katharine, and most fair!
Will you vouchsafe to teach a soldier terms
Such as will enter at a lady's ear,
And plead his love-suit to her gentle heart?
  Kath. Your majesty shall mock at me; I
cannot speak your England.
  K. Hen. O fair Katharine, if you will love
me soundly with your French heart, I will be
glad to hear you confess it brokenly with your
English tongue. Do you like me, Kate?
  Kath. Pardonnez-moi, I cannot tell vat is
like me.
  K. Hen. An angel is like you, Kate, and
you are like an angel.
  *Kath. Que dit-il? que je suis semblable à les
anges?*
  *Alice. Oui, vraiment, sauf votre grace, ainsi
dit-il.*
  K. Hen. I said so, dear Katharine; and I
must not blush to affirm it.
  *Kath. O bon Dieu! les langues des hommes
sont pleines de tromperies.*
  K. Hen. What says she, fair one? that the
tongues of men are full of deceits?
  Alice. Oui, dat de tongues of de mans is be
full of deceits,—dat is de princess.
  K. Hen. The princess is the better English-
woman. I' faith, Kate, my wooing is fit for thy
understanding: I am glad thou canst speak no
better English; for if thou couldst, thou wouldst
find me such a plain king that thou wouldst
think I had sold my farm to buy my crown. I

know no ways to mince it in love, but directly to say I love you: then, if you urge me further than to say, Do you in faith? I wear out my suit. Give me your answer; i' faith, do; and so clap hands and a bargain: how say you, lady?

Kath. Sauf votre honneur, me understand vell.

K. Hen. Marry, if you would put me to verses or to dance for your sake, Kate, why you undid me: for the one I have neither words nor measure, and for the other I have no strength in measure, yet a reasonable measure in strength. If I could win a lady at leap-frog, or by vaulting into my saddle with my armour on my back, under the correction of bragging be it spoken, I should quickly leap into a wife. Or if I might buffet for my love, or bound my horse for her favours, I could lay on like a butcher, and sit like a jack-an-apes, never off. But, before God, Kate, I cannot look greenly, nor gasp out my eloquence, nor I have no cunning in protestation; only downright oaths, which I never use till urged, nor never break for urging. If thou canst love a fellow of this temper, Kate, whose face is not worth sunburning, that never looks in his glass for love of anything he sees there, let thine eye be thy cook. I speak to thee plain soldier: if thou canst love me for this, take me; if not, to say to thee that I shall die is true,—but for thy love, by the Lord, no; yet I love thee too. And while thou livest, dear Kate, take a fellow of plain and uncoined constancy; for he perforce must do thee right, because he hath not the gift to woo in other places: for these fellows of infinite tongue, that can rhyme themselves into ladies' favours, they do always reason themselves out again. What! a speaker is but a prater; a rhyme is but a ballad. A good leg will fall; a straight back will stoop; a black beard will turn white; a curled pate will grow bald; a fair face will wither; a full eye will wax hollow: but a good heart, Kate, is the sun and the moon; or, rather, the sun, and not the moon,—for it shines bright and never changes, but keeps his course truly. If thou would have such a one, take me: and take me, take a soldier; take a soldier, take a king: and what sayest thou, then, to my love? speak, my fair, and fairly, I pray thee.

Kath. Is it possible dat I should love de enemy of France?

K. Hen. No; it is not possible you should love the enemy of France, Kate: but in loving me you should love the friend of France; for I love France so well that I will not part with a village of it; I will have it all mine: and, Kate, when France is mine and I am yours, then yours is France and you are mine.

Kath. I cannot tell vat is dat.

K. Hen. No, Kate? I will tell thee in French; which I am sure will hang upon my tongue like a new-married wife about her husband's neck, hardly to be shook off. *Quand j'ai la possession de France, et quand vous avez la possession de*

moi,—let me see, what then? Saint Denis be my speed!—*donc votre est France et vous êtes mienne.* It is as easy for me, Kate, to conquer the kingdom as to speak so much more French: I shall never move thee in French, unless it be to laugh at me.

Kath. Sauf votre honneur, le Français que vous parlez est meilleur que l'Anglais lequel je parle.

K. Hen. No, faith, is't not, Kate: but thy speaking of my tongue, and I thine, most truly falsely, must needs be granted to be much at one. But, Kate, dost thou understand thus much English,—Canst thou love me?

Kath. I cannot tell.

K. Hen. Can any of your neighbours tell, Kate? I'll ask them. Come, I know thou lovest me: and at night, when you come into your closet, you'll question this gentlewoman about me; and I know, Kate, you will to her dispraise those parts in me that you love with your heart: but, good Kate, mock me mercifully; the rather, gentle princess, because I love thee cruelly. If ever thou be'st mine, Kate,—as I have a saving faith within me tells me thou shalt,—I get thee with scambling, and thou must therefore needs prove a good soldier-breeder: shall not thou and I, between Saint Denis and Saint George, compound a boy, half French, half English, that shall go to Constantinople and take the Turk by the beard? shall we not? what sayest thou, my fair flower-de-luce?

Kath. I do not know dat.

K. Hen. No; 'tis hereafter to know, but now to promise; do but now promise, Kate, you will endeavour for your French part of such a boy; and for my English moiety take the word of a king and a bachelor. How answer you, *la plus belle Katharine du monde, mon très chère et divine déesse?*

Kath. Your *majesté* ave *fausse* French enough to deceive de most *sage damoiselle* dat is *en France.*

K. Hen. Now, fie upon my false French! By mine honour, in true English, I love thee, Kate: by which honour I dare not swear thou lovest me; yet my blood begins to flatter me that thou dost, notwithstanding the poor and untempering effect of my visage. Now, beshrew my father's ambition! he was thinking of civil wars when he got me; therefore was I created with a stubborn outside, with an aspect of iron, that when I come to woo ladies I fright them. But, in faith, Kate, the elder I wax the better I shall appear: my comfort is that old age, that ill layer-up of beauty, can do no more spoil upon my face: thou hast me, if thou hast me, at the worst; and thou shalt wear me, if thou wear me, better and better:—and therefore tell me, most fair Katharine, will you have me? Put off your maiden blushes; avouch the thoughts of your heart with the looks of an empress; take me by the hand and say,—Harry of

England, I am thine: which word thou shalt no sooner bless mine ear withal but I will tell thee aloud, England is thine, Ireland is thine, France is thine, and Henry Plantagenet is thine; who, though I speak it before his face, if he be not fellow with the best king, thou shalt find the best king of good fellows. Come, your answer in broken music,—for thy voice is music and thy English broken; therefore, queen of all, Katharine, break thy mind to me in broken English,—wilt thou have me?

Kath. Dat is as it sall please de *roi mon père.*

K. Hen. Nay, it will please him well, Kate,—it shall please him, Kate.

Kath. Den it sall also content me.

K. Hen. Upon that I kiss your hand, and I call you my queen.

Kath. Laissez, *mon seigneur, laissez, laissez: ma foi, je ne veux point que vous abaissez votre grandeur en baisant la main d'une votre indigne serviteur; excusez-moi, je vous supplie, mon très puissant seigneur.*

K. Hen. Then I will kiss your lips, Kate.

Kath. Les dames et demoiselles pour être baisées devant leur noces, il n'est pas le coutume de France.

K. Hen. Madam, my intrepreter, what says she?

Alice. Dat it is not be de fashion *pour les* ladies of France,—I cannot tell vat is *baiser en* Anglish.

K. Hen. To kiss.

Alice. Your majesty *entendre* bettre *que moi.*

K. Hen. It is not a fashion for the maids in France to kiss before they are married, would she say?

Alice. Oui, vraiment.

K. Hen. O Kate, nice customs court'sy to great kings. Dear Kate, you and I cannot be confined within the weak list of a country's fashion: we are the makers of manners, Kate; and the liberty that follows our places stops the mouth of all find-faults,—as I will do yours for upholding the nice fashion of your country in denying me a kiss: therefore, patiently and yielding. [*Kissing her.*] You have witchcraft in your lips, Kate: there is more eloquence in a sugar touch of them than in the tongues of the French council; and they should sooner persuade Harry of England than a general petition of monarchs.—Here comes your father.

Enter the FRENCH KING *and* QUEEN, BURGUNDY, BEDFORD, GLOSTER, EXETER, WARWICK, WESTMORELAND, *and other* French *and* English Lords.

Bur. God save your majesty! my royal cousin,
Teach you our princess English?

K. Hen. I would have her learn, my fair cousin, how perfectly I love her; and that is good English.

Bur. Is she not apt?

K. Hen. Our tongue is rough, coz, and my condition is not smooth; so that, having neither the voice nor the heart of flattery about me, I cannot so conjure up the spirit of love in her that he will appear in his true likeness.

Bur. Pardon the frankness of my mirth if I answer you for that. If you would conjure in her you must make a circle; if conjure up love in her in his true likeness, he must appear naked and blind. Can you blame her, then, being a maid yet rosed-over with the virgin crimson of modesty, if she deny the appearance of a naked blind boy in her naked seeing self? It were, my lord, a hard condition for a maid to consign to.

K. Hen. Yet they do wink and yield; as love is blind and enforces.

Bur. They are then excused, my lord, when they see not what they do.

K. Hen. Then, good my lord, teach your cousin to consent winking.

Bur. I will wink on her to consent, my lord, if you will teach her to know my meaning: for maids well summered and warm kept are like flies at Bartholomew-tide, blind, though they have their eyes; and then they will endure handling, which before would not abide looking on.

K. Hen. This moral ties me over to time and a hot summer; and so I shall catch the fly, your cousin, in the latter end, and she must be blind too.

Bur. As love is, my lord, before it loves.

K. Hen. It is so: and you may, some of you, thank love for my blindness, who cannot see many a fair French city for one fair French maid that stands in my way.

Fr. King. Yes, my lord, you see them perspectively, the cities turned into a maid; for they are all girdled with maiden walls that war hath never entered.

K. Hen. Shall Kate be my wife?

Fr. King. So please you.

K. Hen. I am content; so the maiden cities you talk of may wait on her: so the maid that stood in the way of my wish shall show me the way to my will.

Fr. King. We have consented to all terms of reason.

K. Hen. Is't so, my lords of England?

West. The king hath granted every article:—
His daughter first; and, in sequel, all,
According to their firm proposed natures.

Exe. Only, he hath not yet subscribed this:
—Where your majesty demands that the King of France, having any occasion to write for matter of grant, shall name your highness in this form and with this addition, in French,—*Notre très cher fils Henry, roi d'Angleterre, héritier de France;* and thus in Latin, *Præclarissimus filius noster Henricus, rex Angliæ et hæres Franciæ.* [denied

Fr. King. Nor this I have not, brother, so
But your request shall make me let it pass.

K. Hen. I pray you, then, in love and dear alliance,

Let that one article rank with the rest;
And thereupon give me your daughter.

   Fr. King. Take her, fair son; and from her
    blood raise up
Issue to me; that the contending kingdoms
Of France and England, whose very shores
    look pale
With envy of each other's happiness,
May cease their hatred; and this dear conjunc-
    tion
Plant neighbourhood and Christian-like accord
In their sweet bosoms, that never war advance
His bleeding sword 'twixt England and fair
    France.

   All. Amen!

   K. Hen. Now, welcome, Kate:—and bear
    me witness all,
That here I kiss her as my sovereign queen.
                     [Flourish.

   Q. Isa. God, the best maker of all marriages,
Combine your hearts in one, your realms in one!
As man and wife, being two, are one in love,
So be there 'twixt your kingdoms such a spousal
That never may ill office or fell jealousy,
Which troubles oft the bed of blessed marriage,
Thrust in between the paction of these king-
    doms,
To make divorce of their incorporate league;
That English may as French, French English-
    men,

Receive each other!—God speak this Amen!

   All. Amen!

   K. Hen. Prepare we for our marriage:—on
    which day,
My Lord of Burgundy, we'll take your oath,
And all the peers', for surety of our leagues.
Then shall I swear to Kate, and you to me;
And may our oaths well kept and prosperous
    be!　　　　　　　　　　　　*[Exeunt.*

Enter Chorus.

Chor. Thus far, with rough and all-unable pen,
   Our bending author hath pursu'd the story;
In little room confining mighty men,　　[glory.
   Mangling by starts the full course of their
Small time, but, in that small, most greatly
    liv'd
   This star of England: Fortune made his
    sword;
By which the world's best garden he achiev'd,
   And of it left his son imperial lord.
Henry the Sixth, in infant bands crown'd king
   Of France and England, did this king suc-
    ceed;
Whose state so many had the managing
   That they lost France and made his England
    bleed:　　　　　　　　　　　　　[sake
Which oft our stage hath shown; and, for their
In your fair minds let this acceptance take.
                       [Exit.

KING HENRY VI.
PART I.

Act II. Sc. 3.

KING HENRY VI.

FIRST PART

DRAMATIS PERSONÆ

KING HENRY THE SIXTH.
DUKE OF GLOSTER, *Uncle to the* KING, *and Protector.*
DUKE OF BEDFORD, *Uncle to the* KING, *and Regent of France.*
THOMAS BEAUFORT, *Duke of Exeter, Great-Uncle to the* KING.
HENRY BEAUFORT, *Great-Uncle to the* KING, *Bishop of Winchester, and afterwards Cardinal.*
JOHN BEAUFORT, *Earl of Somerset, afterwards Duke.*
RICHARD PLANTAGENET, *Eldest son of* RICHARD, *late Earl of Cambridge, afterwards Duke of York.*
EARL OF WARWICK.
EARL OF SALISBURY.
EARL OF SUFFOLK.
LORD TALBOT, *afterwards Earl of Shrewsbury.*
JOHN TALBOT, *his Son.*
EDMUND MORTIMER, *Earl of March.*
MORTIMER'S Keepers.
A Lawyer.
SIR JOHN FASTOLFE.
SIR WILLIAM LUCY.
SIR WILLIAM GLANSDALE.
SIR THOMAS GARGRAVE.
Mayor of London.

WOODVILLE, *Lieutenant of the Tower.*
VERNON, *of the White-rose or York faction.*
BASSET, *of the Red-rose or Lancaster faction.*
CHARLES, *Dauphin, and afterwards King of France.*
REIGNIER, *Duke of Anjou, and Titular King of Naples.*
DUKE OF BURGUNDY.
DUKE OF ALENÇON.
BASTARD OF ORLEANS.
Governor of Paris.
Master-Gunner of Orleans, *and his Son.*
General of the French Forces *in Bordeaux.*
A French Sergeant.
A Porter.
An Old Shepherd, *Father to* JOAN LA PUCELLE.
MARGARET, *Daughter to* REIGNIER, *afterwards married to* KING HENRY.
COUNTESS OF AUVERGNE.
JOAN LA PUCELLE, *commonly called* JOAN OF ARC.

Lords, Warders of the Tower, Heralds, Officers, Soldiers, Messengers, *and several* Attendants *both on the English and French.*

Fiends *appearing to* LA PUCELLE.

SCENE,—*Partly in* ENGLAND, *and partly in* FRANCE.

ACT I.

SCENE I.—*Westminster Abbey.*

Dead March. Corpse of KING HENRY THE FIFTH, *in state, is brought in, attended on by the* DUKES OF BEDFORD, GLOSTER, *and* EXETER, *the* EARL OF WARWICK, *the* BISHOP OF WINCHESTER, Heralds, &c.

Bed. Hung be the heavens with black, yield day to night!
Comets, importing change of times and states,
Brandish your crystal tresses in the sky,
And with them scourge the bad revolting stars
That have consented unto Henry's death!
Henry the Fifth, too famous to live long!
England ne'er lost a king of so much worth.
Glo. England ne'er had a king until his time.
Virtue he had, deserving to command:
His brandish'd sword did blind men with his beams;
His arms spread wider than a dragon's wings;
His sparkling eyes, replete with wrathful fire,
More dazzled and drove back his enemies
Than mid-day sun fierce bent against their faces.
What should I say? his deeds exceed all speech:
He ne'er lift up his hand but conquered.
Exe. We mourn in black: why mourn we not in blood?
Henry is dead, and never shall revive:
Upon a wooden coffin we attend;
And death's dishonourable victory
We with our stately presence glorify,
Like captives bound to a triumphant car.
What! shall we curse the planets of mishap,
That plotted thus our glory's overthrow?
Or shall we think the subtle-witted French
Conjurers and sorcerers, that, afraid of him,
By magic verses have contriv'd his end?
Win. He was a king bless'd of the King of kings,
Unto the French the dreadful judgment-day
So dreadful will not be as was his sight.
The battles of the Lord of hosts he fought:
The church's prayers made him so prosperous.

Glo. The church! where is it? Had not
    church-men pray'd,
His thread of life had not so soon decay'd:
None do you like but an effeminate prince,
Whom, like a school-boy, you may overawe.
    Win. Gloster, whate'er we like, thou art
        protector,
And lookest to command the prince and realm.
Thy wife is proud; she holdeth thee in awe
More than God or religious churchmen may.
    Glo. Name not religion, for thou lov'st the
        flesh;
And ne'er throughout the year to church thou
    go'st,
Except it be to pray against thy foes.
    Bed. Cease, cease these jars and rest your
        minds in peace!
Let's to the altar:—heralds, wait on us:—
Instead of gold, we'll offer up our arms;
Since arms avail not, now that Henry's dead.—
Posterity, await for wretched years,
When at their mother's moisten'd eyes babes
    shall suck;
Our isle be made a marish of salt tears,
And none but women left to wail the dead.—
Henry the Fifth! thy ghost I invocate;
Prosper this realm, keep it from civil broils!
Combat with adverse planets in the heavens!
A far more glorious star thy soul will make
Than Julius Cæsar or bright—

Enter a Messenger.

    Mess. My honourable lords, health to you all!
Sad tidings bring I to you out of France,
Of loss, of slaughter, and discomfiture:
Guienne, Champaigne, Rheims, Orleans,
Paris, Guysors, Poictiers, are all quite lost.
    Bed. What say'st thou, man, before dead
        Henry's corse?
Speak softly; or the loss of those great towns
Will make him burst his lead and rise from
    death.
    Glo. Is Paris lost? is Rouen yielded up?
If Henry were recall'd to life again,
These news would cause him once more yield
    the ghost.
    Exe. How were they lost? what treachery
        was us'd?
    Mess. No treachery but want of men and
        money.
Among the soldiers this is muttered,—
That here you maintain several factions;
And whilst a field should be despatch'd and
    fought,
You are disputing or your generals:
One would have ling'ring wars, with little cost;
Another would fly swift, but wanteth wings;
A third man thinks, without expense at all,
By guileful fair words peace may be obtain'd.
Awake, awake, English nobility!
Let not sloth dim your honours, new-begot;
Cropp'd are the flower-de-luces in your arms;
Of England's coat one half is cut away.
    Exe. Were our tears wanting to this funeral,

These tidings would call forth her flowing tides.
    Bed. Me they concern; regent I am of
        France.—
Give me my steeled coat! I'll fight for France.—
Away with these disgraceful wailing robes!
Wounds will I lend the French, instead of eyes,
To weep their intermissive miseries.

Enter a second Messenger.

    2 Mess. Lords, view these letters, full of bad
        mischance.
France is revolted from the English quite,
Except some petty towns of no import:
The Dauphin Charles is crowned king in
    Rheims;
The Bastard of Orleans with him is join'd;
Reignier, Duke of Anjou, doth take his part;
The Duke of Alençon flieth to his side.
    Exe. The Dauphin crowned king! all fly to
        him!
O, whither shall we fly from this reproach?
    Glo. We will not fly, but to our enemies'
        throats:—
Bedford, if thou be slack I'll fight it out.
    Bed. Gloster, why doubt'st thou of my for-
        wardness?
An army have I muster'd in my thoughts,
Wherewith already France is overrun.

Enter a third Messenger.

    3 Mess. My gracious lords,—to add to your
        laments,   [hearse,—
Wherewith you now bedew King Henry's
I must inform you of a dismal fight
Betwixt the stout Lord Talbot and the French.
    Win. What! wherein Talbot overcame? is't
        so?   [o'erthrown:
    3 Mess. O, no; wherein Lord Talbot was
The circumstance I'll tell you more at large.
The tenth of August last this dreadful lord,
Retiring from the siege of Orleans,
Having full scarce six thousand in his troop,
By three-and-twenty thousand of the French
Was round encompassed and set upon.
No leisure had he to enrank his men;
He wanted pikes to set before his archers;
Instead whereof, sharp stakes, pluck'd out of
    hedges,
They pitched in the ground confusedly,
To keep the horsemen off from breaking in.
More than three hours the fight continued;
Where valiant Talbot, above human thought,
Enacted wonders with his sword and lance:
Hundreds he sent to hell, and none durst stand
    him;
Here, there, and everywhere, enrag'd he flew:
The French exclaim'd the devil was in arms;
All the whole army stood agaz'd on him:
His soldiers, spying his undaunted spirit,
A Talbot! a Talbot! cried out amain,
And rush'd into the bowels of the battle.
Here had the conquest fully been seal'd up
If Sir John Fastolfe had not play'd the coward:
He, being in the vaward,—plac'd behind,

With purpose to relieve and follow them,—
Cowardly fled, not having struck one stroke.
Hence grew the general wreck and massacre;
Enclosed were they with their enemies:
A base Walloon, to win the Dauphin's grace,
Thrust Talbot with a spear into the back;
Whom all France, with their chief assembled
    strength,
Durst not presume to look once in the face.

Bed. Is Talbot slain? then I will slay myself,
For living idly here in pomp and ease,
Whilst such a worthy leader, wanting aid,
Unto his dastard foemen is betray'd.

3 *Mess.* O no, he lives; but is took prisoner,
And Lord Scales with him, and Lord Hunger-
    ford:
Most of the rest slaughter'd or took likewise.

Bed. His ransom there is none but I shall
    pay:
I'll hale the Dauphin headlong from his
    throne,—
His crown shall be the ransom of my friend;
Four of their lords I'll change for one of ours.—
Farewell, my masters; to my task will I;
Bonfires in France forthwith I am to make,
To keep our great Saint George's feast withal:
Ten thousand soldiers with me I will take,
Whose bloody deeds shall make all Europe
    quake.

3 *Mess.* So you had need; for Orleans is be-
    sieg'd;
The English army is grown weak and faint:
The Earl of Salisbury craveth supply,
And hardly keeps his men from mutiny,
Since they, so few, watch such a multitude.

Exe. Remember, lords, your oaths to Henry
    sworn,
Either to quell the Dauphin utterly,
Or bring him in obedience to your yoke.

Bed. I do remember it; and here take my
    leave,
To go about my preparation.   [*Exit.*

Glo. I'll to the Tower, with all the haste I
    can,
To view the artillery and munition;
And then I will proclaim young Henry king.
    [*Exit.*

Exe. To Eltham will I, where the young
    king is,
Being ordain'd his special governor;
And for his safety there I'll best devise. [*Exit.*

Win. Each hath his place and function to
    attend:
I am left out; for me nothing remains.
But long I will not be Jack-out-of-office:
The king from Eltham I intend to steal,
And sit at chiefest stern of public weal.
    [*Exit. Scene closes.*

SCENE II.—FRANCE, *Before Orleans.*

Enter CHARLES, *with his* Forces; ALENCON,
    REIGNIER, *and others.*

Char. Mars his true moving, even as in the
    heavens,

So in the earth, to this day is not known:
Late did he shine upon the English side;
Now we are victors, upon us he smiles.
What towns of any moment but we have?
At pleasure here we lie near Orleans;
Otherwhiles the famish'd English, like pale
    ghosts,
Faintly besiege us one hour in a month.

Alen. They want their porridge and their
    fat bull-beeves:
Either they must be dieted like mules,
And have their provender tied to their mouths,
Or piteous they will look, like drowned mice.

Reig. Let's raise the siege: why live we idly
    here?
Talbot is taken, whom we wont to fear:
Remaineth none but mad-brain'd Salisbury;
And he may well in fretting spend his gall,—
Nor men nor money hath he to make war.

Char. Sound, sound alarum! we will rush on
    them.
Now for the honour of the forlorn French!—
Him I forgive my death that killeth me,
When he sees me go back one foot or flee.
    [*Exeunt.*

*Alarums; excursions; afterwards a retreat. Re-
    enter* CHARLES, ALENÇON, REIGNIER, *and
    others.*

Char. Who ever saw the like? what men
    have I!—
Dogs! cowards! dastards! I would ne'er have
    fled
But that they left me midst my enemies.

Reig. Salisbury is a desperate homicide;
He fighteth as one weary of his life.
The other lords, like lions wanting food,
Do rush upon us as their hungry prey.

Alen. Froissart, a countryman of ours, re-
    cords,
England all Olivers and Rowlands bred
During the time Edward the Third did reign.
More truly now may this be verified;
For none but Samsons and Goliasses
It sendeth forth to skirmish. One to ten!
Lean raw-bon'd rascals! who would e'er sup-
    pose
They had such courage and audacity?

Char. Let's leave this town; for they are
    hair-brain'd slaves,
And hunger will enforce them to be more eager:
Of old I know them; rather with their teeth
The walls they'll tear down than forsake the
    siege.

Reig. I think, by some odd gimmers or de-
    vice,
Their arms are set, like clocks, still to strike on;
Else ne'er could they hold out so as they do.
By my consent, we'll even let them alone.

Alen. Be it so.

Enter the BASTARD OF ORLEANS.

Bast. Where's the Prince Dauphin? I have
    news for him.

Char. Bastard of Orleans, thrice welcome to us.

Bast. Methinks your looks are sad, your cheer appall'd:
Hath the late overthrow wrought this offence?
Be not dismay'd, for succour is at hand:
A holy maid hither with me I bring,
Which, by a vision sent to her from heaven,
Ordained is to raise this tedious siege,
And drive the English forth the bounds of France.
The spirit of deep prophecy she hath,
Exceeding the nine sibyls of old Rome:
What's past and what's to come she can descry.
Speak, shall I call her in? Believe my words,
For they are certain and infallible.

Char. Go, call her in. [*Exit* BASTARD.] But first, to try her skill,
Reignier, stand thou as Dauphin in my place:
Question her proudly; let thy looks be stern:
By this means shall we sound what skill she hath.   [*Retires.*

Re-enter the BASTARD OF ORLEANS, *with* LA PUCELLE.

Reig. Fair maid, is't thou wilt do these wondrous feats?

Puc. Reignier, is't thou that thinkest to beguile me?—   [hind;
Where is the Dauphin?—Come, come from behind;
I know thee well, though never seen before.
Be not amaz'd, there's nothing hid from me:
In private will I talk with thee apart.—
Stand back, you lords, and give us leave awhile.

Reig. She takes upon her bravely at first dash.   [daughter,

Puc. Dauphin, I am by birth a shepherd's daughter,
My wit untrain'd in any kind of art.
Heaven and our Lady gracious hath it pleas'd
To shine on my contemptible estate:
Lo, whilst I waited on my tender lambs,
And to sun's parching heat display'd my cheeks,
God's mother deigned to appear to me,
And in a vision full of majesty
Will'd me to leave my base vocation,
And free my country from calamity:
Her aid she promis'd and assur'd success:
In cómplete glory she reveal'd herself;
And whereas I was black and swart before,
With those clear rays which she infus'd on me,
That beauty am I bless'd with which you see.
Ask me what question thou canst possible,
And I will answer unpremeditated:
My courage try by combat if thou dar'st,
And thou shalt find that I exceed my sex.
Resolve on this,—thou shalt be fortunate
If thou receive me for thy warlike mate.

Char. Thou hast astonish'd me with thy high terms:
Only this proof I'll of thy valour make,—
In single combat thou shalt buckle with me;
And if thou vanquishest, thy words are true:
Otherwise I renounce all confidence.

Puc. I am prepar'd: here is my keen-edg'd sword,
Deck'd with five flower-de-luces on each side;
The which at Touraine, in Saint Katherine's churchyard,
Out of a great deal of old iron I chose forth.

Char. Then come, o' God's name; I fear no woman.

Puc. And while I live I'll ne'er fly from a man.   [*They fight.*

Char. Stay, stay thy hands! thou art an Amazon,
And fightest with the sword of Deborah.

Puc. Christ's mother helps me, else I were too weak.

Char. Whoe'er helps thee, 'tis thou that must help me:
Impatiently I burn with thy desire;
My heart and hands thou hast at once subdu'd.
Excellent Pucelle, if thy name be so,
Let me thy servant and not sovereign be:
'Tis the French Dauphin sueth to thee thus.

Puc. I must not yield to any rites of love,
For my profession's sacred from above:
When I have chased all thy foes from hence,
Then will I think upon a recompense.

Char. Meantime look gracious on thy prostrate thrall.

Reig. My lord, methinks, is very long in talk.

Alen. Doubtless he shrives this woman to her smock;
Else ne'er could he so long protract his speech.

Reig. Shall we disturb him, since he keeps no mean?

Alen. He may mean more than we poor men do know: [tongues.
These women are shrewd tempters with their tongues.

Reig. My lord, where are you? what devise you on?
Shall we give over Orleans, or no?

Puc. Why, no, I say, distrustful recreants!
Fight till the last gasp; I will be your guard.

Char. What she says I'll confirm: we'll fight it out.

Puc. Assign'd am I to be the English scourge.
This night the siege assuredly I'll raise:
Expect Saint Martin's summer, halcyon days,
Since I have entered into these wars.
Glory is like a circle in the water,
Which never ceaseth to enlarge itself,
Till by broad spreading it disperse to naught.
With Henry's death the English circle ends;
Dispersed are the glories it included.
Now am I like that proud insulting ship
Which Cæsar and his fortune bare at once.

Char. Was Mahomet inspired with a dove?
Thou with an eagle art inspired, then.
Helen, the mother of great Constantine,
Nor yet Saint Philip's daughters, were like thee.
Bright star of Venus, fall'n down on the earth,
How may I reverently worship thee enough?

Alen. Leave off delays, and let us raise the siege.

Reig. Woman, do what thou canst to save our honours;
Drive them from Orleans, and be immortaliz'd.
Char. Presently we'll try:—come, let's away about it:—
No prophet will I trust if she prove false.
[*Exeunt.*

SCENE III.—LONDON. *Before the Gates of the Tower.*

Enter the DUKE OF GLOSTER, *with his* Serving-men *in blue coats.*

Glo. I am come to survey the Tower this day: [ance.—
Since Henry's death, I fear, there is convey-
Where be these warders, that they wait not here?
Open the gates: Gloster it is that calls.
[*Servants* knock.
1 *Ward.* [*Within.*] Who's there that knocks so imperiously?
1 *Serv.* It is the noble Duke of Gloster.
2 *Ward.* [*Within.*] Whoe'er he be, you may not be let in.   [tector?—
1 *Serv.* Villains, answer you so the lord pro-
1 *Ward.* [*Within.*] The Lord protect him! so we answer him:
We do no otherwise than we are will'd.
Glo. Who willed you? or whose will stands but mine?
There's none protector of the realm but I.—
Break up the gates, I'll be your warrantize:
Shall I be flouted thus by dunghill grooms?
[GLOSTER'S Servants *rush at the Tower-gates.*
Wood. [*Within.*] What noise is this? what traitors have we here?
Glo. Lieutenant, is it you whose voice I hear?
Open the gates; here's Gloster that would enter.
Wood. [*Within.*] Have patience, noble Duke;
I may not open;
The Cardinal of Winchester forbids:
From him I have express commandment
That thou nor none of thine shall be let in.
Glo. Faint-hearted Woodville, prizest him 'fore me,—
Arrogant Winchester? that haughty prelate
Whom Henry, our late sovereign, ne'er could brook?
Thou art no friend to God or to the king:
Open the gates, or I'll shut thee out shortly.
1 *Serv.* Open the gates unto the lord pro-tector,   [quickly.
Or we'll burst them open if that you come not
[GLOSTER'S Servants *rush again at the Tower-gates.*

Enter WINCHESTER, *with his* Serving-men *in tawny coats.*

Win. How now, ambitious Humphry! what means this?
Glo. Peel'd priest, dost thou command me to be shut out?

Win. I do, thou most usurping proditor,
And not protector of the king or realm.
Glo. Stand back, thou manifest conspirator,
Thou that contriv'dst to murder our dead lord;
Thou that giv'st whores indulgences to sin:
I'll canvass thee in thy broad cardinal's hat,
If thou proceed in this thy insolence.
Win. Nay, stand thou back; I will not budge a foot:
This be Damascus, be thou cursed Cain,
To slay thy brother Abel, if thou wilt.
Glo. I will not slay thee, but I'll drive thee back:
Thy scarlet robes as a child's bearing-cloth
I'll use to carry thee out of this place. .
Win. Do what thou dar'st; I beard thee to thy face.   [face?—
Glo. What! am I dar'd, and bearded to my
Draw, men, for all this privileged place;
Blue-coats to tawny-coats.—Priest, beware your beard;
I mean to tug it, and to cuff you soundly:
Under my feet I'll stamp thy cardinal's hat;
In spite of pope or dignities of church,
Here by the cheeks I'll drag thee up and down.
Win. Gloster, thou wilt answer this before the pope.   [rope!—
Glo. Winchester goose! I cry, a rope! a
Now beat them hence, why do you let them stay?—
Thee I'll chase hence, thou wolf in sheep's array.—
Out, tawny-coats!—Out, scarlet hypocrite!

GLOSTER *and his* Servants *attack the other Party.*
In the tumult, enter the Mayor of London *and* Officers.

May. Fie, lords! that you, being supreme magistrates,
Thus contumeliously should break the peace!
Glo. Peace, mayor! thou know'st little of my wrongs:
Here's Beaufort, that regards nor God nor king,
Hath here distrain'd the Tower to his use.
Win. Here's Gloster, too, a foe to citizens;
One that still motions war, and never peace,
O'ercharging your free purses with large fines;
That seeks to overthrow religion,
Because he is protector of the realm;
And would have armour here out of the Tower,
To crown himself king and suppress the prince.
Glo. I will not answer thee with words, but blows.   [*Here they skirmish again.*
May. Naught rests for me, in this tumultu-ous strife,
But to make open proclamation:—
Come, officer, as loud as e'er thou canst.
Off. [*Reads.*] *All manner of men assembled here in arms this day against God's peace and the king's, we charge and command you, in his highness' name, to repair to your several dwelling-places; and not to wear, handle, or use any sword, weapon, or dagger, henceforward, upon pain of death.*

Glo. Cardinal, I'll be no breaker of the law;
But we shall meet and break our minds at large.
Win. Gloster, we'll meet, to thy. dear cost,
be sure:
Thy heart-blood I will have for this day's work.
May. I'll call for clubs if you will not away:—
This cardinal's more haughty than the devil.
Glo. Mayor, farewell: thou dost but what
thou mayst.
Win. Abominable Gloster! guard thy head;
For I intend to have it ere long.
[*Exeunt severally,* GLO. *and* WIN.,
with their Servants.
May. See the coast clear'd, and then we will
depart.—
Good God, these nobles should such stomachs
bear!
I myself fight not once in forty year. [*Exeunt.*

SCENE IV.—FRANCE. *Before Orleans.*

Enter, on the walls, the Master-Gunner *and
his* Son.

M. Gun. Sirrah, thou know'st how Orleans
is besieg'd,
And how the English have the suburbs won.
Son. Father, I know; and oft have shot at
them,
Howe'er, unfortunate, I missed my aim.
M. Gun. But now thou shalt not. Be thou
rul'd by me:
Chief master-gunner am I of this town;
Something I must do to procure me grace.
The prince's espials have informed me
How the English, in the suburbs close in-
trench'd,
Wont, through a secret grate of iron bars
In yonder tower, to overpeer the city,
And thence discover how with most advantage
They may vex us with shot or with assault.
To intercept this inconvenience,
A piece of ordnance 'gainst it I have plac'd;
And even these three days have I watch'd if I
Could see them.
Now do thou watch, for I can stay no longer.
If thou spy'st any, run and bring me word;
And thou shalt find me at the governor's.
[*Exit.*
Son. Father, I warrant you; take you no
care;
I'll never trouble you if I may spy them.

Enter, in an upper Chamber of a Tower, the
LORDS SALISBURY *and* TALBOT, SIR WILLIAM
GLANSDALE, SIR THOMAS GARGRAVE, *and
others.*

Sal. Talbot, my life, my joy, again return'd!
How wert thou handled being prisoner?
Or by what means gott'st thou to be releas'd?
Discourse, I pr'ythee, on this turret's top.
Tal. The Duke of Bedford had a prisoner
Call'd the brave Lord Ponton de Santrailles;
For him I was exchang'd and ransomed.
But with a baser man of arms by far

Once, in contempt, they would have barter'd
me:
Which I, disdaining, scorn'd; and craved death
Rather than I would be so vile-esteem'd.
In fine, redeem'd I was as I desir'd.
But, O! the treacherous Fastolfe wounds my
heart!
Whom with my bare fists I would execute
If I now had him brought into my power.
Sal. Yet tell'st thou not how thou wert en-
tertain'd.
Tal. With scoffs, and scorns, and contumeli-
ous taunts.
In open market-place produc'd they me,
To be a public spectacle to all:
Here, said they, is the terror of the French,
The scarecrow that affrights our children so.
Then broke I from the officers that led me,
And with my nails digg'd stones out of the
ground
To hurl at the beholders of my shame:
My grisly countenance made others fly;
None durst come near for fear of sudden death.
In iron walls they deem'd me not secure;
So great fear of my name 'mongst them was
spread
That they suppos'd I could rend bars of steel,
And spurn in pieces posts of adamant:
Wherefore a guard of chosen shot I had,
That walk'd about me every minute-while;
And if I did but stir out of my bed,
Ready they were to shoot me to the heart.
Sal. I grieve to hear what torments you en-
dur'd;
But we will be reveng'd sufficiently.
Now it is supper-time in Orleans:
Here, through this grate, I can count each one,
And view the Frenchmen how they fortify:
Let us look in; the sight will much delight
thee.—
Sir Thomas Gargrave and Sir William Glansdale,
Let me have your express opinions
Where is best place to make our battery next.
Gar. I think at the north gate; for there
stand lords.
Glan. And I here, at the bulwark of the
bridge.
Tal. For aught I see, this city must be
famish'd,
Or with light skirmishes enfeebled.
[*Shot from the town.* SAL. *and* SIR
THOMAS GARGRAVE *fall.*
Sal. O Lord, have mercy on us, wretched
sinners!
Gar. O Lord, have mercy on me, woeful man!
Tal. What chance is this that suddenly hath
cross'd us?—
Speak, Salisbury; at least, if thou canst speak:
How far'st thou, mirror of all martial men?
One of thy eyes and thy cheek's side struck
off!—
Accursed tower! accursed fatal hand
That hath contriv'd this woeful tragedy!
In thirteen battles Salisbury o'ercame;

Henry the Fifth he first train'd to the wars;
Whilst any trump did sound or drum struck up,
His sword did ne'er leave striking in the field.—
Yet liv'st thou, Salisbury? though thy speech
doth fail,
One eye thou hast, to look to heaven for grace:
The sun with one eye vieweth all the world.—
Heaven, be thou gracious to none alive
If Salisbury wants mercy at thy hands!—
Bear hence his body; I will help to bury it.
Sir Thomas Gargrave, hast thou any life?
Speak unto Talbot; nay, look up to him.—
Salisbury, cheer thy spirit with this comfort;
Thou shalt not die whiles—
He beckons with his hand, and smiles on me,
As who should say, *When I am dead and gone,
Remember to avenge me on the French.*—
Plantagenet, I will; and like thee, Nero,
Play on the lute, beholding the towns burn:
Wretched shall France be only in my name.
　　　　　[*Thunder heard; afterwards an alarum.*
What stir is this? What tumult's in the
heavens?
Whence cometh this alarum, and the noise?

　　　　　Enter a Messenger.

Mess. My lord, my lord, the French have
gather'd head:
The Dauphin, with one Joan la Pucelle join'd,—
A holy prophetess new risen up,—
Is come with a great power to raise the siege.
　　　　　[SAL. *lifts himself and groans.*
Tal. Hear, hear how dying Salisbury doth
groan!
It irks his heart he cannot be reveng'd.—
Frenchmen, I'll be a Salisbury to you:—
Pucelle or puzzle, dolphin or dogfish,
Your hearts I'll stamp out with my horse's
heels,
And make a quagmire of your mingled brains.—
Convey me Salisbury into his tent,
And then we'll try what these dastard French-
men dare.
　　　　　[*Exeunt, bearing out the bodies.*

SCENE V.—*The same. Before one of the Gates.*

Alarum; skirmishings. Enter TALBOT, *pursuing the* DAUPHIN, *drives him in, and exit:
then enter* JOAN LA PUCELLE, *driving Englishmen before her, and exit after them: then re-
enter* TALBOT.

Tal. Where is my strength, my valour, and
my force?
Our English troops retire, I cannot stay them;
A woman clad in armour chaseth them.
Here, here she comes.

　　　　　Enter LA PUCELLE.

I'll have a bout with thee;
Devil or devil's dam, I'll conjure thee:
Blood will I draw on thee,—thou art a witch,—
And straightway give thy soul to him thou
serv'st.

Puc. Come, come, 'tis only I that must dis-
grace thee.　　　　　[*They fight.*
Tal. Heavens, can you suffer hell so to pre-
vail?
My breast I'll burst with straining of my
courage,
And from my shoulders crack my arms asunder,
But I will chastise this high-minded strumpet.
　　　　　[*They fight again.*
Puc. [*Retiring.*] Talbot, farewell: thy hour
is not yet come:
I must go victual Orleans forthwith.
O'ertake me if thou canst; I scorn thy strength.
Go, go, cheer up thy hunger-starved men;
Help Salisbury to make his testament:
This day is ours, as many more shall be.
　　　　　[LA PUC. *enters the town with* Soldiers.
Tal. My thoughts are whirled like a potter's
wheel;
I know not where I am nor what I do:
A witch by fear, not force, like Hannibal
Drives back our troops, and conquers as she
lists:
So bees with smoke and doves with noisome
stench
Are from their hives and houses driven away.
They call'd us, for our fierceness, English dogs;
Now like to whelps we crying run away.
　　　　　[*A short alarum.*
Hark, countrymen! either renew the fight
Or tear the lions out of England's coat;
Renounce your soil, give sheep in lions' stead:
Sheep run not half so timorous from the wolf,
Or horse or oxen from the leopard,
As you fly from your oft-subdued slaves.
　　　　　[*Alarum. Another skirmish.*
It will not be:—retire into your trenches:
You all consented unto Salisbury's death,
For none would strike a stroke in his revenge.—
Pucelle is enter'd into Orleans,
In spite of us or aught that we could do.
O, would I were to die with Salisbury!
The shame hereof will make me hide my head!
　　　　　[*Alarum. Retreat. Exeunt* TALBOT
　　　　　and Forces, *&c.*

Flourish. Enter on the walls, LA PUCELLE,
　CHARLES, REIGNIER, ALENÇON, *and* Soldiers.

Puc. Advance our waving colours on the
walls;
Rescu'd is Orleans from the English:—
Thus Joan la Pucelle hath perform'd her word.
Char. Divinest creature, Astræa's daughter,
How shall I honour thee for this success?
Thy promises are like Adonis' gardens,
That one day bloom'd and fruitful were the
next.—
France, triumph in thy glorious prophetess!—
Recover'd is the town of Orleans:
More blessed hap did ne'er befall our state.
Reig. Why ring not out the bells aloud,
throughout the town?
Dauphin, command the citizens make bonfires,
And feast and banquet in the open streets,

To celebrate the joy that God hath given us.

Alen. All France will be replete with mirth
and joy
When they shall hear how we have play'd the
men.

Char. 'Tis Joan, not we, by whom the day is
won;
For which I will divide my crown with her;
And all the priests and friars in my realm
Shall in procession sing her endless praise.
A stateli r pyramis to her I'll rear
Than Rhodope's of Memphis ever was:
In memory of 'her when she is dead,
Her ashes, in an urn more precious
Than the rich jewell'd coffer of Darius,
Transported shall be at high festivals
Before the kings and queens of France.
No longer on Saint Denis will we cry,
But Joan la Pucelle shall be France's saint.
Come in, and let us banquet royally,
After this golden day of victory.

[*Flourish. Exeunt.*

ACT II.

Scene I.—*Before Orleans.*

Enter to the Gate a French Sergeant *and two*
Sentinels.

Serg. Sirs, take your places and be vigilant:
If any noise or soldier you perceive
Near to the walls, by some apparent sign
Let us have knowledge at the court of guard.

1 *Sent.* Sergeant, you shall. [*Exit* Sergeant.]
Thus are poor servitors,
When others sleep upon their quiet beds,
Constrain'd to watch in darkness, rain, and
cold.

Enter Talbot, Bedford, Burgundy, *and*
Forces, *with scaling-ladders; their drums
beating a dead march.*

Tal. Lord regent and redoubted Burgundy,—
By whose approach the regions of Artois,
Walloon, and Picardy are friends to us,—
This happy night the Frenchmen are secure,
Having all day carous'd and banqueted:
Embrace we, then, this opportunity,
As fitting best to quittance their deceit,
Contriv'd by art and baleful sorcery.

Bed. Coward of France!—how much he
wrongs his fame,
Despairing of his own arm's fortitude,
To join with witches and the help of hell.

Bur. Traitors have never other company.—
But what's that Pucelle whom they term so
pure?

Tal. A·maid, they say.

Bed. A maid! and be so martial!

Bur. Pray God she prove not masculine ere
long,
If underneath the standard of the French
She carry armour. as she hath begun.

Tal. Well, let them practise and converse
with spirits:

God is our fortress, in whose conquering name
Let us resolve to scale their flinty bulwarks.

Bed. Ascend, brave Talbot; we will follow
thee.

Tal. Not all together: better far, I guess,
That we do make our entrance several ways;
That, if it chance the one of us do fail,
The other yet may rise against their force.

Bed. Agreed: I'll to yon corner.

Bur. And I to this.

Tal. And here will Talbot mount or make
his grave.—
Now, Salisbury, for thee and for the right
Of English Henry, shall this night appear
How much in duty I am bound to both.

[*The* English *scale the walls, crying* St. George!
a Talbot! *and all enter the Town.*

Sent. Arm! arm! the enemy doth make
assault!

The French *leap over the walls in their shirts.
Enter, several ways,* Bastard, Alençon,
Reignier, *half ready and half unready.*

Alen. How now, my lords? what, all unready so?

Bast. Unready! ay, and glad we 'scap'd so
well.

Reig. 'Twas time, I trow, to wake and leave
our beds,
Hearing alarums at our chamber-doors.

Alen. Of all exploits since first I follow'd
arms,
Ne'er heard I of a warlike enterprise
More venturous or desperate than this.

Bast. I think this Talbot be a fiend of hell.

Reig. If not of hell, the heavens, sure, favour
him.

Alen. Here cometh Charles: I marvel how
he sped.

Bast. Tut! holy Joan was his defensive guard.

Enter Charles *and* La Pucelle.

Char. Is this thy cunning, thou deceitful
dame?
Didst thou at first, to flatter us withal,
Make us partakers of a little gain,
That now our loss might be ten times so much?

Puc. Wherefore is Charles impatient with
his friend?
At all times will you have my power alike?
Sleeping or waking, must I still prevail,
Or will you blame and lay the fault on me?
Improvident soldiers! had your watch been
good
This sudden mischief never could have fall'n.

Char. Duke of Alençon, this was your default,
That, being captain of the watch to-night,
Did look no better to that weighty charge.

Alen. Had all your quarters been as safely
kept
As that whereof I had the government,
We had not been thus shamefully surpris'd.

Bast. Mine was secure.

Reig. And so was mine, my lord.

Char. And, for myself, most part of all this
　　night,
Within her quarter and mine own precinct
I was employ'd in passing to and fro,
About relieving of the sentinels:
Then how or which way should they first break
　　in?　　　　　　　　　　　　　　[case,

Puc. Question, my lords, no further of the
How or which way; 'tis sure they found some
　　place
But weakly guarded, where the breach was
　　made.
And now there rests no other shift but this,—
To gather our soldiers, scatter'd and dispers'd,
And lay new platforms to endamage them.

Alarum. Enter an English Soldier, *crying a*
　　Talbot! a Talbot! *They fly, leaving their*
　　clothes behind.

Sold. I'll be so bold to take what they have
　　left.
The cry of Talbot serves me for a sword;
For I have loaden me with many spoils,
Using no other weapon but his name.　　[*Exit.*

SCENE II.—ORLEANS. *Within the Town.*

Enter TALBOT, BEDFORD, BURGUNDY,
　　a Captain, *and others.*

Bed. The day begins to break, and night is
　　fled,
Whose pitchy mantle over-veil'd the earth.
Here sound retreat, and cease our hot pursuit.
　　　　　　　　　　　　[*Retreat sounded.*
Tal. Bring forth the body of old Salisbury,
And here advance it in the market-place,
The middle centre of this cursed town.
Now have I paid my vow unto his soul;
For every drop of blood was drawn from him,
There hath at least five Frenchmen died to-
　　night.
And that hereafter ages may behold
What ruin happen'd in revenge of him,
Within their chiefest temple I'll erect
A tomb, wherein his corpse shall be interr'd:
Upon the which, that every one may read,
Shall be engrav'd the sack of Orleans,
The treacherous manner of his mournful death,
And what a terror he had been to France.
But, lords, in all our bloody massacre,
I muse we meet not with the Dauphin's grace,
His new-come champion, virtuous Joan of Arc,
Nor any of his false confederates.
Bed. 'Tis thought, Lord Talbot, when the
　　fight began,
Rous'd on the sudden from their drowsy beds,
They did, amongst the troops of armed men,
Leap o'er the walls for refuge in the field.
Bur. Myself,—as far as I could well discern
For smoke and dusky vapours of the night,—
Am sure I scar'd the Dauphin and his trull,
When arm in arm they both came swiftly run-
　　ning,
Like to a pair of loving turtle-doves,
That could not live asunder day or night.

After that things are set in order here,
We'll follow them with all the power we have.

Enter a Messenger.

Mess. All hail, my lords! Which of this
　　princely train
Call ye the warlike Talbot, for his acts
So much applauded through the realm of
　　France?
Tal. Here is the Talbot: who would speak
　　with him?　　　　　　　　　[Auvergne,
Mess. The virtuous lady, Countess of
With modesty admiring thy renown,　　[safe
By me entreats, great lord, thou wouldst vouch-
To visit her poor castle where she lies,
That she may boast she hath beheld the man
Whose glory fills the world with loud report.
Bar. Is it even so? Nay, then, I see our wars
Will turn unto a peaceful comic sport,
When ladies crave to be encounter'd with.—
You may not, my lord, despise her gentle suit.
Tal. Ne'er trust me then; for when a world
　　of men
Could not prevail with all their oratory,
Yet hath a woman's kindness overrul'd:—
And therefore tell her I return great thanks,
And in submission will attend on her.—
Will not your honours bear me company?
Bed. No, truly; it is more than manners will:
And I have heard it said, unbidden guests
Are often welcomest when they are gone.
Tal. Well then, alone, since there's no
　　remedy,
I mean to prove this lady's courtesy.—
Come hither, captain. [*Whispers.*] You per-
　　ceive my mind?
Capt. I do, my lord, and mean accordingly.
　　　　　　　　　　　　　　　[*Exeunt.*

SCENE III.—AUVERGNE. *Court of the Castle.*

Enter the COUNTESS *and her* Porter.

Count. Porter, remember what I gave in
　　charge;　　　　　　　　　　　[me.
And when you have done so, bring the keys to
Port. Madam, I will.　　　　　　[*Exit.*
Count. The plot is laid: if all things fall out
　　right,
I shall as famous be by this exploit
As Scythian Tomyris by Cyrus' death.
Great is the rumour of this dreadful knight,
And his achievements of no less account:
Fain would mine eyes be witness with mine ears,
To give their censure of these rare reports.

Enter Messenger *and* TALBOT.

Mess. Madam,
According as your ladyship desir'd,
By message crav'd, so is Lord Talbot come.
Count. And he is welcome. What! is this the
　　man?
Mess. Madam, it is.
Count.　　　　　Is this the scourge of France?
Is this the Talbot, so much fear'd abroad

That with his name the mothers still their babes?
I see report is fabulous and false:
I thought I should have seen some Hercules,
A second Hector, for his grim aspect,
And large proportion of his strong-knit limbs.
Alas, this is a child, a silly dwarf!
It cannot be this weak and writhled shrimp
Should strike such terror to his enemies.

Tal. Madam, I have been bold to trouble you;
But since your ladyship is not at leisure,
I'll sort some other time to visit you. [*Going.*

Count. What means he now?—Go ask him whither he goes.

Mess. Stay, my Lord Talbot; for my lady craves
To know the cause of your abrupt departure.

Tal. Marry, for that she's in a wrong belief,
I go to certify her Talbot's here.

Re-enter Porter *with keys.*

Count. If thou be he, then art thou prisoner.
Tal. Prisoner! to whom?
Count. To me, blood-thirsty lord;
And for that cause I train'd thee to my house.
Long time thy shadow hath been thrall to me,
For in my gallery thy picture hangs:
But now the substance shall endure the like;
And I will chain these legs and arms of thine,
That hast by tyranny these many years
Wasted our country, slain our citizens,
And sent our sons and husbands captive.
Tal. Ha, ha, ha!
Count. Laughest thou, wretch? thy mirth shall turn to moan.
Tal. I laugh to see your ladyship so fond
To think that you have aught but Talbot's shadow
Whereon to practise your severity.
Count. Why, art not thou the man?
Tal. I am indeed.
Count. Then have I substance too.
Tal. No, no, I am but shadow of myself:
You are deceiv'd, my substance is not here;
For what you see is but the smallest part
And least proportion of humanity:
I tell you, madam, were the whole frame here,
It is of such a spacious lofty pitch,
Your roof were not sufficient to contain 't.
Count. This is a riddling merchant for the nonce;
He will be here, and yet he is not here:
How can these contrarieties agree?
Tal. That will I show you presently.
[*He winds a Horn. Drums heard; then a Peal of Ordnance. The Gates being forced, enter* Soldiers.
How say you, madam? are you now persuaded
That Talbot is but shadow of himself?
These are his substance, sinews, arms, and strength,
With which he yoketh your rebellious necks,
Razeth your cities, and subverts your towns,

And in a moment makes them desolate.
Count. Victorious Talbot! pardon my abuse:
I find thou art no less than fame hath bruited,
And more than may be gather'd by thy shape.
Let my presumption not provoke thy wrath;
For I am sorry that with reverence
I did not entertain thee as thou art.
Tal. Be not dismay'd, fair lady; nor misconstrue
The mind of Talbot as you did mistake
The outward composition of his body.
What you have done hath not offended me:
No other satisfaction do I crave
But only—with your patience—that we may
Taste of your wine, and see what cates you have;
For soldiers' stomachs always serve them well.
Count. With all my heart, and think me honoured
To feast so great a warrior in my house.
[*Exeunt.*

SCENE IV.—LONDON. *The Temple Garden.*

Enter the EARLS OF SOMERSET, SUFFOLK, *and* WARWICK; RICHARD PLANTAGENET, VERNON, *and another* Lawyer.

Plan. Great lords and gentlemen, what means this silence?
Dare no man answer in a case of truth?
Suf Within the Temple-hall we were too loud;
The garden here is more convenient. [truth;
Plan. Then say at once if I maintain'd the
Or else was wrangling Somerset in the error?
Suf. Faith, I have been a truant in the law,
And never yet could frame my will to it;
And therefore frame the law unto my will.
Som. Judge you, my lord of Warwick, then, between us. [higher pitch;
War. Between two hawks, which flies the
Between two dogs, which hath the deeper mouth; [temper;
Between two blades, which bears the better
Between two horses, which doth bear him best;
Between two girls, which hath the merriest eye;— [ment;
I have, perhaps, some shallow spirit of judg-
But in these nice sharp quillets of the law,
Good faith, I am no wiser than a daw. [ance:
Plan. Tut, tut, here is a mannerly forbear-
The truth appears so naked on my side
That any purblind eye may find it out.
Som. And on my side it is so well apparell'd,
So clear, so shining, and so evident,
That it will glimmer through a blind man's eye.
Plan. Since you are tongue-tied and so loth to speak,
In dumb significants proclaim your thoughts:
Let him that is a true-born gentleman,
And stands upon the honour of his birth,
If he suppose that I have pleaded truth,
From off this brier pluck a white rose with me.
Som. Let him that is no coward nor no flatterer,

But dare maintain the party of the truth,
Pluck a red rose from off this thorn with me.

War. I love no colours; and, without all
colour
Of base insinuating flattery,
I pluck this white rose with Plantagenet. [set;

Suf. I pluck this red rose with young Somer-
And say withal, I' think he held the right.

Ver. Stay, lords and gentlemen, and pluck
no more
Till you conclude that he upon whose side
The fewest roses are cropp'd from the tree
Shall yield the other in the right opinion.

Som. Good Master Vernon, it is well ob-
jected:
If I have fewest I subscribe in silence.

Plan. And I.

Ver. Then, for the truth and plainness of the
case,
I pluck this pale and maiden blossom here,
Giving my verdict on the white rose side.

Som. Prick not your finger as you pluck it off,
Lest, bleeding, you do paint the white rose red,
And fall on my side so, against your will.

Ver. If I, my lord, for my opinion bleed,
Opinion shall be surgeon to my hurt,
And keep me on the side where still I am.

Som. Well, well, come on; who else?

Law. Unless my study and my books be false,
The argument you held was wrong in you;
                              [*To* SOMERSET.
In sign whereof I pluck a white rose too.

Plan. Now, Somerset, where is your argument?

Som. Here in my scabbard; meditating that
Shall dye your white rose in a bloody red.

Plan. Meantime your cheeks do counterfeit
our roses;
For pale they look with fear, as witnessing
The truth on our side.

Som.   No, Plantagenet,
'Tis not for fear, but anger that thy cheeks
Blush for pure shame to counterfeit our roses,
And yet thy tongue will not confess thy error.

Plan. Hath not thy rose a canker, Somerset?

Som. Hath not thy rose a thorn, Plantagenet?

Plan. Ay, sharp and piercing, to maintain
his truth;
Whiles thy consuming canker eats his falsehood.

Som. Well, I'll find friends to wear my
bleeding roses,
That shall maintain what I have said is true,
Where false Plantagenet dare not be seen.

Plan. Now, by this maiden blossom in my
hand,
I scorn thee and thy faction, peevish boy.

Suf. Turn not thy scorns this way, Plantagenet.

Plan. Proud Poole, I will; and scorn both
him and thee.

Suf. I'll turn my part thereof into thy throat.

Som. Away, away, good William De-la-
Poole!
We grace the yeoman by conversing with him.

War. Now, by God's will, thou wrong'st
him, Somerset;
His grandfather was Lionel Duke of Clarence,
Third son to the third Edward King of England:
Spring crestless yeomen from so deep a root?

Plan. He bears him on the place's privilege,
Or durst not, for his craven heart, say thus.

Som. By him that made me, I'll maintain
my words
On any plot of ground in Christendom.
Was not thy father, Richard Earl of Cambridge,
For treason executed in our late king's days?
And by his treason stand'st not thou attainted,
Corrupted, and exempt from ancient gentry?
His trespass yet lives guilty in thy blood;
And till thou be restor'd thou art a yeoman.

Plan. My father was attach'd, not attainted;
Condemn'd to die for treason, but no traitor;
And that I'll prove on better men than Somer-
set,
Were growing time once ripen'd to my will.
For your partaker Poole, and you yourself,
I'll note you in my book of memory,
To scourge you for this apprehension:
Look to it well, and say you are well warn'd.

Som. Ay, thou shalt find us ready for thee
still;
And know us by these colours for thy foes,—
For these my friends, in spite of thee, shall
wear.

Plan. And, by my soul, this pale and angry
rose,
As cognizance of my blood-drinking hate,
Will I for ever, and my faction, wear,
Until it wither with me to my grave,
Or flourish to the height of my degree.

Suf. Go forward, and be chok'd with thy
ambition!
And so, farewell, until I meet thee next. [*Exit.*

Som. Have with thee, Poole.—Farewell,
ambitious Richard.   [*Exit.*

Plan. How I am brav'd, and must perforce
endure it!   [house,

War. This blot, that they object against your
Shall be wip'd out in the next Parliament,
Call'd for the truce of Winchester and Gloster:
And if thou be not then created York,
I will not live to be accounted Warwick.
Meantime, in signal of my love to thee,
Against proud Somerset and William Poole,
Will I upon thy party wear this rose:
And here I prophesy,—This brawl to-day,
Grown to this faction, in the Temple-garden,
Shall send, between the red rose and the white,
A thousand souls to death and deadly night.

Plan. Good Master Vernon, I am bound to
you,
That you on my behalf would pluck a flower.

Ver. In your behalf still will I wear the same.

Law. And so will I.

Plan. Thanks, gentle sir.
Come, let us four to dinner: I dare say
This quarrel will drink blood another day.
                              [*Exeunt*

SCENE V.—*The same. A Room in the Tower.*

Enter MORTIMER, *brought in in a chair by two* Keepers.

Mor. Kind keepers of my weak decaying age,
Let dying Mortimer here rest himself.—
Even like a man new-haled from the rack,
So fare my limbs with long imprisonment;
And these gray locks, the pursuivants of death,
Nestor-like aged, in an age of care,
Argue the end of Edmund Mortimer. [spent,—
These eyes,—like lamps whose wasting oil is
Wax dim, as drawing to their exigent: [grief;
Weak shoulders, overborne with burdening
And pithless arms, like to a wither'd vine
That droops his sapless branches to the ground:
Yet are these feet,—whose strengthless stay is
    numb,
Unable to support this lump of clay,—
Swift-winged with desire to get a grave,
As witting I no other comfort have.—
But tell me, keeper, will my nephew come?
    I *Keep.* Richard Plantagenet, my lord, will
    come:
We sent unto the Temple, to his chamber;
And answer was return'd that he will come.
    Mor. Enough: my soul shall then be satis-
fied.—
Poor gentleman! his wrong doth equal mine.
Since Henry Monmouth first began to reign,—
Before whose glory I was great in arms,—
This loathsome sequestration have I had;
And even since then hath Richard been ob-
    scur'd,
Depriv'd of honour and inheritance.
But now the arbitrator of despairs,
Just death, kind umpire of men's miseries,
With sweet enlargement doth dismiss me hence:
I would his troubles likewise were expir'd
That so he might recover what was lost.

Enter RICHARD PLANTAGENET.

    I *Keep.* My lord, your loving nephew now
    is come.   [come?
    Mor. Richard Plantagenet, my friend, is he
    Plan. Ay, noble uncle, thus ignobly us'd,
Your nephew, late-despised Richard, comes.
    Mor. Direct mine arms I may embrace his
    neck,
And in his bosom spend my latter gasp:
O, tell me when my lips do touch his cheeks,
That I may kindly give one fainting kiss.—
And now declare, sweet stem from York's great
    stock,
Why didst thou say of late thou wert despis'd?
    Plan. First, lean thine aged back against
    mine arm;
And, in that ease, I'll tell thee my disease.
This day, in argument upon a case,
Some words there grew 'twixt Somerset and me;
Among which terms he us'd his lavish tongue,
And did upbraid me with my father's death:
Which obloquy set bars before my tongue,
Else with the like I had requited him.

Therefore, good uncle, for my father's sake,
In honour of a true Plantagenet,
And for alliance sake, declare the cause
My father, Earl of Cambridge, lost his head.
    Mor. That cause, fair nephew, that impris-
    on'd me,
And hath detain'd me all my flowering youth
Within a loathsome dungeon, there to pine,
Was cursed instrument of his decease.
    Plan. Discover more at large what cause
    that was;
For I am ignorant, and cannot guess.
    Mor. I will, if that my fading breath permit,
And death approach not ere my tale be done.
Henry the Fourth, grandfather to this king,
Depos'd his nephew Richard,—Edward's son,
The first-begotten, and the lawful heir
Of Edward king, the third of that descent:
During whose reign the Percies of the north,
Finding his usurpation most unjust,
Endeavour'd my advancement to the throne:
The reason mov'd these warlike lords to this
Was, for that,—young King Richard thus re-
    mov'd,
Leaving no heir begotten of his body,—
I was the next by birth and parentage;
For by my mother I derived am
From Lionel Duke of Clarence, the third son
To King Edward the Third; whereas he
From John of Gaunt doth bring his pedigree,
Being but fourth of that heroic line.
But mark: as in this haughty great attempt
They laboured to plant the rightful heir,
I lost my liberty, and they their lives.
Long after this, when Henry the Fifth,
Succeeding his father Bolingbroke, did reign,
Thy father, Earl of Cambridge, then deriv'd
From famous Edmund Langley, Duke of York,
Marrying my sister, that thy mother was,
Again, in pity of my hard distress,
Levied an army, weening to redeem
And have install'd me in the diadem:
But, as the rest, so fell that noble earl,
And was beheaded. Thus the Mortimers,
In whom the title rested, were suppress'd.
    Plan. Of which, my lord, your honour is
    the last.
    Mor. True; and thou see'st that I no issue
    have,
And that my fainting words do warrant death:
Thou art my heir; the rest I wish thee gather:
But yet be wary in thy studious care.
    Plan. Thy grave admonishments prevail
    with me:
But yet methinks my father's execution
Was nothing less than bloody tyranny.
    Mor. With silence, nephew, be thou politic;
Strong-fixed is the house of Lancaster,
And, like a mountain, not to be remov'd.
But now thy uncle is removing hence;
As princes do their courts, when they are cloy'd
With long continuance in a settled place.
    Plan. O uncle, would some part of my young
    years

Might but redeem the passage of your age!
Mor. Thou dost then wrong me,—as the
slaughterer doth
Which giveth many wounds when one will kill.
Mourn not, except thou sorrow for my good;
Only, give order for my funeral:
And so, farewell; and fair be all thy hopes,
And prosperous be thy life in peace and war!
                                    [*Dies.*

Plan. And peace, no war, befall thy parting
soul!
In prison hast thou spent a pilgrimage,
And like a hermit overpass'd thy days.—
Well, I will lock his counsel in my breast;
And what I do imagine, let that rest.—
Keepers, convey him hence; and I myself
Will see his burial better than his life.—
    [*Exeunt* Keepers, *bearing out the body of* MOR.
Here dies the dusky torch of Mortimer,
Chok'd with ambition of the meaner sort:—
And for those wrongs, those bitter injuries,
Which Somerset hath offer'd to my house,
I doubt not but with honour to redress;
And therefore haste I to the Parliament,
Either to be restored to my blood,
Or make my ill the advantage of my good.
                                    [*Exit.*

ACT III.

SCENE I.—LONDON. *The Parliament House.*

Flourish. Enter KING HENRY, EXETER, GLO-
STER, WARWICK, SOMERSET, *and* SUFFOLK;
the BISHOP OF WINCHESTER, RICHARD
PLANTAGENET, *and others.* GLOSTER *offers to
put up a bill;* WINCHESTER *snatches it, and
tears it.*

Win. Com'st thou with deep premeditated
lines,
With written pamphlets studiously devis'd,
Humphrey of Gloster? if thou canst accuse,
Or aught intend'st to lay unto my charge,
Do it without invention, suddenly:
As I with sudden and extemporal speech
Purpose to answer what thou canst object.
    Glo. Presumptuous priest! this place com-
mands my patience,
Or thou shouldst find thou hast dishonour'd me.
Think not, although in writing I preferr'd
The manner of thy vile outrageous crimes,
That therefore I have forg'd, or am not able
Verbatim to rehearse the method of my pen:
No, prelate; such is thy audacious wickedness,
Thy lewd, pestiferous, and dissentious pranks,
As very infants prattle of thy pride.
Thou art a most pernicious usurer;
Froward by nature, enemy to peace;
Lascivious, wanton, more than well beseems
A man of thy profession and degree;
And for thy treachery, what's more manifest,—
In that thou laid'st a trap to take my life,
As well at London bridge as at the Tower?
Beside, I fear me, if thy thoughts were sifted,
The king, thy sovereign, is not quite exempt
From envious malice of thy swelling heart.

Win. Gloster, I do defy thee.—Lords,
vouchsafe
To give me hearing what I shall reply.
If I were covetous, ambitious, or perverse,
As he will have me, how am I so poor?
Or how haps it I seek not to advance
Or raise myself, but keep my wonted calling?
And for dissension, who preferreth peace
More than I do,—except I be provok'd?
No, my good lords, it is not that offends;
It is not that that hath incens'd the duke:
It is because no one should sway but he;
No one but he should be about the king;
And that engenders thunder in his breast,
And makes him roar these accusations forth.
But he shall know I am as good—
    Glo.   As good!
Thou bastard of my grandfather!—
    Win. Ay, lordly sir; for what are you, I pray,
But one imperious in another's throne?
    Glo. Am I not protector, saucy priest?
    Win. And am not I a prelate of the church?
    Glo. Yes, as an outlaw in a castle keeps,
And useth it to patronage his theft.
    Win. Unreverent Gloster!
    Glo.   Thou art reverent
Touching thy spiritual function, not thy life.
    Win. Rome shall remedy this.
    War.   Roam thither then.
    Som. My lord, it were your duty to forbear.
    War. Ay, see the bishop be not overborne.
    Som. Methinks my lord should be religious,
And know the office that belongs to such.
    War. Methinks his lordship should be
humbler;
It fitteth not a prelate so to plead.   [near.
    Som. Yes, when his holy state is touch'd so
    War. State holy or unhallow'd, what of that?
Is not his grace protector to the king?
    Plan. Plantagenet, I see, must hold his
tongue,
Lest it be said, *Speak, sirrah, when you should;*
Must your bold verdict enter talk with lords?
Else would I have a fling at Winchester.
                                    [*Aside.*
    K. Hen. Uncles of Gloster and of Winchester,
The special watchmen of our English weal,
I would prevail, if prayers might prevail,
To join your hearts in love and amity.
O, what a scandal is it to our crown
That two such noble peers as ye should jar!
Believe me, lords, my tender years can tell
Civil dissension is a viperous worm
That gnaws the bowels of the commonwealth.
    [*A noise within,* "Down with the tawny
                                    coats."
What tumult's this?
    War.   An uproar, I dare warrant,
Begun through malice of the bishop's men!
    [*A noise again,* "Stones! Stones!"

Enter the Mayor of London, *attended.*

    May. O, my good lords,—and virtuous
Henry,—

Pity the city of London, pity us!
The bishop and the Duke of Gloster's men,
Forbidden late to carry any weapon,
Have fill'd their pockets full of pebble stones,
And, banding themselves in contrary parts,
Do pelt so fast at one another's pate,   [out:
That many have their giddy brains knock'd
Our windows are broke down in every street,
And we, for fear, compell'd to shut our shops.

Enter, skirmishing, the Retainers *of* GLOSTER
and WINCHESTER, *with bloody pates.*

K. Hen. We charge you, on allegiance to
  ourself,   [peace.—
To hold your slaught'ring hands, and keep the
Pray, uncle Gloster, mitigate this strife.
  1 Serv. Nay, if we be
Forbidden stones, we'll fall to it with our teeth.
  2 Serv. Do what ye dare, we are as resolute.
    [*Skirmish again.*
  Glo. You of my household, leave this peevish
  broil,
And set this unaccustom'd fight aside.   [man
  3 Serv. My lord, we know your grace to be a
Just and upright; and for your royal birth
Inferior to none but to his majesty:
And ere that we will suffer such a prince,
So kind a father of the commonweal,
To be disgraced by an inkhorn mate,
We, and our wives and children, all will fight,
And have our bodies slaughter'd by thy foes.
  1 Serv. Ay, and the very parings of our nails
Shall pitch a field when we are dead.
    [*Skirmish again.*
  Glo.   Stay, stay, I say!
And if you love me, as you say you do,
Let me persuade you to forbear awhile.
  K. Hen. O, how this discord doth afflict my
  soul!—
Can you, my Lord of Winchester, behold
My sighs and tears, and will not once relent?
Who should be pitiful if you be not?
Or who should study to prefer a peace,
If holy churchmen take delight in broils?
  War. Yield, my lord protector;—yield,
  Winchester;—
Except you mean, with obstinate repulse,
To slay your sovereign and destroy the realm.
You see what mischief, and what murder too,
Hath been enacted through your enmity;
Then be at peace, except ye thirst for blood.
  Win. He shall submit, or I will never yield.
  Glo. Compassion on the king commands me
  stoop;
Or I would see his heart out, ere the priest
Should ever get that privilege of me.
  War. Behold, my Lord of Winchester, the
  duke
Hath banish'd moody discontented fury,
As by his smoothed brows it doth appear:
Why look you still so stern and tragical?
  Glo. Here, Winchester, I offer thee my hand.
  K. Hen. Fie, uncle Beaufort! I have heard
  you preach

That malice was a great and grievous sin;
And will not you maintain the thing you teach,
But prove a chief offender in the same?
  War. Sweet king!—the bishop hath a kindly
  gird.—
For shame, my Lord of Winchester, relent!
What, shall a child instruct you what to do?
  Win. Well, Duke of Gloster, I will yield to
  thee;
Love for thy love and hand for hand I give.
  Glo. Ay, but, I fear me, with a hollow heart.—
See here, my friends and loving countrymen;
This token serveth for a flag of truce
Betwixt ourselves and all our followers:
So help me God, as I dissemble not!
  Win. So help me God, as I intend it not!
    [*Aside.*
  K. Hen. O loving uncle, kind Duke of
  Gloster,
How joyful am I made by this contract!—
Away, my masters! trouble us no more;
But join in friendship, as your lords have done.
  1 Serv. Content: I'll to the surgeon's.
  2 Serv.   And so will I.
  3 Serv. And I will see what physic the tavern
  affords.   [*Exeunt* Servants, Mayor, &c.
  War. Accept this scroll, most gracious
  sovereign;
Which in the right of Richard Plantagenet
We do exhibit to your majesty.
  Glo. Well urg'd, my Lord of Warwick;—for,
  sweet prince,
And if your grace mark every circumstance,
You have great reason to do Richard right;
Especially for those occasions
At Eltham Place I told your majesty.   [force:
  K. Hen. And those occasions, uncle, were of
Therefore, my loving lords, our pleasure is
That Richard be restored to his blood.
  War. Let Richard be restored to his blood;
So shall his father's wrongs be recompens'd.
  Win. As will the rest, so willeth Winchester.
  K. Hen. If Richard will be true, not that
  alone,
But all the whole inheritance I give
That doth belong unto the house of York,
From whence you spring by lineal descent.
  Plan. Thy humble servant vows obedience
And humble service till the point of death.
  K. Hen. Stoop, then, and set your knee
  against my foot;
And in reguerdon of that duty done
I girt thee with the valiant sword of York:
Rise, Richard, like a true Plantagenet,
And rise created princely Duke of York.   [fall!
  Plan. And so thrive Richard as thy foes may
And as my duty springs, so perish they
That grudge one thought against your majesty!
  All. Welcome, high prince, the mighty Duke
  of York!
  Som. Perish, base prince, ignoble Duke of
  York!   [*Aside.*
  Glo. Now will it best avail your majesty
To cross the seas, and to be crown'd in France:

The presence of a king engenders love
Amongst his subjects and his loyal friends,
As it disanimates his enemies.
   K. Hen. When Gloster says the word, King
      Henry goes;
For friendly counsel cuts off many foes.
   Glo. Your ships already are in readiness.
            [*Flourish. Exeunt all but* EXETER.
   Exe. Ay, we may march in England or in
      France,
Not seeing what is likely to ensue.
This late dissension grown betwixt the peers
Burns under feigned ashes of forg'd love,
And will at last break out into a flame:
As fester'd members rot but by degree,
Till bones and flesh and sinews fall away,
So will this base and envious discord breed.
And now I fear that fatal prophecy
Which in the time of Henry named the Fifth
Was in the mouth of every sucking babe,—
That Henry born at Monmouth should win all,
And Henry born at Windsor should lose all:
Which is so plain that Exeter doth wish
His days may finish ere that hapless time.
                           [*Exit.*

SCENE II.—FRANCE. *Before Rouen.*

Enter LA PUCELLE *disguised, and* Soldiers
*dressed like Countrymen, with sacks upon
their backs.*

   Puc. These are the city-gates, the gates of
      Rouen,
Through which our policy must make a breach:
Take heed, be wary how you place your words;
Talk like the vulgar sort of market-men
That come to gather money for their corn.
If we have entrance,—as I hope we shall,—
And that we find the slothful watch but weak,
I'll by a sign give notice to our friends,
That Charles the Dauphin may encounter
     them.   [the city,
   1 *Sold.* Our sacks shall be a mean to sack
And we be lords and rulers over Rouen;
Therefore we'll knock.   [*Knocks.*
   Guard. [*Within.*] *Qui esi là?*
   Puc. Paysans, pauvres gens de France,—
Poor market-folks that come to sell their corn.
   Guard. [*Opening the gates.*] Enter, go in; the
      market-bell is rung.
   Puc. Now, Rouen, I'll shake thy bulwarks
      to the ground.
        [LA PUCELLE, &c., *enter the Town.*

Enter CHARLES, BASTARD OF ORLEANS,
     ALENÇON, *and* Forces.

   Char. Saint Denis bless this happy stratagem!
And once again we'll sleep secure in Rouen.
   Bast. Here enter'd Pucelle and her practis-
     ants;
Now she is there, how will she specify
Where is the best and safest passage in?
   Alen. By thrusting out a torch from yonder
     tower;   [ing is,—
Which, once discern'd, shows that her mean-

No way to that, for weakness, which she en-
     ter'd.

Enter LA PUCELLE, *on a battlement, holding
out a torch burning.*

   Puc. Behold, this is the happy wedding-torch
That joineth Rouen unto her countrymen,
But burning fatal to the Talbotites.
   Bast. See, noble Charles, the beacon of our
     friend;
The burning torch in yonder turret stands.
   Char. Now shine it like a comet of revenge,
A prophet to the fall of all our foes!
   Alen. Defer no time, delays have dangerous
     ends;
Enter, and cry *The Dauphine!* presently,
And then do execution on the watch.
      [*They enter. Exit* LA PUCELLE *above.*

Alarum. Enter, from the Town, TALBOT *and*
     English Soldiers.

   Tal. France, thou shalt rue this treason with
     thy tears,
If Talbot but survive thy treachery.—
Pucelle, that witch, that damned sorceress,
Hath wrought this hellish mischief unawares,
That hardly we escap'd the pride of France.
                  [*Exeunt into the Town.*

Alarum; excursions. Enter, from the Town,
   BEDFORD, *brought in sick in a chair, with*
   TALBOT, BURGUNDY, *and the* English Forces.
   Then enter on the walls LA PUCELLE,
   CHARLES, BASTARD, ALENÇON, *and others.*

   Puc. Good-morrow, gallants! want ye corn
     for bread?
I think the Duke of Burgundy will fast
Before he'll buy again at such a rate:
'Twas full of darnel;—do you like the taste?
   Bur. Scoff on, vile fiend and shameless cour-
     tezan!
I trust ere long to choke thee with thine own,
And make thee curse the harvest of that corn.
   Char. Your grace may starve, perhaps, be-
     fore that time.   [treason!
   Bed. O let no words, but deeds, revenge this
   Puc. What will you do, good gray-beard?
     break a lance,
And run a tilt at death within a chair? [spite,
   Tal. Foul fiend of France, and hag of all de-
Encompass'd with thy lustful paramours!
Becomes it thee to taunt his valiant age,
And twit with cowardice a man half dead?
Damsel, I'll have a bout with you again,
Or else let Talbot perish with this shame.
   Puc. Are you so hot, sir?—Yet, Pucelle,
     hold thy peace;
If Talbot do but thunder, rain will follow.
     [TALBOT *and the rest consult together.*
God speed the parliament! who shall be the
     speaker?   [field?
   Tal. Dare ye come forth and meet us in the
   Puc. Belike your lordship takes us then for
     fools,

To try if that our own be ours or no.
   Tal. I speak not to that railing Hecaté,
But unto thee, Alençon, and the rest;
Wiil ye, like soldiers, come and fight it out?
   Alen. Signior, no.   [France!
   Tal. Signior, hang!—base muleteers of
Like peasant foot-boys do they keep the walls,
And dare not take up arms like gentlemen.
   Puc. Away, captains! let's get us from the
         walls;
For Talbot means no goodness, by his looks.—
God b' wi' you, my lord! we came but to tell
         you
That we are here.
         [*Exeunt* LA PUC., *&c., from the walls.*
   Tal. And there will we be too, ere it be long,
Or else reproach be Talbot's greatest fame!—
Vow, Burgundy, by honour of thy house,—
Prick'd on by public wrongs sustain'd in
         France,—
Either to get the town again or die;
And I,—as sure as English Henry lives,
And as his father here was conqueror;
As sure as in this late-betrayed town
Great Cœur-de-lion's heart was buried,—
So sure I swear to get the town or die. [vows.
   Bur. My vows are equal partners with thy
   Tal. But ere we go, regard this dying prince,
The valiant Duke of Bedford.—Come, my lord,
We will bestow you in some better place,
Fitter for sickness and for crazy age.
   Bed. Lord Talbot, do not so dishonour me:
Here will I sit before the walls of Rouen,
And will be partner of your weal or woe.
   Bur. Courageous Bedford, let us now per-
         suade you.   [read
   Bed. Not to be' gone from hence; for once I
That stout Pendragon, in his litter, sick
Came to the field, and vanquished his foes:
Methinks I should revive the soldiers' hearts,
Because I ever found them as myself.
   Tal. Undaunted spirit in a dying breast!—
Then be it so:—heavens keep old Bedford safe!
And now no more ado, brave Burgundy,
But gather we our forces out of hand,
And set upon our boasting enemy.
         [*Exeunt into the Town,* BUR., TAL., *and*
              Forces, *leaving* BED. *and others.*

Alarum: excursions. Enter SIR JOHN
         FASTOLFE, *and a* Captain.

   Cap. Whither away, Sir John Fastolfe, in
         such haste?   [flight:
   Fast. Whither away! to save myself by
We are like to have the overthrow again. [bot?
   Cap. What! will you fly, and leave Lord Tal-
   Fast.   Ay,
All the Talbots in the world, to save my life.
                                        [*Exit.*
   Cap. Cowardly knight! ill fortune follow
         thee!   [*Exit into the Town.*
Retreat: excursions. Re-enter, from the town,
   LA PUCELLE, ALENÇON, CHARLES, *&c., and*
      exeunt flying.

   Bed. Now, quiet soul, depart when heaven
         please,
For I have seen our enemies' overthrow.
What is the trust or strength of foolish man?
They that of late were daring with their scoffs
Are glad and fain by flight to save themselves.
         [*Dies, and is carried off in his chair.*

Alarum. Re-enter TALBOT, BURGUNDY, *and*
         others.

   Tal. Lost and recover'd in a day again!
This is a double honour, Burgundy:
Yet heavens have glory for this victory!
   Bur. Warlike and martial Talbot, Burgundy
Enshrines thee in his heart; and there erects
Thy noble deeds, as valour's monuments.
   Tal. Thanks, gentle duke. But where is
         Pucelle now?
I think her old familiar is asleep:
Now where's the Bastard's braves, and Charles
         his gleeks?   [grief
What, all a-mort? Rouen hangs her head for
That such a valiant company are fled.
Now· will we take some order in the town,
Placing therein some expert officers;
And then depart to Paris to the king,
For there young Harry with his nobles lie.
   Bur. What wills Lord Talbot pleaseth Bur
         gundy.
   Tal. But yet, before we go, let's not forget
The noble Duke of Bedford, late deceas'd,
But see his exequies fulfill'd in Rouen:
A braver soldier never couched lance,
A gentler heart did never swa in court;
But kings and mightiest potentates must die,
For that's the end of human misery. [*Exeunt.*

   SCENE III.—*The Plains near Rouen.*

Enter CHARLES, *the* BASTARD, ALENÇON,
         LA PUCELLE, *and* Forces.

   Puc. Dismay not, princes, at this accident,
Nor grieve that Rouen is so recovered:
Care is no cure, but rather corrosive,
For things that are not to be remedied.
Let frantic Talbot triumph for awhile,
And like a peacock sweep along his tail;
We'll pull his plumes and take away his train,
If Dauphin and the rest will be but rul'd.
   Char. We have been guided by thee hitherto,
And of thy cunning had no diffidence:
One sudden foil shall never breed distrust.
   Bast. Search out thy wit for secret policies,
And we will make thee famous through the
         world.
   Alen. We'll set thy statue in some holy place,
And have thee reverenc'd like a blessed saint:
Employ thee, then, sweet virgin, for our good.
   Puc. Then thus it must be; this doth Joan
         devise:
By fair persuasions, mix'd with sugar'd words,
We will entice the Duke of Burgundy
To leave the Talbot and to follow us.
   Char. Ay, marry, sweeting, if we could do
         that,

France were no place for Henry's warriors;
Nor should that nation boast it so with us,
But be extirped from our provinces.

   Alen. For ever should they be expuls'd from
     France,
And not have title of an earldom here.

   Puc. Your honours shall perceive how I will
     work
To bring this matter to the wished end.

                 [Drums heard.
Hark! by the sound of drum you may perceive
Their powers are marching unto Paris-ward.

*An English March. Enter, and pass over at a
   distance,* TALBOT *and his* Forces.

There goes the Talbot, with his colours spread,
And all the troops of English after him.

   A French March. Enter the DUKE OF
    BURGUNDY *and his* Forces.

Now in the rearward comes the duke and his:
Fortune in favour makes him lag behind.
Summon a parley; we will talk with him.
                [A parley sounded.

   Char. A parley with the Duke of Burgundy!
   Bur. Who craves a parley with the Bur-
     gundy?
   Puc. The princely Charles of France, thy
     countryman.
   Bur. What say'st thou, Charles? for I am
     marching hence.
   Char. Speak, Pucelle, and enchant him with
     thy words.   *[France!*
   Puc. Brave Burgundy, undoubted hope of
Stay, let thy humble handmaid speak to thee.
   Bur. Speak on; but be not over-tedious.
   Puc. Look on thy country, look on fertile
     France,
And see the cities and the towns defac'd
By wasting ruin of the cruel foe!
As looks the mother on her lovely babe
When death doth close his tender dying eyes,
See, see the pining malady of France;
Behold the wounds, the most unnatural wounds,
Which thou thyself hast given her woeful breast!
O, turn thy edged sword another way;
Strike those that hurt, and hurt not those that
     help!   *[bosom*
One drop of blood drawn from thy country's
Should grieve thee more than streams of for-
     eign gore:
Return thee, therefore, with a flood of tears,
And wash away thy country's stained spots.
   Bur. Either she hath bewitch'd me with her
     words,
Or nature makes me suddenly relent.
   Puc. Besides, all French and France ex-
     claims on thee,
Doubting thy birth and lawful progeny.
Who join'st thou with but with a lordly nation
That will not trust thee but for profit's sake?
When Talbot hath set footing once in France,
And fashion'd thee that instrument of ill,
Who then but English Henry will be lord.

And thou be thrust out like a fugitive?
Call we to mind,—and mark but this for
     proof,—
Was not the Duke of Orleans thy foe?
And was he not in England prisoner?
But when they heard he was thine enemy,
They set him free, without his ransom paid,
In spite of Burgundy and all his friends.
See, then, thou fight'st against thy countrymen,
And join'st with them will be thy slaughter-
     men.
Come, come, return; return, thou wand'ring
     lord;
Charles and the rest will take thee in their arms.
   Bur. I am vanquished; these haughty words
     of hers
Have batter'd me like roaring cannon-shot,
And made me almost yield upon my knees.—
Forgive me, country, and sweet countrymen!
And, lords, accept this hearty kind embrace:
My forces and my power of men are yours:
So, farewell, Talbot; I'll no longer trust thee.
   Puc. Done like a Frenchman,—turn, and
     turn again!
   Char. Welcome, brave duke! thy friendship
     makes us fresh.   .   *[breasts.*
   Bast. And doth beget new courage in our
   Alen. Pucelle hath bravely play'd her part
     in this,
And doth deserve a coronet of gold.
   Char. Now let us on, my lords, and join our
     powers;
And seek how we may prejudice the foe.
                    [Exeunt.

SCENE IV.—PARIS. *A Room in the Palace.*

Enter KING HENRY, GLOSTER, *and other* Lords,
   VERNON, BASSET, *&c. To them* TALBOT *and
   some of his* Officers.

   Tal. My gracious prince,—and honourable
     peers,—
Hearing of your arrival in this realm,
I have awhile given truce unto my wars,
To do my duty to my sovereign:
In sign whereof, this arm,—that hath reclaim'd
To your obedience fifty fortresses,
Twelve cities, and seven walled towns of
     strength,
Beside five hundred prisoners of esteem,—
Lets fall his sword before your highness' feet,
And with submissive loyalty of heart
Ascribes the glory of his conquest got
First to my God and next unto your grace.
   K. Hen. Is this the Lord Talbot, uncle
     Gloster,
That hath so long been resident in France?
   Glo. Yes, if it please your majesty, my liege.
   K. Hen. Welcome, brave captain and vic-
     torious lord!
When I was young,—as yet I am not old,—
I do remember how my father said
A stouter champion never handled sword.
Long since we were resolved of your truth,
Your faithful service, and your toil in war;

Yet never have you tasted our reward,
Or been reguerdon'd with so much as thanks,
Because till now we never saw your face:
Therefore, stand up; and for these good deserts
We here create you Earl of Shrewsbury;
And in our coronation take your place.

[*Exeunt* K. HEN., GLO., TAL., *and* Nobles.

Ver. Now, sir, to you, that were so hot at
    sea,
Disgracing of these colours that I wear
In honour of my noble Lord of York,—
Dar'st thou maintain the former words thou
    spak'st?

Bas. Yes, sir; as well as you dare patronage
The envious barking of your saucy tongue
Against my lord the Duke of Somerset.

Ver. Sirrah, thy lord I honour as he is.

Bas. Why, what is he? as good a man as
    York.

Ver. Hark ye; not so: in witness, take ye
    that.   [*Strikes him.*

Bas. Villain, thou know'st the law of arms
    is such
That whoso draws a sword 'tis present death,
Or else this blow should broach thy dearest
    blood.
But I'll unto his majesty, and crave
I may have liberty to venge this wrong;
When thou shalt see I'll meet thee to thy cost.

Ver. Well, miscreant, I'll be there as soon
    as you;
And, after, meet you sooner than you would.
                                   [*Exeunt.*

ACT IV.

SCENE I.—PARIS. *A Room of State.*

Enter KING HENRY, GLOSTER, EXETER, YORK,
SUFFOLK, SOMERSET, WINCHESTER, WAR-
WICK, TALBOT, *the* Governor of Paris, *and
others.*

Glo. Lord bishop, set the crown upon his
    head.

Win. God save King Henry, of that name
    the sixth!

Glo. Now, governor of Paris, take your
    oath,—   [Governor *kneels.*
That you elect no other king but him;
Esteem none friends but such as are his friends,
And none your foes but such as shall pretend
Malicious practices against his state:
This shall ye do, so help you righteous God!
                    [*Exeunt* Gov. *and his* Train.

Enter SIR JOHN FASTOLFE.

Fast. My gracious sovereign, as I rode from
    Calais,
To haste unto your coronation,
A letter was deliver'd to my hands,
Writ to your grace from the Duke of Burgundy.

Tal. Shame to the Duke of Burgundy and
    thee!   [next,
I vow'd, base knight, when I did meet thee
To tear the garter from thy craven's leg,—
                              [*Plucking it off.*

Which I have done,—because unworthily
Thou wast installed in that high degree.—
Pardon me, princely Henry, and the rest:
This dastard, at the battle of Patay,
When but in all I was six thousand strong,
And that the French were almost ten to one,—
Before we met, or that a stroke was given,
Like to a trusty squire, did run away:
In which assault we lost twelve hundred men
Myself, and divers gentlemen beside,
Were there surpris'd and taken prisoners.
Then judge, great lords, if I have done amiss;
Or whether that such cowards ought to wear
This ornament of knighthood, yea or no.

Glo. To say the truth, this fact was infamous,
And ill beseeming any common man,
Much more a knight, a captain, and a leader.

Tal. When first this order was ordain'd, my
    lords,
Knights of the garter were of noble birth,
Valiant and virtuous, full of haughty courage,
Such as were grown to credit by the wars;
Not fearing death nor shrinking for distress,
But always resolute in most extremes.
He, then, that is not furnish'd in this sort
Doth but usurp the sacred name of knight,
Profaning this most honourable order,
And should,—if I were worthy to be judge,—
Be quite degraded, like a hedge-born swain
That doth presume to boast of gentle blood.

K. Hen. Stain to thy countrymen, thou
    hear'st thy doom!
Be packing, therefore, thou that wast a knight:
Henceforth we banish thee, on pain of death.
                              [*Exit* FASTOLFE.
And now, my lord protector, view the letter
Sent from our uncle Duke of Burgundy.

Glo. What means his grace, that he hath
    chang'd his style?
                    [*Viewing the superscription.*
No more but, plain and bluntly, *To the King!*
Hath he forgot he is his sovereign?
Or doth this churlish superscription
Pretend some alteration in good-will?
What's here?—[*Reads.*]—*I have, upon especial
    cause,—
Mov'd with compassion of my country's wreck,
Together with the pitiful complaints
Of such as your oppression feeds upon,—
Forsaken your pernicious faction,
And join'd with Charles, the rightful King of
    France.*
O monstrous treachery! Can this be so,—
That in alliance, amity, and oaths,
There should be found such false dissembling
    guile?   [revolt?

K. Hen. What! doth my uncle Burgundy

Glo. He doth, my lord; and is become your
    foe.   [contain?

K. Hen. Is that the worst this letter doth

Glo. It is the worst, and all, my lord, he
    writes.

K. Hen. Why, then, Lord Talbot there shall
    talk with him,

And give him chastisement for this abuse:—
How say you, my lord, are you not content?

Tal. Content, my liege! yes; but that I am
  prevented,   [ploy'd.
I should have begg'd I might have been em-

K. Hen. Then gather strength, and march
  unto him straight:
Let him perceive how ill we brook his treason,
And what offence it is to flout his friends.

Tal. I go, my lord; in heart desiring still
You may behold confusion of your foes. [*Exit.*

Enter VERNON *and* BASSET.

Ver. Grant me the combat, gracious sovereign!   [too!

Bas. And me, my lord, grant me the combat

York. This is my servant: hear him, noble
  prince!   [him!

Som. And this is mine: sweet Henry, favour

K. Hen. Be patient, lords; and give them
  leave to speak.—
Say, gentlemen, what makes you thus exclaim?
And wherefore crave you combat? or with
  whom?

Ver. With him, my lord; for he hath done me
  wrong.

Bas. And I with him; for he hath done me
  wrong.

K. Hen. What is that wrong whereof you
  both complain?
First let me know, and then I'll answer you.

Bas. Crossing the sea from England into
  France,
This fellow here, with envious carping tongue,
Upbraided me about the rose I wear;
Saying the sanguine colour of the leaves
Did represent my master's blushing cheeks
When stubbornly he did repugn the truth
About a certain question in the law
Argu'd betwixt the Duke of York and him;
With other vile and ignominious terms:
In confutation of which rude reproach,
And in defence of my lord's worthiness,
I crave the benefit of law of arms.

Ver. And that is my petition, noble lord:
For though he seem with forged quaint conceit
To set a gloss upon his bold intent,
Yet know, my lord, I was provok'd by him;
And he first took exceptions at this badge,
Pronouncing that the paleness of this flower
Bewray'd the faintness of my master's heart.

York. Will not this malice, Somerset, be left?

Som. Your private grudge, my Lord of York,
  will out,
Though ne'er so cunningly you smother it.

K. Hen. Good Lord, what madness rules in
  brainsick men,
When for so slight and frivolous a cause
Such factious emulations shall arise!—
Good cousins both, of York and Somerset,
Quiet yourselves, I pray, and be at peace.

York. Let this dissension first be tried by
  fight,
And then your highness shall command a peace.

Som. The quarrel toucheth none but us
  alone;
Betwixt ourselves let us decide it them. [set.

York. There is my pledge; accept it, Somer-

Ver. Nay, let it rest where it began at first.

Bas. Confirm it so, mine honourable lord.

Glo. Confirm it so! Confounded be your
  strife!
And perish ye, with your audacious prate!
Presumptuous vassals, are you not asham'd
With this immodest clamorous outráge
To trouble and disturb the king and us?—
And you, my lords,—methinks you do not well
To bear with their perverse objections;
Much less to take occasion from their mouths
To raise a mutiny betwixt yourselves:
Let me persuade you take a better course.

Exe. It grieves his highness:—good my lords,
  be friends.   [combatants:

K. Hen. Come hither, you that would be
Henceforth I charge you, as you love our favour,
Quite to forget this quarrel and the cause.—
And you, my lords, remember where we are;
In France, amongst a fickle wavering nation:
If they perceive dissension in our looks,
And that within ourselves we disagree,
How will their grudging stomachs be provok'd
To wilful disobedience, and rebel!
Beside, what infamy will there arise,
When foreign princes shall be certified
That for a toy, a thing of no regard,
King Henry's peers and chief nobility [France!
Destroy'd themselves and lost the realm of
O, think upon the conquest of my father;
My tender years; and let us not forego
That for a trifle that was bought with blood!
Let me be umpire in this doubtful strife.
I see no reason, if I wear this rose,
        [*Putting on a red rose.*
That any one should therefore be suspicious
I more incline to Somerset than York:
Both are my kinsmen, and I love them both:
As well they may upbraid me with my crown,
Because, forsooth, the King of Scots is crown'd.
But your discretions better can persuade
Than I am able to instruct or teach:
And therefore, as we hither came in peace,
So let us still continue peace and love.—
Cousin of York, we institute your grace
To be our regent in these parts of France:—
And, good my Lord of Somerset, unite
Your troops of horsemen with his bands of
  foot;
And like true subjects, sons of your progenitors,
Go cheerfully together, and digest
Your angry choler on your enemies.
Ourself, my lord protector, and the rest,
After some respite, will return to Calais;
From thence to England; where I hope ere long
To be presented, by your victories,
With Charles, Alençon, and that traitorous
  rout.
    [*Flourish. Exeunt* K. HEN., GLO.,
      SOM., WIN., SUF., *and* BAS.

War. My Lord of York, I promise you, the king
Prettily, methought, did play the orator.
  York. And so he did; but yet I like it not,
In that he wears the badge of Somerset.
  War. Tush, that was but his fancy, blame him not;   [harm.
I dare presume, sweet prince, he thought no
  York. An if I wist he did,—but let it rest;
Other affairs must now be managed.
                [Exeunt YORK, WAR., *and* VER.
  Exe. Well didst thou, Richard, to suppress thy voice:
For had the passions of thy heart burst out,
I fear we should have seen decipher'd there
More rancorous spite, more furious raging broils,
Than yet can be imagin'd or suppos'd.
But howsoe'er, no simple man that sees
This jarring discord of nobility,
This shouldering of each other in the court,
This factious bandying of their favourites,
But that it doth presage some ill event.
'Tis much when sceptres are in children's hands;
But more when envy breeds unkind division;
There comes the ruin, there begins confusion.
                        [Exit.

SCENE II.—FRANCE. *Before Bourdeaux.*

Enter TALBOT, *with his* Forces.

  Tal. Go to the gates of Bourdeaux, trumpeter!
Summon their general unto the wall.

Trumpet sounds a parley. Enter, on the walls, the
  General of the French Forces, *and others.*

English John Talbot, captains, calls you forth,
Servant in arms to Harry King of England;
And thus he would,—Open your city gates;
Be humble to us; call my sovereign yours,
And do him homage as obedient subjects;
And I'll withdraw me and my bloody power:
But if you frown upon this proffer'd peace
You tempt the fury of my three attendants,
Lean famine, quartering steel, and climbing fire;
Who, in a moment, even with the earth
Shall lay your stately and air-braving towers,
If you forsake the offer of their love.
  Gen. Thou ominous and fearful owl of death,
Our nation's terror and their bloody scourge!
The period of thy tyranny approacheth.
On us thou canst not enter but by death;
For, I protest, we are well fortified,
And strong enough to issue out and fight:
If thou retire, the Dauphin, well appointed,
Stands with the snares of war to tangle thee:
On either hand thee there are squadrons pitch'd,
To wall thee from the liberty of flight;
And no way canst thou turn thee for redress
But death doth front thee with apparent spoil,
And pale destruction meets thee in the face.
Ten thousand French have ta'en the sacrament,

To rive their dangerous artillery
Upon no Christian soul but English Talbot.
Lo, there thou stand'st, a breathing valiant man,
Of an invincible unconquer'd spirit!
This is the latest glory of thy praise
That I, thy enemy, due thee withal;
For ere the glass that now begins to run
Finish the process of this sandy hour,
These eyes, that see thee now well coloured,
Shall see thee wither'd, bloody, pale, and dead.
                   [Drum afar off.
Hark! hark! the Dauphin's drum, a warning bell,
Sings heavy music to thy timorous soul;
And mine shall ring thy dire departure out.
       [Exeunt General, *&c. from the Walls.*
  Tal. He fables not; I hear the enemy:—
Out, some light horsemen, and peruse their wings.—
O, negligent and heedless discipline!
How are we park'd and bounded in a pale,—
A little herd of England's timorous deer,
Maz'd with a yelping kennel of French curs!
If we be English deer, be, then, in blood;
Not rascal-like to fall down with a pinch,
But rather, moody-mad and desperate stags,
Turn on the bloody hounds with heads of steel,
And make the cowards stand aloof at bay:
Sell every man his life as dear as mine,
And they shall find dear deer of us, my friends.—   [right,
God and Saint George, Talbot and England's
Prosper our colours in this dangerous fight!
                        [Exeunt.

SCENE III.—*Plains in Gascony.*

Enter YORK, *with* Forces; *to him a* Messenger.

  York. Are not the speedy scouts return'd again,
That dogg'd the mighty army of the Dauphin?
  Mess. They are return'd, my lord; and give it out
That he is march'd to Bourdeaux with his power,
To fight with Talbot: as he march'd along,
By your espials were discovered
Two mightier troops than that the Dauphin led,
Which join'd with him, and made their march for Bourdeaux.
  York. A plague upon that villain Somerset,
That thus delays my promised supply
Of horsemen, that were levied for this siege!
Renowned Talbot doth expect my aid;
And I am louted by a traitor villain,
And cannot help the noble chevalier:
God comfort him in this necessity!
If he miscarry, farewell wars in France.

Enter SIR WILLIAM LUCY.

  Lucy. Thou princely leader of our English strength,
Never so needful on the earth of France,
Spur to the rescue of the noble Talbot,
Who now is girdled with a waist of iron,

And hemm'd about with grim destruction:
To Bourdeaux, warlike duke! to Bourdeaux,
	York!	[honour.
Else, farewell Talbot, France, and England's
	York. O God, that Somerset,—who in proud
		heart
Doth stop my cornets,—were in Talbot's place!
So should we save a valiant gentleman
By forfeiting a traitor and a coward.
Mad ire and wrathful fury makes me weep,
That thus we die, while remiss traitors sleep.
	Lucy. O, send some succour to the distress'd
		lord!
	York. He dies, we lose; I break my warlike
		word;
We mourn, France smiles; we lose, they daily
	get;
All 'long of this vile traitor Somerset.
	Lucy. Then God take mercy on brave Tal-
		bot's soul;	[since
And on his son, young John, who two hours
I met in travel toward his warlike father!
This seven years did not Talbot see his son;
And now they meet where both their lives are
	done.
	York. Alas, what joy shall noble Talbot have
To bid his young son welcome to his grave?
Away! vexation almost stops my breath,
That sunder'd friends greet in the hour of
	death.—
Lucy, farewell: no more my fortune can,
But curse the cause I cannot aid the man.—
Maine, Blois, Poictiers, and Tours are won
	away,
'Long all of Somerset and his delay.
	[*Exit*, with Forces.
	Lucy. Thus, while the vulture of sedition
Feeds in the bosom of such great commanders,
Sleeping neglection doth betray to loss
The conquest of our scarce-cold conqueror,
That ever-living man of memory,
Henry the Fifth:—whiles they each other cross,
Lives, honours, lands, and all, hurry to loss.
	[*Exit*.

SCENE IV.—*Other Plains of Gascony.*

Enter SOMERSET, *with his* Forces; *an* Officer
of TALBOT'S *with him.*

	Som. It is too late; I cannot send them now:
This expedition was by York and Talbot
Too rashly plotted; all our general force
Might with a sally of the very town
Be buckled with: the over-daring Talbot
Hath sullied all his gloss of former honour
By this unheedful, desperate, wild adventure:
York set him on to fight and die in shame.
That, Talbot dead, great York might bear the
	name.
	Off. Here is Sir William Lucy, who with me
Set from our o'er-match'd forces forth for aid.

Enter SIR WILLIAM LUCY.

	Som. How now, Sir William! whither were
		you sent?

	Lucy. Whither, my lord! from bought and
		sold Lord Talbot;
Who, ring'd about with bold adversity,
Cries out for noble York and Somerset,
To beat assailing death from his weak legions:
And whiles the honourable captain there
Drops bloody sweat from his war-wearied limbs,
And, in advantage lingering, looks for rescue,
You, his false hopes, the trust of England's
	honour,
Keep off aloof with worthless emulation.
Let not your private discord keep away
The levied succours that should lend him aid,
While he, renowned noble gentleman,
Yields up his life unto a world of odds:
Orleans the Bastard, Charles, Burgundy,
Alençon, Reignier, compass him about,
And Talbot perisheth by your default.
	Som. York set him on, York should have
		sent him aid.	[claims:
	Lucy. And York as fast upon your grace ex-
Swearing that you withhold his levied horse,
Collected for this expedition.	[the horse:
	Som. York lies; he might have sent and had
I owe him little duty and less love;
And take foul scorn to fawn on him by sending.
	Lucy. The fraud of England, not the force
		of France,
Hath now entrapp'd the noble-minded Talbot:
Never to England shall he bear his life;
But dies betray'd to fortune by your strife.
	Som. Come, go; I will despatch the horse-
		men straight:
Within six hours they will be at his aid.
	Lucy. Too late comes rescue; he is ta'en or
		slain:
For fly he could not, if he would have fled;
And fly would Talbot never, though he might.
	Som. If he be dead, brave Talbot, then,
		adieu!
	Lucy. His fame lives in the world, his shame
		in you.	[*Exeunt.*

SCENE V.—*The English Camp near Bourdeaux.*

Enter TALBOT *and* JOHN *his Son.*

	Tal. O young John Talbot! I did send for
		thee
To tutor thee in stratagems of war,
That Talbot's name might be in thee reviv'd
When sapless age and weak unable limbs
Should bring thy father to his drooping chair.
But,—O malignant and ill-boding stars!—
Now thou art come unto a feast of death,
A terrible and unavoided danger:	[horse;
Therefore, dear boy, mount on my swiftest
And I'll direct thee how thou shalt escape
By sudden flight: come, dally not, begone.
	John. Is my name Talbot? and am I your
		son?
And shall I fly? O, if you love my mother,
Dishonour not her honourable name,
To make a bastard and a slave of me!
The world will say, he is not Talbot's blood
That basely fled when noble Talbot stood.

Tal. Fly to revenge my death, if I be slain.
John. He that flies so will ne'er return again.
Tal. If we both stay we both are sure to die.
John. Then let me stay; and, father, do you
       fly:
Your loss is great, so your regard should be;
My worth unknown, no loss is known in me.
Upon my death the French can little boast;
In yours they will, in you all hopes are lost.
Flight cannot stain the honour you have won;
But mine it will, that no exploit have done;
You fled for vantage, every one will swear;
But if I bow, they'll say it was for fear,
There is no hope that ever I will stay,
If the first hour I shrink and run away.
Here, on my knee, I beg mortality,
Rather than life preserv'd with infamy.
     Tal. Shall all thy mother's hopes lie in one
       tomb?   [womb.
John. Ay, rather than I'll shame my mother's
Tal. Upon my blessing I command thee go.
John. To fight I will, but not to fly the foe.
Tal. Part of thy father may be sav'd in thee.
John. No part of him but will be shame in
       me.   [lose it.
Tal. Thou never hadst renown, nor canst not
John. Yes, your renowned name: shall flight
       abuse it?
     Tal. Thy father's charge shall clear thee
       from that stain.
John. You cannot witness for me, being slain.
If death be so apparent, then both fly.
     Tal. And leave my followers here to fight
       and die?
My age was never tainted with such shame.
     John.. And shall my youth be guilty of such
       blame?
No more can I be sever'd from your side
Than can yourself yourself in twain divide:
Stay, go, do what you will, the like do I;
For live I will not if my father die.   [son,
     Tal. Then here I take my leave of thee, fair
Born to eclipse thy life this afternoon.
Come, side by side together live and die;
And soul with soul from France to heaven fly.
                               [*Exeunt.*

SCENE VI.—*A Field of Battle.*

Alarum: excursions wherein TALBOT'S *Son is
     hemmed about, and* TALBOT *rescues him.*

     Tal. Saint George and victory! fight, sol-
       diers, fight:
The regent hath with Talbot broke his word,
And left us to the rage of France his sword.
Where is John Talbot?—pause, and take thy
       breath;
I gave thee life and rescu'd thee from death.
     John. O, twice my father, twice am I thy son!
The life thou gav'st me first was lost and done,
Till with thy warlike sword, despite of fate,
To my determin'd time thou gav'st new date.
     Tal. When from the Dauphin's crest thy
       sword struck fire,

It warm'd thy father's heart with proud desire
Of bold-fac'd victory. Then leaden age,
Quicken'd with youthful spleen and warlike
       rage,
Beat down Alençon, Orleans, Burgundy,
And from the pride of Gallia rescu'd thee.
The ireful bastard Orleans,—that drew blood
From thee, my boy, and had the maidenhood
Of thy first fight,—I soon encountered,
And, interchanging blows, I quickly shed
Some of his bastard blood; and, in disgrace,
Bespoke him thus,—*Contaminated, base,*
And misbegotten blood I spill of thine,
Mean and right poor, for that pure blood of mine
Which thou didst force from Talbot, my brave
       boy:—
Here, purposing the Bastard to destroy,
Came in strong rescue. Speak, thy father's
       care,—
Art thou not weary, John? how dost thou fare?
Wilt thou yet leave the battle, boy, and fly,
Now thou art seal'd the son of chivalry?
Fly, to revenge my death when I am dead:
The help of one stands me in little stead.
O, too much folly is it, well I wot,
To hazard all our lives in one small boat!
If I to-day die not with Frenchmen's rage,
To-morrow I shall die with mickle age:
By me they nothing gain an if I stay,—
'Tis but the short'ning of my life one day:
In thee thy mother dies, our household's name,
My death's revenge, thy youth, and England's
       fame:
All these, and more, we hazard by thy stay;
All these are sav'd if thou wilt fly away.
     John. The sword of Orleans hath not made
       me smart;   [heart:
These words of yours draw life-blood from my
On that advantage, bought with such a
       shame,—
To save a paltry life, and slay bright fame,—
Before young Talbot from old Talbot fly,
The coward horse that bears me fall and die!
And like me to the peasant boys of France;
To be shame's scorn, and subject of mischance!
Surely, by all the glory you have won,
An if I fly, I am not Talbot's son:
Then talk no more of flight, it is no boot;
If son to Talbot, die at Talbot's foot.   [Crete,
     Tal. Then follow thou thy desperate sire of
Thou Icarus; thy life to me is sweet:
If thou wilt fight, fight by thy father's side;
And, commendable prov'd, let's die in pride.
                               [*Exeunt.*

SCENE VII.—*Another part of the same.*

Alarum: excursions. Enter TALBOT *wounded,
     supported by a* Servant.

     Tal. Where is my other life?—mine own is
       gone;—   [John?—
O, where's young Talbot? where is valiant
Triumphant death, smear'd with captivity,
Young Talbot's valour makes me smile at
       thee:—

When he perceiv'd me shrink and on my knee,
His bloody sword he brandish'd over me,
And like a hungry lion did commence
Rough deeds of rage and stern impatience;
But when my angry guardant stood alone,
Tendering my ruin, and assail'd of none,
Dizzy-ey'd fury and great rage of heart
Suddenly made him from my side to start
Into the clustering battle of the French;
And in that sea of blood my boy did drench
His overmounting spirit; and there died
My Icarus, my blossom, in his pride.

Serv. O my dear lord! lo where your son is borne!

Enter Soldiers, *bearing the body of*
JOHN TALBOT.

Tal. Thou antic death, which laugh'st us here to scorn,
Anon, from thy insulting tyranny,
Coupled in bonds of perpetuity,
Two Talbots, winged through the lither sky,
In thy despite, shall 'scape mortality.—
O thou whose wounds become hard-favour'd death,
Speak to thy father ere thou yield thy breath!
Brave death by speaking, whether he will or no;
Imagine him a Frenchman and thy foe.—
Poor boy! he smiles, methinks, as who should say, [to-day.—
Had death been French, then death had died
Come, come, and lay him in his father's arms:
My spirit can no longer bear these harms.
Soldiers, adieu! I have what I would have,
Now my old arms are young Talbot's grave.
[*Dies.*

Alarums. Exeunt Soldiers *and* Servant, *leaving the two bodies. Enter* CHARLES, ALENÇON, BURGUNDY, BASTARD, LA PUCELLE, *and* Forces.

Char. Had York and Somerset brought rescue in,
We should have found a bloody day of this.

Bast. How the young whelp of Talbot's, raging-wood,
Did flesh his puny sword in Frenchmen's blood!

Puc. Once I encounter'd him, and thus I said,
Thou maiden youth, be vanquish'd by a maid:
But, with a proud majestical high scorn,
He answer'd thus, *Young Talbot was not born
To be the pillage of a giglot wench:*
So, rushing in the bowels of the French,
He left me proudly, as unworthy fight.

Bur. Doubtless he would have made a noble knight:—
See where he lies inhersed in the arms
Of the most bloody nurser of his harms!

Bast. Hew them to pieces, hack their bones asunder, [der.
Whose life was England's glory, Gallia's won-

Char. O, no; forbear! for that which we have fled

During the life, let us not wrong it dead.

Enter SIR WILLIAM LUCY, *attended; a*
French Herald *preceding.*

Lucy. Herald,
Conduct me to the Dauphin's tent, to know
Who hath obtain'd the glory of the day.

Char. On what submissive message art thou sent?

Lucy. Submission, Dauphin! 'tis a mere French word;
We English warriors wot not what it means
I come to know what prisoners thou hast ta'en,
And to survey the bodies of the dead.

Char. For prisoners ask'st thou? hell our prison is.
But tell me whom thou seek'st. [field,

Lucy. But where's the great Alcides of the
Valiant Lord Talbot, Earl of Shrewsbury,—
Created, for his rare success in arms,
Great Earl of Washford, Waterford, and Valence;
Lord Talbot of Goodrig and Urchinfield,
Lord Strange of Blackmere, Lord Verdun of Alton,
Lord Cromwell of Wingfield, Lord Furnival of Sheffield,
The thrice victorious Lord of Falconbridge;
Knight of the noble order of Saint George,
Worthy Saint Michael, and the Golden Fleece;
Great Marshal to Henry the Sixth
Of all his wars within the realm of France?

Puc. Here is a silly-stately style indeed!
The Turk, that two-and-fifty kingdoms hath,
Writes not so tedious a style as this.—
Him that thou magnifiest with all these titles,
Stinking and fly-blown, lies here at our feet.

Lucy. Is Talbot slain,—the Frenchmen's only scourge,
Your kingdom's terror and black Nemesis?
O were mine eye-balls into bullets turn'd,
That I, in rage, might shoot them at your faces!
O that I could but call these dead to life!
It were enough to fright the realm of France:
Were but his picture left among you here,
It would amaze the proudest of you all.
Give me their bodies, that I may bear them hence,
And give them burial as beseems their worth.

Puc. I think this upstart is old Talbot's ghost,
He speaks with such a proud commanding spirit. [here,
For God's sake, let him have 'em; to keep them
They would but stink, and putrefy the air.

Char. Go, take their bodies hence.

Lucy. I'll bear them hence:
But from their ashes shall be rear'd
A phœnix that shall make all France afeard.

Char. So we be rid of them, do with 'em what thou wilt.—
And now to Paris in this conquering vein:
All will be ours, now bloody Talbot's slain.
[*Exeunt.*

ACT V.

SCENE I.—LONDON. *A Room in the Palace.*
Enter KING HENRY, GLOSTER, *and* EXETER.

K. Hen. Have you perus'd the letters from
    the pope,
The emperor, and the Earl of Armagnac?
  Glo. I have, my lord: and their intent is
    this,—
They humbly sue unto your excellence
To have a godly peace concluded
Between the realms of England and of France.
  K. Hen. How doth your grace affect their
    motion?   [means
  Glo. Well, my good lord; and as the only
To stop effusion of our Christian blood,
And stablish quietness on every side. [thought
  K. Hen. Ay, marry, uncle; for I always
It was both impious and unnatural
That such immanity and bloody strife
Should reign among professors of one faith.
  Glo. Beside, my lord, the sooner to effect
And surer bind this knot of amity,
The Earl of Armagnac,—near knit to Charles,
A man of great authority in France,—
Proffers his only daughter to your grace
In marriage, with a large and sumptuous dowry.
  K. Hen. Marriage, uncle! alas, my years are
    young;
And fitter is my study and my books
Than wanton dalliance with a paramour.
Yet, call the ambassadors; and as you please,
So let them have their answers every one:
I shall be well content with any choice
Tends to God's glory and my country's weal.

Enter a Legate *and two* Ambassadors, *with*
WINCHESTER, *now* CARDINAL BEAUFORT, *in
a Cardinal's habit.*

  Exe. What! is my Lord of Winchester in-
    stall'd,
And call'd unto a cardinal's degree?
Then I perceive that will be verified
Henry the Fifth did sometime prophesy,—
If once he come to be a cardinal,
He'll make his cap co-equal with the crown.
  K. Hen. My lords ambassadors, your sev-
    eral suits
Have been consider'd and debated on.
Your purpose is both good and reasonable;
And therefore are we certainly resolv'd
To draw conditions of a friendly peace;
Which by my Lord of Winchester we mean
Shall be transported presently to France.
  Glo. And for the proffer of my lord your
    master,
I have inform'd his highness so at large,
As, liking of the lady's virtuous gifts,
Her beauty, and the value of her dower,
He doth intend she shall be England's queen.
  K. Hen. In argument and proof of which
    contract,

Bear her this jewel [*to the* Amb.], pledge of my
    affection.—
And so, my lord protector, see them guarded
And safely brought to Dover; where, inshipp'd,
Commit them to the fortune of the sea.
    [*Exeunt* K. HEN., GLO., EXE., *and*
    Ambassadors.
  Win. Stay, my lord legate: you shall first
    receive
The sum of money which I promised
Should be delivered to his holiness
For clothing me in these grave ornaments.
  Leg. I will attend upon your lordship's
    leisure.   [*Exit.*
  Win. Now Winchester will not submit, I
    trow,
Or be inferior to the proudest peer.
Humphrey of Gloster, thou shalt well perceive
That neither in birth or for authority
The bishop will be overborne by thee:
I'll either make thee stoop and bend thy knee,
Or sack this country with a mutiny.   [*Exit.*

SCENE II.—FRANCE. *Plains in Anjou.*

Enter CHARLES, BURGUNDY, ALENÇON,
LA PUCELLE, *and* Forces, *marching.*

  Char. These news, my lords, may cheer our
    drooping spirits:
'Tis said the stout Parisians do revolt,
And turn again unto the warlike French.
  Alen. Then march to Paris, royal Charles of
    France,
And keep not back your powers in dalliance.
  Puc. Peace be amongst them if they turn
    to us;
Else ruin combat with their palaces!

Enter a Messenger.

  Mess. Success unto our valiant general,
And happiness to his accomplices!
  Char. What tidings send our scouts? I pr'y-
    thee, speak.
  Mess. The English army, that divided was
Into two parts, is now conjoin'd in one,
And means to give you battle presently.
  Char. Somewhat too sudden, sirs, the warn-
    ing is;
But we will presently provide for them.
  Bur. I trust the ghost of Talbot is not there:
Now he is gone, my lord, you need not fear.
  Puc. Of all base passions fear is most ac-
    curs'd:—   [thine;
Command the conquest, Charles, it shall be
Let Henry fret and all the world repine.
  Char. Then on, my lords; and France be
    fortunate!   [*Exeunt.*

SCENE III.—*The same. Before Angiers.*

Alarums: excursions. Enter LA PUCELLE.

  Puc. The regent conquers and the French-
    men fly,—
Now help, ye charming spells and periapts;
And ye choice spirits that admonish me,
And give me signs of future accidents,—

You speedy helpers, that are substitutes
Under the lordly monarch of the north,
Appear, and aid me in this enterprise!

[*Thunder.*

Enter Fiends.

This speedy and quick appearance argues proof
Of your accustom'd diligence to me.
Now, ye familiar spirits that are cull'd
Out of the powerful legions under earth,
Help me this once, that France may get the
field. [*They walk about and speak not.*
O, hold me not with silence over-long!
Where I was wont to feed you with my blood
I'll lop a member off and give it you,
In earnest of a further benefit,
So you do condescend to help me now.

[*They hang their heads.*

No hope to have redress?—My body shall
Pay recompense if you will grant my suit.

[*They shake their heads.*

Cannot my body nor blood sacrifice
Entreat you to your wonted furtherance?
Then take my soul,—my body, soul, and all,
Before that England give the French the foil.

[*They depart.*

See! they forsake me. Now the time is come
That France must vail her lofty-plumed crest,
And let her head fall into England's lap.
My ancient incantations are too weak,
And hell too strong for me to buckle with:
Now, France, thy glory droopeth to the dust.

[*Exit.*

Alarums. Enter French *and* English, *fighting.*
LA PUCELLE *and* YORK *fight hand to hand:*
LA PUCELLE *is taken. The French fly.*

York. Damsel of France, I think I have you
fast:
Unchain your spirits now with spelling charms,
And try if they can gain your liberty.—
A goodly prize, fit for the devil's grace!
See how the ugly witch doth bend her brows,
As if, with Circe, she would change my shape!

Puc. Chang'd to a worser shape thou canst
not be. [*man;*
York. O, Charles the Dauphin is a proper
No shape but his can please your dainty eye.

Puc. A plaguing mischief light on Charles
and thee!
And may ye both be suddenly surpris'd
By bloody hands, in sleeping on your beds!

York. Fell, banning hag; enchantress, hold
thy tongue! [*awhile.*
Puc. I pr'ythee, give me leave to curse
York. Curse, miscreant, when thou comest
to the stake. [*Exeunt.*

Alarums. Enter SUFFOLK, *leading in* LADY
MARGARET.

Suf. Be what thou wilt, thou art my pris-
oner. [*Gazes on her.*
O fairest beauty, do not fear nor fly!
For I will touch thee but with reverent hands,
And lay them gently on thy tender side.
I kiss these fingers for eternal peace.

[*Kissing her hand.*

Who art thou? say, that I may honour thee.

Mar. Margaret my name, and daughter to
a king,
The king of Naples—whosoe'er thou art.

Suf. An earl I am, and Suffolk am I call'd.
Be not offended, nature's miracle,
Thou art allotted to be ta'en by me:
So doth the swan her downy cygnets save,
Keeping them prisoners underneath her wings.
Yet, if this servile usage once offend,
Go, and be free again as Suffolk's friend.

[*She turns away as going.*

O, stay!—I have no power to let her pass;
My hand would free her, but my heart says no.
As plays the sun upon the glassy streams,
Twinkling another counterfeited beam,
So seems this gorgeous beauty to mine eyes.
Fain would I woo her, yet I dare not speak:
I'll call for pen and ink, and write my mind:
Fie, De-la-Poole! disable not thyself;
Hast not a tongue? is she not here thy prisoner?
Wilt thou be daunted at a woman's sight?
Ay, beauty's princely majesty is such, [*rough*
Confounds the tongue, and makes the senses

Mar. Say, Earl of Suffolk,—if thy name be
so,—
What ransom must I pay before I pass?
For I perceive I am thy prisoner. [*suit*

Suf. How canst thou tell she will deny thy
Before thou make a trial of her love? [*Aside.*

Mar. Why speak'st thou not? what ransom
must I pay? [*woo'd;*

Suf. She's beautiful, and therefore to be
She is a woman, therefore to be won. [*Aside.*

Mar. Wilt thou accept of ransom—yea or no?

Suf. Fond man, remember that thou hast a
wife;
Then how can Margaret be thy paramour?

[*Aside.*

Mar. I were best leave him, for he will not
hear.

Suf. There all is marr'd; there lies a cooling
card. [*Aside.*

Mar. He talks at random; sure, the man is
mad.

Suf. And yet a dispensation may be had.

[*Aside.*

Mar. And yet I would that you would answer me.

Suf. I'll win this Lady Margaret. For whom?
Why, for my king: tush, that's a wooden thing!

[*Aside.*

Mar. He talks of wood: it is some carpenter.

Suf. Yet so my fancy may be satisfied,
And peace established between these realms.
But there remains a scruple in that too;
For though her father be the King of Naples,
Duke of Anjou and Maine, yet is he poor,
And our nobility will scorn the match. [*Aside.*

Mar. Hear ye, captain,—are ye not at
leisure?

Suf. It shall be so, disdain they ne'er so
    much:
Henry is youthful, and will quickly yield.—
                                    [*Aside.*
Madam, I have a secret to reveal.   [a knight,
Mar. What though I be enthrall'd? he seems
And will not any way dishonour me.   [*Aside.*
Suf. Lady, vouchsafe to listen what I say.
Mar. Perhaps I shall be rescued by the
    French;
And then I need not crave his courtesy. [*Aside.*
Suf. Sweet madam, give me hearing in a
    cause—
Mar. Tush! women have been captivate ere
    now.   [*Aside.*
Suf. Lady, wherefore talk you so?
Mar. I cry you mercy, 'tis but *quid* for *quo.*
Suf. Say, gentle princess, would you not
    suppose
Your bondage happy, to be made a queen?
Mar. To be a queen in bondage is more vile
Than is a slave in base servility;
For princes should be free.
Suf.   And so shall you,
If happy England's royal king be free. [me?
Mar. Why, what concerns his freedom unto
Suf. I'll undertake to make thee Henry's
    queen;
To put a golden sceptre in thy hand,
And set a precious crown upon thy head,
If thou wilt condescend to be my—
Mar.   What?
Suf.   His love.
Mar. I am unworthy to be Henry's wife.
Suf. No, gentle madam; I unworthy am
To woo so fair a dame to be his wife,
And have no portion in the choice myself.
How say you, madam,—are you so content?
Mar. An if my father please, I am content.
Suf. Then call our captains and our colours
    forth!—   [*Troops come forward.*
And, madam, at your father's castle-walls
We'll crave a parley, to confer with him.

A Parley sounded. Enter REIGNIER *on the Walls.*

Suf. See, Reignier, see, thy daughter pris-
    oner!
Reig. To whom?
Suf.   To me.
Reig.   Suffolk, what remedy?
I am a soldier, and unapt to weep
Or to exclaim on fortune's fickleness.
Suf. Yes, there is remedy enough, my lord:
Consent,—and for thy honour give consent,—
Thy daughter shall be wedded to my king;
Whom I with pain have woo'd and won thereto;
And this her easy-held imprisonment
Hath gain'd thy daughter princely liberty.
Reig. Speaks Suffolk as he thinks?
Suf.   Fair Margaret knows
That Suffolk doth not flatter, face, or feign.
Reig. Upon thy princely warrant I descend,
To give thee answer of thy just demand.
            [*Exit* REIGNIER *from the Walls.*

Suf. And here I will expect thy coming.

Trumpets sound. Enter REIGNER *below.*

Reig. Welcome, brave earl, into our terri-
    tories;
Command in Anjou what your honour pleases.
Suf. Thanks, Reignier, happy for so sweet a
    child,
Fit to be made companion with a king:
What answer makes your grace unto my suit?
Reig. Since thou dost deign to woo her little
    worth
To be the princely bride of such a lord,
Upon condition I may quietly
Enjoy mine own, the county Maine and Anjou
Free from oppression or the stroke of war,
My daughter shall be Henry's, if he please.
Suf. That is her ransom,—I deliver her;
And those two counties I will undertake
Your grace shall well and quietly enjoy.
Reig. And I again, in Henry's royal name,
As deputy unto that gracious king,
Give thee her hand, for sign of plighted faith.
Suf. Reignier of France, I give thee kingly
    thanks,
Because this is in traffic of a king:— .
And yet, methinks, I could be well content
To be mine own attorney in this case.— [*Aside.*
I'll over, then, to England with this news,
And make this marriage to be solemniz'd.
So, farewell, Reignier: set this diamond safe
In golden palaces, as it becomes.
Reig. I do embrace thee as I would embrace
The Christian prince, King Henry, were he
    here.   [and prayers
Mar. Farewell, my lord: good wishes, praise.
Shall Suffolk ever have of Margaret. [*Going*
Suf. Farewell, sweet madam: but hark you
    Margaret,—
No princely commendations to my king? [maid,
Mar. Such commendations as become a
A virgin, and his servant, say to him.
Suf. Words sweetly plac'd and modestly
    directed.
But, madam, I must trouble you again,—
No loving token to his majesty?   [heart,
Mar. Yes, my good lord,—a pure unspotted
Never yet taint with love, I send the king.
Suf. And this withal.   [*Kisses her.*
Mar. That for thyself:—I will not so pre-
    sume
To send such peevish tokens to a king.
                    [*Exeunt* REIG. *and* MAR.
Suf. O, wert thou for myself!—But, Suffolk,
    stay;
Thou mayst not wander in that labyrinth:
There Minotaurs and ugly treasons lurk.
Solicit Henry with her wondrous praise:
Bethink thee on her virtues that surmount,
And natural graces that extinguish art;
Repeat their semblance often on the seas,
That when thou com'st to kneel at Henry's feet
Thou mayst bereave him of his wits with
    wonder.   [*Exit.*

SCENE IV.—*Camp of the* DUKE OF YORK *in Anjou.*

Enter YORK, WARWICK, *and others.*

York. Bring forth that sorceress, condemn'd to burn.

Enter LA PUCELLE, *guarded, and a* Shepherd.

Shep. Ah, Joan, this kills thy father's heart outright!
Have I sought every country far and near,
And now it is my chance to find thee out
Must I behold thy timeless cruel death?
Ah, Joan, sweet daughter Joan, I'll die with thee!

Puc. Decrepit miser! base ignoble wretch!
I am descended of a gentler blood;
Thou art no father nor no friend of mine.

Shep. Out, out!—My lords, an please you, 'tis not so;
I did beget her, all the parish knows:
Her mother liveth yet, can testify
She was the first fruit of my bachelorship.

War. Graceless, wilt thou deny thy parentage? [been,—

York. This argues what her kind of life hath
Wicked and vile; and so her death concludes.

Shep. Fie, Joan, that thou wilt be so obstacle!
God knows thou art a collop of my flesh;
And for thy sake have I shed many a tear:
Deny me not, I pr'ythee, gentle Joan.

Puc. Peasant, avaunt!—You have suborn'd this man,
Of purpose to obscure my noble birth.

Shep. 'Tis true, I gave a noble to the priest
The morn that I was wedded to her mother.—
Kneel down and take my blessing, good my girl.
Wilt thou not stoop? Now cursed be the time
Of thy nativity! I would the milk [breast
Thy mother gave thee when thou suck'dst her
Had been a little ratsbane for thy sake!
Or else, when thou didst keep my lambs a-field,
I wish some ravenous wolf had eaten thee!
Dost thou deny thy father, cursed drab?
O, burn her, burn her! hanging is too good.
[*Exit.*

York. Take her away; for she hath liv'd too long,
To fill the world with vicious qualities.

Puc. First let me tell you whom you have condemn'd:
Not me begotten of a shepherd swain,
But issu'd from the progeny of kings;
Virtuous and holy; chosen from above,
By inspiration of celestial grace,
To work exceeding miracles on earth.
I never had to do with wicked spirits:
But you,—that are polluted with your lusts,
Stain'd with the guiltless blood of innocents,
Corrupt and tainted with a thousand vices,—
Because you want the grace that others have,
You judge it straight a thing impossible
To compass wonders but by help of devils.

No, misconceived! Joan of Arc hath been
A virgin from her tender infancy,
Chaste and immaculate in very thought;
Whose maiden blood, thus rigorously effus'd,
Will cry for vengeance at the gates of heaven.

York. Ay, ay:—away with her to execution!

War. And hark ye, sirs; because she is a maid,
Spare for no fagots, let there be enow:
Place barrels of pitch upon the fatal stake,
That so her torture may be shortened.

Puc. Will nothing turn your unrelenting hearts?
Then, Joan, discover thine infirmity,
That warranteth by law to be thy privilege.—
I am with child, ye bloody homicides:
Murder not, then, the fruit within my womb,
Although ye hale me to a violent death.

York. Now heaven forfend! the holy maid with child! [wrought:

War. The greatest miracle that e'er ye
Is all your strict preciseness come to this?

York. She and the Dauphin have been juggling:
I did imagine what would be her refuge. [live;

War. Well, go to; we will have no bastards
Especially since Charles must father it. [his:

Puc. You are deceiv'd; my child is none of
It was Alençon that enjoy'd my love.

York. Alençon! that notorious Machiavel!
It dies, an if it had a thousand lives.

Puc. O, give me leave, I have deluded you;
'Twas neither Charles nor yet the duke I nam'd,
But Reignier, King of Naples, that prevail'd.

War. A married man! that's most intolerable.

York. Why, here's a girl!—I think she knows not well—
There were so many—whom she may accuse.

War. It's sign she hath been liberal and free.

York. And yet, forsooth, she is a virgin pure.—
Strumpet, thy words condemn thy brat and thee:
Use no entreaty, for it is in vain.

Puc. Then lead me hence;—with whom I leave my curse:
May never glorious sun reflex his beams
Upon the country where you make abode;
But darkness and the gloomy shade of death
Environ you, till mischief and despair
Drive you to break your necks or hang yourselves! [*Exit, guarded.*

York. Break thou in pieces and consume to ashes,
Thou foul accursed minister of hell!

Enter CARDINAL BEAUFORT, *attended.*

Car. Lord regent, I do greet your excellence
With letters of commission from the king.
For know, my lords, the states of Christendom,
Mov'd with remorse of these outrageous broils,
Have earnestly implor'd a general peace
Betwixt our nation and the aspiring French;

And here at hand the Dauphin and his train
Approacheth, to confer about some matter.
York. Is all our travail turn'd to this effect?
After the slaughter of so many peers,
So many captains, gentlemen, and soldiers,
That in this quarrel have been overthrown,
And sold their bodies for their country's benefit,
Shall we at last conclude effeminate peace?
Have we not lost most part of all the towns,
By treason, falsehood, and by treachery,
Our great progenitors had conquered?—
O Warwick, Warwick! I foresee with grief
The utter loss of all the realm of France.
War. Be patient, York: if we conclude a
    peace,   [nants
It shall be with such strict and severe cove-
As little shall the Frenchmen gain thereby.

Enter CHARLES, *attended;* ALENÇON,
    BASTARD, REIGNIER, *and others.*

Char. Since, lords of England, it is thus
    agreed   [France,
That peaceful truce shall be proclaim'd in
We come to be informed by yourselves
What the conditions of that league must be.
York. Speak, Winchester; for boiling choler
    chokes
The hollow passage of my prison'd voice,
By sight of these our baleful enemies.
Car. Charles, and the rest, it is enacted thus:
That in regard King Henry gives consent,
Of mere compassion and of lenity,
To ease your country of distressful war,
And suffer you to breathe in fruitful peace,—
You shall become true liegemen to his crown:
And, Charles, upon condition thou wilt swear
To pay him tribute and submit thyself,
Thou shalt be plac'd as viceroy under him,
And still enjoy thy regal dignity.   [self?
Alen. Must he be, then, as shadow of him-
Adorn his temples with a coronet,
And yet, in substance and authority,
Retain but privilege of a private man?
This proffer is absurd and reasonless.   [sess'd
Char. 'Tis known already that I am pos-
With more than half the Gallian territories,
And therein reverenc'd for their lawful king:
Shall I, for lucre of the rest unvanquish'd,
Detract so much from that prerogative
As to be call'd but viceroy of the whole?
No, lord ambassador; I'll rather keep
That which I have than, coveting for more,
Be cast from possibility of all.
York. Insulting Charles! hast thou by secret
    means
Us'd intercession to obtain a league,
And now the matter grows to compromise
Stand'st thou aloof upon comparison?
Either accept the title thou usurp'st,
Of benefit proceeding from our king,
And not of any challenge of desert,
Or we will plague thee with incessant wars.
Reig. My lord, you do not well in obstinacy
To cavil in the course of this contráct:

If once it be neglected, ten to one
We shall not find like opportunity.
Alen. To say the truth, it is your policy
To save your subjects from such massacre
And ruthless slaughters as are daily seen
By our proceeding in hostility;
And therefore take this compact of a truce,
Although you break it when your pleasure
    serves.   [*Aside to* CHARLES.
War. How say'st thou, Charles? shall our
    condition stand?
Char. It shall;
Only reserv'd, you claim no interest
In any of our towns of garrison.
York. Then swear allegiance to his majesty,
As thou art knight, never to disobey
Nor be rebellious to the crown of England,—
Thou, nor thy nobles, to the crown of England.
    [CHARLES *and the rest give tokens of fealty.*
So, now dismiss your army when ye please;
Hang up your ensigns, let your drums be still,
For here we entertain a solemn peace. [*Exeunt.*

SCENE V.—LONDON. *A Room in the Palace.*

Enter KING HENRY, *in conference with* SUF-
    FOLK; GLOSTER *and* EXETER *following.*

K. Hen. Your wondrous rare description,
    noble earl,
Of beauteous Margaret hath astonish'd me:
Her virtues, graced with external gifts,
Do breed love's settled passions in my heart:
And like as rigour of tempestuous gusts
Provokes the mightiest hulk against the tide,
So am I driven, by breath of her renown,
Either to suffer shipwreck or arrive
Where I may have fruition of her love.   [tale
Suf. Tush, my good lord,—this superficial
Is but a preface of her worthy praise:
The chief perfections of that lovely dame,—
Had I sufficient skill to utter them,—
Would make a volume of enticing lines,
Able to ravish any dull conceit:
And, which is more, she is not so divine,
So full-replete with choice of all delights,
But, with as humble lowliness of mind,
She is content to be at your command;
Command, I mean, of virtuous chaste intents,
To love and honour Henry as her lord.
K. Hen. And otherwise will Henry ne'er pre-
    sume.
Therefore, my lord protector, give consent
That Margaret may be England's royal queen.
Glo. So should I give consent to flatter sin.
You know, my lord, your highness is betroth'd
Unto another lady of esteem: [tráct,
How shall we, then, dispense with that con-
And not deface your honour with reproach?
Suf. As doth a ruler with unlawful oaths;
Or one that, at a triumph having vow'd
To try his strength, forsaketh yet the lists
By reason of his adversary's odds:
A poor earl's daughter is unequal odds,
And therefore may be broke without offence.

Glo. Why, what, I pray, is Margaret more
    than that?
Her father is no better than an earl,
Although in glorious titles he excel.

Suf. Yes, my lord, her father is a king,
The King of Naples and Jerusalem;
And of such great authority in France
As his alliance will confirm our peace,
And keep the Frenchmen in allegiance.

Glo. And so the Earl of Armagnac may do,
Because he is near kinsman unto Charles.

Exe. Beside, his wealth doth warrant a lib-
    eral dower;
While Reignier sooner will receive than give.

Suf. A dower, my lords! disgrace not so
    your king,
That he should be so abject, base, and poor,
To choose for wealth, and not for perfect love.
Henry is able to enrich his queen,
And not to seek a queen to make him rich:
So worthless peasants bargain for their wives,
As market-men for oxen, sheep, or horse.
Marriage is a matter of more worth
Than to be dealt in by attorneyship;
Not whom we will, but whom his grace affects,
Must be companion of his nuptial bed:
And therefore, lords, since he affects her most,
It most of all these reasons bindeth us
In our opinions she should be preferr'd.
For what is wedlock forced but a hell,
An age of discord and continual strife?
Whereas the contrary bringeth bliss,
And is a pattern of celestial peace.   [king,
Whom should we match with Henry, being a
But Margaret, that is daughter to a king?
Her peerless feature, joined with her birth,
Approves her fit for none but for a king;
Her valiant courage and undaunted spirit,—
More than in women commonly is seen,—
Will answer our hope in issue of a king;
For Henry, son unto a conqueror,

Is likely to beget more conquerors,
If with a lady of so high resolve
As is fair Margaret he be link'd in love.   [me
Then yield, my lords; and here conclude with
That Margaret shall be queen, and none but
    she.

K. Hen. Whether it be through force of your
    report,
My noble Lord of Suffolk, or for that
My tender youth was never yet attaint
With any passion of inflaming love,
I cannot tell; but this I am assur'd.
I feel such sharp dissension in my breast,
Such fierce alarums both of hope and fear,
As I am sick with working of my thoughts.
Take therefore shipping; post, my lord, to
    France;
Agree to any covenants; and procure
That Lady Margaret do vouchsafe to come
To cross the seas to England, and be crown'd
King Henry's faithful and anointed queen:
For your expenses and sufficient charge,
Among the people gather up a tenth.
Be gone, I say; for, till you do return,
I rest perplexed with a thousand cares.—
And you, good uncle, banish all offence:
If you do censure me by what you were,
Not what you are, I know it will excuse
This sudden execution of my will.
And so, conduct me where, from company,
I may resolve and ruminate my grief.   [*Exit.*

Glo. Ay, grief, I fear me, both at first and last.
    [*Exeunt* GLOSTER *and* EXETER.

Suf. Thus Suffolk hath prevail'd; and thus
    he goes,
As did the youthful Paris once to Greece,
With hope to find the like event in love,
But prosper better than the Trojan did.
Margaret shall now be queen, and rule the king;
But I will rule both her, the king, and realm.
    [*Exit.*

KING HENRY VI. PART SECOND.

Act IV. Sc. 2.

KING HENRY VI.

SECOND PART

DRAMATIS PERSONÆ

KING HENRY THE SIXTH.
HUMPHREY, *Duke of Gloster, his Uncle.*
CARDINAL BEAUFORT, *Bishop of Winchester, Great-Uncle to the* KING.
RICHARD PLANTAGENET, *Duke of York.*
EDWARD *and* RICHARD, *his Sons.*
DUKE OF SOMERSET, ⎫
DUKE OF SUFFOLK, ⎪
DUKE OF BUCKINGHAM, ⎬ *of the* KING'S
LORD CLIFFORD, ⎪ *party.*
YOUNG CLIFFORD, *his Son,* ⎭
EARL OF SALISBURY, ⎫ *of the York faction.*
EARL OF WARWICK, ⎭
LORD SCALES, *Governor of the Tower.*
LORD SAY.
SIR HUMPHREY STAFFORD.
WILLIAM STAFFORD, *his Brother.*
SIR JOHN STANLEY.
A Sea Captain, Master, *and* Master's Mate, *and* WALTER WHITMORE.
Two Gentlemen, *Prisoners with* SUFFOLK.
VAUX.
A Herald.

HUME *and* SOUTHWELL, *two Priests*
BOLINGBROKE, *a Conjuror.*
A Spirit *raised by him.*
THOMAS HORNER, *an Armourer.*
PETER, *his Man.*
Clerk of Chatham.
Mayor of Saint Alban's.
SIMPCOX, *an Impostor.*
Two Murderers.
JACK CADE, *a Rebel.*
GEORGE, JOHN, DICK, SMITH *the Weaver,* MICHAEL, *&c., his followers.*
ALEXANDER IDEN, *a Kentish Gentleman.*

MARGARET, *Queen to* KING HENRY.
ELEANOR, *Duchess of Gloster.*
MARGERY JOURDAIN, *a Witch.*
Wife *to* SIMPCOX.

Lords, Ladies, *and* Attendants; Petitioners, Aldermen, *a* Beadle, Sheriff, *and* Officers; Citizens, Prentices, Falconers, Guards, Soldiers, Messengers, &c.

SCENE,—*Dispersedly in various parts of* ENGLAND.

ACT I.

SCENE I.—LONDON. *A Room of State in the Castle.*

Flourish of trumpets: then hautboys. Enter, on one side, KING HENRY, DUKE OF GLOSTER, SALISBURY, WARWICK, *and* CARDINAL BEAUFORT; *on the other,* QUEEN MARGARET, *led in by* SUFFOLK; YORK, SOMERSET, BUCKINGHAM, *and others, following.*

Suf. As by your high imperial majesty
I had in charge at my depart for France,
As procurator to your excellence,
To marry Princess Margaret for your grace;
So, in the famous ancient city Tours,—
In presence of the Kings of France and Sicil,
The Dukes of Orleans, Calaber, Bretagne, and Alencon,
Seven earls, twelve barons, and twenty reverend bishops,
I have perform'd my task, and was espous'd:
And humbly now, upon my bended knee,
In sight of England and her lordly peers,
Deliver up my title in the queen [substance
To your most gracious hands, that are the
Of that great shadow I did represent;
The happiest gift that ever marquis gave,
The fairest queen that ever king receiv'd.

K. Hen. Suffolk, arise.—Welcome, Queen Margaret:
I can express no kinder sign of love [life,
Than this kind kiss.—O Lord, that lends me
Lend me a heart replete with thankfulness!
For thou hast given me, in this beauteous face,
A world of earthly blessings to my soul,
If sympathy of love unite our thoughts.

Q. Mar. Great King of England, and my gracious lord,— [had,
The mutual conference that my mind hath
By day, by night, waking and in my dreams,
In courtly company or at my beads,
With you, mine alder-liefest sovereign,
Makes me the bolder to salute my king
With ruder terms, such as my wit affords
And over-joy of heart doth minister.

K. Hen. Her sight did ravish; but her grace in speech,
Her words y-clad with wisdom's majesty,
Makes me from wondering fall to weeping joys;
Such is the fulness of my heart's content.—
Lords, with one cheerful voice welcome my love.

189

All. [*Kneeling.*] Long live Queen Margaret, England's happiness!

Q. Mar. We thank you all.   .[*Flourish.*

Suf. My lord protector, so it please your grace,
Here are the articles of contracted peace
Between our sovereign and the French King Charles,
For eighteen months concluded by consent.

Glo. [*Reads.*] *Imprimis, It is agreed between the French King Charles and William De-la-Poole, Marquess of Suffolk, ambassador for Henry King of England, that the said Henry shall espouse the Lady Margaret, daughter unto Reignier King of Naples, Sicilia, and Jerusalem; and crown her Queen of England ere the thirtieth of May next ensuing.—Item,—That the duchy of Anjou and the county of Maine shall be released and delivered to the king her father,—*

K. Hen. Uncle, how now!

Glo.   Pardon me, gracious lord;
Some sudden qualm hath struck me at the heart,
And dimm'd mine eyes, that I can read no further.

K. Hen. Uncle of Winchester, I pray read on.

Car. [*Reads.*] *Item,—It is further agreed between them that the duchies of Anjou and Maine shall be released and delivered over to the king her father; and she sent over of the King of England's own proper cost and charges, without having any dowry.*

K. Hen. They please us well.—Lord marquess, kneel down:
We here create thee the first Duke of Suffolk,
And girt thee with the sword.—Cousin of York,
We here discharge your grace from being regent
I' the parts of France, till term of eighteen months
Be full expir'd.—Thanks, uncle Winchester,
Gloster, York, Buckingham, Somerset,
Salisbury, and Warwick;
We thank you all for this great favour done,
In entertainment to my princely queen.
Come, let us in; and with all speed provide
To see her coronation be perform'd.

    [*Exeunt* KING, QUEEN, *and* SUFFOLK.

Glo. Brave peers of England, pillars of the state,
To you Duke Humphrey must unload his grief,—
Your grief, the common grief of all the land.
What! did my brother Henry spend his youth,
His valour, coin, and people in the wars?
Did he so often lodge in open field,
In winter's cold and summer's parching heat,
To conquer France, his true inheritance?
And did my brother Bedford toil his wits

To keep by policy what Henry got?
Have you yourselves, Somerset, Buckingham,
Brave York, Salisbury, and victorious Warwick,
Receiv'd deep scars in France and Normandy?
Or hath mine uncle Beaufort and myself,
With all the learned council of the realm,
Studied so long, sat in the council-house
Early and late, debating to and fro [in awe?
How France and Frenchmen might be kept
And hath his highness in his infancy
Been crown'd in Paris, in despite of foes?
And shall these labours and these honours die?
Shall Henry's conquest, Bedford's vigilance,
Your deeds of war, and all our counsel die?
O peers of England, shameful is this league!
Fatal this marriage! cancelling your fame,
Blotting your names from books of memory,
Razing the characters of your renown.
Defacing monuments of conquer'd France,
Undoing all, as all had never been!

Car. Nephew, what means this passionate discourse,
This peroration with such circumstance?
For France, 'tis ours; and we will keep it still.

Glo. Ay, uncle, we will keep it if we can;
But now it is impossible we should:
Suffolk, the new-made duke that rules the roast,
Hath given the duchy of Anjou and Maine
Unto the poor King Reignier, whose large style
Agrees not with the leanness of his purse.

Sal. Now, by the death of Him that died for all,
These counties were the keys of Normandy:—
But wherefore weeps Warwick, my valiant son?

War. For grief that they are past recovery:
For were there hope to conquer them again
My sword should shed hot blood, mine eyes no tears.
Anjou and Maine! myself did win them both;
Those provinces these arms of mine did conquer:
And are the cities that I got with wounds
Deliver'd up again with peaceful words?
Mort Dieu!   [focate

York. For Suffolk's duke, may he be suf-
That dims the honour of this warlike isle!
France should have torn and rent my very heart
Before I would have yielded to this league.
I never read but England's kings have had
Large sums of gold and dowries with their wives;
And our King Henry gives away his own,
To match with her that brings no vantages.

Glo. A proper jest, and never heard before,

That Suffolk should demand a whole fif-
 teenth
For costs and charges in transporting her!
She should have stay'd in France, and starv'd
 in France,
Before—
 Car. My Lord of Gloster, now you grow
  too hot:
It was the pleasure of my lord the king.
 Glo. My Lord of Winchester, I know your
  mind;
'Tis not my speeches that you do mislike,
But 'tis my presence that doth trouble ye.
Rancour will out: proud prelate, in thy face
I see thy fury: if I longer stay
We shall begin our ancient bickerings.—
Lordings, farewell; and say, when I am gone,
I prophesied France will be lost ere long.
         [*Exit.*
 Car. So, there goes our protector in a rage.
'Tis known to you he is mine enemy;
Nay, more, an enemy unto you all,
And no great friend, I fear me, to the king.
Consider, lords, he is the next of blood,
And heir-apparent to the English crown:
Had Henry got an empire by his marriage,
And all the wealthy kingdoms of the west,
There's reason he should be displeas'd at it.
Look to it, lords; let not his smoothing
 words
Bewitch your hearts; be wise and circum-
 spect.
What though the common people favour him,
Calling him—*Humphrey, the good Duke of
 Gloster;*   [voice,
Clapping their hands, and crying with loud
Jesu maintain your royal excellence!
With *God preserve the good Duke Hum-
 phrey!*
I fear me, lords, for all this flattering gloss,
He will be found a dangerous protector.
 Buck. Why should he then protect our
  sovereign,
He being of age to govern of himself?—
Cousin of Somerset, join you with me,
And altogether, with the Duke of Suffolk,
We'll quickly hoise Duke Humphrey from his
 seat.   [delay;
 Car. This weighty business will not brook
I'll to the Duke of Suffolk presently. [*Exit.*
 Som. Cousin of Buckingham, though
  Humphrey's pride
And greatness of his place be grief to us,
Yet let us watch the haughty cardinal:
His insolence is more intolerable
Than all the princes in the land beside:
If Gloster be displac'd, he'll be protector.
 Buck. Or thou or I, Somerset, will be pro-
  tector,
Despite Duke Humphrey or the cardinal.
   [*Exeunt* BUCKINGHAM *and* SOMERSET.
 Sal. Pride went before, ambition follows
  him.

Whiles these do labour for their own prefer-
 ment,
Behoves it us to labour for the realm.
I never saw but Humphrey Duke of Gloster
Did bear him like a noble gentleman.
Oft have I seen the haughty cardinal,—
More like a soldier than a man o' the church,
As stout and proud as he were lord of all,—
Swear like a ruffian, and demean himself
Unlike the ruler of a commonweal.—
Warwick, my son, the comfort of my age!
Thy deeds, thy plainness, and thy housekeep-
 ing,
Hath won the greatest favour of the com-
 mons,
Excepting none but good Duke Humphrey:—
And, brother York, thy acts in Ireland,
In bringing them to civil discipline;
Thy late exploits done in the heart of France,
When thou wert regent for our sovereign,
Have made thee fear'd and honour'd of the
 people:—
Join we together for the public good
In what we can, to bridle and suppress
The pride of Suffolk and the cardinal,
With Somerset's and Buckingham's ambi-
 tion;
And, as we may, cherish Duke Humphrey's
 deeds
While they do tend the profit of the land.
 War. So God help Warwick, as he loves
  the land
And common profit of his country!
 York. And so says York, for he hath great-
  est cause.
 Sal. Then let's make haste away and look
  unto the main.   [lost,—
 War. Unto the main! O father, Maine is
That Maine which by main force Warwick
 did win,   [last!
And would have kept so long as breath did
Main chance, father, you meant; but I meant
 Maine,—
Which I will win from France, or else be
 slain.
   [*Exeunt* WARWICK *and* SALISBURY.
 York. Anjou and Maine are given to the
  French;
Paris is lost; the state of Normandy
Stands on a tickle point, now they are gone:
Suffolk concluded on the articles;
The peers agreed; and Henry was well pleas'd
To change two dukedoms for a duke's fair
 daughter.
I cannot blame them all: what is 't to them?
'Tis thine they give away, and not their own.
Pirates may make cheap pennyworths of
 their pillage,
And purchase friends, and give to courtezans,
Still revelling like lords till all be gone;
While as the silly owner of the goods
Weeps over them, and wrings his hapless
 hands,

And shakes his head, and trembling stands
    aloof,
While all is shar'd, and all is borne away,
Ready to starve, and dare not touch his own:
So York must sit, and fret, and bite his
    tongue,
While his own lands are bargain'd for and
    sold.
Methinks the realms of England, France, and
    Ireland
Bear that proportion to my flesh and blood
As did the fatal brand Althæa burn'd
Unto the prince's heart of Calydon.
Anjou and Maine both given unto the
    French!
Cold news for me; for I had hope of France,
Even as I have of fertile England's soil.
A day will come when York shall claim his
    own;
And therefore I will take the Nevils' parts,
And make a show of love to proud Duke
    Humphrey,
And, when I spy advantage, claim the crown,
For that's the golden mark I seek to hit:
Nor shall proud Lancaster usurp my right,
Nor hold the sceptre in his childish fist,
Nor wear the diadem upon his head,
Whose church-like humours fit not for a
    crown.
Then, York, be still awhile, till time do serve:
Watch thou and wake, when others be asleep,
To pry into the secrets of the state;
Till Henry, surfeiting in joys of love
With his new bride and England's dear-
    bought queen,
And Humphrey with the peers be fall'n at
    jars:
Then will I raise aloft the milk-white rose,
With whose sweet smell the air shall be per-
    fum'd;
And in my standard bear the arms of York,
To grapple with the house of Lancaster;
And, force perforce, I'll make him yield the
    crown,
Whose bookish rule hath pull'd fair England
    down.
                            [*Exit.*

SCENE II.—LONDON. *A room in the* DUKE
    OF GLOSTER'S *House.*

Enter GLOSTER *and the* DUCHESS.

  Duch. Why droops my lord, like over-
    ripen'd corn
Hanging the head at Ceres' plenteous load?
Why doth the great Duke Humphrey knit
    his brows,
As frowning at the favours of the world?
Why are thine eyes fix'd to the sullen earth,
Gazing on that which seems to dim thy sight?
What see'st thou there? King Henry's dia-
    dem.
Enchas'd with all the honours of the world?

If so, gaze on, and grovel on thy face
Until thy head be circled with the same.
Put forth thy hand, reach at the glorious
    gold:—
What, is 't too short? I'll lengthen it with
    mine;
And, having both together heav'd it up,
We'll both together lift our heads to heaven;
And never more abase our sight so low
As to vouchsafe one glance unto the ground.
  Glo. O Nell, sweet Nell, if thou dost love
    thy lord,
Banish the canker of ambitious thoughts!
And may that thought, when I imagine ill
Against my king and nephew, virtuous
    Henry,
Be my last breathing in this mortal world!
My troublous dream this night doth make
    me sad.
  Duch. What dream'd my lord? tell me,
    and I'll requite it
With sweet rehearsal of my morning's dream.
  Glo. Methought this staff, mine office-
    badge in court,
Was broke in twain; by whom I have forgot,
But, as I think, it was by the cardinal;
And on the pieces of the broken wand
Were plac'd the heads of Edmund Duke of
    Somerset,
And William De-la-Poole, first Duke of Suf-
    folk.
This was my dream; what it doth bode God
    knows.
  Duch. Tut, this was nothing but an argu-
    ment
That he that breaks a stick of Gloster's grove
Shall lose his head for his presumption.
But list to me, my Humphrey, my sweet
    duke:
Methought I sat in seat of majesty
In the cathedral church of Westminster,
And in that chair where kings and queens
    are crown'd;
Where Henry and Dame Margaret kneel'd to
    me,
And on my head did set the diadem.
  Glo. Nay, Eleanor, then must I chide out-
    right:
Presumptuous dame, ill-nurtur'd Eleanor!
Art thou not second woman in the realm,
And the protector's wife, belov'd of him?
Hast thou not worldly pleasure at command,
Above the reach or compass of thy thought?
And wilt thou still be hammering treachery,
To tumble down thy husband and thyself
From top of honour to disgrace's feet?
Away from me, and let me hear no more!
  Duch. What, what, my lord! are you so
    choleric
With Eleanor for telling but her dream?
Next time I'll keep my dreams unto myself,
And not be check'd.
  Glo. Nay, be not angry, I am pleas'd again.

Enter a Messenger.

Mess. My lord protector, 'tis his highness'
pleasure
You do prepare to ride unto Saint Albans,
Whereas the king and queen do mean to
hawk.
Glo. I go.—Come, Nell,—thou wilt ride
with us? [*sently.*
Duch. Yes, my good lord, I'll follow pre-
[*Exeunt* GLOSTER *and* Messenger.
Follow I must; I cannot go before
While Gloster bears this base and humble
mind.
Were I a man, a duke, and next of blood,
I would remove these tedious stumbling-
blocks,
And smooth my way upon their headless
necks:
And, being a woman, I will not be slack
To play my part in fortune's pageant.—
Where are you there, Sir John? nay, fear
not, man,
We are alone; here's none but thee and I.

Enter HUME.

Hume. Jesus preserve your royal majesty!
Duch. What say'st thou? majesty! I am
but grace. [Hume's advice,
Hume. But, by the grace of God and
Your grace's title shall be multiplied.
Duch. What say'st thou, man? hast thou
as yet conferr'd
With Margery Jourdain, the cunning witch,
With Roger Bolingbroke, the conjurer?
And will they undertake to do me good?
Hume. This they have promised,—to show
your highness
A spirit rais'd from depth of under-ground,
That shall make answer to such questions
As by your grace shall be propounded him.
Duch. It is enough; I'll think upon the
questions:
When from Saint Albans we do make return
We'll see these things effected to the full.
Here, Hume, take this reward; make merry,
man,
With thy confederates in this weighty cause.
[*Exit.*
Hume. Hume must make merry with the
duchess' gold;
Marry, and shall. But, how now, Sir John
Hume!
Seal up your lips, and give no words but
mum:
The business asketh silent secrecy.
Dame Eleanor gives gold to bring the witch:
Gold cannot come amiss were she a devil.
Yet have I gold flies from another coast:—
I dare not say from the rich cardinal,
And from the great and new-made Duke of
Suffolk;

Yet I do find it so: for, to be plain,
They, knowing Dame Eleanor's aspiring hu-
mour,
Have hired me to undermine the duchess,
And buzz these conjurations in her brain.
They say,—A crafty knave does need no
broker;
Yet am I Suffolk and the cardinal's broker.
Hume, if you take not heed, you shall go
near
To call them both a pair of crafty knaves.
Well, so it stands; and thus, I fear, at last
Hume's knavery will be the duchess' wreck
And her attainture will be Humphrey's fall:
Sort how it will, I shall have gold for all.
[*Exit.*

SCENE III.—LONDON. *A Room in the Palace.*

Enter PETER *and other* Petitioners.

1 *Pet.* My masters, let's stand close: my
lord protector will come this way by and by,
and then we may deliver our supplications in
the quill.
2 *Pet.* Marry, the Lord protect him, for
he's a good man! Jesu bless him!
1 *Pet.* Here 'a comes, methinks, and the
queen with him. I'll be the first, sure.

Enter SUFFOLK *and* QUEEN MARGARET.

2 *Pet.* Come back, fool; this is the Duke of
Suffolk, and not my lord protector.
Suf. How now, fellow! wouldst anything
with me?
1 *Pet.* I pray, my lord, pardon me: I took
ye for my lord protector.
Q. Mar. [*Glancing at the superscriptions.*]
To my Lord Protector! Are your supplications to his lordship? Let me see them:—
what is thine?
1 *Pet.* Mine is, an 't please your grace,
against John Goodman, my lord cardinal's
man, for keeping my house, and lands, and
wife and all, from me.
Suf. Thy wife too! that is some wrong indeed.—What's yours?—what's here! [*Reads.*]
*Against the Duke of Suffolk, for enclosing
the commons of Melford.*—How now, sir
knave!
2 *Pet.* Alas, sir, I am but a poor petitioner
of our whole township.
Peter. [*Presenting his petition.*] Against
my master, Thomas Horner, for saying that
the Duke of York was rightful heir to the
crown.
Q. Mar. What say'st thou? did the Duke
of York say he was rightful heir to the
crown?
Peter. That my master was? no, forsooth:
my master said that he was; and that the
king was an usurper.
Suf. Who is there? [*Enter* Servants.]—
Take this fellow in, and send for his master

with a pursuivant presently:—we'll hear more of your matter before the king.

[*Exeunt* Servants *with* PETER.

Q. Mar. And as for you, that love to be protected
Under the wings of our protector's grace,
Begin your suits anew, and sue to him.

[*Tears the petitions.*

Away, base cullions!—Suffolk, let them go.
All. Come, let's be gone.

[*Exeunt* Petitioners.

Q. Mar. My lord of Suffolk, say, is this the guise,
Is this the fashion in the court of England?
Is this the government of Britain's isle,
And this the royalty of Albion's king?
What, shall King Henry be a pupil still,
Under the surly Gloster's governance?
Am I a queen in title and in style,
And must be made a subject to a duke?
I tell thee, Poole, when in the city Tours
Thou rann'st a tilt in honour of my love,
And stol'st away the ladies' hearts of France,
I thought King Henry had resembled thee
In courage, courtship, and proportion:
But all his mind is bent to holiness,
To number *Ave-Maries* on his beads:
His champions are, the prophets and apostles;
His weapons, holy saws of sacred writ;
His study is his tilt-yard, and his loves
Are brazen images of canoniz'd saints.
I would the college of the cardinals
Would choose him pope, and carry him to Rome,
And set the triple crown upon his head:—
That were a state fit for his holiness.
Suf. Madam, be patient: as I was cause
Your highness came to England, so will I
In England work your grace's full content.
Q. Mar. Beside the haughty protector, have we Beaufort [ingham,
The imperious churchman, Somerset, Buck-
And grumbling York; and not the least of these
But can do more in England than the king.
Suf. And he of these that can do most of all
Cannot do more in England than the Nevils:
Salisbury and Warwick are no simple peers.
Q. Mar. Not all these lords do vex me half so much
As that proud dame, the lord protector's wife.
She sweeps it through the court with troops of ladies, [phrey's wife:
More like an empress than Duke Hum-
Strangers in court do take her for the queen:
She bears a duke's revenues on her back,
And in her heart she scorns our poverty:
Shall I not live to be aveng'd on her?
Contemptuous base-born callet as she is,
She vaunted 'mongst her minions t' other day

The very train of her worst wearing gown
Was better worth than all my father's lands,
Till Suffolk gave two dukedoms for his daughter.
Suf. Madam, myself have lim'd a bush for her,
And plac'd a quire of such enticing birds
That she will light to listen to the lays,
And never mount to trouble you again.
So, let her rest: and, madam, list to me;
For I am bold to counsel you in this.
Although we fancy not the cardinal,
Yet must we join with him and with the lords,
Till we have brought Duke Humphrey in disgrace.
As for the Duke of York,—this late complaint
Will make but little for his benefit.
So, one by one, we'll weed them all at last,
And you yourself shall steer the happy helm.

Enter KING HENRY, YORK, *and* SOMERSET; DUKE *and* DUCHESS OF GLOSTER, CARDINAL BEAUFORT, BUCKINGHAM, SALISBURY, *and* WARWICK.

K. Hen. For my part, noble lords, I care not which;
Or Somerset or York, all's one to me.
York. If York have ill demean'd himself in France,
Then let him be denay'd the regentship.
Som. If Somerset be unworthy of the place,
Let York be regent; I will yield to him.
War. Whether your grace be worthy, yea or no,
Dispute not that: York is the worthier.
Car. Ambitious Warwick, let thy betters speak.
War. The cardinal's not my better in the field.
Buck. All in this presence are thy betters, Warwick.
War. Warwick may live to be the best of all.
Sal. Peace, son!—and show some reason, Buckingham,
Why Somerset should be preferr'd in this.
Q. Mar. Because the king, forsooth, will have it so.
Glo. Madame, the king is old enough himself
To give his censure: these are no women's matters. [your grace
Q. Mar. If he be old enough, what needs
To be protector of his excellence?
Glo. Madame, I am protector of the realm;
And, at his pleasure, will resign my place.
Suf. Resign it then, and leave thine insolence.

Since thou wert king,—as who is king but thou?—
The commonwealth hath daily run to wreck;
The Dauphin hath prevail'd beyond the seas;
And all the peers and nobles of the realm
Have been as bondmen to thy sovereignty.

Car. The commons hast thou rack'd; the clergy's bags
Are lank and lean with thy extortions.

Som. Thy sumptuous buildings and thy wife's attire
Have cost a mass of public treasury.

Buck. Thy cruelty in execution
Upon offenders hath exceeded law,
And left thee to the mercy of the law.

Q. Mar. Thy sale of offices and towns in France,—
If they were known, as the suspect is great,—
Would make thee quickly hop without thy head.

[*Exit* GLOSTER. *The* QUEEN *drops her fan.*

Give me my fan: what, minion! can you not?

[*Gives the* DUCHESS *a box on the ear.*

I cry you mercy, madam; was it you?

Duch. Was't I? yea, I it was, proud Frenchwoman:
Could I come near your beauty with my nails,
I'd set my ten commandments in your face.

K. Hen. Sweet aunt, be quiet; 'twas against her will.

Duch. Against her will! good king, look to 't in time;
She'll hamper thee, and dandle thee like a baby: [breeches,
Though in this place most master wear no
She shall not strike Dame Eleanor unreveng'd. [*Exit.*

Buck. Lord cardinal, I will follow Eleanor,
And listen after Humphrey, how he proceeds:
She's tickled now; her fume needs no spurs,
She'll gallop fast enough to her destruction.
[*Exit.*

Re-enter GLOSTER.

Glo. Now, lords, my choler being overblown
With walking once about the quadrangle,
I come to talk of commonwealth affairs.
As for your spiteful false objections,
Prove them, and I lie open to the law:
But God in mercy so deal with my soul
As I in duty love my king and country!
But to the matter that we have in hand:—
I say, my sovereign, York is meetest man
To be your regent in the realm of France.

Suf. Before we make election, give me leave
To show some reason, of no little force,
That York is most unmeet of any man.

York. I'll tell thee, Suffolk, why I am unmeet:
First, for I cannot flatter thee in pride;
Next, if I be appointed for the place,
My Lord of Somerset will keep me here,
Without discharge, money, or furniture,
Till France be won into the Dauphin's hands:
Last time, I danc'd attendance on his will
Till Paris was besieg'd, famished, and lost.

War. That can I witness; and a fouler fact
Did never traitor in the land commit.

Suf. Peace, headstrong Warwick!

War. Image of pride, why should I hold my peace?

Enter Servants of SUFFOLK, *bringing in* HORNER *and* PETER.

Suf. Because here is a man accus'd of treason:.
Pray God the Duke of York excuse himself!

York. Doth any one accuse York for a traitor?

K. Hen. What mean'st thou, Suffolk? tell me, what are these?

Suf. Please it your majesty, this is the man
That doth accuse his master of high treason:
His words were these,—that Richard Duke of York
Was rightful heir unto the English crown,
And that your majesty was an usurper.

K. Hen. Say, man, were these thy words?

Hor. An't shall please your majesty, I never said nor thought any such matter: God is my witness, I am falsely accused by the villain.

Pet. By these ten bones, my lords [*holding up his hands,*] he did speak them to me in the garret one night, as we were scouring my Lord of York's armour.

York. Base dunghill villain and mechanical,
I'll have thy head for this thy traitor's speech.—
I do beseech your royal majesty,
Let him have all the rigour of the law.

Hor. Alas, my lord, hang me if ever I spake the words. My accuser is my prentice; and when I did correct him for his fault the other day, he did vow upon his knees he would be even with me: I have good witness of this; therefore I beseech your majesty, do not cast away an honest man for a villain's accusation.

K. Hen. Uncle, what shall we say to this in law?

Glo. This doom, my lord, if I may judge:
Let Somerset be regent o'er the French,
Because in York this breeds suspicion;
And let these have a day appointed them
For single combat in convenient place,
For he hath witness of his servant's malice:
This is the law, and this Duke Humphrey's doom.

K. Hen. Then bé it so.—My Lord of
Somerset,
We make your grace regent over the French.

Som. I humbly thank your royal majesty.

Hor. And I accept the combat willingly.

Pet. Alas, my lord, I cannot fight; for
God's sake, pity my case! the spite of man
prevaileth against me. O Lord, have mercy
upon me! I shall never be able to fight a
blow: O Lord, my heart!

Glo. Sirrah, or you must fight, or else be
hang'd.

K. Hen. Away with them to prison; and
the day [month.—
Of combat shall be the last of the next
Come, Somerset, we'll see thee sent away.
[*Flourish. Exeunt.*

SCENE IV.—*The same. The* DUKE OF
GLOSTER'S *Garden.*

Enter MARGERY JOURDAIN, HUME, SOUTH-
WELL, *and* BOLINGBROKE.

Hume. Come, my masters; the duchess, I
tell you, expects performance of your promises.

Boling. Master Hume, we are therefore
provided: will her ladyship behold and hear
our exorcisms?

Hume. Ay, what else? fear you not her
courage.

Boling. I have heard her reported to be a
woman of an invincible spirit: but it shall be
convenient, Master Hume, that you be by her
aloft, while we be busy below; and so, I
pray you, go in God's name, and leave us.
[*Exit* HUME.] Mother Jourdain, be you
prostrate, and grovel on the earth;—John
Southwell, read you;—and let us to our
work.

Enter DUCHESS *above, and presently* HUME.

Duch. Well said, my masters; and welcome all.
To this gear,—the sooner the better.

Boling. Patience, good lady; wizards know
their times:
Deep night, dark night, the silent of the
night,
The time of night when Troy was set on
fire;
The time when screech-owls cry, and ban-
dogs howl,
And spirits walk, and ghosts break up their
graves,—
That time best fits the work we have in
hand.
Madam, sit you, and fear not: whom we
raise
We will make fast within a hallow'd verge.
[*Here they perform the ceremonies apper-
taining, and make the circle;* BOLING-
BROKE *or* SOUTHWELL *reads,* "Conjuro

te," &c. *It thunders and lightens ter-
ribly; then the* Spirit *riseth.*

Spir. Adsum.

M. Jourd. Asmath,
By the eternal God, whose name and power
Thou tremblest at, answer that I shall ask;
For, till thou speak, thou shalt not pass from
hence. [and done!

Spir. Ask what thou wilt: that I had said

Boling. First of the king: what shall of
him become? [*Reading out of a paper.*

Spir. The duke yet lives that Henry shall
depose;
But him outlive, and die a violent death.
[*As the* Spirit *speaks,* SOUTHWELL
writes the answers.

Boling. What fates await the Duke of
Suffolk?

Spir. By water shall he die and take his
end.

Boling. What shall befall the Duke of
Somerset?

Spir. Let him shun castles;
Safer shall he be upon the sandy plains
Than where castles mounted stand.—
Have done, for more I hardly can endure.

Boling. Descend to darkness and the burn-
ing lake!
False fiend, avoid!
[*Thunder and lightning.* Spirit *descends.*

Enter YORK *and* BUCKINGHAM *hastily, with
their* Guards *and others.*

York. Lay hands upon these traitors and
their trash.—
Beldam, I think we watch'd you at an
inch.—
What, madam, are you there? the king and
commonweal
Are deeply indebted for this piece of pains:
My lord protector will, I doubt it not,
See you well guerdon'd for these good de-
serts.

Duch. Not half so bad as thine to England's king,
Injurious duke, that threatest where's no
cause.

Buck. True, madam, none at all:—what
call you this?
[*Showing her the papers.*
Away with them! let them be clapp'd up
close,
And kept asunder.—You, madam, shall with
us.—
Stafford, take her to thee.—
We'll see your trinkets here all forthcom-
ing.—
All, away!
[*Exeunt, above,* DUCHESS *and* HUME,
guarded, below, SOUTH., BOLING.,
&c., *guarded.*

York. Lord Buckingham, methinks you
watch'd her well:

A pretty plot, well chosen to build upon!
Now, pray, my lord, let's see the devil's writ.
What have we here? [*Reads.*
The duke yet lives that Henry shall depose;
But him outlive, and die a violent death.
Why, this is just,
Aio te, Æacida, Romanos vincere posse.
Well, to the rest:
Tell me what fate awaits the Duke of Suf-
folk?
By water shall he die and take his end.—
What shall betide the Duke of Somerset?
Let him shun castles;
Safer shall he be upon the sandy plains
Than where castles mounted stand.
Come, come, my lords;
These oracles are hardly attain'd,
And hardly understood. [*Albans.*
The king is now in progress toward Saint
With him the husband of this lovely lady:
Thither go these news, as fast as horse can
carry them,—
A sorry breakfast for my lord protector.
  Buck. Your grace shall give me leave, my
Lord of York,
To be the post, in hope of his reward.
  York. At your pleasure, my good lord.—
Who's within there, ho!

Enter c Servant.

Invite my Lords of Salisbury and Warwick
To sup with me to-morrow night.—Away!
[*Exeunt.*

ACT II.

Scene I.—*Saint Albans.*

Enter King Henry, Queen Margaret, Gloster, Cardinal, *and* Suffolk, *with* Falconers *hollaing.*

  Q. Mar. Believe me, lords, for flying at the
brook,
I saw not better sport these seven years' day:
Yet, by your leave, the wind was very high;
And, ten to one, old Joan had not gone out.
  K. Hen. But what a point, my lord, your
falcon made,
And what a pitch she flew above the rest!—
To see how God in all his creatures works!
Yea, man and birds are fain of climbing high.
  Suf. No marvel, an it like your majesty,
My lord protector's hawks do tower so well;
They know their master loves to be aloft,
And bears his thoughts above his falcon's
pitch.
  Glo. My lord, 'tis but a base ignoble mind
That mounts no higher than a bird can soar.
  Car. I thought as much; he would be
above the clouds. [by that?
  Glo. Ay, my lord cardinal,—how think you
Were it not good your grace could fly to
heaven?
  K. Hen. The treasury of everlasting joy!

  Car. Thy heaven is on earth; thine eyes
and thoughts
Beat on a crown, the treasure of thy heart;
Pernicious protector, dangerous peer,
That smooth'st it so with king and common-
weal!
  Glo. What, cardinal, is your priesthood
grown peremptory?
Tantæne animis cælestibus iræ? [malice;
Churchmen so hot? good uncle, hide such
With such holiness can you do it? [comes
  Suf. No malice, sir; no more than well be-
So good a quarrel and so bad a peer.
  Glo. As who, my lord?
  Suf. Why, as you, my lord,
An't like your lordly lord-protectorship.
  Glo. Why, Suffolk, England knows thine
insolence.
  Q. Mar. And thy ambition, Gloster.
  K. Hen. I pr'ythee, peace,
Good queen, and whet not on these furious
peers;
For blessed are the peacemakers on earth.
  Car. Let me be blessed for the peace I
make,
Against this proud protector, with my sword!
  Glo. Faith, holy uncle, would 'twere come
to that [*Aside to* Car.
  Car. Marry, when thou dar'st.
[*Aside to* Glo.
  Glo. Make up no factious numbers for the
matter;
In thine own person answer thy abuse.
[*Aside to* Car.
  Car. Ay, where thou dar'st not peep: an
if thou dar'st,
This evening on the east side of the grove.
[*Aside to* Glo.
  K. Hen. How now, my lords!
  Car. Believe me, cousin Gloster,
Had not your man put up the fowl so sud-
denly,
We had had more sport.—Come with thy
two-hand sword. [*Aside to* Glo.
  Glo. True, uncle.
  Car. Are ye advis'd?—the east side of the
grove? [*Aside to* Glo.
  Glo. Cardinal, I am with you.
[*Aside to* Car.
  K. Hen. Why, how now, uncle Gloster!
  Glo. Talking of hawking; nothing else, my
lord.—
Now, by God's mother, priest, I'll shave your
crown for this,
Or all my fence shall fail. [*Aside to* Car.
  Car. Medice teipsum;
Protector, see to 't well, protect yourself.
[*Aside to* Glo.
  K. Hen. The winds grow high; so do your
stomachs, lords.
How irksome is this music to my heart!
When such strings jar, what hope! of har-
mony?

I pray, my lords, let me compound this strife.

Enter a Townsman *of Saint Albans, crying*
"A Miracle!"

Glo. What means this noise?
Fellow, what miracle dost thou proclaim?
Towns. A miracle! a miracle!
Suf. Come to the king, and tell him what
     miracle.   [bans' shrine,
Towns. Forsooth, a blind man at St. Al-
Within this half hour hath receiv'd his sight;
A man that ne'er saw in his life before.
K. Hen. Now, God be prais'd that to be-
     lieving souls
Gives light in darkness, comfort in despair!

Enter the Mayor of St. Albans *and his*
brethren; and SIMPCOX, *borne between*
two persons in a chair, his WIFE *and a*
multitude following.

Car. Here comes the townsmen on pro-
     cession,
To present your highness with the man.
K. Hen. Great is his comfort in this earth-
     ly vale,
Although by his sight his sin be multiplied.
Glo. Stand by, my masters:—bring him
     near the king;
His highness' pleasure is to talk with him.
K. Hen. Good fellow, tell us here the cir-
     cumstance,
That we for thee may glorify the Lord.
What, hast thou been long blind and now re-
     stor'd?
Simp. Born blind, an't please your grace.
Wife. Ay, indeed, was he.
Suf. What woman is this?
Wife. His wife, an't like your worship.
Glo. Hadst thou been his mother, thou
     couldst have better told.
K. Hen. Where wert thou born?
Simp. At Berwick in the north, an't like
     your grace.
K. Hen. Poor soul, God's goodness hath
     been great to thee:
Let never day nor night unhallow'd pass,
But still remember what the Lord hath done.
Q. Mar. Tell me, good fellow, cam'st thou
     here by chance,
Or of devotion, to this holy shrine?
Simp. God knows, of pure devotion; be-
     ing call'd
A hundred times and oftener, in my sleep,
By good Saint Alban; who said, *Simpcox,*
     come,—
Come, offer at my shrine, and I will help thee.
Wife. Most true, forsooth; and many
     time and oft
Myself have heard a voice to call him so.
Car. What, art thou lame?
Simp. Ay, God Almighty help me!
Suf. How cam'st thou so?
Simp. A fall off a tree.

Wife. A plum-tree, master.
Glo. How long hast thou been blind?
Simp. O, born so, master.
Glo. What, and wouldst climb a tree?
Simp. But that in all my life, when I was
     a youth.   [very dear.
Wife. Too true; and bought his climbing
Glo. Mass, thou lov'dst plums well that
     wouldst venture so.
Simp. Alas, good master, my wife desir'd
     some damsons,
And made me climb, with danger of my life.
Glo. A subtle knave! but yet it shall not
     serve.—   [open them:—
Let me see thine eyes:—wink now;—now
In my opinion yet thou see'st not well.
Simp. Yes, master, clear as day, I thank
     God and Saint Alban.
Glo. Say'st thou me so? What color is this
     cloak of?
Simp. Red, master; red as blood.
Glo. Why, that's well said. What colour is
     my gown of?
Simp. Black, forsooth; coal-black as jet.
K. Hen. Why, then, thou know'st what
     colour jet is of?
Suf. And yet, I think, jet did he never see.
Glo. But cloaks and gowns, before this
     day, a many.
Wife. Never, before this day, in all his
     life.
Glo. Tell me, sirrah, what's my name?
Simp. Alas, master, I know not.
Glo. What's his name?
Simp. I know not.
Glo. Nor his?
Simp. No, indeed, master.
Glo. What's thine own name?
Simp. Saunder Simpcox, an' if it please
     you, master.
Glo. Then, Saunder, sit there, the lyingest
knave in Christendom. If thou hadst been
born blind, thou mightst as well have known
all our names as thus to name the several
colours we do wear. Sight may distinguish of
colours; but suddenly to nominate them all,
it is impossible.—My lords, Saint Alban here
hath done a miracle; and would ye not think
his cunning to be great that could restore
this cripple to his legs again?
Simp. O master, that ye could!
Glo. My masters of Saint Albans, have
you not beadles in your town, and things
called whips?
May. Yes, my lord, if it please your grace.
Glo. Then send for one presently.
May. Sirrah, go fetch the beadle hither
     straight.   [*Exit an* Attendant.
Glo. Now fetch me a stool hither by and
by.
Now, sirrah, if you mean to save yourself
     from whipping, leap me over this stool
     and run away.

Simp. Alas, master, I am not able to stand
alone:
You go about to torture me in vain.

Enter a BEADLE *with whips.*

Glo. Well, sir, we must have you find your
legs. Sirrah beadle, whip him till he
leap over that same stool.

Bead. I will, my lord. Come on, sirrah;
off with your doublet quickly.

Simp. Alas, master, what shall I do? I am
not able to stand.

[*After the* BEADLE *hath hit him once, he
leaps over the stool and runs away;
and they follow and cry, 'A miracle!'*

King. O God, seest Thou this, and bearest
so long?

Queen. It made me laugh to see the villain
run.

Glo. Follow the knave; and take his drab
away.

Wife. Alas, sir, we did it for pure need.

Glo. Let them be whipped through every
market-town, till they come to Berwick, from whence they came.

[*Exeunt* WIFE, BEADLE, MAYOR, *etc.*

Car. Duke Humphrey has done a miracle
to-day.

Suf. True; made the lame to leap and fly
away.

Glo. But you have done more miracles
than I;
You made in a day, my lord, whole towns
to fly.

Enter BUCKINGHAM.

King. What tidings with our cousin Buckingham?

Buck. Such as my heart doth tremble to
unfold.
A sort of naughty persons, lewdly bent,
Under the countenance and confederacy
Of Lady Eleanor, the protector's wife,
The ringleader and head of all this rout,
Have practiced dangerously against your
state,
Dealing with witches and with conjurers:
Whom we have apprehended in the fact;
Raising up wicked spirits from under ground,
Demanding of King Henry's life and death,
And other of your highness' privy-council;
As more at large your grace shall understand.

Car. [*Aside to* GLO.] And so, my lord protector, by this means
Your lady is forthcoming yet at London.
This news, I think, hath turn'd your weapon's edge;
'Tis like, my lord, you will not keep your
hour.

Glo. Ambitious churchman, leave to afflict my heart:
Sorrow and grief have vanquish'd all my
powers;

And, vanquish'd as I am, I yield to thee,
Or to the meanest groom.

King. O God, what mischief's work the
wicked ones,
Heaping confusion on their own heads thereby!

Queen. Gloucester, see here the tainture of
thy nest,
And look thyself be faultless, thou wert best.

Glou. Madam, for myself, to heaven I do
appeal,
How I have loved my king and common-
weal:
And, for my wife, I know not how it stands;
Sorry I am to hear what I have heard:
Noble she is, but if she have forgot
Honor and virtue and conversed with such
As, like to pitch, defile nobility,
I banish her my bed and company,
And give her as a prey to law and shame,
That hath dishonor'd Gloucester's honest
name.

King. Well, for this night we will repose
us here:
To-morrow toward London back again,
To look into this business thoroughly,
And call these foul offenders to their answers,
And poise the cause in justice's equal scales,
Whose beam stands sure, whose rightful
cause prevails. [*Flourish. Exeunt.*

SCENE II.—LONDON. *The* DUKE OF YORK'S
Garden.

Enter YORK, SALISBURY, *and* WARWICK.

York. Now, my good Lords of Salisbury
and Warwick,
Our simple supper ended, give me leave
In this close walk to satisfy myself,
In craving your opinion of my title,
Which is infallible, to England's crown.

Sal. My lord, I long to hear it at full.

War. Sweet York, begin: and if thy claim
be good,
The Nevils are thy subjects to command.

York. Then thus:
Edward the Third, my lords, had seven sons:
The first, Edward the Black Prince, Prince
of Wales;
The second, William of Hatfield, and the
third,
Lionel Duke of Clarence; next to whom
Was John of Gaunt, the Duke of Lancaster;
The fifth was Edmund Langley, Duke of
York;
The sixth was Thomas of Woodstock, Duke
of Gloucester;
William of Windsor was the seventh and
last.
Edward the Black Prince died before his
father,
And left behind him Richard, his only son,
Who after Edward the Third's death reign'd
as king;

Till Henry Bolingbroke, Duke of Lancaster,
The eldest son and heir of John of Gaunt,
Crown'd by the name of Henry the Fourth,
Seized on the realm, deposed the rightful
   king,
Sent his poor queen to France, from whence
   she came,
And him to Pomfret; where, as all you know,
Harmless Richard was murder'd traitorously.
   War. Father, the duke hath told the truth;
Thus got the house of Lancaster the crown.
   York. Which now they hold by force and
   not by right;
For Richard, the first son's heir, being dead,
The issue of the next son should have reign'd.
   Sal. But William of Hatfield died without
   an heir.
   York. The third son, Duke of Clarence,
   from whose line
I claim the crown, had issue, Philippe, a
   daughter,
Who married Edmund Mortimer, Earl of
   March:
Edmund had issue, Roger Earl of March;
Roger had issue, Edmund, Anne and Eleanor.
   Sal. This Edmund, in the reign of Boling-
   broke,
As I have read, laid claim unto the crown;
And, but for Owen Glendower, had been
   king,
Who kept him in captivity till he died.
But to the rest.
   York.   His eldest sister, Anne,
My mother, being heir unto the crown,
Married Richard Earl of Cambridge; who
   was son
To Edmund Langley, Edward the Third's
   fifth son.
By her I claim the kingdom: she was heir
To Roger Earl of March, who was the son
Of Edmund Mortimer, who married Philippe,
Sole daughter unto Lionel Duke of Clarence:
So, if the issue of the elder son
Succeed before the younger, I am king.
   War. What plain proceeding is more plain
   than this?
Henry doth claim the crown from John of
   Gaunt,
The fourth son; York claims it from the
   third.
Till Lionel's issue fails, his should not reign:
It fails not yet, but flourishes in thee
And in thy sons, fair slips of such a stock.
Then, father Salisbury, kneel we together;
And in this private plot be we the first
That shall salute our rightful sovereign
With honor of his birthright to the crown.
   Both. Long live our sovereign Richard,
   England's king!
   York. We thank you, lords. But I am not
   your king
Till I be crown'd, and that my sword be
   stain'd

With heart-blood of the house of Lancaster;
And that's not suddenly to be perform'd,
But with advice and silent secrecy.
Do you as I do in these dangerous days:
Wink at the Duke of Suffolk's insolence,
At Beaufort's pride, at Somerset's ambition,
At Buckingham and all the crew of them,
Till they have snared the shepherd of the
   flock,
That virtuous prince, the good Duke Hum-
   phrey:
'Tis that they seek, and they in seeking that
Shall find their deaths, if York can prophesy.
   Sal. My lord, break we off; we know your
   mind at full.
   War. My heart assures me that the Earl of
   Warwick
Shall one day make the Duke of York a king.
   York. And, Nevil, this I do assure myself:
Richard shall live to make the Earl of War-
   wick
The greatest man in England but the king.
                         [Exeunt.

SCENE III.—*A Hall of Justice.*

Sound trumpets. Enter the KING, *the* QUEEN,
   GLOUCESTER, YORK, SUFFOLK, *and* SALIS-
   BURY; *the* DUCHESS OF GLOUCESTER, MAR-
   GERY JOURDAIN, SOUTHWELL, HUME, *and*
   BOLINGBROKE, *under guard.*

   King. Stand forth, Dame Eleanor Cobham,
   Gloucester's wife:
In sight of God and us, your guilt is great:
Receive the sentence of the law for sins
Such as by God's book are adjudged to death.
You four, from hence to prison back again;
From thence unto the place of execution:
The witch in Smithfield shall be burn'd to
   ashes,
And you three shall be strangled on the gal-
   lows.
You, madam, for you are more nobly born,
Despoiled of your honor in your life,
Shall, after three days' open penance done,
Live in your country here in banishment,
With Sir John Stanley, in the Isle of Man.
   Duch. Welcome is banishment; welcome
   were my death.
   Glo. Eleanor, the law, thou see'st, hath
   judged thee:
I cannot justify whom the law condemns.
         [Exeunt DUCHESS *and other* prisoners,
                              guarded.
Mine eyes are full of tears, my heart of grief.
Ah, Humphrey, this dishonor in thine age
Will bring thy head with sorrow to the
   ground!
I beseech your majesty, give me leave to go;
Sorrow would solace and mine age would
   ease.
   King. Stay, Humphrey Duke of Glouces-
   ter: ere thou go,
Give up thy staff: Henry will to himself

Protector be; and God shall be my hope,
My stay, my guide and lantern to my feet:
And go in peace, Humphrey, no less beloved
Than when thou wert protector to thy king.

Queen. I see no reason why a king of years
Should be to be protected like a child.
God and King Henry govern England's realm.
Give up your staff, sir, and the king his realm.

Glo. My staff? here, noble Henry, is my staff:
As willingly do I the same resign
As e'er thy father Henry made it mine;
And even as willingly at thy feet I leave it
As others would ambitiously receive it.
Farewell, good king: when I am dead and gone,
May honorable peace attend thy throne!
[*Exit.*

Queen. Why, now is Henry king, and Margaret queen;
And Humphrey Duke of Gloucester scarce himself,
That bears so shrewd a maim; two pulls at once;
His lady banish'd, and a limb lopp'd off.
This staff of honor raught, there let it stand
Where it best fits to be, in Henry's hand.

Suf. Thus droops this lofty pine and hangs his sprays;
Thus Eleanor's pride dies in her youngest days.

York. Lords, let him go. Please it your majesty,
This is the day appointed for the combat;
And ready are the appellant and defendant,
The armorer and his man, to enter the lists,
So please your highness to behold the fight.

Queen. Aye, good my lord; for purposely therefore
Left I the court, to see this quarrel tried.

King. O' God's name, see the lists and all things fit: [right!
Here let them end it; and God defend the right!

York. I never saw a fellow worse bested,
Or more afraid to fight, than is the appellant,
The servant of this armorer, my lords.

Enter at one door, HORNER, *the* Armorer, *and his* Neighbors, *drinking to him so much that he is drunk; and he enters with a drum before him and his staff with a sandbag fastened to it; and at the other door* PETER, *his man, with a drum and a sandbag, and* 'Prentices *drinking to him.*

First Neigh. Here, neighbor Horner, I drink to you in a cup of sack: and fear not, neighbor, you shall do well enough.

Sec. Neigh. And here, neighbor, here's a cup of charneco.

Third Neigh. And here's a pot of good double beer, neighbor: drink, and fear not your man.

Hor. Let it come, i' faith, and I'll pledge you all; and a fig for Peter!

First 'Pren. Here, Peter, I drink to thee: and be not afraid.

Sec. 'Pren. Be merry, Peter, and fear not thy master: fight for credit of the 'prentices.

Peter. I thank you all: drink, and pray for me, I pray you; for I think I have taken my last draught in this world. Here, Robin, an if I die, I give thee my apron: and, Will, thou shalt have my hammer: and here, Tom, take all the money that I have. O Lord bless me! I pray God! for I am never able to deal with my master, he hath learnt so much fence already.

Sal. Come, leave your drinking, and fall to blows. Sirrah, what's thy name?

Peter. Peter, forsooth.

Sal. Peter! what more?

Peter. Thump.

Sal. Thump! then see thou thump thy master well.

Hor. Masters, I am come hither, as it were, upon my man's instigation, to prove him a knave and myself an honest man: and touching the Duke of York, I will take my death, I never meant him any ill, nor the king, nor the queen: and therefore, Peter, have at thee with a downright blow!

York. Dispatch: this knave's tongue begins to double. Sound, trumpets, alarum to the combatants!
[*Alarum. They fight, and* PETER *strikes him down.*

Hor. Hold, Peter, hold! I confess, I confess treason.   [*Dies.*

York. Take away his weapon. Fellow, thank God, and the good wine in the master's way.

Peter. O God, have I overcome mine enemy in this presence? O Peter, thou hast prevailed in right!

King. Go, take hence that traitor from our sight;
For by his death we do perceive his guilt:
And God in justice hath reveal'd to us
The truth and innocence of this poor fellow,
Which he had thought to have murder'd wrongfully.
Come, fellow, follow us for thy reward.
[*Sound a flourish. Exeunt.*

SCENE IV.—*A Street.*

Enter GLOUCESTER *and his* Serving-men, *in mourning cloaks.*

Glo. Thus sometimes hath the brightest day a cloud:
And after summer evermore succeeds

Barren winter, with his wrathful nipping
 cold:
So cares and joys abound, as seasons fleet.
Sirs, what's o'clock?
 Serv.   Ten, my lord.
 Glo. Ten is the hour that was appointed
 me
To watch the coming of my punish'd
 duchess:
Uneath may she endure the flinty streets,
To tread them with her tender-feeling feet.
Sweet Nell, ill can thy noble mind abrook
The abject people gazing on thy face,
With envious looks laughing at thy shame,
That erst did follow thy proud chariot-
 wheels,
When thou didst ride in triumph through the
 streets.
But, soft! I think she comes; and I'll prepare
My tear-stain'd eyes to see her miseries.

Enter the DUCHESS OF GLOUCESTER *in a*
 white sheet, and a taper burning in her
 hand; with SIR JOHN STANLEY, *the* Sheriff,
 and Officers.

 Serv. So please your grace, we'll take her
 from the sheriff.
 Glo. No, stir not, for your lives; let her
 pass by.
 Duch. Come you, my lord, to see my open
 shame?
Now thou dost penance too. Look how they
 gaze!
See how the giddy multitude do point,
And nod their heads, and throw their eyes on
 thee!
Ah, Gloucester, hide thee from their hateful
 looks,
And, in thy closet pent up, rue my shame,
And ban thine enemies, both mine and
 thine!
 Glo. Be patient, gentle Nell; forget this
 grief.
 Duch. Ah, Gloucester, teach me to forget
 myself.
For whilst I think I am thy married wife,
And thou a prince, protector of this land,
Methinks I should not thus be led along,
Mail'd up in shame, with papers on my back,
And follow'd with a rabble that rejoice
To see my tears and hear my deep-fet groans.
The ruthless flint doth cut my tender feet,
And when I start, the envious people laugh,
And bid me be advised how I tread.
Ah, Humphrey, can I bear this shameful
 yoke?
Trow'st thou that e'er I'll look upon the
 world,
Or count them happy that enjoy the sun?
No; dark shall be my light and night my
 day;
To think upon my pomp shall be my hell.

Sometime I'll say, I am Duke Humphrey's
 wife,
And he a prince and ruler of the land:
Yet so he ruled, and such a prince he was,
As he stood by whilst I, his forlorn duchess,
Was made a wonder and a pointing-stock
To every idle rascal follower.
But be thou mild and blush not at my shame,
Not stir at nothing till the axe of death
Hang over thee, as, sure, it shortly will;
For Suffolk—he that can do all in all
With her that hateth thee and hates us all—
And York and impious Beaufort, that false
 priest,
Have all limed bushes to betray thy wings,
And, fly thou how thou canst, they'll tangle
 thee:
But fear not thou, until thy foot be snared,
Nor never seek prevention of thy foes.
 Glo. Ah Nell, forbear! thou aimest all
 awry;
I must offend before I be attainted;
And had I twenty times so many foes,
And each of them had twenty times their
 power,
All these could not procure me any scathe,
So long as I am loyal, true and crimeless.
Wouldst have me rescue thee from this re-
 proach?
Why, yet thy scandal were not wiped away,
But I in danger for the breach of law.
Thy greatest help is quiet, gentle Nell:
I pray thee, sort thy heart to patience;
These few days' wonder will be quickly worn.

Enter a Herald.

 Her. I summon your grace to his maj-
 esty's parliament,
Holden at Bury the first of this next month.
 Glo. And my consent ne'er ask'd herein
 before!
This is close dealing. Well, I will be there.
           [*Exit* Herald.
My Nell, I take my leave: and, master sher-
 iff,
Let not her penance exceed the king's com-
 mission,
 Sher. An't please your grace, here my com-
 mission stays,
And Sir John Stanley is appointed now
To take her with him to the Isle of Man.
 Glo. Must you, Sir John, protect my lady
 here?
 Stan. So am I given in charge, may't please
 your grace.
 Glo. Entreat her not the worse in that I
 pray
You use her well: the world may laugh
 again;
And I may live to do you kindness if
You do it her: and so, Sir John, farewell!
 Duch. What, gone, my lord, and bid me
 not farewell!

Glo. Witness my tears, I cannot stay to speak.

[*Exeunt* GLOUCESTER *and* Serving-men.

Duch. Art thou gone too? all comfort go with thee!
For none abides with me: my joy is death,—
Death, at whose name I oft have been afear'd,
Because I wish'd this world's eternity.
Stanley, I prithee, go, and take me hence;
I care not whither, for I beg no favor,
Only convey me where thou art commanded.

Stan. Why, madam, that is to the Isle of Man;
There to be used according to your state.

Duch. That's bad enough, for I am but reproach:
And shall I then be used reproachfully?

Stan. Like to a duchess, and Duke Humphrey's lady;
According to that state you shall be used.

Duch. Sheriff, farewell, and better than I fare,
Although thou hast been conduct of my shame.

Sher. It is my office; and, madam, pardon me.

Duch. Aye, aye, farewell; thy office is discharged.
Come, Stanley, shall we go?

Stan. Madam, your penance done, throw off this sheet,
And go we to attire you for our journey.

Duch. My shame will not be shifted with my sheet:
No, it will hang upon my richest robes,
And show itself, attire me how I can.
Go, lead the way; I long to see my prison.

[*Exeunt.*

ACT III.

SCENE I.—*The Abbey at Bury St. Edmund's.*

Sound a Sennet. Enter KING, QUEEN, CARDINAL BEAUFORT, SUFFOLK, YORK, BUCKINGHAM, SALISBURY *and* WARWICK *to the Parliament.*

King. I muse my Lord of Gloucester is not come
'Tis not his wont to be the hindmost man,
Whate'er occasion keeps him from us now.

Queen. Can you not see? or will ye not observe
The strangeness of his alter'd countenance?
With what a majesty he bears himself,
How insolent of late he is become,
How proud, how peremptory, and unlike himself?
We know the time since he was mild and affable,
And if we did but glance a far-off look,
Immediately he was upon his knee,
That all the court admired him for submission;
But meet him now, and, be it in the morn,
When every one will give the time of day,
He knits his brow and shows an angry eye,
And passeth by with stiff unbowed knee,
Disdaining duty that to us belongs.
Small curs are not regarded when they grin;
But great men tremble when the lion roars;
And Humphrey is no little man in England.
First note that he is near you in descent,
And should you fall, he is the next will mount.
Me seemeth then it is no policy,
Respecting what a rancorous mind he bears,
And his advantage following your decease,
That he should come about your royal person,
Or be admitted to your highness' council.
By flattery hath he won the commons' hearts,
And when he please to make commotion,
'Tis to be feared they all will follow him.
Now 'tis the spring, and weeds are shallow-rooted;
Suffer them now, and they'll o'ergrow the garden,
And choke the herbs for want of husbandry.
The reverent care I bear unto my lord
Made me collect these dangers in the duke.
If it be fond, call it a woman's fear;
Which fear if better reasons can supplant,
I will subscribe and say I wrong'd the duke.
My Lord of Suffolk, Buckingham, and York,
Reprove my allegation, if you can;
Or else conclude my words effectual.

Suf. Well hath your highness seen into this duke;
And, had I first been put to speak my mind,
I think I should have told your grace's tale.
The duchess by his subornation,
Upon my life, began her devilish practices:
Or, if he were not privy to those faults,
Yet, by reputing of his high descent,
As next the king he was successive heir,
As such high vaunts of his nobility,
Did instigate the bedlam brain-sick duchess
By wicked means to frame our sovereign's fall.
Smooth runs the water where the brook is deep;
And in his simple show he harbors treason.
The fox barks not when he would steal the lamb.
No, no, my sovereign; Gloucester is a man
Unsounded yet and full of deep deceit.

Car. Did he not, contrary to form of law,
Devise strange deaths for small offences done?

York. And did he not, in his protectorship,
Levy great sums of money through the realm
For soldiers' pay in France, and never sent it?

By means whereof the towns each day revolted.

Buck. Tut, these are petty faults to faults
unknown,
Which time will bring to light in smooth
Duke Humphrey.

King. My lords, at once: the care you
have of us,
To mow down thorns that would annoy our
foot,
Is worthy praise: but, shall I speak my con-
science,
Our kinsman Gloucester is as innocent
From meaning treason to our royal person,
As is the sucking lamb or harmless dove:
The duke is virtuous, mild and too well given
To dream on evil or to work my downfall.

Queen. Ah, what's more dangerous than
this fond affiance!
Seems he a dove? his feathers are but bor-
row'd,
For he's disposed as the hateful raven:
Is he a lamb? his skin is surely lent him,
For he's inclined as is the ravenous wolf.
Who cannot steal a shape that means deceit?
Take heed, my lord; the welfare of us all
Hangs on the cutting short that fraudful
man.

Enter SOMERSET.

Som. All health unto my gracious sovereign!

King. Welcome, Lord Somerset. What
news from France?

Som. That all your interest in those territories
Is utterly bereft you; all is lost.

King. Cold news, Lord Somerset: but
God's will be done!

York. [*Aside*] Cold news for me; for I
had hope of France
As firmly as I hope for fertile England.
Thus are my blossoms blasted in the bud,
And caterpillars eat my leaves away;
But I will remedy this gear ere long,
Or sell my title for a glorious grave.

Enter GLOUCESTER.

Glo. All happiness unto my lord the king!
Pardon, my liege, that I have stay'd so long.

Suf. Nay, Gloucester, know that thou art
come too soon,
Unless thou wert more loyal than thou art:
I do arrest thee of high treason here.

Glo. Well, Suffolk, thou shalt not see me
blush,
Nor change my countenance for this arrest:
A heart unspotted is not easily daunted.
The purest spring is not so free from mud
As I am clear from treason to my sovereign:
Who can accuse me? wherein am I guilty?

York. 'Tis thought, my lord, that you took
bribes of France,

And, being protector, stay'd the soldiers' pay;
By means whereof his highness hath lost
France.

Glo. Is it but thought so? what are they
that think it?
I never robb'd the soldiers of their pay,
Nor ever had one penny bribe from France
So help me God, as I have watch'd the
night,
Aye, night by night, in studying good for
England!
That doit that e'er I wrested from the king,
Or any groat I hoarded to my use,
Be brought against me at my trial-day!
No; many a pound of mine own proper store,
Because I would not tax the needy commons,
Have I dispursed to the garrisons,
And never ask'd for restitution.

Car. It serves you well, my lord, to say so
much.

Glo. I say no more than truth, so help me
God!

York. In your protectorship you did de-
vise
Strange tortures for offenders never heard of,
That England was defamed by tyranny.

Glo. Why, 'tis well known that, whiles I
was protector,
Pity was all the fault that was in me;
For I should melt at an offender's tears,
And lowly words were ransom for their fault.
Unless it were a bloody murderer,
Or foul felonious thief that fleeced poor pas-
sengers,
I never gave them condign punishment:
Murder, indeed, that bloody sin, I tortured
Above the felon or what trespass else.

Suf. My lord, these faults are easy,
quickly answer'd:
But mightier crimes are laid unto your
charge,
Whereof you cannot easily purge yourself.
I do arrest you in his highness' name;
And here commit you to my lord cardinal
To keep, until your further time of trial.

King. My Lord of Gloucester, 'tis my spe-
cial hope
That you will clear yourself from all suspect:
My conscience tells me you are innocent.

Glo. Ah, gracious lord, these days are
dangerous:
Virtue is choked with foul ambition,
And charity chased hence by rancor's hand;
Foul subordination is predominant,
And equity exiled your highness' land.
I know their complot is to have my life;
And if my death might make this island
happy,
And prove the period of their tyranny,
I would expend it with all willingness:
But mine is made the prologue to their play;
For thousands more, that yet suspect no
peril,

Will not conclude their plotted tragedy.
Beaufort's red sparkling eyes blab his heart's
  malice,
And Suffolk's cloudy brow his stormy hate;
Sharp Buckingham unburthens with his
  tongue
The envious load that lies upon his heart;
And dogged York, that reaches at the moon,
Whose overweening arm I have pluck'd back,
By false accuse doth level at my life:
And you, my sovereign lady, with the rest,
Causeless have laid disgraces on my head,
And with your best endeavor have stirr'd up
My liefest liege to be mine enemy:
Aye, all of you have laid your heads to-
  gether—
Myself had notice of your conventicles—
And all to make away my guiltless life.
I shall not want false witness to condemn
  me,
Nor store of treasons to augment my guilt;
The ancient proverb will be well effected:
'A staff is quickly found to beat a dog.'
  Car. My liege, his railing is intolerable:
If those that care to keep your royal person
From treason's secret knife and traitors'
  rage
Be thus upbraided, chid and rated at,
And the offender granted scope of speech,
'Twill make them cool in zeal unto your
  grace.
  Suf. Hath he not twit our sovereign lady
  here
With ignominious words, though clerkly
  couch'd,
As if she had suborned some to swear
False allegations to o'erthrow his state?
  Queen. But I can give the loser leave to
  chide.
  Glo. Far truer spoke than meant: I lose,
  indeed;
Beshrew the winners, for they play'd me
  false!   [speak.
And well such losers may have leave to
  Buck. He'll wrest the sense and hold us
  here all day:
Lord cardinal, he is your prisoner.
  Car. Sirs, take away the duke, and guard
  him sure.
  Glo. Ah! thus King Henry throws away
  his crutch,
Before his legs be firm to bear his body.
Thus is the shepherd beaten from thy side,
And wolves are gnarling who shall gnaw thee
  first.
Ah, that my fear were false! ah, that it were!
For, good King Henry, thy decay I fear.
                              [*Exit, guarded.*
  King. My lords, what to your wisdom
  seemeth best,
Do or undo, as if ourself were here.
  Queen. What, will your highness leave the
  Parliament?

  King. Aye, Margaret; my heart is drown'd
  with grief,
Whose flood begins to flow within mine eyes,
My body round engirt with misery,
For what's more miserable than discontent?
Ah, uncle Humphrey! in thy face I see
The map of honor, truth and loyalty:
And yet, good Humphrey, is the hour to
  come
That e'er I proved thee false or fear'd thy
  faith.
What louring star now envies thy estate,
That these great lords and Margaret our
  queen
Do seek subversion of thy harmless life?
Thou never didst them wrong nor no man
  wrong;
And as the butcher takes away the calf,
And binds the wretch, and beats it when it
  strays,
Bearing it to the bloody slaughter-house,
Even so remorseless have they borne him
  hence;
And as the dam runs lowing up and down,
Looking the way her harmless young one
  went,
And can do nought but wail her darling's
  loss,
Even so myself bewails good Gloucester's
  case
With sad unhelpful tears, and with dimm'd
  eyes
Look after him and cannot do him good,
So mighty are his vowed enemies.
His fortunes I will weep, and 'twixt each
  groan
Say 'Who's a traitor? Gloucester he is none.'
  [*Exeunt all but* QUEEN, CARDINAL BEAU-
  FORT, SUFFOLK *and* YORK. SOMERSET *re-
  mains apart.*
  Queen. Free lords, cold snow melts with
  the sun's hot beams.
Henry my lord is cold in great affairs,
Too full of foolish pity, and Gloucester's
  show
Beguiles him, as the mournful crocodile
With sorrow snares relenting passengers,
Or as the snake roll'd in a flowering bank,
With shining checker'd slough, doth sting a
  child
That for the beauty thinks it excellent.
Believe me, lords, were none more wise than
  I—
And yet herein I judge mine own with
  good—
This Gloucester should be quickly rid the
  world
To rid us from the fear we have of him.
  Car. That he should die is worthy policy;
But yet we want a color for his death:
'Tis meet he be condemn'd by course of law.
  Suf. But, in my mind, that were no policy:
The commons haply rise, to save his life;

The king will labor still to save his life,
And yet we have but trivial argument,
More than mistrust, that shows him worthy death.

York. So that, by this, you would not have him die.

Suf. Ah, York, no man alive so fain as I!

York. 'Tis York that hath more reason for his death.

But, my lord cardinal, and you, my Lord of Suffolk,
Say as you think, and speak it from your souls:
Were't not all one, an empty eagle were set
To guard the chicken from a hungry kite,
As place Duke Humphrey for the king's protector?   [of death.

Queen. So the poor chicken should be sure

Suf. Madam, 'tis true; and were't not madness, then,
To make the fox surveyor of the fold:
Who being accused a crafty murderer,
His guilt should be but idly posted over,
Because his purpose is not executed.
No; let him die, in that he is a fox,
By nature proved an enemy to the flock,
Before his chaps he stain'd with crimson blood,
As Humphrey, proved by reasons, to my liege.
And do not stand on quillets how to slay him:
Be it by gins, by snares, by subtlety,
Sleeping or waking, 'tis no matter how,
So he be dead; for that is good deceit
Which mates him first that first intends deceit.

Queen. Thrice-noble Suffolk, 'tis resolutely spoke.

Suf. Not resolute, except so much were done;
For things are often spoke and seldom meant:
But that my heart accordeth with my tongue,
Seeing the deed is meritorious,
And to preserve my sovereign from his foe,
Say but the word, and I will be his priest.

Car. But I would have him dead, my lord of Suffolk,
Ere you can take due orders for a priest:
Say you consent and censure well the deed,
And I'll provide his executioner,
I tender so the safety of my liege.

Suf. Here is my hand, the deed is worthy doing.

Queen. And so say I.

York. And I: and now we three have spoke it.
It skills not greatly who impugns our doom.

Enter a Post.

Post. Great lords, from Ireland am I come amain,

To signify that rebels there are up,
And put the Englishmen unto the sword:
Send succors, lords, and stop the rage betime,
Before the wound do grow uncurable;
For, being green, there is great hope of help.

Car. A breach that craves a quick expedient stop!
What counsel give you in this weighty cause?

York. That Somerset be sent as regent thither:
'Tis meet that lucky ruler be employ'd;
Witness the fortune he hath had in France.

Som. If York, with all his far-fet policy,
Had been the regent there instead of me,
He never would have stay'd in France so long.

York. No, not to lose it all, as thou hast done:
I rather would have lost my life betimes
Than bring a burthen of dishonor home,
By staying there so long till all were lost.
Show me one scar character'd on thy skin:
Men's flesh preserved so whole do seldom win.

Queen. Nay, then, this spark will prove a raging fire.
If wind and fuel be brought to feed it with:
No more, good York; sweet Somerset, be still:
Thy fortune, York, hadst thou been regent there,
Might happily have proved far worse than his.

York. What, worse than nought? nay, then, a shame take all!

Som. And, in the number, thee that wishest shame!

Car. My Lord of York, try what your fortune is.
The uncivil kernes of Ireland are in arms,
And temper clay with blood of Englishmen:
To Ireland will you lead a band of men,
Collected choicely, from each county some
And try your hap against the Irishmen?

York. I will, my lord, so please his majesty.

Suf. Why, our authority is his consent,
And what we do establish he confirms:
Then, noble York, take thou this task in hand.

York. I am content: provide me soldiers, lords,
Whiles I take order for mine own affairs.

Suf. A charge, Lord York, that I will see perform'd.
But now return we to the false Duke Humphrey.

Car. No more of him; for I will deal with him,
That henceforth he shall trouble us no more.
And so break off; the day is almost spent:
Lord Suffolk, you and I must talk of that event.

York. My Lord of Suffolk, within four-
teen days
At Bristol I expect my soldiers;
For there I'll ship them all for Ireland.
  Suf. I'll see it truly done, my Lord of
    York.   [*Exeunt all but York.*
  York. Now, York, or never, steel thy fear-
ful thoughts,
And change misdoubt to resolution:
Be that thou hopest to be, or what thou art
Resign to death; it is not worth the en-
joying:
Let pale-faced fear keep with the mean-born
man,
And find no harbor in a royal heart.
Faster than spring-time showers comes
thought on thought,
And not a thought but thinks on dignity.
My brain more busy than the laboring spider
Weaves tedious snares to trap mine enemies.
Well, nobles, well, 'tis politicly done,
To send me packing with an host of men:
I fear me you but warm the starved snake,
Who, cherish'd in your breasts, will sting
your hearts.
'Twas men I lack'd, and you will give them
me:
I take it kindly; yet be well assured
You put sharp weapons in a madman's hands.
Whiles I in Ireland nourish a mighty band,
I will stir up in England some black storm
Shall blow ten thousand souls to heaven or
hell;
And this fell tempest shall not cease to rage
Until the golden circuit on my head,
Like to the glorious sun's transparent beams,
Do calm the fury of this mad-bred flaw.
And, for a minister of my intent,
I have seduced a headstrong Kentishman,
John Cade of Ashford,
To make commotion, as full well he can,
Under the title of John Mortimer.
In Ireland have I seen this stubborn Cade
Oppose himself against a troop of kernes,
And fought so long, till that his thighs with
darts
Were almost like a sharp-quill'd porpentine;
And, in the end being rescued, I have seen
Him caper upright like a wild Morisco,
Shaking the bloody darts as he his bells.
Full often, like a shag-hair'd crafty kerne,
Hath he conversed with the enemy,
And undiscover'd come to me again,
And given me notice of their villanies.
This devil here shall be my substitute;
For that John Mortimer, which now is dead,
In face, in gait, in speech, he doth resemble:
By this I shall perceive the commons' mind,
How they affect the house and claim of York.
Say he be taken, rack'd and tortured,
I know no pain they can inflict upon him
Will make him say I moved him to those
arms.

Say that he thrive, as 'tis great like he will,
Why, then from Ireland come I with my
strength,
And reap the harvest which that rascal
sow'd;
For Humphrey being dead, as he shall be,
And Henry put apart, the next for me.
                              [*Exit.*

SCENE II

*Bury St. Edmund's. A room of state. Enter
    certain* Murderers, *hastily.*

  First Mur. Run to my Lord of Suffolk;
    let him know
We have dispatch'd the duke, as he com-
manded.
  Sec. Mur. O that it were to do! What have
    we done?
Didst ever hear a man so penitent?

Enter SUFFOLK.

  First Mur. Hence comes my lord.
  Suf. Now, sirs, have you dispatch'd this
    thing?
  First Mur. Aye, my good lord, he's dead.
  Suf. Why, that's well said. Go, get you to
    my house;
I will reward you for this venturous deed.
The king and all the peers are here at hand.
Have you laid fair the bed? Is all things
well,
According as I gave directions?
  First Mur. 'Tis, my good lord.
  Suf. Away, be gone. [*Exeunt* Murderers.

Sound trumpets. Enter the KING, *the* QUEEN,
CARDINAL BEAUFORD, SOMERSET, *with* Attendants.

  King. Go, call our uncle to our presence
    straight;
Say we intend to try his grace to-day,
If he be guilty, as 'tis published.
  Suf. I'll call him presently, my noble lord.
                              [*Exit.*
  King. Lords, take your places; and, I pray
    you all,
Proceed no straiter 'gainst our uncle Glouces-
ter
Than from true evidence of good esteem
He be approved in practice culpable.
  Queen. God forbid any malice should pre-
vail,
That faultless may condemn a nobleman!
Pray God he may acquit him of suspicion!
  King. I thank thee, Nell; these words con-
tent me much.

Re-enter SUFFOLK.

How now! why look'st thou pale? why tremblest thou?
Where is our uncle? what's the matter, Suffolk?

Suf. Dead in his bed, my lord; Gloucester
　is dead.
Queen. Marry, God forfend.
Car. God's secret judgment: I did dream
　to-night
The duke was dumb and could not speak a
　word.　　　　　　　[*The* KING *swoons.*
Queen. How fares my lord? Help, lords!
　the king is dead.　　　　　　　[nose.
Som. Rear up his body; wring him by the
Queen. Run, go, help, help! O Henry, ope
　thine eyes!
Suf. He doth revive again: Madam, be
　patient.
King. O heavenly God!
Queen. How fares my gracious lord?
Suf. Comfort, my sovereign! gracious
　Henry, comfort!
King. What, doth my Lord of Suffolk
　comfort me?
Came he right now to sing a raven's note,
Whose dismal tune bereft my vital powers;
And thinks he that the chirping of a wren,
By crying comfort from a hollow breast,
Can chase away the first-conceived sound?
Hide not thy poison with such sugar'd
　words;
Lay not thy hands on me; forbear, I say;
Their touch affrights me as a serpent's sting.
Thou baleful messenger, out of my sight!
Upon thy eye-balls murderous tyranny
Sits in grim majesty, to fright the world.
Look not upon me, for thine eyes are wound-
　ing:
Yet do not go away: come, basilisk,
And kill the innocent gazer with thy sight;
For in the shade of death I shall find joy;
In life but double death, now Gloucester's
　dead.
　Queen. Why do you rate my Lord of Suf-
　folk thus?
Although the duke was enemy to him,
Yet he most Christian-like laments his death:
And for myself, foe as he was to me,
Might liquid tears, or heart-offending groans,
Or blood-consuming sighs recall his life,
I would be blind with weeping, sick with
　groans,
Look pale as primrose with blood-drinking
　sighs,
And all to have the noble duke alive.
What know I how the world may deem of
　me?
For it is known we were but hollow friends:
It may be judged I made the duke away;
So shall my name with slander's tongue be
　wounded,
And princes' courts be fill'd with my re-
　proach.
This get I by his death: aye me, unhappy!
To be a queen, and crown'd with infamy!
　King. Ah, woe is me for Gloucester,
　wretched man!

Queen. Be woe for me, more wretched
　than he is.
What, dost thou turn away and hide thy
　face?
I am no loathsome leper; look on me.
What! art thou, like the adder, waxen deaf?
Be poisonous too and kill thy forlorn queen.
Is all thy comfort shut in Gloucester's tomb?
Why, then, dame Eleanor was ne'er thy joy.
Erect his statuë and worship it,
And make my image but an alehouse sign.
Was I for this nigh wreck'd upon the sea,
And twice by awkward wind from England's
　bank
Drove back again unto my native clime?
What boded this, but well forewarning wind
Did seem to say 'Seek not a scorpion's nest,
Nor set no footing on this unkind shore'?
What did I then, but cursed the gentle gusts,
And he that loosed them forth their brazen
　caves;
And bid them blow towards England's bless-
　ed shore,
Or turn our stern upon a dreadful rock?
Yet Æolus would not be a murderer,
But left that hateful office unto thee:
The pretty-vaulting sea refused to drown
　me,
Knowing that thou wouldst have me drown'd
　on shore,
With tears as salt as sea, through thy un-
　kindness:
The splitting rocks cower'd in the sinking
　sands,
And would not dash me with their ragged
　sides,
Because thy flinty heart, more hard than
　they,
Might in thy palace perish Eleanor.
As far as I could ken thy chalky cliffs,
When from thy shore the tempest beat us
　back,
I stood upon the hatches in the storm,
And when the dusky sky began to rob
My earnest-gaping sight of thy land's view,
I took a costly jewel from my neck—
A heart it was, bound in with diamonds—
And threw it towards thy land: the sea re-
　ceived it,
And so I wish'd thy body might my heart:
And even with this I lost fair England's
　view,
And bid mine eyes be packing with my heart,
And call'd them blind and dusky spectacles,
For losing ken of Albion's wished coast.
How often have I tempted Suffolk's tongue,
The agent of thy foul inconstancy,
To sit and witch me, as Ascanius did,
When he to madding Dido would unfold
His father's acts commenced in burning
　Troy!
Am I not witch'd like her? or thou not false
　like him?

Aye me, I can no more! die, Eleanor!
For Henry weeps that thou dost live so long.

Noise within. Enter WARWICK, SALISBURY,
and many Commons.

  War. It is reported, mighty sovereign,
That good Duke Humphrey traitorously is
    murder'd   [means.
By Suffolk and the Cardinal Beaufort's
The commons, like an angry hive of bees
That want their leader, scatter up and down,
And care not who they sting in his revenge.
Myself have calm'd their spleenful mutiny,
Until they hear the order of his death.
  King. That he is dead, good Warwick, 'tis
    too true;
But how he died God knows, not Henry:
Enter his chamber, view his breathless corpse,
And comment then upon his sudden death.
  War. That shall I do, my liege. Stay, Sal-
    isbury,
With the rude multitude till I return. [*Exit.*
  King. O Thou that judgest all things, stay
    my thoughts,
My thoughts, that labor to persuade my soul
Some violent hands were laid on Hum-
    phrey's life!
If my suspect be false, forgive me, God;
For judgment only doth belong to Thee.
Fain would I go to chafe his paly lips
With twenty thousand kisses, and to drain
Upon his face an ocean of salt tears,
To tell my love unto his dumb deaf trunk,
And with my fingers feel his hand unfeeling:
But all in vain are these mean obsequies;
And to survey his dead and earthy image,
What were it but to make my sorrow great-
    er?

Re-enter WARWICK *and others, bearing*
GLOUCESTER'S *body on a bed.*

  War. Come hither, gracious sovereign,
    view this body.
  King. That is to see how deep my grave is
    made;
For with his soul fled all my worldly solace,
For seeing him I see my life in death.
  War. As surely as my soul intends to live
With that dread King, that took our state
    upon him
To free us from his father's wrathful curse,
I do believe that violent hands were laid
Upon the life of this thrice-famed duke.
  Suf. A dreadful oath, sworn with a solemn
    tongue!
What instance gives Lord Warwick for his
    vow?
  War. See how the blood is settled in his
    face.
Oft have I seen a timely-parted ghost,
Of ashy semblance, meager, pale and blood-
    less,

Being all descended to the laboring heart;
Who, in the conflict that it holds with death,
Attracts the same for aidance 'gainst the
    enemy;
Which with the heart there cools and ne'er
    returneth
To blush and beautify the cheek again.
But see, his face is black and full of blood,
His eye-balls further out than when he lived,
Staring full ghastly like a strangled man;
His hair uprear'd, his nostrils stretch'd with
    struggling;
His hands abroad display'd, as one that
    grasp'd
And tugg'd for life and was by strength sub-
    dued:
Look, on the sheets his hair, you see, is
    sticking;
His well-proportion'd beard made rough and
    rugged,
Like to the summer's corn by tempest lodged
It cannot be but he was murder'd here;
The least of all these signs were probable.
  Suf. Why, Warwick, who should do the
    duke to death?
Myself and Beaufort had him in protection;
And we, I hope, sir, are no murderers.
  War. But both of you were vow'd Duke
    Humphrey's foes,
And you, forsooth, had the good duke to
    keep:
'Tis like you would not feast him like a
    friend;
And 'tis well seen he found an enemy.
  Queen. Then you, belike, suspect these
    noblemen
As guilty of Duke Humphrey's timeless death.
  War. Who finds the heifer dead and bleed-
    ing fresh,
And sees fast by a butcher with an axe,
But will suspect 'twas he that made the
    slaughter?
Who finds the partridge in the puttock's nest,
But may imagine how the bird was dead,
Although the kite soar with unbloodied
    beak?
Even so suspicious is this tragedy.
  Queen. Are you the butcher, Suffolk?
    Where's your knife?
Is Beaufort term'd a kite? Where are his tal-
    ons?
  Suf. I wear no knife to slaughter sleep-
    ing men;
But here's a vengeful sword, rusted with ease.
That shall be scoured in his rancorous heart
That slanders me with murder's crimson
    badge.
Say, if thou darest, proud Lord of Warwick-
    shire,
That I am faulty in Duke Humphrey's death.
  [*Exeunt* CARDINAL, SOMERSET, *and others.*
  War. What dares not Warwick, if false
    Suffolk dare him?

Queen. He dares not calm his contumelious
spirit,
Nor cease to be an arrogant controller,
Though Suffolk dare him twenty thousand
times.
War. Madam, be still; with reverence may
I say;
For every word you speak in his behalf
Is slander to your royal dignity.
Suf. Blunt-witted lord, ignoble in de-
meanor!
If ever lady wrong'd her lord so much.
Thy mother took into her blameful bed
Some stern untutor'd churl, and noble stock
Was graft with crab-tree slip; whose fruit
thou art
And never of the Nevils' noble race.
War. But that the guilt of murder buckles
thee,
And I should rob the deathsman of his fee,
Quitting thee thereby of ten thousand shames,
And that my sovereign's presence makes me
mild,
I would, false murderous coward, on thy
knee
Make thee beg pardon for thy passed speech,
And say it was thy mother that thou
meant'st,
That thou thyself was born in bastardy;
And after all this fearful homage done,
Give thee thy hire and send thy soul to hell,
Pernicious blood-sucker of sleeping men!
Suf. Thou shalt be waking while I shed
thy blood,
If from this presence thou darest go with me.
War. Away even now, or I will drag thee
hence:
Unworthy though thou art, I'll cope with
thee
And do some service to Duke Humphrey's
ghost.
[*Exeunt* SUFFOLK *and* WARWICK.
King. What stronger breastplate than a
heart untainted!
Thrice is he arm'd that hath his quarrel just,
And he but naked, though lock'd up in steel,
Whose conscience with injustice is corrupted.
[*A noise within.*
Queen. What noise is this?

Re-enter SUFFOLK *and* WARWICK, *with their
weapons drawn.*

King. Why, how now, lords! your wrath-
ful weapons drawn
Here in our presence! dare you be so bold?
Why, what tumultuous clamor have we here?
Suf. The traitorous Warwick with the
men of Bury
Set all upon me, mighty sovereign.
Sal. [*to the Commons, entering*] Sirs,
stand apart; the king shall know your mind.
Dread lord, the commons send you word by
me,

Unless Lord Suffolk straight be done to
death.
Or banished fair England's territories,
They will by violence tear him from your
palace,
And torture him with grievous lingering
death.
They say, by him the good Duke Humphrey
died;
They say, in him they fear your highness'
death;
And mere instinct of love and loyalty,
Free from a stubborn opposite intent,
As being thought to contradict your liking,
Makes them thus forward in his banishment.
They say, in care of your most royal person,
That if your highness should intend to sleep,
And charge that no man should disturb your
rest
In pain of your dislike or pain of death,
Yet, notwithstanding such a strait edict,
Were there a serpent seen, with forked
tongue,
That slily glided towards your majesty,
It were but necessary you were waked,
Lest, being suffer'd in that harmful slumber,
The mortal worm might make the sleep
eternal;
And therefore do they cry, though you for-
bid,
That they will guard you, whether you will
or no,
From such fell serpents as false Suffolk is,
With whose envenomed and fatal sting,
Your loving uncle, twenty times his worth,
They say, is shamefully bereft of life.
Commons [*within*]. An answer from the
king, my Lord of Salisbury!
Suf. 'Tis like the commons, rude unpol-
ish'd hinds,
Could send such message to their sovereign:
But you, my lord, were glad to be employ'd,
To show how quaint an orator you are:
But all the honor Salisbury hath won
Is, that he was the lord ambassador
Sent from a sort of tinkers to the king.
Commons [*within*]. An answer from the
king, or we will all break in!
King. Go, Salisbury, and tell them all from
me,
I thank them for their tender loving care,
And had I not been cited so by them,
Yet did I purpose as they do entreat;
For, sure, my thoughts do hourly prophesy
Mischance unto my state by Suffolk's means:
And therefore, by His majesty I swear,
Whose far unworthy deputy I am,
He shall not breathe infection in this air
But three days longer, on the pain of death.
[*Exit Salisbury.*
Queen. O Henry, let me plead for gentle
Suffolk! [Suffolk!
King. Ungentle queen, to call him gentle

No more, I say: if thou dost plead for him,
Thou wilt but add increase unto my wrath.
Had I but said, I would have kept my word,
But when I swear, it is irrevocable.
If, after three days' space, thou here be'st found
On any ground that I am ruler of,
The world shall not be ransom for thy life.
Come, Warwick, come, good Warwick, go with me;
I have great matters to impart to thee.

[Exeunt all but Queen and Suffolk.

Queen. Mischance and sorrow go along with you!
Heart's discontent and sour affliction
Be playfellows to keep you company!
There's two of you; the devil make a third!
And threefold vengeance tend upon your steps!

Suf. Cease, gentle queen, these execrations,
And let thy Suffolk take his heavy leave.

Queen. Fie, coward woman and soft-hearted wretch!
Hast thou not spirit to curse thine enemy?

Suf. A plague upon them! wherefore should I curse them?
Would curses kill, as doth the mandrake's groan,
I would invent as bitter-searching terms,
As curst, as harsh and horrible to hear,
Deliver'd strongly through my fixed teeth,
With full as many signs of deadly hate,
As lean-faced Envy in her loathsome cave:
My tongue should stumble in mine earnest words;
Mine eyes should sparkle like the beaten flint;
Mine hair be fix'd on end, as one distract;
Aye, every joint should seem to curse and ban:
And even now my burthen'd heart would break,
Should I not curse them. Poison be their drink!
Gall, worse than gall, the daintiest that they taste!
Their sweetest shade a grove of cypress trees!
Their chiefest prospect murdering basilisks!
Their softest touch as smart as lizards' stings!
Their music frightful as the serpent's hiss,
And boding screech-owls make the concert full!
All the foul terrors in dark-seated hell—

Queen. Enough, sweet Suffolk; thou torment'st thyself,
And these dread curses, like the sun 'gainst glass,
Or like an overcharged gun, recoil,
And turn the force of them upon thyself.

Suf. You bade me ban, and will you bid me leave?
Now, by the ground that I am banish'd from,
Well could I curse away a winter's night,
Though standing naked on a mountain top,

Where biting cold would never let grass grow,
And think it but a minute spent in sport.

Queen. O, let me entreat thee cease. Give me thy hand,
That I may dew it with my mournful tears;
Nor let the rain of heaven wet this place,
To wash away my woful monuments.
O, could this kiss by printed in thy hand,
That thou mightst think upon these by the seal,
Through whom a thousand sighs are breathed for thee!
So, get thee gone, that I may know my grief;
'Tis but surmised whiles thou art standing by,
As one that surfeits thinking on a want.
I will repeal thee, or, be well assured,
Adventure to be banished myself:
And banished I am, if but from thee.
Go; speak not to me; even now be gone.
O, go not yet! Even thus two friends condemn'd
Embrace and kiss and take ten thousand leaves,
Loather a hundred times to part than die.
Yet now farewell; and farewell life with thee!

Suf. Thus is poor Suffolk ten times banished;
Once by the king, and three times thrice by thee.
'Tis not the land I care for, wert thou thence;
A wilderness is populous enough,
So Suffolk had thy heavenly company:
For where thou art, there is the world itself,
With every several pleasure in the world,
And where thou art not, desolation.
I can no more: live thou to joy thy life;
Myself no joy in nought but that thou livest.

Enter VAUX.

Queen. Wither goes Vaux so fast? what news, I prithee?

Vaux. To signify unto his majesty
That Cardinal Beaufort is at point of death;
For suddenly a grievous sickness took him.
That makes him gasp and stare and catch the air,
Blaspheming God and cursing men on earth.
Sometime he talks as if Duke Humphrey's ghost
Were by his side; sometime he calls the king,
And whispers to his pillow as to him
The secrets of his overcharged soul:
And I am sent to tell his majesty,
That even now he cries aloud for him.

Queen. Go tell this heavy message to the king.   [Exit VAUX.
Aye me! what is this world! what news are these!
But wherefore grieve I at an hour's poor loss,
Omitting Suffolk's exile, my soul's treasure?
Why only, Suffolk, mourn I not for thee.

And with the southern clouds contend in tears,
Theirs for the earth's increase, mine for my sorrows?
Now get thee hence: the king, thou know'st, is coming;
If thou be found by me, thou art but dead.
   Suf. If I depart from thee, I cannot live;
And in thy sight to die, what were it else
But like a pleasant slumber in thy lap?
Here could I breathe my soul into the air,
As mild and gentle as the cradle-babe,
Dying with mother's dug between its lips:
Where, from thy sight, I should be raging mad,
And cry out for thee to close up mine eyes,
To have thee with thy lips to stop my mouth;
So shouldst thou either turn my flying soul,
Or I should breathe it so into thy body,
And then it lived in sweet Elysium.
To die by thee were but to die in jest;
From thee to die were torture more than death:
O, let me stay, befall what may befall!
   Queen. Away! though parting be a fretful corrosive.
It is applied to a deathful wound.
To France, sweet Suffolk: let me hear from thee;
For wheresoe'er thou art in this world's globe,
I'll have an Iris that shall find thee out.
   Suf. I go.
   Queen. And take my heart with thee.
   Suf. A jewel, lock'd into the wofull'st cask
That ever did contain a thing of worth.
Even as a splitted bark, so sunder we:
This way fall I to death.
   Queen.   This way for me.
                [EXEUNT *severally.*

SCENE III.—*A bedchamber.*

Enter the KING, SALISBURY, WARWICK, *to the* CARDINAL *in bed.*

   King. How fares my lord? speak, Beaufort, to thy sovereign.
   Car. If thou be'st death, Ill give thee England's treasure,
Enough to purchase such another island,
So now wilt let me live, and feel no pain.
   King. Ah, what a sign it is of evil life,
Where death's approach is seen so terrible!
   War. Beaufort, it is thy sovereign speaks to thee.
   Car. Bring me unto my trial when you will.
Died he not in his bed? where should he die?
Can I make men live, whether they will or no?
O, torture me no more! I will confess.
Alive again? then show me where he is:
I'll give a thousand pound to look upon him.
He hath no eyes, the dust hath blinded them.

Comb down his hair; look, look! it stands upright,
Like lime-twigs set to catch my winged soul.
Give me some drink; and bid the apothecary
Bring the strong poison that I bought of him.
   King. O thou eternal mover of the heavens,
Look with a gentle eye upon this wretch!
O, beat away the busy meddling fiend
That lays strong siege unto this wretch's soul,
And from his bosom purge this black despair!
   War. See, how the pangs of death do make him grin!
   Sal. Disturb him not; let him pass peaceably.
   King. Peace to his soul, if God's good pleasure be!
Lord Cardinal, if thou think'st on heaven's bliss,
Hold up thy hand, make signal of thy hope.
He dies, and makes no sign. O God, forgive him!
   War. So bad a death argues a monstrous life.
   King. Forbear to judge, for we are sinners all.
Close up his eyes and draw the curtain close;
And let us all to meditation.   [*Exeunt.*

ACT IV.

SCENE I.—*The coast of Kent.*

Alarum. Fight at sea. Ordnance goes off. Enter a CAPTAIN, *a* MASTER, *a* MASTER'S-MATE, WALTER WHITMORE, *and others; with them* SUFFOLK, *and others, prisoners.*

   Cap. The gaudy, blabbing and remorseful day
Is crept into the bosom of the sea;
And now loud-howling wolves arouse the jades
That drag the tragic melancholy night;
Who, with their drowsy, slow and flagging wings,
Clip dead men's graves, and from their misty jaws
Breathe foul contagious darkness in the air.
Therefore bring forth the soldiers of our prize;
For, whilst our pinnace anchors in the Downs,
Here shall they make their ransom on the sand,
Or with their blood stain this discolored shore.
Master, this prisoner freely give I thee;
And thou that art his mate, make boot of this;
The other, Walter Whitmore, is thy share.
   First Gent. What is my ransom, master? let me know.
   Mast. A thousand crowns, or else lay down your head.

Mate. And so much shall you give, or off
goes yours.

Cap. What, think you much to pay two
thousand crowns,
And bear the name and port of gentlemen?
Cut both the villains' throats; for die you
shall:
The lives of those which we have lost in fight
Be counterpoised with such a petty sum!

First Gent. I'll give it, sir; and therefore
spare my life.

Sec. Gent. And so will I, and write home
for it straight.

Whit. I lost mine eye in laying the prize
aboard,
And therefore to revenge it, shalt thou die;
　　　　　　　　　　　　　　　[*To* SUF.
And so should these, if I might have my will.

Cap. Be not so rash; take ransom, let him
live.

Suf. Look on my George; I am a gentleman:
Rate me at what thou wilt, thou shalt be
paid.

Whit. And so am I; my name is Walter
Whitmore.
How now! why start'st thou? what, doth
death affright?

Suf. Thy name affrights me, in whose
sound is death.
A cunning man did calculate my birth,
And told me that by water I should die:
Yet let not this make thee be bloody-minded;
Thy name is Gaultier, being rightly sounded.

Whit. Gaultier or Walter, which it is, I
care not:
Never did base dishonor blur our name,
But with our sword we wiped away the blot;
Therefore, when merchant-like I sell revenge,
Broke be my sword, my arms torn and de-
faced,
And I proclaim'd a coward through the
world!

Suf. Stay, Whitmore; for thy prisoner is
a prince,
The Duke of Suffolk, William de la Pole.

Whit. The Duke of Suffolk, muffled up in
rags!

Suf. Aye, but these rags are no part of the
duke:
Jove sometime went disguised, and why not
I?

Cap. But Jove was never slain, as thou
shalt be.

Suf. Obscure and lowly swain, King Hen-
ry's blood,
The honorable blood of Lancaster,
Must not be shed by such a jaded groom.
Hast thou not kiss'd thy hand and held my
stirrup?
Bare-headed plodded by my foot-cloth
mule,
And thought thee happy when I shook my
head?

How often hast thou waited at my cup,
Fed from my trencher, kneel'd down at the
board,
When I have feasted with Queen Margaret?
Remember it and let it make thee crest-fall'n,
Aye, and allay this thy abortive pride;
How in our voiding lobby hast thou stood
And duly waited for my coming forth?
This hand of mine hath writ in thy behalf,
And therefore shall it charm thy riotous
tongue.

Whit. Speak, captain, shall I stab the forlorn swain?

Cap. First let my words stab him, as he
hath me.

Suf. Base slave, thy words are blunt,
and so art thou.

Cap. Convey him hence and on our long-
boat's side
Strike off his head.

Suf. Thou darest not, for thy own.

Cap. Yes, Pole.

Suf. Pole!

Cap. Pool! Sir Pool! lord!
Aye, kennel, puddle, sink; whose filth and
dirt
Troubles the silver spring where England
drinks.
Now will I dam up this thy yawning mouth,
For swallowing the treasure of the realm:
Thy lips that kiss'd the queen shall sweep
the ground;
And thou that smiledst at good Duke Hum-
phrey's death
Against the senseless winds shalt grin in vain,
Who in contempt shall hiss at thee again:
And wedded be thou to the hags of hell,
For daring to affy a mighty lord
Unto the daughter of a worthless king,
Having neither subject, wealth, nor diadem.
By devilish policy art thou grown great,
And, like ambitious Sylla, overgorged
With gobbets of thy mother's bleeding heart.
By thee Anjou and Maine were sold to
France,
The false revolting Normans thorough thee
Disdain to call us lord, and Picardy
Hath slain their governors, surprised our
forts,
And sent the ragged soldiers wounded home.
The princely Warwick, and the Nevils all,
Whose dreadful swords were never drawn in
vain,
As hating thee, are rising up in arms:
And now the house of York, thrust from the
crown
By shameful murder of a guiltless king,
And lofty proud encroaching tyranny,
Burns with revenging fire; whose hopeful
colors
Advance our half-faced sun, striving to shine,
Under the which is writ 'Invitis nubibus.'
The commons here in Kent are up in arms:
And, to conclude, reproach and beggary

Is crept into the palace of our king,
And all by thee. Away! convey him hence.

Suf. O that I were a god, to shoot forth
thunder
Upon these paltry, servile, abject drudges!
Small things make base men proud: this vil-
lain here,
Being captain of a pinnace, threatens more
Than Bargulus the strong Illyrian pirate.
Drones suck not eagles' blood but rob bee-
hives:
It is impossible that I should die
By such a lowly vassal as thyself.
Thy words move rage and not remorse in
me:
I go of message from the queen to France;
I charge thee waft me safely cross the Chan-
nel.

Cap. Walter,—

Whit. Come, Suffolk, I must waft thee to
thy death.

Suf. Gelidus timor occupat artus: it is thee
I fear.

Whit. Thou shalt have cause to fear before I leave thee.

What, are ye daunted now? now will ye
stoop?

First Gent. My gracious lord, entreat him,
speak him fair.

Suf. Suffolk's imperial tongue is stern and
rough,
Used to command, untaught to plead for
favor.
Far be it we should honor such as these
With humble suit: no, rather let my head
Stoop to the block than these knees bow to
any
Save to the God of heaven and to my king;
And sooner dance upon a bloody pole
Than stand uncover'd to the vulgar groom
True nobility is exempt from fear.
More can I bear than you dare execute.

Cap. Hale him away, and let him talk no
more.

Suf. Come, soldiers, show what cruelty ye
can,
That this my death may never be forgot!
Great men oft die by vile bezonians:
A Roman sworder and banditto slave
Murder'd sweet Tully; Brutus' bastard hand
Stabb'd Julius Cæsar; savage islanders
Pompey the Great; and Suffolk dies by
pirates.

[*Exeunt* WHITMORE *and others with*
SUFFOLK.

Cap. And as for these whose ransom we
have set,
It is our pleasure one of them depart:
Therefore come you with us and let him go.

[*Exeunt all but the* FIRST GENTLEMAN.

Re-enter WHITMORE *with* SUFFOLK'S *body.*

Whit. There let his head and lifeless body
lie,

Until the queen his mistress bury it. [*Exit.*

First Gent. O barbarous and bloody spec-
tacle!
His body will I bear unto the king:
If he revenge it not, yet will his friends;
So will the queen, that living held him dear.

[*Exit with the body.*

SCENE II.—*Blackheath.*

Enter GEORGE BEVIS *and* JOHN HOLLAND

Bevis. Come, and get thee a sword, though
made of a lath: they have been up these
two days.

Holl. They have the more need to sleep
now, then,

Bevis. I tell thee, Jack Cade the clothier
means to dress the commonwealth, and turn
it, and set a new nap upon it.

Holl. So he had need, for 'tis threadbare.
Well, I say it was never merry world in England since gentlemen came up.

Bevis. O miserable age! virtue is not regarded in handicrafts-men.

Holl. The nobility think scorn to go in
leather aprons.

Bevis. Nay, more, the king's council are
no good workmen.

Holl. True; and yet it is said, labor in
thy vocation; which is as much to say as, let
the magistrates be laboring men; and therefore should we be magistrates.

Bevis. Thou hast hit it; for there's no
better sign of a brave mind than a hard hand.

Holl. I see them! I see them! There's
Best's son, the tanner of Wingham,—

Bevis. He shall have the skins of our enemies, to make dog's-leather of.

Holl. And Dick the butcher,—

Bevis. Then is sin struck down like an ox,
and iniquity's throat cut like a calf.

Holl. And Smith the weaver,—

Bevis. Argo, their thread of life is spun.

Holl. Come, come, let's fall in with them.

*Drum. Enter Cade, Dick Butcher, Smith the
Weaver, and a Sawyer, with infinite numbers.*

Cade. We John Cade, so termed of our
supposed father,—

Dick. [*Aside*]. Or rather stealing a cade of
herrings.

Cade. For our enemies shall fall before us,
inspired with the spirit of putting down kings
and princes,—Command silence.

Dick. Silence!

Cade. My father was a Mortimer,—

Dick. [*Aside*] He was an honest man, and
a good bricklayer.

Cade. My mother a Plantagenet,—

Dick. [*Aside*] I know her well; she was a
midwife.

Cade. My wife descended of the Lacies,—

Dick. [*Aside*] She was indeed, a peddler's
daughter, and sold many laces.

Smith [*Aside*] But now of late, not able to travel with her furred pack, she washes bucks here at home.

Cade. Therefore am I of an honorable house.

Dick. [*Aside*] Aye, by my faith, the field is honorable; and there was he born, under a hedge, for his father had never a house but the cage.

Cade. Valiant I am.

Smith [*Aside*] A' must needs; for beggary is valiant.

Cade. I am able to endure much.

Dick. [*Aside*] No question of that; for I have seen him whipped three market-days together.

Cade. I fear neither sword nor fire.

Smith. [*Aside*] He need not fear the sword; for his coat is of proof.

Dick. [*Aside*] But methinks he should stand in fear of fire, being burnt i' the hand for stealing of sheep.

Cade. Be brave, then; for your captain is brave, and vows reformation. There shall be in England seven halfpenny loaves sold for a penny: the three-hooped pot shall have ten hoops; and I will make it felony to drink small beer: all the realm shall be in common; and in Cheapside shall my palfry go to grass: and when I am king, as king I will be,—

All. God save your majesty!

Cade. I thank you, good people: there shall be no money; all shall eat and drink on my score; and I will apparel them all in one livery, that they may agree like brothers, and worship me their lord.

Dick. The first thing we do, let's kill all the lawyers.

Cade. Nay, that I mean to do. Is not this a lamentable thing, that of the skin of an innocent lamb should be made parchment? that parchment, being scribbled o'er, should undo man? Some say the bee stings: but I say, 'tis the bee's wax; for I did but seal once to a thing, and I was never mine own man since. How now! who's there?

Enter some, bringing forward the Clerk of Chatham.

Smith. The clerk of Chatham: he can write and read and cast accompt.

Cade. O monstrous! [copies.

Smith. We took him setting of boys'

Cade. Here's a villain!

Smith. Has a book in his pocket with red letters in 't.

Cade. Nay, then, he is a conjurer.

Dick. Nay, he can make obligations, and write court-hand.

Cade. I am sorry for 't: the man is a proper man, of mine honor; unless I find him guilty, he shall not die. Come hither, sirrah, I must examine thee: what is thy name?

Clerk. Emmanuel.

Dick. They use to write it on the top of letters: 'twill go hard with you.

Cade. Let me alone. Dost thou use to write thy name? or hast thou a mark to thyself, like an honest plain-dealing man?

Clerk. Sir, I thank God, I have been so well brought up that I can write my name.

All. He hath confessed: away with him! he's a villain and a traitor.

Cade. Away with him, I say! hang him with his pen and ink-horn about his neck.

[*Exit one with the Clerk.*

Enter Michael.

Mich. Where's our general?

Cade. Here I am, thou particular fellow.

Mich. Fly, fly, fly! Sir Humphrey Stafford and his brother are hard by, with the king's forces.

Cade. Stand, villain, stand, or I'll fell thee down. He shall be encountered with a man as good as himself: he is but a knight, is a'?

Mich. No.

Cade. To equal him, I will make myself a knight presently. [*Kneels*] Rise up, Sir John Mortimer. [*Rises*] Now have at him!

Enter Sir Humphrey Stafford and his Brother, with drum and soldiers.

Staf. Rebellious hinds, the filth and scum of Kent,
Mark'd for the gallows, lay your weapons down;
Home to your cottages, forsake this groom:
The king is merciful, if you revolt.

Bro. But angry, wrathful, and inclined to blood,
If you go forward; therefore yield, or die.

Cade. As for these silken-coated slaves, I pass not:
It is to you, good people, that I speak,
Over whom, in time to come, I hope to reign;
For I am rightful heir unto the crown.

Staf. Villain, thy father was a plasterer;
And thou thyself a shearman, art thou not?

Cade. And Adam was a gardener.

Bro. And what of that?

Cade. Marry, this: Edmund Mortimer, Earl of March,
Married the Duke of Clarence' daughter, did he not?

Staf. Aye, sir.

Cade. By her he had two children at one birth.

Bro. That's false.

Cade. Aye, there's the question; but I say, 'tis true:
The elder of them, being put to nurse,
Was by a beggar-woman stolen away;
And, ignorant of his birth and parentage,
Became a bricklayer when he came to age:
His son am I; deny it, if you can.

Dick. Nay, 'tis too true; therefore he shall be king.

Smith. Sir, he made a chimney in my father's house, and the bricks are alive at this day to testify it; therefore deny it not.

Staf. And will you credit this base drudge's words,
That speaks he knows not what?

All. Aye, marry, will we; therefore get ye gone.

Bro. Jack Cade, the Duke of York hath taught you this.

Cade. [*Aside*] He lies, for I invented it myself. Go to, sirrah, tell the king from me, that, for his father's sake, Henry the fifth, in whose time boys went to span-counter for French crowns, I am content he shall reign; but I'll be protector over him.

Dick. And furthermore, we'll have the Lord Say's head for selling the dukedom of Maine.

Cade. And good reason; for thereby is England mained, and fain to go with a staff, but that my puissance holds it up. Fellow kings, I tell you that that Lord Say hath gelded the commonwealth, and made it an eunuch: and more than that, he can speak French; and therefore he is a traitor.

Staf. O, gross and miserable ignorance!

Cade. Nay, answer, if you can: the Frenchmen are our enemies; go to, then, I ask but this: can he that speaks with the tongue of an enemy be a good counsellor, or no?   [*head.*

All. No, no; and therefore we'll have his

Bro. Well, seeing gentle words will not prevail,
Assail them with the army of the king.

Staf. Herald, away; and throughout every town   [*Cade;*
Proclaim them traitors that are up with
That those which fly before the battle ends
May, even in their wives' and children's sight,
Be hang'd up for example at their doors:
And you that be the king's friends, follow me.

[*Exeunt the two Staffords, and soldiers.*

Cade. And you that love the commons, follow me.
Now show yourselves men; 'tis for liberty.
We will not leave one lord, one gentleman:
Spare none but such as go in clouted shoon;
For they are thrifty honest men, and such
As would, but that they dare not, take our parts.   [*ward us.*

Dick. They are all in order and march to-

Cade. But then are we in order when we are most out of order. Come, march forward.
[*Exeunt.*

SCENE III.—*Another part of Blackheath.*

Alarums to the fight, wherein both the Staffords are slain. Enter Cade and the rest.

Cade. Where's Dick, the butcher of Ashford?

Dick. Here, sir.

Cade. They fell before thee like sheep and oxen and thou behavedst thyself as if thou hadst been in thine own slaughter-house: therefore thus will I reward thee, the Lent shall be as long again as it is; and thou shalt have a license to kill for a hundred lacking one.

Dick. I desire no more.

Cade. And, to speak truth, thou deservest no less. This monument of the victory will I bear [*putting on Sir Humphrey's brigandine*]; and the bodies shall be dragged at my horse heels till I do come to London, where we will have the mayor's sword borne before us.

Dick. If we mean to thrive and do good, break open the jails and let out the prisoners.

Cade. Fear not that, I warrant thee. Come, let's march toward London.   [*Exeunt.*

SCENE IV.—*London.* The palace.

Enter the King with a supplication, and the Queen with Suffolk's head, the Duke of Buckingham and the Lord Say.

Queen. Oft have I heard that grief softens the mind,
And makes it fearful and degenerate;
Think therefore on revenge and cease to weep,
But who can cease to weep and look on this?
Here may his head lie on my throbbing breast:
But where's the body that I should embrace?

Buck. What answer makes your grace to the rebels' supplication?   [*treat;*

King. I'll send some holy bishop to en-
For God forbid so many simple souls
Should perish by the sword! And I myself,
Rather than bloody war shall cut them short,
Will parley with Jack Cade their general:
But stay, I'll read it over once again.

Queen. Ah, barbarous villains! hath this lovely face
Ruled, like a wandering planet, over me,
And could it not enforce them to relent,
That were unworthy to behold the same?

King. Lord Say, Jack Cade hath sworn to have thy head.

Say. Aye, but I hope your highness shall have his.

King. How now, madam!
Still lamenting and mourning for Suffolk's death?
I fear me, love, if that I had been dead,
Thou wouldest not have mourn'd so much for me.

Queen. No, my love, I should not mourn, but die for thee.

Enter a MESSENGER

King. How now! what news? why comst thou in such haste?

Mess. The rebels are in Southwark; fly my lord!
Jack Cade proclaims himself Lord Mortimer,
Descended from the Duke of Clarence' house,
And calls your grace usurper openly,
And vows to crown himself in Westminster.
His army is a ragged multitude
Of hinds and peasants, rude and merciless:
Sir Humphrey Stafford and his brother's death
Hath given them heart and courage to proceed:
All scholars, lawyers, courtiers, gentlemen,
They call false caterpillars and intend their death.

King. O graceless men! they know not what they do.

Buck. My gracious lord, retire to Killingworth,
Until a power be raised to put them down.

Queen. Ah, were the Duke of Suffolk now alive,
These Kentish rebels would be soon appeased!

King. Lord Say, the traitors hate thee;
Therefore away with us to Killingworth.

Say. So might your grace's person be in danger.
The sight of me is odious in their eyes;
And therefore in this city will I stay,
And live alone as secret as I may.

Enter another MESSENGER.

Mess. Jack Cade hath gotten London Bridge:
The citizens fly and forsake their houses:
The rascal people, thirsting after prey,
Join with the traitor, and they jointly swear
To spoil the city and your royal court.

Buck. Then linger not, my lord; away, take horse.

King. Come, Margaret; God, our hope, will succor us.

Queen. My hope is gone, now Suffolk is deceased.

King. Farewell, my lord: trust not the Kentish rebels.

Buck. Trust nobody, for fear you be betray'd.

Say. The trust I have is in mine innocence,
And therefore am I bold and resolute.
[*Exeunt.*

SCENE V.—LONDON. *The Tower.*

Enter LORD SCALES *upon the Tower, walking.
Then enter two or three* CITIZENS *below.*

Scales. How now! is Jack Cade slain?

First Cit. No, my lord, nor likely to be slain; for they have won the bridge, killing all those that withstand them: the lord mayor craves aid of your honor from the Tower to defend the city from the rebels.

Scales. Such aid as I can spare you shall command;
But I am troubled here with them myself;
The rebels have assay'd to win the Tower.
But get you to Smithfield and gather head,
And thither I will send you Matthew Goffe;
Fight for your king, your country, and your lives;
And so, farewell, for I must hence again.
[*Exeunt.*

SCENE VI.—LONDON. *Cannon Street.*

Enter JACK CADE *and the rest, and strikes his staff on London-stone.*

Cade. Now is Mortimer lord of this city.
And here, sitting upon London-stone, I charge and command that, of the city's cost, the pissing-conduit run nothing but claret wine this first year of our reign. And now henceforward it shall be treason for any that calls me other than Lord Mortimer.

Enter a SOLDIER, *running.*

Sold. Jack Cade! Jack Cade!

Cade. Knock him down there.
[*They kill him.*

Smith. If this fellow be wise, he'll never call ye Jack Cade more: I think he hath a very fair warning.

Dick. My lord, there's an army gathered together in Smithfield.

Cade. Come, then, let's go fight with them: but first, go and set London bridge on fire; and, if you can, burn down the Tower too. Come, let's away.
[*Exeunt.*

SCENE VII.—LONDON. *Smithfield.*

Alarums. MATTHEW GOFFE *is slain, and all the rest. Then enter* JACK CADE, *with his company.*

Cade. So, sirs: now go some and pull down the Savoy; others to the inns of court; down with them all.

Dick. I have a suit upon your lordship.

Cade. Be it a lordship, thou shalt have it for that word.

Dick. Only that the laws of England may come out of your mouth.

Holl. [*Aside*] Mass, 'twill be sore law, then; for he was thrust in the mouth with a spear, and 'tis not whole yet.

Smith. [*Aside*] Nay, John, it will be stinking law; for his breath stinks with eating toasted cheese.

Cade. I have thought upon it, it shall be so. Away burn all the records of the realm: my mouth shall be the parliament of England.

Holl. [*Aside*] Then we are like to have biting statutes, unless his teeth be pulled out.

Cade. And henceforward all things shall be in common.

Enter a Messenger

Mess. My lord, a prize, a prize! here's the
Lord Say, which sold the towns in France; he
that made us pay one and twenty fifteens,
and one shilling to the pound, the last sub-
sidy.

Enter GEORGE BEVIS, *with the* LORD SAY

Cade. Well, he shall be beheaded for it
ten times. Ah, thou say, thou serge, nay,
thou buckram lord! now art thou within
point-blank of our jurisdiction regal. What
canst thou answer to my majesty for giving
up of Normandy unto Monsieur Basimecu,
the dauphin of France? Be it known unto
thee by these presence, even the presence of
Lord Mortimer, that I am the besom that
must sweep the court clean of such filth as
thou art. Thou hast most traitorously corrupted the youth of the realm in erecting a
grammar school: and whereas, before, our
forefathers had no other books but the score
and the tally, thou hast caused printing to be
used, and, contrary to the king, his crown
and dignity, thou hast built a paper-mill. It
will be proved to thy face that thou hast
men about thee that usually talk of a noun
and a verb, and such abominable words as no
Christian ear can endure to hear. Thou hast
appointed justices of peace, to call poor men
before them about matters they were not
able to answer. Moreover, thou hast put
them in prison; and because they could not
read, thou hast hanged them; when, indeed,
only for that cause they have been most
worthy to live. Thou dost ride in a foot-
cloth, dost thou not?

Say. What of that?

Cade. Marry, thou oughtest not to let thy
horse wear a cloak, when honester men than
thou go in their hose and doublets.

Dick. And work in their shirt too; as myself, for example, that am a butcher.

Say. You men of Kent,—

Dick. What say you of Kent?

Say. Nothing but this; 'tis 'bona terra,
mala gens.'

Cade. Away with him, away with him! he
speaks Latin.

Say. Hear me but speak, and bear me
where you will.
Kent, in the Commentaries Cæsar writ,
Is term'd the civil'st place of all this isle:
Sweet is the country, because full of riches;
The people liberal, valiant, active, wealthy;
Which makes me hope you are not void of
pity.
I sold not Maine, I lost not Normandy,
Yet, to recover them, would lose my life.
Justice with favor have I always done;
Prayers and tears have moved me, gifts could
never.

When have I ought exacted at your hands,
But to maintain the king, the realm, and
you?
Large gifts have I bestow'd on learned
clerks,
Because my book preferr'd me to the king,
And seeing ignorance is the curse of God,
Knowledge the wing wherewith we fly to
heaven,
Unless you be possess'd with devilish spirits,
You cannot but forbear to murder me:
This tongue hath parley'd unto foreign kings
For your behoof,—

Cade. Tut, when struck'st thou one blow
in the field?

Say. Great men have reaching hands: oft
have I struck
Those that I never saw and struck them
dead.

Geo. O monstrous coward! what, to come
behind folks?

Say. These cheeks are pale for watching
for your good.

Cade. Give him a box o' the ear and
that will make 'em red again.

Say. Long sitting to determine poor men's
causes
Hath made me full of sickness and diseases.

Cade. Ye shall have a hempen caudle then
and the help of hatchet.

Dick. Why dost thou quiver, man?

Say. The palsy, and not fear, provokes me.

Cade. Nay, he nods at us, as who should
say, I'll be even with you; I'll see if his head
will stand steadier on a pole, or no. Take him
away, and behead him.

Say. Tell me wherein have I offended
most.
Have I affected wealth or honor? speak.
And my chests fill'd up with extorted gold?
Is my apparel sumptuous to behold?
Whom have I injured, that ye seek my
death?
These hands are free from guiltless blood-
shedding,
This breast from harboring foul deceitful
thoughts.
O, let me live!

Cade. [*Aside*] I feel remorse in myself with
his words; but I'll bridle it: he shall die, an
it be but for pleading so well for his life.
Away with him! he has a familiar under his
tongue; he speaks not o' God's name. Go,
take him away, I say, and strike off his head
presently; and then break into his son-in-
law's house, Sir James Cromer, and strike off
his head, and bring them both upon two
poles hither.

All. It shall be done.

Say. Ah, countrymen! if when you make
your prayers,
God should be so obdurate as yourselves,
How would it fare with your departed souls?
And therefore yet relent, and save my life.

Cade. Away with him! and do as I command ye.

[*Exeunt some with* LORD SAY.

The proudest peer in the realm shall not wear a head on his shoulders, unless he pay me tribute; there shall not a maid be married, but she shall pay to me her maidenhead ere they have it: men shall hold of me in capite; and we charge and command that their wives be as free as heart can wish or tongue can tell.

Dick. My lord, when shall we go to Cheapside and take up commodities upon our bills?

Cade. Marry, presently.

All. O, brave!

Re-enter one with the heads.

Cade. But is not this braver? Let them kiss one another, for they loved well when they were alive. Now part them again, lest they consult about the giving up of some more towns in France. Soldiers, defer the spoil of the city until night: for with these borne before us, instead of maces, will we ride through the streets and at every corner have them kiss. Away! [*Exeunt.*

SCENE VIII.—SOUTHWARK.

Alarum and retreat. Enter CADE *and all his rabblement.*

Cade. Up Fish Street! down Saint Magnus Corner! kill and knock down! throw them into Thames! [*Sound a parley.*] What noise is this I hear? Dare any be so bold to sound retreat or parley, when I command them kill?

Enter BUCKINGHAM *and* CLIFFORD, *attended.*

Buck. Aye, here they be that dare and will disturb thee:

Know, Cade, we come ambassadors from the king

Unto the commons whom thou hast misled;

And here pronounce free pardon to them all,

That will forsake thee and go home in peace.

Clif. What say ye, countrymen? will ye relent,

And yield to mercy whilst 'tis offer'd you;

Or let a rebel lead you to your deaths?

Who loves the king and will embrace his pardon,

Fling up his cap, and say 'God save his majesty!'

Who hateth him and honors not his father,

Henry the fifth, that made all France to quake,

Shake he his weapon at us and pass by.

All. God save the king! God save the king!

Cade. What, Buckingham and Clifford, are ye so brave? And you, base peasants, do ye believe him? will you needs be hanged with your pardons about your necks? Hath my

sword therefore broke through London gates, that you should leave me at the White Hart in Southwark? I thought ye would never have given out these arms till you had recovered your ancient freedom; but you are all recreants and dastards, and delight to live in slavery to the nobility. Let them break your backs with burthens, take your houses over your heads, ravish your wives and daughters before your faces: for me, I will make shift for one; and so, God's curse light upon you all!

All. We'll follow Cade, we'll follow Cade!

Clif. Is Cade the son of Henry the Fifth,

That thus you do exclaim you'll go with him?

Will he conduct you through the heart of France,

And make the meanest of you earls and dukes?

Alas, he hath no home, no place to fly to;

Nor knows he how to live but by the spoil,

Unless by robbing of your friends and us.

Were't not a shame, that whilst you live at jar,

The fearful French, whom you late vanquished,

Should make a start o'er seas and vanquish you?

Methinks already in this civil broil

I see them lording it in London streets,

Crying 'Villiago!' unto all they meet.

Better ten thousand base-born Cades miscarry,

Than you should stoop unto a Frenchman's mercy.

To France, to France, and get what you have lost;

Spare England, for it is your native coast:

Henry hath money, you are strong and manly;

God on our side, doubt not of victory.

All. A Clifford! a Clifford! we'll follow the king and Clifford.

Cade. Was ever feather so lightly blown to and fro as this multitude? The name of Henry the Fifth hales them to an hundred mischiefs and makes them leave me desolate. I see them lay their heads together to surprise me. My sword make way for me, for here is no staying. In despite of the devils and hell, have through the very middest of you! and heavens and honor be witness that no want of resolution in me, but only my followers' base and ignominious treasons, make me betake me to my heels. [*Exit.*

Buck. What, is he fled? Go some, and follow him;

And he that brings his head unto the king

Shall have a thousand crowns for his reward.

[*Exeunt some of them.*

Follow me, soldiers: we'll devise a mean

To reconcile you all unto the king.

[*Exeunt.*

SCENE IX.—KENILWORTH CASTLE.

Sound trumpets. Enter KING, QUEEN, *and* SOMERSET, *on the terrace.*

King. Was ever king that joy'd an earthly throne,
And could command no more content than I?
No sooner was I crept out of my cradle
But I was made a king, at nine months old.
Was never subject long'd to be a king
As I do long and wish to be a subject.

Enter BUCKINGHAM *and* CLIFFORD.

Buck. Health and glad tidings to your majesty!
King. Why, Buckingham, is the traitor Cade surprised?
Or is he but retired to make him strong?

Enter below, multitudes, with halters about their necks.

Clif. He is fled, my lord, and all his powers do yield;
And humbly thus, with halters on their necks,
Expect your highness' doom, of life or death.
King. Then, heaven, set ope thy everlasting gates,
To entertain my vows of thanks and praise!
Soldiers, this day have you redeem'd your lives,
And show'd how well you love your prince and country:
Continue still in this so good a mind,
And Henry, though he be infortunate,
Assure yourselves, will never be unkind:
And so, with thanks and pardon to you all,
I do dismiss you to your several countries.
All. God save the king! God save the king!

Enter Messenger.

Mess. Please it your grace to be advertised
The Duke of York is newly come from Ireland,
And with a puissant and mighty power
Of gallowglasses and stout kernes
Is marching hitherward in proud array,
And still proclaimeth, as he comes along,
His arms are only to remove from thee
The Duke of Somerset, whom he terms a traitor.
King. Thus stands my state, 'twixt Cade and York distress'd;
Like to a ship that, having 'scaped a tempest,
Is straightway calm'd and boarded with a pirate: [persed;
But now is Cade driven back, his men dis-
And now is York in arms to second him.
I pray thee, Buckingham, go and meet him,
And ask him what's the reason of these arms.
Tell him I'll send Duke Edmond to the Tower;

And, Somerset, we will commit thee thither,
Until his army be dismiss'd from him.
Som. My lord,
I'll yield myself to prison willingly,
Or unto death, to do my country good.
King. In any case, be not too rough in terms;
For he is fierce and cannot brook hard language.
Buck. I will, my lord; and doubt not so to deal
As all things shall redound unto your good.
King. Come, wife, let's in, and learn to govern better;
For yet may England curse my wretched reign.   [*Flourish. Exeunt.*

SCENE X.—KENT. *Idens' garden.*

Enter CADE.

Cade. Fie on ambition! fie on myself, that have a sword, and yet am ready to famish! These five days have I hid me in these woods and durst not peep out, for all the country is laid for me; but now am I so hungry that if I might have a lease of my life for a thousand years I could stay no longer. Wherefore, on a brick wall have I climbed into this garden, to see if I can eat grass, or pick a sallet another while, which is not amiss to cool a man's stomach this hot weather. And I think this word 'sallet' was born to do me good: for many a time, but for a sallet, my brain-pan had been cleft with a brown bill; and many a time, when I have been dry and bravely marching, it hath served me instead of a quart pot to drink in; and now the word 'sallet' must serve me to feed on.

Enter IDEN

Iden. Lord, who would live turmoiled in the court.
And may enjoy such quiet walks as these?
This small inheritance my father left me
Contenteth me, and worth a monarchy.
I seek not to wax great by others' waning,
Or gather wealth, I care not with what envy:
Sufficeth that I have maintains my state,
And sends the poor well pleased from my gate.
Cade. Here's the lord of the soil come to seize me for a stray, for entering his fee-simple without leave. Ah, villain, thou wilt betray me, and get a thousand crowns of the king by carrying my head to him: but I'll make thee eat iron like an ostrich, and swallow my sword like a great pin, ere thou and I part.
Iden. Why, rude companion, whatsoe'er thou be,
I know thee not; why then should I betray thee?
Is't not enough to break into my garden,
And, like a thief, to come to rob my grounds,
Climbing my walls in spite of me the owner,

But thou wilt brave me with these saucy terms?

Cade. Brave thee! aye, by the best blood that ever was broached, and beard thee too. Look on me well: I have eat no meat these five days; yet, come thou and thy five men, and if I do not leave you all as dead as a door-nail, I pray God I may never eat grass more.

Iden. Nay, it shall ne'er be said, while England stands,
That Alexander Iden, an esquire of Kent,
Took odds to combat a poor famish'd man,
Oppose thy steadfast-gazing eyes to mine,
See if thou canst outface me with thy looks:
Set limb to limb, and thou are far the lesser:
Thy hand is but a finger to my fist,
Thy leg a stick compared with this truncheon;
My foot shall fight with all the strength thou hast;
And if mine arm be heaved in the air,
Thy grave is digg'd already in the earth.
As for words, whose greatness answers words,
Let this my sword report what speech forbears.

Cade. By my valor, the most complete champion that ever I heard! Steel, if thou turn the edge, or cut not out the burly-boned clown in chines of beef ere thou sleep in thy sheath, I beseech God on my knees thou mayst be turned to hobnails.

[*Here they fight.* CADE *falls.*

O, I am slain! famine and no other hath slain me: let ten thousand devils come against me, and give me but the ten meals I have lost, and I'll defy them all. Wither, garden; and be henceforth a burying-place to all that do dwell in this house, because the unconquered soul of Cade is fled.

Iden. Is't Cade that I have slain, that monstrous traitor?
Sword, I will hallow thee for this thy deed,
And hang thee o'er my tomb when I am dead:
Ne'er shall this blood be wiped from thy point;
But thou shalt wear it as a herald's coat,
To emblaze the honor that thy master got.

Cade. Iden, farewell, and be proud of thy victory. Tell Kent from me, she hath lost her best man, and exhort all the world to be cowards; for I, that never feared any, am vanquished by famine, not by valor. [*Dies.*

Iden. How much thou wrong'st me, heaven be my judge.
Die, damned wretch, the curse of her that bare thee;
And as I thrust thy body in with my sword,
So wish I, I might thrust thy soul to hell.
Hence will I drag thee headlong by the heels
Unto a dunghill which shall be thy grave,
And there cut off thy most ungracious head;
Which I will bear in triumph to the king,

Leaving thy trunk for crows to feed upon.
[*Exit.*

ACT V.

SCENE I.—*Fields between Dartford and Blackheath.*

Enter York, and his army of Irish, with drum and colors.

York. From Ireland thus comes York to claim his right,
And pluck the crown from feeble Henry's head:
Ring, bells, aloud; burn, bonfires, clear and bright,
To entertain great England's lawful king.
Ah! sancta majestas, who would not buy thee dear?
Let them obey that know not how to rule;
This hand was made to handle nought but gold.
I cannot give due action to my words,
Except a sword or scepter balance it:
A scepter shall it have, have I a soul,
On which I'll toss the flower-de-luce of France.

Enter BUCKINGHAM.

Whom have we here? Buckingham, to disturb me?
The king hath sent him, sure: I must dissemble.

Buck. York, if thou meanest well, I greet thee well.

York. Humphrey of Buckingham, I accept thy greeting.
Art thou a messenger, or come of pleasure?

Buck. A messenger from Henry, our dread liege,
To know the reason of these arms in peace;
Or why thou, being a subject as I am,
Against thy oath and true allegiance sworn,
Should raise so great a power without his leave,
Or dare to bring thy force so near the court

York. [*Aside*] Scarce can I speak my choler is so great:
O, I could hew up rocks and fight with flint,
I am so angry at these abject terms;
And now, like Ajax Telamonius,
On sheep or oxen could I spend my fury.
I am far better born than is the king,
More like a king, more kingly in my thoughts:
But I must make fair weather yet a while,
Till Henry be more weak and I more strong.—
Buckingham, I prithee, pardon me,
That I have given no answer all this while;
My mind was troubled with deep melancholy. [*hither*
The cause why I have brought this army
Is to remove proud Somerset from the king,
Seditious to his grace and to the state.

Buck. That is too much presumption on thy part:
But if thy arms be to no other end,
The king hath yielded unto thy demand:
The Duke of Somerset is in the Tower.
York. Upon thine honor, is he prisoner?
Buck. Upon mine honor, he is prisoner.
York. Then, Buckingham, I do dismiss my powers.
Soldiers, I thank you all; disperse yourselves;
Meet me to-morrow in Saint George's field,
You shall have pay and everything you wish.
And let my sovereign, virtuous Henry,
Command my eldest son, nay, all my sons,
As pledges of my· fealty and love;
I'll send them all as willing as I live:
Lands, goods, horse, armor, any thing I have,
Is his to use, so Somerset may die.
Buck. York, I commend this kind submission:
We twain will go into his highness' tent.

Enter KING *and* Attendants.

King. Buckingham, doth York intend no harm to us,
That thus he marcheth with thee arm in arm?
York. In all submission and humility
York doth present himself unto your highness.
King. Then what intends these forces thou dost bring?
York. To heave the traitor Somerset from hence,
And fight against that monstrous rebel Cade,
Who since I heard to be discomfited.

Enter IDEN, *with* CADE's *head.*

Iden. If one so rude and of so mean condition
May pass into the presence of a king,
Lo, I present your grace a traitor's head,
The head of Cade, whom I in combat slew.
King. The head of Cade! Great God, how just art Thou!
O, let me view this visage, being dead,
That living wrought me such exceeding trouble.
Tell me, my friend, art thou the man that slew him?
Iden. I was, an't like your majesty.
King. How art thou call'd? and what is thy degree?
Iden. Alexander Iden, that's my name;
A poor esquire of Kent, that loves his king.
Buck. So please it you, my lord, 'twere not amiss
He were created knight for his good service.
King. Iden, kneel down. [*He kneels.*] Rise up a knight.
We give thee for reward a thousand marks,
And will that thou henceforth attend on us.
Iden. May Iden live to merit such a bounty,

And never live but true unto his liege!
[*Rises.*

Enter QUEEN *and* SOMERSET.

King. See, Buckingham, Somerset comes with the queen:
Go, bid her hide him quickly from the duke.
Queen. For thousand Yorks he shall not hide his head,
But boldly stand and front him to his face.
York. How now! is Somerset at liberty?
Then, York, unloose thy long-imprison'd thoughts,
And let thy tongue be equal with thy heart.
Shall I endure the sight of Somerset?
False king! why hast thou broken faith with me,
Knowing how hardly I can brook abuse?
King did I call thee? no, thou art not king,
Not fit to govern and rule multitudes,
Which darest not, no, nor canst not rule a traitor.
That head of thine doth not become a crown;
Thy hand is made to grasp a palmer's staff,
And not to grace an awful princely scepter.
That gold must round engirt these brows of mine,
Whose smile and frown, like to Achilles' spear,
Is able with the change to kill and cure.
Here is a hand to hold a scepter up,
And with the same to act controlling laws.
Give place: by heaven, thou shalt rule no more
O'er him whom heaven created for thy ruler.
Som. O monstrous traitor! I arrest thee, York,
Of capital treason 'gainst the king and crown:
Obey, audacious traitor; kneel for grace.
York. Wouldst have me kneel? first let me ask of these,
If they can brook I bow a knee to man.
Sirrah, call in my sons to be my bail:
[*Exit* Attendant.
I know, ere they will have me go to ward,
They'll pawn their· swords for my enfranchisement.
Queen. Call hither Clifford; bid him come amain,
To say if that the bastard boys of York
Shall be the surety for their traitor father.
[*Exit* BUCKINGHAM.
York. O blood-bespotted Neapolitan,
Outcast of Naples, England's bloody scourge!
The sons of York, thy betters in their birth,
Shall be their father's bail; and bane to those
That for my surety will refuse the boys!

Enter EDWARD *and* RICHARD.

See where they come: I'll warrant they'll make it good.

Enter CLIFFORD *and his son.*

Queen. And here comes Clifford to deny their bail.

Clif. Health and all happiness to my lord the king!   [*Kneels.*

York. I thank thee, Clifford: say, what news with thee?

Nay, do not fright us with an angry look:
We are thy sovereign, Clifford, kneel again;
For thy mistaking so, we pardon thee.

Cliff. This is my king, York, I do not mistake;

But thou mistakest me much to think I do:
To Bedlam with him! is the man grown mad?

King. Aye, Clifford; a bedlam and ambitious humor
Makes him oppose himself against his king.

Cliff. He is a traitor; let him to the Tower,
And chop away that factious pate of his.

Queen. He is arrested, but will not obey;
His sons, he says, shall give their words for him.

York. Will you not, sons?

Edw. Aye, noble father, if our words will serve.

Rich. And if words will not, then our weapons shall.

Clif. Why, what a brood of traitors have we here!

York. Look in a glass, and call thy image so:
I am thy king, and thou a false-heart traitor.
Call hither to the stake my two brave bears,
That with the very shaking of their chains
They may astonish these fell-lurking curs:
Bid Salisbury and Warwick come to me.

Enter the EARLS OF WARWICK *and* SALISBURY.

Clif. Are these thy bears? we'll bait thy bears to death,
And manacle the bear-ward in their chains,
If thou darest bring them to the baiting-place.

Rich. Oft have I seen a hot o'erweening cur
Run back and bite, because he was withheld;
Who, being suffer'd with the bear's fell paw,
Hath clapp'd his tail between his legs and cried:
And such a piece of service will you do,
If you oppose yourselves to match Lord Warwick.

Clif. Hence, heap of wrath, foul indigested lump,
As crooked in thy manners as thy shape!

York. Nay, we shall heat you thoroughly anon.

Clif. Take heed, lest by your heat you burn yourselves.

King. Why, Warwick, hath thy knee forgot to bow?

Old Salisbury, shame to thy silver hair,
Thou mad misleader of thy brain-sick son!
What, wilt thou on thy death-bed play the ruffian,
And seek for sorrow with thy spectacles?
O, where is faith? O, where is loyalty?
If it be banish'd from the frosty head,
Where shall it find a harbor in the earth?
Wilt thou go dig a grave to find out war,
And shame thine honorable age with blood?
Why art thou old, and want'st experience?
Or wherefore dost abuse it, if thou hast it?
For shame! in duty bend thy knee to me,
That bows unto the grave with mickle age.

Sal. My lord, I have consider'd with myself
The title of this most renowned duke;
And in my conscience do repute his grace
The rightful heir to England's royal seat.

King. Hast thou not sworn allegiance unto me?

Sal. I have.

King. Canst thou dispense with heaven for such an oath?

Sal. It is great sin to swear unto a sin.
But greater sin to keep a sinful oath.
Who can be bound by any solemn vow
To do a murderous deed, to rob a man,
To force a spotless virgin's chastity,
To reave the orphan of his patrimony,
To wring the widow from her custom'd right,
And have no other reason for this wrong
But that he was bound by a solemn oath?

Queen. A subtle traitor needs no sophister.

King. Call Buckingham, and bid him arm himself.

York. Call Buckingham, and all the friends thou hast,
I am resolved for death or dignity.

Clif. The first I warrant thee, if dreams prove true.

War. You were best to go to bed and dream again,
To keep thee from the tempest of the field.

Clif. I am resolved to bear a greater storm
Than any thou canst conjure up to-day;
And that I'll write upon thy burgonet,
Might I but know thee by thy household badge.

War. Now, by my father's badge, old Nevil's crest,
The rampant bear chain'd to the ragged staff.
This day I'll wear aloft my burgonet,
As on a mountain top the cedar shows
That keeps his leaves in spite of any storm,
Even to affright thee with the view thereof.

Clif. And from the burgonet I'll rend thy bear,
And tread it under foot with all contempt,
Despite the bear-ward that protects the bear.

Y. Clif. And so to arms, victorious father,
To quell the rebels and their complices.

Rich. Fie! charity, for shame! speak not in spite.

For thou shall sup with Jesu Christ to-night.

Y. Clif. Foul stigmatic, that's more than thou canst tell.

Rich. If not in heaven, you'll surely sup in hell. [*Exeunt severally.*

SCENE II.—*Saint Alban's.*

ALARUMS *to the battle. Enter* WARWICK.

War. Clifford of Cumberland, 'tis Warwick calls:
And if thou dost not hide thee from the bear,
Now, when the angry trumpet sounds alarum,
And dead men's cries do fill the empty air,
Clifford, I say, come forth and fight with me:
Proud northern lord, Clifford of Cumberland,
Warwick is hoarse with calling thee to arms.

Enter YORK.

How now, my noble lord! what, all a-foot?

York. The deadly-handed Clifford slew my steed,
But match to match I have encounter'd·him,
And made a prey for carrion kites and crows
Even of the bonny beast he loved so well.

Enter CLIFFORD.

War. Of one or both of us the time is come.

York. Hold, Warwick, seek thee out some other chase,
For I myself must hunt this deer to death.

War. Then, nobly, York; 'tis for a crown thou fight'st.
As I intend, Clifford, to thrive to-day,
It grieves my soul to leave thee unassail'd.
[*Exit.*

Clif. What seest thou in me, York? why dost thou pause?

York. With thy brave bearing should I be in love,
But that thou are so fast mine enemy.

Clif. Nor should thy prowess want praise and esteem
But that 'tis shown ignobly and in treason.

York. So let it help me now against thy sword,
As I in justice and true right express it.

Clif. My soul and body on the action both! [stantly.

York. A dreadful lay! Address thee in-
[*They fight, and* CLIFFORD *falls.*

Clif. La fin couronne les œuvres. [*Dies.*

York. Thus war hath given thee peace, for thou art still.
Peace with his soul, heaven, if it be thy will!
[*Exit.*

Enter young CLIFFORD.

Y. Clif. Shame and confusion! all is on the rout;
Fear frames disorder, and disorder wounds
Where it should guard. O war, thou son of hell,

Whom angry heavens do make their minister,
Throw in the frozen bosoms of our part
Hot coals of vengeance! Let no soldier fly.
He that is truly dedicate to war
Hath no self-love, nor he that loves himself
Hath not essentially but by circumstance
The name of valor. [*Seeing his dead father*]
O, let the vile world end,
And the premised flames of the last day
Knit earth and heaven together!
Now let the general trumpet blow his blast,
Particularities and petty sounds
To cease! Wast thou ordain'd, dear father,
To lose thy youth in peace, and to achieve
The silver livery of advised age,
And, in thy reverence and thy chair-days, thus
To die in ruffian battle? Even at this sight
My heart is turn'd to stone: and while 'tis mine,
It shall be stony. York not our old men spares;
No more will I their babes: tears virginal
Shall be to me even as the dew to fire,
And beauty that the tyrant oft reclaims
Shall to my flaming wrath be oil and flax.
Henceforth I will not have to do with pity:
Meet I an infant of the house of York,
Into as many gobbets will I cut it
As wild Medea young Absyrtus did:
In cruelty will I seek out my fame.
Come, thou new ruin of old Clifford's house:
As did Æneas old Anchises bear,
So bear I thee upon my manly shoulders;
But then Æneas bare a living load,
Nothing so heavy as these woes of mine.
[*Exit, bearing off his father.*

Enter RICHARD *and* SOMERSET *to fight.*
SOMERSET *is killed.*

Rich. So, lie thou there;
For underneath an alehouse' paltry sign,
The Castle in Saint Alban's, Somerset
Hath made the wizard famous in his death.
Sword, hold thy temper; heart, be wrathful still:
Priests pray for enemies, but princes kill.
[*Exit.*

Fight. Excursions. Enter KING, QUEEN, *and others.*

Queen. Away, my lord! you are slow; for shame, away!

King. Can we outrun the heavens? good Margaret, stay.

Queen. What are you made of? you'll nor fight nor fly:
Now is it manhood, wisdom and defense,
To give the enemy way, and to secure us
By what we can, which can no more but fly.
[*Alarum afar off.*
If you be ta'en, we then should see the bottom
Of all our fortunes: but if we haply scape,

As well we may, if not through your neglect,
We shall to London get, where you are loved,
And where this breach now in our fortunes
    made
May readily be stopp'd.

Re-enter young CLIFFORD.

Y. Clif. But that my heart's on future mis-
    chief set,
I would speak blasphemy ere bid you fly:
But fly you must; uncurable discomfit
Reigns in the hearts of all our present parts.
Away, for your relief! and we will live
To see their day and them our fortune give:
Away, my lord, away! [*Exeunt.*

SCENE III.—*Fields near St. Alban's.*

Alarum. Retreat. Enter YORK, RICHARD,
WARWICK, *and soldiers, with drum and
colors.*

York. Of Salisbury, who can report of him,
That winter lion, who in rage forgets
Aged contusions and all brush of time,
And, like a gallant in the brow of youth,
Repairs him with occasion? This happy day
Is not itself, nor have we won one foot,
If Salisbury be lost.
Rich.   My noble father,
Three times to-day I holp him to his horse,
Three times bestrid him; thrice I led him off,
Persuaded him from any further act:
But still, where danger was, still there I met
    him;

And like rich hangings in a homely house,
So was his will in his old feeble body.
But, noble as he is, look where he comes.

Enter SALISBURY.

Sal. Now, by my sword, well hast thou
    fought to-day;
By the mass, so did we all. I thank you, Rich-
    ard:
God knows how long it is I have to live;
And it hath pleased him that three times to-
    day
You have defended me from imminent death.
Well, lords, we have not got that which we
    have:
'Tis not enough our foes are this time fled,
Being opposites of such repairing nature.
York. I know our safety is to follow them;
For, as I hear, the king is fled to London,
To call a present court of parliament.
Let us pursue him ere the writs go forth.
What says Lord Warwick? shall we after
    them?
War. After them! nay, before them, if we
    can.
Now, by my faith, lords, 'twas a glorious
    day:
Saint Alban's battle won by famous York
Shall be eternized in all age to come.
Sound drums and trumpets, and to London
    all:
And more such days as these to us befall!
                                    [*Exeunt.*

KING HENRY THE SIXTH PART THIRD

Act V. Sc. 5.

KING HENRY VI.

THIRD PART

DRAMATIS PERSONÆ

KING HENRY THE SIXTH.
EDWARD, *Prince of Wales, his Son.*
LOUIS XI., *King of France.*
DUKE OF SOMERSET,
DUKE OF EXETER,
EARL OF OXFORD, *Lords on*
EARL OF NORTHUMBERLAND, *KING*
EARL OF WESTMORELAND, *HENRY'S*
LORD CLIFFORD, *side.*
RICHARD PLANTAGENET, *Duke of York.*
EDWARD, *Earl of March, afterwards*
  KING EDWARD IV.,
EDMUND, *Earl of Rutland, his*
GEORGE, *afterwards Duke of Clarence, Sons.*
RICHARD, *afterwards Duke of Gloster,*
DUKE OF NORFOLK,
MARQUIS OF MONTAGUE,
EARL OF WARWICK, *of the* DUKE OF
EARL OF PEMBROKE, YORK'S *party.*
LORD HASTINGS,
LORD STAFFORD,
SIR JOHN MORTIMER, *Uncles to the* DUKE
SIR HUGH MORTIMER, *of* YORK.

HENRY, *Earl of Richmond, a youth.*
LORD RIVERS, *Brother to* LADY GREY.
SIR WILLIAM STANLEY.
SIR JOHN MONTGOMERY.
SIR JOHN SOMERVILLE.
Tutor to RUTLAND.
Mayor of York.
Lieutenant of the Tower.
A Nobleman.
Two Keepers.
A Huntsman.
A Son *that has killed his Father.*
A Father *that has killed his Son.*

QUEEN MARGARET.
LADY GREY, *afterwards Queen to* EDWARD IV
BONA, *Sister to the French Queen.*

Soldiers, *and other* Attendants *on* KING
  HENRY *and* KING EDWARD, Messengers, Watchmen, &c.

SCENE,—*During part of the Third Act in* FRANCE; *during the rest of the Play in* ENGLAND.

ACT I.

SCENE I.—LONDON. *The Parliament-house.*

Alarum. Enter the DUKE OF YORK, EDWARD, RICHARD, NORFOLK, MONTAGUE, WARWICK, *and Soldiers.*

War. I wonder how the king escaped our
  hands.
York. While we pursued the horsemen of
  the north,
He slily stole away and left his men:
Whereat the great Lord of Northumberland,
Whose warlike ears could never brook retreat,
Cheer'd up the drooping army; and himself,
Lord Clifford and Lord Stafford, all a-breast,
Charged our main battle's front, and breaking in
Were by the swords of common soldiers slain.
  Edw. Lord Stafford's father, Duke of
  Buckingham,
Is either slain or wounded dangerously;
I cleft his beaver with a downright blow:
That this is true, father, behold his blood
  Mont. And, brother, here's the Earl of
  Wiltshire's blood,
Whom I encounter'd as the battles join'd.

Rich. Speak thou for me and tell them
  what I did. [*Throwing down the
  Duke of Somerset's head.*
York. Richard hath best deserved of all
  my sons. [set?
But is your grace dead, my Lord of Somer-
  Norf. Such hope have all the line of John
  of Gaunt!
Rich. Thus do I hope to shake King Hen-
  ry's head.
War. And so do I. Victorious Prince of
  York,
Before I see thee seated in that throne
Which now the house of Lancaster usurps,
I vow by heaven these eyes shall never close.
This is the palace of the fearful king,
And this the regal seat: possess it, York;
For this is thine, and not King Henry's heirs'.
  York. Assist me, then, sweet Warwick, and
  I will;
For hither we have broken in by force.
  Norf. We'll all assist you; he that flies
  shall die.
  York. Thanks, gentle Norfolk: stay by me,
  my lords;
And, soldiers, stay and lodge by me this
  night [*They go up.*

227

War. And when the king comes, offer him
no violence,
Unless he seek to thrust you out perforce.
York. The queen this day here holds her
parliament,
But little thinks we shall be of her council:
By words or blows here let us win our right.
Rich. Arm'd as we are, let's stay within
this house.
War. The bloody parliament shall this be
call'd,
Unless Plantagenet, Duke of York, be king,
And bashful Henry deposed, whose cowardice
Hath made us by-words to our enemies.
York. Then leave me not, my lords; be
resolute:
I mean to take possession of my right.
War. Neither the king, nor he that loves
him best,
The proudest he that holds up Lancaster,
Dare stir a wing, if Warwick shake his bells.
I'll plant Plantagenet, root him up who
dares:
Resolve thee, Richard; claim the English
crown.

Flourish. Enter KING HENRY, CLIFFORD,
NORTHUMBERLAND, WESTMORELAND, EXE-
TER, *and the rest.*

K. Hen. My lords, look where the sturdy
rebel sits,
Even in the chair of state: belike he means,
Back'd by the power of Warwick, that false
peer,
To aspire unto the crown and reign as king.
Earl of Northumberland, he slew thy father,
And thine, Lord Clifford; and you both have
vow'd revenge
On him, his sons, his favorites and his friends.
North. If I be not, heavens be revenged on
me!
Clif. The hope thereof makes Clifford
mourn in steel.
West. What, shall we suffer this? let's
pluck him down:
My heart for anger burns; I cannot brook it.
K. Hen. Be patient, gentle Earl of West-
moreland.
Clif. Patience is for poltroons, such as he:
He durst not sit there, had your father lived.
My gracious lord, here in the parliament
Let us assail the family of York.
North. Well hast thou spoken, cousin: be
it so.
K. Hen. Ah, know you not the city favors
them,
And they have troops of soldiers at their
beck?
Exe. But when the duke is slain, they'll
quickly fly.
K. Hen. Far be the thought of this from
Henry's heart,
To make a shambles of the parliament-
house!

Cousin of Exeter, frowns, words and threats
Shall be the war that Henry means to use.
Thou factious Duke of York, descend my
throne,
And kneel for grace and mercy at my feet;
I am thy sovereign.
York. I am thine.
Exe. For shame, come down: he made thee
Duke of York.
York. 'Twas my inheritance, as the earl-
dom was.
Exe. Thy father was a traitor to the
crown.
War. Exeter, thou art a traitor to the
crown.
In following this usurping Henry.
Clif. Whom should he follow but his nat-
ural king?
War. True, Clifford; and that's Richard
Duke of York.
K. Hen. And shall I stand, and thou sit in
my throne?
York. It must and shall be so: content
thyself.
War. Be Duke of Lancaster; let him be
king.
West. He is both king and Duke of Lan-
caster;
And that the Lord of Westmoreland shall
maintain.
War. And Warwick shall disprove it. You
forget.
That we are those which chased you from
the field,
And slew your fathers, and with colors spread
March'd through the city to the palace gates.
North. Yes, Warwick, I remember it to my
grief;
And, by his soul, thou and thy house shall
rue it.
West. Plantagenet, of thee and these thy
sons,
Thy kinsmen and thy friends, I'll have more
lives
Than drops of blood were in my father's
veins.
Clif. Urge it no more; lest that, instead of
words,
I send thee, Warwick, such a messenger
As shall revenge his death before I stir.
War. Poor Clifford! how I scorn his
worthless threats!
York. Will you we show our title to the
crown?
If not, our swords shall plead it in the field.
K. Hen. What title hast thou, traitor, to
the crown?
Thy father was, as thou art, Duke of York;
Thy grandfather, Roger Mortimer, Earl of
March:
I am the son of Henry the Fifth,
Who made the Dauphin and the French to
stoop,
And seized upon their towns and provinces.

War. Talk not of France, sith thou hast
lost it all.

K. Hen. The lord protector lost it, and not
I:

When I was crown'd I was but nine months
old.

Rich. You are old enough now, and yet,
methinks, you lose.

Father, tear the crown from the usurper's
head.

Edw. Sweet father, do so; set it on your
head.

Mont. Good brother, as thou lovest and
honorest arms,

Let's fight it out and not stand caviling thus.

Rich. Sound drums and trumpets, and the
king will fly.

York. Sons, peace!

K. Hen. Peace, thou! and give King Henry
leave to speak.

War. Plantagenet shall speak first: hear
him, lords;

And be you silent and attentive too,

For he that interrupts him shall not live.

K. Hen. Think'st thou that I will leave my
kingly throne,

Wherein my grandsire and my father sat?

No: first shall war unpeople this my realm;

Ay, and their colors, often borne in France,

And now in England to our heart's great sorrow,

Shall be my winding-sheet. Why faint you,
lords?

My title's good, and better far than his.

War. Prove it, Henry, and thou shalt be
king.

K. Hen. Henry the Fourth by conquest got
the crown.

York. 'Twas by rebellion against his king.

K. Hen. [*Aside*] I know not what to say;
my title's weak.

Tell me, may not a king adopt an heir?

York. What then?

K. Hen. An if he may, then am I lawful
king;

For Richard, in the view of many lords,

Resign'd the crown to Henry the Fourth,

Whose heir my father was, and I am his.

York. He rose against him, being his sovereign,

And made him to resign his crown perforce.

War. Suppose, my lords, he did it uncon-
strain'd,

Think you 'twere prejudicial to his crown?

Exe. No; for he could not so resign his
crown

But that the next heir should succeed and
reign.

K. Hen. Art thou against us, Duke of Exeter?

Exe. His is the right, and therefore pardon
me.

York. Why whisper you, my lords, and
answer not?

Exe. My conscience tells me he is lawful
king.

K. Hen. [*Aside*] All will revolt from me,
and turn to him.

North. Plantagenet, for all the claim thou
lay'st,

Think not that Henry shall be so deposed.

War. Deposed he shall be, in despite of all

North. Thou art deceived; 'tis not thy
southern power,

Of Essex, Norfolk, Suffolk, nor of Kent,

Which makes thee thus presumptuous and
proud,

Can set the duke up in despite of me.

Clif. King Henry, be thy title right or
wrong,

Lord Clifford vows to fight in thy defense:

May that ground gape and swallow me alive,

Where I shall kneel to him that slew my father!

K. Hen. O Clifford, how thy words revive
my heart!

York. Henry of Lancaster, resign thy
crown.

What mutter you, or what conspire you,
lords?

War. Do right unto this princely Duke of
York,

Or I will fill the house with armed men,

And over the chair of state, where now he
sits,

Write up his title with usurping blood.

[*He stamps with his foot, and the Soldiers
show themselves.*

K. Hen. My Lord of Warwick, hear me
but one word:

Let me for this my life-time reign as king.

York. Confirm the crown to me and to
mine heirs,

And thou shalt reign in quiet while thou
livest.

King. I am content: Richard Plantagenet,

Enjoy the kingdom after my decease.

Clif. What wrong is this unto the prince
your son!

War. What good is this to England and
himself!

West. Base, fearful and despairing Henry!

Clif. How hast thou injured both thyself
and us!

West. I cannot stay to hear these articles.

North. Nor I.

Clif. Come, cousin, let us tell the queen
these news.

West. Farewell, faint-hearted and degenerate king,

In whose cold blood no spark of honor bides.

North. Be thou a prey unto the house of
York,

And die in bands, for this unmanly deed!

Clif. In dreadful war mayst thou be overcome,

Or live in peace, abandon'd and despis'd!

[*Exeunt* NORTH., CLIF., *and* WEST.

War. Turn this way, Henry, and regard them not.

Exe. They seek revenge, and therefore will not yield.

K. Hen. Ah, Exeter!

War. Why should you sigh, my lord?

K. Hen. Not for myself, Lord Warwick, but my son,
Whom I unnaturally shall disinherit.
But be it as it may:—I here entail
The crown to thee and to thine heirs for ever;
Conditionally, that here thou take an oath
To cease this civil war, and, whilst I live,
To honour me as thy king and sovereign,
And neither by treason nor hostility
To seek to put me down and reign thyself.

York. This oath I willingly take, and will perform.   [*Coming from the throne.*

War. Long live King Henry!—Plantagenet, embrace him.

K. Hen. And long live thou, and these thy forward sons!

York. Now York and Lancaster are reconcil'd.

Exe. Accurs'd be he that seeks to make them foes!
    [*Sennet. The* LORDS *come forward.*

York. Farewell, my gracious lord; I'll to my castle.

War. And I'll keep London with my soldiers.

Norf. And I to Norfolk with my followers.

Mont. And I unto the sea, from whence I came.
    [*Exeunt* YORK *and his* SONS, WAR.,
    NORF., MONT., Soldiers, *and* Attendants.

K. Hen. And I, with grief and sorrow to the court.

Exe. Here comes the queen, whose looks bewray her anger;
I'll steal away.   [*Going.*

K. Hen. Exeter, so will I.   [*Going.*

Enter QUEEN MARGARET *and the* PRINCE OF WALES.

Q. Mar. Nay, go not from me; I will follow thee.   [*will stay.*

K. Hen. Be patient, gentle queen, and I

Q. Mar. Who can be patient in such extremes?
Ah, wretched man! would I had died a maid,
And never seen thee, never born thee son,
Seeing thou hast prov'd so unnatural a father!
Hath he deserv'd to lose his birthright thus?
Hadst thou but lov'd him half so well as I,
Or felt that pain which I did for him once,
Or nourish'd him as I did with my blood,—
Thou wouldst have left thy dearest heart-
    blood there,   [heir,
Rather than made that savage duke thine
And disinherited thine only son.

Prince. Father, you cannot disinherit me:
If you be king, why should not I succeed?

K. Hen. Pardon me, Margaret;—pardon me, sweet son:—
The Earl of Warwick and the duke enforc'd me.

Q. Mar. Enforc'd thee! art thou king, and wilt be forc'd?
I shame to hear thee speak. Ah, timorous wretch!
Thou hast undone thyself, thy son, and me;
And given unto the house of York such head
As thou shalt reign but by their sufferance.
To entail him and his heirs unto the crown,
What is it, but to make thy sepulchre,
And creep into it far before thy time?
Warwick is chancellor and the lord of Calais;
Stern Falconbridge commands the narrow seas;
The duke is made protector of the realm;
And yet shalt thou be safe? such safety finds
The trembling lamb environed with wolves.
Had I been there, which am a silly woman,
The soldiers should have toss'd me on their pikes
Before I would have granted to that act.
But thou preferr'st thy life before thine honour:
And seeing thou dost, I here divorce myself
Both from thy table, Henry, and thy bed,
Until that act of parliament be repeal'd,
Whereby my son is disinherited.   [colours
The northern lords that have forsworn thy
Will follow mine, if once they see them spread;
And spread they shall be,—to thy foul disgrace,
And utter ruin of the house of York.
Thus do I leave thee.—Come, son, let's away;
Our army is ready; come, we'll after them.

K. Hen. Stay, gentle Margaret, and hear me speak.

Q. Mar. Thou hast spoke too much already: get thee gone   [with me?

K. Hen. Gentle son Edward, thou wilt stay

Q. Mar. Ay, to be murder'd by his enemies.

Prince. When I return with victory from the field
I'll see your grace: till then I'll follow her.

Q. Mar. Come, son, away; we may not linger thus.
    [*Exeunt* QUEEN MARGARET
    and the PRINCE.

K. Hen. Poor queen! how love to me and to her son
Hath made her break out into terms of rage!
Reveng'd may she be on that hateful duke,
Whose haughty spirit, winged with desire,
Will cost my crown, and like an empty eagle
Tire on the flesh of me and my son!
The loss of those three lords torments my heart:
I'll write unto them, and entreat them fair:—
Come, cousin, you shall be the messenger.

Exe. And I, I hope, shall reconcile them
   all.   [*Exeunt.*

SCENE II.—*A Room in Sandal Castle, near
   Wakefield, in Yorkshire.*

Enter EDWARD, RICHARD, *and* MONTAGUE.

Rich. Brother, though I be youngest, give
   me leave.
Edw. No, I can better play the orator.
Mont. But I have reasons strong and forcible.

Enter YORK.

York. Why, how now, sons and brother!
   at a strife?
What is your quarrel? how began it first?
Edw. No quarrel, but a slight contention.
York. About what?
Rich. About that which concerns your
   grace and us,—
The crown of England, father, which is yours.
York. Mine, boy? not till King Henry be
   dead.   [death.
Rich. Your right depends not on his life or
Edw. Now you are heir, therefore enjoy it
   now: [breathe,
By giving the house of Lancaster leave to
It will outrun you, father, in the end.
York. I took an oath that he should
   quietly reign.
Edw. But, for a kingdom, any oath may
   be broken: [year.
I would break a thousand oaths to reign one
Rich. No; God forbid your grace should
   be forsworn.
York. I shall be, if I claim by open war.
Rich. I'll prove the contrary, if you'll hear
   me speak.   [sible.
York. Thou canst not, son; it is impos-
Rich. An oath is of no moment, being not
   took
Before a true and lawful magistrate,
That hath authority over him that swears;
Henry had none, but did usurp the place;
Then, seeing 'twas he that made you to de-
   pose,
Your oath, my lord, is vain and frivolous.
Therefore, to arms. And, father, do but think
How sweet a thing it is to wear a crown;
Within whose circuit is Elysium,
And all that poets feign of bliss and joy.
Why do we linger thus? I cannot rest
Until the white rose that I wear be dy'd
Even in the lukewarm blood of Henry's
   heart.
York. Richard, enough; I will be king, or
   die.—
Brother, thou shalt to London presently,
And whet on Warwick to this enterprise.—
Thou, Richard, shalt to the Duke of Norfolk,
And tell him privily of our intent,—
You, Edward, shall unto my Lord Cobham,
With whom the Kentishmen will willingly
   rise:

In them I trust; for they are soldiers,
Witty, courteous, liberal, full of spirit.—
While you are thus employ'd, what resteth
   more,
But that I seek occasion how to rise,
And yet the king not privy to my drift,
Nor any of the house of Lancaster?

Enter a MESSENGER.

But, stay: what news? Why com'st thou in
   such post?   [earls and lords
Mess. The queen with all the northern
Intend here to besiege you in your castle:
She is hard by with twenty thousand men,
And therefore fortify your hold, my lord.
York. Ay, with my sword. What! think'st
   thou that we fear them?—
Edward and Richard, you shall stay with
   me;—
My brother Montague shall post to London:
Let noble Warwick, Cobham, and the rest,
Whom we have left protectors of the king,
With powerful policy strengthen themselves,
And trust not simple Henry nor his oaths.
Mont. Brother, I go; I'll win them, fear
   it not:
And thus most humbly I do take my leave.
                      [*Exit.*

Enter SIR JOHN *and* SIR HUGH MORTIMER.

York. Sir John and Sir Hugh Mortimer,
   mine uncles!
You are come to Sandal in a happy hour;
The army of the queen mean to besiege us.
Sir John. She shall not need, we'll meet
   her in the field.
York. What, with five thousand men?
Rich. Ay, with five hundred, father, for a
   need:
A woman's general; what should we fear?
            [*A march afar off.*
Edw. I hear their drums: let's set our men
   in order,
And issue forth, and bid them battle straight.
York. Five men to twenty!—though the
   odds be great,
I doubt not, uncle, of our victory.
Many a battle have I won in France,
When as the enemy hath been ten to one:
Why should I not now have the like success?
                  [*Exeunt.*

SCENE III.—*Plains near Sandal Castle.*

Alarum. Enter RUTLAND *and his* TUTOR.

Rut. Ah, whither shall I fly to 'scape their
   hands?
Ah, tutor, look where bloody Clifford comes!

Enter CLIFFORD *and* SOLDIERS.

Clif. Chaplain, away! thy priesthood saves
   thy life.
As for the brat of this accursed duke,
Whose father slew my father,—he shall die.

Tut. And I, my lord, will bear him company.

Clif. Soldiers, away with him!

Tut. Ah, Clifford, murder not this innocent child,

Lest thou be hated both of God and man.

[*Exit, forced off by* SOLDIERS.

Clif. How now! is he dead already? or is it fear

That makes him close his eyes?—I'll open them.

Rut. So looks the pent-up lion o'er the wretch

That trembles under his devouring paws;

And so he walks, insulting o'er his prey,

And so he comes, to rend his limbs asunder.—

Ah, gentle Clifford, kill me with thy sword,

And not with such a cruel threat'ning look!

Sweet Clifford, hear me speak before I die!—

I am too mean a subject for thy wrath:

Be thou reveng'd on men, and let me live.

Clif. In vain thou speak'st, poor boy; my father's blood

Hath stopp'd the passage where thy words should enter.

Rut. Then let my father's blood open it again:

He is a man, and, Clifford, cope with him.

Clif. Had I thy brethren here, their lives and thine

Were not revenge sufficient for me;

No, if I digg'd up thy forefathers' graves,

And hung their rotten coffins up in chains,

It could not slake mine ire nor ease my heart.

The sight of any of the house of York

Is as a fury to torment my soul;

And till I root out their accursed line

And leave not one alive, I live in hell.

Therefore,—   [*Lifting his hand.*

Rut. O let me pray before I take my death!

To thee I pray; sweet Clifford, pity me!

Clif. Such pity as my rapier's point affords.

Rut. I never did thee harm: why wilt thou slay me?

Clif. Thy father hath.

Rut.   But 'twas ere I was born.

Thou hast one son,—for his sake pity me;

Lest in revenge thereof,—sith God is just,—

He be as miserably slain as I.

Ah, let me live in prison all my days;

And when I give occasion of offence

Then let me die, for now thou hast no cause.

Clif. No cause!

Thy father slew my father; therefore, die.

[CLIFFORD *stabs him.*

Rut. Dii faciant, laudis summa sit ista tuæ!   [*Dies.*

Clif. Plantagenet! I come, Plantagenet!

And this thy son's blood cleaving to my blade

Shall rust upon my weapon, till thy blood,

Congeal'd with this, do make me wipe off both.   [*Exit.*

SCENE IV.—*Another part of the Plains near Sandal Castle.*

Alarum. Enter YORK.

York. The army of the queen hath got the field:

My uncles both are slain in rescuing me;

And all my followers to the eager foe

Turn back, and fly, like ships before the wind,

Or lambs pursu'd by hunger-starved wolves.

My sons,—God knows what hath bechanced them: [selves

But this I know,—they have demean'd themselves

Like men born to renown by life or death.

Three times did Richard make a lane to me;

And thrice cried, *Courage, father! fight it out!*

And full as oft came Edward to my side,

With purple falchion, painted to the hilt

In blood of those that had encounter'd him:

And when the hardiest warriors did retire,

Richard cried, *Charge! and give no foot of ground!*

And cried, *A crown, or else a glorious tomb!*

A sceptre, or an earthly sepulchre!

With this we charg'd again: but, out, alas!

We bodg'd again; as I have seen a swan

With bootless labour swim against the tide,

And spend her strength with over-matching waves.   [*A short alarum within.*

Ah, hark! the fatal followers do pursue;

And I am faint, and cannot fly their fury:

And were I strong, I would not shun their fury:

The sands are number'd that make up my life;

Here must I stay, and here my life must end.

Enter QUEEN MARGARET, CLIFFORD, NORTHUMBERLAND, *and Soldiers.*

Come, bloody Clifford,—rough Northumberland,—

I dare your quenchless fury to more rage:

I am your butt, and I abide your shot.

North. Yield to our mercy, proud Plantagenet

Clif. Ay, to such mercy as his ruthless arm

With downright payment, show'd unto my father.

Now Phaeton hath tumbled from his car,

And made an evening at the noontide prick.

York. My ashes, as the phœnix, may bring forth

A bird that will revenge upon you all:

And in that hope I throw mine eyes to heaven,

Scorning whate'er you can afflict me with.

Why come you not? what! multitudes, and fear?

Clif. So cowards fight when they can fly no further;

So doves do peck the falcon's piercing talons;

So desperate thieves, all hopeless of their lives,
Breathe out invectives 'gainst the officers.

York. O Clifford, but bethink thee once again,
And in thy thought o'errun my former time;
And, if thou canst, for blushing, view this face,
And bite thy tongue, that slanders him with cowardice [this!
Whose frown hath made thee faint and fly ere

Clif. I will not bandy with thee word for word,
But buckle with thee blows, twice two for one. [*Draws.*

Q. Mar. Hold, valiant Clifford! for a thousand causes
I would prolong awhile the traitor's life.—
Wrath makes him deaf:—speak thou, Northumberland. [so much

North. Hold, Clifford! do not honour him
To prick thy finger, though to wound his heart:
What valour were it, when a cur doth grin,
For one to thrust his hand between his teeth,
When he might spurn him with his foot away?
It is war's prize to take all 'vantages;
And ten to one is no impeach of valour.

[*They lay hands on* York, *who struggles.*

Clif. Ay, ay, so strives the woodcock with the gin.

North. So doth the cony struggle in the net. [York *is taken prisoner.*

York. So triumph thieves upon their conquer'd booty;
So true men yield, with robbers so o'ermatch'd.

North. What would your grace have done unto him now? [thumberland,

Q. Mar. Brave warriers, Clifford and Northumberland,
Come, make him stand upon this molehill here,
That raught at mountains with outstretched arms,
Yet parted but the shadow with his hand.—
What, was it you that would be England's king?
Was't you that revell'd in our parliament,
And made a preachment of your high descent?
Where are your mess of sons to back you now?
The wanton Edward and the lusty George?
And where's that valiant crook-back prodigy,
Dicky your boy, that with his grumbling voice
Was wont to cheer his dad in mutinies?
Or, with the rest, where is your darling Rutland?
Look, York: I stain'd this napkin with the blood
That valiant Clifford, with his rapier's point,
Made issue from the bosom of the boy:

And if thine eyes can water for his death,
I give thee this to dry thy cheeks withal.
Alas, poor York! but that I hate thee deadly,
I should lament thy miserable state.
I pr'ythee, grieve, to make me merry, York.
What, hath thy fiery heart so parch'd thine entrails
That not a tear can fall for Rutland's death?
Why art thou patient, man? thou shouldst be mad;
And I, to make thee mad, do mock thee thus.
Stamp, rave, and fret, that I may sing and dance.
Thou wouldst be fee'd, I see, to make me sport;
York cannot speak unless he wear a crown.—
A crown for York!—and, lords, bow low to him;—
Hold you his hands whilst I do set it on.

[*Putting a paper crown on his head.*

Ay, marry, sir, now looks he like a king!
Ay, this is he that took King Henry's chair;
And this is he was his adopted heir.—
But how is it that great Plantagenet
Is crown'd so soon, and broke his solemn oath?
As I bethink me, you should not be king
Till our King Henry had shook hands with death.
And will you pale your head in Henry's glory,
And rob his temples of the diadem
Now in his life, against your holy oath?
O, 'tis a fault too, too unpardonable!—
Off with the crown; and, with the crown, his head;
And whilst we breathe take time to do him dead.

Clif. That is my office, for my father's sake.

Q. Mar. Nay, stay; let's hear the orisons he makes.

York. She-wolf of France, but worse than wolves of France, [tooth!
Whose tongue more poisons than the adder's
How ill-seeming is it in thy sex.
To triumph, like an Amazonian trull,
Upon their woes whom fortune captivates!
But that thy face is, visard-like, unchanging,
Made impudent with use of evil deeds,
I would assay, proud queen, to make thee blush:
To tell thee whence thou cam'st, of whom deriv'd,
Were shame enough to shame thee, wert thou not shameless.
Thy father bears the type of King of Naples,
Of both the Sicils, and Jerusalem;
Yet not so wealthy as an English yeoman.
Hath that poor monarch taught thee to insult?
It needs not, nor it boots thee not, proud queen:

Unless the adage must be verified,—
That beggars mounted run their horse to death.
'Tis beauty that doth oft make women proud;
But, God he knows, thy share thereof is small:
'Tis virtue that doth make them most admir'd;
The contrary doth make thee wonder'd at:
'Tis government that makes them seem divine;
The want thereof makes thee abominable:
Thou art as opposite to every good
As the antipodes are unto us,
Or as the south to the septentrion.
O tiger's heart wrapp'd in a woman's hide!
How couldst thou drain the life-blood of the child,
To bid the father wipe his eyes withal.
And yet be seen to bear a woman's face?
Women are soft, mild, pitiful, and flexible;
Thou stern, obdurate, flinty, rough, remorseless.
Bidd'st thou me rage? why, now thou hast thy wish: [thy will:
Wouldst have me weep? why, now thou hast
For raging wind blows up incessant showers,
And when the rage allays, the rain begins.
These tears are my sweet Rutland's obsequies;
And every drop cries vengeance for his death
'Gainst thee, fell Clifford, and thee, false Frenchwoman.   [me so
North. Beshrew me, but his passions move
That hardly can I check my eyes from tears.
York. That face of his the hungry cannibals
Would not have touch'd, would not have stain'd with blood:
But you are more inhuman, more inexorable,—
O, ten times more,—than tigers of Hyrcania.
See ruthless, queen, a hapless father's tears:
This cloth thou dipp'dst in blood of my sweet boy,
And I with tears do wash the blood away.
Keep thou the napkin, and go boast of this:
                    [*He gives back the handkerchief.*
And if thou tell'st the heavy story right,
Upon my soul, the hearers will shed tears;
Yea, even my foes will shed fast-falling tears,
And say, *Alas, it was a piteous deed!*—
There, take the crown, and, with the crown, my curse;
                    [*Giving back the paper crown.*
And in thy need such comfort come to thee
As now I reap at thy too cruel hand!—
Hard-hearted Clifford, take me from the world:
My soul to heaven, my blood upon your heads!   [my kin,
North. Had he been slaughter-man to all

I should not for my life but weep with him,
To see how inly sorrow gripes his soul.
Q. Mar. What, weeping-ripe, my Lord Northumberland?
Think but upon the wrong he did us all,
And that will quickly dry the melting tears.
Clif. Here's for my oath, here's for my father's death.   [*Stabbing him.*
Q. Mar. And here's to right our gentle-hearted king.   [*Stabbing him.*
York. Open thy gate of mercy, gracious God!
My soul flies through these wounds to seek out thee.   [*Dies.*
Q. Mar. Off with his head, and set it on York gates;
So York may overlook the town of York.
                    [*Flourish. Exeunt.*

ACT II.

Scene I.—*A plain near Mortimer's Cross in Herefordshire.*

Drums. Enter Edward *and* Richard, *with their* Forces, *marching.*

Edw. I wonder how our princely father 'scap'd,
Or whether he be 'scap'd away or no
From Clifford's and Northumberland's pursuit:
Had he been ta'en we should have heard the news;   [news;
Had he been slain we should have heard the
Or had he 'scap'd, methinks we should have heard
The happy tidings of his good escape.—
How fares my brother? why is he so sad?
Rich. I cannot joy, until I be resolv'd
Where our right valiant father is become.
I saw him in the battle range about;
And watch'd him how he singled Clifford forth.
Methought he bore him in the thickest troop
As doth a lion in a herd of neat;
Or as a bear, encompass'd round with dogs,—
Who having pinch'd a few, and made them cry,
The rest stand all aloof and bark at him.
So far'd our father with his enemies;
So fled his enemies my warlike father:
Methinks 'tis prize enough to be his son.—
See how the morning ope's her golden gates,
And takes her farewell of the glorious sun!
How well resembles it the prime of youth,
Trimm'd like a younker prancing to his love!
Edw. Dazzle mine eyes, or do I see three suns?
Rich. Three glorious suns, each on a perfect sun;
Not separated with the racking clouds,
But sever'd in a pale clear-shining sky.
See, see! they join, embrace, and seem to kiss,
As if they vow'd some league inviolable:

Now are they but one lamp, one light, one
  sun.
In this the heaven figures some event.
  Edw. 'Tis wondrous strange, the like yet
  never heard of.
I think it cites us, brother, to the field,—
That we, the sons of brave Plantagenet,
Each one already blazing by our meeds,
Should, notwithstanding, join our lights to-
  gether,
And overshine the earth, as this the world
Whate'er it bodes, henceforward will I bear
Upon my target three fair shining suns.
  Rich. Nay, bear three daughters:—by
  your leave I speak it,
You love the breeder better than the male.

Enter a Messenger.

But what are thou, whose heavy looks fore-
  tell
Some dreadful story hanging on thy tongue?
  Mess. Ah, one that was a woeful looker-
  on
When as the noble Duke of York was slain,
Your pricely father and my loving lord!
  Edw. O, speak no more! for I have heard
  too much.
  Rich. Say how he died, for I will hear it
  all.
  Mess. Environed he was with many foes;
And stood against them as the hope of Troy
Against the Greeks that would have enter'd
  Troy.
But Hercules himself must yield to odds;
And many strokes, though with a little axe,
Hew down and fell the hardest-timber'd oak.
By many hands your father was subdu'd;
But only slaughter'd by the ireful arm
Of unrelenting Clifford, and the queen,—
Who crown'd the gracious duke in high de-
  spite,—
Laugh'd in his face; and when with grief he
  wept,
The ruthless queen gave him to dry his
  cheeks
A napkin steeped in the harmless blood
Of sweet young Rutland, by rough Clifford
  slain:
And after many scorns, many foul taunts,
They took his head, and on the gates of York
They set the same; and there it doth remain,
The saddest spectacle that e'er I view'd.
  Edw. Sweet Duke of York, our prop to
  lean upon,—
Now thou art gone, we have no staff, no
  stay!—
O Clifford, boisterous Clifford, thou hast slain
The flower of Europe for his chivalry;
And treacherously hast thou vanquish'd him,
For hand to hand he would have vanquish'd
  thee!—
Now my soul's palace is become a prison:
Ah, would she break from hence, that this
  my body

Might in the ground be closed up in rest!
For never henceforth shall I joy again,
Never, O never shall I see more joy.
  Rich. I cannot weep; for all my body's
  moisture   [heart:
Scarce serves to quench my furnace-burning
Nor can my tongue unload my heart's great
  burden;
For self-same wind that I should speak
  withal
Is kindling coals, that fire all my breast,
And burn me up with flames, that tears
  would quench.
To weep is to make less the depth of grief:
Tears, then, for babes; blows and revenge for
  me!—
Richard, I bear thy name; I'll venge thy
  death,
Or die renowned by attempting it.
  Edw. His name that valiant duke hath left
  with thee;
His dukedom and his chair with me is left.
  Rich. Nay, if thou be that princely eagle's
  bird,
Show thy descent by gazing 'gainst the sun:
For chair and dukedom, throne and kingdom
  say:
Either that is thine, or else thou wert not his.

March. Enter WARWICK *and* MONTAGUE,
  with Forces.

  War. How now, fair lords! What fare?
  what news abroad?   [should recount
  Rich. Great Lord of Warwick, if we
Our baleful news, and at each word's deliv-
  erance
Stab poniards in our flesh till all were told,
The words would add more anguish than the
  'wounds.
O valiant lord, the Duke of York is slain!
  Edw. O Warwick, Warwick! that Plan-
  tagenet
Which held thee dearly as his soul's redemp-
  tion
Is by the stern Lord Clifford done to death.
  War. Ten days ago I drown'd these news
  in tears;
And now, to add more measure to your woes,
I come to tell you things since then befall'n.
After the bloody fray at Wakefield fought,
Where your brave father breath'd his latest
  gasp,
Tidings, as swiftly as the posts could run,
Were brought me of your loss and his depart.
I, then in London, keeper of the king,
Muster'd my soldiers, gather'd flocks of
  friends,
And very well appointed, as I thought,
March'd towards Saint Albans to intercept
  the queen,
Bearing the king in my behalf along;
For by my scouts I was advertised
That she was coming with a full intent
To dash our late decree in parliament

Touching King Henry's oath and your succession.
Short tale to make,—we at St. Albans met,
Our battles join'd, and both sides fiercely fought.
But whether 'twas the coldness of the king,
Who look'd full gently on his warlike queen,
That robb'd my soldiers of their heated spleen;
Or whether 'twas report of her success;
Or more than common fear of Clifford's rigour,
Who thunders to his captives, Blood and death,
I cannot judge: but, to conclude with truth,
Their weapons like to lightning came and went;
Our soldiers',—like the night-owl's lazy flight,
Or like a lazy thrasher with a flail,—
Fell gently down, as if they struck their friends.
I cheer'd them up with justice of our cause,
With promise of high pay and great rewards:
But all in vain; they had no heart to fight,
And we in them no hope to win the day;
So that we fled; the king unto the queen;
Lord George, your brother, Norfolk, and myself,
In haste, post-haste, are come to join with you;
For in the marches here we heard you were
Making another head to fight again.
Edw. Where is the Duke of Norfolk, gentle Warwick?   [England?
And when came George from Burgundy to
War. Some six miles off the duke is with the soldiers;
And for your brother, he was lately sent
From your kind aunt, Duchess of Burgundy,
With aid of soldiers to this needful war.
Rich. 'Twas odds, belike, when valiant Warwick fled:
Oft have I heard his praises in pursuit,
But ne'er till now his scandal of retire.
War. Nor now my scandal, Richard, dost thou hear;   [mine
For thou shalt know this strong right hand of
Can pluck the diadem from faint Henry's head,
And wring the awful sceptre from his fist,
Were he as famous and as bold in war
As he is fam'd for mildness, peace, and prayer.
Rich. I know it well, Lord Warwick; blame me not:
'Tis love I bear thy glories makes me speak.
But in this troublous time what's to be done?
Shall we go throw away our coats of steel,
And wrap our bodies in black mourning-gowns,
Numbering our Ave-Maries with our beads?
Or shall we on the helmets of our foes
Tell our devotion with revengeful arms?

If for the last, say Ay, and to it, lords.
War. Why, therefore Warwick came to seek you out;
And therefore comes my brother Montague.
Attend me, lords. The proud insulting queen,
With Clifford and the haught Northumberland,
And of their feather many more proud birds,
Have wrought the easy-melting king like wax.
He swore consent to your succession,
His oath enrolled in the parliament;
And now to London all the crew are gone,
To frustrate both his oath and what beside
May make against the house of Lancaster.
Their power, I think, is thirty thousand strong:
Now if the help of Norfolk and myself,
With all the friends that thou, brave Earl of March,
Amongst the loving Welshmen canst procure,
Will but amount to five-and-twenty thousand,
Why, *Via!* to London will we march amain;
And once again bestride our foaming steeds,
And once again cry, Charge upon our foes!
But never once again turn back and fly.
Rich. Ay, now methinks I hear great Warwick speak.
Ne'er may he live to see a sunshine day
That cries Retire, if Warwick bid him stay.
Edw. Lord Warwick, on thy shoulder will I lean;
And when thou fail'st,—as God forbid the hour!—
Must Edward fall, which peril heaven forefend!   [of York:
War. No longer Earl of March, but Duke
The next degree is England's royal throne;
For King of England shalt thou be proclaim'd
In every borough as we pass along;
And he that throws not up his cap for joy,
Shall for the fault make forfeit of his head.
King Edward,—valiant Richard,—Montague,—
Stay we no longer, dreaming of renown,
But sound the trumpets and about our task.
Rich. Then, Clifford, were thy heart as hard as steel,—
As thou hast shown it flinty by thy deeds,—
I come to pierce it,—or to give thee mine.
Edw. Then strike up drums:—God and Saint George for us!

Enter a Messenger.

War. How now! what news?
Mess. The Duke of Norfolk sends you word by me,
The queen is coming with a puissant host;
And craves your company for speedy counsel.
War. Why, then it sorts, brave warriors: let's away.   [*Exeunt.*

SCENE II.—*Before York.*

Flourish. Enter KING HENRY, QUEEN MAR-
GARET, *the* PRINCE OF WALES, CLIFFORD,
and NORTHUMBERLAND, *with* Forces.

Q. Mar. Welcome, my lord, to this brave
  town of York.
Yonder's the head of that arch-enemy
That sought to be encompass'd with your
  crown:
Doth not the object cheer your heart, my
  lord?
  K. Hen. Ay, as the rocks cheer them that
  fear their wreck:—
To see this sight, it irks my very soul.—
Withhold revenge, dear God! tis not my
  fault,
Nor wittingly have I infring'd my vow.
  Clif. My gracious liege, this too much
  lenity
And harmful pity must be laid aside.
To whom do lions cast their gentle looks?
Not to the beast that would usurp their den.
Whose hand is that the forest bear doth lick?
Not his that spoils her young before her
  face.
Who scapes the lurking serpent's mortal
  sting?
Not he that sets his foot upon her back.
The smallest worm will turn, being trodden
  on,
And doves will peck in safeguard of their
  brood.
Ambitious York did level at thy crown,
Thou smiling while he knit his angry brows:
He, but a duke, would have his son a king,
And raise his issue, like a loving sire;
Thou, being a king, bless'd with a goodly
  son,
Didst yield consent to disinherit him,
Which argu'd thee a most unloving father.
Unreasonable creatures feed their young;
And though man's face be fearful to their
  eyes,
Yet, in protection of their tender ones,
Who hath not seen them,—even with those
  wings
Which sometime they have us'd with fearful
  flight,—   [nest,
Make war with him that climb'd unto their
Offering their own lives in their young's de-
  fence?
For shame, my liege, make them your prece-
  dent!
Were it not pity that this goodly boy
Should lose his birthright by his father's
  fault,
And long hereafter say unto his child,
*What my great-grandfather and grandsire
  got*
My careless father fondly gave away?
Ah, what a shame were this! Look on the
  boy;
And let his manly face, which promiseth

Successful fortune, steel thy melting heart
To hold thine own, and leave thine own with
  him.   [orator,
  K. Hen. Full well hath Clifford play'd the
Inferring arguments of mighty force.
But, Clifford, tell me, didst thou never hear
That things ill got had ever bad success?
And happy always was it for that son
Whose father for his hoarding went to hell?
I'll leave my son my virtuous deeds behind;
And would my father had left me no more!
For all the rest is held at such a rate
As brings a thousand-fold more care to keep
Than in possession any jot of pleasure.—
Ah, cousin York! would thy best friends did
  know
How it doth grieve me that thy head is here!
  Q. Mar. My lord, cheer up your spirits:
  our foes are nigh;
And this soft courage makes your followers
  faint.
You promis'd knighthood to our forward
  son:
Unsheathe your sword, and dub him pres-
  ently.—
Edward, kneel down.
  K. Hen. Edward Plantagenet, arise a
  knight;
And learn this lesson,—draw thy sword in
  right.
  Prince. My gracious father, by your
  kingly leave,
I'll draw it as apparent to the crown,
And in that quarrel use it to the death.
  Clif. Why, that is spoken like a toward
  prince.

Enter a Messenger.

  Mess. Royal commanders, be in readiness:
For with a band of thirty thousand men
Comes Warwick, backing of the Duke of
  York;
And in the towns, as they do march along,
Proclaims him king, and many fly to him:
Darraign your battle, for they are at hand.
  Clif. I would your highness would depart
  the field: [absent.
The queen hath best success when you are
  Q. Mar. Ay, good my lord, and leave us
  to our fortune.
  K. Hen. Why, that's my fortune too;
  therefore I'll stay.
  North. Be it with resolution, then, to
  fight.   [lords,
  Prince. My royal father, cheer these noble
And hearten those that fight in your defence:
Unsheathe your sword, good father; cry,
  Saint George!

March. Enter EDWARD, GEORGE, RICHARD,
  WARWICK, NORFOLK, MONTAGUE, *and* Soldiers.

  Edw. Now, perjur'd Henry! wilt thou
  kneel for grace,

And set thy diadem upon my head;
Or bide the mortal fortune of the field?

Q. Mar. Go, rate thy minions, proud insulting boy!
Becomes it thee to be thus bold in terms
Before thy sovereign and thy lawful king?

Edw. I am his king, and he should bow
his knee;
I was adopted heir by his consent:
Since when, his oath is broke; for, as I hear,
You, that are king, though he do wear the
crown,
Have caus'd him, by new act of parliament,
To blot out me and put his own son in.

Clif. And reason too:
Who should succeed the father but the son?

Rich. Are you there, butcher?—O, I cannot speak!   [swer thee,

Clif. Ay, crook-back, here I stand to answer or any he the proudest of thy sort.

Rich. 'Twas you that kill'd young Rutland, was it not?

Clif. Ay, and old York, and yet not satisfied.

Rich. For God's sake, lords, give signal to
the fight.   [yield the crown?

War. What say'st thou, Henry, wilt thou

Q. Mar. Why, how now, long-tongu'd
Warwick! dare you speak?
When you and I met at Saint Albans last,
Your legs did better service than your hands.

War. Then 'twas my turn to fly, and now
'tis thine.   [fled.

Clif. You said so much before, and yet you

War. 'Twas not your valour, Clifford,
drove me thence.   [make you stay.

North. No, nor your manhood that durst

Rich. Northumberland, I hold thee reverently.—
Break off the parley; for scarce I can refrain
The execution of my big-swoln heart
Upon that Clifford, that cruel child-killer.

Clif. I slew thy father,—call'st thou him
a child?   [coward,

Rich. Ay, like a dastard and a treacherous
As thou didst kill our tender brother Rutland;
But ere sunset I'll make thee curse the deed.

K. Hen. Have done with words, my lords,
and hear me speak.   [thy lips.

Q. Mar. Defy them, then, or else hold close

K. Hen. I pr'ythee give no limits to my
tongue:
I am a king, and privileg'd to speak.

Clif. My liege, the wound that bred this
meeting here
Cannot be cur'd by words; therefore be still.

Rich. Then, executioner, unsheathe thy
sword:
By him that made us all, I am resolv'd
That Clifford's manhood lies upon his
tongue.

Edw. Say, Henry, shall I have my right,
or no?

A thousand men have broke their fasts today
That ne'er shall dine unless thou yield the
crown.   [head;

War. If thou deny, their blood upon thy
For York in justice puts his armour on.

Prince. If that be right which Warwick
says is right,
There is no wrong, but everything is right.

Rich. Whoever got thee, there thy mother
stands;
For, well I wot, thou hast thy mother's
tongue.

Q. Mar. But thou art neither like thy sire
nor dam;
But like a foul misshapen stigmatic,
Mark'd by the destinies to be avoided,
As venom toads, or lizards' dreadful stings.

Rich. Iron of Naples hid with English
gilt,
Whose father bears the title of a king,—
As if a channel should be call'd the sea,—
Sham'st thou not, knowing whence thou art
extraught,
To let thy tongue detect thy base-born
heart?

Edw. A wisp of straw were worth a thousand crowns,
To make this shameless callet know herself.—
Helen of Greece was fairer far than thou,
Although thy husband may be Menelaus;
And ne'er was Agamemnón's brother
wrong'd
By that false woman as this king by thee.
His father revell'd in the heart of France,
And tam'd the king, and made the dauphin
stoop;
And had he match'd according to his state,
He might have kept that glory to this day;
But when he took a beggar to his bed,
And grac'd thy poor sire with his bridal-day,
Even then that sunshine brew'd a shower for
him
That wash'd his father's fortunes forth of
France,
And heap'd sedition on his crown at home.
For what hath broach'd this tumult but thy
pride?
Hadst thou been meek, our title still had
slept;
And we, in pity of the gentle king,
Had slipp'd our claim until another age.

Geo. But when we saw our sunshine made
thy spring,
And that thy summer bred us no increase,
We set the axe to thy usurping root;   [selves,
And though the edge hath something hit our-
Yet, know thou, since we have begun to
strike
We'll never leave till we have hewn thee
down,
Or bath'd thy growing with our heated
bloods.

Edw. And in this resolution I defy thee;

Not willing any longer conference,
Since thou deniest the gentle king to speak.—
Sound trumpets!—let our bloody colours
wave!—
And either victory or else a grave.
  Q. Mar. Stay, Edward.
  Edw. No, wrangling woman, we'll no
longer stay:
These words will cost ten thousand lives this
day.   [*Exeunt.*

SCENE III.—*A Field of Battle between Tow-
ton and Saxton, in Yorkshire.*

Alarums: excursions. Enter WARWICK.

  War. Forspent with toil, as runners with
a race,
I lay me down a little while to breathe;
For strokes receiv'd and many blows repaid
Have robb'd my strong-knit sinews of their
strength,
And, spite of spite, needs must I rest awhile.

Enter EDWARD, *running.*

  Edw. Smile, gentle heaven! or strike, ungentle death!   [clouded.
For this world frowns, and Edward's sun is
  War. How now, my lord! what hap? what
hope of good?

Enter GEORGE.

  Geo. Our hap is loss, our hope but sad de-
spair;
Our ranks are broke, and ruin follows us:
What counsel give you, whither shall we fly?
  Edw. Bootless is flight,—they follow us
with wings;
And weak we are, and cannot shun pursuit.

Enter RICHARD.

  Rich. Ah, Warwick, why hast thou with-
drawn thyself?
Thy brother's blood the thirsty earth hath
drunk,
Broach'd with the steely point of Clifford's
lance;
And in the very pangs of death he cried,
Like to a dismal clangor heard from far,
*Warwick, revenge! brother, revenge my
death!*
So, underneath the belly of their steeds,
That stain'd their fetlocks in his smoking
blood,
The noble gentleman gave up the ghost.
  War. Then let the earth be drunken with
our blood:
I'll kill my horse, because I will not fly.
Why stand we like soft-hearted women here,
Wailing our losses, whiles the foe doth rage;
And look upon, as if the tragedy
Were play'd in jest by counterfeiting actors?
Here on my knee I vow to God above
I'll·never pause again, never stand still,
Till either death hath clos'd these eyes of
mine

Or fortune given me measure of revenge.
  Edw. O Warwick, I do bend my knee with
thine;
And in this vow do chain my soul to thine!—
And ere my knee rise from the earth's cold
face
I throw my hands, mine eyes, my heart to
thee,
Thou setter-up and plucker-down of kings,—
Beseeching thee, if with thy will it stands
That to my foes this body must be prey,
Yet that thy brazen gates of heaven may
ope,
And give sweet passage to my sinful soul!—
Now, lords, take leave until we meet again,
Where'er it be, in heaven or in earth.
  Rich. Brother, give me thy hand;—and,
gentle Warwick,
Let me embrace thee in my weary arms:
I, that did never weep, now melt with woe
That winter should cut off our spring-time
so.   [lords, farewell.
  War. Away, away! Once more, sweet
  Geo. Yet let us all together to our troops,
And give them leave to fly that will not stay;
And call them pillars that will stand to us;
And if we thrive, promise them such rewards
As victors wear at the Olympian games:
This may plant courage in their quailing
breasts;
For yet is hope of life and victory.—
Forslow no longer, make we hence amain.
     [*Exeunt.*

SCENE IV.—*Another part of the field.*

Excursions. Enter RICHARD *and* CLIFFORD.

  Rich. Now, Clifford, I have singled thee
alone:
Suppose this arm is for the Duke of York,
And this for Rutland; both bound to re-
venge,
Wert thou environ'd with a grazen wall.
  Clif. Now, Richard, I am with thee here
alone:
This is the hand that stabb'd thy father
York;
And this the hand that slew thy brother
Rutland;
And here's the heart that triumphs in their
death,
And cheers these hands that slew thy sire and
brother
To execute the like upon thyself;
And so, have at thee!
     [*They fight.* WAR. *enters;* CLIF. *flies.*
  Rich. Nay, Warwick, single out some
other chase;
For I myself will hunt this wolf to death.
     [*Exeunt.*

SCENE V.—*Another part of the Field.*

Alarum. Enter KING HENRY.

  K. Hen. This battle fares like to the
morning's war,

When dying clouds contend with growing
    light,
What time the shepherd, blowing of his
    nails,
Can neither call it perfect day nor night.
Now sways it this way, like a mighty sea
Forc'd by the tide to combat with the wind;
Now sways it that way, like the selfsame sea
Forc'd to retire by fury of the wind:
Sometime the flood prevails, and then the
    wind;
Now one the better, then another best;
Both tugging to be victors, breast to breast,
Yet neither conqueror nor conquered:
So is the equal poise of this fell war.
Here on this molehill will I sit me down.
To whom God will, there be the victory!
For Margaret my queen, and Clifford too,
Have chid me from the battle; swearing
    both
They prosper best of all when I am thence.
Would I were dead! if God's good will were
    so;
For what is in this world but grief and woe?
O God! methinks it were a happy life
To be no better than a homely swain;
To sit upon a hill, as I do now,
To carve out dials quaintly, point by point,
Thereby to see the minutes how they run,—
How many make the hour full complete;
How many hours bring about the day;
How many days will finish up the year;
How many years a mortal man may live.
When this is known, then to divide the
    times,—
So many hours must I tend my flock;
So many hours must I take my rest;
So many hours must I contemplate;
So many hours must I sport myself;
So many days my ewes have been with
    young;
So many weeks ere the poor fools will
    yean;
So many years ere I shall shear the fleece:
So minutes, hours, days, months, and years,
Pass'd over to the end they were created,
Would bring white hairs unto a quiet grave.
Ah, what a life were this! how sweet! how
    lovely!
Gives not the hawthorn bush a sweeter shade
To shepherds, looking on their silly sheep,
Than doth a rich embroider'd canopy
To kings that fear their subjects' treachery?
O, yes, it doth; a thousand-fold it doth.
And to conclude,—the shepherd's homely
    curds,
His cold thin drink out of his leather bottle,
His wonted sleep under a fresh tree's shade,
All which secure and sweetly he enjoys,
Is far beyond a prince's delicates,
His viands sparkling in a golden cup,
His body couched in a curious bed,
When care, mistrust, and treason wait on
    him.

Alarum. Enter a Son *that has killed his
    Father, bringing in the dead body.*

Son. Ill blows the wind that profits no-
    body.
This man, whom hand to hand I slew in
    fight,
May be possessed with some store of crowns;
And I, that haply take them from him now,
May yet ere night yield both my life and
    them
To some man else, as this dead man doth
    me.—
Who's this?—O God! it is my father's face,
Whom in this conflict I unwares have kill'd.
O heavy times, begetting such events!
From London by the king was I press'd
    forth:
My father, being the Earl of Warwick's man,
Came on the part of York, press'd by his
    master;
And I, who at his hands receiv'd my life,
Have by my hands of life bereaved him.—
Pardon me, God, I knew not what I did!—
And pardon father, for I knew not thee!—
My tears shall wipe away these bloody
    marks;
And no more words till they have flow'd
    their fill.
    K. Hen. O piteous spectacle! O bloody
        times!
Whilst lions war, and battle for their dens,
Poor harmless lambs abide their enmity.—
Weep, wretched man, I'll aid thee tear for
    tear;
And let our hearts and eyes, like civil war,
Be blind with tears, and break o'ercharged
    with grief.

Enter a Father *that has killed his* Son, *with
    the body in his arms.*

    Fath. Thou that so stoutly hast resisted
        me.
Give me thy gold, if thou hast any gold;
For I have bought it with an hundred
    blows.—
But let me see: is this our foeman's face?
Ah, no, no, no, it is mine only son!
Ah, boy, if any life be left in thee,   [arise,
Throw up thine eye! see, see what showers
Blown with the windy tempest of my heart,
Upon thy wounds, that kill mine eye and
    heart!—
O pity, God, this miserable age!—
What stratagems, how fell, how butcherly,
Erroneous, mutinous, and unnatural,
This deadly quarrel daily doth beget!—
O boy, thy father gave thee life too soon,
And hath bereft thee of thy life too late!
    K. Hen. Woe above woe! grief more than
        common grief!   [deeds!—
O that my death would stay these ruthful
O pity, pity, gentle heaven, pity!—
The red rose and the white are on his face,

The fatal colours of our striving houses:
The one his purple blood right well re-
 sembles;
The other his pale cheeks, methinks, pre-
 senteth:
Wither one rose, and let the other flourish;
If you contend, a thousand lives must
 wither.

Son. How will my mother for a father's
 death
Take on with me, and ne'er be satisfied! [son

Fath. How will my wife for slaughter of my
Shed seas of tears, and ne'er be satisfied!

K. Hen. How will the country for these
 woeful chances
Misthink the king, and not be satisfied!

Son. Was ever son so rued a father's
 death?

Fath. Was ever father so bemoan'd his
 son?

K. Hen. Was ever king so griev'd for subjects' woe?
Much is your sorrow; mine ten times so
 much.

Son. I'll bear thee hence, where I may
 weep my fill. [*Exit with the body.*

Fath. These arms of mine shall be thy
 winding-sheet;
My heart, sweet boy, shall be thy sep-
 ulchre,—
For from my heart thine image ne'er shall
 go;
My sighing breast shall be thy funeral bell;
And so obsequious will thy father be,
E'en for the loss of thee, having no more,
As Priam was for all his valiant sons, [will,
I'll bear thee hence; and let them fight that
For I have murder'd where I should not kill.
 [*Exit with the body.*

K. Hen. Sad-hearted men, much overgone
 with care,
Here sits a king more woeful than you are.

Alarums: excursions. Enter QUEEN MAR-
GARET, PRINCE OF WALES, *and* EXETER.

Prince. Fly, father, fly! for all your friends
 are fled,
And Warwick rages like a chafed bull:
Away! for death doth hold us in pursuit

Q. Mar. Mount you, my lord; towards
 Berwick post amain:
Edward and Richard, like a brace of grey-
 hounds
Having the fearful flying hare in sight,
With fiery eyes sparkling for very wrath,
And bloody steel grasp'd in their ireful hands,
Are at our backs; and therefore hence
 amain.

Exe. Away! for vengeance comes along
 with them:
Nay, stay not to expostulate,—make speed;
Or else come after: I'll away before.

K. Hen. Nay, take me with thee, good
 sweet Exeter:

Not that I fear to stay, but love to go
Whither the queen intends. Forward; away!
 [*Exeunt.*

SCENE VI.—*Another part of the Field.*

A loud Alarum. Enter CLIFFORD, *wounded.*

Clif. Here burns my candle out,—ay, here
 it dies,
Which, whiles it lasted, gave King Henry
 light.
O Lancaster, I fear thy overthrow
More than my body's parting with my soul!
My love and fear glu'd many friends to thee;
And, now I fall, thy tough commixtures
 melt.
Impairing Henry, strengthening misproud
 York,
The common people swarm like summer
 flies;
And whither fly the gnats but to the sun?
And who shines now but Henry's enemies?
O Phœbus, hadst thou never given consent
That Phaeton should check thy fiery steeds,
Thy burning car never had scorch'd the
 earth!
And, Henry, hadst thou sway'd as kings
 should do,
Or as thy father and his father did,
Giving no ground unto the house of York,
They never then had sprung like summer
 flies;
I and ten thousand in this luckless realm
Had left no mourning widows for our death;
And thou this day hadst kept thy chair in
 peace.
For what doth cherish weeds but gentle air?
And what makes robbers bold but too much
 lenity?
Bootless are plaints, and cureless are my
 wounds;
No way to fly, nor strength to hold out
 flight:
The foe is merciless, and will not pity;
For at their hands I have deserv'd no pity.
The air hath got into my deadly wounds,
And much effuse of blood doth make me
 faint.
Come, York and Richard, Warwick and the
 rest;
I stabb'd your fathers' bosoms,—split my
 breast.
 [*He faints.*

Alarum and retreat. Enter EDWARD, GEORGE,
RICHARD, MONTAGUE, WARWICK, *and*
Soldiers.

Edw. Now breathe we, lords: good for-
 tune bids us pause, [ful looks.—
And smooth the frowns of war with peace-
Some troops pursue the bloody-minded
 queen,
That led calm Henry, though he were a king,
As doth a sail, fill'd with a fretting gust,
Command an argosy to stem the waves.

But think you, lords, that Clifford fled with them?

War. No, 'tis impossible he should escape;
For though before his face I speak the words,
Your brother Richard mark'd him for the grave:
And, whereso'er he is, he's surely dead.
[CLIFFORD *groans, and dies.*

Edw. Whose soul is that which takes her heavy leave?   [*departing.*

Rich. A deadly groan, like life and death's—

Edw. See who it is; and, now the battle's ended,
If friend or foe, let him be gently us'd.

Rich. Revoke that doom of mercy, for 'tis Clifford;
Who not contented that he lopp'd the branch
In hewing Rutland when his leaves put forth,
But set his murdering knife unto the root
From whence that tender spray did sweetly spring,—
I mean our princely father, Duke of York.

War. From off the gates of York fetch down the head,
Your father's head, which Clifford placed there;
Instead whereof let this supply the room:
Measure for measure must be answered.

Edw. Bring forth that fatal screech-owl to our house,
That nothing sung but death to us and ours:
Now death shall stop his dismal threatening sound,
And his ill-boding tongue no more shall speak.
[Soldiers *bring the body forward.*

War. I think his understanding is bereft.—
Speak, Clifford, dost thou know who speaks to thee?—
Dark cloudy death o'ershades his beams of life,
And he nor sees nor hears us what we say.

Rich. O, would he did! and so, perhaps, he doth:
'Tis but his policy to counterfeit,
Because he would avoid such bitter taunts
Which in the time of death he gave our father.

Geo. If so thou think'st, vex him with eager words.

Rich. Clifford, ask mercy and obtain no grace.

Edw. Clifford, repent in bootless penitence.

War. Clifford, devise excuses for thy faults.

Geo. While we devise fell tortures for thy faults.   [*to York.*

Rich. Thou didst love York, and I am son

Edw. Thou pitiedst Rutland, I will pity thee.   [*you now?*

Geo. Where's Captain Margaret, to fence

War. They mock thee, Clifford: swear as thou wast wont.

Rich. What, not an oath? nay, then the world goes hard
When Clifford cannot spare his friends an oath.—
I know by that he's dead; and, by my soul,
If this right hand would buy two hours' life,
That I in all despite might rail at him,
This hand should chop it off, and with the issuing blood
Stifle the villain whose unstaunched thirst
York and young Rutland could not satisfy.

War. Ay, but he's dead: off with the traitor's head,
And rear it in the place your father's stands.—
And now to London with triumphant march,
There to be crowned England's royal king.
From whence shall Warwick cut the sea to France,
And ask the Lady Bona for thy queen;
So shalt thou sinew both these lands together;
And, having France thy friend, thou shalt not dread
The scatter'd foe that hopes to rise again;
For though they cannot greatly sting to hurt,
Yet look to have them buzz to offend thine ears.
First will I see the coronation;
And then to Brittany I'll cross the sea,
To effect this marriage, so it please my lord.

Edw. Even as thou wilt, sweet Warwick, let it be;
For in thy shoulder do I build my seat,
And never will I undertake the thing
Wherein thy counsel and consent is wanting.—
Richard, I will create thee Duke of Gloster,—
And George, of Clarence;—Warwick, as ourself,
Shall do and undo as him pleaseth best.

Rich. Let me be Duke of Clarence, George of Gloster;
For Gloster's dukedom is too ominous.

War. Tut, that's a foolish observation:
Richard, be Duke of Gloster. Now to London,
To see these honours in possession.
[*Exeunt.*

ACT III

SCENE I.—*A Chase in the North of England.*

Enter two KEEPERS, *with cross-bows in their hands.*

1 *Keep.* Under this thick-grown brake we'll shroud ourselves;
For through this laund anon the deer will come;
And in this covert will we make our stand
Culling the principal of all the deer.

2 *Keep.* I'll stay above the hill, so both may shoot.

1 *Keep.* That cannot be; the noise of thy cross-bow
Will scare the herd, and so my shot is lost.
Here stand we both, and aim we at the best:
And, for the time shall not seem tedious,
I'll tell thee what befell me on a day
In this self-place where now we mean to stand.

2 *Keep.* Here comes a man, let's stay till he be past.

Enter KING HENRY, *disguised, with a prayer-book.*

K. Hen. From Scotland am I stol'n, even of pure love,
To greet mine own land with my wishful sight.
No, Harry, Harry, 'tis no land of thine;
Thy place is fill'd, thy sceptre wrung from thee,
Thy balm wash'd off wherewith thou wast anointed:
No bending knee will call thee Cæsar now,
No humble suitors press to speak for right,
No, not a man comes for redress of thee;
For how can I help them, and not myself?

1 *Keep.* Ay, here's a deer whose skin's a keeper's fee:
This is the *quondam* king; let's seize upon him.

K. Hen. Let me embrace these sour adversities:
For wise men say it is the wisest course.

2 *Keep.* Why linger we? let us lay hands upon him.   [more.

1 *Keep.* Forbear awhile; we'll hear a little

K. Hen. My queen and son are gone to France for aid;
And, as I hear, the great commanding Warwick
Is thither gone, to crave the French king's sister
To wife for Edward: if this news be true,
Poor queen and son, your labour is but lost;
For Warwick is a subtle orator,
And Louis a prince soon won with moving words.   [him;
By this account, then, Margaret may win
For she's a woman to be pitied much:
Her sighs will make a battery in his breast;
Her tears will pierce into a marble heart;
The tiger will be mild while she doth mourn;
And Nero will be tainted with remorse,
To hear and see her plaints, her brinish tears.
Ay, but she's come to beg; Warwick, to give:
She, on his left side, craving aid for Henry;
He, on his right, asking a wife for Edward.
She weeps, and says her Henry is depos'd;
He smiles, and says his Edward is install'd;
That she, poor wretch, for grief can speak no more;   [wrong,
Whiles Warwick tells his title, smooths the

Inferreth arguments of mighty strength,
And in conclusion wins the king from her,
With promise of his sister, and what else,
To strengthen and support King Edward's place.
O Margaret, thus 'twill be; and thou, poor soul,
Art then forsaken, as thou went'st forlorn!

2 *Keep.* Say, what art thou, that talk'st of kings and queens?

K. Hen. More than I seem, and less than I was born to:
A man at least, for less I should not be;
And men may talk of kings, and why not I?

2 *Keep.* Ay, but thou talk'st as if thou wert a king.   [that's enough.

K. Hen. Why, so I am—in mind; and

2 *Keep.* But, if thou be a king, where is thy crown?   [my head,

K. Hen. My crown is in my heart, not on
Not deck'd with diamonds and Indian stones,
Nor to be seen: my crown is call'd content,—
A crown it is that seldom kings enjoy.

2 *Keep.* Well, if you be a king crown'd with content,
Your crown content and you must be contented
To go along with us; for, as we think,
You are the king King Edward hath depos'd;
And we his subjects, sworn in all allegiance,
Will apprehend you as his enemy.

K. Hen. But did you never swear, and break an oath?   [not now.

2 *Keep.* No, never such an oath; nor will

K. Hen. Where did you dwell when I was King of England?

2 *Keep.* Here in this country, where we now remain.

K. Hen. I was anointed king at nine months old;
My father and my grandfather were kings;
And you were sworn true subjects unto me:
And tell me, then, have you not broke your oaths?

1 *Keep.* No;
For we were subjects but while you were king.

K. Hen. Why, am I dead? do I not breathe a man?
Ah, simple men, you know not what you swear!
Look, as I blow this feather from my face,
And as the air blows it to me again,
Obeying with my wind when I do blow,
And yielding to another when it blows,
Commanded always by the greater gust;
Such is the lightness of you common men.
But do not break your oaths; for of that sin
My mild entreaty shall not make you guilty.
Go where you will, the king shall be commanded;
And be you kings; command, and I'll obey.

1 *Keep.* We are true subjects to the king, King Edward.

K. Hen. So would you be again to Henry, If he were seated as King Edward is.

1 *Keep.* We charge you, in God's name and in the king's, To go with us unto the officers.

K. Hen. In God's name, lead; your king's name be obey'd:
And what God will, that let your king perform;
And what he will, I humbly yield unto.

[*Exeunt.*

SCENE II.—LONDON. *A Room in the Palace.*

Enter KING EDWARD, GLOSTER, CLARENCE, *and* LADY GREY.

K. Edw. Brother of Gloster, at Saint Albans' field
This lady's husband, Sir John Grey, was slain,
His lands then seiz'd on by the conqueror:
Her suit is now to repossess those lands;
Which we in justice cannot well deny,
Because in quarrel of the house of York
The worthy gentleman did lose his life.

Glo. Your highness shall do well to grant her suit;
It were dishonour to deny it her.

K. Edw. It were no less; but yet I'll make a pause.

Glo. Yea, is it so?
I see the lady hath a thing to grant,
Before the king will grant her humble suit.

[*Aside to* CLARENCE.

Clar. He knows the game: how true he keeps the wind!   [*Aside to* GLOSTER.

Glo. Silence!   [*Aside to* CLARENCE.

K. Edw. Widow, we will consider of your suit;
And come some other time to know our mind.

L. Grey. Right gracious lord, I cannot brook delay:
May it please your highness to resolve me now;
And what your pleasure is shall satisfy me.

Glo. Ay, widow? then I warrant you all your lands,
An if what pleases him shall pleasure you:
Fight closer, or good faith, you'll catch a blow.   [*Aside.*

Clar. I fear her not, unless she chance to fall.   [*Aside to* GLOSTER.

Glo. God forbid that! for he'll take vantages.   [*Aside to* CLARENCE.

K. Edw. How many children hast thou, widow? tell me.

Clar. I think he means to beg a child of her.   [*Aside to* GLOSTER.

Glo. Nay, whip me, then; he'll rather give her two.   [*Aside to* CLARENCE.

L. Grey. Three, my most gracious lord.

Glo. You shall have four if you'll be ruled by him.   [*Aside.*

K. Edw. 'Twere pity they should lose their father's lands.   [it then.

L. Grey. Be pitiful, dread lord, and grant

K. Edw. Lords, give us leave: I'll try this widow's wit.   [will have leave,

Glo. Ay, good leave have you; for you
Till youth take leave, and leave you to the crutch.

[*Aside, and retires with* CLARENCE.

K. Edw. Now tell me, madam, do you love your children?

L. Grey. Ay, full as dearly as I love myself.

K. Edw. And would you not do much to do them good?   [some harm.

L. Grey. To do them good I would sustain

K. Edw. Then get your husband's lands, to do them good.

L. Grey. Therefore I came unto your majesty.

K. Edw. I'll tell you how these lands are to be got.   [highness' service.

L. Grey. So shall you bind me to your

K. Edw. What service wilt thou do me if I give them?   [me to do.

L. Grey. What you command, that rests in

K. Edw. But you will take exceptions to my boon.

L. Grey. No, gracious lord, except I cannot do it.

K. Edw. Ay, but thou canst do what I mean to ask.   [grace commands.

L. Grey. Why, then, I will do what your

Glo. He plies her hard; and much rain wears the marble.

[*Aside to* CLARENCE.

Clar. As red as fire! nay, then her wax must melt.   [*Aside to* GLOSTER.

L. Grey. Why stops my lord? shall I not hear my task?

K. Edw. An easy task; 'tis but to love a king.

L. Grey. That's soon perform'd, because I am a subject.

K. Edw. Why, then, thy husband's lands I freely give thee.   [sand thanks.

L. Grey. I take my leave with many thou-

Glo. The match is made; she seals it with a curtsy.   [*Aside.*

K. Edw. But stay thee,—'tis the fruits of love I mean.   [loving liege.

L. Grey. The fruits of love I mean, my

K. Edw. Ay, but, I fear me, in another sense.
What love, thinkst thou, I sue so much to get?

L. Grey. My love till death, my humble thanks, my prayers;
That love which virtue begs and virtue grants.

K. Edw. No, by my troth, I did not mean such love.

L. Grey. Why, then, you mean not as I
  thought you did.   [ceive my mind.
K. Edw. But now you partly may per-
L. Grey. My mind will never grant what
  I perceive
Your highness aims at, if I aim aright.
K. Edw. To tell thee plain, I aim to lie
  with thee.
L. Grey. To tell you plain, I had rather
  lie in prison.
K. Edw. Why, then, thou shalt not have
  thy husband's lands.   [my dower;
L. Grey. Why, then, mine honesty shall be
For by that loss I will not purchase them.
K. Edw. Therein thou wrong'st thy chil-
  dren mightily.
L. Grey. Herein your highness wrongs
  both them and me.
But, mighty lord, this merry inclination
Accords not with the sadness of my suit:
Please you dismiss me, either with ay or no.
K. Edw. Ay, if thou wilt say ay to my re-
  quest;
No, if thou dost say no to my demand.
L. Grey. Then, no, my lord. My suit is at
  an end.
Glo. The widow likes him not, she knits
  her brows.   [*Aside to* CLARENCE.
Clar. He is the bluntest wooer in Christen-
  dom.   [*Aside to* GLOSTER.
K. Edw. Her looks do argue her replete
  with modesty;
Her words do show her wit incomparable;
All her perfections challenge sovereignty:
One way or other, she is for a king;
And she shall be my love, or else my queen.—
                     [*Aside.*
Say that King Edward take thee for his
  queen?
L. Grey. 'Tis better said than done, my
  gracious lord:
I am a subject fit to jest withal,
But far unfit to be a sovereign.
K. Edw. Sweet widow, by my state I
  swear to thee
I speak no more than what my soul intends;
And that is to enjoy thee for my love.
L. Grey. And that is more than I will
  yield unto:
I know I am too mean to be your queen,
And yet too good to be your concubine.
K. Edw. You cavil, widow: I did mean
  my queen.
L. Grey. 'Twill grieve your grace my sons
  should call you father.
K. Edw. No more than when my daugh-
  ters call thee mother.
Thou art a widow, and thou hast some chil-
  dren;   [lor,
And, by God's mother, I, being but a bache-
Have other some: why, 'tis a happy thing
To be the father unto many sons.
Answer no more, for thou shalt be my
  queen.

Glo. The ghostly father now hath done
  his shrift.   [*Aside to* CLARENCE.
Clar. When he was made a shriver, 'twas
  for shift.   [*Aside to* GLOSTER.
K. Edw. Brothers, you muse what chat
  we two have had.   [very sad.
Glo. The widow likes it not, for she looks
K. Edw. You'd think it strange if I
  should marry her.
Clar. To whom, my lord?
K. Edw.   Why, Clarence, to myself.
Glo. That would be ten days' wonder at
  the least.
Clar. That's a day longer than a wonder
  lasts.
Glo. By so much is the wonder in ex-
  tremes.
K. Edw. Well, jest on, brothers: I can
  tell you both
Her suit is granted for her husband's lands.

          Enter a Nobleman.

Nob. My gracious lord, Henry your foe is
  taken,
And brought your prisoner to your palace
  gate.
K. Edw. See that he be convey'd unto
  the Tower:—
And go we, brothers, to the man that took
  him,
To question of his apprehension.—
Widow, go you along:—lords, use her hon-
  ourable.
     [*Exeunt* KING EDWARD, LADY GREY,
         CLARENCE, *and* Nobleman.
Glo. Ay, Edward will use women honour-
  ably.—
Would he were wasted, marrow, bones, and
  all,
That from his loins no hopeful branch may
  spring,
To cross me from the golden time I look for!
And yet, between my soul's desire and me,—
The lustful Edward's title buried,—
Is Clarence, Henry, and his son young Ed-
  ward,
And all the unlook'd-for issue of their bodies,
To take their rooms, ere I can place myself:
A cold premeditation for my purpose!
Why, then, I do but dream on sovereignty;
Like one that stands upon a promontory,
And spies a far-off shore where he would
  tread;
Wishing his foot were equal with his eye;
And chides the sea that sunders him from
  thence
Saying he'll lade it dry to have his way:
So do I wish the crown, being so far off;
And so I chide the means that keep me
  from it;
And so I say I'll cut the causes off,
Flattering me with impossibilities.—
My eye's too quick, my heart o'erweens too
  much,

Unless my hand and strength could equal them.

Well, say there is no kingdom, then, for Richard;

What other pleasure can the world afford?

I'll make my heaven in a lady's lap,

And deck my body in gay ornaments,

And witch sweet ladies with my words and looks.

O miserable thought! and more unlikely

Than to accomplish twenty golden crowns!

Why, love forswore me in my mother's womb:

And, for I should not deal in her soft laws,

She did corrupt frail nature with some bribe,

To shrink mine arm up like a wither'd shrub;

To make an envious mountain on my back,

Where sits deformity to mock my body;

To shape my legs of an unequal size;

To disproportion me in every part,

Like to a chaos, or an unlick'd bear-whelp

That carries no impression like the dam.

And am I, then, a man to be belov'd?

O monstrous fault, to harbour such a thought!

Then, since this earth affords no joy to me

But to command, to check, to o'erbear such

As are of better person than myself,

I'll make my heaven to dream upon the crown,

And whiles I live to account this world but hell,

Until my misshap'd trunk that bears this head

Be round empaled with a glorious crown.

And yet I know not how to get the crown,

For many lives stand between me and home:

And I,—like one lost in a thorny wood,

That rents the thorns, and is rent with the thorns,

Seeking a way, and straying from the way;

Not knowing how to find the open air,

But toiling desperately to find it out,—

Torment myself to catch the English crown:

And from that torment I will free myself,

Or hew my way out with a bloody axe.

Why, I can smile, and murder whiles I smile;

And cry content to that which grieves my heart;

And wet my cheeks with artificial tears,

And frame my face to all occasions.

I'll drown more sailors than the mermaid shall;

I'll slay more gazers than the basilisk;

I'll play the orator as well as Nestor;

Deceive more slily than Ulysses could;

And, like a Sinon, take another Troy:

I can add colours to the cameleon;

Change shapes with Proteus for advantages;

And set the murderous Machiavel to school.

Can I do this, and cannot get a crown?

Tut, were it further off, I'll pluck it down!

                       [*Exit.*

SCENE III.—FRANCE. *A Room in the Palace.*

Flourish. Enter LOUIS, *the French King, and* LADY BONA, *attended; the* KING *takes his state. Then enter* QUEEN MARGARET, PRINCE EDWARD *her Son, and the* EARL OF OXFORD.

K. Lou. Fair Queen of England, worthy Margaret,   [*Rising.*

Sit down with us: it ill befits thy state

And birth, that thou shouldst stand while Louis doth sit.   [Margaret

Q. Mar. No, mighty King of France: now

Must strike her sail, and learn awhile to serve

Where kings command. I was, I must confess,

Great Albion's queen in former golden days:

But now mischance hath trod my title down,

And with dishonour laid me on the ground;

Where I must take like seat unto my fortune,

And to my humble seat conform myself.

K. Lou. Why, say, fair queen, whence springs this deep despair?

Q. Mar. From such a cause as fills mine eyes with tears,   [in cares.

And stops my tongue, while heart is drown'd

K. Lou. Whate'er it be, be thou still like thyself,

And sit thee by our side: yield not thy neck   [*Seats her by him.*

To fortune's yoke, but let thy dauntless mind

Still ride in triumph over all mischance.

Be plain, Queen Margaret, and tell thy grief;

It shall be eas'd, if France can yield relief.

Q. Mar. Those gracious words revive my drooping thoughts,

And give my tongue-tied sorrows leave to speak.

Now, therefore, be it known to noble Louis

That Henry, sole possessor of my love,

Is, of a king, become a banish'd man,

And forc'd to live in Scotland a forlorn;

While proud ambitious Edward Duke of York

Usurps the regal title and the seat

Of England's true-anointed lawful king.

This is the cause that I, poor Margaret,—

With this my son, Prince Edward, Henry's heir,—

Am come to crave thy just and lawful aid;

And if thou fail us, all our hope is done:

Scotland hath will to help, but cannot help;

Our people and our peers are both misled,

Our treasure seiz'd, our soldiers put to flight,

And, as thou see'st, ourselves in heavy plight.

K. Lou. Renowned queen, with patience calm the storm,

While we bethink a means to break it off.

Q. Mar. The more we stay the stronger grows our foe.   [succour thee.

K. Lou. The more I stay the more I'll

Q. Mar. O, but impatience waiteth on true sorrow:—

And see where comes the breeder of my sorrow!

Enter WARWICK, *attended.*

K. Lou. What's he approacheth boldly to
our presence?

Q. Mar. Our Earl of Warwick, Edward's
greatest friend.

K. Lou. Welcome, brave Warwick! What
brings thee to France?

[*Descending from his state.* Q. MAR. *rises.*

Q. Mar. Ay, now begins a second storm to
rise;
For this is he that moves both wind and tide.

War. From worthy Edward, King of Al-
bion,
My lord and sovereign, and thy vowed
friend,
I come, in kindness and unfeigned love,—
First, to do greetings to thy royal person;
And then to crave a league of amity;
And lastly, to confirm that amity
With nuptial knot, if thou vouchsafe to
grant
That virtuous Lady Bona, thy fair sister,
To England's king in lawful marriage.

Q. Mar. If that go forward, Henry's hope
is done.

War. And, gracious madam [*to* BONA], in
our king's behalf,
I am commanded, with your leave and fa-
vour,
Humbly to kiss your hand, and with my
tongue
To tell the passion of my sovereign's heart;
Where fame, late entering at his heedful ears,
Hath plac'd thy beauty's image and thy vir-
tue.

Q. Mar. King Louis,—and Lady Bona,—
hear me speak,
Before you answer Warwick. His demand
Springs not from Edward's well-meant hon-
est love,
But from deceit bred by necessity;
For how can tyrants safely govern home
Unless abroad they purchase great alliance?
To prove him tyrant, this reason may suf-
fice,—
That Henry liveth still; but were he dead,
Yet here Prince Edward stands, King
Henry's son.   [and marriage
Look therefore, Louis, that by this league
Thou draw not on thy danger and dis-
honour;
For though usurpers sway the rule awhile,
Yet heavens are just, and time suppresseth
wrongs.

War. Injurious Margaret!

Prince.   And why not queen?

War. Because thy father Henry did usurp;
And thou no more art prince than she is
queen.

Oxf. Then Warwick disannuls great John
of Gaunt,

Which did subdue the greatest part of Spain;
And, after John of Gaunt, Henry the Fourth,
Whose wisdom was a mirror to the wisest;
And, after that wise prince, Henry the Fifth,
Who by his prowess conquered all France:
From these our Henry lineally descends.

War. Oxford, how haps it, in this smooth
discourse,
You told not how Henry the Sixth hath lost
All that which Henry the Fifth had gotten?
Methinks these peers of France should smile
at that.
But for the rest,—you tell a pedigree
Of threescore and two years; a silly time
To make prescription for a kingdom's worth.

Oxf. Why, Warwick, canst thou speak
against thy liege,
Whom thou obey'dst thirty and six years,
And not bewray thy treason with a blush?

War. Can Oxford, that did ever fence the
right,
Now buckler falsehood with a pedigree?
For shame? leave Henry, and call Edward
king.

Oxf. Call him my king by whose injurious
doom
My elder brother, the Lord Aubrey Vere,
Was done to death? and more than so, my
father,
Even in the downfall of his mellow'd years,
When nature brought him to the door of
death?
No, Warwick, no; while life upholds this
arm,
This arm upholds the house of Lancaster.

War. And I the house of York.

K. Lou. Queen Margaret, Prince Edward,
and Oxford,
Vouchsafe, at our request, to stand aside
While I use further conference with Warwick

Q. Mar. Heavens grant that Warwick's
words bewitch him not!

[*Retiring with the* PRINCE *and* OXF.

K. Lou. Now, Warwick, tell me, even
upon thy conscience,
Is Edward your true king? for I were loth
To link with him that were not lawful
chosen.

War. Thereon I pawn my credit and mine
honour.   [eye?

K. Lou. But is he gracious in the people's

War. The more that Henry was unfortunate.

K. Lou. Then further,—all dissembling
set aside,—
Tell me for truth the measure of his love
Unto our sister Bona.

War.   Such it seems
As may beseem a monarch like himself.
Myself have often heard him say, and swear,
That this love was an etrrnal plant,
Whereof the root was fix'd in virtue's ground,
The leaves and fruit maintain'd with beauty's
sun:

Exempt from envy, but not from disdain,
Unless the Lady Bona quit his pain. [resolve.
K. Lou. Now, sister, let us hear your firm
Bona. Your grant or your denial shall be
    mine:—
Yet I confess [to War.] that often ere this
    day,
When I have heard your king's desert re-
    counted,
Mine ear hath tempted judgment to desire.
K. Lou. Then, Warwick, thus,—Our sister
    shall be Edward's;
And now forthwith shall articles be drawn
Touching the jointure that your king must
    make,
Which with her dowry shall be counter-
    pois'd.—
Draw near, Queen Margaret, and be a wit-
    ness
That Bona shall be wife to the English king.
Prince. To Edward, but not to the English
    king.
Q. Mar. Deceitful Warwick! it was thy
    device
By this alliance to make void my suit:
Before thy coming, Louis was Henry's friend.
K. Lou. And still is friend to him and
    Margaret:
But if your title to the crown be weak,—
As may appear by Edward's good success,—
Then 'tis but reason that I be released
From giving aid which late I promised.
Yet shall you have all kindness at my hand
That your estate requires and mine can yield.
War. Henry now lives in Scotland at his
    ease,
Where having nothing, nothing can he lose.
And as for you yourself, our quondam queen,
You have a father able to maintain you;
And better 'twere you troubled him than
    France.
Q. Mar. Peace, impudent and shameless
    Warwick,—
Proud setter-up and puller-down of kings!
I will not hence till, with my talk and tears,
Both full of truth, I make King Louis behold
Thy sly conveyance and thy lord's false love;
For both of you are birds of self-same fea-
    ther.   [A horn is sounded within.
K. Lou. Warwick, this is some post to us
    or thee.

Enter a Messenger.

Mess. My lord ambassador, these letters
    are for you,
Sent from your brother, Marquis Mon-
    tague:—
These from our king unto your majesty:—
And, madam, these for you; from whom I
    know not.
        [To Mar. They all read their letters.
Oxf. I like it well that our fair queen and
    mistress   [his.
Smiles at her news, while Warwick frowns at

Prince. Nay, mark how Louis stamps, as
    he were nettled:
I hope all's for the best.
K. Lou. Warwick, what are thy news?—
    and yours, fair queen? [unhop'd joys.
Q. Mar. Mine, such as fill my heart with
War. Mine, full of sorrow and heart's dis-
    content.   [Lady Grey?
K. Lou. What, has your king married the
And now, to soothe your forgery and his,
Sends me a paper to persuade me patience?
Is this the alliance that he seeks with France?
Dare he presume to scorn us in this manner?
Q. Mar. I told your majesty as much be-
    fore:
This proveth Edward's love and Warwick's
    honesty.   [of heaven,
War. King Louis, I here protest, in sight
And by the hope I have of heavenly bliss,
That I am clear from this misdeed of Ed-
    ward's,—
No more my king, for he dishonours me,
But most himself, if he could see his shame.
Did I forget that by the house of York
My father came untimely to his death?
Did I let pass the abuse done to my niece?
Did I impale him with the regal crown?
Did I put Henry from his native right?
And am I guerdon'd at the last with shame?
Shame on himself! for my desert is honour:
And, to repair my honour lost for him,
I here renounce him, and return to Henry.—
My noble queen, let former grudges pass,
And henceforth I am thy true servitor:
I will revenge his wrong to Lady Bona,
And replant Henry in his former state.
Q. Mar. Warwick, these words have turn'd
    my hate to love;
And I forgive and quite forget old' faults,
And joy that thou becom'st King Henry's
    friend.
War. So much his friend, ay, his unfeigned
    friend,
That if King Louis vouchsafe to furnish us
With some few bands of chosen soldiers,
I'll undertake to land them on our coast,
And force the tyrant from his seat by war.
'Tis not his new-made bride shall succour
    him:
And as for Clarence,—as my letters tell me,—
He's very likely now to fall from him,
For matching more for wanton lust than
    honour,
Or than for strength and safety of our coun-
    try.
Bona. Dear brother, how shall Bona be
    reveng'd
But by thy help to this distressed queen?
Q. Mar. Renowned prince, how shall poor
    Henry live,
Unless thou rescue him from foul despair?
Bona. My quarrel and this English queen's
    are one.   [yours.
War. And mine, fair Lady Bona, joins with

K. Lou. And mine with hers, and thine,
     and Margaret's.
Therefore, at last, I firmly am resolv'd
You shall have aid.
     Q. Mar. Let me give humble thanks for all
          at once.   [in post,
K. Lou. Then, England's messenger, return
And tell false Edward, thy supposed king,
That Louis of France is sending over mas-
     quers
To revel it with him and his new bride:
Thou see'st what's past,—go fear thy king
     withal.
     Bona. Tell him, in hope he'll prove a wid-
          ower shortly,
I'll wear the willow-garland for his sake.
     Q. Mar. Tell him, my mourning-weeds are
          laid aside,
And I am ready to put armour on.
     War. Tell him from me, that he hath done
          me wrong;
And therefore I'll uncrown him ere't be long.
There's thy reward: be gone.   [*Exit* Mess.
K. Lou.   But, Warwick,
Thou and Oxford, with five thousand men,
Shall cross the seas, and bid false Edward
     battle;
And, as occasion serves, this noble queen
And prince shall follow with a fresh supply.
Yet, ere thou go, but answer me one doubt,—
What pledge have we of thy firm loyalty?
     War. This shall assure my constant loy-
          alty,—
That if our queen and this young prince
          agree
I'll join mine eldest daughter, and my joy,
To him forthwith in holy wedlock-bands.
     Q. Mar. Yes, I agree, and thank you for
          your motion.—
Son Edward, she is fair and virtuous,
Therefore delay not,—give thy hand to War-
     wick;
And, with thy hand, thy faith irrevocable,
That only Warwick's daughter shall be thine.
     Prince. Yes, I accept her, for she well de-
          serves it;
And here to pledge my vow, I give my hand.
          [*He gives his hand to* WARWICK.
K. Lou. Why stay we now? These sol-
     diers shall be levied,
And thou, Lord Bourbon, our high-admiral,
Shalt waft them over with our royal fleet.—
I long till Edward fall by war's mischance,
For mocking marriage with a dame of
     France.
          [*Exeunt all but* WARWICK.
     War. I come from Edward as ambassador,
But I return his sworn and mortal foe:
Matter of marriage was the charge he gave
     me,
But dreadful war shall answer his demand.
Had he none else to make a stale but me?
Then none but I shall turn his jest to sorrow.
I was the chief that rais'd him to the crown,

And I'll be chief to bring him down again:
Not that I pity Henry's misery,
But seek revenge on Edward's mockery.
                              [*Exit.*

ACT IV.

SCENE I.—LONDON. *A Room in the Palace.*

Enter GLOSTER, CLARENCE, SOMERSET,
          MONTAGUE, *and others.*

     Glo. Now tell me, brother Clarence, what
          think you
Of this new marriage with the Lady Grey?
Hath not our brother made a worthy choice?
     Clar. Alas, you know, 'tis far from hence
          to France;
How could he stay till Warwick made re-
          turn?
     Som. My lords, forbear this talk; here
          comes the king.
     Glo. And his well-chosen bride.
     Clar. I mind to tell him plainly what I
          think.

Flourish. Enter KING EDWARD, *attended;*
LADY GREY, *as Queen;* PEMBROKE, STAF-
FORD, HASTINGS, *and others.*

     K. Edw. Now, brother of Clarence, how
          like you our choice,
That you stand pensive, as half malcontent?
     Clar. As well as Louis of France or the
          Earl of Warwick;
Which are so weak of courage and in judg-
          ment
That they'll take no offence at our abuse.
     K. Edw. Suppose they take offence with-
          out a cause,
They are but Louis and Warwick: I am Ed-
          ward,
Your king and Warwick's, and must have my
          will.   [king:
     Glo. And shall have your will, because our
Yet hasty marriage seldom proveth well.
     K. Edw. Yea, brother Richard, are you
          offended too?
     Glo. Not I:
No, God forbid that I should wish them
          sever'd
Whom God hath join'd together; ay, and
          'twere pity
To sunder them that yoke so well together.
     K. Edw. Setting your scorns and your
          mislike aside,
Tell me some reason why the Lady Grey
Should not become my wife and England's
          queen:—
And you too, Somerset and Montague,
Speak freely what you think.   [King Louis
     Clar. Then this is mine opinion,—that
Becomes your enemy for mocking him
About the marriage of the Lady Bona.
     Glo. And Warwick, doing what you gave
          in charge,
Is now dishonoured by this new marriage.

K. Edw. What if both Louis and Warwick be appeas'd
By such invention as I can devise?
   Mont. Yet to have join'd with France in such alliance   [monwealth
Would more have strengthen'd this our com-
'Gainst foreign storms than any home-bred marriage.
   Hast. Why, knows not Montague that of itself
England is safe, if true within itself?
   Mont. But the safer when 'tis back'd with France.
   Hast. 'Tis better using France than trusting France:
Let us be back'd with God, and with the seas
Which he hath given for fence impregnable,
And with their helps only defend ourselves;
In them and in ourselves our safety lies.
   Clar. For this one speech Lord Hastings well deserves
To have the heir of the Lord Hungerford.
   K. Edw. Ay, what of that? it was my will and grant;
And for this once my will shall stand for law.
   Glo. And yet methinks your grace hath not done well,
To give the heir and daughter of Lord Scales
Unto the brother of your loving bride;
She better would have fitted me or Clarence:
But in your bride you bury brotherhood.
   Clar. Or else you would not have bestow'd the heir
Of the Lord Bonville on your new wife's son,
And leave your brothers to go speed elsewhere.
   K. Edw. Alas, poor Clarence! is it for a wife
That thou art malcontent? I will provide thee.
   Clar. In choosing for yourself you show'd your judgment,
Which being shallow, you shall give me leave
To play the broker in mine own behalf;
And to that end I shortly mind to leave you.
   K. Edw. Leave me or tarry, Edward will be king,
And not be tied unto his brother's will.
   Q. Eliz. My lords, before it pleas'd his majesty
To raise my state to title of a queen,
Do me but right, and you must all confess
That I was not ignoble of descent;
And meaner than myself have had like fortune.
But as this title honours me and mine,
So your dislikes, to whom I would be pleasing,
Do cloud my joys with danger and with sorrow.
   K. Edw. My love, forbear to fawn upon their frowns:
What danger or what sorrow can befall thee,
So long as Edward is thy constant friend

And their true sovereign, whom they must obey?   [too,
Nay, whom they shall obey, and love thee
Unless they seek for hatred at my hands;
Which if they do, yet will I keep thee safe,
And they shall feel the vengeance of my wrath.
   Glo. I hear, yet say not much, but think the more.   [*Aside.*

Enter a Messenger.

   K. Edw. Now, messenger, what letters or what news
From France?   [few words
   Mess. My sovereign liege, no letters; and
But such as I, without your special pardon,
Dare not relate.
   K. Edw. Go to, we pardon thee: therefore, in brief,   [guess them.
Tell me their words as near as thou canst
What answer makes King Louis unto our letters?
   Mess. At my depart, these were his very words:
Go tell false Edward, thy supposed king,
That Louis of France is sending over masquers
To revel it with him and his new bride.
   K. Edw. Is Louis so brave? belike he thinks me Henry.
But what said Lady Bona to my marriage?
   Mess. These were her words, utter'd with mild disdain:
Tell him, in hope he'll prove a widower shortly,
I'll wear the willow-garland for his sake.
   K. Edw. I blame not her, she could say little less;   [queen?
She had the wrong. But what said Henry's
For I have heard that she was there in place.
   Mess. Tell him, quoth she, *my mourning-weeds are done,*
And I am ready to put armour on.   [zon.
   K. Edw. Belike she minds to play the Ama-
But what said Warwick to these injuries?
   Mess. He, more incens'd against your majesty
Than all the rest, discharg'd me with these words:
Tell him from me, that he hath done me wrong;
And therefore I'll uncrown him ere't be long.
   K. Edw. Ha! durst the traitor breathe out so proud words?
Well, I will arm me, being thus forewarn'd:
They shall have wars, and pay for their presumption.
But say, is Warwick friends with Margaret?
   Mess. Ay, gracious sovereign; they are so link'd in friendship
That young Prince Edward marries Warwick's daughter.
   Clar. Belike the elder; Clarence will have the younger.

Now, brother king, farewell, and sit you fast,
For I will hence to Warwick's other daugh-
ter;
That, though I want a kingdom, yet in mar-
riage
I may not prove inferior to yourself.—
You that love me and Warwick, follow me.
      [*Exit, and* SOMERSET *follows.*
  Glo. Not I:
My thoughts aim at a further matter; I
Stay not for the love of Edward, but the
crown.   [*Aside.*
  K. Edw. Clarence and Somerset both gone
to Warwick!
Yet am I arm'd against the worst can hap-
pen;
And haste is needful in this desperate case.—
Pembroke and Stafford, you in our behalf
Go levy men, and make prepare for war;
They are already, or quickly will be landed:
Myself in person will straight follow you.
              [*Exeunt* PEM. *and* STAF.
But ere I go, Hastings and Montague,
Resolve my doubt. You twain, of all the rest,
Are near to Warwick by blood and by alli-
ance:
Tell me if you love Warwick more than me?
If it be so, then both depart to him;
I rather wish you foes than hollow friends:
But if you mind to hold your true obedience,
Give me assurance with some friendly vow,
That I may never have you in suspect. [true!
  Mont. So God help Montague as he proves
  Hast. And Hastings as he favours Ed-
ward's cause!   [stand by us?
  K. Edw. Now, brother Richard, will you
  Glo. Ay, in despite of all that shall with-
stand you.
  K. Edw. Why, so! then am I sure of vic-
tory.
Now therefore let us hence; and lose no hour
Till we meet Warwick with his foreign power.
                              [*Exeunt.*

SCENE II.—*A Plain in Warwickshire.*

Enter WARWICK *and* OXFORD, *with French
and other* Forces.

  War. Trust me, my lord, all hitherto goes
well;
The common people by numbers swarm to
us.—
But see where Somerset and Clarence come!

Enter CLARENCE *and* SOMERSET.

Speak suddenly, my lords,—are we all
friends?
  Clar. Fear not that, my lord. [Warwick;—
  War. Then, gentle Clarence, welcome unto
And welcome, Somerset.—I hold it coward-
ice
To rest mistrustful where a noble heart
Hath pawn'd an open hand in sign of love;

Else might I think that Clarence, Edward's
brother,
Were but a feigned friend to our proceed-
ings:
But welcome, sweet Clarence; my daughter
shall be thine.
And now, what rests but, in night's cover-
ture,
Thy brother being carelessly encamp'd,
His soldiers lurking in the towns about,
And but attended by a simple guard,
We may surprise and take him at our pleas-
ure?
Our scouts have found the adventure very
easy:
That as Ulysses and stout Diomede
With sleight and manhood stole to Rhesus'
tents
And brought from thence the Thracian fatal
steeds,   [mantle,
So we, well cover'd with the night's black
At unawares may beat down Edward's guard
And seize himself; I say not, slaughter him,
For I intend but only to surprise him.
You that will follow me to this attempt,
Applaud the name of Henry with your
leader.   [*They all cry* "Henry!"
Why, then, let's on our way in silent sort:
For Warwick and his friends, God and Saint
George!   [*Exeunt.*

SCENE III.—EDWARD'S *Camp, near Warwick.*

Enter certain Watchmen, before the KING'S
tent.

  1 Watch. Come on, my masters, each man
take his stand:
The king by this has set him down to sleep.
  2 Watch. What, will he not to bed?
  1 Watch. Why, no: for he hath made a
solemn vow
Never to lie and take his natural rest
Till Warwick or himself be quite suppress'd.
  2 Watch. To-morrow then, belike, shall be
the day,
If Warwick be so near as men report.
  3 Watch. But say, I pray, what nobleman is that
That with the king here resteth in his tent?
  1 Watch. 'Tis the Lord Hastings, the
king's chiefest friend.   [the king
  3 Watch. O, is it so? But why commands
That his chief followers lodge in towns about
him,
While he himself keeps in the cold field?
  2 Watch. 'Tis the more honour, because
more dangerous.   [quietness,
  3 Watch. Ay, but give me worship and
I like it better than a dangerous honour.
If Warwick knew in what estate he stands,
'Tis to be doubted he would waken him.
  1 Watch. Unless our halberds did shut up
his passage.   [royal tent.
  2 Watch. Ay, wherefore else guard we his
But to defend his person from night-foes?

Enter WARWICK, CLARENCE, OXFORD,
SOMERSET, *and Forces.*

War. This is his tent; and see where
stand his guard.
Courage, my masters! honour now or never!
But follow me, and Edward shall be ours.
1 *Watch.* Who goes there?
2 *Watch.* Stay, or thou diest.
[WARWICK *and the rest cry all*—"War-
wick! Warwick!" *and set upon the*
Guard, *who fly crying* "Arm! Arm!"
WARWICK *and the rest following them.*

The drum beating and trumpets sounding,
re-enter WARWICK *and the rest, bringing*
the KING *out in his gown, sitting in a*
chair; GLOSTER *and* HASTINGS *are seen*
flying.
Som.　　　What are they that fly there?
War. Richard and Hastings: let them go;
here is the duke.
K. Edw. The duke! Why, Warwick, when
we parted last
Thou call'dst me king?
War.　　　Ay, but the case is alter'd:
When you disgrac'd me in my embassade,
Then I degraded you from being king,
And come now to create you Duke of York.
Alas, how should you govern any kingdom,
That know not how to use ambassadors;
Nor how to be contented with one wife;
Nor how to use your brothers brotherly;
Nor how to study for the people's welfare;
Nor how to shroud yourself from enemies?
K. Edw. Yea, brother of Clarence, art
thou here too?
Nay, then I see that Edward needs must
down.—
Yet, Warwick, in despite of all mischance,
Of thee thyself and all thy complices,
Edward will always bear himself as king:
Though fortune's malice overthrow my state,
My mind exceeds the compass of her wheel.
War. Then, for his mind, be Edward Eng-
land's king: [*Takes off his crown.*
But Henry now shall wear the English
crown
And be true king indeed; thou but the sha-
dow.—
My Lord of Somerset, at my request,
See that forthwith Duke Edward be con-
vey'd
Unto my brother, Archbishop of York.
When I have fought with Pembroke and
his fellows,
I'll follow you, and tell what answer
Louis and the Lady Bona send to him.—
Now, for awhile farewell, good Duke of
York.
K. Edw. What fates impose, that men
must needs abide;
It boots not to resist both wind and tide.
[*Exit. led out;* SOM. *with him.*

Oxf. What now remains, my lords, for us
to do,
But march to London with our soldiers?
War. Ay, that's the first thing that we
have to do;
To free King Henry from imprisonment,
And see him seated in the regal throne.
[*Exeunt.*

SCENE IV.—LONDON. *A Room in the Palace.*

Enter QUEEN ELIZABETH *and* RIVERS.

Riv. Madam, what makes you in this sud-
den change?
Q. Eliz. Why, brother Rivers, are you yet
to learn
What late misfortune is befall'n King Ed-
ward?
Riv. What, loss of some pitch'd battle
against Warwick?
Q. Eliz. No, but the loss of his own royal
person.
Riv. Then, is my sovereign slain?
Q. Eliz. Ay, almost slain, for he is taken
prisoner;
Either betray'd by falsehood of his guard,
Or by his foe surpris'd at unawares:
And, as I further have to understand,
Is new committed to the Bishop of York,
Fell Warwick's brother, and by that our foe.
Riv. These news, I must confess, are full
·of grief;
Yet, gracious madam, bear it as you may:
Warwick may lose, that now hath won the
day.
Q. Eliz. Till then, fair hope must hinder
life's decay.
And I the rather wean me from despair,
For love of Edward's offspring in my womb:
This is it that makes me bridle passion,
And bear with mildness my misfortune's
cross:
Ay, ay, for this I draw in many a tear,
And stop the rising of blood-sucking sighs,
Lest with my sighs or tears I blast or drown
King Edward's fruit, true heir to the Eng-
lish crown. [become?
Riv. But, madam, where is Warwick, then,
Q. Eliz. I am inform'd that he comes to-
wards London,
To set the crown once more on Henry's
head:
Guess thou the rest; King Edward's friends
must down.
But to prevent the tyrant's violence,—
For trust not him that hath once broken
faith,—·
I'll hence forthwith unto the sanctuary,
To save at least the heir of Edward's right:
There shall I rest secure from force and
fraud.
Come, therefore, let us fly while we may fly:
If Warwick take us, we are sure to die.
[*Exeunt.*

SCENE V.—*A Park near Middleham Castle in Yorkshire.*

Enter GLOSTER, HASTINGS, SIR WILLIAM STANLEY, *and others.*

Glo. Now, my Lord Hastings and Sir
    William Stanley,
Leave off to wonder why I drew you hither
Into this chiefest thicket of the park.
Thus stands the case: you know our king,
    my brother,
Is prisoner to the bishop here, at whose
    hands
He hath good usage and great liberty;
And often, but attended with weak guard,
Comes hunting this way, to disport himself.
I have advértis'd him by secret means
That if about this hour he make this way,
Under the colour of his usual game, [men,
He shall here find his friends, with horse and
To set him free from his captivity.

Enter KING EDWARD *and a* Huntsman.

Hunt. This way, my lord; for this way
    lies the game. [the huntsmen stand.—
K. Edw. Nay, this way, man: see where
Now, brother of Gloster, Lord Hastings, and
    the rest,
Stand you thus close to steal the bishop's
    deer?
Glo. Brother, the time and case requireth
    haste:
Your horse stands ready at the park-corner.
K. Edw. But whither shall we then?
Hast. To Lynn, my lord; and ship from
    thence to Flanders. [my meaning.
Glo. Well guess'd, believe me; for that was
K. Edw. Stanley, I will requite thy for-
    wardness. [to talk.
Glo. But wherefore stay we? 'tis no time
K. Edw. Huntsmen, what say'st thou?
    wilt thou go along?
Hunt. Better do so than tarry and be
    hang'd.
Glo. Come then, away; let's ha' no more
    ado.
K. Edw. Bishop, farewell: shield thee
    from Warwick's frown;
And pray that I may repossess the crown.
                                        [*Exeunt.*

SCENE VI.—*A Room in the Tower.*

Enter KING HENRY, CLARENCE, WARWICK,
SOMERSET, YOUNG RICHMOND, OXFORD,
MONTAGUE, Lieutenant of the Tower, *and*
Attendants.

K. Hen. Master lieutenant, now that God
    and friends
Have shaken Edward from the regal seat,
And turn'd my captive state to liberty,
My fear to hope, my sorrows unto joys,—
At our enlargement what are thy due fees?

Lieut. Subjects may challenge nothing of
    their sovereigns;
But if an humble prayer may prevail,
I then crave pardon of your majesty.
K. Hen. For what, lieutenant? for well-
    using me?
Nay, be thou sure I'll well requite thy kind-
    ness, [ure;
For that it made my imprisonment a pleas-
Ay, such a pleasure as incaged birds
Conceive, when, after many moody thoughts,
At last, by notes of household harmony,
They quite forget their loss of liberty.—
But, Warwick, after God, thou sett'st me
    free,
And chiefly therefore I thank God and thee;
He was the author, thou the instrument.
Therefore, that I may conquer fortune's
    spite,
By living low, where fortune cannot hurt me,
And that the people of this blessed land
May not be punish'd with my thwarting
    stars,—
Warwick, although my head still wear the
    crown,
I here resign my government to thee,
For thou art fortunate in all thy deeds.
War. Your grace hath still been fam'd for
    virtuous;
And now may seem as wise as virtuous
By spying and avoiding fortune's malice,
For few men rightly temper with the stars:
Yet in this one thing let me blame your
    grace
For choosing me when Clarence is in place.
Clar. No, Warwick, thou art worthy of
    the sway,
To whom the heavens, in thy nativity,
Adjudg'd an olive-branch and laurel-crown,
As likely to be blest in peace and war;
And therefore I yield thee my free consent.
War. And I choose Clarence only for pro-
    tector.
K. Hen. Warwick and Clarence, give me
    both your hands:
Now join your hands, and with your hands
    your hearts,
That no dissension hinder government:
I make you both protectors of this land;
While I myself will lead a private life,
And in devotion spend my latter days,
To sin's rebuke and my Creator's praise.
War. What answers Clarence to his sov-
    ereign's will? [consent;
Clar. That he consents if Warwick yield
For on thy fortune I repose myself.
War. Why, then, though loth, yet must I
    be content:
We'll yoke together, like a double shadow
To Henry's body, and supply his place;
I mean, in bearing weight of government,
While he enjoys the honour and his ease
And, Clarence, now then it is more than
    needful

Forthwith that Edward be pronounc'd a
traitor,
And all his lands and goods be confiscate.
  Clar. What else? and that succession be
determin'd.   [his part.
  War. Ay, therein Clarence shall not want
  K. Hen. But, with the first of all your
chief affairs,
Let me entreat,—for I command no more,—
That Margaret your queen, and my son Ed-
ward,
Be sent for, to return from France with
speed;
For till I see them here, by doubtful fear
My joy of liberty is half eclips'd.
  Clar. It shall be done, my sovereign, with
all speed.
  K. Hen. My Lord of Somerset, what
youth is that,
Of whom you seem to have so tender care?
  Som. My liege, it is young Henry, Earl of
Richmond.
  K. Hen. Come hither, England's hope.—If
secret powers
         [*Lays his hand on his head.*
Suggest but truth to my divining thoughts,
This pretty lad will prove our country's bliss.
His looks are full of peaceful majesty;
His head by nature fram'd to wear a crown,
His hand to wield a sceptre; and himself
Likely in time to bless a regal throne.
Make much of him, my lords; for this is he
Must help you more than you are hurt by
me.

Enter a Messenger.

  War. What news, my friend?   [brother,
  Mess. That Edward is escaped from your
And fled, as he hears since, to Burgundy.
  War. Unsavoury news! but how made he
escape?   [of Gloster
  Mess. He was convey'd by Richard Duke
And the Lord Hastings, who attended him
In secret ambush on the forest-side,
And from the bishop's huntsmen rescu'd
him;
For hunting was his daily exercise.
  War. My brother was too careless of his
charge.—
But let us hence, my sovereign, to provide
A salve for any sore that may betide.
      [*Exeunt* KING HENRY, WAR., CLAR.,
        Lieut., *and* Attendants.
  Som. My lord, I like not of this flight of
Edward's:
For doubtless Burgundy will yield him help,
And we shall have more wars before 't be
long.
As Henry's late presaging prophecy
Did glad my heart with hope of this young
Richmond,
So doth my heart misgive me, in these con-
flicts,
What may befall him, to his harm and ours:

Therefore, Lord Oxford, to prevent the
worst,
Forthwith we'll send him hence to Brittany,
Till storms be past of civil enmity.
  Oxf. Ay, for if Edward repossess the
crown,
'Tis like that Richmond with the rest shall
down.
  Som. It shall be so; he shall to Brittany.
Come, therefore, let's about it speedily.
                  [*Exeunt.*

SCENE VII.—*Before York.*

Enter KING EDWARD, GLOSTER, HASTINGS,
       and Forces.

  K. Edw. Now, brother Richard, Lord
Hastings, and the rest,
Yet thus far fortune maketh us amends,
And says that once more I shall interchange
My waned state for Henry's regal crown.
Well have we pass'd, and now repass'd the
seas,
And brought desired help from Burgundy:
What, then, remains, we being thus arriv'd
From Ravenspur haven before the gates of
York,
But that we enter, as into our dukedom?
  Glo. The gates made fast!—Brother, I like
not this;
For many men that stumble at the threshold
Are well foretold that danger lurks within.
  K. Edw. Tush, man, abodements must
not now affright us:
By fair or foul means we must enter in,
For hither will our friends repair to us.
  Hast. My liege, I'll knock once more to
summon them.

Enter, on the Walls, the Mayor of York *and*
       Aldermen.

  May. My lords, we were forewarned of
your coming,
And shut the gates for safety of ourselves;
For now we owe allegiance unto Henry.
  K. Edw. But, master mayor, if Henry be
your king,
Yet Edward at the least is Duke of York.
  May. True, my good lord; I know you for
no less.
  K. Edw. Why, and I challenge nothing but
my dukedom,
As being well content with that alone.
  Glo. But when the fox hath once got in
his nose,
He'll soon find means to make the body
follow.   [*Aside.*
  Hast. Why, master mayor, why stand you
in a doubt?
Open the gates, we are King Henry's friends.
  May. Ay, say you so? the gates shall then
be open'd.   [*Exeunt from above.*
  Glo. A wise stout captain, and soon per-
suaded!   [all were well,
  Hast. The good old man would fain that

So 'twere not 'long of him; but being en-
ter'd,
I doubt not, I, but we shall soon persuade
Both him and all his brothers unto reason.

Re-enter the Mayor *and* Aldermen, *below.*

K. Edw. So, master mayor: these gates
must not be shut
But in the night or in the time of war.
What! fear not, man, but yield me up the
keys; [*Takes his keys.*
For Edward will defend the town and thee.
And all those friends that deign to follow
me.

Drum. Enter MONTGOMERY *and Forces,
marching.*

Glo. Brother, this is Sir John Montgom-
ery,
Our trusty friend, unless I be deceiv'd.
K. Edw. Welcome, Sir John! But why
come you in arms? [of storm,
Mont. To help King Edward in his time
As every loyal subject ought to do.
K. Edw. Thanks, good Montgomery; but
we now forget
Our title to the crown, and only claim
Our dukedom till God please to send the rest.
Mont. Then fare you well, for I will
hence again:
I came to serve a king, and not a duke.—
Drummer, strike up, and let us march away.
[*A march begun.*
K. Edw. Nay, stay, Sir John, awhile; and
we'll debate
By what safe means the crown may be re-
cover'd.
Mont. What talk you of debating? in few
words,—
If you'll not here proclaim yourself our king,
I'll leave you to your fortune, and be gone
To keep them back that come to succour
you:
Why should we fight, if you pretend no title?
Glo. Why, brother, wherefore stand you
on nice points?
K. Edw. When we grow stronger, then
we'll make our claim:
Till then, 'tis wisdom to conceal our mean-
ing.
Hast. Away with scrupulous wit! now
arms must rule.
Glo. And fearless minds climb soonest
unto crowns.
Brother, we will proclaim you out of hand;
The bruit thereof will bring you many
friends.
K. Edw. Then be it as you will; for 'tis
my right,
And Henry but usurps the diadem.
Mont. Ay, now my sovereign speaketh
like himself;
And now will I be Edward's champion.

Hast. Sound trumpet; Edward shall be
here proclaim'd:—
Come, fellow-soldier, make thou proclama-
tion. [*Gives him a paper. Flourish.*
Sold. [*Reads.*] Edward the Fourth, by the
grace of God, King of England and France,
and Lord of Ireland, &c.
Mont. And whoso'er gainsays King Ed-
ward's right,
By this I challenge him to single fight.
[*Throws down his gauntlet.*
All. Long live Edward the Fourth!
K. Edw. Thanks, brave Montgomery;—
and thanks unto you all;
If fortune serve me, I'll requite this kindness.
Now, for this night, let's harbour here in
York;
And when the morning sun shall raise his car
Above the border of this horizon,
We'll forward towards Warwick and his
mates;
For well I wot that Henry is no soldier.—
Ah, froward Clarence! how evil it beseems
thee
To flatter Henry and forsake thy brother!
Yet, as we may, we'll meet both thee and
Warwick.—
Come on, brave soldiers: doubt not of the
day;
And, that once gotten, doubt not of large
pay. [*Exeunt.*

SCENE VIII.—LONDON. *A Room in the
Palace.*

Flourish. Enter KING HENRY, WARWICK,
MONTAGUE, CLARENCE, EXETER, *and* OX-
FORD.

War. What counsel, lords? Edward from
Belgia,
With hasty Germans and blunt Hollanders,
Hath pass'd in safety through the narrow
seas,
And with his troops doth march amain to
London;
And many giddy people flock to him.
Oxf. Let's levy men, and beat him back
again.
Clar. A little fire is quickly trodden out;
Which, being suffer'd, rivers cannot quench.
War. In Warwickshire I have true-heart-
ed friends,
Not mutinous in peace, yet bold in war;
Those will I muster up:—and thou, son
Clarence,
Shalt stir up, in Suffolk, Norfolk, and in
Kent,
The knights and gentlemen to come with
thee:—
Thou, brother Montague, in Buckingham,
Northampton, and in Leicestershire, shalt
find
Men well inclin'd to hear what thou com-
mand'st:—

And thou, brave Oxford, wondrous well be-
lov'd,
In Oxfordshire shalt muster up thy friends.
My sovereign, with the loving citizens,—
Like to his island girt in with the ocean,
Or modest Dian circled with her nymphs,—
Shall rest in London till we come to him.—
Fair lords, take leave, and stand not to
reply.—
Farewell, my sovereign.
   K. Hen. Farewell, my Hector, and my
   Troy's true hope.   [ness' hand.
   Clar. In sign of truth, I kiss your high-
   K. Hen. Well-minded Clarence, be thou
   fortunate!   [my leave.
   Mont. Comfort, my lord;—and so I take
   Oxf. And thus [*kissing* HENRY's *hand*] I
   seal my truth, and bid adieu.
   K. Hen. Sweet Oxford, and my loving
   Montague,
And all at once, once more a happy farewell.
   War. Farewell, sweet lords: let's meet at
   Coventry.
       [*Exeunt* WAR., CLAR., OXF., *and* MONT.
   K. Hen. Here at the palace will I rest
   awhile.
Cousin of Exeter, what thinks your lord-
ship?
Methinks the power that Edward hath in
field
Should not be able to encounter mine.
   Exe. The doubt is, that he will seduce the
   rest.
   K. Hen. That's not my fear; my meed
   hath got me fame:
I have not stopp'd mine ears to their de-
mands,
Nor posted off their suits with slow delays;
My pity hath been balm to heal their
wounds,
My mildness hath allay'd their swelling
griefs,
My mercy dried their water-flowing tears;
I have not been desirous of their wealth,
Nor much oppress'd them with great sub-
sidies,
Nor forward of revenge, though they much
err'd: [than me?
Then why should they love Edward more
No, Exeter, these graces challenge grace;
And, when the lion fawns upon the lamb,
The lamb will never cease to follow him.
    [*Shout within,* "A Lancaster! A Lancaster!"
   Exe. Hark, hark, my lord! what shouts
   are these?

Enter KING EDWARD, GLOSTER, *and* Soldiers.
   Edw. Seize on the shame-fac'd Henry,
   bear him hence;
And once again proclaim us king of Eng-
land.—
You are the fount that makes small brooks
to flow;   [them dry,
Now stops thy spring; my sea shall suck

And swell so much the higher by their ebb.—
Hence with him to the Tower; let him not
speak.
       [*Exeunt some with* KING HENRY.
And, lords, towards Coventry· bend we our
course,
Where peremptory Warwick now remains:
The sun shines hot; and, if we use delay,
Cold biting winter mars our hop'd-for hay.
   Glo. Away betimes, before his forces join,
And take the great-grown traitor unawares:
Brave warriors, march amain towards Cov-
entry.
       [*Exeunt.*

ACT V.

SCENE I.—*Coventry.*

Enter upon the Walls, WARWICK, *the* Mayor
of Coventry, *two* Messengers, *and others.*

   War. Where is the post that came from
   valiant Oxford?
How far hence is thy lord, mine honest fellow?
   1 *Mess.* By this at Dunsmore, marching
   hitherward.
   War. How far off is our brother Montague?—
Where is the post that came from Montague?
   2 *Mess.* By this at Daintry, with a puissant troop.

Enter SIR JOHN SOMERVILLE.

   War. Say, Somerville, what says my lov-
   ing son?
And, by thy guess, how nigh is Clarence
now?   [his forces,
   Som. At Southam I did leave him with
And do expect him here some two hours
hence.   [*Drum heard.*
   War. Then Clarence is at hand; I hear his
   drum.   [am lies;
   Som. It is not his, my lord; here South-
The drum your honour hears marcheth from
Warwick.   [look'd-for friends.
   War. Who should that be? belike un-
   Som. They are at hand, and you shall
   quickly know.

March. Flourish. Enter KING EDWARD,
GLOSTER, *and* Forces.

   K. Edw. Go, trumpet, to the walls, and
   sound a parle.   [the wall!
   Glo. See how the surly Warwick mans
   War. O unbid spite! is sportful Edward
   come?   [seduc'd,
Where slept our scouts, or how are they
That we could hear no news of his repair?
   K. Edw. Now, Warwick, wilt thou ope
   the city gates,
Speak gentle words, and humbly bend thy
knee,
Call Edward king, and at his hands beg
mercy?

And he shall pardon thee these outrages.

War. Nay, rather, wilt thou draw thy forces hence,
Confess who set thee up and pluck'd thee down,
Call Warwick patron, and be penitent?
And thou shalt still remain the Duke of York,

Glo. I thought, at least, he would have said the king;
Or did he make the jest against his will?

War. Is not a dukedom, sir, a goodly gift?

Glo. Ay, by my faith, for a poor earl to give:
I'll do thee service for so good a gift.

War. 'Twas I that gave the kingdom to thy brother.

K. Edw. Why, then, 'tis mine, if but by Warwick's gift.

War. Thou art no Atlas for so great a weight:
And, weakling, Warwick takes his gift again;
And Henry is my king, Warwick his subject.

K. Edw. But Warwick's king is Edward's prisoner:
And, gallant Warwick, do but answer this,—
What is the body when the head is off?

Glo. Alas, that Warwick had no more forecast,
But, whiles he thought to steal the single ten,
The king was slily finger'd from the deck!
You left poor Henry at the bishop's palace,
And, ten to one, you'll meet him in the Tower.

K. Edw. 'Tis even so; yet you are Warwick still.

Glo. Come, Warwick, take the time; kneel down, kneel down:
Nay, when? strike now, or else the iron cools.

War. I had rather chop this hand off at a blow,
And with the other fling it at thy face,
Than bear so low a sail, to strike to thee.

K. Edw. Sail how thou canst, have wind and tide thy friend;
This hand, fast wound about thy coal-black hair,
Shall, whiles thy head is warm and new cut off,
Write in the dust this sentence with thy blood,—
Wind-changing Warwick now can change no more.

Enter OXFORD, *with* Forces, *drum, and colours.*

War. O cheerful colours! see where Oxford comes!

Oxf. Oxford, Oxford, for Lancaster!
[*He and his* Forces *enter the city.*

Glo. The gates are open, let us enter too.

K. Edw. So other foes may set upon our backs.

Stand we in good array; for they no doubt
Will issue out again and bid us battle:
If not, the city being but of small defence,
We'll quickly rouse the traitors in the same.

War. O, welcome, Oxford! for we want thy help.

Enter MONTAGUE, *with* Forces, *drum, and colours.*

Mont. Montague, Montague, for Lancaster!
[*He and his* Forces *enter the city.*

Glo. Thou and thy brother both shall buy this treason
Even with the dearest blood your bodies bear.

K. Edw. The harder match'd, the greater victory:
My mind presageth happy gain and conquest.

Enter SOMERSET, *with* Forces, *drum, and colours.*

Som. Somerset, Somerset, for Lancaster!
[*He and his* Forces *enter the city.*

Glo. Two of thy name, both Dukes of Somerset,
Have sold their lives unto the house of York;
And thou shalt be the third, if this sword hold.

Enter CLARENCE, *with* Forces, *drum and colours.*

War. And lo, where George of Clarence sweeps along,
Of force enough to bid his brother battle;
With whom an upright zeal to right prevails
More than the nature of a brother's love!—
Come, Clarence, come; thou wilt, if Warwick call.

Clar. Father of Warwick, know you what this means?
[*Taking the red rose out of his hat.*
Look here, I throw my infamy at thee:
I will not ruinate my father's house,
Who gave his blood to lime the stones together,
And set up Lancaster. Why, trowst thou, Warwick,
That Clarence is so harsh, so blunt, unnatural,
To bend the fatal instruments of war
Against his brother and his lawful king?
Perhaps thou wilt object my holy oath:
To keep that oath were more impiety
Than Jephtha's, when he sacrific'd his daughter.
I am so sorry for my trespass made,
That, to deserve well at my brother's hands,
I here proclaim myself thy mortal foe;
With resolution wheresoe'er I meet thee,—
As I will meet thee, if thou stir abroad,—
To plague thee for thy foul misleading me.
And so, proud-hearted Warwick, I defy thee.

And to my brother turn my blushing cheeks.—
Pardon me, Edward, I will make amends;
And, Richard, do not frown upon my faults,
For I will henceforth be no more unconstant.
K. Edw. Now welcome more, and ten
     times more belov'd,
Than if thou never hadst deserv'd our hate.
Glo. Welcome, good Clarence; this is
     brother-like.
War. O passing traitor, perjur'd and un-
     just!
K. Edw. What, Warwick, wilt thou leave
     the town and fight?
Or shall we beat the stones about thine ears?
War. Alas, I am not coop'd here for de-
     fence!
I will away towards Barnet presently,
And bid thee battle, Edward, if thou dar'st.
K. Edw. Yes, Warwick, Edward dares,
     and leads the way
Lords, to the field: Saint George and victory.
                              [March. Exeunt.

SCENE II.—A field of Battle near Barnet.

Alarums and excursions. Enter KING ED-
WARD, bringing in WARWICK wounded.

K. Edw. So, lie thou there: die thou, and
     die our fear;
For Warwick was a bug that fear'd us all.—
Now, Montague, sit fast; I seek for thee,
That Warwick's bones may keep thine com-
     pany.   [Exit.
War. Ah, who is nigh? come to me, friend
     or foe,
And tell me who is victor, York or Warwick?
Why ask I that? my mangled body shows,
My blood, my want of strength, my sick
     heart shows,
That I must yield my body to the earth,
And, by my fall, the conquest to my foe.
Thus yields the cedar to the axe's edge,
Whose arms gave shelter to the princely
     eagle,
Under whose shade the ramping lion slept,
Whose top-branch overpeer'd Jove's spread-
     ing tree,
And kept low shrubs from winter's powerful
     wind.
These eyes, that now are dimm'd with
     death's black vail,
Have been as piercing as the mid-day sun,
To search the secret treasons of the world:
The wrinkles in my brows, now fill'd with
     blood,
Were liken'd oft to kingly sepulchres;
For who liv'd king, but I could dig his grave?
And who durst smile when Warwick bent his
     brow?
Lo, now my glory smear'd in dust and
     blood!
My parks, my walks, my manors that I had,
Even now forsake me; and of all my lands
Is nothing left me but my body's length!

Why, what is pomp, rule, reign, but earth
     and dust!
And, live we how we can, yet die we must.

Enter OXFORD and SOMERSET.

Som. Ah, Warwick, Warwick! wert thou
     as we are,
We might recover all our loss again:
The queen from France hath brought a puis-
     sant power;   [thou fly!
Even now we heard the news: ah, couldst
War. Why, then, I would not fly.—Ah,
     Montague,
If thou be there, sweet brother, take my
     hand,
And with thy lips keep in my soul awhile!
Thou lov'st me not; for, brother, if thou
     didst,
Thy tears would wash this cold congealed
     blood
That glues my lips and will not let me speak.
Come quickly, Montague, or I am dead.
Som. Ah, Warwick! Montague hath
     breath'd his last;
And to the latest gasp cried out for War-
     wick,
And said, Commend me to my valiant
     brother.
And more he would have said; and more he
     spoke,
Which sounded like a cannon in a vault,
That might not be distinguish'd; but at last,
I well might hear, deliver'd with a groan,
O, farewell, Warwick!
War. Sweet rest his soul!—fly, lords, and
     save yourselves;
For Warwick bids you all farewell, to meet
     in heav'n.   [Dies.
Oxf. Away, away, to meet the queen's
     great power!
              [Exeunt, bearing off WAR.'s body.

SCENE III.—Another part of the Field.

Flourish. Enter KING EDWARD in triumph;
with CLARENCE, GLOSTER, and the rest.

K. Edw. Thus far our fortune keeps an
     upward course,
And we are grac'd with wreaths of victory.
But in the midst of this bright-shining day
I spy a black, suspicious, threatening cloud,
That will encounter with our glorious sun
Ere he attain his easeful western bed:
I mean, my lords, those powers that the
     queen
Hath rais'd in Gallia have arriv'd our coast,
And, as we hear, march on to fight with us.
Clar. A little gale will soon disperse that
     cloud
And blow it to the source from whence it
     came:
Thy very beams will dry those vapours up;
For every cloud engenders not a storm.
                              [strong,
Glo. The queen is valu'd thirty thousand

And Somerset, with Oxford, fled to her:
If she have time to breathe, be well assur'd,
Her faction will be full as strong as ours.

    K. Edw. We are advértis'd by our loving
        friends   [Tewksbury;
That they do hold their course toward
We, having now the best at Barnet field,
Will thither straight, for willingness rids
    way;   [mented
And as we march, our strength will be aug-
In every county as we go along.—
Strike up the drum; cry, Courage! and
    away.   [*Exeunt.*

SCENE IV.—*Plains near Tewksbury.*

March. Enter QUEEN MARGARET, PRINCE
EDWARD, SOMERSET, OXFORD, *and* Soldiers.

    Q. Mar. Great Lords, wise men ne'er sit
        and wail their loss,
But cheerly seek how to redress their harms.
What though the mast be now blown over-
    board,
The cable broke, the holding-anchor lost,
And half our sailors swallow'd in the flood;
Yet lives our pilot still: is't meet that he
Should leave the helm, and, like a fearful lad,
With tearful eyes add water to the sea,
And give more strength to that which hath
    too much;
Whiles, in his moan, the ship splits on the
    rock,
Which industry and courage might have
    sav'd?
Ah, what a shame! ah, what a fault were
    this!
Say Warwick was our anchor; what of that?
And Montague our top-mast; what of him?
Our slaughter'd friends the tackles; what of
    these?
Why, is not Oxford here another anchor?
And Somerset another goodly mast? [lings?
The friends of France our shrouds and tack-
And, though unskilful, why not Ned and I
For once allow'd the skilful pilot's charge?
We will not from the helm to sit and weep;
But keep our course, though the rough wind
    say no,   [wreck.
From shelves and rocks that threaten us with
As good to chide the waves as speak them
    fair.
And what is Edward but a ruthless sea?
What Clarence but a quicksand of deceit?
And Richard but a ragged fatal rock?
All these the enemies to our poor bark.
Say you can swim; alas, 'tis but a while!
Tread on the sand; why, there you quickly
    sink:
Bestride the rock; the tide will wash you off,
Or else you famish,—that's a threefold death.
This speak I, lords, to let you understand,
If case some one of you would fly from us,
That there's no hop'd-for mercy with the
    brothers,   [and rocks.
More than with ruthless waves, with sands,

Why, courage, then! what cannot be avoided,
'Twere childish weakness to lament or fear.
    Prince. Methinks a woman of this valiant
        spirit
Should, if a coward heard her speak these
    words,
Infuse his breath with magnanimity,
And make him naked foil a man-at-arms.
I speak not this as doubting any here;
For did I but suspect a fearful man,
He should have leave to go away betimes;
Lest in our need he might infect another,
And make him of like spirit to himself.
If any such be here,—as God forbid!—
Let him depart before we need his help.
    Oxf. Women and children of so high a
        courage,
And warriors faint! why, 'twere perpetual
    shame.—
O brave young prince! thy famous grand-
    father
Doth live again in thee: long mayst thou live
To bear his image and renew his glories!
    Som. And he that will not fight for such a
        hope,
Go home to bed, and, like the owl by day,
If he arise, be mock'd and wonder'd at.
    Q. Mar. Thanks, gentle Somerset;—sweet
        Oxford, thanks.   [nothing else.
    Prince. And take his thanks that yet hath

Enter a Messenger.

    Mess. Prepare you, lords, for. Edward is
        at hand,
Ready to fight; therefore be resolute.
    Oxf. I thought no less: it is his policy
To haste thus fast, to find us unprovided.
    Som. But he's deceiv'd; we are in readi-
        ness.
    Q. Mar. This cheers my heart, to see your
        forwardness.   [not budge.
    Oxf. Here pitch our battle; hence we will

Flourish and March. Enter, at a distance,
KING EDWARD, CLARENCE, GLOSTER, *and*
Forces.

    K. Edw. Brave followers, yonder stands
        the thorny wood,   [strength,
Which, by the heavens' assistance and your
Must by the roots be hewn up yet ere night.
I need not add more fuel to your fire;
For well I wot ye blaze to burn them out:
Give signal to the fight, and to it, lords.
    Q. Mar. Lords, knights, and gentlemen,
        what I should say
My tears gainsay; for every word I speak,
Ye see, I drink the water of mine eyes.
Therefore, no more but this:—Henry, your
    sovereign,
Is prisoner to the foe; his state usurp'd,
His realm a slaughter-house, his subjects
    slain,
His statutes cancell'd, and his treasure spent;
And yonder is the wolf that makes this spoil.

You fight in justice: then, in God's name, lords,
Be valiant, and give signal to the fight.
[*Exeunt both armies.*

SCENE V.—*Another part of the Plains.*

Alarums: excursions: and afterwards a retreat. Then enter KING EDWARD, CLARENCE, GLOSTER, *and* Forces, *with* QUEEN MARGARET, OXFORD, *and* SOMERSET, *prisoners.*

K. Edw. Now, here a period of tumultuous broils.
Away with Oxford to Hammes' Castle straight;
For Somerset, off with his guilty head.
[speak.
Go, bear them hence; I will not hear them
Oxf. For my part, I'll not trouble thee with words.   [my fortune.
Som. Nor I, but stoop with patience to
[*Exeunt* OXF. *and* SOM., *guarded.*
Q. Mar. So part we sadly in this troublous world,
To meet with joy in sweet Jerusalem.
K. Edw. Is proclamation made that who finds Edward
Shall have a high reward, and he his life?
Glo. It is; and lo, where youthful Edward comes.

Enter Soldiers, *with* PRINCE EDWARD.

K. Edw. Bring forth the gallant, let us hear him speak.
What, can so young a thorn begin to prick?—
Edward, what satisfaction canst thou make
For bearing arms, for stirring up my subjects,
And all the trouble thou hast turn'd me to?
Prince. Speak like a subject, proud ambitious York!
Suppose that I am now my father's mouth;
Resign thy chair, and where I stand kneel thou,
Whilst I propose the self-same words to thee,
Which, traitor, thou wouldst have me answer to.
Q. Mar. Ah, that thy father had been so resolv'd!
Glo. That you might still have worn the petticoat,
And ne'er have stol'n the breech from Lancaster.
Prince. Let Æsop fable in a winter's night;
His currish riddles sort not with this place.
Glo. By heaven, brat, I'll plague you for that word.   [to men.
Q. Mar. Ay, thou wast born to be a plague
Glo. For God's sake, take away this captive scold.
Prince. Nay, take away this scolding crook-back rather.

K. Edw. Peace, wilful boy, or I will charm your tongue.   [pert.
Clar. Untutor'd lad, thou art too mala-
Prince. I know my duty; you are all undutiful: [George,—
Lascivious Edward,—and thou, perjur'd
And thou, misshapen Dick,—I tell ye all
I am your better, traitors as ye are;—
And thou usurp'st my father's right and mine.
K. Edw. Take that, the likeness of this railer here.   [*Stabs him.*
Glo. Sprawl'st thou? take that, to end thy agony.   [*Stabs him.*
Clar. And there's for twitting me with perjury.   [*Stabs him.*
Q. Mar. O, kill me too!
Glo. Marry, and shall. [*Offers to kill her.*
K. Edw. Hold, Richard, hold; for we have done too much.
Glo. Why should she live, to fill the world with words?
K. Edw. What, doth she swoon? use means for her recovery.
Glo. Clarence, excuse me to the king my brother;
I'll hence to London on a serious matter:
Ere ye come there, be sure to hear some news.
Clar. What? what?
Glo. The Tower! the Tower!   [*Exit.*
Q. Mar. O Ned, sweet Ned! speak to thy mother, boy!   [ers!—
Canst thou not speak?—O traitors! murder-
They that stabb'd Cæsar shed no blood at all,
Did not offend, nor were not worthy blame,
If this foul deed were by to equal it:
He was a man;—this, in respect, a child,—
And men ne'er spend their fury on a child.
What's worse than murderer, that I may name it?
No, no, my heart will burst, an if I speak:—
And I will speak, that so my heart may burst.—
Butchers and villains! bloody cannibals!
How sweet a plant have you untimely cropp'd!
You have no children, butchers! if you had,
The thought of them would have stirr'd up remorse:
But if you ever chance to have a child,
Look in his youth to have him so cut off
As, deathsmen, you have rid this sweet young prince!
K. Edw. Away with her; go, bear her hence perforce.
Q. Mar. Nay, never bear me hence, despatch me here;   [death:
Here, sheathe thy sword, I'll pardon thee my
What, wilt thou not?—then, Clarence, do it thou.   [much ease.
Clar. By heaven, I will not do thee so
Q. Mar. Good Clarence, do; sweet Clarence, do thou do it.

Clar. Didst thou not hear me swear I
   would not do it?

Q. Mar. Ay, but thou usest to forswear
   thyself;
'Twas sin before, but now 'tis charity.
What! wilt thou not?—Where is that devil's
   butcher,   [art thou?
Hard-favour'd Richard?—Richard, where
Thou art not here: murder is thy alms-deed;
Petitioners for blood thou ne'er putt'st back.

K. Edw. Away, I say; I charge ye, bear
   her hence.

Q. Mar. So come to you and yours as to
   this prince!   [*Exit, led out forcibly.*

K. Edw. Where's Richard gone?

Clar. To London, all in post; and, as I
   guess,
To make a bloody supper in the Tower.

K. Edw. He's sudden, if a thing comes in
   his head.   [mon sort
Now march we hence: discharge the com-
With pay and thanks, and let's away to
   London,
And see our gentle queen how well she
   fares,—
By this, I hope, she hath a son for me.
                              [*Exeunt.*

SCENE VI.—LONDON. *A Room in the Tower.*

KING HENRY *is discovered sitting with a
book in his hand, the* Lieutenant *attending.*
Enter GLOSTER.

Glo. Good-day, my lord. What, at your
   book so hard?

K. Hen. Ay, my good lord:—my lord, I
   should say rather;
'Tis sin to flatter, good was little better:
Good Gloster and good devil were alike,
And both preposterous: therefore, not good
   lord.

Glo. Sirrah, leave us to ourselves: we
   must confer.   [*Exit* Lieutenant.

K. Hen. So flies the reckless shepherd
   from the wolf;
So first the harmless sheep doth yield his
   fleece,
And next his throat unto the butcher's
   knife.—
What scene of death hath Roscius now to
   act?

Glo. Suspicion always haunts the guilty
   mind;
The thief doth fear each bush an officer.

K. Hen. The bird that hath been limed in
   a bush,
With trembling wings misdoubteth every
   bush;
And I, the hapless male to one sweet bird,
Have now the fatal object in my eye
Where my poor young was lim'd, was caught,
   and kill'd.

Glo. Why, what a peevish fool was that
   of Crete,
That taught his son the office of a fowl!

And yet, for all his wings, the tool was
   drown'd.

K. Hen. I, Dædalus, my poor boy, Icarus;
Thy father, Minos, that denied our course;
The sun, that sear'd the wings of my sweet
   boy,
Thy brother Edward; and thyself, the sea,
Whose envious gulf did swallow up his life.
Ah, kill me with thy weapon, not with
   words!
My breast can better brook thy dagger's
   point
Than can my ears that tragic history.
But wherefore dost thou come? is't for my
   life?

Glo. Think'st thou I am an executioner?

K. Hen. A persecutor, I am sure, thou art:
If murdering innocents be executing,
Why, then thou art an executioner.

Glo. Thy son I kill'd for his presumption.

K. Hen. Hadst thou been kill'd when first
   thou didst presume,
Thou hadst not liv'd to kill a son of mine.
And thus I prophesy,—that many a thou-
   sand,
Which now mistrust no parcel of my fear,
And many an old man's sigh, and many a
   widow's,
And many an orphan's water-standing
   eye,—
Men for their sons, wives for their hus-
   bands,
And orphans for their parents' timeless
   death,—
Shall rue the hour that ever thou wast born
The owl shriek'd at thy birth,—an evil sign;
The night-crow cried, aboding luckless time;
Dogs howl'd, and hideous tempest shook
   down trees;
The raven rook'd her on the chimney's top,
And chattering pies in dismal discords sung
Thy mother felt more than a mother's pain,
And yet brought forth less than a mother's
   hope,
To wit,—
An indigest deformed lump,
Not like the fruit of such a goodly tree.
Teeth hadst thou in thy head when thou
   wast born,
To signify thou cam'st to bite the world:
And if the rest be true which I have heard,
Thou cam'st—

Glo. I'll hear no more:—die, prophet, in
   thy speech: [*Stabs him.*
For this, amongst the rest, was I ordain'd.

K. Hen. Ay, and for much more slaughter
   after this.
O God forgive my sins and pardon thee!
                              [*Dies.*

Glo. What, will the aspiring blood of Lancaster
Sink in the ground? I thought it would have
   mounted.   [death!
See how my sword weeps for the poor king's

O may such purple tears be alway shed
From those that wish the downfall of our
    house!—
If any spark of life be yet remaining,
Down, down to hell; and say I sent thee
    thither,—   [*Stabs him again.*
I, that have neither pity, love, nor fear.—
Indeed, 'tis true that Henry told me of;
For I have often heard my mother say
I came into the world with my legs forward:
Had I not reason, think ye, to make haste,
And seek their ruin that usurp'd our right:
The midwife wonder'd; and the women
    cried,
O, Jesus bless us, he is born with teeth!
And so I was, which plainly signified
That I should snarl, and bite, and play the
    dog.
Then, since the heavens have shap'd my
    body so,
Let hell make crook'd my mind to answer it.
I have no brother, I am like no brother;
And this word *love*, which greybeards call
    divine,
Be resident in men like one another,
And not in me: I am myself alone.—
Clarence, beware; thou keep'st me from the
    light:
But I will sort a pitchy day for thee;
For I will buzz abroad such prophecies
That Edward shall be fearful of his life:
And then, to purge his fear, I'll be thy death.
King Henry and the prince his son are gone:
Clarence, thy turn is next, and then the rest;
Counting myself but bad till I be best.—
I'll throw thy body in another room,
And triumph, Henry, in thy day of doom.
             [*Exit with the body.*

SCENE VII.—LONDON. *A Room in the Palace.*

Flourish. KING EDWARD *is discovered sitting
    on his throne;* QUEEN ELIZABETH *with the
    infant* PRINCE, CLARENCE, GLOSTER, HAST-
    INGS, *and others, near him.*

K. Edw. Once more we sit in England's
    royal throne.
Repurchas'd with the blood of enemies.
What valiant foemen, like to autumn's corn,
Have we mow'd down in tops of all their
    pride!
Three Dukes of Somerset,—threefold re-
    nown'd
For hardy and undoubted champions;
Two Cliffords, as the father and the son;
And two Northumberlands,—two braver
    men
Ne'er spurr'd their coursers at the trumpet's
    sound;

With them the two brave bears, Warwick
    and Montague,
That in their chains fetter'd the kingly lion,
And made the forest tremble when they
    roar'd.
Thus have we swept suspicion from our seat
And made our footstool of security.—
Come hither, Bess, and let me kiss my boy.—
Young Ned, for thee, thine uncles and my-
    self
Have in our armours watch'd the winter's
    night;
Went all afoot in summer's scalding heat,
That thou mightst repossess the crown in
    peace:
And of our labours thou shalt reap the gain.
    Glo. I'll blast his harvest if your head
    were laid;
For yet I am not look'd on in the world.
This shoulder was ordain'd so thick to heave;
And heave it shall some weight, or break my
    back:—
Work thou the way, -and that shalt execute.
             [*Aside.*
    K. Edw. Clarence and Gloster, love my
    lovely queen;
And kiss your princely nephew, brothers
    both.
    Clar. The duty that I owe unto your ma-
    jesty
I seal upon the lips of this sweet babe.
    K. Edw. Thanks, noble Clarence; worthy
    brother, thanks.
    Glo. And, that I love the tree from whence
    thou sprang'st,
Witness the loving kiss I give the fruit.—
To say the truth, so Judas kiss'd his master,
And cried, all hail! when as he meant all
    harm.   [*Aside.*
    K. Edw. Now am I seated as my soul de-
    lights,
Having my country's peace and brothers'
    loves.
    Clar. What will your grace have done with
    Margaret?
Reignier, her father, to the King of France
Hath pawn'd the Sicils and Jerusalem,
And hither have they sent it for her ransom.
    K. Edw. Away with her, and waft her
    hence to France.
And now what rests but that we spend the
    time
With stately triumphs, mirthful comic shows,
Such as befit the pleasure of the court?
Sound drums and trumpets! farewell, sour
    annoy!
For here, I hope, begins our lasting joy.
             [*Exeunt.*

RICHARD III.

Act IV. Sc. 2.

THE LIFE AND DEATH OF KING RICHARD III.

DRAMATIS PERSONÆ

KING EDWARD THE FOURTH.

EDWARD, *Prince of Wales,*
   afterwards KING ED-
   WARD V.,
RICHARD, *Duke of York,*
GEORGE, *Duke of Clarence,*
RICHARD, *Duke of Gloster,*
   afterwards KING RICH-
   ARD III.,
} *Sons to the* KING.
} *Brothers to the* KING.

A Young Son of Clarence.

HENRY, *Earl of Richmond, afterwards* KING HENRY VII.

CARDINAL BOUCHER, *Archbishop of Canterbury.*

THOMAS ROTHERAM, *Archbishop of York.*

JOHN MORTON, *Bishop of Ely.*

DUKE OF BUCKINGHAM.

DUKE OF NORFOLK.

EARL OF SURREY, *his Son.*

EARL RIVERS, *Brother to* KING EDWARD'S Queen.

MARQUIS OF DORSET *and* LORD GREY, *her Sons.*

EARL OF OXFORD.

LORD HASTINGS.

LORD STANLEY.

LORD LOVEL.

SIR THOMAS VAUGHAN.

SIR RICHARD RATCLIFF.

SIR WILLIAM CATESBY.

SIR JAMES TYRREL.

SIR JAMES BLOUNT.

SIR WALTER HERBERT.

SIR ROBERT BRAKENBURY, *Lieutenant of the* Tower.

CHRISTOPHER URSWICK, *a Priest.*

Another Priest.

Lord Mayor of London.

Sheriff of Wiltshire.

ELIZABETH, *Queen to* KING EDWARD IV.

MARGARET, *Widow to* KING HENRY VI.

DUCHESS OF YORK, *Mother to* KING EDWARD IV., CLARENCE, *and* GLOSTER.

LADY ANNE, *Widow to* EDWARD, *Prince of Wales, Son to* KING HENRY VI.; *afterwards married to the* DUKE OF GLOSTER.

A Young Daughter of Clarence.

Lords, *and other* Attendants; *two* Gentlemen, *a* Pursuivant, Scrivener, Citizens, Murderers, Messengers, Ghosts, Soldiers, &c.

SCENE,—ENGLAND

ACT I.

SCENE I.—LONDON. *A Street.*

Enter GLOSTER.

Glo. Now is the winter of our discontent
Made glorious summer by this sun of York;
And all the clouds that lower'd upon our house
In the deep bosom of the ocean buried.
Now are our brows bound with victorious wreaths;
Our bruised arms hung up for monuments;
Our stern alarums chang'd to merry meetings,
Our dreadful marches to delightful measures.
Grim-visaged war hath smooth'd his wrinkled front;
And now,—instead of mounting barbed steeds
To fright the souls of fearful adversaries,—
He capers nimbly in a lady's chamber
To the lascivious pleasing of a lute.
But I,—that am not shap'd for sportive tricks,
Nor made to court an amorous looking-glass;
I, that am rudely stamp'd, and want love's majesty
To strut before a wanton ambling nymph;
I, that am curtail'd of this fair proportion,
Cheated of feature by dissembling nature,
Deform'd, unfinish'd, sent before my time
Into this breathing world scarce half made up,
And that so lamely and unfashionable
That dogs bark at me as I halt by them;—
Why, I, in this weak piping time of peace,
Have no delight to pass away the time,
Unless to spy my shadow in the sun,
And descant on mine own deformity:
And therefore,—since I cannot prove a lover,
To entertain these fair well-spoken days,—
I am determined to prove a villain,
And hate the idle pleasures of these days.
Plots have I laid, inductions dangerous,
By drunken prophecies, libels, and dreams,
To set my brother Clarence and the king
In deadly hate the one against the other:

And, if King Edward be as true and just
As I am subtle, false, ana treacherous,
This day should Clarence closely be mew'd
　　up,—
About a prophecy, which says that G
Of Edward's heirs the murderer shall be.
Dive, thoughts, down to my soul:—here
　　Clarence comes.

Enter CLARENCE, *guarded, and* BRAKENBURY.

Brother, good-day: what means this armed
　　guard,
That waits upon your grace?
　　Clar.　　　　　　　　　His majesty,
Tendering my person's safety, hath appoint-
　　ed
This conduct to convey me to the Tower.
　　Glo. Upon what cause?
　　Clar.　　　　Because my name is George.
　　Glo. Alack, my lord, that fault is none of
　　yours;
He should, for that, commit your godfath-
　　ers:—
O, belike his majesty hath some intent
That you shall be new-christen'd in the
　　Tower.
But what's the matter, Clarence? may I
　　know?
　　Clar. Yea, Richard, when I know; for I
　　protest
As yet I do not: but, as I can learn,
He hearkens after prophecies and dreams;
And from the cross-row plucks the letter G,
And says a wizard told him that by G
His issue disinherited should be;
And, for my name of George begins with G,
It follows in his thought that I am he.
These, as I learn, and such like toys as these,
Have mov'd his highness to commit me now.
　　Glo. Why, this it is, when men are rul'd by
　　women:—
'Tis not the king that sends you to the
　　Tower;
My Lady Grey, his wife, Clarence, 'tis she
That tempers him to this extremity.
,Vas it not she, and that good man of wor-
　　ship,
Antony Woodville, her brother there,
That made him send Lord Hastings to the
　　Tower,
From whence this present day he is deliv-
　　er'd?
We are not safe, Clarence; we are not safe.
　　Clar. By heaven, I think there is no man
　　secure　　　　　　　　　　　　　　[heralds
But the queen's kindred, and night-walking
'.'hat trudge betwixt the king and Mistress
　　Shore.
Heard you not what an humble suppliant
Lord Hastings was to her for his delivery?
　　Glo. Humbly complaining to her deity
Got my lord chamberlain his liberty.
I'll tell you what,—I think it is our way,
If we will keep in favour with the king,

To be her men, and wear her livery:
The jealous o'er-worn widow and herself,
Since that our brother dubb'd them gentle-
　　women,
Are mighty gossips in this monarchy.
　　Brak. I beseech your graces both to par-
　　don me;
His majesty hath straitly given in charge
That no man shall have private conference,
Of what degree soever, with his brother.
　　Glo. Even so; an please your worship,
　　Brakenbury,
You may partake of anything we say:
We speak no treason, man;—we say the king
Is wise and virtuous; and his noble queen
Well struck in years, fair, and not jealous;—
We say that Shore's wife hath a pretty foot,
A cherry lip, a bonny eye, a passing pleasing
　　tongue;
And the queen's kindred are made gentle-
　　folks:
How say you, sir? can you deny all this?
　　Brak. With this, my lord, myself have
　　naught to do.
　　Glo. Naught to do with Mistress Shore!
　　I tell thee, fellow,
He that doth naught with her, excepting one,
Were best to do it secretly, alone.
　　Brak. What one, my lord?　　[betray me?
　　Glo. Her husband, knave:—Wouldst thou
　　Brak. I beseech your grace to pardon me;
　　and, withal,
Forbear your conference with the noble
　　duke.
　　Clar. We know thy charge, Brakenbury,
　　and will obey.　　　　　　　　　　[obey.—
　　Glo. We are the queen's abjects, and must
Brother, farewell: I will unto the king;
And whatsoe'er you will employ me in,—
Were it to call King Edward's widow sis-
　　ter,—
I will perform it to enfranchise you.
Meantime, this deep disgrace in brotherhood
Touches me deeper than you can imagine.
　　Clar. I know it pleaseth neither of us well.
　　Glo. Well, your imprisonment shall not be
　　long;
I will deliver you, or else lie for you:
Meantime, have patience.
　　Clar.　　　　　I must perforce: farewell.
　　　　[*Exeunt* CLAR., BRAK., *and* Guard.
　　Glo. Go, tread the path that thou shalt
　　ne'er return,
Simple, plain Clarence!—I do love thee so
That I will shortly send thy soul to heaven,
If heaven will take the present at our
　　hands.—
But who comes here? the new-deliver'd
　　Hastings?

Enter HASTINGS.

　　Hast. Good time of day unto my gracious
　　lord!　　　　　　　　　　　　　[berlain!
　　Glo. As much unto my good lord cham-

Well are you welcome to this open air.
How hath your lordship brook'd imprison-
    ment?
  Hast. With patience, noble lord, as pris-
    oners must:
But I shall live, my lord, to give them
    thanks
That were the cause of my imprisonment.
  Glo. No doubt, no doubt; and so shall
    Clarence too;
For they that were your enemies are his,
And have prevail'd as much on him as you.
  Hast. More pity that the eagle should be
    mew'd
While kites and buzzards prey at liberty.
  Glo. What news abroad?
  Hast. No news so bad abroad as this at
    home,—
The king is sickly, weak, and melancholy,
And his physicians fear him mightily.
  Glo. Now, by Saint Paul, this news is bad
    indeed.
O, he hath kept an evil diet long,
And overmuch consum'd his royal person:
'Tis very grievous to be thought upon.
What, is he in his bed?
  Hast.   He is.
  Glo. Go you before, and I will follow you.
                      [*Exit* HASTINGS.
He cannot live, I hope; and must not die
Till George be pack'd with posthorse up to
    heaven.
I'll in, to urge his hatred more to Clarence,
With lies well steel'd with weighty argu-
    ments;
And, if I fail not in my deep intent,
Clarence hath not another day to live:
Which done, God take King Edward to his
    mercy,
And leave the world for me to bustle in!
For then I'll marry Warwick's youngest
    daughter: [father?
What though I kill'd her husband and her
    father?
The readiest way to make the wench amends
Is to become her husband and her father:
The which will I; not all so much for love
As for another secret close intent,
By marrying her, which I must reach unto.
But yet I run before my horse to market:
Clarence still breathes; Edward still lives and
    reigns:
When they are gone, then must I count my
    gains.
                          [*Exit.*

Scene II.—London. *Another Street.*

Enter the Corpse of KING HENRY THE SIXTH,
borne in an open coffin, Gentlemen *bearing
halberds to guard it; and* LADY ANNE *as
mourner.*

  Anne. Set down, set down your honour-
    able load,—
If honour may be shrouded in a hearse,—

Whilst I awhile obsequiously lament
The untimely fall of virtuous Lancaster.—
Poor key-cold figure of a holy king!
Pale ashes of the house of Lancaster!
Thou bloodless remnant of that royal blood!
Be it lawful that I invocate thy ghost,
To hear the lamentations of poor Anne,
Wife to thy Edward, to thy slaughter'd son,
Stabb'd by the self-same hand that made
    these wounds!
Lo, in these windows that let forth thy life,
I pour the helpless balm of my poor eyes:—
O, cursed be the hand that made these holes!
Cursed the heart that had the heart to do it!
Cursed the blood that let this blood from
    hence!
More direful hap betide that hated wretch
That makes us wretched by the death of thee,
Than I can wish to adders, spiders, toads,
Or any creeping venom'd thing that lives!
If ever he have child, abortive be it,
Prodigious, and untimely brought to light,
Whose ugly and unnatural aspèct
May fright the hopeful mother at the view;
And that be heir to his unhappiness!
If ever he have wife, let her be made
More miserable by the death of him
Than I am made by my young lord and
    thee!—
Come, now towards Chertsey with your holy
    load,
Taken from Paul's to be interred there;
And still, as you are weary of the weight,
Rest you, whiles I lament King Henry's corse.
  [*The* Bearers *take up the Corpse and ad-
    vance.*

Enter GLOSTER.

  Glo. Stay, you that bear the corse, and set
    it down.
  Anne. What black magician conjures up
    this fiend,
To stop devoted charitable deeds?
  Glo. Villains, set down the corse; or, by
    Saint Paul,
I'll make a corse of him that disobeys!
  1 *Gent.* My lord, stand back, and let the
    coffin pass.   [command:
  Glo. Unmanner'd dog! stand thou, when I
Advance thy halberd higher than my breast,
Or, by Saint Paul, I'll strike thee to my foot,
And spurn upon thee, beggar, for thy bold-
    ness.
    [*The* Bearers *set down the coffin.*
  Anne. What, do you tremble? are you all
    afraid?
Alas, I blame you not for you are mortal,
And mortal eyes cannot endure the devil.—
Avaunt, thou dreadful minister of hell!
Thou hadst but power over his mortal body,
His soul thou canst not have; therefore be
    gone.
  Glo. Sweet saint, for charity, be not so
    curst.

Anne. Foul devil, for God's sake, hence, and trouble us not;
For thou hast made the happy earth thy hell
Fill'd it with cursing cries and deep exclaims.
If thou delight to view thy heinous deeds,
Behold this pattern of thy butcheries.—
O, gentlemen, see, see! dead Henry's wounds
Open their congeal'd mouths and bleed afresh!
Blush, blush, thou lump of foul deformity;
For 'tis thy presence that exhales this blood
From cold and empty veins, where no blood dwells;
Thy deed, inhuman and unnatural,
Provokes this deluge most unnatural.—
O God, which this blood mad'st, revenge his death!
O earth, which this blood drink'st, revenge his death!   [derer dead;
Either, heaven, with lightning strike the mur-
Or, earth, gape open wide, and eat him quick,
As thou dost swallow up this good king's blood,
Which his hell-govern'd arm hath butchered!
Glo. Lady, you know no rules of charity,
Which renders good for bad, blessings for curses.   [nor man:
Anne. Villain, thou know'st no law of God
No beast so fierce but knows some touch of pity.
Glo. But I know none, and therefore am no beast.   [truth!
Anne. O wonderful, when devils tell the
Glo. More wonderful when angels are so angry.—
Vouchsafe, divine perfection of a woman,
Of these supposed evils to give me leave,
By circumstance, but to acquit myself.
Anne. Vouchsafe, diffus'd infection of a man,
For these known evils but to give me leave,
By circumstance, to curse thy cursed self.
Glo. Fairer than tongue can name thee, let me have
Some patient leisure to excuse myself.
Anne. Fouler than heart can think thee, thou canst make
No excuse current, but to hang thyself.
Glo. By such despair I should accuse my-self.
Anne. And by despairing shalt thou stand excus'd;
For doing worthy vengeance on thyself,
That didst unworthy slaughter upon others.
Glo. Say that I slew them not?
Anne. Then say they were not slain:
But dead they are, and, devilish slave, by thee.
Glo. I did not kill your husband.
Anne.   Why, then he is alive.
Glo. Nay, he is dead; and slain by Ed-ward's hand.
Anne. In thy foul throat thou liest: Queen Margaret saw

Thy murderous falchion smoking in his blood;
The which thou once didst bend against her breast,
But that thy brothers beat aside the point.
Glo. I was provoked by her slanderous tongue,
That laid their guilt upon my guiltless shoul-ders.
Anne. Thou wast provoked by thy bloody mind,
That never dreamt on aught but butcheries:
Didst thou not kill this king?
Glo.   I grant ye.
Anne. Dost grant me, hedgehog? then, God grant me too
Thou mayst be damned for that wicked deed!
O, he was gentle, mild, and virtuous.
Glo. The fitter for the King of Heaven, that hath him.   [never come.
Anne. He is in heaven, where thou shalt
Glo. Let him thank me, that holp to send him thither;
For he was fitter for that place than earth.
Anne. And thou unfit for any place but hell.
Glo. Yes, one place else, if you will hear me name it.
Anne. Some dungeon.
Glo.   Your bed-chamber.
Anne. Ill rest betide the chamber where thou liest!
Glo. So will it, madam, till I lie with you.
Anne. I hope so.
Glo. I know so.—But, gentle Lady Anne,—
To leave this keen encounter of our wits,
And fall somewhat into a slower method,—
Is not the causer of the timeless deaths
Of these Plantagenets, Henry and Edward,
As blameful as the executioner?
Anne. Thou wast the cause and most ac-curs'd effect.
Glo. Your beauty was the cause of that effect;
Your beauty, that did haunt me in my sleep
To undertake the death of all the world,
So I might live one hour in your sweet bos-om.
Anne. If I thought that, I tell thee, ho-micide,
These nails should rend that beauty from my cheeks.   [beauty's wreck.
Glo. These eyes could not endure that
You should not blemish it if I stood by:
As all the world is cheered by the sun,
So I by that; it is my day, my life.
Anne. Black night o'ershade thy day, and death thy life!   [art both.
Glo. Curse not thyself, fair creature; thou
Anne. I would I were, to be reveng'd on thee.
Glo. It is a quarrel most unnatural.
To be reveng'd on him that loveth thee.

Anne. It is a quarrel just and reasonable,
To be reveng'd on him that kill'd my husband.

Glo. He that bereft thee, lady, of thy husband,
Did it to help thee to a better husband.

Anne. His better doth not breathe upon
the earth.   [could.

Glo. He lives that loves thee better than he

Anne. Name him.

Glo.   Plantagenet.

Anne.   Why, that was he.

Glo. The self-same name, but one of better
nature.

Anne. Where is he?

Glo.   Here. [*She spits at him.*] Why
dost thou spit at me?   [thy sake!

Anne. Would it were mortal poison, for

Glo. Never came poison from so sweet a
place.

Anne. Never hung poison on a fouler toad.
Out of my sight! thou dost infect mine eyes.

Glo. Thine eyes, sweet lady, have infected
mine.

Anne. Would they were basilisks, to strike
thee dead!   [at once;

Glo. I would they were, that I might die
For now they kill me with a living death.
Those eyes of thine from mine have drawn
salt tears,   [drops:
Sham'd their aspécts with store of childish
These eyes, which never shed remorseful tear,
No, when my father York and Edward wept,
To hear the piteous moan that Rutland made
When black-fac'd Clifford shook his sword
at him;
Nor when thy warlike father, like a child,
Told the sad story of my father's death,
And twenty times made pause, to sob and
weep,
That all the standers-by had wet their
cheeks,
Like trees bedash'd with rain; in that sad
time
My manly eyes did scorn an humble tear;
And what these sorrows could not thence
exhale,
Thy beauty hath, and made them blind with
weeping.
I never su'd to friend nor enemy; [ing word;
My tongue could never learn sweet smooth-
But, now thy beauty is propos'd my fee,
My proud heart sues, and prompts my
tongue to speak.
                [*She looks scornfully at him.*
Teach not thy lip such scorn; for it was
made
For kissing, lady, not for such contempt.
If thy revengeful heart cannot forgive,
Lo, here I lend thee this sharp-pointed
sword;
Which if thou please to hide in this true
breast,
And let the soul forth that adoreth thee,

I lay it naked to the deadly stroke,
And humbly beg the death upon my knee.
Nay, do not pause; for I did kill King
Henry,—
                [*He lays his breast open; she offers
                at it with his sword.*
But 'twas thy beauty that provoked me.
Nay, now despatch; 'twas I that stabb'd
young Edward,—
                [*She again offers at his breast.*
But 'twas thy heavenly face that set me on.
                [*She lets fall the sword.*
Take up the sword again, or take up me.

Anne. Arise, dissembler: though I wish thy
death,
I will not be thy executioner.

Glo. Then bid me kill myself, and I will do
it.

Anne. I have already.

Glo.   That was in thy rage:
Speak it again, and, even with the word,
This hand, which for thy love did kill thy
love,
Shall, for thy love, kill a far truer love;
To both their deaths shalt thou be accessary.

Anne. I would I knew thy heart.

Glo. 'Tis figured in my tongue.

Anne. I fear me both are false.

Glo. Then never man was true.

Anne. Well, well, put up your sword.

Glo. Say, then, my peace is made.

Anne. That shalt thou know hereafter.

Glo. But shall I live in hope?

Anne. All men, I hope, live so.

Glo. Vouchsafe to wear this ring.

Anne. To take is not to give.
                [*She puts on the ring.*

Glo. Look, how this ring encompasseth
thy finger,
Even so thy breast encloseth my poor heart;
Wear both of them, for both of them are
thine.
And if thy poor devoted servant may
But beg one favour at thy gracious hand,
Thou dost confirm his happiness for ever.

Anne. What is it?

Glo. That it may please you leave these
sad designs
To him that hath more cause to be a
mourner,
And presently repair to Crosby Place;
Where,—after I have solemnly interr'd
At Chertsey monastery, this noble king,
And wet his grave with my repentant tears,—
I will with all expedient duty see you:
For divers unknown reasons, I beseech you,
Grant me this boon.   [joys me too

Anne. With all my heart; and much it
To see you are become so penitent.—
Tressel and Berkley, go along with me.

Glo. Bid me farewell.

Anne.   'Tis more than you deserve;
But since you teach me how to flatter you,

Imagine I have said farewell already.

[*Exeunt* LADY ANNE, TRESS., *and* BERK.

Glo. Sirs, take up the corse.

Gent.   Towards Chertsey, noble lord?

Glo. No, to White Friars; there attend my
      coming.

[*Exeunt the rest, with the Corpse.*

Was ever woman in this humour woo'd?
Was ever woman in this humour won?
I'll have her; but I will not keep her long.
What! I, that kill'd her husband and his
      father,
To take her in her heart's extremest hate;
With curses in her mouth, tears in her eyes,
The bleeding witness of her hatred by;
Having God, her conscience, and these bars
      against me,
And I no friends to back my suit withal,
But the plain devil and dissembling looks,
And yet to win her,—all the world to noth-
      ing!
Ha!
Hath she forgot already that brave prince,
Edward, her lord, whom I, some three
      months since,
Stabb'd in my angry mood at Tewksbury?
A sweeter and a lovelier gentleman,—
Fram'd in the prodigality of nature,
Young, valiant, wise, and, no doubt, right
      royal,—
The spacious world cannot again afford:
And will she yet abase her eyes on me,
That cropp'd the golden prime of this sweet
      prince,
And made her widow to a woeful bed?
On me, whose all not equals Edward's
      moiety?
On me, that halt and am misshapen thus?
My dukedom to a beggarly denier,
I do mistake my person all this while:
Upon my life, she finds, although I cannot,
Myself to be a marvellous proper man.
I'll be at charges for a looking-glass;
And entertain a score or two of tailors,
To study fashions to adorn my body:
Since I am crept in favour with myself,
I will maintain it with some little cost.
But first I'll turn yon fellow in his grave;
And then return lamenting to my love.—
Shine out, fair sun, till I have bought a glass,
That I may see my shadow as I pass. [*Exit.*

SCENE III.—LONDON. *A Room in the Palace.*

Enter QUEEN ELIZABETH, LORD RIVERS,
      and LORD GREY.

Riv. Have patience, madam: there's no
      doubt his majesty
Will soon recover his accustom'd health.

Grey. In that you brook it ill, it makes
      him worse: [comfort,
Therefore, for God's sake, entertain good
And cheer his grace with quick and merry
      words.

Q. Eliz. If he were dead, what would be-
      tide on me?

Grey. No other harm but loss of such a
      lord.

Q. Eliz. The loss of such a lord includes
      all harms.   [a goodly son,

Grey. The heavens have bless'd you with
To be your comforter when he is gone.

Q. Eliz. Ah, he is young; and his minority
Is put unto the trust of Richard Gloster,
A man that loves not me, nor none of you.

Riv. Is it concluded he shall be protector?

Q. Eliz. It is determin'd, not concluded
      yet:
But so it must be, if the king miscarry.

Enter BUCKINGHAM *and* STANLEY.

Grey. Here come the Lords of Bucking-
      ham and Stanley.   [grace!

Buck. Good time of day unto your royal

Stan. God make your majesty joyful as
      you have been!

Q. Eliz. The Countess Richmond, good
      my Lord of Stanley,
To your good prayer will scarcely say amen.
Yet, Stanley, notwithstanding she's your
      wife,
And loves not me, be you, good lord, as-
      sur'd
I hate not you for her proud arrogance.

Stan. I do beseech you, either not believe
The envious slanders of her false accusers;
Or, if she be accus'd on true report,
Bear with her weakness, which I think pro-
      ceeds
From wayward sickness, and no grounded
      malice.   [Lord of Stanley?

Q. Eliz. Saw you the king to-day, my

Stan. But now the Duke of Buckingham
      and I
Are come from visiting his majesty.

Q. Eliz. What likelihood of his amend-
      ment, lords?

Buck. Madam, good hope; his grace
      speaks cheerfully.

Q. Eliz. God grant him health! Did you
      confer with him?   [atonement

Buck. Ay, madam: he desires to make
Between the Duke of Gloster and your
      brothers,
And between them and my lord chamber-
      lain;
And sent to warn them to his royal presence.

Q. Eliz. Would all were well!—but that
      will never be:
I fear our happiness is at the height.

Enter GLOSTER, HASTINGS, *and* DORSET.

Glo. They do me wrong, and I will not
      endure it:—
Who are they that complain unto the king
That I, forsooth, am stern, and love them
      not?
By Holy Paul, they love his grace but lightly

That fill his ears with such dissentious ru-
　　mours.
Because I cannot flatter and speak fair,
Smile in men's faces, smooth, deceive, and
　　cog,
Duck with French nods and apish courtesy,
I must be held a rancourous enemy.
Cannot a plain man live, and think no harm,
But thus his simple truth must be abus'd
By silken, sly insinuating Jacks? [your grace?
　Grey. To whom in all this presence speaks
　Glo. To thee, that hast nor honesty nor
　　grace.
When have I injur'd thee? when done thee
　　wrong?—
Or thee?—or thee?—or any of your faction?
A plague upon you all! His royal grace,—
Whom God preserve better than you would
　　wish!—
Cannot be quiet scarce a breathing while,
But you must trouble him with lewd com-
　　plaints.　　　　　　　　　　[the matter.
　Q. Eliz. Brother of Gloster, you mistake
The king, on his own royal disposition,
And not provok'd by any suitor else—
Aiming, belike, at your interior hatred,
That in your outward action shows itself
Against my children, brothers, and myself—
Makes him to send; that thereby he may
　　gather
The ground of your ill-will, and so remove
　　it.
　Glo. I cannot tell: the world is grown so
　　bad,
That wrens may prey where eagles dare not
　　perch:
Since every Jack became a gentleman,
There's many a gentle person made a Jack.
　Q. Eliz. Come, come, we know your mean-
　　ing, brother Gloster;
You envy my advancement, and my
　　friends';
God grant we never may have need of you!
　Glo. Meantime, God grants that we have
　　need of you:
Our brother is imprison'd by your means,
Myself disgrac'd, and the nobility
Held in contempt; while great promotions
Are daily given to ennoble those
That scarce, some two days since, were worth
　　a noble.　　　　　　　　　[careful height
　Q. Eliz. By Him that raised me to this
From that contented hap which I enjoy'd,
I never did incense his majesty
Against the Duke of Clarence, but have been
An earnest advocate to plead for him.
My lord, you do me shameful injury,
Falsely to draw me in these vile suspects.
　Glo. You may deny that you were not the
　　mean
Of my Lord Hastings' late imprisonment.
　Riv. She may, my lord; for,—
　Glo. She may, Lord Rivers?—why, who
　　knows not so?

She may do more, sir, than denying that:
She may help you to many fair preferments;
And then deny her aiding hand therein,
And lay those honours on your high desert.
What may she not? She may, ay, marry, may
　　she,—
　Riv. What, marry, may she?　　　　[king,
　Glo. What, marry, may she! marry with a
A bachelor, a handsome stripling too:
I wis your grandam had a worser match.
　Q. Eliz. My Lord of Gloster, I have too
　　long borne
Your blunt upbraidings and your bitter
　　scoffs:
By heaven, I will acquaint his majesty
Of those gross taunts that oft I have en-
　　dur'd.
I had rather be a country servant-maid
Than a great queen, with this condition,—
To be so baited, scorn'd, and stormed at.

　　　Enter QUEEN MARGARET, *behind*.

Small joy have I in being England's queen.
　Q. Mar. And lessen'd be that small, God,
　　I beseech Him!
Thy honour, state, and seat is due to me.
　Glo. What! threat you me with telling of
　　the king?
Tell him, and spare not: look, what I have
　　said
I will avouch in presence of the king:
I dare adventure to be sent to the Tower.
'Tis time to speak,—my pains are quite for-
　　got.
　Q. Mar. Out, devil! I remember them too
　　well:
Thou kill'dst my husband Henry in the
　　Tower,
And Edward, my poor son, at Tewksbury.
　Glo. Ere you were queen, ay, or your hus-
　　band king,
I was a pack-horse in his great affairs;
A weeder-out of his proud adversaries,
A liberal rewarder of his friends:
To royalize his blood I spilt mine own.
　Q. Mar. Ay, and much better blood than
　　his or thine.　　　　　　　　　[band Grey
　Glo. In all which time you and your hus-
Were factious for the house of Lancaster;—
And, Rivers, so were you: was not your hus-
　　band
In Margaret's battle at Saint Albans slain?
Let me put in your minds, if you forget,
What you have been ere this, and what you
　　are;
Withal, what I have been, and what I am.
　Q. Mar. A murderous villain, and so still
　　thou art.　　　　　　　　　　[Warwick;
　Glo. Poor Clarence did forsake his father,
Ay, and forswore himself,—which Jesu par-
　　don!—
　Q. Mar. Which God revenge!　　[crown;
　Glo. To fight on Edward's party, for the
And for his meed, poor lord, he is mew'd up.

I would to God my heart were flint, like
　　Edward's,
Or Edward's soft and pitiful, like mine:
I am too childish-foolish for this world.
　　Q. Mar. Hie thee to hell for shame, and
　　　leave this world,
Thou cacodemon! there thy kingdom is.
　　Riv. My Lord of Gloster, in those busy
　　　days
Which here you urge to prove us enemies,
We follow'd then our lord, our sovereign
　　king:
So should we you, if you should be our king.
　　Glo. If I should be!—I had rather be a
　　　pedler:
Far be it from my heart, the thought there-
　　of!
　　Q. Eliz. As little joy, my lord, as you sup-
　　　pose
You should enjoy, were you this country's
　　king,—
As little joy you may suppose in me,
That I enjoy, being the queen thereof.
　　Q. Mar. As little joy enjoys the queen
　　　thereof;
For I am she, and altogether joyless.
I can no longer hold me patient.—
　　　　　　　　　　　　　　[*Advancing.*
Hear me, you wrangling pirates, that fall out
In sharing that which you have pill'd from
　　me!
Which of you trembles not that looks on
　　me?
If not that, I being queen, you bow like
　　subjects,　　　　　　　　[rebels?—
Yet that, by you depos'd, you quake like
Ah, gentle villain, do not turn away!
　　Glo. Foul wrinkled witch, what mak'st
　　　thou in my sight?　　　　　[marr'd,
　　Q. Mar. But repetition of what thou hast
That will I make before I let thee go.
　　Glo. Wert thou not banished on pain of
　　　death?
　　Q. Mar. I was; but I do find more pain in
　　　banishment
Than death can yield me here by my abode.
A husband and a son thou ow'st to me,—
And thou a kingdom,—all of you allegiance:
This sorrow that I have, by right is yours;
And all the pleasures you usurp are mine.
　　Glo. The curse my noble father laid on
　　　thee,
When thou didst crown his warlike brows
　　with paper,　　　　　　　　[eyes;
And with thy scorns drew'st rivers from his
And then, to dry them, gav'st thé duke a
　　clout
Steep'd in the faultless blood of pretty Rut-
　　land;—
His curses, then from bitterness of soul
Denounc'd against thee, are all fallen upon
　　thee;
And God, not we, hath plagu'd thy bloody
　　deed.

　　Q. Eliz. So just is God, to right the inno-
　　　cent.
　　Hast. O, 'twas the foulest deed to slay
　　　that babe,
And the most merciless that e'er was heard
　　of.
　　Riv. Tyrants themselves wept when it was
　　　reported.
　　Dor. No man but prophesied revenge for
　　　it.
　　Buck. Northumberland, then present,
　　　wept to see it.　　　　[fore I came,
　　Q. Mar. What, were you snarling all be-
Ready to catch each other by the throat,
And turn you all your hatred now on me?
Did York's dread curse prevail so much with
　　heaven
That Henry's death, my lovely Edward's
　　death,
Their kingdom's loss, my woeful banish-
　　ment,
Could all but answer for that peevish brat?
Can curses pierce the clouds and enter
　　heaven?—
Why, then, give way, dull clouds, to my
　　quick curses!—
Though not by war, by surfeit die your king,
As ours by murder, to make him a king!
Edward thy son, that now is Prince of
　　Wales,
For Edward my son, that was Prince of
　　Wales,
Die in his youth by like untimely violence!
Thyself a queen, for me that was a queen,
Outlive thy glory, like my wretched self!
Long mayst thou live to wail thy children's
　　loss;
And see another, as I see thee now,
Deck'd in thy rights, as thou art stall'd in
　　mine!
Long die thy happy days before thy death;
And, after many lengthen'd hours of grief,
Die neither mother, wife, nor England's
　　queen!—
Rivers and Dorset, you were standers by,—
And so wast thou, Lord Hastings,—when my
　　son　　　　　　　　　　　[pray him,
Was stabb'd with bloody daggers: God, I
That none of you may live your natural age,
But by some unlook'd accident cut off!
　　Glo. Have done thy charm, thou hateful
　　　wither'd hag.
　　Q. Mar. And leave out thee? stay, dog, for
　　　thou shalt hear me.
If heaven have any grievous plague in store,
Exceeding those that I can wish upon thee,
O, let them keep it till thy sins be ripe,
And then hurl down their indignation
On thee, the troubler of the poor world's
　　peace!
The worm of conscience still be-gnaw thy
　　soul!
Thy friends suspect for traitors while thou
　　liv'st,

And take deep traitors for thy dearest
  friends!
No sleep close up that deadly eye of thine,
Unless it be while some tormenting dream
Affrights thee with a hell of ugly devils!
Thou elvish-mark'd, abortive, rooting hog!
Thou that wast seal'd in thy nativity
The slave of nature and the son of hell!
Thou slander of thy heavy mother's womb!
Thou loathed issue of thy father's loins!
Thou rag of honour! thou detested—
  Glo. Margaret.
  Q. Mar   Richard!
  Glo.   Ha!
  Q. Mar.   I call thee not.
  Glo. I cry thee mercy, then; for I did
  think
That thou hadst call'd me all those bitter
  names.
  Q. Mar. Why, so I did; but look'd for no
  reply.
O, let me make the period to my curse!
  Glo. 'Tis done by me, and ends in—Mar-
  garet.
  Q. Eliz. Thus have you breath'd your
  curse against yourself.
  Q. Mar. Poor painted queen, vain flourish
  of my fortune!
Why strew'st thou sugar on that bottled
  spider,
Whose deadly web ensnareth thee about?
Fool, fool! thou whett'st a knife to kill thy-
  self.
The day will come that thou shalt wish for
  me
To help thee curse this poisonous bunch-
  back'd toad.
  Hast. False-boding woman, end thy fran-
  tic curse,
Lest to thy harm thou move our patience.
  Q. Mar. Foul shame upon you! you have
  all mov'd mine.
  Riv. Were you well serv'd, you would be
  taught your duty.   [do me duty,
  Q. Mar. To serve me well, you all should
Teach me to be your queen, and you my
  subjects:
O, serve me well, and teach yourselves that
  duty!
  Dor. Dispute not with her,—she is lunatic.
  Q. Mar. Peace, master marquis, you are
  malapert:
Your fire-new stamp of honour is scarce cur-
  rent:
O, that your young nobility could judge
What 'twere to lose it, and be miserable!
They that stand high have many blasts to
  shake them;
And if they fall they dash themselves to
  pieces.
  Glo. Good counsel, marry:—learn it, learn
  it, marquis.
  Dor. It touches you, my lord, as much as
  me.

  Glo. Ay, and much more: but I was born
  so high
Our aery buildeth in the cedar's top,
And dallies with the wind, and scorns the
  sun.
  Q. Mar. And turns the sun to shade;—
  alas! alas!—
Witness my son, now in the shade of death;
Whose bright out-shining beams thy cloudy
  wrath
Hath in eternal darkness folded up.
Your aery buildeth in our aery's nest:—
O God, that see'st it, do not suffer it;
As it was won with blood, lost be it so!
  Buck. Peace, peace, for shame, if not for
  charity.   [to me:
  Q. Mar. Urge neither charity nor shame
Uncharitably with me have you dealt,
And shamefully. my hopes by you are
  butcher'd.
My charity is outrage, life my shame,—
And in my shame still live my sorrow's rage!
  Buck. Have done, have done.   [thy hand,
  Q. Mar. O princely Buckingham, I'll kiss
In sign of league and amity with thee:
Now fair befall thee and thy noble house!
Thy garments are not spotted with our
  blood,
Nor thou within the compass of my curse.
  Buck. Nor no one here; for curses never
  pass
The lips of those that breathe them in the
  air.
  Q. Mar. I will not think but they ascend
  the sky,
And there awake God's gentle sleeping
  peace.
O Buckingham, take heed of yonder dog!
Look, when he fawns he bites; and when he
  bites,
His venom tooth will rankle to the death:
Have not to do with him, beware of him;
Sin, death, and hell have set their marks on
  him,
And all their ministers attend on him.
  Glo. What doth she say, my Lord of
  Buckingham?   [lord.
  Buck. Nothing that I respect, my gracious
  Q. Mar. What, dost thou scorn me for my
  gentle counsel?
And soothe the devil that I warn thee from?
O, but remember this another day,
When he shall split thy very heart with sor-
  row,
And say, poor Margaret was a prophetess!—
Live each of you the subjects to his hate,
And he to yours, and all of you to God's!
                                  [*Exit.*
  Hast. My hair doth stand on end to hear
  her curses.   [at liberty.
  Riv. And so doth mine: I muse why she's
  Glo. I cannot blame her: by God's holy
  mother,
She hath had too much wrong; and I repent

My part thereof that I have done to her.

Q. Eliz. I never did her any, to my knowledge.   [wrong.

Glo. Yet you have all the vantage of her
I was too hot to do somebody good,
That is too cold in thinking of it now.
Marry, as for Clarence, he is well repaid;
He is frank'd up to fatting for his pains;
God pardon them that are the cause thereof!

Riv. A virtuous and a Christian-like conclusion,
To pray for them that have done scathe to us.

Glo. So do I ever, being well advis'd;
For had I curs'd now, I had curs'd myself.   [*Aside.*

Enter CATESBY.

Cates. Madam, his majesty doth call for you,—
And for your grace,—and you, my noble lords.

Q. Eliz. Catesby, I come.—Lords, will you go with me?

Riv. We wait upon your grace.
                              [*Exeunt all but* GLOSTER.

Glo. I do the wrong, and first begin to brawl.
The secret mischiefs that I set abroach
I lay unto the grievous charge of others.
Clarence,—whom I, indeed, have cast in darkness,—
I do beweep to many simple gulls;
Namely, to Stanley, Hastings, Buckingham;
And tell them 'tis the queen and her allies
That stir the king against the duke my brother.
Now, they believe it; and withal whet me
To be revenged on Rivers, Vaughan, Grey:
But then I sigh; and, with a piece of Scripture,
Tell them that God bids us do good for evil:
And thus I clothe my naked villany
With odd old ends stol'n forth of holy writ;
And seem a saint when most I play the devil.—
But, soft! here come my executioners.

Enter two Murderers.

How now, my hardy, stout-resolved mates!
Are you now going to despatch this thing?

1 Murd. We are, my lord, and come to have the warrant,
That we may be admitted where he is.

Glo. Well thought upon;—I have it here about me: [*Gives the warrant.*
When you have done, repair to Crosby Place.
But, sirs, be sudden in the execution,
Withal obdurate, do not hear him plead;
For Clarence is well-spoken, and perhaps
May move your hearts to pity, if you mark him.

1 Murd. Tut, tut, my lord, we will not stand to prate;

Talkers are no good doers: be assur'd
We go to use our hands, and not our tongues.

Glo. Your eyes drop millstones when fools' eyes fall tears:
I like you, lads;—about your business straight;
Go, go, despatch.

1 Murd.   We will, my noble lord.
                              [*Exeunt.*

SCENE IV.—LONDON. *A Room in the Tower.*

Enter CLARENCE *and* BRAKENBURY.

Brak. Why looks your grace so heavily to-day?

Clar. O, I have pass'd a miserable night,
So full of fearful dreams, of ugly sights,
That, as I am a Christian faithful man,
I would not spend another such a night
Though 'twere to buy a world of happy days.—
So full of dismal terror was the time!

Brak. What was your dream, my lord? I
        pray you, tell me.   [the Tower,

Clar. Methought that I had broken from
And was embark'd to cross to Burgundy;
And, in my company, my brother Gloster;
Who from my cabin tempted me to walk
Upon the hatches: thence we look'd toward England,
And cited up a thousand heavy times,
During the wars of York and Lancaster,
That had befall'n us. As we pac'd along
Upon the giddy footing of the hatches,
Methought that Gloster stumbled; and, in falling,   [board
Struck me, that thought to stay him, over-
Into the tumbling billows of the main.
O Lord! methought what pain it was to drown!
What dreadful noise of water in mine ears!
What sights of ugly death within mine eyes!
Methought I saw a thousand fearful wrecks;
A thousand men that fishes gnaw'd upon;
Wedges of gold, great anchors, heaps of pearl,
Inestimable stones, unvalu'd jewels,
All scatter'd in the bottom of the sea: [holes
Some lay in dead men's skulls; and in those
Where eyes did once inhabit there were crept,
As 'twere in scorn of eyes,—reflecting gems,
That woo'd the slimy bottom of the deep,
And mock'd the dead bones that lay scatter'd by.

Brak. Had you such leisure in the time of death
To gaze upon the secrets of the deep? [strive

Clar. Methought I had; and often did I
To yield the ghost: but still the envious flood
Stopp'd in my soul, and would not let it forth
To find the empty, vast, and wandering air;
But smother'd it within my panting bulk,
Which almost burst to belch it in the sea.

Brak. Awak'd you not with this sore
 agony?
 Clar. No, no, my dream was lengthen'd
 after life;
O, then began the tempest to my soul!
I pass'd, methought, the melancholy flood
With that grim ferryman which poets write
 of,
Unto the kingdom of perpetual night.
The first that there did greet my stranger
 soul
Was my great father-in-law, renowned War-
 wick;
Who cried aloud, *What scourge for perjury*
Can this dark monarchy afford false Clar-
 ence?
And so he vanish'd: then came wandering by
A shadow like an Angel, with bright hair
Dabbled in blood; and he shriek'd out aloud,
Clarence is come,—false, fleeting, perjur'd
 Clarence,—
That stabb'd me in the field by Tewks-
 bury;—
Seize on him, Furies, take him to your tor-
 ments!
With that, methought, a legion of foul fiends
Environ'd me, and howled in mine ears
Such hideous cries that, with the very noise,
I trembling wak'd, and for a season after
Could not believe but that I was in hell,—
Such terrible impression made my dream.
 Brak. No marvel, lord, though it affright-
 ed you;
I am afraid, methinks, to hear you tell it.
 Clar. O Brakenbury, I have done those
 things
That now give evidence against my soul,
For Edward's sake; and see how he requites
 me!— [thee,
O God! If my deep prayers cannot appease
But thou wilt be aveng'd on my misdeeds,
Yet execute thy wrath in me alone,—
O, spare my guiltless wife and my poor chil-
 dren!—
Keeper, I pr'ythee, sit by me awhile;
My soul is heavy, and I fain would sleep.
 Brak. I will, my lord; God give your grace
 good rest!—
 [CLARENCE *reposes himself on a chair.*
Sorrow breaks seasons and reposing hours,
Makes the night morning, and the noontide
 night.
Princes have but their titles for their glories,
An outward honour for an inward toil;
And, for, unfelt imaginations,
They often feel a world of restless cares:
So that, between their titles and low name,
There's nothing differs but the outward
 fame.

 Enter the two Murderers.

1 *Murd.* Ho! who's here?
 Brak. What wouldst thou, fellow? and
 how cam'st thou thither?

1 *Murd.* I would speak with Clarence, and
I came hither on my legs.
 Brak. What, so brief?
 2 *Murd.* 'Tis better, sir, than to be te-
 dious.—
Let him see our commission: talk no more.
 [*A paper is delivered to* BRAK., *who reads
 it.*
 Brak. I am, in this, commanded to deliver
The noble Duke of Clarence to your
 hands:—
I will not reason what is meant hereby,
Because I will be guiltless of the meaning.
There lies the duke asleep,—and there the
 keys;
I'll to the king, and signify to him
That thus I have resign'd to you my
 charge.
 1 *Murd.* You may, sir; 'tis a point of
wisdom: fare you well.
 [*Exit* BRAKENBURY.
 2 *Murd.* What, shall we stab him as he
sleeps?
 1 *Murd.* No; he'll say 'twas done cowardly, when he wakes.
 2 *Murd.* When he wakes! why, fool, he
shall never wake until the great judgment-
day.
 1 *Murd.* Why, then he'll say we stabb'd
him sleeping.
 2 *Murd.* The urging of that word judgment hath bred a kind of remorse in me.
 1 *Murd.* What, art thou afraid?
 2 *Murd.* Not to kill him, having a warrant for it; but to be damned for killing
him, from the which no warrant can defend
me.
 1 *Murd.* I thought thou hadst been resolute.
 2 *Murd.* So I am, to let him live.
 1 *Murd.* I'll back to the Duke of Gloster,
and tell him so.
 2 *Murd.* Nay, I pr'ythee, stay a little: I
hope my holy humour will change; it was
wont to hold me but while one tells twenty.
 1 *Murd.* How dost thou feel thyself now?
 2 *Murd.* Faith, some certain·dregs of conscience are yet within me.
 1 *Murd.* Remember our reward, when the
deed's done.
 2 *Murd.* Zounds, he dies: I had forgot the
reward.
 1 *Murd.* Where's thy conscience now?
 2 *Murd.* In the Duke of Gloster's purse.
 1 *Murd.* So, when he opens his purse to
give us our reward, thy conscience flies
out.
 2 *Murd.* 'Tis no matter; let it go; there's
few or none will entertain it.
 1 *Murd.* What if it come to thee again?
 2 *Murd.* I'll not meddle with it,—it makes
a man a coward; a man cannot steal, but
it accuseth him; a man cannot swear, but it

checks him; a man cannot lie with his neighbour's wife, but it detects him: 'tis a blushing shame-faced spirit that mutinies in a man's bosom, it fills one full of obstacles: it made me once restore a purse of gold that by chance I found; it beggars any man that keeps it: it is turned out of all towns and cities for a dangerous thing; and every man that means to live well endeavours to trust to himself and live without it.

1 Murd. Zounds, it is even now at my elbow, persuading me not to kill the duke.

2 Murd. Take the devil in thy mind, and believe him not: he would insinuate with thee but to make thee sigh.

1 Murd. I am strong-framed, he cannot prevail with me.

2 Murd. Spoke like a tall fellow that respects his reputation. Come, shall we fall to work?

1 Murd. Take him on the costard with the hilts of thy sword, and then throw him into the malmsey-butt in the next room.

2 Murd. O excellent device! and make a sop of him.

1 Murd. Soft! he wakes.

2 Murd. Strike!

1 Murd. No, we'll reason with him.

Clar. Where art thou, keeper? give me a cup of wine.

1 Murd. You shall have wine enough, my lord, anon.

Clar. In God's name, what art thou?

1 Murd. A man, as you are.

Clar. But not, as I am, royal.

1 Murd. Nor you, as we are, loyal.

Clar. Thy voice is thunder, but thy looks are humble.

1 Murd. My voice is now the king's, my looks mine own.

Clar. How darkly and how deadly dost thou speak!
Your eyes do menace me: why look you pale?
Who sent you hither? Wherefore do you come?

Both Murd. To, to, to—

Clar. To murder me?

Both Murd. Ay, ay.

Clar. You scarcely have the hearts to tell me so,
And therefore cannot have the hearts to do it.
Wherein, my friends, have I offended you?

1 Murd. Offended us you have not, but the king.

Clar. I shall be reconcil'd to him again.

2 Murd. Never, my lord; therefore prepare to die.

Clar. Are you drawn forth among a world of men
To slay the innocent? What is my offence?
What is the evidence that doth accuse me?

Where lawful quest have given their verdict up
Unto the frowning judge? or who pronounc'd
The bitter sentence of poor Clarence's death?
Before I be convict by course of law,
To threaten me with death is most unlawful.
I charge you, as you hope to have redemption
By Christ's dear blood shed for our grievous sins,
That you depart, and lay no hands on me:
The deed you undertake is damnable.

1 Murd. What we will do, we do upon command.

2 Murd. And he that hath commanded is our king.   [kings

Clar. Erroneous vassals! the great King of
Hath in the table of his law commanded
That thou shalt do no murder: will you then
Spurn at his edict, and fulfil a man's?
Take heed; for he holds vengeance in his hand,
To hurl upon their heads that break his law.

2 Murd. And that same vengeance doth he hurl on thee
For false forswearing, and for murder too:
Thou didst receive the sacrament to fight
In quarrel of the house of Lancaster.

1 Murd. And, like a traitor to the name of God,
Didst break that vow; and with thy treacherous blade
Unripp'dst the bowels of thy sovereign's son.

2 Murd. Whom thou wast sworn to cherish and defend.

1 Murd. How canst thou urge God's dreadful law to us,
When thou hast broke it in such dear degree?

Clar. Alas! for whose sake did I that ill deed?
For Edward, for my brother, for his sake:
He sends you not to murder me for this;
For in that sin he is as deep as I.
If God will be avenged for the deed,
O, know you yet, he doth it publicly:
Take not the quarrel from his powerful arm;
He needs no indirect nor lawless course
To cut off those that have offended him.

1 Murd. Who made thee, then, a bloody minister
When gallant-springing brave Plantagenet,
That princely novice, was struck dead by thee?

Clar. My brother's love, the devil, and my rage.   [thy faults,

1 Murd. Thy brother's love, our duty, and
Provoke us hither now to slaughter thee.

Clar. If you do love my brother, hate not me;
I am his brother, and I love him well.
If you are hir'd for meed, go back again,
And I will send you to my brother Gloster,

Who shall reward you better for my life
Than Edward will for tidings of my death.

   2 *Murd.* You are deceiv'd, your brother
    Gloster hates you.   [me dear:
   Clar. O, no, he loves me, and he holds
Go you to him from me.

   Both Murd.   Ay, so we will.

   Clar. Tell him, when that our princely
    father York
Bless'd his three sons with his victorious arm,
And charg'd us from his soul to love each
    other,
He little thought of this divided friendship:
Bid Gloster think on this, and he will weep.

   1 *Murd.* Ay, millstones; as he lesson'd us
    to weep.

   Clar. O, do not slander him, for he is kind.

   1 *Murd.* Right as snow in harvest.—Come,
    you deceive yourself:
'Tis he that sends us to destroy you here.

   Clar. It cannot be; for he bewept my for-
    tune,
And hugg'd me in his arms, and swore, with
    sobs,
That he would labour my delivery.

   1 *Murd.* Why, so he doth, when he deliv-
    ers you
From this earth's thraldom to the joys of
    heaven.

   2 *Murd.* Make peace with God, for you
    must die, my lord.

   Clar. Have you that holy feeling in your
    souls,
To counsel me to make my peace with God,
And are you yet to your own souls so blind
That you will war with God by murdering
    me?—
O, sirs, consider, they that set you on
To do this deed will hate you for the deed.

   2 *Murd.* What shall we do?

   Clar.   Relent, and save your souls.

   1 *Murd.* Relent! 'tis cowardly and wom-
    anish.   [ilish.

   Clar. Not to relent is beastly, savage, dev-
Which of you, if you were a prince's son,
Being pent from liberty, as I am now,—
If two such murderers as yourself came to
    you,—
Would not entreat for life?—
My friend, I spy some pity in thy looks;
O, if thine eye be not a flatterer,
Come thou on my side, and entreat for me,
As you would beg, were you in my distress:
A begging prince what beggar pities not?

   2 *Murd.* Look behind you, my lord.

   1 *Murd.* Take that, and that: if all this
    will not do,   [*Stabs him.*
I'll drown you in the malmsey-butt within.
         [*Exit with the body.*

   2 *Murd.* A bloody deed, and desperately
    despatch'd!
How fain, like Pilate, would I wash my
    hands
Of this most grievous guilty murder done!

Re-enter First Murderer.

   1 *Murd.* How now, what mean'st thou,
    that thou help'st me not?
By heaven, the duke shall know how slack
    you have been.   [his brother!

   2 *Murd.* I would he knew that I had sav'd
Take thou the fee, and tell him what I say;
For I repent me that the duke is slain. [*Exit.*

   1 *Murd.* So do not I: go, coward as thou
    art.—
Well, I'll go hide the body in some hole,
Till that the duke give order for his burial:
And when I have my meed, I will away;
For this will out, and then I must not stay.
          [*Exit.*

ACT II.

SCENE I.—LONDON. *A Room in the Palace.*

Enter KING EDWARD, *led in sick;* QUEEN
ELIZABETH, DORSET, RIVERS, HASTINGS,
BUCKINGHAM, GREY, *and others.*

   K. Edw. Why, so;—now have I done a
    good day's work:—
You peers, continue this united league:
I every day expect an embassage
From my Redeemer, to redeem me hence;
And now in peace my soul shall part to
    heaven,
Since I have made my friends at peace on
    earth.
Rivers and Hastings, take each other's hand;
Dissemble not your hatred, swear your love.

   Riv. By heaven, my soul is purg'd from
    grudging hate;
And with my hand I seal my true heart's
    love.

   Hast. So thrive I, as I truly swear the
    like!

   K. Edw. Take heed you dally not before
    your king;
Lest he that is the supreme King of kings
Confound your hidden falsehood, and award
Either of you to be the other's end.

   Hast. So prosper I, as I swear perfect
    love!

   Riv. And I, as I love Hastings with my
    heart!

   K. Edw. Madam, yourself are not exempt
    from this,—
Nor you, son Dorset,—Buckingham, nor
    you;—
You have been factious one against the other.
Wife, love Lord Hastings, let him kiss your
    hand;
And what you do, do it unfeignedly.

   Q. Eliz. There, Hastings; I will never more
    remember
Our former hatred, so thrive I and mine!

   K. Edw. Dorset, embrace him;—Hastings,
    love lord marquis.   [test,

   Dor. This interchange of love I here pro-
Upon my part shall be inviolable.

Hast. And so swear I. [*Embraces* DORSET.

K. Edw. Now, princely Buckingham, seal
  thou this league
With thy embracements to my wife's allies,
And make me happy in your unity.

Buck. Whenever Buckingham doth turn
  his hate
Upon your grace [*to the* QUEEN], but with
  all duteous love
Doth cherish you and yours, God punish me
With hate in those where I expect most love!
When I have most need to employ a friend,
And most assured that he is a friend,
Deep, hollow, treacherous, and full of guile,
Be he unto me!—this do I beg of heaven
When I am cold in love to you or yours.
                [*Embracing* RIVERS, &c.

K. Edw. A pleasing cordial, princely
  Buckingham,
Is this thy vow unto my sickly heart.
There wanteth now our brother Gloster here,
To make the blessed period of this peace.

Buck. And, in good time, here comes the
  noble duke.

Enter GLOSTER.

Glo. Good-morrow to my sovereign king
  and queen;
And, princely peers, a happy time of day!

K. Edw. Happy, indeed, as we have spent
  the day.
Gloster, we have done deeds of charity;
Made peace of enmity, fair love of hate,
Between these swelling wrong-incensed peers.

Glo. A blessed labour, my most sovereign
  lord.—
Among this princely heap, if any here,
By false intelligence or wrong surmise,
Hold me a foe;
If I unwittingly, or in my rage,
Have aught committed that is hardly borne
By any in this presence, I desire
To reconcile me to his friendly peace:
'Tis death to me to be at enmity;
I hate it, and desire all good men's love.—
First, madam, I entreat true peace of you,
Which I will purchase with my duteous serv-
  ice;—
Of you, my noble cousin Buckingham,
If ever any grudge were lodg'd between us;—
Of you, and you, Lord Rivers, and of Dor-
  set,
That all without desert have frown'd on me;
Of you, Lord Woodville, and, Lord Scales, of
  you;—
Dukes, earls, lords, gentlemen;—indeed, of
  all.
I do not know that Englishman alive
With whom my soul is any jot at odds
More than the infant that is born to-night;
I thank my God for my humility.   [after:—

Q. Eliz. A holiday shall this be kept here-
I would to God all strifes were well compounded.—

My sovereign lord, I do beseech your highness
To take our brother Clarence to your grace.

Glo. Why, madam, have I offer'd love for
  this,
To be so flouted in this royal presence?
Who knows not that the gentle duke is dead?
                [*They all start.*
You do him injury to scorn his corse.

K. Edw. Who knows not he is dead! who
  knows he is?   [this!

Q. Eliz. All-seeing heaven, what a world is

Buck. Look I so pale, Lord Dorset, as the
  rest?   [the presence

Dor. Ay, my good lord; and no man in
But his red colour hath forsook his cheeks.

K. Edw. Is Clarence dead? the order was
  revers'd.   [died,

Glo. But he, poor man, by your first order
And that a winged mercury did bear;
Some tardy cripple bore the countermand
That came too lag to see him buried.
God grant that some, less noble and less
  royal,
Nearer in bloody thoughts, but not in blood,
Deserve not worse than wretched Clarence
  did,
And yet go current from suspicion!

Enter STANLEY.

Stan. A boon, my sovereign, for my service done!   [of sorrow.

K. Edw. I pr'ythee, peace: my soul is full

Stan. I will not rise unless your highness
  hear me.

K. Edw. Then say at once what is it thou
  request'st.

Stan. The forfeit, sovereign, of my serv-
  ant's life;
Who slew to-day a riotous gentleman
Lately attendant on the Duke of Norfolk.

K. Edw. Have I a tongue to doom my
  brother's death,
And shall that tongue give pardon to a
  slave?
My brother kill'd no man,—his fault was
  thought,
And yet his punishment was bitter death.
Who su'd to me for him? who, in my wrath,
Kneel'd at my feet, and bid me be advis'd?
Who spoke of brotherhood? who spoke of
  love?
Who told me how the poor soul did forsake
The mighty Warwick, and did fight for me?
Who told me, in the field at Tewksbury,
When Oxford had me down, he rescu'd me,
And said, *Dear brother, live, and be a king?*
Who told me, when we both lay in the field
Frozen almost to death, how he did lap me
Even in his garments, and did give himself,
All thin and naked, to the numb-cold night?
All this from my remembrance brutish wrath
Sinfully pluck'd, and not a man of you
Had so much grace to put it in my mind.

But when your carters or your waiting-vas-
    sals
Have done a drunken slaughter, and defac'd
The precious image of our dear Redeemer,
You straight are on your knees for pardon,
    pardon;
And I, unjustly too, must grant it you:—
But for my brother not a man would speak,—
Nor I, ungracious, speak unto myself
For him, poor soul. The proudest of you all
Have been beholden to him in his life;
Yet none of you would once beg for his
    life.—
O God, I fear thy justice will take hold
On me, and you, and mine, and yours, for
    this!
Come, Hastings, help me to my closet.
Ah, poor Clarence!
        [*Exeunt* KING, QUEEN, HAST., RIV.,
            DOR., *and* GREY.
  Glo. This is the fruit of rashness!—Mark'd
    you not
How that the guilty kindred of the queen
Look'd pale when they did hear of Clarence'
    death?
O, they did urge it still unto the king!
God will revenge it.—Come, lords, will you
    go
To comfort Edward with our company?
  Buck. We wait upon your grace. [*Exeunt.*

SCENE II.—*Another Room in the Palace.*

Enter the DUCHESS OF YORK, *with a Son and*
    Daughter *of* CLARENCE.

  Son. Good grandam, tell us, is our father
    dead?
  Duch. No, boy.   [your breast,
  Daugh. Why do you weep so oft, and beat
And cry, *O Clarence, my unhappy son!*
  Son. Why do you look on us, and shake
    your head,
And call us orphans, wretches, castaways,
If that our noble father be alive?   [both;
  Duch. My pretty cousins, you mistake me
I do lament the sickness of the king,
As loth to lose him, not your father's death;
It were lost sorrow to wail one that's lost.
  Son. Then you conclude, my grandam, he
    is dead.
The king mine uncle is to blame for this:
God will revenge it; whom I will importune
With earnest prayers all to that effect.
  Daugh. And so will I.
  Duch. Peace, children, peace! the king
    doth love you well:
Incapable and shallow innocents,   [death.
You cannot guess who caus'd your father's
  Son. Grandam, we can; for my good
    uncle Gloster
Told me, the king, provok'd to it by the
    queen,
Devis'd impeachments to imprison him:
And when my uncle told me so, he wept,
And pitied me. and kindly kiss'd my cheek;

Bade me rely on him as on my father,
And he would love me dearly as his child.
  Duch. Ah, that deceit should steal such
    gentle shape,
And with a virtuous visard hide deep vice!
He is my son; ay, and therein my shame;
Yet from my dugs he drew not this deceit.
  Son. Think you my uncle did dissemble,
    grandam?
  Duch. Ay, boy.   [is this?
  Son. I cannot think it.—Hark! what noise

  Enter QUEEN ELIZABETH, *distractedly;*
    RIVERS *and* DORSET *following her.*

  Q. Eliz. Ah, who shall hinder me to wail
    and weep,
To chide my fortune, and torment myself?
I'll join with black despair against my soul,
And to myself become an enemy. [patience?
  Duch. What means this scene of rude im-
  Q. Eliz. To make an act of tragic violence:
Edward, my lord, thy son, our king, is
    dead.—
Why grow the branches when the root is
    gone?
Why wither not the leaves. that want their
    sap?—
If you will live, lament; if die, be brief,
That our swift-winged souls may catch the
    king's;
Or, like obedient subjects, follow him
To his new kingdom of perpetual rest.
  Duch. Ah, so much interest have I in thy
    sorrow
As I had title in thy noble husband!
I have bewept a worthy husband's death,
And liv'd by looking on his images:
But now two mirrors of his princely sem-
    blance
Are crack'd in pieces by malignant death,
And I for comfort have but one false glass,
That grieves me when I see my shame in him.
Thou art a widow; yet thou art a mother,
And hast the comfort of thy children left:
But death hath snatch'd my husband from
    mine arms,   [hands,—
And pluck'd two crutches from my feeble
Clarence and Edward. O, what cause have
    I,—
Thine being but a moiety of my moan,—
To overgo thy woes and drown thy cries?
  Son. Ah, aunt, you wept not for our fath-
    er's death!
How can we aid you with our kindred tears?
  Daugh. Our fatherless distress was left
    unmoan'd,
Your widow-dolour likewise be unwept!
  Q. Eliz. Give me no help in lamentation;
I am not barren to bring forth complaints:
All springs reduce their currents to mine
    eyes,
That I, being govern'd by the watery moon,
May send forth plenteous tears to drown the
    world!

Ah for my husband, for my dear Lord Edward!

Chil. Ah for our father, for our dear Lord
Clarence!   [and Clarence!

Duch. Alas for both, both mine, Edward

Q. Eliz. What stay had I but Edward?
and he's gone.   [and he's gone.

Chil. What stay had we but Clarence?

Duch. What stays had I but they? and
they are gone.   [loss!

Q. Eliz. Was never widow had so dear a

Chil. Were never orphans had so dear a
loss!

Duch. Was never mother had so dear a
loss!

Alas, I am the mother of these griefs!
Their woes are parcell'd, mine are general.
She for an Edward weeps, and so do I;
I for a Clarence weep, so doth not she:
These babes for Clarence weep, and so do I;
I for an Edward weep, so do not they:—
Alas, you three, on me, threefold distress'd,
Pour all your tears! I am your sorrow's
nurse,
And I will pamper it with lamentation.

Dor. Comfort, dear mother: God is much
displeas'd
That you take with unthankfulness his do-
ing:
In common worldly things 'tis call'd ungrate-
ful,
With dull unwillingness to repay a debt
Which with a bounteous hand was kindly
lent;
Much more to be thus opposite with heaven,
For it requires the royal debt it lent you.

Riv. Madam, bethink you, like a careful
mother,   [for him;
Of the young prince your son: send straight
Let him be crown'd; in him your comfort
lives:
Drown desperate sorrow in dead Edward's
grave,
And plant your joys in living Edward's
throne.

Enter GLOSTER, BUCKINGHAM, STANLEY,
HASTINGS, RATCLIFFE, *and others.*

Glo. Sister, have comfort: all of us have
cause
To wail the dimming of our shining star;
But none can cure their harms by wailing
them.—
Madam, my mother, I do cry your mercy;
I did not see your grace:—humbly on my
knee
I crave your blessing.   [in thy breast,

Duch. God bless thee; and put meekness
Love, charity, obedience, and true duty!

Glo. Amen; and make me die a good old
man!—
That is the butt end of a mother's blessing;
I marvel that her grace did leave it out.
                              [*Aside.*

Buck. You cloudy princes and heart-sor-
rowing peers,
That bear this heavy mutual load of moan,
Now cheer each other in each other's love:
Though we have spent our harvest of this
king,
We are to reap the harvest of his son.
The broken rancour of your high-swoln
hearts,
But lately splinter'd, knit, and join'd to-
gether,
Must gently be preserv'd, cherish'd, and
kept:
Me seemeth good that, with some little train.
Forthwith from Ludlow the young prince be
fet
Hither to London, to be crown'd our king.

Riv. Why with some little train, my Lord
of Buckingham?

Buck. Marry, my lord, lest, by a multi-
tude,
The new-heal'd wound of malice should
break out;
Which would be so much the more danger-
ous
By how much the estate is green and yet un-
govern'd:
Where every horse bears his commanding
rein,
And may direct his course as please himself,
As well the fear of harm as harm apparent,
In my opinion, ought to be prevented.

Glo. I hope the king made peace with all
of us;
And the compact is firm and true in me.

Riv. And so in me; and so, I think, in all:
Yet, since it is but green, it should be put
To no apparent likelihood of breach,
Which haply by much company might be
urg'd:
Therefore I say with noble Buckingham,
That it is meet so few should fetch the
prince.

Hast. And so say I.

Glo. Then be it so; and go we to deter-
mine
Who they shall be that straight shall post to
Ludlow.
Madam,—and you, my mother,—will you go
To give your censures in this business?
              [*Exeunt all but* BUCK. *and* GLO.

Buck. My lord, whoever journeys to the
prince,
For God's sake, let not us two stay at home;
For by the way I'll sort occasion,
As index to the story we late talk'd of,
To part the queen's proud kindred from the
prince.

Glo. My other self, my counsel's consis-
tory,
My oracle, my prophet!—my dear cousin,
I, as a child, will go by thy direction.
Toward Ludlow then, for we'll not stay be-
hind.   [*Exeunt.*

SCENE III.—LONDON. *A Street.*

Enter two Citizens, *meeting.*

1 *Cit.* Good-morrow, neighbour: whither
away so fast?

2 *Cit.* I promise you, I scarcely know myself:
Hear you the news abroad?

1 *Cit.*   Yes,—that the king is dead.

2 *Cit.* Ill news, by'r lady: seldom comes
the better:
I fear, I fear 'twill prove a giddy world.

Enter a third Citizen.

3 *Cit.* Neighbours, God speed!

1 *Cit.*   Give you good-morrow, sir.

3 *Cit.* Doth the news hold of good King
Edward's death?   [while!

2 *Cit.* Ay, sir, it is too true; God help the

3 *Cit.* Then, masters, look to see a troublous world.

1 *Cit.* No, no, by God's good grace, his son
shall reign.   [by a child!

3 *Cit.* Woe to that land that's govern'd

2 *Cit.* In him there is a hope of govern-
ment,
Which, in his nonage, council under him,
And, in his full and ripen'd years, himself,
No doubt, shall then, and till then, govern
well.

1 *Cit.* So stood the state when Henry the
Sixth
Was crown'd in Paris but at nine months old.

3 *Cit.* Stood the state so? No, no, good
friends, God wot;
For then this land was famously enrich'd
With politic grave counsel; then the king
Had virtuous uncles to protect his grace.

1 *Cit.* Why, so hath this, both by his father and mother.

3 *Cit.* Better it were they all came by his
father,
Or by his father there were none at all;
For emulation now, who shall be nearest,
Will touch us all too near if God prevent
not.
O, full of danger is the Duke of Gloster!
And the queen's sons and brothers haught
and proud:
And were they to be rul'd, and not to rule,
This sickly land might solace as before.

1 *Cit.* Come, come, we fear the worst; all
will be well.

3 *Cit.* When clouds are seen, wise men put
on their cloaks;
When great leaves fall, then winter is at
hand;
When the sun sets, who doth not look for
night?
Untimely storms make men expect a dearth.
All may be well; but, if God sort it so,
'Tis more than we deserve or I expect.

2 *Cit.* Truly, the hearts of men are full of
fear:
You cannot reason almost with a man
That looks not heavily and full of dread.

3 *Cit.* Before the days of change, still is it
so:
By a divine instinct men's minds mistrust
Ensuing danger; as, by proof, we see
The water swell before a boisterous storm.
But leave it all to God.—Whither away?

2 *Cit.* Marry, we were sent for to the justices.

3 *Cit.* And so was I: I'll bear you company.   [*Exeunt.*

SCENE IV.—LONDON. *A Room in the Palace.*

Enter the ARCHBISHOP OF YORK, *the young*
DUKE OF YORK, QUEEN ELIZABETH, *and*
the DUCHESS OF YORK.

Arch. Last night, I hear, they at Northampton lay;
And at Stony-Stratford will they be to-
night:
To-morrow or next day they will be here.

Duch. I long with all my heart to see the
prince:
I hope he is much grown since last I saw him.

Q. Eliz. But I hear no; they say my son
of York
Has almost overta'en him in his growth.

York. Ay, mother; but I would not have
it so.

Duch. Why, my young cousin? it is good
to grow.   [at supper,

York. Grandam, one night, as we did sit
My Uncle Rivers talk'd how I did grow
More than my brother: *Ay*, quoth my uncle
Gloster,   [*apace:*
Small herbs have grace, great weeds do grow
And since, methinks, I would not grow so
fast,
Because sweet flowers are slow, and weeds
make haste.   [did not hold

Duch. Good faith, good faith, the saying
In him that did object the same to thee:
He was the wretched'st thing when he was
young,
So long a growing, and so leisurely,
That, if his rule were true, he should be
gracious.

Arch. And so no doubt he is, my gracious
madam.

Duch. I hope he is; but yet let mothers
doubt.

York. Now, by my troth, if I had been
remember'd,
I could have given my uncle's grace a flout,
To touch his growth nearer than he touch'd
mine.

Duch. How, my young York? I pr'ythee,
let me hear it.

York. Marry, they say my uncle grew so
fast
That he could gnaw a crust at two hours
old:
'Twas full two years ere I could get a tooth.

Grandam, this would have been a biting jest.

Duck. I pr'ythee, pretty York, who told thee this?

York Grandam, his nurse.

Duck. His nurse! why she was dead ere thou wast born.

York. If 'twere not she, I cannot tell who told me. [too shrewd.

Q. Eliz. A parlous boy:—go to, you are

Arch. Good madam, be not angry with the child.

Q. Eliz. Pitchers have ears.

Arch. Here comes a messenger.

Enter a Messenger.

What news? [to report.

Mess. Such news, my lord, as grieves me

Q. Eliz. How doth the prince?

Mess. Well, madam, and in health.

Duch. What is thy news?

Mess. Lord Rivers and Lord Grey are sent to Pomfret,

With them Sir Thomas Vaughan, prisoners.

Duch. Who hath committed them?

Mess. The mighty dukes Gloster and Buckingham.

Q. Eliz. For what offence?

Mess. The sum of all I can, I have disclos'd;

Why or for what the nobles were committed

Is all unknown to me, my gracious lady.

Q. Eliz. Ah me, I see the ruin of my house!

The tiger now hath seiz'd the gentle hind;

Insulting tyranny begins to jet

Upon the innocent and awless throne:—

Welcome, destruction, blood, and massacre!

I see, as in a map, the end of all. [days!

Duch. Accurs'd and unquiet wrangling

How many of you have mine eyes beheld?

My husband lost his life to get the crown;

And often up and down my sons were toss'd,

For me to joy and weep their gain and loss:

And being seated, and domestic broils

Clean over-blown, themselves, the conquerors,

Make war upon themselves; brother to brother,

Blood to blood, self against self:—O, preposterous

And frantic outrage, end thy damned spleen;

Or let me die, to look on death no more!

Q. Eliz. Come, come, my boy; we will to sanctuary.—

Madam, farewell.

Duch. Stay, I will go with you.

Q. Eliz. You have no cause.

Arch. My gracious lady, go. [To the QUEEN.

And thither bear your treasure and your goods.

For my part, I'll resign unto your grace

The seal I keep; and so betide to me

As well I tender you and all of yours!

Come, I'll conduct you to the sanctuary.

[Exeunt.

ACT III.

SCENE I.—LONDON. *A Street.*

The trumpets sound. Enter the PRINCE OF WALES, GLOSTER, BUCKINGHAM, CATESBY, CARDINAL BOUCHIER, *and others.*

Buck. Welcome, sweet prince, to London, to your chamber.

Glo. Welcome, dear cousin, my thought's sovereign:

The weary way hath made you melancholy.

Prince. No, uncle; but our crosses on the way

Have made it tedious, wearisome, and heavy:

I want more uncles here to welcome me.

Glo. Sweet prince, the untainted virtue of your years

Hath not yet div'd into the world's deceit:

No more can you distinguish of a man

Than of his outward show; which, God he knows,

Seldom or never jumpeth with the heart.

Those uncles which you want were dangerous;

Your grace attended to their sugar'd words,

But look'd not on the poison of their hearts:

God keep you from them, and from such false friends!

Prince. God keep me from false friends! but they were none. [to greet you.

Glo. My lord, the mayor of London comes

Enter the Lord Mayor *and his* Train.

May. God bless your grace with health and happy days!

Prince. I thank you, good my lord;—and thank you all. [Exeunt Mayor, &c.

I thought my mother and my brother York

Would long ere this have met us on the way:

Fie, what a slug is Hastings, that he comes not

To tell us whether they will come or no!

Buck. And, in good time, here comes the sweating lord.

Enter HASTINGS.

Prince. Welcome, my lord: what, will our mother come?

Hast. On what occasion, God he knows, not I,

The queen your mother and your brother York

Have taken sanctuary: the tender prince

Would fain have come with me to meet your grace,

But by his mother was perforce withheld.

Buck. Fie, what an indirect and peevish course

Is this of hers?—Lord cardinal, will your grace

Persuade the queen to send the Duke of York
Unto his princely brother presently?
If she deny, Lord Hastings, go with him,
And from her jealous arms pluck him per-
force.
    Card. My Lord of Buckingham, if my
    weak oratory
Can from his mother win the Duke of York,
Anon expect him here; but if she be obdurate
To mild entreaties, God in heaven forbid
We should infringe the holy privilege
Of blessed sanctuary! not for all this land
Would I be guilty of so great a sin.   [lord,
    Buck. You are too senseless-obstinate, my
Too ceremonious and traditional:
Weigh it but with the grossness of this age,
You break not sanctuary in seizing him.
The benefit thereof is always granted
To those whose dealings have deserv'd the
    place,
And those who have the wit to claim the
    place:
This prince hath neither claim'd it nor de-
    serv'd it;
And therefore, in mine opinion, cannot have
    it:
Then, taking him from hence that is not
    there,
You break no privilege nor charter there.
Oft have I heard of sanctuary-men;
But sanctuary-children ne'er till now.
    Card. My lord, you shall o'errule my mind
    for once.—
Come on, Lord Hastings, will you go with
    me?
    Hast. I go, my lord.
    Prince. Good lords, make all the speedy
    haste you may.
               [Exeunt CAR. *and* HAST.
Say, uncle Gloster, if our brother come,
Where shall we sojourn till our coronation?
    Glo. Where it seems best unto your royal
    self.
If I may counsel you, some day or two
Your highness shall repose you at the
    Tower:
Then where you please, and shall be thought
    most fit
For your best health and recreation.
    Prince. I do not like the Tower, of any
    place—
Did Julius Cæsar build that place, my lord?
    Glo. He did, my gracious lord, begin that
    place;
Which, since, succeeding ages have re-edi-
    fied.
    Prince. Is it upon record, or else reported
Successively from age to age, he built it?
    Buck. Upon record, my gracious lord.
    Prince. But say, my lord, it were not reg-
    ister'd,   [age,
Methinks the truth should live from age to
As 'twere retail'd to all posterity,
Even to the general all-ending day.

    Glo. So wise so young, they say, do **never**
    live long.   *[Aside.*
    Prince. What say you, uncle?   [long.—
    Glo. I say, without characters, fame **lives**
Thus, like the formal vice, Iniquity,
I moralize two meanings in one word. *[Aside.*
    Prince. That Julius Cæsar was a famous
    man;
With what his valour did enrich his wit,
His wit set down to make his valour live:
Death makes no conquest of this conqueror;
For now he lives in fame, though not in
    life.—
I'll tell you what, my cousin Buckingham,—
    Buck. What, my gracious lord?
    Prince. And if I live until I be a man,
I'll win our ancient right in France again,
Or die a soldier, as I liv'd a king.
    Glo. Short summers lightly have a for-
    ward spring.   *[Aside.*
    Buck. Now, in good time, here comes the
    Duke of York.

Enter YORK, HASTINGS, *and the* CARDINAL.

    Prince. Richard of York! how fares our
    loving brother?   [you now.
    York. Well, my dread lord; so must I call
    Prince. Ay brother,—to our grief, as it is
    yours:
Too late he died that might have kept that
    title,
Which by his death hath lost much majesty.
    Glo. How fares our cousin, noble Lord of
    York?   [lord,
    York. I thank you, gentle uncle. O, my
You said that idle weeds are fast in growth:
The prince my brother hath outgrown me
    far.
    Glo. He hath, my lord.
    York.   And therefore is he idle?
    Glo. O, my fair cousin, I must not say so.
    York. Then is he more beholding to you
    than I.
    Glo. He may command me as my sover-
    eign;
But you have power in me as in a kinsman.
    York. I pray you, uncle, give me this
    dagger.
    Glo. My dagger, little cousin? with all my
    heart.
    Prince. A beggar, brother?
    York. Of my kind uncle, that I know will
    give;
And being but a toy, which is no grief to give.
    Glo. A greater gift than that I'll give my
    cousin.   [to it.
    York. A greater gift! O, that's the sword
    Glo. Ay, gentle cousin, were it light
    enough.
    York. O then, I see, you will part but
    with light gifts;
In weightier things you'll say a beggar nay.
    Glo. It is too weighty for your grace to
    wear.

York. I weigh it lightly, were it heavier.
Glo. What, would you have my weapon, little lord?　　　　[you call me.
York. I would, that I might thank you as
Glo. How?
York. Little.　　　　[cross in talk:—
Prince. My Lord of York will still be
Uncle, your grace knows how to bear with him.
York. You mean, to bear me, not to bear with me:—
Uncle, my brother mocks both you and me;
Because that I am little, like an ape,
He thinks that you should bear me on your shoulders.　　　　[reasons!
Buck. With what a sharp-provided wit he
To mitigate the scorn he gives his uncle,
He prettily and aptly taunts himself:
So cunning and so young is wonderful.
Glo. My gracious lord, wil't please to pass along?
Myself and my good cousin Buckingham
Will to your mother, to entreat of her
To meet you at the Tower, and welcome you.
York. What, will you go unto the Tower, my lord?　　　　[it so.
Prince. My lord protector needs will have
York. I shall not sleep in quiet at the Tower.
Glo. Why, what should you fear? [ghost:
York. Marry, my uncle Clarence' angry
My grandam told me he was murder'd there.
Prince. I fear no uncles dead.
Glo. Nor none that live, I hope.　　[fear.
Prince. An if they live, I hope I need not
But come, my lord; and with a heavy heart,
Thinking on them, go I unto the Tower.

[*Sennet. Exeunt* PRINCE, YORK, HAST.,
　　　　CAR., *and* Attendants.

Buck. Think you, my lord, this little prating York
Was not incensed by his subtle mother
To taunt and scorn you thus opprobriously?
Glo. No doubt, no doubt: O, 'tis a parlous boy;
Bold, quick, ingenious, forward, capable:
He is all the mother's, from the top to toe.
Buck. Well, let them rest.—Come hither, Catesby.　　　　[intend
Thou art sworn as deeply to effect what we
As closely to conceal what we impart:
Thou know'st our reasons urg'd upon the way;—
What think'st thou? is it not an easy matter
To make William Lord Hastings of our mind,
For the instalment of this noble duke
In the seat royal of this famous isle? [prince
Cate. He for his father's sake so loves the
That he will not be won to aught against him.
Buck. What think'st thou then of Stanley? will not he?
Cate. He will do all in all as Hastings doth.

Buck. Well, then, no more but this: go, gentle Catesby,　　　　[ings
And, as it were far off, sound thou Lord Hast-
How he doth stand affected to our purpose;
And summon him to-morrow to the Tower,
To sit about the coronation.
If thou dost find him tractable to us.
Encourage him, and tell him all our reasons:
If he be leaden, icy, cold, unwilling,
Be thou so too; and so break off the talk,
And give us notice of his inclination:
For we to-morrow hold divided councils,
Wherein thyself shalt highly be employ'd.
Glo. Commend me to Lord William: tell him, Catesby,
His ancient knot of dangerous adversaries
To-morrow are let blood at Pomfret Castle;
And bid my lord, for joy of this good news,
Give Mistress Shore one gentle kiss the more.
Buck. Good Catesby, go, effect this business soundly.　　　　[heed I can.
Cate. My good lords both, with all the
Glo. Shall we hear from you, Catesby, ere we sleep?
Cate. You shall, my lord.
Glo. At Crosby Place, there shall you find us both.　　　　[*Exit* CATESBY.
Buck. Now, my lord, what shall we do if we perceive
Lord Hastings will not yield to our complots?
Glo. Chop off his head, man;—somewhat we will do:—
And look, when I am king, claim thou of me
The earldom of Hereford, and all the movables
Whereof the king my brother was possess'd.
Buck. I'll claim that promise at your grace's hand.　　　　[kindness.
Glo. And look to have it yielded with all
Come, let us sup betimes, that afterwards
We may digest our complots in some form.

　　　　　　　　　　　　[*Exeunt.*

SCENE II.—*Before* LORD HASTINGS' *House.*

Enter a Messenger.

Mess. My lord, my lord!—　　[*Knocking.*
Hast. [*Within.*] Who knocks?
Mess. One from the Lord Stanley.
Hast. [*Within.*] What is't o'clock?
Mess. Upon the stroke of four.

Enter HASTINGS.

Hast. Cannot my Lord Stanley sleep these tedious nights?
Mess. So it appears by that I have to say.
First, he commends him to your noble self.
Hast. What then?　　　　[night
Mess. Then certifies your lordship that this
He dreamt the boar had razed off his helm:
Besides, he says there are two councils held;
And that may be determin'd at the one

Which may make you and him to rue at the
other.　　　　　　　　　[pleasure,—
Therefore he sends to know your lordship's
If you will presently take horse with him,
And with all speed post with him toward the
north,
To shun the danger that his soul divines.

Hast. Go, fellow, go, return unto thy lord;
Bid him not fear the separated councils:
His honour and myself are at the one,
And at the other is my good friend Catesby;
Where nothing can proceed that toucheth us
Whereof I shall not have intelligence.
Tell him his fears are shallow, without in-
stance:
And for his dreams, I wonder he's so simple
To trust the mockery of unquiet slumbers:
To fly the boar before the boar pursues,
Were to incense the boar to follow us,
And make pursuit where he did mean no
chase.
Go, bid thy master rise and come to me;
And we will both together to the Tower,
Where, he shall see, the boar will use us
kindly.

Mess. I'll go, my lord, and tell him what
you say.　　　　　　　　　[*Exit.*

Enter CATESBY.

Cate. Many good-morrows to my noble
lord!

Hast. Good-morrow, Catesby; you are
early stirring:　　　　　　[state?
What news, what news, in this our tottering

Cate. It is a reeling world indeed, my lord;
And I believe will never stand upright
Till Richard wear the garland of the realm.

Hast. How! wear the garland! dost thou
mean the crown?

Cate. Ay, my good lord.

Hast. I'll have this crown of mine cut
from my shoulders
Before I'll see the crown so foul misplac'd.
But canst thou guess that he doth aim at it?

Cate. Ay, on my life; and hopes to find
you forward
Upon his party for the gain thereof:
And thereupon he sends you this good
news,—
That this same very day your enemies,
The kindred of the queen, must die at Pom-
fret.

Hast. Indeed, I am no mourner for that
news,
Because they have been still my adversaries:
But that I'll give my voice on Richard's side,
To bar my master's heirs in true descent,
God knows I will not do it to the death.

Cate. God keep your lordship in that gracious mind!

Hast. But I shall laugh at this a twelve
month hence,—　　　　　　[hate,
That they who brought me in my master's
I live to look upon their tragedy.

Well, Catesby, ere a fortnight make me older,
I'll send some packing that yet think not on't.

Cate. 'Tis a vile thing to die, my gracious
lord,
When men are unprepar'd, and look not for
it.

Hast. O monstrous, monstrous! and so falls
it out
With Rivers, Vaughan, Grey: and so 'twill do
With some men else that think themselves as
safe
As thou and I; who, as thou know'st, are dear
To princely Richard and to Buckingham.

Cate. The princes both make high account
of you,—
For they account his head upon the bridge.
　　　　　　　　　　　　[*Aside.*

Hast. I know they do; and I have well
deserv'd it.

Enter STANLEY.

Come on, come on; where is your boar-spear,
man?
Fear you the boar, and go so unprovided?

Stan. My lord, good-morrow; and good-
morrow, Catesby:—
You may jest on, but, by the holy rood,
I do not like these several councils, I.

Hast. My lord, I hold my life as dear as
you do yours;
And never in my days, I do protest,
Was it more precious to me than 'tis now:
Think you, but that I know our state secure,
I would be so triumphant as I am?

Stan. The lords at Pomfret, when they
rode from London,　　　　[sure,—
Were jocund, and suppos'd their states were
And they, indeed, had no cause to mistrust;
But yet, you see, how soon the day o'ercast!
This sudden stab of rancour I misdoubt;
Pray God, I say, I prove a needless coward!
What, shall we toward the Tower? the day
is spent.

Hast. Come, come, have with you.—Wot
you what, my lord?
To-day the lords you talk of are beheaded.

Stan. They, for their truth, might better
wear their heads　　　　　[hats,—
Than some that have accus'd them wear their
But come, my lord, let's away.

Enter a Pursuivant.

Hast. Go on before; I'll talk with this good
fellow.　　　　[*Exeunt* STAN. *and* CATE.
How now, sirrah! how goes the world with
thee?　　　　　　　　　　[to ask.

Purs. The better that your lordship please

Hast. I tell thee, man, 'tis better with me
now　　　　　　　　　　[we meet:
Than when thou mett'st me last where now
Then was I going prisoner to the Tower,
By the suggestion of the queen's allies;
But now, I tell thee,—keep it to thyself,—
This day those enemies are put to death,

And I in better state than e'er I was.

Purs. God hold it, to your honour's good
content!   [for me.

Hast. Gramercy, fellow: there, drink that
                    [*Throwing him his purse.*

Purs. I thank your honour.   [*Exit.*

Enter a Priest.

Pr. Well met, my lord; I am glad to see
your honour.

Hast. I thank thee, good Sir John, with all
my heart.
I am in your debt for your last exercise;
Come the next Sabbath, and I will content
you.

Enter BUCKINGHAM

Buck. What, talking with a priest, lord
chamberlain!
Your friends at Pomfret, they do need the
priest;
Your honour hath no shriving-work in hand.

Hast. Good faith, and when I met this holy
man,
The men you talk of came into my mind,—
What, go you toward the Tower?

Buck. I do, my lord; but long I cannot
stay there:
I shall return before your lordship thence.

Hast. Nay, like enough, for I stay dinner
there.

Buck. And supper too, although thou
know'st it not.   [*Aside.*
Come, will you go?

Hast. I'll wait upon your lordship.
                                    [*Exeunt.*

SCENE III.—POMFRET. *Before the Castle.*

Enter RATCLIFF, *with a* Guard, *conducting*
RIVERS, GREY, *and* VAUGHAN *to execution.*

Riv. Sir Richard Ratcliff, let me tell thee
this,—
To-day shalt thou behold a subject die
For truth, for duty, and for loyalty.

Grey. God bless the prince from all the
pack of you!
A knot you are of damned blood-suckers.

Vaugh. You live that shall cry woe for this
hereafter.

Rat. Despatch; the limit of your lives is
out.

Riv. O Pomfret, Pomfret! O thou bloody
prison.
Fatal and ominous to noble peers!
Within the guilty closure of thy walls
Richard the Second here was hack'd to death:
And, for more slander to thy dismal seat,
We give thee up our guiltless blood to drink.

Grey. Now Margaret's curse is fallen upon
our heads,
When she exclaim'd on Hastings, you, and I,
For standing by when Richard stabb'd her
son.

Riv. Then curs'd she Richard, then curs'd
she Buckingham,
Then curs'd she Hastings:—O, remember,
God,
To hear her prayer for them, as now for us!
And for my sister and her princely sons,
Be satisfied, dear God, with our true blood,
Which, as thou know'st, unjustly must be
spilt!

Rat. Make haste; the hour of death is expiate.

Riv. Come, Grey,—come, Vaughan,—let
us here embrace:
Farewell, until we meet again in heaven.
                                    [*Exeunt.*

SCENE IV.—LONDON. *A Room in the Tower.*

BUCKINGHAM, STANLEY, HASTINGS, *the*
BISHOP OF ELY, RATCLIFF, LOVEL, *and
others, sitting at a table:* Officers of the
Council *attending.*

Hast. Now, noble peers, the cause why we
are met
Is to determine of the coronation.
In God's name, speak,—when is the royal
day?

Buck. Are all things ready for that royal
time?

Stan. They are; and wants but nomination.

Ely. To-morrow, then, I judge a happy
day.

Buck. Who knows the lord protector's mind
herein?
Who is most inward with the noble duke?

Ely. Your grace, we think, should soonest
know his mind.

Buck. We know each other's faces: for our
hearts,
He knows no more of mine than I of yours;
Nor I of his, my lord, than you of mine.—
Lord Hastings, you and he are near in love.

Hast. I thank his grace, I know he loves
me well;
But for his purpose in the coronation
I have not sounded him, nor he deliver'd
His gracious pleasure any way therein:
But you, my noble lords, may name the time;
And in the duke's behalf I'll give my voice,
Which, I presume, he'll take in gentle part.

Ely. In happy time, here comes the duke
himself.

Enter GLOSTER.

Glo. My noble lords and cousins all, good-
morrow.
I have been long a sleeper; but I trust
My absence doth neglect no great design
Which by my presence might have been con-
cluded.

Buck. Had you not come upon your cue,
my lord,   [part,—
William Lord Hastings had pronounc'd your
I mean, your voice,—for crowning of the
king.

Glo. Than my Lord Hastings no man
　　might be bolder;　　　　　[well.—
His lordship knows me well, and loves me
My lord of Ely, when I was at last in Hol-
　　born
I saw good strawberries in your garden there:
I do beseech you send for some of them.
　　Ely. Marry, and will, my lord, with all my
　　　　heart.　　　　　　　　　　[*Exit.*
　　Glo. Cousin of Buckingham, a word with
　　　you.　　　　　　[*Takes him aside.*
Catesby hath sounded Hastings in our busi-
　　ness,
And finds the testy gentleman so hot
That he will lose his head ere give consent
His master's child, as worshipfully he terms
　　it,
Shall lose the royalty of England's throne.
　　Buck. Withdraw yourself awhile; I'll go
　　　with you.　　[*Exeunt* GLO. *and* BUCK.
　　Stan. We have not yet set down this day
　　　of triumph.
To-morrow, in my judgment, is too sudden;
For I myself am not so well provided
As else I would be, were the day prolong'd.

　　　Re-enter BISHOP OF ELY.

　　Ely. Where is my lord the Duke of Glos-
　　ter?
I have sent for these strawberries.
　　Hast. His grace looks cheerfully and
　　smooth this morning;
There's some conceit or other likes him well
When that he bids good-morrow with such
　　spirit.
I think there's ne'er a man in Christendom
Can lesser hide his love or hate than he;
For by his face straight shall you know his
　　heart.
　　Stan. What of his heart perceive you in his
　　face
By any livelihood he showed to-day?
　　Hast. Marry, that with no man here he is
　　offended;
For, were he, he had shown it in his looks.

　　　Re-enter GLOSTER *and* BUCKINGHAM.

　　Glo. I pray you all, tell me what they de-
　　serve
That do conspire my death with devilish
　　plots
Of damned witchcraft, and that have pre-
　　vail'd
Upon my body with their hellish charms?
　　Hast. The tender love I bear your grace,
　　my lord,
Makes me most forward in this princely pres-
　　ence
To doom the offenders: whosoe'er they be,
I say, my lord, they have deserved death.
　　Glo. Then be your eyes the witness of their
　　evil:
Look how I am bewitch'd; behold, mine arm
Is, like a blasted sapling, wither'd up:

And this is Edward's wife, that monstrous
　　witch,
Consorted with that harlot-strumpet Shore,
That by their witchcraft thus have marked
　　me.
　　Hast. If they have done this deed, my no-
　　　ble lord,—　　　　　　[strumpet,
　　Glo. If! thou protector of this damned
Talk'st thou to me of *ifs?*—Thou art a
　　traitor:—
Off with his head!—now, by Saint Paul I
　　swear,
I will not dine until I see the same.—
Lovel and Ratcliff:—look that it be done:—
The rest, that love me, rise and follow me.
　　　[*Exeunt all except* HAST., LOV., *and*
　　　　　　　　　RATCLIFF.
　　Hast. Woe, woe, for England! not a whit
　　for me;
For I, too fond, might have prevented this.
Stanley did dream the boar did raze his
　　helm;
And I did scorn it, and disdain to fly.
Three times to-day my foot-cloth horse did
　　stumble,
And started, when he look'd upon the Tower,
As loth to bear me to the slaughter-house.
O, now I need the priest that spake to me:
I now repent I told the pursuivant,
As too triumphing, how mine enemies
To-day at Pomfret bloodily were butcher'd,
And I myself secure in grace and favour.
O Margaret, Margaret, now thy heavy curse
Is lighted on poor Hastings' wretched head.
　　Rat. Come, come, despatch; the duke
　　would be at dinner:
Make a short shrift; he longs to see your
　　head.
　　Hast. O momentary grace of mortal men,
Which we more hunt for than the grace of
　　God!
Who builds his hope in air of your good looks,
Lives like a drunken sailor on a mast,
Ready, with every nod, to tumble down
Into the fatal bowels of the deep.
　　Lov. Come, come, despatch; 'tis bootless
　　to exclaim.　　　　　　　　[land!
　　Hast. O bloody Richard!—miserable Eng-
I prophesy the fearfull'st time to thee
That ever wretched age hath look'd upon.—
Come, lead me to the block; bear him my
　　head:
They smile at me who shortly shall be dead.
　　　　　　　　　　　　　　[*Exeunt.*

SCENE V.—LONDON. The Tower Walls.

Enter GLOSTER *and* BUCKINGHAM *in rusty
　　armour, marvellous ill-favoured.*

　　Glo. Come, cousin, canst thou quake and
　　change thy colour,
Murder thy breath in middle of a word,
And then again begin, and stop again,
As if thou wert distraught and mad with
　　terror?

Buck. Tut, I can counterfeit the deep
    tragedian;
Speak and look back, and pry on every side,
Tremble and start at wagging of a straw,
Intending deep suspicion: ghastly looks
Are at my service, like enforced smiles;
And both are ready in their offices,
At any time, to grace my stratagems.
But what, is Catesby gone?   [along.
  Glo. He is; and, see, he brings the mayor

Enter the Lord Mayor *and* CATESBY.

  Buck. Lord mayor,—
  Glo. Look to the drawbridge there!
  Buck. Hark! a drum.
  Glo. Catesby, o'erlook the walls.
  Buck. Lord Mayor, the reason we have
    sent,—
  Glo. Look back, defend thee,—here are
    enemies.
  Buck. God and our innocency defend and
    guard us!
  Glo. Be patient, they are friends,—Ratcliff
    and Lovel.

Enter LOVEL *and* RATCLIFF, *with* HASTINGS'
head.

  Lov. Here is the head of that ignoble
    traitor,
The dangerous and unsuspected Hastings.
  Glo. So dear I lov'd the man that I must
    weep.
I took him for the plainest harmless creature
That breath'd upon the earth a Christian;
Made him my book, wherein my soul re-
    corded
The history of all her secret thoughts:
So smooth he daub'd his vice with show of
    virtue
That, his apparent open guilt omitted,—
I mean, his conversation with Shore's wife,—
He liv'd from all attainder of suspect.
  Buck. Well, well, he was the covert'st shel-
    ter'd traitor
That ever liv'd.—
Would you imagine, or almost believe,—
Were't not that by great preservation
We live to tell it you,—the subtle traitor
This day had plotted, in the council-house,
To murder me and my good Lord of Gloster!
  May. Had he done so?   [fidels?
  Glo. What! think you we are Turks or In-
Or that we would, against the form of law,
Proceed thus rashly in the villain's death,
But that the extreme peril of the case,
The peace of England and our persons' safety,
Enforc'd us to this execution?
  May. Now, fair befall you! he deserv'd his
    death;   [ceeded,
And your good graces both have well pro-
To warn false traitors from the like attempts.
I never look'd for better at his hands
After he once fell in with Mistress Shore.

  Buck. Yet had we not determin'd he
    should die
Until your lordship came to see his end;
Which now the loving haste of these our
    friends,
Something against our meaning, hath pre-
    vented:
Because, my lord, we would have had you
    heard
The traitor speak, and timorously confess
The manner and the purpose of his treasons;
That you might well have signified the same
Unto the citizens, who haply may
Misconstrue us in him, and wail his death.
  May. But, my good lord, your grace's
    word shall serve
As well as I had seen, and heard him speak:
And do not doubt, right noble princes both.
But I'll acquaint our duteous citizens
With all your just proceedings in this case.
  Glo. And to that end we wish'd your lord-
    ship here,
To avoid the censures of the carping world.
  Buck. But since you come too late of our
    intent,
Yet witness what you hear we did intend:
And so, my good lord mayor, we bid fare-
    well.   [*Exit* LORD MAYOR.
  Glo. Go, after, after, cousin Buckingham.
The mayor towards Guildhall hies him in all
    post:—
There, at your meetest vantage of the time,
Infer the bastardy of Edward's children:
Tell them how Edward put to death a citizen,
Only for saying he would make his son
Heir to the crown; meaning, indeed, his
    house,
Which, by the sign thereof, was termed so.
Moreover, urge his hateful luxury,
And bestial appetite in change of lust;
Which stretch'd unto their servants, daugh-
    ters, wives,
Even where his raging eye or savage heart,
Without control, listed to make a prey.
Nay, for a need, thus far come near my per-
    son:—   [child
Tell them, when that my mother went with
Of that insatiate Edward, noble York,
My princely father, then had wars in France;
And, by true computation of the time,
Found that the issue was not his begot;
Which well appeared in his lineaments,
Being nothing like the noble duke my father:
Yet touch this sparingly, as 'twere far off;
Because, my lord, you know my mother lives.
  Buck. Doubt not, my lord, I'll play the
    orator
As if the golden plea for which I plead
Were for myself: and so, my lord, adieu.
  Glo. If you thrive well, bring them to Bay-
    nard's Castle;
Where you shall find me well accompanied
With reverend fathers and well learned bish-
    ops.

Buck. I go; and towards three or four o'clock
Look for the news that the Guildhall affords.
                                        [*Exit.*
Glo. Go, Lovel, with all speed to Doctor
    Shaw.—   [them both
Go thou [*to* CATE.] to Friar Penker;—bid
Meet me within this hour at Baynard's Castle.
                        [*Exeunt* Lov. *and* CATE.
Now will I in, to take some privy order
To draw the brats of Clarence out of sight;
And to give notice that no manner of person
Have any time recourse unto the prices.
                                        [*Exit.*

SCENE VI.—LONDON. *A Street.*

Enter a Scrivener.

Scriv. Here is the indictment of the good
    Lord Hastings;
Which in a set hand fairly is engross'd,
That it may be to-day read o'er in Paul's.
And mark how well the sequel hangs to-
    gether:—
Eleven hours I have spent to write it over,
For yesternight by Catesby was it sent me;
The precedent was full as long a-doing:
And yet within these five hours Hastings
    liv'd,
Untainted, unexamin'd, free, at liberty.
Here's a good world the while! Who is so
    gross
That cannot see this palpable device!
Yet who so bold but says he sees it not!
Bad is the world; and all will come to naught
When such ill dealing must be seen in thought.
                                        [*Exit.*

SCENE VII.—LONDON. *Court of Baynard's
        Castle.*

Enter GLOSTER *and* BUCKINGHAM, *meeting.*

Glo. How now, how now! what say the
    citizens?
Buck. Now, by the holy mother of our
    Lord,
The citizens are mum, say not a word.
Glo. Touch'd you the bastardy of Ed-
    ward's children?   [Lucy,
Buck. I did; with his contract with Lady
And his contract by deputy in France;
The insatiate greediness of his desires,
And his enforcement of the city wives;
His tyranny for trifles; his own bastardy,—
As being got, your father then in France,
And his resemblance, being not like the duke:
Withal I did infer your lineaments,—
Being the right idea of your father,
Both in your form and nobleness of mind;
Laid open all your victories in Scotland,
Your discipline in war, wisdom in peace,
Your bounty, virtue, fair humility;
Indeed, left nothing fitting for your purpose
Untouch'd or slightly handled in discourse:
And when my oratory drew toward end
I bid them that did love their country's good

Cry, *God save Richard, England's royal king!*
Glo. And did they so?   [a word;
Buck. No, so God help me, they spake not
But, like dumb statuas or breathing stones,
Star'd each on other, and look'd deadly pale.
Which when I saw, I reprehended them;
And ask'd the mayor what meant this wilful
    silence:
His answer was,—the people were not us'd
To be spoke to but by the recorder.
Then he was urg'd to tell my tale again,—
*Thus saith the duke, thus hath the duke in-
    ferr'd*
But nothing spoke in warrant from himself.
When he had done, some followers of mine
    own,
At lower end of the hall, hurl'd up their caps,
And some ten voices cried, *God save King
    Richard!*
And thus I took the vantage of those few,—
Thanks, gentle citizens and friends, quoth I;
*This general applause and cheerful shout
Argues your wisdom and your love to Rich-
    ard:*
And even here brake off and came away.
Glo. What tongueless blocks were they!
    would they not speak?   [come?
Will not the mayor, then, and his brethren,
Buck. The mayor is here at hand. Intend
    some fear;
Be not you spoke with but by mighty suit:
And look you get a prayer-book in your
    hand,
And stand between two churchmen, good my
    lord;
For on that ground I'll make a holy descant:
And be not easily won to our requests;
Play the maid's part,—still answer nay, and
    take it.
Glo. I go; and if you plead as well for
    them
As I can say nay to thee for myself,
No doubt we bring it to a happy issue.
Buck. Go, go, up to the leads; the lord
    mayor knocks.   [*Exit* GLOSTER.

Enter the Lord Mayor, Aldermen, *and*
    Citizens.

Welcome, my lord: I dance attendance here;
I think the duke will not be spoke withal.

Enter, from the Castle, CATESBY.

Now, Catesby,—what says your lord to my
    request?   [ble lord,
Cate. He doth entreat your grace, my no-
To visit him to-morrow or next day:
He is within, with two right reverend fath-
    ers,
Divinely bent to meditation:
And in no worldly suit would he be mov'd,
To draw him from his holy exercise.
Buck. Return, good Catesby, to the gra-
    cious duke;
Tell him, myself, the mayor and aldermen.

In deep designs, in matter of great moment,
No less importing than our general good,
Are come to have some conference with his
　　grace.
　Cate. I'll signify so much unto him straight.
　　　　　　　　　　　　　　　　　　[*Exit.*
　Buck. Ah, ha, my lord, this prince is not
　　an Edward!
He is not lolling on a lewd day-bed
But on his knees at meditation;
Not dallying with a brace of courtezans,
But meditating with two deep divines;
Not sleeping, to engross his idle body,
But praying, to enrich his watchful soul:
Happy were England would this virtuous
　　prince
Take on himself the sovereignty thereof:
But, sure, I fear, we shall not win him to it.
　May. Marry, God defend his grace should
　　say us nay!　　　　　　　　　[again.
　Buck. I fear he will. Here Catesby comes

Re-enter CATESBY.

Now, Catesby, what says his grace?
　Cate. He wonders to what end you have
　　assembled
Such troops of citizens to come to him:
His grace not being warn'd thereof before,
He fears, my lord, you mean no good to him.
　Buck. Sorry I am my noble cousin should
Suspect me, that I mean no good to him:
By heaven, we come to him in perfect love;
And so once more return and tell his grace.
　　　　　　　　　　　　　　[*Exit* CATESBY.
When holy and devout religious men
Are at their beads, 'tis much to draw them
　　thence,—
So sweet is zealous contemplation.

Enter GLOSTER, *in a Gallery above, between two* BISHOPS. CATESBY *returns.*

　May. See, where his grace stands 'tween
　　two clergymen!　　　　　　　[prince,
　Buck. Two props of virtue for a Christian
To stay him from the fall of vanity:
And, see, a book of prayer in his hand,—
True ornament to know a holy man.—
Famous Plantagenet, most gracious prince,
Lend favourable ear to our requests;
And pardon us the interruption
Of thy devotion and right Christian zeal.
　Glo. My lord, there needs no such apology:
I rather do beseech you pardon me,
Who, earnest in the service of my God,
Deferr'd the visitation of my friends. [sure?
But, leaving this, what is your grace's plea-
　Buck. Even that, I hope, which pleaseth
　　God above,
And all good men of this ungovern'd isle.
　Glo. I do suspect I have done some offence
That seems disgracious in the city's eye;
And that you come to reprehend my ignor-
　　ance.

　Buck. You have, my lord: would it might
　　please your grace,
On our entreaties, to amend your fault!
　Glo. Else wherefore breathe I in a Chris-
　　tian land?　　　　　　　　　[resign
　Buck. Know, then, it is your fault that you
The supreme seat, the throne majestical,
The scepter'd office of your ancestors,
Your state of fortune and your due of birth,
The lineal glory of your royal house,
To the corruption of a blemish'd stock:
Whilst, in the mildness of your sleepy
　　thoughts,—
Which here we waken to our country's
　　good,—
This noble isle doth want her proper limbs;
Her face defac'd with scars of infamy,
Her royal stock graft with ignoble plants,
And almost shoulder'd in the swallowing gulf
Of dark forgetfulness and deep oblivion.
Which to recure, we heartily solicit
Your gracious self to take on you the charge
And kingly government of this your land;—
Not as protector, steward, substitute,
Or lowly factor for another's gain;
But as successively, from blood to blood,
Your right of birth, your empery, your own.
For this, consorted with the citizens
Your very worshipful and loving friends,
And, by their vehement instigation,
In this just suit come I to move your grace.
　Glo. I cannot tell if to depart in silence
Or bitterly to speak in your reproof
Best fitteth my degree or your condition:
If not to answer, you might haply think
Tongue-tied ambition, not replying, yielded
To bear the golden yoke of sovereignty,
Which fondly you would here impose on me;
If to reprove you for this suit of yours,
So season'd with your faithful love to me,
Then, on the other side, I check'd my friends.
Therefore,—to speak, and to avoid the first,
And then, in speaking, not to incur the last,—
Definitively thus I answer you.
Your love deserves my thanks; but my desert
Unmeritable shuns your high request.
First, if all obstacles were cut away,
And that my path were even to the crown,
As the ripe revenue and due of birth,
Yet so much is my poverty of spirit,
So mighty and so many my defects, [ness,—
That I would rather hide me from my great-
Being a bark to brook no mighty sea,—
Than in my greatness covet to be hid,
And in the vapour of my glory smother'd.
But, God be thank'd, there is no need of
　　me,—
And much I need to help you, were there
　　need;—
The royal tree hath left us royal fruit,
Which, mellow'd by the stealing hours of
　　time,
Will well become the seat of majesty,
And make, no doubt, us happy by his reign.

On him I lay that you would lay on me,—
The right and fortune of his happy stars;
Which God defend that I should wring from
   him!   [your grace;
  Buck. My lord, this argues conscience in
But the respects thereof are nice and trivial,
All circumstances well considered.
You say that Edward is your brother's son:
So say we too, but not by Edward's wife;
For first was he contract to Lady Lucy,—
Your mother lives a witness to his vow,—
And afterward by substitute betroth'd
To Bona, sister to the King of France.
These both put off, a poor petitioner,
A care-craz'd mother to a many sons,
A beauty-waning and distressed widow,
Even in the afternoon of her best days,
Made prize and purchase of his wanton eye,
Seduc'd the pitch and height of his degree
To base declension and loath'd bigamy:
By her, in his unlawful bed, he got
This Edward, whom our manners call the
   prince.
More bitterly could I expostulate,
Save that, for reverence to some alive,
I give a sparing limit to my tongue.
Then, good my lord, take to your royal self
This proffer'd benefit of dignity;
If not to bless us and the land withal,
Yet to draw forth your noble ancestry
From the corruption of abusing time
Unto a lineal true-derived course,
  May. Do, good my lord; your citizens en-
   treat you.
  Buck. Refuse not, mighty lord, this prof-
   fer'd love.   [ful suit!
  Cate. O, make them joyful, grant their law-
  Glo. Alas, why would you heap those
   cares on me?
I am unfit for state and majesty:—
I do beseech you, take it not amiss;
I cannot nor I will not yield to you.
  Buck. If you refuse it,—as, in love and
   zeal,
Loth to depose the child, your brother's son—
As well we know your tenderness of heart,
And gentle, kind, effeminate remorse,
Which we have noted in you to your kin-
   dred,
And equally, indeed, to all estates,—
Yet know, whe'r you accept our suit or no,
Your brother's son shall never reign our king;
But we will plant some other in the throne,
To the disgrace and downfall of your house:
And in this resolution here we leave you.—
Come, citizens, we will entreat no more.
   [*Exeunt* BUCK., *the* Mayor *and* Citizens
            retiring.
  Cate. Call them again, sweet prince, ac-
   cept their suit:
If you deny them, all the land will rue it.
  Glo. Will you enforce me to a world of
   cares?
Call them again.

           [CATE. *goes to the* Mayor, *&c., and then exit.*
I am not made of stone,
But penetrable to your kind entreaties,
Albeit against my conscience and my soul.

Re-enter BUCKINGHAM *and* CATESBY, *the*
      Mayor, *&c, coming forward.*

Cousin of Buckingham,—and sage, grave
   men,
Since you will buckle fortune on my back,
To bear her burden, whe'r I will or no,
I must have patience to endure the load:
But if black scandal or foul-fac'd reproach
Attend the sequel of your imposition,
Your mere enforcement shall acquittance me
From all the impure blots and stains thereof;
For God he knows, and you may partly see,
How far I am from the desire of this.
  May. God bless your grace! we see it, and
   will say it.
  Glo. In saying so, you shall but say the
   truth.
  Buck. Then I salute you with this royal
   title,—
Long live King Richard, England's worthy
   king!
  All. Amen.   [crown'd?
  Buck. To-morrow may it please you to be
  Glo. Even when you please, for you will
   have it so.
  Buck. To-morrow, then, we will attend
   your grace:
And so, most joyfully, we take our leave.
  Glo. Come, let us to our holy work
   again.—
            [*To the* Bishops.
Farewell, my cousin;—farewell, gentle
   friends.   [*Exeunt.*

ACT IV.

SCENE I.—LONDON. *Before the Tower.*

Enter, on one side, QUEEN ELIZABETH, DUCH-
ESS OF YORK, *and* MARQUIS OF DORSET; *on
the other,* ANNE DUCHESS OF GLOSTER,
leading LADY MARGARET PLANTAGENET,
CLARENCE'S *young Daughter.*

  Duch. Who meets us here?—my niece
   Plantagenet
Led in the hand of her kind aunt of Gloster?
Now, for my life, she's wandering to the
   Tower,
On pure heart's love, to greet the tender
   princes.—
Daughter, well met.
  Anne.   God gives your graces both
A happy and a joyful time of day!
  Q. Eliz. As much to you, good sister!
   Whither away?
  Anne. No further than the Tower; and, as
   I guess,
Upon the like devotion as yourselves,
To gratulate the gentle princes there.

Q. Eliz. Kind sister, thanks: we'll enter all
    together:—
And, in good time, here the lieutenant comes.

Enter BRAKENBURY.

Master lieutenant, pray you, by your leave,
How doth the prince, and my young son of
    York?
Brak. Right well, dear madam. By your
    patience,
I may not suffer you to visit them;
The king has strictly charg'd the contrary.
Q. Eliz. The king! who's that?
Brak.   I mean the lord protector.
Q. Eliz. The lord protect him from that
    kingly title!
Hath he set bounds between their love and
    me?
I am their mother; who shall bar me from
    them?
Duch. I am their father's mother, I will
    see them.   [mother:
Anne. Their aunt I am in law, in love their
Then bring me to their sights; I'll bear thy
    blame,
And take thy office from thee, on my peril.
Brak. No, madam, no,—I may not leave
    it so:
I am bound by oath, and therefore pardon
    me.   [*Exit.*

Enter STANLEY.

Stan. Let me but meet you, ladies, one
    hour hence,
And I'll salute your grace of York as mother
And reverend looker-on of two fair queens.—
Come, madam, you must straight to West-
    minster,
         [*To the* DUCHESS OF GLOSTER.
There to be crowned Richard's royal queen.
Q. Eliz. Ah, cut my lace asunder,   [beat,
That my pent heart may have some scope to
Or else I swoon with this dead-killing news!
Anne. Despiteful tidings! O unpleasing
    news!
Dor. Be of good cheer: mother, how fares
    your grace?   [gone!
Q. Eliz. O Dorset, speak not to me, get thee
Death and destruction dog thee at the heels;
Thy mother's name is ominous to children.
If thou wilt outstrip death, go cross the seas,
And live with Richmond, from the reach of
    hell:
Go, hie thee, hie thee from this slaughter-
    house,
Lest thou increase the number of the dead;
And make me die the thrall of Margaret's
    curse,
Nor mother, wife, nor England's counted
    queen.
Stan. Full of wise care is this your coun-
    sel, madam.—
Take all the swift advantage of the hours;
You shall have letters from me to my son

In your behalf, to meet you on the way:
Be not ta'en tardy by unwise delay.
Duch. O ill-dispersing wind of misery!—
O my accursed womb, the bed of death!
A cockatrice hast thou hatch'd to the world,
Whose unavoided eye is murderous.
Stan. Come, madam, come; I in all haste
    was sent.
Anne. And I with all unwillingness will
    go.—
O, would to God that the inclusive verge
Of golden metal that must round my brow
Were red-hot steel, to sear me to the brain!
Anointed let me be with deadly venom,
And die ere men can say God save the Queen!
Q. Eliz. Go, go, poor soul, I envy not thy
    glory;
To feed my humour, wish thyself no harm.
Anne. No, why?—When he that is my
    husband now
Came to me, as I follow'd Henry's corse;
When scarce the blood was well wash'd from
    his hands
Which issu'd from my other angel husband,
And that dead saint which then I weeping
    follow'd;
O, when, I say, I look'd on Richard's face,
This was my wish,—*Be thou,* quoth I, *ac-*
    curs'd
For making me, so young, so old a widow!
And when thou wedd'st, let sorrow haunt thy
    bed;
And be thy wife,—if any be so mad,—
More miserable by the life of thee   [*death!*
Than thou hast made me by my dear lord's
Lo, ere I can repeat this curse again,
Within so small a time, my woman's heart
Grossly grew captive to his honey words,
And prov'd the subject of mine own soul's
    curse,—
Which hitherto hath held mine eyes from
    rest;
For never yet one hour in his bed
Did I enjoy the golden dew of sleep,
But with his timorous dreams was still
    awak'd.
Besides, he hates me for my father Warwick;
And will, no doubt, shortly be rid of me.
Q. Eliz. Poor heart, adieu! I pity thy com-
    plaining.
Anne. No more than with my soul I mourn
    for yours.   [glory!
Q. Eliz. Farewell, thou woeful welcomer of
Anne. Adieu, poor soul, that tak'st thy
    leave of it!
Duch. Go thou to Richmond, and good
    fortune guide thee!—   [*To* DORSET.
Go thou to Richard, and good angels tend
    thee!—   [*To* ANNE.
Go thou to sanctuary, and good thoughts
    possess thee! [*To* QUEEN ELIZABETH.
I to my grave, where peace and rest lie with
    me!
Eighty odd years of sorrow have I seen,

And each hour's joy wreck'd with a week of
    teen.
  Q. Eliz. Stay yet, look back with me unto
    the Tower.—
Pity, you ancient stones, those tender babes,
Whom envy hath immur'd within your walls!
Rough cradle for such little pretty ones!
Rude ragged nurse, old sullen playfellow
For tender princes, use my babies well!
So foolish sorrow bids your stones farewell.
                        [*Exeunt.*

SCENE II.—LONDON. *A Room of State in the
    Palace.*

Flourish of trumpets. RICHARD, *as King, upon
  his throne;* BUCKINGHAM, CATESBY, *a Page,
  and others.*

  K. Rich. Stand all apart.—Cousin of Buck-
    ingham,—
  Buck. My gracious sovereign?
  K. Rich. Give me thy hand. Thus high, by
    thy advice
And thy assistance, is King Richard seated:—
But shall we wear these glories for a day?
Or shall they last, and we rejoice in them?
  Buck. Still live they, and for ever let them
    last!
  K. Rich. Ah, Buckingham, now do I play
    the touch.
To try if thou be current gold indeed:—
Young Edward lives;—think now what I
    would speak.
  Buck. Say on, my loving lord.
  K. Rich. Why, Buckingham, I say, I
    would be king.
  Buck. Why, so you are, my thrice-re-
    nowned liege.   [ward lives.
  K. Rich. Ha! am I king? 'tis so: but Ed-
  Buck. True, noble prince.
  K. Rich.   O bitter consequence,
That Edward still should live,—true, noble
    prince!—
Cousin, thou wast not wont to be so dull:—
Shall I be plain?—I wish the bastards dead;
And I would have it suddenly perform'd.
What say'st thou now? speak suddenly, be
    brief.
  Buck. Your grace may do your pleasure.
  K. Rich. Tut, tut, thou art all ice, thy
    kindness freezes:
Say, have I thy consent that they shall die?
  Buck. Give me some little breath, some
    pause, dear lord,
Before I positively speak in this:
I will resolve your grace immediately. [*Exit.*
  Cate. The king is angry: see, he gnaws his
    lip.   [*Aside.*
  K. Rich. I will converse with iron-witted
    fools   [*Descends from his throne.*
And unrespective boys; none are for me
That look into me with considerate eyes:
High-reaching Buckingham grows circum-
    spect.
Boy!—

  Page. My lord?
  K. Rich. Know'st thou not any whom cor-
    rupting gold
Would tempt into a close exploit of death?
  Page. I know a discontented gentleman,
Whose humble means match not his haughty
    spirit:
Gold were as good as twenty orators,
And will, no doubt, tempt him to anything.
  K. Rich. What is his name?
  Page.   His name, my lord, is Tyrrel.
  K. Rich. I partly know the man: go, call
    him hither, boy.   [*Exit* Page.
The deep-revolving witty Buckingham
No more shall be the neighbour to my coun-
    sels:
Hath he so long held out with me untir'd,
And stops he now for breath?—well, be it so.

         Enter STANLEY.

How now, Lord Stanley! what's the news?
  Stan. Know, my loving lord,
The Marquis Dorset, as I hear, is fled
To Richmond, in the parts where he abides.
  K. Rich. Come hither Catesby: rumour it
    abroad
That Anne, my wife, is very grievous sick;
I will take order for her keeping close:
Inquire me out some mean poor gentleman
Whom I will marry straight to Clarence'
    daughter;—
The boy is foolish, and I fear not him.—
Look, how thou dream'st!—I say again, give
    out
That Anne my queen is sick, and like to die:
About it; for it stands me much upon,
To stop all hopes whose growth may dam-
    age me.   [*Exit* CATESBY.
I must be married to my brother's daughter,
Or else my kingdom stands on brittle glass:—
Murder her brothers, and then marry her!
Uncertain way of gain! But I am in
So far in blood that sin will pluck on sin:
Tear-falling pity dwells not in this eye.

    Re-enter Page, *with* TYRREL.

Is thy name Tyrrel?
  Tyr. James Tyrrel, and your most obedient
    subject.
  K. Rich. Art thou, indeed?
  Tyr.   Prove me, my gracious lord.
  K. Rich. Dar'st thou resolve to kill a
    friend of mine?   [enemies.
  Tyr. Please you. But I had rather kill two
  K. Rich. Why, then, thou hast it: two
    deep enemies,
Foes to my rest, and my sweet sleep's dis-
    turbers,
Are they that I would have thee deal upon:—
Tyrrel, I mean those bastards in the Tower.
  Tyr. Let me have open means to come to
    them,
And soon I'll rid you from the fear of them.

K. Rich. Thou sing'st sweet music. Hark, come hither, Tyrrel:
Go, by this token:—rise, and lend thine ear:
                          [*Whispers.*
There is no more but so:—say it is done,
And I will love thee, and prefer thee for it.
Tyr. I will despatch it straight.   [*Exit.*

Re-enter BUCKINGHAM.

Buck. My lord, I have consider'd in my mind
The late demand that you did sound me in.
K. Rich. Well, let that rest. Dorset is fled to Richmond.
Buck. I hear the news, my lord.
K. Rich. Stanley, he is your wife's son:—well, look to it.   [by promise,
Buck. My lord, I claim the gift, my due
For which your honour and your faith is pawn'd;
The earldom of Hereford, and the movables,
Which you have promised I shall possess.
K. Rich. Stanley, look to your wife: if she convey
Letters to Richmond, you shall answer it.
Buck. What says your highness to my just request?   [Sixth
K. Rich. I do remember me,—Henry the
Did prophesy that Richmond should be king,
When Richmond was a little peevish boy.
A king!—perhaps,—
Buck. My lord,—
K. Rich. How chance the prophet could not at that time   [him?
Have told me, I being by, that I should kill
Buck. My lord, your promise for the earl-dom,—   [Exeter,
K. Rich. Richmond!—When last I was at
The mayor in courtesy show'd me the castle,
And call'd it Rouge-mont: at which name I started,
Because a bard of Ireland told me once
I should not live long after I saw Richmond.
Buck. My lord,—
K. Rich. Ay, what's o'clock?   [in mind
Buck. I am thus bold to put your grace
Of what you promis'd me.
K. Rich.   Well, but what's o'clock?
Buck. Upon the stroke of ten.
K. Rich.   Well, let it strike.
Buck. Why let it strike?
K. Rich. Because that, like a Jack, thou keep'st the stroke
Betwixt thy begging and my meditation.
I am not in the giving vein to-day.
Buck. Why, then resolve me whether you will or no.   [the vein.
K. Rich. Thou troublest me; I am not in
        [*Exeunt* K. RICH. *and* Train.
Buck. And is it thus? repays he my deep service   [this?
With such contempt? made I him king for
O, let me think on Hastings, and be gone

To Brecknock while my fearful head is on!
                         [*Exit.*

SCENE III.—LONDON. *Another Room in the Palace.*

Enter TYRREL.

Tyr. The tyrannous and bloody act is done,—
The most arch deed of piteous massacre
That ever yet this land was guilty of.
Dighton and Forrest, whom I did suborn
To do this piece of ruthless butchery,
Albeit they were flesh'd villains, bloody dogs,
Melting with tenderness and mild compassion,   [story.
Wept like two children in the death's sad
O thus, quoth Dighton, *lay the gentle babes,—*   [other
Thus, thus, quoth Forrest, *girdling one an-*
Within their alabaster innocent arms:
Their lips were four red roses on a stalk,
Which in their summer beauty kiss'd each other.
A book of prayers on their pillow lay;
Which one, quoth Forrest, *almost chang'd my mind;*
But, O, the devil,—there the villain stopp'd;
When Dighton thus told on,—*we smothered*
The most replenished sweet work of nature
That from the prime creation e'er she fram'd.—   [remorse
Hence both are gone; with conscience and
They could not speak; and so I left them both,
To bear this tidings to the bloody king:—
And here he comes:—

Enter KING RICHARD.

        All health, my sovereign lord!
K. Rich. Kind Tyrrel, am I happy in thy news?   [charge
Tyr. If to have done the thing you gave in
Beget your happiness, be happy then,
For it is done.
K. Rich. But didst thou see them dead?
Tyr. I did, my lord.
K. Rich.   And buried, gentle Tyrrel?
Tyr. The chaplain of the Tower hath buried them;
But where, to say the truth, I do not know.
K. Rich. Come to me, Tyrrel, soon, at after supper,   [death.
When thou shalt tell the process of their
Meantime, but think how I may do thee good,
And be inheritor of thy desire.
Farewell till then.
Tyr.   I humbly take my leave. [*Exit.*
K. Rich. The son of Clarence have I pent up close;   [marriage;
His daughter meanly have I matched in
The sons of Edward sleep in Abraham's bosom,   [night.
And Anne my wife hath bid the world good-

Now, for I know the Bretagne Richmond
　　aims
At young Elizabeth, my brother's daughter,
And by that knot looks proudly on the
　　crown,
To her go I, a jolly thriving wooer.

Enter RATCLIFF.

Rat. My lord,—
K. Rich. Good news or bad, that thou
　　com'st in so bluntly?　　[Richmond;
Rat. Bad news, my lord: Morton is fled to
And Buckingham, back'd with the hardy
　　Welshmen,
Is in the field, and still his power increaseth.
K. Rich. Ely with Richmond troubles me
　　more near　　[strength.
Than Buckingham and his rash-levied
Come,—I have learn'd that fearful com-
　　menting
Is leaden servitor to dull delay;　　[gary:
Delay leads impotent and snail-pac'd beg-
Then fiery expedition be my wing,
Jove's Mercury, and herald for a king!
Go, muster men: my counsel is my shield;
We must be brief when traitors brave the
　　field.　　[*Exeunt.*

SCENE IV.—LONDON. *Before the Palace.*

Enter QUEEN MARGARET.

Q. Mar. So, now prosperity begins to mel-
　　low,
And drop into the rotten mouth of death,
Here in these confines slily have I lurk'd,
To watch the waning of mine enemies.
A dire induction am I witness to,
And will to France; hoping the consequence
Will prove as bitter, black, and tragical.—
Withdraw thee, wretched Margaret: who
　　comes here?　　[*Retires.*

Enter QUEEN ELIZABETH *and the* DUCHESS OF
　　YORK.

Q. Eliz. Ah, my poor princes! ah, my ten-
　　der babes!
My unblown flowers, new-appearing sweets!
If yet your gentle souls fly in the air,
And be not fix'd in doom perpetual,
Hover about me with your airy wings,
And hear your mother's lamentation!
Q. Mar. Hover about her; say, that right
　　for right　　[night.
Hath dimm'd your infant morn to aged
Duch. So many miseries have craz'd my
　　voice
That my woe-wearied tongue is still and
　　mute.—
Edward Plantagenet, why art thou dead?
Q. Mar. Plantagenet doth quit Plantage-
net, Edward for Edward pays a dying debt.
Q. Eliz. Wilt thou, O God, fly from such
　　gentle lambs,
And throw them in the entrails of the wolf?

When didst thou sleep when such a deed was
　　done?　　[sweet son.
Q. Mar. When holy Harry died, and my
Duch. Dead life, blind sight, poor mortal-
　　living ghost,　　[life usurp'd,
Woe's scene, world's shame, grave's due by
Brief abstract and record of tedious days,
Rest thy unrest on England's lawful earth,
　　　　　[*Sitting down.*
Unlawfully made drunk with innocent
　　blood!
Q. Eliz. Ah, that thou wouldst as soon af-
　　ford a grave
As thou canst yield a melancholy seat!
Then would I hide my bones, not rest them
　　here.
Ah, who hath any cause to mourn but we?
　　　　　[*Sitting down by her.*
Q. Mar. If ancient sorrow be most rev-
　　erent,
Give mine the benefit of seniory,
　　　　　[*Coming forward.*
And let my griefs frown on the upper hand.
If sorrow can admit society,
　　　　　[*Sitting down with them.*
Tell o'er your woes again by viewing mine:—
I had an Edward, till a Richard kill'd him;
I had a Henry, till a Richard kill'd him:
Thou hadst an Edward, till a Richard kill'd
　　him;　　[him.
Thou hadst a Richard, till a Richard kill'd
Duch. I had a Richard too, and thou didst
　　kill him;
I had a Rutland too, thou holp'st to kill him.
Q. Mar. Thou hadst a Clarence too, and
　　Richard kill'd him　　[crept
From forth the kennel of thy womb hath
A hell-hound that doth hunt us all to death:
That dog, that had his teeth before his eyes,
To worry lambs and lap their gentle blood;
That foul defacer of God's handiwork;
That excellent grand tyrant of the earth,
That reigns in galled eyes of weeping souls,—
Thy womb let loose, to chase us to our
　　graves.—
O upright, just, and true-disposing God,
How do I thank thee that this carnal cur
Preys on the issue of his mother's body,
And makes her pew-fellow with others'
　　moan!　　[woes!
Duch. O Harry's wife, triumph not in my
God witness with me, I have wept for thine.
Q. Mar. Bear with me; I am hungry for
　　revenge,
And now I cloy me with beholding it.
Thy Edward he is dead, that kill'd my Ed-
　　ward;
Thy other Edward dead to quit my Edward;
Young York is but boot, because both
　　they
Match not the high perfection of my loss:
Thy Clarence he is dead that stabb'd my Ed-
　　ward;
And the beholders of this frantic play,

The adulterate Hastings, Rivers, Vaughan,
    Grey,
Untimely smother'd in their dusky graves.
Richard yet lives, hell's black intelligencer;
Only reserv'd their factor to buy souls,
And send them thither:—but at hand, at
    hand,
Ensues his piteous and unpitied end: [pray,
Earth gapes, hell burns, fiends roar, saints
To have him suddenly convey'd from
    hence.—
Cancel his bond of life, dear God, I pray,
That I may live to say, The dog is dead!
  Q. Eliz. O, thou didst prophesy the time
    would come
That I should wish for thee to help me curse
That bottled spider, that foul bunch-back'd
    toad!   [of my fortune;
  Q. Mar. I call'd thee then, vain flourish
I call'd thee then, poor shadow, painted
    queen;
The presentation of but what I was,
The flattering index of a direful pageant;
One heav'd a-high, to be hurl'd down below;
A mother only mock'd with two fair babes;
A dream of what thou wast; a garish flag,
To be the aim of every dangerous shot;
A sign of dignity, a breath, a bubble;
A queen in jest, only to fill the scene.
Where is thy husband now? where be thy
    brothers?   [joy?
Where be thy two sons? wherein dost thou
Who sues, and kneels, and says, God save
    the queen?   [thee?
Where be the bending peers that flatter'd
Where be the thronging troops that fol-
    low'd thee?
Decline all this, and see what now thou art:
For happy wife, a most distressed widow;
For joyful mother, one that wails the name;
For one being su'd to, one that humbly sues;
For queen, a very caitiff crown'd with care;
For one that scorn'd at me, now scorn'd of
    me;
For one being fear'd of all, now fearing one;
For one commanding all, obey'd of none.
Thus hath the course of justice wheel'd
    about,
And left thee but a very prey to time:
Having no more but thought of what thou
    wast,   [art.
To torture thee the more, being what thou
Thou didst usurp my place, and dost thou
    not
Usurp the just proportion of my sorrow?
Now thy proud neck bears half my bur-
    den'd yoke;   [head,
From which even here I slip my wearied
And leave the burden of it all on thee.
Farewell, York's wife, and queen of sad mis-
    chance:—   [France.
These English woes shall make me smile in
  Q. Eliz. O thou well skill'd in curses, stay
    awhile.

And teach me how to curse mine enemies!
  Q. Mar. Forbear to sleep the night, and
    fast the day;
Compare dead happiness with living woe;
Think that thy babes were fairer than they
    were,
And he that slew them fouler than he is:
Bettering thy loss makes the bad-causer
    worse;
Revolving this will teach thee how to curse.
  Q. Eliz. My words are dull; O, quicken
    them with thine!
  Q. Mar. Thy woes will make them sharp,
    and pierce like mine.   [*Exit.*
  Duch. Why should calamity be full of
    words?   [woes,
  Q. Eliz. Windy attorneys to their client
Airy succeeders of intestate joys,
Poor breathing orators of miseries [impart
Let them have scope: though what they do
Help nothing else, yet do they ease the heart.
  Duch. If so, then be not tongue-tied: go
    with me,   [smother
And in the breath of bitter words let's
My damned son, that thy two sweet sons
    smother'd.   [*Drum within.*
I hear his drum:—be copious in exclaims.

Enter KING RICHARD *and his* Train,
    marching.

  K. Rich. Who intercepts me in my expe-
    dition?   [thee,
  Duch. O, she that might have intercepted
By strangling thee in her accursed womb,
From all the slaughters, wretch, that thou
    hast done!
  Q. Eliz. Hidst thou that forehead with a
    golden crown,   [right,
Where should be branded, if that right were
The slaughter of the prince that ow'd that
    crown,   [brothers?
And the dire death of my poor sons and
Tell me, thou villain-slave, where are my
    children?   [brother Clarence?
  Duch. Thou toad, thou toad, where is thy
And little Nèd Plantagenet, his son?
  Q. Eliz. Where is the gentle Rivers, Vaugh-
    han, Grey?
  Duch. Where is kind Hastings?
  K. Rich. A flourish, trumpets! strike
    alarum, drums!   [women
Let not the heavens hear these tell-tale
Rail on the Lord's anointed: strike, I say!
     [*Flourish. Alarums.*
Either be patient, and entreat me fair,
Or with the clamorous report of war
Thus will I drown your exclamations.
  Duch. Art thou my son?   [yourself.
  K. Rich. Ay, I thank God, my father, and
  Duch. Then patiently hear my impa-
    tience.   [condition,
  K. Rich. Madam, I have a touch of your
That cannot brook the accent of reproof.
  Duch. O, let me speak!

K Rich. Do, then; but I'll not hear.

Duch. I will be mild and gentle in my words. [in haste.

K. Rich. And brief, good mother; for I am

Duch. Art thou so hasty? I have stay'd for thee,

God knows, in torment and in agony.

K. Rich. And came I not at last to comfort you? [it well

Duch. No, by the holy rood, thou know'st

Thou cam'st on earth to make the earth my hell.

A grievous burden was thy birth to me;

Tetchy and wayward was thy infancy;

Thy schobl-days frightful, desperate, wild, and furious [venturous;

Thy prime of manhood daring, bold, and

Thy age confirm'd, proud, subtle, sly, and bloody, [hatred:

More mild, but yet more harmful, kind in

What comfortable hour canst thou name

That ever grac'd me in thy company?

K. Rich. Faith, none but Humphrey Hour, that call'd your grace

To breakfast once forth of my company.

If I be so disgracious in your eye,

Let me march on and not offend you, madam.—

Strike up the drum.

Duch. I pr'ythee, hear me speak.

K. Rich. You speak too bitterly.

Duch. Hear me a word;

For I shall never speak to thee again.

K. Rich. So. [ordinance

Duch. Either thou wilt die by God's just

Ere from this war thou turn a conqueror;

Or I with grief and extreme age shall perish,

And never look upon thy face again.

Therefore take with thee my most heavy curse;

Which in the day of battle tire thee more

Than all the complete armour that thou wear'st!

My prayers on the adverse party fight;

And there the little souls of Edward's children

Whisper the spirits of thine enemies,

And promise them success and victory.

Bloody thou art, bloody will be thy end;

Shame serves thy life and doth thy death attend. [*Exit.*

Q. Eliz. Though far more cause, yet much less spirit to curse

Abides in me; I say amen to her. [*Going.*

K. Rich. Stay, madam, I must talk a word with you. [blood

Q. Eliz. I have no more sons of the royal

For thee to slaughter: for my daughters, Richard,— [queens;

They shall be praying nuns, not weeping

And therefore level not to hit their lives.

K. Rich. You have a daughter call'd Elizabeth,

Virtuous and fair, royal and gracious.

Q. Eliz. And must she die for this? O let her live, [beauty;

And I'll corrupt her manners, stain her

Slander myself as false to Edward's bed;

Throw over her the veil of infamy: [ter,

So she may live unscarr'd of bleeding slaugh-

I will confess she was not Edward's daughter.

K. Rich. Wrong not her birth; she is of royal blood. [so.

Q. Eliz. To save her life I'll say she is not

K. Rich. Her life is safest only in her birth. [brothers.

Q. Eliz. And only in that safety died her

K. Rich. Lo, at their births good stars were opposite. [contrary.

Q. Eliz. No, to their lives bad friends were

K. Rich. All unavoided is the doom of destiny. [destiny:

Q. Eliz. True, when avoided grace makes

My babes were destined to a fairer death

If grace had bless'd thee with a fairer life.

K. Rich. You speak as if that I had slain my cousins. [uncle cozen'd

Q. Eliz. Cousins, indeed; and by their

Of comfort, kingdom, kindred, freedom, life.

Whose hand soever lanc'd their tender hearts,

Thy head, all indirectly, gave direction:

No doubt the murderous knife was dull and blunt

Till it was whetted on thy stone-hard heart,

To revel in the entrails of my lambs. [tame,

But that still use of grief makes wild grief

My tongue should to thy ears not name my boys [eyes;

Till that my nails were anchor'd in thine

And I, in such a desperate bay of death,

Like a poor bark, of sails and tackling reft,

Rush all to pieces on thy rocky bosom.

K. Rich. Madam, so thrive I in my enterprise

And dangerous success of bloody wars,

As I intend more good to you and yours

Than ever you or yours by me were harm'd!

Q. Eliz. What good is cover'd with the face of heaven,

To be discover'd, that can do me good?

K. Rich. The advancement of your children, gentle lady. [their heads?

Q. Eliz. Up to some scaffold, there to lose

K. Rich. No, to the dignity and height of honour,

The high imperial type of this earth's glory.

Q. Eliz. Flatter my sorrows with report of it; [honour,

Tell me what state, what dignity, what

Canst thou demise to any child of mine?

K. Rich. Even all I have; ay, and myself and all

Will I withal endow a child of thine;

So in the Lethe of thy angry soul [wrongs

Thou drown the sad remembrance of those

Which thou supposest I have done to thee.

Q. Eliz. Be brief. lest that the process of thy kindness

Last longer telling than thy kindness' date.

K. Rich. Then know, that from my soul I
love thy daughter.   [with her soul.

Q. Eliz. My daughter's mother thinks it

K. Rich. What do you think?

Q. Eliz. That thou dost love my daughter
from thy soul: [brothers;
So from thy soul's love didst thou love her
And from my heart's love I do thank thee
for it.   [meaning:

K. Rich. Be not so hasty so confound my
I mean that with my soul I love thy daugh-
ter,   [land.
And do intend to make her Queen of Eng-

Q. Eliz. Well, then, who dost thou mean
shall be her king?

K. Rich. Even he that makes her queen:
who else should be?

Q. Eliz. What, thou?   [madam?

K. Rich. I, even I: what think you of it,

Q. Eliz. How canst thou woo her?

K. Rich.   That I would learn of you,
As one being best acquainted with her humour.

Q. Eliz. And wilt thou learn of me?

K. Rich.   Madam, with all my heart.

Q. Eliz. Send to her, by the man that slew
her brothers,
A pair of bleeding hearts; thereon engrave
Edward and York; then haply will she weep:
Therefore present to her,—as sometime Mar-
garet   [blood,—
Did to thy father, steep'd in Rutland's
A handkerchief; which, say to her, did drain
The purple sap from her sweet brothers'
bodies,
And bid her wipe her weeping eyes withal,
If this inducement move her not to love,
Send her a letter of thy noble deeds;
Tell her thou mad'st away her uncle Clar-
ence,
Her uncle Rivers; ay, and for her sake
Mad'st quick conveyance with her good aunt
Anne.   [not the way

K. Rich. You mock me, madam; this is
To win your daughter.

Q. Eliz.   There is no other way;
Unless thou couldst put on some other shape,
And not be Richard that hath done all this.

K. Rich. Say that I did all this for love of
her?   [choose but hate thee,

Q. Eliz. Nay, then indeed she cannot
Having bought love with such a bloody spoil.

K. Rich. Look, what is done cannot be
now amended:
Men shall deal unadvisedly sometimes,
Which after-hours give leisure to repent.
If I did take the kingdom from your sons,
To make amends I'll give it to your daughter.
If I have kill'd the issue of your womb,
To quicken your increase I will beget
Mine issue of your blood upon your daugh-
ter:

A grandam's name is little less in love
Than is the doating title of a mother;
They are as children but one step below,
Even of your mettle, of your very blood;
Of all one pain,—save for a night of groans
Endur'd of her, for whom you bid like sor-
row.
Your children were vexation to your youth;
But mine shall be a comfort to your age.
The loss you have is but a son being king,
And by that loss your daughter is made
queen.
I cannot make you what amends I would,
Therefore accept such kindness as I can.
Dorset your son, that with a fearful soul
Leads discontented steps in foreign soil,
This fair alliance quickly shall call home
To high promotions and great dignity: [wife,
The king, that calls your beauteous daughter
Familiarly shall call thy Dorset brother;
Again shall you be mother to a king,
And all the ruins of distressful times
Repair'd with double riches of content.
What! we have many goodly days to see:
The liquid drops of tears that you have shed
Shall come again, transform'd to orient pearl,
Advantaging their loan with interest
Of ten-times-double gain of happiness.
Go, then, my mother, to thy daughter go;
Make bold her bashful years with your ex-
perience;
Prepare her ears to hear a wooer's tale:
Put in her tender heart the aspiring flame
Of golden sovereignty; acquaint the princess
With the sweet silent hours of marriage joys:
And when this arm of mine hath chastised
The petty rebel, dull-brain'd Buckingham,
Bound with triumphant garlands will I come,
And lead thy daughter to a conqueror's bed;
To whom I will retail my conquest won,
And she shall be sole victress, Cæsar's Cæsar

Q. Eliz. What were I best to say? her
father's brother
Would be her lord? or shall I say her uncle?
Or he that slew her brothers and her uncles?
Under what title shall I woo for thee,
That God, the law, my honour, and her love
Can make seem pleasing to her tender years?

K. Rich. Infer fair England's peace by this
alliance.   [still-lasting war.

Q. Eliz. Which she shall purchase with

K. Rich. Tell her the king, that may command, entreats.   [king's King forbids.

Q. Eliz. That at her hands which the

K. Rich. Say she shall be a high and
mighty queen.   [doth.

Q. Eliz. To wail the title, as her mother

K. Rich. Say I will love her everlastingly.

Q. Eliz. But how long shall that title,
ever, last?   [life's end.

K. Rich. Sweetly in force unto her fair

Q. Eliz. But how long fairly shall her
sweet life last?

K. Rich. As long as heaven and nature lengthens it.

Q. Eliz. As long as hell and Richard likes of it.   [ject low.

K. Rich. Say I, her sovereign, am her sub-

Q. Eliz. But she, your subject, loathes such sovereignty.

K. Rich. Be eloquent in my behalf to her.

Q. Eliz. An honest tale speeds best being plainly told.   [ing tale.

K. Rich. Then, plainly to her tell my lov-

Q. Eliz. Plain and not honest is too harsh a style.   [too quick.

K. Rich. Your reasons are too shallow and

Q. Eliz. O, no, my reasons are too deep and dead;—   [graves.
Too deep and dead, poor infants, in their

K. Rich. Harp not on that string, madam; that is past.   [strings break.

Q. Eliz. Harp on it still shall I till heart-

K. Rich. Now, by my George, my garter, and my crown,—   [third usurp'd.

Q. Eliz. Profan'd, dishonour'd, and the

K. Rich. I swear,—

Q. Eliz. By nothing; for this is no oath:
Thy George, profan'd hath lost his holy honour;   [virtue;
Thy garter, blemish'd, pawn'd his knightly
Thy crown, usurp'd, disgrac'd his kingly glory.   [believ'd,
If something thou wouldst swear to be
Swear, then, by something that thou hast not wrong'd.

K. Rich. Now, by the world,—

Q. Eliz. 'Tis full of thy foul wrongs.

K. Rich. My father's death,—

Q. Eliz. Thy life hath that dishonour'd.

K. Rich. Then, by myself,—

Q. Eliz. Thyself is self-misus'd.

K. Rich. Why, then, by God,—

Q. Eliz.   God's wrong is most of all.
If thou hadst fear'd to break an oath by him,
The unity the king thy brother made
Had not been broken, nor my brother slain:
If thou hadst fear'd to break an oath by him,
The imperial metal, circling now thy head,
Had grac'd the tender temples of my child;
And both the princes had been breathing here,
Which now, two tender bedfellows for dust,
Thy broken faith hath made a prey for worms.
What canst thou swear by now?

K. Rich.   The time to come.

Q. Eliz. That thou hast wrong'd in the time o'erpast;
For I myself have many tears to wash
Hereafter time, for time past wronged by thee   [slaughter'd,
The children live whose parents thou hast
Ungovern'd youth, to wail it in their age;
The parents live whose children thou hast butcher'd,

Old barren plants, to wail it with their age.
Swear not by time to come; for that thou hast
Misus'd ere used, by times ill-us'd o'erpast.

K. Rich. As I intend to prosper and repent!
So thrive I in my dangerous attempt
Of hostile arms! myself myself confound!
Heaven and fortune bar me happy hours!
Day, yield me not thy light; nor, night, thy rest!
Be opposite all planets of good luck
To my proceeding!—if, with pure heart's love,
Immaculate devotion, holy thoughts,
I tender not thy beauteous princely daughter!
In her consists my happiness and thine;
Without her, follows to myself and thee;
Herself, the land, and many a Christian soul,
Death, desolation, ruin, and decay:
It cannot be avoided but by this;
It will not be avoided but by this.
Therefore, dear mother,—I must call you so,—
Be the attorney of my love to her:
Plead what I will be, not what I have been;
Not my deserts, but what I will deserve:
Urge the necessity and state of times,
And be not peevish found in great designs.

Q. Eliz. Shall I be tempted of the devil thus?   [good.

K. Rich. Ay, if the devil tempt you to do

Q. Eliz. Shall I forget myself to be myself?   [wrong yourself.

K. Rich. Ay, if your self's remembrance

Q. Eliz. But thou didst kill my children.

K. Rich. But in your daughter's womb I bury them: [breed
Where, in that nest of spicery, they shall
Selves of themselves, to your recomforture.

Q. Eliz. Shall I go win my daughter to thy will?   [deed.

K. Rich. And be a happy mother by the

Q. Eliz. I go.—Write to me very shortly,
And you shall understand from me her mind.

K. Rich. Bear her my true love's kiss; and so, farewell.
                    [*Kissing her. Exit* Q. ELIZ.
Relenting fool, and shallow changing woman!

Enter RATCLIFF; CATESBY *following.*

How now! what news?

Rat. Most mighty sovereign, on the western coast
Rideth a puissant navy; to the short
Throng many doubtful hollow-hearted friends,
Unarm'd, and unresolv'd to beat them back:
'Tis thought that Richmond is their admiral;
And there they hull, expecting but the aid
Of Buckingham to welcome them ashore.

K. Rich. Some light-foot friend post to
the Duke of Norfolk:—
Ratcliff, thyself,—or Catesby; where is he?
Cate. Here, my good lord.
K. Rich.   Catesby, fly to the duke.
Cate. I will, my lord, with all convenient
haste.   [Salisbury:
K. Rich. Ratcliffe, come hither:—post to
When thou com'st thither,—Dull, unmindful
villain,   [*To* CATESBY.
Why stay'st thou here, and go'st not to the
duke?   [highness' pleasure,
Cate. First, mighty liege, tell me your
What from your grace I shall deliver to him.
K. Rich. O, true, good Catesby:—bid him
levy straight   [make,
The greatest strength and power he can
And meet me suddenly at Salisbury.
Cate. I go.   [*Exit.*
Rat. What, may it please you, shall I do
at Salisbury?   [before I go?
K. Rich. Why, what wouldst thou do there
Rat. Your highness told me I should post
before.

Enter STANLEY.

K. Rich. My mind is chang'd.—Stanley,
what news with you?
Stan. None good, my liege, to please you
with the hearing.
Nor none so bad but well may be reported.
K. Rich. Hoyday, a riddle! neither good
nor bad!
What need'st thou run so many miles about,
When thou mayst tell thy tale the nearest
way?
Once more, what news?
Stan.   Richmond is on the seas.
K. Rich. There let him sink, and be the
seas on him!
White-liver'd runagate, what doth he there?
Stan. I know not, mighty sovereign, but
by guess.
K. Rich. Well, as you guess?
Stan. Stirr'd up by Dorset, Buckingham,
and Morton,   [crown.
He makes for England here, to claim the
K. Rich. Is the chair empty? is the sword
unsway'd?
Is the king dead? the empire unpossess'd?
What heir of York is there alive but we?
And who is England's king but great York's
heir?
Then, tell me, what makes he upon the seas?
Stan. Unless for that, my liege, I cannot
guess.   [your liege,
K. Rich. Unless for that he comes to be
You cannot guess wherefore the Welshman
comes.
Thou wilt revolt, and fly to him I fear.
Stan. No, mighty liege; therefore mistrust
me not.   [beat him back?
K. Rich. Where is thy power, then, to
Where be thy tenants and thy followers?

Are they not now upon the western shore,
Safe-conducting the rebels from their ships?
Stan. No, my good lord, my friends are in
the north.   [in the north,
K. Rich. Cold friends to me: what do they
When they should serve their sovereign in
the west?   [mighty king:
Stan. They have not been commanded,
Pleaseth your majesty to give me leave,
I'll muster up my friends, and meet your
grace   [please.
Where and what time your majesty shall
K. Rich. Ay, ay, thou wouldst be gone to
join with Richmond;
But I'll not trust thee.
Stan.   Most mighty sovereign,
You have no cause to hold my friendship
doubtful:
I never was nor never will be false.
K. Rich. Go, then, and muster men. But
leave behind   [be firm,
Your son, George Stanley: look your heart
Or else his head's assurance is but frail.
Stan. So deal with him as I prove true to
you.   [*Exit.*

Enter a Messenger.

Mess. My gracious sovereign, now in
Devonshire,
As I by friends am well advertised,
Sir Edward Courtney, and the haughty pre-
late,
Bishop of Exeter, his elder brother,
With many more confederates, are in arms.

Enter a second Messenger.

2 Mess. In Kent, my liege, the Guilfords
are in arms;
And every hour more competitors   [strong.
Flock to the rebels, and their power grows

Enter a third Messenger.

3 Mess. My lord, the army of great
Buckingham,—
K. Rich. Out on ye, owls! nothing but
songs of death?   [*He strikes him.*
There, take thou that till thou bring better
news.   [jesty
3 Mess. The news I have to tell your ma-
Is, that by sudden floods and fall of waters,
Buckingham's army is dispers'd and scat-
ter'd:
And he himself wander'd away alone,
No man knows whither.
K. Rich.   I cry you mercy:
There is my purse to cure that blow of thine.
Hath any well-advised friend proclaim'd
Reward to him that brings the traitor in?
3 Mess. Such proclamation hath been
made, my liege.

Enter a fourth Messenger.

4 Mess. Sir Thomas Lovell and Lord Marquis Dorset,

'Tis said, my liege, in Yorkshire are in arms.
But this good comfort bring I to your high-
　　ness,—
The Bretagne navy is dispers'd by tempest:
Richmond, in Dorsetshire, sent out a boat
Unto the shore, to ask those on the banks
If they were his assistants, yea or no;
Who answer'd him they came from Bucking-
　　ham
Upon his party: he, mistrusting them,
Hois'd sail, and made his course again for
　　Bretagne.　　　　　　　[up in arms;
K. Rich. March on, march on, since we are
If not to fight with foreign enemies,
Yet to beat down these rebels here at home.

Re-enter CATESBY.

Cate. My liege, the Duke of Buckingham
　　is taken,—　　　　　　　[Richmond
That is the best news: that the Earl of
Is with a mighty power landed at Milford
Is colder news, but yet they must be told.
K. Rich. Away towards Salisbury! while
　　we reason here
A royal battle might be won and lost:—
Some one take order Buckingham be brought
To Salisbury; the rest march on with me.
　　　　　　　　　　　[*Flourish. Exeunt.*

SCENE V.—*A Room in* LORD STANLEY'S
　　　　House.

Enter STANLEY *and* SIR CHRISTOPHER,
　　　URSWICK.

Stan. Sir Christopher, tell Richmond this
　　from me:—
That in the sty of the most deadly boar
My son George Stanley is frank'd up in hold:
If I revolt, off goes young George's head;
The fear of that holds off my present aid.
So, get thee gone: commend me to thy lord;
Withal say that the queen hath heartily con-
　　sented
He should espouse Elizabeth her daughter.
But tell me, where is princely Richmond
　　now?　　　　　　　　　　[in Wales.
Chris. At Pembroke, or at Ha'rford-west,
Stan. What men of name resort to him?
Chris. Sir Walter Herbert, a renowned
　　soldier;
Sir Gilbert Talbot, Sir William Stanley;
Oxford, redoubted Pembroke, Sir James
　　Blunt,
And Rice ap Thomas, with a valiant crew;
And many other of great name and worth:
And towards London do they bend their
　　power,
If by the way they be not fought withal.
Stan. Well, hie thee to thy lord; I kiss his
　　hand;
These letters will resolve him of my mind.
Farewell.　　　[*Gives papers to* SIR CHRIS.
　　　　　　　　　　　　　　[*Exeunt.*

ACT V.

SCENE I.—SALISBURY. *An open place.*

Enter the Sheriff *and* Guard, *with* BUCK-
　　INGHAM, *led to execution.*

Buck. Will not King Richard let me speak
　　with him?
Sher. No, my good lord; therefore be
　　patient.　　　　　　　[Grey, and Rivers,
Buck. Hastings, and Edward's children,
Holy King Henry, and thy fair son Edward,
Vaughan, and all that have miscarried
By underhand corrupted foul injustice,—
If that your moody discontented souls [hour,
Do through the clouds behold this present
Even for revenge mock my destruction!—
This is All-Souls' day, fellows, is it not?
Sher. It is, my lord.
Buck. Why, then, All-Souls' day is my
　　body's doomsday.　　　　　　[time
This is the day which in King Edward's
I wish'd might fall on me, when I was found
False to his children or his wife's allies;
This is the day wherein I wish'd to fall
By the false faith of him whom most I
　　trusted;
This, this All-Souls' day to my fearful soul
Is the determin'd respite of my wrongs;
That high All-Seer which I dallied with
Hath turn'd my feigned prayer on my head,
And given in earnest what I begg'd in jest.
Thus doth he force the swords of wicked men
To turn their own points on their masters'
　　bosoms:　　　　　　　　[neck,
Thus Margaret's curse falls heavy on my
When he, quoth she, *shall split thy heart with*
　　sorrow,
Remember Margaret was a prophetess.—
Come, sirs, convey me to the block of shame;
Wrong hath but wrong, and blame the due
　　of blame.　　　　　　　　　[*Exeunt.*

SCENE II.—*Plain near Tamworth.*

Enter, with drum and colours, RICHMOND,
　　OXFORD, SIR JAMES BLUNT, SIR WALTER
　　HERBERT, *and others, with* Forces, *march-
　　ing.*

Richm. Fellows in arms, and my most
　　loving friends,
Bruis'd underneath the yoke of tyranny,
Thus far into the bowels of the land
Have we march'd on without impediment;
And here receive we from our father Stanley
Lines of fair comfort and encouragement.
The wretched, bloody, and usurping boar,
That spoil'd your summer fields and fruitful
　　vines,　　　　　　　　　his trough
Swills your warm blood like wash, and makes
In your embowell'd bosoms,—this foul swine
Lies now even in the centre of this isle,
Near to the town of Leicester, as we learn:
From Tamworth thither is but one day's
　　march.　　　　　　　　[friends
In God's name, cheerly on courageous

To reap the harvest of perpetual peace
By this one bloody trial of sharp war.
 Oxf. Every man's conscience is a thousand
  swords,
To fight against that bloody homicide.
 Herb. I doubt not but his friends will turn
  to us.   [friends for fear,
 Blunt. He hath no friends but what are
Which in his dearest need will fly from him.
 Richm. All for our vantage. Then, in
   God's name, march: [wings;
True hope is swift, and flies with swallows'
Kings it makes gods, and meaner creatures
  kings.   [*Exeunt.*

  SCENE III.—*Bosworth Field.*

Enter KING RICHARD *and* Forces; *the* DUKE
OF NORFOLK, EARL OF SURREY, *and others.*

 K. Rich. Here pitch our tents, even here
  in Bosworth field.—
My Lord of Surrey, why look you so sad?
 Sur. My heart is ten times lighter than my
  looks.
 K. Rich. My Lord of Norfolk,—
 Nor.   Here, most gracious liege.
 K. Rich. Norfolk, we must have knocks;
  ha! must we not?   [ing lord.
 Nor. We must both give and take, my lov-
 K. Rich. Up with my tent! Here will I lie
  to-night;
  [Soldiers *begin to set up the* KING's *tent.*
But where to-morrow? Well, all's one for
  that.—   [tors?
Who hath descried the number of the trai-
 Nor. Six or seven thousand is their utmost
  power.   [account:
 K. Rich. Why, our battalia trebles that
Besides, the king's name is a tower of
  strength,
Which they upon the adverse faction want.—
Up with the tent!—Come, noble gentlemen,
Let us survey the vantage of the ground;—
Call for some men of sound direction:—
Let's lack no discipline, make no delay;
For, lords, to-morrow is a busy day.
         [*Exeunt.*

Enter, on the other side of the Field, RICH-
MOND, SIR WILLIAM BRANDON, OXFORD,
and other Lords. *Some of the* Soldiers *pitch*
RICHMOND's *tent.*

 Richm. The weary sun hath made a
  golden set,
And by the bright track of his fiery car
Gives token of a goodly day to-morrow.—
Sir William Brandon, you shall bear my stan-
  dard.—
Give me some ink and paper in my tent:
I'll draw the form and model of our battle,
Limit each leader to his several charge,
And part in just proportion our small
  power.—
My Lord of Oxford,—you, Sir William Bran-
  don,—

And you, Sir Walter Herbert,—stay with
  me.—
The Earl of Pembroke keeps his regiment:—
Good Captain Blunt, bear my good-night to
  him,
And by the second hour in the morning
Desire the earl to see me in my tent:
Yet one thing more, good captain, do for
  me,—
Where is Lord Stanley quarter'd, do you
  know?
 Blunt. Unless I have mista'en his colours
  much,—
Which well I am assur'd I have not done,—
His regiment lies half a mile at least
South from the mighty power of the king.
 Richm. If without peril it be possible,
Sweet Blunt, make some good means to speak
  with him,
And give him from me this most needful
  note.
 Blunt. Upon my life, my lord, I'll under-
  take it;
And so, God give you quiet rest to-night!
 Richm. Good-night, good Captain Blunt.
  —Come, gentlemen,
Let us consult upon to-morrow's business:
In to my tent; the air is raw and cold.
     [*They withdraw into the tent.*

Enter, to his tent, KING RICHARD, NORFOLK,
  RATCLIFF, *and* CATESBY.

 K. Rich. What is't o'clock?
 Cate.   It's supper-time, my lord;
It's six o'clock.
 K. Rich.   I will not sup to-night.—
Give me some ink and paper.—
What, is my beaver easier than it was?
And all my armour laid into my tent?
 Cate. It is, my liege; and all things are in
  readiness.
 K. Rich. Good Norfolk, hie thee to thy
  charge;
Use careful watch, choose trusty sentinels.
 Nor. I go, my lord.
 K. Rich. Stir with the lark to-morrow,
  gentle Norfolk.
 Nor. I warrant you, my Lord. [*Exit*
 K. Rich. Ratcliff,—
 Rat. My lord?
 K. Rich. Send out a pursuivant-at-arms
To Stanley's regiment; bid him bring his
  power
Before sunrising, lest his son George fall
Into the blind cave of eternal night.—
Fill me a bowl of wine.—Give me a watch.—
Saddle white Surrey to the field to-mor-
  row.—
Look that my staves be sound, and not too
  heavy.—
Ratcliff,—
 Rat. My lord?
 K. Rich. Saw'st thou the melancholy Lord
  Northumberland?

Rat. Thomas the Earl of Surrey and himself,
Much about cock-shut time, from troop to troop
Went through the army, cheering up the soldiers.
  K. Rich. So, I am satisfied.—Give me a bowl of wine:
I have not that alacrity of spirit
Nor cheer of mind that I was wont to have.
Set it down.—Is ink and paper ready?
  Rat. It is, my lord.
  K. Rich. Bid my guard watch; leave me.
Ratcliff, about the mid of night come to my tent
And help to arm me. Leave me, I say.
        [K. RICH. *retires into his tent. Exeunt*
            RATCLIFF *and* CATESBY.

RICHMOND'S *tent opens, and discovers him and his Officers, &c.*

                Enter STANLEY.

  Stan. Fortune and victory sit on thy helm!
  Richm. All comfort that the dark night can afford
Be to thy person, noble father-in-law!
Tell me, how fares our loving mother?
  Stan. I, by attorney, bless thee from thy mother,
Who prays continually for Richmond's good:
So much for that.—The silent hours steal on,
And flaky darkness breaks within the east.
In brief,—for so the season bids us be,—
Prepare thy battle early in the morning,
And put thy fortune to the arbitrement
Of bloody strokes and mortal-staring war.
I, as I may,—that which I would I cannot,—
With best advantage will deceive the time,
And aid thee in this doubtful stroke of arms:
But on thy side I may not be too forward,
Lest, being seen, thy brother, tender George,
Be executed in his father's sight.
Farewell: the leisure and the fearful time
Cuts off the ceremonious vows of love
And ample interchange of sweet discourse,
Which so-long-sunder'd friends should dwell upon:
God give us leisure for these rites of love!
Once more, adieu: be valiant, and speed well!
  Richm. Good lords, conduct him to his regiment:
I'll strive, with troubled thoughts, to take a nap,
Lest leaden slumber peise me down to-morrow,
When I should mount with wings of victory:
Once more, good-night, kind lords and gentlemen.
        [*Exeunt* Lords, *&c., with* STAN.
O Thou whose captain I account myself,
Look on my forces with a gracious eye;
Put in their hands thy bruising irons of wrath,

That they may crush down with a heavy fall
The usurping helmets of our adversaries!
Make us thy ministers of chastisement,
That we may praise thee in thy victory!
To thee I do commend my watchful soul
Ere I let fall the windows of mine eyes:
Sleeping and waking, O, defend me still!
        [*Sleeps.*

The Ghost *of* PRINCE EDWARD, *son to* HENRY THE SIXTH, *rises between the two tents.*

  Ghost. Let me sit heavy on thy soul to-morrow!   [*To* KING RICHARD.
Think how thou stabb'dst me in my prime of youth
At Tewksbury: despair, therefore, and die!—
Be cheerful, Richmond; for the wronged souls
Of butcher'd princes fight in thy behalf:
King Henry's issue, Richmond, comforts thee.

The Ghost *of* KING HENRY THE SIXTH *rises.*

  Ghost. When I was mortal, my anointed body   [*To* KING RICHARD.
By thee was punched full of deadly holes:
Think on the Tower and me: despair, and die,—
Harry the Sixth bids thee despair and die!—
Virtuous and holy, be thou conqueror!
        [*To* RICHMOND.
Harry, that prophesied thou shouldst be king,
Doth comfort thee in sleep: live, and flourish!

The Ghost *of* CLARENCE *rises.*

  Ghost. Let me sit heavy on thy soul to-morrow!
        [*To* KING RICHARD.
I, that was wash'd to death with fulsome wine,
Poor Clarence, by thy guile betray'd to death!
To-morrow in the battle think on me,
And fall thy edgeless sword: despair, and die!—
Thou offspring of the house of Lancaster,
        [*To* RICHMOND.
The wronged heirs of York do pray for thee:
Good angels guard thy battle! live, and flourish!

The Ghosts *of* RIVERS, GREY, *and* VAUGHAN *rise.*

  G. of R. Let me sit heavy on thy soul to-morrow,   [*To* KING RICHARD.
Rivers, that died at Pomfret! despair, and die!
  G. of G. Think upon Grey, and let thy soul despair!   [*To* KING RICHARD.
  G. of V. Think upon Vaughan, and, with guilty fear,
Let fall thy lance: despair, and die!—
        [*To* KING RICHARD.

All Three. Awake, and think our wrongs in
   Richard's bosom   [*To* RICHMOND.
Will conquer him!—awake, and win the day!

    The Ghost *of* HASTINGS *rises.*

Ghost. Bloody and guilty, guiltily awake,
             [*To* KING RICHARD.
And in a bloody battle end thy days!
Think on Lord Hastings: despair, and die!—
Quiet untroubled soul, awake, awake!
             [*To* RICHMOND.
Arm, fight, and conquer, for fair England's
   sake!

The Ghosts *of the two young* Princes *rise.*

Ghosts. Dream on thy cousins smother'd
   in the Tower:
Let us be lead within thy bosom, Richard,
And weigh thee down to ruin, shame, and
   death!   [*die*!—
Thy nephews' souls bid thee despair and
Sleep, Richmond, sleep in peace, and wake
   in joy;
Good angels guard thee from the boar's an-
   noy!
Live, and beget· a happy race of kings!
Edward's unhappy sons do bid thee flourish.

   The Ghost *of* QUEEN ANNE *rises.*

Ghost. Richard, thy wife, that wretched
   Anne thy wife,
That never slept a quiet hour with thee,
Now fills thy sleep with perturbations:
To-morrow in the battle think on me,
And fall thy edgeless sword: despair, and
   die!—
   Thou quiet soul, sleep thou a quiet sleep;
             [*To* RICHMOND.
Dream of success and happy victory:
Thy adversary's wife doth pray for thee.

   The Ghost *of* BUCKINGHAM *rises.*

Ghost. The first was I that help'd thee to
   the crown;   [*To* KING RICHARD.
The last was I that felt thy tyranny:
O, in the battle think on Buckingham,
And die in terror of thy guiltiness!
Dream on, dream on of bloody deeds and
   death:
Fainting, despair; despairing, yield thy
   breath!—
I died for hope ere I could lend thee aid:
             [*To* RICHMOND.
But cheer thy heart, and be thou not dis-
   may'd:
God and good angels fight on Richmond's
   side;
And Richard falls in height of all his pride.
   [*The* Ghosts *vanish.* K. RICH. *starts*
     out of his dream.
  K. Rich. Give me another horse,—bind up
   my wounds,—
Have mercy, Jesu!—Soft! I did but
   dream.—

O coward conscience, how dost thou afflict
   me!—
The lights burn blue.—It is now dead mid-
   night.
Cold fearful drops stand on my trembling
   flesh.
What, do I fear myself? there's none else by:
Richard loves Richard; that is, I am I.
Is there a murderer here? No;—yes; I am:
Then fly. What, from myself? Great reason
   why,—
Lest I revenge. What,—myself upon myself!
Alack, I love myself. Wherefore! for any
   good
That I myself have done unto myself?
O, no! alas, I rather hate myself
For hateful deeds committed by myself!
I am a villain: yet I lie, I am not.
Fool, of thyself speak well:—fool, do not
   flatter.
My conscience hath a thousand several
   tongues,
And every tongue brings in a several tale,
And every tale condemns me for a villain.
Perjury, perjury, in the high'st degree;
Murder, stern murder, in the dir'st degree;
All several sins, all us'd in each degree,
Throng to the bar, crying all, Guilty! guilty!
I shall despair. There is no creature loves me;
And if I die no soul shall pity me:
Nay, wherefore should they,—since that I
   myself
Find in myself no pity to myself?
Methought the souls of all that I had mur-
   der'd
Came to my tent; and every one did threat
To-morrow's vengeance on the head of Rich-
   ard.

     Enter RATCLIFF.

  Rat. My lord,—
  K. Rich. Who's there?   [village-cock
  Rat. Ratcliff, my lord; 'tis I. The early
Hath twice done salutation to the morn;
Your friends are up, and buckle on their
   armour.
  K. Rich. O Ratcliff, I have dream'd a fear-
   ful dream!—   [all true?
What thinkest thou,—will our friends prove
  Rat. No doubt, my lord.
  K. Rich.   O Ratcliff, I fear, I fear,—
  Rat. Nay, good my lord, be not afraid of
   shadows.   [night
  K. Rich. By the apostle Paul, shadows to-
Have struck more terror to the soul of Rich-
   ard
Than can the substance of ten thousand
   soldiers
Armed in proof and led by shallow Rich-
   mond.
It is not yet near day. Come, go with me;
Under our tents I'll play the eaves-dropper,
To hear if any mean to shrink from me.
     [*Exeunt* K. RICH. *and* RATCLIFF.

RICHMOND *wakes. Enter* OXFORD *and others.*

Lords. Good-morrow, Richmond!
Richm. Cry mercy, lords and watchful
    gentlemen,
That you have ta'en a tardy sluggard here.
Lords. How have you slept, my lord?
Richm. The sweetest sleep and fairest-
    boding dreams
That ever enter'd in a drowsy head
Have I since your departure had, my lords.
Methought their souls whose bodies Rich-
    ard murder'd
Came to my tent, and cried on victory:
I promise you, my heart is very jocund
In the remembrance of so fair a dream.
How far into the morning is it, lords?
Lords. Upon the stroke of four.
Richm. Why, then, 'tis time to arm and
    give direction.—
         [*He advances to the* Troops.
More than I have said, loving countrymen,
The leisure and enforcement of the time
Forbids to dwell on: yet remember this,—
God and our good cause fight upon our side;
The prayers of holy saints and wronged
    souls,
Like high-rear'd bulwarks, stand before our
    faces;
Richard except, those whom we fight against
Had rather have us win than him they fol-
    low: [men,
For what is he they follow? truly, gentle-
A bloody tyrant and a homicide;   [lish'd;
One rais'd in blood, and one in blood estab-
One that made means to come by what he
    hath,
And slaughter'd those that were the means
    to help him;
A base foul stone, made precious by the foil
Of England's chair, where he is falsely set;
One that hath ever been God's enemy:
Then, if you fight against God's enemy,
God will, in justice, ward you as his soldiers;
If you do sweat to put a tyrant down,
You sleep in peace, the tyrant being slain;
If you do fight against your country's foes,
Your country's fat shall pay your pains the
    hire;
If you do fight in safeguard of your wives,
Your wives shall welcome home the con-
    querors;
If you do free your children from the sword,
Your children's children quit it in your age.
Then, in the name of God and all these rights,
Advance your standards, draw your willing
    swords.
For me, the ransom of my bold attempt
Shall be this cold corpse on the earth's cold
    face;
But if I thrive, the gain of my attempt
The least of you shall share his part thereof.
Sound drums and trumpets boldly and
    cheerfully;

God and Saint George! Richmond and vic-
    tory!   [*Exeunt.*

Re-enter KING RICHARD, RATCLIFF,
    Attendants, *and* Forces.

K. Rich. What said Northumberland as
    touching Richmond?
Rat. That he was never trained up in
    arms.
K. Rich. He said the truth: and what said
    Surrey then?   [purpose.
Rat. He smil'd, and said, the better for our
K. Rich. He was in the right; and so, in-
    deed, it is.   [*Clock strikes.*
Tell the clock there.—Give me a calendar.—
Who saw the sun to-day?
Rat.   Not I, my lord.
K. Rich. Then he disdains to shine; for by
    the book
He should have brav'd the east an hour ago:
A black day will it be to somebody.—
Ratcliff,—
Rat. My lord?
K. Rich. The sun will not be seen to-day;
The sky doth frown and lower upon our
    army.
I would these dewy tears were from the
    ground.
Not shine to-day! Why, what is that to me
More than to Richmond? for the selfsame
    heaven
That frowns on me looks sadly upon him.

Enter NORFOLK.

Nor. Arm, arm, my lord; the foe vaunts in
    the field.   [my horse;—
K. Rich. Come, bustle, bustle; caparison
Call up Lord Stanley, bid him bring his
    power:
I will lead forth my soldiers to the plain,
And thus my battle shall be ordered:—
My forward shall be drawn out all in length,
Consisting equally of horse and foot;
Our archers shall be placed in the midst:
John Duke of Norfolk, Thomas Earl of Sur-
    rey,
Shall have the leading of this foot and
    horse.
They thus directed, we ourself will follow
In the main battle; whose puissance on ei-
    ther side
Shall be well winged with our chiefest horse.
This, and Saint .George to boot!—What
    think'st thou, Norfolk?
Nor. A good direction, warlike sover-
    eign.—
This found I on my tent this morning.
             [*Giving a scroll.*
K. Rich. [*Reads.*] *Jocky of Norfolk, be
    not too bold,
    For Dickon thy master is bought and
    sold.*
A thing devised by the enemy.—
Go, gentlemen, every man unto his charge:

Let not our babbling dreams affright our
    souls;
Conscience is but a word that cowards use,
Devis'd at first to keep the strong in awe:
Our strong arms be our conscience, swords
    our law.
March on, join bravely, let us to't pell-mell;
If not to heaven, then hand in hand to hell.—
What shall I say more than I have inferr'd?
Remember whom you are to cope withal;—
A sort of vagabonds, rascals, and runaways,
A scum of Bretagnes, and base lackey peas-
    ants,
Whom their o'er-cloyed country vomits forth
To desperate ventures and assur'd destruc-
    tion.
You sleeping safe, they bring you to unrest;
You having lands, and bless'd with beau-
    teous wives,
They would restrain the one, distain the
    other.
And who doth lead them but a paltry fellow,
Long kept in Bretagne at our mother's cost?
A milk sop, one that never in his life
Felt so much cold as over shoes in snow?
Let's whip these stragglers o'er the seas
    again;
Lash hence these over-weening rags of
    France,
These famish'd beggars, weary of their lives;
Who, but for dreaming on this fond exploit,
For want of means, poor rats, had hang'd
    themselves:
If we be conquer'd, let men conquer us,
And not these bastard Bretagnes; whom our
    fathers   [thump'd,
Have in their own land beaten, bobb'd, and
And, on record, left them the heirs of shame.
Shall these enjoy our lands? lie with our
    wives?
Ravish our daughters?—Hark! I hear their
    drum.   [Drum afar off.
Fight, gentlemen of England! fight, bold
    yeomen!
Draw, archers, draw your arrows to the
    head!
Spur your proud horses hard, and ride in
    blood;
Amaze the welkin with your broken staves!

      Enter a Messenger.

What says Lord Stanley? will he bring his
    power?
Mess. My lord, he doth deny to come.
K. Rich. Off with his son George's head!
Nor. My lord, the enemy is pass'd the
    marsh:
After the battle let George Stanley die.
  K. Rich. A thousand hearts are great
    within my bosom:
Advance our standards, set upon our foes;
Our ancient word of courage, fair Saint
    George,
Inspire us with the spleen of fiery dragons!

Upon them! Victory sits on our helms.
               [*Exeunt.*

SCENE IV.—*Another part of the Field.*
Alarum: excursions. Enter NORFOLK *and*
    Forces; *to him* CATESBY.

Cate. Rescue, my Lord of Norfolk, rescue,
    rescue!
The king enacts more wonders than a man,
Daring an opposite to every danger:
His horse is slain, and all on foot he fights,
Seeking for Richmond in the throat of death.
Rescue, fair lord, or else the day is lost!

    Alarum. Enter KING RICHARD.

K. Rich. A horse! a horse! my kingdom
    for a horse!
Cate. Withdraw, my lord; I'll help you to
    a horse.
K. Rich. Slave, I have set my life upon a
    cast,
And I will stand the hazard of the die:
I think there be six Richmonds in the field;
Five have I slain to-day instead of him.—
A horse! a horse! my kingdom for a horse!
               [*Exeunt.*

    SCENE V.—*Another part of the Field.*
Alarums. Enter, from opposite sides, KING
    RICHARD *and* RICHMOND; *and exeunt
    fighting. Retreat, and flourish. Then re-
    enter* RICHMOND, *with* STANLEY *bearing
    the crown, and divers other* Lords *and*
    Forces.

Richm. God and your arms be prais'd,
    victorious friends;
The day is ours, the bloody dog is dead.
  Stan. Courageous Richmond, well hast
    thou acquit thee!
Lo, here, this long-usurped royalty
From the dead temples of this bloody wretch
Have I pluck'd off, to grace thy brows with-
    al:
Wear it, enjoy it, and make much of it.
  Richm. Great God of heaven, say Amen
    to all!—
But, tell me, is young George Stanley living?
  Stan. He is, my lord, and safe in Leicester
    town,   [draw us.
Whither, if it please you, we may now with-
  Richm. What men of name are slain on
    either side?
  Stan. John Duke of Norfolk, Walter Lord
    Ferrers,   [Brandon.
Sir Robert Brakenbury, and Sir William
  Richm. Inter their bodies as becomes their
    births:
Proclaim a pardon to the soldiers fled
That in submission will return to us:
And then, as we have ta'en the sacrament,
We will unite the white rose and the red:—
Smile heaven upon this fair conjunction,
That long hath frown'd upon their enmity!
What traitor hears me, and says not Amen?

England hath long been mad, and scarr'd
    herself;
The brother blindly shed the brother's blood,
The father rashly slaughter'd his own son,
The son, compell'd, been butcher to the sire:
All this divided York and Lancaster,
Divided in their dire division,—
O, now let Richmond and Elizabeth,
The true succeeders of each royal house,
By God's fair ordinance conjoin together!
And let their heirs,—God, if thy will be so,—
Enrich the time to come with smooth'd-
    fac'd peace,
With smiling plenty, and fair prosperous
    days!
Abate the edge of traitors, gracious Lord,
That would reduce these bloody days again,
And make poor England weep in streams of
    blood!
Let them not live to taste this land's increase
That would with treason wound this fair
    land's peace!
Now civil wounds are stopp'd, peace lives
    again:
That she may long live here, God say Amen!
                [*Exeunt.*

HENRY THE EIGHTH

Act III. Sc. 2.

KING HENRY VIII.

DRAMATIS PERSONÆ

KING HENRY THE EIGHTH.
CARDINAL WOLSEY.
CARDINAL CAMPEIUS.
CAPUCIUS, *Ambas. from the Emperor* CHARLES V.
CRANMER, *Archbishop of Canterbury.*
DUKE OF NORFOLK.
DUKE OF BUCKINGHAM.
DUKE OF SUFFOLK.
EARL OF SURREY.
Lord Chamberlain. Lord Chancellor.
GARDINER, *Bishop of Winchester.*
BISHOP OF LINCOLN.
LORD ABERGAVENNY.
LORD SANDS.
SIR HENRY GUILDFORD.
SIR THOMAS LOVELL.
SIR ANTHONY DENNY.
SIR NICHOLAS VAUX.
Secretaries *to* WOLSEY.
CROMWELL, *Servant to* WOLSEY.

GRIFFITH, *Gent.-Usher to* QUEEN KATHARINE.
Three Gentlemen.
DR. BUTTS, *Physician to the* KING.
Garter King-at-Arms.
Surveyor *to the* DUKE OF BUCKINGHAM.
BRANDON, *and a* Sergeant-at-Arms.
Doorkeeper of the Council Chamber.
Porter, *and his* Man.
Page *to* GARDINER. A Crier.

QUEEN KATHARINE, *Wife to* KING HENRY, *afterwards divorced.*
ANNE BULLEN, *her Maid of Honour, afterwards Queen.*
An Old Lady, *Friend to* ANNE BULLEN.
PATIENCE, *Woman to* QUEEN KATHARINE.
Several Lords and Ladies *in the Dumb Shows;* Women *attending upon the* QUEEN; Scribes, Officers, Guards, *and other* Attendants; Spirits.

SCENE,—*Chiefly in* LONDON *and* WESTMINSTER; *once at* KIMBOLTON.

PROLOGUE.

I come no more to make you laugh: things now
That bear a weighty and a serious brow,
Sad, high, and working, full of state and woe,
Such noble scenes as draw the eye to flow,
We now present. Those that can pity, here
May, if they think it well, let fall a tear;
The subject will deserve it. Such as give
Their money out of hope they may believe,
May here find truth too. Those that come to see
Only a show or two, and so agree
The play may pass, if they be still and willing,
I'll undertake may see away their shilling
Richly in two short hours. Only they
That come to hear a merry bawdy play,
A noise of targets, or to see a fellow
In a long motley coat guarded with yellow,
Will be deceiv'd; for, gentle hearers, know,
To rank our chosen truth with such a show
As fool and fight is, beside forfeiting
Our own brains, and the opinion that we bring,
To make that only true we now intend,
Will leave us never an understanding friend.
Therefore, for goodness' sake, and as you are known

The first and happiest hearers of the town,
Be sad, as we would make ye: think ye see
The very persons of our noble story
As they were living; think you see them great,
And follow'd with the general throng and sweat
Of thousand friends; then, in a moment, see
How soon this mightiness meets misery:
And if you can be merry then I'll say
A man may weep upon his wedding-day.

ACT I.

SCENE I.—LONDON. *An Ante-chamber in the Palace.*

Enter the DUKE OF NORFOLK *at one door; at the other, the* DUKE OF BUCKINGHAM *and the* LORD ABERGAVENNY.

Buck. Good-morrow, and well met. How have you done
Since last we saw in France?
Nor.　　　　　I thank your grace,
Healthful; and ever since a fresh admirer
Of what I saw there.
Buck.　　　　　An untimely ague
Stay'd me a prisoner in my chamber, when
Those suns of glory, those two lights of men,
Met in the vale of Andren.
Nor.　　　　　'Twixt Guynes and Arde:

I was then present, saw them salute on
    horseback;   [clung
Beheld them, when they lighted, how they
In their embracement, as they grew together;
Which had they, what four thron'd ones
    could have weigh'd
Such a compounded one?
    Buck.   All the whole time
I was my chamber's prisoner.
    Nor.   Then you lost
The view of earthly glory: men might say,
Till this time pomp was single, but now mar-
    ried
To one above itself. Each following day
Became the next day's master, till the last
Made former wonders it's: to-day the
    French,
All clinquant, all in gold, like heathen gods,
Shone down the English; and to-morrow
    they
Made Britain India: every man that stood
Show'd like a mine. Their dwarfish pages
    were
As cherubims, all gilt: the madams too,
Not us'd to toil, did almost sweat to bear
The pride upon them, that their very labour
Was to them as a painting: now this masque
Was cried incomparable; and the ensuing
    night
Made it a fool and beggar. The two kings,
Equal in lustre, were now best, now worst,
As presence did present them; him in eye,
Still him in praise: and, being present both,
'Twas said they saw but one; and no dis-
    cerner
Durst wag his tongue in censure. When these
    suns,—   [challeng'd
For so they phrase 'em,—by their heralds
The noble spirits to arms, they did perform
Beyond thought's compass: that former
    fabulous story,
Being now seen possible enough, got credit,
That Bevis was believ'd.
    Buck.   O, you go far.
    Nor. As I belong to worship, and affect
In honour honesty, the tract of everything
Would by a good discourser lose some life,
Which action's self was tongue to. All was
    royal;
To the disposing of it naught rebell'd,
Order gave each thing view; the office did
Distinctly his full function.
    Buck.   Who did guide—
I mean, who set the body and the limbs
Of this great sport together, as you guess?
    Nor. One, certes, that promises no element
In such a business.
    Buck.   I pray you, who, my lord?
    Nor. All this was order'd by the good dis-
    cretion
Of the right reverend Cardinal of York.
    Buck. The devil speed him! no man's pie is
    freed

From his ambitious finger. What had he
To do in these fierce vanities? I wonder
That such a keech can with his very bulk
Take up the rays o' the beneficial sun,
And keep it from the earth.
    Nor.   Surely, sir,
There's in him stuff that puts him to these
    ends;   [grace
For, being not propp'd by ancestry, whose
Chalks successors their way; nor call'd upon
For high feats done to the crown; neither
    allied
To eminent assistants; but, spider-like,
Out of his self-drawing web, he gives us note
The force of his own merit makes his way;
A gift that heaven gives for him, which buys
A place next to the king.
    Aber.   I cannot tell
What heaven hath given him,—let some
    graver eye
Pierce into that; but I can see his pride
Peep through each part of him: whence has
    he that?
If not from hell, the devil is a niggard;
Or has given all before, and he begins
A new hell in himself.
    Buck.   Why the devil,
Upon this French going-out, took he upon
    him,
Without the privity o' the king, to appoint
Who should attend on him? He makes up
    the file
Of all the gentry; for the most part such
To whom as great a charge as little honour
He meant to lay upon: and his own letter,
The honourable board of council out,
Must fetch him in the papers.
    Aber.   I do know
Kinsmen of mine, three at the least, that
    have
By this so sicken'd their estates that never
They shall abound as formerly.
    Buck.   O, many [on 'em
Have broke their backs with laying manors
For this great journey. What did this vanity
But minister communication of
A most poor issue?
    Nor.   Grievingly I think,
The peace between the French and us not
    values
The cost that did conclude it.
    Buck.   Every man,
After the hideous storm that follow'd, was
A thing inspir'd; and, not consulting, broke
Into a general prophecy,—That this tempest,
Dashing the garment of this peace, aboded
The sudden breach on 't.
    Nor.   Which is budded out;
For France hath flaw'd the league, and hath
    attach'd
Our merchants' goods at Bourdeaux.
    Aber.   Is it therefore
The ambassador is silenc'd?

Nor.　　　　　　　　　　Marry, is 't.

Aber. A proper title of a peace; and pur-
　chas'd

At a superfluous rate!

Buck.　　　　　Why, all this business

Our reverend cardinal carried.

Nor.　　　　　　　　Like it your grace,

The state takes notice of the private differ-
　ence

Betwixt you and the cardinal. I advise you,—

And take it from a heart that wishes to-
　wards you

Honour and plenteous safety,—that you read

The cardinal's malice and his potency

Together; to consider further, that

What his high hatred would effect wants not

A minister in his power. You know his na-
　ture,

That he's revengeful; and I know his sword

Hath a sharp edge: it's long, and, 't may be
　said,

It reaches far; and where 'twill not extend,

Thither he darts it. Bosom up my counsel,

You'll find it wholesome.—Lo, where comes
　that rock

That I advise you shunning.

*Enter CARDINAL WOLSEY, the purse borne be-
fore him, certain of the Guard, and two
Secretaries with papers. The CARDINAL in
his passage fixeth his eye on BUCKINGHAM,
and BUCKINGHAM on him, both full of disdain.*

Wol. The Duke of Buckingham's sur-
　veyor? ha?

Where's his examination?

1 Secr.　　　　　　Here, so please you.

Wol. Is he in person ready?

1 Secr.　　　　　Ay, please your grace.

Wol. Well, we shall then know more; and
　Buckingham

Shall lessen this big look.

　　　　　　　[*Exeunt WOLSEY and Train.*

Buck. This butcher's cur is venom-
　mouth'd, and I

Have not the power to muzzle him; there-
　fore best

Not wake him in his slumber. A beggar's
　book

Outworths a noble's blood.

Nor.　　　　What, are you chaf'd?

Ask God for temperance; that's the ap-
　pliance only

Which your disease requires.

Buck.　　　　　I read in 's looks

Matter against me; and his eye revil'd

Me, as his abject object: at this instant

He bores me with some trick: he's gone to
　the king;

I'll follow, and outstare him.

Nor.　　　　　　Stay, my lord,

And let your reason with your choler ques-
　tion

What 'tis you go about: to climb steep hills

Requires slow pace at first: anger is like

A full-hot horse, who being allow'd his way,

Self-mettle tires him. Not a man in Eng-
　land

Can advise me like you: be to yourself

As you would to your friend.

Buck.　　　　　　　I'll to the king;

And from a mouth of honour quite cry down

This Ipswich fellow's insolence; or proclaim

There's difference in no persons.

Nor.　　　　　　　　Be advis'd;

Heat not a furnace for your foe so hot

That it do singe yourself: we may outrun,

By violent swiftness, that which we run at,

And lose by over-running. Know you not,

The fire that mounts the liquor till 't run
　o'er,

In seeming to augment it wastes · it? Be
　advis'd:

I say again, there is no English soul

More stronger to direct you than yourself,

If with the sap of reason you would quench

Or but allay the fire of passion.

Buck.　　　　　　　　Sir,

I am thankful to you; and I'll go along

By your prescription: but this top-proud
　fellow,—

Whom from the flow of gall I name not, but

From sincere motions,—by intelligence,

And proofs as clear as founts in July, when

We see each grain of gravel, I do know

To be corrupt and treasonous.

Nor.　　　　　　Say not treasonous.

Buck. To the king I'll say't; and make my
　vouch as strong

As shore of rock. Attend. This holy fox,

Or wolf, or both,—for he is equal ravenous

As he is subtle, and as prone to mischief

As able to perform 't; his mind and place

Infecting one another, yea, reciprocally,—

Only to show his pomp as well in France

As here at home, suggests the king our master

To this last costly treaty, the interview,

That swallow'd so much treasure, and like a
　glass

Did break i' the rinsing.

Nor.　　　　Faith, and so it did.

Buck. Pray, give me favour, sir. This cun-
　ning cardinal

The articles o' the combination drew

As himself pleas'd; and they were ratified

As he cried, Thus let be: to as much end

As give a crutch to the dead: but our count-
　cardinal

Has done this, and 'tis well; for worthy
　Wolsey,

Who cannot err, he did it. Now this fol-
　lows,—

Which, as I take it, is a kind of puppy

To the old dam treason,—Charles the em-
　peror,

Under pretence to see the queen his aunt,—

For 'twas indeed his colour, but he came
To whisper Wolsey,—here makes visitation:
His fears were that the interview betwixt
England and France might, through their
    amity,
Breed him some prejudice; for from this
    league
Peep'd harms that menac'd him: he privily
Deals with our cardinal; and, as I trow,—
Which I do well; for I am sure the emperor
Paid ere he promis'd; whereby his suit was
    granted
Ere it was ask'd;—but when the way was
    made,
And pav'd with gold, the emperor thus de-
    sir'd,—
That he would please to alter the king's
    course,
And break the foresaid peace. Let the king
    know,—
As soon he shall by me,—that thus the
    cardinal
Does buy and sell his honour as he pleases,
And for his own advantage.
    Nor.   I am sorry
To hear this of him; and could wish he were
Something mistaken in 't.
    Buck.   No, not a syllable:
I do pronounce him in that very shape
He shall appear in proof.

Enter BRANDON, *a* Sergeant-at-Arms *before
    him, and two or three of the* Guard.

    Bran. Your office, sergeant; execute it.
    Serg.   Sir,
My lord the Duke of Buckingham, and Earl
Of Hereford, Stafford, and Northampton, I
Arrest thee of high treason, in the name
Of our most sovereign king.
    Buck.   Lo, you, my lord,
The net has fall'n upon me! I shall perish
Under device and practice.
    Bran.   I am sorry
To see you ta'en from liberty, to look on
The business present: 'tis his highness' pleas-
    ure
You shall to the Tower.
    Buck.   It will help me nothing
To plead mine innocence; for that dye is on
    me
Which makes my whit's part black. The will
    of heaven
Be done in this and all things!—I obey.—
O my Lord Aberga'ny, fare you well!
    Bran. Nay, he must bear you company.—
    The king   [*To* ABERGAVENNY.
Is pleas'd you shall to the Tower, till you
    know
How he determines further.
    Aber.   As the duke said,
The will of heaven be done, and the king's
    pleasure
By me obey'd!
    Bran.   Here is a warrant from

The king to attach Lord Montacute; and
    the bodies
Of the duke's confessor, John de la Car,
One Gilbert Peck, his chancellor,—
    Buck.   So, so;
These are the limbs o' the plot:—no more, I
    hope.
    Bran. A monk o' the Chartreux.
    Buck.   O, Nicholas Hopkins?
    Bran.   He.
    Buck. My surveyor is false; the o'er-great
    cardinal   [already:
Hath show'd him gold; my life is spann'd
I am the shadow of poor Buckingham,
Whose figure even this instant cloud puts on,
By darkening my clear sun.—My lord, fare-
    well.   [*Exeunt*

SCENE II.—LONDON. *The Council Chamber*

Cornets. Enter KING HENRY, CARDINAL
    WOLSEY, *the Lords of the Council,* SIR
    THOMAS LOVELL, *Officers, and Attendants.
    The* KING *enters, leaning on the* CARD-
    INAL'S *shoulder.*

    K. Hen. My life itself, and the best heart
    of it,   [level
Thanks you for this great care: I stood i' the
Of a full-charg'd confederacy, and give
    thanks
To you that choked it.—Let be call'd before
    us
That gentleman of Buckingham's: in person
I'll hear him his confessions justify;
And point by point the treasons of his master
He shall again relate.
    [*The* KING *takes his state. The* Lords *of
    the* Council *take their several places. The*
    CARDINAL *places himself under the*
    KING'S *feet, on his right side.*

A noise within, crying, "Room for the
    Queen!" *Enter* QUEEN KATHARINE, *ushered
    by the* DUKES OF NORFOLK *and* SUFFOLK:
    she kneels. The KING *riseth from his state,
    takes her up, kisses, and placeth her by
    him.*

    Q. Kath. Nay, we must longer kneel: I am
    a suitor.   [half your suit
    K. Hen. Arise, and take place by us:—
Never name to us; you have half our power:
The other moiety, ere you ask, is given;
Repeat your will, and take it.
    Q. Kath.   Thank your majesty.
That you would love yourself, and in that
    love
Not unconsider'd leave your honour, nor
The dignity of your office, is the point
Of my petition.
    K. Hen. Lady mine, proceed.
    Q. Kath. I am solicited, not by a few,
And those of true condition, that your sub-
    jects
Are in great grievance: there have been com-
    missions

Sent down among 'em which have flaw'd the
　　heart
Of all their loyalties:—wherein, although,
My good lord cardinal, they vent reproaches
Most bitterly on you, as putter-on
Of these exactions, yet the king our master,—
Whose honour Heaven shield from soil!—
　　even he escapes not
Language unmannerly, yea, such which
　　breaks
The sides of loyalty, and almost appears
In loud rebellion.

Nor　　　Not almost appears,—
It doth appear; for, upon these taxations,
The clothiers all, not able to maintain
The many to them 'longing, have put off
The spinsters, carders, fullers, weavers, who,
Unfit for other life, compell'd by hunger
And lack of other means, in desperate man-
　　ner
Daring the event to the teeth, are all in up-
　　roar,
And danger serves among them.

K. Hen.　　　　　　　Taxation!
Wherein? and what taxation?—My lord
　　cardinal,
You that are blam'd for it alike with us,
Know you of this taxation?

Wol.　　　　　Please you, sir,
I know but of a single part, in aught
Pertains to the state; and front but in that
　　file
Where others tell steps with me.

Q. Kath.　　　　No, my lord,
You know no more than others; but you
　　frame
Things that are known alike; which are not
　　wholesome　　　　　　[yet must
To those which would not know them, and
Perforce be their acquaintance. These ex-
　　actions,
Whereof my sovereign would have note, they
　　are
Most pestilent to the hearing; and to bear
　　'em
The back is sacrifice to the load. They say
They are devis'd by you; or else you suffer
Too hard an exclamation.

K. Hen.　　　　　Still exaction!
The nature of it? in what kind, let's know,
Is this exaction?

Q. Kath.　　I am much too venturous
In tempting of your patience; but am bold-
　　en'd
Under your promis'd pardon. The subjects'
　　grief
Comes through commissions, which compel
　　from each
The sixth part of his substance, to be levied
Without delay; and the pretence for this
Is nam'd your wars in France: this makes
　　bold mouths;
Tongues spit their duties out, and cold hearts
　　freeze

Allegiance in them; their curses now
Live where their prayers did: and it's come
　　to pass
This tractable obedience is a slave
To each incensed will. I would your highness
Would give it quick consideration, for
There is no primer business.

K. Hen.　　　　　　By my life,
This is against our pleasure.

Wol.　　　　　And for me,
I have no further gone in this than by
A single voice; and that not pass'd me but
By learned approbation of the judges. If I
　　am
Traduc'd by ignorant tongues, which neither
　　know
My faculties nor person, yet will be
The chronicles of my doing,—let me say
'Tis but the fate of place, and the rough
　　brake
That virtue must go through. We must not
　　stint
Our necessary actions, in the fear
To cope malicious censurers; which ever,
As ravenous fishes, do a vessel follow
That is new-trimm'd, but benefit no further
Than vainly longing. What we oft do best,
By sick interpreters, once weak ones, is
Not ours, or not allow'd; what worst, as oft
Hitting a grosser quality, is cried up
For our best act. If we shall stand still,
In fear our motion will be mock'd or carp'd
　　at,
We should take root here where we sit, or sit
State-statutes only.

K. Hen.　　　Things done well
And with a care exempt themselves from
　　fear;
Things done without example, in their issue
Are to be fear'd. Have you a precedent
Of this commission? I believe, not any.
We must not rend our subjects from our laws,
And stick them in our will. Sixth part of
　　each?
A trembling contribution! Why, we take
From every tree lop, bark, and part o' the
　　timber;
And, though we leave it with a root, thus
　　hack'd,
The air will drink the sap. To every county
Where this is question'd send our letters, with
Free pardon to each man that has denied
The force of this commission: pray, look to't;
I put it to your care.

Wol.　　　　A word with you.
　　　　　　　　　　[*To the* Secretary.
Let there be letters writ to every shire,
Of the king's grace and pardon. The griev'd
　　commons
Hardly conceive of me; let it be nois'd
That through our intercession this revoke-
　　ment
And pardon comes: I shall anon advise you
Further in the proceeding.　[*Exit* Secretary.

Enter Surveyor.

Q. Kath. I am sorry that the Duke of Buckingham
Is run in your displeasure.

K. Hen.   It grieves many:
The gentleman is learn'd, and a most rare speaker;
To nature none more bound; his training such
That he may furnish and instruct great teachers,
And never seek for aid out of himself. Yet see,
When these so noble benefits shall prove
Not well dispos'd, the mind growing once corrupt,
They turn to vicious forms, ten times more ugly
Then ever they were fair. This man so complete,   [we,
Who was enroll'd 'mongst wonders, and when
Almost with ravish'd list'ning, could not find
His hour of speech a minute; he, my lady,
Hath into monstrous habits put the graces
That once were his, and is become as black
As if besmear'd in hell. Sit by us; you shall hear—
This was his gentleman in trust,—of him
Things to strike honour sad.—Bid him recount
The fore-recited practices; whereof
We cannot feel too little, hear too much.

Wol. Stand forth, and with bold spirit relate what you,
Most like a careful subject, have collected
Out of the Duke of Buckingham.

K. Hen.   Speak freely.

Surv. First, it was usual with him, every day
It would infect his speech,—that if the king
Should without issue die, he'll carry it so
To make the sceptre his: these very words
I have heard him utter to his son-in-law,
Lord Aberga'ny; to whom by oath he menac'd
Revenge upon the cardinal.

Wol.   Please your highness, note
This dangerous conception in this point.
Not friended by his wish, to your high person
His will is most malignant; and it stretches
Beyond you to your friends.

Q. Kath.   My learn'd lord cardinal,
Deliver all with charity.

K. Hen.   Speak on:
How grounded he his title to the crown
Upon our fail? to this point hast thou heard him
At any time speak aught?

Surv.   He was brought to this
By a vain prophecy of Nicholas Hopkins.

K. Hen. What was that Hopkins?

Surv.   Sir, a Chartreux friar,
His confessor; who fed him every minute
With words of sovereignty.

K. Hen.   How know'st thou this?

Surv. Not long before your highness sped to France,
The Duke being at the Rose, within the parish
Saint Lawrence Poultney, did of me demand
What was the speech among the Londoners
Concerning the French journey: I replied,
Men fear'd the French would prove perfidious,
To the king's danger. Presently the duke
Said, 'twas the fear, indeed; and that he doubted
'Twould prove the verity of certain words
Spoke by a holy monk; *That oft,* says he,
*Hath sent to me, wishing me to permit
John de la Car, my chaplain, a choice hour
To hear from him a matter of some moment:
Whom after under the confession's seal
He solemnly had sworn, that what he spoke
My chaplain to no creature living but
To me should utter, with demure confidence
This pausingly ensu'd,—Neither the king nor's heirs,
Tell you the duke, shall prosper: bid him strive
To gain the love o' the commonalty: the duke
Shall govern England.*

Q. Kath.   If I know you well,
You were the duke's surveyor, and lost your office
On the complaint o' the tenants: take good heed
You charge not in your spleen a noble person,
And spoil your nobler soul: I say, take heed;
Yes, heartily beseech you.

K. Hen.   Let him on:—
Go forward.

Surv. On my soul, I'll speak but truth.
I told my lord the duke, by the devil's illusions
The monk might be deceiv'd; and that 'twas dangerous for him
To ruminate on this so far, until
It forg'd him some design, which, being believ'd,
It was much like to do: he answer'd, *Tush,
It can do me no damage;* adding further,
That, had the king in his last sickness fail'd,
The cardinal's and Sir Thomas Lovell's heads
Should have gone off.

K. Hen. Ha! what, so rank? Ah-ha!
There's mischief in this man:—Canst thou say further?

Surv. I can, my liege.

K. Hen.   Proceed.

Surv.   Being at Greenwich.
After your highness had reprov'd the duke
About Sir William Blomer,—

K. Hen.   I remember
Of such a time:—being my sworn servant,
The duke retain'd him his.—But on; what hence?

Surv. If, quoth he, *I for this had been committed,*

As, to the Tower, I thought,—I would have play'd
The part my father meant to act upon
The usurper Richard; who, being at Salisbury,
Made suit to come in's presence; which, if granted,
As he made semblance of his duty, would
Have put his knife into him.

K. Hen.   A giant traitor!

Wol. Now, madam, may his highness live in freedom,
And this man out of prison?

Q. Kath.   God mend all!

K. Hen. There's something more would out of thee; what say'st?

Surv. After *the duke his father*, with *the knife*,   [*dagger*,
He stretch'd him, and, with one hand on his
Another spread on's breast, mounting his eyes,
He did discharge a horrible oath; whose tenor
Was, were he evil us'd, he would out-go
His father by as much as a performance
Does an irresolute purpose.

K. Hen.   There's his period,
To sheath his knife in us. He is attach'd;
Call him to present trial: if he may
Find mercy in the law, 'tis his; if none,
Let him not seek't of us: by day and night,
He is a daring traitor to the height. [*Exeunt.*

SCENE III.—LONDON. *A Room in the Palace.*

Enter the Lord Chamberlain *and* LORD SANDS.

Cham. Is't possible the spells of France should juggle
Men into such strange mysteries?

Sands.   New customs,
Though they be never so ridiculous,
Nay, let them be unmanly, yet are follow'd.

Cham. As far as I see, all the good our English
Have got by the late voyage is but merely
A fit or two o' the face; but they are shrewd ones;
For when they hold them, you would swear directly
Their very noses had been counsellors
To Pepin or Clotharius, they keep state so.

Sands. They have all new legs, and lame ones: one would take it,
That never saw 'em pace before, the spavin
Or springhalt reign'd among 'em.

Cham.   Death! my lord,
Their clothes are after such a pagan cut too,
That sure they have worn out Christendom.

Enter SIR THOMAS LOVELL.

                        How now?
What news, Sir Thomas Lovell?

Lov.   'Faith, my lord,
I hear of none, but the new proclamation
That's clapp'd upon the court-gate.

Cham.   What is't for?

Lov. The reformation of our travell'd gallants,
That fill the court with quarrels, talk, and tailors.

Cham. I am glad 'tis there: now I would pray our monsieurs
To think an English courtier may be wise,
And never see the Louvre.

Lov.   They must either—
For so run the conditions—leave those remnants
Of fool and feather that they got in France,
With all their honourable points of ignorance   [works;
Pertaining thereunto,—as fights and fireworks,
Abusing better men than they can be,
Out of a foreign wisdom,—renouncing clean
The faith they have in tennis, and tall stockings,
Short blister'd breeches, and those types of travel,
And understand again, like honest men;
Or pack to their old playfellows: there, I take it,
They may, *cum privilegio*, wear away
The lag end of their lewdness, and be laugh'd at.

Sands. 'Tis time to give 'em physic, their diseases
Are grown so catching.

Cham.   What a loss our ladies
Will have of these trim vanities!

Lov.   Ay, marry,
There will be woe indeed, lords: the sly whoresons
Have got a speeding trick to lay down ladies;
A French song and a fiddle has no fellow.

Sands. The devil fiddle 'em! I am glad they're going,—
For, sure, there's no converting of 'em:—now
An honest country lord, as I am, beaten
A long time out of play, may bring his plainsong,
And have an hour of hearing; and, by'r Lady,
Held current music too.

Cham.   Well said, Lord Sands;
Your colt's tooth is not cast yet.

Sands.   No, my lord;
Nor shall not, while I have a stump.

Cham.   Sir Thomas,
Whither were you a-going?

Lov.   To the cardinal's:
Your lordship is a guest too.

Cham.   O, 'tis true;
This night he makes a supper, and a great one,
To many lords and ladies; there will be
The beauty of this kingdom, I'll assure you.

Lov. That churchman bears a bounteous mind indeed,
A hand as fruitful as the land that feeds us;
His dews fall everywhere.

Cham.   No doubt he's noble;
He had a black mouth that said other of him.

Sands. He may, my lord,—has where-
with al; in him   [trine:
Sparing would show a worse sin than ill doc-
Men of his way should be most liberal;
They are set here for examples.
   Cham.   True, they are so;
But few now give so great ones. My barge
stays;   [Thomas,
Your lordship shall along.—Come, good Sir
We shall be late else; which I would not be,
For I was spoke to, with Sir Henry Guild-
ford,
This night to be comptrollers.
   Sands.   I am your lordship's.
              [*Exeunt.*

SCENE IV.—LONDON. *The Presence Chamber*
in York Place.

Hautboys. A small table under a state for the
CARDINAL, *a longer table for the guests.*
Enter, at one door, ANNE BULLEN, *and*
divers Lords, Ladies, *and* Gentlewomen, *as*
guests; at another door, enter SIR HENRY
GUILDFORD.

   Guild. Ladies, a general welcome from his
grace
Salutes ye all; this night he dedicates
To fair content and you: none here, he hopes,
In all this noble bevy, has brought with her
One care abroad; he would have all as merry
As, first, good company, good wine, good wel-
come   [tardy:
Can make good people.—O, my lord, you are

Enter Lord Chamberlain, LORD SANDS, *and*
SIR THOMAS LOVELL.

The very thought of this fair company
Clapp'd wings to me.
   Cham. You are young, Sir Henry Guild-
ford.
   Sands. Sir Thomas Lovell, had the cardinal
But half my lay-thoughts in him, some of
these
Should find a running banquet ere they
rested;
I think would better please 'em: by my life,
They are a sweet society of fair ones.
   Lov. O, that your lordship were but now
confessor
To one or two of these!
   Sands   I would I were;
They should find easy penance.
   Lov.   Faith, how easy?
   Sands. As easy as a down-bed would afford
it.
   Cham. Sweet ladies, will it please you sit?
Sir Harry,   [this:
Place you that side; I'll take the charge of
His grace is ent'ring.—Nay, you must not
freeze;   [weather:—
Two women plac'd together makes cold
My Lord Sands, you are one will keep 'em
waking;
Pray, sit between these ladies.

   Sands.   By my faith,
And thank your lordship.—By your leave,
sweet ladies:
    [*Seats himself between* ANNE BULLEN
          and another Lady.
If I chance to talk a little wild, forgive
me;
I had it from my father.
   Anne.   Was he mad, sir?
   Sands. O, very mad, exceeding mad, in love
too:
But he would bite none; just as I do now,—
He would kiss you twenty with a breath.
              [*Kisses her.*
   Cham.   Well said, my lord.—
So, now you're fairly seated.—Gentlemen,
The penance lies on you if these fair ladies
Pass away frowning.
   Sands.   For my little cure,
Let me alone.

   Hautboys. Enter CARDINAL WOLSEY,
     attended; and takes his state.

   Wol. Ye're welcome, my fair guests: that
noble lady
Or gentleman that is not freely merry
Is not my friend: this, to confirm my wel-
come;
And to you all, good health.   [*Drinks.*
   Sands.   Your grace is noble:—
Let me have such a bowl may hold my
thanks,
And save me so much talking.
   Wol.   My Lord Sands,
I am beholden to you: cheer your neigh-
bours.—
Ladies, you are not merry:—gentlemen,
Whose fault is this?
   Sands.   The red wine first must rise
In their fair cheeks, my lord; then we shall
have 'em
Talk us to silence.
   Anne.   You are a merry gamester,
My Lord Sands,
   Sands.   Yes, if I make my play.
Here's to your ladyship: and pledge it, ma-
dam,
For 'tis to such a thing,—
   Anne.   You cannot show me.
   Sands. I told your grace they would talk
anon.
    [*Drum and trumpets: Chambers*
        discharged within.
   Wol.   What's that?
   Cham. Look out there, some of ye.
            [*Exit* a Servant.
   Wol.   What warlike voice,
And to what end, is this?—Nay, ladies, fear
not;
By all the laws of war ye're privileg'd.

       Re-enter Servant.

   Cham. How now! what is 't?
   Serve.   A noble troop of strangers,—

For so they seem; they have left their barge,
　　　and landed;
And hither make, as great ambassadors
From foreign princes.
　Wol.　　　　　Good lord chamberlain,
Go, give 'em welcome, you can speak the
　　　French tongue;
And, pray receive 'em nobly, and conduct
　　　'em
Into our presence, where this heaven of
　　　beauty
Shall shine at full upon them.—Some attend
　　　him.
　　[*Exit* Chamberlain *attended. All arise,
　　　　and tables removed.*
You have now a broken banquet: but we'll
　　　mend it.
A good digestion to you all: and once more
I shower a welcome on you;—welcome all.

Hautboys. Enter the KING, *and others, as
　maskers, habited like shepherds, with*
　Torchbearers, *ushered by the* Lord Cham-
　berlain. *They pass directly before the* CAR-
　DINAL, *and gracefully salute him.*

A noble company! what are their pleasures?
　Cham.　Because they speak no English, thus
　　　they pray'd
To tell your grace,—that, having heard by
　　　fame
Of this so noble and so fair assembly
This night to meet here, they could do no less,
Out of the great respect they bear to beauty,
But leave their flocks; and, under your fair
　　　conduct,
Crave leave to view these ladies, and entreat
An hour of revels with 'em.
　Wol.　　　　　Say, lord chamberlain,
They have done my poor house grace; for
　　　which I pray 'em　　　[pleasures.
A thousand thanks, and pray 'em take their
　　[*Ladies chosen for the dance. The* KING
　　　　chooses ANNE BULLEN.
　K. Hen.　The fairest hand I ever touch'd!
　　　　O beauty,
Till now I never knew thee! [*Music. Dance.*
　Wol.　My lord,—
　Cham.　　　　Your grace?
　Wol.　Pray tell them thus much from me:—
There should be one amongst them, by his
　　　person,
More worthy this place than myself; to
　　　whom,
If I but knew him, with my love and duty
I would surrender it.
　Cham.　　　I will, my lord.
　　　　[*Goes to the Maskers, and returns.*
　Wol.　What say they?
　Cham.　　　Such a one, they all confess,
There is indeed; which they would have your
　　　grace
Find out, and he will take it.
　Wol.　　　　Let me see, then.—
　　　　　　[*Comes from his state.*

By all your good leaves, gentlemen;—here I'll
　　　make
My royal choice.
　K. Hen.　　Ye have found him, cardinal:
　　　　　　　　[*Unmasking.*
You hold a fair assembly; you do well, lord:
You are a churchman, or I'll tell you, car-
　　　dinal,
I should judge now unhappily.
　Wol.　　　　　　I am glad
Your grace is grown so pleasant.
　K. Hen.　　　My lord chamberlain,
Pr'ythee, come hither: what fair lady's that?
　Cham.　An't please your grace, Sir Thomas
　　　Bullen's daughter,—　　　[women.
The Viscount Rochford,—one of her highness'
　K. Hen.　By heaven, she is a dainty one.—
　　　Sweetheart,
I were unmannerly to take you out,
And not to kiss you.—A health, gentlemen!
Let it go round.
　Wol.　Sir Thomas Lovell, is the banquet
　　　ready
I' the privy chamber?
　Lov.　　　　Yes, my lord.
　Wol.　　　　　　Your grace,
I fear, with dancing is a little heated.
　K. Hen.　I fear, too much.
　Wol.　　　There's fresher air, my lord,
In the next chamber.　　　[sweet partner,
　K. Hen.　Lead in your ladies, every one:—
I must not yet forsake you:—let's be
　　　merry:—
Good my lord cardinal, I have half a dozen
　　　healths
To drink to these fair ladies, and a measure
To lead 'em once again; and then let's dream
Who's best in favour.—Let the music knock
　　　it.　　　　[*Exeunt, with trumpets.*

ACT II.

SCENE I.—LONDON. *A Street.*

Enter two Gentlemen, *meeting.*

　1 *Gent.*　Whither away so fast?
　2 *Gent.*　　　　O, God save ye!
E'en to the hall, to hear what shall become
Of the great Duke of Buckingham.
　1 *Gent.*　　　　I'll save you
That labour, sir. All's now done, but the
　　　ceremony
Of bringing back the prisoner.
　2 *Gent.*　　　Where you there?
　1 *Gent.*　Yes, indeed, was I.
　2 *Gent.*　Pray, speak what has happen'd.
　1 *Gent.*　You may guess quickly what.
　2 *Gent.*　　　Is he found guilty?
　1 *Gent.*　Yes, truly is he, and condemn'd
　　　upon't.
　2 *Gent.*　I am sorry for't.
　1 *Gent.*　　　So are a number more.
　2 *Gent.*　But pray, how pass'd it?　[duke
　1 *Gent.*　I'll tell you in a little. The great
Came to the bar; where to his accusations
He pleaded still not guilty, and alleg'd

Many sharp reasons to defeat the law.
The king's attorney, on the contrary,
Urg'd on the examinations proofs, confessions
Of divers witnesses; which the duke desir'd
To have brought, *vivâ voce*, to his face:
At which appear'd against him his surveyor;
Sir Gilbert Peck, his chancellor; and John
    Car,
Confessor to him; with that devil-monk,
Hopkins, that made this mischief.

  2 Gent.   That was he
That fed him with his prophecies?

  1 Gent.   The same.
All these accus'd him strongly; which he fain
Would have flung from him, but, indeed, he
    could not:
And so his peers, upon this evidence,
Have found him guilty of high treason. Much
He spoke, and learnedly, for life; but all
Was either pitied in him or forgotten.

  2 Gent. After all this, how did he bear
    himself?

  1 Gent. When he was brought again to the
    bar to hear   [stirr'd
His knell rung out, his judgment,—he was
With such an agony, he sweat extremely,
And something spoke in choler, ill, and hasty;
But he fell to himself again, and sweetly
In all the rest show'd a most noble patience.

  2 Gent. I do not think he fears death.

  1 Gent.   Sure, he does not,
He never was so womanish; the cause
He may a little grieve at.

  2 Gent.   Certainly
The cardinal is the end of this.

  1 Gent.   'Tis likely,
By all conjectures: first, Kildare's attainder,
Then deputy of Ireland; who remov'd,
Earl Surrey was sent thither, and in haste too,
Lest he should help his father.

  2 Gent.   That trick of state
Was a deep envious one.

  1 Gent.   At his return
No doubt he will requite it. This is noted,
And generally,—whoever the king favours
The cardinal instantly will find employment,
And far enough from court too.

  2 Gent.   All the commons
Hate him perniciously, and, o' my conscience,
Wish him ten fathom deep: this duke as much
They love and dote on; call him bounteous
    Buckingham,
The mirror of all courtesy,—

  1 Gent.   Stay there, sir,
And see the noble ruin'd man you speak of.

Enter BUCKINGHAM *from his arraignment;
  Tip-staves before him; the axe with the
  edge towards him; halberds on each side:
  with him* SIR THOMAS LOVELL, SIR NICH-
OLAS VAUX, SIR WILLIAM SANDS, *and common people.*

  2 Gent. Let's stand close, and behold him.
  Buck.   All good people,

You that thus far have come to pity me,
Hear what I say, and then go home and lose
    me.
I have this day receiv'd a traitor's judgment,
And by that name must die: yet, heaven bear
    witness,
And if I have a conscience, let it sink me,
Even as the axe falls, if I be not faithful!
The law I bear no malice for my death;
'T has done, upon the premises, but justice:
But those that sought it I could wish more
    Christians:
Be what they will, I heartily forgive 'em:
Yet let 'em look they glory not in mischief,
Nor build their evils on the graves of great
    men;
For then my guiltless blood must cry against
    'em.
For further like in this world I ne'er hope,
Nor will I sue, although the king have mercies
More than I dare make faults. You few that
    lov'd me,
And dare be bold to weep for Buckingham,
His noble friends and fellows, whom to leave
Is only bitter to him, only dying,
Go with me, like good angels, to my end;
And as the long divorce of steel falls on me
Make of your prayers one sweet sacrifice,
And lift my soul to heaven.—Lead on, o'
    God's name.

  Lov. I do beseech your grace, for charity,
If ever any malice in your heart
Were hid against me, now to forgive me
    frankly.

  Buck. Sir Thomas Lovell, I as free forgive
    you
As I would be forgiven: I forgive all;
There cannot be those numberless offences
'Gainst me that I cannot take peace with: no
    black envy
Shall make my grave.—Commend me to his
    grace;
And if he speak of Buckingham, pray tell him
You met him half in heaven: my vows and
    prayers
Yet are the king's; and, till my soul forsake,
Shall cry for blessings on him: may he live
Longer than I have time to tell his years!
Ever belov'd and loving may his rule be!
And when old time shall lead him to his end,
Goodness and he fill up one monument!

  Lov. To the water side I must conduct
    your grace;
Then give my charge up to Sir Nicholas Vaux,
Who undertakes you to your end.

  Vaux.   Prepare there,
The duke is coming: see the barge be ready;
And fit it with such furniture as suits
The greatness of his person.

  Buck.   Nay, Sir Nicholas,
Let it alone; my state now will but mock me.
When I came hither I was lord high constable
And Duke of Buckingham; now, poor Ed-
    ward Bohun:

Yet I am richer than by base accusers,
That never knew what truth meant: I now
  seal it;
And with that blood will make 'em one day
  groan for't.
My noble father, Henry of Buckingham,
Who first rais'd head against usurping Rich-
  ard,
Flying for succour to his servant Banister,
Being distress'd, was by that wretch betray'd,
And without trial fell; God's peace be with
  him!
Henry the Seventh succeeding, truly pitying
My father's loss, like a most royal prince,
Restor'd me to my honours, and out of ruins
Made my name once more noble. Now his
  son,
Henry the Eighth, life, honour, name, and all
That made me happy, at one stroke has taken
For ever from the world. I had my trial,
And must needs say a noble one; which
  makes me
A little happier than my wretched father:
Yet thus far we are one in fortunes,—both
Fell by our servants, by those men we lov'd
  most;
A most unnatural and faithless service!
Heaven has an end in all: yet, you that hear
  me,
This from a dying man receive as certain:—
Where you are liberal of your loves and
  counsels,
Be sure you be not loose; for those you make
  friends   [ceive
And give your hearts to, when they once per-
The least rub in your fortunes, fall away
Like water from ye, never found again
But where they mean to sink ye. All good
  people,   [hour
Pray for me! I must now forsake ye: the last
Of my long weary life is come upon me.
Farewell: [sad,
And when you would say something that is
Speak how I fell.—I have done; and God for-
  give me!

       Exeunt BUCKINGHAM *and* Train.
  1 *Gent.* O, this is full of pity!—Sir, it calls,
I fear, too many curses on their heads
That were the authors.
  2 *Gent.*   If the duke be guiltless,
'Tis full of woe: yet I can give you inkling
Of an ensuing evil, if it fall,
Greater than this.
  1 *Gent.*   Good angels, keep it from us!
Where may it be? You do not doubt my
  faith, sir?   [quire
  2 *Gent.* This secret is so weighty, 'twill re-
A strong faith to conceal it.
  1 *Gent.*   Let me have it;
I do not talk much.
  2 *Gent.*   I am confident;
You shall, sir: did you not of late days hear
A buzzing of a separation
Between the king and Katharine?

  1 *Gent.*   Yes, but it held not:
For when the king once heard it, out of anger
He sent command to the lord mayor straight
To stop the rumour, and allay those tongues
That durst disperse it.
  2 *Gent.*   But that slander, sir,
Is found a truth now: for it grows again
Fresher than e'er it was; and held for certain
The king will venture at it. Either the cardi-
  nal,
Or some about him near, have, out of malice
To the good queen, possess'd him with a
  scruple
That will undo her: to confirm this too,
Cardinal Campeius is arriv'd, and lately;
As all think, for this business.
  1 *Gent.*   'Tis the cardinal;
And merely to revenge him on the emperor
For not bestowing on him, at his asking,
The archbishopric of Toledo, this is purpos'd.
  2 *Gent.* I think you have hit the mark: but
  is't not cruel   [cardinal
That she would feel the smart of this? The
Will have his will, and she must fall.
  1 *Gent.*   'Tis woeful.
We are too open here to argue this;
Let's think in private more.   [*Exeunt.*

SCENE II.—LONDON. *An Ante-chamber in the
  Palace.*

Enter the Lord Chamberlain *reading a letter.*

  Cham. My lord,—The horses your lordship sent for, with all the care I had, I saw
*well chosen, ridden, and furnished. They were
young and handsome, and of the best breed in
the north. When they were ready to set out
for London, a man of my lord cardinal's, by
commission and main power, took 'em from
me; with this reason,—His master would be
served before a subject, if not before the
king; which stopped our mouths, sir.*
I fear he will indeed: well, let him have them:
He will have all, I think.

Enter the DUKES OF NORFOLK *and* SUFFOLK.

  Nor. Well met, my Lord Chamberlain.
  Cham. Good-day to both your graces.
  Suf. How is the king employ'd?
  Cham.   I left him private,
Full of sad thoughts and troubles.
  Nor.   What's the cause?
  Cham. It seems the marriage with his
  brother's wife
Has crept too near his conscience.
  Suf.   No, his conscience
Has crept too near another lady.
  Nor.   'Tis so:
This is the cardinal's doing, the king-cardinal:
That blind priest, like the eldest son of for-
  tune,
Turns what he lists. The king will know
  him one day.
  Suf. Pray God he do! he'll never know
  himself else.

Nor. How holily he works in all his busi-
    ness!
And with what zeal! for, now he has crack'd
    the league   [great-nephew,
Between us and the emperor, the queen's
He dives into the king's soul, and there scat-
    ters
Dangers, doubts, wringing of the conscience,
Fears, and despairs,—and all these for his
    marriage:
And out of all these to restore the king,
He counsels a divorce; a loss of her
That, like a jewel, has hung twenty years
About his neck, yet never lost her lustre;
Of her that loves him with that excellence
That angels love good men with; even of her
That, when the greatest stroke of fortune
    falls,   [pious?
Will bless the king: and is not this course
Cham. Heaven keep me from such counsel!
    'Tis most true   [speaks 'em,
These news are everywhere; every tongue
And every true heart weeps for't: all that
    dare
Look into these affairs see this main end,—
The French king's sister. Heaven will one day
    open
The king's eyes, that so long have slept upon
This bold bad man.
Suf.   And free us from his slavery.
Nor. We had need pray,
And heartily, for our deliverance;
Or this imperious man will work us all
From princes into pages: all men's honours
Lie like one lump before him, to be fashion'd
Into what pitch he please.
Suf.   For me, my lords,
I love him not, nor fear him; there's my
    creed:
As I am made without him, so I'll stand,
If the king please; his curses and his blessings
Touch me alike, they are breath I not believe
    in
I knew him, and I know him; so I leave him
To him that made him proud, the pope.
Nor.   Let's in;
And with some other business put the king
From these sad thoughts that work too much
    upon him:—
My lord, you'll bear us company?
Cham.   Excuse me;
The king has sent me other-where: besides,
You'll find a most unfit time to disturb him:
Health to your lordships.
Nor.   Thanks, my good lord chamberlain.
         [*Exit* Lord Chamberlain.

NORFOLK *opens a folding door. The* KING *is
    discovered sitting, and reading pensively.*
Suf. How sad he looks! sure, he is much
    afflicted.
K. Hen. Who is there, ha?
Nor.   Pray God he be not angry.

K. Hen. Who's there, I say? How dare
    you thrust yourselves
Into my private meditations?
Who am I, ha?
Nor. A gracious king, that pardons all of-
    fences   [way
Malice ne'er meant: our breach of duty this
Is business of estate; in which we come
To know your royal pleasure.
K. Hen.   Ye are too bold;
Go to; I'll make you know your times of
    business:
Is this an hour for temporal affairs, ha?

         Enter WOLSEY *and* CAMPEIUS.

Who's there? my good lord cardinal?—O my
    Wolsey,
The quiet of my wounded conscience,
Thou art a cure fit for a king.—You're wel-
    come,   [*To* CAMPEIUS.
Most reverend learned sir, into our kingdom:
Use us and it.—My good lord, have great
    care
I be not found a talker.   [*To* WOLSEY.
Wol.   Sir, you cannot.
I would your grace would give us but an hour
Of private conference.
K. Hen.   We are busy; go.
         [*To* NORFOLK *and* SUFFOLK.
Nor. [*Aside to* SUF.] This priest has no
    pride in him!
Suf. [*Aside to* NOR.]   Not to speak of:
I would not be so sick though for his place:
But this cannot continue.
Nor. [*Aside to* SUF.] If it do,
I'll venture one have-at-him.
Suf. [*Aside to* NOR.]   I another.
         [*Exeunt* NOR. *and* SUF.
Wol. Your grace has given a precedent of
    wisdom
Above all princes, in committing freely
Your scruple to the voice of Christendom.
Who can be angry now? what envy reach
    you?   [her,
The Spaniard, tied by blood and favour to
Must now confess, if they have any goodness,
The trial just and noble. All the clerks,
I mean the learned ones, in Christian king-
    doms,
Have their free voices: Rome the nurse of
    judgment,
Invited by your noble self, hath sent
One general tongue unto us, this good man,
This just and learned priest, Cardinal Cam-
    peius,—   [ness.
Whom once more I present unto your high-
K. Hen. And once more in mine arms I bid
    him welcome,
And thank the holy conclave for their loves:
They have sent me such a man I would have
    wish'd for.   [strangers' loves,
Cam. Your grace must needs deserve all
You are so noble. To your highness' hand

I tender my commission;—by whose vir-
tue,—   [lord
The court of Rome commanding,—you, my
Cardinal of York, are join'd with me their
servant,
In the unpartial judging of this business.
    K. Hen. Two equal men. The queen shall
be acquainted   [Gardiner?
Forthwith for what you come.—Where's
    Wol. I know your majesty has always
lov'd her
So dear in heart, not to deny her that
A woman of less place might ask by law,
Scholars allow'd freely to argue for her.
    K. Hen. Ay, and the best she shall have;
and my favour   [Cardinal,
To him that does best: God forbid else.
Pr'ythee, call Gardiner to me, my new secre-
tary:
I find him a fit fellow.   [Exit WOLSEY.

        Re-enter WOLSEY with GARDINER.

    Wol. [Aside to GARD.] Give me your hand:
much joy and favour to you;
You are the king's now.
    Gard. [Aside to WOL.] But to be com-
manded   [rais'd me.
For ever by your grace, whose hand has
    K. Hen. Come hither, Gardiner.
                    [They converse apart.
    Cam. My Lord of York, was not one Doc-
tor Pace
In this man's place before him?
    Wol.   Yes, he was.
    Cam. Was he not held a learned man?
    Wol.   Yes, surely.
    Cam. Believe me, there's an ill opinion
spread, then,
Even of yourself, lord cardinal.
    Wol.   How! of me?
    Cam. They will not stick to say you envied
him;   [ous,
And fearing he would rise, he was so virtu-
Kept him a foreign man still; which so
griev'd him
That he ran mad and died.
    Wol.   Heaven's peace be with him!
That's Christian care enough: for living mur-
murers
There's places of rebuke. He was a fool;
For he would needs be virtuous: that good
fellow,
If I command him, follows my appointment:
I will have none so near else. Learn this,
brother,
We live not to be grip'd by meaner persons.
    K. Hen. Deliver this with modesty to the
queen.   [Exit GARDINER.
The most convenient place that I can think of
For such receipt of learning is Black-Friars;
There ye shall meet about this weighty busi-
ness:—
My Wolsey, see it furnish'd—O, my lord,

Would it not grieve an able man to leave
So sweet a bedfellow? But, conscience, con-
science,—
O, 'tis a tender place! and I must leave her.
                                    [Exeunt.

SCENE III.—LONDON. An Ante-chamber in the
        QUEEN'S Apartments.

        Enter ANNE BULLEN and an Old Lady.

    Anne. Not for that neither: here's the pang
that pinches:—   [and she
His highness having liv'd so long with her,
So good a lady that no tongue could ever
Pronounce dishonour of her,—by my life,
She never knew harm-doing;—O, now, after
So many courses of the sun enthron'd,
Still growing in a majesty and pomp,—the
which
To leave a thousand-fold more bitter than
'Tis sweet at first to acquire,—after this proc-
ess,
To give her the avaunt! it is a pity
Would move a monster.
    Old L.   Hearts of most hard temper
Melt and lament for her.
    Anne.   O, God's will! much better
She ne'er had known pomp: though it be
temporal,
Yet, if that quarrel, fortune, do divorce
It from the bearer, 'tis a sufferance panging
As soul and body's severing.
    Old L.   Alas, poor lady!
She's a stranger now again.
    Anne.   So much the more
Must pity drop upon her. Verily,
I swear, 'tis better to be lowly born,
And range with humble livers in content,
Than to be perk'd up in a glistering grief,
And wear a golden sorrow.
    Old L.   Our content
Is our best having
    Anne   By my troth and maidenhead,
I would not be a queen.
    Old L.   Beshrew me, I would,
And venture maidenhead for't; and so would
you,
For all this spice of your hypocrisy:
You, that have so fair parts of woman on
you,
Have too a woman's heart; which ever yet
Affected eminence, wealth, sovereignty;
Which, to say sooth, are blessings;—and
which gifts,—
Saving your mincing,—the capacity
Of your soft cheveril conscience would receive
If you might please to stretch it.
    Anne.   Nay, good troth,—
    Old L. Yes, troth and troth; you would
not be a queen?   [heaven.
    Anne. No, not for all the riches under
    Old L. 'Tis strange: a threepence bowed
would hire me,
Old as I am, to queen it: but, I pray you,

What think you of a duchess? have you limbs
To bear that load of title?

Anne.   No, in truth.

Old L. Then you are weakly made: pluck
off a little;
I would not be a young count in your way
For more than blushing comes to: if your
back
Cannot vouchsafe this burden, 'tis too weak
Ever to get a boy.

Anne.   How you do talk!
I swear again I would not be a queen
For all the world.

Old L.   In faith, for little England
You'd venture an emballing: I myself
Would for Carnarvonshire, although there
long'd   [comes here?
No more to the crown but that. Lo, who

Enter the Lord Chamberlain.

Cham. Good-morrow, ladies. What wer't
worth to know
The secret of your conference?

Anne.   My good lord,
Not your demand; it values not your asking:
Our mistress' sorrows we were pitying.

Cham. It was a gentle business,. and be-
coming
The action of good women: there is hope
All will be well.

Anne.   Now, I pray God, amen!

Cham. You bear a gentle mind, and heav-
enly blessings   [lady,
Follow such creatures. That you may, fair
Perceive I speak sincerely, and high note's
Ta'en of your many virtues, the king's ma-
jesty   [and
Commends his good opinion of you to you,
Does purpose honour to you no less flowing
Than Marchioness of Pembroke; to which
title
A thousand pound a year, annual support,
Out of his grace he adds.

Anne.   I do not know
What kind of my obedience I should tender;
More than my all is nothing: nor my prayers
Are not words duly hallow'd, nor my wishes
More worth than empty vanities; yet prayers
and wishes
Are all I can return. Beseech your lordship,
Vouchsafe to speak my thanks and my obedi-
ence,   [ness;
As from a blushing handmaid, to his high-
Whose health and royalty I pray for.

Cham.   Lady,
I shall not fail to approve the fair conceit
The king hath of you.—I have perus'd her
well;   [*Aside.*
Beauty and honour in her are so mingled
That they have caught the king: and who
knows yet
But from this lady may proceed a gem
To lighten all this isle?—I'll to the king
And say I spoke with you.

Anne.   My honour'd lord.
[*Exit* Lord Chamberlain.

Old L. Why, this it is; see, see!
I have been begging sixteen years in court,—
Am yet a courtier beggarly,—nor could
Come pat betwixt too early and too late
For any suit of pounds; and you, O fate!
A very fresh-fish here,—fie, fie, fie upon
This compell'd fortune!—have your mouth
filled up
Before you open it.

Anne.   This is strange to me.

Old L. How tastes it? is it bitter? forty
pence, no.
There was a lady once,—'tis an old story,—
That would not be a queen, that would she
not,   [it?
For all the mud in Egypt:—have you heard

Anne. Come, you are pleasant.

Old L.   With your theme I could
O'ermount the lark. The Marchioness of
Pembroke!
A thousand pounds a year for pure respect!
No other obligation! By my life,   [train
That promises more thousands: honour's
Is longer than his foreskirt. By this time
I know your back will bear a duchess:—say,
Are you not stronger than you were?

Anne.   Good lady,
Make yourself mirth with your particular
fancy,
And leave me out on't. Would I had no being,
If this salute my blood a jot: it faints me
To think what follows.
The queen is comfortless, and we forgetful
In our long absence: pray, do not deliver
What here you have heard to her.

Old L.   What do you think me?
[*Exeunt.*

SCENE IV.—LONDON. *A Hall in* BLACK-FRIARS.

Trumpet, sennet, and cornets. Enter two Ver-
gers, *with short silver wands; next them,*
two Scribes, *in the habits of doctors; after*
them, the ARCHBISHOP OF CANTERBURY
alone; after him, the BISHOPS OF LINCOLN,
ELY, ROCHESTER, *and* SAINT ASAPH; *next*
them, with some small distance, follows a
Gentleman *bearing the purse, with the great*
seal, and a Cardinal's hat; then two Priests,
bearing each a silver cross; then a Gentle-
man-usher *bareheaded, accompanied with a*
Sergeant-at-Arms *bearing a silver mace;*
then two Gentlemen *bearing two great sil-*
ver pillars; after them, side by side, the
two Cardinals, WOLSEY *and* CAMPEIUS;
two Noblemen *with the sword and mace.*
Then enter the KING *and* QUEEN *and their*
Trains. *The* KING *takes place under the*
cloth of state; the two Cardinals *sit under*
him as judges. The QUEEN *takes place at*
some distance from the KING. *The* Bishops
place themselves on each side the court, in
manner of a consistory; between them the

Scribes. *The* Lords *sit next the* Bishops. *The* Crier *and the rest of the* Attendants *stand in convenient order about the hall.*

Wol. Whilst our Commission from Rome is read,
Let silence be commanded.
　K. Hen.　　　　　　What's the need?
It hath already publicly been read,
And on all sides the authority allow'd;
You may, then, spare that time.
　Wol.　　　　　　Be't so.—Proceed.
　Scribe. Say, Henry King of England, come into the court.
　Crier. Henry King of England, &c.
　K. Hen. Here.
　Scribe. Say, Katharine Queen of England, come into the court.
　Crier. Katharine Queen of England, &c.
[*The* QUEEN *makes no answer, rises out of her chair, goes about the court, comes to the* KING, *and kneels at his feet; then speaks.*
　Q. Kath. Sir, I desire you do me right and justice;
And to bestow your pity on me: for
I am a most poor woman, and a stranger,
Born out of your dominions; having here
No judge indifferent, nor no more assurance
Of equal friendship and proceeding. Alas, sir,
In what have I offended you? what cause
Hath my behaviour given to your displeasure,
That thus you should proceed to put me off,
And take your good grace from me? Heaven witness,
I have been to you a true and humble wife,
At all times to your will conformable:
Even in fear to kindle your dislike,　[sorry
Yea, subject to your countenance,—glad or
As I saw it inclin'd. When was the hour
I ever contradicted your desire,　[friends
Or made it not mine too? Or which of your
Have I not strove to love, although I knew
He were mine enemy? what friend of mine
That had to him deriv'd your anger, did I
Continue in my liking? nay, gave notice
He was from thence discharg'd? Sir, call to mind
That I have been your wife, in this obedience,
Upward of twenty years, and have been blest
With many children by you: if, in the course
And process of this time, you can report,
And prove it too, against mine honour aught,
My bond to wedlock or my love and duty,
Against your sacred person, in God's name,
Turn me away; and let the foul'st contempt
Shut door upon me, and so give me up
To the sharp'st kind of justice. Please you, sir,
The king, your father, was reputed for
A prince most prudent, of an excellent　[nand,
And unmatch'd wit and judgment: Ferdi-
My father, King of Spain, was reckon'd one
The wisest prince that there had reign'd by many
A year before: it is not to be question'd

That they had gather'd a wise council to them
Of every realm, that did debate this business,
Who deem'd our marriage lawful: wherefore I humbly
Beseech you, sir, to spare me, till I may
Be by my friends in Spain advis'd; whose counsel
I will implore; if not, i' the name of God,
Your pleasure be fulfill'd!
　Wol.　　　　You have here, lady,—
And of your choice,—these reverend fathers; men
Of singular integrity and learning,
Yea, the elect o' the land, who are assembled
To plead your cause: it shall be therefore bootless
That longer you desire the court; as well
For your own quiet as to rectify
What is unsettled in the king.
　Cam.　　　　　　His grace
Hath spoken well and justly: therefore, madam,
It's fit this royal session do proceed;
And that, without delay, their arguments
Be now produc'd and heard.
　Q. Kath.　　　　　Lord cardinal,—
To you I speak.
　Wol.　　Your pleasure, madam?
　Q. Kath.　　　　　　　Sir,
I am about to weep; but, thinking that
We are a queen,—or long have dream'd so,—certain
The daughter of a king, my drops of tears
I'll turn to sparks of fire.
　Wol.　　　　　Be patient yet.
　Q. Kath. I will, when you are humble; nay, before,
Or God will punish me. I do believe,
Induc'd by potent circumstances, that
You are mine enemy; and make my challenge
You shall not be my judge: for it is you
Have blown this coal betwixt my lord and me,—　　　　　　　　　[again,
Which God's dew quench! Therefore I say
I utterly abhor, yea, from my soul　[more,
Refuse you for my judge; whom, yet once
I hold my most malicious foe, and think not
At all a friend to truth.
　Wol.　　　　I do profess
You speak not like yourself; who ever yet
Have stood to charity, and display'd the effects
Of disposition gentle, and of wisdom
O'ertopping woman's power. Madam, you do me wrong:
I have no spleen against you, nor injustice
For you or any: how far I have proceeded,
Or how far further shall, is warranted
By a commission from the consistory,
Yea, the whole consistory of Rome. You charge me
That I have blown this coal: I do deny it:
The king is present: if it be known to him
That I gainsay my deed, how may he wound,

And worthily, my falsehood! yea, as much
As you have done my truth. If he know
That I am free of your report, he knows
I am not of your wrong. Therefore in him
It lies to cure me: and the cure is, to   [before
Remove these thoughts from you: the which
His highness shall speak in, I do beseech [ing,
You, gracious madam, to unthink your speak-
And to say so no more.

    Q. Kath.   My lord, my lord,
I am a simple woman, much too weak
To oppose your cunning. You're meek and
        humble-mouth'd;   [ing,
You sign your place and calling, in full seem-
With meekness and humility; but your heart
Is crammed with arrogancy, spleen, and pride.
You have, by fortune and his highness' fa-
    vours,   [mounted
Gone slightly o'er low steps, and now are
Where powers are your retainers; and your
    words,
Domestics to you, serve your will as't please
Yourself pronounce their office. I must tell
    you,
You tender more your person's honour than
Your high profession spiritual: that again
I do refuse you for my judge; and here,
Before you all, appeal unto the pope,
To bring my whole cause 'fore his holiness,
And to be judg'd by him.
    [She curtsies to the KING, *and offers to*
                        depart.

    Cam.   The queen is obstinate,
Stubborn to justice, apt to accuse it, and
Disdainful to be tried by it: 'tis not well.
She's going away.

    K. Hen.   Call her again.

    Crier. Katherine Queen of England, come
into the court.

    Grif. Madam, you are call'd back.

    Q. Kath. What need you note it? pray
you, keep your way;   [help,
When you are call'd, return.—Now the Lord
They vex me past my patience! Pray you,
    pass on:
I will not tarry; no, nor ever more
Upon this business my appearance make
In any of their courts.
    [Exeunt QUEEN, GRIF., *and her other*
                    Attendants.

    K. Hen.   Go thy ways, Kate:
That man i' the world who shall report he has
A better wife, let him in naught be trusted
For speaking false in that: thou art, alone,—
If thy rare qualities, sweet gentleness,
Thy meekness saint-like, wife-like govern-
    ment—
Obeying in commanding—and thy parts
Sovereign and pious else, could speak thee
    out,—   [born;
The queen of earthly queens:—she's noble
And like her true nobility she has
Carried herself towards me.

    Wol.   Most gracious sir,
In humblest manner I require your highness
That it shall please you to declare, in hearing
Of all these ears,—for where I am robb'd and
    bound,
There must I be unloos'd; although not there
At once and fully satisfied,—whether ever I
Did broach this business to your highness; or
Laid any scruple in your way, which might
Induce you to the question on't? or ever
Have to you,—but with thanks to God for
    such   [might
A royal lady,—spake one the least word that
Be to the prejudice of her present state,
Or touch of her good person?

    K. Hen.   My lord cardinal,
I do excuse you; yea, upon mine honour,
I free you from't. You are not to be taught
That you have many enemies, that know not
Why they are so, but, like to village curs,
Bark when their fellows do: by some of these
The queen is put in anger. You are excus'd:
But will you be more justified? you ever
Have wish'd the sleeping of this business;
    never   [der'd, oft,
Desir'd it to be stirr'd; but oft have hin-
The passages made toward it:—on my hon-
    our,
I speak my good lord cardinal to this point,
And thus far clear him. Now, what mov'd me
    to't,   [tion:—
I will be bold with time and your atten-
Then mark the inducement. Thus it came;—
    give heed to't:—
My conscience first receiv'd a tenderness,
Scruple, and prick, on certain speeches ut-
    ter'd   [ambassador;
By the Bishop of Bayonne, then French
Who had been hither sent on the debating
A marriage 'twixt the Duke of Orleans and
Our daughter Mary: I' the progress of this
    business,
Ere a determinate resolution, he,—
I mean the bishop,—did require a respite;
Wherein he might the king his lord advertise
Whether our daughter were legitimate,
Respecting this our marriage with the do-
    wager,   [shook
Sometimes our brother's wife. This respite
The bosom of my conscience, enter'd me,
Yea, with a splitting power, and made to
    tremble   [way
The region of my breast; which forc'd such
That many maz'd considerings did throng,
And press'd in with this caution. First, me-
    thought
I stood not in the smile of heaven; who had
Commanded nature that my lady's womb,
If it conceiv'd a male child by me, should
Do no more offices of life to't than   [issue
The grave does to the dead; for her male
Or died where they were made, or shortly
    after

This world had air'd them: hence I took a
   thought
This was a judgment on me; that my king-
   dom,
Well worthy the best heir o' the world,
   should not
Be gladded in't by me: then follows that
I weigh'd the danger which my realms stood
   in
By this my issue's fail; and that gave to me
Many a groaning throe. Thus hulling in
The wild sea of my conscience, I did steer
Toward this remedy, whereupon we are
Now present here together; that's to say,
I meant to rectify my conscience,—which
I then did feel full sick, and yet not well,—
By all the reverend fathers of the land,
And doctors learn'd:—first, I began in private
With you, my Lord of Lincoln; you remem-
   ber
How under my oppression I did reek
When I first mov'd you.
   Lin.   Very well, my liege.
   K. Hen. I have spoke long: be pleas'd
   yourself to say
How far you satisfied me.
   Lin.   So please your highness,
The question did at first so stagger me,—
Bearing a state of mighty moment in 't,
And consequence of dread,—that I committed
The daring'st counsel which I had to doubt;
And did entreat your highness to this course
Which you are running here.
   K. Hen.   I then mov'd you,
My Lord of Canterbury; and got your leave
To make this present summons:—unsolicited
I left no reverend person in this court;
But by particular consent proceeded
Under your hands and seals: therefore, go on;
For no dislike i' the world against the person
Of the good queen, but the sharp thorny
   points
Of my alleged reasons, drive this forward:
Prove but our marriage lawful, by my life
And kingly dignity, we are contented
To wear our mortal state to come with her,
Katharine our queen, before the primest
   creature
That's paragon'd o' the world.
   Cam.   So pleasure your highness,
The queen being absent, 'tis a needful fitness
That we adjourn this court till furtherday:
Meanwhile must be an earnest motion
Made to the queen to call back her appeal
She intends unto his holiness.
               [*They rise to depart.*
   K. Hen.   I may perceive
These cardinals trifle with me: I abhor
This dilatory sloth and tricks of Rome
               [*Aside.*
My learn'd and well-belov'd servant, Cran-
   mer,
Pr'ythee, return! with thy approach, I know,

My comfort comes along. Break up the court:
I say, set on.
        [*Exeunt in manner as they entered.*

ACT III.

   Scene I.—London. *Palace at Bridewell.*
    A Room in the Queen's *Apartment.*
The Queen *and some of her* Women *at work.*

   Q. Kath. Take thy lute, wench: my soul
   grows sad with troubles;   [*working.*
Sing and disperse 'em if thou canst: leave

SONG.

Orpheus with his lute made trees,
  And the mountain-tops that freeze,
    Bow themselves, when he did sing:
To his music plants and flowers
Ever sprung; as sun and showers
    There had made a lasting spring.

Everything that heard him play,
Even the billows of the sea,
    Hung their heads and then lay by.
In sweet music is such art:
Killing care and grief of heart
    Fall asleep, or, hearing, die.

     Enter a Gentleman.

   Q. Kath. How now?   [great cardinals
   Gent. An't please your grace, the two
Wait in the presence.
   Q. Kath.   Would they speak with me?
   Gent. They will'd me say so, madam.
   Q. Kath.   Pray their graces
To come near. [*Exit* Gent.) What can be
   their business   [vour?
With me, a poor weak woman, fallen from fa-
I do not like their coming, now I think on't.
They should be good men; their affairs as
   righteous:
But all hoods make not monks.

    Enter Wolsey *and* Campeius.

   Wol.   Peace to your highness!
   Q. Kath. Your graces find me here part of
   a housewife;   [pen.
I would be all, against the worst may hap-
What are your pleasures with me, reverend
   lords?   [withdraw
   Wol. May it please you, noble madam, to
Into your private chamber, we shall give you
The full cause of our coming.
   Q. Kath.   Speak it here;
There's nothing I have done yet, o' my con-
   science,
Deserves a corner: would all other women
Could speak this with as free a soul as I do!
My lords, I care not,—so much I am happy
Above a number,—if my actions   ['em,
Were tried by every tongue, every eye saw
Envy and base opinion set against 'em,
I know my life so even. If your business
Seek me out, and that way I am wife in,
Out with it boldly: truth loves open dealing.

Wol. *Tanta est erga te mentis integritas,*
  regina serenissima,—
  Q. Kath. O, good my lord, no Latin;
I am not such a truant since my coming
As not to know the language I have lived in:
A strange tongue makes my cause more
  strange, suspicious;   [thank you,
Pray, speak in English: here are some will
If you speak truth, for their poor mistress'
  sake,—   [cardinal,
Believe me, she has had much wrong: lord
The willing'st sin I ever yet committed
May be absolv'd in English.
  Wol.   Noble lady,
I am sorry my integrity should breed,—
And service to his majesty and you,—
So deep suspicion, where all faith was meant.
We come not by the way of accusation
To taint that honour every good tongue
  blesses,
Nor to betray you any way to sorrow,—
You have too much, good lady; but to know
How you stand minded in the weighty dif-
  ference
Between the king and you; and to deliver,
Like free and honest men, our just opinions,
And comforts to your cause.
  Cam.   Most honour'd madam,
My Lord of York,—out of his noble nature,
Zeal and obedience he still bore your grace,—
Forgetting, like a good man, your late censure
Both of his truth and him,—which was too
  far,—
Offers, as I do, in a sign of peace,
His service and his counsel.
  Q. Kath.   To betray me. [*Aside.*
My lords, I thank you both for your good-
  wills;   [prove so!
Ye speak like honest men,—pray God ye
But how to make ye suddenly an answer,
In such a point of weight, so near mine
  honour,—   [wit,
More near my life, I fear,—with my weak
And to such men of gravity and learning,
In truth, I know not. I was set at work
Among my maids; full little, God knows,
  looking
Either for such men or such business.
For her sake that I have been,—for I feel
The last fit of my greatness,—good your
  graces,
Let me have time and counsel for my cause:
Alas, I am a woman, friendless, hopeless!
  Wol. Madam, you wrong the king's love
  with these fears:
Your hopes and friends are infinite.
  Q. Kath.   In England
But little for my profit: can you think, lords,
That any Englishman dare give me counsel?
Or be a known friend, 'gainst his highness'
  pleasure,—   [est,—
Though he be grown so desperate to be hon-
And live a subject? Nay, forsooth, my
  friends,

They that must weigh out my afflictions,
They that my trust must grow to, live not
  here:
They are, as all my other comforts, far hence,
In mine own country, lords.
  Cam.   I would your grace
Would leave your griefs, and take my counsel.
  Q. Kath. How, sir?
  Cam. Put your main cause into the king's
  protection;   [much
He's loving and most gracious: 'twill be
Both for your honour better and your cause;
For if the trial of the law o'ertake ye
You'll part away disgrac'd.
  Wol.   He tells you rightly.
  Q. Kath. Ye tell me what ye wish for both,
  —my ruin:
Is this your Christian counsel? out upon ye!
Heaven is above all yet; there sits a Judge
That no king can corrupt.
  Cam.   Your rage mistakes us.
  Q. Kath. The more shame for ye: holy
  men I thought ye,
Upon my soul, two reverend cardinal vir-
  tues
But cardinal sins and hollow hearts I fear ye:
Mend them, for shame, my lords. Is this your
  comfort?
The cordial that ye bring a wretched lady,—
A woman lost among ye, laugh'd at, scorn'd?
I will not wish ye half my miseries;
I have more charity: but say I warn'd ye;
Take heed, for heaven's sake, take heed, lest
  at once
The burden of my sorrows fall upon ye.
  Wal. Madam, this is a mere distraction;
You turn the good we offer into envy.
  Q. Kath. Ye turn me into nothing: woe
  upon ye,   [me,—
And all such false professors! would you have
If you have any justice, any pity,
If ye be anything but churchmen's habits,—
Put my sick cause into his hands that hates
  me?
Alas! has banish'd me his bed already,
His love too long ago! I am old, my lords,
And all the fellowship I hold now with him
Is only my obedience. What can happen
To me above this wretchedness? all your
  studies
Make me a curse like this.
  Cam.   Your fears are worse.
  Q. Kath. Have I liv'd thus long,—let me
  speak myself,   [one?
Since virtue finds no friends,—a wife, a true
A woman,—I dare say without vain-glory,—
Never yet branded with suspicion?
Have I with all my full affections
Still met the king? lov'd him next heaven?
  obey'd him?
Been, out of fondness, superstitious to him?
Almost forgot my prayers to content him?
And am I thus rewarded? 'tis not well, lords.
Bring me a constant woman to her husband,

One that ne'er dream'd a joy beyond his
  pleasure;
And to that woman, when she has done most,
Yet will I add an honour,—a great patience.
  Wol. Madam, you wander from the good
    we aim at.   [so guilty,
  Q. Kath. My lord, I dare not make myself
To give up willingly that noble title
Your master wed me to: nothing but death
Shall e'er divorce my dignities.
  Wol.   Pray, hear me.
  Q. Kath. Would I had never trod this Eng-
    lish earth,
Or felt the flatteries that grow upon it!
Ye have angels' faces, but heaven knows your
    hearts.
What will become of me now, wretched lady?
I am the most unhappy woman living.—
Alas, poor wenches, where are now your for-
    tunes?   [*To her* Women.
Shipwreck'd upon a kingdom, where no pity,
No friends, no hope; no kindred weep for
    me;
Almost no grave allow'd me:—like the lily,
That once was mistress of the field and flour-
    ish'd,
I'll hang my head and perish.
  Wol.   If your grace
Could but be brought to know our ends are
    honest,   [good lady,
You'd feel more comfort: why should we,
Upon what cause, wrong you? alas, our
    places,
The way of our profession is against it:
We are to cure such sorrows, not to sow 'em,
For goodness' sake, consider what you do;
How you may hurt yourself, ay, utterly
Grow from the king's acquaintance, by this
    carriage.
The hearts of princes kiss obedience,
So much they love it; but to stubborn spirits
They swell, and grow as terrible as storms.
I know you have a gentle-noble temper.
A soul as even as a calm: pray, think us
Those we profess, peace-makers, friends, and
    servants.   [your virtues
  Cam. Madam, you'll find it so. You wrong
With these weak women's fears: a noble
    spirit,
As yours was put into you, ever casts
Such doubts, as false coin, from it. The king
    loves you;
Beware you lose it not: for us, if you please
To trust us in your business, we are ready
To use our utmost studies in your service.
  Q. Kath. Do what ye will, my lords: and,
    pray, forgive me
If I have us'd myself unmannerly;
You know I am a woman, lacking wit
To make a seemly answer to such persons.
Pray, do my service to his majesty:
He has my heart yet; and shall have my
    prayers   [fathers,
While I shall have my life. Come, reverend

Bestow your counsels on me; she now begs
That little thought, when she set footing here,
She should have bought her dignities so dear.
                                  [*Exeunt.*

SCENE II.—LONDON. *Ante-chamber to the
    KING'S Apartment in the Palace.*

Enter the DUKE OF NORFOLK, *the* DUKE OF
    SUFFOLK, *the* EARL OF SURREY, *and the*
    Lord Chamberlain.

  Nor. If you will now unite in your com-
    plaints,   [dinal
And force them with a constancy, the car-
Cannot stand under them: if you omit
The offer of this time, I cannot promise
But that you shall sustain more new disgraces,
With these you bear already.
  Sur.   I am joyful
To meet the least occasion that may give me
Remembrance of my father-in-law, the duke,
To be reveng'd on him.
  Suf.   Which of the peers
Have uncontemn'd gone by him, or at least
Strangely neglected? when did he regard
The stamp of nobleness in any person
Out of himself?
  Cham. My lords, you speak your pleas-
    ures:
What he deserves of you and me I know;
What we can do to him,—though now the
    time   [not
Gives way to us,—I much fear. If you can-
Bar his access to the king, never attempt
Anything on him; for he hath a witchcraft
Over the king in's tongue.
  Nor.   O, fear him not;
His spell in that is out: the king hath found
Matter against him that for ever mars
The honey of his language. No, he's settled.
Not to come off, in his displeasure
  Sur.   Sir,
I should be glad to hear such news as this
Once every hour.
  Nor.   Believe it, this is true;
In the divorce his contrary proceedings
Are all unfolded; wherein he appears
As I would wish mine enemy.
  Sur.   How came
His practices to light?
  Suf.   Most strangely.
  Sur.   O, how, how?
  Suf. The cardinal's letters to the pope mis-
    carried,   [read
And came to the eye o' the king: wherein was
How that the cardinal did entreat his holiness
To stay the judgment o' the divorce; for if
It did take place, *I do,* quoth he, *perceive
My king is tangled in affection to
A creature of the queen's, Lady Anne Bullen.*
  Sur. Has the king this?
  Suf.   Believe it.
  Sur.   Will this work?
  Cham. The king in this perceives him how
    he coasts

And hedges his own way. But in this point
All his tricks founder, and he brings his
    physic
After his patient's death: the king already
Hath married the fair lady.
  Sur.   Would he had!
  Suf. May you be happy in your wish, my
    lord!
For, I profess, you have it.
  Sur.   Now, all my joy
Trace the conjunction!
  Suf.   My amen to't!
  Nor.   All men's!
  Sur. There's order given for her corona-
    tion:
Marry, this is yet but young, and may be left
To some ears unrecounted.—But, my lords,
She is a gallant creature, and complete
In mind and feature: I persuade me, from her
Will fall some blessing to this land, which
    shall
In it be memoriz'd.
  Sur.   But will the king
Digest this letter of the cardinal's?
The Lord forbid!
  Nor.   Marry, amen!
  Suf.   No, no;
There be more wasps that buzz about his nose
Will make this sting the sooner. Cardinal
    Campeius
Is stol'n away to Rome; hath ta'en no leave;
Has left the cause o' the king unhandled; and
Is posted, as the agent of our cardinal,
To second all his plot. I do assure you
The king cried Ha! at this.
  Cham.   Now, God incense him,
And let him cry Ha! louder!
  Nor.   But, my lord,
When returns Cranmer?
  Suf. He is return'd, in his opinions; which
Have satisfied the king for his divorce,
Together with all famous colleges
Almost in Christendom: shortly, I believe,
His second marriage shall be publish'd, and
Her coronation. Katharine no more
Shall be call'd queen, but princess dowager
And widow to Prince Arthur.
  Nor.   This same Cranmer's
A worthy fellow, and hath ta'en much pain
In the king's business.
  Suf.   He has; and we shall see him
For it an archbishop.
  Nor.   So I hear.
  Suf.   'Tis so.—
The cardinal!

Enter WOLSEY *and* CROMWELL.

  Nor.   Observe, observe, he's moody.
  Wol. The packet, Cromwell,
Gave't you the king?
  Crom. To his own hand, in's bedchamber.
  Wol. Look'd he o' the inside of the paper?
  Crom.   Presently
He did unseal them: and the first he view'd,

He did it with a serious mind; a heed
Was in his countenance. You he bade
Attend him here this morning.
  Wol.   Is he ready
To come abroad?
  Crom.   I think by this he is.
  Wol. Leave me awhile. [*Exit* CROMWELL.
It shall be to the Duchess of Alencon,
The French king's sister: he shall marry
    her.—   [him:
Anne Bullen! No; I'll no Anne Bullens for
There's more in't than fair visage.—Bullen!
No, we'll no Bullens.—Speedily I wish
To hear from Rome.—The Marchioness of
    Pembroke!
  Nor. He's discontented.
  Suf.   May be he hears the king
Does whet his anger to him.
  Sur.   Sharp enough,
Lord, for thy justice!   [knight's daughter,
  Wol. The late queen's gentlewoman, a
To be her mistress' mistress! the queen's
    queen!—   [it;
This candle burns not clear: 'tis I must snuff
Then out it goes.—What though I know her
    virtuous
And well deserving? yet I know her for
A spleeny Lutheran; and not wholesome to
Our cause, that she should lie i' the bosom of
Our hard-rul'd king. Again, there is sprung
    up
An heretic, an arch one, Cranmer; one
Hath crawl'd into the favour of the king,
And is his oracle.
  Nor.   He is vex'd at something.
  Sur. I would 'twere something that would
    fret the string,
The master-cord on's heart!
  Suf.   The king, the king!

Enter the KING, *reading a schedule, and*
    LOVELL.

  K. Hen. What piles of wealth hath he ac-
    cumulated   [the hour
To his own portion! and what expense by
Seems to flow from him! How, i' the name
    of thrift,
Does he rake this together?—Now, my lords,
Saw you the cardinal?
  Nor.   My lord, we have
Stood here observing him: some strange com-
    motion
Is in his brain: he bites his lip and starts;
Stops on a sudden, looks upon the ground,
Then lays his finger on his temple; straight
Springs out into fast gait; then stops again,
Strikes his breast hard; and anon he casts
His eye against the moon: in most strange
    postures
We have seen him set himself.
  K. Hen.   It may well be;
There is a mutiny in's mind. This morning
Papers of state he sent me to peruse,
As I requir'd: and wot you what I found

There,—on my conscience, put unwittingly?
Forsooth, an inventory, thus importing,—
The several parcels of his plate, his treasure,
Rich stuffs, and ornaments of household;
　　which
I find at such proud rate that it out-speaks
Possession of a subject.
　　Nor.　　　　　　It's heaven's will:
Some spirit put this paper in the packet
To bless your eye withal.
　　K. Hen.　　　　　　If we did think
His contemplation were above the earth,
And fix'd on spiritual object, he should still
Dwell in his musings: but I am afraid
His thinkings are below the moon, not worth
His serious considering.
　　[*He takes his seat and whispers* LOVELL,
　　　　who goes to WOLSEY.
　　Wol.　　　　　　Heaven forgive me!
Ever God bless your highness!
　　K. Hen.　　　　　　Good, my lord,
You are full of heavenly stuff, and bear the
　　inventory
Of your best graces in your mind; the which
You were now running o'er: you have scarce
　　time
To steal from spiritual leisure a brief span
To keep your earthly audit: sure, in that
I deem you an ill husband, and am glad
To have you therein my companion.
　　Wol.　　　　　　　　Sir,
For holy offices I have a time; a time
To think upon the part of business which
I bear i' the state; and nature does require
Her times of preservation, which perforce
I, her frail son, amongst my brethren mortal,
Must give my tendance to.
　　K. Hen.　　　　　You have said well.
　　Wol. And ever may your highness yoke to-
　　gether,
As I will lend you cause, my doing well
With my well saying!
　　K. Hen.　　　　'Tis well said again;
And 'tis a kind of good deed to say well:
And yet words are no deeds. My father lov'd
　　you:
He said he did; and with his deed did crown
His word upon you. Since I had my office
I have kept you next my heart; have not
　　alone　　　　　　　　　　　[home,
Employ'd you where high profits might come
But par'd my present havings to bestow
My bounties upon you.
　　Wol. What should this mean?　　[*Aside.*
　　Sur. The Lord increase this business!
　　　　　　　　　　[*Aside to others.*
　　K. Hen.　　　　Have I not made you
The prime man of the state? I pray you, tell
　　me　　　　　　　　　　　　[true:
If what I now pronounce you have found
And, if you may confess it, say withal
If you are bound to us or no. What say you?
　　Wol. My sovereign, I confess your royal
　　graces,

Shower'd on me daily, have been more than
　　could
My studied purposes requite; which went
Beyond all man's endeavours:—my endeav-
　　ours
Have ever come too short of my desires,
Yet fill'd with my abilities: mine own ends
Have been mine so that evermore they
　　pointed
To the good of your most sacred person and
The profit of the state. For your great graces
Heap'd upon me, poor undeserver, I
Can nothing render but allegiant thanks;
My prayers to heaven for you; my loyalty,
Which ever has and ever shall be growing,
Till death, that winter, kill it.
　　K. Hen.　　　　　Fairly answer'd;
A loyal and obedient subject is
Therein illustrated: the honour of it
Does pay the act of it: as, i' the contrary,
The foulness is the punishment. I presume
That, as my hand has open'd bounty to you,
My heart dropp'd love, my power rain'd
　　honour, more
On you than any; so your hand and heart,
Your brain, and every function of your
　　power,　　　　　　　　　　　[duty,
Should, notwithstanding that your bond of
As 'twere in love's particular, be more
To me, your friend, than any.
　　Wol.　　　　　　I do profess
That for your highness' good I ever labour'd
More than mine own; that am, have, and
　　will be,—　　　　　　　　　　[to you,
Though all the world should crack their duty
And throw it from their soul; though perils
　　did　　　　　　　　　　　　[and
Abound as thick as thought could make 'em,
Appear in forms more horrid.—yet my duty,
As doth a rock against the chiding flood,
Should the approach of this wild river break,
And stand unshaken yours.
　　K. Hen.　　　　　'Tis nobly spoken:
Take notice, lords, he has a loyal breast,
For you have seen him open't.—Read o'er
　　this;　　　　　　　[*Giving him papers.*
And after, this: and then to breakfast with
What appetite you have.
　　[*Exit, frowning upon* CARDINAL WOLSEY:
　　　the Nobles *throng after him, smiling
　　　and whispering.*
　　Wol.　　　　　What should this mean?
What sudden anger's this? how have I reap'd
　　it?
He parted frowning from me, as if ruin
Leap'd from his eyes: so looks the chafed lion
Upon the daring huntsman that has gall'd
　　him;
Then makes him nothing. I must read this
　　paper;
I fear, the story of his anger.—'Tis so;
This paper has undone me:—'tis the account
Of all that world of wealth I have drawn to-
　　gether

For mine own ends; indeed, to gain the pope-
dom,
And fee my friends in Rome. O negligence,
Fit for a fool to fall by! What cross devil
Made me put this main secret in the packet
I sent the king? Is there no way to cure this?
No new device to beat this from his brains?
I know 'twill stir him strongly; yet I know
A way, if it take right, in spite of fortune,
Will bring me off again.—What's this—*To the
Pope?*
The letter, as I live, with all the business
I writ to 's holiness. Nay then, farewell!
I have touch'd the highest point of all my
greatness;
And from that full meridian of my glory
I haste now to my setting: I shall fall
Like a bright exhalation in the evening,
And no man see me more.

Re-enter the DUKES OF NORFOLK *and* SUF-
FOLK, *the* EARL OF SURREY, *and the* Lord
Chamberlain.

Nor. Hear the king's pleasure, cardinal:
who commands you
To render up the great seal presently
Into our hands; and to confine yourself
To Asher House, my Lord of Winchester's,
Till you hear further from his highness.
Wol.   Stay,—
Where's your commission, lords? words can-
not carry
Authority so weighty.
Suf.   Who dare cross 'em,
Bearing the king's will from his mouth ex-
pressly?
Wol. Till I find more than will or words to
do it,—
I mean your malice,—know, officious lords,
I dare and must deny it. Now I feel
Of what coarse metal ye are moulded,—envy:
How eagerly ye follow my disgraces,
As if it fed ye! and how sleek and wanton
Ye appear in everything may bring my ruin!
Follow your envious courses, men of malice;
You have Christian warrant for them, and,
no doubt,
In time will find their fit rewards. That seal,
You ask with such a violence, the king,—
Mine and your master,—with his own hand
gave me;—
Bade me enjoy it, with the place and honours,
During my life; and, to confirm his goodness,
Tied it by letters-patents: now, who'll take
it?
Sur. The king, that gave it.
Wol.   It must be himself then.
Sur. Thou art a proud traitor, priest.
Wol.   Proud lord, thou liest:
Within these forty hours Surrey durst better
Have burnt that tongue than said so.
Sur.   Thy ambition,
Thou scarlet sin, robb'd this bewailing land
Of noble Buckingham, my father-in-law:

The heads of all thy brother cardinals,—
With thee and all thy best parts bound to-
gether,—
Weigh'd not a hair of his. Plague of your
policy!
You sent me deputy for Ireland;
Far from his succour, from the king, from all
That might have mercy on the fault thou
gav'st him;
Whilst your great goodness, out of holy pity,
Absolv'd him with an axe.
Wol.   This, and all else
This talking lord can lay upon my credit,
I answer, is most false. The duke by law
Found his deserts: how innocent I was
From any private malice in his end,
His noble jury and foul cause can witness.
If I lov'd many words, lord, I should tell you
You have as little honesty as honour,
That in the way of loyalty and truth
Toward the king, my ever royal master,
Dare mate a sounder man than Surrey can
be,
And all that love his follies.
Sur.   By my soul,
Your long coat, priest, protects you; thou
shouldst feel
My sword i' the life-blood of thee else.—My
lords,
Can ye endure to hear this arrogance?
And from this fellow? If we live thus tamely,
To be thus jaded by a piece of scarlet,
Farewell, nobility; let his grace go forward,
And dare us with his cap like larks.
Wol.   All goodness
Is poison to thy stomach.
Sur.   Yes, that goodness
Of gleaning all the land's wealth into one,
Into your own hands, cardinal, by extortion;
The goodness of your intercepted packets
You writ to the pope against the king: your
goodness,   [ous.—
Since you provoke me, shall be most notori-
My Lord of Norfolk,—as you are truly noble,
As you respect the common good, the state
Of our despis'd nobility, our issues,
Who, if he live, will scarce be gentlemen,—
Produce the grand sum of his sins, the articles
Collected from his life:—I'll startle you
Worse than the sacring bell, when the brown
wench
Lay kissing in your arms, lord cardinal.
Wol. How much, methinks, I could despise
this man,
But that I am bound in charity against it!
Nor. Those articles, my lord, are in the
king's hand:
But, thus much, they are foul ones.
Wol.   So much fairer
And spotless shall mine innocence arise,
When the king knows my truth.
Sur.   This cannot save you
I thank my memory I yet remember
Some of these articles; and out they shall.

Now, if you can blush and cry guilty, card-
  inal,
You'll show a little honesty.
  Wol.   Speak on, sir,
I dare your worst objections: if I blush,
It is to see a nobleman want manners.
  Sur. I'd rather want those than my head.—
  Have at you!
First, that, without the king's assent or know-
  ledge,
You wrought to be a legate; by which power
You maim'd the jurisdiction of all bishops.
  Nor. Then, that in all you writ to Rome,
  or else
To foreign princes, *Ego et Rex meus* [king
Was still inscrib'd; in which you brought the
To be your servant.
  Suf. Then, that, without the knowledge,
Either of king or council, when you went
Ambassador to the emperor, you made bold
To carry into Flanders the great seal.
  Sur. Item, you sent a large commission
To Gregory de Cassalis, to conclude,
Without the king's will or the state's allow-
  ance,
A league between his highness and Ferrara.
  Suf. That, out of mere ambition, you have
  caus'd
Your holy hat to be stamp'd on the king's
  coin.
  Sur. Then, that you have sent innumerable
  substance,   [science,
By what means got I leave to your own con-
To furnish Rome, and to prepare the ways
You have for dignities; to the mere undoing
Of all the kingdom. Many more there are,
Which, since they are of you, and odious,
I will not taint my mouth with.
  Cham.   O my lord,
Press not a falling man too far! 'tis virtue:
His faults lie open to the laws; let them,
Not you, correct him. My heart weeps to see
  him
So little of his great self.
  Sur.   I forgive him. [pleasure is,—
  Suf. Lord Cardinal, the king's further
Because all those things you have done of late,
By your power legatine within this kingdom,
Fall into the compass of a *præmunire*,—
That therefore such a writ be sued against
  you;
To forfeit all your goods, lands, tenements,
Chattels, and whatsoever, and to be
Out of the king's protection:—this is my
  charge.
  Nor. And so we'll leave you to your medi-
  tations
How to live better. For your stubborn an-
  swer
About the giving back the great seal to us,
The king shall know it, and, no doubt, shall
  thank you.
So fare you well, my little good lord cardinal.
          [*Exeunt all but* WOLSEY.

  Wol. So farewell to the little good you
  bear me.
Farewell, a long farewell, to all my greatness!
This is the state of man: to-day he puts forth
The tender leaves of hope; to-morrow blos-
  soms,
And bears his blushing honours thick upon
  him;
The third day comes a frost, a killing frost,
And,—when he thinks, good easy man, full
  surely
His greatness is a-ripening,—nips his root,
And then he falls, as I do. I have ventur'd,
Like little wanton boys that swim on blad-
  ders,
This many summers in a sea of glory;
But far beyond my depth: my high-blown
  pride
At length broke under me; and now has left
  me,
Weary and old with service, to the mercy
Of a rude stream, that must for ever hide me.
Vain pomp and glory of this world, I hate ye:
I feel my heart new opened. O, how wretched
Is that poor man that hangs on prince's fa-
  vours!   [to,
There is, betwixt that smile we would aspire
That sweet aspect of princes, and their ruin,
More pangs and fears than wars or women
  have:
And when he falls, he falls like Lucifer,
Never to hope again.

          Enter CROMWELL, *amazedly.*
                    Why, how now, Cromwell!
  Crom. I have no power to speak, sir.
  Wol.   What, amaz'd
At my misfortunes? can thy spirit wonder
A great man should decline? Nay, an you
  weep,
I am fallen indeed.
  Crom.   How does your grace?
  Wol.   Why, well;
Never so truly happy, my good Cromwell.
I know myself now; and I feel within me
A peace above all earthly dignities,
A still and quiet conscience. The king has
  cur'd me,
I humbly thank his grace; and from these
  shoulders,
These ruin'd pillars, out of pity, taken
A load would sink a navy,—too much hon-
  our:
O, 'tis a burden, Cromwell, 'tis a burden
Too heavy for a man that hopes for heaven!
  Crom. I am glad your grace has made that
  right use of it.   [thinks,—
  Wol. I hope I have: I am able now, me-
Out of a fortitude of soul I feel,—
To endure more miseries and greater far
Than my weak-hearted enemies dare offer.
What news abroad?
  Crom.   The heaviest and the worst
Is your displeasure with the king.

Wol.   God bless him!
Crom. The next is that Sir Thomas More is
        chosen
Lord Chancellor in your place.
Wol.   That's somewhat sudden:
But he's a learned man. May he continue
Long in his highness' favour, and do justice,
For truth's sake and his conscience; that his
        bones,
When he has run his course and sleeps in
        blessings,
May have a tomb of orphans' tears wept on
        'em!
What more?
Crom. That Cranmer is return'd with wel-
        come,
Install'd Lord Archbishop of Canterbury.
Wol. That's news indeed.
Crom.   Last, that the Lady Anne,
Whom the king has in secrecy long married,
This day was view'd in open as his queen,
Going to chapel; and the voice is now
Only about her coronation.
Wol. There was the weight that pull'd me
        down. O Cromwell,
The king has gone beyond me: all my glories
In that one woman I have lost for ever:
No sun shall ever usher forth mine honours,
Or gild again the noble troops that waited
Upon my smiles. Go, get thee from me, Crom-
        well;
I am a poor fallen man, unworthy now
To be thy lord and master: seek the king;
That sun, I pray, may never set! I have told
        him   [thee;
What and how true thou art: he will advance
Some little memory of me will stir him,—
I know his noble nature,—not to let
Thy hopeful service perish too: good Crom-
        well,
Neglect him not; make use now, and pro-
        vide
For thine own future safety.
Crom.   O my lord,
Must I then leave you? must I needs forego
So good, so noble, and so true a master?
Bear witness, all that have not hearts of iron,
With what a sorrow Cromwell leaves his lord.
The king shall have my service; but my
        prayers
For ever and for ever shall be yours.
Wol. Cromwell, I did not think to shed a
        tear
In all my miseries; but thou hast forc'd me,
Out of thy honest truth, to play the woman.
Let's dry our eyes: and thus far hear me,
        Cromwell;
And,—when I am forgotten, as I shall be,
And sleep in dull cold marble, where no men-
        tion
Of me more must be heard of,—say I taught
        thee;
Say Wolsey,—that once trod the ways of
        glory,

And sounded all the depths and shoals of
        honour,—
Found thee a way, out of his wreck, to rise
        in;
A sure and safe one, though thy master miss'd
        it.
Mark but my fall, and that that ruin'd me.
Cromwell, I charge thee, fling away ambition:
By that sin fell the angels; how can man,
        then,
The image of his Maker, hope to win by it?
Love thyself last: cherish those hearts that
        hate thee;
Corruption wins not more than honesty.
Still in thy right hand carry gentle peace,
To silence envious tongues. Be just, and fear
        not:
Let all the ends thou aim'st at be thy coun-
        try's,
Thy God's, and truth's; then, if thou fall'st,
        O Cromwell,
Thou fall'st a blessed martyr! Serve the king;
And,—pr'ythee, lead me in:
There take an inventory of all I have,
To the last penny; 'tis the king's: my robe,
And my integrity to heaven, is all
I dare now call mine own. O Cromwell,
        Cromwell!
Had I but serv'd my God with half the zeal
I serv'd my king, he would not in mine age
Have left me naked to mine enemies.
Crom. Good sir, have patience.
Wol.   So I have. Farewell
The hopes of court! my hopes in heaven do
        dwell.   [*Exeunt.*

ACT IV.

SCENE I.—*A Street in Westminster.*

Enter two Gentlemen, *meeting.*

1 *Gent.* You are well met once again.
2 *Gent.*   So are you.
1 *Gent.* You come to take your stand here,
        and behold
The Lady Anne pass from her coronation?
2 *Gent.* 'Tis all my business. At our last
        encounter
The Duke of Buckingham came from his
        trial.
1 *Gent.* 'Tis very true: but that time of-
        fer'd sorrow;
This, general joy.
2 *Gent.*   'Tis well: the citizens,
I am sure, have shown at full their royal
        minds;
As, let 'em have their rights, they are ever
        forward,
In celebration of this day with shows,
Pageants, and sights of honour.
1 *Gent.*   Never greater,
Nor, I'll assure you, better taken sir.
2 *Gent.* May I be bold to ask what that
        contains,
That paper in your hand?

1 Gent. Yes; 'tis the list
Of those that claim their offices this day,
By custom of the coronation.
The Duke of Suffolk is the first, and claims
To be high-steward; next, the Duke of Nor-
folk,
He to be earl marshal: you may read the
rest.
2 Gent. I thank you, sir; had I not known
those customs,
I should have been beholden to your paper.
But, I beseech you, what's become of Kath-
arine,
The princess dowager? how goes her busi-
ness?
1 Gent. That I can tell you too. The Arch-
bishop
Of Canterbury, accompanied with other
Learned and reverend fathers of his order,
Held a late court at·Dunstable, six miles off
From Ampthill, where the princess lay; to
which
She was often cited by them, but appear'd
not:
And, to be short, for not appearance and
The king's late scruple, by the main assent
Of all these learned men, she was divorc'd,
And the late marriage made of none effect:
Since which she was remov'd to Kimbolton,
Where she remains now sick.
2 Gent. Alas, good lady!—
[*Trumpets.*
The trumpets sound: stand close, the queen is
coming.

THE ORDER OF THE PROCESSION.

A lively flourish of trumpets: then enter,

1. Two Judges.
2. Lord Chancellor, with the purse and mace before
   him. [*Music.*
3. Choristers singing.
4. Mayor of London, bearing the mace. Then Garter, in his coat of arms, and on his head a gilt
   copper crown.
5. Marquis Dorset, bearing a sceptre of gold, on his
   head a demi-coronal of gold. With him, the
   Earl of Surrey, bearing the rod of silver with
   the dove, crowned with an earl's coronet. Collars of SS.
6. Duke of Suffolk, in his robe of estate, his coronet
   on his head, bearing a long white wand, as
   high-steward. With him, the Duke of Norfolk,
   with the rod of marshalship, a coronet on his
   head. Collars of SS.
7. A canopy borne by four of the Cinque-ports; under it the Queen in her robe; her hair richly
   adorned with pearl, crowned. On each side of
   her, the Bishops of London and Winchester.
8. The old Duchess of Norfolk, in a coronal of gold,
   wrought with flowers, bearing the Queen's
   train.
9. Certain Ladies or Countesses, with plain circlets
   of gold without flowers.

A royal train, believe me.—These I know:—
Who's that that bears the sceptre?
1 Gent. Marquis Dorset:

And that the Earl of Surrey, with the rod.
2 Gent. A bold brave gentleman. That
should be
The Duke of Suffolk?
1 Gent. 'Tis the same,—high-steward.
2 Gent. And that my Lord of Norfolk?
1 Gent. Yes.
2 Gent. Heaven bless thee!
[*Looking on the* QUEEN.
Thou hast the sweetest face I ever look'd
on.—
Sir, as I have a soul, she is an angel;
Our king has all the Indies in his arms,
And more and richer, when he strains that
lady:
I cannot blame his conscience.
1 Gent. They that bear
The cloth of honour over her are four barons
Of the Clinque-ports.
2 Gent. Those men are happy; and so are
all are near her.
I take it, she that carries up the train
Is that old noble lady, Duchess of Norfolk.
1 Gent. It is; and all the rest are countesses.
2 Gent. Their coronets say so. These are
stars indeed;
And sometimes falling ones.
1 Gent. No more of that.
[*Exit Procession, with a great flourish
of trumpets.*

Enter a third Gentleman.

God save you, sir! where have you been broil-
ing? [where a finger
3 Gent. Among the crowd i' the abbey;
Could not be wedg'd in more: I am stifled
With the mere rankness of their joy.
2 Gent. You saw
The ceremony?
3 Gent. That I did.
1 Gent. How was it?
3 Gent. Well worth the seeing.
2 Gent. Good sir, speak it to us.
3 Gent. As well as I am able. The rich
stream
Of lords and ladies, having brought the queen
To a prepar'd place in the choir, fell off
A distance from her: while her grace sat down
To rest awhile, some half an hour or so,
In a rich chair of state, opposing freely
The beauty of her person to the people.
Believe me, sir, she is the goodliest woman
That ever lay by man: which when the peo-
ple
Had the full view of, such a noise arose
As the shrouds make at sea in a stiff tempest,
As loud, and to as many tunes: hats, cloaks,—
Doublets, I think,—flew up; and had their
faces
Been loose, this day they had been lost. Such
joy
I never saw before. Great-bellied women,
That had not half a week to go, like rams

In the old time of war, would shake the press,
And make 'em reel before 'em. No man living
Could say, *This is my wife*, there; all were woven
So strangely in one piece.

   2 Gent.   But what follow'd?

   3 Gent. At length her grace rose, and with modest paces   [saintlike,
Came to the altar; where she kneel'd, and,
Cast her fair eyes to heaven, and pray'd devoutly.
Then rose again, and bow'd her to the people:
When by the Archbishop of Canterbury
She had all the royal makings of a queen;
As holy oil, Edward Confessor's crown,
The rod, and bird of peace, and all such emblems,
Laid nobly on her: which perform'd, the choir,
With all the choicest music of the kingdom,
Together sung *Te Deum*. So she parted,
And with the same full state pac'd back again
To York Place, where the feast is held.

   1 Gent.   Sir,
You must no more call it York Place, that's past:
For, since the cardinal fell, that title's lost:
'Tis now the king's, and call'd Whitehall.

   3 Gent.   I know it;
But 'tis so lately alter'd that the old name
Is fresh about me.

   2 Gent.   What two reverend bishops
Were those that went on each side of the queen?

   3 Gent. Stokesly and Gardiner; the one of Winchester,—
Newly preferr'd from the king's secretary,—
The other, London.

   2 Gent.   He of Winchester
Is held no great good lover of the archbishop's,
The virtuous Cranmer.

   3 Gent.   All the land knows that:
However, yet there is no great breach; when it comes,   [from him.
Cranmer will find a friend will not shrink

   2 Gent. Who may that be, I pray you?

   3 Gent.   Thomas Cromwell,
A man in much esteem with the king, and truly
A worthy friend.—The king
Has made him master o' the jewel-house,
And one, already, of the privy council.'

   2 Gent. He will deserve more.

   3 Gent.   Yes, without all doubt.—
Come, gentlemen, ye shall go my way, which
Is to the court, and there ye shall be my guests:
Something I can command. As I walk thither
I'll tell ye more.

   Both.   You may command us, sir.
                        [*Exeunt.*

SCENE II.—*Kimbolton.*

Enter KATHARINE, *Dowager, sick; led between* GRIFFITH *and* PATIENCE.

   Grif. How does your grace?

   Kath.   O Griffith, sick to death!
My legs, like loaden branches, bow to the earth,
Willing to leave their burden. Reach a chair:—
So,—now, methinks, I feel a little ease.
Didst thou not tell me, Griffith, as thou ledd'st me,
That the great child of honour, Cardinal Wolsey,
Was dead?

   Grif. Yes, madam; but I think your grace.
Out of the pain you suffer'd, gave no ear to 't.

   Kath. Pr'ythee, good Griffith, tell me how he died:
If well, he stepp'd before me, happily,
For my example.

   Grif.   Well, the voice goes, madam:
For after the stout Earl Northumberland
Arrested him at York, and brought him forward,—
As a man sorely tainted,—to his answer,
He fell sick suddenly, and grew so ill
He could not sit his mule.

   Kath.   Alas, poor man!

   Grif. At last, with easy roads, he came to Leicester,   [abbot,
Lodg'd in the abbey; where the reverend
With all his covent, honourably receiv'd him;
To whom he gave these words,—O, *father abbot,*
An old man, broken with the storms of state,
Is come to lay his weary bones among ye;
Give him a little earth for charity!
So went to bed; where eagerly his sickness
Pursu'd him still: and three nights after this,
About the hour of eight,—which he himself
Foretold should be his last,—full of repentance,
Continual meditations, tears, and sorrows,
He gave his honours to the world again,
His blessed part to heaven, and slept in peace.

   Kath. So may he rest; his faults lie gently on him!   [him,
Yet thus far, Griffith, give me leave to speak
And yet with charity. He was a man
Of an unbounded stomach, ever ranking
Himself with princes; one that, by suggestion,
Tied all the kingdom: simony was fair play;
His own opinion was his law: i' the presence
He would say untruths; and be ever double
Both in his words and meaning: he was never,
But where he meant to ruin, pitiful:
His promises were, as he then was, mighty;
But his performance, as he is now, nothing:

Of his own body he was ill, and gave
The clergy ill example.
Grif.   Noble madam,
Men's evil manners live in brass; their vir-
tues
We write in water. May it please your high-
ness
To hear me speak of his good now!
Kath.   Yes, good Griffith;
I were malicious else.
Grif.   This cardinal,
Though from an humble stock, undoubtedly
Was fashion'd to much honour from his
cradle.
He was a scholar, and a ripe and good one;
Exceeding wise, fair-spoken, and persuading:
Lofty and sour to them that lov'd him not;
But to those men that sought him sweet as
summer.
And though he were unsatisfied in getting,—
Which was a sin,—yet in bestowing, madam,
He was most princely: ever witness for him
Those twins of learning that he rais'd in you,
Ipswich and Oxford! one of which fell with
him,
Unwilling to outlive the good that did it;
The other, though unfinish'd, yet so famous,
So excellent in art, and still so rising,
That Christendom shall ever speak his vir-
tue.
His overthrow heap'd happiness upon him;
For then, and not till then, he felt himself,
And found the blessedness of being little:
And, to add greater honours to his age
Than man could give him, he died fearing
God.
Kath. After my death I wish no other
herald,
No other speaker of my living actions,
To keep mine honour from corruption,
But such an honest chronicler as Griffith.
Whom I most hated living, thou hast made
me,
With thy religious truth and modesty,
Now in his ashes honour: peace be with
him!—
Patience, be near me still; and set me lower:
I have not long to trouble thee.—Good Grif-
fith,
Cause the musicians play me that sad note
I nam'd my knell, whilst I sit meditating
On that celestial harmony I go to.
                        [*Sad and solemn music.*
Grif. She is asleep; good wench, let's sit
down quiet,
For fear we wake her:—softly, gentle Pa-
tience.

THE VISION. *Enter, solemnly tripping one after another, six Personages clad in white robes, wearing
on their heads garlands of bays, and golden vizards
on their faces; branches of bays or palm in their
hands. They first congee unto her, then dance; and,
at certain changes, the first two hold a spare garland*
*over her head; at which the other four make reverent
courtesies; then the two that held the garland deliver
the same to the other next two, who observe the same
order in their changes, and holding the garland over
her head: which done, they deliver the same garland
to the last two, who likewise observe the same order:
at which,—as it were by inspiration,—she makes in
her sleep signs of rejoicing, and holdeth up her
hands to heaven: and so in their dancing they vanish,
carrying the garland with them. The music con-
tinues.*

Kath. Spirits of peace, where are ye? Are
ye all gone?
And leave me here in wretchedness behind
ye?
Grif. Madam, we are here.
Kath.   It is not you I call for:
Saw ye none enter since I slept?
Grif.   None, madam.
Kath. No? Saw you not, even now, a
blessed troop
Invite me to a banquet; whose bright faces
Cast thousand beams upon me, like the sun?
They promis'd me eternal happiness;
And brought me garlands, Griffith, which I
feel
I am not worthy yet to wear: I shall,
Assuredly.   [*dreams*
Grif. I am most joyful, madam, such good
Possess your fancy.
Kath.   Bid the music leave,
They are harsh and heavy to me.
                        [*Music ceases.*
Pat.   Do you note
How much her grace is alter'd on the sud-
den?
How long her face is drawn? how pale she
looks,
And of an earthy cold? Mark you her eyes!
Grif. She is going, wench: pray, pray.
Pat.   Heaven comfort her!

Enter a Messenger.

Mess. An't like your grace,—
Kath.   You are a saucy fellow:
Deserve we no more reverence?
Grif.   You are to blame,
Knowing she will not lose her wonted great-
ness,
To use so rude behaviour: go to, kneel.
Mess. I humbly do entreat your highness'
pardon;   [*staying*
My haste made me unmannerly. There is
A gentleman, sent from the king, to see you.
Kath. Admit him entrance, Griffith: but
this fellow
Let me ne'er see again.
                        [*Exeunt* GRIFFITH *and* Messenger.

Re-enter GRIFFITH, *with* CAPUCIUS.

                        If my sight fail not,
You should be lord ambassador from the
emperor,
My royal nephew, and your name Capucius.

Cap. Madam, the same,—your servant.
Kath.   O, my Lord,
The times and titles now are alter'd strange-
ly
With me since first you knew me. But, I
     pray you,
What is your pleasure with me?
Cap.   Noble lady,
First, mine own service to your grace; the
     next,
The king's request that I would visit you;
Who grieves much for your weakness,.and by
     me
Sends you his princely commendations,
And heartily entreats you take good com-
     fort.
Kath. O, my good lord, that comfort comes
     too late;
'Tis like a pardon after execution:
That gentle physic, given in time, had cur'd
     me;
But now I am past all comforts here, but
     prayers.
How does his highness?
Cap.   Madam, in good bealth.
Kath. So may he ever do! and ever flour-
     ish,
When I shall dwell with worms, and my poor
     name
Banish'd the kingdom!—Patience, is that let-
     ter
I caus'd you write yet sent away?
Pat.   No, madam.
               [*Giving it to* KATHARINE.
Kath. Sir, I most humbly pray you to de-
     liver
This to my lord the king.
Cap.   Most willing, madam.
Kath. In which I have commended to his
     goodness   [daughter,—
The model of our chaste loves, his young
The dews of heaven fall thick in blessings on
     her!—
Beseeching him to give her virtuous breed-
     ing;
She is young, and of a noble modest na-
     ture,—
I hope she will deserve well;—and a little
To love her for her mother's sake, that lov'd
     him,
Heaven knows how dearly. My next poor
     petition
Is, that his noble grace would have some pity
Upon my wretched women, that so long
Have follow'd both my fortunes faithfully:
Of which there is not one, I dare avow,—
And now 1 should not lie,—but will deserve,
For virtue and true beauty of the soul,
For honesty and decent carriage,
A right good husband, let him be a noble;
And, sure, those men are happy that shall
     have them.
The last is, for my men,—they are the poor-
     est,

But poverty could never draw 'em from
     me,—
That they may have their wages duly paid
     'em,
And something over to remember me by:
If heaven had pleas'd to have given me long-
     er life
And able means, we had not parted thus.
These are the whole contents:—and, good my
     lord,
By that you love the dearest in this world,
As you wish Christian peace to souls de-
     parted,
Stand these poor people's friend, and urge
     the king
To do me this last right.
Cap.   By heaven, I will,
Or let me lose the fashion of a man!   [me
Kath. I thank you, honest lord. Remember
In all humility unto his highness:
Say his long trouble now is passing.   [him,
Out of this world, tell him, in death I bless'd
For so I will.—Mine eyes grow dim.—Fare-
     well,
My lord.—Griffith, farewell.—Nay, Patience,
You must not leave me yet: I must to bed;
Call in more women.—When I am dead, good
     wench,
Let me be us'd with honour: strew me over
With maiden flowers, that all the world may
     know
I was a chaste wife to my grave: embalm me,
Then lay me forth: although unqueen'd, yet
     like
A queen, and daughter to a king, inter me.
I can no more. [*Exeunt, leading* KATHARINE.

ACT V.

SCENE I.—LONDON. *A Gallery in the Palace.*

Enter GARDINER, *Bishop of Winchester, a*
     Page *with a torch before him.*

Gar. It's one o'clock, boy, is 't not?
Boy.   It has struck.
Gar. These should be hours for necessities,
Not for delights; times to repair our nature
With comforting repose, and not for us
To waste these times.

Enter SIR THOMAS LOVELL.

               Good hour of night, Sir Thomas!
Whither so late?
Lov. Came you from the king, my Lord?
Gar. I did, Sir Thomas; and left him at
     primero
With the Duke of Suffolk.
Lov.   I must to him too,
Before he go to bed. I'll take my leave.
Gar. Not yet, Sir Thomas Lovell. What's
     the matter?
It seems you are in haste: an if there be
No great offence belongs to 't, give your
     friend

Some touch of your late business: affairs that
  walk,—
As they say spirits do,—at midnight, have
In them a wilder nature than the business
That seeks despatch by day.

Lov.   My lord, I love you;
And durst commend a secret to your ear
Much weightier than this work. The queen's
  in labour,
They say in great extremity; and fear'd
She'll with the labour end.

Gar.   The fruit she goes with
I pray for heartily, that it may find [Thomas,
Good time, and live: but for the stock, Sir
I wish it grubb'd up now.

Lov.   Methinks I could
Cry thee amen; and yet my conscience says
She's a good creature, and, sweet lady, does
Deserve our better wishes.

Gar.   But, sir, sir,—
Hear me, Sir Thomas: you are a gentleman
Of mine own way; I know you wise, relig-
  ious;
And, let me tell you, it will ne'er be well,—
'Twill not, Sir Thomas Lovell, take 't of
  me,—
Till Cranmer, Cromwell, her two hands, and
  she,
Sleep in their graves.

Lov.   Now, sir, you speak of two
The most remark'd i' the kingdom. As for
  Cromwell,—   [master
Beside that of the jewel-house, he's made
O' the rolls, and the king's secretary; fur-
  ther, sir,
Stands in the gap and trade of more prefer-
  ments,
With which the time will load him. The arch-
  bishop
Is the king's hand and tongue; and who dare
  speak
One syllable against him?

Gar.   Yes, yes, Sir Thomas,
There are that dare; and I myself have ven-
  tur'd
To speak my mind of him: and indeed this
  day,
Sir,—I may tell it you,—I think I have
Incens'd the lords o' the council, that he is,—
For so I know he is, they know he is,—
A most arch heretic, a pestilence   [moved,
That does infect the land: with which they
Have broken with the king; who hath so far
Given ear to our complaint,—of his great
  grace
And princely care; foreseeing those fell mis-
  chiefs
Our reasons laid before him,—hath com-
  manded
To-morrow morning to the council-board
He be convented. He's a rank weed, Sir
  Thomas,
And we must root him out. From your
  affairs

I hinder you too long: good night, Sir
  Thomas.

Lov. Many good nights, my lord: I rest
  your servant.
                    [*Exeunt* GARDINER *and* Page.

As LOVELL *is going out, enter the* KING *and
  the* DUKE OF SUFFOLK.

K. Hen. Charles, I will play no more to-
  night;
My mind's not on 't; you are too hard for
  me.

Suf. Sir, I did never win of you before.

K. Hen. But little, Charles;
Nor shall not, when my fancy's on my play.—
Now, Lovell, from the queen what is the
  news?

Lov. I could not personally deliver to her
What you commanded me, but by her woman
I sent your message; who return'd her thanks
In the greatest humbleness, and desir'd your
  highness
Most heartily to pray for her.

K. Hen.   What say'st thou, ha?
To pray for her? what, is she crying out?

Lov. So said her woman: and that her
  sufferance made   .
Almost each pang a death.

K. Hen.   Alas, good lady!

Suf. God safely quit her of her burden, and
With gentle travail, to the gladding of
Your highness with an heir!

K. Hen.   'Tis midnight, Charles;
Pr'ythee, to bed; and in thy prayers remem-
  ber
The estate of my poor queen. Leave me
  alone;
For I must think of that which company
Will not be friendly to.

Suf.   I wish your highness
A quiet night; and my good mistress will
Remember in my prayers.

K. Hen.   Charles, good-night.
                              [*Exit* SUFFOLK.

Enter SIR ANTHONY DENNY.

Well, sir, what follows?   [bishop,

Den. Sir, I have brought my lord the arch-
As you commanded me.

K. Hen.   Ha! Canterbury?

Den. Ay, my good lord.

K. Hen. 'Tis true: where is he, Denny?

Den. He attends your highness' pleasure.

K. Hen.   Bring him to us.
                              [*Exit* DENNY.

Lov. This is about that which the bishop
  spake:
I am happily come hither.   [*Aside.*

Re-enter DENNY, *with* CRANMER.

K. Hen. Avoid the gallery.
                    [LOVELL *seems to stay.*
                    Ha! I have said. Be gone.
What!   [*Exeunt* LOVELL *and* DENNY.

Cran. I am fearful:—wherefore frowns he
    thus?
'Tis his aspect of terror. All's not well. [*Aside.*
K. Hen. How now, my lord? you do de-
    sire to know
Wherefore I sent for you.
Cran.   It is my duty
To attend your highness' pleasure.
K. Hen.   Pray you, arise,
My good and gracious Lord of Canterbury.
Come, you and I must walk a turn together;
I have news to tell you: come, come, give me
    your hand.
Ah, my good lord, I grieve at what I speak,
And am right sorry to repeat what follows:
I have, and most unwillingly, of late
Heard many grievous, I do say, my lord,
Grievous complaints of you; which, being
    consider'd,
Have mov'd us and our council that you shall
This morning come before us; where, I know,
You cannot with such freedom purge your-
    self
But that, till further trial in those charges
Which will require your answer, you must
    take
Your patience to you, and be well contented
To make your house our Tower: you a bro-
    ther of us,
It fits we thus proceed, or else no witness
Would come against you.
Cran.   I humbly thank your highness;
And am right glad to catch this good occasion
Most thoroughly to be winnow'd, where my
    chaff
And corn shall fly asunder: for I know
There's none stands under more calumnious
    tongues
Than I myself, poor man.
K. Hen.   Stand up, good Canterbury:
Thy truth and thy integrity is rooted
In us, thy friend: give me thy hand, stand
    up:
Pr'ythee, let's walk. Now, by my holy-dame,
What manner of man are you? My lord, I
    look'd
You would have given me your petition that
I should have ta'en some pains to bring to-
    gether
Yourself and your accusers; and to have
    heard you,
Without indurance, further.
Cran.   Most dread liege,
The good I stand on is my truth and honesty:
If they shall fail, I, with mine enemies, [not,
Will triumph o'er my person; which I weigh
Being of those virtues vacant. I fear nothing
What can be said against me.
K. Hen.   Know you not
How your state stands i' the world, with the
    whole world?
Your enemies are many, and not small; their
    practices
Must bear the same proportion; and not ever

The justice and the truth o' the question
    carries
The due o' the verdict with it: at what ease
Might corrupt minds procure knaves as
    corrupt
To swear against you? such things have been
    done.
You are potently oppos'd; and with a malice
Of as great size. Ween you of better luck,
I mean in perjur'd witness, than your Master,
Whose minister you are, whiles here he liv'd
Upon this naughty earth? Go to, go to;
You take a precipice for no leap of danger,
And woo your own destruction.
Cran.   God and your majesty
Protect mine innocence, or I fall into
The trap is laid for me!
K. Hen.   Be of good cheer;
They shall no more prevail than we give way
    to.
Keep comfort to you; and this morning see
You do appear before them: if they shall
    chance,
In charging you with matters, to commit you,
The best persuasions to the contrary
Fail not to use, and with what vehemency
The occasion shall instruct you: if entreaties
Will render you no remedy, this ring
Deliver them, and your appeal to us
There make before them.—Look, the good
    man weeps!
He's honest, on mine honour. God's bless'd
    mother!
I swear he is true-hearted; and a soul
None better in my kingdom.—Get you gone,
And do as I have bid you. [*Exit* CRANMER.]
    —He has strangled
His language in his tears.

Enter an Old Lady.

Gent. [*Within.*] Come back: what mean
    you?
Old L. I'll not come back; the tidings that
    I bring   [angels
Will make my boldness manners.—Now, good
Fly o'er thy royal head, and shade thy
    person
Under their blessed wings!
K. Hen.   Now, by thy looks
I guess thy message. Is the queen deliver'd?
Say ay; and of a boy.
Old L.   Ay, ay, my liege;
And of a lovely boy: the God of Heaven
Both now and ever bless her!—'tis a girl,—
Promises boys hereafter. Sir, your queen.
Desires your visitation, and to be
Acquainted with this stranger; 'tis as like you
As cherry is to cherry.
K. Hen.   Lovell,—

Re-enter LOVELL.

Lov.   Sir?
K. Hen. Give her an hundred marks. I'll
    to the queen.   [*Exit.*

Old L. An hundred marks! By this light,
　I'll ha' more.
An ordinary groom is for such payment.
I will have more, or scold it out of him.
Said I for this, the girl was like to him?
I will have more, or else unsay 't; and now,
While it is hot, I'll put it to the issue.
　　　　　　　　　　　　　　[*Exeunt.*

SCENE II.—*Lobby before the Council Chamber.*

Enter CRANMER; Servants, Door-keeper, &c.,
　　　attending.

Cran. I hope I am not too late; and yet
　the gentleman
That was sent to me from the council pray'd
　me
To make great haste. All fast? what means
　this?—Ho!
Who waits there?—Sure, you know me?
D. Keep.　　　　　　　　　　Yes, my lord;
But yet I cannot help you.
Cran. Why?
D. Keep. Your grace must wait till you be
　call'd for.

Enter DOCTOR BUTTS.

Cran.　　　　　　　　　　　　　　So.
Butts. [*Aside.*] This is a piece of malice. I
　am glad
I came this way so happily: the king
Shall understand it presently.　　[*Exits.*
Cran. [*Aside.*]　　　　　　　'Tis Butts,
The King's physician: as he pass'd along,
How earnestly he cast his eyes upon me!
Pray, heaven, he sound not my disgrace! For
　certain,
This is of purpose laid by some that hate
　me,—
God turn their hearts! I never sought their
　malice,—　　　　　　　[to make me
To quench mine honour: they would shame
Wait else at door, a fellow-counsellor,
Among boys, grooms, and lackeys. But their
　pleasures
Must be fulfill'd, and I attend with patience.

The KING *and* BUTTS *appear at a window
　above.*

Butts. I'll show your grace the strangest
　sight,—
K. Hen.　　　　　　　What's that, Butts?
Butts. I think your highness saw this many
　a day.
K. Hen. Body o' me, where is it?
Butts.　　　　　　　　There my lord:
The high promotion of his grace of Canter-
　bury;
Who holds his state at door, 'mongst pur-
　suivants,
Pages, and footboys.
K. Hen.　　　　　　Ha! 'tis he indeed:
Is this the honour they do one another?

'Tis well there's one above them yet. I had
　thought
They had parted so much honesty among
　'em,—
At least good manners,—as not thus to
　suffer
A man of his place, and so near our favour,
To dance attendance on their lordships' plea-
　sures,
And at the door too, like a post with packets.
By holy Mary, Butts, there's knavery:
Let 'em alone, and draw the curtain close;
We shall hear more anon.　　　　[*Exeunt.*

The Council Chamber.

Enter the Lord Chancellor, *the* DUKE OF
　SUFFOLK, *the* DUKE OF NORFOLK, EARL
　OF SURREY, Lord Chamberlain, GARDINER,
　and CROMWELL. *The* Chancellor *places
　himself at the upper end of the table on
　the left hand; a seat being left void above
　him, as for the* ARCHBISHOP OF CANTER-
　BURY. *The rest seat themselves in order on
　each side.* CROMWELL *at the lower end, as
　Secretary.*

Chan. Speak to the business, master secre-
　tary:
Why are we met in council?
Crom.　　　　　　　　Please your honours,
The chief cause concerns his grace of Canter-
　bury.
Gar. Has he had knowledge of it?
Crom.　　　　　　　　　　　　　Yes.
Nor.　　　　　　　　Who waits there?
D. Keep. Without, my noble lords?
Gar.　　　　　　　　　　　　　Yes.
D. Keep.　　　　　　　My lord archbishop;
And has done half an hour, to know your
　pleasures.
Chan. Let him come in.
D. Keep.　　　　Your grace may enter now.
　　　[CRAN. *approaches the Council-table.*
Chan. My good lord archbishop, I am very
　sorry
To sit here at this present, and behold
That chair stand empty: but we all are men
In our own natures frail, and capable
Of our flesh; few are angels: out of which
　frailty　　　　　　　　　　[teach us,
And want of wisdom, you, that best should
Have misdemean'd yourself, and not a little,
Toward the king first, then his laws, in filling
The whole realm, by your teaching and your
　chaplains,—
For so we are inform'd,—with new opinions,
Divers and dangerous; which are heresies,
And, not reform'd, may prove pernicious.
Gar. Which reformation must be sudden
　too,
My noble lords; for those that tame wild
　horses
Pace 'em not in their hands to make 'em
　gentle,

But stop their mouths with stubborn bits, and
    spur 'em,
Till they obey the manage. If we suffer,—
Out of our easiness, and childish pity
To one man's honour,—this contagious sick-
    ness,
Farewell all physic: and what follows then?
Commotions, uproars, with a general taint
Of the whole state: as, of late days, our
    neighbours,
The upper Germany, can dearly witness,
Yet freshly pitied in our memories.

Cran. My good lords, hitherto in all the
    progress
Both of my life and office, I have labour'd,
And with no little study, that my teaching
And the strong course of my authority
Might go one way, and safely; and the end
Was ever to do well: nor is there living,—
I speak it with a single heart, my lords,—
A man that more detests, more stirs against,
Both in his private conscience and his place,
Defacers of a public peace, than I do.
Pray heaven, the king may never find a heart
With less allegiance in it! Men that make
Envy and crooked malice nourishment
Dare bite the best. I do beseech your lord-
    ships
That, in this case of justice, my accusers,
Be what they will, may stand forth face to
    face,
And freely urge against me.

Suf.   Nay, my lord,
That cannot be: you are a counsellor,
And, by that virtue, no man dare accuse you.

Gar. My lord, because we have business of
    more moment,   [pleasure,
We will be short with you. 'Tis his highness'
And our consent, for better trial of you,
From hence you be committed to the Tower;
Where, being but a private man again,
You shall know many dare accuse you boldly,
More than, I fear, you are provided for.

Cran. Ah, my good Lord of Winchester,
    I thank you;   [pass
You are always my good friend; if your will
I shall both find your lordship judge and
    juror,
You are so merciful: I see your end,—
'Tis my undoing: love and meekness, lord,
Become a churchman better than ambition:
Win straying souls with modesty again,
Cast none away. That I shall clear myself,
Lay all the weight ye can upon my patience,
I make as little doubt as you do conscience
In doing daily wrongs. I could say more,
But reverence to your calling makes me
    modest.

Gar. My lord, my lord, you are a sectary.
That's the plain truth: your painted gloss
    discovers,   [weakness.
To men that understand you, words and

Crom. My Lord of Winchester, you are a
    little,

By your good favour, too sharp; men so
    noble,
However faulty, yet should find respect
For what they have been: 'tis a cruelty
To load a falling man.

Gar.   Good master secretary,
I cry your honour mercy; you may, worst
Of all this table, say so.

Crom.   Why, my lord?

Gar. Do not I know you for a favourer
Of this new sect? ye are not sound.

Crom.   Not sound?

Gar. Not sound, I say.

Crom.   Would you were half so honest!
Men's prayers then would seek you, not their
    fears.

Gar. I shall remember this bold language.

Crom.   Do.
Remember your bold life too.

Chan.   This is too much;
Forbear, for shame, my lords.

Gar.   I have done.

Crom.   And I.

Chan. Then thus for you, my lord: it
    stands agreed,
I take it, by all voices, that forthwith
You be conveyed to the Tower a prisoner;
There to remain till the king's further
    pleasure
Be known unto us:—are you all agreed,
    lords?

All. We are.

Cran.   Is there no other way of mercy,
But I must needs to the Tower, my lords?

Gar.   What other
Would you expect? You are strangely
    troublesome.—
Let some o' the guard be ready there.

Enter Guard.

Cran.   For me?
Must I go like a traitor thither?

Gar.   Receive him,
And see him safe i' the Tower.

Cran.   Stay, good my lords.
I have a little yet to say. Look there, my
    lords;
By virtue of that ring I take my cause
Out of the gripes of cruel men, and give it
To a most noble judge, the king my master.

Cham. This is the king's ring.

Sur.   'Tis no counterfeit.

Suf. 'Tis the right ring, by heaven: I told
    ye all,   [rolling,
When we first put this dangerous stone a-
'Twould fall upon ourselves.

Nor.   Do you think, my lords,
The king will suffer but the little finger
Of this man to be vex'd?

Chan.   'Tis now too certain:
How much more is his life in value with him?
Would I were fairly out on 't!

Crom.   My mind gave me,
In seeking tales and informations

Against this man,—whose honesty the devil
And his disciples only envy at,—
Ye blew the fire that burns ye: now have at
    ye.

Enter the KING *frowning on them; he takes
    his seat.*

  Gar. Dread sovereign, how much are we
    bound to heaven
In daily thanks, that gave us such a prince;
Not only good and wise, but most religious:
One that, in all obedience, makes the church
The chief aim of his honour; and, to
    strengthen
That holy duty, out of dear respect,
His royal self in judgment comes to hear
The cause betwixt her and this great offender.
  K. Hen. You were ever good at sudden
    commendations,
Bishop of Winchester. But know, I come not
To hear such flattery now, and in my pres-
    ence;
They are too thin and bare to hide offences.
To me you cannot reach: you play the
    spaniel,
And think with wagging of your tongue to
    win me;
But whatsoe'er thou tak'st me for, I am sure
Thou hast a cruel nature, and a bloody.—
Good man [*to* CRANMER], sit down. Now let
    me see the proudest,
He that dares most, but wag his finger at
    thee:
By all that's holy, he had better starve
Than but once think this place becomes thee
    not.
  Sur. May it please your grace,—
  K. Hen. No, sir, it does not please me.
I had thought I had had men of some under-
    standing
And wisdom of my council; but I find none.
Was it discretion, lords, to let this man,
This good man,—few of you deserve that
    title,—
This honest man, wait like a lousy footboy
At chamber door? and one as great as you
    are?
Why, what a shame was this! Did my com-
    mission
Bid ye so far forget yourselves? I gave ye
Power as he was a counsellor to try him,
Not as a groom: there's some of ye, I see,
More out of malice than integrity,
Would try him to the utmost, had ye mean;
Which ye shall never have while I live.
  Chan.   Thus far,
My most dread sovereign, may it like your
    grace   [pos'd
To let my tongue excuse all. What was pur-
Concerning his imprisonment was rather,—
If there be faith in men,—meant for his trial,
And fair purgation to the world, than
    malice,—
I'm sure in me.

  K. Hen. Well, well, my lords, respect him;
Take him, and use him well, he's worthy of
    it.
I will say thus much for him,—if a prince
May be beholding to a subject, I
Am, for his love and service, so to him.
Make me no more ado, but all embrace him:
Be friends, for shame, my lords!—My Lord
    of Canterbury,
I have a suit which you must not deny me;
That is, a fair young maid that yet wants
    baptism,
You must be godfather, and answer for her.
  Cran. The greatest monarch now alive may
    glory
In such an honour: how may I deserve it,
That am a poor and humble subject to you?
  K. Hen. Come, come, my lord, you'd spare
    your spoons: you shall have
Two noble partners with you: the old Duch-
    ess of Norfolk
And Lady Marquis Dorset: will these please
    you?
Once more, my Lord of Winchester, I charge
    you,
Embrace and love this man.
  Gar.   With a true heart
And brother-love I do it.
  Cran.   And let heaven
Witness how dear I hold this confirmation.
  K. Hen. Good man, those joyful tears show
    thy true heart:
The common voice, I see, is verified
Of thee, which says thus,—*Do my Lord of
    Canterbury
A shrewd turn, and he is your friend for
    ever.*—
Come, lords, we trifle time away; I long
To have this young one made a Christian.
As I have made ye one, lords, one remain;
So I grow stronger, you more honour gain.
                                    [*Exeunt.*

SCENE III.—*The Palace Yard.*

Noise and tumult within. Enter Porter *and
    his* Man.

  Port. You'll leave your noise anon, ye
rascals: do you take the court for Paris garden? ye rude slaves, leave your gaping.
  [*Within*] Good master porter, I belong to
the larder.
  Port. Belong to the gallows, and be
hanged, you rogue! is this a place to roar in?
—Fetch me a dozen crab-tree staves, and
strong ones: these are but switches to them.
—I'll scratch your heads: you must be see-
ing christenings? do you look for ale and
cakes here, you rude rascals?
  Man. Pray, sir, be patient: 'tis as much
    impossible,—
Unless we sweep them from the door with
    cannons,—
To scatter 'em as 'tis to make 'em sleep
On May-day morning; which will never be:

We may as well push against Paul's as stir 'em.

Port. How got they in, and be hang'd?

Man. Alas, I know not; how gets the tide in?
As much as one sound cudgel of four foot,—
You see the poor remainder;—could distribute,
I made no spare, sir.

Port.   You did nothing, sir.

Man. I am not Samson, nor Sir Guy, nor Colbrand,
To mow 'em down before me: but if I spar'd any
That had a head to hit, either young or old,
He or she, cuckold or cuckold-maker,
Let me ne'er hope to see a chine again;
And that I would not for a cow, God save her!

[*Within.*] Do you hear, master porter?

Port. I shall be with you presently, good master puppy.—Keep the door close, sirrah.

Man. What would you have me do?

Port. What should you do, but knock them down by the dozens? Is this Moorfields to muster in? or have we some strange Indian with the great tool come to court, the women so besiege us? Bless me, what a fry of fornication is at door! On my Christian conscience, this one christening will beget a thousand: here will be father, godfather, and all together.

Man. The spoons will be the bigger, sir. There is a fellow somewhat near the door, he should be a brazier by his face, for, o' my conscience, twenty of the dog-days now reign in 's nose; all that stand about him are under the line, they need no other penance: that fire-drake did I hit three times on the head, and three times was his nose discharged against me; he stands there, like a mortar-piece, to blow us. There was a haberdasher's wife of small wit near him, that railed upon me till her pink'd porringer fell off her head, for kindling such a combustion in the state. I miss'd the meteor once, and hit that woman, who cried out *Clubs!* when I might see from far some forty truncheoners draw to her succour, which were the hope of the Strand, where she was quartered. They fell on; I made good my place: at length they came to the broomstaff to me; I defied them still: when suddenly a file of boys behind them, loose shot delivered such a shower of pebbles, that I was fain to draw mine honour in, and let them win the work: the devil was amongst them, I think, surely.

Port. These are the youths that thunder at a play-house and fight for bitten apples; that, no audience, but the Tribulation of Tower-hill or the limbs of Limehouse, their dear brothers, are able to endure. I have some of them in *Limbo Patrum*, and there they are like to dance these three days; besides the running banquet of two beadles that is to come.

Enter the Lord Chamberlain.

Cham. Mercy o'me, what a multitude are here!   [coming,
They grow still too; from all parts they are
As if we kept a fair here! Where are these porters,
These lazy knaves?—Ye have made a fine hand, fellows.
There's a trim rabble let in: are all these
Your faithful friends o' the suburbs? We shall have   [ladies,
Great store of room, no doubt, left for the
When they pass back from the christening.

Port.   An't please your honour,
We are but men; and what so many may do,
Not being torn a pieces, we have done:
An army cannot rule 'em.

Chan.   As I live,
If the king blame me for't, I'll lay ye all
By the heels, and suddenly; and on your heads
Clap round fines for neglect: you're lazy knaves;
And here ye lie baiting of bombards, when
Ye should do service. Hark! the trumpets sound;
They are come already from the christening:
Go, break among the press, and find a way out
To let the troop pass fairly; or I'll find
A Marshalsea shall hold you play these two months.

Port. Make way there for the princess.

Man.   You great fellow,
Stand close up, or I'll make your head ache.

Port. You i' the camlet, get up o' the rail;
I'll pick you o'er the pales else.   [*Exeunt.*

SCENE IV.—The Palace.

Enter trumpets, sounding; then two Aldermen, Lord Mayor, Garter, CRANMER, DUKE OF NORFOLK, *with his marshal's staff,* DUKE OF SUFFOLK, *two* Noblemen *bearing great standing-bowls for the christening gifts; then four* Noblemen *bearing a canopy, under which the* DUCHESS OF NORFOLK, *godmother, bearing the child richly habited in a mantle, &c. Train borne by a* Lady; *then follows the* MARCHIONESS OF DORSET, *the other godmother, and* Ladies. *The troop pass once about the stage, and* Garter *speaks.*

Gart. Heaven, from thy endless goodness, send prosperous life, long, and ever-happy, to the high and mighty princess of England, Elizabeth!

Flourish. Enter KING *and* Train.

Cran. [*kneeling.*] And to your royal grace and the good queen,
My noble partners and myself thus pray;—

All comfort, joy, in this most gracious lady,
Heaven ever laid up to make parents happy,
May hourly fall upon ye!
   K. Hen. Thank you, good lord archbishop.
What is her name?
   Cran.   Elizabeth.
   K. Hen.   Stand up, lord.—
            [*The* KING *kisses the child.*
With this kiss take my blessing: God protect
   thee!
Into whose hand I give thy life.
   Cran.   Amen.
   K. Hen. My noble gossips, ye have been
   too prodigal.
I thank ye heartily; so shall this lady,
When she has so much English.
   Cran.   ·Let me speak, sir,
For heaven now bids me; and the words I
   utter   [truth.
Let none think flattery, for they'll find 'em
This royal infant,—Heaven still move about
   her!—
Though in her cradle, yet now promises
Upon this land a thousand thousand blessings,
Which time shall bring to ripeness: she shall
   be,—   [ness,—
But few now living can behold that good-
A pattern to all princes living with her,
And all that shall succeed: Saba was never
More covetous of wisdom and fair virtue
Than this pure soul shall be: all princely
   graces,
That mould up such a mighty piece as this is,
With all the virtues that attend the good,
Shall still be doubled on her: truth shall nurse
   her,
Holy and heavenly thoughts still counsel her:
She shall be lov'd and fear'd: her own shall
   bless her;
Her foes shake like a field of beaten corn,
And hang their heads with sorrow: good
   grows with her:
In her days every man shall eat in safety,
Under his own vine, what he plants; and
   sing
The merry songs of peace to all his neigh-
   bours:
God shall be truly known; and those about
   her
From her shall read the perfect ways of hon-
   our,
And by those claim their greatness, not by
   blood.   [when
Nor shall this peace sleep with her: but as
The bird of wonder dies, the maiden phœnix,
Her ashes new create another heir,
As great in admiration as herself;
So shall she leave her blessedness to one,—
When heaven shall call her from this cloud of
   darkness,—
Who from the sacred ashes of her honour
Shall star-like rise, as great in fame as she was,

And so stand fix'd: peace, plenty, love, truth,
   terror,
That were the servants to this chosen infant,
Shall then be his, and like a vine grow to him:
Wherever the bright sun of heaven shall shine,
His honour and the greatness of his name
Shall be, and make new nations: he shall
   flourish,
And, like a mountain cedar, reach his
   branches
To all the plains about him:—our children's
   children
Shall see this and bless Heaven.
   K. Hen.   Thou speak'st wonders.
   Cran. She shall be, to the happiness of
   England,
An aged princess; many days shall see her,
And yet no day without a deed to crown it.
Would I had known no more! but she must
   die,
She must, the saints must have her,—yet a
   virgin;
A most unspotted lily shall she pass
To the ground, and all the world shall mourn
   . her.
   K. Hen. O lord archbishop,
Thou hast made me now a man; never, before
This happy child, did I get anything:
This oracle of comfort has so pleas'd me
That when I am in heaven I shall desire
To see what this child does, and praise my
   Maker.—
I thank ye all.—To you, my good lord mayor,
And you, good brethren, I am much behold-
   ing;
I have received much honour by your pres-
   ence,
And ye shall find me thankful.—Lead the
   way, lords:—   [ye,
Ye must all see the queen, and she must thank
She will be sick else. This day, no man think
Has business at his house; for all shall stay:
This little one shall make it holiday. [*Exeunt.*

EPILOGUE.

'Tis ten to one this play can never please
All that are here: some come to take their
   ease,
And sleep an act or two; but those, we fear,
We have frightened with our trumpets; so,
   'tis clear,
They'll say 'tis naught: others to hear the city
Abus'd extremely, and to cry,—*That's witty!*
Which we have not done neither: that, I fear,
All the expected good we're like to hear
For this play at this time, is only in
The merciful construction of good women;
For such a one we show'd 'em: if they smile,
And say 'twill do, I know, within awhile
All the best men are ours; for 'tis ill hap
If they hold when their ladies bid 'em clap.

VENUS AND ADONIS

'Vilia miretur vulgus, mihi flavus Apollo
Pocula Castalia plena ministret aqua.'—OVID.

TO THE

RIGHT HONOURABLE HENRY WRIOTHESLY,

EARL OF SOUTHAMPTON, AND BARON OF TITCHFIELD.

RIGHT HONOURABLE,
I KNOW not how I shall offend in dedicating my unpolished lines to your lordship, nor how the world will censure me for choosing so strong a prop to support so weak a burthen: only if your honour seem but pleased, I account myself highly praised, and vow to take advantage of all idle hours till I have honoured you with some graver labour. But if the first heir of my invention prove deformed, I shall be sorry it had so noble a godfather, and never after ear so barren a land, for fear it yield me still so bad a harvest. I leave it to your honourable survey, and your honour to your heart's content; which I wish may always answer your own wish, and the world's hopeful expectation.
Your Honour's in all duty,
WILLIAM SHAKESPEARE.

EVEN as the sun with purple-colour'd face
Had ta'en his last leave of the weeping morn,
Rose-cheek'd Adonis hied him to the chase;
Hunting .he lov'd, but love he laugh'd to
    scorn;
  Sick-thoughted Venus makes amain unto
      him
  And like a bold-fac'd suitor 'gins to woo
      him.

'Thrice fairer than myself,' thus she began,
'The field's chief flower, sweet above compare,
Stain to all nymphs, more lovely than a man,
More white and red than doves or roses are;
  Nature that made thee, with herself at
      strife,
  Saith that the world hath ending with thy
      life.

'Vouchsafe, thou wonder, to alight thy steed,
And rein his proud head to the saddle-bow;
If thou wilt deign this favour, for thy meed
A thousand honey-secrets shalt thou know:
  Here come and sit, where never serpent
      hisses,
  And being set I'll smother thee with kisses;

'And yet not cloy thy lips with loath'd satiety,
But rather famish them amid their plenty,
Making them red and pale with fresh variety,
Ten kisses short as one, one long as twenty:
  A summer's day will seem an hour but
      short,
  Being wasted in such time-beguiling sport.'

With this she seizeth on his sweating palm,

The precedent of pith and livelihood,
And, trembling in her passion, calls it balm,
Earth's sovereign salve to do a goddess good:
  Being so enrag'd, desire doth lend her force,
  Courageously to pluck him from his horse.

Over one arm the lusty courser's rein,
Under her other was the tender boy,
Who blush'd and pouted in a full disdain,
With leaden appetite, unapt to toy;
  She red and hot as coals of glowing fire,
  He red for shame, but frosty in desire.

The studded bridle on a ragged bough
Nimbly she fastens; (O how quick is love!)
The steed is stalled up, and even now
To tie the rider she begins to prove:
  Backward she push'd him, as she would be
      thrust,
  And govern'd him in strength, though not
      in lust.

So soon was she along, as he was down,
Each leaning on their elbows and their hips:
Now doth she stroke his cheek, now doth he
    frown,
And 'gins to chide, but soon she stops his
    lips;
  And kissing speaks, with lustful language
      broken,
  'If thou wilt chide, thy lips shall never
      open.'

He burns with bashful shame; she with her
    tears
Doth quench the maiden burning of his
    cheeks:

Then with her windy sighs, and golden hairs,
To fan and blow them dry again she seeks:
He saith she is immodest, blames her 'miss;
What follows more she murders with a kiss.

Even as an empty eagle, sharp by fast,
Tires with her beak on feathers, flesh, and
bone,
Shaking her wings, devouring all in haste,
Till either gorge be stuff'd, or prey be gone;
Even so she kiss'd his brow, his cheek, his
chin,
And where she ends she doth anew begin.

Forc'd to content, but never to obey,
Panting he lies, and breatheth in her face;
She feedeth on the steam, as on a prey,
And calls it heavenly moisture, air of grace,
Wishing her cheeks were gardens full of
flowers,
So they were dew'd with such distilling
showers.

Look how a bird lies tangled in a net,
So fastened in her arms Adonis lies;
Pure shame and aw'd resistance made him
fret,
Which bred more beauty in his angry eyes;
Rain added to a river that is rank,
Perforce will force it overflow the bank.

Still she entreats, and prettily entreats,
For to a pretty ear she tunes her tale;
Still is he sullen, still he low'rs and frets,
'Twixt crimson shame, and anger ashy pale;
Being red, she loves him best; and being
white,
Her best is better'd with a more delight.

Look how he can, she cannot choose but love;
And by her fair immortal hand she swears
From his soft bosom never to remove,
Till he take truce with her contending tears,
Which long have rain'd, making her cheeks
all wet;
And one sweet kiss shall pay this countless
debt.

Upon this promise did he raise his chin,
Like a dive-dapper peering through a wave,
Who, being look'd on, ducks as quickly in;
So offers he to give what she did crave;
But when her lips were ready for his pay,
He winks, and turns his lips another way.

Never did passenger in summer's heat
More thirst for drink, than she for this good
turn:
Her help she sees, but help she cannot get;
She bathes in water, yet her fire must burn:
'O, pity,' 'gan she cry, 'flint-hearted boy!
'Tis but a kiss I beg; why art thou coy?

'I have been woo'd, as I entreat thee now,
Even by the stern and direful god of war,
Whose sinewy neck in battle ne'er did bow,
Who conquers where he comes, in every jar;
Yet hath he been my captive and my slave,
And begg'd for that which thou unask'd
shalt have.

'Over my altars hath he hung his lance,
His batter'd shield, his uncontrolled crest,
And for my sake hath learn'd to sport and
dance,
To toy, to wanton, dally, smile, and jest;
Scorning his churlish drum and ensign red,
Making my arms his field, his tent my bed.

'Thus he that overrul'd I oversway'd,
Leading him prisoner in a red-rose chain:
Strong-temper'd steel his stronger strength
obey'd,
Yet was he servile to my coy disdain.
O, be not proud, nor brag not of thy might,
For mastering her that foil'd the god of
fight!

'Touch but my lips with those fair lips of
thine,
(Though mine be not so fair, yet are they
red.)
The kiss shall be thine own as well as mine:—
What seest thou in the ground? hold up thy
head;
Look in mine eyeballs, there thy beauty
lies:
Then why not lips on lips, since eyes in
eyes?

'Art thou asham'd to kiss? then wink again,
And I will wink, so shall the day seem night:
Love keeps his revels where there are but
twain;
Be bold to play, our sport is not in sight:
These blue-vein'd violets whereon we lean
Never can blab, nor know not what we
mean.

'The tender spring upon thy tempting lip
Shows thee unripe; yet mayst thou well be
tasted;
Make use of time, let not advantage slip;
Beauty within itself should not be wasted:
Fair flowers that are not gather'd in their
prime
Rot and consume themselves in little time.

'Were I hard-favour'd, foul, or wrinkled-old,
Ill-nurtur'd, crooked, churlish, harsh in voice,
O'er-worn, despised, rheumatic, and cold,
Thick-sighted, barren, lean, and lacking juice,
Then mightst thou pause, for then I were
not for thee;
But having no defects, why dost thou abhor me?

'Thou canst not see one wrinkle in my brow;
Mine eyes are grey, and bright, and quick in
    turning;
My beauty as the spring doth yearly grow,
My flesh is soft and plump, my marrow burn-
    ing;
    My smooth moist hand, were it with thy
        hand felt,
    Would in thy palm dissolve, or seem to
        melt.

'Bid me discourse, I will enchant thine ear,
Or, like a fairy, trip upon the green,
Or, like a nymph, with long dishevell'd hair,
Dance on the sands, and yet no footing seen:
    Love is a spirit all compact of fire,
    Not gross to sink, but light, and will aspire.

'Witness this primrose bank whereon I lie!
These forceless flowers like sturdy trees sup-
    port me;
Two strengthless doves will draw me through
    the sky,
From morn to night, even where I list to
    sport me:
    Is love so light, sweet boy, and may it be
    That thou shouldst think it heavy unto
        thee?

'Is thine own heart to thine own face affect-
    ed?
Can thy right hand seize love upon thy left?
Then woo thyself, be of thyself rejected,
Steal thine own freedom, and complain on
    theft.
    Narcissus so himself himself forsook,
    And died to kiss his shadow in the brook.

'Torches are made to light, jewels to wear,
Dainties to taste, fresh beauty for the use,
Herbs for their smell, and sappy plants to
    bear;
Things growing to themselves are growth's
    abuse:
    Seed spring from seeds, and beauty breed-
        eth beauty,
    Thou wast begot,—to get it is thy duty.

'Upon the earth's increase why shouldst thou
    feed,
Unless the earth with thy increase be fed?
By law of Nature thou are bound to breed,
That thine may live, when thou thyself art
    dead;
    And so in spite of death thou dost survive,
    In that thy likeness still is left alive.'

By this the love-sick queen began to sweat,
For, where they lay, the shadow had forsook
    them,
And Titan, 'tired in the mid-day heat,
With burning eye did hotly overlook them;
    Wishing Adonis had his team to guide,
    So he were like him, and by Venus' side.

And now Adonis, with a lazy spright,
And with a heavy, dark, disliking eye,
His lowering brows o'erwhelming his fair
    sight,
Like misty vapours when they blot the sky,
    Souring his cheeks, cries, 'Fie, no more of
        love!
    The sun doth burn my face; I must re-
        move.'

'Ah me,' quoth Venus, 'young, and so unkind!
What bare excuses mak'st thou to begone!
I'll sigh celestial breath, whose gentle wind
Shall cool the heat of this descending sun;
    I'll make a shadow for thee of my hairs;
    If they burn too, I'll quench them with my
        tears.

'The sun that shines from heaven shines but
    warm,
And lo, I lie between that sun and thee:
The heat I have from thence doth little harm,
Thine eye darts forth the fire that burneth
    me:
    And were I not immortal, life were done,
    Between this heavenly and earthly sun.

'Art thou obdurate, flinty, hard as steel,
Nay, more than flint, for stone at rain relent-
    eth?
Art thou a woman's son, and canst not feel
What 'tis to love? how want of love torment-
    eth?
    O had thy mother borne so hard a mind,
    She had not brought forth thee, but died
        unkind.

'What am I, that thou shouldst contemn me
    this?
Or what great danger dwells upon my suit?
What were thy lips the worse for one poor
    kiss;
Speak, fair; but speak fair words, or else be
    mute:
    Give me one kiss, I'll give it thee again,
    And one for interest, if thou wilt have
        twain.

'Fie, lifeless picture, cold and senseless stone,
Well-painted idol, image dull and dead,
Statue contenting but the eye alone,
Thing like a man, but of no woman bred;
    Thou art no man, though of a man's com-
        plexion,
    For men will kiss even by their own direc-
        tion.'

This said, impatience chokes her pleading
    tongue,
And swelling passion doth provoke a pause;
Red cheeks and fiery eyes blaze forth her
    wrong;
Being judge in love, she cannot right her
    cause:

And now she weeps, and now she fain
would speak,
And now her sobs do her intendments
break.

Sometimes she shakes her head, and then his
hand,
Now gazeth she on him, now on the ground;
Sometimes her arms infold him like a band;
She would, he will not in her arms be bound;
    And when from thence he struggles to be
gone,
    She locks her lily fingers one in one.

'Fondling,' she saith, 'since I have hemm'd
thee here,
Within the circuit of this ivory pale,
I'll be a park, and thou shalt be my deer;
Feed where thou wilt, on mountain or in
dale:
    Graze on my lips; and if those hills be dry,
    Stray lower, where the pleasant fountains
lie.

'Within this limit is relief enough,
Sweet bottom-grass, and high delightful plain,
Round rising hillocks, brakes obscure and
rough,
To shelter thee from tempest and from rain;
    Then be my deer, since I am such a park;
    No dog shall rouse thee, tho' a thousand
bark.'

At this Adonis smiles as in disdain,
That in each cheek appears a pretty dimple:
Love made those hollows, if himself were
slain,
He might be buried in a tomb so simple;
    Foreknowing well if there he came to lie,
    Why there Love liv'd and there he could
not die.

These lovely caves, these round enchanting
pits,
Open'd their mouths to swallow Venus' liking:
Being mad before, how doth she now for
wits?
Struck dead at first, what needs a second
striking?
    Poor queen of love, in thine own law for-
lorn,   [scorn!
    To love a cheek that smiles at thee in

Now which way shall she turn? what shall
she say?
Her words are done, her woes the more increasing,
The time is spent, her object will away,
And from her twining arms doth urge releas-
ing:
    'Pity'—she cries,—'some favour—some re-
morse—'
    Away he springs, and hasteth to his horse.

But lo, from forth a copse that neighbours
by,
A breeding jennet, lusty, young, and proud,
Adonis' trampling courser doth espy,
And forth she rushes, snorts, and neighs
aloud:
    The strong-neck'd steed, being tied unto a
tree,
    Breaketh his rein, and to her straight goes
he.

Imperiously he leaps, he neighs, he bounds,
And now his woven girths he breaks asunder;
The bearing earth with his hard hoof he
wounds,
Whose hollow womb resounds like heaven's
thunder;
    The iron bit he crushes 'tween his teeth,
    Controlling what he was controlled with.

His ears up-prick'd; his braided hanging
mane
Upon his compass'd crest now stand on end;
His nostrils drink the air, and forth again,
As from a furnace, vapours doth he send:
    His eye, which scornfully glisters like fire,
    Shows his hot courage and his high desire.

Sometimes he trots, as if he told the steps,
With gentle majesty, and modest pride;
Anon he rears upright, curvets, and leaps,
As who should say, lo! thus my strength is
tried;
    And this I do to captivate the eye
    Of the fair breeder that is standing by.

What recketh he his rider's angry stir,
His flattering 'holla,' or his 'Stand, I say'?
What cares he now for curb, or pricking
spur?
For rich caparisons, or trapping gay?
    He sees his love, and nothing else he sees,
    Nor nothing else with his proud sight
agrees.

Look, when a painter would surpass the life,
In limning out a well-porportion'd steed,
His art with nature's workmanship at strife,
As if the dead the living should exceed;
    So did this horse excel a common one,
    In shape, in courage, colour, pace, and bone.

Round-hoof'd, short-jointed, fetlocks shag
and long,
Broad breast, full eye, small head, and nostril
wide,
High crest, short ears, straight legs, and passing strong,
Thin mane, thick tail, broad buttock, tender
hide:
    Look what a horse should have, he did not
lack,
    Save a proud rider on so proud a back.

Sometime he scuds far off, and there he
  stares;
Anon he starts at stirring of a feather;
To bid the wind a base he now prepares,
And whe'r he run, or fly, they knew not
  whether;
  For thro' his mane and tail the high wind
    sings,
  Fanning the hairs, who wave like feather'd
    wings.

He looks upon his love and neighs unto her;
She answers him as if she knew his mind:
Being proud, as females are, to see him woo
  her,
She puts on outward strangeness, seems un-
  kind;
  Spurns at his love, and scorns the heat he
    feels,
  Beating his kind embracements with her
    heels.

Then, like a melancholy malecontent,
He vails his tail, that, like a falling plume,
Cool shadow to his melting buttock lent;
He stamps, and bites the poor flies in his
  fume:
  His love, perceiving how he is enrag'd,
  Grew kinder, and his fury was assuag'd.

His testy master goeth about to take him;
When lo, the unback'd breeder, full of fear,
Jealous of catching, swiftly doth forsake him,
With her the horse, and left Adonis there:
  As they were mad unto the wood they hie
    them,
  Out-stripping crows that strive to over-fly
    them.

All swoln with chasing, down Adonis sits,
Banning his boisterous and unruly beast;
And now the happy season once more fits,
That love-sick Love by pleading may be
  blest;
  For lovers say the heart hath treble wrong,
  When it is barr'd the aidance of the tongue.

An oven that is stopp'd, or river stay'd,
Burneth more hotly, swelleth with more rage:
So of concealed sorrow may be said;
Free vent of words love's fire doth assuage;
  But when the heart's attorney once is mute,
  The client breaks, as desperate in his suit.

He sees her coming, and begins to glow,
Even as a dying coal revives with wind,
And with his bonnet hides his angry brow;
Looks on the dull earth with disturbed mind,
  Taking no notice that she is so nigh,
  For all askaunce he holds her in his eye.
O what a sight it was, wistly to view

How she came stealing to the wayward boy!
To note the fighting conflict of her hue!
How white and red each other did destroy!
  But now her cheek was pale, and by and by
  It flash'd forth fire, as lightning from the
    sky.

Now was she just before him as he sat,
And like a lowly lover down she kneels;
With one fair hand she heaveth up his hat,
Her other tender hand his fair cheek feels:
  His tenderer cheek receives her soft hand's
    print
  As apt as new-fallen snow takes any dint.

O what a war of looks was then between
    them!
Her eyes, petitioners, to his eyes suing:
His eyes saw her eyes as they had not seen
    them;
Her eyes woo'd still, his eyes disdain'd the
    wooing:
  And all this dumb play had his acts made
    plain
  With tears, which, chorus-like, her eyes did
    rain.

Full gently now she takes him by the hand,
A lily prison'd in a gaol of snow,
Or ivory in an alabaster band;
So white a friend engirts so white a foe:
  This beauteous combat, wilful and unwill-
    ing,
  Show'd like two silver doves that sit a-bill-
    ing.

Once more the engine of her thoughts began:
'O fairest mover on this mortal round,
Would thou wert as I am, and I a man,
My heart all whole as thine, thy heart my
    wound;
  For one sweet look thy help I would assure
    thee,
  Though nothing but my body's bane would
    cure thee.'

'Give me my hand,' saith he, 'why dost thou
    feel it?'
'Give me my heart,' saith she, 'and thou shalt
    have it;
O give it me lest thy hard heart do steel it,
And being steel'd, soft sighs can never grave
    it;
  Then love's deep groans I never shall re-
    gard,
  Because Adonis' heart hath made mine
    hard.'

'For shame,' he cries, 'let go, and let me go;
My day's delight is past, my horse is gone,
And 'tis your fault I am bereft him so;
I pray you hence, and leave me here alone:

For all my mind, my thought, my busy
    care,
Is how to get my palfrey from the mare.'

Thus she replies: 'Thy palfrey, as he should,
Welcomes the warm approach of sweet desire.
Affection is a coal that must be cool'd;
Else, suffer'd, it will set the heart on fire:
    The sea hath bounds, but deep desire hath
      none,
    Therefore no marvel though thy horse be
      gone.

'How like a jade he stood, tied to the tree,
Servilely master'd with a leathern rein!
But when he saw his love, his youth's fair fee,
He held such petty bondage in disdain;
    Throwing the base thong from his bending
      crest,
    Enfranchising his mouth, his back, his
      breast.

'Who sees his true love in her naked bed,
Teaching the sheets a whiter hue than white,
But, when his glutton eye so full hath fed,
His other agents aim at like delight?
    Who is so faint that dare not be so bold
    To touch the fire, the weather being cold?

'Let me excuse thy courser, gentle boy;
And learn of him, I heartily beseech thee,
To take advantage on presented joy;
Though I were dumb, yet his proceedings
    teach thee.
    O learn to love; the lesson is but plain,
    And, once made perfect, never lost again.'

'I know not love,' quoth he, 'nor will not
    know it,
Unless it be a boar, and then I chase it:
'Tis much to borrow, and I will not owe it;
My love to love is love but to disgrace it;
    For I have heard it is a life in death,
    That laughs, and weeps, and all but with a
      breath.

'Who wears a garment shapeless and un-
    finish'd?
Who plucks the bud before one leaf put
    forth?
If springing things be any jot diminish'd,
They wither in their prime, prove nothing
    worth:
    The colt that's back'd and burthen'd being
      young
    Loseth his pride, and never. waxeth strong.

'You hurt my hand with wringing; let us
    part,
And leave this idle theme, this bootless chat:
Remove your siege from my unyielding
    heart;
To love's alarm it will not ope the gate.

Dismiss your vows, your feigned tears,
    your flattery;
For where a heart is hard, they make no
    battery.'

'What! canst thou talk,' quoth she, 'hast thou
    a tongue?
O would thou hadst not, or I had no hearing!
Thy mermaid's voice hath done me double
    wrong;
I had my load before, now press'd with bear-
    ing:
    Melodious discord, heavenly tune harsh
      sounding,
    Ear's deep-sweet music, and heart's deep-
      sore wounding.

'Had I no eyes, but ears, my ears would love
That inward beauty and invisible:
Or, were I deaf, thy outward parts would
    move
Each part in me that were but sensible:
    Though neither eyes nor ears, to hear nor
      see,
    Yet should I be in love, by touching thee.

'Say that the sense of feeling were bereft me,
And that I could not see, nor hear, nor touch,
And nothing but the very smell were left me,
Yet would my love to thee be still as much;
    For from the still'tory of thy face excelling
    Comes breath perfum'd, that breedeth love
      by smelling.

'But O, what banquet wert thou to the taste,
Being nurse and feeder of the other four!
Would they not wish the feast might ever
    last,
And bid Suspicion double-lock the door?
    Lest Jealousy, that sour unwelcome guest.
    Should, by his stealing in, disturb the
      feast.'

Once more the ruby-colour'd portal open'd,
Which to his speech did honey passage yield;
Like a red morn, that ever yet betoken'd
Wreck to the seaman, tempest to the field,
    Sorrow to shepherds, woe unto the birds,
    Gusts and foul flaws to herdmen and to
      herds.

This ill presage advisedly she marketh:
Even as the wind is hush'd before it raineth,
Or as the wolf doth grin before it barketh,
Or as the berry breaks before it staineth,
    Or like the deadly bullet of a gun,
    His meaning struck her ere his words
      begun.

And at his look she flatly falleth down,
For looks kill love, and love by looks re-
    viveth:
A smile recures the wounding of a frown,

But blessed bankrupt, that by love so
  thriveth!
The silly-boy, believing she is dead, [red;
Claps her pale cheek, till clapping makes it

And all-amaz'd brake off his late intent,
For sharply he did think to reprehend her,
Which cunning love did wittily prevent:
Fair fall the wit that can so well defend her!
  For on the grass she lies as she were slain,
  Till his breath breatheth life in her again.

He wrings her nose, he strikes her on the
  cheeks,
He bends her fingers, holds her pulses hard;
He chafes her lips, a thousand ways he seeks
To mend the hurt that his unkindness
  marr'd;
  He kisses her; and she, by her good will,
  Will never rise so he will kiss her still.

The night of sorrow now is turn'd to day:
Her two blue windows faintly she upheaveth,
Like the fair sun, when in his fresh array
He cheers the morn, and all the world re-
  lieveth:
  And as the bright sun glorifies the sky,
  So is her face illumin'd with her eye:

Whose beams upon his hairless face are fix'd,
As if from thence they borrow'd all their
  shine.
Were never four such lamps together mix'd,
Had not his clouded with his brows' repine;
  But hers, which thro' the crystal tears gave
  light,
  Shone like the moon in water seen by night.

'O, where am I?' quoth she, 'in earth or
  heaven,
Or in the ocean drench'd, or in the fire?
What hour is this? or morn, or weary even?
Do I delight to die, or life desire?
  But now I liv'd, and life was death's
  annoy;
  But now I died, and death was lively joy.

'O thou didst kill me;—kill me once again:
Thy eyes' shrewd tutor, that hard heart of
  thine,
Hath taught them scornful tricks, and such
  disdain   [mine;
That they have murder'd this poor heart of
  And these mine eyes, true leaders to their
  queen,
  But for thy piteous lips no more had seen.

'Long may they kiss each other, for this cure!
O never let their crimson liveries wear!
And as they last, their verdure still endure,
To drive infection from the dangerous year!
  That the star-gazers, having writ on death,
  May say the plague is banished by thy
  breath.

'Pure lips, sweet seals in my soft lip im-
  printed,
What bargains may I make, still to be seal-
  ing?
To sell myself I can be well contented,
So thou wilt buy, and pay, and use good
  dealing;
  Which purchase if thou make, for fear of
  slips,
  Set thy seal-manual on my wax-red lips.

'A thousand kisses buys my heart from me;
And pay them at thy leisure, one by one.
What is ten hundred touches unto thee?
Are they not quickly told, and quickly gone?
  Say, for non-payment that the debt should
  double,
  Is twenty hundred kisses such a trouble?'

'Fair queen,' quoth he, 'if any love you owe
  me,
Measure my strangeness with my unripe
  years;
Before I know myself seek not to know me;
No fisher but the ungrown fry forbears:
  The mellow plum doth fall, the green sticks
  fast,
  Or being early pluck'd is sour to taste.

'Look, the world's comforter, with weary
  gait,
His day's hot task hath ended in the west:
The owl, night's herald, shrieks,—'tis very
  late;
The sheep are gone to fold, birds to their
  nest;
  And coal-black clouds that shadow
  heaven's light
  Do summon us to part, and bid good night.

'Now let me say "good night," and so say
  you;
If you will say so, you shall have a kiss.'
'Good night,' quoth she; and, ere he says
  'adieu,'
The honey fee of parting tender'd is:
  Her arms do lend his neck a sweet em-
  brace;
  Incorporate then they seem; face grows to
  face.

Till, breathless, he disjoin'd, and backward
  drew
The heavenly moisture, that sweet coral
  mouth,
Whose precious taste her thirsty lips well
  knew,
Whereon they surfeit, yet complain on
  drouth:
  He with her plenty press'd, she faint with
  dearth,
  (Their lips together glued,) fall to the
  earth.

Now quick Desire hath caught the yielding
      prey,
And glutton-like she feeds, yet never filleth;
Her lips are conquerors, his lips obey,
Paying what ransom the insulter willeth;
      Whose vulture thought doth pitch the price
        so high,
      That she will draw his lips' rich treasûre
        dry.

And having felt the sweetness of the spoil,
With blindfold fury she begins to forage;
Her face doth reek and smoke, her blood
      doth boil,
And careless lust stirs up a desperate cour-
      age;
      Planting oblivion, beating reason back,
      Forgetting shame's pure blush, and hon-
        our's wrack.

Hot, faint, and weary, with her hard em-
      bracing,
Like a wild bird being tam'd with too much
      handling,
Or as the fleet-foot roe that's tir'd with
      chasing,
Or like the froward infant still'd with
      dandling,
      He now obeys, and now no more resisteth,
      While she takes all she can, not all she
        listeth.

What wax so frozen but dissolves with tem-
      pering,
And yields at last to every light impression?
Things out of hope are compass'd oft with
      venturing,
Chiefly in love, whose leave exceeds commis-
      sion:
      Affection faints not like a pale-fac'd cow-
        ard,
      But then wooes best when most his choice
        is froward.

When he did frown, O had she then gave
      over,
Such nectar from his lips she had not suck'd.
Foul words and frowns must not repel a
      lover;
What though the rose have prickles, yet 'tis
      pluck'd:
      Were beauty under twenty locks kept fast,
      Yet love breaks through, and picks them
        all at last.

For pity now she can no more detain him;
The poor fool prays her that he may depart:
She is resolv'd no longer to restrain him;
Bids him farewell, and look well to her heart,
      The which, by Cupid's bow she doth pro-
        test,
      He carries thence incaged in his breast.

'Sweet boy,' she says, 'this night I'll waste in
      sorrow,
For my sick heart commands mine eyes to
      watch.
Tell me, love's master, shall we meet to-
      morrow?
Say, shall we? shall we? wilt thou make the
      match?'
      He tells her, no; to-morrow he intends
      To hunt the boar with certain of his
        friends.

'The boar!' quoth she, whereat a sudden pale,
Like lawn being spread upon the blushing
      rose,
Usurps her cheeks; she trembles at his tale,
And on his neck her yoking arms she throws:
      She sinketh down, still hanging by his
        neck,
      He on her belly falls, she on her back.

Now is she in the very lists of love,
Her champion mounted for the hot encoun-
      ter:
All is imaginary she doth prove,
He will not manage her, although he mount
      her;
      That worse than Tantalus' is her annoy,
      To clip Elysium, and to lack her joy.

Even as poor birds, deceiv'd with painted
      grapes,
Do surfeit by the eye, and pine the maw,
Even so she languisheth in her mishaps,
As those poor birds that helpless berries saw:
      The warm effects which she in him finds
        missing,
      She seeks to kindle with continual kissing.

But all in vain; good queen, it will not be:
She hath assay'd as much as may be prov'd;
Her pleading hath deserv'd a greater fee;
She's Love, she loves, and yet she is not
      lov'd.
      'Fie, fie,' he says, 'you crush me; let me
        go;
      You have no reason to withhold me so.'

'Thou hadst been gone,' quoth she, 'sweet
      boy, ere this,   [the boar.
But that thou told'st me thou wouldst hunt
O be advis'd! thou know'st not what it is
With javelin's point a churlish swine to gore,
      Whose tushes never sheath'd he whetteth
        still,
      Like to a mortal butcher, bent to kill.

'On his bow-back he hath a battle set
Of bristly pikes, that ever threat his foes;
His eyes like glowworms shine when he doth
      fret:
His snout digs sepulchres where'er he goes;

Being mov'd, he strikes whate'er is in his way,
And whom he strikes his cruel tushes slay.

'His brawny sides, with hairy bristles arm'd,
Are better proof than thy spear's point can enter;
His short thick neck cannot be easily harm'd;
Being ireful on the lion he will venture:
    The thorny brambles and embracing bushes,
    As fearful of him, part; through whom he rushes.

'Alas, he nought esteems that face of thine,
To which Love's eyes pay tributary gazes;
Nor thy soft hands, sweet lips, and crystal eyne,
Whose full perfection all the world amazes;
    But having thee at vantage, (wondrous dread!)
    Would root these beauties as he roots the mead.

'O, let him keep his loathsome cabin still!
Beauty hath nought to do with such foul fiends:
Come not within his danger by thy will:
They that thrive well take counsel of their friends.
    When thou didst name the boar, not to dissemble,   [tremble.
    I fear'd thy fortune, and my joints did

'Didst thou not mark my face? Was it not white?
Saw'st thou not signs of fear lurk in mine eye?
Grew I not faint? And fell I not downright?
Within my bosom, whereon thou dost lie,
    My boding heart pants, beats, and takes no rest,
    But, like an earthquake, shakes thee on my breast.

'For where Love reigns, disturbing Jealousy
Doth call himself Affection's sentinel;
Gives false alarms, suggesteth mutiny,
And in a peaceful hour doth cry, "kill, kill;"
    Distempering gentle Love in his desire,
    As air and water do abate the fire.

'This sour informer, this bate-breeding spy,
This canker that eats up love's tender spring,
This carry-tale, dissentious Jealousy,
That sometime true news, sometime false doth bring,
    Knocks at my heart, and whispers in mine ear,
    That if I love thee I thy death should fear:

'And, more than so, presenteth to mine eye
The picture of an angry-chafing boar,

Under whose sharp fangs on his back doth lie
An image like thyself, all stain'd with gore;
    Whose blood upon the fresh flowers being shed
    Doth make them droop with grief, and hang the head.

'What should I do, seeing thee so indeed,
That tremble at the imagination?
The thought of it doth make my faint heart bleed,
And fear doth teach it divination:
    I prophesy thy death, my living sorrow,
    If thou encounter with the boar to-morrow.

'But if thou needs will hunt, be rul'd by me;
Uncouple at the timorous flying hare,
Or at the fox, which lives by subtilty,
Or at the roe, which no encounter dare:
    Pursue these fearful creatures o'er the downs,
    And on thy well-breath'd horse keep with thy hounds.

'And when thou hast on foot the purblind hare,
Mark the poor wretch, to overshoot his troubles,
How he outruns the wind, and with what care
He cranks and crosses, with a thousand doubles:
    The many musits through the which he goes
    Are like a labyrinth to amaze his foes.

'Sometime he runs among a flock of sheep,
To make the cunning hounds mistake their smell,
And sometime where earth-delving conies keep,
To stop the loud pursuers in their yell;
    And sometime sorteth with a herd of deer;
    Danger deviseth shifts; wit waits on fear:

'For there his smell with others being mingled,
The hot scent-snuffing hounds are driven to doubt,
Ceasing their clamorous cry till they have singled
With much ado the cold fault cleanly out;
    Then do they spend their mouths: Echo replies,
    As if another chase were in the skies.

'By this, poor Wat, far off upon a hill,
Stands on his hinder legs with listening ear
To hearken if his foes pursue him still;
Anon their loud alarums he doth hear;

And now his grief may be compared well
To one sore sick that hears the passing
   bell.

'Then shalt thou see the dew-bedabbled
   wretch
Turn, and return, indenting with the way;
Each envious briar his weary legs doth
   scratch,
Each shadow makes him stop, each murmur
   stay:
   For misery is trodden on by many,
   And being low never reliev'd by any.

'Lie quietly, and hear a little more;
Nay, do not struggle, for thou shalt not rise:
To make thee hate the hunting of the boar,
Unlike myself thou hear'st me moralize,
   Applying this to that, and so to so;
   For love can comment upon every woe.

'Where did I leave?'—'No matter where,'
   quoth he;
'Leave me, and then the story aptly ends:
The night is spent.'—'Why, what of that?'
   quoth she.
'I am,' quoth he, 'expected of my friends;
And now 'tis dark, and going I shall fall.'
'In night,' quoth she, 'desire sees best of
   all.

'But if thou fall, O then imagine this,
The earth in love with thee thy footing
   trips,
And all is but to rob thee of a kiss. [thy lips
Rich preys make true men thieves: so do
   Make modest Dian cloudy and forlorn,
   Lest she should steal a kiss, and die for-
    sworn.

'Now of this dark night I perceive the rea-
   son:
Cynthia for shame obscures her silver shine,
Till forging nature be condemn'd of treason,
For stealing moulds from heaven that were
   divine,   [despite,
   Wherein she fram'd thee in high heaven's
   To shame the sun by day, and her by night.

'And therefore hath she brib'd the Destinies,
To cross the curious workmanship of nature,
To mingle beauty with infirmities,
And pure perfection with impure defeature;
   Making it subject to the tyranny
   Of mad mischances and much misery;

'As burning fevers, agues pale and faint,
Life-poisoning pestilence, and frenzies wood,
The marrow-eating sickness, whose attaint
Disorder breeds by heating of the blood:
   Surfeits, imposthumes, grief, and damn'd
    despair,
   Swear Nature's death for framing thee so
    fair.

'And not the least of all these maladies,
But in one minute's fight brings beauty
   under:
Both favour, savour, hue, and qualities,
Whereat the impartial gazer late did won-
   der,
   Are on the sudden wasted, thaw'd and
    done,   [sun.
   As mountain-snow melts with the midday

'Therefore, despite of fruitless chastity,
Love-lacking vestals, and self-loving nuns,
That on the earth would breed a scarcity
And barren dearth of daughters and of sons,
   Be prodigal: the lamp that burns by night
   Dries up his oil to lend the world his light.

'What is thy body but a swallowing grave,
Seeming to bury that posterity   [have,
Which by the rights of time thou needs must
If thou destroy them not in dark obscurity?
   If so, the world will hold thee in disdain,
   Sith in thy pride so fair a hope is slain.

'So in thyself thyself art made away;
A mischief worse than civil home-bred strife,
Or theirs whose desperate hands themselves
   do slay
Or butcher-sire, that reaves his son of life.
   Foul cankering rust the hidden treasure
    frets,
   But gold that's put to use more gold be-
    gets.'

'Nay, then,' quoth Adon, 'you will fall again
Into your idle over-handled theme;
The kiss I gave you is bestow'd in vain,
And all in vain you strive against the stream;
   For by this black-fac'd night, desire's foul
    nurse,   [worse.
   Your treatise makes me like you worse and

'If love have lent you twenty thousand
   tongues,
And every tongue more moving than your
   own,
Bewitching like the wanton mermaid's songs,
Yet from mine ear the tempting tune is
   blown;
   For know, my heart stands armed in mine
    ear,
   And will not let a false sound enter there;

'Lest the deceiving harmony should run
Into the quiet closure of my breast;
And then my little heart were quite undone,
In his bedchamber to be barr'd of rest.
   No, lady, no; my heart longs not to groan,
   But soundly sleeps, while now it sleeps
    alone.

'What have you urg'd that I cannot reprove?
The path is smooth that leadeth on to danger;

I hate not love, but your device in love,
That lends embracements unto every strang-
er.
  You do it for increase; O strange excuse!
  When reason is the bawd to lust's abuse.

'Call it not love, for love to heaven is fled,
Since sweating lust on earth usurp'd his
  name;
Under whose simple semblance he hath fed
Upon fresh beauty, blotting it with blame; .
  Which the hot tyrant stains, and soon be-
    reaves,
  As caterpillars do the tender leaves.

'Love comforteth like sunshine after rain,
But lust's effect is tempest after sun;
Love's gentle spring doth always fresh remain,
Lust's winter comes ere summer half be done.
  Love surfeits not; lust like a glutton dies:
  Love is all truth; lust full of forged lies.

'More I could tell, but more I dare not say;
The text is old, the orator too green.
Therefore, in sadness, now I will away;
My face is full of shame, my heart of teen;
  Mine ears that to your wanton talk at-
    tended,
  Do burn themselves for having so offended.'

With this he breaketh from the sweet embrace
Of those fair arms which bound him to her
  breast,
And homeward through the dark laund runs
  apace;
Leaves Love upon her back deeply distress'd.
  Look how a bright star shooteth from the
    sky,
  So glides he in the night from Venus' eye;

Which after him she darts, as one on shore
Gazing upon a late-embarked friend,
Till the wild waves will have him seen no
  more,
Whose ridges with the meeting clouds con-
  tend;
  So did the merciless and pitchy night
  Fold in the object that did feed her sight.

Whereat amaz'd, as one that unaware
Hath dropp'd a precious jewel in the flood,
Or 'stonish'd as night-wanderers often are,
  Their light blown out in some mistrustful
    wood;
  Even so confounded in the dark she lay,
  Having lost the fair discovery of her way.

And now she beats her heart, whereat it
  groans,
That all the neighbour-caves, as seeming
  troubled,
Make verbal repetition of her moans;
Passion on passion deeply is redoubled:

'Ah me!' she cries, and twenty times, 'woe,
  woe!'
And twenty echoes twenty times cry so.

She, marking them, begins a wailing note,
And sings extemp'rally a woeful ditty;
How love makes young men thrall, and old
  men dote;
How love is wise in folly, foolish-witty:
  Her heavy anthem still concludes in woe,
  And still the choir of echoes answer so.

Her song was tedious, and outwore the night,
For lovers' hours are long, though seeming
  short:
If pleas'd themselves, others, they think, de-
  light
In such like circumstance, with such like
  sport:
  Their copious stories, oftentimes begun,
  End without audience, and are never done.

For who hath she to spend the night withal,
But idle sounds resembling parasites,
Like shrill-tongued tapsters answering every
  call,
Soothing the humour of fantastic wits?
  She says, ''tis so:' they answer all, ''tis so;'
  And would say after her, if she said 'no.'

Lo! here the gentle lark, weary of rest,
From his moist cabinet mounts up on high,
And wakes the morning, from whose silver
  breast
The sun ariseth in his majesty;
  Who doth the world so gloriously behold,
  The cedar-tops and hills seem burnish'd
    gold.

Venus salutes him with this fair good-mor-
  row:
'O thou clear god, and patron of all light,
From whom each lamp and shining star doth
  borrow
The beauteous influence that makes him
  bright,
  There lives a son, that suck'd an earthly
    mother,
  May lend thee light, as thou dost lend to
    other.'

This said, she hasteth to a myrtle grove,
Musing the morning is so much o'erworn,
And yet she hears no tidings of her love:
She hearkens for his hounds, and for his
  horn:
  Anon she hears them chant it lustily,
  And all in haste she coasteth to the cry.

And as she runs, the bushes in the way
Some catch her by the neck, some kiss her
  face,
Some twine about her thigh to make her stay;

She wildly breaketh from their strict embrace,
Like a milch doe, whose swelling dugs do
ache,
Hasting to feed her fawn, hid in some
brake.

By this she hears the hounds are at a bay,
Whereat she starts, like one that spies an
adder
Wreath'd up in fatal folds, just in his way,
The fear whereof doth make him shake and
shudder;
Even so the timorous yelping of the hounds
Appals her senses, and her spright con-
founds.

For now she knows it is no gentle chase,
But the blunt boar, rough bear, or lion proud,
Because the cry remaineth in one place,
Where fearfully the dogs exclaim aloud:
Finding their enemy to be so curst,
They all strain court'sy who shall cope him
first.

This dismal cry rings sadly in her ear,
Through which it enters to surprise her heart,
Who, overcome by doubt and bloodless fear,
With cold-pale weakness numbs each feeling
part:
Like soldiers, when their captain once doth
yield,
They basely fly, and dare not stay the field.

Thus stands she in a trembling ecstasy;
Till, cheering up her senses sore-dismay'd,
She tells them 'tis a causeless fantasy,
And childish error that they are afraid;
Bids them leave quaking, bids them fear no
more;—
And with that word she spied the hunted
boar;

Whose frothy mouth, bepainted all with red,
Like milk and blood being mingled ·both to-
gether,
A second fear through all her sinews spread,
Which madly hurries her she knows not
whither:
This way she runs, and now she will no
further,   [ther:
But back retires, to rate the boar for mur-

A thousand spleens bear her a thousand
ways;
She treads the path that she untreads again;
Her more than haste is mated with delays,
Like the proceedings of a drunken brain,
Full of respect, yet nought at all respecting
In hand with all things, nought at all effect-
ing.

Here kennell'd in a brake she finds a hound,
And asks the weary caitiff for his master;
And, there another licking of his wound,

'Gainst venom'd sores the only sovereign
plaster;
And here she meets another sadly scowling,
To whom she speaks, and he replies with
howling.

When he hath ceas'd his ill-resounding noise,
Another flap-mouth'd mourner, black and
grim,
Against the welkin volleys out his voice;
Another and another answer him,
Clapping their proud tails to the ground
below,
Shaking their scratch'd ears, bleeding as
they go.

Look, how the world's poor people are
amaz'd
At apparitions, signs, and prodigies,
Whereon with fearful eyes they long have
gaz'd,
Infusing them with dreadful prophecies:
So she at these sad signs draws up her
breath,
And, sighing it again, exclaims on Death.

'Hard-favour'd tyrant, ugly, meagre, lean,
Hateful divorce of love,' (thus chides she
Death,)
'Grim-grinning ghost, earth's worm, what
dost thou mean
To stifle beauty, and to steal his breath,
Who when he liv'd, his breath and beauty
set
Gloss on the rose, smell to the violet?

'If he be dead,—O no, it cannot be,
Seeing his beauty, thou shouldst strike at it—
O yes, it may; thou hast no eyes to see,
But hatefully at random dost thou hit.
Thy mark is feeble age; but thy false dart
Mistakes that aim, and cleaves an infant's
heart.

'Hadst thou but bid beware, then he had
spoke,
And hearing him thy power had lost his
power.
The Destinies will curse thee for this stroke;
They bid thee crop a weed, thou pluck'st a
flower:
Love's golden arrow at him should have
fled,   [dead.
And not Death's ebon dart, to strike him

'Dost thou drink tears, that thou provok'st
such weeping?
What may a heavy groan advantage thee?
Why hast thou cast into eternal sleeping
Those eyes that taught all other eyes to see?
Now Nature cares not for thy mortal
vigour,
Since her best work is ruin'd with thy
rigour.'

Here overcome, as one full of despair,
She vail'd her eyelids, who, like sluices,
 stopp'd
The crystal tide that from her two cheeks
 fair
In the sweet channel of her bosom dropp'd;
 But through the floodgates breaks the sil-
 ver rain, [again.
 And with his strong course opens them

O how her eyes and tears did lend and borrow!
Her eyes seen in the tears, tears in her eye;
Both crystals, where they view'd each other's
 sorrow,
Sorrow, that friendly sighs sought still to
 dry;
 But like a stormy day, now wind, now
 rain,
 Sighs dry her cheeks, tears make them
 wet again.

Variable passions throng her constant woe,
As striving who should best become her
 grief;
All entertain'd, each passion labours so
That every present sorrow seemeth chief,
 But none is best; then join they all to-
 gether,
 Like many clouds consulting for foul
 weather.

By this, far off she hears some huntsmen
 hollo:
A nurse's song ne'er pleas'd her babe so
 well:
The dire imagination she did follow
This sound of hope doth labour to expel;
 For now reviving joy bids her rejoice,
 And flatters her it is Adonis' voice.

Whereat her tears began to turn their tide,
Being prison'd in her eye, like pearls in glass;
Yet sometimes falls an orient drop beside,
Which her cheek melts, as scorning it should
 pass,
 To wash the foul face ·of the sluttish
 ground,
 Who is but drunken when she seemeth
 drown'd.

O hard-believing love, how strange it seems
Not to believe, and yet too credulous!
Thy weal and woe are both of them ex-
 tremes,
Despair and hope make thee ridiculous:
 The one doth flatter thee in thoughts un-
 likely,
 In likely thoughts the other kills thee
 quickly.

Now she unweaves the web that she hath
 wrought;
Adonis lives, and Death is not to blame;

It was not she that called him all-to naught:
Now she adds honours to his hateful name;
 She clepes him king of graves, and grave
 for kings,
 Imperious supreme of all mortal things.

'No, no,' quoth she, 'sweet Death, I did but
 jest;
Yet pardon me, I felt a kind of fear,
When as I met the boar, that bloody beast,
Which knows no pity, but is still severe;
 Then, gentle shadow (truth I must con-
 fess),
 I rail'd on thee, fearing my love's decease.

''Tis not my fault: the boar provok'd my
 tongue;
Be wreak'd on him, invisible commander;
'Tis he, foul creature, that hath done thee
 wrong;
I did but act, he's author of thy slander:
 Grief hath two tongues, and never woman
 yet
 Could rule them both, without ten wo-
 men's wit.'

Thus, hoping that Adonis is alive,
Her rash suspect she doth extenuate;
And that his beauty may the better thrive,
With Death she humbly doth insinuate;
 Tells him of trophies, statues, tombs; and
 stories
 His victories, his triumphs, and his glories.

'O Jove,' quoth she, 'how much a fool was I
To be of such a weak and silly mind,
To wail his death who lives, and must not
 die,
Till mutual overthrow of mortal kind!
 For he being dead, with him is beauty
 slain,
 And, beauty dead, black chaos comes
 again.

'Fie, fie, fond love, thou art so full of fear
As one with treasure laden, hemm'd with
 thieves,
Trifles, unwitnessed with eye or ear,
Thy coward heart with false bethinking
 grieves.'
 Even at this word she hears a merry horn,
 Whereat she leaps that was but late for-
 lorn.

As falcon to the lure away she flies;
The grass stoops not, she treads on it so
 light;
And in her haste unfortunately spies
The foul boar's conquest on her fair delight;
 Which seen, her eyes, as murder'd with the
 view,
 Like stars asham'd of day, themselves
 withdrew.

Or, as the snail, whose tender horns being
    hit,
Shrinks backward in his shelly cave with
    pain,
And there, all smother'd up, in shade doth
    sit,
Long after fearing to creep forth again;
    So, at his bloody view, her eyes are fled
    Into the deep dark cabins of her head;

Where they resign their office and their light
To the disposing of her troubled brain;
Who bids them still consort with ugly night,
And never wound the heart with looks
    again;
    Who, like a king perplexed in his throne,
    By their suggestion gives a deadly groan.

Whereat each tributary subject quakes:
As when the wind, imprison'd in the ground,
Struggling for passage, earth's foundation
    shakes,
Which with cold terror doth men's minds
    confound,
    The mutiny each part doth so surprise,
    That from their dark beds once more leap
    her eyes;

And, being open'd, threw unwilling light
Upon the wide wound that the boar had
    trench'd
In his soft flank; whose wonted lily white
With purple tears, that his wound wept, was
    drench'd:
    No flower was nigh, no grass, herb, leaf, or
    weed,   [to bleed.
    But stole his blood, and seem'd with him

This solemn sympathy poor Venus noteth;
Over one shoulder doth she hang her head;
Dumbly she passions, franticly she doteth;
She thinks he could not die, he is not dead.
    Her voice is stopp'd, her joints forget to
    bow;
    Her eyes are mad that they have wept till
    now.

Upon his hurt she looks so steadfastly,
That her sight dazzling makes the wound
    seem three;
And then she reprehends her mangling eye
That makes more gashes where no breach
    should be:
    His face seems twain, each several limb is
    doubled;   [troubled.
    For oft the eye mistakes, the brain being

'My tongue cannot express my grief for one,
And yet,' quoth she, 'behold two Adons
    dead!
My sighs are blown away, my salt tears
    gone,

Mine eyes are turn'd to fire, my heart to
    lead;
    Heavy heart's lead melt at mine eyes' red
    fire!
    So shall I die by drops of hot desire.

'Alas, poor world, what treasure hast thou
    lost!
What face remains alive that's worth the
    viewing?   [boast
Whose tongue is music now? what canst thou
Of things long since, or anything ensuing?
    The flowers are sweet, their colours fresh
    and trim;
    But true-sweet beauty liv'd and died with
    him.

'Bonnet nor veil henceforth no creature
    wear!
Nor sun nor wind will ever strive to kiss
    you:
Having no fair to lose, you need not fear;
The sun doth scorn you, and the wind doth
    hiss you:
    But when Adonis liv'd, sun and sharp air
    Lurk'd like two thieves to rob him of his
    fair;

'And therefore would he put his bonnet on,
Under whose brim the gaudy sun would
    peep;
The wind would blow it off, and, being gone,
Play with his locks; then would Adonis
    weep:
    And straight, in pity of his tender years,
    They both would strive who first should
    dry his tears.

'To see his face the lion walk'd along
Behind some hedge, because he would not
    fear him:
To recreate himself, when he hath sung,
The tiger would be tame and gently hear
    him:
    If he had spoke the wolf would leave his
    prey,
    And never fright the silly lamb that day.

'When he beheld his shadow in the brook,
The fishes spread on it their golden gills;
When he was by, the birds such pleasure
    took
That some would sing, some other in their
    bills
    Would bring him mulberries, and ripe-red
    cherries;   [berries.
    He fed them with his sight, they him with

'But this foul, grim, and urchin-snouted
    boar,
Whose downward eye still looketh for a
    grave,

Ne'er saw the beauteous livery that he wore;
Witness the entertainment that he gave;
If he did see his face, why then I know
He thought to kiss him, and hath kill'd
    him so.

' 'Tis true, 'tis true; thus was Adonis slain;
He ran upon the boar with his sharp
    spear,
Who did not whet his teeth at him again,
But by a kiss thought to persuade him
    there;
    And nuzzling in his flank the loving swine
    Sheath'd, unaware, the tusk in his soft
        groin.

'Had I been tooth'd like him, I must con-
    fess,
With kissing him I should have kill'd him
    first;
But he is dead, and never did he bless
My youth with his; the more am I accurst.'
    With this she falleth in the place she stood,
    And stains her face with his congealed
        blood.

She looks upon his lips, and they are pale;
She takes him by the hand, and that is
    cold;
She whispers in his ears a heavy tale,
As if they heard the woeful words she told:
    She lifts the coffer-lids that close his eyes,
    Where, lo! two lamps, burnt out, in dark-
        ness lies:

Two glasses where herself herself beheld
A thousand times, and now no more reflect;
Their virtue lost, wherein they late ex-
    cell'd,
And every beauty robb'd of his effect:
    'Wonder of time,' quoth she, 'this is my
        spite,
    That you being dead the day should yet
        be light.

'Since thou art dead, lo! here I prophesy,
Sorrow on love hereafter shall attend;
It shall be waited on with jealousy,
Find sweet beginning but unsavoury end;
    Ne'er settled equally, but high or low;
    That all love's pleasure shall not match
        his woe.

'It shall be fickle, false, and full of fraud;
Bud and be blasted in a breathing while;
The bottom poison, and the top o'erstraw'd
With sweets that shall the truest sight be-
    guile:
    The strongest body shall it make most
        weak,
    Strike the wise dumb, and teach the fool
        to speak.

'It shall be sparing, and too full of riot,
Teaching decrepit age to tread the measures;
The staring ruffian shall it keep in quiet,
Pluck down the rich, enrich the poor with
    treasures:
    It shall be raging mad, and silly mild,
    Make the young old, the old become a
        child.

'It shall suspect where is no cause of fear;
It shall not fear where it should most mis-
    trust;
It shall be merciful, and too severe,
And most deceiving when it seems most
    just;
    Perverse it shall be where it shows most
        toward,
    Put fear to valour, courage to the coward

'It shall be cause of war and dire events,
And set dissension 'twixt the son and sire;
Subject and servile to all discontents,
As dry combustious matter is to fire;
    Sith in his prime death doth my love de-
        stroy,
    They that love best their love shall not
        enjoy.'

By this, the boy that by her side lay kill'd
Was melted like a vapour from her sight,
And in his blood that on the ground lay
    spill'd,
A purple flower sprung up, chequer'd with
    white,
    Resembling well his pale cheeks, and the
        blood
    Which in round drops upon their white-
        ness stood.

She bows her head, the new-sprung flower
    to smell,
Comparing it to her Adonis' breath;
And says, within her bosom it shall dwell,
Since he himself is reft from her by death:
    She crops the stalk, and in the breach
        appears
    Green dropping sap, which she compares
        to tears.

'Poor flower,' quoth she, 'this was thy
    father's guise,
(Sweet issue of a more sweet-smelling sire,)
For every little grief to wet his eyes,
To grow unto himself was his desire,
    And so 'tis thine; but know, it is as good
    To wither in my breast as in his blood.

'Here was thy father's bed, here in my breast;
Thou art the next of blood, and 'tis thy
    right:
Lo! in this hollow cradle take thy rest,
My throbbing heart shall rock thee day and
    night:

There shall not be one minute in an hour
Wherein I will not kiss my sweet love's
    flower.'

Thus weary of the world, away she hies,
And yokes her silver doves; by whose swift
    aid

Their mistress, mounted, through the empty
    skies
In her light chariot quickly is convey'd,
    Holding their course to Paphos, where
        their queen
    Means to immure herself, and not be
        seen.

THE RAPE OF LUCRECE

TO THE

RIGHT HONOURABLE HENRY WRIOTHESLY,

EARL OF SOUTHAMPTON, AND BARON OF TITCHFIELD.

THE love I dedicate to your Lordship is without end; whereof this pamphlet, without beginning, is but a superfluous moiety. The warrant I have of your honourable disposition, not the worth of my untutored lines, makes it assured of acceptance. What I have done is yours, what I have to do is yours; being part in all I have, devoted yours. Were my worth greater my duty would show greater: meantime, as it is, it is bound to your Lordship, to whom I wish long life, still lengthened with all happiness,

Your Lordship's in all duty,
WILLIAM SHAKESPEARE.

THE ARGUMENT.

LUCIUS TARQUINIUS (for his excessive pride surnamed Superbus), after he had caused his own father-in-law, Servius Tullius, to be cruelly murdered, and, contrary to the Roman laws and customs, not requiring or staying for the people's suffrages, had possessed himself of the kingdom, went, accompanied with his sons and other noblemen of Rome, to besiege Ardea. During which siege, the principal men of the army meeting one evening at the tent of Sextus Tarquinius, the king's son, in their discourses after supper, every one commended the virtues of his own wife; among whom, Collatinus extolled the incomparable chastity of his wife Lucretia. In that pleasant humour they all posted to Rome; and intending by their secret and sudden arrival to make trial of that which every one had before avouched, only Collatinus finds his wife (though it were late in the night) spinning amongst her maids: the other ladies were all found dancing and revelling, or in several disports. Whereupon the noblemen yielded Collatinus the victory, and his wife the fame. At that time Sextus Tarquinius, being inflamed with Lucrece's beauty, yet smothering his passions for the present, departed with the rest back to the camp; from whence he shortly after privily withdrew himself, and was (according to his estate) royally entertained and lodged by Lucrece at Collatium. The same night he treacherously stealeth into her chamber, violently ravished her, and early in the morning speedeth away. Lucrece, in this lamentable plight, hastily despatcheth messengers, one to Rome for her father, another to the camp for Collatine. They came, the one accompanied with Junius Brutus, the other with Publius Valerius; and, finding Lucrece attired in mourning habit, demanded the cause of her sorrow. She, first taking an oath of them for her revenge, revealed the actor and whole manner of his dealing, and withal suddenly stabbed herself. Which done, with one consent they all vowed to root out the whole hated family of the Tarquins; and, bearing the dead body to Rome, Brutus acquainted the people with the doer and manner of the vile deed, with a bitter invective against the tyranny of the king; wherewith the people were so moved, that with one consent and a general acclamation the Tarquins were all exiled, and the state government changed from kings to consuls.

FROM the besieged Ardea all in post,
Borne by the trustless wings of false desire,
Lust-breathed Tarquin leaves the Roman host,
And to Collatium bears the lightless fire
Which, in pale embers hid, lurks to aspire,
  And girdle with embracing flames the waist
  Of Collatine's fair love, Lucrece the chaste.

Haply that name of chaste unhapp'ly set
This bateless edge on his keen appetite;

When Collatine unwisely did not let
To praise the clear unmatched red and white
Which triumph'd in that sky of his delight,
  Where mortal stars, as bright as heaven's beauties,
  With pure aspects did him peculiar duties.

For he the night before, in Tarquin's tent,
Unlock'd the treasure of his happy state,
What priceless wealth the heavens had him lent
In the possession of his beauteous mate;

Reckoning his fortune at such high-proud
    rate,
  That kings might be espoused to more
    fame,
  But king nor peer to such a peerless dame.

O happiness enjoy'd but of a few!
And, if possess'd, as soon decay'd and done
As is the morning's silver-melting dew
Against the golden splendour of the sun!
An expir'd date, cancell'd ere well begun:
  Honour and beauty, in the owner's arms,
  Are weakly fortress'd from a world of
    harms.

Beauty itself doth of itself persuade
The eyes of men without an orator;
What needeth then apologies be made
To set forth that which is so singular?
Or why is Collatine the publisher
  Of that rich jewel he should keep unknown
  From thievish ears, because it is his own?

Perchance his boast of Lucrece's sovereignty
Suggested this proud issue of a king;
For by our ears our hearts oft tainted be:
Perchance that envy of so rich a thing,
Braving compare, disdainfully did sting
  His high-pitch'd thoughts, that meaner
    men should vaunt,
  That golden hap which their superiors
    want.

But some untimely thought did instigate
His all-too-timeless speed, if none of those:
His honour, his affairs, his friends, his state,
Neglected all, with swift intent he goes
To quench the coal which in his liver glows.
  O rash false heat, wrapp'd in repentant
    cold,
  Thy hasty spring still blasts, and ne'er
    grows old!

When at Collatium this false lord arriv'd,
Well was he welcom'd by the Roman dame,
Within whose face beauty and virtue striv'd
Which of them both should underprop her
    fame:
When virtue bragg'd, beauty would blush
    for shame;
  When beauty boasted blushes, in despite
  Virtue would stain that or with silver
    white.

But beauty, in that white intituled,
From Venus' doves doth challenge that fair
    field:
Then virtue claims from beauty beauty's
    red,
Which virtue gave the golden age, to gild
Their silver cheeks, and call'd it then their
    shield;
  Teaching them thus to use it in the fight,—

When shame assail'd, the red should fence
    the white.

This heraldry in Lucrece' face was seen,
Argued by beauty's red, and virtue's white:
Of either's colour was the other queen,
Proving from world's minority their right:
Yet their ambition makes them still to fight;
  The sovereignty of either being so great,
  That oft they interchange each other's
    seat.

This silent war of lilies and of roses
Which Tarquin view'd in her fair face's field,
In their pure ranks his traitor eye encloses;
Where, lest between them both it should be
    kill'd,
The coward captive vanquished doth yield
  To those two armies that would let him
    go,
  Rather than triumph in so false a foe.

Now thinks he that her husband's shallow
    tongue
(The niggard prodigal that prais'd her so)
In that high task hath done her beauty
    wrong,
Which far exceeds his barren skill to show:
Therefore that praise which Collatine doth
    owe,
  Enchanted Tarquin answers with surmise,
  In silent wonder of still-gazing eyes.

This earthly saint, adored by this devil,
Little suspecteth the false worshipper;
For unstain'd thoughts do seldom dream on
    evil;
Birds never lim'd no secret bushes fear:
So guiltless she securely gives good cheer
  And reverend welcome to her princely
    guest,
  Whose inward ill no outward harm ex-
    press'd:

For that he colour'd with his high estate,
Hiding base sin in plaits of majesty;
That nothing in him seem'd inordinate,
Save sometime too much wonder of his eye,
Which, having all, all could not satisfy;
  But, poorly rich, so wanteth in his store
  That cloy'd with much he pineth still for
    more.

But she, that never cop'd with stranger eyes,
Could pick no meaning from their parling
    looks,
Nor read the subtle-shining secrecies
Writ in the glassy margents of such books;
She touch'd no unknown baits, nor fear'd no
    hooks;
  Nor could she moralize his wanton sight,
  More than his eyes were open'd to the
    light.

He stories to her ears her husband's fame,
Won in the fields of fruitful Italy;
And decks with praises Collatine's high
  name,
Made glorious by his manly chivalry,
With bruised arms and wreaths of victory;
  Her joy with heav'd-up hand she doth
    express,
  And, wordless, so greets heaven for his
    success.

Far from the purpose of his coming thither
He makes excuses for his being there.
No cloudy show of stormy blustering
  weather
Doth yet in his fair welkin once appear;
Till sable Night, mother of Dread and Fear,
  Upon the world dim darkness doth dis-
    play,
  And in her vaulty prison stows the day.

For then is Tarquin brought unto his bed,
Intending weariness with heavy spright;
For, after supper, long he questioned
With modest Lucrece, and wore out the
  night:
Now leaden slumber with life's strength doth
  fight;
  And every one to rest themselves betake,
  Save thieves, and cares, and troubled
    minds, that wake.

As one of which doth Tarquin lie revolving
The sundry dangers of his will's obtaining;
Yet ever to obtain his will resolving,
Though weak-built hopes persuade him to
  abstaining;
Despair to gain doth traffic oft for gaining;
  And when great treasure is the meed pro-
    pos'd,
  Though death be adjunct, there's no death
    suppos'd.

Those that much covet are with gain so fond
That what they have not, that which they
  possess
They scatter and unloose it from their bond,
And so, by hoping more, they have but less;
Or, gaining more, the profit of excess
  Is but to surfeit, and such griefs sustain,
  That they prove bankrupt in this poor-rich
    gain.

The aim of all is but to nurse the life
With honour, wealth, and ease, in waning
  age;
And in this aim there is such thwarting
  strife,
That one for all, or all for one we gage;
As life for honour in fell battles' rage;
  Honour for wealth; and oft that wealth
    doth cost
  The death of all, and all together lost.

So that in vent'ring ill we leave to be
The things we are, for that which we ex-
  pect;
And this ambitious foul infirmity,
In having much, torments us with defect
Of that we have: so then we do neglect
  The thing we have, and, all for want of
    wit,
  Make something nothing, by augmenting
    it.

Such hazard now must doting Tarquin make,
Pawning his honour to obtain his lust;
And for himself himself he must forsake:
Then where is truth if there be no self-trust?
When shall he think to find a stranger just,
  When he himself himself confounds, be-
    trays
  To slanderous tongues, and wretched hate-
    ful days?

Now stole upon the time the dead of night,
When heavy sleep had clos'd up mortal eyes;
No comfortable star did lend his light, [cries;
No noise but owls' and wolves' death-boding
Now serves the season that they may sur-
  prise
  .The silly lambs; pure thoughts are dead
    and still, [kill.
  While lust and murder wake to stain and

And now this lustful lord leap'd from his
  bed,
Throwing his mantle rudely o'er his arm;
Is madly toss'd between desire and dread;
Th' one sweetly flatters, th' other feareth
  harm;
But honest Fear, bewitch'd with lusts's foul
  charm,
  Doth too too oft betake him to retire,
  Beaten away by brain-sick rude Desire.

His falchion on a flint he softly smiteth,
That from the cold stone sparks of fire do
  fly,
Whereat a waxen torch forthwith he light-
  eth,
Which must be lode-star to his lustful eye:
And to the flame thus speaks advisedly:
  'As from this cold flint I enforc'd this fire,
  So Lucrece must I force to my desire.'

Here pale with fear he doth premeditate
The dangers of his loathsome enterprise,
And in his inward mind he doth debate
What following sorrow may on this arise;
Then looking scornfully, he doth despise
  His naked armour of still-slaughter'd lust,
  And justly thus controls his thoughts un-
    just:

'Fair torch, burn out thy light, and lend it
  not
To darken her whose light excelleth thine!

And die, unhallow'd thoughts, before you
blot
With your uncleanness that which is divine!
Offer pure incense to so pure a shrine:
  Let fair humanity abhor the deed
  That spots and stains love's modest snow-
    white weed.

'O shame to knighthood and to shining
  arms!
O foul dishonour to my household's grave!
O impious act, including all foul harms!
A martial man to be soft fancy's slave;
True valour still a true respect should have;
  Then my digression is so vile, so base,
  That it will live engraven in my face.

'Yea, though I die, the scandal will survive,
And be an eyesore in my golden coat;
Some loathsome dash the herald will con-
  trive,
To cipher me how fondly I did dote;
That my posterity, sham'd with the note,
  Shall curse my bones, and hold it for no
    sin
  To wish that I their father had not been.

'What win I if I gain the thing I seek?
A dream, a breath, a froth of fleeting joy:
Who buys a minute's mirth to wail a week?
Or sells eternity to get a toy?
For one sweet grape who will the vine de-
  stroy?
  Or what fond beggar, but to touch the
    crown,
  Would with the sceptre straight be
    strucken down?

'If Collatinus dream of my intent,
Will he not wake, and in a desperate rage
Post hither, this vile purpose to prevent?
This siege that hath engirt his marriage,
This blur to youth, this sorrow to the sage,
  This dying virtue, this surviving shame,
  Whose crime will bear an ever-during
    blame?

'O what excuse can my invention make
When thou shalt charge me with so black a
  deed?
Will not my tongue be mute, my frail joints
  shake?
Mine eyes forego their light, my false heart
  bleed?
The guilt being great, the fear doth still
  exceed;
  And extreme fear can neither fight nor fly,
  But, coward-like, with trembling terror
    die.

'Had Collatinus kill'd my son or sire,
Or lain in ambush to betray my life,

Or were he not my dear friend, this desire
Might have excuse to work upon his wife;
As in revenge or quittal of such strife:
  But as he is my kinsman, my dear friend,
  The shame and fault finds no excuse nor
    end.

'Shameful it is;—ay, if the fact be known:
Hateful it is;—there is no hate in loving;
I'll beg her love;—but she is not her own;
The worst is but denial, and reproving:
My will is strong, past reason's weak re-
  moving.
  Who fears a sentence or an old man's saw
  Shall by a painted cloth be kept in awe.'

Thus, graceless, holds he disputation
'Tween frozen conscience and hot-burning
  will,
And with good thoughts makes dispensation,
Urging the worser sense for vantage still;
Which in a moment doth confound and kill
  All pure effects, and doth so far proceed,
  That what is vile shows like a virtuous
    deed.

Quoth he, 'She took me kindly by the hand,
And gaz'd for tidings in my eager eyes,
Fearing some hard news from the warlike
  band
Where her beloved Collatinus lies.
O how her fear did make her colour rise!
  First red as roses that on lawn we lay,
  Then white as lawn, the roses took away.

'And how her hand, in my hand being
  lock'd,
Forc'd it to tremble with her loyal fear;
Which struck her sad, and then it faster
  rock'd,
Until her husband's welfare she did hear;
Whereat she smiled with so sweet a cheer,
  That had Narcissus seen her as she stood,
  Self-love had never drown'd him in the
    flood.

'Why hunt I then for colour or excuses?
All orators are dumb when beauty pleadeth;
Poor wretches have remorse in poor abuses;
Love thrives not in the heart that shadows
  dreadeth:
Affection is my captain, and he leadeth;
  And when his gaudy banner is display'd,
  The coward fights, and will not be dis-
    may'd.

'Then, childish fear, avaunt! debating, die!
Respect and reason wait on wrinkled age!
My heart shall never countermand mine
  eye;
Sad pause and deep regard beseem the sage;
My part is youth and beats these from the
  stage.

Desire my pilot is, beauty my prize;
Then who fears sinking where such treasure lies?'

As corn o'ergrown by weeds, so heedful fear
Is almost chok'd by unresisted lust.
Away he steals with opening, listening ear,
Full of foul hope, and full of fond mistrust;
Both which, as servitors to the unjust,
So cross him with their opposite persuasion,
That now he vows a league, and now invasion.

Within his thought her heavenly image sits,
And in the selfsame seat sits Collatine:
That eye which looks on her confounds his wits;
That eye which him beholds, as more divine,
Unto a view so false will not incline;
But with a pure appeal seeks to the heart,
Which once corrupted takes the worser part;

And therein heartens up his servile powers,
Who, flatter'd by their leader's jocund show,
Stuff up his lust, as minutes fill up hours;
And as their captain, so their pride doth grow,
Paying more slavish tribute than they owe.
By reprobate desire thus madly led,
The Roman lord marcheth to Lucrece' bed.

The locks between her chamber and his will,
Each one by him enforc'd retires his ward;
But as they open they all rate his ill,
Which drives the creeping thief to some regard,
The threshold grates the door to have him heard;
Night-wand'ring weasels shriek to see him there;
They fright him, yet he still pursues his fear.

As each unwilling portal yields him way,
Through little vents and crannies of the place
The wind wars with his torch, to make him stay,
And blows the smoke of it into his face,
Extinguishing his conduct in this case;
But his hot heart, which fond desire doth scorch,
Puffs forth another wind that fires the torch:

And being lighted, by the light he spies
Lucretia's glove, wherein her needle sticks;
He takes it from the rushes where it lies,
And griping it, the needl his finger pricks:
As who should say this glove to wanton tricks

Is not inur'd; return again in haste;
Thou seest our mistress' ornaments are chaste.

But all these poor forbiddings could not stay him;
He in the worst sense construes their denial:
The doors, the wind, the glove that did delay him,
He takes for accidental things of trial;
Or as those bars which stop the hourly dial,
Who with a lingering stay his course doth let,
Till every minute pays the hour his debt.

'So, so,' quoth he, 'these lets attend the time,
Like little frosts that sometime threat the spring,
To add a more rejoicing to the prime,
And give the sneaped birds more cause to sing.
Pain pays the income of each precious thing
Huge rocks, high winds, strong pirates, shelves and sands,
The merchant fears, ere rich at home he lands.'

Now is he come unto the chamber door
That shuts him from the heaven of his thought,
Which with a yielding latch, and with no more,
Hath barr'd him from the blessed thing he sought.
So from himself impiety hath wrought,
That for his prey to pray he doth begin,
As if the heaven should countenance his sin.

But in the midst of his unfruitful prayer,
Having solicited the eternal power,
That his foul thoughts might compass his fair fair,
That they would stand auspicious to the hour,
Even there he starts:—quoth he, 'I must deflower; [fact.
The powers to whom I pray abhor this
How can they then assist me in the act?

'Then Love and Fortune be my gods, my guide!
My will is back'd with resolution: [tried,
Thoughts are but dreams till their effects be
The blackest sin is clear'd with absolution;
Against love's fire fear's frost hath dissolution.
The eye of heaven is out, and misty night
Covers the shame that follows sweet delight.'

This said, his guilty hand pluck'd up the latch,
And with his knee the door he opens wide:

The dove sleeps fast that this night-owl will
    catch;
Thus treason works ere traitors be espied.
Who sees the lurking serpent steps aside;
    But she, sound sleeping, fearing no such
        thing,
    Lies at the mercy of his mortal sting.

Into the chamber wickedly he stalks,
And gazeth on her yet unstained bed.
The curtains being close, about he walks,
Rolling his greedy eyeballs in his head:
By their high treason is his heart misled;
    Which gives the watchword to his hand
        full soon,
    To draw the cloud that hides the silver
        moon.

Look, as the fair and fiery-pointed sun,
Rushing from forth a cloud, bereaves our
    sight;
Even so, the curtain drawn, his eyes begun
To wink, being blinded with a greater light:
Whether it is that she reflects so bright,
    That dazzleth them, or else some shame
        supposed;   [enclosed.
    But blind they are, and keep themselves

O, had they in that darksome prison died,
Then had they seen the period of their ill!
Then Collatine again by Lucrece' side
In his clear bed might have reposed still:
But they must ope, this blessed league to
    kill;
    And holy-thoughted Lucrece to their sight
    Must sell her joy, her life, her world's
        delight.

Her lily hand her rosy cheek lies under,
Cozening the pillow of a lawful kiss;
Who therefore angry, seems to part in sun-
    der,
Sweiling on either side to want his bliss;
Between whose hills her head entombed is:
    Where, like a virtuous monument, she
        lies,
    To be admir'd of lewd unhallow'd eyes.

Without the bed her other fair hand was,
On the green coverlet; whose perfect white
Show'd like an April daisy on the grass,
With pearly sweat, resembling dew of night.
Her eyes, like marigolds, had sheath'd their
    light,
    And canopied in darkness sweetly lay,
    Till they might open to adorn the day.

Her hair, like golden threads, play'd with
    her breath;
O modest wantons! wanton modesty!
Showing life's triumph in the map of death,
And death's dim look in life's mortality:

Each in her sleep themselves so beautify,
    As if between them twain there were no
        strife,
    But that life liv'd in death, and death in
        life.

Her breasts, like ivory globes circled with
    blue,
A pair of maiden worlds unconquered,
Save of their lord no bearing yoke they
    knew,
And him by oath they truly honoured.
These worlds in Tarquin new ambition bred:
    Who like a foul usurper went about
    From this fair throne to heave the owner
        out.

What could he see but mightily he noted?
What did he note but strongly he desir'd?
What he beheld on that he firmly doted,
And in his will his wilful eye he tir'd.
With more than admiration he admir'd
    Her azure veins, her alabaster skin,
    Her coral lips, her snow-white dimpled
        chin.

As the grim lion fawneth o'er his prey,
Sharp hunger by the conquest satisfied,
So o'er this sleeping soul doth Tarquin stay,
His rage of lust by gazing qualified;
Slack'd, not suppress'd; for standing by her
    side,
    His eye, which late this mutiny restrains,
    Unto a greater uproar tempts his veins:

And they, like straggling slaves for pillage
    fighting,
Obdurate vassals, fell exploits effecting,
In bloody death and ravishment delighting,
Nor children's tears, nor mother's groans re-
    specting,
Swell in their pride, the onset still expecting:
    Anon his beating heart, alarum striking,
    Gives the hot charge, and bids them do
        their liking.

His drumming heart cheers up his burning
    eye,
His eye commends the leading to his hand;
His hand, as proud of such a dignity, [stand
Smoking with pride, march'd on to make his
On her bare breast, the heart of all her land;
    Whose ranks of blue veins, as his hand did
        scale,
    Left their round turrets destitute and pale.

They, mustering to the quiet cabinet
Where their dear governess and lady lies,
Do tell her she is dreadfully beset,
And fright her with confusion of their cries:
She, much amaz'd, breaks ope her lock'd-up
    eyes,
    Who, peeping forth this tumult to behold,

Are by his flaming torch dimm'd and con-
troll'd.

Imagine her as one in dead of night
From forth dull sleep by dreadful fancy
waking,
That thinks she hath beheld some ghastly
sprite,
Whose grim aspect sets every joint a shak-
ing;
What terror 'tis! but she, is worser taking,
From sleep disturbed, heedfully doth view
The sight which makes supposed terror
true.

Wrapp'd and confounded in a thousand
fears,
Like to a new-kill'd bird she trembling lies;
She dares not look; yet, winking, there ap-
pears
Quick-shifting antics, ugly in her eyes:
Such shadows are the weak brain's forger-
ies:
Who, angry that the eyes fly from their
lights,
In darkness daunts them with more dread-
ful sights.

His hand, that yet remains upon her breast,
(Rude ram, to batter such an ivory wall!)
May feel her heart, poor citizen, distress'd,
Wounding itself to death, rise up and fall,
Beating her bulk, that his hand shakes
withal.
This moves in him more rage, and lesser
pity,
To make the breach, and enter this sweet
city.

First, like a trumpet, doth his tongue begin
To sound a parley to his heartless foe,
Who o'er the white sheet peers her whiter
chin,
The reason of this rash alarm to know,
Which he by dumb demeanour seeks to
show;
But she with vehement prayers urgeth still
Under what colour he commits this ill.

Thus he replies: 'The colour in thy face
(That even for anger makes the lily pale,
And the red rose blush at her own disgrace)
Shall plead for me, and tell my loving tale:
Under that colour am I come to scale
Thy never-conquer'd fort: the fault is
thine,
For those thine eyes betray thee unto mine.

'Thus I forestall thee, if thou mean to chide:
Thy beauty hath ensnar'd thee to this night,
Where thou with patience must my will
abide,
My will that marks thee for my earth's
delight,

Which I to conquer sought with all my
might;
But as reproof and reason beat it dead,
By thy bright beauty was it newly bred.

'I see what crosses my attempt will bring;
I know what thorns the growing rose de-
fends;
I think the honey guarded with a sting:
All this, beforehand, counsel comprehends:
But will is deaf, and hears no heedful
friends;
Only he hath an eye to gaze on beauty
And dotes on what he looks, 'gainst law or
duty.

'I have debated, even in my soul,
What wrong, what shame, what sorrow I
shall breed;
But nothing can Affection's course control,
Or stop the headlong fury of his speed.
I know repentant tears ensue the deed,
Reproach, disdain, and deadly enmity;
Yet strive I to embrace mine infamy.'

This said, he shakes aloft his Roman blade,
Which, like a falcon towering in the skies,
Coucheth the fowl below with his wing's
shade,
Whose crooked beak threats if he mount he
dies:
So under his insulting falchion lies
Harmless Lucretia, marking what he tells
With trembling fear, as fowl hear falcon's
bells.

'Lucrece,' quoth he, 'this night I must enjoy
thee:
If thou deny, then force must work my way
For in thy bed I purpose to destroy thee;
That done, some worthless slave of thine I'll
slay,
To kill thine honour with thy life's decay;
And in thy dead arms do I mean to place
him,
Swearing I slew him, seeing thee embrace
him.

'So thy surviving husband shall remain
The scornful mark of every open eye;
Thy kinsmen hang their heads at this dis-
dain,
Thy issue blurr'd with nameless bastardy:
And thou, the author of their obloquy,
Shall have thy trespass cited up in rhymes,
And sung by children in succeeding times.

'But if thou yield I rest thy secret friend:
The fault unknown is as a thought unacted;
A little harm, done to a great good end,
For lawful policy remains enacted.
The poisonous simple sometimes is com-
pacted

In a pure compound; being so applied,
His venom in effect is purified.

'Then, for thy husband and thy children's
sake,
Tender my suit: bequeath not to their lot
The shame that from them no device can
take,
The blemish that will never be forgot;
Worse than a slavish wipe, or birth-hour's
blot:
  For marks descried in men's nativity
  Are nature's faults, not their own infamy.'

Here with a cockatrice' dead-killing eye
He rouseth up himself, and makes a pause;
While she, the picture of pure piety,
Like a white hind under the grype's sharp
claws,
Pleads in a wilderness, where are no laws,
  To the rough beast that knows no gentle
  right,
  Nor aught obeys but his foul appetite:

But when a black-fac'd cloud the world doth
threat,
In his dim mist the aspiring mountains hiding,
From earth's dark womb some gentle gust
doth get,
Which blows these pitchy vapours from their
biding,
Hindering their present fall by this divid-
ing;
  So his unhallow'd haste her words delays,
  And moody Pluto winks while Orpheus
  plays.

Yet, foul night-waking cat, he doth but
dally,
While in his holdfast foot the weak mouse
panteth;
Her sad behaviour feeds his vulture folly,
A swallowing gulf that even in plenty want-
eth:
His ear her prayers admits, but his heart
granteth
  No penetrable entrance to her plaining:
  Tears harden lust, though marble wear
  with raining.

Her pity-pleading eyes are sadly fix'd
In the remorseless wrinkles of his face;.
Her modest eloquence with sighs is mix'd,
Which to her oratory adds more grace.
She puts the period often from his place,
  And 'midst the sentence so her accent
  breaks,
  That twice she doth begin ere once she
  speaks.

She conjures him by high almighty Jove,
By knighthood, gentry, and sweet friend-
ship's oath,
By her untimely tears, her husband's love,
By holy human law, and common troth,
By heaven and earth, and all the power of
both,
  That to his borrow'd bed he make retire,
  And stoop to honour, not to foul desire.

Quoth she, 'Reward not hospitality. [tended;
With such black payment as thou hast pre-
Mud not the fountain that gave drink to
thee;
Mar not the thing that cannot be amended;
End thy ill aim, before thy shoot be ended:
  He is no woodman that doth bend his bow
  To strike a poor unseasonable doe.

'My husband is thy friend, for his sake
spare me;
Thyself art mighty, for thine own sake leave
me;
Myself a weakling, do not then ensnare me;
Thou look'st not like deceit; do not deceive
me;
My sighs, like whirlwinds, labour hence to
heave thee.
  If ever man were mov'd with woman's
  moans,
  Be moved with my tears, my sighs, my
  groans:

'All which together, like a troubled ocean,
Beat at thy rocky and wreck-threatening
heart;
To soften it with their continual motion;
For stones dissolv'd to water do convert.
O, if no harder than a stone thou art,
  Melt at my tears, and be compassionate!
  Soft pity enters at an iron gate.

'In Tarquin's likeness I did entertain thee;
Hast thou put on his shape to do him
shame?
To all the host of heaven I complain me,
Thou wrong'st his honour, wound'st his
princely name.
Thou art not what thou seem'st; and if the
same,
  Thou seem'st not what thou art, a god, a
  king;
  For kings like gods should govern every-
  thing.

'How will thy shame be seeded in thine age,
'When thus thy vices bud before thy spring!
If in thy hope thou dar'st do such outrage,
What dar'st thou not when once thou art a
king!
O be remember'd, no outrageous thing
  From vassal actors can be wip'd away;
  Then kings' misdeeds cannot be hid ·in
  clay.

'This deed will make thee only lov'd for
fear,

But happy monarchs still are fear'd for love:
With foul offenders thou perforce must bear,
When they in thee the like offences prove:
If but for fear of this thy will remove;
    For princes are the glass, the school, the
        book,   [look.
    Where subjects' eyes do learn, do read, do

'And wilt thou be the school where Lust
    shall learn?
Must he in thee read lectures of such shame:
Wilt thou be glass, wherein it shall discern
Authority for sin, warrant for blame,
To privilege dishonour in thy name?
    Thou back'st reproach against long-lived
        laud,
    And mak'st fair reputation but a bawd.

'Hast thou command? by him that gave it
    thee,
From a pure heart command thy rebel will:
Draw not thy sword to guard iniquity,
For it was lent thee all that brood to kill.
Thy princely office how canst thou fulfil,
    When, pattern'd by thy fault, foul Sin
        may say,   [way?
    He learn'd to sin, and thou didst teach the

'Think but how vile a spectacle it were
To view thy present trespass in another.
Men's faults do seldom to themselves ap-
    pear;
Their own transgressions partially they
    smother:
This guilt would seem death-worthy in thy
    brother,
    O how are they wrapp'd in with in-
        famies,
    That from their own misdeeds askaunce
        their eyes!

'To thee, to thee, my heav'd-up hands appeal,
Not to seducing lust, thy rash relier;
I sue for exil'd majesty's repeal;
Let him return and flattering thoughts retire:
His true respect will 'prison false desire,
    And wipe the dim mist from thy doting
        eyne,   [mine.'
    That thou shalt see thy state, and pity

'Have done,' quoth he; 'my uncontrolled tide
Turns not, but swells the higher by this let.
Small lights are soon blown out, huge fires
    abide,
And with the wind in greater fury fret:
The petty streams that pay a daily debt
    To their salt sovereign, with their fresh
        falls' haste,
    Add to his flow, but alter not his taste.'

'Thou art,' quoth she, 'a sea, a sovereign
    king;
And lo, there falls into thy boundless flood

Black lust, dishonour, shame, misgoverning,
Who seek to stain the ocean of thy blood.
If all these petty ills shall charge thy good,
    Thy sea within a puddle's womb is hears'd,
    And not the puddle in thy sea dispers'd.

'So shall these slaves be king, and thou their
    slave;
Thou nobly base, they basely dignified;
Thou their fair life, and they thy fouler
    grave;
Thou loathed in their shame, they in thy
    pride:
The lesser things should not the greater hide;
    The cedar stoops not to the base shrub's
        foot,
    But low shrubs wither at the cedar's root.

'So let thy thoughts, low vassals to thy
    state'—
'No more,' quoth he; 'by heaven, I will not
    hear thee:
Yield to my love; if not, enforced hate,
Instead of love's coy touch, shall rudely tear
    thee;
That done, despitefully I mean to bear thee
    Unto the base bed of some rascal groom,
    To be thy partner in this shameful doom.'

This said, he sets the foot upon the light,
For light and lust are deadly enemies;
Shame folded up in blind concealing night,
When most unseen, then most doth tyrannize.
The wolf hath seiz'd his prey, the poor lamb
    cries
    Till with her own white fleece her voice
        controll'd
    Entombs her outcry in her lips' sweet fold:

For with the nightly linen that she wears
He pens her piteous clamours in her head;
Cooling his hot face in the chastest tears
That ever modest eyes with sorrow shed.
O, that prone lust should stain so pure a
    bed!
    The spots whereof could weeping purify,
    Her tears should drop on them perpetually.

But she hath lost a dearer thing than life,
And he hath won what he would lose again.
This forced league doth force a further strife,
This momentary joy breeds months of pain,
This hot desire converts to cold disdain:
    Pure Chastity is rifled of her store,
    And Lust, the thief, far poorer than before.

Look, as the full-fed hound or gorged hawk,
Unapt for tender smell or speedy flight,
Make slow pursuit, or altogether balk
The prey wherein by nature they delight;
So surfeit-taking Tarquin fares this night:
    His taste delicious, in digestion souring,
    Devours his will that liv'd by foul devour-
        ing.

O deeper sin than bottomless conceit
Can comprehend in still imagination!
Drunken desire must vomit his receipt,
Ere he can see his own abomination.
While lust is in his pride no exclamation
    Can curb his heat, or rein his rash desire,
    Till, like a jade, self-will himself doth tire.

And then with lank and lean discolour'd
    cheek,
With heavy eye, knit brow, and strengthless
    pace,
Feeble desire, all recreant, poor, and meek,
Like to a bankrupt beggar wails his case:
The flesh being proud, desire doth fight with
    grace,
    For there it revels; and when that decays,
    The guilty rebel for remission prays.

So fares it with this faultful lord of Rome,
Who this accomplishment so hotly chas'd;
For now against himself he sounds his doom,
That through the length of times he stands
    disgrac'd:
Besides, his soul's fair temple is defac'd;
    To whose weak ruins muster troops of
    cares,
    To ask the spotted princess how she fares.

She says, her subjects with foul insurrection
Have batter'd down her consecrated wall,
And by their mortal fault brought in subjec-
    tion
Her immortality, and make her thrall
To living death, and pain perpetual;
    Which in her prescience she controlled still,
    But her foresight could not forestall their
    will.

Even in this thought through the dark night
    he stealeth,
A captive victor that hath lost in gain;
Bearing away the wound that nothing
    healeth,
The scar that will, despite of cure, remain,
Leaving his spoil perplex'd in greater pain.
    She bears the load of lust he left behind,
    And he the burthen of a guilty mind.

He like a thievish dog creeps sadly thence;
She like a wearied lamb lies panting there;
He scowls, and hates himself for his offence;
She, desperate, with her nails her flesh doth
    tear;
He faintly flies, sweating with guilty fear;
    She stays, exclaiming on the direful night;
    He runs, and chides his vanish'd, loath'd
    delight.

He thence departs a heavy convertite;
She there remains a hopeless castaway:
He in his speed looks for the morning light;
She prays she never may behold the day;

'For day,' quoth she, 'night's scapes doth
    open lay;
And my true eyes have never practis'd how
To cloak offences with a cunning brow.

'They think not but that every eye can see
The same disgrace which they themselves
    behold;
And therefore would they still in darkness be,
To have their unseen sin remain untold;
For they their guilt with weeping will un-
    fold,
    And grave, like water, that doth eat in
    steel,
    Upon my cheeks what helpless shame I
    feel.'

Here she exclaims against repose and rest,
And bids her eyes hereafter still be blind.
She wakes her heart by beating on her breast,
And bids it leap from thence, where it may
    find
Some purer chest, to close so pure a mind.
    Frantic with grief thus breathes she forth
    her spite
    Against the unseen secrecy of night:

'O comfort-killing night, image of hell!
Dim register and notary of shame!
Black stage for tragedies and murders fell!
Vast sin-concealing chaos! nurse of blame!
Blind muffled bawd! dark harbour for de-
    fame!
    Grim cave of death, whispering conspira-
    tor,
    With close-tongued treason and the rav-
    isher!

'O hateful, vaporous, and foggy night,
Since thou art guilty of my cureless crime,
Muster thy mists to meet the eastern light,
Make war against proportion'd course of
    time!
Or if thou wilt permit the sun to climb
    His wonted height, yet ere he go to bed,
    Knit poisonous clouds about his golden
    head.

'With rotten damps ravish the morning air;
Let their exhal'd unwholesome breaths make
    sick
The life of purity, the supreme fair,
Ere he arrive his weary noontide prick;
And let thy misty vapours march so thick,
    That in their smoky ranks his smother'd
    light,
    May set at noon, and make perpetual
    night.

'Were Tarquin night (as he is but night's
    child),
The silver-shining queen he would distain;
Her twinkling handmaids too, by him defil'd,

Through night's black bosom should not peep
  again;
So should I have copartners in my pain:
  And fellowship in woe doth woe assuage,
  As palmers' chat makes short their pil-
    grimage.

'Where now I have no one to blush with me,
To cross their arms, and hang their heads
    with mine,
To mask their brows, and hide their infamy;
But I alone alone must sit and pine,
Seasoning the earth with showers of silver
    brine,
  Mingling my talk with tears, my grief with
    groans,
  Poor wasting monuments of lasting moans.

'O night, thou furnace of foul-reeking smoke,
Let not the jealous day behold that face
Which underneath thy black all-hiding cloak
Immodestly lies martyr'd with disgrace!
Keep still possession of thy gloomy place,
  That all the faults which in thy reign are
    made,
  May likewise be sepulchred in thy shade!

'Make me not object to the tell-tale day!
The light will show, character'd in my brow,
The story of sweet chastity's decay,
The impious breach of holy wedlock vow:
Yea, the illiterate, that know not how
  To 'cipher what is writ in learned books,
  Will quote my loathsome trespass in my
    looks.

'The nurse, to still her child, will tell my
    story,
And fright her crying babe with Tarquin's
    name;
The orator, to deck his oratory,
Will couple my reproach to Tarquin's shame:
Feast-finding minstrels, tuning my defame,
  Will tie the hearers to attend each line,
  How Tarquin wronged me, I Collatine.

'Let my good name, that senseless reputation,
For Collatine's dear love be kept unspotted:
If that be made a theme for disputation,
The branches of another root are rotted,
And undeserv'd reproach to him allotted,
  That is as clear from this attaint of mine,
  As I, ere this, was pure to Collatine.

'O unseen shame! invisible disgrace!
O unfelt sore! crest-wounding, private scar!
Reproach is stamp'd in Collatinus' face,
And Tarquin's eye may read the mot afar,
How he in peace is wounded, not in war.
  Alas, how many bear such shameful blows,
  Which not themselves but he that gives
    them knows!

'If, Collatine, thine honour lay in me,
From me by strong assault it is bereft.
My honey lost, and I, a drone-like bee,
Have no perfection of my summer left,
But robb'd and ransack'd by injurious theft:
  In thy weak hive a wandering wasp hath
    crept,   [kept.
  And suck'd the honey which thy chaste bee

'Yet am I guilty of thy honour's wrack,—
Yet for thy honour did I entertain him;
Coming from thee, I could not put him back,
For it had been dishonour to disdain him:
Besides of weariness he did complain him,
  And talk'd of virtue:—O, unlook'd for evil,
  When virtue is profan'd in such a devil!

'Why should the worm intrude the maiden
    bud?
Or hateful cuckoos hatch in sparrows' nests?
Or toads infect fair founts with venom
    mud?
Or tyrant folly lurk in gentle breasts?
Or kings be breakers of their own behests?
  But no perfection is so absolute,
  That some impurity doth not pollute.

'The aged man that coffers up his gold
Is plagued with cramps, and gouts, and pain-
    ful fits,
And scarce hath eyes his treasure to behold,
But like still-pining Tantalus he sits,
And useless barns the harvest of his wits;
  Having no other pleasure of his gain
  But torment that it cannot cure his pain.

'So then he hath it, when he cannot use it,
And leaves it to be master'd by his young;
Who in their pride do presently abuse it:
Their father was too weak, and they too
    strong,
To hold their cursed-blessed fortune long,
  The sweets we wish for turn to loathed
    sours,
  Even in the moment that we call them
    ours.

'Unruly blasts wait on the tender spring;
Unwholesome weeds take root with precious
    flowers;
The adder hisses where the sweet birds sing;
What virtue breeds iniquity devours:
We have no good that we can say is ours,
  But ill-annexed Opportunity
  Or kills his life, or else his quality.

'O Opportunity! thy guilt is great:
'Tis thou that execut'st the traitor's treason;
Thou sett'st the wolf where he the lamb
    may get;
Whoever plots the sin, thou 'point'st the sea-
    son;

'Tis thou that spurn'st at right, at law, at
    reason;
And in thy shady cell, where none may
    spy him,
  Sits Sin, to seize the souls that wander by
    him.

'Thou mak'st the vestal violate her oath;
Thou blow'st the fire when temperance is
    thaw'd;
Thou smother'st honesty, thou murther'st
    troth;
Thou foul abettor! thou notorious bawd!
Thou plantest scandal, and displacest laud:
  Thou ravisher, thou traitor, thou false
    thief,
  Thy honey turns to gall, thy joy to grief!

'Thy secret pleasure turns to open shame,
Thy private feasting to a public fast;
Thy smoothing titles to a ragged name;
Thy sugar'd tongue to bitter wormwood
    taste:
Thy violent vanities can never last.
  How comes it then, vile Opportunity,
  Being so bad, such numbers seek for thee?

'When wilt thou be the humble suppliant's
    friend,
And bring him where his suit may be ob-
    tain'd?
When wilt thou sort an hour great strifes to
    end?
Or free that soul which wretchedness hath
    chain'd?
Give physic to the sick, ease to the pain'd?
  The poor, lame, blind, halt, creep, cry out
    for thee;
  But they ne'er meet with Opportunity.

'The patient dies while the physician sleeps;
The orphan pines while the oppressor feeds;
Justice is feasting while the widow weeps;
Advice is sporting while infection breeds;
Thou grant'st no time for charitable deeds:
  Wrath, envy, treason, rape, and murder's
    rages,
  Thy heinous hours wait on them as their
    pages.

'When truth and virtue have to do with thee,
A thousand crosses keep them from thy aid;
They buy thy help: but Sin ne'er gives a fee,
He gratis comes; and thou art well appay'd
As well to hear as grant what he hath said.
  My Collatine would else have come to me
  When Tarquin did, but he was stay'd by
    thee.

'Guilty thou art of murder and of theft;
Guilty of perjury and subornation;
Guilty of treason, forgery, and shift;
Guilty of incest, that abomination:

An accessary by thine inclination
  To all sins past, and all that are to come,
  From the creation to the general doom.

'Mis-shapen Time, copesmate of ugly night,
Swift subtle post, carrier of grisly care,
Eater of youth, false slave to false delight,
Base watch of woes, sin's packhorse, virtue's
    snare;
Thou nursest all, and murtherest all that are.
  O hear me then, injurious, shifting Time!
  Be guilty of my death, since of my crime.

'Why hath thy servant, Opportunity,
Betray'd the hours thou gav'st me to repose?
Cancell'd my fortunes and enchained me
To endless date of never-ending woes?
Time's office is to fine the hate of foes;
  To eat up errors by opinion bred,
  Not spend the dowry of a lawful bed.

'Time's glory is to calm contending kings,
To unmask falsehood, and bring truth to
    light,
To stamp the seal of time in aged things,
To wake the morn, and sentinel the night,
To wrong the wronger till he render right;
  To ruinate proud buildings with thy hours,
  And smear with dust their glittering golden
    towers:

'To fill with worm-holes stately monuments,
To feed oblivion with decay of things,
To blot old books, and alter their contents,
To pluck the quills from ancient ravens'
    wings,
To dry the old oak's sap, and cherish springs;
  To spoil antiquities of hammer'd steel,
  And turn the giddy round of Fortune's
    wheel;

'To show the beldame daughters of her
    daughter,
To make the child a man, the man a child,
To slay the tiger that doth live by slaughter,
To tame the unicorn and lion wild,
To mock the subtle, in themselves beguil'd;
  To cheer the ploughman with increaseful
    crops,
  And waste huge stones with little water-
    drops.

'Why work'st thou mischief in thy pilgrim-
    age,
Unless thou couldst return to make amends?
One poor retiring minute in an age
Would purchase thee a thousand thousand
    friends,
Lending him wit that to bad debtors lends:
  O, this dread night, wouldst thou one hour
    come back,
  I could prevent this storm, and shun thy
    wrack!

'Thou ceaseless lackey to eternity,
With some mischance cross Tarquin in his
  flight:
Devise extremes beyond extremity,
To make him curse this cursed crimeful
  night:
Let ghastly shadows his lewd eyes affright,
  And the dire thought of his committed evil
  Shape every bush a hideous shapeless devil.

'Disturb his hours of rest with restless
  trances,
Afflict him in his bed with bedrid groans;
Let there bechance him pitiful mischances,
To make him moan, but pity not his moans:
Stone him with harden'd hearts, harder than
  stones;
  And let mild women to him lose their
  mildness,
  Wilder to him than tigers in their wildness.

'Let him have time to tear his curled hair,
Let him have time against himself to rave,
Let him have time of Time's help to despair,
Let him have time to live a loathed slave,
Let him have time a beggar's orts to crave;
  And time to see one that by alms doth live
  Disdain to him disdained scraps to give.

'Let him have time to see his friends his foes,
And merry fools to mock at him resort;
Let him have time to mark how slow time
  goes
In time of sorrow, and how swift and short
His time of folly and his time of sport:
  And ever let his unrecalling crime
  Have time to wail the abusing of his time.

'O Time, thou tutor both to good and bad,
Teach me to curse him that thou taught'st
  this ill!
At his own shadow let the thief run mad!
Himself himself seek every hour to kill!
Such wretched hands such wretched blood
  should spill:
  For who so base would such an office have
  As slanderous death's-man to so base a
  slave?

'The baser is he, coming from a king,
To shame his hope with deeds degenerate.
The mightier man, the mightier is the thing
That makes him honour'd, or begets him
  hate;
For greatest scandal waits on greatest state.
  The moon being clouded presently is miss'd,
  But little stars may hide them when they
  list.

'The crow may bathe his coal-black wings in
  mire,
And unperceiv'd fly with the filth away,
But if the like the snow-white swan desire,

The stain upon his silver down will stay.
Poor grooms are sightless night, kings glorious
  day.
  Gnats are unnoted whersoe'er they fly,
  But eagles gaz'd upon with every eye.

'Out, idle words, servants to shallow fools!
Unprofitable sounds, weak arbitrators!
Busy yourselves in skill-contending schools,
Debate where leisure serves with dull de-
  baters;
To trembling clients be you mediators:
  For me, I force not argument a straw,
  Since that my case is past the help of law.

'In vain I rail at Opportunity,
At Time, at Tarquin, and uncheerful night;
In vain I cavil with my infamy,
In vain I spurn at my confirm'd despite:
This helpless smoke of words doth me no
  right.
  The remedy indeed to do me good,
  Is to let forth my foul, defiled blood.

'Poor hand, why quiver'st thou at this de-
  cree?
Honour thyself to rid me of this shame;
For if I die my honour lives in thee,
But if I live thou liv'st in my defame:
Since thou couldst not defend thy loyal dame,
  And was afear'd to scratch her wicked foe,
  Kill both thyself and her for yielding so.'

This said, from her betumbled couch she
  starteth,
To find some desperate instrument of death:
But this no-slaughter-house no tool im-
  parteth,
To make more vent for passage of her breath,
Which thronging through her lips so van-
  isheth
  As smoke from Ætna, that in air consumes,
  Or that which from discharged cannon
  fumes.

'In vain,' quoth she, 'I live, and seek in vain
Some happy mean to end a hapless life.
I fear'd by Tarquin's falchion to be slain,
Yet for the self-same purpose seek a knife:
But when I fear'd I was a loyal wife;
  So am I now:—O no, that cannot be;
  Or that true type hath Tarquin rifled me.

'O! that is gone for which I sought to live,
And therefore now I need not fear to die.
To clear this spot by death, at least I give
A badge of fame to slander's livery;
A dying life to living infamy;
  Poor helpless help, the treasure stolen away,
  To burn the guiltless casket where it lay!

'Well, well, dear Collatine, thou shalt not
  know

The stained taste of violated troth;
I will not wrong thy true affection so
To flatter thee with an infringed oath;
This bastard graff shall never come to
    growth:
  He shall not boast who did thy stock pol-
      lute
  That thou art doting father of his fruit.

'Nor shall he smile at thee in secret thought,
Nor laugh with his companions at thy state;
But thou shalt know thy interest was not
    bought
Basely with gold, but stolen from forth thy
    gate.
  For me, I am the mistress of my fate,
  And with my trespass never will dispense,
  Till life to death acquit my forc'd offence.

'I will not poison thee with my attaint,
Nor fold my fault in cleanly-coin'd excuses;
My sable ground of sin I will not paint,
To hide the truth of this false night's abuses:
  My tongue shall utter all; mine eyes like
      sluices,
    As from a mountain-spring that feeds a
        dale,
    Shall gush pure streams to purge my im-
      pure tale.'

By this, lamenting Philomel had ended
The well-tun'd warble of her nightly sorrow,
And solemn night with slow-sad gait de-
    scended
To ugly hell; when lo, the blushing morrow
Lends light to all fair eyes that light will
    borrow:
  But cloudy Lucrece shames herself to see
  And therefore still in night would clois-
      ter'd be.

Revealing day through every cranny spies,
And seems to point her out where she sits
    weeping,
To whom she sobbing speaks: 'O eye of eyes,
Why pryest thou through my window? leave
    thy peeping;
Mock with thy tickling beams eyes that are
    sleeping:
  Brand not my forehead with thy piercing
      light,
  For day hath nought to do what's done by
      night.'

Thus cavils she with everything she sees:
True grief is fond and testy as a child,
Who wayward once, his mood with nought
    agrees.
Old woes, not infant sorrows, bear them mild;
Continuance tames the one; the other wild,
  Like an unpractis'd swimmer plunging still
  With too much labour drowns for want of
      skill.

So she, deep-drenched in a sea of care,
Holds disputation with each thing she views,
And to herself all sorrow doth compare;
No object but her passion's strength renews;
And as one shifts, another straight ensues:
  Sometime her grief is dumb and hath no
      words;   [fords.
  Sometime 'tis mad, and too much talk af-

The little birds that tune their morning's joy
Make her moans mad with their sweet mel-
    ody.
For mirth doth search the bottom of annoy;
Sad souls are slain in merry company:
Grief best is pleas'd with grief's society:
  True sorrow then is feelingly suffic'd
  When with like semblance it is sym-
      pathiz'd.

'Tis double death to drown in ken of shore;
He ten times pines that pines beholding food;
To see the salve doth make the wound ache
    more;
Great grief grieves most at that would do it
    good;
Deep woes roll forward like a gentle flood,
  Who, being stopp'd, the bounding banks
      o'erflows:
  Grief dallied with nor law nor limit knows.

'You mocking birds,' quoth she, 'your tunes
    entomb
Within your hollow-swelling feather'd
    breasts,
And in my hearing be you mute and dumb!
(My restless discord loves no stops nor rests;
A woeful hostess brooks not merry guests:)
  Relish your nimble notes to pleasing ears;
  Distress like dumps when time is kept with
      tears.

'Come, Philomel, that sing'st of ravishment,
Make thy sad grove in my dishevell'd hair.
As the dank earth weeps at thy languishment,
So I at each sad strain will strain a tear,
And with deep groans the diapason bear:
  For burthen-wise I'll hum on Tarquin still,
  While thou on Tereus descant'st better
      skill.

'And whiles against a thorn thou bear'st thy
    part,
To keep thy sharp woes waking, wretched I,
To imitate thee well, against my heart
Will fix a sharp knife, to affright mine eye;
Who, if it wink, shall thereon fall and die.
  These means, as frets upon an instrument,
  Shall tune our heartstrings to true lan-
      guishment.

'And for, poor bird, thou sing'st not in the
    day,
As shaming any eye should thee behold,

Some dark deep desert, seated from the way,
That knows nor parching heat nor freezing
cold,
We will find out; and there we will unfold
To creatures stern sad tunes, to change
their kinds:
Since men prove beasts, let beasts bear
gentle minds.'

As the poor frighted deer, that stands at gaze,
Wildly determining which way to fly,
Or one encompass'd with a winding maze,
That cannot tread the way out readily;
So with herself is she in mutiny,
To live or die which of the twain were
better,
When life is sham'd, and Death reproach's
debtor.

'To kill myself,' quoth she, 'alack! what were
it,
But with my body my poor soul's pollution?
They that lose half with greater patience
bear it
Than they whose whole is swallow'd in con-
fusion.
That mother tries a merciless conclusion
Who, having two sweet babes, when death
takes one,
Will slay the other, and be nurse to none.

'My body or my soul, which was the dearer?
When the one pure, the other made divine.
Whose love of either to myself was nearer?
When both were kept for heaven and Colla-
tine.
Ah, me! the bark peel'd from the lofty pine,
His leaves will wither, and his sap decay;
So must my soul, her bark being peel'd
away.

'Her house is sack'd, her quiet interrupted,
Her mansion batter'd by the enemy;
Her sacred temple spotted, spoil'd, corrupted,
Grossly engirt with daring infamy:
Then let it not be call'd impiety
If in this blemish'd fort I make some hole
Through which I may convey this troubled
soul.

'Yet die I will not till my Collatine
Have heard the cause of my untimely death;
That he may vow, in that sad hour of mine,
Revenge on him that made me stop my
breath.
My stained blood to Tarquin I'll bequeath,
Which by him tainted shall for him be
spent,
And as his due writ in my testament.

'My honour I'll bequeath unto the knife
That wounds my body so dishonoured.
'Tis honour to deprive dishonour'd life;

The one will live, the other being dead:
So of shame's ashes shall my fame be bred;
For in my death I murther shameful
scorn:
My shame so dead, mine honour is new-
born.

'Dear lord of that dear jewel I have lost,
What legacy shall I bequeath to thee?
My resolution, Love, shall be thy boast,
By whose example thou reveng'd mayst be.
How Tarquin must be used, read it in me:
Myself, thy friend, will kill myself, thy
foe;
And, for my sake, serve thou false Tar-
quin so.

'This brief abridgment of my will I make:
My soul and body to the skies and ground;
My resolution, husband, do thou take;
Mine honour be the knife's that makes my
wound;
My shame be his that did my fame con-
found;
And all my fame that lives disbursed be
To those that live, and think no shame of
me.

'Thou, Collatine, shalt oversee this will;
How was I overseen that thou shalt see it!
My blood shall wash the slander of mine ill;
My life's foul deed my life's fair end shall
free it.
Faint not, faint heart, but stoutly say, "so
be it."
Yield to my hand; my hand shall conquer
thee;
Thou dead, both die, and both shall vic-
tors be.

This plot of death when sadly she had laid,
And wip'd the brinish pearl from her bright
eyes,
With untun'd tongue she hoarsely call'd her
maid,
Whose swift obedience to her mistress hies;
For fleet-wing'd duty with thought's feathers
flies.
Poor Lucrece' cheeks unto her maid seem
so
As winter meads when sun doth melt their
snow.

Her mistress she doth give demure good-
morrow,
With soft-slow tongue, true mark of modesty,
And sorts a sad look to her lady's sorrow,
(For why? her face wore sorrow's livery,)
But durst not ask of her audaciously
Why her two suns were cloud-eclipsed so,
Nor why her fair cheeks over-wash'd with
woe.

But as the earth doth weep, the sun being
  set,
Each flower moisten'd like a melting eye;
Even so the maid with swelling drops 'gan
  wet
Her circled eyne, enforc'd by sympathy
Of those fair suns, set in her mistress' sky,
  Who in a salt-wav'd ocean quench their
    light,
  Which makes the maid weep like the dewy
    night.

A pretty while these pretty creatures stand,
Like ivory conduits coral cisterns filling:
One justly weeps; the other takes in hand
No cause, but company, of her drops spilling:
  Their gentle sex to weep are often willing;
  Grieving themselves to guess at others'
    smarts,
  And then they drown their eyes, or break
    their hearts.

For men have marble, women waxen minds,
And therefore are they form'd as marble
  will;
The weak oppress'd, the impression of
  strange kinds
Is form'd in them by force, by fraud, or
  skill:
  Then call them not the authors of their ill,
  No more than wax shall be accounted evil,
  Wherein is stamp'd the semblance of a
    devil.

Their smoothness, like a goodly champaign
  plain,
Lays open all the little worms that creep;
In men, as in a rough-grown grove, remain
Cave-keeping evils that obscurely sleep:
  Through crystal walls each little mote will
    peep:
  Though men can cover crimes with bold
    stern looks,
  Poor women's faces are their own faults'
    books.

No man inveigh against the wither'd flower,
But chide rough winter that the flower hath
  kill'd!
Not that devour'd, but that which doth de-
  vour
Is worthy blame. O, let it not be hild
Poor women's faults that they are so fulfill'd
  With men's abuses! those proud lords, to
    blame,
  Make weak-made women tenants to their
    shame.

The precedent whereof in Lucrece view,
Assail'd by night with circumstances strong
Of present death, and shame that might en-
  sue
By that her death, to do her husband wrong:

Such danger to resistance did belong,
  That dying fear through all her body
    spread;
  And who cannot abuse a body dead?

By this, mild Patience bid fair Lucrece speak
To the poor counterfeit of her complaining:
'My girl,' quoth she, 'on what occasion break
Those tears from thee, that down thy cheeks
  are raining?
  If thou dost weep for grief of my sustaining,
  Know, gentle wench, it small avails my
    mood:
  If tears could help, mine own would do me
    good.

'But tell me, girl, when went'—(and there
  she stay'd
Till after a deep groan) 'Tarquin from
  hence?'
  Madam, ere I was up,' replied the maid,
'The more to blame my sluggard negligence:
  Yet with the fault I thus far can dispense;
  Myself was stirring ere the break of day,
  And, ere I rose, was Tarquin gone away.

'But, lady, if your maid may be so bold,
She would request to know your heaviness.'
'O peace!' quoth Lucrece; 'if it should be
  told,
The repetition cannot make it less;
For more it is than I can well express:
  And that deep torture may be call'd a hell,
  When more is felt than one hath power to
    tell.

'Go, get me hither paper, ink, and pen—
Yet save that labour, for I have them here.
What should I say?—One of my husband's
  men
Bid thou be ready, by and by, to bear
A letter to my lord, my love, my dear;
  Bid him with speed prepare to carry it:
  The cause craves haste, and it will soon be
    writ.'

Her maid is gone, and she prepares to
  write,
First hovering o'er the paper with her quill:
Conceit and grief an eager combat fight;
What wit sets down is blotted straight with
  will:
  This is too curious-good, this blunt and ill:
  Much like a press of people at a door,
  Throng her inventions, which shall be be-
    fore.

At last she thus begins:—'Thou worthy lord
Of that unworthy wife that greeteth thee,
Health to thy person! next vouchsafe to af-
  ford
(If ever, love, thy Lucrece thou wilt see)
Some present speed to come and visit me:

So I commend me from our house in grief;
My woes are tedious, though my words
are brief.'

Here folds she up the tenor of her woe,
Her certain sorrow writ uncertainly.
By this short schedule Collatine may know
Her grief, but not her grief's true quality;
She dares not thereof make discovery,
  Lest he should hold it her own gross abuse,
  Ere she with blood had stain'd her stain'd
    excuse.

Besides, the life and feeling of her passion
She hoards, to spend when he is by to hear
  her;
When sighs, and groans, and tears may grace
  the fashion
Of her disgrace, the better so to clear her
From that suspicion which the world might
  bear her
  To shun this blot, she would not blot the
    letter   [better.
  With words, till action might become them

To see sad sights moves more than hear them
  told;
For then the eye interprets to the ear
The heavy motion that it doth behold,
When every part a part of woe doth bear.
'Tis but a part of sorrow that we hear:
  Deep sounds make lesser noise than shal-
    low fords,   [of words.
  And sorrow ebbs, being blown with wind

Her letter now is seal'd, and on it writ,
'At Ardea to my lord with more than haste;'
The post attends, and she delivers it,
Charging the sour-fac'd groom to hie as fast
As lagging fowls before the northern blast.
  Speed more than speed but dull and slow
    she deems:
  Extremity still urgeth such extremes.

The homely villain court'sies to her low;
And blushing on her, with a steadfast eye
Receives the scroll, without or yea or no,
And forth with bashful innocence doth hie.
But they whose guilt within their bosoms lie
  Imagine every eye beholds their blame;
  For Lucrece thought he blush'd to see her
    shame;

When, silly groom! God wot, it was defect
Of spirit, life, and bold audacity.
Such harmless creatures have a true respect
To talk in deeds, while others saucily
Promise more speed, but do it leisurely:
  Even so, this pattern of the worn-out age
  Pawn'd honest looks, but laid no words to
    gage.

His kindled duty kindled her mistrust,
That two red fires in both their faces blaz'd;

She thought he blush'd as knowing Tarquin's
  lust,
And, blushing with him, wistly on him gaz'd;
Her earnest eye did make him more amaz'd:
  The more she saw the blood his cheeks
    replenish,   [blemish.
  The more she thought he spied in her some

But long she thinks till he return again,
And yet the duteous vassal scarce is gone.
The weary time she cannot entertain,
For now 'tis stale to sigh, to weep, and
    groan:
  So woe hath wearied woe, moan tired moan,
  That she her plaints a little while doth
    stay,
  Pausing for means to mourn some newer
    way.

At last she calls to mind where hangs a piece
Of skilful painting, made for Priam's Troy;
Before the which is drawn the power of
    Greece,
For Helen's rape the city to destroy,
Threat'ning cloud-kissing Ilion with annoy;
  Which the conceited painter drew so
    proud,
  As heaven (it seem'd) to kiss the turrets
    bow'd.

A thousand lamentable objects there,
In scorn of Nature, Art gave lifeless life:
Many a dry drop seem'd a weeping tear,
Shed for the slaughter'd husband by the
    wife:
  The red blood reek'd to show the painter's
    strife;
  And dying eyes gleam'd forth their ashy
    lights,
  Like dying coals burnt out in tedious
    nights.

There might you see the labouring pioneer
Begrim'd with sweat, and smeared all with
    dust;
And from the towers of Troy there would
    appear
The very eyes of men through loopholes
    thrust,
Gazing upon the Greeks with little lust:
  Such sweet observance in this work was
    had,
  That one might see those far-off eyes look
    sad.

In great commanders grace and majesty
You might behold, triumphing in their faces;
In youth, quick bearing and dexterity;
And here and there the painter interlaces
Pale cowards, marching on with trembling
    paces;
  Which heartless peasants did so well re-
    semble,

That one would swear he saw them quake
and tremble.

In Ajax and Ulysses, O what art
Of physiognomy might one behold!
The face of either 'cipher'd either's heart;
Their face their manners most expressly told:
In Ajax' eyes blunt rage and rigour roll'd;
  But the mild glance that sly Ulysses lent
Show'd deep regard and smiling govern-
    ment.

There pleading might you see grave Nestor
    stand,
As't were encouraging the Greeks to fight;
Making such sober action with his hand
That it beguil'd attention, charm'd the
    sight:
In speech, it seem'd, his beard all silver
    white
  Wagg'd up and down, and from his lips
    did fly
Thin winding breath, which purl'd up to
    the sky.

About him were a press of gaping faces,
Which seem'd to swallow up his sound ad-
    vice;
All jointly listening, but with several graces,
As if some mermaid did their ears entice;
Some high, some low, the painter was so
    nice:
  The scalps of many, almost hid behind,
  To jump up higher seem'd to mock the
    mind.

Here one man's hand lean'd on another's
    head,
His nose being shadow'd by his neighbour's
    ear;
Here one being throng'd bears back, all
    boll'n and red;
Another smother'd seems to pelt and swear;
And in their rage such signs of rage they
    bear,
  As, but for loss of Nestor's golden words,
  It seem'd they would debate with angry
    swords.

For much imaginary work was there;
Conceit deceitful, so compact, so kind,
That for Achilles' image stood his spear,
Grip'd in an armed hand; himself, behind,
Was left unseen, save to the eye of mind:
  A hand, a foot, a face, a leg, a head,
  Stood for the whole to be imagined.

And from the walls of strong-besieged Troy
When their brave hope, bold Hector,
    march'd to field,
Stood many Trojan mothers, sharing joy
To see their youthful sons bright weapons
    wield:

And to their hope they such odd action
    yield,
That through their light joy seemed to
    appear
(Like bright things stain'd) a kind of
    heavy fear.

And, from the strond of Dardan where they
    fought,
To Simois' reedy banks, the red blood ran,
Whose waves to imitate the battle sought
With swelling ridges; and their ranks began
To break upon the galled shore, and then
  Retire again, till meeting greater ranks
  They join, and shoot their foam at Simois'
    banks.

To this well-painted piece is Lucrece come,
To find a face where all distress is stell'd.
Many she sees where cares have carved
    some,
But none where all distress and dolour
    dwell'd,
Till she despairing Hecuba beheld,
  Staring on Priam's wounds with her old
    eyes,
  Which bleeding under Pyrrhus' proud foot
    lies.

In her the painter had anatomiz'd
Time's ruin, beauty's wrack, and grim care's
    reign;
Her cheeks with chaps and wrinkles were
    disguis'd;
Of what she was no semblance did remain:
Her blue blood, chang'd to black in every
    vein,
  Wanting the spring that those shrunk
    pipes had fed,
  Show'd life imprison'd in a body dead.

On this sad shadow Lucrece spends her eyes,
And shapes her sorrow to the beldame's
    woes,
Who nothing wants to answer her but cries,
And bitter words to ban her cruel foes:
The painter was no god to lend her those;
  And therefore Lucrece swears he did her
    wrong,
  To give her so much grief, and not a
    tongue.

'Poor instrument,' quoth she, 'without a
    sound,
I'll tune thy woes with my lamenting tongue:
And drop sweet balm in Priam's painted
    wound,
And rail on Pyrrhus that hath done him
    wrong,
And with my tears quench Troy that burns
    so long;
  And with my knife scratch out the angry
    eyes
  Of all the Greeks that are thine enemies.

THE RAPE OF LUCRECE

'Show me the strumpet that began this stir,
That with my nails her beauty I may tear.
Thy heat of lust, fond Paris, did incur
This load of wrath that burning Troy doth
    bear;
Thy eye kindled the fire that burneth here:
  And here in Troy, for trespass of thine
    eye,
  The sire, the son, the dame, and daugh-
    ter, die.

'Why should the private pleasure of some
    one
Become the public plague of many mo?
Let sin, alone committed, light alone
Upon his head that hath transgressed so.
Let guiltless souls be freed from guilty woe:
  For one's offence why should so many
    fall,
  To plague a private sin in general?

'Lo, here weeps Hecuba, here Priam dies,
Here manly Hector· faints, here Troilus
    swounds;
Here friend by friend in bloody channel lies,
And friend to friend gives unadvised wounds,
And one man's lust these many lives con-
    founds:
  Had doting Priam check'd his son's de-
    sire,
  Troy had been bright with fame, and not
    with fire.

Here feelingly she weeps Troy's painted
    woes:
For sorrow, like a heavy-hanging bell,
Once set on ringing, with his own weight
    goes;
Then little strength rings out the doleful
    knell:
So Lucrece set a-work sad tales doth tell
  To pencill'd pensiveness and colour'd sor-
    row;
  She lends them words, and she their looks
    doth borrow.

She throws her eyes about the painting
    round,
And whom she finds forlorn she doth la-
    ment:
At last she sees a wretched image bound,
That piteous looks to Phrygian shepherds
    lent;
His face, though full of cares, yet show'd
    content:
  Onward to Troy with the blunt swains he
    goes,
  So mild that Patience seem'd to scorn his
    woes.

In him the painter labour'd with his skill
To hide deceit, and give the harmless show
An humble gait, calm looks, eyes wailing
    still,

A brow unbent, that seem'd to welcome
    woe;
Cheeks neither red nor pale, but mingled so
  That blushing red no guilty instance gave,
  Nor ashy pale the fear that false hearts
    have.

But, like a constant and confirmed devil,
He entertain'd a show so seeming just,
And therein so ensconc'd his secret evil,
That jealousy itself could not mistrust
False-creeping craft and perjury should
    thrust
  Into so bright a day such black-fac'd
    storms,
  Or blot with hell-born sin such saint-like
    forms.

The well-skill'd workman this mild image
    drew
For perjur'd Sinon, whose enchanting story
The credulous old Priam after slew; [glory
Whose words, like wildfire, burnt the shining
Of rich-built Ilion, that the skies were sorry,
  And little stars shot from their fixed
    places,
  When their glass fell wherein they view'd
    their faces.

This picture she advisedly perus'd,
And chid the painter for his wondrous skill;
Saying, some shape in Sinon's was abus'd,
So fair a form lodg'd not a mind so ill;
And still on him she gaz'd, and gazing still,
  Such signs of truth in his plain face she
    spied,
  That she concludes the picture was belied.

'It cannot be,' quoth she, 'that so much
    guile'—
(She would have said) 'can lurk in such a
    look;'
But Tarquin's shape came in her mind the
    while,
And from her tongue 'can lurk' from 'can-
    not' took;
'It cannot be' she in that sense forsook,
  And turn'd it thus: 'It cannot be, I find,
  But such a face should bear a wicked
    mind:

'For even as subtle Sinon here is painted,
So sober-sad, so weary, and so mild,
(As if with grief or travail he had fainted,)
To me came Tarquin armed; so beguil'd
With outward honesty, but yet defil'd
  With inward vice: as Priam him did cher-
    ish,
  So did I Tarquin; so my Troy did perish.

'Look, look, how listening Priam wets his
    eyes,
To see those borrow'd tears that Sinon
    sheds.

Priam, why art thou old, and yet not wise?
For every tear he falls a Trojan bleeds;
His eye drops fire, no water thence proceeds;
  Those round clear pearls of his that move thy pity
  Are balls of quenchless fire to burn thy city.

'Such devils steal effects from lightless hell;
For Sinon in his fire doth quake with cold,
And in that cold hot-burning fire doth dwell;
These contraries such unity do hold
Only to flatter fools, and make them bold;
  So Priam's trust false Sinon's tears doth flatter,
  That he finds means to burn his Troy with water.'

Here, all enrag'd, such passion her assails,
That patience is quite beaten from her breast.
She tears the senseless Sinon with her nails,
Comparing him to that unhappy guest
Whose deed hath made herself herself detest;
  At last she smilingly with this gives o'er;
  'Fool! fool!' quoth she, 'his wounds will not be sore.'

Thus ebbs and flows the current of her sorrow,
And time doth weary time with her complaining.
She looks for night, and then she longs for morrow,
And both she thinks too long with her remaining:
Short time seems long in sorrow's sharp sustaining.
  Though woe be heavy, yet it seldom sleeps;
  And they that watch see time how slow it creeps.

Which all this time hath overslipp'd her thought,
That she with painted images hath spent;
Being from the feeling of her own grief brought
By deep surmise of others' detriment;
Losing her woes in shows of discontent.
  It easeth some, though none it ever cur'd,
  To think their dolour others have endur'd.

But now the mindful messenger, come back,
Brings home his lord and other company;
Who finds his Lucrece clad in mourning black;
And round about her tear-distained eye
Blue circles stream'd, like rainbows in the sky.

These water-galls in her dim element
Foretell new storms to those already spent.

Which when her sad-beholding husband saw,
Amazedly in her sad face he stares:
Her eyes, though sod in tears, look'd red and raw,
Her lively colour kill'd with deadly cares.
He hath no power to ask her how she fares,
  But stood like old acquaintance in a trance,
  Met far from home, wondering each other's chance.

At last he takes her by the bloodless hand,
And thus begins: 'What uncouth ill event
Hath thee befallen, that thou dost trembling stand?
Sweet love, what spite hath thy fair colour spent?
Why art thou thus attir'd in discontent?
  Unmask, dear dear, this moody heaviness,
  And tell thy grief, that we may give redress.'

Three times with sighs she gives her sorrow fire,
Ere once she can discharge one word of woe:
At length address'd to answer his desire,
She modestly prepares to let them know
Her honour is ta'en prisoner by the foe;
  While Collatine and his consorted lords
  With sad attention long to hear her words

And now this pale swan in her watery nest
Begins the sad dirge of her certain ending:
'Few words,' quoth she, 'shall fit the trespass best,
Where no excuse can give the fault amending:
In me more woes than words are now depending;   [long,
  And my laments would be drawn out too
  To tell them all with one poor tired tongue.

'Then be this all the task it hath to say:--
Dear husband, in the interest of thy bed
A stranger came, and on that pillow lay
Where thou wast wont to rest thy weary head;
And what wrong else may be imagined
  By foul enforcement might be done to me,
  From that, alas! thy Lucrece is not free.

'For in the dreadful dead of dark midnight,
With shining falchion in my chamber came
A creeping creature, with a flaming light,
And softly cried, Awake, thou Roman dame,
And entertain my love; else lasting shame
  On thee and thine this night I will inflict,
  If thou my love's desire do contradict.

'For some hard-favour'd groom of thine, quoth he,
Unless thou yoke thy liking to my will,
I'll murder straight, and then I'll slaughter thee,
And swear I found you where you did fulfil
The loathsome act of lust, and so did kill
   The lechers in their deed: this act will be
   My fame, and thy perpetual infamy.

'With this I did begin to start and cry,
And then against my heart he set his sword,
Swearing, unless I took all patiently,
I should not live to speak another word:
So should my shame still rest upon record,
   And never be forgot in mighty Rome
   The adulterate death of Lucrece and her groom.

'Mine enemy was strong, my poor self weak,
And far the weaker with so strong a fear:
My bloody judge forbade my tongue to speak;
No rightful plea might plead for justice there:
His scarlet lust came evidence to swear
   That my poor beauty had purloin'd his eyes,
   And when the judge is robb'd, the prisoner dies.

'O teach me how to make mine own excuse!
Or, at the least, this refuge let me find;
Though my gross blood be stain'd with this abuse,
Immaculate and spotless is my mind;
That was not forc'd; that never was inclin'd
   To accessary yieldings, but still pure
   Doth in her poison'd closet yet endure.'

Lo here, the hopeless merchant of this loss,
With head declin'd, and voice damm'd up with woe,
With sad-set eyes, and wretched arms across,
From lips new-waxen pale begins to blow
The grief away that stops his answer so:
   But wretched as he is he strives in vain;
   What he breathes out his breath drinks up again.

As through an arch the violent roaring tide
Outruns the eye that doth behold his haste;
Yet in the eddy boundeth in his pride
Back to the strait that forc'd him on so fast;
In rage sent out, recall'd in rage, being past:
   Even so he sighs, his sorrows make a saw,
   To push grief on, and back the same grief draw.

Which speechless woe of his poor she attendeth,
And his untimely frenzy thus awaketh:
'Dear lord, thy sorrow to my sorrow lendeth

Another power; no flood by raining slaketh.
My woe too sensible thy passion maketh
   More feeling-painful: let it then suffice
   To drown one woe, one pair of weeping eyes.

'And for my sake, when I might charm thee so,
For she that was thy Lucrece,—now attend me;
Be suddenly revenged on my foe, [fend me
Thine, mine, his own; suppose thou dost de-
From what is past: the help that thou shalt lend me
   Comes all too late, yet let the traitor die;
   For sparing justice feeds iniquity.

'But ere I name him, you, fair lords,' quoth she,
(Speaking to those that came with Colla-tine)
'Shall plight your honourable faiths to me,
With swift pursuit to venge this wrong of mine;
For 'tis a meritorious fair design
   To chase injustice with revengeful arms:
   Knights, by their oaths, should right poor ladies' harms.'

At this request, with noble disposition
Each present lord began to promise aid,
As bound in knighthood to her imposition,
Longing to hear the hateful foe bewray'd.
But she, that yet her sad task hath not said,
   The protestation stops. 'O speak,' quoth she, [me?
   'How may this forced stain be wip'd from

'What is the quality of mine offence,
Being constrain'd with dreadful circum-stance?
May my pure mind with the foul act dis-pense,
My low-declined honour to advance?
May any terms acquit me from this chance?
   The poison'd fountain clears itself again;
   And why not I from this compelled stain?'

With this, they all at once began to say,
Her body's stain her mind untainted clears;
While with a joyless smile she turns away
The face, that map which deep impression bears
Of hard misfortune, carv'd in it with tears.
   'No, no,' quoth she, 'no dame, hereafter living,
   By my excuse shall claim excuse's giving.'

Here with a sigh, as if her heart would break,
She throws forth Tarquin's name: 'He, he,'
   she says, [not speak;
But more than 'he' her poor tongue could
Till after many accents and delays,

Untimely breathings, sick and short assays,
   She utters this: 'He, he, fair lords, 'tis he,
   That guides this hand to give this wound
      to me.'

Even here she sheathed in her harmless
      breast
A harmful knife, that thence her soul un-
      sheath'd:
That blow did bail it from the deep unrest
Of that polluted prison where it breath'd:
Her contrite sighs unto the clouds bequeath'd
   Her winged sprite, and through her
      wounds doth fly
   Life's lasting date from cancell'd destiny.

Stone-still, astonish'd with this deadly deed,
Stood Collatine and all his lordly crew;
Till Lucrece' father that beholds her bleed,
Himself on her self-slaughter'd body threw;
And from the purple fountain Brutus drew
   The murderous knife, and as it left the
      place,
   Her blood, in poor revenge, held it in
      chase;

And bubbling from her breast, it doth
      divide
In two slow rivers, that the crimson blood
Circles her body in on every side,
Who like a late-sack'd island vastly stood
Bare and unpeopled, in this fearful flood.
   Some of her blood still pure and red re-
      main'd,
   And some look'd black, and that false
      Tarquin stain'd.

About the mourning and congealed face
Of that black blood a watery rigol goes,
Which seems to weep upon the tainted
      place:
And ever since, as pitying Lucrece' woes,
Corrupted blood some watery token shows;
   And blood untainted still doth red abide,
   Blushing at that which is so putrefied.

'Daughter, dear daughter,' old Lucretius
      cries,
'That life was mine which thou hast here
      depriv'd.
If in the child the father's image lies,
Where shall I live now Lucrece is unliv'd?
Thou wast not to this end from me deriv'd.
   If children predecease progenitors,
   We are their offspring, and they none of
      ours.

'Poor broken glass, I often did behold
In thy sweet semblance my old age new
      born;
But now that fair fresh mirror, dim and old,
Shows me a barebon'd death by time out-
      worn;

O, from thy cheeks my image thou hast
      torn!
And shiver'd all the beauty of my glass,
That I no more can see what once I was.

'O time, cease thou thy course, and last no
      longer,
If they surcease to be that should survive.
Shall rotten death make conquest of the
      stronger,
And leave the faltering feeble souls alive?
The old bees die, the young possess their
      hive:
   Then live, sweet Lucrece, live again, and
      see
   Thy father die, and not thy father thee!'

By this starts Collatine as from a dream,
And bids Lucretius give his sorrow place;
And then in key-cold Lucrece' bleeding
      stream
He falls, and bathes the pale fear in his face,
And counterfeits to die with her a space;
   Till manly shame bids him possess his
      breath,
   And live, to be revenged on her death.

The deep vexation of his inward soul
Hath serv'd a dumb arrest upon his tongue;
Who, mad that sorrow should his use con-
      trol,
Or keep him from heart-easing words so
      long,
Begins to talk; but through his lips do
      throng
   Weak words, so thick come, in his poor
      heart's aid,
   That no man could distinguish what he
      said.

Yet sometime Tarquin was pronounced
      plain,
But through his teeth, as if the name he tore.
This windy tempest, till it blow up rain,
Held back his sorrow's tide, to make it
      more;
At last it rains, and busy winds give o'er:
   Then son and father weep with equal
      strife,
   Who should weep most for daughter or
      for wife.

The one doth call her his, the other his,
Yet neither may possess the claim they lay,
The father says, 'She's mine,' 'O, mine she
      is,'
Replies her husband: 'do not take away
My sorrow's interest; let no mourner say
   He weeps for her, for she was only mine,
   And only must be wail'd by Collatine.'

'O,' quoth Lucretius, 'I did give that life
Which she too early and too late hath
      spill'd'

'Woe, woe,' quoth Collatine, 'she was my wife,
I ow'd her, and 'tis mine that she hath kill'd.'
'My daughter!' and 'My wife!' with clamours fill'd
  The dispers'd air, who, holding Lucrece' life,
  Answer'd their cries, 'My daughter!' and 'My wife!'

Brutus, who pluck'd the knife from Lucrece' side,
Seeing such emulation in their woe,
Began to clothe his wit in state and pride,
Burying in Lucrece' wound his folly's show.
He with the Romans was esteemed so
  As silly jeering idiots are with kings,
  For sportive words, and uttering foolish things.

But now he throws that shallow habit by,
Wherein deep policy did him disguise;
And arm'd his long-hid wits advisedly,
To check the tears in Collatinus' eyes.
'Thou wronged lord of Rome,' quoth he, 'arise;
  Let my unsounded self, suppos'd a fool,
  Now set thy long-experienc'd wit to school.

'Why, Collatine, is woe the cure for woe?
Do wounds help wounds, or grief help grievous deeds?
Is it revenge to give thyself a blow,
For his foul act by whom thy fair wife bleeds?
Such childish humour from weak minds proceeds:
  Thy wretched wife mistook the matter so,
  To slay herself, that should have slain her foe.

'Courageous Roman, do not steep thy heart
In such relenting dew of lamentations,
But kneel with me, and help to bear thy part,
To rouse our Roman gods with invocations,
That they will suffer these abominations,
  (Since Rome herself in them doth stand disgrac'd,)
  By our strong arms from forth her fair streets chas'd.

'Now by the Capitol that we adore,
And by this chaste blood so unjustly stain'd,
By heaven's fair sun that breeds the fat earth's store,
By all our country rights in Rome maintain'd,
And by chaste Lucrece' soul that late complain'd
  Her wrongs to us, and by this bloody knife,
  We will revenge the death of this true wife.'

This said, he struck his hand upon his breast,
And kiss'd the fatal knife to end his vow;
And to his protestation urg'd the rest,
Who, wondering at him, did his words allow;
Then jointly to the ground their knees they bow;
  And that deep vow which Brutus made before,
  He doth again repeat, and that they swore.

When they had sworn to this advised doom,
They did conclude to bear dead Lucrece thence;
To show her bleeding body thorough Rome,
And so to publish Tarquin's foul offence:
Which being done with speedy diligence,
  The Romans plausibly did give consent
  To Tarquin's everlasting banishment.

SONNETS

TO . THE . ONLIE . BEGETTER . OF
THESE . INSUING . SONNETS .
MR. W. H. ALL . HAPPINESSE .
AND . THAT . ETERNITIE .
PROMISED .

BY .

OUR . EVER - LIVING . POET .
WISHETH .
THE . WELL - WISHING .
ADVENTURER . IN .
SETTING .
FORTH .

T. T.

I.

From fairest creatures we desire increase,
That thereby beauty's rose might never die,
But as the riper should by time decrease,
His tender heir might bear his memory:
But thou, contracted to thine own bright
    eyes,
Feed'st thy light's flame with self-substantial
    fuel,
Making a famine where abundance lies,
Thyself thy foe, to thy sweet self too cruel.
Thou that art now the world's fresh orna-
    ment,
And only herald to the gaudy spring,
Within thine own bud buriest thy content,
And, tender churl, mak'st waste in niggard-
    ing.
  Pity the world, or else this glutton be,
  To eat the world's due, by the grave and
    thee.

II.

When forty winters shall besiege thy brow,
And dig deep trenches in thy beauty's field,
Thy youth's proud livery, so gaz'd on now,
Will be a tatter'd weed, of small worth
    held:
Then being ask'd where all thy beauty lies,
Where all the treasure of thy lusty days;
To say, within thine own deep sunken eyes,
Were an all-eating shame and thriftless
    praise.
How much more praise deserv'd thy beauty's
    use,
If thou couldst answer—'This fair child of
    mine

Shall sum my count, and make my old ex-
    cuse—'
Proving his beauty by succession thine!
  This were to be new-made when thou art
    old,
  And see thy blood warm when thou
    feel'st it cold.

III.

Look in thy glass, and tell the face thou
    viewest,
Now is the time that face should form an-
    òther;
Whose fresh repair if now thou not renew-
    est,
Thou dost beguile the world, unbless some
    mother.
For where is she so fair whose unear'd womb
Disdains the tillage of thy husbandry?
Or who is he so fond will be the tomb
Of his self-love, to stop posterity?
Thou art thy mother's glass, and she in thee
Calls back the lovely April of her prime:
So thou through windows of thine age shalt
    see,
Despite of wrinkles, this thy golden time.
  But if thou live, remember'd not to be,
  Die single, and thine image dies with thee.

IV.

Unthrifty loveliness, why dost thou spend
Upon thyself thy beauty's legacy?
Nature's bequest gives nothing, but doth
    lend,
And, being frank, she lends to those are free.

Then, beauteous niggard, why dost thou abuse
The bounteous largess given thee to give?
Profitless usurer, why dost thou use
So great a sum of sums, yet canst not live?
For having traffic with thyself alone,
Thou of thyself thy sweet self dost deceive,
Then how, when nature calls thee to be gone,
What acceptable audit canst thou leave?
    The unus'd beauty must be tomb'd with thee,
    Which, used, lives th' executor to be.

V.

Those hours that with gentle work did frame
The lovely gaze where every eye doth dwell,
Will play the tyrants to the very same,
And that unfair which fairly doth excel;
For never-resting time leads summer on
To hideous winter, and confounds him there;
Sap check'd with frost, and lusty leaves quite gone,
Beauty o'ersnow'd, and bareness everywhere:
Then, were not summer's distillation left,
A liquid prisoner pent in walls of glass,
Beauty's effect with beauty were bereft,
Nor it, nor no remembrance what it was.
    But flowers distill'd, though they with winter meet,   [lives sweet.
    Leese but their show; their substance still

VI.

Then let not winter's ragged hand deface
In thee thy summer, ere thou be distill'd:
Make sweet some phial; treasure thou some place
With beauty's treasure, ere it be self-kill'd.
That use is not forbidden usury,
Which happies those that pay the willing loan;
That's for thyself to breed another thee,
Or ten times happier, be it ten for one;
Ten times thyself were happier than thou art,
If ten of thine ten times refigur'd thee:
Then what could Death do if thou shouldst depart,
Leaving thee living in posterity?
    Be not self-will'd, for thou art much too fair
    To be Death's conquest and make worms thine heir.

VII.

Lo, in the orient when the gracious light
Lifts up his burning head, each under eye
Doth homage to his new-appearing sight,
Serving with looks his sacred majesty;
And having climb'd the steep-up heavenly hill,
Resembling strong youth in his middle age,
Yet mortal looks adore his beauty still,
Attending on his golden pilgrimage;
But when from high-most pitch, with weary car,
Like feeble age, he reeleth from the day,
The eyes, 'fore duteous, now converted are
From his low tract, and look another way:
    So thou, thyself, outgoing in thy noon,
    Unlook'd on diest, unless thou get a son.

VIII.

Music to hear, why hear'st thou music sadly?
Sweets with sweets war not, joy delights in joy,
Why lov'st thou that which thou receiv'st not gladly?
Or else receiv'st with pleasure thine annoy?
If the true concord of well-tuned sounds
By unions married, do offend thine ear,
They do but sweetly chide thee, who confounds
In singleness the parts that thou shouldst bear.
Mark how one string, sweet husband to another,
Strikes each in each by mutual ordering;
Resembling sire and child and happy mother,
Who, all in one, one pleasing note do sing:
    Whose speechless song, being many, seeming one,
    Sings this to thee, 'thou single wilt prove none.'

IX.

Is it for fear to wet a widow's eye
That thou consum'st thyself in single life?
Ah! if thou issueless shalt hap to die,
The world will wail thee, like a makeless wife:
The world will be thy widow, and still weep
That thou no form of thee hast left behind,
When every private widow well may keep,
By children's eyes, her husband's shape in mind.
Look, what an unthrift in the world doth spend
Shifts but his place, for still the world enjoys it:
But beauty's waste hath in the world an end,
And kept unus'd, the user so destroys it.
    No love toward others in that bosom sits,
    That on himself such murderous shame commits.

X.

For shame! deny that thou bear'st love to any,
Who for thyself art so unprovident.

Grant if thou wilt thou art belov'd of many,
But that thou none lov'st is most evident;
For thou art so possess'd with murderous hate,
That 'gainst thyself thou stick'st not to conspire,
Seeking that beauteous roof to ruinate,
Which to repair should be thy chief desire.
O change thy thought, that I may change my mind!
Shall hate be fairer lodg'd than gentle love?
Be, as thy presence is, gracious and kind,
Or to thyself, at least, kind-hearted prove;
　Make thee another self, for love of me,
　That beauty still may live in thine or thee.

XI.

As fast as thou shalt wane, so fast thou grow'st
In one of thine, from that which thou departest.
And that fresh blood which youngly thou bestow'st,
Thou mayst call thine, when thou from youth convertest.
Herein lives wisdom, beauty, and increase:
Without this folly, age, and cold decay.
If all were minded so the times should cease,
And threescore years would make the world away.
Let those whom Nature hath not made for store,
Harsh, featureless, and rude, barrenly perish:
Look whom she best endow'd, she gave the more;　　[bounty cherish;
Which bounteous gift thou shouldst in
She carv'd thee for her seal, and meant thereby
Thou shouldst print more, nor let that copy die.

XII.

When I do count the clock that tells the time,
And see the brave day sunk in hideous night;
When I behold the violet past prime,
And sable curls, all silver'd o'er with white;
When lofty trees I see barren of leaves,
Which erst from heat did canopy the herd,
And summer's green all girded up in sheaves,
Borne on the bier with white and bristly beard;
Then of thy beauty do I question make,
That thou among the wastes of time must go,
Since sweets and beauties do themselves forsake,
And die as fast as they see others grow;
　And nothing 'gainst Time's scythe can make defence　　[thee hence.
　Save breed, to brave him when he takes

XIII.

O that you were yourself: but, love, you are
No longer yours than you yourself here live:
Against this coming end you should prepare,
And your sweet semblance to some other give.
So should that beauty which you hold in lease
Find no determination: then you were
Yourself again, after yourself's decease,
When your sweet issue your sweet form should bear.
Who lets so fair a house fall to decay,
Which husbandry in honour might uphold
Against the stormy gusts of winter's day,
And barren rage of death's eternal cold?
　O! none but unthrifts:—Dear my love, you know
　You had a father; let your son say so.

XIV.

Not from the stars do I my judgment pluck;
And yet methinks I have astronomy,
But not to tell of good or evil luck,
Of plagues, of dearths, or season's quality:
Nor can I fortune to brief minutes tell,
Pointing to each his thunder, rain, and wind,
Or say with princes if it shall go well,
By oft predict that I in heaven find:
But from thine eyes my knowledge I derive,
And (constant stars) in them I read such art,
As truth and beauty shall together thrive,
If from thyself to store thou wouldst convert:
　Or else of thee this I prognosticate,
　Thy end is truth's and beauty's doom and date.

XV.

When I consider every thing that grows
Holds in perfection but a little moment,
That this huge state presenteth nought but shows
Whereon the stars in secret influence comment;
When I perceive that men as plants increase,
Cheered and check'd even by the self-same sky;
Vaunt in their youthful sap, at height decrease,
And wear their brave state out of memory;
Then the conceit of this inconstant stay
Sets you most rich in youth before my sight,
Where wasteful time debateth with decay,
To change your day of youth to sullied night;
　And, all in war with Time, for love of you,
　As he takes from you, I engraft you new.

XVI.

But wherefore do not you a mightier way
Make war upon this bloody tyrant, Time?
And fortify yourself in your decay
With means more blessed than my barren
rhyme?
Now stand you on the top of happy hours;
And many maiden gardens, yet unset,
With virtuous wish would bear your living
flowers,
Much liker than your painted counterfeit:
So should the lines of life that life repair,
Which this, Time's pencil, or my pupil pen,
Neither in inward worth, nor outward fair,
Can make you live yourself in eyes of men.
But give away yourself keeps yourself still;
And you must live, drawn by your own
sweet skill.

XVII.

Who will believe my verse in time to come,
If it were fill'd with your most high deserts?
Though yet, Heaven knows, it is but as a
tomb
Which hides your life, and shows not half
your parts.
If I could write the beauty of your eyes,
And in fresh numbers number all your
graces,
The age to come would say, this poet lies,
Such heavenly touches ne'er touch'd earthly
faces.
So should my papers, yellow'd with their
age,
Be scorn'd, like old men of less truth than
tongue;
And your true rights be term'd a poet's rage,
And stretched metre of an antique song:
But were some child of yours alive that
time,   [rhyme.
You should live twice;—in it, and in my

XVIII.

Shall I compare thee to a summer's day?
Thou art more lovely and more temperate:
Rough winds do shake the darling buds of
May,   [date:
And summer's lease hath all too short a
Sometime too hot the eye of heaven shines,
And often is his gold complexion dimm'd;
And every fair from fair sometime declines,
By chance, or nature's changing course, un-
trimm'd;
But thy eternal summer shall not fade,
Nor lose possession of that fair thou owest;
Nor shall Death brag thou wander'st in his
shade,
When in eternal lines to time thou growest;
So long as men can breathe, or eyes can
see,
So long lives this, and this gives life to
thee

XIX.

Devouring Time, blunt thou the lion's paws,
And make the earth devour her own sweet
brood;
Pluck the keen teeth from the fierce tiger's
jaws,
And burn the long-liv'd phœnix in her blood;
Make glad and sorry seasons, as thou fleets,
And do whate'er thou wilt, swift-footed
Time,
To the wide world, and all her fading
sweets;
But I forbid thee one most heinous crime:
O carve not with thy hours my love's fair
brow,
Nor draw no lines there with thine antique
pen;
Him in thy course untainted do allow,
For beauty's pattern to succeeding men.
Yet, do thy worst, old Time: despite thy
wrong,
My love shall in my verse ever live young.

XX.

A woman's face, with nature's own hand
painted,
Hast thou, the master-mistress of my pas-
sion;
A woman's gentle heart, but not acquainted
With shifting change, as is false woman's
fashion;
An eye more bright than theirs, less false in
rolling,
Gilding the object whereupon it gazeth;
A man in hue, all hues in his controlling,
Which steals men's eyes, and women's souls
amazeth.
And for a woman wert thou first created;
Till Nature, as she wrought thee, fell a-dot-
ing,
And by addition me of thee defeated,
By adding one thing to my purpose nothing.
But since she prick'd thee out for women's
pleasure,
Mine be thy love, and thy love's use their
treasure.

XXI.

So is it not with me as with that muse,
Stirr'd by a painted beauty to his verse;
Who heaven itself for ornament doth use,
And every fair with his fair doth rehearse;
Making a couplement of proud compare,
With sun and moon, with earth and sea's
rich gems,   [rare
With April's first-born flowers, and all things
That heaven's air in this huge rondure hems.
O let me, true in love, but truly write,
And then believe me, my love is as fair
As any mother's child, though not so bright
As those gold candles fix'd in heaven's air:

Let them say more that like of hearsay
    well;
I will not praise, that purpose not to sell.

XXII.

My glass shall not persuade me I am old,
So long as youth and thou are of one date;
But when in thee time's furrows I behold,
Then look I death my days should expiate.
For all that beauty that doth cover thee
Is but the seemly raiment of my heart,
Which in thy breast doth live, as thine in
    me;
How can I then be elder than thou art?
O therefore, love, be of thyself so wary,
As I not for myself but for thee will;
Bearing thy heart, which I will keep so chary
As tender nurse her babc from faring ill.
    Presume not on thy heart when mine is
      slain;
    Thou gav'st me thine, not tc give back
      again.

XXIII.

As an unperfect actor on the stage,
Who with his fear is put besides his part
Or some fierce thing replete with too much
    rage,
Whose strength's abundance weakens his own
    heart;
So I, for fear of trust, forget to say
The perfect ceremony of love's rite,
And in mine own love's strength seem to de-
    cay,
O'ercharg'd with burthen of mine own love's
    might.
O let my books be, then, the eloquence
And dumb presagers of my speaking breast;
Who plead for love, and look for recom-
    pense
More than that tongue that more hath more
    express'd.
    O learn to read what silent love hath writ:
    To hear with eyes belongs to love's fine
    wit.

XXIV.

Mine eye hath play'd the painter, and hath
    stell'd
Thy beauty's form in table of my heart;
My body is the frame wherein 'tis held,
And perspective it is best painter's art.
For through the painter must you see his
    skill,
To find where your true image pictur'd lies,
Which in my bosom's shop is hanging still,
That hath his windows glazed with thine
    eyes.
Now see what good turns eyes for eyes have
    done:
Mine eyes have drawn thy shape, and thine
    for me   [the sun
Are windows to my breast, where-through

Delights to peep, to gaze therein on thee;
    Yet eyes this cunning want to grace their
      art,
    They draw but what they see, know not
      the heart.

XXV.

Let those who are in favour with their stars,
Of public honour and proud titles boast,
Whilst I, whom fortune of such triumph
    bars,
Unlook'd for joy in that I honour most.
Great princes' favourites their fair leaves
    spread
But as the marigold at the sun's eye;
And in themselves their pride lies buried,
For at a frown they in their glory die.
The painful warrior famoused for fight,
After a thousand victories once foil'd,
Is from the book of honour razed quite,
And all the rest forgot for which he toil'd:
    Then happy I, that love and am belov'd
    Where I may not remove, nor be remov'd.

XXVI.

Lord of my love, to whom in vassalage
Thy merit hath my duty strongly knit,
To thee I send this written embassage,
To witness duty, not to show my wit.
Duty so great, which wit so poor as mine
May make seem bare, in wanting words to
    show it;
But that I hope some good conceit of thine
In thy soul's thought, all naked, will bestow
    it:
Till whatsoever star that guides by moving,
Points on me graciously with fair aspect,
And puts apparel on my tatter'd loving,
To show me worthy of thy sweet respect:
    Then may I dare to boast how I do love
      thee,
    Till then, not show my head where thou
      mayst prove me.

XXVII.

Weary with toil, I haste me to my bed,
The dear repose for limbs with travel tir'd;
But then begins a journey in my head,
To work my mind, when body's work's ex-
    pir'd:
For then my thoughts (from far where I
    abide)
Intend a zealous pilgrimage to thee,
And keep my drooping eyelids open wide,
Looking on darkness which the blind do see:
Save that my soul's imaginary sight
Presents thy shadow to my sightless view,
Which, like a jewel hung in ghastly night,
Makes black night beauteous, and her old
    face new.
    Lo, thus, by day my limbs, by night my
      mind
    For thee, and for myself, no quiet find.

XXVIII.

How can I then return in happy plight,
That am debarr'd the benefit of rest?
When day's oppression is not eas'd by night,
But day by night and night by day oppress'd?
And each, though enemies to either's reign,
Do in consent shake hands to torture me,
The one by toil, the other to complain
How far I toil, still farther off from thee.
I tell the day, to please him, thou art bright,
And dost him grace when clouds do blot the heaven:
So flatter I the swart-complexion'd night;
When sparkling stars twire not, thou gild'st the even.
  But day both daily draw my sorrows longer,
  And night doth nightly make grief's strength seem stronger.

XXIX.

When in disgrace with fortune and men's eyes,
I all alone beweep my outcast state, [cries,
And trouble deaf Heaven with my bootless
And look upon myself, and curse my fate,
Wishing me like to one more rich in hope,
Featur'd like him, like him with friends possess'd,
Desiring this man's art, and that man's scope,
With what I most enjoy contented least;
Yet in these thoughts myself almost despising,
Haply I think on thee,—and then my state
(Like to the lark at break of day arising
From sullen earth) sings hymns at heaven's gate;
  For thy sweet love remember'd such wealth brings,
  That then I scorn to change my state with kings.

XXX.

When to the sessions of sweet silent thought
I summon up remembrance of things past,
I sigh the lack of many a thing I sought,
And with old woes new wail my dear times' waste:
Then can I drown an eye, unus'd to flow,
For precious friends hid in death's dateless night.
And weep afresh love's long-since cancell'd woe,
And moan the expense of many a vanish'd sight.
Then can I grieve at grievances foregone,
And heavily from woe to woe tell o'er
The sad account of fore-bemoaned moan,
Which I new pay as if not paid before.
  But if the while I think on thee, dear friend,
  All losses are restor'd, and sorrows end.

XXXI.

Thy bosom is endeared with all hearts,
Which I by lacking have supposed dead;
And there reigns love and all love's loving parts,
And all those friends which I thought buried.
How many a holy and obsequious tear
Hath dear religious love stolen- from mine eye,
As interest of the dead, which now appear
But things remov'd, that hidden in thee lie!
Thou art the grave where buried love doth live,
Hung with the trophies of my lovers gone,
Who all their parts of me to thee did give;
That due of many now is thine alone:
  Their images I lov'd I view in thee,
  And thou (all they) hast all the all of me.

XXXII.

If thou survive my well-contented day,
When that churl Death my bones with dust shall cover,
And shalt by fortune once more re-survey
These poor rude lines of thy deceased lover,
Compare them with the bettering of the time;
And though they be outstripp'd by every pen,
Reserve them for my love, not for their rhyme,
Exceeded by the height of happier men.
O then vouchsafe me but this loving thought!
'Had my friend's muse grown with this growing age,
A dearer birth than this his love had brought,
To march in ranks of better equipage:
  But since he died, and poets better prove,
  Theirs for their style I'll read, his for his love.'

XXXIII.

Full many a glorious morning have I seen
Flatter the mountain-tops with sovereign eye,
Kissing with golden face the meadows green,
Gilding pale streams with heavenly alchymy;
Anon permit the basest clouds to ride
With ugly rack on his celestial face,
And from the forlorn world his visage hide,
Stealing unseen to west with this disgrace:
Even so my sun one early morn did shine
With all triumphant splendour on my brow;
But out! alack! he was but one hour mine,
The region cloud hath mask'd him from me now.
  Yet him for this my love no whit disdaineth;
  Suns of the world may stain, when heaven's sun staineth.

XXXIV.

Why didst thou promise such a beauteous day,

And make me travel forth without my cloak,
To let base clouds o'ertake me in my way,
Hiding thy bravery in their rotten smoke?
'Tis not enough that through the cloud thou
    break,
To dry the rain on my storm-beaten face,
For no man well of such a salve can speak,
That heals the wound, and cures not the dis-
    grace:
Nor can thy shame give physic to my grief;
Though thou repent, yet I have still the loss:
The offender's sorrow lends but weak relief
To him that bears the strong offence's cross,
    Ah! but those tears are pearl which thy
        love sheds,
    And they are rich, and ransom all ill deeds.

XXXV.

No more be griev'd at that which thou hast
    done:
Roses have thorns, and silver fountains mud,
Clouds and eclipses stain both moon and sun,
And loathsome canker lives in sweetest bud.
All men make faults, and even I in this,
Authorising thy trespass with compare,
Myself corrupting, salving thy amiss,
Excusing thy sins more than thy sins are:
For to thy sensual fault I bring in sense,
(Thy adverse party is thy advocate,)
And 'gainst myself a lawful plea commence:
Such civil war is in my love and hate,
    That I an accessary needs must be
        To that sweet thief which sourly robs
            from me.

XXXVI.

Let me confess that we two must be twain,
Although our undivided loves are one:
So shall those blots that do with me remain,
Without thy help, by me be borne alone.
In our two loves there is but one respect,
Though in our lives a separable spite,
Which though it alter not love's sole effect,
Yet doth it steal sweet hours from love's
    delight.
I may not evermore acknowledge thee,
Lest my bewailed guilt should do thee
    shame;
Nor thou with public kindness honour me,
Unless thou take that honour from thy
    name:
    But do not so; I love thee in such sort,
    As, thou being mine, mine is thy good re-
        port.

XXXVII.

As a decrepit father takes delight
To see his active child do deeds of youth,
So I, made lame by fortune's dearest spite,
Take all my comfort of thy worth and
    truth;
For whether beauty, birth, or wealth, or wit,
Or any of these all, or all, or more,
Entitled in thy parts do crowned sit,
I make my love engrafted to this store:
So then I am not lame, poor, nor despis'd,
Whilst that this shadow dost such substance
    give,
That I in thy abundance am suffic'd,
And by a part of all thy glory live.
    Look, what is best, that best I wish in
        thee;
    This wish I have; then ten times happy
        me!

XXXVIII.

How can my muse want subject to invent,
While thou dost breathe, that pour'st into
    my verse
Thine own sweet argument, too excellent
For every vulgar paper to rehearse?
O, give thyself the thanks, if aught in me
Worthy perusal stand against thy sight;
For who's so dumb that cannot write to thee,
When thou thyself dost give invention light?
Be thou the tenth muse, ten times more in
    worth
Than those old nine which rhymers invocate;
And he that calls on thee, let him bring forth
Eternal numbers to outlive long date.
    If my slight muse do please these curious
        days,   [praise.
    The pain be mine, but thine shall be the

XXXIX.

O, how thy worth with manners may I sing,
When thou art all the better part of me?
What can mine own praise to mine own self
    bring?
And what is 't but mine own, when I praise
    thee?
Even for this let us divided live,
And our dear love lose name of single one,
That by this separation I may give
That due to thee, which thou deserv'st alone.
O absence, what a torment wouldst thou
    prove,
Were it not thy sour leisure gave sweet leave
To entertain the time with thoughts of love,
(Which time and thoughts so sweetly doth
    deceive,)
    And that thou teachest how to make one
        twain,
    By praising him here, who doth hence re-
        main!

XL.

Take all my loves, my love, yea, take them
    all;
What hast thou then more than thou hadst
    before?
No love, my love, that thou mayst true love
    call;
All mine was thine, before thou hadst this
    more.
Then if for my love thou my love receivest,

I cannot blame thee for my love thou usest;
But yet be blam'd, if thou thyself deceivest
By wilful taste of what thyself refusest.
I do forgive thy robbery, gentle thief,
Although thou steal thee all my property;
And yet, love knows, it is a greater grief
To bear love's wrong, than hate's known in-
jury.
 Lascivious grace, in whom all ill well
  shows,
 Kill me with spites; yet we must not be
  foes.

XLI.

Those pretty wrongs that liberty commits
When I am sometime absent from thy heart,
Thy beauty and thy years full well befits,
For still temptation follows where thou art.
Gentle thou art, and therefore to be won,
Beauteous thou art, therefore to be assail'd;
And when a woman wooes, what woman's
 son
Will sourly leave her till she have prevail'd?
Ah me! but yet thou mightst my seat for-
 bear,
And chide thy beauty and thy straying
 youth,
Who lead thee in their riot even there
Where thou art forc'd to break a twofold
 truth;
 Hers, by thy beauty tempting her to thee,
 Thine, by thy beauty being false to me.

XLII.

That thou hast her, it is not all my grief,
And yet it may be said I lov'd her dearly;
That she hath thee, is of my wailing chief,
A loss in love that touches me more nearly.
Loving offenders, thus I will excuse ye:—
Thou dost love her, because thou knew'st I
 love her;
And for my sake even so doth she abuse me,
Suffering my friend for my sake to approve
 her.
If I lose thee, my loss is my love's gain,
And, losing her, my friend hath found that
 loss;
Both find each other, and I lose both twain,
And both for my sake lay on me this cross:
 But here's the joy; my friend and I are
  one;
 Sweet flattery! then she loves but me
  alone.

XLIII.

When most I wink, then do mine eyes best
 see,
For all the day they view things unrespected;
But when I sleep, in dreams they look on
 thee,
And, darkly bright, are bright in dark directed;

Then thou whose shadow shadows doth
 make bright,
How would thy shadow's form form happy
 show
To the clear day with thy much clearer light,
When to unseeing eyes thy shade shines so!
How would (I say) mine eyes be blessed
 made
By looking on thee in the living day,
When in dead night thy fair imperfect shade
Through heavy sleep on sightless eyes doth
 stay?
 All days are nights to see, till I see thee,
 And nights, bright days, when dreams do
  show thee me.

XLIV.

If the dull substance of my flesh were
 thought,
Injurious distance should not stop my way;
For then, despite of space, I would be
 brought
From limits far remote, where thou dost stay.
No matter then, although my foot did stand
Upon the farthest earth remov'd from thee,
For nimble thought can jump both sea and
 land,
As soon as think the place where he would be.
But ah! thought kills me, that I am not
 thought,
To leap large lengths of miles when thou art
 gone,
But that, so much of earth and water
 wrought,
I must attend time's leisure with my moan;
 Receiving nought by elements so slow
 But heavy tears, badges of either's woe:

XLV.

The other two, slight air and purging fire,
Are both with thee, wherever I abide;
The first my thought, the other my desire,
These present-absent with swift motion slide.
For when these quicker elements are gone
In tender embassy of love to thee,
My life, being made of four, with two alone
Sinks down to death, oppress'd with melan-
 choly;
Until life's composition be recur'd
By those swift messengers return'd from thee,
Who even but now come back again, assur'd
Of thy fair health, recounting it to me:
 This told, I joy; but then no longer glad,
 I send them back again, and straight grow
  sad.

XLVI.

Mine eye and heart are at a mortal war,
How to divide the conquest of thy sight;
Mine eye my heart thy picture's sight would
 bar,
My heart mine eye the freedom of that right.

My heart doth plead that thou in him dost lie,
(A closet never pierc'd with crystal eyes,)
But the defendant doth that plea deny,
And says in him thy fair appearance lies.
To 'cide this title is impannelled
A quest of thoughts, all tenants to the heart;
And by their verdict is determined
The clear eye's moiety, and the dear heart's part:
  As thus; mine eye's due is thine outward part,
  And my heart's right thine inward love of heart.

XLVII.

Betwixt mine eye and heart a league is took,
And each doth good turns now unto the other:
When that mine eye is famish'd for a look,
Or heart in love with sighs himself doth smother,
With my love's picture then my eye doth feast,
And to the painted banquet bids my heart;
Another time mine eye is my heart's guest,
And in his thoughts of love doth share a part:
So, either by thy picture or my love,
Thyself away art present still with me;
For thou not farther than my thoughts canst move,
And I am still with them, and they with thee;
  Or if they sleep, thy picture in my sight
  Awakes my heart to heart's and eye's delight.

XLVIII.

How careful was I when I took my way,
Each trifle under truest bars to thrust,
That, to my use, it might unused stay
From hands of falsehood, in sure wards of trust!
But thou, to whom my jewels trifles are,
Most worthy comfort, now my greatest grief,
Thou, best of dearest, and mine only care,
Art left the prey of every vulgar thief.
Thee have I not lock'd up in any chest,
Save where thou art not, though I feel thou art,
Within the gentle closure of my breast,
From whence at pleasure thou mayst come and part;
  And even thence thou wilt be stolen I fear,
  For truth proves thievish for a prize so dear.

XLIX.

Against that time, if ever that time come,
When I shall see thee frown on my defects,
Whenas thy love hath cast his utmost sum,
Call'd to that audit by advis'd respects;
Against that time, when thou shalt strangely pass,
And scarcely greet me with that sun, thine eye,
When love, converted from the thing it was,
Shall reasons find of settled gravity;
Against that time do I ensconce me here
Within the knowledge of mine own desert,
And this my hand against myself uprear,
To guard the lawful reasons on thy part:
  To leave poor me thou hast the strength of laws,
  Since, why to love, I can allege no cause.

L.

How heavy do I journey on the way,
When what I seek—my weary travel's end—
Doth teach that ease and that repose to say,
'Thus far the miles are measur'd from thy friend!'
The beast that bears me, tired with my woe,
Plods dully on, to bear that weight in me,
As if by some instinct the wretch did know
His rider lov'd not speed, being made from thee:
The bloody spur cannot provoke him on
That sometimes anger thrusts into his hide,
Which heavily he answers with a groan,
More sharp to me than spurring to his side;
  For that same groan doth put this in my mind,
  My grief lies onward, and my joy behind.

LI.

Thus can my love excuse the slow offence
Of my dull bearer, when from thee I speed:
From where thou art why should I haste me thence?
Till I return, of posting is no need.
O what excuse will my poor beast then find,
When swift extremity can seem but slow?
Then should I spur, though mounted on the wind;
In winged speed no motion shall I know:
Then can no horse with my desire keep pace;
Therefore desire, of perfect'st love being made,
Shall neigh (no dull flesh) in his fiery race;
But love, for love, thus shall excuse my jade;
  Since from thee going he went wilful slow,
  Towards thee I'll run, and give him leave to go.

LII.

So am I as the rich, whose blessed key
Can bring him to his sweet up-locked treasure,
The which he will not every hour survey,
For blunting the fine point of seldom pleasure.
Therefore are feasts so solemn and so rare,
Since seldom coming, in the long year set,

Like stones of worth they thinly placed are,
Or captain jewels in the carcanet.
So is the time that keeps you, as my chest,
Or as the wardrobe which the robe doth hide,
To make some special instant special-blest,
By new unfolding his imprison'd pride.
  Blessed are you, whose worthiness gives
    scope,
  Being had, to triumph, being lack'd, to
    hope.

LIII.

What is your substance, whereof are you
    made,
That millions of strange shadows on you
    tend?
Since every one hath, every one, one's shade,
And you, but one, can every shadow lend.
Describe Adonis, and the counterfeit
Is poorly imitated after you;
On Helen's cheek all art of beauty set,
And you in Grecian tires are painted new;
Speak of the spring, and foison of the year;
The one doth shadow of your beauty show,
The other as your bounty doth appear,
And you in every blessed shape we know.
  In all external grace you have some part,
  But you like none, none you, for constant
    heart.

LIV.

O how much more doth beauty beauteous
    seem,
By that sweet ornament which truth doth
    give!
The rose looks fair, but fairer we it deem
For that sweet odour which doth in it live.
The canker-blooms have full as deep a dye
As the perfumed tincture of the roses,
Hang on such thorns, and play as wantonly
When summer's breath their masked buds
    discloses:
But, for their virtue only is their show,
They live unwoo'd, and unrespected fade;
Die to themselves. Sweet roses do not so;
Of their sweet deaths are sweetest odours
    made:
  And so of you, beauteous and lovely
    youth,
  When that shall fade, by verse distils your
    truth.

LV.

Not marble, nor the gilded monuments
Of princes, shall outlive this powerful rhyme;
But you shall shine more bright in these
    contents
Than unswept stone, besmear'd with sluttish
    time.
When wasteful war shall statues overturn,
And broils root out the work of masonry,
Nor Mars his sword nor war's quick fire
    shall burn

The living record of your memory.
'Gainst death and all-oblivious enmity
Shall you pace forth; your praise shall still
    find room,
Even in the eyes of all posterity
That wear this world out to the ending
    doom.
  So, till the judgment that yourself arise,
  You live in this, and dwell in lovers' eyes.

LVI.

Sweet love, renew thy force; be it not said,
Thy edge should blunter be than appetite,
Which but to-day by feeding is allay'd,
To-morrow sharpen'd in his former might:
So, love, be thou; although to-day thou fill
Thy hungry eyes, even till they wink with
    fulness,
To-morrow see again, and do not kill
The spirit of love with a perpetual dulness.
Let this sad interim like the ocean be
Which parts the shore, where two contract-
    ed-new
Come daily to the banks, that, when they see
Return of love, more blest may be the view;
  Or call it winter, which, being full of care,
  Makes summer's welcome thrice more
    wish'd, more rare.

LVII.

Being your slave, what should I do but tend
Upon the hours and times of your desire?
I have no precious time at all to spend,
Nor services to do, till you require.
Nor dare I chide the world-without-end
    hour,
Whilst I, my sovereign, watch the clock for
    you,
Nor think the bitterness of absence sour,
When you have bid your servant once adieu;
Nor dare I question with my jealous thought
Where you may be, or your affairs suppose,
But, like a sad slave, stay and think of
    nought,
Save, where you are how happy you make
    those:
  So true a fool is love, that in your will
  (Though you do anything) he thinks no
    ill.

LVIII.

That God forbid, that made me first your
    slave,
I should in thought control your times of
    pleasure,
Or at your hand the account of hours to
    crave,
Being your vassal, bound to stay your lei-
    sure!
O, let me suffer (being at your beck)
The imprison'd absence of your liberty,
And patience, tame to sufferance, bide each
    check

Without accusing you of injury.
Be where you list; your charter is so strong,
That you yourself may privilege your time:
Do what you will, to you it doth belong
Yourself to pardon of self-doing crime.
  I am to wait, though waiting so be hell;
  Not blame your pleasure, be it ill or well.

LIX.

If there be nothing new, but that which is
Hath been before, how are our brains be-
    guil'd,
Which labouring for invention bear amiss
The second burthen of a former child!
O, that record could with a backward look,
Even of five hundred courses of the sun,
Show me your image in some antique book,
Since mind at first in character was done!
That I might see what the old world could
    say
To this composed wonder of your frame;
Whether we are mended, or whe'r better
    they,
Or whether revolution be the same.
  O! sure I am, the wits of former days
  To subjects worse have given admiring
    praise.

LX.

Like as the waves make towards the pebbled
    shore,
So do our minutes hasten to their end;
Each changing place with that which goes
    before.
In sequent toil all forwards do contend.
Nativity, once in the main of light,
Crawls to maturity, wherewith being
    crown'd,
Crooked eclipses 'gainst his glory fight,
And Time, that gave, doth now his gift con-
    found.
Time doth transfix the flourish set on youth,
And delves the parallels in beauty's brow;
Feeds on the rarities of nature's truth,
And nothing stands but for his scythe to
    mow.
  And yet, to times in hope, my verse shall
    stand,
  Praising thy worth, despite his cruel hand.

LXI.

Is it thy will thy image should keep open
My heavy eyelids to the weary night?
Dost thou desire my slumbers should be
    broken,
While shadows, like to thee, do mock my
    sight?
Is it thy spirit that thou send'st from thee
So far from home, into my deeds to pry;
To find out shames and idle hours in me,
The scope and tenor of thy jealousy?
O no! thy love, though much, is not so
    great:

It is my love that keeps mine eye awake;
Mine own true love that doth my rest defeat,
To play the watchman ever for thy sake:
  For thee watch I, whilst thou dost wake
    elsewhere,
From me far off, with others all-too-near.

LXII.

Sin of self-love possesseth all mine eye,
And all my soul, and all my every part;
And for this sin there is no remedy,
It is so grounded inward in my heart.
Methinks no face so gracious is as mine,
No shape so true, no truth of such account,
And for myself mine own worth to define,
As I all other in all worths surmount.
But when my glass shows me myself indeed,
Beated and chopp'd with tann'd antiquity,
Mine own self-love quite contrary I read,
Self so self-loving were iniquity.
  'Tis thee (myself) that for myself I praise,
  Painting my age with beauty of thy days.

LXIII.

Against my love shall be, as I am now,
With Time's injurious hand crush'd and o'er-
    worn;
When hours have drain'd his blood, and fill'd
    his brow
With lines and wrinkles; when his youthful
    morn
Hath travell'd on to age's steepy night;
And all those beauties, whereof now he's
    king,
Are vanishing or vanish'd out of sight,
Stealing away the treasure of his spring;
For such a time do I now fortify
Against confounding age's cruel knife,
That he shall never cut from memory
My sweet love's beauty, though my lover's
    life.
  His beauty shall in these black lines be
    seen,
  And they shall live, and he in them, still
    green.

LXIV.

When I have seen by Time's fell hand de-
    fac'd
The rich-proud cost of outworn buried age;
When sometime lofty towers I see down-
    ras'd,
And brass eternal, slave to mortal rage;
When I have seen the hungry ocean gain
Advantage on the kingdom of the shore,
And the firm soil win of the wat'ry main,
Increasing store with loss, and loss with
    store;
When I have seen such interchange of state,
Or state itself confounded to decay;
Ruin hath taught me thus to ruminate—
That Time will come and take my love
    away.

This thought is as a death, which cannot choose
But weep to have that which it fears to lose.

LXV.

Since brass, nor stone, nor earth, nor boundless sea,
But sad mortality o'ersways their power,
How with this rage shall beauty hold a plea,
Whose action is no stronger than a flower?
O, how shall summer's honey breath hold out
Against the wreckful siege of battering days,
When rocks impregnable are not so stout,
Nor gates of steel so strong, but time decays?
O fearful meditation! where, alack!
Shall Time's best jewel from Time's chest lie hid?
Or what strong hand can hold his swift foot back?
Or who his spoil of beauty can forbid?
    O none, unless this miracle have might,
    That in black ink my love may still shine bright.

LXVI.

Tir'd with all these, for restful death I cry,—
As, to behold desert a beggar born,
And needy nothing trimm'd in jollity,
And purest faith unhappily forsworn,
And gilded honour shamefully misplac'd,
And maiden virtue rudely strumpeted,
And right perfection wrongfully disgrac'd,
And strength by limping sway disabled,
And art made tongue-tied by authority,
And folly (doctor-like) controlling skill,
And simple truth miscall'd simplicity,
And captive good attending captain ill:
    Tir'd with all these, from these would I be gone,
    Save that, to die, I leave my love alone.

LXVII.

Ah! wherefore with infection should he live,
And with his presence grace impiety,
That sin by him advantage should achieve,
And lace itself with his society?
Why should false painting imitate his cheek,
And steal dead seeing of his living hue?
Why should poor beauty indirectly seek
Roses of shadow, since his rose is true?
Why should he live now Nature bankrupt is,
Beggar'd of blood to blush through lively veins?
For she hath no exchequer now but his,
And, proud of many, lives upon his gains.
    O, him she stores, to show what wealth she had
    In days long since, before these last so bad.

LXVIII.

Thus is his cheek the map of days outworn,

When beauty liv'd and died as flowers do now,
Before these bastard signs of fair were born,
Or durst inhabit on a living brow;
Before the golden tresses of the dead,
The right of sepulchres, were shorn away,
To live a second life on second head,
Ere beauty's dead fleece made another gay:
In him those holy antique hours are seen,
Without all ornament, itself, and true,
Making no summer of another's green,
Robbing no old to dress his beauty new;
    And him as for a map doth Nature store,
    To show false Art what beauty was of yore.

LXIX.

Those parts of thee that the world's eye doth view
Want nothing that the thought of hearts can mend:
All tongues (the voice of souls) give thee that due,
Uttering bare truth, even so as foes commend.
Thine outward thus with outward praise is crown'd;
But those same tongues that give thee so thine own,
In other accents do this praise confound,
By seeing farther than the eye hath shown.
They look into the beauty of thy mind,
And that, in guess, they measure by thy deeds;
Then (churls) their thoughts, although their eyes were kind,
To thy fair flower add the rank smell of weeds:
    But why thy odour matcheth not thy show,
    The solve is this,—that thou dost common grow.

LXX.

That thou art blam'd shall not be thy defect.
For slander's mark was ever yet the fair;
The ornament of beauty is suspect,
A crow that flies in heaven's sweetest air.
So thou be good, slander doth but approve
Thy worth the greater, being woo'd of time;
For canker vice the sweetest buds doth love,
And thou present'st a pure unstained prime.
Thou hast pass'd by the ambush of young days,
Either not assail'd, or victor being charg'd;
Yet this thy praise cannot be so thy praise,
To tie up envy, evermore enlarg'd:
    If some suspect of ill mask'd not thy show,
    Then thou alone kingdoms of hearts shouldst owe:

LXXI.

No longer mourn for me when I am dead

Than you shall hear the surly sullen bell
Give warning to the world that I am fled
From this vile world, with vilest worms to
    dwell:
Nay, if you read this line, remember not
The hand that writ it; for I love you so,
That I in your sweet thoughts would be for-
    got,
If thinking on me then should make you
    woe.
O, if (I say) you look upon this verse,
When I perhaps compounded am with clay,
Do not so much as my poor name rehearse;
But let your love even with my life decay:
    Lest the wise world should look into your
        moan,
    And mock you with me after I am gone.

LXXII.

O, lest the world should task you to recite
What merit liv'd in me, that you should love
After my death,—dear love, forget me quite,
For you in me can nothing worthy prove;
Unless you would devise some virtuous lie,
To do more for me than mine own desert,
And hang more praise upon deceased I
Than niggard truth would willingly impart:
O, lest your true love may seem false in this,
That you for love speak well of me untrue,
My name be buried where my body is,
And live no more to shame nor me nor you.
    For I am sham'd by that which I bring
        forth,
    And so should you, to love things nothing
        worth.

LXXIII.

That time of year thou mayst in me behold
When yellow leaves, or none, or few, do hang
Upon those boughs which shake against the
    cold,
Bare ruin'd choirs, where late the sweet birds
    sang.
In me thou seest the twilight of such day
As after sunset fadeth in the west,
Which by and by black night doth take
    away,
Death's second self, that seals up all in rest.
In me thou seest the glowing of such fire,
That on the ashes of his youth doth lie,
As the death-bed whereon it must expire,
Consum'd with that which it was nourish'd
    by.
    This thou perceiv'st which makes thy love
        more strong,
    To love that well which thou must leave
        ere long:

LXXIV.

But be contented: when that fell arrest
Without all bail shall carry me away,
My life hath in this line some interest,
Which for memorial still with thee shall stay.

When thou reviewest this, thou dost review
The very part was consecrate to thee.
The earth can have but earth, which is his
    due;
My spirit is thine, the better part of me:
So then thou hast but lost the dregs of life,
The prey of worms, my body being dead;
The coward conquest of a wretch's knife,
Too base of thee to be remembered.
    The worth of that, is that which it con-
        tains,
    And that is this, and this with thee re-
        mains.

LXXV.

So are you to my thoughts, as food to life,
Or as sweet-season'd showers are to the
    ground,
And for the peace of you I hold such strife
As 'twixt a miser and his wealth is found:
Now proud as an enjoyer, and anon
Doubting the filching age will steal his
    treasure;
Now counting best to be with you alone,
Then better'd that the world may see my
    pleasure:
Sometime all full with feasting on your sight,
And by and by clean starved for a look;
Possessing or pursuing no delight,
Save what is had or must from you be took.
    Thus do I pine and surfeit day by day.
    Or gluttoning on all, or all away.

LXXVI.

Why is my verse so barren of new pride?
So far from variation or quick change?
Why, with the time, do I not glance aside
To new-found methods and to compounds
    strange?
Why write I still all one, ever the same,
And keep invention in a noted weed,
That every word doth almost tell my name,
Showing their birth, and where they did
    proceed?
O know, sweet love, I always write of you,
And you and love are still my argument;
So all my best is dressing old words new,
Spending again what is already spent;
    For as the sun is daily new and old,
    So is my love still telling what is told.

LXXVII.

Thy glass will show thee how thy beauties
    wear,
Thy dial how thy precious minutes waste;
The vacant leaves thy mind's imprint will
    bear,
And of this book this learning mayst thou
    taste.
The wrinkles which thy glass will truly show,
Of mouthed graves will give thee memory;
Thou by thy dial's shady stealth mayst know
Time's thievish progress to eternity.

Look what thy memory cannot contain,
Commit to these waste blanks, and thou shalt find
Those children nurs'd, deliver'd from thy brain,
To take a new acquaintance of thy mind.
These offices, so oft as thou wilt look,
Shall profit thee, and much enrich thy book.

LXXVIII.

So oft have I invok'd thee for my muse,
And found such fair assistance in my verse,
As every alien pen hath got my use,
And under thee their poesy disperse.
Thine eyes, that taught the dumb on high to sing,
And heavy ignorance aloft to fly,
Have added feathers to the learned's wing,
And given grace a double majesty.
Yet be most proud of that which I compile,
Whose influence is thine, and born of thee:
In others' works thou dost but mend the style,
And arts with thy sweet graces graced be;
But thou art all my art, and dost advance
As high as learning my rude ignorance.

LXXIX.

Whilst I alone did call upon thy aid,
My verse alone had all thy gentle grace;
But now my gracious numbers are decay'd,
And my sick muse doth give another place.
I grant, sweet love, thy lovely argument
Deserves the travail of a worthier pen;
Yet what of thee thy poet doth invent,
He robs thee of, and pays it thee again.
He lends thee virtue, and he stole that word
From thy behaviour; beauty doth he give,
And found it in thy cheek; he can afford
No praise to thee but what in thee doth live.
Then thank him not for that which he doth say,
Since what he owes thee thou thyself dost pay.

LXXX.

O, how faint when I of you do write,
Knowing a better spirit doth use your name,
And in the praise thereof spends all his might,
To make me tongue-tied, speaking of your fame!
But since your worth (wide as the ocean is)
The humble as the proudest sail doth bear,
My saucy bark, inferior far to his,
On your broad main doth wilfully appear.
Your shallowest help will hold me up afloat,
Whilst he upon your soundless deep doth ride;
Or, being wreck'd, I am a worthless boat,
He of tall building, and of goodly pride:
Then if he thrive, and I be cast away,
The worst was this;—my love was my decay.

LXXXI.

Or I shall live your epitaph to make,
Or you survive when I in earth am rotten;
From hence your memory death cannot take,
Although in me each part will be forgotten.
Your name from hence immortal life shall have,   [die:
Though I, once gone, to all the world must
The earth can yield me but a common grave,
When you entombed in men's eyes shall lie.
Your monument shall be my gentle verse,
Which eyes not yet created shall o'er-read;
And tongues to be, your being shall rehearse,
When all the breathers of this world are dead;
You still shall live (such virtue hath my pen)
Where breath most breathes,—even in the mouths of men.

LXXXII.

I grant thou wert not married to my muse,
And therefore mayst without attaint o'erlook
The dedicated words which writers use
Of their fair subject, blessing every book.
Thou art as fair in knowledge as in hue,
Finding thy worth a limit past my praise;
And therefore art enforc'd to seek anew
Some fresher stamp of the time-bettering days.
And do so, love; yet when they have devis'd
What strained touches rhetoric can lend,
Thou truly fair wert truly sympathiz'd
In true plain words, by thy true-telling friend,
And their gross painting might be better us'd
Where cheeks need blood; in thee it is abus'd.

LXXXIII.

I never saw that you did painting need,
And therefore to your fair no painting set.
I found, or thought I found, you did exceed
The barren tender of a poet's debt:
And therefore have I slept in your report
That you yourself, being extant, well might show
How far a modern quill doth come too short,
Speaking of worth, what worth in you doth grow.
This silence for my sin you did impute,
Which shall be most my glory, being dumb;
For I impair not beauty being mute,
When others would give life, and bring a tomb,
There lives more life in one of your fair eyes
Than both your poets can in praise devise.

LXXXIV.

Who is it that says most? which can say
more
Than this rich praise,—that you alone are
you?
In whose confine immured is the store
Which should example where your equal
grew?
Lean penury within that pen doth dwell,
That to his subject lends not some small
glory;
But he that writes of you, if he can tell
That you are you, so dignifies his story,
Let him but copy what in you is writ,
Not making worse what nature made so
clear,
And such a counterpart shall fame his wit,
Making his style admired everywhere.
    You to your beauteous blessings add a
    curse,
    Being fond on praise, which makes your
    praises worse.

LXXXV.

My tongue-tied muse in manners holds her
still,
While comments of your praise, richly com-
pil'd,
Reserve their character with golden quill,
And precious phrase by all the muses fil'd.
I think good thoughts, while others write
good words,
And, like unlettered clerk, still cry 'Amen'
To every hymn that able spirit affords,
In polish'd form of well-refined pen.
Hearing you prais'd, I say, ' 'Tis so, 'tis true,'
And to the most of praise add something
more;
But that is in my thought, whose love to
you,
Though words come hindmost, holds his rank
before.
    Then others for the breath of words re-
    spect,
    Me for my dumb thoughts, speaking in
    effect.

LXXXVI.

Was it the proud full sail of his great verse,
Bound for the prize of all-too-precious you,
That did my ripe thoughts in my brain in-
hearse,
Making their tomb the womb wherein they
grew?
Was it his spirit, by spirits taught to write
Above a mortal pitch, that struck me dead?
No, neither he, nor his compeers by night
Giving him aid, my verse astonished.
He, nor that affable familiar ghost
Which nightly gulls him with intelligence,
As victors, of my silence cannnot boast;
I was not sick of any fear from thence.

But when your countenance fil'd up his
line,
Then lack'd I matter; that enfeebled mine.

LXXXVII.

Farewell! thou art too dear for my possess-
ing,
And like enough thou know'st thy estimate:
The charter of thy worth gives thee releas-
ing;
My bonds in thee are all determinate.
For how do I hold thee but by thy grant-
ing?
And for that riches where is my deserving?
The cause of this fair gift in me is wanting,
And so my patent back again is swerving.
Thyself thou gav'st, thy own worth then not
knowing,
Or me, to whom thou gav'st it, else mistak-
ing;
So thy great gift, upon misprision growing,
Comes home again, on better judgment mak-
ing.
    Thus have I had thee, as a dream doth
    flatter,
    In sleep a king, but, waking, no such
    matter.

LXXXVIII.

When thou shalt be dispos'd to set me light,
And place my merit in the eye of scorn,
Upon thy side against myself I'll fight,
And prove thee virtuous, though thou art
forsworn:
With mine own weakness being best ac-
quainted,
Upon thy part I can set down a story
Of faults conceal'd, wherein I am attainted;
That thou, in losing me, shall win much
glory:
And I by this will be a gainer too;
For bending all my loving thoughts on thee,
The injuries that to myself I do,
Doing thee vantage, double-vantage me.
    Such is my love, to thee I so belong,
    That for thy right myself will bear all
    wrong.

LXXXIX.

Say that thou didst forsake me for some
fault,
And I will comment upon that offence:
Speak of my lameness, and I straight will
halt;
Against thy reasons making no defence.
Thou canst not, love, disgrace me half so ill,
To set a form upon desired change,
As I'll myself disgrace: knowing thy will,
I will acquaintance strangle, and look
strange,
Be absent from thy walks; and in my
tongue

Thy sweet-beloved name no more shall
    dwell;
Lest I (too much profane) should do it
    wrong,
And haply of our old acquaintance tell.
    For thee, against myself I'll vow debate,
    For I must ne'er love him whom thou dost
    hate.

XC.

Then hate me when thou wilt; if ever, now;
Now while the world is bent my deeds to
    cross,
Join with the spite of fortune, make me bow,
And do not drop in for an after-loss:
Ah! do not, when my heart hath scap'd this
    sorrow,
Come in the rearward of a conquer'd woe;
Give not a windy night a rainy morrow,
To linger out a purpos'd overthrow.
If thou wilt leave me, do not leave me last,
When other petty griefs have done their
    spite,
But in the onset come; so shall I taste
At first the very worst of fortune's might;
    And other strains of woe, which now seem
    woe,
    Compar'd with loss of thee will not seem
    so.

XCI.

Some glory in their birth, some in their skill,
Some in their wealth, some in their body's
    force;
Some in their garments, though new-fangled
    ill;
Some in their hawks and hounds, some in
    their horse;
And every humour hath his adjunct pleasure,
Wherein it finds a joy above the rest;
But these particulars are not my measure,
All these I better in one general best.
Thy love is better than high birth to me,
Richer than wealth, prouder than garments'
    cost,
Of more delight than hawks and horses be;
And, having thee, of all men's pride I boast.
    Wretched in this alone, that thou mayst
    take
    All this away, and me most wretched
    make.

XCII.

But do thy worst to steal thyself away,
For term of life thou art assured mine;
And life no longer than thy love will stay,
For it depends upon that love of thine.
Then need I not to fear the worst of wrongs,
When in the least of them my life hath end.
I see a better state to me belongs
Than that which on thy humour doth de-
    pend;

Thou canst not vex me with inconstant
    mind,
Since that my life on thy revolt doth lie.
O what a happy title do I find,
Happy to have thy love, happy to die!
    But what's so blessed-fair that fears no
    blot?—
    Thou mayst be false, and yet I know it
    not:

XCIII.

So shall I live, supposing thou art true,
Like a deceived husband; so love's face
May still seem love to me, though alter'd
    new;
Thy looks with me, thy heart in other place:
For there can live no hatred in thine eye,
Therefore in that I cannot know thy change.
In many's looks the false heart's history
Is writ, in moods and frowns and wrinkles
    strange;
But heaven in thy creation did decree
That in thy face sweet love should ever
    dwell;
Whate'er thy thoughts or thy heart's work-
    ings be,
Thy looks should nothing thence but sweet-
    ness tell.
    How like Eve's apple doth thy beauty
    grow,
    If thy sweet virtue answer not thy show?

XCIV.

They that have power to hurt and will do
    none,
That do not do the thing they most do show,
Who, moving others, are themselves as stone,
Unmoved, cold, and to temptation slow;
They rightly do inherit Heaven's graces,
And husband nature's riches from expense;
They are the lords and owners of their faces,
Others but stewards of their excellence.
The summer's flower is to the summer sweet
Though to itself it only live and die;
But if that flower with base infection meet,
The basest weed outbraves his dignity:
    For sweetest things turn sourest by their
    deeds:
    Lilies that fester smell far worse than
    weeds.

XCV.

How sweet and lovely dost thou make the
    shame,
Which, like a canker in the fragrant rose,
Doth spot the beauty of thy budding name!
O, in what sweets dost thou thy sins enclose!
That tongue that tells the story of thy days,
Making lascivious comments on thy sport,
Cannot dispraise but in a kind of praise:
Naming thy name blesses an ill report.
O, what a mansion have those vices got
Which for their habitation chose out thee!

Where beauty's veil doth cover every blot,
And all things turn to fair, that eyes can see!
   Take heed, dear heart, of this large privi-
     lege;
   The hardest knife ill-used doth lose his
     edge.

XCVI.

Some say thy fault is youth, some wanton-
   ness;
Some say thy grace is youth and gentle
   sport;
Both grace and faults are lov'd of more and
   less:
Thou mak'st faults graces that to thee resort.
As on the finger of a throned queen
The basest jewel will be well esteem'd;
So are those errors that in thee are seen
To truths translated, and for true things
   deem'd.
How many lambs might the stern wolf be-
   tray,
If like a lamb he could his looks translate!
How many gazers mightst thou lead away,
If thou wouldst use the strength of all thy
   state!
   But do not so; I love thee in such sort,
   As, thou being mine, mine is thy good re-
     port.

XCVII.

How like a winter hath my absence been.
From thee, the pleasure of the fleeting year!
What freezings have I felt, what dark days
   seen!
What old December's bareness everywhere!
And yet this time remov'd was summer's
   time,
The teeming autumn, big with rich increase,
Bearing the wanton burden of the prime,
Like widow'd wombs after their lords' de-
   cease;
Yet this abundant issue seem'd to me
But hope of orphans, and unfather'd fruit;
For summer and his pleasures wait on thee,
And, thou away, the very birds are mute;
   Or, if they sing, 'tis with so dull a cheer,
   That leaves look pale, dreading the win-
     ter's near.

XCVIII.

From you have I been absent in the spring,
When proud-pied April, dress'd in all his
   trim,
Hath put a spirit of youth in everything,
That heavy Saturn laugh'd and leap'd with
   him.
Yet nor the lays of birds, nor the sweet smell
Of different flowers in odour and in hue,
Could make me any summer's story tell,
Or from their proud lap pluck them where
   they grew:
Nor did I wonder at the lilies white,

Nor praise the deep vermilion in the rose;
They were but sweet, but figures of delight,
Drawn after you, you pattern of all those.
   Yet seem'd it winter still, and you, away,
   As with your shadow I with these did
     play:

XCIX.

The forward violet thus did I chide;—
Sweet thief, whence didst thou steal thy
   sweet that smells,
If not from my love's breath? The purple
   pride
Which on thy soft cheek for complexion
   dwells,
In my love's veins thou hast too grossly dy'd,
The lily I condemned for thy hand,
And buds of marjoram had stolen thy hair:
The roses fearfully on thorns did stand,
One blushing shame, another white despair;
A third, nor red nor white, had stolen of
   both,
And to his robbery had annex'd thy breath;
But for his theft, in pride of all his growth
A vengeful canker eat him up to death.
   More flowers I noted, yet I none could see,
   But sweet or colour it had stolen from
     thee.

C.

Where art thou, Muse, that thou forgett'st
   so long
To speak of that which gives thee all thy
   might?
Spend'st thou thy fury on some worthless
   song,
Darkening thy power, to lend base subjects
   light?
Return, forgetful Muse, and straight redeem
In gentle numbers time so idly spent;
Sing to the ear that doth thy lays esteem,
And gives thy pen both skill and argument.
Rise; resty Muse, my love's sweet face sur-
   vey,
If Time have any wrinkle graven there;
If any, be a satire to decay,
And make Time's spoils despised everywhere.
   Give my love fame faster than Time wastes
     life;
   So thou prevent'st his scythe and crooked
     knife.

CI.

O truant Muse, what shall be thy amends
For thy neglect of truth in beauty dy'd?
Both truth and beauty on my love depends;
So dost thou too, and therein dignified.
Make answer, Muse: wilt thou not haply say,
'Truth needs no colour with his colour fix'd,
Beauty no pencil, beauty's truth to lay;
But best is best, if never intermix'd?'—
Because he needs no praise, wilt thou be
   dumb?

Excuse not silence so; for it lies in thee
To make him much outlive a gilded tomb,
And to be prais'd of ages yet to be.
    Then do thy office, Muse; I teach thee how
    To make him seem long hence as he shows
    now.

CII.

My love is strengthen'd, though more weak
    in seeming;
I love not less, though less the show appear;
That love is merchandiz'd whose rich esteem-
    ing
The owner's tongue doth publish everywhere.
Our love was new, and then but in the
    spring,
When I was wont to greet it with my lays;
As Philomel in summer's front doth sing,
And stops her pipe in growth of riper days:
Not that the summer is less pleasant now
Than when her mournful hymns did hush the
    night,
But that wild music burthens every bough,
And sweets grown common lose their dear
    delight.
    Therefore, like her, I sometime hold my
    tongue,
    Because I would not dull you with my
    song.

CIII.

Alack! what poverty my Muse brings forth,
That having such a scope to show her pride,
The argument, all bare, is of more worth,
Than when it hath my added praise beside.
O blame me not if I no more can write!
Look in your glass, and there appears a face
That over-goes my blunt invention quite,
Dulling my lines, and doing me disgrace.
Were it not sinful, then, striving to mend,
To mar the subject that before was well?
For to no other pass my verses tend,
Than of your graces and your gifts to tell;
    And more, much more, than in my verse
    can sit,
    Your own glass shows you, when you look
    in it.

CIV.

To me, fair friend, you never can be old,
For as you were when first your eye I eyed,
Such seems your beauty still. Three winters'
    cold
Have from the forests shook three summers'
    pride;
Three beauteous springs to yellow autumn
    turn'd
In process of the seasons have I seen;
Three April perfumes in three hot Junes
    burn'd,
Since first I saw you fresh, which yet are
    green.
Ah! yet doth beauty, like a dial-hand,

'Steal from his figure, and no pace perceiv'd;
So your sweet hue, which methinks still doth
    stand,
Hath motion, and mine eye may be deceiv'd.
    For fear of which, hear this, thou age un-
    bred,
    Ere you were born, was beauty's summer
    dead.

CV.

Let not my love be call'd idolatry,
Nor my beloved as an idol show,
Since all alike my songs and praises be,
To one, of one, still such, and ever so.
Kind is my love to-day, to-morrow kind,
Still constant in a wondrous excellence;
Therefore my verse, to constancy confin'd,
One thing expressing, leaves out difference.
Fair, kind, and true, is all my argument,
Fair, kind, and true, varying to other words;
And in this change is my invention spent,
Three themes in one, which wondrous scope
    affords.
    Fair, kind, and true, have often liv'd alone,
    Which three, till now, never kept seat in
    one.

CVI.

When in the chronicle of wasted time
I see descriptions of the fairest wights,
And beauty making beautiful old rhyme,
In praise of ladies dead and lovely knights,
Then in the blazon of sweet beauty's best,
Of hand, of foot, of lip, of eye, of brow,
I see their antique pen would have express'd
Even such a beauty as you master now.
So all their praises are but prophecies
Of this our time, all you prefiguring;
And, for they look'd but with divining eyes,
They had not skill enough your worth to
    sing:
    For we, which now behold these present
    days,
    Have eyes to wonder, but lack tongues to
    praise.

CVII.

Not mine own fears, nor the prophetic soul
Of the wide world dreaming on things to
    come,
Can yet the lease of my true love control,
Suppos'd as forfeit to a confin'd doom.
The mortal moon hath her eclipse endur'd,
And the sad augurs mock their own presage:
Incertainties now crown themselves assur'd,
And peace proclaims olives of endless age.
Now with the drops of this most balmy time
My love looks fresh, and Death to me sub-
    scribes,
Since spite of him I'll live in this poor rhyme,
While he insults o'er dull and speechless
    tribes.

And thou in this shalt find thy monument,
When tyrants' crests and tombs of brass
    are spent.

CVIII.

What's in the brain that ink may character,
Which hath not figur'd to thee my true
    spirit?
What's new to speak, what new to register,
That may express my love, or thy dear
    merit?
Nothing, sweet boy; but yet, like prayers di-
    vine,
I must each day say o'er the very same;
Counting no old thing old, thou mine, I
    thine.
Even as when first I hallow'd thy fair name.
So that eternal love in love's fresh case
Weighs not the dust and injury of age,
Nor gives to necessary wrinkles place,
But makes antiquity for aye his page;
    Finding the first conceit of love there bred,
    Where time and outward form would show
      it dead.

CIX.

O, never say that I was false of heart,
Though absence seem'd my flame to qualify!
As easy might I from myself depart,
As from my soul, where in thy breast doth
    lie:
That is my home of love: if I have rang'd,
Like him that travels, I return again;
Just to the time, not with the time ex-
    chang'd,—
So that myself bring water for my stain.
Never believe, though in my nature reign'd
All frailties that besiege all kinds of blood,
That it could so preposterously be stain'd,
To leave for nothing all thy sum of good;
    For nothing this wide universe I call,
    Save thou, my rose; in it thou art my all.

CX.

Alas, 'tis true, I have gone here and there,
And made myself a motley to the view,
Gor'd mine own thoughts, sold cheap what is
    most dear,
Made old offences of affections new.
Most true it is, that I have look'd on truth
Askance and strangely; but, by all above,
These blenches gave my heart another youth,
And worst essays prov'd thee my best of
    love.
Now all is done, save what shall have no
    end:
Mine appetite I never more will grind
On newer proof, to try an older friend,
A God in love, to whom I am confined.
    Then give me welcome, next my heaven the
      best,   [breast.
    Even to thy pure and most most loving

CXI.

O, for my sake do you with Fortune chide,
The guilty goddess of my harmful deeds,
That did not better for my life provide,
Than public means, which public manners
    breeds.
Thence comes it that my name receives a
    brand,
And almost thence my nature is subdued
To what it works in, like the dyer's hand:
Pity me then, and wish I were renew'd;
Whilst, like a willing patient, I will drink
Potions of eysell, 'gainst my strong infection;
No bitterness that I will bitter think,
Nor double penance, to correct correction.
    Pity me then, dear friend, and I assure ye,
    Even that your pity is enough to cure me.

CXII.

Your love and pity doth the impression fill
Which vulgar scandal stamp'd upon my
    brow;
For what care I who calls me well or ill,
So you o'ergreen my bad, my good allow?
You are my all-the-world, and I must strive
To know my shames and praises from your
    tongue;
None else to me, nor I to none alive,
That my steel'd sense or changes, right or
    wrong.
In so profound abysm I throw all care
Of other's voices, that my adder's sense
To critic and to flatterer stopped are.
Mark how with my neglect I do dispense;—
    You are so strongly in my purpose bred,
    That all the world besides methinks are
      dead.

CXIII.

Since I left you, mine eye is in my mind;
And that which governs me to go about
Doth part his function, and is partly blind,
Seems seeing, but effectually is out;
For it no form delivers to the heart
Of bird, of flower, or shape, which it doth
    latch;
Of his quick objects hath the mind no part,
Nor his own vision holds what it doth catch;
For if it see the rud'st or gentlest sight,
The most sweet favour, or deformed'st crea-
    ture,
The mountain or the sea, the day or night,
The crow, or dove, it shapes them to your
    feature.
    Incapable of more, replete with you,
    My most true mind thus maketh mine
      untrue.

CXIV.

Or whether doth my mind being crown'd
    with you,
Drink up the monarch's plague, this flattery,

Or whether shall I say mine eye saith true;
And that your love taught it this alchymy,
To make of monsters and things indigest
Such cherubins as your sweet self resemble,
Creating every bad a perfect best,
As fast as objects to his beams assemble?
O, 'tis the first; 'tis flattery in my seeing,
And my great mind most kingly drinks it
up:
Mine eye well knows what with his gust is
'greeing,
And to his palate doth prepare the cup:
  If it be poison'd, 'tis the lesser sin
    That mine eye loves it, and doth first
    begin.

CXV.

Those lines that I before have writ, do lie;
Even those that said I could not love you
dearer;
Yet then my judgment knew no reason why
My most full flame should afterwards burn
clearer.
But reckoning time, whose million'd acci-
dents
Creep in 'twixt vows, and change decrees of
kings,
Tan sacred beauty, blunt the sharp'st in-
tents,
Divert strong minds to the course of alter-
ing things;
Alas! why, fearing of Time's tyranny,
Might I not then say, 'Now I love you
best,'
When I was certain o'er incertainty,
Crowning the present, doubting of the rest?
  Love is a babe; then might I not say so,
    To give full growth to that which still
    doth grow?

CXVI.

Let me not to the marriage of true minds
Admit impediments. Love is not love
Which alters when it alteration finds,
Or bends with the remover to remove:
O no; it is an ever-fixed mark,
That looks on tempests, and is never shaken;
It is the star to every wandering bark,
Whose worth's unknown, although his
height be taken.
Love's not Time's fool, though rosy lips and
cheeks
Within his bending sickle's compass come;
Love alters not with his brief hours and
weeks,
But bears it out even to the edge of doom.
  If this be error, and upon me prov'd,
  I never writ, nor no man ever lov'd.

CXVII.

Accuse me thus; that I have scanted all
Wherein I should your great deserts repay;
Forgot upon your dearest love to call,

Whereto all bonds do tie me day by day;
That I have frequent been with unknown
minds,
And given to time your own dear-purchas'd
right;
That I have hoisted sail to all the winds
Which should transport me farthest from
your sight.
Book both my wilfulness and errors down,
And on just proof surmise accumulate,
Bring me within the level of your frown,
But shoot not at me in your waken'd hate:
  Since my appeal says, I did strive to prove
  The constancy and virtue of your love.

CXVIII.

Like as, to make our appetites more keen,
With eager compounds we our palate urge;
As, to prevent our maladies unseen,
We sicken to shun sickness, when we purge;
Even so, being full of your ne'er-cloying
sweetness,
To bitter sauces did I frame my feeding,
And, sick of welfare, found a kind of meet-
ness
To be diseas'd, ere that there was true need-
ing.
Thus policy in love, to anticipate
The ills that were not, grew to faults as-
sured,
And brought to medicine a healthful state,
Which, rank of goodness, would by ill be
cured.
  But thence I learn, and find the lesson
  true,
  Drugs poison him that so fell sick of you.

CXIX.

What potions have I drunk of Siren tears,
Distill'd from limbecs foul as hell within,
Applying fears to hopes, and hopes to fears,
Still losing when I saw myself to win!
What wretched errors hath my heart com-
mitted,
Whilst it hath thought itself so blessed
never!
How have mine eyes out of their spheres
been fitted,
In the distraction of this madding fever!
O benefit of ill! now I find true
That better is by evil still made better;
And ruin'd love, when it is built anew,
Grows fairer than at first, more strong, far
greater.
  So I return rebuk'd to my content,
  And gain by ill thrice more than I have
  spent.

CXX.

That you were once unkind, befriends me
now,
And for that sorrow, which I then did feel,
Needs must I under my transgression bow,

Unless my nerves were brass or hammer'd
  steel.
For if you were by my unkindness shaken,
As I by yours, you have pass'd a hell of
  time;
And I, a tyrant, have no leisure taken
To weigh how once I suffer'd in your crime.
O that our night of woe might have remem-
  ber'd
My deepest sense, how hard true sorrow
  hits,
And soon to you, as you to me, then ten-
  der'd
The humble salve which wounded bosoms
  fits!
  But that your trespass now becomes a
    fee;
  Mine ransoms yours, and yours must ran-
    som me.

CXXI.

'Tis better to be vile than vile esteem'd,
When not to be receives reproach of being,
And the just pleasure lost, which is so
  deem'd
Not by our feeling, but by others' seeing.
For why should others' false adulterate eyes
Give salutation to my sportive blood?
Or on my frailties why are frailer spies,
Which in their wills count bad what I think
  good?
No.—I am that I am; and they that level
At my abuses, reckon up their own:
I may be straight, though they themselves
  be bevel;
By their rank thoughts my deeds must not
  be shown;
  Unless this general evil they maintain,—
  All men are bad, and in their badness
    reign.

CXXII.

Thy gift, thy tables, are within my brain
Full character'd with lasting memory
Which shall above that idle rank remain,
Beyond all date, even to eternity:
Or at the least so long as brain and heart
Have faculty by nature to subsist;
Till each to raz'd oblivion yield his part
Of thee, thy record never can be miss'd.
That poor retention could not so much hold,
Nor need I tallies thy dear love to score;
Therefore to give them from me was I bold,
To trust those tables that receive thee more:
  To keep an adjunct to remember thee,
  Were to import forgetfulness in me.

CXXIII.

No! Time, thou shalt not boast that I do
  change:
Thy pyramids built up with newer might
To me are nothing novel, nothing strange;
They are but dressings of a former sight.

Our dates are brief, and therefore we admire
What thou dost foist upon us that is old;
And rather make them born to our desire,
Than think that we before have heard them
  told.
Thy registers and thee I both defy,
Not wondering at the present nor the past;
For thy records and what we see do lie,
Made more or less by thy continual haste:
  This I do vow, and this shall ever be,
  I will be true, despite thy scythe and thee.

CXXIV.

If my dear love were but the child of state,
It might for Fortune's bastard be unfath-
  er'd,
As subject to Time's love, or to Time's hate,
Weeds among weeds, or flowers with flowers
  gather'd.
No, it was builded far from accident;
It suffers not in smiling pomp, nor falls
Under the blow of thralled discontent,
Whereto the inviting time our fashion calls:
It fears not policy, that heretic,
Which works on leases of short-number'd
  hours,
But all alone stands hugely politic,
That it nor grows with heat, nor drowns
  with showers.
  To this I witness call the fools of time,
  Which die for goodness, who have liv'd
    for crime.

CXXV.

Were it aught to me I bore the canopy,
With my extern the outward honouring,
Or laid great bases for eternity,
Which prove more short than waste or ruin-
  ing?
Have I not seen dwellers on form and favour
Lose all, and more, by paying too much
  rent,
For compound sweet foregoing simple
  savour,
Pitiful thrivers, in their gazing spent?
No;—let me be obsequious in thy heart,
And take thou my oblation, poor but free,
Which is not mix'd with seconds, knows no
  art,
But mutual render, only me for thee.
  Hence, thou suborn'd informer! a true
    soul,
  When most impeach'd, stands least in thy
    control.

CXXVI.

O thou, my lovely boy, who in thy power
Dost hold Time's fickle glass, his sickle,
  hour;
Who hast by waning grown, and therein
  show'st
Thy lovers withering, as thy sweet self
  grow'st!

If Nature, sovereign mistress over wrack,
As thou goest onwards, still will pluck thee
    back,
She keeps thee to this purpose, that her skill
May time disgrace, and wretched minutes
    kill.
Yet fear her, O thou minion of her pleasure;
She may detain, but not still keep her treas-
    ure:
    Her audit, though delay'd, answer'd must
      be,
    And her quietus is to render thee.

CXXVII.

In the old age black was not counted fair,
Or if it were, it bore not beauty's name;
But now is black beauty's successive heir,
And beauty slander'd with a bastard shame:
For since each hand hath put on nature's
    power,
Fairing the foul with art's false borrow'd
    face,
Sweet beauty hath no name, no holy hour,
But is profan'd, if not lives in disgrace.
Therefore my mistress' eyes are raven black,
Her eyes so suited; and they mourners seem
At such, who, not born fair, no beauty lack,
Slandering creation with a false esteem:
    Yet so they mourn, becoming of their
      woe,
    That every tongue says, beauty should
      look so.

CXXVIII.

How oft, when thou, my music, music
    play'st,
Upon that blessed wood whose motion
    sounds
With thy sweet fingers, when thou gently
    sway'st
The wiry concord that mine ear confounds,
Do I envy those jacks, that nimble leap
To kiss the tender inward of thy hand,
Whilst my poor lips, which should that har-
    vest reap,
At the wood's boldness by thee blushing
    stand!
To be so tickled, they would change their
    state
And situation with those dancing chips,
O'er whom thy fingers walk with gentle
    gait,
Making dead wood more bless'd than living
    lips.
    Since saucy jacks so happy are in this,
    Give them thy fingers, me thy lips to kiss.

CXXIX.

The expense of spirit in a waste of shame
Is lust in action; and till action, lust
Is perjur'd, murderous, bloody, full of
    blame,
Savage, extreme, rude, cruel, not to trust;

Enjoy'd no sooner, but despised straight;
Past reason hunted; and no sooner had,
Past reason hated, as a swallow'd bait,
On purpose laid to make the taker mad:
Mad in pursuit, and in possession so;
Had, having, and in quest to have, extreme;
A bliss in proof,—and prov'd, a very woe;
Before, a joy propos'd; behind, a dream:
    All this the world well knows; yet none
      knows well
    To shun the heaven that leads men to this
      hell.

CXXX.

My mistress' eyes are nothing like the sun;
Coral is far more red than her lips' red:
If snow be white, why then her breasts are
    dun;
If hairs be wires, black wires grow on her
    head.
I have seen roses damask'd, red and white,
But no such roses see I in her cheeks;
And in some perfumes is there more delight
Than in the breath that from my mistress
    reeks.
I love to hear her speak,—yet well I know
That music hath a far more pleasing sound;
I grant I never saw a goddess go,—
My mistress when she walks, treads on the
    ground;
    And yet, by heaven, I think my love as
      rare
    As any she belied with false compare.

CXXXI.

Thou art as tyrannous, so as thou art,
As those whose beauties proudly make them
    cruel;
For well thou know'st to my dear doting
    heart
Thou art the fairest and most precious
    jewel,
Yet, in good faith, some say that thee be-
    hold,
Thy face hath not the power to make love
    groan:
To say they err, I dare not be so bold,
Although I swear it to myself alone,
And, to be sure that is not false I swear,
A thousand groans, but thinking on thy
    face,
One on another's neck, do witness bear
Thy black is fairest in my judgment's place.
    In nothing art thou black, save in thy
      deeds,
    And thence this slander, as I think, pro-
      ceeds.

CXXXII.

Thine eyes I love, and they, as pitying me,
Knowing thy heart torments me with dis-
    dain,
Have put on black, and loving mourners be,

Looking with pretty ruth upon my pain.
And truly not the morning sun of heaven
Better becomes the grey cheeks of the east,
Nor that full star that ushers in the even
Doth half that glory to the sober west,
As those two mourning eyes become thy
    face:
O, let it then as well beseem thy heart
To mourn for me, since mourning doth thee
    grace,
And suit thy pity like in every part.
  Then will I swear beauty herself is black,
  And all they foul that thy complexion lack.

CXXXIII.

Beshrew that heart that makes my heart to
    groan   [me!
For that deep wound it gives my friend and
Is't not enough to torture me alone,
But slave to slavery my sweet'st friend must
    be?
Me from myself thy cruel eye hath taken,
And my next self thou harder hast en-
    gross'd;
Of him, myself, and thee, I am forsaken;
A torment thrice three-fold thus to be
    cross'd.
Prison my heart in thy steel bosom's ward,
But then my friend's heart let my poor
    heart bail;
Who e'er keeps me, let my heart be his
    guard;
Thou canst not then use rigour in my goal:
  And yet thou wilt; for I, being pent in
    thee
  Perforce am thine, and all that is in me.

CXXXIV.

So now I have confess'd that he is thine,
And I myself am mortgag'd to thy will;
Myself I'll forfeit, so that other mine
Thou wilt restore, to be my comfort still:
But thou wilt not, nor he will not be free,
For thou art covetous, and he is kind;
He learn'd but, surety-like, to write for me,
Under that bond that him as fast doth bind.
The statute of thy beauty thou wilt take,
Thou usurer, that putt'st forth all to use,
And sue a friend, came debtor for my sake;
So him I lose through my unkind abuse.
  Him have I lost; thou hast both him and
    me;
  He pays the whole, and yet am I not free.

CXXXV.

Whoever hath her wish, thou hast thy will,
And will to boot, and will in over-plus;
More than enough am I that vex thee still,
To thy sweet will making addition thus.
Wilt thou, whose will is large and spacious,
Not once vouchsafe to hide my will in thine?
Shall will in others seem right gracious,
And in my will no fair acceptance shine?

The sea, all water, yet receives rain still,
And in abundance addeth to his store;
So thou, being rich in will, add to thy will
One will of mine, to make thy large will
    more.
  Let no unkind, no fair beseechers kill;
  Think all but one, and me in that one
    Will.

CXXXVI.

If thy soul check thee that I come so near,
Swear to thy blind soul that I was thy
    Will,
And will, thy soul knows, is admitted there;
Thus far for love, my love-suit, sweet, fulfil.
Will will fulfil the treasure of thy love,
Ay, fill it full with wills, and my will one,
In things of great receipt with ease we
    prove;
Among a number one is reckon'd none.
Then in the number let me pass untold,
Though in thy stores' account I one must
    be;
For nothing hold me, so it please thee hold
That nothing me, a something sweet to thee;
  Make but my name thy love, and love
    that still,   [*Will.*
  And then thou lov'st me,—for my name is

CXXXVII.

Thou blind fool, Love, what dost thou to
    mine eyes,
That they behold, and see not what they
    see?
They know what beauty is, see where it
    lies,
Yet what the best is, take the worst to be.
If eyes, corrupt by over-partial looks,
Be anchor'd in the bay where all men ride,
Why of eyes' falsehood hast thou forged
    hooks,
Whereto the judgment of my heart is tied?
Why should my heart think that a several
    plot,
Which my heart knows the wide world's
    common place?
Or mine eyes, seeing this, say this is not,
To put fair truth upon so foul a face?
  In things right true my heart and eyes
    have err'd,   [transferr'd.
  And to this false plague are they now

CXXXVIII.

When my love swears that she is made of
    truth,
I do believe her, though I know she lies;
That she might think me some untutor'd
    youth,
Unlearned in the world's false subtleties.
Thus vainly thinking that she thinks me
    young,
Although she knows my days are past the
    best,

Simply I credit her false-speaking tongue;
On both sides thus is simple truth supprest,
But wherefore says she not she is unjust?
And wherefore say not I that I am old?
O, love's best habit is in seeming trust,
And age in love loves not to have years
    told:
  Therefore I lie with her, and she with me,
  And in our faults by lies we flatter'd be.

CXXXIX.

O, call not me to justify the wrong
That thy unkindness lays upon my heart;
Wound me not with thine eye, but with thy
    tongue;
Use power with power, and slay me not by
    art.
Tell me thou lov'st elsewhere; but in my
    sight,
Dear heart, forbear to glance thine eye
    aside.
What need'st thou wound with cunning,
    when thy might
Is more than my o'erpress'd defence can
    'bide?
Let me excuse thee: ah! my love well knows
Her pretty looks have been mine enemies;
And therefore from my face she turns my
    foes,
That they elsewhere might dart their in-
    juries:
  Yet do not so: but since I am near slain,
  Kill me outright with looks, and rid my
    pain.

CXL.

Be wise as thou art cruel; do not press
My tongue-tied patience with too much
    disdain;
Lest sorrow lend me words, and words ex-
    press
The manner of my pity-wanting pain.
If I might teach thee wit, better it were,
Though not to love, yet, love, to tell me so;
(As testy sick men, when their deaths be
    near,
No news but health from their physicians
    know;)
For, if I should despair, I should grow mad,
And in my madness might speak ill of thee:
Now this ill-wresting world is grown so
    bad,
Mad slanderers by mad ears believed be.
  That I may not be so, nor thou belied,
  Bear thine eyes straight, though thy proud
    heart go wide.

CXLI.

In faith I do not love thee with mine eyes,
For they in thee a thousand errors note;
But 'tis my heart that loves what they de-
    spise,
Who in despite of view is pleased to dote.

Nor are mine ears with thy tongue's tune
    delighted;
Nor tender feeling, to base touches prone,
Nor taste nor smell, desire to be invited
To any sensual feast with thee alone:
But my five wits, nor my five senses can
Dissuade one foolish heart from serving thee
Who leaves unsway'd the likeness of a man,
Thy proud heart's slave and vassal wretch
    to be:
  Only my plague thus far I count my gain,
  That she that makes me sin, awards me
    pain.

CXLII.

Love is my sin, and thy dear virtue hate,
Hate of my sin, grounded on sinful loving:
O, but with mine compare thou thine own
    state,
And thou shalt find it merits not reproving;
Or, if it do, not from those lips of thine,
That have profan'd their scarlet ornaments,
And seal'd false bonds of love as oft as
    mine;
Robb'd others' beds' revenues of their rents.
Be it lawful I love thee, as thou lov'st those
Whom thine eyes woo as mine importune
    thee:
Root pity in thy heart, that, when it grows,
Thy pity may deserve to pitied be.
  If thou dost seek to have what thou dost
    hide,
  By self-example mayst thou be denied!

CXLIII.

Lo, as a careful housewife runs to catch
One of her feather'd creatures broke away,
Sets down her babe, and makes all swift
    despatch
In pursuit of the thing she would have
    stay;
Whilst her neglected child holds her in
    chace,
Cries to catch her whose busy care is bent
To follow that which flies before her face,
Not prizing her poor infant's discontent;
So runn'st thou after that which flies from
    thee,
Whilst I thy babe chase thee afar behind;
But if thou catch thy hope, turn back to
    me,
And play the mother's part, kiss me, be
    kind:
  So will I pray that thou mayst have thy
    Will,
  If thou turn back, and my loud crying
    still.

CXLIV.

Two loves I have of comfort and despair,
Which like two spirits do suggest me still;
The better angel is a man right fair,
The worser spirit a woman, colour'd ill.

To win me soon to hell, my female evil
Tempteth my better angel from my side,
And would corrupt my saint to be a devil,
Wooing his purity with her foul pride.
And whether that my angel be turn'd fiend,
Suspect I may, yet not directly tell;
But, being both from me, both to each
   friend,
I guess one angel in another's hell.
   Yet this shall I ne'er know, but live in
     doubt,
   Till my bad angel fire my good one out.

CXLV.

Those lips that Love's own hand did make
Breath'd forth the sound that said, 'I hate,'
To me that languish'd for her sake:
But when she saw my woeful state,
Straight in her heart did mercy come,
Chiding that tongue, that ever sweet
Was used in giving gentle doom;
And taught it thus anew to greet:
'I hate' she alter'd with an end,
That follow'd it as gentle day
Doth follow night, who like a fiend
From heaven to hell is flown away.
   'I hate' from hate away she threw,
   And sav'd my life, saying—'not you.'

CXLVI.

Poor soul, the centre of my sinful earth,
Fool'd by these rebel powers that thee ar-
   ray,
Why dost thou pine within, and suffer
   dearth,
Painting thy outward walls so costly gay?
Why so large cost, having so short a lease,
Dost thou upon thy fading mansion spend?
Shall worms, inheritors of this excess,
Eat up thy charge? Is this thy body's end?
Then, soul, live thou upon thy servant's
   loss,
And let that pine to aggravate thy store;
Buy terms divine in selling hours of dross;
Within be fed, without be rich no more:
   So shalt thou feed on Death, that feeds on
     men,   [ing then.
   And, Death once dead, there's no more dy-

CXLVII.

My love is as a fever, longing still
For that which longer nurseth the disease;
Feeding on that which doth preserve the ill,
The uncertain sickly appetite to please.
My reason, the physician to my love,
Angry that his prescriptions are not kept,
Hath left me, and I desperate now approve
Desire is death, which physic did except.
Past cure I am, now reason is past care,
And frantic mad with evermore unrest;
My thoughts and my discourse as mad men's
   are,
At random from the truth vainly express'd;

For I have sworn thee fair, and thought
   thee bright,
Who art as black as hell, as dark as night.

CXLVIII.

O me! what eyes hath love put in my head,
Which have no correspondence with true
   sight!
Or, if they have, where is my judgment
   fled,
That censures falsely what they see aright?
If that be fair whereon my false eyes dote,
What means the world to say it is not so?
If it be not, then love doth well denote
Love's eye is not so true as all men's: no,
How can it? O how can Love's eye be true,
That is so vex'd with watching and with
   tears?
No marvel then though I mistake my view;
The sun itself sees not till heaven clears.
   O cunning Love! with tears thou keep'st
     me blind,
   Lest eyes well-seeing thy foul faults should
     find.

CXLIX.

Canst thou, O cruel! say I love thee not,
When I, against myself, with thee partake?
Do I not think on thee, when I forgot
Am of myself, all tyrant, for thy sake?
Who hateth thee that I do call my friend?
On whom frown'st thou that I do fawn
   upon?
Nay if thou low'rst on me, do I not spend
Revenge upon myself with present moan?
What merit do I in myself respect,
That is so proud thy service to despise,
When all my best doth worship thy defect,
Commanded by the motion of thine eyes?
   But, love, hate on, for now I know thy
     mind;
   Those that can see thou lov'st, and I am
     blind.

CL.

O, from what power hast thou this power-
   ful might,
With insufficiency my heart to sway?
To make me give the lie to my true sight,
And swear that brightness doth not grace
   the day?
Whence hast thou this becoming of things
   ill,
That in the very refuse of thy deeds
There is such strength and warrantise of
   skill,
That in my mind, thy worst all best ex-
   ceeds?
Who taught thee how to make me love thee
   more,
The more I hear and see just cause of hate?
O, though I love what others do abhor,

With others thou shouldst not abhor my
 state;
 If thy unworthiness rais'd love in me,
 More worthy I to be belov'd of thee.

CLI.

Love is too young to know what conscience
 is:
Yet who knows not, conscience is born of
 love?
Then, gentle cheater, urge not my amiss,
Lest guilty of my faults thy sweet self prove.
For thou betraying me, I do betray
My nobler part to my gross body's trea-
 son;
My soul doth tell my body that he may
Triumph in love; flesh stays no farther
 reason;
But, rising at thy name, doth point out thee
As his triumphant prize. Proud of this
 pride,
He is contented thy poor drudge to be,
To stand in thy affairs, fall by thy side,
 No want of conscience hold it that I call
 Her—love, for whose dear love I rise and
 fall.

CLII.

In loving thee thou know'st I am forsworn,
But thou art twice forsworn, to me love
 swearing;
In act thy bed-vow broke, and new faith
 torn,
In vowing new hate after new love bearing.
But why of two oaths' breach do I accuse
 thee,
When I break twenty? I am perjur'd most;
For all my vows are oaths but to misuse
 thee,
And all my honest faith in thee is lost:
For I have sworn deep oaths of thy deep
 kindness,
Oaths of thy love, thy truth, thy constancy;
And, to enlighten thee, gave eyes to blind-
 ness,

Or made them swear against the thing they
 see;
 For I have sworn thee fair: more perjur'd I,
 To swear, against the truth, so foul a lie!

CLIII.

Cupid lay by his brand, and fell asleep:
A maid of Dian's this advantage found,
And his love-kindling fire did quickly steep
In a cold valley-fountain of that ground;
Which borrow'd from this holy fire of love
A dateless lively heat, still to endure,
And grew a seething bath, which yet men
 prove
Against strange maladies a sovereign cure.
But at my mistress' eye Love's brand new-
 fir'd,
The boy for trial needs would touch my
 breast;
I, sick withal, the help of bath desir'd,
And thither hied, a sad distemper'd guest,
 But found no cure: the bath for my help
 lies
 Where Cupid got new fire,—my mistress'
 eyes.

CLIV.

The little love-god, lying once asleep
Laid by his side his heart-inflaming brand,
Whilst many nymphs that vow'd chaste life
 to keep
Came tripping by; but in her maiden hand
The fairest votary took up that fire
Which many legions of true hearts had
 warm'd:
And so the general of hot desire
Was sleeping by a virgin hand disarm'd.
This brand she quenched in a cool well by,
Which from Love's fire took heat perpetual,
Growing a bath and healthful remedy
For men diseas'd; but I, my mistress' thrall,
 Came there for cure, and this by that I
 prove,
 Love's fire heats water, water cools not
 love.

A LOVER'S COMPLAINT

From off a hill whose concave womb re-worded
A plaintful story from a sistering vale,
My spirits to attend this double voice ac-corded,
And down I laid to list the sad-tun'd tale;
Ere long espied a fickle maid full pale,
Tearing of papers, breaking rings a-twain,
Storming her world with sorrow's wind and rain.

Upon her head a platted hive of straw,
Which fortified her visage from the sun,
Whereon the thought might think sometime it saw
The carcase of a beauty spent and done.
Time had not scythed all that youth begun,
Nor youth all quit; but, spite of Heaven's fell rage,
Some beauty peep'd through lattice of sear'd age.

Oft did she heave her napkin to her eyne,
Which on it had conceited characters,
Laund'ring the silken figures in the brine
That season'd woe had pelleted in tears,
And often reading what contents it bears;
As often shrieking undistinguish'd woe,
In clamours of all size, both high and low.

Sometimes her levell'd eyes their carriage ride;
As they did battery to the spheres intend;
Sometimes diverted their poor balls are tied
To th' orbed earth: sometimes they do extend
Their view right on; anon their gazes lend
To every place at once, and nowhere fix'd,
The mind and sight distractedly commix'd.

Her hair, nor loose, nor tied in formal plat,
Proclaim'd in her a careless hand of pride;
For some, untuck'd, descended her sheav'd hat,
Hanging her pale and pined cheek beside;
Some in her threaden fillet still did bide,
And, true to bondage, would not break from thence,
Though slackly braided in loose negligence.

A thousand favours from a maund she drew
Of amber, crystal, and of bedded jet,
Which one by one she in a river threw,
Upon whose weeping margent she was set;
Like usury, applying wet to wet,
Or monarch's hands, that let not bounty fall
Where want cries 'some,' but where excess begs all.

Of folded schedules had she many a one,
Which she perus'd, sigh'd, tore, and gave the flood;
Crack'd many a ring of posied gold and bone,
Bidding them find their sepulchres in mud;
Found yet mo letters sadly penn'd in blood,
With sleided silk feat and affectedly
Enswath'd, and seal'd to curious secresy.

These often bath'd she in her fluxive eyes,
And often kiss'd, and often gave to tear;
Cried, 'O false blood, thou register of lies,
What unapproved witness dost thou bear!
Ink would have seem'd more black and damned here!'
This said, in top of rage the lines she rents,
Big discontent so breaking their contents.

A reverend man that graz'd his cattle nigh,
Sometime a blusterer, that the ruffle knew
Of court, of city, and had let go by
The swiftest hours, observed as they flew,
Towards this afflicted fancy fastly drew;
And, privileg'd by age, desires to know
In brief, the grounds and motives of her woe.

So slides he down upon his grained bat,
And comely-distant sits he by her side;
When he again desires her, being sat,
Her grievance with his hearing to divide:
If that from him there may be aught applied
Which may her suffering ecstasy assuage,
'Tis promis'd in the charity of age.

'Father,' she says, 'though in me you behold
The injury of many a blasting hour,
Let it not tell your judgment I am old;
Not age, but sorrow, over me hath power:
I might as yet have been a spreading flower,
Fresh to myself, if I had self-applied
Love to myself, and to no love beside.

'But woe is me! too early I attended
A youthful suit (it was to gain my grace)
Of one by nature's outwards so commended,
That maiden's eyes stuck over all his face:
Love lack'd a dwelling, and made him her place;

And when in his fair parts she did abide,
She was new lodg'd, and newly deified.

'His browny locks did hang in crooked
  curls;
And every light occasion of the wind
Upon his lips their silken parcels hurls.
What's sweet to do, to do will aptly find:
Each eye that saw him did enchant the
  mind;
For on his visage was in little drawn,
What largeness thinks in paradise was sawn.

'Small show of man was yet upon his chin;
His phœnix down began but to appear,
Like unshorn velvet, on that termless skin,
Whose bare out-bragg'd the web it seem'd
  to wear;
Yet show'd his visage by that cost more
  dear;
And nice affections wavering stood in doubt
If best 'twere as it was, or best without.

'His qualities were beauteous as his form,
For maiden-tongued he was, and thereof
  free;
Yet, if men mov'd him, was he such a storm
As oft 'twixt May and April is to see,
When winds breathe sweet, unruly though
  they be.
His rudeness so with his authoriz'd youth
Did livery falseness in a pride of truth.

'Well could he ride, and often men would
  say
That horse his mettle from his rider takes:
Proud of subjection, noble by the sway,
What rounds, what bounds, what course,
  what stop he makes!
And controversy hence a question takes,
Whether the horse by him became his deed,
Or he his manage by the well-doing steed.

'But quickly on this side the verdict went;
His real habitude gave life and grace
To appertainings and to ornament,
Accomplish'd in himself, not in his case:
All aids, themselves made fairer by their
  place,
Can for additions; yet their purpos'd trim
Piec'd not his grace, but were all grac'd by
  him.

'So on the tip of his subduing tongue
All kind of arguments and question deep,
All replication prompt, and reason strong,
For his advantage still did wake and sleep:
To make the weeper laugh, the laugher
  weep,
He had the dialect and different skill,
Catching all passions in his craft of will;

'That he did in the general bosom reign

Of young, of old; and sexes both enchanted,
To dwell with him in thoughts, or to re-
  main
In personal duty, following where he
  haunted:
Consents bewitch'd, ere he desire, have
  granted;
And dialogued for him what he would say,
Ask'd their own wills, and made their wills
  obey.

'Many there were that did his picture get,
To serve their eyes, and in it put their mind;
Like fools that in the imagination set
The goodly objects which abroad they find
Of lands and mansions, theirs in thought
  assign'd;
And labouring in mo pleasures to bestow
  them,
Than the true gouty landlord which doth
  owe them:

'So many have, that never touch'd his hand,
Sweetly suppos'd them mistress of his heart.
My woeful self, that did in freedom stand,
And was my own fee-simple, (not in part,)
What with his heart in youth, and youth in
  art,
Threw my affections in his charmed power,
Reserv'd the stalk, and gave him all my
  flower.

'Yet did I not, as some my equals did,
Demand of him, nor being desired yielded;
Finding myself in honour so forbid,
With safest distance I mine honour shielded:
Experience for me many bulwarks builded
Of proofs new-bleeding, which remain'd the
  foil
Of this false jewel, and his amorous spoil.

'But ah! who ever shunn'd by precedent
The destin'd ill she must herself assay?
Or forc'd examples, 'gainst her own content,
To put the by-pass'd perils in her way?
Counsel may stop a while what will not
  stay;
For when we rage, advice is often seen
By blunting us to make our wits more
  keen.

'Nor gives it satisfaction to our blood,
That we must curb it upon others' proof,
To be forbid the sweets that seem so good,
For fear of harms that preach in our be-
  hoof.
O appetite, from judgment stand aloof!
The one a palate hath that needs will taste,
Though reason weep, and cry It is thy last.

'For further I could say, This man's untrue,
And knew the patterns of his foul beguiling;

Heard where his plants in others' orchards
  grew,
Saw how deceits were gilded in his smiling;
Knew vows were ever brokers to defiling;
Thought characters and words, merely but
  art,
And bastards of his foul adulterate heart.

'And long upon these terms I held my city,
Till thus he 'gan besiege me: Gentle maid,
Have of my suffering youth some feeling
  pity
And be not of my holy vows afraid:
That's to you sworn, to none was ever said;
For feasts of love I have been call'd unto,
Till now did ne'er invite, nor never vow.

'All my offences that abroad you see
Are errors of the blood, none of the mind;
Love made them not; with acture they may
  be,
Where neither party is nor true nor kind:
They sought their shame that so their shame
  did find;
And so much less of shame in me remains,
By how much of me their reproach con-
  tains.

'Among the many that mine eyes have seen,
Not one whose flame my heart so much as
  warm'd,
On my affection put to the smallest teen,
Or any of my leisures ever charm'd:
Harm have I done to them, but ne'er was
  harm'd;
Kept hearts in liveries, but mine own was
  free,
And reign'd, commanding in his monarchy.

'Look here what tributes wounded fancies
  sent me,
Of paled pearls, and rubies red as blood;
Figuring that they their passions likewise
  lent me
Of grief and blushes, aptly understood
In bloodless white and the encrimson'd
  mood;
Effects of terror and dear modesty,
Encamp'd in hearts, but fighting outwardly.

'And lo! behold the talents of their hair,
With twisted metal amorously impleach'd,
I have receiv'd from many a several fair,
(Their kind acceptance weepingly be-
  seech'd,)
With the annexions of fair gems enrich'd,
And deep-brain'd sonnets that did amplify
Each stone's dear nature, worth, and
  quality.

'The diamond, why 'twas beautiful and hard,
Whereto his invis'd properties did tend;
The deep-green emerald, in whose fresh re-
  gard

Weak sights their sickly radiance do amend;
The heaven-hued sapphire and the opal blend
With objects manifold; each several stone,
With wit well blazon'd, smil'd or made some
  moan.

'Lo! all these trophies of affections hot,
Of pensiv'd and subdued desires the tender,
Nature hath charg'd me that I hoard them
  not,
But yield them up where I myself must ren-
  der,
That is, to you, my origin and ender:
For these, of force, must your oblations be,
Since I their altar, you enpatron me.

'O then advance of yours that phraseless
  hand,
Whose white bears down the airy scale of
  praise;
Take all these similes to your own command,
Hallow'd with sighs that burning lungs did
  raise;
What me your minister, for you obeys,
Works under you; and to your audit comes
Their distract parcels in combined sums.

'Lo! this device was sent me from a nun,
Or sister sanctified of holiest note;
Which late her noble suit in court did shun,
Whose rarest havings made the blossoms
  dote;
For she was sought by spirits of richest coat,
But kept cold distance, and did thence re-
  move,
To spend her living in eternal love.

'But O, my sweet, what labour is 't to leave
The thing we have not, mastering what not
  strives?
Paling the place which did no form receive,
Playing patient sports in unconstrained
  gyves:
She that her fame so to herself contrives,
The scars of battle 'scapeth by the flight,
And makes her absence valiant, not her
  might.

'O pardon me, in that my boast is true;
The accident which brought me to her eye,
Upon the moment did her force subdue,
And now she would the caged cloister fly:
Religious love put out religion's eye:
Not to be tempted, would she be immur'd,
And now, to tempt all, liberty procur'd.

'How mighty then you are, O hear me tell!
The broken bosoms that to me belong
Have emptied all their fountains in my well,
And mine I pour your ocean all among:
I strong o'er them, and you o'er me being
  strong,
Must for your victory us all congest,
As compound love to physic your cold breast.

'My parts had power to charm a sacred nun,
Who, disciplin'd and dieted in grace,
Believ'd her eyes when they to assail begun,
All vows and consecrations giving place.
O most potential love! vow, bond, nor space,
In thee hath neither sting, knot, nor confine,
For thou art all, and all things else are thine.

'When thou impressest, what are precepts
    worth
Of stale example? When thou wilt inflame,
How coldly those impediments stand forth,
Of wealth, of filial fear, law, kindred, fame!
Love's arms are peace, 'gainst rule, 'gainst
    sense, 'gainst shame,
And sweetens, in the suffering pangs it bears,
The aloes of all forces, shocks, and fears.

'Now all these hearts that do on mine de-
    pend,
Feeling it break, with bleeding groans they
    pine,
And supplicant their sighs to you extend,
To leave the battery that you make 'gainst
    mine,
Lending soft audience to my sweet design,
And credent soul to that strong-bonded oath,
That shall prefer and undertake my troth.

'This said, his watery eyes he did dismount,
Whose sights till then were levell'd on my
    face;
Each cheek a river running from a fount
With brinish current downward flow'd apace:
O how the channel to the stream gave grace!
Who, glaz'd with crystal, gate the glowing
    roses
That flame through water which their hue
    encloses.

'O father, what a hell of witchcraft lies
In the small orb of one particular tear!
But with the inundation of the eyes
What rocky heart to water will not wear?
What breast so cold that is not warmed
    here?
O cleft effect! cold modesty, hot wrath,

Both fire from hence and chill extincture
    hath!

'For lo! his passion, but an art of craft,
Even there resolv'd my reason into tears;
There my white stole of chastity I daff'd,
Shook off my sober guards, and civil fears;
Appear to him, as he to me appears, [bore,
All melting; though our drops this difference
His poison'd me, and mine did him restore.

'In him a plenitude of subtle matter,
Applied to cautels, all strange forms receives,
Of burning blushes or of weeping water,
Or swooning paleness ; and he takes and
    leaves,
In either's aptness, as it best deceives,
To blush at speeches rank, to weep at woes,
Or to turn white and swoon at tragic shows;

'That not a heart which in his level came
Could scape the hail of his all-hurting aim,
Showing fair nature is both kind and tame;
And, veil'd in them, did win whom he would
    maim:
Against the thing he sought he would ex-
    claim;
When he most burn'd in heart-wish'd luxury,
He preach'd pure maid, and prais'd cold
    chastity.

'Thus merely with the garment of a Grace
The naked and concealed fiend he cover'd,
That the unexperienc'd gave the tempter
    place,
Which, like a cherubin, above them hover'd.
Who, young and simple, would not be so
    lover'd?
Ah me! I fell; and yet do question make
What I should do again for such a sake.

'O, that infected moisture of his eye,
O, that false fire which in his cheek so
    glow'd,
O, that forc'd thunder from his heart did fly,
O, that sad breath his spongy lungs bestow'd,
O, all that borrow'd motion, seeming ow'd,
Would yet again betray the fore-betray'd,
And new pervert a reconciled maid!'

THE PASSIONATE PILGRIM

I.

Did not the heavenly rhetoric of thine eye,
'Gainst whom the world could not hold argument,
Persuade my heart to this false perjury?
Vows for thee broke deserve not punishment.
A woman I forswore; but I will prove,
Thou being a goddess, I forswore not thee:
My vow was earthly, thou a heavenly love;
Thy grace being gain'd cures all disgrace in me.
My vow was breath, and breath a vapour is;
Then, thou fair sun, that on this earth doth shine,
Exhale this vapour vow; in thee it is:
If broken, then it is no fault of mine.
  If by me broke, what fool is not so wise
  To lose an oath, to win a paradise?

II.

Sweet Cytherea, sitting by a brook
With young Adonis, lovely, fresh, and green,
Did court the lad with many a lovely look,
Such looks as none could look but beauty's queen.
She told him stories to delight his ear;
She show'd him favours to allure his eye;
To win his heart, she touch'd him here and there:
Touches so soft still conquer chastity.
But whether unripe years did want conceit,
Or he refus'd to take her figur'd proffer,
The tender nibbler would not touch the bait,
But smile and jest at every gentle offer:
  Then fell she on her back, fair queen, and toward;
  He rose and ran away; ah, fool too froward!

III.

If love make me forsworn, how shall I swear to love?
O never faith could hold, if not to beauty vow'd:
Though to myself forsworn, to thee I'll constant prove;   [osiers bow'd.
Those thoughts, to me like oaks, to thee like
Study his bias leaves, and makes his book thine eyes,   [comprehend.
Where all those pleasures live that art can
If knowledge be the mark, to know thee shall suffice;   [commend;
Well learned is that tongue that well can thee
All ignorant that soul that sees thee without wonder;

Which is to me some praise, that I thy parts admire:
Thine eye Jove's lightning seems, thy voice his dreadful thunder,
Which (not to anger bent) is music and sweet fire.
  Celestial as thou art, O do not love that wrong,
  To sing the heavens' praise with such an earthly tongue.

IV.

Scarce had the sun dried up the dewy morn,
And scarce the herd gone to the hedge for shade,
When Cytherea, all in love forlorn,
A longing tarriance for Adonis made,
Under an osier growing by a brook,
A brook where Adon used to cool his spleen.
Hot was the day; she hotter that did look
For his approach, that often there had been.
Anon he comes, and throws his mantle by,
And stood stark naked on the brook's green brim;
That sun look'd on the world with glorious eye,
Yet not so wistly as this queen on him:
  He, spying her, bounc'd in, whereas he stood;
  O Jove, quoth she, why was not I a flood?

V.

Fair is my love, but not so fair as fickle;
Mild as a dove, but neither true nor trusty;
Brighter than glass, and yet, as glass is, brittle;
Softer than wax, and yet, as iron, rusty:
  A lily pale, with damask die to grace her,
  None fairer, nor none falser to deface her.

Her lips to mine how often hath she join'd,
Between each kiss her oaths of true love swearing!
How many tales to please me hath she coin'd,
Dreading my love, the loss thereof still fearing!
  Yet in the midst of all her pure protestings,
  Her faith, her oaths, her tears, and all were jestings.

She burn'd with love, as straw with fire flameth,
She burn'd out love, as soon as straw out burneth;   [framing,
She fram'd the love, and yet she foil'd the
She bade love last, and yet she fell a turning.

Was this a lover, or a lecher whether?
Bad in the best, though excellent in neither.

VI.

If music and sweet poetry agree,
As they must needs, the sister and the
    brother,
Then must the love be great 'twixt thee and
    me,
Because thou lov'st the one, and I the other.
Dowland to thee is dear, whose heavenly
    touch
Upon the lute doth ravish human sense;
Spencer to me, whose deep conceit is such,
As, passing all conceit, needs no defence.
Thou lov'st to hear the sweet melodious
    sound
That Phœbus' lute, the queen of music,
    makes;
And I in deep delight am chiefly drown'd,
Whenas himself to singing he betakes.
    One god is god of both, as poets feign;
    One knight loves both, and both in thee
    remain.

VII.

Fair was the morn, when the fair queen of
    love,
*   *   *   *   *   *
Paler for sorrow than her milk-white dove,
For Adon's sake, a youngster proud and
    wild;
Her stand she takes upon a steep-up hill:
Anon Adonis comes with horn and hounds;
She, silly queen, with more than love's good
    will,
Forbade the boy he should not pass those
    grounds;
Once, quoth she, did I see a fair sweet youth
Here in these brakes deep-wounded with a
    boar,
Deep in the thigh, a spectacle of ruth!
See in my thigh, quoth she, here was the
    sore:
    She showed hers; he saw more wounds
    than one,
    And blushing fled, and left her all alone.

VIII.

Sweet rose, fair flower, untimely pluck'd,
    soon vaded,
Pluck'd in the bud, and vaded in the spring!
Bright orient pearl, alack! too timely shaded!
Fair creature, kill'd too soon by death's sharp
    sting!
    Like a green plum that hangs upon a tree,
    And falls, through wind, before the fall
    should be.

I weep for thee, and yet no cause I have;
For why? thou left'st me nothing in thy will.
And yet thou left'st me more than I did
    crave;

For why? I craved nothing of thee still:
O yes, dear friend, I pardon crave of thee;
Thy discontent thou didst bequeath to me.

IX.

Venus, with Adonis sitting by her,
Under a myrtle shade, began to woo him:
She told the youngling how god Mars did
    try her,
And as he fell to her, she fell to him.
Even thus, quoth she, the warlike god em-
    brac'd me;
And then she clipp'd Adonis in her arms:
Even thus, quoth she, the warlike god un-
    lac'd me;
As if the boy should use like loving charms.
Even thus, quoth she, he seized on my lips,
And with her lips on his did act the seizure;
And as she fetched breath, away he skips,
And would not take her meaning nor her
    pleasure.
Ah! that I had my lady at this bay,
To kiss and clip me till I run away!

X.

Crabbed age and youth
    Cannot live together;
Youth is full of pleasance,
    Age is full of care;
Youth like summer morn,
    Age like winter weather;
Youth like summer brave,
    Age like winter bare.
Youth is full of sport,
Age's breath is short,
    Youth is nimble, age is lame:
Youth is hot and bold,
Age is weak and cold;
    Youth is wild, and age is tame.
Age, I do abhor thee,
Youth, I do adore thee;
    O, my love, my love is young!
Age, I do defy thee;
O sweet shepherd, hie thee,
    For methinks thou stay'st too long.

XI.

Beauty is but a vain and doubtful good,
A shining gloss, that vadeth suddenly;
A flower that dies, when first it 'gins to bud;
A brittle glass, that's broken presently:
    A doubtful good, a gloss, a glass, a flower,
    Lost, vaded, broken, dead within an hour.

And as goods lost are seld or never found,
As vaded gloss no rubbing will refresh,
As flowers dead lie wither'd on the ground,
As broken glass no cement can redress,
    So beauty, blemish'd once, for ever's lost,
    In spite of physic, painting, pain, and cost.

XII.

Good night, good rest. Ah! neither be my
    share:

She bade good night, that kept my rest
    away;
And daff'd me to a cabin hang'd with care,
To descant on the doubts of my decay.
  Farewell, quoth she, and come again to-
    morrow;
  Farewell I could not, for I supp'd with
    sorrow.

Yet at my parting sweetly did she smile,
In scorn or friendship, nill I construe
  whether:
'T may be, she joy'd to jest at my exile,
'T may be, again to make me wander
  thither:
  Wander, a word for shadows like myself,
  As take the pain, but cannot pluck the pelf.

XIII.

Lord, how mine eyes throw gazes to the east!
My heart doth charge the watch; the morning rise

Doth cite each moving sense from idle rest.
Not daring trust the office of mine eyes,
  While Philomela sits and sings, I sit and
    mark,
  And wish her lays were tuned like the lark;

For she doth welcome daylight with her ditty,
And drives away dark dismal-dreaming night:
The night so pack'd, I post unto my pretty;
Heart hath his hope, and eyes their wished
    sight;   [sorrow;
  Sorrow chang'd to solace, solace mix'd with
  For why? she sigh'd, and bade me come
    tomorrow.

Were I with her, the night would post too
    soon;
But now are minutes added to the hours;
To spite me now, each minute seems a moon;
Yet not for me, shine sun to succour flowers!
  Pack night, peep day; good day, of night
    now borrow;   [tomorrow.
  Short, night, to-night, and length thyself

SONNETS TO SUNDRY NOTES OF MUSIC

It was a lording's daughter, the fairest one
    of three,   [be.
That liked of her master as well as well might
Till looking on an Englishman, the fairest
    that eye could see,
  Her fancy fell a turning.
Long was the combat doubtful, that love with
    love did fight,   [knight;
To leave the master loveless, or kill the gallant
To put in practice either, alas it was a spite
  Unto the silly damsel.   [pain,
But one must be refused, more mickle was the
That nothing could be used, to turn them
    both to gain,   [ed with disdain:
For of the two the trusty knight was wound-
  Alas, she could not help it!   [of the day,
Thus art, with arms contending, was victor
Which by a gift of learning did bear the maid
    away;
Then lullaby, the learned man hath got the
    lady gay;
  For now my song is ended.

II.

On a day (alack the day!),
Love, whose month was ever May,
Spied a blossom passing fair,
Playing in the wanton air:
Through the velvet leaves the wind,
All unseen, 'gan passage find;
That the lover, sick to death,
Wish'd himself the heaven's breath.
Air, quoth he, thy cheeks may blow;
Air, would I might triumph so!
But, alas, my hand hath sworn
Ne'er to pluck thee from thy thorn:
Vow, alack, for youth unmeet,
Youth, so apt to pluck a sweet,
Thou for whom Jove would swear
Juno but an Ethiope were;
And deny himself for Jove,
Turning mortal for thy love.

III.

My flocks feed not,
My ewes breed not,
My rams speed not,
  All is amiss:
Love is dying,
Faith's defying,
Heart's denying,
  Causer of this.
All my merry jigs are quite forgot,

All my lady's love is lost, God wot:
Where her faith was firmly fix'd in love,
There a nay is plac'd without remove.
One silly cross
Wrought all my loss;
  O frowning Fortune, cursed, fickle dame!
For now I see,
Inconstancy
  More in women than in men remain.

In black mourn I,
All fears scorn I,
Love hath forlorn me,
  Living in thrall:
Heart is bleeding,
All help needing,
(O cruel speeding!)
  Fraughted with gall.
My shepherd's pipe can sound no deal,
My wether's bell rings doleful knell;
My curtail dog, that wont to have play'd,
Plays not at all, but seems afraid;
With sighs so deep,
Procures to weep,
  In howling-wise, to see my doleful plight.
How sighs resound
Through heartless ground,   [fight!
  Like a thousand vanquish'd men in bloody

Clear wells spring not,
Sweet birds sing not,
Green plants bring not
  Forth; they die:
Herds stand weeping,
Flocks all sleeping,
Nymphs back peeping
  Fearfully.
All our pleasure known to us poor swains,
All our merry meetings on the plains,
All our evening sport from us is fled,
All our love is lost, for Love is dead.
Farewell, sweet lass,
Thy like ne'er was   [moan:
  For a sweet content, the cause of all my
Poor Coridon
Must live alone,
  Other help for him I see that there is none.

IV.

Whenas thine eye hath chose the dame,
And stall'd the deer that thou shouldst
    strike,
Let reason rule things worthy blame,

As well as fancy, partial might:
  Take counsel of some wiser head,
  Neither too young, nor yet unwed.

And when thou com'st thy tale to tell,
Smooth not thy tongue with filed talk,
Lest she some subtle practice smell;
(A cripple soon can find a halt:)
  But plainly say thou lov'st her well,
  And set her person forth to sell.

What though her frowning brows be bent,
Her cloudy looks will calm ere night;
And then too late she will repent,
That thus dissembled her delight;
  And twice desire, ere it be day,
  That which with scorn she put away.

What though she strive to try her
    strength,
And ban and brawl, and say thee nay,
Her feeble force will yield at length,
When craft hath taught her thus to say:
  'Had women been so strong as men,
  In faith you had not had it then.'

And to her will frame all thy ways;
Spare not to spend,—and chiefly there
Where thy desert may merit praise,
By ringing in thy lady's ear:
  The strongest castle, tower, and town,
  The golden bullet beats it down.

Serve always with assured trust,
And in thy suit be humble, true;
Unless thy lady prove unjust,
Press never thou to choose anew:
  When time shall serve, be thou not
      slack
  To proffer, though she put thee back.

The wiles and guiles that women work,
Dissembled with an outward show,
The tricks and toys that in them lurk,
The cock that treads them shall not
    know.
  Have you not heard it said full oft,
  A woman's nay doth stand for
      nought?

Think women still to strive with men,
To sin, and never for to saint:
There is no heaven, by holy then,
When time with age shall them attaint.
  Were kisses all the joys in bed,
  One woman would another wed.

But soft; enough,—too much I fear,
Lest that my mistress hear my song;
She'll not stick to round me i' th' ear,
To teach my tongue to be so long:
  Yet will she blush, here be it said,
  To hear her secrets so bewray'd.

V.

Live with me, and be my love,
And we will all the pleasures prove
That hills and valleys, dales and fields,
And all the craggy mountains yields.

There will we sit upon the rocks,
And see the shepherds feed their flocks.
By shallow rivers, by whose falls
Melodious birds sing madrigals.

There will I make thee a bed of roses,
With a thousand fragrant posies,
A cap of flowers and a kirtle
Embroider'd all with leaves of myrtle.

A belt of straw and ivy buds,
With coral clasps and amber studs;
And if these pleasures may thee move,
Then live with me, and be my love.

LOVE'S ANSWER

If that the world and love were young,
And truth in every shepherd's tongue,
These pretty pleasures might me move
To live with thee and be thy love.

VI.

As it fell upon a day,
In the merry month of May,
Sitting in a pleasant shade
With a grove of myrtles made,
Beasts did leap, and birds did sing,
Trees did grow, and plants did spring:
Everything did banish moan,
Save the nightingale alone:
She, poor bird, as all forlorn,
Lean'd her breast up-till a thorn,
And there sung the dolefull'st ditty
That to hear it was great pity:
Fie, fie, fie, now would she cry,
Teru, Teru, by and by:
That to hear her so complain,
Scarce I could from tears refrain;
For her griefs so lively shown,
Made me think upon mine own.
Ah thought I, thou mourn'st in vain;
None take pity on thy pain:
Senseless trees, they cannot hear thee;
Ruthless bears, they will not cheer thee.
King Pandion, he is dead;
All thy friends are lapp'd in lead;
All thy fellow-birds do sing,
Careless of thy sorrowing.
Even so, poor bird, like thee,
None alive will pity me.
Whilst as fickle fortune smil'd,
Thou and I were both beguil'd.
Every one that flatters thee
Is no friend in misery
Words are easy like the wind;
Faithful friends are hard to find.

Every man will·be thy friend,
Whilst thou hast wherewith to spend;
But if store of crowns be scant,
No man will supply thy want.
If that one be prodigal,
Bountiful they will him call:
And with such-like flattering
'Pity but he were a king.'
If he be addict to vice,
Quickly him they will entice;
If to women he be bent,
They have him at commandement;

But if fortune once do frown,
Then farewell his great renown:
They that fawn'd on him before,
Use his company no more.
He that is thy friend indeed,
He will help thee in thy need;
If thou sorrow, he will weep;
If thou wake, he cannot sleep:
Thus of every grief in heart
He with thee doth bear a part.
These are certain signs to know
Faithful friend from flattering foe.

THE PHŒNIX AND THE TURTLE

LET the bird of loudest lay,
On the sole Arabian tree,
Herald sad and trumpet be,
To whose sound chaste wings obey.

But thou, shrieking harbinger,
Foul pre-currer of the fiend,
Augur of the fever's end,
To this troop come thou not near.

From this session interdict
Every fowl of tyrant wing,
Save the eagle, feather'd king:
Keep the obsequy so strict.

Let the priest in surplice white,
That defunctive music can,
Be the death-divining swan,
Lest the requiem lack his right.

And thou, treble-dated crow,
That thy sable-gender mak'st
With the breath thou giv'st and tak'st,
'Mongst our mourners shalt thou go.

Here the anthem doth commence:
Love and constancy is dead;
Phœnix and the turtle fled
In a mutual flame from hence.

So they lov'd, as love in twain
Had the essence but in one;
Two distincts, division none:
Number there in love was slain.

Hearts remote, yet not asunder;
Distance, and no space was seen
'Twixt the turtle and his queen;
But in them it were a wonder.

So between them love did shine,
That the turtle saw his right
Flaming in the phœnix' sight:
Either was the other's mine.

Property was thus appall'd,
That the self was not the same;
Single nature's double name
Neither two nor one was call'd.

Reason, in itself confounded,
Saw division grow together;
To themselves yet either-neither,
Simple were so well compounded

That it cried how true a twain
Seemeth this concordant one!
Love hath reason, reason none
If what parts can so remain.

Whereupon it made this threne
To the phœnix and the dove,
Co-supremes and stars of love;
As chorus to their tragic scene.

THRENOS.

Beauty, truth, and rarity,
Grace in all simplicity,
Here enclos'd in cinders lie.

Death is now the phœnix' nest;
And the turtle's loyal breast
To eternity doth rest,

Leaving no posterity:—
'Twas not their infirmity,
It was married chastity.

Truth may seem, but cannot be:
Beauty brag, but 'tis not she;
Truth and beauty buried be.

To this urn let those repair
That are either true or fair;
For these dead birds sigh a prayer.